GROVE'S
DICTIONARY OF MUSIC
AND MUSICIANS

*Supplementary Volume
to the Fifth Edition*

GROVE'S
DICTIONARY OF MUSIC
AND MUSICIANS

Supplementary Volume to the Fifth Edition

EDITED BY

ERIC BLOM

ASSOCIATE EDITOR

DENIS STEVENS

NEW YORK

ST. MARTIN'S PRESS INC

First Edition, planned and edited by SIR GEORGE GROVE,
D.C.L., in four volumes, with an Appendix edited by
J. A. Fuller-Maitland, and an Index by Mrs. Edmond
Wodehouse, 1878, 1880, 1883, 1899.
Second Edition, edited by J. A. FULLER-MAITLAND, in five
volumes, 1900.
Third Edition, edited by H. C. COLLES, in five volumes,
1927.
Fourth Edition, edited by H. C. COLLES, in five volumes,
with Supplementary Volume, 1940.
Fifth Edition, edited by ERIC BLOM, in nine volumes, 1954;
with Supplementary Volume, 1961.
Reprinted 1966, 1968, 1970, 1973.

ST MARTIN'S PRESS INC
175 Fifth Avenue New York NY 10010

MACMILLAN AND COMPANY LIMITED
Little Essex Street London WC 2
also Bombay Calcutta Madras Melbourne

THE MACMILLAN COMPANY OF CANADA LIMITED
70 Bond Street Toronto 2

PRINTED IN THE UNITED STATES OF AMERICA
By
Halliday Lithograph Corporation
West Hanover, Massachusetts

PUBLISHER'S NOTE

ERIC BLOM had assembled the bulk of the material for this Supplementary Volume, and had even corrected some of the galleys, before his death on the 11th April, 1959. This sad event deprived the world of music of one of the kindest, most tolerant, and least tyrannical editors it has known. An account of his life, together with an appreciation of his work, may be found in this Supplement, and all who knew him or corresponded with him about matters pertaining to GROVE will be able to round out the picture from their own experiences and recollections.

In the Preface which was found among his papers and is here printed as he left it, Dr. Blom mentions his gratitude to the many people who helped him in the preparation of this Volume. His Publishers hope that readers will continue to send suggestions for additions or amendments, which may be incorporated eventually in the Sixth Edition of GROVE.

Finally, the Publishers must express their gratitude to Mr. Denis Stevens who took over the editing of this Volume after Eric Blom's sudden death, and who has carried out his difficult task most competently and expeditiously.

PREFACE

THE first thing to bear in mind about this Supplement is that it does not constitute a new edition of Grove's Dictionary. A sixth edition will doubtless appear in due time and it may differ from the fifth in some respects as well as, no doubt, be up to its own date.

To bring the fifth edition of 1954 completely up to date has not been the principal aim in the planning of the present volume. No consistent attempt has been made, for instance, to complete all the catalogues of composers' and authors' works down to the year 1960, or indeed any year between 1954 and now; for that *would* have meant a sixth edition, and turned out so costly that few of those who spent a considerable amount of money on the main body of the work not very long ago would have been inclined to invest in it. Besides, no work of this kind ever is completely up to date, and to make it much larger as well as more expensive than it is now would have caused such delay in its production that once again all kinds of new information would have missed the boat.

Nevertheless, catalogues have in a great many cases been improved, and important new works, as well as many not so important, have been entered so far as information has been available. There has, however, been no systematic search for such information from letter A to letter Z, partly because of insurmountable difficulties, and partly, again, in order to avoid both delay and inflation. What *has* been added, though admittedly in an inevitably haphazard, hand-to-mouth kind of way, will often, I am sure, be found very useful, so much so that the absence of other accessions will, I hope, be thought excusable as well as understandable.

Addenda, as the title-page indicates, have not been the only purpose for which this volume was planned. No less important, if less pleasing to the Editor, are *Corrigenda*. In any work of reference giving thousands of items of factual information, gathered by fallible human beings from often equally fallible sources, mistakes are bound to appear in abundance, and most of them, unfortunately, remain undiscovered until the work has been published and gone through the hands of a multitude of users, who may or may not make their grievances known to the publishers or the Editor. It is an immense advantage if they do, needless to say, and I should like here to thank all those who have had the kindness and, I may add, the public spirit to give me the benefit of their complaints.

Corrections, all the same, no more constitute the major part of this volume than do additions to the entries in the main body of Grove V; and I am glad to be able to say that actual misprints have been found to be almost infinitesimally few in proportion to the eight million words or so contained in the 1954 edition. What pleases me even more is that there has been extremely little criticism of the technical articles, which have practically all stood the severe tests of scholarly scrutiny they must have undergone during these last four years and more. Most of the mistakes discovered are in the biographical entries, where in the nature of the case they were indeed much more liable to occur. The doings of all sorts of musicians, in the past and even in the present, are far more difficult to pin down without fear of error than the facts of musical science, provided that these are investigated by such scholarship as I have been fortunate to enlist for the new treatment of technical subjects or the revision of earlier articles on them.

The contributions to the Supplement may be divided into four main categories in, I think, roughly the following proportions :

1. Corrections — one quarter.
2. Additions to existing articles — one quarter.
3. New entries of persons or subjects previously omitted — one quarter.
4. New discoveries — one quarter.

On the third category I need not comment : the new entries will be found at a glance through the pages of the volume and, I hope, justify themselves on the whole, though they may err a little on the side of generosity of admission and no doubt a little more in the matter of still persisting omission. But the discoveries I cannot refrain from commenting on briefly, especially as, I should like to point out, they often look inconspicuous in our pages, seeing that it may take but a single line to publish some fact or other that may be of positively sensational importance.

Detailed new information on the early life of Peter Philips, before he settled in the Netherlands, for example, or the fascinating new facts about the Lanier family, is sure to be welcome ; and it may be found amusing as well as useful to find that, among other English families of musicians, the fifth edition had one Eccles too few and one Tomkins too many. Then, more than once, it will be discovered that two musicians of the past now turn out to be one and the same person, while on the other hand the biography of one has all too long covered the facts concerning two different people. There are other sensational corrections, such as the information that Jean Alain, previously described as a " French or Netherlands composer ", was in fact an Englishman, John Aleyn ; or that Heinrich Schütz, always said to have been born on 8 October 1585 (baptized on the 9th), was much more likely to have been four days older ; and so on — how far on a glance at the pages that follow will soon reveal.

The numerous deaths that have occurred since 1954 have, of course, all been entered, so far as they have come to my notice, and I think I may claim that the gathering of this kind of information has been done systematically and comprehensively. The same may, I think, be claimed for the bibliographies, which have been brought up to date from a variety of sources. Here I wish to acknowledge gratefully that the quarterly book-lists published by the American ' Musical Quarterly ' have been most helpful, even where they have merely confirmed information gathered previously.

No attempt has been made to alter present to past tenses in the articles on persons deceased since 1954. This would have merely cluttered up the Supplement, wastefully, pedantically and tiresomely, with corrections the need for which is self-evident.

Cross references have been vastly improved. The technical problems of page make-up made it impossible to achieve the ideal in this respect at the time the fifth edition went through its final stages. The entries on instruments, for instance, do not always show references to illustrations of them in that edition, and since plates grouping a number of different instruments of a given family may appear in a plate remote from that of the articles on them, often not even in the same volume, these new guides to pictorial reproductions, without which no instrument can be well described, will be found convenient. Even more valuable will be the numerous new references to works by a given composer appearing in various miscellaneous collections, the full catalogues of which are entered under their own heads. Any reader who wishes to study such music by an old composer as may have been published in one or more of these collections, will now be shown at a glance where to find it.

Actually at two glances, I should say, since inevitably the new supplementary information still remains separated from the main entries. And here I should like to recommend a simple expedient by which the Supplement may be made incalculably more useful to users of Grove. If they will take the trouble, once and for all, to go through the nine volumes of the fifth edition and mark with a cross or an asterisk (perhaps with the aid of a small rubber stamp) all the places for which corrections are indicated, with convenient page, column and line reference in the Supplement, they will save themselves all the further trouble of referring to it for information that may not be there. They may even like to go a little farther and mark small corrections, such as a wrong date or a misprint in the main entry, leaving only the larger *addenda* and *corrigenda* to be looked up in the new volume. I am sorry to suggest inflicting some editorial work on the owners of the fifth edition; but it is obvious that there is no way of relieving them of some small effort, which I am sure will amply be repaid by infinitely increasing the value of the Supplement.[1]

It remains for me to tender my thanks to all those who have, in greater or smaller measure, helped to make this Supplement what it is. They are so numerous that it would be utterly impossible to mention them all by name; but I am as deeply indebted to those who may only have pointed out a single mistake in a letter as to those who have very kindly sent whole lists of corrections and additional information. Among them are, of course, those marked * * in the revised list of Contributors found on pp. xi-xxxii of this volume; but there have been countless others whom I can only thank collectively but, I trust they will understand, none the less warmly.

Two voluntary collaborators, however, I must mention by name, for they have sent me an almost endless amount of information on which they must have done extremely hard and often exasperating work, all for their sheer love of and interest in Grove. They are Mr. Nicolas Slonimsky, who has given me literally hundreds of corrected dates of birth and death for musicians of all periods, all based on unassailable documentary evidence, including certificates laboriously gathered from church or municipal records all over the world; and Mr. Frank Walker, whose researches into the biographies of many old and more recent musicians, especially but not exclusively Italian, have often yielded startling new information that may be implicitly trusted. I may here add that, however disturbing some of our new dates of birth and death may appear, they may be safely accepted even against the conflicting evidence of other works of reference. True, we must allow for human fallibility in

---

[1] The more usual alternative of referring to the Supplement as a matter of course when looking up entries in the main volumes may recommend itself to some readers, especially when the required information is not at first found there, as the Supplement contains a large amount of new material.

remembering the possibility of misprints, but even that is very small, having been guarded against by checking and double-checking of proofs.

Others who have been very helpful in supplying new scholarly or factual information are Mr. Thurston Dart, Mr. Robert Donington, Mr. Donald W. MacArdle, Mr. Gilbert Reaney and Mr. Denis Stevens; these I must mention at the risk of being invidious, for many others have been almost equally assiduous. I can only assure them that they take an equal share of my gratitude.

ERIC BLOM

LONDON, 1959

CONTRIBUTORS

INCLUDING THOSE RETAINED FROM PREVIOUS EDITIONS

(Contributors marked * are new to the Fifth Edition ; those marked ** are new to the Supplement ; those marked † are deceased)

ABRAHAM, PROFESSOR GERALD, M.A., F.T.C.L.	G. A.
ABRAHAMSEN, ERIK, Ph.D.	E. A.
ALDRICH, RICHARD	R. A.
ALFONSO, FRANCISCO	F. A.
*ANDREWS, H. K., M.A., D.Mus.	H. K. A.
ANDREWS, HILDA F., D.Mus.	H. F. A.
*ANGLÈS, REV. MONSIGNOR HIGINI, Ph.D.	H. A. (ii)
ANTCLIFFE, HERBERT	H. A.
*APRAHAMIAN, FELIX	F. A. (ii)
†ARKWRIGHT, G. E. P.	G. E. P. A.
†ARMBRUSTER, CARL	C. A.
*ARNOLD, DENIS M., M.A., B.Mus.	D. M. A.
†ARNOLD, F. T.	F. T. A.
*ASHWORTH, A. H.	A. H. A.
*†AVERY, KENNETH	K. A.
BACKUS, EDYTHE N.	E. N. B.
**BAILLIE, HUGH, M.A.	H. B. (ii)
*BAINES, ANTHONY	A. B.
*BAKE, PROFESSOR ARNOLD A., M.A. (Oxon.), D.Litt. (Utrecht)	A. A. B.
*BALZER, JÜRGEN, M.A.	J. B. (ii)
*BANNER, BARBARA D., B.Mus., A.R.C.M.	B. D. B.
†BAPTIE, DAVID	D. B.
*BARBEAU, MARIUS, Ph.D.	M. B. (ii)
*BARBLAN, PROFESSOR GUGLIELMO	G. B.
*BARTLETT, K. W.	K. W. B.
BARTOŠ, JOSEF, Ph.D.	J. B.
*BATE, PHILIP A. T.	P. B.
*BECKETT, JULIAN N. F.	J. N. F. B.
†BENNETT, J. R. STERNDALE	J. R. S. B.
**BERGMANN, WALTER, Ph.D.	W. B.
†BLAIKLEY, D. J.	D. J. B.
†BLOM, ERIC, C.B.E., D.Litt., Hon. R.A.M. (Editor of the Fifth Edition)	E. B.
*BOALCH, DONALD H., M.A.	D. H. B.
*BONACCORSI, PROFESSOR ALFREDO	A. B. (ii)
†BONAVIA, FERRUCCIO	F. B.
BORREL, E.	E. B. (ii)
†BORWICK, LEONARD	L. B.
*†BOSTON, JOHN LYNN	J. L. B.
BOULT, SIR ADRIAN C., M.A., D.Mus., &c.	A. C. B.
†BOUVET, CHARLES	C. B.
**†BRAILOIU, PROFESSOR CONSTANTIN	C. B. (ii)

xi

BREHMER, REIDER, Ph.D.   .   .   .   .   .   R. B.
BRODER, NATHAN   .   .   .   .   .   .   N. B.
BROMAN, STEN .   .   .   .   S. B.
*BROWN, ARTHUR, M.A.   .   .   .   .   .   A. B. (iii)
*BROWN, MAURICE J. E.   .   .   .   .   .   M. J. E. B.
*BRYANT, RAYMOND, M.A.   .   .   .   .   .   R. B. (ii)
†BUCK, SIR PERCY C., D.Mus.   .   .   .   .   P. C. B.
†BURRELL, HON. MRS. M.   .   .   .   .   .   M. B.
†BUTLER, HUGH   .   .   .   .   .   .   H. B.
†BUTTERWORTH, GEORGE S. KAYE   .   .   .   .   G. S. K. B.

†CALVOCORESSI, M. D. .   .   .   .   .   .   M. D. C.
†CAPELL, RICHARD   .   .   .   .   .   .   R. C.
†CAPSTICK, J. W.   .   .   .   .   .   .   J. W. C.
*CARNER, MOSCO, Ph.D.   .   .   .   .   .   M. C.
**CARPITELLA, PROFESSOR DIEGO   .   .   .   .   D. C.
†CARR, MRS. WALTER .   .   .   .   .   .   M. C. C.
CARRITT, R. GRAHAM   .   .   .   .   .   R. G. C.
*†CARSE, ADAM, F.R.A.M.   .   .   .   .   .   A. C. (iii)
†CASELLA, ALFREDO   .   .   .   .   .   .   A. C. (ii)
*ČERNUŠÁK, PROFESSOR GRACIAN   .   .   .   .   G. Č.
†CHADFIELD, EDWARD .   .   .   .   .   .   E. C.
*CHAMPION, C. MAX   .   .   .   .   .   .   C. M. C.
†CHAPPELL, WILLIAM .   .   .   .   .   .   W. C.
*CHERBULIEZ, PROFESSOR ANTOINE-ÉLIE, Ph.D.   .   A.-E. C.
†CHITTY, ALEXIS   .   .   .   .   .   .   A. C.
†CHOUQUET, GUSTAVE .   .   .   .   .   .   G. C.
*CLARKE, CYRIL   .   .   .   .   .   .   C. C.
*CLIFFORD, HUBERT, D.Mus. .   .   .   .   .   H. C. (ii)
COATES, HENRY, M.A., Ph.D.   .   .   .   .   H. C.
†COBBETT, W. W.   .   .   .   .   .   .   W. W. C.
*COCHOFEL, JOÃO JOSÉ, Ph.D.   .   .   .   .   J. J. C.
*COCKS, WILLIAM A.   .   .   .   .   .   .   W. A. C.
†COLERIDGE, A. D.   .   .   .   .   .   .   A. D. C.
†COLLES, H. C., D.Mus. (Editor of the Third and Fourth
    Editions)   .   .   .   .   H. C. C.
**COLLINS, WALTER S., Ph.D. .   .   .   .   .   W. S. C.
*CORBET, AUGUST, Ph.D.   .   .   .   .   .   A. L. C.
†CORDER, FREDERICK   .   .   .   .   .   .   F. C.
*CORRÊA DE AZEVEDO, PROFESSOR L. H.   .   .   L. H. C. DE A.
*CRAUFURD, J. G.   .   .   .   .   .   .   J. G. C.
†CRAWFORD, MAJOR GEORGE ARTHUR   .   .   .   G. A. C.
CREIGHTON, T. R. M. .   .   .   .   .   .   T. R. M. C.
CREIGHTON, WALTER R.   .   .   .   .   .   W. R. C.
*CROFT, A. J. .   .   .   .   A. J. C.
*CROSSLEY-HOLLAND, PETER, M.A., B.Mus. (Oxon.)   .   P. C.-H.
*CUDWORTH, C. L.   .   .   .   .   .   .   C. L. C.
†CUMMINGS, W. H.   .   .   .   .   .   .   W. H. C.
†CUNNINGHAM, G. D., Mus.D., F.R.C.O.   .   .   G. D. C.
†CUSINS, SIR WILLIAM GEORGE   .   .   .   .   W. G. C.

*DALE, KATHLEEN   .   .   .   .   .   .   K. D.
*†DALLEY-SCARLETT, ROBERT, D.Mus.   .   .   .   R. D.-S.

DALY, WILLIAM H. . . . . . . W. H. D.
*DAMERINI, PROFESSOR ADELMO . . . . A. D. (ii)
DANIELS, H. G. . . . . . . H. G. D.
*DANNEMANN, ERNA, Ph.D. . . . . . E. D. (ii)
†DANNREUTHER, EDWARD . . . . . E. D.
*DART, THURSTON, M.A., A.R.C.M. . . . . R. T. D.
†DAVID, PAUL . . . . P. D.
†DAVIES, SIR H. WALFORD, K.C.V.O., Mus.D. . . H. W. D.
*DAVIES, JOHN H. . . . . . . J. H. D.
†DAVISON, J. W. . . . . . . J. W. D.
*DEAN, WINTON, M.A. . . . . . W. D.
DEAS, PROFESSOR STEWART . . . . . S. D.
*DELLA CORTE, PROFESSOR ANDREA . . . . A. D. C. (ii)
†DENT, PROFESSOR EDWARD J. . . . . . E. J. D.
*DEUTSCH, PROFESSOR OTTO ERICH . . . . O. E. D.
†DIX, L. M'C. L. . . . . . . L. M. L. D.
*DONINGTON, ROBERT, B.A., B.Litt. (Oxon.) . . R. D.
*DONOSTIA, REV. P. . . . . . . P. D. (ii)
DÖRFEL, ALFRED . . . . . . A. D.
DYSON, SIR GEORGE, M.A., D.Mus., LL.D. . . G. D.

EDDY, CLARENCE . . . . . . C. E.
*EDMUNDS, CHRISTOPHER, Mus.D. . . . . C. M. E.
†EDWARDS, F. G. . . . . . . F. G. E.
†EDWARDS, H. SUTHERLAND . . . . . H. S. E.
EHINGER, HANS, Ph.D. . . . . . H. E.
ELLINWOOD, LEONARD, Ph.D. . . . . L. E.
ELLISTON, THOMAS . . . . . . T. E.
ELSNER, EMILIE . . . . . . E. E. (ii)
†ENGEL, CARL . . . . C. E. (ii)
ENTHOVEN, H. E., Ph.D. . . . . . H. E. E.
ERLEBACH, RUPERT, A.R.C.M. . . . . R. E.
†EVANS, EDWIN . . . . E. E.
*EVANS, THOMAS, M.A., Mus.B. (Cantab.) . . . T. E. (ii)

*FARMER, HENRY GEORGE, Ph.D., D.Litt., Mus.D.
  (h.c.). . . . . H. G. F.
†FELLOWES, REV. EDMUND H., D.Mus., C.H. . . E. H. F.
†FERRARI, GUSTAVE . . . . . . G. F.
*FIELDEN, THOMAS P., D.Mus. . . . . T. P. F.
*FISCHER, KURT VON, Ph.D. . . . . . K. V. F.
†FITZSIMMONS, A. W. . . . . . . A. W. F.
*FLEISCHMANN, PROFESSOR ALOYS . . . . A. F. (ii)
†FLOOD, WILLIAM HENRY GRATTAN . . . . W. H. G. F.
†FORD, WALTER . . . . . . W. F.
**FORD, WYN K. . . . . . . W. K. F.
*FORTUNE, NIGEL, B.A., Mus.D. . . . . N. F. (ii)
†FOSS, HUBERT J. . . . . . . H. J. F.
†FOX STRANGWAYS, A. H., M.A. . . . . A. H. F. S.
*FRANKLYN, CHARLES A. H., M.A., M.D., M.R.C.S.,
  F.L.S., &c. . . . . C. A. H. F.
*FRASER, NORMAN . . . . . . N. F.

†Frere, Rt. Rev. Walter H. . . . . W. H. F.
†Friedländer, Max, Ph.D. . . . . . M. F.
*Fry, Allen . . . . A. F.
†Fuller-Maitland, J. A. (Editor of the Second Edition) . J. A. F.-M.

†Galpin, Rev. Canon F. W., LL.D. . . . . F. W. G.
*Gardner, B. Bellamy . . . . . B. B. G.
Gatti, Guido M. . . . . . . G. M. G.
†Gatty, Nicholas Comyn, Mus.D. . . . . N. C. G.
†Gehring, Franz, Ph.D. . . . . . F. G.
Geiringer, Professor Karl, Ph.D. . . . K. G.
*Gerson-Kiwi, Edith, Ph.D. . . . . . E. G.-K.
Gervais, Terence White . . . . . T. W. G.
*Glanville-Hicks, Peggy . . . . . P. G.-H.
Goddard, Scott . . . . . . S. G.
Godfery, Major M. van Someren . . . M. V. S. G.
**Godman, Stanley . . . . . . S. G. (ii)
*Goldbeck, Fred . . . . . . F. E. G.
*Gorer, Richard . . . . . . R. G.
*Gough, Hugh, B.Sc. (Econ.) . . . . H. G. (ii)
†Grace, Harvey, Mus.D. . . . . . H. G.
*Gradenwitz, Peter, Ph.D. . . . . . P. G.
†Graves, Charles L. . . . . . . C. L. G.
*Graves, Perceval . . . . . . P. G. (ii)
Griffith, J. C. . . . . . . J. C. G.
**Grindea, Miron . . . . . . M. G.
†Grove, Sir George (Editor of the First Edition) . G.
**Gurvin, Professor Olav, Ph.D. . . . O. G.

Haapanen, Toivo, Ph.D. . . . . T. H. (ii)
*Halfpenny, Eric . . . . . . E. H.
*Halski, Czesław R. . . . . . . C. R. H.
Hamilton, H. V. . . . . . . H. V. H.
Harding, Rosamond E. M., Ph.D. . . . R. E. M. H.
Harrison, Mrs. Robert . . . . . B. H.
*Harthan, J. P. . . . . . . J. P. H.
Hartnoll, Phyllis, M.A., L. ès L. . . . P. H.
Hasse, Karl . . . . K. H. (ii)
Haward, Lawrence W. . . . . . L. W. H.
†Hayes, Gerald, O.B.E. . . . . . G. H. (ii)
*Hedley, Arthur . . . . . . A. H. (iii)
†Helmore, Rev. T. . . . . . . T. H.
†Henderson, W. J. . . . . . . W. J. H.
†Henderson, William . . . . . W. H.
*Herbage, Julian . . . . . . J. H. (iii)
†Herbert, George . . . . . . G. H.
†Heron-Allen, E. . . . . . . E. H.-A.
†Hill, Arthur F. . . . . . . A. F. H.
Hind, Harold C., D.Mus., F.T.C.L., L.R.A.M., A.R.C.M. H. C. H.
†Hipkins, A. J. . . . . . . A. J. H.
†Hipkins, Edith J. . . . . . . E. J. H. (ii)
†Hobday, Claude . . . . . . C. H.
*Hodsdon, Alec . . . . . . A. H. (iv)

*Holland, A. K.   .   .   .   .   .   . A. K. H.
†Hopkins, Edward John   .   .   .   . E. J. H.
*Horton, John, B.A., B.Mus. (Dunelm)   .   . J. H. (ii)
*Howard, H. Michael, M.A.   .   .   .   . H. M. H.
Howes, Frank, M.A., C.B.E., F.R.C.M., Hon. R.A.M. . F. S. H.
*†Hudec, Professor Konštantín, Ph.D.   .   .   . K. H.
†Hudson, Rev. Canon T. Percy (Canon Pemberton)   . T. P. H.
†Hueffer, Francis   .   .   .   .   .   . F. H.
Hughes, Rev. Dom Anselm, O.S.B.   .   .   . A. H.
Hughes-Hughes, A. .   .   .   .   .   . A. H.-H.
†Hull, A. Eaglefield, Mus.D.   .   .   .   . A. E. H.
†Hullah, John   .   .   .   .   .   . J. H.
†Hume, Duncan   .   .   .   .   .   . D. H.
Hume, W.   .   .   .   . W. H. (ii)
*Hunt, Edgar H.   .   .   .   .   .   . E. H. H.
Hurst, Kathleen D.   .   .   .   .   . K. D. H.
†Husk, William H.   .   .   .   .   . W. H. H.
Hussey, Dyneley   .   .   .   .   . D. H. (ii)
Huth, Arno, Ph.D. .   .   .   .   .   . A. H. (ii)

*Iliff, James, B.Mus. (Lond.)   .   .   .   . J. I.
*†Irving, Ernest, Hon. R.A.M.   .   .   .   . K. E. I.

*Jackson, George Pullen, Ph.D.   .   .   . G. P. J.
*Jacob, Gordon, D.Mus., F.R.C.M., Hon. R.A.M.   . G. J.
*James, F. E. Skone, B.A., B.C.L. (Oxon.)   .   . F. E. S. J.
James, Ivor, F.R.C.M., Hon. R.A.M.   .   . I. J.
James, Philip, C.B.E. .   .   .   .   .   . P. J.
**Jeans, Susi (Lady Jeans)   .   .   .   . S. J.
†Jenks, F. H.   .   .   .   .   .   . F. H. J.
Jeppesen, Professor Knud, Ph.D.   .   .   . K. J.
†Jullien, Adolphe   .   .   .   .   . A. J.

Kalcsik, H. J.   .   .   .   .   .   . H. J. K.
†Kalisch, Alfred   .   .   .   .   . A. K.
*Karpeles, Maud   .   .   .   .   . M. K. (ii)
Kastner, Santiago .   .   .   .   .   . S. K.
*Katzarova, Professor Raina   .   .   . R. K.
*Keeler, G. A.   .   .   .   .   .   . G. A. K.
*Keller, Hans   .   .   .   .   .   . H. K. (ii)
†Kelly, Cuthbert   .   .   .   .   . C. K.
*†Kelsey, Franklyn   .   .   .   .   . F. K. (ii)
*Keys, Professor Ivor, M.A., D.Mus., F.R.C.O. .   . I. K. (ii)
†Kidson, Frank   .   .   .   .   .   . F. K.
*King, A. Hyatt, M.A.   .   .   .   .   . A. H. K.
*Kirby, Professor Percival R., M.A., D.Litt., F.R.C.M.,
     &c. .   .   .   . P. R. K.
†Klein, Herman   .   .   .   .   .   . H. K.
Knyvett, Greville L.   .   .   .   .   . G. L. K.
Kolodin, Irving   .   .   .   .   .   . I. K.
Krall, E.   .   .   .   . E. K.
†Krehbiel, H. E.   .   .   .   .   .   . H. E. K.
†Kufferath, Maurice   .   .   .   .   . M. K.

*LANGWILL, LYNDESAY G., C.A., Hon. F.T.C.L. . . L. G. L.
LE FLEM, PAUL . . . . . . P. L. F.
†LEGGE, ROBIN H. . . . . . . R. H. L.
†LEVIEN, J. MEWBURN . . . . . . J. M. L.
*LEWIS, PROFESSOR ANTHONY C., M.A., Mus.B. (Cantab.). A. C. L
†LINCOLN, H. J. . . . . . . H. J. L.
*LINDSAY, MAURICE . . . . . . M. L.
†LITCHFIELD, R. B. . . . . . . R. B. L.
*†LLOYD, LL. S., C.B., M.A. (Cantab.) . . . LL. S. L.
LOEB, SYLVIA . . . . . . S. L. (iii)
†LOEWENBERG, ALFRED, Ph.D. . . . . A. L.
*LOGAN, SINCLAIR, Mus.B., F.R.C.O. . . . S. L. (ii)
*LOPES GRAÇA, FERNANDO . . . . F. L. G.
*†LORD, HERBERT . . . . . . H. L.
†LUCAS, STANLEY . . . . . . S. L.

**MACCALLUM, FRANK K. . . . . . F. K. M.
†MACKESON, REV. CHARLES . . . . C. M.
†MACLEAN, CHARLES, D.Mus. . . . . C. M. (ii)
*†McNAUGHT, WILLIAM, B.A. (Oxon.), Hon. R.A.M. . W. M.
†MACZEWSKY, A. . . . . . . A. M.
*MAINWARING, JAMES, D.Litt., F.B.Ps.S. . . J. M. (iii)
*MANN, WILLIAM . . . . . . W. S. M.
*MARCEL-DUBOIS, CLAUDIE . . . . C. M.-D.
MARK, JEFFRY . . . . . . J. M. (ii)
†MARSHALL, JULIAN . . . . . . J. M.
†MARSHALL, MRS. JULIAN . . . . F. A. M.
†MARTINEAU, RUSSELL . . . . . . R. M.
*MASON, COLIN . . . . C. M. (iii)
†MAZZUCATO, GIANNANDREA . . . . G. M.
*MEADMORE, W. S. . . . . . . W. S. M. (i)
†MEE, REV. J. H. . . . . . . J. H. M.
*MELLERS, WILFRID H., M.A. (Cantab.) . . W. H. M.
MENGELBERG, RUDOLF . . . . R. M. (ii)
*MICHAELIDES, SOLON, Ph.D. . . . . S. M.
MIDDLETON, LOUISA . . . . . L. M. M.
†MILNE, REV. J. R. . . . . . . J. R. M.
*MOBERG, PROFESSOR CARL-ALLAN . . . C.-A. M.
MOHR, ERNST . . . . . . E. M.
*MONTAGU-NATHAN, M. . . . . . M. M.-N.
**MOORE, STEPHEN S. . . . . . S. S. M.
*MOOSER, R. ALOYS . . . . . R. A. M.
†MORRIS, R. O., D.Mus. . . . . . R. O. M.
MURRAY, D. L. . . . . . . D. L. M.
MYERS, ROLLO H. . . . . . . R. H. M.

NEGUS, V. E., F.R.C.S. . . . . V. E. N.
†NEWMARCH, ROSA . . . . . . R. N.
*NEWTON, RICHARD, M.A., B.Litt. (Oxon.) . . R. N. (ii)
*NOBLE, JEREMY . . . . . . J. N.
†NORLIND, TOBIAS, Ph.D. . . . . T. N.
NORTHCOTE, SYDNEY, Mus.D. . . . . S. N.

†Oakeley, E. M. . . . . . . E. M. O.
†Oakeley, Sir Herbert S. . . . . . H. S. O.
*Ó'Broin, Éimear, B.A., B.Mus. . . . . É. Ó'B.
Oldman, C. B., M.A., F.S.A., Hon. Mus. Doc., Edinburgh C. B. O.
*Oransay, Gültekin . . . . . . G. O.
*O'Sullivan, Donal, M.A. (Dublin), Litt.D. . . D. O'S.
†Ouseley, Rev. Sir Frederick A. Gore, Bart. . . F. A. G. O.

*Panassié, Hugues . . . . . . H. P. (iii)
*Paoli, Professor Rodolfo . . . . . R. P. (ii)
†Pardon, Sidney H. . . . . . . S. H. P.
*Parker, D. C. . . . . D. C. P.
†Parr, Henry . . . . H. P.
†Parratt, Sir Walter . . . . . W. P. (ii)
†Parry, Sir C. Hubert H., Bart. . . . . C. H. H. P.
Paucitis, K. . . . . K. P.
†Payne, Edward John . . . . . E. J. P.
†Pearson, Rev. H. . . . . . . H. P. (ii)
*Pegge, R. Morley . . . . . . R. M. P.
†Pember, Edward H. . . . . . . E. H. P.
†Pemberton, Rev. Canon T. P. (formerly Hudson) . T. P. P.
†Pereyra, Marie Louise . . . . . M. L. P.
*Perkins, Francis D. . . . . . . F. D. P.
*Pettis, Ashley . . . . . . A. P.
Phillimore, C. M. . . . . . . C. M. P.
*†Phillips, Stanley . . . . . . S. P.
*Picken, Laurence, M.A., Ph.D. . . . . L. P.
Piggott, F. . . . . F. P.
Pincherle, Marc . . . . . . M. P.
*Pine, Edward, M.A. . . . . . . E. P. (iii)
*Pirrotta, Professor Nino . . . . . N. P.
†Pohl, C. Ferdinand . . . . . . C. F. P.
†Pole, William . . . . . . W. P.
†Polonaski, E. . . . . E. P. (ii)
†Pontigny, Victor de . . . . . v. de P.
†Poole, Reginald Lane . . . . . R. L. P.
*Porter, Maurice M. . . . . . M. M. P.
*Priestley, Rachel . . . . . . R. P.
**Priestman, Brian . . . . . . B. P.
*Pritchard, T. C. L., M.A., Mus.D. . . . T. C. L. P.
†Prod'homme, J. G. . . . . . J. G. P.
†Prout, Ebenezer, D.Mus. . . . . E. P.
*Prynne, Col. Michael W., O.B.E., R.E. . . . M. W. P.
†Pulling, Rev. W. . . . . . . W. P. (iii)
†Purday, Charles H. . . . . . . C. H. P.

†Racster, Olga (Baroness Olga de Wagstaffe) . . O. R.
*Radcliffe, Philip F., M.A., Mus.B. . . . P. F. R.
Raugel, Félix . . . . . . F. R.
*Ravell, John . . . . J. R.
**Reaney, Gilbert, M.A. . . . . . G. R. (iii)
Redlich, Hans F., Ph.D. . . . . . H. F. R.
†Reed, William Henry . . . . . W. H. R.

b

REESE, GUSTAVE	G. R.
REICH, WILLI, Ph.D.	W. R.
REISS, PROFESSOR JÓZEF W.	J. W. R.
*†RENDALL, F. G., M.A., F.S.A.	F. G. R.
†RICCI, LUIGI	L. R.
RICE, EDWARD H.	E. H. R.
*RICHARDSON, E. G., B.A., Ph.D., D.Sc.	E. G. R.
*RIHTMAN, PROFESSOR CVJETKO	C. R.
†RIMBAULT, EDWARD F.	E. F. R.
†RIZZELLI, F.	F. R. (ii)
*ROBERTSON, A. E., B.Sc., A.M.I.E.E.	A. E. R.
*ROBERTSON, ALEC, F.R.A.M.	A. R. (ii)
†ROCKSTRO, W. S.	W. S. R.
ROGER, KURT, Ph.D.	K. R.
*†ROKSETH, PROFESSOR YVONNE	Y. R.
*RONCAGLIA, PROFESSOR GINO	G. R. (ii)
**ROSENTHAL, HAROLD	H. D. R.
*ROY, LÉO	L. R. (ii)
RUDGE, OLGA	O. R. (ii)
*†RUDNEV, PROFESSOR ANDREJ	A. R.
*RUSSELL, JOHN F.	J. F. R.
*RUSSELL, RAYMOND	R. R.
*RUTHERFORD, KENNETH	K. S. R.
*RUTZ, HANS	H. R.
SAMAZEUILH, GUSTAVE	G. S.
*SANDS, MOLLIE	M. S. (ii)
*SANDVIK, O. M., Ph.D.	O. M. S.
*SARTORI, PROFESSOR CLAUDIO	C. S. (iii)
*SAYGUN, PROFESSOR A. ADNAN	A. A. S. (ii)
SCHAEFFER, MYRON	M. S.
*SCHIØRRING, NILS, Ph.D.	N. S. (ii)
**SCHJELDERUP-EBBE, DAG	D. S.-E.
*†SCHOLES, PERCY A., M.A., O.B.E., D.Litt., Hon. D.Mus. (Oxon.)	P. A. S.
†SCOTT, MARION M., A.R.C.M.	M. M. S.
**SEAMAN, GERALD	G. S. (ii)
SEARLE, HUMPHREY	H. S. (ii)
*SEEGER, CHARLES, A.D. (Harvard)	C. S. (ii)
SHAW, HAROLD WATKINS, M.A.	H. W. S.
SHAWE-TAYLOR, DESMOND	D. S.-T.
*†SHERA, F. H., M.A., Mus.M. (Cantab.), Emeritus Professor (Sheffield)	F. H. S.
*†SHINN, FREDERICK GEORGE, D.Mus. (Dunelm), F.R.C.O., F.R.C.M., Hon. R.A.M.	F. G. S.
SIEBER, P. O., Ph.D.	P. O. S.
†SIGTENHORST MEYER, BERNARD VAN DEN	B. v. d. s. m.
SINCLAIR, HON. MRS.	G. A. S.
SLONIMSKY, NICOLAS	N. S.
†SMIJERS, PROFESSOR A. A.	A. A. S.
*SMITH, CARLETON SPRAGUE, Ph.D.	C. S. S.
SMITH, WARREN STOREY	W. S. S.
*SMITH, WILLIAM C.	W. C. S.
*SMOLDON, WILLIAM L., Ph.D., B.Mus., F.T.C.L.	W. L. S.

SMYTHE, BARBARA . . . . . . B. S.
*SOCIETY FOR CULTURAL RELATIONS WITH THE U.S.S.R. . S.C.R.
†SONNECK, O. G. . . . . . . O. G. S.
†ŠOUREK, OTAKAR, Dr. Ing. . . . . . O. Š.
†SOUTHGATE, T. L. . . . . . . T. L. S.
SPALDING, PROFESSOR WALTER R. . . . . W. R. S.
**SPINK, IAN, B.Mus., F.T.C.L. . . . . I. S.
†SPITTA, PHILIPP . . . . . . P. S.
SPURLING, S. J. . . . . . . S. J. S.
†SQUIRE, WILLIAM BARCLAY . . . . . W. B. S.
†STAINER, C. . . . . C. S.
†STAINER, SIR JOHN . . . . . . J. S.
†STAINER, J. F. R. . . . . . . J. F. R. S.
*STANTON, PROFESSOR W. K., M.A., D.Mus. (Oxon.) . W. K. S.
*STARKIE, PROFESSOR WALTER, C.B.E., Litt.D. . . W. S.
†STARMER, W. W. . . . . . . W. W. S.
*STEGMANN, G. F. . . . . . . G. F. S.
*STEVENS, DENIS W., M.A. (Oxon.), F.S.A. . . . D. W. S.
*STEVENS, JOHN, M.A. (Cantab.) . . . . J. S. (ii)
STEVENSON, E. IRENAEUS PRIME . . . . E. I. P. S.
*STEVENSON, ROBERT, Ph.D. . . . . R. S.
†STEWART, SIR ROBERT P. . . . . . R. P. S.
*STOCK, W. H. . . . . W. H. S. (ii)
†STONE, WILLIAM H. . . . . . . W. H. S.
†STRAETEN, E. VAN DER . . . . . E. v. d. s.
†STREATFEILD, R. A. . . . . . . R. A. S.
STROBEL, HEINRICH . . . . . . H. S.
*STURLEY, K. R., Ph.D., M.I.E.E. . . . . K. R. S.
*SUMNER, W. L., D.Sc. . . . . . W. L. S. (ii)
*SWAN, PROFESSOR ALFRED J. . . . . . A. S.

*TAYLOR, ERIC R., B.Mus., M.A. (Oxon.) . . . E. R. T.
†TAYLOR, FRANKLIN . . . . . . F. T.
*TAYLOR, KENDALL . . . . . . K. T.
†TERRY, CHARLES SANFORD . . . . . C. S. T.
*TERRY, WALTER, B.A. . . . . . W. T.
†TESSIER, ANDRÉ . . . . . . A. T.
†THAYER, ALEXANDER WHEELOCK . . . . A. W. T.
THISTLETON, FRANK . . . . . . F. T. (iii)
THOMAS, BERTHA . . . . . . B. T.
*THOMAS, JUAN MARÍA . . . . . J. M. T.
*THOMPSON-ALLEN, AUBREY, F.I.S.O.B., F.I.M.I.T. . A. T.-A.
†THOMPSON, HERBERT, D.Litt. . . . . H. T.
*THORNTON-PETT, PETER . . . . . P. T.-P.
†TIBY, PROFESSOR OTTAVIO . . . . . O. T.
TILLYARD, PROFESSOR H. JULIUS W., D.Litt. . . H. J. W. T.
*TOOZE, JOHN . . . . J. T.
TOYE, FRANCIS, C.B.E. . . . . . F. T. (ii)
*TRACEY, HUGH T. . . . . . . H. T. T.
†TREND, PROFESSOR J. B. . . . . . J. B. T.

VALERA, TERRY DE . . . . . . T. de V.
†VALLAS, LÉON . . . . L. V.
†VAUGHAN WILLIAMS, RALPH, Mus.D., O.M. . . R. V. W.

Vešelý, Richard . . . . . . R. V.
Vetterl, Karel, Ph.D. . . . . . K. V.

*Wailes, Marylin . . . . . . M. W.
*Wakeling, Donald R. . . . . D. R. W.
†Walker, Ernest, D.Mus. . . . . . E. W.
*Walker, Frank . . . . . . F. W. (ii)
†Wallace, William . . . . . . W. W.
†Walrond, S. H. . . . . . . S. H. W.
*Ward, Martha Kingdon . . . . M. K. W.
Warner, Sylvia Townsend . . . . . S. T. W.
Watson, Edward . . . . . . E. W. (ii)
†Webb, P. G. L. . . . . . . P. G. L. W.
*Weissmann, John S. . . . . . J. S. W.
Wellesz, Egon, C.B.E., M.A. (Oxon.), D.Mus.
　(h.c. Oxon.) . . . . E. J. W.
*Werner, Professor Eric, Ph.D. . . . E. W. (iii)
†Westlake, Frederick . . . . . F. W.
Westrup, Professor J. A., D.Mus. . . . J. A. W.
*Whates, Harold R. G. . . . . . H. R. G. W.
Whitehead, H. A. . . . . . . H. A. W.
†Whitehouse, W. E. . . . . . . W. E. W.
*†Whitworth, Reginald, M.B.E. . . . R. W.
†Williams, C. F. Abdy . . . . . C. F. A. W.
Willsher, Harry M., M.A., D.Litt. . . . H. M. W.
†Wilson, C. W. . . . . . . C. W. W.
*Winnington-Ingram, Professor R. P., M.A. . R. P. W.-I.
Winsor, Curtin . . . . . . C. W.
*Wiora, Professor Walter, Ph.D. . . . W. W. (ii)
†Wodehouse, Mrs. Edmund . . . . A. H. W.
†Wood, J. Muir . . . . . . J. M. W.
†Wooldridge, H. E. . . . . . . H. E. W.
*Worsthorne, Simon Towneley, M.A., D.Phil. . S. T. W. (ii)
†Wyndham, H. Saxe . . . . . . H. S. W.

*Young, Percy M., M.A., Mus.D. . . . P. M. Y.
*Young, Robert W., B.Sc., Ph.D. . . . R. W. Y.

*Zoder, Professor Raimund . . . . . R. Z.

CONTRIBUTORS
ALPHABETICAL LIST OF INITIALS BY WHICH
THEIR ARTICLES ARE SIGNED

(For degrees and titles see the list of surnames)

A. A. B.	Arnold A. Bake
A. A. S.	A. A. Smijers
A. A. S. (ii)	A. Adnan Saygun
A. B.	Anthony Baines
A. B. (ii)	Alfredo Bonaccorsi
A. B. (iii)	Arthur Brown
A. C.	Alexis Chitty
A. C. (ii)	Alfredo Casella
A. C. (iii)	Adam Carse
A. C. B.	Adrian C. Boult
A. C. L.	Anthony C. Lewis
A. D.	Alfred Dörfel
A. D. (ii)	Adelmo Damerini
A. D. C.	A. D. Coleridge
A. D. C. (ii)	Andrea Della Corte
A.-E. C.	Antoine-Élie Cherbuliez
A. E. H.	A. Eaglefield Hull
A. E. R.	A. E. Robertson
A. F.	Allen Fry
A. F. (ii)	Aloys Fleischmann
A. F. H.	Arthur F. Hill
A. H.	Anselm Hughes
A. H. (ii)	Arno Huth
A. H. (iii)	Arthur Hedley
A. H. (iv)	Alec Hodsdon
A. H. A.	A. H. Ashworth
A. H. F. S.	A. H. Fox Strangways
A. H.-H.	A. Hughes-Hughes
A. H. K.	A. Hyatt King
A. H. W.	Mrs. Edmund Wodehouse
A. J.	Adolphe Jullien
A. J. C.	A. J. Croft
A. J. H.	A. J. Hipkins
A. K.	Alfred Kalisch
A. K. H.	A. K. Holland
A. L.	Alfred Loewenberg
A. L. C.	August Corbet
A. M.	A. Maczewsky
A. P.	Ashley Pettis
A. R.	Andrej Rudnev
A. R. (ii)	Alec Robertson
A. S.	Alfred J. Swan
A. T.	André Tessier
A. T.-A.	Aubrey Thompson-Allen

A. W. F.	A. W. Fitzsimmons
A. W. T.	Alexander Wheelock Thayer
B. B. G.	B. Bellamy Gardner
B. D. B.	Barbara D. Banner
B. H.	Mrs. Robert Harrison
B. P.	Brian Priestman
B. S.	Barbara Smythe
B. T.	Bertha Thomas
B. v. d. s. m.	Bernard van den Sigtenhorst Meyer
C. A.	Carl Armbruster
C. A. H. F.	Charles A. H. Franklyn
C.-A. M.	Carl-Allan Moberg
C. B.	Charles Bouvet
C. B. (ii)	Constantin Brailoiu
C. B. O.	C. B. Oldman
C. C.	Cyril Clarke
C. E.	Clarence Eddy
C. E. (ii)	Carl Engel
C. F. A. W.	C. F. Abdy Williams
C. F. P.	Carl Ferdinand Pohl
C. H.	Claude Hobday
C. H. H. P.	C. Hubert H. Parry
C. H. P.	Charles H. Purday
C. K.	Cuthbert Kelly
C. L. C.	C. L. Cudworth
C. L. G.	Charles L. Graves
C. M.	Charles Mackeson
C. M. (ii)	Charles Maclean
C. M. (iii)	Colin Mason
C. M. C.	C. Max Champion
C. M.-D.	Claudie Marcel-Dubois
C. M. E.	Christopher Edmunds
C. M. P.	C. M. Phillimore
C. R.	Cvjetko Rihtman
C. R. H.	Czesław R. Halski
C. S.	C. Stainer
C. S. (ii)	Charles Seeger
C. S. (iii)	Claudio Sartori
C. S. S.	Carleton Sprague Smith
C. S. T.	Charles Sanford Terry
C. W.	Curtin Winsor
C. W. W.	C. W. Wilson
D. B.	David Baptie
D. C.	Diego Carpitella
D. C. P.	D. C. Parker
D. H.	Duncan Hume
D. H. (ii)	Dyneley Hussey
D. H. B.	Donald H. Boalch

D. J. B.	D. J. Blaikley
D. L. M.	D. L. Murray
D. M. A.	Denis M. Arnold
D. O'S.	Donal O'Sullivan
D. R. W.	Donald R. Wakeling
D. S.-E.	Dag Schjelderup-Ebbe
D. S.-T.	Desmond Shawe-Taylor
D. W. S.	Denis W. Stevens
E. A.	Erik Abrahamsen
E. B.	Eric Blom
E. B. (ii)	E. Borrel
E. C.	Edward Chadfield
E. D.	Edward Dannreuther
E. D. (ii)	Erna Dannemann
E. E.	Edwin Evans
E. E. (ii)	Emilie Elsner
E. F. R.	Edward F. Rimbault
E. G.-K.	Edith Gerson-Kiwi
E. G. R.	E. G. Richardson
E. H.	Eric Halfpenny
E. H.-A.	E. Heron-Allen
E. H. F.	Edmund H. Fellowes
E. H. H.	Edgar H. Hunt
E. H. P.	Edward H. Pember
E. H. R.	Edward H. Rice
E. I. P. S.	E. Irenaeus Prime Stevenson
E. J. D.	Edward J. Dent
E. J. H.	Edward John Hopkins
E. J. H. (ii)	Edith J. Hipkins
E. J. P.	Edward John Payne
E. J. W.	Egon Wellesz
E. K.	E. Krall
E. M.	Ernst Mohr
E. M. O.	E. M. Oakeley
E. N. B.	Edythe N. Backus
É. Ó'B.	Éimear Ó'Broin
E. P.	Ebenezer Prout
E. P. (ii)	E. Polonaski
E. P. (iii)	Edward Pine
E. R. T.	Eric R. Taylor
E. v. d. s.	E. van der Straeten
E. W.	Ernest Walker
E. W. (ii)	Edward Watson
E. W. (iii)	Eric Werner
F. A.	Francisco Alfonso
F. A. (ii)	Felix Aprahamian
F. A. G. O.	Frederick A. Gore Ouseley
F. A. M.	Mrs. Julian Marshall
F. B.	Ferruccio Bonavia
F. C.	Frederick Corder
F. D. P.	Francis D. Perkins

F. E. G.	FRED GOLDBECK
F. E. S. J.	F. E. SKONE JAMES
F. G.	FRANZ GEHRING
F. G. E.	F. G. EDWARDS
F. G. R.	F. G. RENDALL
F. G. S.	FREDERICK GEORGE SHINN
F. H.	FRANCIS HUEFFER
F. H. J.	F. H. JENKS
F. H. S.	F. H. SHERA
F. K.	FRANK KIDSON
F. K. (ii)	FRANKLYN KELSEY
F. K. M.	FRANK K. MACCALLUM
F. L. G.	FERNANDO LOPES GRAÇA
F. P.	F. PIGGOTT
F. R.	FÉLIX RAUGEL
F. R. (ii)	F. RIZZELLI
F. S. H.	FRANK HOWES
F. T.	FRANKLIN TAYLOR
F. T. (ii)	FRANCIS TOYE
F. T. (iii)	FRANK THISTLETON
F. T. A.	F. T. ARNOLD
F. W.	FREDERICK WESTLAKE
F. W. (ii)	FRANK WALKER
F. W. G.	F. W. GALPIN

G.	GEORGE GROVE
G. A.	GERALD ABRAHAM
G. A. C.	GEORGE ARTHUR CRAWFORD
G. A. K.	G. A. KEELER
G. A. S.	HON. MRS. SINCLAIR
G. B.	GUGLIELMO BARBLAN
G. C.	GUSTAVE CHOUQUET
G. Č.	GRACIAN ČERNUŠÁK
G. D.	GEORGE DYSON
G. D. C.	G. D. CUNNINGHAM
G. E. P. A.	G. E. P. ARKWRIGHT
G. F.	GUSTAVE FERRARI
G. F. S.	G. F. STEGMANN
G. H.	GEORGE HERBERT
G. H. (ii)	GERALD HAYES
G. J.	GORDON JACOB
G. L. K.	GREVILLE L. KNYVETT
G. M.	GIANNANDREA MAZZUCATO
G. M. G.	GUIDO M. GATTI
G. O.	GÜLTEKIN ORANSAY
G. P. J.	GEORGE PULLEN JACKSON
G. R.	GUSTAVE REESE
G. R. (ii)	GINO RONCAGLIA
G. R. (iii)	GILBERT REANEY
G. S.	GUSTAVE SAMAZEUILH
G. S. (ii)	GERALD SEAMAN
G. S. K. B.	GEORGE S. KAYE BUTTERWORTH

H. A.	. . . . .	HERBERT ANTCLIFFE
H. A. (ii) .	. . . .	HIGINI ANGLÈS
H. A. W. .	. . . .	H. A. WHITEHEAD
H. B.	. . . .	HUGH BUTLER
H. B. (ii) .	. . . .	HUGH BAILLIE
H. C.	. . . .	HENRY COATES
H. C. (ii) .	. . . .	HUBERT CLIFFORD
H. C. C. .	. . . .	H. C. COLLES
H. C. H. .	. . . .	HAROLD C. HIND
H. D. R. .	. . . .	HAROLD ROSENTHAL
H. E.	. . . .	HANS EHINGER
H. E. E. .	. . . .	H. E. ENTHOVEN
H. E. K. .	. . . .	H. E. KREHBIEL
H. E. W. .	. . . .	H. E. WOOLDRIDGE
H. F. A. .	. . . .	HILDA F. ANDREWS
H. F. R. .	. . . .	HANS F. REDLICH
H. G.	. . . .	HARVEY GRACE
H. G. (ii) .	. . . .	HUGH GOUGH
H. G. D. .	. . . .	H. G. DANIELS
H. G. F. .	. . . .	HENRY GEORGE FARMER
H. J. F. .	. . . .	HUBERT J. FOSS
H. J. K. .	. . . .	H. J. KALCSIK
H. J. L. .	. . . .	H. J. LINCOLN
H. J. W. T.	. . . .	H. JULIUS W. TILLYARD
H. K.	. . . .	HERMAN KLEIN
H. K. (ii) .	. . . .	HANS KELLER
H. K. A. .	. . . .	H. K. ANDREWS
H. L.	. . . .	HERBERT LORD
H. M. H. .	. . . .	H. MICHAEL HOWARD
H. M. W. .	. . . .	HARRY M. WILLSHER
H. P.	. . . .	HENRY PARR
H. P. (ii) .	. . . .	H. PEARSON
H. P. (iii)	. . . .	HUGUES PANASSIÉ
H. R.	. . . .	HANS RUTZ
H. R. G. W.	. . . .	HAROLD R. G. WHATES
H. S.	. . . .	HEINRICH STROBEL
H. S. (ii) .	. . . .	HUMPHREY SEARLE
H. S. E. .	. . . .	H. SUTHERLAND EDWARDS
H. S. O. .	. . . .	HERBERT S. OAKELEY
H. S. W. .	. . . .	H. SAXE WYNDHAM
H. T.	. . . .	HERBERT THOMPSON
H. T. T. .	. . . .	HUGH TRACEY
H. V. H. .	. . . .	H. V. HAMILTON
H. W. D. .	. . . .	H. WALFORD DAVIES
H. W. S. .	. . . .	HAROLD WATKINS SHAW
I. J.	. . . .	IVOR JAMES
I. K.	. . . .	IRVING KOLODIN
I. K. (ii) .	. . . .	IVOR KEYS
I. S.	. . . .	IAN SPINK
J. A. F.-M.	. . . .	J. A. FULLER-MAITLAND
J. A. W. .	. . . .	J. A. WESTRUP
J. B.	. . . .	JOSEF BARTOŠ

J. B. (ii)	.	.	.	.	JÜRGEN BALZER
J. B. T.	.	.	.	.	J. B. TREND
J. C. G.	.	.	.	.	J. C. GRIFFITH
J. F. R.	.	.	.	.	JOHN F. RUSSELL
J. F. R. S.	.	.	.	.	J. F. R. STAINER
J. G. C.	.	.	.	.	J. G. CRAUFURD
J. G. P.	.	.	.	.	J. G. PROD'HOMME
J. H.	.	.	.	.	JOHN HULLAH
J. H. (ii)	.	.	.	.	JOHN HORTON
J. H. (iii)	.	.	.	.	JULIAN HERBAGE
J. H. D.	.	.	.	.	JOHN H. DAVIES
J. H. M.	.	.	.	.	J. H. MEE
J. I.	.	.	.	.	JAMES ILIFF
J. J. C.	.	.	.	.	JOÃO JOSÉ COCHOFEL
J. L. B.	.	.	.	.	JOHN L. BOSTON
J. M.	.	.	.	.	JULIAN MARSHALL
J. M. (ii)	.	.	.	.	JEFFRY MARK
J. M. (iii)	.	.	.	.	JAMES MAINWARING
J. M. L.	.	.	.	.	J. MEWBURN LEVIEN
J. M. T.	.	.	.	.	JUAN MARÍA THOMAS
J. M. W.	.	.	.	.	J. MUIR WOOD
J. N.	.	.	.	.	JEREMY NOBLE
J. N. F. B.	.	.	.	.	JULIAN N. F. BECKETT
J. P. H.	.	.	.	.	J. P. HARTHAN
J. R.	.	.	.	.	JOHN RAVELL
J. R. M.	.	.	.	.	J. R. MILNE
J. R. S. B.	.	.	.	.	J. R. STERNDALE BENNETT
J. S.	.	.	.	.	JOHN STAINER
J. S. (ii)	.	.	.	.	JOHN STEVENS
J. S. W.	.	.	.	.	JOHN S. WEISSMANN
J. T.	.	.	.	.	JOHN TOOZE
J. W. C.	.	.	.	.	J. W. CAPSTICK
J. W. D.	.	.	.	.	J. W. DAVISON
J. W. R.	.	.	.	.	JÓZEF W. REISS
K. A.	.	.	.	.	KENNETH AVERY
K. D.	.	.	.	.	KATHLEEN DALE
K. D. H.	.	.	.	.	KATHLEEN D. HURST
K. E. I.	.	.	.	.	ERNEST IRVING
K. G.	.	.	.	.	KARL GEIRINGER
K. H.	.	.	.	.	KONŠTANTÍN HUDEC
K. H. (ii)	.	.	.	.	KARL HASSE
K. J.	.	.	.	.	KNUD JEPPESEN
K. P.	.	.	.	.	K. PAUCITIS
K. R.	.	.	.	.	KURT ROGER
K. R. S.	.	.	.	.	K. R. STURLEY
K. S. R.	.	.	.	.	KENNETH RUTHERFORD
K. T.	.	.	.	.	KENDALL TAYLOR
K. V.	.	.	.	.	KARL VETTERL
K. V. F.	.	.	.	.	KURT VON FISCHER
K. W. B.	.	.	.	.	K. W. BARTLETT
L. B.	.	.	.	.	LEONARD BORWICK
L. E.	.	.	.	.	LEONARD ELLINWOOD

L. G. L.	LYNDESAY G. LANGWILL
L. H. C. de A.	L. H. CORRÊA DE AZEVEDO
LL. S. L.	LL. S. LLOYD
L. M. L. D.	L. M'C. L. DIX
L. M. M.	LOUISA MIDDLETON
L. P.	LAURENCE PICKEN
L. R.	LUIGI RICCI
L. R. (ii)	LÉO ROY
L. V.	LÉON VALLAS
L. W. H.	LAWRENCE W. HAWARD
M. B.	HON. MRS. M. BURRELL
M. B. (ii)	MARIUS BARBEAU
M. C.	MOSCO CARNER
M. C. C.	MRS. WALTER CARR
M. D. C.	M. D. CALVOCORESSI
M. F.	MAX FRIEDLÄNDER
M. G.	MIRON GRINDEA
M. J. E. B.	MAURICE J. E. BROWN
M. K.	MAURICE KUFFERATH
M. K. (ii)	MAUD KARPELES
M. K. W.	MARTHA KINGDON WARD
M. L.	MAURICE LINDSAY
M. L. P.	MARIE LOUISE PEREYRA
M. M. N.	M. MONTAGU-NATHAN
M. M. P.	MAURICE M. PORTER
M. M. S.	MARION M. SCOTT
M. P.	MARC PINCHERLE
M. S.	MYRON SCHAEFFER
M. S. (ii)	MOLLIE SANDS
M. V. S. G.	M. VAN SOMEREN GODFERY
M. W.	MARYLIN WAILES
M. W. P.	MICHAEL W. PRYNNE
N. B.	NATHAN BRODER
N. C. G.	NICHOLAS COMYN GATTY
N. F.	NORMAN FRASER
N. F. (ii)	NIGEL FORTUNE
N. P.	NINO PIRROTTA
N. S.	NICOLAS SLONIMSKY
N. S. (ii)	NILS SCHIØRRING
O. E. D.	OTTO ERICH DEUTSCH
O. G.	OLAV GURVIN
O. G. S.	O. G. SONNECK
O. M. S.	O. M. SANDVIK
O. R.	OLGA RACSTER
O. R. (ii)	OLGA RUDGE
O. Š.	OTAKAR ŠOUREK
O. T.	OTTAVIO TIBY
P. A. S.	PERCY A. SCHOLES
P. B.	PHILIP BATE
P. C. B.	PERCY C. BUCK
P. C.-H.	PETER CROSSLEY-HOLLAND

P. D.	PAUL DAVID
P. D. (ii)	P. DONOSTIA
P. F. R.	PHILIP F. RADCLIFFE
P. G.	PETER GRADENWITZ
P. G. (ii)	PERCEVAL GRAVES
P. G.-H.	PEGGY GLANVILLE-HICKS
P. G. L. W.	P. G. L. WEBB
P. H.	PHYLLIS HARTNOLL
P. J.	PHILIP JAMES
P. L. F.	PAUL LE FLEM
P. M. Y.	PERCY M. YOUNG
P. O. S.	P. O. SIEBER
P. R. K.	PERCIVAL R. KIRBY
P. S.	PHILIPP SPITTA
P. T.-P.	PETER THORNTON-PETT
R. A.	RICHARD ALDRICH
R. A. M.	R. ALOYS MOOSER
R. A. S.	R. A. STREATFEILD
R. B.	REIDER BREHMER
R. B. (ii)	RAYMOND BRYANT
R. B. L.	R. B. LITCHFIELD
R. C.	RICHARD CAPELL
R. D.	ROBERT DONINGTON
R. D.-S.	ROBERT DALLEY-SCARLETT
R. E.	RUPERT ERLEBACH
R. E. M. H.	ROSAMOND E. M. HARDING
R. G.	RICHARD GORER
R. G. C.	R. GRAHAM CARRITT
R. H. L.	ROBIN H. LEGGE
R. H. M.	ROLLO H. MYERS
R. K.	RAINA KATZAROVA
R. L. P.	REGINALD LANE POOLE
R. M.	RUSSELL MARTINEAU
R. M. (ii)	RUDOLF MENGELBERG
R. M. P.	R. MORLEY PEGGE
R. N.	ROSA NEWMARCH
R. N. (ii)	RICHARD NEWTON
R. O. M.	R. O. MORRIS
R. P.	RACHEL PRIESTLEY
R. P. (ii)	RODOLFO PAOLI
R. P. S.	ROBERT P. STEWART
R. P. W.-I.	R. P. WINNINGTON-INGRAM
R. R.	RAYMOND RUSSELL
R. S.	ROBERT STEVENSON
R. T. D.	THURSTON DART
R. V.	RICHARD VEŠELY
R. V. W.	RALPH VAUGHAN WILLIAMS
R. W.	REGINALD WHITWORTH
R. W. Y.	ROBERT W. YOUNG
R. Z.	RAIMUND ZODER
S. B.	STEN BROMAN
S.C.R.	SOCIETY FOR CULTURAL RELATIONS WITH THE U.S.S.R.

S. D.	.	.	.	. STEWART DEAS
S. G.	.	.	.	. SCOTT GODDARD
S. G. (ii) .	.	.	.	. STANLEY GODMAN
S. H. P.	.	.	.	. SIDNEY H. PARDON
S. H. W.	.	.	.	. S. H. WALROND
S. J.	.	.	.	. SUSI JEANS (LADY JEANS)
S. J. S.	.	.	.	. S. J. SPURLING
S. K.	.	.	.	. SANTIAGO KASTNER
S. L.	.	.	.	. STANLEY LUCAS
S. L. (ii) .	.	.	.	. SINCLAIR LOGAN
S. L. (iii) .	.	.	.	. SYLVIA LOEB
S. M.	.	.	.	. SOLON MICHAELIDES
S. N.	.	.	.	. SYDNEY NORTHCOTE
S. P.	.	.	.	. STANLEY PHILLIPS
S. S. M.	.	.	.	. STEPHEN S. MOORE
S. T. W.	.	.	.	. SYLVIA TOWNSEND WARNER
S. T. W. (ii)	.	.	.	. SIMON TOWNELEY WORSTHORNE

T. C. L. P.	.	.	.	. T. C. L. PRITCHARD
T. de V.	.	.	.	. TERRY DE VALERA
T. E.	.	.	.	. THOMAS ELLISTON
T. E. (ii) .	.	.	.	. THOMAS EVANS
T. H.	.	.	.	. T. HELMORE
T. H. (ii) .	.	.	.	. TOIVO HAAPANEN
T. L. S.	.	.	.	. T. L. SOUTHGATE
T. N.	.	.	.	. TOBIAS NORLIND
T. P. F.	.	.	.	. THOMAS P. FIELDEN
T. P. H.	.	.	.	. T. PERCY HUDSON
				(Canon Pemberton)
T. P. P.	.	.	.	. T. P. PEMBERTON
				(formerly Hudson)
T. R. M. C.	.	.	.	. T. R. M. CREIGHTON
T. W. G.	.	.	.	. TERENCE WHITE GERVAIS

V. de P.	.	.	.	. VICTOR DE PONTIGNY
V. E. N.	.	.	.	. V. E. NEGUS

W. A. C.	.	.	.	. WILLIAM A. COCKS
W. B.	.	.	.	. WALTER BERGMANN
W. B. S.	.	.	.	. WILLIAM BARCLAY SQUIRE
W. C.	.	.	.	. WILLIAM CHAPPELL
W. C. S.	.	.	.	. WILLIAM C. SMITH
W. D.	.	.	.	. WINTON DEAN
W. E. W.	.	.	.	. W. E. WHITEHOUSE
W. F.	.	.	.	. WALTER FORD
W. G. C.	.	.	.	. WILLIAM GEORGE CUSINS
W. H.	.	.	.	. WILLIAM HENDERSON
W. H. (ii)	.	.	.	. W. HUME
W. H. C.	.	.	.	. W. H. CUMMINGS
W. H. D.	.	.	.	. WILLIAM H. DALY
W. H. F.	.	.	.	. WALTER H. FRERE
W. H. G. F.	.	.	.	. WILLIAM HENRY GRATTAN FLOOD
W. H. H.	.	.	.	. WILLIAM H. HUSK
W. H. M.	.	.	.	. WILFRID H. MELLERS

W. H. R.	WILLIAM HENRY REED
W. H. S.	WILLIAM H. STONE
W. H. S. (ii)	W. H. STOCK
W. J. H.	W. J. HENDERSON
W. K. F.	WYN K. FORD
W. K. S.	W. K. STANTON
W. L. S.	WILLIAM L. SMOLDON
W. L. S. (ii)	W. L. SUMNER
W. M.	WILLIAM McNAUGHT
W. P.	WILLIAM POLE
W. P. (ii)	WALTER PARRATT
W. P. (iii)	W. PULLING
W. R.	WILLI REICH
W. R. C.	WALTER R. CREIGHTON
W. R. S.	WALTER R. SPALDING
W. S.	WALTER STARKIE
W. S. C.	WALTER S. COLLINS
W. S. M.	WILLIAM S. MANN
W. S. M. (ii)	W. S. MEADMORE
W. S. R.	W. S. ROCKSTRO
W. S. S.	WARREN STOREY SMITH
W. T.	WALTER TERRY
W. W.	WILLIAM WALLACE
W. W. (ii)	WALTER WIORA
W. W. C.	W. W. COBBETT
W. W. S.	W. W. STARMER
Y. R.	YVONNE ROKSETH

ABBREVIATIONS

A.B.A.	. .	' Altbachisches Archiv '
A.M.F.	. .	' Archiv für Musikforschung '
A.M.W.	. .	' Archiv für Musikwissenschaft '
A.M.Z.	. .	' Allgemeine musikalische Zeitung '
A.R.C.M.	. .	Associate of the Royal College of Music
B. & H.	. .	Breitkopf & Härtel
B.-G..	. .	Bach-Gesellschaft (collected edition of J. S. Bach's works)
B.J.-B.	. .	' Bach-Jahrbuch '
B.M..	. .	British Museum
B.M.S. Ann.	.	British Musical Society's Annual
Baldwin	. .	Commonplace Book of John Baldwin
Barnard	. .	First Book of Selected Church Music, ed. by John Barnard, 1641
Bibl. Nat.	. .	Bibliothèque Nationale, Paris
Bodl. Lib.	. .	Bodleian Library, Oxford
Bodl. Mus. Sch.	.	Oxford Music School Collection (now in the Bodleian Library)
C.B.E.	. .	Commander of the British Empire
C.U.P.	. .	Cambridge University Press
Caius.	. .	Caius College, Cambridge
Ch. Ch.	. .	Christ Church, Oxford
Ch. Ch. O.B.	.	Organ Book at Christ Church, Oxford
Corp. Script. Mus..		' Corpus Scriptorum de Musica '
D.B.E.	. .	Dame of the British Empire
D.T.B.	. .	' Denkmäler der Tonkunst in Bayern '
D.D.T.	. .	' Denkmäler deutscher Tonkunst '
D.N.B.	. .	' Dictionary of National Biography '
D.T.Ö.	. .	' Denkmäler der Tonkunst in Österreich '
Durh.	. .	Durham Cathedral
Ely .	. .	Ely Cathedral
F.R.C.O.	. .	Fellow of the Royal College of Organists
Fétis .	. .	Fétis's ' Biographie universelle ' (with Supplement)
Fitzw.	. .	Fitzwilliam Library, Cambridge
G.S.M.	. .	Guildhall School of Music, London
Harl.	. .	Harleian Manuscripts, British Museum
I.M.G.	. .	Internationale Musik Gesellschaft
I.S.C.M.	. .	International Society for Contemporary Music
I.S.M.	. .	Incorporated Society of Musicians
J.M.P.	. .	' Jahrbuch der Musikbibliothek Peters '
L.R.A.M.	. .	Licentiate of the Royal Academy of Music
Lambeth	. .	Lambeth Palace, London
M. & L.	. .	' Music & Letters '
M.B.E.	. .	Member of the British Empire
M.f.M.	. .	' Monatshefte für Musikgeschichte '
M.G.G.	. .	' Musik in Geschichte und Gegenwart '
M.M.R.	. .	' The Monthly Musical Record '
M.Q.	. .	' The Musical Quarterly '

M. Rev.	'The Music Review'
Mus. Ant.	'The Musical Antiquary'
Mus. Ant. Soc.	Musical Antiquarian Society
Mus. T.	'The Musical Times'
N.B.-G.	Neue Bach-Gesellschaft
N.O.H.M.	'New Oxford History of Music'
N.Z.M.	'Neue Zeitschrift für Musik'
O.B.E.	Officer of the British Empire
O.H.M.	'Oxford History of Music'
O.U.P.	Oxford University Press
PH	Peterhouse College, Cambridge
Proc. Mus. Ass.	Proceedings of the Musical Association
Proc. Roy. Mus. Ass.	Proceedings of the Royal Musical Association
Q.-L.	Eitner's 'Quellen-Lexikon'
R.A.M.	Royal Academy of Music, London
R.C.M.	Royal College of Music, London
R.C.O.	Royal College of Organists, London
R. de M.	'Revue de Musicologie'
Rass. Mus.	'La Rassegna Musicale'
Rev. Mus.	'Revue Musicale'
Riv. Mus. It.	'Rivista Musicale Italiana'
Roy. Lib.	Royal Library (now in the British Museum)
Roy. MSS	Royal Collection Manuscripts, British Museum
S.I.M.	'Sammelbände der Internationalen Musikgesellschaft'
S.M.W.	'Studien zur Musikwissenschaft'
S.T.M.	'Svensk Tidskrift för Musikforskning'
Schw. Mz.	'Schweizerische Musikzeitung'
Sadler	Sadler Partbooks (now in the Bodleian Library, Oxford)
St. G. Ch.	St. George's Chapel, Windsor
Tenb.	St. Michael's College, Tenbury
Tenb. O.B.	Batten Organ Book (in St. Michael's College Library, Tenbury)
Wimb.	Wimborne Minster
Worc.	Worcester Cathedral
Yk.	York Minster
Z.I.M.	'Zeitschrift der Internationalen Musikgesellschaft'
Z.M.W.	'Zeitschrift für Musikwissenschaft'

ADDENDA & CORRIGENDA

VOL. I

Page Col.

1 ii **A KEMPIS,** *entry should read:*
A KEMPIS, Jean Florent (Nicolas). *See*
A' KEMPIS (p. 79).

(cancel all the rest)

2 i **AARON, P.**
Add at end, before signature:

Modern facsimile reprints are announced
to appear in ' Documenta Musicologica ',
' Toscanello ' (Vol. 1) and ' Lucidario ' (Vol.
2).

3 ii **ABBEY GLEE CLUB**
Par. 5, ll. 2-3 *should read:*

1932 and its affairs were wound up. The
music formerly belonging to the Abbey and
Adelphi Glee Clubs was presented to the
British Museum in 1959.

H. C. C., adds.

4 i **ABBOTT**
Par. 2, ll. 14-15 *should read:*

she formed her own operatic company, of
which her husband, Eugene Wetherell, whom
she had married in 1875, became manager.
Its

9 ii **ABELL**
l. 1. 1650 *should read:*
1653

10 i **ABENDROTH**
Par. 1, l. 2 *should read:*

o/M., 19 Jan. 1883; *d.* Jena, 29 May 1956).

ii **ABER** (*d.* London, 21 May 1960).
Par 2, l. 19 *should read:*

London. In 1958 the President of the
Federal Republic of Germany awarded him
the Grand Cross of Merit.

14 i **ABRAHAM**
Par. 2, ll. 11-13 *should read:*

collaborated with M. D. Calvocoressi in
' Masters of Russian Music ' (1936), and

ii *Add Par. 3, after* l. 1:
' Studies in Russian Music ' (1935).

Page Col.

14 ii *Add Par.* 5, *after* l. 3:
' Grieg ' (1948).

Add after **ABRAHAM, John**

ABRAHAM, Paul (*b.* Apatin, 2 Nov.
1892).
Hungarian composer. He studied in Budapest and became professor of theory there. He
wrote a cello Concerto and some chamber
music, but excelled in the composition of light
music and made a success with several operettas from 1928 onwards. One of them, ' Victoria and her Hussar ', was produced at the
Shaftesbury Theatre in London on 17 Sept.
1931. He lived in Berlin at that time, but his
music was banned by the Nazi rule and he
emigrated to the U.S.A. Being penniless and
friendless, he fell on evil days, lost his reason
and was confined to a mental hospital; but a
Paul Abraham Society was formed in W.
Germany and in 1956 he was sent back there
to be cared for. His music is gaining ground
again. ' Victoria ' has appeared on a long-
playing record and has also been filmed, as
well as two other operettas, ' Flower of
Hawaii ' and ' Ball at the Savoy '. He also
wrote a Requiem, concertos, orchestral and
chamber music, &c. E. B.

15 ii **ÁBRÁNYI, Emil,**
CATALOGUE:
CHORAL WORKS
l. 3. Szegedi *should read:*
Szeged

18 i **ABSIL,** CATALOGUE
STAGE WORKS
l. 3 *should read:*

' Le Chapeau chinois ', comedy in 1 act (lib. by Franc-
Nohain) (1944).
' Le Miracle de Pan ', ballet (1949).
' Les Voix de la mer ', opera in 3 acts (lib. by R. Lyr)
(1951).
' Les Météores ', ballet (1951).

RADIO MUSIC

' Ulysse et les sirènes ' (J. Bruyr) (1939).
' Pierre Breughel l'ancien ' (R. Lyr) (1950).

19 ii **ACADÉMIE DE MUSIQUE**
Par. 2, ll. 8-9 *should read:*

the space of twelve years. Nearly a century
before this, in 1570, similar privileges had

22   i   *After* Par. 6, ending " commune of Paris ", *add* new par. :

In 1953–54, under the directorship of Maurice Lehmann, great stress was laid on elaborately spectacular productions, which included Rameau's ' Les Indes galantes ', Mozart's ' Magic Flute ' and Weber's ' Oberon '.

   ii   *Add before* **ACAEN** :

(These two articles are restored by request from the 4th edition.)

ACADEMY OF ANCIENT MUSIC. An English association formed in London about 1710, at the Crown and Anchor Tavern in the Strand, by a body of distinguished instrumentalists, professional and amateur, including the Earl of Abercorn, Henry Needler, Mulso and other gentlemen, for the study and practice of vocal and instrumental works. An important feature in the scheme was the formation of a library of printed and manuscript music.

The Academy met with the utmost success under the direction of Pepusch, the gentlemen and boys of St. Paul's Cathedral and the Chapel Royal taking part in the performances. In 1728 Greene left the Academy and established a rival institution at the Devil Tavern, Temple Bar ; but this existed for only a few years, and the old Academy continued its work, with Needler as leader of the orchestra. In 1734 there was a second secession from the Academy, Gates retiring and taking with him the children of the Chapel Royal. After passing through one season without any treble voices the Academy issued invitations to parents to place their children under the instruction of Pepusch, one of the conditions being that they should sing at the concerts. A subscription list was also opened to provide the necessary funds, and among those who supported the Academy were Handel and Geminiani, the latter of whom frequently played at its concerts.

The death of Pepusch in 1752 was a serious loss to the institution, but the doctor bequeathed to it the most valuable portion of his library. The Academy closed its career in 1792 under the conduct of Arnold, who had been appointed its director in 1789.

C. M.

ACADEMY OF VOCAL MUSIC.[1] An English society started in London on " Fryday,

[1] Percy A. Scholes, in his book on Hawkins, takes the view that this association was identical with the Academy of Ancient Music. Dr. Scholes says that the information given by F. G. E. " clearly applies to the same body under its primitive name (the same persons being mentioned as founders), and this gives its date of foundation as 1725/6 [which is indeed that given in the present article] : this article is based on the Minute Book of the said Academy from its foundation to 1731, which is now in the British Museum ".

Jan. 7, 172⅚, at the Crown Tavern, against St. Clement's Church, in yᵉ Strand ", according to the original minute-book presented to the British Museum by Vincent Novello (Add. MSS 11,732). The meetings were held fortnightly from 7 to 9 P.M. At the first, the thirteen persons who paid a subscription of half a crown each included King, Gates, S. Wesley, Pepusch, Greene and Galliard. The expenses of that evening included—

	s.	d.
A coach for yᵉ children [the choristers of St. Paul's Cathedral]	2	0
Wine and bread	10	6
For the use of yᵉ room, fire, and candles . .	5	0
The Drawer	1	0

A fortnight later the names of Flintoft and Crofts appear — they each paid half a guinea — and among subsequent names of subscribers those of Bononcini, Haym, Geminiani, Senesino and Dieupart. In 1729 the sixty-nine subscribers included Hogarth, Festing, Robinson and Randall. On 1 June 1727 Steffani was elected President.

The last entry in the minute-book (from which these particulars are derived) contains various resolutions drawn up on 26 May 1731, one of them being " By yᵉ composition of the Ancients is meant of such as lived before yᵉ end of the 16th century " ; another, " That Dr. Pepusch be desired to demand of Dr. Green the Six Motetts yᵉ Bishop of Spiga [Steffani] sent the Academy ". The name of Handel is absent from the roll of members.

Vincent Novello has endorsed the manuscript to the effect that the Academy of Vocal Music afterwards became the King's Concerts of Ancient Music, but this has never been confirmed, nor has the conjecture that this society was identical with the Academy of Ancient Music, though the definition of " Ancients " quoted above lends it some support.   F. G. E., rev.

26   i   **ACCOLTUHUS**
      l. 1 *should read* :

ACCOLUTHUS

29   ii   **ACCORDATURA**
      l. 2 *should read* :

which a string instrument is usually tuned. The word is thus the antonym of *scordatura*, used for unusual tunings temporarily adopted for special effects.

31   i   **ACKERMANN**
      Par. 2, l. 11 *should read* :

there. He was conductor-in-chief at the Zürich Opera in 1948–53 and in the latter year became *Generalmusikdirektor* at the Cologne Opera.

31   i   **ACKTÉ**
Par. 2, l. 13.   *After* ' Lohengrin '
add :
, Elisabeth in ' Tannhäuser '

ii   **ACOURT**
Par. 1, l. 1 *should read* :
ACOURT, Jo. de (*b.* ? ; *d.* ?).

Par. 2, ll. 2-4 *should read* :
is to be identified with " Haucourt " and " Jo
de Alte Curie " (Chantilly MS 1047, f. 15') ;
his surviving works may be found in Oxford,
Bodl. Can. misc. 213 and Chantilly MS 1047.
The Oxford rondeau has been reprinted

44   ii   **ACOUSTICS**
Add to BIBL. :
STEPHANI, HERMANN, ' Zur Psychologie des musika-
lischen Hörens ' (Ratisbon, 1956).

ACOUSTICS OF BUILDINGS
Add to BIBL. :
CONTURIE, L., ' L'Acoustique dans les bâtiments:
théorie et application ' (Paris, 1955).

47   i   **ADAGIO**
Par. 1.   *Add at end* :
A superlative form, *adagissimo*, is occasionally
met with in a context implying an extremely
slow tempo.

ii   **ADALBERT**
Par. 1, l. 1.   **Swięty** *should read* :
Święty

l. 3 *should read* :
23 Apr. 997).

Add after **ADALBERT** :
ADAM, ? (*b.* ? ; *d.* ?).
French 14th–15th-century composer. He
has been identified with only some degree of
certainty as one of the following : Adam
Fabri, clerk at Notre-Dame, Paris, in 1415 ;
Adam Maigret, first chaplain to Charles VI
in 1422 ; Erasmus Adam, a *cantor* mentioned
in a motet from the Aosta manuscript. His
three Rondeaux all have third-influenced
melodies in the *cantus* and are written in
tempus perfectum diminutum throughout. They
are three-voice works with text in the *cantus*
only, but, while ' Tout à coup ' has very much
the same rhythms in *cantus* and *tenor* and a
leaping trumpet-like *contratenor*, in ' A temps
vendra ' the *cantus* is livelier than the *tenor*
and *contratenor*, which are clearly linked and
even begin imitatively. ' Au grief hermitage '
has simpler lower parts, mostly moving with
dotted crotchets on the beat. Adam's extant
work is published in Vol. II of ' Early Fifteenth-Century Music ', edited by Gilbert
Reaney (Amer. Inst. of Musicology, 1958).
G. R. (iii).

48   —   **ADAM**
List of Works, *after* ' Lambert Simnel '
add :
(only partly by Adam).

50   ii   **ADAM OF FULDA**
Add at end :
See also Chorwerk, Vol. 32 (modern reprint of hymns).

51   ii   **ADAMOWSKI, Tymoteusz**
Par. 1, l. 2 *should read* :
24 Mar. 1858 ; *d.* Boston, Mass., 18 Apr.
1943).

ADAMS, Charles
Par. 1, ll. 1-2.   Dates *should read* :
(*b.* Charlestown, Mass., 9 Feb. 1843 ; *d.*
Charlestown, 4 July 1900).

52   i   **ADAMS, Suzanne**
Par. 1, l. 2 *should read* :
28 Nov. 1872 ; *d.* London, 5 Feb. 1953).

Par. 2, l. 6 *should read* :
in 1898, winning decided favour. She seems to
have studied

ii   Par. 2, l. 1 *should read* :
who appears to have greatly admired her
brilliant yet flexible

59   ii   *Add before* **ADLGASSER** :
ADLER, Larry. *See* MOUTH ORGAN.

60   i   **ADLUNG**
l. 1 *should read* :
Four of Adlung's works are of lasting value

l. 6 *should read* :
(Leipzig, 1783).   (2) ' Fragmente einiger
Gedanken des musikalischen Zuschauers '
(1766), a little book containing much that is
useful on the subject of contemporary performing practice, including some very interesting cadenzas.   (3) ' Musica mechanica or-

l. 13.   (3) *should read* :
(4)

Par. 2, l. 3 *should read* :
was published at Cassel in 1931. A modern
facsimile reprint of the ' Anleitung ' appeared
in ' Documenta Musicologica ', Series I, Vol.
iv.

61   i   **AEGIDIUS (Egidio)**
Par. 2 *should read* :
French or Italian 14th-century composer.
He is probably to be identified with Aegidius
de Merino and the " Egidius Augustinus " of
Chantilly MS 1047. His works are to be

found in this manuscript, in Modena Bibl. Est.
MS M.5.24 and Florence, Bibl. Laur. MS
Pal. 87.   R. T. D.

BIBL.—REANEY, GILBERT, 'The Manuscript Chantilly,
Musée Condé 1047' ('Musica Disciplina', VIII,
1954, pp. 68-69).

63 ii **AEROPHOR**
        l. 1.   1912 *should read*:
1911

64 i   **AESCHBACHER**
        Par. 1, l. 1.   **Walter** *should read*:
Walther

Aeschylus
Before Kirby *insert*:
Huybrechts ('Agamemnon', do.).

65 ii **AESTHETICS**
        Add to BIBL.:

ALEXANDER, SAMUEL, 'Beauty and Other Forms of
Value' (London, 1933).
BULLOUGH, EDWARD, 'Aesthetics: Lectures and Essays'
(Stanford, California, 1957).
HOWES, FRANK, 'The Foundations of Musical Aesthe-
tics' (Proc. Roy. Mus. Ass., Vol. LXXXIII,
1956-57).
LANGER, SUZANNE, 'Form and Feeling' (New York,
1952; London, 1953).
'Philosophy in a New Key' (Cambridge, Mass.,
1942).
LEE, VERNON, 'Music and its Lovers' (London, 1932).
MILA, MASSIMO, 'L' esperienza musicale e l' estetica'
(Turin, 1956).
OSBORN, HAROLD, 'Æsthetics and Criticism' (London,
1955).
'Theory of Beauty' (London, 1952).
RONGA, LUIGI, 'Arte e gusto nella musica dall' ars nova
a Debussy' (Milan, 1956).
SERVIEN, PIUS, 'Estétique: musique, peinture, poésie,
science' (Paris, 1953).

AFANASIEV
Par. 1, l. 1 *should read*:
AFANASSIEV

l. 2 *should read*:
Tobolsk, 12 Jan. 1821; d. St. Petersburg, 3
June 1898).

Par. 2, l. 15 *should read*:
Italy. In 1870 he composed one

66 i   Par. 1, *cancel* l. 1.
        l. 2 *should read*:
of the first string quartets (there were three by
Alabiev and a few others before this) by native
composers,

l. 7.   Afanasiev *should read*:
Afanassiev

Par. 2, l. 4.   Afanasiev *should read*:
Afanassiev

l. 5 *should read*:
form and on 5 Dec. 1870 his 'Ammelat Bek',
to a

66 i   l. 17.   Afanasiev *should read*:
Afanassiev

l. 30.   Afanasiev *should read*:
Afanassiev

Par. 3, l. 3.   Afanasiev *should read*:
Afanassiev

ii *Add after* **AFFILARD**:
AFFLIGEN(ENSIS), John (Johannes).
See COTTON, JOHN.

AFRANIO
l. 1 *should read*:
AFRANIO (Afranio Albonese) (*b.* Pavia, *c.* 1480; *d.* ? Ferrara, *c.* 1560).

l. 2 *should read*:
Italian inventor. He was a

67 ii **AFZELIUS**
        Par. 1, l. 2.   Västergöttland *should
        read*:
Västergötland

68 i   **AGAZZARI**
        Par. 6, l. 3 *should read*:
of the Council of Trent. 'Del suonare . . .'
has been reprinted in facsimile (Milan, 1933)
and a very full summary of its contents, in
English, appears in F. T. Arnold's 'The Art
of Accompaniment from a Thorough-Bass'
(London, 1931), pp. 67-74, with comments
by Arnold.
Agazzari's pastoral

Add at end:
BIBL.—BARBLAN, GUGLIELMO, 'Contributo a una biografia di Agostino Agazzari' (Florence, 1956).

70 i   **AGNEW**
        Par. 2, l. 1 *should read*:
Australian composer. He was largely self-
taught, but studied in London from 1923. He
returned to Australia in 1934.

l. 3 *should read*:
'Poem' for voice and orchestra, 4 pianoforte

ii **AGOSTINI, Paolo**
    Par. 1, l. 1.   Valerano *should read*:
Vallerano

Par. 2, l. 7 *should read*:
Vatican Chapel on 16 Feb. 1626.

71 i   **AGRELL**
        BIBL., l. 1.   over *should read*:
över

72   ii   **AGRICOLA, Martin**
FUNCK
    BIBL., l. 1. FUNK *should read*:

    See also Rhaw *should read*:
See also Publikationen G.M.F., Vol. 20 (modern ed. of
'Musica instrumentalis'). Rhau.

74   ii   **AGUILERA DE HEREDIA**
    Add at end:
See also Eslava (modern reprint of Magnificat).

75   i   **AHLE, Johann Rudolph**
    Add at end:
See also Denkmäler (2), Vol. 5 (modern ed.).

    ii   **ÅHLSTRÖM, Olof**
    Par. 1, l. 3 *should read*:
Aug. 1835).

76   i   *Add to* BIBL. :
WIBERG, A., 'Olof Åhlströms Musiktryckeri' (S.T.M.,
    1949).
'Striden om Olof Åhlströms Musiktryckeriprivi-
    legium' (S.T.M., 1952).

77   i   **AICHINGER**
    Par. 3, l. 1 *should read*:
Pieces by Aichinger appeared in the tablature
book of songs by Bernhard Schmid the younger
(1607). A Litany, a 'Stabat Mater' and
various

    AIDA
    ll. 5-6 *should read*:
by Camille Du Locle. Written for the inauguration of the theatre built in Cairo to
celebrate the opening of the Suez Canal[3], and
produced there on

    Add footnote:
[3] It was not actually the first opera performed at the
theatre; the 'Revue et Gazette musicale' for 19 Nov.
1871 reports that it was opened with Meyerbeer's
'Huguenots'.

    ii   **AIKIN**
    Par. 1, l. 9. Dictionary[3] *should read*:
Dictionary[4]
    Footnote 3 *becomes* 4.

78   i   **AINSWORTH**
    Add at end:
BIBL.—FROST, M., 'English and Scottish Psalm and
    Hymn Tunes' (London, 1953), pp. 394-405.

    AIR
    BIBL., l. 1 *should read*:
WARLOCK, PETER, 'The

79   i   **AIR DE COUR**
    Add at end:
See also Publications Soc. Franç., Vols. 3 & 4
(modern reprints).

80   i   **AKHRON**
    Par. 1, l. 1. Losdzeye *should read*:
Lozdzieje, Poland,

---

85   i   *Add after* **ALA**:
Alabaster, William. *See* Rubbra (2 sonnets).

    ii   **ALABIEV**
    Par. 3, l. 21 *should read*:
and Marcella Sembrich, Liszt made a

    ALAIN, Jean
    l. 1 *should read*:
ALAIN, Jean. *See* ALEYN, JOHN.

    Delete Pars. 1 and 2 and footnote.

86   i   *Delete* ll. 1-3 and BIBL.

    ALAIN, Jehan
    Par. 1, l. 2 *should read*:
en-Laye, 3 Feb. 1911; d. Petits-Puits nr.
Saumur, 20 June

87   i   **ALANI** } *should read*:
    ALANUS }
ALANUS, Johannes. *See* ALEYN, JOHN.

    ii   **ALBANESI, Carlo**
    Transfer article to stand after
    ALBANESE, Licia

    ALBANESI, Licia
    Par. 1, l. 1 *should read*:
ALBANESE, Licia (*b.* Bari, 22 July 1913).

    Par. 2, l. 10 *should read*:
House in New York on 9 Feb. 1940. Before
that, in 1937, she had sung Nanetta in 'Falstaff' and Liù in 'Turandot' at Covent
Garden in London. She has

    l. 12 *should read*:
ever since 1940, singing mainly lyric parts of
the

88   i   *Transfer* **ALBANESI** *from p. 87 to*
    stand before **ALBANI.**

    ALBANI
    Par. 2, l. 15 *should read*:
gested by Lamperti, the name of Albani, from
the city of Albany, N.Y., where she had begun
her career. She

    ii   **ALBÉNIZ**
    Par. 2, ll. 15-16 *should read*:
embarked for Puerto Rico. His father, who
was sent to Cuba as a customs inspector,
caught him there by coincidence and had him
arrested as a disobedient child, but eventually
allowed him to continue his tour. He made
his way to the U.S.A., supporting

88   ii   l. 26 *should read*:

Brassin. In 1877 he appears to have been in New York for a brief period. But his ambition was to become a

89   i   Par. 1, ll. 6-8 *should read*:

in the matter of idiom. After a tour in Europe and America, and appearing with great success as

90   i   BIBL., l. 4. inquita *should read*: inquieta

Add to BIBL.:

LAPLANE, GABRIEL, 'Albéniz: sa vie, son œuvre' (Paris, 1956).

92   ii   **ALBERT, Heinrich**
Par. 2, l. 2. nephew *should read*: cousin

93   i   Par. 3, l. 3. Schütz " *should read*:
Schütz " [1],

l. 18. 'Arien' [1] *should read*:
'Arien' [2]

Par. 4, l. 12. continuo.[2] *should read*:
continuo.[3]

Add footnote:

[1] In spite of this it has been established that he and Schütz were cousins.

Change footnotes 1 & 2 *to* 2 & 3.

Add to BIBL.:

'Festschrift zur Ehrung von Heinrich Albert', ed. by Günther Kraft (Weimar, 1954).

94   ii   *Add after* **ALBERTINI**:

ALBERTIS, Gaspar de (Gaspare Alberti) (*b.* ? Padua, *c.* 1480; *d.* Bergamo, *c.* 1563).
Italian composer. In 1502 he was a singer in the basilica of Santa Maria Maggiore at Bergamo. In Dec. 1524 he was granted an increase in his salary to provide a book of masses and another of motets, and to instruct four clerics in polyphonic singing; in Apr. 1541, when his students were increased to twelve, he received a further rise. In Aug. 1550 he was relieved of his duties on account of old age. He returned to the church as choirmaster in Apr. 1552, but was again dismissed two years later. In 1560, however, he was given a special grant to relieve him in his great age. His music survives in three choir-books which he refused to surrender to the church on his first retirement, but must later have presented, since at his death they were transferred to the new choirmaster, Pietro Pincio.
The choir-books contain the following works composed by or ascribed to Albertis:

14 Psalms *a* 4, 7 Psalms for double choir, 15 Lamentations *a* 4 (4 anonymous), 7 Magnificats (2 for double choir), 11 motets *a* 4, 1 motet *a* 6, 5 motets *post passionem* (2 anonymous), 5 Masses, 3 Passions and a Litany *a* 4.   E. B.[1]

BIBL.—JEPPESEN, KNUD, 'A Forgotten Master of the early 16th Century: Gaspar de Albertis' (M.Q., XLIV, July 1958, p. 311).

[1] Details from Knud Jeppesen's article (*see* BIBL.).

95   i   **ALBICASTRO**
Par. 2, l. 16 *should read*:

in 1921 by Beckmann. The Swiss Musicological Society published a modern edition of the concertos in 1957.
E. V. D. S., adds.

96   i   **ALBONESE**
Par. 3 *should read*:
See also Afranio. Phagotus.

ALBONI
Par. 2, ll. 1-2 *should read*:
Italian contralto singer. She met

ll. 10-11 *should read*:
appearance at Bologna on 3 Oct. 1842, in Pacini's 'Saffo'. In the

ii   Par. 3, l. 2 *should read*:
fully 2½ octaves, from g to c''', was perfectly

Add at end:
BIBL.—POUGIN, A., 'Marietta Alboni' (Paris, 1912).

97   ii   **ALBRECHTSBERGER**
Add to BIBL.:

SCHRAMEK-KIRCHNER, A. M., 'Johann Georg Albrechtsbergers Fugenkompositionen in seinen Werken für Tasteninstrumente' (Vienna, 1954).

99   ii   **ALDEBURGH FESTIVAL**
ll. 15-16 *should read*:

about a week. Britten's work naturally figures in the musical part of the programme, but does not unduly predominate, and

101   i   **ALDRICH, Henry**
Par. 2, l. 13 *should read*:
Nov. 1681; B.A. 1685. The date of Talbott's manuscript is *c.* 1695-98.   R. D.

ii   **ALDRICH, Richard**
Par. 4, l. 12 *should read*:
in the possession of his heirs. A volume of collected criticism, 'Concert Life in New York, 1902-1923', was published posthumously in 1941.

ALDROVANDINI
Par. 1, l. 3 *should read*:
9 Feb. 1707).

102   i   **ALEMBERT**
Par. 2, l. 2 *should read*:

He was a foundling christened after the
Church of Saint-Jean-le-Rond, on the steps of
which he had been abandoned by his un-
married mother.   He was educated at the
Mazarin College

ii   Par. 1, l. 7.   J. A. Serré *should
read*:

Jean-Adam Serre

103   i   **ALESSANDRI, Felice**
Par. 1, l. 1.   1742 *should read*:

1747

104   i   **ALESSANDRO, R. d'**
Par. 1, l. 2 *should read*:

17 Mar. 1911; *d.* Lausanne, 17 Mar. 1959).

106   i   *Add before* **ALEXIS**

ALEXANIAN, Dirian (*b.* Constantinople,
1881; *d.* Chamonix, 27 June 1954).
Armenian cellist.   He studied under Grütz-
macher in Germany and settled in Paris,
where he made a great reputation, especially
as a teacher at the École Normale de
Musique.   He wrote a book on cello playing.

E. B.

Add before **ALFANO** :

ALEYN, John (*b.* ? ; *d.* ?, 1373).
English composer and theorist.   He was a
member of the Chapel Royal from the middle
of the 14th century until his death.   The fact
that he held livings at Rochester and was sent
into Kent to borrow money from heads of
religious houses, at the instigation of Edward
III, may indicate that he was a native of that
county.   He seems to have been one of the
king's favourite musicians, for documentary
evidence between 1361 and 1370 shows that
he enjoyed many lucrative ecclesiastical
appointments.   Under royal grants he held
successively prebends in St. Paul's, London ;
St. George's, Windsor ; Bradstead, Kent ;
Royal Free Chapel, Exeter Castle ; Nayleston,
Lincoln ; Shoreham, Kent ; Wells Cathedral ;
Otteford, Kent.   He managed to hold on to
his Windsor canonry and was also made a
canon of Exeter Cathedral in 1370.   On his
death he left a vellum roll containing polyphonic music to the choir at Windsor.

Two of Aleyn's compositions survive : a
' Gloria ' for 3 voices in the ' Old Hall Manuscript ' (1, 7) and an isorhythmic motet, ' Sub
Arturo plebs / Fons citharizancium / In omnem terram ', for 2 voices and instrument. The
' Gloria ' is a simple setting in *conductus* style,
without *cantus firmus*, and its use of perfect
prolation as well as its general style indicates

a fairly early date, possibly as early as the
middle of the 14th century.

The motet may well belong to the same
period, though the notation and rhythm of
the individual voice-parts are highly complex.
One reason for this may be the subject of the
two motet texts, which deal respectively with
practical musicians and theorists.   At the very
end of the list of theorists, the composer brings
in his own name, with a humble and charming
plea for recognition :

> Illis licet infimus
> Johannes Alanus
> sese recommendat,
> quatenus ab invidis
> ipsum sonis validis
> laus horum defendat.

Aleyn is not otherwise known as a theorist,
but the tenor of this motet is cited in a late
14th-century treatise written at Florence and
now preserved in the Biblioteca Medicea
Laurenziana (Redi 71, f. 24).   The motet
is found complete at Chantilly, Musée Condé,
1047 (f. 70 v) and at Bologna, Biblioteca G. B.
Martini, Q 15 (f. 225 v).   A facsimile of the
former copy is given in Wolf's ' Musikalische
Schrifttafeln ', and a transcription, with col-
lation of both sources, in D.T.Ö., LXXVI, 9.
Coussemaker published the text of the *triplum*
only in ' Les Harmonistes du XIVᵉ siècle ',
without, however, offering information about
the musicians concerned.

This has now been supplied by Brian
Trowell, who suggests that the motet was
written for some important ceremony, such
as the Garter celebrations at Windsor on
or around St. George's Day 1358.   In 1356
the Black Prince's Victory at Poitiers and the
capture of the King of France had given the
English good reason to rejoice, and the text
of the motet does indeed mention rejoicing
among the people and the patronage of a
warlike prince.   Most of the musicians were
either members of the Chapel Royal or
musically inclined ecclesiastics living in the
provinces.

Among the theorists whose names are de-
claimed by the singer of the motetus one finds
Tubal, Pythagoras, Boethius, St. Gregory,
Guido, Franco and finally Aleyn, a catholic if
somewhat odd collection of people.   The instrumental part supporting the upper voices
consists of a most appropriate plainsong Communion, " In omnem terram exivit sonus
eorum et in fines orbis ", and it has been
suggested that the work as a whole, besides
being noteworthy for certain effects mainly
apparent to the eye [1], has more than a touch
of propaganda in at least one of its texts.

D. W. S.

BIBLIOGRAPHY

BUKOFZER, MANFRED, ' Studies in Medieval and Renais-
    sance Music ' (New York, 1950).

[1] *See* EYE MUSIC.

CARAPETYAN, ARMEN, ' A Fourteenth-Century Florentine Treatise in the Vernacular' (' Musica Disciplina ', IV, 1950).
DANNEMANN, ERNA, ' Die spätgotische Musiktradition in Frankreich und Burgund vor dem Auftreten Dufays' (Strasbourg, 1936).
FICKER, RUDOLF VON, ed., ' Sieben Trienter Codices : Sechste Auswahl' (D.T.Ö., LXXVI, 1933).
LABORDE, LÉON DE, ' Les Ducs de Bourgogne' (Paris, 1849).
RAMSBOTHAM, ALEXANDER, ed., ' The Old Hall Manuscript', Vol. I (London, 1933).
REANEY, GILBERT, ' The Manuscript Chantilly, Musée Condé 1047' (' Musica Disciplina ', VIII, 1954).
TOULMIN-SMITH, LUCY, ed., ' Expeditions to Prussia and the Holy Land made by Henry, Earl of Derby' (London, 1894).
TROWELL, BRIAN, ' A Fourteenth-Century Ceremonial Motet and its Composer' (' Acta Musicologica ', Vol. XXIX, 1957).
' Some English Contemporaries of Dunstable ' (Proc. Roy. Mus. Ass., LXXXI, 1954-55).
WOLF, JOHANNES, ' Musikalische Schrifttafeln ' (Leipzig, 1923).

106   i   **ALFANO**
Par. 1, l. 2 should read :

1876; d. San Remo, 26 Oct. 1954).

Par. 2, ll. 9-10 should read :

Conservatorio di Santa Cecilia in Rome. In 1950 he was acting director of the

108   ii   **ALFONSO EL SABIO**
Add at end :

See also Publicacions Catalunya, Vol. 15 (modern ed. of ' Cantigas de Santa María ').

110   i   **ALIÓ**
Par. 1, ll. 1-2. Dates should read :

(b. Barcelona, 21 Mar. 1862; d. Barcelona, 31 Mar. 1908).

112   ii   **ALKAN**
Add after Op. 17 :

17a. Finale, for pf. duet.

Op. 26b. Morceau should read :
moresca

Op. 32 should read :

32. 4 Impromptus (cf. Op. 26b & c), 2e recueil d'Impromptus, 3 airs variés à 5 et 7 temps '.

113   i   Add after l. 2 :

{ ' Caprice ou étude.'
{ Chord Study, C ma.
' 2e Concerto da Camera ', C# mi.

ll. 6-7.   Cancel entry
PIANOFORTE AND ORCHESTRA

114   ii   **ALLEGRI, Domenico**
Par. 1, l. 1.   Date should read :

Rome, 1585; (delete c.)

115   i   **ALLEGRI, Gregorio**
Par. 2, ll. 15-16 should read :

(1770) wrote down the notes from memory after hearing the Miserere sung, and Choron managed to insert

116   i   **ALLEGRI, L.**
Add at end, before signature :

A modern facsimile reprint of ' Il primo libro ' is to appear in ' Documenta Musicologica ', Vol. 3.

119   ii   **ALLIN**
Par. 1, l. 2 should read :

ance of unusual distinction. He also appeared in the international seasons there in 1926-27, 1932-33 and 1938, especially as Fasolt and Hunding.

Par. 2, l. 10 should read :

formances of ' Figaro ' at Glyndebourne (1934).

l. 12 should read :

as professor of singing at the R.A.M. He was created C.B.E. in 1958.

122   ii   **ALMQUIST**
Add to BIBL. :

BERGSTRAND, ARNE, ' Songes : litteraturhistoriska studier i C. L. Almquists diktsamling ' (Uppsala, 1953).

123   i   **ALNAES**
Par. 1, l. 1.   **Ervind** should read :
Eyvind

l. 2.   25 Dec. should read :
24 Dec.

Par. 2, l. 2.   Ivar should read :
Iver

l. 3.   1892-93 should read :
1892-95.

ii   **ALPAERTS**
Par. 1, l. 2 should read :

1876; d. Antwerp, 5 Oct. 1954).

Par. 2, ll. 20-22 should read :

Flemish Opera at Antwerp. He was a member of the Académie Royale de Belgique.

124   i   **CATALOGUE**
l. 19 should read :

4 String Quartets.
' Avondmuziek ' for 8 woodwind insts.

125   ii   **ALSEN**
Par. 2, l. 14 should read :

appointed Kammersänger in 1947. He appeared at the Metropolitan in New York in 1938-39 and at Covent Garden in London in 1947.

126   i   Add before **ALTE MEISTER** :

ALTE CURIE, Jo. de.   See ACOURT. HAUCOURT.

Altenberg
l. 2 should read :

orch., 3 with pf.). Wellesz (song).

126 ii **ALTÈS, E. E.**
Par. 1, l. 2 *should read*:
1830 ; *d.* Saint-Dyé nr. Blois, 8 July 1899).

127 i **ALTÈS, J. H.**
Par. 1, l. 2 *should read*:
1826 : *d.* Paris, 24 July 1895).

ii **ALTNIKOL**
Par. 4, ll. 8-9 *should read*:
printed, and his addition to Bach's last manuscript, 'The Art of Fugue', of the chorale 'Vor deinen Tron', at the composer's dictation is his last claim to fame.

128 ii **ALVAREZ, Marguerite d'**
Par. 2, ll. 1-2 *should read*:
  English contralto singer of noble Peruvian parentage, her full name being Margarita Amelia Alvarez de Rocafuerte. Her mother was French. After some experience in French provincial opera she made her operatic début in New
l. 6 *should read*:
she first appeared in London, making her début at the London Opera House (Stoll) in Massenet's 'Hérodiade', and also made a name as a concert

After l. 9 *add*:
In 1914 she sang at Covent Garden.

Add at end:
BIBL.—ALVAREZ, MARGUERITE D', 'Forsaken Altars' (London, 1954).

129 i **ALWYN**
Par. 2, l. 19 *should read*:
interest in most contemporary music. Among Alwyn's orchestral works the most important are three symphonies, the third of which was first performed in London in Oct. 1956.

131 i **AMATI (1)**
Par. 1, l. 2 *should read*:
d. Cremona, ? 1). He was the first member

Add footnote:
¹ He must have died after 1611, as he became a widower in that year, according to Piccolellis (*see* BIBL.).

ii Par 2, l. 2. 1564. *should read*:
1564.¹

Add footnote:
¹ They are now in the Ashmolean Museum at Oxford, part of a gift of instruments made by Messrs. Hill. *See* Thurston Dart, 'The Instruments in the Ashmolean Museum' ('Galpin Society Journal', VII, 1954), pp. 7-10.

132 i **(4) Nicolo Amati**
Par. 1, l. 1. Sept. *should read*:
Dec.

132 i l. 2. Aug. *should read*:
Apr.

ii **AMATI**
Add at end:
BIBL.—PICCOLELLIS, A., 'Liutai antichi e moderni' (Florence, 1886).

AMATO, Pasquale
Par. 2. *After* l. 10 *add*:
of which he was a member from 1908 to 1921,

l. 15 *should read*:
illness checked his career. He created the part of Jack Rance in the production of Puccini's 'Fanciulla del West' there in 1910. He was in England

134 ii **AMBROS, Vladimír**
Par. 1, l. 2 *should read*:
ravia, 18 Sept. 1891 ; *d.* Prostějov, 12 May 1956).

Par. 2, l. 7 *should read*:
place. After that time he devoted his activi-

l. 11 *should read*:
blended in his works. His later com-

135 i *Add before* **AMBROSIO** :
  AMBROSIAN SINGERS. English choir founded in 1952 by John McCarthy and Denis Stevens. A fully professional body from the very beginning, the choir has specialized in broadcasting and recording, although it has occasionally appeared in public. The male voices are chosen from the choral establishment of the most eminent of London churches and cathedrals, and the interpretation of medieval and renaissance polyphony has always been a particular feature of the choir's repertory. As an exclusively male-voice ensemble, they began their career by providing a complex and difficult series of illustrations to programmes on 'Early Western Music' broadcast by the B.B.C. At a later stage, sopranos and contraltos were added and the repertory was gradually advanced so that eventually modern works, including several first performances, appeared alongside the classical and pre-classical items.
  Their chief conductor is Denis Stevens, whose musical and musicological training assures a high standard of textual accuracy and correctness in performance practice. In 1956 he chose from the Singers a group of six soloists who concentrated under his direction on sacred and secular music of the renaissance, performing fluently in French, Latin, German, Italian and Spanish. The Ambrosian Consort (as this smaller group is known) has frequently appeared in public both in London and in the provinces and has made numerous

gramophone recordings, more especially for American companies. The Singers and Consort have been heard either separately or together in television and broadcast programmes such as 'Monteverdi and his Contemporaries', 'Thomas Tomkins', 'Secular Music of the Renaissance', 'The Cries of London', 'Royal Music', 'Italian Court Music', 'Masters of the Late Renaissance', and 'Festival Music of the Middle Ages'.

E. B.

135   i   **AMBROSIO**
Par. 1, l. 2 *should read*:

June 1871 ; d. Nice, 29 Dec. 1914).

136   i   **AMENGUAL**
Par. 1, l. 2 *should read*:

2 Sept. 1911 ; d. Santiago, 2 Aug. 1954).

ii   *Add after* **AMERBACH**:

AMERICAN INSTITUTE OF MUSICOLOGY, PUBLICATIONS OF THE. A valuable series of reprints of old music and treatises on music, published in the following series (shown abbreviated in the list below):

'Corpus Mensurabilis Musicae';
'Corpus Scriptorum de Musica';
'Musicological Studies and Documents';
'Miscellanea'.

The following volumes have appeared so far (1960):

C.M.M. 1, Guillaume Dufay, 'Opera omnia', ed. by G. de Van & H. Besseler.
C.M.M. 2, Guillaume de Machaut, Mass, ed. by G. de Van.
C.M.M. 3, Adriaan Willaert, 'Opera omnia', ed. by H. Zenck & W. Gerstenberg.
C.M.M. 4, Jacobus Clemens non Papa, 'Opera omnia', ed. by K. P. Bernet Kempers.
C.M.M. 5, Antoine Brumel, 'Opera omnia', ed. by Armen Carapetyan.
C.M.M. 6, Nicolas Gombert, 'Opera omnia', ed. by J. Schmidt-Görg.
C.M.M. 7, Jacobus Barbireau, 'Opera omnia', ed. by Bernhard Meier.
C.M.M. 8, 'The Music of Fourteenth-Century Italy', ed. by Nino Pirrotta.
C.M.M. 9, Johannes Regis, 'Opera omnia', ed. by C. W. H. Lindenburg.
C.M.M. 10, Franchinus Gafurius, 'The Collected Musical Works', ed. by L. Finscher.
C.M.M. 11, 'Early Fifteenth-Century Music', ed. by G. Reaney.
C.M.M. 12, Giovanni Gabrieli, 'Opera omnia', ed. by D. Arnold.
C.M.M. 13, 'Missa Tornacensis', ed. by C. van den Borren.
C.M.M. 14, Cipriano de Rore, 'Opera omnia', ed. B. Meier.
C.M.M. 15, Loyset Compère, 'Opera omnia', ed. by L. Finscher.
C.M.M. 16, Robert Carver, 'Opera omnia', ed. by D. Stevens.
C.M.M. 17, Robert Fayrfax, 'Opera omnia', ed. by E. B. Warren.
C.S.M. 1, Johannes Affligemensis (Cotto), 'De Musica cum tonario', ed. by J. Smits de Waesberghe.
C.S.M. 2, Aribo, 'De Musica', ed. by J. Smits de Waesberghe.
C.S.M. 3, Jacques de Liège, 'Speculum Musicae', ed. by Roger Bragard.
C.S.M. 4, Guido d' Arezzo, 'Micrologus', ed. by J. Smits de Waesberghe.

C.S.M. 5, Anon : 'Notitia del valore delle Note Canto Misurato', ed. by A. Carapetyan.
C.S.M. 6, Ugolino of Orvieto, 'Declaratio Musicae Disciplinae', ed. by A. Seay.
M.S.D. 1, 'Cymbala' (Bells in the Middle Ages), ed. by J. Smits de Waesberghe.
M.S.D. 2, 'The Worcester Fragments', ed. by L. Dittmer.
Misc. 1. Claude Le Jeune, Airs (1608), ed. by D. P. Walker
Misc. 2, 'A Textbook of Melody', by J. S. van Waesberghe.

136   ii   **AMERICAN MUSICOLOGICAL SOCIETY**
Par. 2, l. 15 *should read*:
history and science.

Add at end :

The Society's 'Journal', which has been issued three times a year since 1948, contains much valuable material. The A.M.S. has also published Vol. II of Okeghem's collected works, edited by Dragan Plamenac and, jointly with the Royal Musical Association and 'Musica Britannica', John Dunstable's complete works, edited by Manfred Bukofzer.

H. C. C., adds.

137   ii   *Add before* **AMES** :
" AMERICAN " QUARTET (Dvořák). *See* " NIGGER " QUARTET.

Add before **AMES** :
Amerling, Conrad. *See* Berg (Alban, song).

138   ii   **AMIOT**
Par. 1, l. 2 *should read*:
8 Feb. 1718 ; d. Peking, 8 Oct. 1793).

139   i   **AMMERBACH**
Par. 1, l. 2.   27 Jan. *should read* :
29 Jan.

140   ii   **AMOROSIUS**
Headline should read:
AMOROSIO

Par. 1, l. 1 *should read* :
AMOROSIO, Simone (b. ? ; d. ?).

Par. 2, l. 1 *should read* :

Italian 16th–17th-century composer, also known under the latinized form of his name, Simon Amorosius. He

141   i   *Add after* **AMPHICORD** :
AMPHITHEATROF, Daniele (b. St. Petersburg, 29 Oct. 1901).

Italian naturalized composer and conductor of Russian birth. He completed the greater part of his studies in Italy, where his family settled at the Ligurian Riviera while he was still in his infancy. In 1937 he emigrated to the U.S.A., where at present (1959) he lives at Beverly Hills. The influence of his first masters, Wihtol in St. Petersburg and Křička in Prague, is seen in his work to have been overridden by that of Respighi, whose composition course he attended at the Conservatorio di Santa Cecilia in Rome, where he took his diploma in 1924. Between 1938 and 1941 he was engaged in a very active career as conductor in Rome and Turin, at the Italian radio, at Minneapolis and elsewhere.

Among Amphitheatrof's important compositions, which show brilliant orchestral display and a modern taste, may be mentioned the early symphonic poems ' Il miracolo delle rose ', ' Poema del mare ' and ' Panorama americano ' (into which he tried to introduce jazz elements), a ' De profundis ' for chorus and orchestra, a pianoforte Concerto and several chamber-music works. He has also written much music for films.   G. M. G.

141   i   **AMPHITHEATROF, Massimo**
Par. 2, l. 1 *should read*:

Italian violoncellist of Russian parentage, brother of the preceding.

144   i   **ANCIENT CONCERTS**
Par. 2, l. 8 *should read*:

Charles Knyvett acted for him.   He was succeeded by

l. 10 *should read*:

death in 1831, when William Knyvett, Charles's son, who had been

ii   Par. 2.   Last line *should read*:

name of B.A.C.H., now regarded as spurious.

145   ii   **ANCONA**
Par. 2, ll. 1-2 *should read*:

After 1900 Ancona only once appeared in London, as Scarpia and Telramund in 1904, but sang for several seasons in 1893–97 at the

Add before **Anczyc**:

ANCYZ (or Anglez).   A Polish name given to the English country dance, which reached Poland through France and became very popular among the gentry of the 18th century.   C. R. H.

147   i   *Add before* **ANDERSEN, Anton Jörgen**:

ANDERS, Peter (*b.* Essen, 1 July 1908; *d.* Hamburg, 10 Sept. 1954).
German tenor singer.   He first appeared on the stage in 1931 and was engaged for the Heidelberg Municipal Theatre in 1932. He progressed by way of Darmstadt, Cologne and

Hanover to the Munich State Opera (1937–1941). During the second world war he appeared in Vienna and Berlin.   On its conclusion he joined the Berlin State Opera and in 1948 that of Hamburg. He sang both heroic and lyrical parts and was also well known as an interpreter of *Lieder*, both at recitals and on gramophone records.   He died of injuries received in a motor accident.   E. B.

147   i   **Andersen, Hans**
Add after l. 2 :

Borowski (' Little Match Girl ', recitation).

l. 6 *should read*:

(' Liti Kjersti ', melodrama).   Egk (' Chinesische Nachtigall ', ballet). Enna (3 operas, melo-

Add after **Andersen, Hans** :

ANDERSEN, Karl (August) (*b.* Oslo, 29 Sept. 1903).
Norwegian violoncellist and composer.   He studied the cello with H. Becker in Berlin (1921–24), theory with Iver Holter in Oslo and H. Grabner in Germany.   Since 1924 he has been cellist in the Oslo Philharmonic Orchestra.   He is also a well-known composition teacher.   His works include a Suite (1937) and a ' Festforspill ' for orchestra, a Symphony for chamber orchestra and various chamber works.   D. S.-E.

ii   **ANDERSON, Marian**
Add at end :

On 18 Jan. 1955 she made her début at the New York Metropolitan Opera as Ulrica in Verdi's ' Ballo in maschera '.

Add to BIBL. :

BIBL.—ANDERSON, MARIAN, ' My Lord, what a Morning : an Autobiography ' (New York, 1956).

148   i   **ANDERSSON, Folke**
Par. 2, ll. 8-9 *should read*:

1922 to 1934, appeared in 1926 at concerts in America,

153   i   *Add after* **ANDREOZZI** :

ANDRÉSEN, Ivar (*b.* Oslo, 27 July 1896 ; *d.* Stockholm, 6 Nov. 1940).
Norwegian bass singer.   He studied in Stockholm, where he made his début as the King in ' Aida ' in 1919.   He became a member of the Dresden State Opera in the 1920s and of the Berlin State Opera in 1935.   He was regularly heard at Bayreuth between 1927 and 1936 as King Mark, Gurnemanz, Pogner, the Landgrave and Fasolt, and was made a German *Kammersänger*. Andrésen made his Covent Garden début in 1928, and during the next four seasons sang the leading Wagnerian bass parts in London, as well as Sarastro in Bruno Walter's 1931 production of ' Die

Zauberflöte ', a part he repeated at Glyndebourne in 1935, together with Osmin. He
was also heard at the Metropolitan, New
York, from 1930 to 1932. He possessed a
beautiful voice, noble in sound and was an
artist of the first rank.   H. D. R.

153   i   *Add after* **Andrewes** :
ANDREWS, Herbert Kennedy (*b.* Com-
ber, Co. Down, 10 Aug. 1904).
Irish organist, composer and musical
scholar. He was educated at Bedford School
and New College, Oxford, and studied music
at the R.C.M. in London. He holds the
degrees of M.A., D.Mus. (Oxon.), F.R.C.O.
and A.R.C.M. He was organist and choirmaster at Beverley Minster in 1934–38 and
at New College, Oxford, in 1938–56, and in
1944 he became a Fellow of that College. He
is now lecturer in music at Oxford University.
Andrews has an outstanding gift of writing
on technical matters in a way that combines
lucid and interesting exposition with stimu-
lating readability. His contributions to this
Dictionary are notable examples, and no less
so are his two books, ' The Oxford Harmony ',
Vol. II (1950), and ' An Introduction to the
Technique of Palestrina ' (1958). He has
also published articles and reviews, and his
compositions include church music, partsongs
and solo songs.   E. B.

154   ii   **ANDRZEJOWSKI**
           Par. 1, l. 1.   ?, 1880 ; *should read* :
Kobryń, 1880 ;

155   i   **ANERIO, F.**
           Par. 4, ll. 8-9, *delete, except*
N. F. (ii).

       ii   **ANERIO, G. F.**
           Par. 1, ll. 10-15 *should read* :
live in Rome. He

           ll. 26-27 *should read* :
Roman family of Giacomo Avila. He afterwards entered the service of King Sigismund
III of Poland at Cracow and died on his way
back from there to Italy.

156   i   *Add to* BIBL. :
EITNER, ROBERT, ' Giovanni Francesco Anerio '
(M.f.M., XIX, 1887, p. 17).

           BIBL.   l. 12 *should read* :
lisches Jahrbuch, 1886, p. 51 ff. ; 1891, p. 97 ff. &
1895, p. 93 ff.).

       ANET (2)
           Par. 2, l. 16.   Leczinski *should
           read* :
Leszczinski

156   ii   **ANGELI**
           Par. 1, l. 2 *should read* :
1868 ;   *d.* San Michele nr. Verona, 28 Oct.
1940).

157   i   **ANGELICA**
           Add to BIBL. :
LESURE, F., ' The Angélique in 1653 ' (' Galpin Society
Journal ', VI, 1953), p. 111.

       ii   **ANGLEBERT, J.-B.-H.**
           Par. 1, l. 2 *should read* :
(*b.* Paris, 5 Sept. 1661 ; *d.* Paris, 9 Mar. 1747).

158   i   **ANGLEBERT, J.-H.**
           Par. 1, l. 2.   1635 *should read* :
1628

           Par. 5, ll. 5-6 *should read* :
positions are published in ' Publications de la
Société Française de Musicologie ', Vol. 8,
edited by Roesgen-

       ii   *Add before* **ANGLIA** :
ANGLEZ. *See* ANCYZ.

160   i   **ANNIBALE**
           Par. 1, l. 2.   end of *should read* :
15

       ii   *Add at end* :
See also Lyrebird Press (ed. of 13 organ ricercari).

161   i   **ANNUNZIO**
           Add to BIBL. :
' Le Martyre de Saint Sébastien : d' Annunzio et
Debussy ' (' Revue Musicale ', special No. 234,
Paris, 1957).

       ANROOY
           Par. 2, l. 11.   St. Petersburg *should
           read* :
Moscow

       ii   *Add after* **Anseaume** :
ANSELMI, Giorgio (*b.* Parma, ? [1] ; *d.* ?,
c. 1440–43).
Italian theorist, astrologer and philosopher.
Two of his astrological treatises are preserved
at the Vatican and the musical treatise, dated
1424, at Milan. The latter is mentioned by
Anselmi's grandson in some early 16th-
century epigrams as ' Dialoghi de harmonia '.
This it in fact is, since apparently the three
sections of the work correspond to three days
of discussion at the baths of Corsena between
Giorgio and his teacher Petrus Rubeus. Whatever the importance of Petrus, who is also
known as a composer, it is clear that he does
most of the talking, while Giorgio in the main
puts the questions. The treatise is divided
into sections on cosmic music, the notes of

[1] It must have been before 1386, the year in which
his father died.

the scale (*harmonia instrumentalis*) and practical music. The second part deals with the intervallic system according to the ancient cithara and the modern monochord, while the third is concerned with " practical " matters such as the hexachords, the church modes, measured music and counterpoint. There are interesting references to changes in the quality of the voice to accommodate different emotions. These are indicative of the humanistic traits which appear in the work, which, however, is medieval in its often factual approach to the subject. It is clear, for instance, that Anselmi appreciates the difference in sound between organ pipes of differing diameter. His treatise seems to have had considerable influence on Gafori, who actually owned and annotated the only existing manuscript some time between 1484 and 1492.

G. R. (iii).

BIBL.—HANDSCHIN, JACQUES, ' Anselmi's Treatise on Music annotated by Gafori ' (' Musica Disciplina ', II, 1948).
' Zur Behandlung des Mensurproblems im Mittelalter ' (in ' Gedenkschrift J. Handschin ', Berne, 1957).

161   ii   **ANSELMI, Giuseppe**
Par. 1, l. 1.   Catania *should read*:
Nicolosi

162   i   Par. 1, l. 17.   ' La Tosca ' *should read*:
' Tosca '.

ANSERMET
Par. 3, l. 12 *should read*:
introduction to what was then the composer's later manner.

ii   **ANSON**
Par. 1, l. 2 *should read*:
Wellington, New Zealand, 18 Oct. 1894; *d.* London, 4 Aug. 1958).

Par. 3 *should read*:
Anson is the author of the section on ' Improvisation ', the third volume of a series of text-books edited by Sir George Dyson, ' Musicianship for Students ', to which he also contributed ' Extempore Pianoforte Accompaniment '. His compositions include:

163   ii   **ANSSEAU**
Par. 2, l. 8 *should read*:
critics, and he reappeared in 1920, 1926, 1928 and 1929. In 1923–28 he was at the Chicago Opera.

Par. 3.   *Delete* ll. 1-2.

l. 4 *should read*:
Conservatoire in 1939, when he retired from the stage.

164   ii   **ANTEGNATI (5)**
ll. 1-2.   Dates *should read*:
(*b.* Brescia, 1549; *d.* Brescia, 16 Nov. 1624),

165   i   **ANTHEIL**
Par. 1, l. 2 *should read*:
July 1900; *d.* New York, 12 Feb. 1959).

Par. 2, ll. 13-15 *should read*:
1924, was produced in Paris on 19 June 1926 and first performed in New York on 10 Apr. 1927. It was scored for xylophones, electric

ii   Par. 2, l. 9.   ' Transatlantique '. *should read*:
' Transatlantic '.

Add to OPERAS, after ' The Rascal ':
' Volpone ' (after Ben Jonson), prod. Los Angeles, 9 Jan. 1953.
' The Brothers ', prod. Denver, 28 July 1954.
' The Wish ', prod. Louisville, 2 Apr. 1955.

166   i   **CATALOGUE**
SONGS
Add under heading:
' Nightpiece ' (contributed to ' Joyce Book ', 1932).

168   ii   **ANTHOLOGIE SONORE**
l. 11.   have *should read*:
has

Add at end:
They have been re-issued as LP records in France and the U.S.A.

172   i   **ANTIPHONAL**
Add at end:
See also Paléographie Mus. (for modern reprints).

173   i   *Add before* **ANTTI**:
ANTONIUS ROMANUS (*b.* ? Rome, ? ; *d.* ?).
Italian 14th–15th-century composer. He obviously worked in Venice, for two of his three motets are for the election of Venetian doges, namely Tommaso Mocenigo (1414) and Francesco Foscari (1423), while the third is in honour of Giovanni Francesco Gonzaga of Mantua. All are for four voices and one is isorhythmic. The rest of his output consists of three Mass movements, *i.e.* 2 Glorias and a Credo, and an incomplete *ballata*. One of the motets is in A. Schering's ' Geschichte der Musik in Beispielen ' (1931).

G. R. (iii).

ii   **ANTWERP**
Par. 2, ll. 8-10 *should read*:
Flor Alpaerts (1933–41), Jef van Hoof (1941–1944) and Lodewijk de Vocht (1944–52). In 1952 Flor Peeters was appointed.

174 ii **APEL**
Par. 3, l. 12. 800–1600 ' *should
read* :
900–1600 '

Add at end :

Apel is joint editor with A. T. Davison of the
' Historical Anthology of Music ' (1947).

178 ii **AP RHYS**
Transfer to before **APRILE.**

APRILE
Par. 1, l. 2. 29 Oct. 1732 *should
read* :
28 Oct. 1731 [4] ;

Add footnote :

[4] The birth certificate, although dated 29 Oct. 1731,
distinctly states " nato il 28 ottobre ".

179 i **APTHORP**
Par. 2, ll. 14-15 *should read* :
Music Lovers ' (1894), ' By the Way, being
a Collection of Short Essays about Music and
Art in General ', 2 vols. (1898), ' The Opera,

188 ii **ARANYI, Jelly d'**
Par. 1, l. 1. 3 May *should read* :
30 May

Par. 2, l. 15. 1923 *should read* :
1913.

Add before **ARBEAU** :

ARBATSKY, Yury Ivanovich (*b*. Moscow, 15 Apr. 1911).
Russian musicologist. He left Russia in
1924 and went to live in Prague, where he
began his musical education with a pupil of
Rimsky-Korsakov, studying composition with
Lopatnikov. His first appointment was that
of musical director at Belgrade Cathedral.
In 1930 he gained the Rakhmaninov scholarship at the Leipzig Conservatory. On leaving
that institution he co-operated in the organization of the Paris branch of the Belaiev publishing concern, performing a similar service
for that of Wilhelm Zimmerman, son of the
proprietor of the well-known Russian musical
edition. Returning to Prague, he entered the
University, from which he graduated with a
diploma in philosophy. He was elected
scientific correspondent of Prague University.
Spending the period of the second world
war in Prague, Arbatsky was given access to
the Soviet Union's secret musical archives
and to the then unpublished works of the
famous Kastalsky. In 1949 he took up residence in the U.S.A., where he spent much of
his time examining the musical archives in
the Newberry Library at Chicago. For his
services to science he was awarded the Guggen-
heim Prize in 1955. He is the author of a

Study of Russian Musical History, published
in Russian in New York by the Chekhov
publishing concern.   M. M-N.

189 ii **ARBÓS**
Par. 1, ll. 2-3 *should read* :
24 Dec. 1863 [1] ; *d*. San Sebastián, 2 June
1939 [2]).

l. 5 *should read* :
terio, the eminent violinist. Through his

Add footnotes :
[1] According to the birth certificate, quoted by Moltó
(*see* Bibl.).
[2] According to the certificate of death.

191 i **ARCADELT**
Par. 2, ll. 5-6. ' Années ', pp.
25-29, *should read* :
' Trésor musical ', X and XXV–XXIX

Add after See also :
Chorwerk, Vol. 58 (modern reprint of madrigals).

Add after See also at end :
Collectio O.M.B., Vols. 8, 12 (modern ed.).

ARCHAMBEAU
Par. 1, l. 2 *should read* :
28 Sept. 1879 ; *d*. Villefranche-sur-Mer, 29
Dec. 1955).

193 i **ARCHIVES DES MAÎTRES DE
L'ORGUE**
List, Vol. 3, l. 4. noës *should read* :
noëls

ii **ARCHLUTE**
Add at end:
PLATE 42, Vol. V, p. 432, No. 5.

195 i **ARENSKY**
List of Works, *add after* Symphony No. 2 :
Variations on a Theme of Tchaikovsky, for stgs
(Op. 35*a*).[1]

Add after ' The Wolves ' :
Pf. Trio No. 2, F mi. (Op. 73).

Add footnote :
[1] Arranged from the string Quartet No. 2.

ARGENTA MAZA
Par. 1, l. 2 *should read* :
Urdiales, Santander, 19 Nov. 1913 ; *d*. nr.
Madrid, 21 Jan. 1958).

196 ii Footnote, Vol. I *should read* :
Vol. II

201 i **Aristophanes**
ll. 13-14 *should read* :
ballet). Leigh (' Frogs ', incid. m.). Lincke ' Lysistrata ', operetta). Mellers (' Lysistrata ', incid. m. and
' Extravaganza ' for chamber m.) Mil-

202   i   **ARKOR**
Par. 2, ll. 7-10 *should read*:

held that position for seventeen years.   In
1931 he appeared at the Opéra-Comique in
Paris and in 1934 he made an American tour.

203   i   **ARMA**
Par. 1, l. 2 *should read*:

haus) (*b*. Budapest, 22 Oct. 1905).

206   i   **ARMONICA**
Par. 2, ll. 3-4 *should read*:

Mozart's exquisite Adagio and Rondo for
armonica, flute, oboe, viola and cello (K. 617),
which he com-

ii   Par. 2, l. 36.   Goosens *should read*:
Goossens
Add to BIBL.:
GEISSLER, HORST WOLFRAM, 'Die Glasharmonica'
(Munich, 1953).

207   i   **ARMSTRONG**
Par. 1, l. 1 *should read*:

**ARMSTRONG, (Sir) Thomas (Henry
Wait)**
ii   Par. 2, l. 23 *should read*:

'Craftsmanship in Music'.   In 1957 Armstrong succeeded Sir Reginald Thatcher as
Principal of the R.A.M. in London, and he
was knighted in 1958.

208   i   **ARNAUD, Yvonne**
Par. 1, l. 2 *should read*:

deaux, 20 Dec. 1890; *d*. London, 20 Sept.
1958).

209   i   **ARNE**
Par. 2, ll. 6-7.   19 Dec. 1733
should read:

12 Jan. 1734

Par. 3, ll. 24-25 *should read*:

tree ", " Blow, blow, thou winter wind " and
" When daisies pied ", the last introduced
into that play from ' Love's Labour's Lost '.

214   i   *Add to* ORCHESTRAL WORKS (*after*
8 Overtures):

4 ' New Overtures or Symphonies ' (in B.M.).

Add to See also, l. 7 (*before* Oldham):
Musica Britannica, Vol. 3 (modern ed. of ' Comus ').

215   ii   **ARNELL**
Add to Catalogue (*after* BALLETS):
TELEVISION OPERA
' Love in Transit ' (lib. by Hal Burton).

ORCHESTRAL WORKS
Add at end:
— Symphony No. 5 (1954).
' Landscapes and Figures ' (1956).

215   ii   *Add after* SOLO INSTRUMENT AND
ORCHESTRA:
VOICE AND ORCHESTRA
' Ode to the West Wind ' (Shelley) for soprano (1954).

216   i   *Add after* **ARNLJOT**:
ARNOLD, Denis (Midgley) (*b*. Sheffield, 15 Dec. 1926).
English musicologist.   He studied at Sheffield University under F. H. Shera in 1944–
1948, took the B.A. in 1947, the B.Mus. in
1948 and the M.A. in 1950 with a thesis on
Thomas Weelkes.   In 1950–51 he held an
Italian State Scholarship, and he also took
the A.R.C.M. as a pianoforte performer in
1948.   In 1951 he was appointed lecturer in
music in the Department of Extra-Mural
Studies at Queen's University, Belfast.   His
connections with Italy were strengthened by
a series of ten lecture-recitals of English virginal music given for the British Council
in the principal Italian cities and an invitation to give one of the lectures celebrating
the quatercentenary of Giovanni Gabrieli at
the Venice Conservatory in Sept. 1957.   The
American Institute of Musicology appointed
him editor of that master's ' Opera omnia '
(Vol. I, 1956; Vol. II, 1958).
Apart from many articles on Italian subjects contributed to M.G.G., Arnold has
published the following:
' Thomas Weelkes and the Madrigal ' (M. & L., 1950).
' Giovanni Croce and the Concertato Style ' (M.Q.,
1953).
' Giovanni Croce and the English Madrigal ' (M. & L.,
1954).
' Notes on the Monteverdi Vespers ' (M.M.R., 1956).
' Gastoldi and the English Ballett ' (M.M.R., 1957).
' " Seconda   Pratica ":   Monteverdi's   Madrigals '
(M. & L., 1957).
' Ceremonial Music in Venice at the Time of the
Gabrielis ' (Proc. Roy. Mus. Ass., Vol. LXXXII).
E. B.

217   ii   **ARNOLD, J. H.**
Par. 1, l. 2 *should read*:

London, 29 May 1887; *d*. Stanmore, Middle-
sex, 19 June 1956).

ARNOLD, Malcolm
List of Works
Add at top:
Ballet ' Solitaire ' (1956).

220   ii   **ARNOLDSON, Sigrid**
Par. 3, l. 20.   Maurice Fischof,
should read:

Arnold Fischof,

221   i   *Add after* **ARON**:
Arp, Hans. *See* Vogel (' Arpiade ').

ARPEGGIO
Par. 1.   *Add at end*:

The forms *arpeggiando* and *arpeggiato* are also
met with in rehearsal and in scores.

226   i   **ARRANGEMENT**
          Par. 4 *and*

      ii Par. 1, *delete.*
          (The contributor was mistaken:
          Brahms first arranged the ori-
          ginal string Quintet as a Sonata
          for two pianofortes, and the
          final version is the pianoforte
          Quintet. Unfortunately the
          numbering of these versions is
          misleading, the final quintet
          version being Op. 34 and the
          Sonata Op. 34b.)

229   i   **ARRIETA**
          Par. 3, ll. 4-5 *should read:*

1849), ' Isabella la Cattolica, ossia La con-
quista di Granada ' (1850, revised 1855), the
librettos by

233   ii **ARS NOVA**
          See also should read:

See also Lyrebird Press (modern eds.). Notation.

234   ii **ART OF FUGUE**
          Add to BIBL.:

LEONHARDT, GUSTAV M., ' The Art of Fugue ' (The
Hague, 1952).

235   ii **ARTEAGA**
          Par. 2, ll. 14-16 *should read:*

left an Italian manuscript treatise on the
rhythm of the ancients, which is in the National
Historic Archives in Madrid and was published there in 1944 by P. Miguel Batllori.
Its title is ' Del ritmo sonoro e del ritmo muto
nella musica degli antichi '.

242   ii **ASKENASE**
          Par. 1, l. 2 *should read:*

with Sauer in 1919. He also studied composition with Joseph Marx. He made his début
in

          l. 10 *should read:*

and settled in Brussels, where in 1954 he
became professor at the Conservatoire Royal.

243   i   **ASSAFIEV**
          Par. 1, l. 3. June *should read:*
July

244   i   *Add before* **Asseyev:**

ASSASSINIO NELLA CATTEDRALE.
Opera in 2 acts by Pizzetti. Libretto by the
Composer, based on T. S. Eliot's play ' Mur-
der in the Cathedral ', Italian translation by
Alberto Castelli. Produced Milan, Teatro
alla Scala, 1 Mar. 1958.

          Add after **ASSHETON:**

Assier, Maurice d'. *See* Delvincourt (6 songs).

247   i   **ASTORGA**
          Add to BIBL.:

TIBY, OTTAVIO, ' Emanuele d' Astorga: aggiunte e
correzioni da apportare alle ricerche del Prof.
Hans Volkmann ' (' Acta Musicologica ', XXV, iv,
1953).

      ii **ATHALIA**
          l. 2 *should read:*

Humphreys, based on Racine's tragedy, music
by Handel. The score was

248   ii **ATKINS**
          Par. 2, l. 22 *should read:*

preface to ' Worcester Mediaeval Harmony '
is to

          Add before **ATONALITY:**

ATKINS (Atkinson), John (*b.* ?; *d.*
London, 1671).
     English violinist and composer. He entered
the royal band as a violinist in 1660 and
served up to the beginning of the year of his
death. Playford did not print any of his songs,
but several (mostly drinking-songs) survive
in the following manuscripts: B.M. Add.
MS 29,396; New York Public Library,
Drexel MSS 4275; and especially 4041,
which, since it is primarily a source of pre-
Commonwealth play-songs, may indicate that
the composer (like John Gamble) was a
theatre musician. His style is typical of the
younger Commonwealth song-writers; less
emotional than Henry Lawes, but still
declamatory in a sort of *parlando* style.

                                              I. S.

249   ii **ATTAIGNANT**
          Par. 1, l. 6 *should read:*

Rokseth. They were the first printed books
of organ music to be published in France. All
the leading composers of the

          Add at end:
          See also Lyrebird Press (modern ed. of 13 books of
          motets).

250   i   **ATTERBERG**
          List of works, l. 11 *should read:*
' Aladdin ', Op. 43, opera, prod. Stockholm, 18 Mar.
1941.

      ii **Atterbom**
          ll. 1-2. *division should be:*
' Sjö-kvinnan '

256   i   **AUBÉRY DU BOULLEY**
          Par. 1, l. 3 *should read:*

28 Jan. 1870).

257   ii **AUCASSIN ET NICOLETTE**
          l. 1. *Add after See:*

CASTELNUOVO-TEDESCO (opera).

257   ii   **Auden**
l. 1 *should read*:

Auden, W. H.   *See* Berio ('Nones').   Bernstein
('Age of Anxiety').

259   ii   **AUGUSTINE**
Par. 2, l. 4 *should read*:

metres of the early Christian period. There
is an English translation by R. Catesby Talia-
fero (1939) and a German one by C. J. Perl
(1737).

Add before See also:

BIBL.—EDELSTEIN, H., 'Die Musikanschauung Augus-
tins' (Freiburg i/B, 1928).
HOFFMANN, W., 'Philosophische Interpretation der
Augustin-Schrift "De musica"' (Freiburg i/B,
1930).

Add after See also:

Dallapiccola ('Canti di liberazione', choral work).

265   ii   **AURIC**
FRENCH FILMS
l. 13. 'L'Heureux Retour' *should read*:

'L'Éternel Retour' (Cocteau).

Add after this:

'La Symphonie pastorale' (after André Gide).
'La Belle et la bête' (Cocteau).
'Orphée' (Cocteau).
'La Fête à Henriette.'

266   i   SONGS
l. 5.   (1920) *should read*:
(1918).

268   ii   **AUSTIN, Sumner**
Add at end:

In 1952 he was responsible for the first English
stage production of Berg's 'Wozzeck' at
Covent Garden.

AUSTRAL, Florence
Add at end:

In 1937–39 she appeared as a guest artist at
Sadler's Wells Theatre in London as Brünnhilde, Aida and Santuzza.

270   i   **AUSTRALIA**
Par. 3.   *Add at end*:

Goossens resigned in 1956, and was succeeded
by Sir Bernard Heinze in 1957.

Par. 4.   *Add at end*:

There are now four permanent members on
the music staff.

Par. 6, ll. 3 & 4 *should read*:

stone Choral Society conducted by Albert
Keats.

Par. 7, l. 11 *should read*:

Under the direction of Nicolai Malko, with

ii   Par. 2.   *Delete paragraph.*

c

270   ii   Par. 3.   *Add at end*:

The University Pro Musica Society, conducted by Professor Peart, has produced
operas and concerts since 1949.

Add new paragraph after Par. 5 :

A scheme for an opera house was first
mooted in 1954 by the late Premier, Cahill.
A site was selected, and an international
competition held for the best design. The
site is one of the finest in Sydney, Bennelong
Point, right on the main harbour front, looking out to Circular Quay and the Bridge;
the winning design, by the Dane, Jorn Utzon,
takes full advantage of it with an uncom-
promisingly modern building, with soaring
concrete shell domes echoing the sails of
yachts. It will doubtless be one of the most
interesting opera and concert buildings in the
world. There will be four auditoriums : a
main hall, holding 2800 for symphony concerts, but with an adjustable stage area which
will reduce it to 1700 for operatic productions ;
a second theatre holding 1100; a small
experimental theatre holding 430; and a
chamber music room for 310. Besides this,
there are the usual service rooms, dressing
rooms and a restaurant. Building is already
under way, and the whole project will be
complete in 1963.

Par. 6, ll. 6-11 *should read*:

equipped conservatory is now functioning
under control from the Sydney Conservatorium, and concerts are given in the newly-
completed War Memorial Cultural Centre.

Par. 7, l. 6 *should read*:

conducted by Kurt Woess and the University

271   i   Par. 2, last two lines *should read*:

cathedral organist is now Lance Hardy.

ii   Par. 4.   *Add at end*:

Dr. R. Dalley-Scarlett died in 1959. His
valuable collection of early Handel prints
and other music went to the University of
Sydney, Fisher Library.

Par. 5, ll. 9-12 *should read*:

Rudolf Pekarek. John Farnsworth Hall, his
predecessor, now conducts the West Australian
Symphony Orchestra.

272   i   Par. 5.   *Delete paragraph.*

Par. 6 *should read*:

The Brisbane Conservatory was established in
1959. Its first Director, Dr. William Love-
lock, has since resigned.

ii   Par. 1.   *Delete last sentence.*

272 ii Par. 3. *After this add new paragraph*:

Adelaide held its first International Festival of the Arts, with music and drama prominent, in 1960.

Par. 4. *Add at end*:

Henry Krips now conducts the permanent South Australian Symphony Orchestra.

Par. 6. *Delete first sentence and replace by*:

Frank Callaway was appointed Professor of Music at the University of W.A. in 1959.

274 ii **AVERY, John**
Par 1. (*b.* ?; *should read*:
(*b.* Stroud, Gloucestershire, ?;

Par. 2, l. 4 *should read*:

the fact that an organ of his was inaugurated at Stroud on 18 Apr. 1798 (when he was called " a Native of this Parish ") and that he died while engaged in finishing

l. 7 *should read*:

Westminster Abbey are his work.   Apart from that at Stroud, the organs

275 i **AVISON**
Par. 1, l. 2. bapt. Feb. *should read*:
bapt. 16 Feb.

277 ii *Add before* **AYLWARD, Theodore**:

AYLWARD (Ayleward, Yleward), Richard (*b.* Winchester, 1626; *d.* Norwich, 15 Oct. 1669).

English organist and composer.   He was the son of a Minor Canon at Winchester Cathedral and became a chorister in the cathedral choir under Christopher Gibbons. He was the first organist to be appointed at Norwich Cathedral after the Restoration, and his name appears in the cathedral audit book for the first time in 1661.   In 1664 his post was taken over by Thomas Gibbs, but when Gibbs died two years later, Aylward was again appointed and seems to have held the post until his death.   F. Blomefield (1701–1752) mentions in his ' History of Norfolk ' the tombstone of Richard Aylward, which bore the arms of " A saltier between four griffins heads erased " and was " lately removed ". He also gives the inscription :

Here lyeth interred the body of Richard Yleward, Organist of this place, who was born at Winchester and died here the 15th of October, An. Dom. 1669.

Here lyes a perfect Harmonie,
Of Faith & Truth & Loyaltie,
And whatsoever Vertues can,
Be reckoned up, was in this Man,
His sacred Ashes here abide,
Who in God's Service Liv'd & dy'd.
But now by Death advanced higher,
To serve in the Celestial Quire.
God save the King.

A set of eight part-books and an organ book containing services, anthems and chants by Aylward are at the Rowe Music Library, King's College, Cambridge (MS 9-17).   They belonged to him and contain many of his works.   The organ book is probably in holograph.   At the same library there are scores compiled by Dr. John Beckwith (*c.* 1760–1809) which could have been made from the above part-books (MS 267).   Both the part-books and the Beckwith scores belonged to Dr. A. H. Mann, formerly organist of King's College and an ex-chorister of Norwich Cathedral.   Canon Boston [1] mentions a note of Mann's referring to the scores made by Beckwith :

I have in my library a complete Service and 12 Anthems and one incomplete by Richard Aylward written in score by Dr. Beckwith. . . . I bought them in an old bookshop in Norwich.

Aylward's anthem ' The King shall rejoice ' was especially composed for the Restoration.   His Morning and Evening Service in D major consists of Te Deum, Benedicite, Litany, Responses, Creed, Preces, Magnificat and Nunc Dimittis.   The Responses and Litany are printed in Jebb's ' Choral Responses ' (1857), Vol. II, p. 33.

J. E. West [2] mentions some organ pieces in a manuscript belonging to Dr. W. H. Cummings and Eitner [3] some in MS Sydcote, West Dulwich Library.   These have not been traced so far.   A few virginal pieces are in the Lambeth Palace Library (MS 1040) and some more in a MS volume of harpsichord pieces (B.M., R.C.M. 1154) transcribed by E. Dannreuther from MSS once in the Taphouse collection.   s. J.

[1] Canon Noel Boston, ' The Musical History of Norwich Cathedral ' (Norwich, 1939).
[2] J. E. West, S.I.M., Year XII, p. 215.
[3] ' Quellen-Lexicon.'

278 i **AYRTON (1)**
Par. 1, l. 1 *should read*:

(1) **William Ayrton** (*b.* Ripon, [bapt. 18 Nov.] 1726; *d.*

AYRTON (2)
Par. 1, l. 1 *should read*:

(2) **Edmund Ayrton** (*b.* Ripon, [bapt. 19 Nov.] 1734; *d.*

280 ii **BABBINI** *should read*:
BABINI
Transfer to p. 281, after **BABIN.**

281 i Par. 2, l. 9 *should read*:
Matteo Babini ' (Bologna, 1821).

BABBITT
Par. 3, ll. 6-7. *Delete* ' Composition for Five Brass Instruments ' (1953),

281   ii   **BABINI**
           Transfer from p. 280, after **BABIN.**

283   ii   **BABYLONIAN MUSIC**
           Add at end :

BIBL.—FALKENSTEIN, ADAM & SODEN, WOLFRAM VON (eds.), ' Sumerische und akkadische Hymnen und Gebete ' (Zürich, 1953).

284   i   **BACCALONI**
          Par. 2, ll. 14-16 *should read* :

countries, including England, where he appeared at the Covent Garden Opera in London in 1928–29. In the U.S.A. he

ll. 18-25 *should read* :

1930. He also sang at Glyndebourne in 1936–1939 and San Francisco in 1938, and made many appearances at the Teatro Colón in Buenos Aires in 1931–40 and at Philadelphia, where his first part was Bartolo in ' Figaro ' on 3 Dec. 1940. He has been one of the principals of the Metropolitan Opera in New York ever since 7 Dec. 1940, with a large list of parts in Italian,

Bacchelli
l. 2 *should read* :

opera). Veretti (' Medico volante ', lib.; ' Galante tiratore ', scen.).

286   i   **BACH**
          Par. 3. *Add at end* :
BIBL.—GEIRINGER, KARL, ' The Bach Family ' (New York, Toronto & Oxford, 1954).

290   Page Heading:
           Relations *should read* :
Relatives

      i   **BACH (15)**
          Par. 1, l. 11 *should read* :
1690 ", also exists and has been recorded.

          BACH (17)
          l. 2 *should read* :
b. 27 Aug. 1674; d. ? London, 1740, taught the clavier at Erfurt,

292   Page Heading:
           Add :
of Johann Sebastian

293   i   **BACH (30)**
          Add at end :
BIBL.—FREYSE, CONRAD, ' Die Ohrdrufer Bache in der Silhouette : Johann Sebastian Bachs ältester Bruder Johann Christoph und seine Nachkommen ' (Cassel, 1955).

304   i   **BACH (32)**
          Add to footnote 1 :
' also Besseler (*see* Bibl.).

308   i   **BACH (J. S.)**
          Add to BIBL. (ENGLISH).

DICKINSON, A. E. F., ' Bach's Fugal Works : with an Account of Fugue before and after Bach ' (London, 1956).

BIBL., l. 20 *should read* :
' The Art of Bach ' (London, 1936;

Add after l. 23 :
' Notes on Bach's Organ Works : a Companion to the Revised Novello Edition ' (London, 1957).

Add to BIBL. :
GEIRINGER, KARL, ' The Bach Family ' (New York, Toronto & Oxford, 1954).

      ii   l. 17. *Add after* Motets '
, Musical Pilgrim series

Add after l. 18 :
' The Passions ', Musical Pilgrim series, 2 vols. (Oxford, 1926).

Under SCHWEITZER.
translated from the French by *should read* :
translated by

Under SPITTA.
(London, 1889). *should read* :
(London, 1889 ; new ed. New York & London, 1952).

Add to BIBL. :
TAYLOR, STAINTON DE B., ' The Chorale Preludes of J. S. Bach : a Handbook ' (Oxford, 1942).

Under TERRY.
l. 3, (Oxford, 1915–21). *should read* :
(Cambridge, 1915–21).

BIBL. TERRY, l. 12. (Oxford, 1932). *should read* :
(Oxford, 1932 ; reprint, 1958).

Add to BIBL. (ENGLISH) :
TUSLER, ROBERT L., ' The Style of J. S. Bach's Chorale Preludes ' (Berkeley, Cal., Los Angeles & Cambridge, 1956).

Add to BIBL. (GERMAN) :
BESSELER, HEINRICH, ' Fünf echte Bildnisse Johann Sebastian Bachs ' (Cassel & Basel, 1956).
CZACZKES, LUDWIG, ' Analyse des wohltemperierten Klavieres : Form und Aufbau der Fuge bei Bach ' (Vienna & Würzburg, 1956).

309   i   *Add to* BIBL. :
DAVID, JOHANN NEPOMUK, ' Die zweistimmigen Inventionen von Johann Sebastian Bach ' (Göttingen, 1957).
DÜRR, ALFRED, ' Zur Chronologie der Leipziger Vokalwerke J. S. Bachs ' (Berlin & Cassel, 1957).
HUBER, ANNA GETRUD, ' Johann Sebastian Bach : seine Schüler und Interpreten. Querschnitt durch die Geschichte der Bach-Interpretation ', Vol. I (Zürich, London & New York, 1958).

BIBL. *under* NEUMANN.
l. 2 *should read* :
Bachs ' (Leipzig, 1947 ; 2nd ed. 1953).

      ii   SCHMIEDER, LUDWIG.
           Delete entry.

           SCHMIEDER, WOLFGANG.
           l. 3 *should read* :
Sebastian Bach ' (Leipzig & Wiesbaden, 1950).

309 ii SCHWEBSCH.
l. 2 should read :
(Stuttgart, 1931; 2nd ed. 1955).

Add to BIBL.:
SCHWEITZER, ALBERT, 'J. S. Bach' (augmented translation of the French work) (Leipzig, 1908).

BIBL. (FRENCH.)
Add 2nd work by DUFOURCQ :
'Un Architecte de la musique : Jean Sébastien Bach, génie allemand — génie latin ? ' (Paris, 1954).

Add at end :
ITALIAN
TAGLIAVINI, LUIGI FERDINANDO, 'Studi sui testi delle cantate sacre di J. S. Bach' (Padua, 1957).
VALABREGA, CESARE, 'Giovanni Sebastiano Bach' (Parma, 1950).

315   Scored for, ll. 18-19. 'Wir müssen . . .',
         should read :
S.A.T.B., chor., fl., 2 ob., 2 ob. d'a., ob. da c., stgs., org. concertante & cont.

320 — CATALOGUE
        CLAVIER WORKS
        Col. 2, l. 22. 1731. should read :
1726-31.
        Col. 2, l. 39. (" English " Suites), c. 1725.
        should read :
c. 1720.

321   Page Heading:
         should read :
BACH (J. S.) : Wives — (Wilhelm Friedemann)

i   See also, ll. 34-35. Villa Lobos should read :
Villa-Lobos

326 i BACH, C. P. E., CATALOGUE
        SONGS, heading should read :
SONGS [1]
        l. 5. ' Cramers übersetzte should read :
' [J. A.] Cramers übersetzte
        l. 10 should read :
c. 100 other songs (nearly 300 in all, but some doubtful), including settings of Gellert, Hagedorn, Hölty, Ewald von Kleist, Klopstock, Lessing and J. H. Voss.

Add footnote :
[1] A complete list is given by Gudrun Busch in ' C. Ph. E. Bach und seine Lieder ', Vol. II : Appendix (Ratisbon, 1957).

ii Add to BIBL. :
BUSCH, GUDRUN, ' C. Ph. E. Bach und seine Lieder ', 2 vols. (Ratisbon, 1957).
CRICKMORE, LEON, ' C. P. E. Bach's Harpsichord Concertos ' (M. & L., XXXIX, 1958, p. 227).

327 i BACH (34)
        See also, l. 2 should read :
of). Bebung. Denkmäler (5) I, Vol. 18 (modern ed. of Symphonies). Sonata, pp. 897-98. Symphony, pp.

328 ii BACH (36)
        Par 2, l. 25 should read :
mann, is in D.D.T., Vol. LVI, together with modern editions of ' Die Kindheit Jesu ' and ' Die Auferweckung des Lazarus '.

331 ii BACH (38)
        Add to BIBL. :
SADIE, STANLEY, 'The Wind Music of J. C. Bach' (M. & L., XXXVII, 1956, p. 107).

See also, between ll. 1 & 2 add :
Denkmäler (5) I, Vol. 3 (modern ed. of 6 Quintets).

l. 6 should read :
pp. 900-1. Sondheimer Ed., Vols. 8, 17, 34 (modern ed. of var. works). Symphony, p. 212.

338 i BACH TRUMPET
        See TRUMPET. should read :
See TRUMPET; PLATE 74, Vol. VIII, p. 562, No. 10.

340 i BACILLY
        Par. 2, l. 16 should read :
with vocal embellishments.

Add at end :
A modern facsimile reprint of ' Remarques curieuses ' is to be published in ' Documenta Musicologica ', Vol. 4.   E. V. d. s., adds.

ii BACKER-GRØNDAHL, A.
    Par. 2, l. 3. (1866) should read :
(1865–67)
    l. 4. (1867) should read :
(1871)
    l. 8 should read :
former is ' Mot Kveld ' (' Towards Evening '), and she also set a

Add at end :
BIBL.—SANDVIK, O. M., 'Agathe og O. A. Gröndahl, 1847–1947 ' (Oslo, 1948).

341 i BACKER-GRØNDAHL, F.
        Par. 1, l. 2 should read :
Christiania, 15 Oct. 1885 ; d. Oslo, 21 June 1959).

344 i BAEYENS
        Par. 2, l. 6 should read :
Dead Poet ', 1920), incidental music for Maeterlinck's ' The Blue Bird ' (1951) ; the oratorio ' Lofzang
        l. 8 should read :
6 Symphonies and the orch. works ' Entrata ' (1917), ' Niobe '
        l. 12 should read :
breve ' (1927) ; chamber music incl. 5 stg. Quartets and wind Quintet. He also wrote pf. works and

ii BAGGE, Selmar
    Par. 1, l. 2. 17 July should read :
16 July

350   ii   **BAGPIPE**
Par. 4 *should read*:

The small mouth-blown *dudy* was borrowed from Poland by Germany, where it was called *Dudey* in the 17th century and had a melodic compass from e♭" to d'''.[1]

Par 5, l. 1.   *koza should read*:
kobza

Par. 5, l. 1.   *koziol* [1] *should read*:
koziol [2]

Add footnote:
[1] Curt Sachs, ' Reallexikon der Musikinstrumente', p. 122.
Footnote 1 becomes 2.

354   ii   *See also should read*:
See also Biniou. Musette. *PLATE* 34, Vol. IV, p. 500, No. 5.

BAGUER
Par. 1, l. 1.   **Carles** *should read*:
Carlos

l. 2 *should read*:
d. Barcelona, 29 Feb. 1808).

BAHR-MILDENBURG
Par. 2, l. 28.   Shakespeare *should read*:
Makepeace

355   ii   **BAILLIE, Isobel**
Par. 2, ll. 8-9 *should read*:
California (1933). She is not an operatic artist, but sang Amor in Gluck's ' Orfeo' at Covent Garden in 1937.
The character of Isobel

358   i   **BAINTON**
Par 1, l. 2 *should read*:
14 Feb. 1880; d. Sydney, 8 Dec. 1956).

ii   **BAIRD**
Par. 1, l. 2 *should read*:
wiecki, 26 July 1928).

359   ii   **BAKER, Dalton**
Par. 2, l. 1 *should read*:
English baritone singer and conductor. He was trained at the

ll. 6-7 *should read*:
London performance of Elgar's ' The Kingdom ' in 1906 and in that of Bantock's

ll. 9-10 *should read*:
Canada, where he taught singing at the Toronto Rugeley Conservatory for twenty years. In 1934 he settled at Vancouver as teacher and choral conductor.

360   i   **BAKER, Theodore**
Par. 2, l. 7.   Slominsky *should read*:
Slonimsky

367   i   **BALAKIREV**
Add to BIBL. :
MONTAGU-NATHAN, M., ' Balakirev's Letters to Calvocoressi' (M. & L., XXXV, 1954, p. 347).

368   i   PIANOFORTE TRANSCRIPTIONS
Delete
Alabiev :
        ' The Nightingale '.

ii   **Balázs**
l. 2.   ' Woodcut Prince ' *should read*:
' Wooden Prince '

369   i   **BALBI**
Par. 1, l. 1.   Venice, ?, *should read*:
Venice, 1545 [1]

Add footnote:
[1] Deduced from a letter written by Costanzo Porta to Cardinal Borromeo on 7 Nov. 1579, quoted in Garbelotto's book on that composer, in which he recommends Balbi as *maestro di cappella* for Milan and says that he is thirty-four years of age.

ii   *Add before* **BALDUIN** :
BALDOVINO, Amedeo (*b.* Alexandria, Egypt, 5 Feb. 1916).
Violoncellist and composer of Italian parentage. He took diplomas for cello playing in 1930 and for composition in 1940 at the Conservatory of Bologna.
                                        G. M. G.

370   i   *Add before* **BALELLI** :
BALE, Alfonso.   *See* BALES.

Add after **BALELLI** :
BALES (Bale, Ball, Balls), Alfonso (*b.* London, ? ; *d.* London, 1635).
English lutenist and composer. It was probably Alfonso rather than his father, (?) Richard, who was the Mr. Balls who composed ' Chloris sighed and sung and wept ', one of the most famous declamatory ayres of pre-Commonwealth times. No fewer than six manuscript versions of it have survived (two is average), and Bannister and Lowe printed it in their ' New Ayres and Dialogues ' (1678), p. 88 — a late publication which nevertheless drew upon some early sources not available to Playford, or overlooked by him. The song itself is a perfect example of the affective style current in the 1620s, and many of the manuscripts are typically and profusely ornamented. Another song, the Charon dialogue from Beaumont and Fletcher's ' Mad Lover ', is also attributed to him in B.M. Add. MS 10,337.
Both father and son were London Waits ; Richard from 1603 to 1622 and Alfonso from

1613 to 1635. The latter was one of Prince Charles's musicians sometime before 1625 and served as one of the king's lutes and voices up to 1635, in which year he died, John Wilson taking his place.

The manuscripts containing 'Chloris sighed' are: B.M. Add. MSS (a) 11,608 (the only ascribed version); (b) 10,337; (c) Trinity College, Dublin, MS F. 5. 13; (d) Ch. Ch. MS 87; (e) Bodl. Lib. MS Don. C. 57; (f) New York Public Library, Drexel MS 4175: (b) and (f) supply virginal and lute accompaniments respectively.   I. S.

372   i   **BALFOUR, Henry Lucas**
            Par. 1, l. 2 *should read*:

Oct. 1859; *d.* Croydon, Surrey, 27 Dec. 1946).

        ii   *Add after* **BALIUS Y VILA**:
BALL (Balls), Alfonso. See BALES.

375   i   **BALLAD**
            Add to BIBL.:

LAWS, G. MALCOLM, 'American Balladry from British Broadsides: a Guide for Students and Collectors of Traditional Song' (Philadelphia, 1957).

377   i   *Add to* BIBL.:

MEIERHANS, LYDIA, 'Die Ballata' (Berne, 1956).

378   i   **BALLARD (family)**
            Add to BIBL.:

LESURE, FRANÇOIS & THIBAULT, GENEVIÈVE, 'Bibliographie des éditions d'Adrien Le Roy et Robert Ballard (1551-1598)' (Paris, 1955).

389   ii   **BALLET**
            Par. 2, l. 18 *should read*:

mann and Frederick Ashton. Since 1948 John Cranko has done distinguished work as choreographer.

        Par. 3, ll. 14-15 *should read*:

Petit to music by Chabrier and 'Ballet Imperial' (choreography by Balanchine), an ingenious pastiche of the Russian

392   i   *Add to* BIBL.:

CHUJOY, ANATOLE, 'The New York City Ballet' (New York, 1953).
CLARKE, MARY, 'The Sadler's Wells Ballet: a History and an Appreciation' (London, 1955).
DREW, DAVID, (ed.), 'The Decca Book of Ballet' (London, 1958).
FRANKS, ARTHUR HENRY, 'Twentieth-Century Ballet' (London, 1954).
GUEST, IVOR FORBES, 'Romantic Ballet in England: its Development, Fulfilment and Decline' (London, 1954).
'The Ballet of the Second Empire: 1847-1858' (London, 1955).
'The Ballet of the Second Empire, 1858-1870' (London, 1953).
LIFAR, SERGE, 'Serge de Diaghilev: sa vie, son œuvre, sa légende' (Monaco, 1954).
MONTAGU-NATHAN, M., 'Mlle Camargo' (London, 1932).

REYNA, FERDINANDO, 'Les Origines du ballet' (Paris, 1955).
'The History of the Russian Ballet from its Origins to the Present Day', trans. by Arnold Haskell (London, 1954).
SEARLE, HUMPHREY, 'Ballet Music: an Introduction' (London, 1958).
WILSON, G. B. L., 'A Dictionary of Ballet' (Harmondsworth, 1957).

394   i   **BALLETT**
            Par. 4, l. 1 *should read*:

"Balletto" is used by Frescobaldi in his keyboard music for an allegro and by Bach for another, both in

395   i   *Add after* **Balocchi**:
Balog, István. See Mátray ('Gyuró Czerni', incid. m.).

        ii   **BALTZAR**
            Par. 1, ll. 1-2 *should read*:

In 1661 Baltzer joined the king's celebrated band of 24 violins, but there is no evidence that he was its leader.[1] He

            Add footnote:
[1] *See* Westrup, 'Purcell', p. 29, note.

        BAMPTON
        Par. 3, l. 4 *should read*:

Dresden and appeared in the title-part of 'Aida' at Warsaw; but in 1937, at Covent Garden in London, she reverted to Amneris in the same work. Her first appearance as a soprano

396   ii   **BANCHIERI**
            Par. 1, l. 1.   1567 *should read*:

3 Sept. 1568

            Par. 2, ll. 3-7 *should read*:

of Giuseppe Guami. He took holy orders on 8 Sept. 1589 and lived at the monastery of SS. Bartolomeo e Ponziano at Lucca in 1592, at that of San Benedetto at Siena in 1593, at that of San Michele in Bosco near Bologna, known as Monte Oliveto, in 1594-1600, and he became organist at the church there in 1596. In 1600-4 he was

            l. 10.   *Full stop at end of line.*

            ll. 11-12 *should read*:

In 1604 he was organist at the monastery of San Pietro at Gubbio, in 1605-6 at that of Sant' Elena at Venice, in 1606-8 at that of Santa Maria in Organo at Verona, and in 1608 he returned to resume his former post at San Michele in Bosco near Bologna, where he remained until his death. He became abbot in 1620. He did

397   ii   *Add to* BIBL.:

BIBL.—CAPACCIOLI, E., 'Precisazioni biografiche su Adriano Banchieri' (Riv. Mus. It., Oct.–Dec. 1954).

397   ii   *See also*, l. 1 *should read* :

See also Amfiparnaso. Classici Musica Italiana, Vol. 1 (modern ed. of choral works). Ghizzolo (letter to and song

399   ii   **BANDROWSKI**
Dates *should read* :

(*b.* Lubaczówka, Galicia, 22 Apr. 1860 ; *d.* Cracow, 28 May 1913).

403   ii   **BANJO**
Add to BIBL. :

NATHAN, HANS, ' Early Banjo Tunes and American Syncopation ' (M.Q., XLII, 1956, p. 455).

404   i   **BANNISTER**
Par. 1, l. 1. ? *should read* :

Oxford, 18 Mar.

ii   **BANTI**
Par. 3, ll. 1-4 *should read* :

Banti's larynx (of extraordinary size) was examined and reported on after her death by three physiologists, by permission of her husband, the dancer

411   —   **BANTOCK,** CATALOGUE
PIANOFORTE SOLO
ll. 6-11 *should read* :

425   ii   Par. 1, ll. 4-5 *should read* :

1935 and 1936, he won Pulitzer Travelling Fellowships and in 1958 the Pulitzer Prize for his opera ' Vanessa '. During the second world war he

426   i   BIBL. *should read* :

BIBL.—BRODER, NATHAN, ' Samuel Barber ' (New York & London, 1954).
' The Music of Samuel Barber ' (M.Q., XXIV, 1948, p. 325).

CATALOGUE
Add under heading :

Op.   OPERA
— ' Vanessa ' (lib. by Gian Carlo Menotti), prod. New York, Metropolitan Opera, 15 Jan. 1958.

SOLO INSTRUMENTS AND OR-
CHESTRA
Op. 14. (1939). *should read* :
(1940).

ii   **BARBI**
Par. 1, l. 2 *should read* :

d. Rome, 4 Sept. 1948).

427   i   Par. 3, l. 5 *should read* :

to the Marchese Pietro Tomasi della Torretta, who was Italian ambassador to London from 1922 to 1927.

Title	Composed	Published
' Strathspey : Monymusk.'	1917.	
' Two Scottish Pieces '	1917.	1918.
1. Quickstep : The Hills of Glenorchy.		
2. Reel : The Bobers of Brechin.		
' Three Scottish Scenes '	1917–18.	
1. Quickstep : The Cameron Highlanders.		
2. Pibroch : The Gathering of Clan Chattan.		
3. Reel : Timour the Tartar.		

l. 13. (*see* Orchestral Works). *should read* :
(*see* Incidental Music).

l. 34 *should read* :

| ' Arabian Nights ', 7 pieces in 3 albums. | 1919–20. | 1920. |

422   i   **BARALLA**
Par. 1, ll. 1-2 *should read* :

BARALLI, (Don) Raffaello (*b.* Camigliano, Lucca, 25 June 1862 ; *d.* ?, 1922).

423   ii   **BARBARINO**
Add to BIBL. :

FORTUNE, NIGEL, ' Italian Secular Monody from 1600 to 1635 : an Introductory Survey ' (M.Q., XXXIX, 1953, p. 171).

424   ii   **BARBÉ**
Add at end :

See also Collectio O.M.B., Vol. 12 (modern ed.).

425   i   **BARBER, Samuel**
Par. 1, l. 1. Westchester *should read* :

West Chester

ii   **BARBIERI**
Par. 2, l. 4 *should read* :

and appearing again in 1945–48, and in 1949 during the

428   i   **BARBIREAU**
Add at end :

See also Amer. Inst. Musicol. (C.M.M.), Vol. 7 (modern ed. of complete works).

ii   **BARBIROLLI**
Par. 4, l. 28 *should read* :

from at home and abroad. Between 1951 and 1954 he appeared as guest conductor at Covent Garden in London.

430   i   **BARBLAN, Otto**
Par. 1, l. 2. 19 Dec. *should read* :

20 Dec.

430   i   Par. 3, l. 8 *should read* :

1938 was declared a national language by

ll. 11-12 *should read* :

work is the music he composed for the festival play commemorating the battle of Calven (1499), for solo voices, chorus and

ii   **BARBOUR**
Par. 1, l. 2 *should read* :

burg, Pennsylvania, 31 Mar. 1897).

Par. 2, l. 22 *should read* :

State College. In 1957 he was elected president of the American Musicological Society.

431   i   **BARCEWICZ**
Par. 1, l. 2 *should read* :

16 Apr. 1858 ; *d.* Warsaw, 1 Sept. 1929).

435   i   **BÄRENREITER-VERLAG**
Par. 1, l. 10 *should read* :

communities. With the aid of Walther Hensel (*d.* 1956)

435-36   **BARGAGLIA**
Cancel the whole entry and replace as follows :

Bargaglia, Scipione. Previously entered in this Dictionary and other musical works of reference, he is now known to have been no composer at all, but a 17th-century poet, and he is wrongly mentioned as a Neapolitan contrapuntist by Cerreto.[1] According to Burney the word " concerto " occurs for the first time in his work ' Trattenimenti ossia divertimenti . . . da suonare ' (Venice, 1587) ; but Alfred Einstein pointed out that this title cannot be one used in the 16th century, and that it had either been misquoted or that the year of publication was 1687. The word " concerto ", he maintained, is equally impossible at the earlier date, at any rate for an instrumental work. Einstein, indeed, regarded the facts given by all musical dictionaries about Bargaglia as highly suspicious. The book in question contains no musical notation and does not use the word " concerto ", but " concento ", according to Egon F. Kenton (' A Lexicographical Communication on a Non-existent Composer ' in ' Acta Musicologica ', 1954).
E. B.

[1] He is found described as " gentil' huomo sanese " and was in fact born at Siena in 1540.

437   i   **BARING-GOULD**
Add at end :

BIBL.—PURCELL, WILLIAM, ' Onward Christian Soldiers ', biography (London, 1957).

438   i   **Barker, George**
Add to l. 2 :
Finzi (song).

441   i   **BARNARD**
Par. 1, l. 2 *should read* :

bassus cantoris part of the printed edition is in the Manchester Free

449   i   **BAROQUE INTERPRETATION**
Par. 2, l. 12 *should read* :

mere metaphor. Most instruments, including

452   i   Par. 3, l. 3. seems *should read* :
seem

454   i   *Add to* BIBL. :
PINCHERLE, MARC, ' On the Rights of the Interpreter in the Performance of 17th- and 18th-Century Music ' (M.Q., XLIV, Apr. 1958, p. 145).

455   i   **BARRAUD**
OPERAS
l. 2. (1938) *should read* :
(1938), prod. Paris, Opéra-Comique, 26 June 1948.

l. 4 *should read* :
based on Cervantes) (1950), prod. Paris, Opéra, 15 Apr. 1955.

ii   *Add at end* :
BIBL.—ROSTAND, CLAUDE, ' Tendencies and Contrasts in the Music of Henry Barraud ' (' Tempo ', No. 44, 1957).

457   ii   **BARRETT, W. A.**
Par. 2. *Add at end* :

One of his most important publications was ' English Glees and Part-Songs — an Enquiry into their Historical Development ' (1886).

458   i   **BARRIENTOS**
Par. 1, l. 4 *should read* :

opera-houses in Europe (including London, Covent Garden, in 1903) and America she

BARRIOS
Par. 1, l. 2. 1886). *should read* :
1882).

460   ii   **BARTERED BRIDE**
l. 8. Covent Garden *should read* :
Drury Lane

461   ii   **BARTHÉLEMON**
Par. 1, l. 1 *should read* :
BARTHÉLEMON [1], **François Hippolyte**

l. 2. London, 23 *should read* :
London, 20

Add footnote :
[1] His daughter, Cecilia Maria Henslowe, in her preface to a selection from his ' Jefte in Masfa ' published in 1827, spells his name with two acute accents, Barthélémon ; but this should be accepted with caution, being unconfirmed elsewhere. On the other hand, Mrs. Henslowe's statement " On the 20th of July 1828 will be accomplished the 20th anniversary of his decease " establishes the date of his death more certainly than that in the ' Dictionary of National Biography ' (23 July).

462   i   Par. 2, l. 22 *should read* :
In 1827 his daughter,

463   i   **BARTLEMAN**
Par. 2, l. 2 *should read* :
probably in Westminster, and there is little doubt that he was the son of Barthélemon. He was educated

464 i **BARTÓK**
Par. 3, l. 14.   1891 *should read*:
1901

467 i Par. 4, ll. 9-11 *should read*:
been widely blamed, although his last publishers did their best to help him even by
subterfuges with his royalties, which, however,
his pride forbade him to countenance when
he discovered them. It is too early yet to

l. 20 *should read*:
commissioned a new string Quartet, to be
published by Boosey & Hawkes, for which

472 i *Add to* BIBL.:
BARTÓK, BÉLA, 'Eigene Schriften und Erinnerungen',
   ed. by Willi Reich (Basel & Stuttgart, 1958).
'Béla Bartók: l'homme et l'œuvre', ed. by Albert
   Richard (Rev. Mus., No. 224, 1955).
DEMÉNY, JÁNOS (ed.), 'Bartók Béla Levelei: Magyar,
   Román, Slovák, Dokumentmok' (Budapest, 1955).
ENGELMANN, HANS ULRICH, 'Béla Bartóks "Mikro-
   kosmos": Versuch einer Typologie neuer Musik'
   (Würzburg, 1953).
FASSETT, AGATHA, 'Béla Bartók's Last Years; The
   Naked Face of Genius' (London, 1958).
GERSON-KIWI, EDITH, 'Béla Bartók — Scholar in Folk
   Music' (M. & L., XXXVIII, 1957, p. 149).

ii *Add after* l. 6 (LENDVAI):
'Bartók stílusa' (Budapest, 1955).

l. 19 *should read*:
gage (Paris, 1949; Eng. trans. by G. S. Fraser &
Erik de Mauny, London, 1953).

Add to BIBL.

MORIEUX, SERGE, 'Béla Bartók' (Paris, 1955).
PERLE, GEORGE, 'Symmetrical Formations in the String
   Quartets of Bartók' (M. Rev., XVI, 1955, p. 300).
SZABOLCSI, BENCE (ed.), 'Bartók, sa vie et son œuvre',
   symposium (Budapest, 1956).
TRAIMER, ROSWITHA, 'Béla Bartóks Kompositions-
   technik, dargestellt an seinen sechs Streich-
   quartetten' (Ratisbon, 1956).

473 — CATALOGUE
l. 4 (*Title*) *should read*:
'Cantata profana: The Enchanted Stag.

ORCHESTRAL WORKS
Col. 2, l. 20. Nos. 7-15 *should read*:
Nos. 6-12, 14 & 15

476 — SONGS
Col. 2, l. 12. *Delete* (unpublished).

Col. 3, l. 7. Béla Balázs and others
                     should read:
Composer.

Add before **Bartolini**:
BARTOLETTI, Bruno (*b*. Sesto Fiorentino, Florence, 10 June 1926).
Italian conductor. He studied at the Conservatory "L. Cherubini" at Florence, became assistant conductor to the Maggio
Musicale and made his first operatic appearance at the Florentine Teatro Comunale in
1952. He has conducted opera and symphony
concerts at important theatres (Scala, Milan;
Opera, Rome) and concert halls (Rome,
Amsterdam, etc.).   G. M. G.

476 ii *Add after* **BARTOLINI**:
BARTOLOMEO DA BOLOGNA (*b*.? Bologna, ?; *d*. ?).
Italian 15th-century composer. He lived
early in the century and was a prior of the
Benedictine order. His small output of seven
works is very varied and consists of 3 secular
works on Italian texts, *i.e.* 2 *ballate* and a
rondeau, and 4 Latin pieces, of which two are
Mass movements and two complex compositions in the late 14th-century French
manner in *ballade* and *virelai* form respectively.
Moreover, both Mass movements, a Gloria
and a Credo, are based on Bartolomeo's own
ballate ' Vince con lena ' and ' Morir desio ',
providing early examples of parody technique. All seven compositions are for three
voices.
'Vince con lena' is in Stainer's 'Dufay
and his Contemporaries' (1898), the *virelai*
in J. Wolf's 'Geschichte der Mensural-
Notation' (1904), the Gloria and Credo in
C. van den Borren's 'Polyphonia Sacra'
(1932).   G. R. (iii).

478 ii **BARYTON (1)**
l. 2 *should read*:
BORDONE. *PLATE* 67, Vol. VIII, p. 146 (ii),
No. 2.

BARYTON (Fr.)
Entry should read:
BARYTON (Fr.). *See* BARITONE (2); also
a French name for the bass oboe, an instrument pitched an octave below the normal
oboe but quite distinct from the Heckelphone.

Add before **BAS-DESSUS**:
BARZUN, Jacques (*b*. Paris, 30 Nov.
1907).
French historian and writer on music. He
went to the U.S.A. in 1919 and studied at
Columbia University in New York, where he
took the A.B. in 1927 and the Ph.D. in 1932.
He became lecturer in history there in 1927
and professor in 1945. Among his books concerned with music are ' Darwin, Marx,
Wagner' (Boston, 1941) and ' Berlioz and
the Romantic Century', 2 vols. (Boston, 1950),
an exhaustively documented work. He is
also the editor and translator of ' New Letters
of Berlioz ' (New York, 1954) and published
a new translation of that master's ' Evenings
with the Orchestra ' (New York, 1956).
                                     E. B.

Add after **BAS-DESSUS**:
BASCHNE, Josef ⎫
                        ⎬ *See* BASZNY, JÓZEF.
BASCHNY, Josef ⎭

479   ii   **BASEL**
Par. 3, ll. 1-3 *should read*:
The Municipal Theatre, opened in 1834, was under the direction of Dr. Friedrich Schramm until 1954, when he was succeeded by Hermann Wedekind. It receives a handsome

Par. 4, l. 12 *should read*:
15 teachers and 222 pupils in 1950. August Wenzinger has been its director since 1954.

481   i   **BASS CLARINET**
Add at end of line:
PLATE 12, Vol. II, p. 321, Nos. 1 & 2.

BASS DRUM
Add at end of line:
PLATE 49, Vol. VI, p. 622, No. 1.

BASS FLUTE
l. 2 *should read*:
Stops. *PLATE* 21, Vol. III, p. 176, No. 17.

ii   **BASS-HORN**
See also, l. 2 *should read*:
Serpent. *PLATE* 59, Vol. VII, p. 712, No. 6.

BASS TRUMPET
Add at end of line:
PLATE 74, Vol. VIII, p. 562, No. 16.

Casa some time after 1598. His successor in that post was appointed on 5 Sept. 1617. Most of

484   i   **BASSE DE MUSETTE**
Add at end:
See PLATE 3, No. 2, p. 488.

ii   **BASSET HORN (1)**
Add at end of line:
PLATE 12, Vol. II, p. 321, Nos. 3 & 4.

485   i   **BASSIRON**
Add at end:
See also Collectio O.M.B., Vol. 8 (modern ed.).

BASSON D'AMOUR
Add at end:
See PLATE 3, No. 1, p. 488.

488   i   **BASSOON**
Par. 3, l. 8.   Phagotum *should read*:
Phagotus

l. 10.   (1480– *should read*:
(*c.* 1480–

opp.   **Plate**
l. 1 of caption *should read*:
RARE BASSOONS AND OBOES

PLATE 3, captions *should read*:

**BASSON D'AMOUR, BASSE DE MUSETTE, BARYTONE OBOE
AND RARE BASSOON**
(all in Bernisches Historisches Museum, Berne)

1. Basson d'Amour, spherical brass bell and pirouette, 18th century, inscribed 1.1R.   2. Basse de Musette with pirouette, 18th century, inscribed 1.1R, both from Gurzelen Church, Canton of Berne.   3. Barytone (Oboe) by Piatet & Benoit of Lyons (1836–55).   4. Bassoon (no name), early 19th century.

482   i   **BASSANI, G. B.**
Add at end, before signature:
A modern facsimile reprint of ' Motetti, madrigali e canzoni francese ' is to be published in ' Documenta Musicologica ', Vol. 5.

Add at end:
Bibl.—Haselbach, Richard, ' Giovanni Battista Bassani: Werkkatalog, Bibliographie und künstlerische Würdigung ' (Cassel & Basel, 1955).
See also Classici Musica Italiana, Vol. 2 (modern ed. of choral works).

BASSANO, G.
Par. 1.   *d.* ?). *should read*:
d. ?, prob. Aug. or Sept. 1617).

Par. 2, l. 1 *should read*:
Italian singer and composer. He

l. 5 *should read*:
(1595) and director of the instrumentalists, in which capacity he succeeded Girolamo Dalla

494   ii   **BASTON, Josquin**
Add at end:
Sss also Collectio O.M.B., Vol. 12 (modern ed.).

Add after **BASTON**:
BASZNY [1], **Józef** (*b.* Bohemia, ? ; *d.* Lwów, 1844).
Bohemian flautist, composer and bandmaster. As a young man he emigrated to Kiev and shortly afterwards went to Lwów, where he settled permanently. He became chorus master at the Cathedral and deputy director of the Music Society. Besides several cantatas he composed operatic works: ' Twardowski na Krzemionkach ' (' Mr. Twardowski at Krzemionki '), a comic opera in 5 acts to a libretto by J. N. Kamiński, produced at Lwów on 22 June 1825; ' Więzienie Jana Kazimierza we Francji ' (' The Imprisonment of Jan Casimir in France ') to a German libretto

[1] Also known as Baschne, Baschny, Buschne and Buszny.

based on A. Oppeln-Bronikowski's novel ' Der gallische Kerker ' (1827) ; and a 3-act vaude-ville, ' Skalmierzanki (' The Maidens of Skalmierz '), to a libretto by Kamiński, produced at Lwów on 5 Dec. 1828 with an enormous success. Within a year it was performed all over Poland, and it was revived at Poznań in 1939.   C. R. H.

494   ii   **BATE, S.**
Par. 1, l. 2. 1913). *should read* :

1911 ; *d.* London, 19 Oct. 1959).

496   ii   **BATES, Joah**
Par. 3, l. 3 *should read* :

Alfred H. Littleton. A pleasant portrait sketch of him is in the University Music School, Downing Place, Cambridge.
                 W. H. H., adds.

504   i   **BATTISTINI**
Par. 1, l. 1. 27 Nov. *should read* :
27 Feb.

506   ii   **BAUER, Ernst**
Par. 1, l. 1. **Ernst** *should read* :
Ernest

1889). *should read* :
1889 ; *d.* Neuchâtel, 11 Mar. 1956).

507   i   **BAUER, Marion**
Par. 1, l. 2 *should read* :

Walla, Washington, 15 Aug. 1887 ; *d.* South Hadley, Mass., 9 Aug. 1955).

    ii   CATALOGUE
CHAMBER MUSIC
Add after l. 3 :
' Pan ', choreographic sketch for 7 insts. & pf. (1937).

Baumbach
See Busoni (song). *should read* :
See Berg (Alban, song). Busoni (song).

509   i   **BAX**
Footnote. l. 5 *should read* :
(*see* Bibl.) there was no Irish strain in him. On the other hand he may have been of remote Dutch descent (*see* Eyck, Jacob van, whose mother " belonged to the noble family of Bax ").

    ii   Par. 4, l. 1. 1906 *should read* :
1916
         Par. 4, l. 4. two for violin *should read* :
three for violin

511   ii   CATALOGUE
CHORAL WORKS
After l. 12, transfer *from p. 512* :
' Five Greek Folksongs ' (trans. by M. D. Calvocoressi) (1944).
and add :
  1. The Miracle of St. Basil.
  2. The Bridesmaids' Song.

3. In Far-off Malta.
4. The Happy Tramp.
5. A Pilgrim's Chant.

511   ii   *After* l. 17 *add* :
Magnificat for S.A.T.B. & Organ (prob. 1949).
    Also ' To Russia ' for chorus & orch. (MS) and ' Five Fantasies on Polish Christmas Carols ' (trans. by Jan Sliwinski) for unison treble voices & stgs.
  1. God is born.
  2. In Nightly Stillness.
  3. In the Manger He is lying.
  4. Lullay, dear Jesus.
  5. Merrily to Bethlehem.

ORCHESTRAL WORKS
Add at end :
Also, in MS, ' Festival Overture ', ' Threnody and Scherzo ', ' Spring Fire ' and Suite ' Malta G.C.'.

SOLO INSTRUMENT AND OR-CHESTRA
Add at end :
Concerto for pf., left hand (1950).
' Concertante ' for 3 solo insts. :
  1. English Horn.
  2. Clarinet.
  3. Horn.

VOICE AND ORCHESTRA
ll. 5-6 *should read* :
' The Bard of Dimbovitza ', song cycle (Carmen Silva) (1915).

CHAMBER MUSIC
ll. 4-5 *should read* :
' An Irish Elegy ' (' In Memoriam ') for Eng. horn, harp & stgs. (1917).

512   i   *Add at end* :
Also Trio in B♭ ma. for va., cello & pf. and Trio for vn., va. & pf.

PIANOFORTE SOLO
Add at end :
' Two Lyrical Pieces ' (from ' Oliver Twist ' film) (1948).
    Also ' Paean ' and 7 Variations on ' Dame get up and bake your pies '.

    ii   SONGS
Add last item but one, after ' Out and Away ' :
' Watching the Needleboats ' (contributed to ' Joyce Book ', 1932).

transfer last 2 ll. to p. 511 (see above).

Add after **Bax, Clifford** :
Baxter, K. M. *See* Le Fleming (' Your Trumpets, Angels ', incid. m.).

516   i   **BAYREUTH**
l. 15-18 *should read* :
1954 : ' Tannhäuser ' (6). Keilberth.
        ' Lohengrin ' (7). Jochum.
        ' Ring ' (2). Keilberth.
        ' Parsifal ' (4). Knappertsbusch.

Add at end, before signature :
1955 : ' Der fliegende Holländer ' (6). Knap-pertsbusch, Keilberth.
        ' Tannhäuser ' (7). André Cluytens.
        ' Ring ' (2). Keilberth.
        ' Parsifal ' (4). Knappertsbusch.

1956 : ' Der fliegende Holländer ' (7). Keilberth.
' Meistersinger ' (8). Cluytens.
' Ring ' (2). Keilberth. Knappertsbusch.
' Parsifal ' (4). Knappertsbusch.
1957 : ' Tristan ' (6). Wolfgang Sawallisch.
' Meistersinger ' (8). Cluytens.
' Ring ' (2). Knappertsbusch.
' Parsifal ' (4). Knappertsbusch, Cluytens.
1958 : ' Lohengrin ' (5). Cluytens.
' Tristan ' (4). Sawallisch.
' Meistersinger ' (5). Cluytens.
' Ring ' (2). Knappertsbusch.
' Parsifal ' (4). Knappertsbusch.

517   i   **BEACH**
Par. 1, l. 1. **Mary** *should read* :
Marcy

518   ii   *Add after* **BEAT (4)** :
BEAT (5). *See* ACOUSTICS (p. 39).

519   i   **BEAULAIGNE**
Delete whole entry and replace by :
BEAULAIGUE[1], Barthélemy (*b.* ?, *c.*
1540 ; *d.* ?).
French composer. He was a choirboy in
the cathedral church of Marseilles and was
only fifteen years of age when he wrote the
dedication to his 13 chansons and 14 motets
printed by Robert Granjon in 1559. The
collection is addressed to Diane de Poitiers,
Duchesse de Valentinois, and the only known
part-books are preserved in the Paris Bibliothèque Nationale. Three of the chansons
were written for the prior of Capua, who has
been identified as Leone Strozzi (*d.* 1554), and
one of the motets is in praise of the Cardinal
of Lorraine, who passed through Marseilles
on his way to Rome in 1555.
The chansons are for the usual four voices,
but the motets vary from five to eight voices.
Most of the latter are written for use in church
and two are in praise of saints particularly
honoured at Marseilles. The motets, as compared with the homophonic chansons, are
imitative and learned, sometimes employing
long-note *cantus firmi*, sometimes not. In one
case a retrograde canon is employed and
double pedals are frequent at the final
cadence.   G. R. (iii).

BIBL.—AUDA, A., ' Barthélemy Beaulaigue : poète et
musicien prodige ' (Brussels, 1957).

[1] Not Beaulaigne, as in Grove V.

ii   **BEAUMARCHAIS**
Par. 4, l. 6 *should read* :
[' Figaro '], do.). Herberigs (' Mariage de Rosine ',
opera). Morlacchi (' Barbiere di Siviglia ',

520   i   *Add after* **BEAUVARLET** :
Beauvoir, Roger de. *See* Berlioz (song).

522   ii   **BECK, Franz**
Par. 2, l. 14 *should read* :
Arts. He founded the first Bordeaux

523   i   *Add at end* :
See also Sondheimer Ed., Vols. 20, 21 & 43 (modern
ed. of symphonies).

524   i   **BECKER, C. F.**
Par. 1, l. 1. Date *should read* :
(*b.* Leipzig, 17 July

Par. 3, l. 2 *should read* :
lischen Literatur . . .' (1836).

Cancel ll. 3-5.

526   i   **BECKMANN**
Par. 1, l. 2 *should read* :
1883 ; *d.* Berlin, 14 Nov. 1948).

527   i   **BEDFORD, CATALOGUE**
ORCHESTRAL WORKS
Add at end :
Symph. Poem ' Hamadryad ' (1930) ; also a version
for chamber orch.

528   i   **BEDYNGHAM**
Par. 2, l. 3 *should read* :
" Longstrides ". In certain choirbooks com-

Par. 5, ll. 2-3 *should read* :
' Salva Jesu' for 3 voices.
' Vidi Domine' for 2 voices.

529   i   **BEECHAM**
Par. 1, l. 28 *should read* :
married the English pianist Betty Humby (*d.*
1958),

End l. *should read* :
Festival. In 1951 he returned to Covent
Garden with ' Die Meistersinger ' and a
revival of Balfe's ' Bohemian Girl '. In 1957
he was created a Companion of Honour.

530   i   **BEER-WALDBRUNN** *should*
read :
BEER-WALBRUNN

Par. 1, l. 2. Munich, 23 *should read* :
Munich, 22

BIBL., l. 1. -Waldbrunn ' *should read* :
-Walbrunn ',

Beerbohm
Add at end of See also :
Tranchell (' Zuleika ', mus. comedy).

542   i   **BEETHOVEN**
Par. 3, ll. 7-8 *should read*:
over oppressed Europe. Ries reported more than thirty years later that one day, when he was in Beethoven's rooms, and

ll. 11-15 *should read*:

himself emperor. Angrily, says Ries, Beethoven tore off the title-page bearing his dedication to the great liberator: " Now he too [the words are reported by Ries] will trample on all the rights of man and indulge only his ambition ". But the title-page still exists in Vienna, with Napoleon's name inked out by Beethoven, some time after the proclamation, for in a letter to Breitkopf & Härtel dated 26 Aug. 1804 he still refers to it as " eigentlich Bonaparte genannt ".

547   i   Par. 1, l. 21 *should read*:

in favour of Therese von Brunswick, with her sister Josephine coming second and with the

573   i   *Add to* BIBL. :

BLOM, ERIC, 'Beethoven's Diabelli Variations' in 'Classics: Major and Minor' (London, 1958).
COCKSHOOT, JOHN V., 'The Fugue in Beethoven's Piano Music' (London, 1959).

ii   *Add to* BIBL. :

HESS, WILLY, 'Beethoven' (Zürich, 1956).

Add second work by HOPKINSON & OLDMAN to BIBL. :

'Thomson's Collection of National Song, with special reference to Haydn and Beethoven: Addenda and Corrigenda' (Edinburgh Bibl. Soc. Transactions, Vol. III, Part ii, Edinburgh, 1954).

Add to BIBL.

HIRSCH, PAUL & OLDMAN, C. B., 'Contemporary English Editions of Beethoven' (M. Rev., XIV, 1953, p. 1).
MACARDLE, DONALD W. & MISCH, LUDWIG, 'New Beethoven Letters' (Norman, Oklahoma, 1957).
NETTL, PAUL, 'Beethoven Encyclopedia' (New York, 1956).
STERBA, EDITHA & RICHARD, 'Beethoven and his Nephew: a Psychological Study of their Relationship', trans. by Willard R. Trask (New York, 1954; London, 1957).

574   i   *Add to* BIBL. (FRENCH) :

MASSIN, JEAN & BRIGITTE, 'Ludwig van Beethoven' (Paris, 1955).

ii   *Entry* HESS, WILLY, *should read*:

HESS, WILLY, 'Beethovens Oper " Fidelio " und ihre drei Fassungen' (Zürich, 1953).
'Verzeichnis der nicht in der Gesamtausgabe veröffentlichten Werke Ludwig van Beethovens' (Wiesbaden, 1957).

Add to BIBL. :

KINSKY, GEORG, 'Das Werk Beethovens: thematisch-bibliographisches Verzeichnis' (posth., ed. by Hans Halm) (Leipzig, 1955).
LEY, STEPHAN, 'Wahrheit, Zweifel und Irrtum in der Kunde von Beethovens Leben' (Wiesbaden & Leipzig, 1955).

575   i   *Add to* BIBL. :

RIEZLER, WALTER, 'Beethoven' (Zürich, 1936).

575   ii   *Add to* BIBL. :

SCHÖNEWOLF, KARL, 'Beethoven in der Zeitwende', 2 vols. (Halle, 1953).

578 —   Col. *Original Publisher*, l. 9. Hetlinger *should read*:
Haslinger

597   i   **BEGGAR'S OPERA**
Par. 6, ll. 2-4 *should read*:
in vocal score in 1920. A later version was made by Edward J. Dent in 1940–41 and published in vocal score in 1954. It treats the music in an elaborately

ii   *Add to* BIBL. :

HINRICHSEN, MAX (ed.), 'Ninth Music Book, containing " John Gay and the Ballad Opera " (" The Beggar's Opera ") ' (London, 1956).

598   i   **BEHR**
Par. 1, l. 2 *should read*:
1876 ; *d.* Lugano, 30 Jan. 1959).

ii   **BEINUM**
Par. 1, l. 2 *should read*:
Arnhem, 3 Sept. 1901 ; *d.* Amsterdam, 13 Apr. 1959).

599   i   Par. 2, l. 16 *should read*:
1948–49. In 1957 the University of Amsterdam conferred the honorary degree of Ph.D. on him.

604   i   **BELLA, J. L.**
Add to BIBL. :
ZAVARSKÝ, ERNEST, 'Ján Levoslav Bella : život a dielo' (Bratislava, 1955).

605   ii   **BELLENGUES**
Add at end:
His extant work is published in Vol. II of 'Early Fifteenth-Century Music', edited by Gilbert Reaney (Amer. Inst. of Musicology, 1958).

606   i   **BELLERMANN (2)**
l. 2.   4 Feb. *should read*:
5 Feb.

ii   **BELL' HAVER**
Par. 1, l. 2 *should read*:
Venice, ? Oct. 1587).

Par. 2, ll. 1-2 *should read*:

Italian organist and composer. He was first organist at St. Mark's, Venice, from 30 Oct. 1586 to 1 Oct. 1587,

l. 4 *should read*:

being followed on 30 Oct. 1588

607   i   **BELLI, Domenico**
Add to BIBL. :

FORTUNE, NIGEL, ' Italian Secular Monody from 1600 to 1635: an Introductory Survey ' (M.Q., XXXIX, 1953, p. 171).

608   i   **BELLINCIONI**
Add at end:

BIBL.—BELLINCIONI, GEMMA, ' Io ed il palco-scenico ' (Milan, 1920).

BELLINI
Par. 2, ll. 7-9 *should read :*

directed at that time by Zingarelli. Another of Bellini's fellow-pupils was

     ii   Par. 3, l. 3.   il sarà ', *should read :*

il sarà '¹,
         l. 8.   London.¹ *should read*

London.²

Add footnote :

¹ A mysterious work of which all that is known comes from Alberto Cametti's 'Un poeta melodrammatico romano. . . . Jacopo Ferretti e i musicisti del suo tempo ' (Milan, n.d., extract from the ' Gazzetta Musicale di Milano ', 1897). He says that among Ferretti's MS papers was an undated 1-act libretto, ' Il fu ed il sarà ', performed with music by Bellini at the wedding of Camillo Giuliani, P.A. (*pastore arcado*) and Carolina Persiani (Rome, 18 Feb. 1832). There is no reference to this work in Bellini's letters. He left Milan early in Jan. 1832 for Naples, perhaps by way of Rome, and may have composed Ferretti's libretto there ; or, as Cametti suggests, some music by him may have been fitted to the text. The cast of allegorical figures mentioned by Cametti suggests that the work was a dramatic cantata rather than an opera.   F. W. (ii)

Footnote 1 becomes 2.

609   i   Par. 1, ll. 31-32 *should read :*

succumbed to an illness from which he had suffered for some time. This was not consumption, as had long been supposed, but a disease of the digestive organs, including a large abscess in the liver and ulcers in the intestine.¹

Add footnote :

¹ This appears clearly from the ' Epistolario ', ed. by L. Cambi (*see* Bibl.) ; also Frank Walker's article listed there).

Footnotes 1 & 2 become 2 & 3.

     ii   BIBL. FRACAROLI *should read :*

FRACCAROLI

Add to BIBL.:

SCHLITZER, FRANCO (ed.), ' Tommaso Traetta, Leonardo Leo, Vincenzo Bellini: notizie e documenti ' (Siena, 1952).
WALKER, FRANK, ' Giuditta Turina and Vincenzo Bellini ' (M. & L., XL, 1959, p. 19).

610   —   LIST OF OPERAS
             Col. 1, l. 9.   sarà.' *should read :*
sarà.' ¹
             Col. 2, l. 14.   ? *should read :*
Jacopo Ferretti.

             Col. 3, l. 17 *should read :*
Privately performed, Rome, 18 Feb. 1832.

Add footnote :
¹ *See* footnote 1, p. 608.

610   ii   **BELLMAN**
             BIBL., l. 3.   un Bellmans *should read :*
om Bellmans

611   i   BIBL., l. 3.   musikalsk *should read :*
musikalisk

Add to BIBL. :

ZUCKMAYER, KARL, ' Ulla Winblad, oder Musik und Leben des Carl Michael Bellman ' (Frankfort o/M., 1953).

Add after **Belloc, Hilaire** :

Belloc Lowndes, Marie Adelaide.   *See* Tate (' Lodger ', opera).

Add at bottom :

BELLS.   *See* CARILLON.   CHANGE-RINGING.

612   i   **BELSHAZZAR**
     Par. 1, l. 4 *should read :*
1745.¹

Add footnote :

¹ The story, told in various sources, that ' The Daily Advertiser ' announced the work as ' Belteshazzar ' is untrue (*see* Winton Dean, ' Handel's Dramatic Oratorios and Masques ', Oxford, 1959).

613   ii   **BENDA (1)**
     Footnote 2, l. 6 should read :

' Tonkünstlerlexikon Berlins ' (1860–61). Paul Nettl's ' Forgotten Musicians ' (New York, 1951) draws on it.

615   ii   **BENDA (2)**
     See also, l. 2 should read :

Musica Antiqua Bohemica, Vol. 10 (modern ed. of Concerto for pf. & stgs.). Neefe (son-in-law). Sondheimer Ed., Vol. 24 (modern ed. of symphony).

616   ii   **BENDER**
     Par. 2, ll. 14-15 *should read :*

kavalier ' under Bruno Walter. In 1927 he sang Rocco in ' Fidelio ' and Osmin in ' Die Entführung ' there. In 1922–27 he was

618   i   **BENEDETTI**
     Add to BIBL. :

FORTUNE, NIGEL, ' Italian Secular Monody from 1600 to 1635: an Introductory Survey ' (M.Q., XXXIX, 1953, p. 171).

     BIBL., l. 2 *should read :*

(diss., unpubl., Leipzig, 1923).

620   ii   **BENET, John**
     Add at end :

It has been suggested that " Benet ", an abbreviation for " Benedict " or " Benedictine ", may be of significance in identifying John Benet with John Dunstable. No details of Benet's life are known, although eighteen of his works have been preserved and one of them, a ' Sanctus ', appears in the Aosta Manuscript with the attribution " Bennet " and in Trent 90 with the name " Dunstable ". If there were more than one direct instance of such overlapping, allied with incontrovertible evidence that Dunstable himself was a

member of the Order of St. Benedict, this ingenious theory would carry more weight. Its
sponsor, Brian Trowell, has drawn up a list,
with concordances, of Benet's works, omitting
the motet ' Gaude tu baptista Christi ', which
appears in Bologna, Liceo Musicale 37
(=Biblioteca G. B. Martini, Q 15) with the
ascription Benenoit. This is presumably a
scribal error for (Guillaume) Benoit.

D. W. S.

BIBL.—BESSELER, HEINRICH, ' Bourdon und Fauxbourdon ' (Leipzig, 1950).
BUKOFZER, MANFRED, ' Studies in Medieval and Renaissance Music ' (New York, 1950).
TROWELL, BRIAN, ' Some English Contemporaries of
Dunstable ' (Proc. Roy. Mus. Ass., LXXXI, 1954–
1955).

620 ii   *Add at end:*

Modern reprints appear in D.T.Ö., Vol. XXXI, and
Johannes Wolf's ' Geschichte der Mensural-Notation '.

621 ii   **BENGTSSON, Ingmar**
Par. 2, l. 18. Wadstone *should
read:*
Wadstena

628 ii   **BENOIT-BERBIGUIER**   *should
read:*
BENOÎT-BERBIGUIER

629 i   **BENOIT, Peter**
Par. 2, l. 12 *should read:*
Mountain Village ', produced 14 Dec. 1856),
which attained

630 i   *Add to* BIBL.:

DOULIEZ, PAUL, ' Peter Benoit ' (Bloemendaal, 1954).

ii   **BENTZON, JØRGEN**
Par. 1, l. 2 *should read:*
Feb. 1897; *d.* Hørsholm, 9 July 1951).

631 ii   **BENTZON, N. V.**
ORCHESTRAL MUSIC
Add at end:
Symphony No. 4 (' Metamorphoses ', Op. 55) 1949.

632 i   **BERARDI**
ll. 6-8 *should read:*
church of Santa Maria Trastevere in Rome.
He wrote a number of compositions and
important theoretical works. Modern facsimile reprints of ' Ragionamenti musicali '
(1681) and ' Miscellana musicale ' (1689) are
to appear in ' Documenta Musicologica ',
Vols. 6 & 7.   E. V. D. S., adds.

634 i   **BERCHEM**
Add at end of Par. 4:
A Mass, ' Auspice ', appears in Vol. XXVI of the
collected edition of Philippe de Monte's works (Düsseldorf, 1935).

BIBL., l. 4. Z.f.M. *should read:*
Z.M.W.

635 i   **BEREZOVSKY**
Par. 1, l. 2 *should read:*
burg, 17 May 1900; *d.* New York, 27 Aug.
1953).

List of works. l. 21 *should read:*
Suite for woodwind 5tet, Op. 11 (1930).

638 ii   **BERG, Alban**
Add to BIBL.:
JOUVE, P. J. & FANO, M., ' Wozzeck, ou Le Nouvel
Opéra ' (Paris, 1953).

Add after l. 8 (2nd work by Leibowitz):
' Schoenberg and his School ' (New York, 1949).

Add to BIBL.:
MITCHELL, DONALD, ' The Character of Lulu: Wede-
kind's and Berg's Conception Compared ' (M. Rev.,
XV, 1954, p. 268).
REDLICH, H. F., ' Alban Berg: the Man and his Music '
(London, 1957).

CATALOGUE
OPERAS
l. 1. ' Wozzeck ' (lib. *should read:*
' Wozzeck ', Op. 7 (lib.

639 i   *Add before* ORCHESTRA:
CHORAL WORKS
Compositions for 6-8-part chorus (1907, lost).

VIOLIN AND ORCHESTRA
l. 2 *should read:*
(Manon Gropius) (1935).

VOICE AND ORCHESTRA
Add after l. 2:
1. Seele wie bist du schöner.
2. Sahst du nach dem Gewitterregen.
3. Über die Grenzen des All.
4. Nichts ist gekommen.
5. Hier ist Friede.

CHAMBER MUSIC
Add under heading:
Fugue on 3 subjects for stg. 5tet & pf. (1907, lost).

PIANOFORTE SOLO
Add under heading:
12 Variations on an Original Theme (1908, MS).

SONGS
Add under heading:
Early Songs (1900–5, MS)
1. Heilige Himmel (F. Evers).
2. Herbstgefühl (Siegfried Fleischer).
3. Unter den Linden (Walther von der Vogelweide).
4. Spielleute (Henrik Ibsen).
5. Wo der Goldregen steht (Lorenz).
6. Lied des Schiffermädels (Otto Julius Bierbaum).
7. Abschied (Monsterberg).
8. Liebeslied (Dolorosa).
9. Über den Nächten (Dolorosa).
10. Sehnsucht I (Hohenberg).
11. Sternenfall (Wilhelm).
12. Er klagt, dass der Frühling (Arno Holz).
13. Ich und du (Busse).
14. Über Nacht (Rognetti).
15. Verlassen (Bohemian folksong).
16. Traurigkeit (Altenberg).
17. Hoffnung (Altenberg).
18. Flötenspielerin (Altenberg).
19. Spaziergang (Alfred Mombert).
20. Soldatenbraut (Eduard Mörike).
21. So regnet es sich langsam ein (Caesar Flaischlen).
22. Grenzen der Menschheit (Goethe).

23. Ballade des äusseren Lebens (Hugo von Hofmannsthal).
24. Im Walde (Bjørnstjerne Bjørnson).
25. Viel Träume (Amerling).
26. Tiefe Sehnsucht (Detlev von Liliencron).
27. Über den Berg (Busse).
28. Am Strande (G. Scherer).
29. Reiselied (Hofmannsthal).
30. Spuk (Friedrich Hebbel).
31. Aus Pfingsten (Evers).
32. Winter (Johannes Schlaf).
33. O wär mein Lieb ein Röslein rot (Robert Burns).
34. Sehnsucht II (Hohenberg).
35. Ich liebe dich (Christian Grabbe).
36. Ferne Lieder (Friedrich Rückert).
37. Ich will die Fluren meiden (Rückert).
38. Geliebte Schöne (Heinrich Heine).
39. Schattenleben (Graf).
40. Am Abend (Emanuel Geibel).
41. Wenn Gespenster auferstehn (Felix Dörmann).
42. Vom Ende (Marie Madeleine).
43. Vorüber (Wiesbacher).
44. Scheidelied (Rudolf Baumbach).
45. Eure Weisheit (Fischer).
46. Schlummerlose Nacht (Greif).
47. Nachtgesang (Bierbaum).
48. Es wandelt, was wir schauen (Joseph von Eichendorff).
49. Liebe (Rainer Maria Rilke).
50. Wandert, ihr Wolken (Avenarius).
51. Im Morgengrauen (Stieler).
52. Grabschrift (Jakoboswki).
53. Traum (Semmler).
54. Furcht (Palma).
55. Augenblicke (Hamerling).
56. Trinklied (Rückl).
57. Fromm (Gustav Falke).
58. Leben (Evers).
59. Näherin (Rilke).
60. Erster Verlust (Goethe).
61. Süss sind mir die Schollen des Tales (Knodt).
62. Der milde Herbst anno 45 (Max Mell).
63. Menschenherz (Delle Grazie).
64. Holophan (Wallpach).
65. Mignon (Goethe).
66. Läuterung (Hohenberg).
67. Die Sorglichen (Falke).
68. Das stille Königreich (Busse).
69. Trinklied (Henckell).

639   ii   **BERG, (C.) N.**
              Par. 1, l. 2 *should read*:

9 Feb. 1879; d. Stockholm, 15 Oct. 1957).

640   i   **BERG, Natanael**
             Par. 2, l. 6.   ' Ganoveva ' *should read*:

' Genoveva '

641   i   *Add before* **BERGER, Francesco**:
BERGER, Erna (b. Dresden, 19 Oct. 1900).
German soprano singer. She studied the pianoforte with Heta Boeckel and then voice with Melita Hitzl at Dresden. She was awarded a scholarship by the Richard Wagner Verein, and in order to finance further study, she applied for an audition with Fritz Busch, then *Generalmusikdirektor* of the Dresden State Opera. As a result she was offered a contract with the Dresden company, making her début in the 1926–27 season as the First Boy in ' Die Zauberflöte ', following it up with the Shepherd in ' Tannhäuser ' and Olympia in ' Tales of Hoffmann'. After only eighteen months she was entrusted with the creation of the title-part in Graener's ' Hanneles Himmelfahrt '. Following a successful performance as Annchen in ' Der Freischütz ' she was engaged by Siegfried Wagner for the 1929 Bayreuth Festival, where she sang the Shepherd in ' Tannhäuser ', the First Rhinemaiden and the Waldvogel. She returned to Bayreuth in 1930 and 1931, and in 1932 was heard at the Salzburg Festival as Blondchen in ' Die Entführung '. From 1930 to 1932 she was a member of the Berlin Städtische Oper under Carl Ebert, and in 1934 she made her Covent Garden début as Marcellina in ' Fidelio ' and returned to London in 1935, 1938 (Queen of Night, Sophie, Constanze) and after the war between 1949 and 1951 when she was heard as Gilda as well as Sophie and Queen of Night again. She sang at the Metropolitan Opera, New York, from 1949 to 1951, and continued to appear in opera in Germany and Austria until the end of the 1954–55 season. More recently she has devoted herself to *Lieder* singing and teaching.

Erna Berger's voice retained its youthful freshness and girlish quality throughout her long career. She enchanted her listeners as Sophie, Zerlina and Blondchen, threading a string of pearly notes on to a pure *legato* line. In the days when dramatic coloratura singers were virtually non-existent, her Queen of Night and Constanze were considered unapproachable; and her purely sung and innocent Gilda was one of the best of its day.

H. D. R.

642   i   **BERGLUND**
             Par. 2, l. 14 *should read*:

U.S.A.   In 1945–49 he was at the New York Metropolitan Opera.   He specializes in Wagner, and among

      ii   **BERGMANN**
             Par. 1, l. 2.   Saxony, 1821 ; *should read*:

Saxony, 11 Apr. 1821 ;

644   i   *Add before* **BÉRIOT**:
BERIO, Luciano (b. Oneglia, 10 Oct. 1925).
Italian composer. He first studied under his father and then at the Conservatory " G. Verdi " in Milan under Ghedini, taking his diploma in composition. He also studied with Dallapiccola in the U.S.A. Among his works are a ballet, ' Mimusic No. 2 ' (1953), ' Nones ' (1953) and ' Mutazioni ' (1956) for orchestra, Variations for chamber orchestra (1953), Quartets for woodwind instruments (1949–1951), the opera ' Allez, hop ! ' (Venice, 1959). ' Nones ' is based on a Passion poem by W. H. Auden, of which two versions exist:

one in the form of an oratorio and another a set of orchestral variations on instrumental portions of the work.

During the last few years Berio has devoted himself to electrophonic music : he conducts at the Milan radio a studio especially occupied with the problems of that music. He has written technical and aesthetic essays of exceptional insight on this subject, particularly in the Milanese review ' Incontri musicali ' promoted and edited by him, among other contributors to which are qualified supporters of vanguard music such as Boulez, Pousseur and Stockhausen.   G. M. G.

645   ii   **BERKELEY**
Par. 4, l. 6 *should read* :

Stratford production of ' The Tempest'. He was created C.B.E. in 1957.

646   i   CATALOGUE
Beginning of list *should read* :
OPERAS
Op.
43. ' Nelson ' (libretto by Alan Pryce-Jones) (1953), prod. London, Sadler's Wells Theatre, 22 Sept. 1954.
45. ' A Dinner Engagement ' (lib. by Paul Dehn), prod. Aldeburgh Festival, 17 June 1954.
— ' Ruth ' (lib. by Eric Crozier), prod. London, Scala Theatre, 2 Oct. 1956.

CHAMBER MUSIC
Add to section :
44. Sonata for vn., horn & pf. (1954).

ii   *Delete See also l. at end.*

649   i   **BERLIN**
Par. 2, l. 26. has lost *should read* :
had lost

ll. 30-31 *should read* :

members of the orchestra either joined the Städtische Opera or accepted engagements elsewhere in western Germany. But in 1952–1954 Kleiber conducted a number of performances and was appointed General Musical Director. He resigned in 1955, when Franz Konwitschny became Musical Director and Max Burghardt Intendant.

650   i   Par. 1, ll. 5-7 *should read* :
Berlin. Two important first productions took place during this period : Werner

l. 9 *should read* :

ballet ' Die weisse Rose ' (1951). Fricsay left during the 1951-52 season, and Blech, Rother and Leopold Ludwig were among the succeeding conductors. In 1954 Carl Ebert was appointed Intendant in succession to Tietjen, Richard Kraus became Musical Director and Wolfgang Martin first conductor. New pro-

D

ductions since 1951 have included Boris Blacher's ' Preussiches Märchen ', and there have been revivals of Busoni's ' Doktor Faust ' and Schillings's ' Mona Lisa '.

650   i   Par. 4, l. 12 *should read* :
' Die Kluge '. In the 1954-55 season the first Berlin performance of Strauss's ' Frau ohne Schatten ' was given, conducted by the Musical Director of the theatre, Meinhard von Zallinger.

653   i   *Add to* BIBL. :
FETTING, HUGO, ' Geschichte der deutschen Staatsoper ' (Berlin, 1955).

654   ii   **BERLIOZ**
Par. 2, ll. 28-29 *should read* :
Cléopâtre '. And this when the Opéra saw the triumph of Rossini's

ll. 32-33 *should read* :
Harriet's country, and the following year, during the revolutionary days of

655   i   Par. 3, l. 11. *Delete* Remove its dramatic *and the rest of the par.*

Par. 4, l. 6 *should read* :
fixed for 5 Dec. of that year, the very day on which

661   ii   Par. 3, l. 37 *should read* :
never yet been performed in Paris in its

670   i   BIBL. l. 8 *should read* :
BOSCHOT, ADOLPHE, ' Le " Faust " de Berlioz ' (Paris, 1927).
(*Delete first two titles*)

ii   BIBL. l. 5 *should read* :
1913 ; Vols. I & II, new ed., 1946 ; Vol. III, 1950).

Add to BIBL :
BARRAUD, HENRY, ' Hector Berlioz ' (Paris, 1955).
COLLET, ROBERT, ' Berlioz : Different Angles of Approach to his Work ' (' The Score ', No. 10, Dec. 1945).
COURT, GLYN, ' Berlioz and Alfred de Vigny ' (M. & L., XXXVII, 1956, p. 118).
' Hector Berlioz : 1803–1869 ', ed. by Albert Richard (Rev. Mus. No. 233, 1956).
' Revue Musicale ', No. 234, 1956 (Berlioz number).
VALENSI, THÉODORE, ' Le Chevalier Quandmême Berlioz ' (Nice, 1955).
' Fin et gloire de Berlioz ' (Nice, 1956).

671   —   CATALOGUE
Col. *Title*, l. 19. (' Messe des *should read* :
(' Grande Messe des

672   —   SONGS WITH PIANOFORTE
Col. *Words*
l. 1. *Add* :
Albert D***

Col. *Words*
672 — l. 11. *Add*:
Charles Brizeux.

673 — l. 9. *Add*:
Léon Guérin.

l. 12. *Add*:
Alexandre Dumas, sen.

l. 13. *Add*:
Roger de Beauvoir.

l. 14. *Add*:
Adolphe de Leuven.

l. 16. *Add*:
Brizeux.

l. 17. *Add*:
A. de Bouclon.

l. 18. *Add*:
Bouclon.

674 i **BERMUDO**
Add at end, before signature :
A modern facsimile reprint of the ' Declara-
ción ' (1555 ed.), edited by M. Santiago
Kastner, was published in the ' Documenta
Musicologica ' series of the International
Society for Musicology (Cassel, 1958).

ii **BERNAC**
Par. 1, l. 1 *should read* :
BERNAC, Pierre [1] (*b.* Paris, 12 Jan. 1899).

Par. 2, ll. 1-2 *should read* :
French baritone singer. He studied with
Reinhold von Warlich at Salzburg and began
his artistic

l. 11. four days *should read* :
five days

Add footnote :
[1] His real surname was Bertin, but he changed it to
avoid confusion with the actor Pierre Bertin.

675 ii **BERNAL JIMÉNEZ**
Par. 1, l. 2 *should read* :
16 Feb. 1910; *d.* León, Mexico, 26 July
1956).

Add before **BERNARD** :
Bernanos, Georges. *See* Poulenc (' Dialogues des
Carmélites ', opera).

682 i **BERNET KEMPERS**
Par. 3, l. 1. 1919 *should read* :
1929

683 i **BERNHARD**
Add at end :
See also Denkmäler (2), Vol. 6 (modern ed.).

Add at end :
See also Chorwerk (modern reprint of Mass).

683 i **BERNIER, Nicolas**
Par. 1, l. 2 *should read* :
1664 ; *d.* Paris, ? 8 July 1734 [2]).

Par. 2, l. 18 *should read* :
libraries. He married Marais's daughter
Marguerite Pélagie.

Add footnote :
[2] The date of death given as 5 Sept. 1734 in earlier
editions must be wrong, since his widow obtained a privilege for a posthumous edition of his cantatas on 5 Aug.
1734. Titon du Tillet gives the above date as that of
his death, but that too seems rather uncertain, as Marguerite Pélagie was remarried, to Roger van Hove, on
5 Aug. 1734. Titon du Tillet is usually trustworthy, but
his " 1734 " may possibly be a misprint for 1733 or 1724.

684 i **BERNSTEIN**
Par. 2, l. 9 *should read* :
Vienna, Paris and Scheveningen. In the
seasons of 1953–54 and 1954–55 he conducted
at the Milan Teatro alla Scala.

Par. 2. *Add at end* :
In 1958 he succeeded Mitropoulos as con-
ductor-in-chief of the New York Philharmonic
Orchestra.

685 i **BERSAG HORN**
Add at end :
PLATE 14, Vol. II, p. 446, No. 10.

686 ii **BERTI**
Add to BIBL. :
FORTUNE, NIGEL, ' Italian Secular Monody from 1600 to
1635 : an Introductory Survey ' (M.Q., XXXIX,
1953, p. 171).

BIBL. l. 5 *should read* :
(2nd ed., Leipzig, 1955), p. 69f.

690 i **BERTONI**
Add to See also
Classici Musica Italiana, Vol. 16 (modern ed.)

Add after **BERTONI** :
BERTRAND, Antoine de (*b.* Fontanges,
Cantal, *c.* 1545; *d.* ?).
French composer. He produced seven
books of chansons for 4 voices : two entitled
' Les Amours de P. de Ronsard ' (1576, reprinted 1578, 1587), two entitled ' Sonets
chrestiens ' (1580) and three entitled simply
' Chansons ' (1578, reprinted 1587). He was
in advance of his time in his use of chromaticism.
Modern editions of chansons by Bertrand
appeared in H. Expert's ' Monuments de la
musique française au temps de la Renaissance ', Vols. IV-VII.   E. B.

BERTRAND, J. G.
Par. 1, l. 2. Paris, 1880 *should
read* :
Paris, 9 Feb. 1880

692 ii **BERWALD**
Add to BIBL.:
CASTEGREN, NILS, ' Musikaliska Konstföreningen och Franz Berwald ' (S.T.M., 1953).
NORDBERG, G. O. (ed.), ' Franz och Mathilde Berwald: Brew och Dagboksblad ' (Stockholm, 1955).

693 i **BESEKIRSKY (i)**
Par. 1, l. 2. *d.* ?, *should read*:
d. Moscow,

695 i **BESSELER**
Par. 2, l. 13 *should read*:
in 1949, but in 1956 he accepted a similar post at Leipzig. He contributed the section ' Die

697 i **BEST**
Add to BIBL.:
CARR, J. ARTHUR, ' Hatton and Best of Liverpool ' (' Liverpool Libraries, Museums and Arts Committee Bulletin ', Vol. I, No. 2, Oct. 1951).

Add before **BETLY**:

BETHUNE, Thomas Greene (*b.* Muscogee County, Georgia, U.S.A., 25 May 1849; *d.* Hoboken, New Jersey, 13 June 1908).
American Negro musical prodigy, known as " Blind Tom ". He was born blind and was all but an imbecile, but from the age of four developed an extraordinary gift of reproducing from memory on the pianoforte compositions he had once heard, until he was able thus to memorize works of any length and complexity. He was taken on a tour in Europe in his early twenties. He had no technical knowledge of music and was not emotionally affected by it; he merely reproduced what he heard mechanically in an inexplicable way. E. B.

BETTINELLI
Par. 3 (works). *Add at end*:
' Tre ricercari e toccata ' for pf.

698 i **BEVIN**
Par. 2, ll. 3-8 *should read*:
tion under Tallis. He was admitted as vicar-choral at Wells Cathedral on 10 May 1579; but on 2 Jan. 1580 he and another vicar-choral, Thomas Goolde, were suspended " until they mend their ways " for not having communicated. A Roman tendency has been inferred, but it may be that they were simply lax in their religious duty, as was quite common at the time, and neither man seems to have been under a disability for any length of time. At any rate, Bevin is recorded as having been present at a meeting of vicars in Mar. 1581, and at the next annual election he was elected a Senior. In 1583 Goolde and another, styled " Vicars-choral ", leased property to Bevin and some others. Bevin signed a Wells charter in 1584. Arch-

698 ii *Signature should read*:
J. M. (ii), adds. W. K. F.

699 i **BEYDTS**
Par. 1, l. 2 *should read*:
(*b.* Bordeaux, 29 June 1895; *d.* Candéran, 16 Sept. 1953).

ii **BEYRON**
Par. 2. *Insert after* l. 25:
the 1946–47 season he sang Tristan, with Flagstad as Isolde, at the Milan Teatro alla Scala. In

701 i **BIANCHI, P. A.**
Par. 2, l. 4 *should read*:
Austria in 1597. His works comprise

(*delete* In 1609 . . . at Venice.)

702 i **BIBER**
Par. 3, ll. 1-2 *should read*:
Sonatas for violin and clavier are published in D.T.Ö., Vols. V, 2 and XII, 2. An engraved

Insert after Par. 3:
Biber wrote a set of 15 sonatas for violin and continuo which are interesting specimens of early programme music. They represent the following incidents of the Mystery of the Cross:

1. Gabriel's annunciation to Mary.
2. Mary visits Elizabeth.
3. The Adoration.
4. The Presentation.
5. Jesus in the Temple at the age of twelve.
6. Christ on the Mount of Olives.
7. The Scourging.
8. The Crown of Thorns.
9. Christ bears the Cross.
10. The Crucifixion.
11. The Resurrection (using the Easter melody ' Surrexit Christus hodie ').
12. The Ascension.
13. Whit Sunday.
14. The Assumption.
15. The Crowning of the Virgin Mary.

There are momentary glimpses of realism, such as the lashing violin effects in No. 7, the rushing scale passages in the sonatas dealing with visits of angels, the curious attempt to imitate wind in No. 13 and the suggestion of earth tremors in No. 10. For the most part the sonatas aim at reflecting the general emotion of each title through the medium of dance forms: many contain a sarabande, courante, allemande, gavotte and gigue, many with doubles. There is an unsatisfactory edition of these sonatas by Alfred Heust.

E. B.

ii **Bickerstaffe**
l. 3 *should read*:
libs.). Entführung aus dem Serail (source of lib.). Ephesian Matron (Dibdin, lib.). Lampe (J. F.,

704 i **Bierbaum**
See Dieren *should read*:
See Berg (Alban, 2 songs). Dieren

BIERDIAJEW
Par. 1, l. 2 *should read*:
7 Mar. 1885; *d.* Warsaw, 28 Nov. 1956).

705 i **BIGGS**
Par. 1, l. 7 *should read*:
others. Biggs has edited many early organ works.

709 ii **BINCHOIS**
Par. 2, ll. 11-12. Duke of Norfolk *should read*:
Duke of Suffolk

710 ii *See also should read*:
See also Chanson (mus. ex.). Chorwerk, Vol. 22 (modern reprint of songs). Dufay (meeting with).

711 i **BINDER**
Par. 1, l. 2. Dresden, Jan. *should read*:
Dresden, 1 Jan.

ii **BINET**
(*d.* Trélex-sur-Nyon, 24 Feb. 1960).

715 i **BIRCHENSHA**
Par. 1, l. 3 *should read*:
while Ch. Ch. has twelve voluntaries for violin and bass (MS 1016-17) and the Bodleian Library Suites *a* 3 (E. 410-14).

717 i **BIRMINGHAM**
Par. 1, l. 7 *should read*:
training provided. Edmunds retired in 1956 and Sir Steuart Wilson was appointed full-time Principal. Gordon Clinton succeeded him in 1960.

719 ii *Insert after* Par. 2:
In 1955 the City of Birmingham Symphony Orchestra, as it then came to be called, made what was a new departure among English provincial orchestras by commissioning three important orchestral works from Sir Arthur Bliss, Edmund Rubbra and Michael Tippett. In May of that year the orchestra made a tour in Holland under Schwarz.

Add before Par. 3:
In 1957 Schwarz was appointed conductor-in-chief of the B.B.C. Symphony Orchestra in succession to Sir Malcolm Sargent, and he was succeeded in Birmingham by Andrzej Panufnik, Sir Adrian Boult and Meredith Davies.

720 ii After Par. 1, signature C. M. E. *should read*:
H. C. C., adds.

BIRNBACH, K. J.
Par. 2. *Add after* l. 1:
He was a pupil of Dittersdorf and wrote 2 operas (1783), several symphonies, 2 pianoforte concertos, an oratorio and some church music.

721 ii **BISHOP, Ann**
Par. 2, l. 2. singing-master *should read*:
drawing-master

Par. 3, l. 8. 1855 *should read*:
1856

727 i **BIZET**
Par. 2, ll. 7, 9 and 13 and Par. 3, l. 19. Zimmerman *should read*:
Zimmermann

741 ii BIBL. l. 36 *should read*:
(London, 1926; rev. 1951).

Add to BIBL. :
CURTISS, MINA, 'Bizet and his World' (New York, 1958; London, 1959).
SHANET, HOWARD, 'Bizet's Suppressed Symphony' (M.Q., XLIV, 1958, p. 461).

746 i **BJÖRLING, Johan**
Par. 1, l. 2. 1911 *should read*:
1907

BJÖRLING, Jussi
(*d.* Stockholm, 9 Sept. 1960).
Par. 2, l. 16 *should read*:
from 1931 to 1939. In the latter year he sang Manrico in 'Trovatore' at Covent Garden in London. He has sung as guest at

ll. 18-19 *should read*:
(Metropolitan, New York, 1938-41, 1945-54) and sang in London again in 1951 and 1952. His voice

ii **BJÖRLING, Sigurd**
Par. 2, ll. 16-17 *should read*:
court. In 1951 he sang Wotan, Kurwenal and Amfortas at Covent Garden in London, and he was the first post-war Wotan at Bayreuth that year. In 1952-53 he was at the New York Metropolitan Opera. Among

Bjørnson
l. 2 *should read*:
Solbakken', film m.). Bax (song). Berg (Alban, song). Delius (4 songs).

747   i   **BLACHER,** CATALOGUE
Par. 3. *Delete and substitute heading* :
CATALOGUE OF WORKS
Then add :
OPERA
Op.
43. ' Abstrakte Oper No. 1 ' (lib. by Werner Egk) (1953).

STAGE WORKS
l. 1. *Delete Op.*

After l. 6 *cancel rest of par. and add* :
30. ' Preussisches Märchen ', opera (lib. by Heinz von Cramer).
33. ' Chiarina ', ballet.
34. ' Lysistrata ', ballet after Aristophanes.
35. ' Hamlet ', ballet after Shakespeare.
50. ' Der Mohr von Venedig ', ballet after Shakespeare's ' Othello '.
—   ' Romeo und Julia ', chamber opera after Shakespeare.
Much incidental and radio music.

CHORAL WORKS
49. Cantata ' Träume vom Tod und vom Leben '.
—   ' Der Grossinquisitor ', dramatic oratorio after Dostoyesvky.

ORCHESTRAL WORKS
After Op. 17 add :
20. Concerto for stg. orch.

| | ' Tobias and the Angel ' | | Christopher Hassall |

After Op. 26 *add* :
44. ' Orchester-Ornament.'
45. ' Studie in Pianissimo.'
46. ' Zwei Inventionen.'

l. 9. 30. Partita *should read* :
—   Partita for stgs. & perc.

Add at end :
—   ' Music for Cleveland ', for 40th Anniversary of Cleveland Orchestra (1958).

SOLO INSTRUMENT AND OR-CHESTRA *should read* :
SOLO INSTRUMENTS AND ORCHESTRA

Op. 28 *should read* :
28. Pf. Concerto No. 1.

Then add :
29. Vn. Concerto.
36. Concerto for clar., bassoon, horn, trumpet, harp & stgs.
42. Pf. Concerto No. 2.
48. Concerto for va.
—   ' Dialog ' for flute, vn., pf. & stgs.

CHAMBER MUSIC
ll. 6-7 *should read* :
31. Divertimento for trumpet, tromb. & pf.
32. Stg. Quartet No. 4.

Then add :
38. Divertimento for flute, oboe, clar. & bassoon.
41. Epitaph for stg. 4tet (in memory of Franz Kafka) (1951).
SOLO VIOLIN
40. Sonata.

PIANOFORTE MUSIC
Add :
37. ' Ornamente : 7 Studien über variable Metren.'
39. Sonata.

747   i   SONGS
Add :
47. ' Francesca da Rimini ' (after Dante) for sop. & vn.

748   i   **BLADDER PIPE**
Add to See also :
PLATE 34, Vol. IV, p. 500, No. 4.

754   i   **BLANÍK**
l. 2 *should read* :
Poem). *See* SMETANA (' Má Vlast ').

758   i   **BLECH, Leo**
Par. 1.   1871). *should read* :
1871 ;   *d.* Berlin, 24 Aug. 1958).

759   i   *Add after* **BLIND OCTAVES** :
BLIND TOM. *See* BETHUNE, THOMAS GREENE.

761   —   **BLISS,** CATALOGUE
OPERA
Add :
B.B.C. Television, 19 May 1960.

ii   *Add at bottom* :
Variations on a Theme by Blow (1955).

762   i   CHAMBER MUSIC
l. 19 *should read* :
String Quartet No. 1 (1923–24).

After l. 22 *add* :
String Quartet No. 2 (1953).
' Elegiac Sonnet ' (Cecil Day Lewis) for tenor, stg. 4tet & pf. (1954).

PIANOFORTE MUSIC
Add at end :
Sonata (1953).

SONGS
Add after l. 12.
' Simples ' (contributed to ' Joyce Book ', 1932).

ii   **BLITHEMAN**
Par. 6, l. 1 *should read* :
This is reprinted in its entirety in Vol. 1 of ' Musica Britannica '. The " meane " is printed in the appendix to

Add :
BIBL.—LOWINSKY, EDWARD, ' English Organ Music of the Renaissance ' (M.Q., XXXIX, 1953).

763   ii   **BLITZSTEIN**
OPERAS
l. 8 *should read* :
' Regina ', on Lillian Hellman's novel ' The Little Foxes ' (1947–48).

BLOCH
Par. 1.   *Add* :
d. Portland, Oregon, 15 July 1959).

764   ii   Par. 1, l. 9.   12 Dec. *should read*:
20 Dec.

766   i   ORCHESTRAL WORKS
Add at end:
Symphony, E♭ ma. (1954-55).

SOLO INSTRUMENT AND OR-
CHESTRA
Add at end:
' Proclamation ' for trumpet (1955).

ii   CHAMBER MUSIC
Add:
Stg. Quartet No. 4 (1954).
Stg. Quartet No. 5 (1956).
' Suite Modale ' for flute & pf. (1956).
3 Suites for cello solo (1956-57).
Quintet No. 2 for stgs. & pf. (1957).
2 Suites for violin solo (1958).

767   ii   **BLOCKX**
Par. 2, l. 14.   30 Oct. *should read*:
10 Oct.

768   i   **BLODEK**
Par. 1, l. 2.   1860–71 *should read*:
1860.

Par. 2, l. 2.   17 Oct. *should read*:
17 Nov.

Add before **BLOMDAHL**:

BLOM, Eric (Walter) (*b*. Berne, 20 Aug.
1888; *d*. London, 11 Apr. 1959).
English critic, scholar and author. He was
Danish by descent, Swiss by birth, and British
by choice, domicile and naturalization. His
education was mostly private in German-
speaking Switzerland — hence his command
of the German language, which enabled him
to make English translations of Specht's ' Life
of Brahms ', Weissman's ' Music come to
Earth ', and of the libretto of Mozart's ' The
Impresario '. But he had the gift of tongues,
for he picked up Danish, English, Italian and
French while still a young man. He was
largely self-taught in music and began to
acquire a vast store of musical knowledge during his first years in London. He first became
known to the British public as a writer of
programme notes, which were conspicuous
for their wealth of accurate knowledge. This
was in 1919, when he began to assist Rosa
Newmarch in providing annotations for Sir
Henry Wood's concerts. Thereafter he was
prominent in English musical life for 40 years,
most of them spent in London but the 15 years
between 1931 and 1946 in Birmingham as
music critic to ' The Birmingham Post '.
Blom's first appointment as a critic was to
' The Manchester Guardian ', for which he
wrote notices of London events from 1923 to
1931. Like Ernest Newman, to whose career
Blom's bore some resemblance and ran
parallel, he moved from the Manchester to
the Birmingham paper and thence to ' The

Observer ' in London, serving as chief music
critic from 1949 to 1953, and continuing his
weekly contributions to the day of his death.
He returned to London in 1946 to begin his
work as editor of the fifth edition of the present
Dictionary.
As a critic Blom was judicious in general
but not without idiosyncrasies to give character
— and wit — to his writing. He had a liking
for the byways of music, so that his first published book bore the title ' Stepchildren of
Music ' (1923) and his last, ' Classics Major
and Minor ', which contained reprinted
essays on such minor composers as Dussek.
He had a fastidious taste, not only in music
but in drama and painting, but his criticism
was less of the connoisseur, wine-tasting kind
than that of the scholar. The scrupulousness
of his mind, which informed his journalism
throughout his career, made him also a good
editor.
Editorship took Blom into three different
fields of activity. As musical adviser to the
publishing firm of Dent he became general
editor of the ' Master Musicians ' series of
biographies and discovered a number of
young writers to whom he gave their first
opportunity of authorship. His connection
with Dent also led him into lexicography.
The first edition of ' Everyman's Dictionary
of Music ' came out in 1947 and has since
been twice revised. At the opposite extreme
of method to set against the abbreviations and
compactness of a single pocket-size manual
was the fifth edition of the present Dictionary
which came out in nine volumes in 1954.
Blom set his mark on it by a more systematic
provision of lists, tables and bibliographies
and other purely reference features while preserving its literary character as determined by
Grove himself. His journalism and his
encyclopaedic learning were linked in his
editorship of the quarterly periodical ' Music
and Letters '. He took over the editorship
from its founder, A. H. Fox-Strangways, in
1937 and continued to edit it until 1950, when
because of his pre-occupation with this
Dictionary he retired, only to return in 1954,
when its then proprietor and editor, Richard
Capell, died. He thus gave 18 years of
voluntary service to a journal of international
standing.
Because of these unceasing demands on his
time Blom wrote no big book, but his Mozart
biography, contributed to his own ' Master
Musicians ' series, bears eloquent testimony
to his quality as author. His great love of
Mozart led him to bring out a popular edition
of a selection of the composer's letters in
Emily Anderson's translation, for the Mozart
bicentenary in 1956. His book ' The Limitations of Music ' (1928) was a study in aesthetics in which he cleared his mind on the

principles of criticism. His 'Romance of the Piano' (also 1928) was a useful little history for popular consumption, whereas various small studies in 'The Musical Pilgrim' series and elsewhere were analytical, early examples of a type of criticism relating value judgments to technical features which has become increasingly favoured as a counterpoise to that which describes the adventures of the soul among the masterpieces.

For his public service to music in these forms and for the committee work which falls to public-spirited persons in music as in other spheres of life, Blom was made C.B.E. in 1955 and was awarded a D.Litt. by Birmingham University in the same year. F. S. H.

BOOKS
'Stepchildren of Music' (London, 1923). Essays on curious, unfamiliar and forgotten works.
'Tchaikovsky: Orchestral Works' ('Musical Pilgrim' series) (Oxford, 1927).
'The Limitations of Music' (London, 1928). A theory of aesthetics with special reference to Mozart.
'The Romance of the Piano' (London, 1928).
'Strauss's "Rose Cavalier"' ('Musical Pilgrim' series) (Oxford, 1930).
'Mozart' ('Master Musicians' series) (London, 1935; Ger. trans. Zürich, 1953).
'The Music Lover's Miscellany' (London, 1935). An anthology of literary references to music.
'Beethoven's Pianoforte Sonatas Discussed' (London, 1938). Detailed analyses of the 32 sonatas interspersed with essays bearing on various aspects of the subject.
'A Musical Postbag' (London, 1941). A selection of the weekly essays contributed to 'The Birmingham Post'.
'Music in England' (Pelican Books) (Harmondsworth, 1942; Ger. trans. Hamburg, 1947; It. trans. Florence, 1954).
'Some Great Composers' (Oxford, 1944; Braille transcription, 1954).
'Everyman's Dictionary of Music' (London, 1947; rev. ed., 1954). A concise book of reference in 1 vol.
'Classics: Major and Minor, with other Musical Ruminations' (London, 1958).

CONTRIBUTIONS TO COLLECTIVE WORKS
'An Essay on Performance and Listening' in 'The Musical Companion' ed. by Alfred Bacharach (London, 1934).
'Strauss', 'Sullivan' and 'Vaughan Williams' in 'The International Cyclopedia of Music and Musicians' ed. by Oscar Thompson (New York, 1939).
'Vaughan Williams' in David Ewen's 'Book of Modern Composers' (New York, 1942).
'Works for Solo Instrument and Orchestra' in 'Tchaikovsky: a Symposium' ed. by Gerald Abraham (London, 1945).
'The Piano Music' in 'Sibelius: a Symposium' ed. by Gerald Abraham (London, 1947).
'The Future of Music' in 'The Prospect before us' (London, 1948).

TRANSLATIONS
'Johannes Brahms' by Richard Specht (London, 1930).
'Music come to Earth' by Adolf Weissmann (London, 1930).
Mozart's 'Impresario' (prod. Arts Theatre, Cambridge, 1937).
'Schubert: a Documentary Biography' ed by O. E. Deutsch (London, 1946).

775 i BLOW
See also, l. 3. Add:
Lyrebird Press (modern eds. of 2 sonatas & 'Venus and Adonis'). Musica Britannica, Vol. 7 (modern ed. of anthems).

776 i BLUME
BOOKS
l. 12 should read:
(Cassel, 1947; Eng. trans., Oxford, 1950).

ii Blunden
l. 2 should read:
Day', choral ode; 'White-flowering Days', chorus; 2 songs). Garland for the Queen (Finzi,

778 i Boccaccio
l. 3. 'Boccaceries' for orch. should read:
'Boccaceries' for pf. or orch.

779 ii BOCCHERINI
See also, l. 2. Add before Tasche:
Classici Musica Italiana, Vol. 3 (modern ed. of sonatas). Sondheimer Ed., Vols. 1, 3, 4, 9, 11, 32, 36, 44, 45 (do. of var. works).

780 i Add after BOCK:
BOCKELMANN, Rudolf (August Louis Wilhelm) (b. Bodenteich nr. Lüneburg, 2 Apr. 1890; d. Dresden, 10 Oct. 1958).

German bass-baritone singer. He was educated at Celle and at the University of Leipzig, and studied singing with Oscar Lassner from 1920 to 1923. He was engaged at the Leipzig Opera in 1921–26, making his début as the Herald in 'Lohengrin', as leading Heldenbariton at Hamburg in 1926–32, and at the Berlin State Opera in 1932–45. He sang regularly at Bayreuth from 1928, when he was heard as Gunther and Kurwenal, until 1942, and was considered one of the finest interpreters of Hans Sachs and Wotan of his generation. He was heard, too, at Covent Garden in 1929 and 1930, and then yearly from 1934 to 1938; and he also sang with the Chicago Civic Opera in 1930–31. Bockelmann found it difficult to resume his career after the war, and apart from a few appearances at Hamburg and the German provinces, he devoted his time to teaching at Hamburg. He was made a German Kammersänger.

Rudolf Bockelmann was one of the best German singers, in a period rich in fine artists. He had a beautiful voice, of sympathetic quality, and was able to sustain with ease the exhausting parts of Sachs and Wotan. Although an outstanding Wotan, dignified and authoritative, his personality never quite suited him to those moments of towering rage that occur in the last act of 'Walküre' and in several passages in 'Siegfried'. On the other hand his warm mellow voice, his feeling for poetry and his artistry combined to make his Hans Sachs one of the greatest ever heard.

H. D. R.

ii BODANZKY
Par. 2, l. 9 should read:
Opera. He was

782 i **BOEHM, Karl**
Par. 2, l. 24 *should read*:
posers, Mozart and Strauss. From 1941 he
was at the Vienna State Opera, from which
he resigned in 1954, but where he was nominated *Generalmusikdirektor* for the reopening of
the house in 1955.

ii Par. 1, l. 6 *should read*:
von Pinsk '. In 1949 he conducted Berg's
' Wozzeck ' at Naples. He also introduced in
several

783 i **BOEHM, Theobald**
Par. 2. l. 4. William Gordon
should read:
James Gordon

See also. Gordon (W., *should read*:
Gordon (James,

ii **BOËLLMANN**
Add:
BIBL.—DUFOURCQ, N., ' La Musique d'orgue française
de Jehan Titelouze à Jehan Alain ' (Paris, 1949).

784 i **BOËLY**
Add:
BIBL.—DUFOURCQ, N., ' La Musique d'orgue française
de Jehan Titelouze à Jehan Alain ' (Paris, 1949).

BOELZA
Par. 1. Keltzy, Poland, 1904
should read:
Kielce, Poland, 8 Feb. 1904).

ii **BOERO**
Par. 1, l. 2 *should read*:
1884 ; *d.* Buenos Aires, 10 Aug. 1958).

785 ii **BOGATIREV**
Par. 1, l. 1 *should read*:
BOGATIREV, Anatoly Vassilevich (*b.*
Vitebsk, 13 Aug.

788 i *Add after* **BOHN**:
BOHNEN, Michael (*b.* Cologne, 2 May
1887).
German bass-baritone singer. He was
educated privately and studied music under
Fritz Steinbach and Schulz-Dornburg at the
Cologne Conservatory. He made his début
at Düsseldorf in 1910 as Caspar in ' Freischütz '. Engagements followed at Wiesbaden (1912–13), the Berlin Court Opera
(1913–21), the Metropolitan, New York
(1922–33) and the Deutsches Opernhaus,
Berlin (1933–45). After the war he was
appointed Intendant of the Städtische Oper,
Berlin, a post he held until 1947. Bohnen
also sang at Bayreuth in 1914 (Hunding and

Daland), at Drury Lane in the Beecham
season the same year as Baron Ochs and
Sarastro, and at Salzburg. His sole Covent
Garden appearance was in 1914, when he
was called from Drury Lane to substitute for
an indisposed singer as Heinrich in ' Lohengrin '. Bohnen was gifted with a large voice
of extensive range which enabled him to cope
with both bass and baritone parts. He was
just as much at home as Scarpia and Amonasro
as he was singing Baron Ochs and Mephistopheles. He was a highly gifted and individual
actor who was compared on more than one
occasion with Shaliapin, not least for his
exaggerations and the musical liberties he
often took. He was often attracted by parts
that lay outside the normal repertory, and
while a member of the Metropolitan, New
York, sang Francesco in Schillings's ' Mona
Lisa ' and the title-part in Křenek's ' Jonny
spielt auf '.   H. D. R.

788 i **BÖHNER**
Par. 2, l. 6. Kittl *should read*:
Kittl

ii **BOHNKE**
Par. 1, l. 2. Berlin, *should read*:
Pasewalk, Pomerania,

Par. 2, l. 13 *should read*:
pieces for violin and pianoforte. Bohnke and
his wife were killed in a motoring accident.

790 ii **BOIELDIEU**
Par. 2, ll. 18-19 *should read*:
softened by his second wife, the singer Jenny
Philis-Bertin, whom he had married on 22 Jan.

BIBL., l. 5. FAURE, *should read*:
FAVRE,

791 i **BOIELDIEU, A. L. V.**
Par. 1, l. 2. ?, *should read*:
Paris,

Par. 2, ll. 1-2 *should read*:
French composer, illegitimate son of the
preceding and Thérèse Regnault, a singer at
the Paris Opéra-Comique. He was educated
at the

792 i **BOISMORTIER**
Par. 2, l. 11 *should read*:
fashionable instruments during the 1730s. He
was also an important composer for the
harpsichord : his ' Quatre Suites de pièces de
clavecin ' (1736) were reprinted in 1959,
edited by Erwin R. Jacobi.

Signature should read:
A. L., adds.

793   i   **BOITO**
Par. 2, ll. 18-21 *should read*:
unsuccessfully performed at Turin; he wrote

     ii   Par. 1, l. 7.   written rapidly *should
read*:
rapidly completed

794   i   *Add before* Par. 1:
In 1871-72 [1] Boito was busy with words
and music for a new opera, ' Ero e Leandro ',
of which later he destroyed the music and
handed the text to Luigi Mancinelli.

     Add footnote:
[1] Not during 1861-68, as previously stated, and as
disproved by Nardi (*see* BIBL.).

     ii   Par. 2, ll. 7-8 *should read*:
conda ' (Ponchielli), ' Pier Luigi Farnese '
(Palumbo) and ' Iràm ' (Dominicetti). The

795   ii   BIBL. ll. 7-8 *should read*:
1942), containing the first

               l. 10.   Dominiceto *should read*:
Dominicetti

     Add to BIBL.:
VAJRO, MASSIMILIANO, ' Arrigo Boito ' (Brescia, 1955).

796   i   *See also*, l. 9.   alle nazioni ', *should read*:
delle nazioni ',

799   i   *Add before* **BOLOGNA, M. A. da:**
BOLOGNA, Jacopo da.   See JACOPO DA
BOLOGNA.

801   ii   **BONAVENTURA, Arnaldo**
Par. 1, l. 2 *should read*:
28 July 1862;   *d.* Florence, 7 Oct. 1952).

802   ii   **BOND, Capel**
Par. 1.   Dates *should read*:
(*b.* Gloucester, [bapt. 14 Dec.] 1730;   *d.*
Coventry, 14 Feb. 1790).

     Par 2, l. 1 *should read*:
English organist and composer. Son of a
bookseller, he was apprenticed to Martin
Smith, organist of Gloucester Cathedral, in
1742. He seems to have been sub-organist
there for some time, but later was appointed
organist of St. Michael's and Holy Trinity
Churches at Coventry, where he remained
until his death.
Bond con-

BONDEVILLE
Par. 3, l. 4 *should read*:
at the Paris Opéra-Comique on 19 June 1935.
The same theatre produced on 1 June 1951 his

three-act opera ' Madame Bovary ', to a
libretto by René Fauchois based on Flaubert's
novel. His

802   ii   l. 8 *should read*:
(first performance, Lamoureux, 29 Mar. 1933)
and
           ll. 10-11 *should read*:
1934), forming a ' Triptyque ' after Rimbaud's ' Illuminations '. He has also written a

805   i   **BONNO**
     Add at end:
See also Fitzwilliam Music (reprint of sacred works).

     ii   **BONNY BOOTS**
     Add after signature:
According to a conjecture arrived at by
Thurston Dart, and mentioned in Hotson's
book ' The First Night of Twelfth Night ',
there is now a high degree of probability that
Bonny Boots is to be identified with Robert
Hales, for whom, at Elizabeth I's express
wish, a song was especially included in that
play.   E. B.

BONONCINI (Buononcini)
should read:
BONONCINI (Buononcini [2]**).**

     Par. 2, l. 3 *should read*:
d. Modena, 19 Oct. 1678).

     l. 4 *should read*:
is said to have been a pupil of Giovanni Paolo
Colonna at

     l. 7 *should read*:
an early age, but this has been disproved.[3]
In 1668 he joined the Accademia

     l. 9.   sons were born.[2] *should read*:
sons were born.[4]

     Add Footnote 2:
[2] This spelling was actually used as an alternative by
some of his contemporaries, but Gino Roncaglia, in
' La Cappella . . .' (*see* BIBL.), says it is incorrect.

     Add Footnote 3:
[3] By Roncaglia, *op. cit.*

     Footnote 2 becomes 4.

806   i   **BONONCINI (2)**
l. 2 *should read*:
18 July 1670; *d.* Vienna, 9 July 1747 [2]), com-

     Footnote 2. l. 2 should read:
at Bologna is wrong. Place and date have been estab-
lished by Karl Hueber in a paper, ' Gli ultimi anni di
G. Bononcini, published in ' Atti e memorie della
Accademia di Scienze. Lettere e Arti di Modena ', Vol.
XII, 1954.

807   i   Par. 2.   *Delete last sentence* (No further facts . . . forgotten).

808   i   l. 24.   Calfurnia *should read*:
Calpurnia

ii   *See also. Add to* l. 1:
Fitzwilliam Music (reprint of sacred works).

BONONCINI (3)
l. 2.   1675 *should read*:
1677

809   i   *Add to* BIBL.:
HUEBER, KURT, ' Die Wiener Opern Giovanni Bononcinis von 1697-1710 ' (Vienna, 1955).
RONCAGLIA, GINO, ' La cappella musicale del duomo di Modena ' (Florence, 1957).

l. 1 *should read*:
' L. A. Muratori : la musica

810   ii   **BONTEMPI**
Par. 1, ll. 1-2 *should read*:

BONTEMPI-ANGELINI, Giovanni Andrea (*b.* Perugia, 1624; *d.* Perugia, 1 June

811   i   **BOON**
Par. 1, l. 2.   Halland län *should read*:
Hallands län

812   i   **BOOSEY & HAWKES**
Par. 3, l. 14 *should read*:
manufacture.   Very far-reaching developments occurred in this department during the 1940s.

Add at end, before signature:
In 1946 the firm made itself responsible for the lease, rent and house expenses of the Royal Opera, Covent Garden, when that famous London theatre was reopened.

ii   **BORCHARD**
Par. 1, l. 2.   1892 *should read*:
1882.

Par. 2, l. 7 *should read*:
patronized by Queen Alexandra, before whom he played on 4 June 1908), Germany,

813   i   **BORCHGREVINCK**
Add at end:
See also Vereniging, Vol. 34 (reprint of orchestral works).

814   i   **BORDES**
BIBL., l. 1.   ALIBERT *should read*:
ALBERT

816   ii   **BORGIOLI**
(*d.* Florence, 13 Sept. 1960).
Par. 2, l. 16 *should read*:
London.   In 1946-48 he was adviser to the Pomeroy opera company at the Cambridge

Theatre in London, where he produced ' Il barbiere di Siviglia ' and ' La Bohème '.

817   i   *Add after* **BORJON**:
BORKH, Inge(borg) (*b.* Mannheim, 26 May 1921).
German soprano singer.   She is the daughter of a Swiss diplomat and a Viennese soprano. She was educated at Geneva, and when she was fourteen became a member of Max Reinhardt's seminary attached to the Burg theatre in Vienna.   Two years later she made her début as a young actress at Linz ; but after two years on the straight stage she decided to become a singer.   A period of study in Italy followed, first at Milan with Muratti, then at Florence.   She next went to the Mozarteum at Salzburg in 1939-41. Borkh's first engagement was at Lucerne, where she made her début in the 1940-41 season as Czipra in Johann Strauss's ' Zigeunerbaron '.   She remained there until 1944 and was then engaged at Berne, where she remained until 1951, singing such parts as Agathe, Leonore in ' Fidelio ', Aida and Marie in ' Wozzeck '.   In 1951 she created a sensation at Basel with her interpretation of Magda Sorel in the German language première of ' The Consul '.   A call to Paris, soon after, to replace Ljuba Welitsch as Salome, found her singing opposite the Stuttgart baritone Alexander Welitsch (no relation to the soprano), and shortly afterwards she married him.   She was then invited to sing Senta and Salome at Munich and Leonore, Magda and Elektra in Berlin.   In the summer of 1952 she sang Freia and Sieglinde at Bayreuth and Leonore in ' Fidelio ' with the Hamburg Opera at Edinburgh.   Borkh's American début took place in the autumn of 1953 at San Francisco, where she sang Elektra and Turandot ; the latter part she has also sung in Italy.   She has returned regularly to San Francisco, singing also Lady Macbeth and Elsa.   London heard her for the first time in the autumn of 1955, when she appeared with the Stuttgart Opera at the Royal Festival Hall in her highly individualized interpretation of Elektra. She sang Salome at Covent Garden in 1959.
Inge Borkh has a clear, bright voice, light in colour and more Italianate than German in sound.   It is well produced and easily stands the strain of such exhausting parts as Elektra, Salome and Turandot, which one generally associates with a more dramatic voice.   Indeed it was generally agreed after her London Elektra appearances that the part had rarely been sung with so pure a tone.   Her intense and highly individual acting is not universally approved of; but this, coupled with her intelligence and musicality, has resulted in her being invited to sing such diverse parts as Silvana in Respighi's ' La

fiamma ' at La Scala, Eglantine in Weber's
' Euryanthe ' at Florence and Edinburgh, and
Cathleen in Egk's ' Irische Legende ', which
she created in Salzburg in 1955.

H. D. R.

819   i   **BORODIN**
Par. 1, l. 2.   12 Nov. *should read*:
11 Nov.

ii   Par. 2, l. 30.   Mendelev *should
read*:
Mendeleyev

821   i   Par. 1, l. 8.   (a work believed
should read:
(a work once believed

ii   Par. 3, l. 20 *should read*:
edition.¹

Add footnote :
¹ The set was orchestrated by N. Tcherepnin under
the title of ' Tati-Tati ' in 1937.

824   i   l. 2 *should read*:
cello (publ. 1949 ; the first and fourth movements are
arranged from a Haydn pianoforte sonata).

825   ii   **BOROVSKY**
Par. 1, l. 23 *should read*:
London.   In 1956 he was appointed pianoforte professor at Boston University.   As a
pianist he combines a

BOROWSKI
Par. 1, l. 2 *should read*:
shire, 10 Mar. 1872 ; *d.* Chicago, 6 Sept.
1956).

Par. 2, l. 13 *should read*:
Northwestern University, Evanston, Ill., and
from 1937 to 1942 he was Professor of Musicology there.   He then became musical editor
of the ' Chicago Sun '.   He also wrote programme notes for the Chicago Symphony
Orchestra.   Bo-

List of Works.   *Delete last 3 lines and
replace by* :
' Requiem for a Child ' for orch. (1944).
' The Little Match Girl ' (after Hans Andersen) for
narrator & orch. (1943).
Pf. Concerto (1913).
3 String Quartets (1930–44).
3 Organ Sonatas.
Pf. works, songs, etc.

826   ii   **BORREN**
Par. 1.   *Add after* l. 2 :
' Polyphonia sacra ' (1932).

Par. 3, l. 13 *should read*:
logical Society.   In 1944 a volume of tributes,
' Mélanges ', edited by Suzanne Clercx and
A. van der Linden, was published to celebrate
his seventieth birthday.   It contains a complete list of his articles and reviews (*c.* 400).

826   ii   **BØRRESEN**
Par. 1, l. 2 *should read*:
Copenhagen, 2 June 1876 ; *d.* Copenhagen, 6
Oct. 1954).

827   i   **BORTKIEVICH**
Par. 1, l. 2 *should read*:
(*b.* Kharkov, 22 Feb. 1877; *d.* Vienna, 25
Oct. 1952).

828   i   **BOS**
Par. 1, ll. 1-2 *should read*:
BOS, Coenraad V. (*b.* Leyden, 7 Dec.
1875; *d.* Chappaqua, N.Y., 5 Aug. 1955).

829   i   **BOSCHOT**
Par. 1, l. 2 *should read*:
Bois, Seine, 4 May 1871 ; *d.* Neuilly nr. Paris,
1 June 1955).

Par. 2, l. 13 *should read*:
and translated into German, Italian and
Spanish.

ii   Par. 1, l. 7 *should read*:
(1935) ; ' Musiciens poètes ' (1937) ; ' Portraits de musiciens ' (1946).

BOSCOOP
Add at end:
See also Vereniging, Vol. 22 (reprint of 50 Psalms).

BOSCOVICH
Par. 1, l. 2 *should read*:
Klausenburg, Transylvania, 16 Aug. 1907).

830   i   **BOSETTI**
Par. 2, ll. 5-7 *should read*:
soprano parts.   She appeared in London, at
Covent Garden, in 1905 and 1907.   She excelled as Zerlina in ' Don Giovanni ' and in
1913 she reappeared in

ii   **BOSQUET**
Add at end:
His extant work is published in Vol. II of
' Early Fifteenth-Century Music ', edited by
Gilbert Reaney (Amer. Inst. of Musicology,
1958).

836   ii   **BOSTON**
Par. 4, ll. 16-17 *should read*:
Harrison Keller, who succeeded Goodrich's
successor, Quincy Porter, as acting director
in 1946.   He served as director from 1947 to
1958.   A students' orchestra has been formed

837   ii   *Add before* **BOTE & BOCK** :
BOSWORTH & CO.   The music-publish-
ing firm of Bosworth & Co. Ltd. was founded

at Leipzig in 1889. Arthur Edwin Bosworth, the founder, served his apprenticeship with Edgar Horne of Derby, leaving there to join the firm of J. B. Cramer & Co. in London. He afterwards went to Chappell & Co., where he met Sullivan, who persuaded him to go to Leipzig to protect and propagate the Gilbert and Sullivan operettas in German-speaking countries. Branches were established in Brussels, London, Zürich and Vienna. After the founder's death in 1923, the business was carried on by his sons, Laurence Owen Bosworth and Arthur Ferdinand Bosworth. During the second world war the London premises were totally destroyed by bombing in 1940, but a new building of a modern design has since been opened at 14 Heddon Street, London, W.1.

Bosworth & Co. specialize in educational and numerous popular orchestral works and are proprietors of the Steingräber Edition for the British Empire. Their catalogue incorporates those of Laudy, London ; Wickens, London ; Blaha, Vienna (including popular songs by Gruber and Komzak) ; Carl Kratochwill, Vienna ; Josef Chmel, Vienna (original publisher of Lehár's 'Gold and Silver' waltz) ; Roehr, Berlin (orchestral editions) ; and L'Art Belge, Brussels (including works by Joseph Jongen). Their own publications include works by Bantock, Mackenzie, Stanford ; 'Cathedral Music', ed. by Frederick Bridge and Stanley Roper ; Ševčík's Violin Method ; popular Viennese operettas by Heuberger and Zeller, &c.

E. B.

837   ii   **BOTSTIBER**
                Par. 1, l. 2.   1942 *should read* :
1941

838   ii   **BOTTESINI**
                Par. 1, l. 2 *should read* :
bardy, 22 Dec. 1821 [1] ; *d.* Parma, 7 July

Add footnote :

[1] According to the birth certificate, as stated in his monograph by Carniti (*see* Bibl.), who found it at Crema Cathedral.

839   i   **BOTTRIGARI**
                Par. 2, ll. 1-3 *should read* :

Italian scholar, the illegitimate son of a nobleman, but legitimatized at the age of seven. He studied music under Bartolomeo Spontone. In *c.* 1575–86 he lived at

ii   Par. 1, ll. 3-4 *should read* :

pseudonym of Alemanno Benelli (Venice, 1594), an anagram of the name of his friend Annibale Melone, with whom has been wrongly said to have studied music. It was reprinted under his own name

839   ii   Par. 2, l. 3.   Melone *should read* :
melone

l. 11 *should read* :

valuable library. Modern facsimile reprints of ' Il melone ' and ' Il patricio ' are to be published in ' Documenta Musicologica ', Vols. 9 & 10.   E. B.

840   i   *Add after* **Boucicault** :
Bouclon, A. de.   *See* Berlioz (2 songs).

        ii   **BOUGHTON**
                Par. 1, l. 2 *should read* :

23 Jan. 1878 ;   *d.* London, 25 Jan. 1960).

844   i   **BOULANGER**
                Par. 1, l. 24 *should read* :

that Society. In 1940–46 she lived in the U.S.A. as lecturer and teacher. In 1948 she became director of the American Conservatory at Fontainebleau.

        BOULEZ
                Par. 1, l. 2.   1926 *should read* :
1925

                Add at bottom :
' Le Marteau sans maître ' (Char) for contralto and chamber orch. (1954).

845   i   **BOULT**
                Par. 3, l. 14 *should read* :

monic Orchestra. He relinquished this post in Mar. 1957, without, however, giving up work with this and other orchestras, and became Hon. Musical Adviser to the L.P.O. and conductor of the City of Birmingham Symphony Orchestra.

846   i   **BOURGEOIS**
                Par. 1, l. 1.   Name *should read* :
BOURGEOIS, Louis (Loys)

848   ii   Par. 6, l. 3.   xxxiv [5] *should read* :
xxxiv

                Par. 6, l. 5 *should read* :
Siméon. Genève, 1550.[5]

                Footnote 5 *should read* :
A modern facsimile reprint appeared in ' Documenta Musicologica ', Series I, Vol. vi.

                Par. 7, ll. 1-2 *should read* :

This treatise, in twelve chapters, follows Ornithoparcus in proposing to abandon the

                Par. 3, l. 5 *should read* :

melody, while 32 certainly and perhaps as many as 36 are adapted from secular

849 ii **BOURGUIGNON**
Par. 1, l. 2 *should read*:
28 May 1890).

Par. 3, l. 1 *should read*:

His works include an opera, ' Tradimento ' ;
a ballet, ' La Mort d'Orphée ' ; an oratorio,
' La Nuit ' ·

850 i **BOURNEMOUTH**
Add at end:

The concerts are now held in a new hall
on the site of the old Winter Gardens, originally built for sports. In 1954 the corporation,
not for the first time, decided to do without
the orchestra ; but whereas before it had
yielded to public opinion and restored it, a
newly formed Western Orchestral Society
now made itself responsible, the corporation,
however, contributing a subsidy, which is supplemented by an Arts Council grant and another from the Winter Gardens Society. The
orchestra thus no longer belongs exclusively
to Bournemouth, and it visits other sizable
towns in south-western England, which contribute to its upkeep.

851 i **BOUTMY (2)**
Add at end:
See also Monumenta Mus. Belg., Vol. 5 (modern ed.
of harpsichord works).

852 i **BOUVET**
Par. 1, l. 2. 19 July *should read*:
22 May

ii **BOVICELLI**
Par. 2, l. 5 *should read*:

his time, ' Regole passaggi di musica ', which
is of great historical interest, as

l. 11 *should read*:

p. 945. A modern facsimile reprint of the
' Regole ', edited by Nanie Bridgman, was
published in the ' Documenta Musicologica ',
Series I, Vol. xii, of the International Society
for Musicology (Cassel, 1958).

853 i **BOVY**
Par. 2, l. 11. until 1939. *should
read*:
until 1938.

857 i **BOWER**
Par. 2, ll. 31-32 *should read*:

He was Honorary Associate Director of the
Royal School of Church Music until 1952 and
President of

863 ii **BOYCE**
Add before CATALOGUE :
BIBL.—TAYLOR, ERIC, ' William Boyce and the Theatre '
(M. Rev., XIV, 1953, p. 275).

864 ii INSTRUMENTAL MUSIC
*Concerto (MS Son's sale) *should read*:
Concerto Grosso in B minor (B.M. Add. MS 17836).
Concerti Grossi in B flat, E minor, D minor (unfinished),
    D minor (Bodleian, MS Mus. Sch. D 230 a-c).

865 i *See also*. l. 3 *should read*:
arr. & ed.). Musica Britannica, Vol. 13 (modern ed.
of overtures).

BOYD NEEL ORCHESTRA
See NEEL *should read*:

See NEEL. PHILOMUSICA OF LONDON.

Add before **BOYDEN** :

BOYDELL, Brian (*b.* Dublin, 17 Mar.
1917).
Irish composer, conductor and lecturer.
After early schooling in Dublin and at Rugby,
he studied for a year at the Evangelisches
Kirchenmusikalisches Institut at Heidelberg.
In 1935 he became exhibitioner at Clare College, Cambridge, where he took a first-class
honours degree in natural science. Subsequently he studied at the R.C.M. in London
and finally at the Royal Irish Academy of
Music, taking the L.R.I.A.M. in singing and
proceeding to Mus.B. at Dublin University
in 1942. In 1944–52 he was professor of
singing at the R.I.A.M. In 1942 he succeeded Havelock Nelson as conductor of the
Dublin Orchestral Players. Since 1946 he
has been lecturer in music for the Royal
Dublin Society's extension lecture scheme,
and since 1955 also lecturer under the Forás
Éireann-Shaw Trust. He has been a frequent
guest conductor with the Radio Éireann
Symphony Orchestra and others, and a con-
ductor-lecturer for children's orchestral concerts organized by Ceol Cumann na nóg in
Dublin. In 1955 he conducted one of Sir
Robert Mayer's children's concerts in London ; the same year, and again in 1957, he
gave concerts of works by himself and other
Irish composers with the C.B.C. Symphony
Orchestra at Toronto. He has broadcast
over 400 talks on music from Radio Éireann
and is a successful adjudicator at music
festivals, having twice covered the Canadian
circuit.
As a composer Boydell typifies the reaction
against the folksong influence in the work of
the preceding generation of Irish composers,
for he has, on the whole, followed a central
European tendency. His orchestral works
include ' In Memoriam Mahatma Gandhi '
(1948), ' Megalithic Ritual Dances ' (1956)
and ' Meditation and Fugue ' (1956). His
violin Concerto, perhaps his finest work, won
the Radio Éireann Carolan Prize in 1954 ;
another solo work is ' Elegy and Capriccio '
for clarinet and strings (1956). His chamber
music includes a string Trio (1944), a string

Quartet which won the Carolan Prize in 1950 and a ' Divertimento for Three Music-Makers ' (1954). He has also written a number of distinctive smaller works, including ' Five Joyce Songs ' (1946).   A. F. (ii).

866   i   *Add after* **BRACES** :
BRADBURY, Ernest.   *See* Leeds, Vol. V, p. 108 ii.

868   i   **BRADFORD**
Par. 1, ll. 9-10 *should read* :
the work. In 1926 St. George's Hall became a cinema, but it was purchased by the municipality in 1949 to serve again as a

870   ii   **BRAHMS**
Par. 2, l. 9 *should read* :
appeared under the assumed names of G. W. Marks and Karl Würth, and by

877   i   Par. 3, l. 3 *should read* :
was a string Quintet with two cellos [1] and re-
Add footnote :
[1] A conjectural reconstruction of this by Sebastian H. Brown was performed in London by the Mangeot Quartet on 15 Oct. 1946.

890   ii   Bibl., English. l. 5 *should read* :
(Oxford, 1929 ; reprinted in Tovey's ' Essays and Lectures on Music ').

Add to Bibl. (German) :
Kross, Siegfried, ' Die Chorwerke von Johannes Brahms ' (Berlin-Halensee, 1958).

German. *Add at end* :
Thematic catalogues of Brahms's works were published by Simrock of Berlin in 1887, 1897, 1902 & 1904.

French. *Add at end* :
Rostand, Claude, ' Brahms ' (Paris, 1954).

906   ii   **BRAIN, Aubrey**
Par. 1, l. 2 *should read* :
12 July 1893 ; *d.* London, 21 Sept. 1955).

907   i   Par. 5, l. 3 *should read* :
as professor at the R.A.M.

Cancel rest of par.

ii   **BRAIN, Dennis**
Par. 1, l. 1.   1921). *should read* :
1921 ; *d.* Hatfield, 1 Sept. 1957).

Par. 3, ll. 11-12 *should read* :
French type. He ranked beyond question with the finest instrumentalists.
Brain was killed in a motoring accident on a return journey of some 400 miles after the Edinburgh Festival of 1957, at which he had

appeared with the Philharmonia and with the wind chamber-music team that bears his name and won international fame for the perfection of its concerted playing.
R. M. P., adds.

908   i   **BRAITHWAITE**
Par. 1, l. 6 *should read* :
and, from 1949 to 1952, to conducting the Covent

909   i   **BRANDENBURG CONCERTOS**
Par. 1, ll. 4-6 *should read* :
instruments in four cases and with solo string instruments only in the cases of Nos. 3 and 6, which however, are usually performed by massed strings nowadays. All the concertos were intended to be

ii   Par. 1 *should read* :
played with a harpsichord continuo, with the probable exception of No. 5, which has a solo harpsichord part. The omission of such a continuo is not only unhistorical, but destroys the carefully planned textures of Bach's writing (*e.g.* in No. 4, where for much of the first and last movements the continuo line is independent of the bass line). In Nos. 1 and 2 the *ripieni* need more than one player to a part if the solo instruments are to be adequately supported. In Nos. 3 and 6 Bach intended solo players throughout. In No. 4 the *ripieno* parts should ideally be played by single instruments. In No. 5 the music is the better for several players to each of the *ripieni*.

Par. 3 *should read* :
No.
1. F major, for violino piccolo, 3 oboes, 2 horns, bassoon and *ripieno* of 2 vns., viola, cello and *continuo.*
2. F major, for vn., recorder, oboe, trumpet and *ripieno* of 2 vns., viola and violone, with cello and *continuo.*
3. G major, for 3 vns., 3 violas, 3 cellos, with violone and *continuo.*
4. G major, for vn. and 2 recorders and *ripieno* of 2 vns., viola and violone, cello and *continuo.*
5. D major, for flute, vn. and harpsichord *concertato,* with *ripieno* of vn., viola, cello and violone.
6. B♭ major, for 2 violas, 2 *viole da gamba,* cello, violone and *continuo.*

Add Par. 4 :
A beautiful facsimile of the complete set in full score, edited by P. Wackernagel, was published at Leipzig in 1955.
R. T. D.

BRANDL
Par. 1, l. 2.   14 Sept. 1760 *should read* :
14 Nov. 1760

910   i   *After* **BRANDT, Jan** *add* :
BRANDT, Jobst vom.   *See* Brant, Jobst.

912 i **BRANT, H. D.**
Par. 1, l. 1 *should read* :
BRANT, Henry Dreyfus (*b.* Montreal,

ii List of Works. *Add after* ' In Zuru ' :
Cantata ' Spanish Underground ' (1947).

Add after ' Dedication in Memory...' :
' Music for an Imaginary Ballet ' for orch. (1947).

BRANT, Jobst
Par. 1. Dates *should read* :
(*b.* Waldershof nr. Marktredwitz, 28 Oct.
1517; *d.* Brand nr. Marktredwitz, 22 Jan.
1570).
Par. 2, l. 1 *should read* :
German composer. G. For-

913 i **BRANZELL**
Par. 2, l. 14 *should read* :
1935, 1937 and 1938. In 1924 she made her
début at the

ll. 16-17 *should read* :
engaged until 1944 and reappeared in 1950–
1951. She sang as guest at the Munich State
Opera between 1926 and 1938; at

i **BRASS BAND**
Par. 1, l. 2. 18th century *should read* :
19th century

916 i Par. 7, ll. 1-5 *should read* :
Three English periodicals devoted to the
movement must be mentioned : ' The British
Bandsman ' (weekly), ' The Brass Band News '
(monthly) and ' Musical Progress and Mail '
(monthly, discontinued). Three publishers
(one continu-

918 ii **BRAUNFELS**
Par. 1, l. 2 *should read* :
19 Dec. 1882 ; *d.* Cologne, 19 Mar. 1954).

919 i SOLO AND ORCHESTRA
ll. 1-3 *should read* :
8. ' Hexensabbath ' for pf.
21. Pf. Concerto No. 1, A ma.
29. Pf. Concerto No. 2.

BRAVNICAR
Par. 1, l. 2 *should read* :
venia, 24 Feb. 1897).

922 i **BREHME**
Par. 1, l. 2 *should read* :
1904 ; *d.* Stuttgart, 10 Nov. 1957).

928 ii Page heading, BRETON *should read* :
BRETÓN

928 ii **BRETON, Tomás**
Par. 1, l. 1. Surname *should read* :
BRETÓN

Par. 3, l. 2. Breton's *should read* :
Bretón's

930 ii **BREWER**
Par. 1, l. 3 *should read* :
Mar. 1928).

Par. 3, l. 9 *should read* :
the B.Mus. at Dublin and later the Lambeth
D.Mus. was conferred on him. In the mean-

932 ii **BRIARD**
Add at end :
Bibl.—Meyer, K., ' Music Printing, 1473–1934 ', in
' Dolphin ' (New York, 1935).

934 ii **BRIDGE,** CATALOGUE :
PIANOFORTE SOLO
Add after l. 2 :
Capriccio No. 2, F♯ mi. (1905).

l. 21. *Delete this.*

936 i **Bridges**
l. 4 *should read* :
(B., song). Davies (W. H., song). Finzi (' In terra pax '
& 7 partsongs ; 1 song).

ii *Add after* **Bridgewater** :
BRIDGMAN, Nanie (*b.* Angoulême, 2
Feb. 1907).
French musicologist, librarian and contralto
singer. She studied musical history with
André Pirro at the Paris Sorbonne and gained
the Certificat d'Histoire de la Musique in
1928, the Licence ès Lettres in 1930 and the
Diplôme d'Études Supérieures in 1946. The
diploma was awarded for a thesis on music
at the court of Henry VIII. She studied singing at the Paris Conservatoire with Claire
Croiza and more recently took up oriental
languages, gaining the diploma of the School
of Oriental Languages in Paris in 1949
(Serbo-Croatian). A librarian in the Music
Department of the Bibliothèque Nationale
since 1945, she has since produced valuable
studies and articles on French and Italian
music of the 16th century in the ' Annales
Musicologiques ', R. de M., M.Q., ' Collectanea historiae musicae ', M.G.G., etc.
More recently she has been entrusted with
the direction of the French group of the
Répertoire des Sources Musicales, for which
her bibliographical knowledge and work make
her particularly suitable. She has also sponsored the Fiori Musicali, a group of performers who give concerts of older music,
and was on the panel of specialists who
transcribed 16th-century chansons for the
volume edited by François Lesure.

G. R. (iii).

938   ii   **BRIQUET**
Add at end:

His extant work is published in Vol. II of 'Early Fifteenth-Century Music', edited by Gilbert Reaney (Amer. Inst. of Musicology, 1958).

939   i   **BRISTOL MADRIGAL SOCIETY**
Delete Par. 3 *and replace by*:

After the death of Hunt in 1945, Alwyn Surplice, organist of Bristol Cathedral, became

952   ii   **BRITTEN**
Add to Bibl. :

BROWN, DAVID, 'Stimulus and Form in Britten's Work' (M. & L., XXXIX, 1958, p. 218).
LINDLAR, HEINRICH (ed.), 'Benjamin Britten' ('Musik der Zeit', No. 7) (Bonn, 1954).
STEIN, ERWIN, 'Britten's New Opera for Children: "Noye's Fludde"' ('Tempo', No. 48, 1958).

l. 37 *should read*:
his Life and Works' (London, 1954).

CATALOGUE :
OPERAS
Add at end:

54	'The Turn of the Screw'	Myfanwy Piper, based on Henry James's novel.	Venice, Teatro La Fenice, 14 Sept. 1954.
59	'Noye's Fludde' (1 act).	Chester Mystery Play.	Orford, Suffolk, 18 June 1958.
64	'A Midsummer Night's Dream'	Shakespeare.	Aldeburgh, 11 June 1960.

Add after this:

BALLET

Op.	Title	Choreography	Production
—	'The Prince of the Pagodas', ballet in 3 acts.	John Cranko.	London, Covent Garden Theatre, 1 Jan. 1957.

954   —   SOLO VOICES AND ORCHESTRA
Add at end:

Op.	Title	Words	Scored for	Composed
60	'Nocturne'		Tenor, 7 solo insts. & stgs.	1958.
	1. On a poet's lips I slept.	Shelley.		
	2. Below the thunders of the upper deep.	Tennyson.		
	3. Encinctured with a twine of leaves.	Coleridge.		
	4. Midnight's bell.	Middleton.		
	5. But that night when on my bed I lay.	Wordsworth.		
	6. She sleeps on soft last breaths.	Wilfred Owen.		
	7. What is more gentle than a wind in summer?	Keats.		
	8. When most I wink, then do mine eyes best see.	Shakespeare.		

CHAMBER MUSIC
Add at end:

| 55 | Canticle No. 3, 'Still falls the rain' (Edith Sitwell). | | Tenor, horn & pf. | | 1954. |

956   —   SONGS
Add at end:

| 58 | 6 Songs from the Chinese, for voice & guitar. | | Trans. Arthur Waley. | | 1958. | |

conductor, and activities, suspended during the 1939–45 war, were resumed, cathedral boys and male altos being replaced by women sopranos and contraltos. In 1949, when Surplice went to Winchester, his successor, Clifford Harker, took over the conductorship. The Society took part in the 1950 Bristol Bach Festival and in 1955 Herbert Byard became conductor. Under him the Society performs Byrd's masses, other 16th- and 17th-century church music, Bach's motets, occasionally choral works with orchestra such as Handel's Dettingen Te Deum, etc., but the main purpose is still the performance of madrigals. Bath and other places near Bristol are occasionally visited.

956   i   Page heading *should read*:
BRITTON

(*Delete*: Works).

ii   **BRITTON**
Add at end:

See also Collections, Private (Vol. II, p. 373, par. 1 & note 2, for information on library and sale catalogue).

957   ii   **Brizeux**
l. 1. *Add to* See :
Berlioz (2 songs).

958   ii   **BROADWOOD**
ll. 1-2 *should read*:

BROADWOOD, John (*b*. ?, 13 May 1798; *d*. Capel, Surrey, 26 Jan. 1864).

958   ii   Par. 2, l. 2.   brother *should read*:
half-brother

959   i   **BROADWOOD, Lucy**
Par. 1, l. 1.   *b. ?*; *should read*:
b. London, 9 Aug. 1858 ;

Brockes
l. 3.   Music (ex.). *should read*:
Music (text).

ii   **BROCKWAY**
List of works, ll. 2-3.   chorus a *cappella*
should read:
chorus *a cappella*

960   i   **BRODER**
l. 4.   1951 *should read*:
1954

961   i   *Add after* **BROEMEL**
BROKEN CHOIRS.   *See* CORI SPEZZATI.

ii   **BROMAN**
Par. 3, l. 6.   forskning en *should
read*:
forskningen

Add at end:
BIBL.—LUNDERQVIST, T., ' Sten Broman, musiker och
texikav ' (' Musikrevy ', 1954, No. 1, Stockholm).

962   ii   **Brontë, Emily**
l. 2 *should read*:
incid., m. for Fr. stage version).   Floyd (C., do., opera).
Herrmann (B., do.

963   i   **BROS**
Par. 1, ll. 1-2.   Dates *should read*:
(*b.* Tortosa, 5 May 1776 ; *d.* Oviedo, 12 Mar.
1852).

964   ii   *Add after* **Broughton**:
**BROUWENSTIJN, Gré (Gerarda Dem-
phina)** (*b.* Den Helder, 26 Aug. 1915).
Dutch soprano singer. She studied as a
child with the help of a wealthy patron after
being expelled from the school choir on
account of too high-pitched a voice, and she
continued an intensive course under various
teachers. She became leading dramatic
soprano at the Amsterdam Opera and has
sung in Rome, Vienna, Stuttgart, Antwerp
and Brussels, and in 1953 made her first
appearance in London, at Covent Garden,
as Amelia in Verdi's ' Ballo in maschera ',
singing in English. In 1955 and 1956 she
also sang in the Italian performances of
' Otello ' there, with great distinction, under
Rafael Kubelík, with whom she also appeared
in a broadcast performance at the Royal

Festival Hall in Dvořák's ' Rusalka '. In
1954, 1955 and 1956 she was engaged for
Bayreuth by Wieland Wagner. In 1956 she
received the Oranje Nassau Order from the
Queen of the Netherlands.

Gré Brouwenstijn's voice is admirably
suited both to lyrical and to dramatic soprano
parts, if perhaps a little too heroic for the
former and not quite enough so for the latter.
It is beautifully smooth in quality and even
throughout a wide range, and if she shows no
overwhelming power at moments of climax,
they never betray the least vocal strain. She
is not especially remarkable for her acting,
which is nevertheless perfectly adequate to
the parts she undertakes.   E. B.

964   ii   **BROWN**
Par. 1, l. 2 *should read*:
Furness, 15 June 1874 ; *d.* Holywood, Co.
Down, 2 Feb. 1955).

965   ii   **BROWN, Maurice**
ll. 16-17 *should read*:
(London, 1954) and a second, large-scale work
on the composer, perhaps the most important
modern book of its kind in any language, was
finished in 1956 (London, 1958). An important article on Schubert manuscripts appeared
in M. & L., Vol. XXXVIII, Oct. 1957.
E. B.

966   i   **BROWNE, John**
Last line *should read*:
five-part settings.   The modern edition of
this choirbook (' Musica Britannica ', Vols.
10-12, ed. by F. Ll. Harrison) includes all
Browne's extant works and gives some additional information on him.
J. M. (ii), adds.

BROWNE, Richard
Par. 2, ll. 2-8 *should read*:
at Worcester Cathedral, where he appears to
have spent the whole of his career, serving as
chorister there in 1639, sub-deacon in 1642-43,
minor canon from 1644 and organist from
1662. He was buried in the north aisle of the
cathedral nave.[2]

There was another Richard Browne, details
of whose career have been confused with those
of the above and cannot be disentangled from
them with certainty. He was " admitted
vicar-choral and organist for a year of probation " at Wells Cathedral on 26 Mar. 1614
and became perpetual vicar-choral a year
later. The accounts of the Keeper of the
Fabric for 1619-20 show a receipt for 2s. 6d.
from " Mr. Browne, the organist ", but thereafter there is no definite record of him, unless
he is the " Mr. Browne " who appears in the
cathedral accounts at Winchester in 1627-39.

E

The following compositions by a Richard Browne preserved in the library of the R.C.M. (now in the British Museum) appear all to be the work of the latter man, since entries in these part-books were probably discontinued long before the first Civil War.

Signature should read:

J. M. (ii), rev. w. k. f.

966   ii   **Browning, E. B.**
l. 2 *should read:*

Tedesco (3 songs). Du Plessis (sonnets for mezzo-soprano & pf.). Elgar (' Sea Pictures ', No. 3, voice

BROWNLEE
Par. 2, l. 15 *should read:*

Covent Garden, where he sang again in 1930 and 1934-36, he became best known by such

Par. 3, l. 5 *should read:*

he became a regular member in 1936. In 1935 he was

968   i   **BRUCH**
l. 10 *should read:*

Nidrei ' and the Scottish Fantasy ², in

CATALOGUE :
OPERAS
Op. 16, Geibel.² *should read:*

Geibel.³

14 Apr. *should read:*

14 June

CHORAL WORKS
Add after Op. 34 :

64. Hymn on biblical words for solo voices, chorus & orch.

Add footnote :

² The following Scottish tunes are used in this work : 1st movement, ' Auld Robin Morris '; Scherzo, ' Hey the dusty miller ' (modified) ; Andante, ' I'm a' down for lack o' Johnnie '; Finale, ' Hey tutti taitie ' (' Scots wha hae ').

Footnote 2.   ² The libretto *should read:*

³ The libretto

ii   SOLO INSTRUMENTS AND OR-CHESTRA
Delete Op. 64.

972   i   **BRUCKNER**
Par. 2, l. 9. *Urfassung should read:*
original version

Par. 3, ll. 14 & 26. Loewe *should read:*
Löwe

l. 23. *Urfassungen should read:*
original versions

ii Par. 1, l. 1. *Urfassungen should read:*
original versions

Par. 2, l. 15 *should read:*

ruption. From 1950 onwards a revised collected edition has been in progress, issued by

the Austrian National Library, edited by Leopold Nowak. It is sometimes at variance with Robert Haas's editions.

972   ii   Bibl. l. 13, 1934). *should read:*
1934 ; new ed., Vienna, 1952).

Add to Bibl. (2nd work by Engel) :
' The Symphonies of Anton Bruckner ' (New York, 1955).

973   i   *Add to* Bibl. :
Krohn, Ilmari, ' Anton Bruckners Sinfonien : eine Untersuchung über Formenbau und Stimmungsgehalt ', Vol. I : Symphonies 1-3 (Helsingfors, 1955).

ii   Bibl. Redlich entries, l. 1 *should read:*

Redlich, H. F., ' Bruckner and Brahms Quintets in F ' (M. & L., XXVI, July 1955).
' Bruckner and Mahler ' (' Master Musicians ' series) (London, 1955).

Add after l. 4 :

Introduction to a revision of Symphony IV (4th version) in Eulenburg Miniature Score (London, 1955).
' The Finale of Bruckner's Symphony IX ' (M.M.R., LXXIV, 1949).

l. 5. *Delete* Redlich, H. F.

l. 29. Neuchâtel *should read:*
Brussels

974   —   CATALOGUE
LARGE-SCALE SACRED WORKS
Col. 1, l. 7. soprano *should read:*
soloists

Col. 2, l. 3. 1881–82 *should read:*
1881.

Col. 4, l. 1. 1890 publ. *should read:*
Publ. 1892 by composer ; rev. 1924 (J. V. Woess) ; orig. version (1864), ed. L. Nowak, publ. 1957.

l. 3. 1894 publ. *should read:*
1st version (1867–68) unpubl. ; 2nd version (1881), ed. R. Haas, publ. 1944 ; 3rd version (1883) unpubl. ; 4th version publ. 1890 by composer.

975   —   ORCHESTRAL WORKS
Symphony No. 1, col. 6, l. 3. Haas). *should read:*
Haas) ; rev. ed., L. Nowak, 1954.

Symphony No. 4, col. 6, l. 2. Haas). *should read:*
Haas) ; version 2/3, rev. ed., L. Nowak, 1954.

Symphony No. 5, col. 6, l. 2. Haas). *should read:*
Haas) ; 3rd version, rev. ed., L. Nowak, 1951.

Symphony No. 6, col. 6, l. 2. Haas-A. Orel). *should read:*
Haas-A. Orel) ; rev. ed. (based on autograph), L. Nowak, 1952.

Symphony No. 7, col. 6, l. 2. (ed. R. Haas). *should read:*
(ed. R. Haas) ; rev. ed. (based on autograph) L. Nowak, 1954.

Symphony No. 8, col. 6, l. 2. (ed. R. Haas). *should read:*
(ed. R. Haas) ; 2nd version (1886–87), rev. ed., L. Nowak, 1955.

Symphony No. 9, col. 6, l. 3. Orel). *should read:*
Orel) ; rev. ed. (based on autograph), L. Nowak, 1951.

976 i CHAMBER MUSIC
Add after l. 1 :

String Quartet, C mi., composed 1863; first publ., ed.
L. Nowak, 1956.

977 i BRUDIEU
Add at end :

See also Publicacions Catalunya, Vol. 1 (modern ed.
of Madrigals in Requiem).

Brueghel
l. 1 *should read :*

Brueghel (Breughel), Pieter. *See* Absil (' Pierre
Breughel l'ancien ', radio m.). Brusselmans (' Brueghe-
liaanse

l. 3 *should read :*

Schoemaker (ballet & orch. suite).

ii BRUHNS
Add at end :

See also Denkmäler (5) I (modern ed. of collected
works, 2 vols.).

978 i BRUMAGNE
Par. 1, l. 2. Brussels, Mar. *should
read :*

Brussels, 17 Mar.

979 i BRUMEL, Antoine
Add at end :

See also Amer. Inst. Musicol. (C.M.M.), Vol. 5
(modern ed. of complete works). Maîtres Musiciens, Vol.
8 (modern ed. of Mass).

985 i BRUNNER, H.
Par. 1, l. 1.   1898). *should read :*

1898; *d.* Basel, 29 September 1958).

ii *Add before* **Bruno :**

BRUNNER, Ulric (*b.* Guilsborough,
Northamptonshire, 30 July 1882; *d.* London,
1 May 1956).
English schoolmaster and musical educationist. He was educated at Towcester
Grammar School and Culham Training College, and served in the Northampton Yeo-
manry in France and Italy as captain in
1914–18. He held a number of school
appointments in Warwickshire and in 1921
became headmaster of St. Mary's School,
Bridgnorth. In 1926 he drew up the scheme
for non-competitive schools' music festivals,
the first festival being held at Bridgnorth in
1927. In 1939 he became the first chairman
of the Schools' Music Association and after
the 1939–45 war served for several years as
its hon. secretary. During the latter part of
the war he worked for some time in the
Ministry of Labour and National Service
(Appointments Office, Birmingham), and
afterwards became secretary of the City of
Birmingham Symphony Orchestra, being
largely instrumental in putting this orchestra
on a permanent footing. In 1952 he received

the honour of O.B.E. for national service to
music.   S. S. M.
See also Schools' Music Association. Schools' Music
Festivals.

985 ii BRUNSWICK
Par. 3, l. 4 *should read :*

the United States Section of the I.S.C.M. In
1946 he became chairman of the Music
Department in the College of the City of New
York. He

986 i *Add before* **BRUSSELMANS :**

BRUSCANTINI, Sesto (*b.* Porto Civita-
nova, Macerata, 10 Dec. 1919).
Italian bass-baritone singer. He originally
studied law and then turned to music, studying
with Luigi Ricci in Rome. He made his
début at La Scala, Milan, in Mar. 1949 as
Geronimo in ' Il matrimonio segreto '. He
sang several parts for the Italian radio, including Don Pasquale, Sulpice and Don Procopio
(Bizet), and was then engaged for Glyndebourne, where he made his début as Alfonso
in ' Così fan tutte ' in 1950. He returned to
Glyndebourne regularly until 1956 singing
Guglielmo (' Così '), Dandini, Figaro (Rossini
and Mozart), Music Master (' Ariadne ', in
German) and Raimbaud (' Comte Ory ', in
French).   While at Glyndebourne he met
Sena Jurinac, whom he married in 1953.
Bruscantini, without possessing an outstanding
voice, has made a place for himself as a
stylist and musician. He is one of the few
Italians able to sing Mozart adequately, and
his enunciation and excellent sense of timing
make him one of the best *buffo* artists since
Stabile.   H. D. R.

BRUSSELMANS
Par. 2, l. 8 *should read :*

the ballets ' Les Néréides ' (1911) and ' Ker-
messe flamande ' (1912); the oratorio ' Jesus '
(1936), cantatas; 2

988 ii BRUSTAD
Par. 7. *Add before* ' Snow White ' :
Opera ' Atlantis ' (1945).

Add after ' Snow White ' :
Symphony No. 1 (1948).

989 i BRYAN
Par. 1, l. 2 *should read :*

1895; *d.* London, 19 Nov. 1957).

**BRYANSTON SCHOOL OF
MUSIC**
l. 1 *should read :*

BRYANSTON SCHOOL OF MUSIC.
See Summer School of Music.

Transfer article to Vol. VIII, p. 188.

990 ii **BRZEZIŃSKI**
Par. 1, l. 2. Warsaw, 1944 *should read* :

Warsaw, 6 Aug. 1944

991 i **BUCCHI**
Par. 2, l. 7. *After the following insert* :

comic opera ' Il contrabasso ' (on a story by Tchekhov), produced Florence, Maggio Musicale, 20 May 1954 ;

l. 12 *should read* :

cantata for voice and nine instruments (1946), a string Quartet (written for the Quartetto Italiano),

992 i **Büchner, Georg**
Add at end :
Zeisl (' Leonce und Lena ', opera).

BUCHNER, Johann
Par. 1, l. 1 *should read* :

BUCHNER (Bucher, Puchner), Hans

l. 3 *should read* :
d. Zürich, c. 1538).

Par. 2, l. 8 *should read* :
ing Protestantism. He went to

ll. 10-11 *should read* :

autograph theoretical treatise entitled ' Fundamentum ' is preserved in the town library. It is a Latin work on playing and writing for the organ and contains 35 pieces for the instrument, 18 of which were reprinted in V.M.W., V, i.

Par. 3. *Delete* l. 5.

l. 6 *should read* :
E. v. d. s., adds.

994 i **BÜCKEN**
Par. 3. *Add after* l. 4 :
' Die Musik der Nationen ' (1937).

Insert after ' R. Schumann ' :
' Musik der Deutschen ' (Cologne, 1941).

1007 ii **BUKOFZER**
Par. 1, l. 2 *should read* :

27 Mar. 1910; d. Oakland, California, 7 Dec. 1955).

1008 i Par. 2, l. 4 *should read* :
logy of the American Council of Learned

Par. 5, ll. 3-4 *should read* :

motets by Dufay (1949), and brought out a collected edition of John Dunstable.

1009 i **BULL**
Par. 10, ll. 2-3 *should read* :

where for about a year he became one of the organists in the archduke's chapel, under Géry de Ghersem. He received the high salary of 250 florins *per tercio*, but left at the end of 1614.

ii Par. 7, l. 2 *should read* :
organ or virginals [4] are in

Footnote 4 should read :

[4] In a manuscript book now in the Fitzwilliam Museum at Cambridge there are also some 50 pieces for viols, but their authenticity is extremely doubtful, since the book was a miscellany bound for Bull in which many other composers are represented.

1010 i *Add to* BIBL. :
DART, R. T., ' John Bull's " Chapel " ' (M. & L., July 1959).
HOPPE, H., ' John Bull in the Archduke Albert's Service ' (M. & L., April 1954).
VAN DER MEER, JOHN HENRY, ' The Keyboard Works in the Vienna Bull Manuscript ' (' Tijdschrift voor Muziekwetenschap ', Vol. XVIII, Part ii, p. 72).

l. 4 *should read* :
catalogue below is compiled).

Delete l. 5 *and replace by* :
MELLERS, WILFRID, ' John Bull and English Keyboard Music ' (M.Q., XL, July-Oct. 1954).

ii List. ' Te lucis ' entry, mund *should read* :
mundi

' Tellucis irgens ' *should read* :
' Telluris ingens '

See also. l. 1 *should read* :
See also Ashwell. English Musicians Abroad. Musica Britannica, Vol. 14 (modern ed. of keyboard music).

1011 ii **BULL, Ole**
Par. 3, ll. 1-10 *should read* :

Only relatively few of his numerous compositions appear to have been published. Among them are a set of ' Variazioni di bravura ', ' La preghiera d' una madre ', ' Polacca guerriera ' (his *cheval de bataille*), ' La Mélancolie ' and ' A Visit to the Mountain Chalet ', which includes his most celebrated melody, ' Sæterjentens Søndag ' (often performed in an arrangement for strings by Svendsen). The titles of others, such as ' The

1012 i BIBL., l. 1. folkemusik ' *should read* :
folkemusikk '

l. 8. ' Evantyret *should read* :
' Eventyret

l. 9. i utdreg ' *should read* :
i utdrag '

Add to BIBL. :
LINGE, OLA, ' Ole Bull : livshistoria, mannen, kunstnaren ' (Oslo, 1953).

1017   ii   *Add after* **BURDEN** :

BURELL, John (*b.* ? ; *d.* ?, 1437).

English singer and composer. He was active during the early 15th century and is mentioned, with Damett, Sturgeon and Cooke, in the Wardrobe Books of the royal household for the year 1413.[1] This was the year of Henry V's accession, and thereafter Burell frequently accompanied the monarch as a member of the Chapel Royal to the courts of France and Burgundy. It is not improbable that he may be identified with Johannes Bodoil, whose compositions are found in continental sources compiled during the century. In 1415 he went with the Chapel to Harfleur and was on the sick-list there. He returned to England in the following year and was granted a corrody at Meaux Abbey by royal warrant, perhaps as a reward for service abroad. As in so many cases, the warrant was grudgingly honoured " to avoid the king's wrath and in obedience to his verbal command " [2], but the annuity of five marks was granted to Burell in return for his aid and counsel, and there is no reason to suspect that he neglected his duties. Indeed, Meaux became an important centre of liturgical polyphony as time went on, and some part of this may have been due to Burell's interest in the Abbey and its music.

A further grant was made to him in 1417, that of the prebend of Norton, in Hereford Cathedral, and apparently he did not resign it until 1436.[3] When Catherine of Valois was crowned in 1421, Burell was among those members of the Chapel awarded four ells of scarlet cloth for use as ceremonial robes.[4] Soon afterwards he was granted the prebend of East Merden in Chichester Cathedral, perhaps as a result of the translation of Thomas Polton, Bishop of Hereford, to Chichester in 1422. Burell was permitted, however, to exchange this prebend for one in York Minster in 1424.[5] In view of the resignation of the Hereford prebend in 1436, and the termination of the corrody at Meaux in 1437, it is likely that Burell died about that time.

Two works by Burell are to be found in the ' Old Hall Manuscript ': a ' Gloria ' and a ' Credo '. The ' Gloria ' (I, 17) is a three-voice setting in *conductus* style, contrasts in metre to some extent supplanting those of texture, which are ruled out by the style of writing. Similar characteristics are apparent in the ' Credo ' (II, 58), which uses almost identical clef-positions and ends (like the ' Gloria ') on G. Two contrasting metres are employed alternately — O C O C O — and

similar evidence of careful planning may be seen in the alternate choice of G and D as finals for the individual sections of the work. Since both ' Gloria ' and ' Credo ' have in common such features as *conductus* style mode, clef-positions, number of voices and attribution, it is not unlikely that they form a Mass pair. This custom of pairing ' Gloria ' and ' Credo ' (as well as ' Sanctus ' and ' Agnus ') was well known if not widespread before 1420.   D. W. S.

BIBLIOGRAPHY

BUKOFZER, MANFRED, ' Studies in Medieval and Renaissance Music ' (New York, 1950).
GREENE, RICHARD L., ' Two Medieval Musical Manuscripts ' (Journ. Amer. Musicol. Soc., VII, 1954).
RAMSBOTHAM, ALEXANDER, ed., ' The Old Hall Manuscript ', Vols. I & II (London, 1933 & 1935).
TROWELL, BRIAN, ' Some English Contemporaries of Dunstable ' (Proc. Roy. Mus. Ass., LXXXI, 1954–1955).

1024   i   **BURGUNDIAN SCHOOL**
           Add at end :

See also Lyrebird Press (modern ed. of 15th-century music).

1025   i   **BURIAN**
           Par. 2, l. 10 *should read* :

at Dresden, also in that in Paris. He sang in London, at Covent Garden, in 1904-5, 1910 and 1914.

BURKE
Par. 2, l. 16 *should read* :

pheles, Prince Igor, Amfortas and Pogner. He was at the New York Metropolitan Opera in 1922-25.

ii   **BURKHARD**
     Par. 1, l. 2 *should read* :

Bienne, Canton Berne, 18 Apr. 1900 ; *d.* Zürich, 18 June 1955).

1027   i   CATALOGUE
           Add to CHORAL WORKS WITH INSTRUMENTS :

96. Psalm CLXVIII for unison chorus & insts. (1954).

Add to UNACCOMPANIED CHORAL WORKS :

97. ' Die Sintflut ' (1954-55).

Add to ORCHESTRAL WORKS :

95. Divertimento for stgs. (1954).

Add to SOLO INSTRUMENTS AND ORCHESTRA :

93. Viola Concerto (1953).
94. ' Concertino ' for 2 flutes, harpsichord & stgs. (1954).

Add to CHAMBER MUSIC :

92. Serenade for flute & clar. (1953).

ii   *Add before* PIANOFORTE MUSIC :

SOLO FLUTE

98. Suite (1955).

¹ Public Record Office, E 101/406/21.
² Patent Rolls, Henry VI, 1436-41.
³ Patent Rolls, Henry V, 1416-22 ; ' Fasti Ecclesiae Anglicanae ', I.
⁴ Public Record Office, E 101/407/4.
⁵ Patent Rolls, Henry VI, 1422-29.

1027　ii　*Add to* PIANOFORTE MUSIC:
99. 6 Preludes (1955).

Add to BIBL.:
MOHR, ERNST, 'Willy Burkhard: Leben und Werk'
(Zürich, 1957).
ZÚRLINDEN, MAX, 'Willy Burkhard' (Zürich & Stuttgart, 1956).

BURLE MARX
Par. 1, l. 2 *should read*:
23 July 1902).

1031　ii　**BURNEY**
Par. 4, l. 5 *should read*:
experiences.[1] His manuscript copy of the omitted

Par. 7, l. 5 *should read*:
vols. in 1935 (American ed., 1957). The chapters on
the Music of the

Add footnote:
[1] A modern facsimile reprint is to appear in 'Documenta Musicologica', Vol. 11.

1032　i　**Burns**
l. 2 *should read*:
(partsongs). Bax (song). Berg (Alban, song). Bishop
(H., 'Jolly Beggars',

1035　i　**BUSBY**
Add at end:
BIBL.—SPENCE, K. G. F., 'The Learned Doctor Busby'
(M. & L., XXXVII, 1956, p. 141).

ii　**BUSCH (1)**
Par. 2, l. 10 *should read*:
Edinburgh (*hon. causa*). He conducted in the
U.S.A. in 1941 and 1942, was guest conductor of the New York Philharmonic in
1942–45, and conducted opera at the Colón
Theatre in Buenos Aires (1933–36, 1943–45)
and afterwards at the New York Metropolitan
Opera (1945–49).

BUSCH (2)
Par. 1, l. 2. Guildford *should read*:
Guilford

Par. 4, l. 6 *should read*:
chief initiators of the Lucerne Festival. In
1940 he settled in New York.

1037　i　*Add before* BUSCOPIUS:
BUSCHNE, Josef. *See* BASZNY, JÓZEF.

ii　**BUSH**
Par. 1, l. 21. 31 May *should read*:
6 Sept.

Par. 2, l. 12 *should read*:
'Keynote', Vol. I, No. 4), he had used, if

ll. 16-17 *should read*:
thematically significant, is an attempted compromise between the twelve-note method of

1037　ii　Par. 2, l. 21 *should read*:
deeply interested, although he now rejects it,
and tonality, in a broad Hindemithian sense,
on the other.

1039　i　List of works
OPERA *should read*:
OPERAS
l. 4 *should read*:
— 'Wat Tyler' (lib. by Nancy Bush) (1950), prod.
Leipzig, Städtisches Theater, 6 Sept. 1953.

Add after l. 5:
— 'Men of Blackmoor' (lib. by Nancy Bush), prod.
Weimar, Nationaltheater, 18 Nov. 1956.

ii　HORN AND PIANOFORTE
Add after Op. 36:
— 2 Pieces (1954).

PIANOFORTE MUSIC
46. 'Variations, Nocturne and Finale on an English
Sea-Song.'
49. Suite, 'Mr. Playford's Times'.

1043　i　**BUSONI**
BIBL., l. 10. (Florence, 1941) *should read*:
(Milan, 1954).

Add after l. 12:
'The Essence of Music and Other Papers', trans.
by Rosamond Ley (London, 1957).

Add to BIBL.:
BUSONI, GERDA, 'Erinnerungen an Ferruccio Busoni',
ed. by Friedrich Schnapp (Berlin, 1958).
GERVAIS, TERENCE WHITE, 'Busoni encore significatif'
('Cahiers français de la musique', No. 1, Mar.
1957).
'Busoni's Continued Significance' ('Chesterian',
July 1953).
'Busoni's Possible Influence' ('Chesterian', Jan.
1953).

ii　l. 18. 1927 *should read*:
1937

Add to BIBL.:
STEVENSON, RONALD, 'Busoni—the Legend of a Prodigal' ('The Score', No. 15, Mar. 1956, p. 15).

1047　i　**Busse**
See Radó *should read*:
See Berg (Alban, 3 songs). Radó

ii　**BÜSSER**
Par. 2, l. 6 *should read*:
Opéra-Comique and president of the Académie des Beaux-Arts in 1947. He published
a 'Précis de composition' in 1943.

1048　i　*Add after* **Bussine**:
BUSZNY, Józef. *See* BASZNY.

1050　i　**BUTTERWORTH**
Par. 2, ll. 15-18 *should read*:
themes, was produced by Boult at West Kirby,
Cheshire, on 27 Feb. 1914, conducted by the
composer at Oxford the next day and first
heard in London at one of F. B. Ellis's concerts
on 20 Mar.

1050   ii **BUTTING**
ORCHESTRAL WORKS
Add after Op. 29 :
6 Symphonies had been written by 1945.

1051   i **BUTTSTETT, J. H.**
BIBL., l. 2. 1935 *should read* :
1934.

1053   i **BUUS**
Add at end :
See also Collectio O.M.B., Vol. 8 (modern ed.).

1054   i **BUXHEIM ORGAN BOOK**
Par. 1, l. 7 *should read* :
the extensive article by Eitner. A facsimile
of the manuscript, edited by Bertha Antonia
Wallner, was published in ' Documenta Musicologica ' (Series II, Vol. i) in 1955, and her
transcription followed in 1958–59, as Vols.
37-39 of ' Das Erbe Deutscher Musik '.

D. W. S.

Add to BIBL. :
BEDBROOK, G. S., ' The Buxheim Keyboard Manuscript '
(M. Rev., XIV, 1953, p. 288).

BIBL. *Add after* l. 3 :
' Das Buxheimer Orgelbuch.' Facsimile ed. by Bertha
Antonio Wallner (Cassel & Basel, 1955).

BUXTEHUDE
Par. 1, ll. 1-2 *should read* :

BUXTEHUDE, Diderik (Diderich, Ger.
Dietrich) (*b.* Oldesloe, Holstein, 1637 ; *d.*
Lübeck, 9 May

Footnote. l. 8 *should read* :
name the Swedish equivalent of which is Jöns. What is
more, the birthplace is now considered both by Moser
and by Sørensen (*see* Bibl.) to have been most likely
Oldesloe, and since Holstein was at that time under
Danish rule (Holsten), he must still be regarded as of
Danish birth ; moreover, the Lübeck Magazine for July
1707 says that he *Patriam agnoscit Daniam.*

1055   i Par. 1, l. 5 *should read* :
at Klecken in 1925. An edition of 19 suites,
6 sets of variations and some other hitherto
unknown works for clavichord (from a manuscript discovered in Denmark) was published
by Hansen of Copenhagen (ed. Bangert) in
1941, and 4 more suites for clavichord by
Engstrøm & Sødring there (ed. Lundgren).
Merseburger of Leipzig have published some
church cantatas for the first time.

C. F. P., rev. & adds.

BIBL. *Add after* l. 8 GRUSNICK) :
' Zur Chronologie von Dietrich Buxtehudes Vokal-
werken ' (' Musikforschung ', Vol. X, 1957, p. 75).

Add to BIBL. :
HEDAR, JOSEF, ' Dietrich Buxtehudes Orgelwerke '
(Stockholm & Frankfort o/M., 1951).
HUTCHINS, FARLEY K., ' Dietrich Buxtehude : the Man,
his Music, his Era ' (Paterson, N.J., 1955).
LORENZ, HELMUT, ' Die Klaviermusik Dietrich Buxte-
hudes ' (A.f.M., XI, 3, p. 238).
MOSER, HANS JOACHIM, ' Dietrich Buxtehude : der
Mann und sein Werk ' (Berlin, 1957).
SØRENSEN, SØREN, ' Diderich Buxtehudes vokale kirke-
musik : studier til den evangeliske kirkekantates
udviklingshistorie ', 2 vols. (Copenhagen, 1958).

1055   i BIBL. l. 19 *should read* :
' Dietrich Buxtehude ' (Cassel, 1937 ; new ed. Cassel
& Basel, 1952).

Add to See also :
Denkmäler (2), Vol. XI (modern ed. of trio sonatas) ;
Vol. XIV (do. of ' Abendmusiken ' & cantatas).

Add at end, before See also
LIST OF CANTATAS [1]
FOR A SOLO VOICE
(with strings and continuo unless
otherwise mentioned)

' Also hat Gott die Welt geliebet ', G ma., soprano (St.
John).
' Dies ist der Tag, den der Herr gemacht hat ' (frag-
ment), G ma., soprano.
' Dixit Dominus Domino meo ', C ma., soprano or
tenor (Psalm 110).
' Herr, nun lässt du deinen Diener ', C ma., tenor (St.
Luke).
' Herr, wenn ich nur dich hab ', G ma., soprano (Ps. 73).
' Ich bin die Auferstehung und das Leben ', C ma.,
bass, 2 cornetts, 2 trumpets, bassoon, stgs. & cont.
(St. John).
' Ich bin eine zu Saron ', A ma., bass (Song of Songs).
' Ich sprach in meinem Herzen ', C ma., soprano, stgs.,
bassoon & cont. (Ecclesiastes).
' Jubilate Domino ', D ma., alto (Ps. 98).
' Lauda anima mea ', C ma., soprano (Ps. 146).
' Laudate Dominum ', E ma., soprano (Ps. 117).
' Lobe den Herrn, meine Seele ', A ma., tenor (Ps. 103).
' Mein Herz ist bereit ', F ma., bass (Ps. 57).
' O clemens, O mitis, O coelestis Pater ', C mi., soprano
(paraphrase of St. Luke).
' Quemadmodum desiderat cervus ', F ma., tenor
(paraphrase of Ps. 42).
' Schaffe in mir, Gott, ein rein Herz ', B♭ ma., soprano
(Ps. 51).
' Sicut Moses exaltavit serpentum ', D ma., soprano
(St. John).
' Singet dem Herrn ein neues Lied ', C ma., soprano
(Ps. 98).

FOR TWO SOLO VOICES
(with strings and continuo unless
otherwise mentioned)

' Herr, ich lasse dich nicht ', B♭ ma., T.B., trombone,
stgs. & cont. (Gen.).
' Laudate pueri ', D mi., S.S. (Ps. 113).
' Salve Jesu Patris gnate ', D ma., S.S. (?).

FOR THREE SOLO VOICES

' Afferte Domino gloriam honorem ', F ma., S.S.B. &
cont. (Ps. 96, 31, 34).
' Aperite mihi portas justitiae ', F ma., A.T.B., vns. &
cont. (Ps. 118).
' Canite Jesu nostro ', F ma., S.S.B., stgs. & cont. (?).
' Cantate Domino canticum novum ', G ma., S.S.B. &
cont. (Ps. 96).
' In te Domine speravi ', C ma., S.A.B. & cont. (Ps. 71
or 31).

FOR 4- OR 5-PART CHORUS
(with strings and continuo unless
otherwise mentioned)

' Accedite gentes ', C ma., S.S.A.T.B. (paraphrase of
var. Psalms).
' Der Herr ist mit mir ', C mi., S.A.T.B. (Ps. 118).
' Domine salvum fac regem et exaudi ', A mi.,
S.S.A.T.B. (Ps. 20).
' Ecce nunc benedicite Domino ', G ma., A.T.T.B.
(Ps. 134).
' Fürwahr, er trug unsere Krankheit ', C mi., S.S.A.T.B.
(Isaiah).
' Nun danket alle Gott ', C ma., S.S.A.T.B., 2 cornetts,
bassoon, 2 trumpets, stgs. & cont. (?).

---

[1] Based on the detailed Catalogue in Sørensen (*see*
Bibl.), Vol. I, pp. 27-43.

WITH ONE ARIA [1]
(with strings and continuo unless
otherwise mentioned)

' Drei schöne Dinge sind ', F ma., soprano & bass.
' Eins bitte ich vom Herrn ', C ma., S.S.A.T.B., 2 flutes,
stgs. & cont. (words of aria by Christian Weselo-
vius).
' Fürchtet euch nicht ', F ma., soprano & bass (aria:
words Adam Olearius).
' Gott fähret auf mit Jauchzen ', C ma., 2 sopranos,
bass, 2 cornetts, 2 trumpets, 2 trombones, bassoon,
stgs. & cont. (aria: words Johann Rist).
' Herr, auf dich traue ich ', A mi., soprano (aria?).
' Herr, wenn ich nur dich habe ', G ma., soprano (aria:
words, Anna Sophia, Landgravine of Hesse-
Darmstadt).
' Ich habe Lust abzuscheiden ', C mi., 2 sopranos, bass,
bassoon, stgs. & cont. (aria: words Johann
Niedling).
' Ich habe Lust abzuscheiden ', C mi., 2 sopranos &
bass (2nd setting).
' Ich halte es dafür ', G mi., soprano & bass (aria:
words Johannes Flitner).
' Ich suchte des Nachts in meinem Bette ', G mi., tenor,
bass, 2 oboes, stgs. & cont. (aria?).
' Ist es recht, dass man dem Kaiser Zinse gebe ', B♭ ma.,
S.S.A.T.B. (aria?).
' Je höher du bist ', B mi., 2 sopranos & bass (aria?).
' Membra Jesu Nostri ', cycle of 7 cantatas (arias from
' Rhytmica oratio ') :
  1. Ecce super montes, C mi., S.S.A.T.B.
  2. Ad ubera portabimini, E♭ ma., S.S.A.T.B.
  3. Quid sunt plagae istae, G mi., S.S.A.T.B.
  4. Surge amica mea, D mi., S.S.A.T.B.
  5. Sicut modo geniti, A mi., A.T.B.
  6. Vulnerasti cor meum, E mi., S.S.B.
  7. Illustra faciem tuam, E mi., S.S.A.T.B.
' Nichts soll uns scheiden von der Liebe Gottes ', D mi.,
soprano, alto & bass (aria?).
' O dulcis Jesu ', E mi., soprano (aria?).

WITH ARIAS AND CHORALES

' Alles, was ihr tut mit Worten ', G ma., S.A.T.B. &
stgs.
' Frohlocket mit Händen, alle Völker ', C ma.,
S.S.A.T.B., 2 trumpets, stgs. & cont.
' Gott, hilf mir ', C mi., S.A.T.B., stgs. & cont.
' Man singet mit Freuden vom Sieg ', C ma., S.S.A.T.B.,
2 trumpets, 2 trombones, bassoon, stgs. & cont.

CHORALE CANTATAS WITHOUT INTERPOLATIONS [2]

' All solch dein Güt wir preisen ', C mi., S.S.A.T.B.
(Paul Eber : Joachim Magdeburg).
' Befiel dem Engel, dass er komm ', A mi., S.A.T.B.
(Erasmus Alberus : Johann Spangenberg).
' Du Friedefürst, Herr Jesu Christ ', G ma., 2 sopranos,
bass, bassoon, stgs. & cont. (Jacob Ebert: Bartho-
lomäus Gesius).
' Du Friedefürst, Herr Jesu Christ ', B♭ ma., S.S.A.T.B.
(id.).
' Erhalt uns, Herr, bei deinem Wort ', A mi., S.A.T.B.
(Luther : Klug ; Luther : Gutknecht ; ? : Johann
Walther ; ? Hans Thomissøn).
' Gen Himmel zu dem Vater mein ', G ma., soprano
(Luther : ?).
' Herren vår Gud ', E. Phrygian, S.A.T.B. (Danish
paraphrase on Ps. 26 : Burchard Waldis).
' Herzlich lieb hab ich dich ', C ma., S.S.A.T.B. (Martin
Schalling : ?).
' Herzlich tut mich verlangen ', E. Phrygian, soprano
(C. Knoll : Hans Leo Hassler).
' In dulci jubilo ', F ma., 2 sopranos & bass (Klug : do.).
' Jesu, meine Freude ', E mi., 2 sopranos & bass (Johann
Franck : Johann Crüger).
' Nimm vom uns, Herr ', E mi., S.A.T.B., bassoon, stgs.
& cont. (Martin Moller : Schumann [1539]).
' Nun lasst uns Gott dem Herren ', C ma., S.A.T.B.
(Ludwig Helmbold : Crüger).

' Wachet auf, ruft, uns die Stimme ', D ma., 2 sopranos,
bass, bassoon, stgs. & cont. (Philipp Nicolai : do.).
' Walts Gott, mein Werk ich lasse ', C mi., S.A.T.B.
(Michael Ziegenspeck : Hassler).
' Wär Gott nicht mit uns diese Zeit ', G mi., S.A.T.B.
(Luther : Walther).

CHORALE CANTATAS WITH INTERPOLATIONS

' Erbarm dich mein, O Herre Gott ', E mi., S.A.T.B.,
bassoon, stgs. & cont. (E. Hegenwald : Walther).
' Heut triumphieret Gottes Sohn ', C ma., S.S.A.T.B.,
bassoon, 2 trumpets, stgs. & cont. (Basilius Förtsch :
Gesius).
' Ihr lieben Christen, freut euch nun ', D ma., 3 cornetts,
2 trumpets, 2 muted trumpets, 3 trombones, stgs.
& cont. (Alberus : ?).
' O Gott, wir danken deiner Güt ', A mi., S.S.A.T.B.
(Nicolas Boye : ?).
' Wo soll ich fliehen hin ? ', G mi. S.A.T.B. (Johann
Heermann : Regnart [? F. or J.] ; Bartholomäus
Ringwald : ?).

SONG CANTATAS FOR SOLO VOICES [3]

' An Filius non est Dei ', (?), B mi., alto, tenor, bass, 3
trombones & stgs.
' Att du Jesu vill mig höra ' (?), C mi., soprano.
' Bedenke Mensch das Ende ' (Salomon Liskow), G mi.,
2 sopranos & bass.
' Entreisst euch, meine Sinnen ', (?), D mi., soprano.
' Fallax mundus ornat vultus ' (?), C mi., soprano.
' Jesu dulcis memoria ' (Jubilus S. Bernardi), E mi.,
2 sopranos.
' Jesu dulcis memoria ' (do.), G ma., alto, tenor & bass.
' Jesu, komm, mein Trost und Lachen ' (Ernst Christoph
Homburg), C mi., alto, tenor & bass.
' Jesu, meine Freud und Lust ' (Angelus Silesius [Johann
Scheffler]), A ma., alto.
' Jesulein, du Tausendschön ' (?), C ma., alto, tenor,
bass, bassoon & stgs.
' Kommst du, kommst du, Licht der Heiden ' (Hom-
burg), B♭ ma., 2 sopranos & bass.
' Lauda Sion Salvatorem ' (Thomas Aquinas), A mi.,
2 sopranos & bass.
' Liebster, meine Seele saget ' (Homburg), C ma., 2
sopranos.
' Mein Gemüt erfreuet sich ' (?), C ma., soprano, alto,
bass, vns., cornetts, regal & cont.
' Meine Seele willtu ruhn ' (Silesius), G ma., 2 sopranos
& bass.
' Nun freut euch ihr Frommen ' (Silesius), C ma., 2
sopranos.
' O fröhliche Stunden ' (Johann Rist), A ma., soprano.
' O Gottes Stadt ' (Rist), C mi., soprano.
' O Jesu mi dulcissime ' (Bernardi), E mi., 2 sopranos
& bass.
' O lux beata Trinitas ' (?), A mi., 2 sopranos, vns. &
bassoon.
' O wie selig sind ' (J. W. Petersen), A mi., alto & bass.
' Salve desiderium ' (?), C mi., 2 sopranos, bass, bassoon,
stgs. & cont.
' Surrexit Christus hodie ' (?), G ma., 2 sopranos, bass,
bassoon, stgs. & cont.
' Wachet auf, ruft uns die Stimme ' (Nicolai), C ma.,
alto, tenor & bass.
' Was frag ich nach der Welt ' (Georg Michael Pfeffer-
korn), C ma., soprano, alto & bass.
' Was mich auf dieser Welt betrübt ' (Michael Franck),
G ma., soprano.
' Welt, packe dich ' (Justus Sieber), A ma., 2 sopranos &
bass.
' Wenn ich, Herr Jesu, habe dich ' (Anna Sophia of
Hesse Darmstadt), E mi., alto.
' Wie schmeckt es so lieblich und wohl ' (Heinrich
Müller), D ma., soprano, alto & bass.
' Wie soll ich dich empfangen ' (Paul Gerhardt), A mi.,
2 sopranos, bass, bassoon, stgs. & cont.
' Wo ist doch mein Freund geblieben ' (?), B♭ ma.,
soprano, bass, bassoon, stgs. & cont.

CHORAL SONG CANTATAS

' Das neugeborne Kindelein ' (Cyriacus Schneegass),
A mi., S.A.T.B., bassoon, stgs. & cont.

---

[1] Voices fully written out are solos ; those abbreviated
S.A.T.B. are choral.
[2] Names in brackets are those of the poets and the
composers of the chorales, shown in that order.

[3] Names in brackets are those of the poets of the songs
on which the cantatas are based.

'Dein edles Herz ' (Rist), C mi., S.A.T.B.
'Du Lebensfürst, Herr Jesu Christ' (Rist), C mi.,
 S.A.T.B.
'Jesu, meiner Freuden Meister' (Moritz Rachelius),
 C mi., S.A.T.B.
'Jesu, meines Lebens Leben' (Homburg), D mi.,
 S.A.T.B.
'O fröhliche Stunden ', C ma., S.S.A.B.
'Pange lingua gloriosi' (Thomas Aquinas), E mi.,
 S.S.A.B.
'Schwinget euch himmelan ' (?), C ma., S.S.A.T.B.
'Wie wird erneut, wie wird erfreuet' (?), C ma.,
 S.S.A.T.T.B., 3 cornetts, 3 trumpets, 2 trombones,
 harpsichord, stgs. & organ cont.

SACRED PARODY SONG CANTATAS [1]

'Erfreue dich, Erde, der Himmel erschallt ' (?), 2
 sopranos, alto, bass, trumpets, drums, stgs. &
 organ cont.
'Klinget mit Freuden, ihr klaren Klarinen ' (?), C ma.,
 2 sopranos, bass, trumpets, stgs. & cont.

[1] Words altered from secular cantata texts by unknown
poets.

1067   ii   **BYRD**
           See also. l. 5 *should read*:
milit. band). Lyrebird Press (modern ed. of keyboard
music). Non nobis Domine (? B.'s comp.).

Byron
  l. 23 *should read*:
partsong). Maillart ('Lara', opera). Marsick (A., do.).
Masson (E.,

1068   i   *Add after* **BYSTRÖM**:

BYTTERING, ? (*b.* ? ; *d.* ?).
English 14th-15th-century singer and composer. He may have been one of the 24 members of the Chapel Royal of Henry V, some of
whom sang before the French envoys on 1
July 1415, the occasion being that of the marriage negotiations between Henry and Catherine of Valois. Five years later, when the
marriage took place, the festivities were en-
livened by the contributions of artists and
musicians. A picture of the royal bride and
bridegroom is preserved in the British Museum
(Cotton, Julius, E. IV, f. 22), and the tenor of
Byttering's motet 'En Katherinae solennia/
Virginalis contio' is taken from the respond
for St. Catherine ('Virgo flagellatur') whose
verse begins "Sponsus amat sponsam".
There is no proof that this work was performed in 1420, when the wedding took place,
but it is significant that Byttering chose only
that part of the respond which could be related to a marriage ceremony. Stylistically
the motet belongs to this period, and it is not
unreasonable to assume that Byttering's
activities as a composer were then at their
height.
The bulk of his music is preserved in the
'Old Hall Manuscript', though there are
two concordances, one at York (Diocesan
Registry, now in the Borthwick Institute of
Historical Research) and another at Aosta
(Seminario Maggiore). There are two settings of 'Gloria', two of 'Credo', the motet

mentioned above, and the antiphon 'Nescient
Mater '. This slender corpus is sufficient to
show that Byttering was a composer of considerable skill and that, apart from his remarkable melodic gifts, he had a keen sense of
liturgical style, both traditional and experimental. The fact that one 'Gloria ' in 'Old
Hall ' (I, 39) is found in an Italian manuscript
is also an indication that Byttering's music,
like that of so many of his contemporaries,
enjoyed a wide continental audience.
His four extant mass sections are all in
" free treble " or " ballade mass " style. The
'Gloria ' (I, 39) is set for alto voice and two
supporting instruments, except at the words
"Domine Fili ", where the instrumentalist
responsible for the lowest part stops playing
and sings instead. This work is rich in
imitative passages and triplet coloration, besides being notable for its metrical contrasts,
some of which are reminiscent of Italian *ars
nova* subtleties. It may possibly be paired with
the 'Credo ' (II, 149), also for alto and two
instruments, which uses exactly the same clef-
positions as the 'Gloria' and indulges in
similar proportional quirks after the Italian
style, especially at the words " et homo factus
est " and " Amen ".
The second 'Gloria ' (I, 47) appears at
first glance to be scored for the same combination as the Mass pair mentioned above,
but in fact the uppermost voice contains a
hidden canon, first discovered in 1948 by
Oliver Strunk. The text of the 'Gloria ' is
thus telescoped and shared between two
voices, often with striking dramatico-liturgical
effect, as when " Domine Deus Rex coelestis "
has superimposed upon it " Deus Pater omni-
potens ", which in turn is echoed by " Domine
Fili unigenite ". The actual texture of the
piece, as well as its imitative characteristics, is
matched exactly by the 'Credo ' (II, 203),
which also employs two alto voices and two
instruments. Other features in common are
the final on D and the nearly similar clef-
positions. Here, then, is another possible
Mass pair. An additional attribute of the
'Credo ' is its loosely used isorhythmic technique, recalling late 14th-century Italian
style.
A strictly isorhythmic tenor is to be found
in the motet 'En Katherinae solennia ',
(III, 145), where there are two *taleae* thrice
repeated in increasing diminution. This instrumental tenor supports two voices, an alto
and a tenor, each of whom sings a distinct and
different text, though both are in honour of
St. Catherine of Alexandria. Apparently
much less complex is the antiphon 'Nesciens
Mater ' for three voices in *conductus* style
(I, 157). But the plainsong is handled in an
especially subtle manner, for instead of appearing in one voice throughout the composition,

it is found first in one voice, then in another, a phenomenon sometimes termed " migrant *cantus firmus* ". Thus no single voice is tied to the contour of the plainsong, and the impression is one of freedom and inventiveness. Byttering, indeed, is nothing if not inventive, yet he combines with his many-sided ingenuity a sure instinct for beauty of melodic line and sonority of texture.   D. W. S.

BIBLIOGRAPHY

BELLAGUET, L. F., ' Chronique du religieux de Saint-Denis ' (Paris, 1839–52).
BUKOFZER, MANFRED, ' Studies in Medieval and Renaissance Music ' (New York, 1950).

RAMSBOTHAM, ALEXANDER, ed., ' The Old Hall Manuscript ', Vols. I-III (completed by H. B. Collins and Dom Anselm Hughes) (London, 1933–38).
STRUNK, OLIVER, ' The Music of the Old Hall Manuscript — A Postscript ' (in Bukofzer, *op. cit.*).

1078   i   **BYZANTINE MUSIC**
         Add to BIBL. :

WELLESZ, EGON, ' Byzantine Music and its Place in the Liturgy ' (Proc. Roy. Mus. Ass., LXXXI, 1954–1955).
' The Music of the Byzantine Church ' (Cologne, 1959).

   ii   *See also should read* :

See also Lyrebird Press (modern ed.). Notation, p. 110.

VOL. II

Page Col.

2 ii **CABANILLES, Juan**
Par. 5, l. 6 *should read*:

(1935) ; III 25 *tientos* (1936). The complete organ works are in Publicacions Catalunya, Vols. IV, VIII and XIII.   H. A. (ii).

3 ii **CABEZÓN (1)**
Par. 1, l. 1 *should read*:

Matajudíos nr. Burgos, 1510 ; *d.*

4 ii *Add to* BIBL.:

DART, THURSTON, ' Cavazzoni and Cabezón ' (M. & L., XXXVI, 1955, p. 2).
JEPPESEN, K., ' Cavazzoni–Cabezón ' (J.A.M.S., VIII, 1955, p. 81).

Add at end:
See also Hispaniae Schola, Vols. 3, 4, 7 & 8 (modern reprints).

5 i **CABO**
Add at end:
See also Eslava (modern reprint of ' Memento Domine ').

ii **CACCINI**
Par. 2, l. 16. (10 Feb. 1662)
should read:

(10 Feb. 1622)

7 i Par. 2, l. 42 *should read*:

3665) are possibly his work [4] ; and there appear to be motets in MS L 76 at the monastery of Kremsmünster.[5] He is repre-

Add footnote:
[5] *Cf.* A. Kellner, ' Musikgeschichte des Stiftes Kremsmünster ' (Cassel & Basel, 1956), p. 189.

ii Par. 3, l. 9. remarks [5] *should read*:
remarks [6]

l. 20. ance.[6] *should read*:
ance.[7]

Footnotes 5 & 6 become 6 & 7.

Add to BIBL.:

FORTUNE, NIGEL, ' A Florentine Manuscript and its Place in Italian Song ' (Acta Musicol., XXIII, 1951, p. 124).
' Italian Secular Monody from 1600 to 1635 : an Introductory Survey ' (M.Q., XXXIX, 1953, p. 171).
' Italian 17th-century Singing ' (M. & L., XXXV, 1954, p. 206).
GANDOLFI, RICCARDO, ' Alcune considerazioni intorno alla riforma melodrammatica a proposito di Giulio Caccini detto Romano ' (Riv. Mus. It., III, 1896, p. 714).
GHISI, FEDERICO, ' Un Aspect inédit des intermèdes de 1589 à la cour médicéenne ' (' Les Fêtes de la Renaissance ', Paris, 1956, p. 145).
MAZE, NANCY, ' Tenbury MS 1018 : a Key to Caccini's Art of Embellishment ' (abstract in J.A.M.S., IX, 1956, p. 61).

PIRROTTA, NINO, ' Temperaments and Tendencies in the Florentine Camerata ' (M.Q., XL, 1954, p. 169).
' Tragédie et comédie dans la Camerata fiorentina ' (' Musique et poésie au XVIe siècle ', Paris, 1954, p. 287).

8 i *Add to* BIBL.:

WALKER, D. P., ' La Musique des intermèdes florentins de 1589 et l'humanisme ' (' Les Fêtes de la Renaissance ', Paris, 1956, p. 133).

See also, l. 2. *Add*:
Classici Musica Italiana, Vol. 4 (modern ed. of arias).

l. 3. *Add*:
Publikationen G.M.F., Vol. 9 (modern ed. of ' Euridice ').

12 ii **CADENCE**
Add to BIBL.:
BAIRSTOW, E. C., ' The Evolution of Musical Form ' (London, 1943).
O.H.M., Vol. I.

13 i **CADENZA**
Add at end:
See also Concerto, p. 394.

14 i **CADMAN, CATALOGUE**
PIANOFORTE MUSIC
Add after l. 2 :
' Three Moods ' (1919)
1. A Nubian Face on the Nile.
2. To a Vanishing Race.
3. The Pompadour's Fan.

16 ii **CAFFI**
Par. 1, l. 2 *should read*:

1778 ; *d.* Padua, 24 Jan. 1874).

Par. 2, l. 10 *should read*:

A ' Storia della musica teatrale in Venezia durante la sua Repubblica ' remained in manuscript.

19 i *Add before* **CALAH** :

CAKEWALK. A grotesque, strutting dance of negro origin, extremely popular in Paris during the first decade of the twentieth century. Debussy immortalized it in his ' Golliwogs' Cakewalk ' (Suite, ' Children's Corner ').

CALAMITÀ DE' CUORI
l. 1 *should read*:

CALAMITA [1] DE' CUORI, LA (Opera).

Add footnote:
[1] Not *calamità*, as frequently spelt in non-Italian works : " magnet ", not " calamity ".

l. 2 *should read*:

See GALUPPI. GOLDONI.

19 ii **CALDARA**
Par. 2, l. 5. XXVI *should read*:
XIII
Add after See also Astorga :
Chorwerk, Vol. 25 (modern reprint of madrigals & canons).

20 ii **CALESTANI**
Add at end:
BIBL.—FORTUNE, NIGEL, ' Italian Secular Monody from 1600 to 1635: an Introductory Survey ' (M.Q., XXXIX, 1953, p. 171).

21 ii **CALKIN**
(5), l. 3 *should read*:
singer, cousin of the preceding, son of (2). He studied

(6), ll. 2-3 *should read*:
Mar. 1827 ; *d.* ?, 1905), composer, organist and pianist, brother of the preceding. Taught by his father, he

(7), l. 2 *should read*:
1829 ; *d.* ?, 1911), violoncellist and teacher, brother

CALLAS
Name *should read*:
CALLAS, Maria (Meneghini-Callas, formerly **Calogeropoulos)**

24 ii **CALVOCORESSI**
Par. 3, ll. 4-5 *should read*:
Among several biographical books was one on Mussorgsky (1908)

ll. 7-8 *should read*:
Spanish and German. But a much more important work on the same composer, ' Modest Mussorgsky: his Life and Works ', at which he had worked for many years and which was ready for publication in 1938, was put into safe keeping in Paris at the outbreak of war, having been sent there for publication by a firm owned by Kussevitsky. This concern having come to an end and Calvocoressi having died before the end of the war, the manuscript was lost sight of for a long time, to be eventually unearthed and published in London in 1956. Meanwhile a smaller work on Mussorgsky, written for the ' Master

29 i **CAMERATA**
Add at end:
BIBL.—PIRROTTA, NINO, ' Temperaments and Tendencies in the Florentine Camerata ' (M.Q., XL, 1954, p. 169).

See also. l. 2 *should read*:
Istituzioni, Vol. 4 (modern reprints, Galilei, &c.). Peri.

29 ii **CAMERON**
Par. 3, l. 24 *should read*:
standard classics. He was created C.B.E. in 1957.

30 i *Add before* **CAMILLA** :
CAMILIERI, Lorenzo (*b.* Corfu, 1878 ; *d.* New York, 20 Apr. 1956).
American conductor, teacher and composer of Greek birth. He entered the Naples Conservatory at the age of fourteen and took a diploma in 1895. Having conducted and taught in Athens for a time, he visited England and France as conductor and accompanied the singer Maria Barrientos on a tour. In Nov. 1914 he settled in New York as a teacher of singing ; in 1921 he became an American citizen, and he then organized singing classes and formed the People's Chorus. His compositions were mainly choral. E. B.

ii **CAMPAGNOLI**
Par. 1, l. 2 *should read*:
di Ferrara, 10 Sept. 1751 ; *d.* Neustrelitz,

Par. 2, l. 2 *should read*:
the violin from Dall' Occa, a pupil of Lolli's,

CAMPANA
Par. 2, l. 6 *should read*:
1838 ; another, ' Giulio d' Este ', at

ll. 8-9 *should read*:
ence, 1842 ; ' Luisa di Francia ', Rome, 1844. ' Giulio d' Este ' was revived at Milan in or about 1850.

31 i **CAMPANINI**
Par. 1, l. 2 *should read*:
1845 ; *d.* Vigatto, 14 Nov. 1896 [1]).

Footnote should read:
[1] According to the official death certificate 13 Nov., given by ' The Athenaeum ', is wrong.

ii **CAMPBELL**
Par. 4, l. 13 *should read*:
company and orchestra. The first stage performance was given by the Dundee Operatic Society on 12 Mar. 1956.

32 i **CAMPIAN**
Par. 1, ll. 1-2. *b.* London *should read*:
b. Witham, Essex,

34 ii **CAMPIONI**
Add at end:
BIBL.—FLOROS, CONSTANTIN, ' Carlo Antonio Campioni als Instrumentalkomponist ' (Vienna, 1955).

37   ii   **CAMPRA**
BIBL. ll. 6-7 *should be* ll. 4-5 (work by LA LAURENCIE, not by MASSON).

Add to BIBL. :
BARTHÉLEMY, MAURICE, 'André Campra : sa vie et son œuvre : étude biographique' (Paris, 1957).

41   ii   **CANIS**
Add at end:
See also Collectio O.M.B., Vol. 8 (modern ed.).

42   ii   **CANNABICH (2)**
Add to See also :
Sondheimer Ed., Vol. 35 (modern ed. of Symphony).

44   ii   **CANON (1)**
Par. 3 *should read* :

The word " canon " is also sometimes applied, quite incorrectly, to a species of vocal composition properly called a " round ". The habit still persists, especially in Germany, of referring to the " canons " in ' Così fan tutte ' (" E nel tuo, nel mio bicchiero ") and ' Fidelio ' (" Mir ist so wunderbar "), which are, of course, the two most famous operatic examples of rounds, where lengthy melodies are sung by each voice in turn, one after the other, with different counter-melodies against them at each recurrence, and do not overlap with themselves, as in a canon.

46   ii   **CANTATA**
BIBL., SCHMITZ. l. 2 *should read* :
kantate ' (Leipzig, 1914 ; 2nd ed. 1955).

47   i   **CANTE HONDO**
Add at end:
BIBL.—BALOUCH, AZIZ, ' Cante jondo : su origen y evolución ' (Madrid, 1955).
MANFREDI CANO, DOMINGO, ' Geografia del cante jondo ' (Madrid, 1955).

CANTELLI
Par. 1, l. 2 *should read* :
1920 ; *d.* Paris, 24 Nov. 1956 [1]).

Add footnote :
[1] At Orly airport, in an Italian air liner which crashed soon after taking off.

ii   Par. 1, l. 15 *should read* :
burgh Festival of 1950 and the same year appeared

CANTELOUBE
Par 1, l. 2. Anonnay *should read* :
Annonay

l. 3 *should read* :
Oct. 1879 ; *d.* Paris, 4 Nov. 1957).

48   ii   **CANTO CARNASCIALESCO**
Add after See also :
Chorwerk, Vol. 43 (modern reprints).

52   i   **CAPELL**
Par. 2, l. 7. *Add* :
It was resumed by Blom after Capell's death.

Add at end:
BIBL.—' Richard Capell : 1885–1954' (M. & L., XXXV, 1954, p. 277).

ii   *Add after* **CAPET** :
CAPETA, Jacomi. *See* JACOMI.

55   ii   *Add after* **CAPRON** :
CAPUANA, Franco (*b.* Fano, 29 Sept. 1894).
Italian conductor and composer. He studied composition at the Naples Conservatory under Camillo de Nardis, taking his diploma in 1915, and the same year he began his career as a conductor, which led to his appearance at the major Italian theatres, in Buenos Aires and in many important concert-halls. He has also been conductor of the Teatro alla Scala in Milan (1937–40), the Teatro Regio of Turin, the Opera in Rome, conductor of the Orchestra Stabile Sinfonica at Naples (1930–32) and elsewhere. His compositions include works for orchestra, a cantata, ' Attollite portas ' for solo voices, chorus and orchestra (Milan, 1932), a musical fable, an operetta, etc.   G. M. G.

56   ii   *Add after* **CARA** :
CARACCIOLO, Franco (*b.* Bari, 29 Mar. 1920).
Italian conductor. He studied at the Naples Conservatory, where he took diplomas in pianoforte playing and composition. He then attended Bernardino Molinari's finishing course for conductors at the Accademia di Santa Cecilia in Rome. He has conducted concerts in Italy and abroad, giving up large portions of his programmes to modern music, especially Italian. He has been conductor of the Associazione " Alessandro Scarlatti " at Naples since 1949.   G. M. G.

58   i   **CARAPELLA**
Par. 2, l. 2. Marchesi's *should read* :
Marchese's

60   i   **CARDUS**
Add at end :
A volume of reprinted essays, ' Talking of Music ', appeared in 1957.

61   i   **CAREY, B. A.**
Par. 2, l. 25 *should read* :
voices. He was made an honorary Doctor of Music by the Moravian College of Women in 1937.

61   ii   **CAREY, Clive**
Par. 3, l. 22 *should read*:
there in that capacity in 1947.   He was
created C.B.E. in 1955.

CAREY, Henry
Par. 1, l. 2.   4 Oct. *should read*:
5 Oct.

Par. 2, l. 7.   Marquis *should read*:
Marquess

67   ii   **CARICATURE**
Add to BIBL.:

CROFT-MURRAY, EDWARD, 'Venetian Caricatures' in
'Venetian Drawings of the XVII & XVIII
Centuries in the Collection of Her Majesty the
Queen at Windsor Castle', with Anthony Blunt
(London, 1957). Contains numerous reproductions
of opera singers.
SELIGMAN, JANEY, 'Figures of Fun: the Caricature-
Statuettes of Jean-Pierre Dantan' (Oxford, 1957).

70   ii   **CARILLON (1)**
Add to BIBL.:

DART, THURSTON, 'The Ghent Chime Book' (' Galpin
Society Journal', VI, 1953, p. 70).

BIBL. l. 4 *should read*:

Bells: their History and Music' (Princeton, N.J.,
1948).

Add to BIBL.:

PALUEL-MARMONT, ALBERT PIERRE, 'Cloches et caril-
lons: leur histoire, leur fabrication, leurs légendes'
(Paris, 1953).

73   ii   **CARISSIMI**
Add to BIBL.:

MASSENKEIL, GÜNTHER, 'Die oratorische Kunst in den
lateinischen Historien und Oratorien Giacomo
Carissimis' (Mainz, 1952).

Add to See also:

Classici Musica Italiana, Vol. 5 (extracts from oratorios). Denkmäler (1), Vol. 2 (do.). Fitzwilliam
Music (do. of sacred works).

74   i   **CARL ROSA OPERA COM-
PANY**
Par. 4, l. 9 *should read*:

Carl Rosa Trust.   Mrs. Phillips retired in
1957, and a committee was formed under the
chairmanship of Sir Donald Wolfit, with Mr.
Alan Bohun as secretary and Professor Humphrey Procter-Gregg as artistic director. They
all resigned in July 1958, however, owing to
insurmountable difficulties with which the
artistic director found himself confronted. In
order to keep the artists together, and to ex-
plore future possibilities, an independent provincial tour was then arranged under the
directorship of Proctor-Gregg, with the support of the Arts Council, which proved highly
successful.

75   i   *Add before* **CARMEN**:

CARMELITES, THE (Poulenc).   *See*
DIALOGUES DES CARMÉLITES.

75   ii   **CARMEN, Johannes**
Add to BIBL.:

REANEY, GILBERT, 'Early Fifteenth-Century Music
Vol. I (New York, 1955).

76   ii   **CARNER**
Par. 2, l. 15 *should read*:

symposia.   His study of Bartók's string quartets, contributed to the Pelican Book ' Chamber Music' edited by Alec Robertson, is
important.
In 1958, in time for the centenary of
Puccini's birth, appeared what is Carner's
most substantial work so far, ' Puccini: a
Critical Biography ', by far the most important book on the composer in English and altogether the most detailed and penetrating
study of his work, with an account of his life
showing unusual psychological insight.

88   i   **CAROL**
BIBL.   *Change order of sections*:

DANISH
DUTCH AND FLEMISH
ITALIAN

Add at end:

POLISH

BARAŃSKI, F., ' Kolendy' (Lwów, 1899).
BRODNICKI, A., ' Symfonie anyelskie' (Cracow, 1913).
DACHNOWSKI, K., ' Symphonie anyelskie abo Kolenda'
(Cracow, 1630).
DOBRZYCKI, S., ' O kolędach' (Poznań, 1923).
' Kolędy polskie a czeskie' (Poznań, 1930).
GWOŹDZIOWSKI, J. A., ' Największa kantyczka' (Wie-
liczka, 1938).
KLONOWSKI, T., ' Szczeble do nieba' (Cracow, 1867).
KOLBERG, O., ' Lud', publ. in series (Cracow & Warsaw,
1857–90).
MIODUSZEWSKI, M., ' Kolendy i pastorałki' (Cracow,
1843).
NIEWIADOMSKI, S., ' Kolendy' (Lwów, 1912).
RYBICKI, F., ' W żłobie leży' (Warsaw, 1946).
SIEMIEŃSKI, L., ' Wigilia i Kantyczki' (Warsaw, 1881).
SURZYŃSKI, J., ' Polskie pieśni Kościoła Katol.' (Poznań,
1887).
TARNOWSKI, S., ' O kolędach' (Cracow, 1894).
WINDAKIEWICZ, S., ' Dramat liturgiczny w Polsce'
(Cracow, 1902).

Add to See also:

Musica Britannica, Vol. 4 (modern ed. of medieval
carols).

89   i   **CAROLAN**
Add to BIBL.:

O'SULLIVAN, DONAL, ' Carolan: the Life, Times and
Music of an Irish Harper', 2 Vols. (London, 1958)

ii   *Add after* **CARON**:

CAROSIO, Margherita (*b*. Genoa, 7 June
1908).
Italian soprano singer.   She began her
musical studies at her birthplace, Genoa, at
the age of five, under the guidance of her
father, himself a composer and singing-teacher
(he wrote the ' Inno dell' anno santo' in 1950).
When she was sixteen she had gained diplomas
for singing, pianoforte and harmony at the
Paganini Conservatory of Genoa.   She also

studied the violin and has appeared at concerts. At the same time she took lessons in painting with Maragliano and Motto, and also she holds diplomas in anatomy and physiology. Her operatic début was made at Novi Ligure in 1927 in the title-part of ' Lucia di Lammermoor '. The following summer brought her to Covent Garden, where she sang Musetta and Feodor in ' Boris Godunov ' opposite Shaliapin. Also singing at Covent Garden that season was Aureliano Pertile, leading tenor of La Scala, who recommended her to Toscanini. She made her Scala début in Mar. 1929 as Oscar in ' Un ballo in maschera '. From 1931 until 1939 and again from 1946 until 1952 she never missed a Scala season, and the list of parts she sang there shows her amazing versatility: Gnese and Gasparina in Wolf-Ferrari's ' Il campiello ', Aminta in Strauss's ' Die schweigsame Frau ', Walter in ' La Wally ', Vivetta in ' L' Arlesiana ', Norina, Gretel, Leïla, Pamina, Elvira in 'I Puritani ' and the Princess in ' Sadko '. Perhaps two things more than anything else helped to establish her reputation in Italy: her creating the part of the Slave Girl, Egloge, in Mascagni's ' Nerone ' in 1935, and her many appearances with Tito Schipa, who found her a most sympathetic partner in such parts as Adina, Amina and Rosina.

It was not really until after the second world war that Margherita Carosio became an international figure. When she returned to Covent Garden in 1946 with the San Carlo Opera it was immediately recognized that the pre-war Italian light soprano had become a finished artist capable of sustaining vocally and dramatically one of the most demanding parts in the repertory, Violetta in ' Traviata '. Her almost classical portrayal of Nedda in ' Pagliacci ' and her polished Rosina in ' Il barbiere di Siviglia ' were no less applauded. After Violetta perhaps her greatest success in London was her Adina in ' L' elisir d' amore ', which she sang with the Scala Company at Covent Garden in 1950, when her neatly executed *fioriture* and evenly produced voice were much admired. Her piquant charm, exquisite phrasing and superb musicianship make her a most suitable interpreter of the works of Donizetti, and she was especially chosen to participate in the Donizetti centenary celebrations at Bergamo in 1948, singing in the seldom performed ' Betly '.

H. D. R.

91   i   **CARPENTER, J. A.,** List of Works
BALLETS   BALLET *should read:*

BALLET
l. 2 *should read:*
' Krazy Kat ' (1922, rev. 1939).

91   i   CHORAL WORKS
l. 1 *should read:*
' Song of Faith ' for chorus & orch. (1931, rev. 1937).

Add to ORCHESTRAL WORKS:
' Carmel Concerto ' (1948).

ii   *Add after* **CARPIO VALDÉS:**
CARPITELLA, Diego (*b.* Reggio di Calabria, 12 June 1924).
Italian musicologist. He studied at the University of Rome and took the laureate in musical history there. He teaches at the Conservatorio di Musica di Santa Cecilia in Rome and also at the Accademia Nazionale di Danza, and he is on the staff of the Centro Nazionale Studi di Musica Popolare shared by the Accademia di Santa Cecilia and Radiotelevisione Italiana. He is a member of the Società Italiana di Etnografia and the I.S.C.M., and corresponding member of the International Folk Music Council.

Carpitella is a pioneer in research into Italian folk music, a subject which, except for some distinguished regional work (in Sicily, for example), has suffered great neglect in its own country. Between 1952 and 1958 he collected and recorded for the Centro Nazionale some 3,000 folksongs all over Italy. He has published articles on the subject in specialist journals (Rass. Mus., ' Lares ', ' Società ', etc.) and given numerous lectures, not only in many Italian centres, but also in Switzerland, Germany, Denmark, Finland and Norway. In collaboration with A. Lomax he brought out the Italian edition of Bartók's writings on folk music, and in 1957 he published a gramophone anthology of Italian folk music for the Columbia World Library of Folk and Primitive Music. A printed anthology by him is in preparation (1959).

E. B.

93   ii   Page heading *should read:*
CARRENO

95   ii   **Carroll, Lewis**
l. 5. Kelly *should read:*
Kelley

96   i   **CARSE**
Par. 1, l. 2 *should read:*
19 May 1878 ; *d.* Gt. Missenden, 2 Nov. 1958).

97   ii   **CARTER, Elliott**
Add before CATALOGUE :
BIBL.—GOLDMAN, RICHARD FRANKO, ' The Music of Elliott Carter ' (M.Q., XLIII, 1957, p. 151).

98   i   CHORAL WORKS
l. 2 *should read:*
' Harvest Home ' and ' To Music ' (Herrick) for unaccomp. chorus (1937).

98   i   ORCHESTRAL WORKS
         Add at end:
Variations (1955–56).

CHAMBER MUSIC
Add at end:
Sonata for flute, oboe, cello & harpsichord (1952).

ONE INSTRUMENT AND PIANO-
FORTE
Add before Cello Sonata:
' Elegy ' for viola or cello (1943).

99   i   **CARUSO**
         Par. 2, l. 10 *should read*:
other operas.   It is said that he was first
offered that of Cavaradossi in ' Tosca ' by
Puccini, who, however, afterwards changed his
mind for some reason.   Little was heard of
Caruso in

     ii   Par. 2, l. 10 *should read*:
duet in the dungeon at the end of ' Aida '.
Among his most successful parts were those
of Éléazar in Halévy's ' La Juive ' and Nemorino in Donizetti's ' L' elisir d' amore ', the
last he was to sing at the Metropolitan.

         Par. 3.   Last lines *should read*:
politan.   He died of pleurisy.
   Caruso was one of the first singers to make
a great success on the gramophone.   His
records, for the most part reissued with superimposed electrically recorded accompaniments, are still remarkable and instructive.
                                   s. h. p., adds.

100   i   **CARVALHO, E. de**
          Par. 1, l. 2 *should read*:
Ceara, Brazil, 28 June 1912).

102   i   **CARVER**
          Add at end:
See also American Institute of Musicology, C.M.M. 16.
' Musica Britannica ', Vol. 15 (for ' O bone Jesu ' and
Mass ' L'homme armé ').

      ii   **CASADESUS (1)**
           l. 2 *should read*:
(*b*. Paris, 2 Dec. 1870; *d*. Suresnes nr. Paris,
27 June 1954),

          CASADESUS (5)
          l. 2 *should read*:
7 Apr. 1899), pianist, cousin of the preceding.

          l. 9 *should read*:
servatory, Fontainebleau.   In 1914 he settled
in the U.S.A.   He composed two Symphonies,
a pianoforte Concerto,

104   i   **CASALS**
          Par. 3, l. 6 *should read*:
never returned to his native soil, except for
one day in 1955, when he attended a relative's
funeral.   Instead, he

      ii   Par. 1, l. 6 *should read*:
chamber music in 1950.   In 1955 he visited
his mother's home at Puerto Rico and stopped
at Mexico City long enough to conduct an
orchestral concert.

          Add to Bibl.:
Corredor, José María, ' Conversations avec Casals:
   souvenirs et opinions d'un musicien ' (Paris, 1955);
   Eng. trans. by André Mangeot, ' Conversations
   with Casals ' (London, 1956).

          Casanova, G. J.
          l. 3 *should read*:
(G. meeting with).   Lincke (operetta).

          Add to Bibl. (2nd work by Nettl):
' The Other Casanova ' (New York, 1950).

106   i   **CASAVOLA**
          Par. 1, l. 2 *should read*:
13 July 1891; *d*. Bari, 7 July 1955).

107   i   **CASELLA**
          Add to Bibl.:
d'Amico, Fedele & Gatti, Guido M. (ed.), ' Alfredo
   Casella ' (Milan, 1958).
Casella, Alfredo, ' Music in my Time : Memoirs ',
   trans. & ed. by Spencer Norton (Norman, Oklahoma, 1955).

      ii   OPERAS
          l. 7 *should read*:
Venice, Teatro Goldoni, 6 Sept. 1932.

111   ii   **CASTANETS**
           Par. 2, ll. 2-3 *should read*:
a Spanish flavour, such as Glinka's ' Jota
aragonesa ', Bizet's ' Carmen '

          Add at end:
(*PLATE* 49, Vol. VI, p. 622, No. 3.)

112   i   *Add after* **CASTELLAIN**:
Castellan de Castellani, Pierozzo.   *See* Malipiero
(G. F., ' Figliuol prodigo ', opera).

113   ii   **CASTELNUOVO-TEDESCO**
           OPERAS
           l. 7.   (1938). *should read*:
(1938), prod. Florence, 2 June 1951.

          Add at end:
' Il mercante di Venezia ', lib. by Composer, based on
   Shakespeare's ' Merchant of Venice ' (1957).
' All's Well that Ends Well ', lib. by Composer, based
   on Shakespeare's play (1958).

114   ii   **CASTÉRA**
           Par. 1, l. 2 *should read*:
3 Apr. 1873; *d*. Angoumi nr. Dax, 9 Oct.
1955).

114 ii **Casti**
l. 1. Libretto. Salieri *should read*:
Libretto. Paisiello (' Re Teodoro ', lib.). Salieri

119 i **CATALANI, Alfredo**
Par. 1, ll. 10-11 *should read*:
(text by Boito), was performed in July 1875.
His first public appearance was with
            Par. 2, l. 1. ' Dejanire ' *should read*:
' Dejanice '
            Add to BIBL. :
GATTI, CARLO, ' Catalani: la vita e le opere ' (Milan, 1953).

122 ii **CATEL**
Par. 3, l. 13. Solfèges *should read*:
Solféges

123 i **CATELANI**
Par. 1, l. 2. 15 Sept. *should read*:
5 Sept.

CATHEDRAL MUSIC
(Anglican)
Add after Par. 1 :

For a thorough understanding of cathedral organization in post-Reformation times, some acquaintance with medieval practice is necessary, since the medieval organization is presupposed in the later, although some alterations were made. Thus we find that the *Statuta Antiqua* of Wells Cathedral were copied in 1634, in connection with Archbishop Laud's visitation.

One of the changes made in medieval cathedral organization in post-Reformation times was in the status of the dean compared with the chapter: formerly he was merely the president, *primus inter pares*. The chapter did not hesitate to lodge complaints against him, as is shown by the protracted dispute at Lincoln in the 15th century. Not until later did his position sometimes become that of an autocrat; in days when a secular cathedral was less of a diocesan mother church than a private collegiate establishment, this would have been intolerable.

The primary musical function in the chapter, however, was assumed by the office of precentor (cantor, chanter), who had the general overseeing both of the music in the choir and of the musicians who made it. Besides the singers, the musical establishment included an organist and a master of the choristers whose duty it was to house the boys as well as to ensure that their education, both musical and otherwise, was sufficient. Bishop Cosin's visitation articles at Durham in 1662 indicate his duties as envisaged at the Restoration in a cathedral where music was highly developed :

Doth the Master of the Quiristers (or Organist) diligently teach and instructe the tenn young choristers every day

F

in their schoole ? Doth he attend Divyne service dayly in the Quire habit, as others the Singing-clerkes doe, and looke that all the Quiristers doe the same, every one keeping their gownes and surplices cleane, and behaveing themselves orderly, reverently, and decently, dureing the whole tyme of Divyne servyce in the Quire ?

The two posts of organist and master of the choristers, however, were originally quite distinct. At Lincoln the offices were not combined until the time of Byrd, and there were instances previously of holders of the latter post resigning on appointment as organist. At Salisbury, where the post in later times was held by a singing-man, the positions do not appear to have been combined until John Farrant, who had been master of the choristers since 1571, became organist also from 1587. Nevertheless, his successor was not capable of executing the duties of both offices, and he was relieved of the post of organist when the younger John Farrant was appointed as the junior vicar choral and organist in 1600. At Laud's visitation in 1634 it was stated that the posts were held by two of the seven singing-men ; there were six vicars choral in holy orders and six choristers. Some of the choir were said to be " not able ". At Wells, where of old " the Principal master of the Choristers " had been expected to be in priest's orders, the first regular amalgamation of the two offices appears to have been in 1625, when the dean, acting as the precentor's proxy, dismissed the master for inefficiency and appointed John Okeover, who had been organist since 1620, in his stead. There had been a previous instance of the amalgamation in 1507, but this seems to have been not a double appointment, but an arrangement made with the good will of all concerned. At Westminster Abbey the posts were separate at the beginning of the Commonwealth, although previously they had been combined.

The choristers themselves seem to have declined in numbers after the Reformation, owing, no doubt, to financial hardship. The earliest records at Gloucester Cathedral suggest that the strength was maintained at eight boys, with six singing-men and a master of the choristers. It is interesting to observe that here the master is apparently assumed to be the organist ; no mention of the latter appears in the *Stipendia Soluta* of the treasurer's accounts, whereas the master is referred to as the organist in the chapter minutes. Evidence of financial hardship is also available at Gloucester, for the singing-men complained at the episcopal visitation of 1661 that their stipend of 10 li was barely sufficient for a livelihood.

The same numbers occur in the musical establishment at Chester from the time of Henry VIII. But, whereas there were twelve boys at York in the last quarter of the 16th century, at Westminster the Elizabethan statutes gave the number of boys as ten, and that number was maintained until the Commonwealth. At Wells at that time there were six, but there were ten boys at Windsor in 1586. The marginal notes in the two " relations " of journeys undertaken in 1634–1635 contained in B.M. MS Lansdowne 213 [1] show the regular number of choristers in cathedral establishments at that period to have been six or eight, although Exeter, Worcester and Durham are shown as having ten boys each. Such marginalia in this source should not, however, be taken without reserve : Canterbury is shown as having forty choristers and Chester three. But there seem to have been only four at Winchester in 1680, although the statutes given to the cathedral by Charles I allow for six. These statutes show also that the organist was to be their master.

On the other hand, the number of choristers at Salisbury seems to have varied from fourteen to sixteen in the 15th century, decreasing to twelve, ten and six ; only in 1713 was the number increased to eight. At Lincoln it appears that there were only twelve boys provided for on the foundation in 1264, but at Exeter there were to be fourteen. Elsewhere the number varied from five to twelve. The numbers of the choristers at Chichester varied as follows : 1232, ten ; 1481, twelve, when the number was reduced to eight until 1670. By 1710 there were six, and they remained at this number until 1804. [2] A chapter minute of this cathedral dated 10 October 1591 records that six men undertook not to remove their sons from the choir without the consent of the dean and chapter before the expiration of a period of seven years from the date when the boys joined the choir.

It should not be assumed that nomenclature was consistent ; B.M. Lans. 213, for instance, refers to " some Queristers, & Singing Boyes " in the " fayre Church " at Newark-on-Trent, and, although the names commonly used for the part-books were *Medius, Contratenor, Tenor* and *Bassus, Decani* (= of the Dean's side) and *Cantoris* (= of the Precentor's side), with the further designation *Primus* and *Secundus* when required, yet B.M. MS Harley 6346 and Bodleian MS Rawl. poet. 23 speak of " Treble ", " Meane ", and further " 2 Children & a Meane ", in naming the voices used in various verse anthems.

The provision of music books seems to have been frequently the duty of the organist, for it was he who commonly, but by no means invariably, had the task of writing them out. Unfortunately details of the music in the actual possession of the various cathedrals in earlier times is none too plentiful ; the long

series of part-books covering a period of centuries at Durham Cathedral is unique, and very little remains elsewhere. In the inventories made at Gloucester in 1610 and at Winchester in 1633 and 1661, no mention is made of music books, although the former of the Winchester list has a blank page headed " Setts of Songbookes for ye Quyre ", and it would seem that music books were not highly valued. This is supported by the state in which music of this and later times has been found recently in Gloucester Cathedral, embedded in a pile of rubbish. However, inventories of music exist at Chichester for 1621 and 1767 [3] and at Canterbury for various years. It is evident that anthologies as well as pieces and collections by individual composers were kept, both printed and in MS, and Barnard's ' First Book of Selected Church Music ' (1641) was widely used. In 1665 the chapter of Winchester Cathedral ordered " A set of printed singing books for the service of the Quire . . . with a quire of ruled paper to every booke ", so that additions could be made to the music in the books, " & be sure the organ part be among them ". Presumably this referred to Barnard, although other collections, such as Tomkins's ' Musica Deo Sacra ' and Amner's ' Sacred Hymnes ', had appeared ; the first two at least of these were in use a century after they were published.

In addition to the organ, other instruments were used at cathedral services. Lans. 213 records that at Lincoln the travellers " heard theire solemne Service, the Organe, wth other Instrum[ts], suited to most excellent voyces ", and at Exeter they heard " Vialls, and other sweet Instruments " in addition to the organ. The records seem to suggest that no other instrumentalist save the organist was paid a regular stipend, and that the most commonly used additional instruments were the cornett and the sackbut ; but from the passing references made to them in the records, and from the remuneration they received—at Wells the two players, one for each instrument, received ten shillings a quarter—it would appear that they were employed only occasionally, although it is clear from a minute of the Durham chapter of 22 Nov. 1633, that such instruments were in daily use in the cathedral at that time, and that John Cosin, Bishop of Durham after the Restoration and previously a prebendary, approved of their use ; furthermore, it seems that they were in regular use at Gloucester after the Restoration. The evidence available is insufficient to show that other instruments were used on any other than special occasions. At York the city waits played in the minster twice in 1624, and " the Oxford musicke " played in Gloucester

---

[1] Ed. by L. G. Wickham Legg ; one published with introduction, London, 1904 ; the other in ' Camden Miscellany ' (London, 1936).

[2] ' Sussex Archaeological Collections ', 78, p. 144.

[3] Printed in C. E. Welch, ' Two Cathedral Organists ' (Chichester, 1957).

Cathedral at " the Summer Assizes " of 1639. In 1618 instrumental music was played in Chester Cathedral on 5 Nov. It is quite clear that special significance was attached to this occasion, as a day for thanksgiving. Special music was composed for it; part-books of the 17th century contain numerous anthems headed " Gunpowder ", or with a similar title, and the earlier of the Chichester inventories show that that cathedral had separate books containing music for this day. Special prominence was accorded also to the anniversary of the Restoration in 1660.

The quality of performance obtaining at cathedral establishments varied considerably. The travelogues in B.M. Lans. 213 referred to above bear sufficient witness for their time, for their author varies in his appraisal of the music he heard. There is other evidence for the neglect of cathedral music at this time; for example, Archbishop Laud's injunctions of 1635 to Lichfield Cathedral contain the observation : " 1. That the two payre of organs in your Church which are much defective be speedily amended . . .". Even in the Chapel Royal the performances in the following century left much to be desired.

The inferiority of musical performances in cathedral services was doubtless due, at least in part, to low standards of morality and of conventional behaviour. Cathedral records show that neglect of duty was common. These low standards were not peculiar to the post-Reformation period : there is evidence of similar laxity in the middle ages.[1]

It was not until the latter part of the 17th century that music by foreign composers, as distinct from foreign-born musicians domiciled in England, began to appear in the cathedral repertory. The earliest adaptations appear to have been largely the work of Henry Aldrich. A century later the influx of foreign compositions was appreciable, but in earlier times the repertory of each cathedral consisted both of works by celebrated musicians and of pieces by local composers which were mostly confined to their own locality. Latin texts were not proscribed, since the use of that language is permitted in collegiate foundations, where it might be presumed to be understood.

[1] Cf. G. G. Coulton, ' Life in the Middle Ages ' (Cambridge, 1935), I, 95 ff.

123   ii   Par. 2, ll. 4-5 should read :

establishments there were anything from twelve to fifty-two Prebendaries and perhaps a dozen Priest-

124   i   Add before BIBL. :

Early in the 19th century cathedral choristers suffered scandalous neglect at the hands of deans and chapters, and the treatment meted out to those children of tender years

by the masters set over them was often brutal. Maria Hackett (1783–1874) devoted her time and means to ameliorating the condition of choristers in all parts of the kingdom, by personal visitations to the various cathedrals, and by her pen in vigorously waging war with deans and chapters, and bringing them to a sense of their duties. Miss Hackett had the satisfaction to see the realization, to a very large extent, of the object to which she had devoted her beneficent life.

124   i   Signature should read :

E. H. F. & W. K. F.

BIBLIOGRAPHY

ATKINS, I., ' Early Occupants of the Office of Organist and Master of the Choristers of the Cathedral . . . Worcester ' (Worcester, 1918).
BUMPUS, J. S., ' A History of English Cathedral Music, 1549–1889 ' (London, n.d.).
EDWARDS, K., ' The English Secular Cathedrals in the Middle Ages ' (Manchester, 1948).
FELLOWES, E. H., ' English Cathedral Music from Edward VI to Edward VII ' (London, 1941).
HARRISON, F. LL., ' Music in Medieval Britain ' (London, 1958).
NICHOLSON, S. H., ' Quires and Places where they sing ' (London, 1932).
PINE, E., ' The Westminster Abbey Singers ' (London, 1953).
ROBERTSON, D. H., ' Sarum Close ' (London, 1938).
SRAWLEY, J. H., ' The Origin and Growth of Cathedral Foundations ' (Lincoln Minster Pamphlets No. 1, 1951).
THOMPSON, A. H., ' Cathedral Churches of England ' (London, 1925).
' Song-Schools in the Middle Ages ' (Church Music Society Occasional Papers No. 14, London, 1942 [1]).
' The English Clergy and their Organization in the Later Middle Ages ' (Oxford, 1947).
WOODFILL, W. L., ' Musicians in English Society ' (Princeton, 1953).

[1] Other papers in this series contain relevant information.

CATHEDRAL MUSIC (Collections)

l. 2. BERNARD should read :

BARNARD

CATLEY, Ann

Par. 1, ll. 1-2.   nr. Brentford should read :

Little Ealing nr. Brentford

ii   Par. 1, ll. 6-7 should read :

in 1784. She died at the house of Major General Francis Lascelles, the father of her eight children, at Little Ealing, naming him sole executor in her will dated 13 Oct. 1788, but in an affidavit was described as " spinster ".

126   ii   **CAVAILLÉ-COLL**
BIBL., l. 2. orgues should read :
origines

127   ii   **CAVALIERI, E. de'**
Add to See also :

Classici Musica Italiana, Vol. 10 (extracts from ' Rap. presentazione ').

128   i   **CAVALIERI, Lina**
Par. 2, l. 22 *should read*:
Chicago. In 1913 she married the tenor Lucien Mura-

132   i   **CAVALLI**
Add to See also:
Publikationen G.M.F., Vol. 11 (modern ed. of 'Giasone ').

ii   **CAVAZZONI, G.**
Add at end:
See also Classici Musica Italiana, Vol. 6 (modern ed.).

CAVAZZONI, M. A.
Add at end:
BIBL.—DART, THURSTON, ' Cavazzoni and Cabezón ' (M. & L., XXXVI, 1955, p. 2).
JEPPESON, KNUD, ' Cavazzoni-Cabezón ' (Journ. Amer. Musicol. Soc., VIII, 1955, p. 81 ; *see also ibid.* p. 148).

133   i   **CAVOS**
Par. 2, ll. 9-12 & par. 3, ll. 1-3 *should read*:
army into Venice, and on 16 Nov. 1799 his 4-act ballet ' Il sotterraneo ' was produced there (together with Nasolini's opera ' Le feste d' Iside '). He had by this time left Venice, however, for on 1 Apr. 1799 he was engaged as conductor by the Imperial Theatres in St. Petersburg. He remained in Russia to the end of his life.
In 1803 he wrote additional music for a Russian

ii   *Add at end, before See also*:
BIBL.—MOOSER, R. ALOYS, ' Annales de la musique et des musiciens en Russie au XVIIIᵉ siècle ', 3 vols. (Geneva, 1948-52).

134   ii   *Add after* **CEBALLOS**:
CEBEDEM. The name of a Belgian organization for the propagation and preservation of modern Belgian music. It was founded in Brussels in 1951 on the model of the Dutch institution " Donemus ", and its full name is Centre Belge de Documentation Musicale. It has a library consisting of microfilms and photostats of unpublished work by contemporary Belgian composers. From these conducting and study scores as well as vocal scores and orchestral parts are made as required. CeBeDem publishes a series of short monographs on Belgian composers with complete catalogues of their works.   A. L. C.

CEBELL
l. 10 *should read*:
name, which also appears as Cibell, Sybel, Sebell, &c., was unknown until recently, but the tune of two songs, ' Lard, how men can claret drink ' (*c.* 1707) and ' Pray now, John, let Jug prevail ' (*c.* 1710) (B.M., G. 305 &

H. 1601), is described as " the Old Cibell ", and has been found (*see* Bibl.) to be identical with an air and bass called ' Descente de Cybelle ' which occurs in Lully's opera ' Atys ', at the end of the first act, where the scene is set in the temple of Cybele.   R. T. D.
BIBL.—DART, THURSTON, ' The Cibell ' (' Revue Belge de Musicologie ', VI, 1952, Fasc. 1).

135   i   **CECCHINO**
Par. 1, l. 2 *should read*:
1580 ; *d.* Hvar [Lesina], 1644).

Par. 2, ll. 2-3.   Spalato (Split) *should read*:
Split (Spalato)

l. 5.   Lesina *should read*:
Hvar

l. 8 *should read*:
for he claims to have reached Op. 27. He was certainly one of the leading composers in Dalmatia in the first half of the 17th century, especially of sacred music in the new *concertato* style. His

Add at end:
BIBL.—PLAMENAC, DRAGAN, ' Music of the 16th and 17th Centuries in Dalmatia ' (' Papers read at the International Congress of Musicology held at New York, September 11th to 16th 1939 ', New York, 1944, p. 49).
' Toma Cecchini kapelnik stolhih crkava u Splitu i Hvaru u prvoj polovini XVII stoljeća ' (' Rad Jugoslavenske Akademije Znanosti i Umjetnosti ', p. 77).

136   ii   **CECILIAN FESTIVALS**
Add to BIBL. :
HUSK, W. H., ' An Account of the Musical Celebrations on St. Cecilia's Day ' (London, 1857).

137   ii   *Add after* **CELIBIDACHE**:
CELIS, Frits (*b.* Antwerp, 11 Apr. 1929).
Belgian conductor. He studied at the Royal Flemish Conservatory at Antwerp under K. Candael and M. de Jong (counterpoint and fugue) and at the Conservatoire Royal of Brussels under R. Defossez (conducting). In 1955 he was appointed second conductor of the Théâtre Royal de la Monnaie there, with the ballet company of which he had an outstanding success at the Festival of Aix-en-Provence in 1956.   A. L. C.

140   i   *Add after* **CENTRAL MUSIC LIBRARY**:
CENTRE BELGE DE DOCUMENTATION MUSICALE. *See* CEBEDEM.

ii   **ČERNOHORSKÝ**
Add at end:
See also Musica Antiqua Bohemica, Vol. 3 (modern ed. of organ pieces).

141 ii *Add before* **CERRETO** :

CERQUETTI, Anita (*b.* Montecosaro nr. Macerata, 13 Apr. 1931). Italian soprano singer. She studied at the Liceo Musicale Morlacchi at Perugia. While still a student she participated in the Concorso Nazionale di Canto at Bologna in 1950, winning first place ; and the following year, when only twenty, she won a similar competition organized by the Centro Sperimentale at Spoleto, making her début there as Aïda. Appearances in Milan followed, and in 1953 she was heard as Aïda and Leonora in ' Trovatore ' at the Verona Arena. This was the beginning of her international career, and engagements followed at the leading Italian opera-houses, as well as in Spain, Portugal, France and Switzerland. In 1955 she made her American début with the Lyric Opera of Chicago, as Amelia in ' Un ballo in maschera ', and in the autumn of 1957 she sang Pallas Athene in Gluck's ' Paride ed Elena ' in New York, and Norma in Philadelphia. Cerquetti's début at the Milan Scala took place in the spring of 1958 as Abigaille in Verdi's ' Nabucco '. Her scheduled Covent Garden appearances in the summer of the same year were cancelled owing to her having contracted a sudden appendicitis.

Cerquetti's repertory further includes La Gioconda, Elisabeth de Valois (' Don Carlos '), Elvira (' Ernani '), Donna Anna, Tosca and Santuzza. Her voice is rare among Italian sopranos of to-day : not only is it large in size and capable of great dramatic intensity, but it also is one of great natural beauty, brilliant at the top and rich and warm in its middle and lower registers. Her secure vocal technique and brilliance of attack mark her out as one of the finest Italian singers since the second world war. H. D. R.

142 i **CERTON**
Add at end, before signature:
GUILLAUME MORLAYE : ' Psaumes de Pierre Certon réduits pour chant et luth (1554) ' ed. by Richard de Morcourt (Paris, 1957).

Add after signature :
See also Collectio O.M.B., Vol. 12 (modern ed.). Monuments Mus. Franç., Vol. 2 (modern reprint of Masses).

ii **CERVELAT**
l. 2. *Add* :
(*PLATE* 15, Vol. II, p. 447, No. 12.)

144 i **CESARIS**
Add to BIBL. :
REANEY, GILBERT, ' Early Fifteenth-Century Music ', Vol. I (New York, 1955).

CESTI
Footnote. ll. 4-6 *should read :*
tonio " is a mistake, accounted for as follows by Nino Pirrotta in ' La scuola romana ' (Siena, 1953), pp.

57-58, and ' L' orchestra ' (Florence, 1954), p. 156 : at Innsbruck Cesti was created Marchese di Leombria, and the abbreviation of this title, " March. Antonio Cesti ", appears on the scores of the last period of his life. The libretto of

144 i l. 10 *should read :*
Cavalier Cesti " or " Sig. Cav. Antonio Cesti ". Two original letters of the composer that have recently come to light are both signed " A. Cesti ".

146 ii Par. 2, l. 2. Vol. XII *should read :*
Vol. XI

l. 4 *should read :*
' Il pomo d' oro ' : D.T.Ö., Vols. III-IV.

CATALOGUE
11th title *should read :*
' Il pomo d' oro.' [1]

Add footnote :
[1] For modern edition *see* DENKMÄLER (3), Vols. III-IV.

147 ii **CEVALLOS**
Add at end :
See also Hispaniae Schola, Vol. 6 (modern reprint).

149 ii **CHABRIER**
See also, l. 2. Bourée *should read :*
Bourrée

151 ii *Add before* **CHAIR** :

CHAILLY, Luciano (*b.* Ferrara, 19 Jan. 1920). Italian composer. He took diplomas for violin playing at Ferrara in 1941 and for composition at the Milan Conservatory in 1945 ; he is also laureate in literature of Bologna University (1943). He has written numerous concert works, including 9 ' Sonate tritematiche ' for orchestra, for chorus and orchestra, for violin and pianoforte, for pianoforte solo, for string instruments, etc., and the operas ' Ferrovia sopraelevata ', 6 episodes by D. Buzzati (produced at Bergamo in 1955), ' Una domanda di matrimonio ', one act, after Tchekhov (Milan, Piccola Scala. 1957), ' Il canto del cigno ', one act, after Tchekhov (Bologna, Teatro Comunale, 1957) and ' La riva delle sirti ', prologue and 3 acts (Monte Carlo, 1959). Chailly is also a musical contributor to periodicals and reviews.
G. M. G.

155 i **CHAMBER MUSIC**
Add to BIBL. :
NEWMAN, WILLIAM S., ' The Sonata in the Baroque Era ' (Chapel Hill, North Carolina, 1959).
ROBERTSON, ALEC (ed.), ' Chamber Music ' (Pelican Books) (Harmondsworth, 1957).
ROWEN, RUTH H., ' Early Chamber Music ' (New York, 1949).
ULRICH, HOMER, ' Chamber Music ' (New York, 1948).

156 ii **CHAMBONNIÈRES**
Add at end, before signature :
An admirable modern edition of the complete harpsichord works, ' Œuvres complètes

de Chambonnières ', edited by Paul Brunold and André Tessier, was published in Paris in 1925.

156 ii *Add before* **CHAMINADE** :
CHAMBURE, Comtesse de. *See* THI-BAULT, GENEVIÈVE.

157 ii **CHAMPION (4)**
l. 1. Dates *should read* :
(*b.* ?, *c.* 1570 ; *d.* ?, *c.* 1640).

ll. 3-4 *should read* :
of " Sieur de la Chapelle ", a courtesy title given him as lord of the manor of a village known as La Chapelle.

166 i **CHANSON**
Par. 1, 1. 10 *should read* :
ballade in canon is unusual.[2] But owing to the

Add footnote :

[2] The canon at two bars' interval in each voice can be studied in Gilbert Reaney's version, shown in his article ' The Ballads, Rondeaux and Virelais of Guillaume de Machaut : Melody, Rhythm and Form ' (' Acta Musicologica ', Vol. XXVII, pp. 57-58).

Footnotes' references and footnotes 2-10 become 3-11.

168 ii ll. 31-32. A *virelai* by Ciconia, ' Or *should read* :
An anonymous *virelai*, ' Or

171 i Par. 3, l. 1. Jeppeson *should read* : Jeppesen

Add at end :

BIBL.—ZINGERLE, HANS, ' Zur Entwicklung der Rhythmik und Textbehandlung in der Chanson von *c.* 1470 bis *c.* 1530 ' (Innsbruck, 1954).

172 i *Add after See also* :

Chorwerk, Vol. 61 (modern reprints from Jacques Moderne). Publikationen G.M.F., Vol. 27 (modern ed. of 60 chansons).

175 i **CHANTER**
ll. 2-5 *should read* :
pipe, the finger-pipe bored with holes which, when opened or closed, produce a series of notes. The larger pipes with a greater bore, called drones, are not equipped with lateral holes and skirl a constant bass accompaniment on unvarying notes to the melody produced by the chanter.   C. R. H.

176 i **CHANTING**
Par. 1, 1. 11. Abbott's *should read* : Abbot's

176 ii Par. 4, 1. 14 *should read* :
have been sown, and they are germinating. Two works that have done much to help are ' The Parish Psalter ', edited by Sir Sydney Nicholson, and ' The Worcester Psalter ', edited by Sir Ivor Atkins.

178 ii **CHAPEL ROYAL**
Par. 2, 1. 20. in his honour, *should read* :
in his honour [1],

Add footnote :

[1] This is somewhat questionable, since Weelkes died two years before Charles's accession, but the anthem may have been written for him as prince.

180 i Par. 1, 1 3 *should read* :
St. James's Palace) which records

184 i **Char**
l. 1. (2 works). *should read* :
(3 works).

CHARACTER NOTATION
Heading should read :

CHARACTER NOTATION (or Shape Notation).

185 ii *Add after* **CHARDINY** :
CHARITÉ, ? (*b.* ? ; *d.* ?).
French 14th–15th-century composer. He may be one of three men : Jehan Carité, canon of Laon, who like Briquet was a member of the court of love formed by Charles VI in 1401 ; Jacques Carité, who received a payment from the Duc de Berry in 1416 ; or Johannes Caritatis, a chaplain of the Duc de Berry, who received a prebend at Saint-Donatien, Bruges, in 1406, which he lost in 1411. Charité's tritextual Rondeau in the Oxford manuscript is noteworthy for its clear delimitation of vocal and instrumental phrases in all its parts. His extant work is published in Vol. II of ' Early Fifteenth-Century Music ' edited by Gilbert Reaney (Amer. Inst. of Musicology, 1958) and by Stainer in ' Dufay and his Contemporaries ' (1898).

G. R. (iii).

186 ii **CHARLES**
Par. 1, 1. 4. 1756 *should read* :
1754

CHARPENTIER
Par. 1, 1. 2 *should read* :
Meurthe, 25 June 1860 ; *d.* Paris, 18 Feb. 1956).

190 ii **CHASINS**
Par. 6. *Add at end* :
Pf. Concerto No. 2, F♯ mi.

191   i   **Chaucer**
l. 8.   *Add*:

Troilus and Cressida (Walton).

l. 10.   *Add*:

Walton ('Troilus and Cressida', opera).

CHAUSSON
Par. 1, l. 2 *should read*:

20 Jan.[2] 1855; d. Limay nr. Mantes-la-Jolie,

Add footnote:

[2] Not 21 Jan., which is the date of the birth certificate, where it is stated that he was " né la veille ".

ii   Par. 2, ll. 3-4 *should read*:

for the first time at Nancy in Dec. 1896 and the Symphony in Paris on 18 Apr. 1898.

Add to BIBL. :

BARRICELLI, PIERRE & WEINSTEIN, LEO, 'Ernest Chausson: the Composer's Life and Works' (Norman, Oklahoma, 1955).

192   i   CATALOGUE :
ORCHESTRAL WORKS
l. 2.   (1882). *should read*:
(1882–83).

BIBL., l. 5.   (Paris, 1921). *should read*:
(Paris, 1911).

VOICE AND ORCHESTRA
l. 3.   (Jean Cros) *should read*:
(Charles Cros)

ii   *Add after Op.* 13 :
14. 'La Caravane' (Théophile Gautier) (1887).

Op. 36, l. 2.   Jhouney) *should read*:
Jounet)

ii   **CHÁVEZ**
Par 2, l. 2 *should read*:

child of a Mexican father and a mother who was one quarter Indian ;

l. 5.   fifteen *should read*:
ten

l. 8.   twenty *should read*:
eighteen

Par. 3, l. 1 *should read*:

In Sept. 1922 Chávez went to Europe, where he remained until May 1923. He

193   i   Par. 1, l. 1 *should read*:

lived in New York from Dec. 1923 to Mar. 1924 and again from Sept. 1926 to July 1928 ; the rest of the time in 1922–28 he was in Mexico. He became

ll. 8-11 *should read*:

productive tropical lands. The last scene, originally entitled 'Revolt of the Machines' by the painter Diego Rivera, was omitted from the performance of the ballet, which was

193   i   Par. 1, l. 16 *should read*:

gonos' ('Hexagons') for voice and pianoforte (so called because the poems consist of 6-line stanzas),

Par. 2, ll. 9-11 *should read*:

on 29 Sept. 1934. Another work belonging to this period, rather misleadingly called 'Republican Overture', was light music based on three popular Mexican 19th-century tunes.

194   i   CATALOGUE
CHORAL WORKS
l. 4.   'Arból que te *should read*:
'Arbolucu te

ORCHESTRAL WORKS
l. 1.   (1920). *should read*:
(1915–18).

PIANOFORTE MUSIC
l. 1.   (1920). *should read*:
(1919).

l. 13.   (1950). *should read*:
(1949).

200   ii   **CHERUBINI**
Delete from BIBL. : ESPRIL, 'Les Voyages de Cherubini, ou L'Enfance de Mozart' (the title is 'Voyages de Chérubin'!).

201   —   LIST OF OPERAS
Col. 4, l. 21.   German text. *should read*:
A German translation of an Italian libretto by an unknown author set by the composer.

201   i   *Add to See also,* l. 3 :
Classici Musica Italiana, Vol. 7 (extracts from 'Deux Journées').

206   i   **CHEVREUILLE**
Par. 3.   *Add before* l. 1 :
'Atta Troll', chamber opera in 1 act (after Heine) (1952).

Add after l. 1 :
Ballet 'Le Bal chez la portière' (1954).

l. 8 *should read*:
Symphonies Nos. 1 (1939) & 3 (1951).

Add after l. 8 :
'Symphonie des souvenirs' (No. 2, 1944).
Short Symphony (No. 4, 1952).
'Symphonie printanière' (No. 5, 1954).

l. 9 *should read*:
2 Pf. Concertos (1937 & 1952).

l. 11 *should read*:
2 Vn. Concertos (1941 & 1953).

208   i   **CHICAGO**
Par. 6, l. 5 *should read*:

tion, which no longer exists, was given its later name in 1910.

(Change whole paragraph to past tense.)

208 ii Par. 1, l. 3 *should read*:

North Western University, but came to an end in 1932. It gave a series

(*Change rest of paragraph to past tense.*)

Par. 3, l. 11 *should read*:

Wild, who succeeded him, but who died in 1929.

213 ii **CHILE**
Par. 1, l. 33. Malcuszinsky *should read*:

Malcuzinsky

214 ii *Add after* **CHILESOTTI**:

CHILMEAD, Edmund (*b.* Stow-on-the-Wold, Gloucestershire, 1610; *d.* London, [buried 19] Feb. 1654).

English scholar and musician. He was one of the clerks of Magdalen College, Oxford, from 1629 to 1634 (Wood says from 1625), from which college he graduated B.A. in Feb. 1629. He took his M.A. from Christ Church in Dec. 1631 and served as a petty canon there until 1648, when he was ejected by the Commonwealth. Thus deprived of a livelihood he took lodgings in London; not, as Wood informs us, with Thomas East, who had been dead since 1609, but perhaps in East's old house, the Black Horse in Aldersgate Street. Here he is said to have started a weekly music meeting. Wood adds that he was sheltered for a time by Sir Henry Holbrooke, Garter King at Arms, in whose translation of Procopius (1653) he assisted.

As a scholar Chilmead deserves special mention on account of his treatise ' De Musica Antiqua Graeca ', which was printed posthumously with his ' Annotationes in Eratosthenem et Hymnos Dionysii ' in the Oxford edition of Aratus in 1672. Hawkins uses it in his ' History ', and it is notable for the fact that it contains transcriptions of supposed specimens of Greek music. Two of these were rendered into a sort of plainsong, and the last into modern notation. It follows that given by Athanasius Kircher in his ' Musurgia Universalis ' (1650): the Pindaric ' Golden Lyre ' ode, which Kircher claimed to have discovered in the monastery of San Salvatore in Sicily, but which is now believed by most scholars to have been forged by him. However, it demonstrates how up-to-date Chilmead was in his sources.

His translations have been republished as recently as 1889 and show the range of his interests (*see* D.N.B. for these). Nor can the harsh necessity of earning a living after 1648 be the sole cause of their production (though it was a contributory factor), for they were begun while he was still at Oxford. In 1632

and 1634 he copied out music books for the choir at Magdalen and catalogued the Greek manuscripts in the Bodleian Library in 1636. He also wrote a treatise called ' De Sonis ', but this seems to have been lost.

Chilmead's compositions are few and not very distinguished. Four songs are included in Edward Lowe's Autograph (B.M. Add. MS 29,396) and a couple of instrumental pieces in Add. MS 31,429. Since Lowe was organist at Christ Church while Chilmead was there, these songs probably date from 1634 to 1648 and were written perhaps for college plays — two, possibly three, are known to be play-songs.   I. S.

248 i **CHINESE MUSIC**
Add to BIBL.:

KORNFELD, FRITZ, ' Die tonale Struktur chinesischer Musik ' (Mödling nr. Vienna, 1955).
PICKEN, K., N.O.H.M., Vol. I (Oxford, 1957).
REINHARD, KURT, ' Chinesische Musik ' (Eisenach & Cassel, 1956).

ii *Add before* **CHINNER**:

CHINESE WOOD BLOCK. A slotted oblong block of wood emitting a hollow sound when struck with a light stick. Originally used only in dance-bands, it has occasionally appeared in the symphony orchestra.

249 ii *Add before* **Chirico**:

CHIRBURY, Robert (*b.* ?; *d.* ?, *c.* 1456). English singer and composer. He was a member of the Chapel Royal in the reigns of Henry V and Henry VI, and subsequently chaplain of St. George's, Windsor. His name occurs first in the Wardrobe Books of the royal household in 1421 [1], appearing for several years following together with the names of Damett, Sturgeon, Cooke and Burell. He was a chaplain of Windsor in 1455, and since nothing is heard of him thereafter it is possible that he died during the following year.

Four of his works are preserved in the ' Old Hall Manuscript ': a ' Credo ', two settings of ' Sanctus ' and one of ' Agnus Dei '. All are for three voices and in *conductus* style. The ' Credo ' (II, 36) is apparently an early work, as stylistic and palæographic estimates confirm, but in spite of its lack of metrical contrast it displays a well-developed sense of modal colour and makes considerable use of faburden style. Similar characteristics are found in the earlier of the two ' Sanctus ' settings (III, 34), which is reproduced in facsimile as the frontispiece to Vol. III of the ' Old Hall Manuscript '. A notable feature of this work is the division of the *cantus firmus* (Sarum 7) between all three voices.

The other ' Sanctus ' (III, 22) and the single setting of ' Agnus Dei ' (III, 116) may

[1] Public Record Office, E 101/407/4.

well constitute a Mass pair, since they have many points in common: same composer, clef-positions, style, opening chord, threefold metrical scheme. Moreover, in both works the intonations are set in three-part harmony, as opposed to the other 'Sanctus', where they are written out for solo voice. The opening of the 'Agnus Dei', with its chromatically rising uppermost voice (C, C♯, D), is frequently cited as an early example of transition, but the even more extended example in the Fountains Fragment (B.M. Add. MS 40,011 B), an 'Agnus Dei' on f. 11v which begins F(♯), G, G♯, A, shows that this was by no means unusual at the time. Chirbury's 'Agnus Dei' is based on Sarum 3, the chant being divided among all three voices.

D. W. S.

BIBL.—BUKOFZER, MANFRED, ' Studies in Medieval and Renaissance Music ' (New York, 1950).
HUGHES, DOM ANSELM, Introductions to Vols. II & III of the ' Old Hall Manuscript ' (*see* below).
RAMSBOTHAM, ALEXANDER, ed., ' The Old Hall Manuscript ', Vols. II & III (London, 1935 & 1938).

263   i   **CHOPIN**
         Add to BIBL. :

BOURNIQUEL, CAMILLE, ' Chopin ' (' Solfèges ' series No. 5) (Paris, 1957).
BROWN, MAURICE J. E., ' The Posthumous Publication of Chopin's Songs ' (M.Q., XLII, Jan. 1956, p. 51).
HOLCMAN, JAN, ' The Legacy of Chopin ' (New York, 1954).
KOBYLAŃSKA, KRYSTYNA (ed.), ' Chopin in his own Land : Documents and Souvenirs ' (New York, 1956).
LONG, ESMOND R., ' A History of the Therapy of Tuberculosis and the Case of Frederic Chopin ' (Lawrence, Kansas, 1956).

KELLEY   BIBL., l. 57. KELLY *should read* :

264   —   **CHOPIN**, CATALOGUE
         Last l., col. 1 *should read* :
Bolero, C ma.-A mi.

         Col. 2, l. 10. Wlad. *should read* :
Václav

265   —   l. 40, col. 1 *should read* :
Ballade, F ma.-A mi.

266   —   *Footnote* 4. as " Op. 15 " *should read* :
as Franchomme's Op. 15.

267   ii   **CHOPIN INTERNATIONAL COMPETITION**
         Add at end :

The fifth competition was held in Warsaw in 1955. 77 pianists from 27 countries contested.

First Prize—Adam Harasiewicz (Poland).
Second Prize—Bernard Ringeissen (France).
Third Prize—Fou Tsong (China).
Fourth Prize—Vladimir Aszkenasi (U.S.S.R.).

In 1960 the sixth competition took place in Warsaw (the 150th anniversary of Chopin's

birth) and 76 pianists from 30 countries took part.

First Prize—Maurizio Pollini (Italy).
Second Prize—Irina Zaritskaya (U.S.S.R.).
Third Prize—Tania Achot-Haroutounian (Iran).
Fourth Prize—Li Miu-chan (China).

267   ii   **CHOPSTICKS**
         Par. 3, l. 9 *should read* :

variation of his own. The set was orchestrated by N. Tcherepnin in 1937 under the title of ' Tati-Tati '.

268   i   **CHORAGUS**
         Signature C. A. F. *should read* :
H. C. C.

269   ii   **CHORAL SYMPHONY**
         Add to BIBL. :

GROVE, GEORGE, ' Beethoven and his Nine Symphonies ' (London, 1896).
VAUGHAN WILLIAMS, R., ' Some Thoughts on Beethoven's Choral Symphony, with Other Writings on Musical Subjects ' (Oxford, 1955).

CHORALE
         Par. 3, l. 1 *should read* :

THE GREGORIAN CHORALE. *See* GREGORIAN MUSIC & PLAINSONG.

         Delete the rest of the par.

270   i   Par. 1.   *Delete* ll. 1-16.

         l. 17 *should read* (new par.) :

In Germany short vernacular hymns were early admitted

274   ii   *Add to* BIBL. :

BLINDOW, MARTIN, ' Die Choralbegleitung des 18. Jahrhunderts in der evangelischen Kirche Deutschlands ' (Ratisbon, 1957).
JAMMERS, EWALD, ' Der mittelalterliche Choral : Art und Herkunft ' (Mainz, 1954).

         (2nd book by JOHNER) :

' Wort und Ton im Choral : ein Beitrag zur Aesthetik des gregorianischen Gesanges ' (Leipzig, 1953).

275   i   *Add to* BIBL. :

WILSON, ARCHIBALD W., ' The Chorale ' (London, 1920).

278   i   *Add before* **Chottin** :

CHORWERK, DAS. A collection of old vocal music, either intended to be or capable of being performed chorally, published in 52 numbers up to 1939 by the Georg Kallmeyer Verlag and now reprinted, with the addition of a further 12 issues and others in preparation, under the editorship of Friedrich Blume and Kurt Gudewill, by the Möseler Verlag of Wolfenbüttel. The British agents are Novello & Co. A number of the works in the series have never been published in modern editions elsewhere. The following issues were ready in 1957:

1. Josquin des Prés, 'Missa Pange lingua', ed. F. Blume.
2. Jacobus Vaet, 6 Motets, ed. E. H. Meyer.
3. Josquin des Prés & others, Secular Choruses, ed. F. Blume.
4. Johannes Okeghem, 'Missa Mi-Mi', ed. H. Besseler.
5. Adriaen Willaert & others, Italian Madrigals, ed. W. Wiora.
6. Thomas Stoltzer, 37th Psalm, ed. O. Gombosi.
7. Henricus Isaac, 'Missa Carminum', ed. R. Heyden.
8. Willaert & others, Italian Folksongs, ed. Hertzmann.
9. Heinrich Finck, 8 Hymns, ed. R. Gerber.
10. Giovanni Gabrieli, 3 Motets, ed. H. Besseler.
11. Pierre de La Rue, Requiem and Motet, ed. F. Blume.
12. Johann Hermann Schein, 6 German Motets, ed. A. Adrio.
13. Orlande de Lassus, Madrigals and Chansons, ed. H. Besseler.
14. Lassus, Hassler, Schein, Sweelinck & H. Praetorius, 7 Chromatic Motets, ed. F. Blume.
15. Johannes Lupi, 10 Secular Choruses, ed. H. Albrecht.
16. Johann Theile & Christoph Bernhard, 2 Short Masses, ed. R. Gerber.
17. Henry Purcell, 5 Anthems, ed. F. Blume.
18. Josquin des Prés, 4 Motets, ed. F. Blume.
19. Guillaume Dufay, 12 Sacred and Secular Works, ed. H. Besseler.
20. Josquin des Prés, 'Missa Da Pacem', ed. F. Blume.
21. Heinrich Finck, 'Missa in Summis', ed. K. Hasse.
22. Gilles Binchois, 16 Secular Songs, ed. W. Gurlitt.
23. Josquin des Prés, 3 Gospel Motets, ed. F. Blume.
24. Melchior Franck, 5 Motets from the Song of Solomon, ed. A. A. Abert.
25. Antonio Caldara, Madrigal & 18 Canons, ed. K. Geiringer.
26. Thomas Selle, St. John Passion, ed. R. Gerber.
27. Christoph Demantius, German St. John Passion, ed. F. Blume.
28. Gallus Dressler, 5 Motets, ed. M. Ruetz.
29. Peter Schöffer, Song Book of 1513, ed. K. Hasse.
30. Josquin, Le Maistre, Regnart, Vento, Utendahl & Hollander, 8 Motets, ed. H. Osthoff.
31. Aulen, Mass for 3 Voices, ed. H. Birtner.
32. German Masters of the 15th Century, 12 Hymns (Heinrich Finck, Adam von Fulda & others), ed. R. Gerber.
33. Josquin des Prés, 3 Psalms, ed. F. Blume.
34. Lassus, 'St. Peter's Tears of Repentance' (Part I), ed. H. J. Therstappen.
35. Italian Madrigals by Nordic Pupils of Gabrieli (J. Grabbe, M. Pedersøn & H. Nielsen), ed. R. Gerber.
36. Johann Hermann Schein & Christoph Demantius, 116th Psalm, ed. A. Adrio.
37. Lassus, 'St. Peter's Tears of Repentance' (Part II), ed. H. J. Therstappen.
38. Melchior Franck, 'Musikalische Bergkreyen', ed. B. Grusnick.
39. Christoph Demantius, German Motets, ed. A. A. Abert.
40. Alessandro Grandi, 3 Concert Motets, ed. F. Blume.
41. Lassus, 'St. Peter's Tears of Repentance' (Part III), ed. H. J. Therstappen.
42. Josquin des Prés, 'Missa de beata Virgine', ed. F. Blume.
43. Renaissance Carnival Songs, ed. K. Westphal.
44. Johannes Hähnel, Easter Mass on the Hymn, 'Christ is arisen', ed. F. Blume & W. Schulze.
45. German Songs from Foreign Sources, ed. H. Funck.
46. Johannes Martini, 3 Hymns, ed. R. Gerber.
47. Balthasar Harzer (Resinarius), St. John Passion, ed. F. Blume & W. Schulze.
48. Lassus, 'Prophetiae Sibyllarum', ed. H. J. Therstappen.
49. Guillaume Dufay, Hymns, ed. R. Gerber.
50. Johannes Georg Kühnhausen, St. Matthew Passion, ed. A. Adrio.
51. Lambert de Sayve & Michael Praetorius, 'Teutsche Liedlein', ed. F. Blume.
52. Augustin Pfleger, Passion Music on the Seven Last Words, ed. F. Stein.
53. Melchior Franck, 3 Quodlibets, ed. K. Gudewill.
54. Josquin, Arcadelt, Cipriano de Rore, Willaert, 5 Virgil Motets, ed. H. Osthoff.
55. Loyset Compère, 'Missa Alles regrets', ed. L. Finscher.
56. Missa anonyma II from the Breslau Codex Mf. 2016, ed. F. Feldmann.
57. Josquin des Prés, 3 Motets, ed. H. Osthoff.
58. Jakob Arcadelt & others, 6 Italian Madrigals, ed. B. Meier.
59. Willaert, Selected Motets, ed. W. Gerstenberg.
60. Henricus Isaac & Ludwig Senfl, 2 settings of 'Salve Regina', ed. W. Gurlitt.
61. French Chansons from the collections of Jacques Moderne, ed. H. Albrecht.
62. Senfl, Selected Motets, ed. W. Gerstenberg.
63. Secular songs from Georg Forster's 'Frische teutsche Liedlein III–V', ed. K. Gudewill.
64. Josquin des Prés, Motets, ed. H. Osthoff.

279   i   *Add after* **CHRISTO, L. de**:

CHRISTOFF, Boris (*b.* Sofia, 19 May 1919).

Bulgarian bass singer. Originally intended for the legal profession, he studied at Sofia and took his degree in law. He was always interested in singing, and joined the famous Gussala Choir as an amateur. During one of the concerts by the choir, in which he sang as a soloist, he was heard by King Boris of Bulgaria, who was so impressed by the young bass's voice that he encouraged him to study singing with a view to making it his career, providing funds to enable him to go to Rome in 1941 to study with Riccardo Stracciari. He then moved to Salzburg to continue his studies with Muratti. His teacher did not long after, and the end of the war found Christoff in a displaced persons' camp in the Tyrol. He returned to Italy and in 1946 made his début as a concert singer. In Mar. 1946 he made his stage début as Colline in 'La Bohème' during a short season at the Teatro Adriano, Rome. The following season he was heard as Pimen in 'Boris Godunov' at both Rome and the Scala. His first Boris did not follow for another two years; this was in London, where he was making his début at Covent Garden, and it took place without the benefit of full rehearsals. A few weeks later (Dec. 1950) Christoff sang Boris at the Scala, and since then has been a frequent interpreter of this part and others in the Russian repertory in the Italian, Spanish and Portuguese opera-houses. He is equally at home in the German and Italian repertory, and his parts include Rocco in 'Fidelio', the King in 'Lohengrin', King Mark in 'Tristan' the Landgrave in 'Tannhäuser', Hagen in 'Götterdämmerung', the title-part in Handel's 'Giulio Cesare', most of the leading bass parts in Verdi as well as Mephistopheles in both the Gounod and Boito operas. He has appeared at the Teatro Colón, Buenos Aires, and with the Chicago and San Francisco opera companies.

Boris Christoff has been hailed by many people as Shaliapin's successor; perhaps there is an element of truth in this, for Christoff, like Shaliapin, has become identified with the great singing-acting parts in the Russian repertory. But there the comparison must end, for Christoff, unlike Shaliapin, is careful to avoid excesses and exaggerations, and also, unlike his Russian predecessor, he is an outstanding Verdi singer. His voice is not by nature a very large one, but it is of fine penetrating quality, smooth, round and perfectly under control. He is not afraid of singing softly, and his performance of Philip's great monologue in ' Don Carlos ' during the Covent Garden Centenary celebrations in the summer of 1958 was a consummate piece of soft sustained singing, ending with the most ravishing *pianissimo*. He is able to produce a feeling of tension whenever he is on the stage and his seemingly perfect judgment of the exact way in which to colour a phrase, by producing the exact weight of tone required, coupled with his ability to give words their fullest meaning, place him with Gobbi, who, incidentally, is his brother-in-law, as one of the few really great singing actors of the day.

H. D. R.

281   i   **CHROMATICISM**
Add new paragraph after Par. 4 :

A composer very little younger than Wagner, César Franck, developed a highly chromatic idiom that is the most strongly characteristic feature of his style, and so intensely individual as to be instantly recognizable and quite independent of Wagner.

     ii   *Signature* G. D. *should read :*
G. D., adds.

287   ii   **CHURCH, MUSIC OF THE EARLY**
         Par. 2, l. 13.   inexorably *should read :*
in general

291   i   **CHURCH MUSIC SOCIETY**
         Par. 5, l. 7 *should read :*
Society gave considerable assist-

         ll. 9-12 *should read :*
able music for parish churches until 1946, when the Musical Advisory Board of the Royal Society for Church Music was appointed.

     ii   Par. 1, l. 8 *should read :*
reprints and pamphlets.

         Delete rest of l. 8 *and* ll. 9-10.

         CHVÁLA
         Par 2.   Penultimate line *should read :*
Musik ' (1882-87), helped to introduce the

294   ii   **CIANCHETTINI (1)**
         l. 6 *should read :*
and several sonatas for the pianoforte. Her husband, with his partner Sperati, published in 1807-9 the first scores of Beethoven's Symphonies Nos. 1-3 as well as four symphonies and two overtures by Mozart. He was also the editor and publisher of a book of canons by Martini.

         CIANCHETTINI (2)
         Cancel ll. 20-23.

         CIARAMELLA
         Add :
(*PLATE* 60, Vol. VII, p. 746, No. 7.)

295   ii   *Add before* **Cicognini, G. A. :**
CIBELL.   *See* CEBELL.

         CICONIA
         Par. 1, l. 2 *should read :*
(*b.* Liège [2], *c.* 1335; *d.* Padua, Dec.[3] 1411).

         Add footnote :
     [3] Between 15 and 24 Dec.

296   i   Par. 1, ll. 1-12 *should read :*
Walloon theorist and composer. He was in Italy between 1358 and 1367, back at Liège between 1372 and 1401, and lived at Padua from 1402 till his death. He was a canon of Padua and

         Par. 4, l. 3 *should read :*
dated 1411 ; manuscripts of it are at Faenza, Pisa and Venice,

         l. 6 *should read :*
at Bologna, and it also occurs in manuscripts at Florence and Rome ; and ' Incipit praephatio nove

         Par. 5, l. 1 *should read :*
Of his compositions, which include 10 motets, some 10 Mass movements and at least 16 secular works, 7 pieces of the *ordinarium*

         Add to BIBL. :
CLERCX, S., ' Johannes Ciconia de Leodio ' (Congress Report of Int. Mus. Soc., Utrecht, 1952). ' Johannes Ciconia théoricien ' (' Annales musicologiques ', Vol. III, 1955, pp. 39-75). ' Johannes Ciconia: un musicien liégeois et son temps ', 2 vols. (Brussels, 1960).

297   ii   **CIKKER**
         Add at end :
BIBL.—ŠAMKO, JOZEF, ' Ján Cikker ' (Bratislava, 1955).

298   i   *Add before* **CIMA, G. P. :**
CILLARIO, Carlo Felice (*b.* San Rafael, Mendoz, Argentina, 7 Feb. 1915).
Argentine violinist and conductor. He studied in Buenos Aires and afterwards at the

Conservatory of Bologna, where he took diplomas for violin and composition. At first appearing as concert violinist in Italy and elsewhere, he began his career as conductor at the Opera of Odessa. Later he was conductor of the Philharmonic Orchestra in Bucharest, but returned to Italy, where he first appeared at the Teatro Duse at Bologna, conducting Rossini's ' Barbiere '. In 1947 he was appointed permanent conductor of the symphony orchestra attached to the National University of Tucumán. But he left Argentina for Italy again, where he conducts opera and concerts. G. M. G.

298 ii **CIMADORO**
Par. 4, ll. 1-3 *should read*:

Cimadoro arranged six Mozart symphonies and three pianoforte concertos for flute and strings (2 violins, 2 violas, cello and double bass). The symphonies are K. 385, 425, 504, 541, 550 and 551, and the concertos K. 466, 503 and 595.[4] They were published by Monzani & Hill in London, in which firm Cimadoro was a partner till 1805. He wrote

Add footnote:
[4] The Symphonies K. 250 297 and 319 were arranged for the same combination by Girolamo Masi.

301 i **CIMAROSA**
CANTATAS
Delete l. 1.

Add after l. 10:
1800. ' Il giorno felice ' (with Gnecco).

CIMBALOM
Add:
(*PLATE* 17, Vol. II, p. 798.)

309 ii **CINTI-DAMOREAU**
Par. 2, l. 5 *should read*:
age of fifteen, Mlle Cinti, as she now called

310 i Par. 1, ll. 1-4 *should read*:
herself, made her first appearance there in ' Una cosa rara ' on 8 Jan. 1816.[1] By the end of Catalani's management (Apr. 1818) she had attained the rank of *seconda donna* and scored her first notable success in Gnecco's ' Carolina e Filandro ' on 11 Oct. 1817. She was one of the few members of the old company to be re-engaged when a new one was formed in Mar. 1819, and from then on she sang regularly at the Théâtre Louvois. On 22 Feb. 1821 she took over the part of Rosina in Rossini's ' Barbiere ' in the temporary absence of Mme Fodor-Mainvielle, but did not otherwise yet appear in principal

310 i Par. 1, l. 7 *should read*:
now appeared as *prima donna* (Ninetta in ' La gazza ladra ', 5 Nov. 1822; Amenaida in ' Tancredi ', 19 Nov. 1822). She

Add footnote:
[1] *See* ' Journal de Paris ', 10 Jan. 1816.

311 i **CISNEROS**
Par. 1, l. 2 *should read*:
foot) (*b.* New York, 1 Nov. 1878; *d.* New York, 3 Feb. 1934).

ii **CITHER**
Add:
(*PLATE* 22, Vol. III, p. 848, No. 2.)

312 i **CITOLE**
Add:
(*PLATE* 69, Vol. VIII, p. 146 [iv], No. 1.)

CITTERN
Add:
(*PLATE* 69, Vol. VIII, p. 146 [iv], No. 1.)

314 ii **CLAPP**
Par. 1, l. 2 *should read*:
4 Aug. 1888; *d.* Iowa City, 9 Apr. 1954).

Par. 2, l. 29 *should read*:
tion he held till his death. He greatly contributed

315 ii **CLARI, G.**
Add at end:
See also Fitzwilliam Music (reprints of sacred works).

323 ii **CLARINET**
Par. 2, l. 18. ♭♮' *should read*:
b♮'

329 i **CLARINET (1)**
Add at end:
See also Mock Trumpet.

ii **CLARION**
Add:
(*PLATE* 32, Vol. IV, p. 492, No. 8.)

330 i **CLARKE, Douglas**
(*b.* ?, 1893). *should read*:
(*b.* Reading, 4 Apr. 1893).

Par. 2, l. 18 *should read*:
became conductor of the Montreal Symphony Orchestra,

l. 21 *should read*:
University. He retired from both these posts. He introduced new works by

335   i   **CLASSICI MUSICA ITALIANA**
should read :

I CLASSICI DELLA MUSICA ITALIANA [1]

[1] The large-scale works in this collection are represented by extracts only.

Vol. 2. Bassani, C. B. *should read* :
Bassani, G. B.

Vol. 33. Turrini *should read* :
Turini

   ii   **Claudel**
l. 2. *Add* :
Dupré (' Chemin de la Croix ' for organ).

!. 6 *should read* :
Koechlin (song). Milhaud, ' Christophe Colomb ', opera & incid. m. for adapt. ; ' Protée ', incid. m. [2 versions] ;

Claudius
l. 2 *should read* :
ner (motet). David (J. N., do.). Gál (do.) Gerstberger

l. 6. Schoeck 17 songs) *should read* :
Schoeck (poems for voice & orch. ; 17 songs).

336   i   **CLAUSULA**
Par. 3, l. 8.   non-liturgical *should read* :

para-liturgical

Add :
BIBL.—APEL, W., ' From St. Martial to Notre Dame ' (J.A.M.S., II, 1949).
BUKOFZER, M., ' Interrelations between Conductus and Clausula ' (' Annales Musicologiques ', I, 1953).
GENNRICH, F., ' Sankt Viktor Clausulae und ihre Motetten ' (Darmstadt, 1953).
WAITE, WILLIAM, ' The Rhythm of Twelfth-Century Polyphony ' (New Haven, 1954).
' Discantus, Copula, and Organum ' (J.A.M.S., V, 1952).

CLAVÉ
Par. 1.   Dates *should read* :
(*b.* Barcelona, 21 Apr. 1824 ; *d.* Barcelona, 24 Feb. 1874).

339   i   **CLAVICHORD**
Add to BIBL. :
BOALCH, DONALD, ' Makers of the Harpsichord and Clavichord : 1440 to 1840 ' (London & Cardiff, 1956).

See also. l. 2 *should read* :
Clavier (*PLATE* 7, Vol. II, Frontispiece ; *PLATES* 37 & 38, Vol. IV, p. 736).

   ii   **CLAVICOR**
Par. 2, l. 4 *should read* :
1850s. (*PLATE* 14, Vol. II, p. 446, No. 9.)

343   ii   **CLEMENS NON PAPA**
Add at end :
See also Amer. Inst. Musicol. (C.M.M.), Vol. 4 (modern ed. of complete works). Collectio O.M.B., Vols. 1-3, 5, 8, 10, 12 (modern ed.). Vereniging, Vol. 44 (reprint of motet).

345   ii   **CLEMENTI**
Par. 1, l. 8 *should read* :
the house of his protector, Stapleton Iwerne, near Blandford [2], Dorset. Then,

Par. 2, l. 2.   Paris [2] ; *should read* :
Paris [3] ;

Add footnote :
[2] This is asserted with fair certainty by A. Henry Higginson in his book on Peter Beckford (London, 1957), pp. 84 & 121. Earlier editions of Grove had, more vaguely, " Wiltshire " and did not give the house any name.

Footnote 2 *becomes* 3.

346   i   Par. 2, l. 2 *should read* :
in 1785 and a visit to Vienna in 1799 Clementi spent all his time from 1782

347   ii   Par. 3, ll. 8-9.   the present librarian *should read* :
the librarian

349   i   *See also.* Add to l. 2 :
Classici Musica Italiana, Vol. 8 (modern ed. of sonatas).

350   i   **CLÉRAMBAULT**
Add at end :
See also Lyrebird Press (modern ed. of 14 pieces).

   ii   **CLEVE**
Add at end :
See also Collectio O.M.B., Vol. 4 (modern ed.).

CLEVELAND
Par. 4, ll. 5-6 *should read* :
succeeded by Arthur Rodzinski, who in turn was followed by Georg Szell in 1946.

351   i   Par. 6, l. 6 *should read* :
time. For the celebration of the orchestra's fortieth anniversary in 1958 the conductor, George Szell, commissioned ten American and foreign composers to compose special works for first performance at Cleveland. They included Blacher, Creston, Einem, Etler, Hanson, Martinů, Mennin and Walton.

   ii   **CLICQUOT (2)**
l. 1.   Dates *should read* :
(*b.* Paris, 3 Nov. 1678 ; *d.* Paris, 1744).

352   i   **CLICQUOT (4)**
l. 2.   1791 *should read* :
24 May 1790

Add to BIBL. :
DUFOURCQ, NORBERT, ' Les Cliquot ' (Paris, 1942).

   ii   **CLIFFORD**
Par. 1, l. 2 *should read* :
dale, Australia, 31 May 1904 ; *d.* Singapore, 4 Sept. 1959).

355   i   **CLOSSON**
César
Par. 3, l. 5. Césare *should read*:

356   i   *Add before* **CLUZEAU MORTET**:
CLUYTENS, André (*b.* Antwerp, 26 Mar.
1905).
Belgian conductor. He was educated at
the Royal Flemish Conservatory of Antwerp
in 1914–22, gaining first prize for pianoforte
in 1921 and for harmony and counterpoint
the following year. In 1922 he was appointed
chorus master at the Théâtre Royal, Antwerp,
a position he held until 1927, when he became
first conductor there. He then held the following appointments: first conductor at
Capitole, Toulouse, 1932; Lyons, 1935;
Bordeaux, 1938; Paris Opéra, 1944; Paris
Opéra-Comique, 1947. In 1949 he was
appointed chief conductor of the orchestra of
the Societé des Concerts du Conservatoire,
of which organization he is Vice-President.
For his services to French music he has been
made a Chevalier de la Légion d'Honneur.
Subsequently he was appointed chief conductor of the Orchestre National de France,
and he has conducted concerts all over
Europe (including Russia) and the U.S.A.
Cluytens's work both in the concert-hall
and opera-house came to the notice of Wieland
Wagner, who engaged him to conduct the
new 'Tannhäuser' production at Bayreuth in
1955 at short notice, in place of the indisposed
Markevitch. He returned to direct 'Meistersinger' in 1956 and 'Lohengrin' in 1958.
He is the first conductor of the French school
to have established himself at Bayreuth and
is also much admired in Vienna, where he
has conducted the Philharmonic on many
occasions.
Cluytens's approach to Wagner does not
please everybody. Many find his 'Meistersinger' untraditional as to tempi, rhythm and
emphasis; his romantic and lyrical 'Tannhäuser' is much preferred, but on the whole
he seems temperamentally unsuited to German
music. His interpretation of the French
repertory, however, is an entirely different
matter.   H. D. R.

357   i   **COATES, Eric**
Par. 1, l. 2 *should read*:
shire, 27 Aug. 1886; *d.* Chichester, 21 Dec.
1957).

ii   **COATES, Henry**
Par. 2, l. 17 *should read*:
the death of Dr. George Oldroyd in 1951.

361   i   **COCHLAEUS**
Par. 2. *Add after* l. 1:
In 1504 he entered Cologne University, be-
came *Baccalaureus* in 1505, *Magister* in 1507

and Professor in the Faculty of Arts in 1509.
Through the influence of friends he was ap-
pointed rector of the St. Lorenz School at
Nuremberg in 1510.

361   i   l. 5 *should read*:
Frankfort o/M. Glarean was one of his pupils.

Par. 3, ll. 2–3 *should read*:
Luther. He wrote a

ii   **COCLICO**
Add at end, before signature:
A modern facsimile reprint of the 'Com-
pendium musices' appeared in 'Documenta
Musicologica', Series I, Vol. ix.

Cocteau
l. 1 *should read*:
Cocteau, Jean. *See* Auric ('Éternel Retour', 'La
Belle et la bête', 'Orphée' &

Add at end:
BIBL.—RAŠÍN, VERA, '"Les Six" and Jean Cocteau'
(M. & L., XXXVIII, 1957, p. 164).

362   ii   **CODA**
Add before See also:
BIBL.—SUDER, ALEXANDER L., 'Die Coda bei Haydn,
Mozart und Beethoven als Resultante verschiede-
ner Gestaltungsprinzipien' (Munich, 1951).

363   ii   **COELHO, M. R.**
Add at end:
The complete works of Coelho, edited by
M. S. Kastner, were chosen to inaugurate
the series of Portuguese musical monuments
('Portugaliae Musica') in 1960.

364   i   **COENEN, Willem**
Par. 1, l. 2. London, *should read*:
Lugano,

Par. 2, l. 9 *should read*:
and songs. He lived in London for forty years,
but retired to Lugano, where he died.

365   ii   **COHEN, Alexander**
Par. 1, l. 2 *should read*:
1884; *d.* Birmingham, 17 Dec. 1953).

Par. 3, ll. 2–3 *should read*:
City of Birmingham Orchestra, and from that
time lived in Birmingham permanently,

Par. 4, ll. 10–12 *should read*:
But he contrived to equip himself to give the
public the

366   i   Par. 1, l. 6 *should read*:
concert-giver. He was often assisted by his
wife, Doris Watkins, a highly gifted soprano
and pianist.

366   i   **COHEN, Harriet**
Add at end, before signature:

The Harriet Cohen International Music Awards, of which Sir Arnold Bax was the founder and first president, organizes annual competitions for performers, composers and musicologists on a large, cosmopolitan scale, offering prizes in the form of medals and purses.

ii   **COHEN, Louis**
Par. 1, l. 2 *should read*:

1894; *d.* Liverpool, 25 Nov. 1956).

367   ii   *Add before* **COKE, R. S.**:

COKE, John (*b.* ?; *d.* London, 1507). English composer. He was parish clerk of St. Olave's Church, Hart Street, London, and master of the guild of London church musicians, the Fraternity of St. Nicholas, in 1501. It was probably he who wrote the Mass 'Venit dilectus', one of the "York Masses", preserved at the Borthwick Institute, York.   H. B. (ii).

COKE, R. S.
Par. 2, l. 17 *should read*:

based on Shelley (first performed at the Scala Theatre, London, 5 Nov. 1959), 3 symphonies, 4 symphonic

Par. 2, l. 20 *should read*:

painting by Corot), 6 pianoforte Concertos, 3

l. 27 *should read*:

pianoforte, and over 80 songs, including cycle 'The Gardener' (Tagore). Nearly all

370   i   **Coleridge, S. T.**
l. 3 *should read*:

Brian (songs). Britten ('Nocturne', No. 3). Coleridge-Taylor ('Kubla Khan',

371   ii   **COLERIDGE-TAYLOR (3)**
Add at end:

As a conductor Avril Coleridge-Taylor is gifted with technique and authority. She formed a symphony orchestra under her own name which for six years gave employment to many musicians, and later she became conductor of the New World Singers and of the City Orchestra, the latter of which gave its first concert in July 1958, at St. Paul's Church, Covent Garden. In 1955 she visited South Africa, where she introduced modern works by British and American composers, visited schools and colleges, and started a scheme for music and ballet in parks which was taken up by Johannesburg and spread to other parts of the Union.

372   ii   *Add at top of col.*:
COLLABORATIONS. *See* COLLECTIVE WORKS.

373   i   **COLLARD**
l. 4. with W. F. *should read*:
with F. W.

COLLECTIO OPERUM MUSI-CORUM
Vol. XII
l. 2 *should read*:
Claudin (de Sermisy).

l. 4 *should read*:
Lupi, J. (Leleu).

l. 8 *should read*:
Barbé, A.

375   i   **COLLECTIVE WORKS**
l. 15. Goosens *should read*:
Goossens

ii   *See also. Add to* l. 1:
Diabelleries.

376   ii   **COLLES**
Par. 2, ll. 3-4 *should read*:
tised at Bridgnorth, but came from Somerset and belonged to a family of Irish origin.[1] Eager to devote himself to music,

Add footnote:
[1] Henry Colles's grandfather, also called Abraham, who had gone to Dublin from Kilkenny, was an eminent surgeon and discovered what is still known as the "Colles fracture".

378   i   **COLLINGWOOD**
Par. 2, l. 7 *should read*:
linck's tragedy. The order of C.B.E. was bestowed on him in 1948.

Add at end:
BIBL.—GLOVER, CEDRIC, 'Lawrance Collingwood' (M.Q., XII, Apr. 1926).

380   i   **Colman, George, sen.**
Add to l. 4:
Handel, p. 51 ('Arianna e Teseo', ? adapt.).

381   i   *Add after* **COLOMBE, LA**:

COLOMBI, Giuseppe (*b.* Modena, ? 1635; *d.* Modena, 28 Sept. 1694). Italian violinist and composer. He became *vicemaestro di cappella* to the Modenese court in 1674 and *maestro di cappella* of Modena Cathedral in 1678. Five books of composition by him were printed and 22 other works are in manuscript in the Biblioteca Estense at Modena. A 'Ciaccona' for violin and continuo has been published with pianoforte accompaniment by Gino Roncaglia.

E. B.

BIBL.—RONCAGLIA, GINO, ' G. Colombi e la vita musicale modenese durante il regno di Francesco II d' Este ' (Accad. di Sc., Lett. e Arti, Modena, 1952). ' La cappella musicale del duomo di Modena ' (Florence, 1957).

381   ii   **COLONNA, G. P.**
Add at end:
See also Fitzwilliam Music (reprint of sacred works).

384   ii   **COMES, J. B.**
Par. 1, l. 2 *should read:*
29 Feb. 1568 ; *d.* Valencia, 5 Jan. 1643).

385   i   *Add at end:*
BIBL.—PALAU, MANUEL, ' La obra del músico valenciano Juan Bautista Comes ' (Madrid, 1944).
See also Eslava (modern reprint of ' Hodie nobis ').

387   ii   **COMPÈRE**
Add to BIBL. :
FINSCHER, L., ' Loyset Compère and his Works ' (' Musica Disciplina ', XII, 1958 ; XIII, 1959 ; XIV, 1960).

Add at end:
See also Chorwerk, Vol. 55 (modern reprint of ' Missa Alles regrets '). American Institute of Musicology, C.M.M. 15.

389   i   **COMPOSITION**
Add to BIBL. :
HALL, RICHARD, ' Some Reflexions on the Teaching of Musical Composition ' (' The Score ', No. 18, Dec. 1956, p. 30).
HUTCHINGS, ARTHUR, ' The Invention and Composition of Music ' (London, 1958).

ii   **COMPTON**
Par. 1, l. 2.   1876). *should read:*
1874 ; *d.* London, 6 Apr. 1957).

390   ii   **COMUS**
Par. 3, l. 4 *should read:*
Temple Hall, London (Mar. 1923). A modern reprint of the whole of Arne's setting, edited by Julian Herbage, appeared in ' Musica Britannica ', Vol. 3.

Signature should read:

F. K., adds.

392   ii   **CONCERTO**
Footnote 2, ll. 4-5 should read:
orchestre ', Chausson's Concerto for violin, piano and string quartet, and Stravinsky's Concerto for 2 pianos.

395   ii   Par. 1, ll. 24-25 *should read:*
century ; Alban Berg's for violin, piano and 13 wind instruments, and Arthur Bliss's for piano, tenor voice, xylophone and strings, are salient examples

396   i   BIBL. l. 22 *should read:*
piano ', 2 vols. (Paris, 1939 ; Eng. ed., London, 1948 ; Norman, Oklahoma, 1954).

l. 31 *should read:*
da Mozart ai contemporanei ' (Milan, 1954).

Add to BIBL. :
BOYDEN, DAVID D., ' When is a Concerto not a Concerto ? ' (M.Q., XLIII, 1957, p. 220).

397   i   *Add after* **CONCORD** :
CONCOURS REINE ÉLISABETH DE BELGIQUE. An international musical competition held annually in Brussels under the patronage of H.M. Queen Elisabeth of Belgium. Open by turns to violinists, pianists and composers, it was founded in 1951 as a continuation and extension of the pre-war Concours Eugène Ysaÿe. The following is a list of the winners of the *premier prix*:

1951 (violin) : Leonid Kogan — U.S.S.R.
1952 (pianoforte) : Leo Fleisher — U.S.A.
1953 (composition) : Michał Spisak — Poland.
1954 No competition.
1955 (violin) : Berl Senofsky — U.S.A.
1956 (pianoforte) : Vladimir Askenazy — U.S.S.R.
1957 (composition) : Chamber Orchestra: Michał Spisak — Poland. Symphony Orchestra: Grazio Fiume — Italy.

A. L. C.

CONCRETE MUSIC. See ADDENDA, Vol. IX, *should read:*

CONCRETE MUSIC (Fr. Musique concrète). The invention of Pierre Schaeffer of Paris. He began work on it in 1948 under the auspices of the Club d'Essai of the Radiodiffusion Française. At first it was merely the use of musical or natural sounds from available gramophone records, rearranged in a new order to suit the purpose intended. In this process the individual sounds could be played backwards or the speed of the record could be considerably increased or decreased to produce corresponding differences in pitch as well as in quality. After 1950 Schaeffer's work was aided and simplified by the construction of new kinds of apparatus using magnetophone tape instead of discs : this made it easier both to record new sounds and to alter or distort sounds already recorded. At the same time Schaeffer's experimental group, consisting of himself, Pierre Henry and the engineer Jacques Poullin, was put on a permanent basis within the framework of the French Radio.

Schaeffer calls this type of music " concrete " because it starts from already existing sounds, unlike normal music, which begins from an abstract idea in the composer's mind and has first to be written down and then performed before it becomes sound. In concrete music the " composing " process is the choice of the sounds to be used, their alteration or distortion, if required, and their rearrangement to form a whole. An example of the result of this process is Schaeffer's ' Symphonie pour un homme seul ' — a representation of a number of sounds heard by a solitary man. The work lasts about twenty minutes and is in ten movements with titles such as ' Partita ', ' Scherzo ', ' Stretto ', ' Erotica ' and ' Eroica '. Each movement creates a mood-picture based on a loose association of ideas, and the sounds are arranged in rhythmical patterns which correspond to normal musical shapes; it is in fact in the fields of rhythm and sound-colour that concrete music has made its most striking contributions so far. It has also been used in films, such as Schaeffer's own ' Mascarade ' and ' Leonardo da Vinci ' (the latter in collaboration with Pierre Henry), and he has also composed an *opéra-ballet concrète* on the subject of Orpheus, produced at the Donau-eschingen Festival of 1953. Other French composers, including Messiaen and Boulez, have also shown interest in concrete music and created some pieces in this medium, which, though still at an experimental stage, does represent a new means of expression that may be of technical assistance to artistic creation, particularly in music for radio, film and theatre (especially ballet). H. S. (ii).

BIBL.—SCHAEFFER, PIERRE, ' A la recherche d'une musique concrète ' (Paris, 1952).
(ed.), ' Vers une musique expérimentale ' (Rev. Mus., No. 236, 1957).
See also Electrophonic Music.

404　　ii　　**CONDUCTING**
Add to BIBL. :

GROSBAYNE, BENJAMIN, ' Techniques of Modern Orchestral Conducting ' (Cambridge, Mass. & London, 1956).

BIBL. *Add to* INGHELBRECHT :
Eng. trans., ' The Conductor's World ' (London, 1953).

405　　i　　*Add to* BIBL. :
SAMINSKY, LAZARE, ' Essentials of Conducting ' (London, 1958).

Delete article on **CONDUCTUS** *and replace by the following* :

CONDUCTUS. Generic term usually applied to the monodic and polyphonic Latin song which flourished in the 12th and early 13th centuries. Purely secular music does not generally come under this heading, though the subject-matter may vary from light-hearted songs of rejoicing to works which can be fitted into the framework of the liturgy. The word conductus is employed first with

reference to introductions to the reading in the Compostela codex, and this use is continued in the New Year's Office of Sens and Beauvais. Introductions or tropes to the ' Benedicamus ', however, are simply labelled ' Benedicamus ' in the Compostela and St. Martial sources, though such works form a very important part of the Notre-Dame conductus repertoire. Nevertheless the processional nature of the early conductus at least is clear from its use in ' The Play of Daniel ' for songs performed when characters come on or go off. Undoubtedly the processional meaning became secondary in the 13th century and the general meaning of a song in Latin took precedence. It is possible to consider early Latin songs dating back to the 9th century, such as the lament on the death of Charlemagne, as conductus, and certainly such works must form the origin of the conductus dealing with state events (*e.g.* ' Redit aetas aurea ' in honour of the coronation of Richard the Lion Heart). The word conductus itself, however, is of later date.

The musical form is as varied as that of the text, which is often strophic but may be through-composed. A frequent system is to have fresh music for groups of stanzas, for instance 1-2, 3-4, 5-6, but the groupings are not necessarily regular, as in this example. It is not unusual to find the sequence form adopted, and indeed paired stanzas may suggest secular origin, *i.e.* the music may originally be secular while the Latin words are new. This is the case with ' Veritas, equitas ', a conductus with triple rather than double versicles and Latin words by Chancellor Philippe of Paris University (*d.* 1236), which had a chequered history. Originally one of the few Provençal lays, it was then provided with French words by Gautier de Coincy and finally with Latin ones for the conductus fascicles of the Notre - Dame and Fauvel manuscripts. ' O mens, cogita ', another fine work, suggests lay origin, but no source has yet been found for it. Such monodic works were called *simplex* by the theorists of the 13th century, as against the polyphonic pieces, which could be in two, three or four parts. Both monodic and polyphonic works may be entirely syllabic or have melismas at beginning and end. One of the most extended works of all, complete with long melismatic sections, is the ' Salvatoris hodie ' attributed to Pérotin by the 13th-century theorist known as Anon. IV. This is a three-voice piece, but, of the three compositions mentioned as Pérotin's by Anon. IV, the other two extant works are for one and two voices respectively (' Beata viscera ' and ' Dum sigillum '). In spite of the fact that the conductus style is generally note-against-note, it is not uncommon in the melismas to find the held-note

G

style of organum, *i.e.* the lower part holds one note while the upper part moves about rapidly. Similarly voices may conclude a phrase simultaneously in a melisma, or may overlap so that both voices conclude the phrase at a different place. Although it is not generally appreciated, imitation is common between voices in the Notre-Dame organa, and the same is true of the conductus. An expert like Handschin considers motivic imitation in one and the same voice earlier than that between individual voices, though both techniques were employed simultaneously. He has also noted the non-literal repetition of a syllabic section in a succeeding melisma, and a tendency to ritornello treatment in conductus melismas.

In spite of the importance of the polyphonic conductus in the works of the Notre Dame school, the conductus was evidently monodic in the first place. In the works of the St. Martial school a composition may be monodic in one source, generally the earlier one, and polyphonic in another. Two-voice writing was the norm in the first half of the 12th century, but towards the end of the century three-part writing became frequent. Four-part writing occurs in only a handful of compositions and remained exceptional. The note-against-note writing is interesting harmonically, but the process of composition evidently remained the art of combining successively invented voices. Franco of Cologne's statement that the cantus firmus must be a newly invented melody rather than a pre-existing plainchant has been widely echoed in medieval and modern writings, but there is clear evidence now that even in the conductus borrowed material was used at times, even if it was in paraphrased form.

The main reason why so few conductus have been published is that the transcription of the syllabic sections is still uncertain. One school of thought feels that modal rhythm must apply, while another prefers a prevailing fifth mode. Under the latter system, and it must be made clear that the fifth mode is really a series of even beats as against the longs and shorts of genuine modal rhythm (modes 1-4), each syllable has a beat and ligatures are worked out within this framework in longs and shorts. Lengthening of the lower note may be required where there are many notes in the upper voice against one note of the lower one, but this generally occurs only at cadences. The Spanish MS of Las Huelgas is a useful guide to conductus notation, since it contains many pieces in 14th-century mensural notation, which, however, must be followed with caution since the source is a late one.

The conductus declined in the second half of the 13th century when the motet was in great favour, and retained its hold only in secular songs like Adam de la Halle's Rondeaux, three-part works in note-against-note style. In England note-against-note style was always popular, and even the 15th-century carol, written in Latin or English, is essentially in conductus style. The 14th-century Italian madrigal has the opening and concluding melismas of the conductus, but syllabic style for the rest, identical text in all parts and a certain predominance of the upper part. In 14th-century France the conductus must have been considered archaic harmonically, for the 'Roman de Fauvel' contains only monodic ones, mainly from the Notre-Dame repertoire, including the lower voices only of some pieces. The aged Jacobus of Liège, writing about 1330, complains that organa and conductus are neglected, while motets and secular songs are alone cultivated.

G. R. (iii)

BIBLIOGRAPHY

Angles, H., 'El Còdex Musical de Las Huelgas' (Barcelona, 1931), 3 vols.
Apel, W., 'The Notation of Polyphonic Music, 900-1600' (Cambridge, Mass., 4th ed., 1949).
Bukofzer, M. F., 'Interrelations between Conductus and Clausula' ('Annales Musicologiques', I, 1953).
Ellinwood, L., 'The Conductus' (M.Q., XXVII, 1941).
Geering, A., 'Die Organa und mehrst. Conductus in den Hss. des deutschen Sprachgebietes' (Bern, 1952).
Gröninger, E., 'Repertoire-Untersuchungen zum mehrstimmigen Notre Dame-Conductus' (Cologne, 1939).
Handschin, J., 'Conductus-Spicilegien' (A.M.W., IX, 1952).
'Notizen über die Notre Dame-Conductus' ('Bericht über den musikwissenschaftlichen Kongress zu Leipzig', 1925-26).
'The Summer Canon and its Background' ('Musica Disciplina', III, 1949 and V, 1951).
Hughes, Dom A., ed., 'New Oxford History of Music', II (London, 1954).
Prado, Dom G., 'Liber Sancti Jacobi, Codex Calixtinus' (Santiago de Compostela, 1944), Vols. 2-3.
Spanke, H., 'Die Londoner St. Martial-Conductus Handschrift' and H. Anglès, 'La música del Ms. de Londres, British Museum, Add. MS 36881' in 'Bulletí de la Biblioteca de Catalunya', VIII, 1928-32).
Wooldridge, H. E., 'The Oxford History of Music', I (London, 1901).

406   i   **CONFALONIERI**

Par. 3, l. 7 *should read*:

Cherubini (' Prigionia di un artista : il romanzo di Luigi Cherubini ', 1948), in whose work he specializes

407   i   **CONRAD VON ZABERN**

Add at end:

Bibl.—Gümpel, K.-W., 'Das Tastenmonochord Conrads von Zabern' (A.M.W., Vol. XII, 1955).
'Die Musiktraktate Conrads von Zabern' (*ibid.*, Vol. XIII, 1956).

412   i   **CONSORT**

Bibl. l. 1 *should read*:

Dart, Thurston, 'Jacobean Consort Music' (Proc. Roy. Mus. Ass., Vol. LXXXI, 1954-55).
'Morley's Consort Lessons of

413   ii   **CONSORT OF VIOLS**
Add at end :
See also Musica Britannica, Vol. 9 (modern ed. of Jacobean consort music).

CONSTANTINESCU
Par. 1, l. 2 *should read :*
30 June 1909).

414   i   *Add after* **CONSUELO** :

CONTADINA ASTUTA, LA. Intermezzi in 2 parts by Pergolesi, now better known as ' Livietta e Tracollo '.[1] Libretto by Tommaso Mariani. Produced Naples, Teatro San Bartolommeo, 25 Oct. 1734. 1st perf. abroad, Dresden (as ' Il finto pazzo '), 5 Aug. 1747. 1st in Britain, Edinburgh (as ' Tracollo '), 11 July 1763. Modern revival : London, R.A.M. (trans. by M. and E. Radford), 6 Mar. 1933.

Add footnote :
[1] Originally performed between the acts of his serious opera ' Adriano in Siria '.

415   i   *Add after* **CONTI, I. M.** :

CONTILLI, Gino (*b.* Rome, 19 Apr. 1907). Italian composer. He studied at the " Santa Cecilia " Conservatory in Rome under Respighi. Since 1942 he has been director of and professor of composition at the Liceo Musicale " A. Laudamo " at Messina. His most important compositions are a ' Sinfonia italiana ' and a Concerto for orchestra, ' La notte ', lyric suite for one voice and instruments, etc. During recent years he has made use of twelve-note technique (' 4 studietti dodecafonici ' for pianoforte, etc.).

G. M. G.

416   i   **CONTREBASSE-À-ANCHE**
l. 2 *should read :*
BASSOON. (*PLATE* 14, Vol. II, p. 446, No. 11.)

418   ii   **COOKE, Arnold**
Add to BIBL. (2nd work by CLAPHAM) :
' Arnold Cooke : the Achievement of Twenty Years ' (' Music Survey ', Vol. III, 1951).

420   ii   *Add before* **COOKE, Nathaniel** :

COOKE, John (*b.* ? ; *d.* ?, 1456).
English composer. He was clerk of the Chapel Royal during the reigns of Henry V and Henry VI. Grants to him are shown in the Patent Rolls and Close Rolls until 1455, after which his name does not reappear. Eight of his works are to be found in the ' Old Hall Manuscript ' ; of these, five are Mass sections and three are motets.

There is considerable stylistic contrast in the four settings of ' Gloria ', proving that Cooke was as conversant with the simpler *conductus* style as he was with the " free treble "

style, or even the progressive method of alternating duet passages with sections in four-part harmony scored for voices and instruments. The two settings of ' Gloria ' in *conductus* style (I, 1 and I, 28) exhibit many similar characteristics, not the least important being a strikingly symmetrical plan of changes in time-signature. This feature is also found in another ' Gloria ' (I, 138), which is set out for tenor and two instruments. An unusual aspect of this work is found near the end, where the words " in gloria Dei Patris. Amen " are sung to the same music as " Laudamus te . . . glorificamus te ".

The fourth ' Gloria ' (I, 124) is skilfully set out for one solo alto voice (accompanied by one instrument) and two *ripieno* alto voices supported by two instruments. These sections *a 2* and *a 4* alternate regularly throughout the work, heightening the liturgical text by contrasts in texture, though not in metre, which remains as *tempus imperfectum* from beginning to end. For the climax, the three altos join forces, and with the support of the two instruments an imposing edifice in five-part harmony is created for the section " Quoniam tu solus Sanctus " until the " Amen ", in which the instrumentalists join, singing instead of playing. When this brief five-part section begins, altos 1 and 2 sing " Quoniam . . ." while alto 3 sings " Jesu Christe . . .", an example of telescoping which is found in much bolder form in Cooke's ' Credo ' (II, 252). Here the entire text is telescoped, as in certain Credo settings by Lionel Power, Swynford and Damett. Three instruments are called for ; two double the alto and tenor voices, while the third plays the *cantus-firmus*-like lower part. Occasional tricks of mensural notation producing syncopated or proportional effects demonstrate Cooke's not inconsiderable knowledge of theory.

Only one of his motets, the antiphon ' Ave regina coelorum ' (I, 161), is actually liturgical : it is in *conductus* style, with a symmetrical scheme of mensural contrasts, as well as hints of relief in texture by the occasional scaling down to two voices. The final " Alleluia " shows that it was composed for use in Paschal time. Also in *conductus* style is the processional hymn against the plague, ' Stella coeli exstirpavit ' (I, 168). The striking chromatic sequence at the outset of this hymn is more than likely to be inspired by its gruesome subject : certainly there is no similar example in European music of the 15th century.

Besides composing this musical challenge to the plague, Cooke wrote a paraliturgical motet for use in time of war. ' Alma proles regia / Christi miles inclite ' (III, 46) has for its tenor an optional part of the Rogationtide litany, " Ab inimicis nostris defende nos Christe ", identified by Manfred Bukofzer.

This phrase is directed to be sung, according to the Sarum Processional, only during war-time, and this fact allied to the prayers to the Virgin Mary and to St. George in the upper voices may assist in narrowing down the period during which the work might have been composed.

Although the Feast of St. George had been taken over from the Roman Kalendar, it was not until after Agincourt that the grade of the Feast was raised and the saint venerated as Patron of England. The year 1416, which saw the change in grade, may well have brought forth " occasional " works such as Cooke's motet, and the one which immediately precedes it in the manuscript, Damett's ' Salvatoris mater pia / Sancte Georgi, Deo care ', also invoking the intercession of the Virgin Mary and St. George. The treaties of Canterbury and Calais in 1416 caused a lull in hostilities, however, and it was not until the following year that Henry V began his Norman campaign. It is unlikely, therefore, that the motet was written before September 1417, or later than May 1420, when the Treaty of Troyes reconciled the monarchs of England and France.

Later outbreaks of war might equally well claim this motet, but for the fact that St. George rapidly became a popular cult, and subsequent music written in his honour was invariably couched in the form of the carol, which if not necessarily popular, is a good deal more simple than the two isorhythmic motets by Damett and Cooke. The latter is for alto and tenor voices, with one instrument, which plays the *cantus firmus* three times in successively diminishing mensural values. The writing is of a dignified and unadorned nature entirely suitable for a solemn festival, now praising and now calling upon the new-found patron-saint, who is begged to vouchsafe either victory or glory, after death, in the heavenly kingdom.   D. W. S.

BIBLIOGRAPHY
BUKOFZER, MANFRED, ' Studies in Medieval and Renaissance Music ' (New York, 1950).
GREENE, RICHARD L., ' Two Medieval Musical Manuscripts ' (Journ. Amer. Musicol. Soc., VII, 1954).
HARVEY, JOHN, ' Gothic England ' (London, 1947).
RAMSBOTHAM, ALEXANDER, ed., ' The Old Hall Manuscript ', Vols. I-III (London, 1933-38).

422 ii COOPER, Emil
Par. 1 & par. 2, ll. 1-2 *should read* :

COOPER, Emil (*b*. Kherson, 20 Dec. 1877).
Russian conductor. He received his first lessons from his father,

423 ii COOPER, Gerald
Par. 1, l. 25 *should read* :

ham Palace Road, London. The British Union Catalogue of Music, published in two volumes in 1957, owed a great deal to Cooper's very generous financial support.   E. B.

423 ii COOPER, Martin
Par. 3, l. 16 *should read* :

Master ' series (London, 1952). In 1958 he published ' The Concise Encyclopedia of Music and Musicians '.   E. B.

424 i COOPER, Robert
l. 1 *should read* :

COOPER, Robert. *See* COWPER.

Cancel rest of entry and footnote.

ii COOPERSMITH
Add at end, before signature :
A complete thematic catalogue of Handel's works was desposited by Coopersmith in manuscript in the Widener Library at Harvard University.

425 i COPENHAGEN
Par. 3, *add at end* :

In 1957 Bruno Bartoletti was appointed conductor of the Royal Opera.

428 ii COPLAND
BIBL. l. 5 *should read* :
' Aaron Copland ' (New York, 1950 ; Oxford, 1953).

Add to BIBL. :
SMITH, JULIA FRANCES, ' Aaron Copland : his Work and Contribution to American Music ' (New York, 1955).

Add below CATALOGUE OF WORKS :
OPERA
' The Tender Land ' (libretto by Horace Everett), prod. New York, 1 Apr. 1954.

429 ii SONGS
Add at end :
' Old American Songs ', Set I (1950).
' Old American Songs ', Set II (1952).

430 i COPULA. *should read* :
COPULA (1).

Add :
BIBL.—WAITE, WILLIAM, ' Discantus, Copula, and Organum ' (J.A.M.S., V, 1952).

Add at end :

(2). An 8-ft. organ flute stop specified by Mozart in his Church Sonatas K. 244 and 245.[1]

Add footnote :
[1] For details *see* ORGAN STOPS, Vol. VI, p. 351.

COPYRIGHT (BRITISH).[1]
should read :
COPYRIGHT (BRITISH).[2]

Footnote 1 becomes 2.

434   ii   **COQ D'OR**
l. 2.   COCKEREL *should read* :
WEATHERCOCK

435   i   **COR ANGLAIS (1)**
l. 2 *should read* :
46, Vol. VI, p. 160, Nos. 3 & 4).

436   ii   *Add before* **CORDANS** :

CORBRAND (Corbronde), William (*b.* ? ; *d.* ? London, ?).
English 14th–15th-century singer and composer. He was chaplain at Bokingfeld Chapel, Kent, in 1481–93 and rented a house from the London Carpenters' Company in 1501–10. In the latter year he sang in the choirs of All Hallows, London Wall. There is a record of a payment of £3 6s. 8d. made in 1515 to " oone Corbronde a syngyng man " by the hand of William Cornyshe. Motets for 2 voices by him, ' In manus tuas ' and ' Confitemini ', are in Pepys MS 1236 at Magdalene College, Cambridge.

                              H. B. (ii).

437   i   **CORDER, F.**
Par. 4, l. 12.   ' Modern Composition ' *should read* :
' Modern Musical Composition '

    ii   **CORDIER, Baude**
Par. 1, l. 1.   Rheims, *c.* 1400 ;
should read :
Rheims, *c.* 1380 ;

Delete paragraph 2 and signature and substitute :

French 14th–15th-century composer. What is known of his life comes from a few words of one of his own Rondeau texts. He came from Rheims and his works were famous from there to Rome. The title *Maistre*, which is given to him in this poem and in other pieces from the Oxford manuscript, confirms that he was a *magister artium*. His only sacred composition, an ' Et in terra ', is in the cantilena style so popular in the early 15th century. It is attributed to him only in the Bologna manuscript, which also contains one of his secular compositions. If he had been at the schismatic pope's court at Avignon, his name would doubtless have been at the head of this ' Et in terra ' in the Apt manuscript, but in fact the piece is anonymous there. The Apt version must be the earlier one, however, since the Bologna " Amen " is new and appears to be composed in a more recent style.
    Cordier's ten secular works are all Rondeaux with the exception of the Ballade ' Dame excellent [*sic*] '. Apart from the Bologna Rondeau and two Rondeaux which form later additions

to the corpus of the important Chantilly codex, all the secular compositions occur in the Oxford manuscript, so important for the secular output of Dufay. Cordier must have flourished about 1400, for his songs belong partly to the complex late 14th-century style exemplified in the Chantilly manuscript and partly to the new, simple style, generally in 6-8 time, in which the early songs of Dufay are written. The complexity of ' Amans, amés ' is in many ways unsurpassed, for, although it takes up only 15 bars in modern transcription, its three voices contain 23 mensuration signs. Of the two Chantilly compositions one is written in the shape of a heart and the other is the first known example of a circular canon, the latter showing acquaintance with the Italian *caccia*. In spite of the attractive melodies of these compositions, they still show complex notational subtleties which disappear in such Rondeaux as ' Ce jour de l'an ' and ' Je suy celui '. Duple rhythms appear in one of the Rondeaux, but they are more common in sacred works at this period, as in the ' Et in terra '. Obviously, however, Cordier was primarily a secular composer, and as such he is an important precursor of Dufay, who doubtless imitated such Rondeaux as ' Ce jour de l'an '. Cordier's extant work is published in Vol. I of ' Early Fifteenth-Century Music ', edited by Gilbert Reaney (Amer. Inst. of Musicology, 1955).

                              G. R. (iii).

438   i   **CORELLI**
Par. 3, l. 9.   Filharmonica *should read* :
Filarmonica

l. 10.   Bragnoli *should read* :
Brugnoli

    ii   Par. 2, l. 11 *should read* :
foot. Mainwaring, in his Memoirs of Handel,

439   i   Par. 4, l. 5 *should read* :
an orchestra of 150 musicians, no doubt the famous Roman Accademia of 1687. The King of

    ii   Par. 2, ll. 6–9 *should read* :
health began to fail. His last work was dedicated to his admirer John William, Prince Palatine of the Rhine. He died in Rome on 8 Jan. 1713 and was buried

440   i   Par. 5, l. 6 *should read* :
per l' organo, Op. 3 (Modena, 1689). The same arranged by Geminiani as *concerti grossi*.

    ii   BIBL., l. 8.   (Paris, 1933) *should read* :
(Paris, 1933 ; rev. 1954). Eng. trans. by Hubert E. M. Russell (New York, 1956).

440   ii   *Add to* BIBL. :
RINALDI, M., ' Arcangelo Corelli ' (Milan, 1953).

See also, l. 1.   *Add*:
Classici Musica Italiana, Vol. 9 (modern ed. of sonatas). Denkmäler (1), Vol. 3 (modern ed. of works).

l. 5.   *Add*:
Sondheimer Ed., Vols. 39-41 (modern ed. of vn. sonatas).

441   i   **CORELLI PLAYERS**
l. 7 *should read*:
music by Steffani, Leclair and Tele-

Add after **CORFINI**:
CORI SPEZZATI (Ital. = broken choirs). Groups of singers placed in different parts of a building; also the music composed for them. The practice goes back to Jewish and early Christian liturgical music, but the Italian term *cori spezzati* belongs to the 16th century and the polychoral music which became popular at that time. While its history may be traced back to psalmody, its more immediate ancestry is the double-choir polyphony of the 15th century. Such music as that in two choir-books of the second half of that century at Modena or Josquin's 8-part motet ' Lugebat David ' was no doubt performed with two choirs on opposite sides of the church. It was nearly always composed for extraordinary and festive occasions.

The popularity of *cori spezzati* at the beginning of the 16th century seems to have been greatest in and about Venice. At Treviso, Padua and Bergamo there were a number of composers interested in such polychoral music, and several new developments came about. In the work of Francesco Santacroce who was in the service of Treviso Cathedral about 1515-29, instead of the structure of the music being dependent on the alternate verses of the text, the composer thinks more of the sheer effectiveness of rapidly changing choirs:

In his polychoral music Santacroce also seeks a new balance between homophony and imitative counterpoint. He still uses imitation a little, but for long stretches a simple chordal style prevails, giving great clarity to the words and relying for musical variety almost entirely on the alternating choirs. The music is much simpler to perform than double-choir polyphony and of surprising " modernity " in its harmonic progressions.

It was probably from such works that Willaert learned the possibilities of *cori spezzati*, and it was his famous psalm settings for double choir published by Gardano which led to the vogue for polychoral music in the later part of the 16th century. In some ways these settings are more advanced than Santacroce's, although the harmony is simple and diatonic. As Zarlino was to point out, the choirs have complete harmony in themselves, an important rule when the two bodies of singers are at some distance from each other.

These works were highly popular, perhaps because they fulfilled the requirements of the Council of Trent, and there were many imitations. The Vesper psalms were especially popular material, and it is possible to trace polychoral settings of them from Willaert well into the 17th century.

In the twenty years following the publication of Willaert's works the composition of polychoral music increased tremendously. Not only the immediate pupils of Willaert found the style attractive, but several other composers living outside northern Italy composed motets for two choirs. The most important of these was Lassus. He used *cori spezzati* less for psalm settings and liturgical pieces than for great ceremonial motets, some with secular Latin texts in praise of his patrons. In contrast to Willaert, Lassus tends to use the *tutti* of the two choirs a great deal, and in order to gain true contrapuntal independence for each voice his music sometimes becomes very complicated in rhythm. The result is a lack of clarity in the words, but a much

greater brilliance in sound, which was probably made even greater by the use of instruments. Lassus also extended the use of *cori spezzati* to secular music in the vernacular and was one of the earliest composers of dialogues and echo music. In none of these works does Lassus adhere to the Willaertian rules about the completeness of choirs. His main resemblance to the older composer is in the slow movement of his dialogue technique, the long phrases being made necessary by contrapuntal elaboration; and in the simplicity of the choral alteration, each choir taking up the movement from the other without much interlocking or overlapping.

The greatest of the Lassus pupils was, perhaps, Andrea Gabrieli. A native of Venice, the elder Gabrieli combines the natural vivacity of the earlier Italian composers with the seriousness of Willaert and Lassus's love of sonority. Like Lassus he usually set ceremonial texts rather than psalms. Nearly all his polychoral motets were written for use at the great Venetian festivals.

Sometimes one choir consists of upper voices only while the other may be a *coro grave*, and the tessitura of the uppermost and lowest parts is often such as to require instruments. In one or two works certain choirs are marked to be performed *a cappella*, which implies that others are essentially a mixture of voices and instruments.

Bassano, Donato, Croce, Bell'haver and Giovanni Gabrieli all followed the example of Andrea Gabrieli. All took for granted his harmonic and dialogue style, and his wide contrast between the various groups of voices and instruments. It is a tribute to his modernity and imagination that few of these composers could add any really novel feature in an age full of innovations. Only his nephew and Giovanni Croce, in fact, are at all in advance of Andrea's 'Concerti' of 1587. The earliest works of both these composers are close to his in style. Croce extended the use of *cori spezzati* to the composition of parody masses. In these as well as in his double-choir motets the dialogue technique and diatonic harmonies are quite clearly derived from the older composer. Giovanni Gabrieli is also a close follower of his uncle. Very little of his church music is written for single choir, and most of the texts set by him were those set by Andrea and published in 1587. In the younger Gabrieli's 'Sacrae Symphoniae' (1597) he used the choral and instrumental groupings and general harmonic idiom of his uncle. The contrasts between the groups are now sharper and instruments are essential in many works. The place of solo voices is now more distinct, even though there are no solo or instrumental idioms to be found. The work of Giovanni Gabrieli was to

complete the fame of *cori spezzati*. Almost every composer of church music used his techniques, and the employment of soloists and a full orchestra in different parts of a church was widely imitated. A further development was the separation of the soloists from each other. Ignatio Donati recommends in his 'Sacri Concentus' (1612) a method which he calls "distant singing". The famous 'Vesperi della Beata Vergine' of Monteverdi use effects of this kind very freely. The complexity which can be reached is seen in a posthumously published setting of the psalm 'Laudate pueri' by Croce. In this work the four soloists are split up to give echoes of one another. In addition there is a *ripieno* choir in another part of the church and yet a further group consisting of trombones accompanying an alto voice.

In Venice and its surrounding state polychoral music declined and by 1630 it was no longer the main form of ceremonial music. Its popularity continued, however, for a short time in both Rome and Germany. In Rome Palestrina had composed and published motets for two choirs as early as 1572. The texts chosen for setting indicate that the music was intended for great ceremonial occasions, but although this might denote the influence of Venetian composers, the actual style shows less interest in the resources of *cori spezzati* than in the greater sonority made possible by eight voices. There is little contrast between the choirs, and although a free dialogue style sometimes is used, the main interest is in imitative counterpoint. A later volume published in 1575 shows the composer to have become more modern, using triple-time passages, homophonic dialogue between harmonically complete choirs and so on. Even so, the more characteristic and powerful passages, such as the beginning of 'Surge Illuminare', are dependent on counterpoint rather than polychoral devices. There are long imitative phrases and independent, interesting melodic lines, both of which the Venetian composers completely ignored in the later part of the century.

Palestrina's pupils and imitators continued to follow his style for many years. Victoria, whose first polychoral compositions were also published in 1572, began in a manner very close to that of Palestrina, although in some of his later works written after his return to Spain he approached the Venetian composers in general style, if without the sumptuousness of their orchestral technique.

Soriano, Agostino, Abbatini and several other composers in Rome continued to compose for *cori spezzati* well into the 17th century. The most famous of them was Orazio Benevoli, whose work approaches the Venetian composers in its scale, although remaining truly contrapuntal and Roman in general style. Benevoli chose mainly choirs of equal range and ignored the more brilliant possibilities of dynamic contrasts. He uses octave doublings and occasional un-Palestrinian dissonance, but his attitude is firmly based on 16th-century idiom. This is true even of his splendid Mass for 53 voices written for the consecration of Salzburg Cathedral.

In Germany the vogue for separated choirs was of great importance in the 17th century. The style was well known there from the time of Lassus and encouraged by a number of Andrea Gabrieli's pupils, of whom the most distinguished were Hans Leo Hassler and Aichinger. Two other composers must be mentioned as of some importance. Schütz, having studied with Giovanni Gabrieli, was very fond of polychoral devices and had much the same talent for using space as part of the musical pattern. In his earlier works he is clearly indebted to Venetian models, but later he went farther in the dramatic use of *cori spezzati*. Michael Praetorius, although not capable of such power, is important because he explored the possibilities given by space with Germanic thoroughness and codified them in his comprehensive treatise ' Syntagma Musicum '.

Bach still used the device, long after it had ceased to be generally popular, mainly in his festival works, such as the St. Matthew Passion and the motets. In these there are genuine space effects, but in general he uses such divisions more because they make for increased sonority. This also applies to the few later examples, such as the ' Te Deum ' of Berlioz or Walton's ' Belshazzar's Feast ', where the wide separation of performers is incidental and forced upon the composer by the very size of his resources.   D. M. A.

BIBL.—ALESSI, G. D', ' Precursors of Adriano Willaert in the Practice of Coro Spezzato ' (Journ. Amer. Musicol. Soc., V [1950], p. 187 ff.).
ARNOLD, DENIS, ' The Significance of " Cori spezzati " ' (M. & L., XL, 1959, p. 4).
' Andrea Gabrieli und die Entwicklung der " Corispezzati " ' (' Musikforschung ', XII, 1959).
HERTZMANN, E., ' Zur Frage der Mehrchörigkeit in der ersten Hälfte des 16. Jahrhunderts ' (Z.M.W., XII [1929–30], p. 138 ff.).
ZENCK, H., ' Adrian Willaerts " Salmi spezzati " (1550) ' (' Musikforschung ', II [1949], p. 97 ff.).

441   ii   **CORKINE**
Add at end :

Evidence that Corkine went to Poland in 1617 is found in

A passe for the sayd Geo Vincent to goe over to the Prince of Poland and to carry over with him to the sayd Prince, his master these musitians Richard Jones, Wm. Corkin, Donatus O'Chaine, Thomas White, Wm. Jackson, Tho. Sutton, Valentine Flood and John Wayd.

(22 June 1617. Acts of P.C. of England, New Series, 1616–17).   s. j.

444   ii   **CORNELYS**
Par. 4, l. 13 *should read :*

hands.³ This enterprise nearly ruined her, and

Add footnote :

³ This information, coming from Casanova, may be thought suspect, but it is confirmed by the list of subscribers to ' Cent Contredanses ' by Robert Daubat, published in 1757; they include " Mlle [*sic*] Pompeati, directrice des spectacles en Flandre ". The list is given by Paul Bergmans in his ' Variétés musicologiques ', Series I (Ghent, 1891).

446   i   **CORNET**
Par. 2, l. 18. Isaac Levy *should read :*

Jules Levy

450   ii   **CORNETT**
Add at end :

(*PLATES* 15, Vol. II, p. 447 & 31, Vol. IV, p. 448, No. 3.)

451   ii   **CORNU**
Par. 3, l. 4 *should read :*

music by Grétry.² (*PLATE* 6, Vol. I, p. 1004, No. 2.)

452   ii   **CORNYSHE**
Par. 3, l. 5 *should read :*

she morneth ' (duet), ' A Robyn ' ⁵, ' Trolly, lolly lolly

Par. 4, l. 13. Skelton ⁵ *should read :*

Skelton

Add footnote :

⁵ Words by Wyatt, song used by Shakespeare in ' Twelfth Night '; *see* Ivy L. Mumford, ' Musical Settings to the Poems of Sir Thomas Wyatt ' (M. & L., XXXVII, 1956, p. 315).

Footnote 5 becomes 6.

454   ii   *Add before* **Corradi** :

CORPUS SCRIPTORUM DE MUSICA. A series of reprints of old treatises on music published by the American Institute of Musicology, which has its headquarters in New York and at Dallas, Texas, and branches in London, Paris and Cassel. *See* AMERICAN INSTITUTE OF MUSICOLOGY.

462   i   **COSTELEY**
Add at end :

See also Florilège, Vol. 4 (modern ed. of chansons). Maîtres Musiciens, Vols. 3, 18 & 19 (do. of various works).

463   i   **COTTON, John**
l. 1 *should read :*

COTTON (Cotto, Cottonius), John (Johannes Affligemensis, John of Affligem) (*b.* ? ; *d.* ?).

463   i   Par. 2, l. 2 *should read*:

the author of a treatise, 'De Musica cum tonario', dating from

     ii   *Add at end*:

See also Corp. Script. Mus., Vol. 1 (modern ed. of treatise).

COTUMACCI
Par. 1, l. 2 *should read*:

Villa Santa Maria, Chieti, 1709 [1]; *d.* Naples, 29 July 1785).

Par. 2, l. 12 *should read*:

where he taught until his own death.

(*delete* ll. 13-16)

Add footnote:

[1] According to U. Prota Giurleo; Schmidl had already pointed out that he must have been born well after 1698, the date previously accepted by some authorities, since, if that had been correct, he would have been still teaching at the age of eighty-seven.

481   i   **COUNTERPOINT**
      Add to BIBL.:

PROCTOR, LELAND H., 'Tonal Counterpoint' (Dubuque, Iowa, 1957).
SEARLE, HUMPHREY, 'Twentieth-Century Counterpoint' (London, 1954).

498   i   **COUPERIN (4)**
      CATALOGUE:
      Col. 1, l. 1 *should read*:
'Épitaphe du paresseux': "Jean s'en alla" (La Fontaine).

      Add to See also, l. 1:

Denkmäler (1), Vol. 4 (modern ed. of suites).

      l. 2:

Lyrebird Press (complete ed.).

499   ii   **COUPERIN (10)**
      Add at end:

See also Lyrebird Press (modern ed. of 'La Chaumière').

      COUPERIN (11)
      Add to BIBL.:

CITRON, PIERRE, 'Couperin' ('Solfèges' series) (Paris, 1956).

      BIBL., l. 24. (Rev. Mus. 1902-3). *should read*:
(Paris, 1913).

503   i   **COURTOIS**
      Add at end:

See also Maîtres Musiciens, Vol. 5 (modern ed. of chansons).

506   i   **COVENT GARDEN THEATRE**
      Par. 4, l. 6 *should read*:

general administrator and Karl Rankl musical

506   i   Par. 4, ll. 8-9 *should read*:

& Hawkes took upon themselves the responsibility for the lease, rent and house expenses, while for the production of opera and ballet a very

507   i   Par. 3, l. 11 *should read*:

building was opened on 15 May 1858; and also, perhaps, that other famous opera-houses (*e.g.* the Teatro della Pergola at Florence) are no better situated. That

      Add to BIBL.:

ROSENTHAL, HAROLD, 'Two Centuries of History at Covent Garden' (London, 1958).

509   ii   **COWELL**
      Par. 2, l. 3. four symphonies
      should read:

at least thirteen symphonies

511   ii   **COWPER, Robert**
      Delete entry.

512   ii   **CRACOVIA CIVITAS**
      l. 15. It is a kind of monody
      should read:

It is a monody

513   i   **CRAMER (2)**
      Par. 2, ll. 7-8 *should read*:

1824 he established the firm of Cramer, Addison & Beale, music publishers, having been first in

     ii   *Add to* BIBL.:

BROCKLEHURST, J. BRIAN, 'The Studies of J. B. Cramer and his Predecessors' (M. & L., XXXIX, 1958, p. 236).

514   i   **CRAMER (3)**
      Par. 1, l. 3 *should read*:

to William IV in 1834, succeeding Christian (also known as Christopher)

     ii   **CRAMER, C. F.**
      Par. 2, l. 2. philosophy *should read*:

philology

515   ii   **CRANMER**
      Par. 1, l. 2 *should read*:

mingham, 5 May 1885; *d.* Harlech, 20 Aug. 1954).

516   ii   *Add after* **Crawfurd**:

      CRAWLEY, Sybil. *See* NIELSEN, FLORA.

517   ii   **CRECQUILLON**
      Add to See also:

Collectio O.M.B., Vols. 10, 12 (modern eds.).

518 i **CRESTON**
Par. 2, ll. 1-2 *should read*:

American composer of Italian origin. He comes of a poor family named Guttoveggio and was christened Giuseppe. He was obliged

ii CATALOGUE
ORCHESTRAL WORKS
Add at end:

68. 'Toccata' for 40th Anniversary of Cleveland Orchestra (1958).

519 ii **CRIST**
Par. 2, l. 31 *should read*:

harmony. He wrote a book, 'The Art of Setting Words to Music' (New York, 1944).
N. B.

536 i **CRITICISM**
Add to BIBL.:

DEMMERY, MORTON, 'The Hybrid Critic' (M. & L., XXXVII, 1956, p. 128).
LACHNER, CORBINIAN, 'Die Musikkritik: Versuch einer Grundlegung' (Munich, 1954).
STUCKENSCHMIDT, HANS, 'Glanz und Elend der Musikkritik: der Verfall des musikalischen Geschmacks' (Berlin, 1957).

537 ii **CROCE**
Par. 3, ll. 7-8 *should read*:

madrigal 'Ove tra l' herbe' for 'Il trionfo di Dori' was printed in Book II of 'Musica Transalpina' and provided one of the models for the madrigals in 'The Triumphes of Oriana';

BIBL. l. 1 *should read*:

BIBL.—ARNOLD, DENIS, 'Croce and the English Madrigal' (M. & L., XXXV, 1954, p. 309).
'Giovanni Croce and the Con-

539 ii *Add before* **CROIZA**:

CROIX SONORE (Instrument). *See* OBUKHOV.

540 ii **Cros, Charles**
See Gramophone (invention). *should read*:

See Chausson ('Chanson perpétuelle'). Gramophone (invention).

Cancel entry **Cros, Jean.**

541 ii **CROSS, Joan**
Par. 2, l. 33 *should read*:

tion production of Britten's 'Gloriana'. The order of C.B.E. was bestowed on her in 1951.

549 ii **CRUSELL**
BIBL., l. 5. Svenks *should read*:
Svensk
l. 7. forlag *should read*:
förlag
ll. 10-11 *should read*:
vall, 1918).
'Några brev från Bernard Crusell' (S.T.M., 1949).

551 i **CRWTH**
Add at end:

(*PLATE* 31, Vol. IV, p. 488, No. 1.)

552 i **CRYPTOGRAPHY**
Par. 2, l. 8 *should read*:

in Schumann's 'Carnaval', which represent the musical letters in his surname (S.[E♭ = es]C. H. A.), Ravel's Minuet

l. 12 *should read*:

heading. The motto in Alban Berg's Chamber Symphony, "Aller guten Dinge . . . [sind drei]", is followed by a theme constructed on the musical letters in " Arnold Schönberg, Anton Webern and Alban Berg ".[2]

Add footnote:
[2] Quoted in H. F. Redlich, 'Alban Berg: the Man and his Music', p. 112.

554 i **CSÁRDÁS**
Par. 2, l. 13. Borbály *should read*:
Borbély

ii Par. 1, l. 5. Jószef *should read*:
József

555 ii **CSERMÁK**
BIBL., l. 25. TARA *should read*:
TÁRA

COLLECTIONS
l. 1. AGOST *should read*:
ÁGOST

557 i **CUCLIN**
Date *should read*:

(*b.* Galatz, 5 Apr. 1885).

ii *Add after* **CUDMORE**:

CUDWORTH, Charles (bapt. **Cyril Leonard**) (*b.* Cambridge, 30 Oct. 1908). English musical bibliographer, lecturer and author. Largely self-taught, he became assistant in various University departments and libraries at Cambridge between 1930 and 1946. In the latter year he was appointed Sub-Librarian of the Cambridge University Music School and in 1957 Curator of the Pendlebury Library, Cambridge University Faculty of Music. He has been extra-mural lecturer for the University and for the W.E.A. since 1938 and is well known as an adult-education lecturer in the eastern counties. The hon. M.A.Cantab. was conferred on him and he was made a member of Gonville and Caius College in 1958.

Cudworth is the author of librettos for Patrick Hadley's 'Fen and Flood' (1955) and 'Connemara' (1958). As a musicologist he has specialized in 18th-century music, particularly instrumental and largely English, and he has frequently broadcast on such subjects. He lectured to the Royal Musical

Association on 'The English Symphonists of the 18th Century' (Proc. Roy. Mus. Ass., 1951-52) and published a 'Thematic Index of Eighteenth-Century English Overtures and Symphonies' (London, 1953). His large number of articles include regular contributions to 'Music' (1951-54) and 'Record News' (from 1953). Among other important articles are:

'Notes on the Instrumental Works attributed to Pergolesi' (M. & L., XXX, 1949).
'Cadence galante: the Story of a Cliché' (M.M.R., LXXIX, 1949).
'Pergolesi, Ricciotti and the Duke of Bentinck' (I.G.M., Utrecht Congress, Amsterdam, 1953).
'The English Organ Concerto' ('The Score', No. 8, 1953).
'Baroque, Rococo, Galant, Classic' (M.M.R., LXXXIII, 1953).
'An Essay on John Marsh' (M. & L., XXXVI, 1955).
'Baptist's Vein: French Orchestral Music and its Influence, 1650-1750' (Proc. Roy. Mus. Ass., Vol. LXXXIII, 1956-57).
'Handel and the French Style' (M. & L., XL, 1959).

E. B.

559   i   **CUI**
            CATALOGUE:
            OPERAS
            l. 6 *should read:*
perf. St. Petersburg, 19 Dec. 1878.

        ii   l. 12 *should read:*
scene), 1 act, prod. Moscow, 23 Nov. 1901.

                l. 14. 15 Dec. *should read:*
16 Nov.

565   i   **CURZON, Clifford**
            Par. 3, l. 3 *should read:*
given recitals. In 1958 the order of C.B.E. was bestowed on him.   D. H. (ii).

566   ii   **CUTELL**
            Par. 2, ll. 2-5 *should read:*
author of a vernacular treatise on English descant, which is preserved in MS 842 of the Bodleian Library at Oxford.
                                    W. H. H., rev.

567   i   **CUVELIER**
            Par. 2, ll. 1-7 *should read:*
French 14th-15th-century writer and musician (?). He is the author of one of the last great epic poems of the middle ages, the 'Chronique de Bertrand du Guesclin', and may be identical with the Jacquemart Le Cuvelier mentioned by the anonymous author of an early 15th-century treatise on versification, 'Règles de la seconde rhétorique'. This man came from Tournai and was *faiseur* to Charles V, *i.e.* probably a minstrel. One Jó. Cuvelier is represented by three *ballades* preserved in MS Chantilly (Musée Condé 1047), whose repertory dates mainly from the 1380s.

567   i   Par. 2. *Add at end:*
One of his works is addressed to Gaston Phebus, Count of Foix, who died in 1391.
                        E. D. (ii) & G. R. (iii).

570   ii   **CYMBALS**
            Par. 1, l. 2 *should read:*
rarely met with. The writer possesses a pair

            Add at end:
(*PLATES* 34, Vol. IV, p. 492, No. 4; 35, Vol. IV, p. 504, No. 2; 49, Vol. VI, p. 622, No. 3.)

            Add after **CYMON:**
Cynewulf. *See* Fricker ('Vision of Judgment').

572   ii   **CZERNY**
            Par. 1, ll. 14-15 *should read:*
London. She was followed by Liszt, then in his tenth year [1], whose father placed him in Czerny's

            Add footnote:
[1] In his MS Reminiscences Czerny says that this was in 1819, when the boy was about eight years of age, but it is clear that his memory played him false and that the date was 1821.

576   i   *Add after* **DAL GAUDIO:**
DAL MONTE, Toti (Antonietta Meneghelli) (*b.* Treviso, 27 June 1893).
Italian soprano singer. Originally a pianoforte student at the Liceo Benedetto Marcello in her native city, she sustained an injury to her left hand which prevented her from completing her keyboard studies. Her father then took her to Barbara Marchisio, a famous contralto of the 1850s and 1860s, who was living in retirement at Mira. The young Dal Monte sang her the Jewel Song from 'Faust' and was immediately accepted as a pupil. In 1916 she made her début at the Scala, Milan, in the small part of Biancafiore in Zandonai's 'Francesca da Rimini'. She then spent a further period of study, this time in stagecraft, with Antonio Pini-Corsi. After appearances in the Italian provinces as Norina, Cio-Cio-San and Lauretta, which seemed to indicate that she was going to become a *soprano lirico*, she sang the soprano part in Beethoven's ninth Symphony at Turin under Toscanini. The conductor invited her to La Scala to sing Gilda during the 1921-22 season, and from then onwards she decided to concentrate on the *soprano leggiero* repertory — Lucia, Rosina, Amina, Linda di Chamounix, with occasional excursions into more lyric parts like Lodoletta in Mascagni's opera of that name and Violetta. She sang regularly at the Scala, in Rome, Naples and elsewhere in Italy. In America she was with the Chicago Opera from 1924 to 1928, but only

spent one season at the Metropolitan, 1924–25. Likewise she sang only once at Covent Garden, in 1925, as Lucia and Rosina, after which she was chosen by Melba as one of the members of the opera company the great soprano took to Australia on her farewell tour. She did, however, make several recital appearances in London and was one of the last Italian " divas " to delight audiences in old-fashioned Patti-like concerts. She was married to the tenor Enzo de Muro Lomanto, who died in 1952. In recent years she has enjoyed a brief period as an actress, and she now devotes her time to teaching.   **H. D. R.**

576 i **DALAYRAC**
          Par. 1, l. 2. 13 June *should read* :
8 June

581 ii **DALLA CASA, N.**
          Par. 1. *d. ?*). *should read* :

d. Venice, Jan. or Feb. 1616).

          Par. 2, l. 1 *should read* :

Italian musician, probably

          l. 3 *should read* :

the Venetian Seignory's musicians. His successor, Alvise Grani, in the wind band of St. Mark's was appointed on 8 Feb. 1616. He wrote

582 i **DALLAM**
          Add at end :
BIBL.—MAYES, STANLEY, 'An Organ for the Sultan' (London, 1956).

      ii **DALLAPICCOLA**
          Add at end :
BIBL.—NATHAN, HANS, 'The Twelve-Tone Compositions of Luigi Dallapiccola' (M.Q., XLIV, July 1958, p. 289).
VLAD, ROMAN, 'Dallapiccola: 1948–1955' ('The Score', No. 15, Mar. 1956, p. 39).
'Luigi Dallapiccola', trans. by Cynthia Jolly (Milan, 1957).

583 i CATALOGUE
          CHORAL WORKS
          Add at end :
'Job', *sacra rappresentazione* for speaker, solo voices, chorus & orch. (1949–50).
'Canti di liberazione' (St. Augustine, etc.) for chorus & orch. (1952–55).

          ORCHESTRAL WORKS
          Add at end :
'Due pezzi per orchestra' (1946–47).
'Variazioni per orchestra' (1953–54).
'Piccola musica notturna' (1954).

          VOICE AND CHAMBER
          ORCHESTRA
          Add at end :
'Tre poemi' (James Joyce, Michelangelo, Eugenio Montale) (1949).
Cantata 'An Mathilde' (Heine) for mezzo-soprano (1952–55).
'Concerto per la Notte di Natale dell' anno 1956' (Jacopone de Todi) with soprano (1956–57).

583 i VOCAL CHAMBER MUSIC
          Add at end :
'Goethe-Lieder' (from Goethe's 'West-östlicher Divan') for mezzo-soprano & 3 clars. (1952–53).
'Cinque canti' (S. Quasimodo, from Greek poems) for baritone & 8 insts. (1956).

          PIANOFORTE MUSIC
          Add at end :
'Quaderno musicale di Annalibera' (1st version, 1952 ; 2nd version, 1953).

584 ii **DALLEY-SCARLETT**
          Par. 1, l. 2 *should read* :
chester, 16 Apr. 1890 ; *d.* Brisbane, 31 July 1959).

585 ii **DALMORÈS**
          l. 8. 'Salomé' *should read* :
'Sapho'

587 i *Add after* **DAMERINI** :

DAMETT, Thomas (*b.* ? ; *d.* ?, 1437).
English singer and composer. He entered Winchester College as a Commoner in the first years of the fifteenth century, and left the College in May 1407. From a dispensation dated 5 Mar. 1421/22 it is clear that Damett was the illegitimate son of a wealthy gentleman living in the southern counties. A previous dispensation from Rome had enabled Damett to take holy orders and to hold benefices. He was some time chaplain of the Chapel Royal in the reigns of Henry V and Henry VI. He became rector of the parish church of Stockton, Wiltshire, in 1413. Later he went to London and joined the brilliant group of composer-clerics then attached to the Chapel Royal, serving at Harfleur and taking part in royal journeys to the courts of France and Burgundy. It is worthy of note that two of his compositions make use of texts found among the sequences of Sarum Missals in Paris and Bologna. Both manuscripts were of English origin, were taken abroad (probably by members of the Chapel Royal) and used there by generations of English singers and composers. The texts in question, ' Salvatoris mater pia ' and ' Salve virgo sacra parens ', are not found in Sarum books written in and for England.

In 1418 Henry V presented Damett with the prebend of Rugmere in St. Paul's Cathedral, and a similar appointment followed in 1431, when the composer was granted a prebend in St. George's Chapel, Windsor. Damett's music is preserved mainly in the ' Old Hall Manuscript ', though there are two fragments in the Bodleian Library (University College 192) corresponding with the two ' Credo ' settings in the main source. Among the nine works extant there are examples of *conductus* style, ballade-Mass and isorhythmic motet, showing that Damett was conversant with the main trends of music in the first third of the 15th century, though he did not venture beyond the bounds of three-part texture as some of his more ambitious colleagues did.

Of four settings of ' Gloria in excelsis ' two are in *conductus* style (I, 22; III, [13]) and two are composed after the manner of the ballade-Mass or " free-treble " style (I, 132; I, 144). The settings in *conductus* style seek contrasts in metre, since the texture is invariable, but even in the first and perhaps most simple setting there is some use of mensural tricks, in this instance a passage in *subsesquitertia* proportion. Damett was evidently a learned man, who lost no opportunity of displaying his learning, which is fortunately of the kind that helps rather than hinders the music itself. Both of the ballade-Mass pieces are set for tenor and two instruments; a distinctive feature of I, 144 is the alternation between this combination and short duo sections for tenor and bass voices.

The two ' Credo ' settings are very similar in style, both being scored for alto, tenor and one instrument, which plays a *cantus-firmus*-like tune (apparently non-liturgical) throughout. There is a similar distinction to that already noted in the ' Gloria ' compositions in ballade-Mass style, for the second ' Credo ' also makes extensive use of duet sections. Both works (II, 93; II, 261) illustrate the words " tertia die " with triplet figuration in the uppermost voice.

Alternating duet and trio sections also characterize the antiphon for Vespers of the B.V.M., ' Beata Dei Genitrix ' (I, 164), whose " Alleluia " indicates use in Paschal time. This short but very beautiful piece is in *conductus* style and makes occasional but effective use of faburden. The work printed as ' Salve porta paradisi ' (I, 166) is actually the second stanza of the sequence beginning ' Salve virgo sacra parens '. The first stanza was presumably chanted in unison and followed by Damett's setting of stanza 2, which closes with the acclamation " Mater Christi " instead of continuing the sequence text.

A comparable case of branching off is found in the isorhythmic motet ' Salvatoris mater pia / Sancte Georgi / Benedictus Mariae Filius qui ve ' (III, 40), where the text of the upper voice again corresponds with that of the sequence, only to diverge after the third verse in order to bring in references to Henry V. The middle voice also mentions Henry, though it is largely concerned with the praise of St. George (as is the corresponding voice in Cooke's ' Alma proles regia '), and it may not be unreasonable to associate these motets with one and the same occasion. Another important association is that of Damett's tenor and the tenor of Sturgeon's ' Salve mater

Domini ', which completes the odd syllable thus: " [n]it in nomine Domini ". Both motets are therefore linked by one tenor, broken in the middle, which is based on Sanctus 3 of the Sarum Gradual. It may also be noted that among the items which Damett left to his mother in the will proved on 14 Apr. 1437 (P. C. C. Luffenham, f. 21) there is " a silver cup chased and covered with writing and ' Benedictus qui venit in nomine Domini '."   D. W. S.

BIBL.—BUKOFZER, MANFRED, ' Studies in Medieval and Renaissance Music ' (New York, 1950).
HARVEY, JOHN, ' Gothic England ' (London, 1947).
RAMSBOTHAM, ALEXANDER, ed., ' The Old Hall Manuscript ', Vols. I-III (London, 1933–38).

587   i   *Add before* **DAMMEN** :

D'AMICO, Fedele (*b.* Rome, 27 Dec. 1912).

Italian music critic. He was a pupil of Casella for pianoforte and composition. He has long occupied the columns of musical criticism in newspapers and reviews, displaying profound knowledge and a combative spirit especially in the domain of modern music. He is joint secretary of the Istituto Italiano per la Storia della Musica and directed the musical section of the ' Enciclopedia dello spettacolo ' from the beginning till 1957, a work edited by his father, Silvio d' Amico, a noted theatrical historian and critic, until his death. D' Amico has published monographs of Rossini (1939), Mussorgsky (1942) and Goffredo Petrassi (1942). He is also responsible for translations of opera librettos (Janáček, Henze, Menotti, etc.).   G. M. G.

ii   **DAMROSCH (1)**
Par. 1, l. 18.   1850–60 *should read* :
1858–60
Par. 2, l. 7.   1874 *should read* :
1873

590   i   **DANCLA**
Par. 1, l. 2.   1818 *should read* :
1817

592   i   *Add after* **DANKOWSKI** :

DANKS, Harry (*b.* Dudley, Worcestershire, 18 May 1912).

English violist. He attended a Church of England school and learnt the violin in his youth with little professional teaching, attaining such proficiency as to be able to join the City of Birmingham Orchestra. In 1930 its conductor, Leslie Heward, persuaded him to change over to the viola, an instrument h studied very thoroughly and for a long peric with Lional Tertis. In 1937 he joined th. B.B.C. Symphony Orchestra at the last viola desk, and after national service during the 1939–45 war he rejoined it in 1946, being offered the post of principal viola. His next step was to make an exhaustive study of the viol family, and he directed the London Consort of Viols, in which he played treble viol. More important still was his special devotion to the viola d' amore and his close study of its repertory. He has given radio recitals on this instrument on the Continent, broadcasting from Stockholm, Copenhagen, Bergen, Brussels and Hilversum. An article by him on the viola d' amore was published in ' Music & Letters ' (Jan. 1957), and he has also contributed to ' The Strad ' and to the American quarterly ' Symphony '. E. B.

594   i   **Dante Alighieri**
l. 2. *Add* :

Blacher (' Francesca da Rimini ', sop. & vn.).

l. 24 *should read* :
(' Francesca da R.', opera). Rossini (do., ' Recitativo rit-

595   ii   **DAQUIN**
Par. 3, l. 5. violins, *should read* :
violons,

Add to BIBL. :
DUFOURCQ, NORBERT, ' La Musique d'orgue française ' (Paris, 1949).

598   ii   **DARMSTADT HOLIDAY COURSES.** *See* ADDENDA, Vol. IX, p. 573 *should read* :

DARMSTADT HOLIDAY COURSES.
A series of musical events taking place annually in July at Darmstadt-Kranichstein and officially entitled Internationale Ferienkurse für neue Musik. They are organized, under the patronage of the Hessian Minister of Culture and with the support of the Hessian Ministry of the Interior, by the Kranichstein Musical Institute, with the collaboration of the Darmstadt State Theatre. The artistic director is Dr. Wolfgang Steinecke. The courses began in 1946. They have attracted an increasing number of international musicians and encouraged new composers of any nationality who have something new to say. The tendencies are progressive to the point of including electrophonic music and *musique concrète*, but the choice is by no means narrowly exclusive, as is shown by a list of 193 composers from some twenty-five different countries whose works were performed between 1946 and 1954. Living or recently dead composers receive nearly all the attention, since this is the special aim of the courses, but rare and interesting works of the past also find a place in the programmes : in 1953, for instance, Orazio Vecchi's ' Amfiparnaso ' was performed for the first time in Germany. Special courses in performance and interpretation are held for young students under the guidance of eminent musicians. E. B.

See also Concrete Music. Electrophonic Music.

602   i   **Davenant, William**
l. 6. masque). *should read* :
& ' Britannia Triumphans ', masques).

603   i   **DAVICO**
Add at end :
BIBL.—VALABREGA, CESARE, ' La musica da camera di Vincenzo Davico ' (Rome, 1953).

605   ii   **DAVID, Ferdinand**
Par. 1, l. 1. 19 June *should read* :
19 Jan.
l. 2. 19 July *should read* :
14 July

606   ii   **DAVID, J. N.**
Par. 3, ORCHESTRA. *Add after* l. 4 :
Symphony No. 5.
Symphony No. 6 (1956).
Symphony No. 7, Op. 49 (1957).

Add at end :
Vn. Concerto (1936).

Par. 4, CHORAL WORKS. *Add at end* :
' Requiem chorale.'
Cycle to words by great Europeans, Op. 34, incl. Motet ' Empfangen und genährt ' (Matthias Claudius). Motet ' Komm, Trost der Welt ' (Hans Jakob von Grimmelshausen).

609   ii   *Add before* **Davies, Aneurin** :

DAVIES, (Albert) Meredith (*b.* Birkenhead, 30 July 1922).
English organist and conductor. He was educated at the Stationers' Company School and afterwards studied at the R.C.M. in London, where he was a Junior Exhibitioner in 1930 and took the A.R.C.M. for pianoforte performance in 1938. He went to Keble College, Oxford, with an Organ Scholarship in 1940, taking the B.A., and the B.Mus. in 1946. The same year he took the F.R.C.O. (Read and Limpus Prizes) and in 1949 he obtained the Silver Medal of the Worshipful Company of Musicians.
Davies was appointed organist of St. Albans Cathedral in 1947 and of Hereford Cathedral in 1949. He twice conducted the Three Choirs Festivals, held in that town in 1952 and 1955, with unusual distinction, and unlike most organists, even those of the Festival towns, he made a special study of conducting, visiting the Accademia di S. Cecilia in Rome for that purpose in 1954 and 1956. There he obtained the Diploma del Corso di Perfezionamento di Direzione d' Orchestra.
In 1956 Davies left Hereford to become organist, in succession to H. K. Andrews, at New College, Oxford, of which he is a Fellow.
E. B.

614   i   **DAVIES, Tudor**
Par. 1, l. 2 *should read* :
Wales, 12 Nov. 1892 ; *d.* Penault, Monmouth, 2 Apr. 1958).

616   ii   **DAVY**
Par. 1, l. 1.   55 *should read*:
something over 50

List of Works
ll. 7 & 11.   Tenor *should read*
Countertenor

620   ii   **DEAN**
Par. 1, ll. 13-15 *should read*:
substantial book entitled ' Handel's Dramatic
Oratorios and Masques ' which was published
in 1959.

621   i   **DEAS**
Par. 1, l. 13 *should read*:
the Sheffield Chamber Orchestra (until 1955
Sheffield Bach Orchestra).

625   i   **DEBUSSY**
BIBL.   *Add after* l. 20:
' Lettres inéditées à André Caplet (1908–1914) ', ed.
by Edward Lockspeiser (Monaco, 1957).

ii   *Add*:
ESTRADE-GUERRA, O. D', ' Les Manuscrits de " Pelléas et
Mélisande " de Claude Debussy ' (Rev. Mus., No.
235, 1957).
' Le Martyre de Saint-Sébastien ' (Rev. Mus., No. 234,
1957).
GERVAIS, FRANÇOISE, ' La Notion d'arabesque chez
Debussy ', Rev. Mus. No. 241 (Paris, 1958).

KOECHLIN.   1927). *should read*:
1927 & 1956).

Add:
SEROFF, VICTOR I., ' Debussy : Musician of France '
(New York, 1956 ; London, 1957).
VALLERY-RADOT, P., ' Lettres de Claude Debussy à sa
femme Emma ' (Paris, 1957).

628   TWO PIANOFORTES, FOUR HANDS
l. 3.   A. Kussevitsky *should read*:
S. Kussevitsky.[5]

SONGS
ll. 10, 11 & 13.   Footnote figures *should
read*:
6, 7 & 8.

Add footnote :
[5] The initial appears wrongly as " A " in the dedication.

Footnote figures 5, 6 & 7 *should read*:
6, 7 & 8

632   i   **DEFAUW**
Par. 1, l. 2 *should read*:
1885; *d.* Gary, Indiana, 1960).

Par. 2, ll. 17-18 *should read*:
in 1940, going first to Canada and in

l. 21.   1949 *should read*:
1947.

633   ii   **DEGREES IN MUSIC**
Par. 6, ll. 2-3 *should read*:

at Cambridge, Mus.B. in 1463 (Henry
Habyngton) and Mus.D. in 1463 or earlier
(Thomas Saintwix), and at Oxford, B.Mus. in
1505 and D.Mus. in 1511.

634   ii   Par. 1, l. 17 *should read*:
(Oxford offered Haydn the degree on his first

635   i   Par. 2.   *Delete* ll. 21-29 *and insert*:
At Oxford academic residence is now a
necessary qualification for a degree in music.
Courses of musical study within the University
are required, and much fuller provision is
made for such courses than formerly.

Par. 3, l. 1 *should read*:
The regulations at present (1957) are as
follows :

ii   *Delete* Par. 1 *and insert*:
For the B.A. degree.—In 1952 a Final
Honour School of Music was instituted making
possible, for the first time, a B.A. degree with
music as the sole subject.
The following examinations must be passed :
(*a*) The Qualifying Examination (which may
be passed before commencing residence) consisting of harmony and counterpoint and a
viva voce examination. (*b*) The Preliminary
Examination, the subjects being : four-part
harmony and counterpoint, history of music
and formal analysis, acoustics, figured bass,
score-reading and keyboard harmony. (*c*)
The Final Honour School, the subjects being :
five-part harmony and counterpoint, fugue,
orchestration, history of music, prescribed
scores, a foreign language and a *viva voce*
examination including score-reading and
history of music.
Every B.A. in Music is entitled to proceed
to the M.A. degree 21 terms after matriculation.
For the B.Mus. degree.—Before 1952 a
candidate for the B.Mus. degree was required
to gain a B.A. degree before his B.Mus. could
be awarded. The work for these two degrees
was to a certain extent done concurrently, the
music examinations exempting from two
Groups of the Pass School, leaving only one
language Group to be passed in order to
qualify for the B.A. degree.
The B.Mus. degree is now open only to
B.A.'s who have gained a first or second class
in the Final Honour School of Music. Every
candidate must pass an examination in composition for voices or instruments, or both
together, and must also submit at the time
of entry for the examination a musical
" exercise " of his own unaided composition,
which must be *either* a work for chorus and
orchestra, small or large, *or* an orchestral

work in one or more movements *or* a chamber work for not less than four instruments in not less than three movements. No one may enter for the examination until three terms after passing the final honour school.

635   ii   Par. 2, l. 13 *should read*:

instruments; song cycle; (*f*) sonata for not less than two

l. 23 *should read*:

positions selected from prescribed lists.

Delete ll. 24-27 *and insert*:

For the Diploma in Music.—This diploma was instituted in 1946. A candidate must pass the Qualifying Examination and *either* be qualified for the B.A. degree *or* have passed two Groups of the Pass School which together with the diploma would qualify him for the B.A. The subjects are: ear tests, four-part harmony and counterpoint, musical form, outlines of musical history and *either* a practical test *or* an approved thesis *or* an examination on an approved period of foreign music.

ll. 28-32 *should read*:

Fees (excluding college fees: Qualifying Examination, £2; B.A. examinations and degree, £17 : 10s.; B.Mus. examinations and degree, £24; D.Mus. examinations and degree, £35; Diploma examination, £4.

636   i   *Delete* Pars. 3 (The present regulations are as follows:) *and* 4, *and insert*:

The Faculty Board of Music made a report to the University of Cambridge dated 25 Apr. 1945. The Board recommended the establishment of a Music Tripos and fresh Regulations for the Mus.B. degree. On 7 Oct. 1954 new regulations came into force entitled Music Tripos (awarded by Graces 4 of 8 Feb. 1952 and 3 of 23 Jan. 1954). These regulations are very complex and detailed, and cover 4½ pages of small print. A candidate can obtain the B.A. (Honours) by way of both parts of the Music Tripos or one part of the Music Tripos together with Honours in another Tripos. A B.A. may be admitted to the M.A. degree not less than six years from the end of his first term of residence, if two years have elapsed since he was admitted to the B.A. degree. By Grace 6 of 26 Nov. 1953 Regulation 6 for the Music Tripos was amended so as to read:

In both Parts the names of students who obtain honours shall be arranged in three classes, of which the second shall be in two divisions. The names of the first and third classes and in each division of the second class shall be arranged in alphabetical order.

New Regulations were issued at the same time for the Mus.M. degree (more than a page)

and also for the Mus.D. degree (2 pages). Copies of these Regulations should be obtained from the University Registry. A Bachelor in Music may be admitted to the degree of Master in Music at the end of three years after his admittance to the Mus.B. degree. Any person may be a candidate for the degree of Doctor in Music who is a graduate of the University and who *either* is of not less than eight years' standing from his first degree in the University *or* is of not less than two years' standing from admission to his first degree of the University if that degree is the degree of Master of Arts conferred on him under Statute B, III, 6; provided that he is of not less than eight years' standing from admission to his first degree of some other University. A fee of £21 for the Chest must be paid at each application made by a candidate. If the application is granted, this sum shall form part of the University fee for the degree: such applications shall be referred to the Degree Committee of the Faculty of Music. If referees are not appointed the fee of £21 shall be returned: if referees are appointed each referee shall receive 10 guineas for the Chest.

Supplementary Regulations.—Fees to be paid by candidates for examination and for degrees: Mus.B., £6 (for persons matriculated before the Easter Term 1915, £8), or £4 if the candidate has already taken the degree of Bachelor in any other Faculty; Mus.M., £8 (£12 for persons matriculated before Easter Term 1915); Mus.D., £25. For admission or readmission to each part of the Mus.M. examination, £3.

636   ii   *Delete* Par. 1 *and* Par. 2, ll. 1-9.

Par. 2, ll. 10-16 *should read*:

Academic residence is now required as a condition for the granting of a degree in music, and courses of musical study within the University are obligatory.

637   i   Par. 2, ll. 13-15 *should read*:

for Matriculation, £5, registration fee, £10; for the Mus.B. examinations and degree, £12 (£5 to a B.A.); for the Mus.D. examinations and degree, £40.

Par. 3, l. 3 *should read*:

ship dates from 1902.

Delete rest of Par. 3 *and* Pars. 4 *and* 5.

ii   *Delete* Pars. 1-3 *and insert*:

Candidates for the degree of Bachelor in Music are required to satisfy the minimum University and Faculty entrance requirements, and pass the Intermediate and Final Examinations. The Intermediate Examination comprises papers in history of music and form and analysis, in harmony and in counterpoint in not more than four parts, vocal and instrumental, and an oral test of general musical knowledge including elementary acoustics as affecting musical instruments. The Final Examination comprises: (a) papers in harmony and counterpoint, tests being given for voices, which may include the setting of words, in four or five parts, and for strings or organ in four or five parts in various styles; fugue, including canonic writing; orchestration; history of music (on a prescribed special period); two special subjects; (b) an oral examination including a critical analysis of two prescribed works and questions on instruments found in a normal symphony orchestra; (c) a practical test of ability to play on the piano from an orchestral score previously studied for twenty minutes, to transpose a chorus and supply correct harmonic support, and to play at sight a vocal score or single instrument of a string quartet.

Candidates for the degree of Doctor in Music are required to have obtained the B.Mus. degree at least two academic years previously. The D.Mus. degree examination comprises: (1) a written examination in harmony and composition, up to eight parts, vocal and instrumental; fugue in not more than five parts on a given subject, vocal or instrumental; counterpoint and canon; orchestration and history of music including critical knowledge in some detail of the great standard compositions; (2) an oral test with reference to knowledge of standard works; (3) an exercise, being either a work for chorus and full orchestra (with or without solo voices) or a symphony for full orchestra in the usual four movements.

The degree of Doctor of Philosophy (Ph.D.) is also offered in the Faculty of Music.

Fees: for Intermediate and B.Mus. examinations, £12 : 12s.; for D.Mus. examination, £21.

Degrees are conferred on both internal and external students.

637   ii   Par. 4, l. 2.   1831 ; *should read*: 1832 ;

Delete Pars. 5 and 6.

638   i-ii. *Delete whole page and substitute*:

The degrees of Bachelor and Doctor in Music are offered in the Faculty of Music, the Board of which is advisory to the Board of the Faculty of Arts for the degree of B.A. with Honours in Music.

Regulations for the B.Mus. degree.—(1) First Examination in harmony, counterpoint and history of music. (2) Second Examination in harmony and composition, counter-

point, fugue, canon, history of music and prescribed works. (3) An exercise, which must include composition for combined instruments, or for voices with orchestra, but may include a dissertation.

Regulations for the D.Mus. degree.—(1) An examination in composition, orchestration, counterpoint and canon and the history of music, together with a general paper and a *viva voce* examination. (2) An exercise which must include large-scale composition but may include a dissertation.

The degrees of B.A. with Honours in Music, M.A. and Ph.D. are not available to non-resident students. Residence is not required for the degrees of B.Mus. and D.Mus.

The fees are as follows:

For the B.Mus. degree.—Entrance examination or exemption from it, £2 ; admission as a Student in Music, £2 ; first Examination in Music or exemption from it, £3 ; second Examination in Music, £3 ; on submitting an Exercise, £3 ; admission to the degree, £5. For the D.Mus. degree.—Examination for D.Mus., £4 ; on submitting an Exercise, £5 ; admission to the degree, £15.

UNIVERSITY OF EDINBURGH.—The Reid Professorship of Music dates from 1839. Regulations for degrees in music were instituted in 1893 (Mus.Bac. and Mus.Doc.) ; these were revised in 1930 when the Mus.Bac. with Honours was introduced as an alternative to the ordinary degree. New regulations for all degrees in music were adopted in 1954, the short titles being then officially designated B.Mus. and D.Mus. respectively. No external degrees are granted.

Regulations for the ordinary B.Mus.—For admission to the course the Attestation Certificate of the Scottish Universities Entrance Board is required. There are three statutory examinations, the Qualifying Examination and the First and Second Degree Examinations. The full course is four years, but those who pass the Qualifying Examination before commencing study at the University are exempted from the first year. (1) The Qualifying Examination includes (a) diatonic four-part harmony; (b) general knowledge of music; (c) ear-tests; (d) playing at sight on the pianoforte; (e) keyboard harmony. (2) The First Degree Examination includes (a) four-part harmony; (b) three-part counterpoint; (c) outlines of history of music; (d) musical form; (e) acoustics; (f) keyboard harmony; (g) score-reading and transposition; (h) performance. (3) The Second Degree Examination includes (a) five-part harmony; (b) four-part counterpoint and fugue; (c) special periods of history of music ; (d) musical form ; (e) orchestration and knowledge of prescribed scores ; (f) score-reading and playing from figured bass ; and (g)

H

original composition (three small-scale compositions).

Regulations for B.Mus. with Honours.—Before admission to an honours course the candidate must have passed the Second Examination for the ordinary degree with merit in those subjects which are specially relevant to the honours course proposed. The course is normally one year. The subjects of the Final Examination for Honours in Composition are: five-part counterpoint (16th-century styles), four-part fugue, canon, five-part harmony, orchestration, critical analysis. The candidate must also submit an original composition, *either* for chorus and orchestra *or* an orchestral work *or* an ensemble chamber work in not less than three movements. The Final Examination for Honours in History of Music (for which foreign language qualifications are required) includes these subjects: general history of music, one special period, history of music in England and Scotland, history of European musical instruments and notation, and a prescribed book (French or German). In addition the candidate must submit a short thesis or research work in transcribing and editing (with commentary) an approved manuscript.

Regulations for the D.Mus. degree.—The degree may be conferred in three departments: candidates must be not less than twenty-five years of age. Bachelors in Music of other Universities recognized for the purpose by the University Court may be admitted as candidates for this degree upon certain conditions, which include the proviso that they shall engage in special study or research for not less than one academical year as matriculated students of the University of Edinburgh in the Faculty of Music. (1) Candidates as *Composers* must submit one or more extended compositions according to a prescribed classification, and will be examined in (a) counterpoint in six or more parts; (b) fugal-writing in five or more parts; (c) orchestration; (d) history of music. (2) Candidates as *Executants* must satisfy the examiners that they possess an extensive repertory and will be required to show technical skill and artistic judgment in the performance of solo and ensemble work in different styles, selected partly by the candidate and partly by the examiners. They will also be examined in sight-reading and playing from orchestral scores, in general history of music and in the history and music of their special instrument. (3) Candidates as *Theorists* or *Historians* must present one or more treatises on theoretical or historical subjects, the result of research and original thought. They will also be examined in history of music and in theory of music.

The research degree of Ph.D. may also be taken in the Faculty of Music. This normally requires a minimum of two years' full-time study under supervision on a subject previously approved by the Senate.

The fees for the B.Mus. (Ordinary and Honours) are £35 p.a. for each year of the course (no separate examination or graduation fee); for the D.Mus. examination, £20.

UNIVERSITY OF BIRMINGHAM.—Founded by Royal Charter in 1900. The first Professor of Music was Sir Edward Elgar, who held the Chair from 1905 to 1908, being succeeded by Sir Granville Bantock. The Department of Music (including the Music Library) is housed in the Barber Institute of Fine Arts, situated at Edgbaston. The University awards the degrees of Bachelor in Music (B.Mus.), Master in Music (M.Mus.) and Doctor in Music (D.Mus.); music may also be taken for the degrees of M.A. and Ph.D.

Regulations for the B.Mus. degree.—There is a special School of Music in which the degree of B.Mus. with Honours can be obtained. Candidates must have satisfied the requirements of the Joint Matriculation Board for entry upon a degree course, and have obtained a General Certificate of Education showing three subjects (of which Music should normally be one) passed at advanced level; they must also satisfy the Professor of Music that they have an adequate power of performance on some musical instrument and sufficient facility in harmony and counterpoint to satisfy the requirements of the course. The course for the degree of B.Mus. with Honours extends over three consecutive years and embraces the following subjects: (1) Music offered as the Honours subject; (2) English or a foreign language studied for two years. (Music may also be offered as a subject of study for the degree of B.A. in General subjects.)

Degree of M.Mus.—Bachelors in Music of Birmingham or another approved University may become candidates for the degree of M.Mus. either by (a) attending a course of study or research, approved by the Professor of Music, extending over a period of one session, (b) passing a written and oral examination or (c) either (i) presenting not fewer than three original compositions for different musical combinations or (ii) presenting a thesis or other literary work upon some musical subject.

Degree of D.Mus.—Bachelors in Music of Birmingham University may be admitted to Doctor in Music after five academic years from B.Mus.; Masters in Music of Birmingham University admitted after not less than three academic years from M.Mus.

The fees are as follows:

For the B.Mus. degree, inclusive annual fee (covering membership, lecture and class fees, and examination fees), £35 : 1s. p.a.;

for the M.Mus. degree, £15 basic fee for the whole course plus £10 annual charge, together with membership fee of £5 : 5s. each session and examination fee of £6 : 6s.; for the D.Mus. degree, examination fee £25.

639 i Par. 3, l. 11 *should read*:

year. The M.A. in music can be taken after this without taking the B.A. The Mus.M. requires, besides the ex-

Delete entry UNIVERSITY OF MAN-CHESTER *and substitute new article*:

UNIVERSITY OF MANCHESTER.—The first degrees in Music were conferred in 1894. The regulations for the degree of Mus.D. were revised in 1936 and those for the degree of Mus.B. (both Ordinary and Honours) in 1936 and 1956.

Mus.B.—All candidates for the degree of Mus.B. must have passed or have been exempted from the Matriculation Examination of the Northern Universities' Joint Board and must subsequently have attended for at least three academic years approved courses of study, certain of which are given in the Royal Manchester College of Music. Attendance includes such practical musical experience in the University and in the Royal Manchester College of Music as the Board of the Faculty may require.

The examination is divided into the Preliminary, the Part One and the Final Examinations. The Preliminary and the Part One Examinations both include harmony, counterpoint and the literary and historical background of music ; in addition the Preliminary also covers form, analysis and general musical history, and the Part One a prescribed period of musical history and the principles of instrumentation. Both examinations must be completed at least one academic year before the candidate can present himself for the Final Examination.

In the Final Examination, candidates must choose a special subject, which may be *either* (*a*) composition *or* (*b*) performance *or* (*c*) performance with conducting *or* (*d*) history and criticism ; examination is by means of a written paper (fugue, standard instrumental works or orchestral technique and repertory or history and criticism) and by the submission of vocal and instrumental compositions or a recital programme or a thesis on an approved subject. In addition all candidates take the following written papers : (i) vocal and instrumental writing up to five parts in a variety of styles ; (ii) orchestral arrangement ; (iii) an essay paper ; (iv) musical dictation, together with a *viva voce* examination including score-reading and questions on a group of prescribed works.

Candidates of appropriate standard may be admitted to the courses for the degree with Honours not later than the beginning of their third academic year. They must take the Final Honours Examination at the end of that year if *one* special subject is offered, but they may offer *two* special subjects and take the Final Examination a year later. A higher standard is required than that for the ordinary degree and certain additional tests are imposed.

All candidates for the degree must complete satisfactorily a course in acoustics and musical terms and must show proficiency in a foreign language (for Honours students a full course of Intermediate standard is required).

Mus.D.—Graduates in music of the University of at least four years' standing who have pursued in the University subsequent to graduation an approved course during at least one academic year, and graduates in music of other approved Universities of at least four years' standing who have pursued in the University during at least two academic years a similar course of study, may present themselves for the degree of Doctor of Music. They must satisfy the Board of the Faculty that they have achieved work of high musical distinction and scholarship in one of four branches : (*a*) composition, (*b*) performance, (*c*) performance with conducting, (*d*) history and criticism. Candidates in composition must submit original work and also pass an examination in the technique of composition (including eight-part counterpoint and orchestration) and in score-reading and knowledge of the works of the great masters, and in special historical aspects of music. Candidates in performance must perform selected items from two approved programmes, must take certain written or oral examinations and also pass an examination in score-reading, etc. and musical history. Candidates offering performance with conducting must satisfy the Board of ability and experience in directing rehearsals and performances of an approved high standard of choral and orchestral music and also pass an examination in score-reading, etc. and musical history. Candidates in musical history and criticism must submit a literary work or works and will be examined, as above, in score-reading, etc. and musical history and must present such further essay or undergo such further examination as the Board may prescribe.

Particulars regarding fees may be obtained on application to the Registrar, The University, Manchester 13.

639 ii Par. 8, l. 6 *should read*:

former, there was formerly a " Dublin Corporation Professor of

639   ii   Par. 9, l. 1 *should read*:

Regulations for the B.Mus. degree at Uni-

l. 3 *should read*:

tion, including four-

640   i   *Add after* Par. 1 :

The B.Mus. degree may be conferred either as a Pass Degree or as a Degree with Honours. The D.Mus. degree: before sitting for the examination the candidate must submit an exercise in original composition; this may be *either* a symphony for full orchestra *or* a concerto for solo instrument with orchestra *or* a work for voices and full orchestra.

Fees: for the B.Mus. degree, £8; for the D.Mus. degree, £11.

Par. 2, l. 1 *should read*:

Regulations for the B.Mus. degree at Uni-

Par. 3, l. 1 *should read*:

General regulations for the D.Mus. degree.

Par. 4, ll. 2-5 *should read*:

1893. There are Professors of Music at three of the constituent colleges (Aberystwyth, Bangor and Cardiff). Candidates must satisfy the University entrance requirements.

Par. 5 *should read*:

Regulations for the B.Mus. degree.—All candidates pursue courses for one year in Part I in theory of music, history of music and analysis, together with one of the following: Latin, English, Welsh, French, German, Italian, Physics. For a pass degree, candidates pursue courses for a further two years and are examined in theory of music, history of music and composition, and submit an exercise for strings or for voices or for both. For an honours degree, candidates pursue courses for a further two years after Part I, and are examined in theory and practice of music, and submit a composition for chamber music ensemble or for orchestra or for choir and orchestra.

Par. 6, l. 1 *should read*:

Regulations for the M.Mus. degree.—(1)

l. 5 *should read*:

and fugue. (2) A written examination in eight-part

ii   Par. 2, l. 1 *should read*:

Regulations for the D.Mus. degree.—Origi-

ll. 5-9 *should read*:

phony. Fees: for the B.Mus. degree, annual composite fee, £55; for the M.Mus. examination, £10; for the D.Mus. examination, £25.

640   ii   Par. 3, ll. 1-2 *should read*:

UNIVERSITY COLLEGE OF WALES (ABER-YSTWYTH). UNIVERSITY COLLEGE OF NORTH WALES (BANGOR). UNIVERSITY COLLEGE OF SOUTH WALES AND MONMOUTHSHIRE (CAR-DIFF).—The degree of Bachelor in Music B.Mus.) can

ll. 7-8 *should read*:

dates preparing for the degrees of M.Mus. and D.Mus.

Par. 4, l. 3.   Mus.B. *should read*:

B.Mus.

ll. 4-6 *should read*:

was instituted in 1931. The M.A. in music can be taken after this without taking the B.A. The degree

l. 7.   Mus.D. *should read*:

D.Mus.

ll. 8-12 *should read*:

candidates must be graduates of Sheffield and are required to submit either a composition exercise or a thesis and to pass an examination in history and prescribed works. In 1934 music became one of the

Par. 5, ll. 5-12 *should read*:

£20,000 for its foundation. The first Professor was W. G. Whittaker, who held office from 1930 to 1941. He was succeeded by Sir Ernest Bullock, who resigned in 1952. Both held the Principalship of the Royal Scottish Academy of Music in association with the Chair, but the posts were separated in 1953, when Robin Orr became Professor.

Par. 6, ll. 1 and 3.   Mus.B. *should read*:

B.Mus.

ll. 2 and 8.   Mus.D. *should read*:

D.Mus.

640-41   *Insert between pages*:

UNIVERSITY OF BRISTOL.—The Stanley Hugh Badock Chair of Music was created in 1946, and in 1951 the University approved the institution of degrees of Bachelor of Music (B.Mus.) and Doctor of Music (D.Mus.). Music may also be taken as a subject for the general degree of B.A., awarded as a pass degree or an honours degree.

The examinations for the B.A. (Music) degree are: First Part (at end of first year): 2-part counterpoint; 4-part harmony; a special period in musical history; knowledge of prescribed scores; musical dictation; playing at sight; transposition. Final Part (at end of third year): counterpoint and harmony in not more than 4 parts; double counterpoint; 2-part canon; knowledge of prescribed scores and of a special subject; reduction of a classical score; history of music and form; playing at sight from figured bass, vocal score, string quartet score. Membership of the University Choral Society and/or Orchestra is expected.

The examinations of the B.Mus. degree are: (1) an original composition: (a) string quartet or pianoforte quintet; (b) song cycle with strings, strings and pianoforte or orchestra; (c) overture for orchestra; (d) extended work for not less than 5 voices in polyphonic style; (e) extended work not covered by (a-d) as approved by the Professor of Music. (2) The following subjects, if (1) is approved: (i) counterpoint in not more than 5 parts; (ii) harmony in not more than 5 parts; (iii) fugue, including double counterpoint and canon; (iv) orchestration; (v) general musical history and special period (2 papers); (vi) sight-reading at keyboard of vocal and orchestral score and figured or unfigured bass; (vii) analysis of prescribed scores; (viii) one of the following: (a) essay on musical subject approved by the Professor; (b) instrumental or vocal performance of high standard; (c) lecture on subject approved by the Professor; (d) orchestral, choral or madrigal conducting. (ix) viva voce examination.

The D.Mus. degree may be conferred on persons who not less than five years previously have attained the University degree of B.Mus. or some other qualification approved by the Senate. The examinations are: (1) 2 or 3 original compositions chosen from (a) symphony; (b) concerto; (c) extended work for chorus and orchestra; (d) extended chamber work; (e) overture; (f) extended unaccompanied vocal work. (2) The following subjects, if (1) is approved: (i) vocal and instrumental counterpoint; (ii) harmony; (iii) vocal and instrumental fugue; (iv) form and structure; (v) orchestration; (vi) history of music; (vii) critical analysis of prescribed works; (viii) viva voce examinations.

Fees: particulars to be obtained from the Registrar, University of Bristol.

UNIVERSITY OF HULL.—Founded by Royal Charter on 6 Sept. 1955. The University confers in Music the degrees of B.Mus. and D.Mus., and the Ph.D. degree may be taken in music; but although it has power to award these degrees, detailed regulations have not yet (1958) been drafted. There is a lecturer in charge of the Department of Music. The academical robes for the Hull degrees of B.Mus. and D.Mus. are unsurpassed in beauty by those of any other musical degree in the world; those for Ph.D. (Music) are similar to the Hull Ph.D. in any other Faculty, distinguished by cream-coloured cord and button,

cords and tassels on the yoke of the gown and robe, and the round caps, respectively.

641   i   Par. 1, l. 16.   Mus.D. *should read*: D.Mus.

Par. 2, l. 22 *should read*:

is possible that sooner or later this

ii   Par. 1, l. 2 *should read*:

endorsed and enrolled. The title " Lambeth Degree ", although a convenience, is really a misnomer. All Lambeth degrees are actually Crown grants under the Great Seal of the Realm. The Archbishop's Instrument nominates the candidate to a certain degree, but contains a voiding clause stating that unless this instrument is duly confirmed by H.M. Royal Letters-Patent, it is null and void in effect. This implies that if for some reason or other the Archbishop's instrument were not so confirmed and enrolled in the Crown Office, the degree would not have been conferred. The Archbishop usually confers the degree in the library of Lambeth Palace and hoods the recipient.

645   ii   Par. 2, l. 4.   (Ch.M.) *should read*: (CHM)

l. 7 *should read*:

(A.D.C.M.).

(*delete* ll. 8-9)

646   ii   *Add after* **DEL MEL**:

DEL MONACO, Mario (b. Florence, 27 July 1915).

Italian tenor singer. He was the son of a city councillor of Pesaro, in which town he was brought up. He was educated at the local Conservatory, where he studied pianoforte, harmony, and the theory and history of music. His teachers were Luisa Melai-Palazzini and Arturo Melocchi. He also spent much time at the local art academy, where he studied sculpture and painting. When he was thirteen he sang (non-professionally) on the stage of the Teatro Beniamino Gigli at Mondaldo, where he appeared in Massenet's cantata for voice and orchestra, ' Narcisse '. When he was twenty he was invited by Tullio Serafin to enter a competition for a place in the studio attached to the Teatro dell' Opera, Rome. He gained the place from eighty competitors. He was never happy studying with voice-teachers and after six months decided to have no teacher but himself, relying on personal study and listening to gramophone records of the great singers of the past. His first appearance was as Turiddu at Pesaro in 1939, but what the tenor himself regards as his professional début was his appearance as

Pinkerton at the Teatro Puccini, Milan, on 1 Jan. 1941. During the 1943–44 season, when the Scala was performing at Como, Del Monaco sang Rodolfo in 'La Bohème'. But during most of the period 1938–44 he was in the army.

It was during the 1945–46 season that the foundations of Del Monaco's international career were laid: Radamès at the Verona Arena, Andrea Chénier at Trieste, Pinkerton in Milan and Cavaradossi, Canio, Pinkerton and Rodolfo at Covent Garden with the San Carlo Opera. Four full years of appearances in Italy, South America, Egypt, Spain, Portugal, Sweden and Switzerland followed. Then, in 1950, came his débuts in Buenos Aires and at San Francisco. He joined the Metropolitan Opera, New York, for the 1951–52 season and has been one of the most popular singers there ever since. He divides his time principally between America and Milan, but also appears as a guest artist in Vienna, Lisbon and Barcelona.

Mario del Monaco possesses a thrilling natural voice of enormous power and great dramatic intensity. His declamatory style is reminiscent of Pertile's, but as yet he has not displayed the musical feeling and style of that artist. His tendency to sing at all times at nothing below *mezzo-forte* has been adversely commented upon. Yet he can, when in the mood, give a moving and sensitive performance. In recent seasons (1957 and 1958) his interpretation of Otello has been especially praised for its sincerity and feeling, as well as for its sheer vocal splendour.   H. D. R.

647   i   **DELAGE**
             Par. 3, l. 6 *should read*:

mage à Manuel de Falla' and 'Danse'; 'Le Bateau ivre' (after Rimbaud) for orch.; a

Add after **DELAGE**:

DELALANDE, Michel-Richard.   *See*
LALANDE.[1]

             Add footnote:
[1] On this spelling *see* footnote, Vol. V, p. 24.

De la Mare
l. 6 *should read*:
Sleep', partsong). Finzi (song). Fricker (2 madrigals). Garland for

             l. 11 *should read*:
Labunski (F. R., cantata). Le Fleming ('A Quiet Company', song cycle). Milford (children's cantata). Thompson (R., song).

DELANEY
Par. 1, l. 2 *should read*:

Maryland, 24 July 1903; *d.* Santa Barbara, Cal., 21 Sept. 1956).

648   ii   **DE LARA, Adelina**
              Add at end:
BIBL.—DE LARA, ADELINA, 'Finale' (London, 1955).

DE LARA, Isidore
Par. 1, l. 2. Paris, 2 Aug. *should read*:
Paris, 2 Sept.

649   i   **DELÂTRE, J. P. C.**
             Add at end:
See also Collectio O.M.B., Vol. 1 modern ed.).

651   —   **DELIBES**
             CATALOGUE :
             BALLETS
             l. 1. (with Minkus). *should read*:
(with Minkus).[3]

        i   *Add footnote*:
[3] Also known as 'Naïla', the name of the principal character, described as "the spirit of the spring".

        ii   **DELIUS**
              Par. 2, l. 8 *should read*:
so profound that at the age of twenty-two he left

              l. 10 *should read*:
planter in Florida, where he arrived in Apr. 1884. In this remote seclusion he

658   i   **DELLA CASA**
             Par. 1, l. 2. Berne, 1919). *should read*:
Berne, 2 Feb. 1919)

             Par. 2, l. 2 *should read*:
Margarete Haeser, who was her only teacher. She made her stage début in the title-part of 'Madama Butterfly' at Solothurn and Bienne in 1941 and two years later joined the Zürich Municipal Theatre, where she remained until 1950. In the meantime she began a re-

             l. 17 *should read*:
bourne as the Countess in 'Figaro', and later that year she was heard at Munich as Sophie in 'Rosenkavalier' and her most famous part, Arabella in Strauss's opera. London heard her in this part in 1953 and New York in 1957. In 1952 she was made an Austrian *Kammersängerin*, and she is now a regular member of the Vienna State Opera.

             Signature should read:
                     K. V. F., adds. H. D. R.

DELLA CIAIA
Par. 1, l. 2. *For* Jan. *read*:
15 Jan.

659   i   **DELLE SEDIE**
Par. 1, l. 2.   1824 *should read* :
1822

660   ii   **DELLO JOIO**
Add at top of col. :
OPERA
' The Ruby ' (libretto by the composer on Lord Dunsany's ' A Night at the Inn '), prod. Indiana University, 13 May 1955.

661   ii   **DEL PUENTE**
Dates *should read* :
(*b.* Naples, 30 Jan. 1841 ; *d.* Philadelphia, 25 May 1900).

662   i   **DELVINCOURT**
Par. 1, l. 2 *should read* :
Jan. 1888 ; *d.* Bivio di Albinia, Obertello [Grosseto], 5 Apr.

Par. 3, l. 10 *should read* :
Opéra on 15 Dec. 1948.

Cancel the rest and replace by :
CATALOGUE OF WORKS
OPERAS
' Lucifer ', mystery (1940), prod. Paris, Opéra, 15 Dec. 1948.
' La Femme à barbe ', farce (1936), prod. Versailles, 2 June 1938 ; rev. version Paris, Opéra-Comique, 29 Oct. 1954.

BALLET
' Bal vénitien ' (*see* Chamber Music), stage version prod. Paris, Opéra-Comique, 1942.

INCIDENTAL MUSIC
' Oedipus Rex ' by Sophocles (1938).

FILM MUSIC
La Croisade jaune ' (1934).

CHORAL WORKS
' Hodie Christus natus ' for chorus, oboes, bassoons & organ (1909).
' Aurore ' for women's voices & pf. or orch. (1910).
Cantata ' Acis et Galathée ' (1910).
' Nuit tombante ' for chorus & pf. or orch. (1911).
Cantata ' Yanitza ' (1911).
Cantata ' Fulvia ' (1912).
' La Source ' for women's voices & pf. or orch. (1912).
Cantata ' Faust et Hélène ' (1913, Prix de Rome).
' Ave, verum corpus ' for solo voices, chorus, stg. 5tet & organ (1918).
3 Unaccompanied Choruses (1932)
  1. Capriol.
  2. Huîtres de prairie.
  3. Lavandière.
Symph. poem with chorus ' Automne ' (1937, Exhibition).
' Salut solennel ' for 4 solo voices, chorus & orch. (1948).

ORCHESTRAL WORKS
Symph. poem ' Typhaon ' (1914).
' Radio-Sérénade ' (1914).
Choreographic poem ' Offrande à Siva ' (1921).
' Boccaceries ', arr. from pf. pieces (1924).
' Onchets ' (1929).
' Bal vénitien ', orch. version (*see* Chamber Music) (1931).
' Poème chorégraphique ' (1931).

VOICE AND ORCHESTRA
' Thestylis ' (1908).
' Ce monde de rosée', 14 songs, orch. version (1934).

CHAMBER MUSIC
Quintet for stgs. & pf. (1907).
Trio for vn., cello & pf. (1909).
' Bal vénitien ', suite for vn., viola, cello, flute, bassoon & trumpet (1927).
String Quartet (1951–54).

VIOLIN AND PIANOFORTE
Duo (1908).
Sonata (1919).
' Danseries ' (1933–34).

PIANOFORTE MUSIC
' Boccaceries ' (1922).
5 Pieces (1923).
Suite (1924).
' Croquembouches ', 12 pieces (1926).
' Heures juvéniles ', 12 pieces (1928).
' Images pour les contes du temps passé', 4 hands (1934).

ORGAN MUSIC
' Marche d'église ' (1910).
2 Pieces (1913)
  1. Méditation.
  2. Sortie de fête.

SONGS
' Sommeil d'enfant ' (1912).
' Six Poèmes de Maurice d'Assier ' (1918).
' Ce monde de rosée', 14 songs (1925).
' Chansons de la ville et des champs ', 6 songs on 18th-century tunes (1934).
' Quatre Chansons de Clément Marot ' (1935).
' Pater Noster ' for baritone & organ (1948).
' Un éventail, un sourire ' (1948).

662   ii   **DEMANTIUS**
Add at end :
BIBL.—EGGEBRECHT, HANS HEINRICH, ' Ein Musiklexikon von Christoph Demantius ' (' Musikforschung,' Vol. X, 1957, 1, 48).
See also Chorwerk, Vols. 27, 36, 39 (modern reprints).
Denkmäler (5), II (modern ed.).

663   ii   **DEMUTH**
Par. 2, l. 29 *should read* :
of the Paris Conservatoire. In 1954 he was nominated Chevalier de la Légion d'Honneur. He is also a Membre Correspondant de l'Institut,

664   i   Par. 1, l. 27 *should read* :
two short motives.
Since 1952 Demuth has written a good deal of organ music at the suggestion of the B.B.C. The organ ' Symphony ' of 1957 is described as " Homage to C. M. Widor ", and all his organ works, while entirely individual, follow French rather than English aesthetics.   C. M. (iii).

CATALOGUE
Add to OPERAS :
' Rogue Scapin ' (lib. by Wilfrid Grantham) (1954).

CHORAL WORKS
l. 1. *Add* :
(1952).
l. 2. *Add* :
(1953).
Add at end :
Requiem for unaccomp. chorus (1954).

664   ii   *Add to* ORCHESTRAL WORKS:

Symphony for stgs. (1952).
'Ouverture à la française' (1952).
'Variations symphoniques' (1954).
'François Villon' (1956).
Symphony (1956–57).
Partita (1958).
Concert Overture (1958).

SOLO INSTRUMENTS AND
ORCHESTRA
Add at end:
'Mouvement symphonique' for ondes Martenot (1952).
'Ballade' for viola (1953).
Cello Concerto (1956).
'Sinfonietta' for orch. & pf. (1958).

CHAMBER MUSIC
Add at end:
'Lyric Trio' for flute, oboe & pf. (1953).
Suite for flute, oboe & harpsichord (1954).
Quartet for flute, vn. cello & pf. (1955).
'Le Souper du Roi' for wind, drums & harpsichord (1956).
'Divertissement' for flute, vn., cello & pf. (1957).
'Pastoral Fantasy' for vn., viola, cello & pf. (1957).
'Primavera' for flute, vn., cello & pf. (1958).

VIOLIN AND PIANOFORTE
Add at end:
'Sonate de printemps' (1955).

Add after TWO PIANOFORTES:
ORGAN
'Suite pour la Trinité' (1952).
'Livre d'orgue' (1953).
'Pastorale' (1956).
Symphony (1957).
'Cantiones Sacrae' Nos. 1–7 (1957–58).
2 Preludes and Fugues (1957).
3 Chorals (1957).
'Fanfare and Procession', with 3 trumpets (1958).

BOOKS ON MUSIC
l. 11 *should read*:
'A Course in Musical Composition', 4 parts (1950–58).

l. 12 *should read*:
'Musical Trends in the 20th Century' (London, 1952).

Add at end:
'Musical Forms and Textures' (1953).
'French Piano Music' (1958).

665   ii   DENKMÄLER
Add after Par. 1:

The Denkmäler series had been difficult to obtain in recent years, but reprints were announced in 1956–57.

666   i   (2) Denkmäler deutscher Tonkunst
List
X, l. 2.   D. A. Schmierer *should read*:
J. A. Schmierer

669   i   DENT
Par. 1, l. 2 *should read*:

Yorkshire, 16 July 1876; *d.* London, 22 Aug. 1957).

670   i   Par. 1, l. 34 *should read*:

Cambridge (1947). In 1953 he was one of the first two musicians to be elected a Fellow of the British Academy.

670   i   Bibl. l. 2 *should read*:

graphy' (M. Rev., VII, 1946, p. 242: rev. ed., Cambridge, 1956).

ii   DENTICE (2)
l. 8 *should read*:

for 5 voices.[1]

Add footnote:
[1] *See* Hist. MS Commission, Report on Pepys MSS, Challoner-Dudley Letters, p. 30.

DENZA
Par. 1, l. 1.   Castellamare *should read*:

Castellammare

672   i   DERING
Add to Bibl.:

Brennecke, Ernest, 'The "Country Cryes" of Richard Deering' (M.Q., XLII, 1956, p. 366).

674   i   Deschamps
l. 3 *should read*:

Niedermeyer (songs). Rossini (song ['Péchés de vieillesse']).

675   i   DESMOND
Par. 2, l. 28 *should read*:

well as in the U.S.A. She was created a C.B.E. in 1949.

676   i   DESSUS
Entry should read:

DESSUS (Fr., noun = top). The 17th-century French name for the ordinary violin of the period, with the highest string tuned to e″.

ii   DESTOUCHES
Par. 1, l. 2 *should read*:

Paris, [bapt. 6 Apr.] 1672; *d.* Paris, 3 Feb. 1749).

680   i   DEUTSCH
Par. 3, l. 6.   continues *should read*:

continued

Par. 4, l. 8 *should read*:

the editorship in 1950 and returned to Vienna in 1954.

Add at end:

Deutsch made a new German translation of Sullivan's 'Mikado', originally intended for a production by the Vienna State Opera in 1958.

Bibl.—'Österreichische Musikzeitschrift', special number, autumn 1958.

681   ii   **DEVIENNE**
           Par. 3, l. 7. Jemmapes *should
           read*:
Jemappes

682   i   *Add after* **DEVISENARIE** :
DEVREESE, Frederic (*b*. Amsterdam, 2
June 1929).
   Belgian composer. He was born in Holland
during his father's membership of the Concertgebouw Orchestra in Amsterdam. He later
studied under his father at the Mechlin Music
School and afterwards at the Conservatoire
Royal in Brussels. In 1949, at the early age
of twenty, he received a special award from
the city of Ostend for the composition of a
pianoforte Concerto, the success of which
earned him a scholarship for further study in
Amsterdam, with Pizzetti in Rome, and in
Vienna. Apart from the pianoforte Concerto
his works include a remarkable violin Concerto and the ballet ' Mascarade ', produced
at the Aix-en-Provence Festival of 1956 and
afterwards staged at the Théâtre Royal de la
Monnaie in Brussels.   A. L. C.

DEVREESE, Godefroid
Par. 1, l. 1. **Godefroid** *should
read*:
Godfried

Par. 2, l. 1 *should read*:
   Belgian violinist, violist, conductor and
composer, father of the preceding.

ll. 5-14 *should read*:
Orchestra at Ostend. In 1919-20 he was
conductor of the Royal French Theatre at
Antwerp, in 1920-21 of the Théâtre du Parc
in Brussels and in 1921-23 of the French
Opera at The Hague. In 1924 he declined
an offer to become second conductor at
Monaco, preferring to enter the Amsterdam
Concertgebouw Orchestra as leader of the
second violins. He was also the viola in the
Concertgebouw String Quartet. He remained
in Amsterdam until 1930, when he was
appointed director of the Mechlin Conservatory.

DEZÈDE
Par. 1, l. 2 *should read*:
(*b*. ?, *c.* 1745; *d*. Paris, 11 Sept. 1792).

ii   Par. 3, ll. 1-2 *should read*:
   Dèzede died in Paris in 1792 ; the ' Almanach des Spectacles ' published

683   i   *Add after* **DHOOGE** :
DI STEFANO, Giuseppe. *See* STEFANO.

DIABELLERIES. The title, suggesting
" devilries " and alluding to Beethoven's

" Diabelli " variations, given to a set of
variations for 11 instruments by a group of
English composers, on a light song by Alfred
Scott-Gatty, " Where's my little basket
gone ? ", chosen by Ralph Vaughan Williams ;
first performed in London by the Macnaghten
New Music Group on 16 May 1955. There is
a setting of the theme by Vaughan Williams
followed by 7 variations (Howard Ferguson,
Alan Bush, Alan Rawsthorne, Elisabeth
Lutyens, Elizabeth Maconchy, Gerald Finzi
and Grace Williams) and a finale by Gordon
Jacob.

683   i   **DIABELLI**
           Par. 3, l. 11 *should read*:
the publications of the extinct firms of
Matthias Artaria,

      ii   *Add after* **DIALOGUE** :
DIALOGUES DES CARMÉLITES. Opera
in 3 acts by Poulenc. Libretto based on
Georges Bernanos's film version of Gertrud
von Le Fort's novel ' Last on the Scaffold '.
Produced Milan, Teatro alla Scala, 26 Jan.
1957. 1st perf. in England, London, Covent
Garden Theatre, 16 Jan. 1958.

691   ii   **DICTIONARIES**
           Par. 4, l. 1. Janovska *should read*:
Janovka

693   i   Par. 2, l. 24. (1946) *should read*:
(1946, rev. 1954)

      ii   Par. 1, l. 2 *should read*:
mative work. ' Musikens Hvem, Hvad,
Hvor ' (3 vols., Copenhagen, 1950) is valuable.

Par. 2, ll. 1-2 *should read*:
Dutch.—The only general dictionaries of
substance are the ' Geillustreerd Muziek Lexi-
con ' by G. Keller & Philip Kruseman (1932 ;
Supp. 1949) and H. A. Viotta's very good
' Lexicon

Par. 3, l. 1. ' Musikiin *should read*:
' Musiikin

l. 5 *should read*:
musicians and institutions. ' Suomen Sävel-
täjiä ' (Helsingfors, 1945) is a biographical
dictionary listing 90 composers.

694   ii   Par. 2, l. 20. (1896, 1914) *should
           read*:
(1896, 1904)

695   i   Par. 1, l. 11 *should read*:
Turin, 1944). An excellent small work is
Cesare Valabrega's ' Il piccolo dizionario
musicale per tutti ' (Rome, 1949 ; 2nd ed.
1952).

696   i   *Russia*, l. 5. 'Volshaya *should read*: 'Bolshaya

697   ii   Par. 2, l. 19 *should read*: dei musicisti' was first published in 1887–89. A reprint began to appear in parts at

l. 20. in 1937 *should read*: in 1926

698   ii   Par. 2, ll. 1–5 *should read*: *Hungary.*—J. Hagh's 'Magyar zenészti lexicon. Encyklopediai kézikönyv' (Budapest, 1880) still holds the field; but there is a work dealing more adequately with modern Hungarian musicians: 'Zenei Lexikon', ed. by Bence Szabolcsi and Aladár Tóth (2 vols., Budapest, 1931; enlarged ed. 1935).

Par. 3, ll. 10–11 *should read*: 1500–1700' (2 vols., Berlin, 1892); the section 'Collections', revised by Alfred Ein-

Par. 4, l. 8 *should read*: (Paris, 1874). Chybiński's 'Słownik muzyków dawnej Polski' (Cracow, 1949) is important.

Poland.   Cancel entry and replace by:

Poland.—Information about composers and other musicians is included in many general dictionaries and encyclopedias. The musical dictionaries proper are here shown in chronological order:

Potocki, Ignacy, ' Mały słowniczek muzyczny' (Warsaw, 1818).
Sowiński, Albert, 'Les Musiciens polonais et slaves: dictionnaire biographique' (Paris, 1857).
'Słownik muzyków polskich dawnych i nowoczesnych' (Warsaw, 1874).
Surzyński, Józef, Abbé, 'Spis alfabetyczny muzyków polskich', a pamphlet (Poznań, 1889).
Roguski, Gustaw, 'Słowniczek znakomitych muzyków' (Warsaw, 1906).
Frączkiewicz, Aleksander, 'Spis kompozytorów polskich' (Cracow, 1948).
Chybiński, Adolf, 'Słownik muzyków dawnej Polski' ('A Dictionary of Musicians in Ancient Poland') (Cracow, 1948–49).
Reiss, Józef W., 'Podręczna Encyklopedia Muzyki' (2 vols.) (Letters A-K only) (Cracow, 1949).
Szulc, Zdzisław, 'Słownik lutników polskich' (Poznán, 1953).
Habela, J., 'Słowniczek muzyczny' (Cracow, 1956).
Schäffer, Bogusław, 'Almanach polskich kompozytorów współczesnych' (Cracow, 1956).

699   i   Par. 3, ll. 14–17 *should read*: The most comprehensive work, brought up to date periodically and now under the editorship of Nicolas Slonimsky, is Baker's 'Biographical Dictionary of Musicians' (1900, 1905, 1919, 1940, 1958). The American supplement to "Grove" (1920) is now sadly out of date. Canada is fairly well

704   i   **DIEREN,** CATALOGUE PIANOFORTE MUSIC
Op. 4a. should read:
6 Sketches.

706   i   **DIETRICH**
BIBL. l. 3 *should read*:
Reformation' (Leipzig, 1928), *see* DENKMÄLER (4), Vol. III.

Add at end:
See also Denkmäler (5) I, Vol. 23 (modern ed.).

DIETSCH
Add at end:
BIBL.—HARASZTI, E., 'Pierre-Louis Dietsch und seine Oper' (' Musikforschung', VIII, 1955, p. 39).

ii   **DIEUPART**
Footnote 5.   l. 4 should read:
seems to be known. There is, however, a unique copy in the Rowe Music Library, King's College, Cambridge, of 'Six Sonatas for a Flute [*i.e.* recorder] and a Through Bass compos'd by Mr Dieupart' (Walsh & Hare, London), which is almost certainly an English edition of the same work.

707   i   Par. 2, l. 15 & (new) Par. 3 *should read*:
England.
A complete modern edition of Dieupart's extant works, in 2 vols., 'Six Suites pour clavecin' and 'Airs et chansons', edited by Paul Brunold, appeared in Paris in 1934.
w. h. h., adds.

Add at end:
See also Lyrebird Press (modern ed.).

709   ii   *Add after* **DIONIGI**

DIPLACUSIS. The name of a phenomenon well known to psychologists and to some physiologists. It refers to the fact that the two ears of many human beings, if not all, hear a sound of a given frequency of vibrations as of two different frequencies, when received by each ear separately. The phenomenon, of course, does not affect musicians from a practical point of view, but the present writer has discovered what does not appear to have been observed before, that when two tuning-forks of identical frequency are sounded simultaneously, one before one ear and the second before the other, beats are generated. No explanation can be given for this, but it seems reasonable to conjecture that it is due to some unaccountable process in the brain.

P. R. K.

BIBL.—KIRBY, PERCIVAL R., ' Bilateral Variation between the Ears in Pitch Discrimination ' (' South African Medical Journal ', 1956).

709   ii   **DIRECT**
Par. 1, l. 1.   *tractulus should read* :
custos

710   i   **DIRGE**
l. 4 *should read* :
the opening words of the first antiphon of the

712   ii   **DISCANTUS SUPRA LIBRUM**
Add at end :
See also Descant.

Add before **DISTIN & SONS** :
DI STEFANO, Giuseppe. *See* STEFANO.

713   ii   **DITAL HARP**
Add after HARP-LUTE.
(*PLATE* 70, Vol. VIII, p. 146 [v], No. 5.)

715   i   **DITTERSDORF**
BIBL. l. 4 *should read* :
1896). Extracts in Paul Nettl's, ' Forgotten Musicians ' (New York, 1951).

Add to See also, l. 1 :
Denkmäler (3), Vol. 43 (modern ed. of instrumental works).

719   ii   *Add before* **DODD** :
DOCUMENTA MUSICOLOGICA. A series of facsimile reprints of important old music and theoretical works serving as source-material for musical scholarship, published by the Bärenreiter-Verlag of Cassel, represented by Novello & Co. in London. The series is published in two sections, containing printed and manuscript works respectively; the former has so far (1959) grown considerably larger. The contents are as follows :

I. PRINTED WORKS

i. Georg Rhau, ' Enchiridion utriusque Musicae practicae I '.
ii. Johann Joachim Quantz, ' Versuch einer Anweisung die flûte traversière zu spielen '.
iii. Johann Gottfried Walther, ' Musikalisches Lexikon '.
iv. Jacob Adlung, ' Anleitung zu der musikalischen Gelahrtheit '.
v. Johann Mattheson, ' Der vollkommene Capellmeister '.
vi. Loys Bourgeois, ' Le droict chemin de musique '.
vii. Paschal de L'Estocart, ' Cent-cinquante Pseaumes de David '.
viii. F. B. C. Majer, ' Museum musicum '.
ix. Adrien Petit Coclico, ' Compendium musices '.
x. Joachim Burmeister, ' Musica poetica '.
xi. Juan Bermudo, ' Declaración de instrumentos musicales '.
xii. Giovanni Battista Bovicelli, ' Regole passaggi di musica 1594 '.
xiii. Francisco Salinas, ' De musica '.

xiv. Michael Praetorius, ' Syntagma musicum ', Vol. II, ' De Organographia '.
xv. do. Vol. III, ' Termini musici '.

II. MANUSCRIPTS

i. The Buxheim Organ-Book.
ii. ' Codex Escorial '.

The following further volumes are planned for publication as need and opportunity may arise. Although it is unlikely that many, if any, of these will be ready before the present Supplement appears, reference to the titles (and cross-references under the entries concerned) will doubtless prove serviceable in the future.

1. Pietro Aaron, ' Toscanello de la musica '.
2. Pietro Aaron, ' Lucidario in musica '.
3. Lorenzo Allegri, ' Il primo libro delle musiche '.
4. Bénigne de Bacilly, ' Remarques curieuses sur l'art de bien chanter '.
5. Giovanni Bassani, ' Motetti, madrigali e canzoni francese '.
6. Angelo Berardi, ' Ragionamenti musicali '.
7. Angelo Berardi, ' Miscellana musicale '.
8. (Not announced.)
9. Ercole Bottrigari, ' Il melone '.
10. Ercole Bottrigari, ' Il patricio '.
11. Charles Burney, ' The Present State of Music in France and Italy '.
12. Hermann Finck, ' Practica musica '.
13. Franchinno Gafuri, ' Theoricum opus armonice discipline '.
14. Franchinno Gafuri, ' Practica musicae '.
15. Franchinno Gafuri, ' Angelicum ac divinum opus musicae '.
16. Lampadius, ' Compendium musices '.
17. Johann Mattheson, ' Das neu-eröffnete Orchester '.
18. Marin Mersenne, ' Harmonie universelle '.
19. Pablo Minguet, ' Reglas y advertencias '.
20. Friedrich Erhardt Niedt, ' Musicalische Handleitung '.
21. Friedrich Erhardt Niedt, ' Handleitung zur Variation '.
22. Friedrich Erhardt Niedt, ' Musikalischer Handleitung dritter und letzter Theil '.
23. Erhart Oeglin, ' Liederbuch '.
24. Andreas Ornitoparchus, ' Musicae Activae Micrologus '.
25. Pietro Pontio, ' Ragionamenti di musica '.
26. Michael Praetorius, ' Syntagma musicum ', Vol. I.
27. Schoefer-Apiarius, ' Fünff und sechzig teutscher Lieder '.
28. Claudius Sebastiani, ' Bellum musicale '.
29. Cipriano de Rore, ' Tutti madrigali '.
30. Daniel Gottlob Türk, ' Klavierschule '.
31. Stefano Vanneo, ' Recanetum de musica aurea '.
32. Nicolo Vicentino, ' L'antica musica ridotta alla moderna prattica '.
33. Sebastian Virdung, ' Musica getutscht '.
34. Lodovica Zacconi, ' Prattica di musica '.
35. Johannes Zangerus, ' Practicae musicae praecepta '.

E. B.

721   i   **Dodsley**
Add ll. 1-2 :
Monsigny (' Roi et le fermier ').

722   i   **DOHNÁNYI**
Par. 1, l. 2 *should read* :
Poszony [Pressburg], 27 July 1877; d. New York, 11 Feb. 1960).

    ii   Par. 1, l. 13 *should read* :
sity, Tallahassee.

723   i   **CATALOGUE** :
ORCHESTRAL WORKS
Op. 33*b*. *should read* :
32*b*.

723   i   SOLO INSTRUMENT AND OR-
             CHESTRA
             l. 3 *should read*:
— Vn. Concerto No. 1.

       Add after Op. 25. :
— Vn. Concerto No. 2.

       Add at end:
— Pf. Concerto No. 2, B mi.

             VIOLIN AND PIANOFORTE
             Op. 33*c. should read*:
32*c.*

       ii   PIANOFORTE MUSIC
             Op. 33*a. should read*:
32*a.*

       Add before **DOLBY** :

DOKTOR UND APOTHEKER (Dittersdorf). *See* DOCTOR UND APOTHEKER.

726   i   **DOLMETSCH**
             Par. 1, ll. 10-11 *should read*:
easily in fine adjustment.

             Par. 2, l. 10.   harmony.[2] *should
             read*:
harmony.[1]

             (*Delete Footnote* 1 *and change figure of* 2 *to* 1).

       ii   *Add to* BIBL. :
DOLMETSCH, MABEL, ' Personal Recollections of Arnold
  Dolmetsch' (London, 1958).

727   i   *Add before* **DOMINANT** :
DOMGRAF-FASSBÄNDER, Willi (*b.*
Aachen, 19 Feb. 1897).
   German baritone singer. He was educated
at the Cathedral School at Aachen, where his
family had sent him to study church music.
He was heard by Erich Orthmann, conductor
of the Aachen Opera, singing a solo part in a
concert of church music and was immediately
engaged for the local opera-house, where he
made his début in 1922. Engagements followed at the Deutsches Opernhaus, Berlin,
at Düsseldorf and at Stuttgart ; and in 1928
he was engaged as first lyric baritone at the
Berlin State Opera, where he remained until
the end of the war. He was first heard in
England at Glyndebourne on the opening
night of the first season in 1934, when he sang
Figaro. He appeared again at Glyndebourne
in 1935 and 1937 as Figaro, Guglielmo and
Papageno. After the war he made appearances in Hanover, Vienna, Munich and
Nuremberg, where he is now *Oberspielleiter*.
He has recently scored a great personal
success as Peer Gynt in Werner Egk's opera of
that name and in the title-part of ' Wozzeck '.
   Domgraf-Fassbänder possesses a warm and
pleasing natural baritone, which makes his
Mozart singing particularly appealing. His
mercurial personality and good looks were

an added attraction in a small theatre like
Glyndebourne.   H. D. R.

728   ii   **DON JUAN DE MAÑARA**
             l. 2 *should read*:
GOOSSENS. TOMASI (H.).

       DON PASQUALE
       ll. 2-3 *should read*:
Donizetti. Libretto by Giovanni Ruffini,
published as by " M.A.".[1]

       Add footnote :
   [1] Not by " Michele Accursi " (G. Ruffini), as previously stated from information in Loewenberg's ' Annals
of Opera ' and the B.M. Catalogue. Ruffini did not
use the name of " Michele Accursi " as a pseudonym, as
the inverted commas seem to suggest. Accursi was a
different person, Donizetti's agent in Paris, and when the
libretto was published as by " M.A." it was assumed to
be his. But the real author was Ruffini, as letters to his
mother show. He explained : " Non ho messo il nome
mio, si intende, perchè, fatto con quella fretta e in certo
qual modo essendo stata paralizzata la mia libertà
d' azione dal Maestro, a così dire non lo riconosco per
mio ". (*See* A. Lazzari, ' Giovanni Ruffini, Gaetano
Donizetti e il Don Pasquale ', in ' Rassegna Nazionale ',
Florence, 1 Oct. and 16 Oct. 1915.)   F. W. (ii).

       DONALDA
       Par. 1, l. 2.   1884 *should read*:
1882

729   i   Par. 2, l. 19 *should read*:
Comique, Paris. She founded the Opera
Guild at Montreal and in 1954 McGill University conferred an honorary doctorate on
her.

734   ii   **DONIZETTI**
             Add to BIBL. :
BOSSI, LEA, ' Donizetti ' (Brescia, 1956).
GEDDO, ANGELO, ' Donizetti: l' uomo, le musiche '
  (Bergamo, 1956).
WALKER, FRANK, ' The Librettist of " Don Pasquale " '
  (M.M.R., Nov.-Dec. 1958).

             BIBL. ll. 27-30 *should read*:
lario' (Bergamo, 1948). Supersedes all previous collections of Donizetti letters.

735   —   CATALOGUE OF OPERAS
             Col. 2, l. 19 *should read*:
Giuseppe Checcherini, based on a play of the same
name by Stefano Scatizzi.[1]

             Add footnote :
   [1] Discovered by Jeremy Commons : *see* his article,
' Emilia di Liverpool ', M. & L., XL, 1959, p. 207.

736   —   Col. 2, ll. 45-46 *should read*:
Giovanni Ruffini [1], based on

             Col. 3, l. 35 *should read*:
Comp. 1831 ; prod. Milan, Teatro alla Scala, 10

             Add footnote :
   [1] For correction of the original statement *see* DON
PASQUALE.

737   i   **DONOSTIA**
      Par. 1, l. 2 *should read*:
Sebastián, 10 Jan. 1886; *d.* Lecaroz, Navarre,
30 Aug. 1957).

738   i   **DONOVAN**
      Par. 2, l. 4. 1950 *should read*:
1928

      l. 6 *should read*:
at Yale University School of Music, and in
1947 he was appointed to a full professorship.
He is

      ll. 7 & 9. Newhaven *should read*:
New Haven

      ii **DONZELLI**
      Par. 2, l. 14 *should read*:
Italien, until the spring of 1831. But he was
in Italy intermittently during those years:
in a letter to Rossini of 7 Feb. 1826, for instance, he says he is going to Bologna immediately after his appearances at Venice.
His contract with the Théâtre-Italien [1] included an agreement that money should be
advanced to him to enable him to break his
contract with Barbaia, and an unpublished
letter from Rossini to that impresario [2] shows
that the composer, in 1827, was trying to heal
a breach between him and Donzelli caused by
this action.

      Add footnotes:
[1] Dated 4 Apr. 1826; offered for sale in an autograph dealer's catalogue.
[2] In the Biblioteca Comunale, Forlì.

741   i   **DORET**
      Par. 1, l. 1. 1927. *should read*:
prod. Paris, Nov. 1926.

      DÖRFEL *should read*:
DÖRFFEL

      Par. 3, l. 1. Dörfel *should read*:
Dörffel

742   ii **DORN**
      BIBL., l. 1. HAUCH *should read*:
RAUH

743   i   *Add after* **D'ORTIGUE**:
DÖRUMSGAARD, Arne (Oddvar) (*b.*
Fredrikstad, 7 Dec. 1921).
Norwegian composer. He studied composition with Karl Andersen at Oslo. Since
1949 he has been living in Paris. He has
written *c.* 100 songs and some pianoforte
pieces, but has become known chiefly for his
editions and arrangements of songs of the
Renaissance and Baroque periods, many of
which have been sung and recorded by
artists such as Kirsten Flagstad and Gérard

Souzay. Dörumsgaard is also an admirable
translator of Japanese and Chinese poetry.
                                        O. G.

745   i   **DOTZAUER**
      Par. 1, l. 2. ? *should read*:
Dresden

752   ii **DOUBLE TONGUEING**
      ll. 2-5 *should read*:
articulation applicable especially to the flute
as well as the cornet and some other brass
instruments. On the clarinet it is possible but
difficult, on the bassoon and particularly the
oboe it is even harder. Single tongueing
signifies the

753   i   Par. 1, ll. 5-8 *should read*:
stead of repeated action. It is the introduction
of the mouthpiece into the cavity of the mouth
which makes such an alternation so difficult
in the three instruments named above, but it
is much easier

      Par. 2, l. 3 *should read*:
two tongues instead of one.   w. h. s., rev.

756   i   **DOWLAND, John**
      Par. 2, l. 1. In 1606 *should read*:
In 1609

758   i   *Add to See also*, l. 4:
Musica Britannica, Vol. 6 (modern ed. of ayres).

      ii **DOWNES, Olin**
      Par. 1, l. 2 *should read*:
Ill., 27 Jan. 1886; *d.* New York, 22 Aug.
1955).

      Add at end:
BIBL.—' Olin Downes on Music: a Selection from his
      Writings during the Half-Century 1906–1955 ', ed.
      by Irene Downes (New York, 1957).

759   i   *Add before* **Doyer**:
DOYEN, Jean (*b.* Paris, 1907).
French pianist. He started his musical
studies at the age of five, first with his mother,
a singer at the Opéra, then at the Paris
Conservatoire in the class of Marguerite
Long, where he was awarded the first pianoforte prize in 1922. He made his début in
1924 at the Colonne concerts and became
soloist of several symphonic associations in
Paris. He also gave a number of recitals
annually both in France and abroad. In
1931 he made his London début at a concert
conducted by Gabriel Pierné. He broadcasts
regularly in France and is considered one of
the best exponents of modern French pianoforte music, particularly Fauré, Debussy and
Ravel. At the celebrations of the seventy-
ninth birthday of Vincent d'Indy the

composer chose Doyen as pianist for his 'Symphonie cévenole'. In 1937 he was awarded the Prix Gabriel Fauré and in 1938 the Grand Prix du Disque.   A. H. (ii).

761   i   **DRAGHI, G. B.**
Par. 4, l. 2 *should read*:
after 1690 are scanty, but there is reason to

ll. 4-5 *should read*:
(who returned to Portugal in 1692) shortly after 1700, but not before 1694, when, as "John Baptista Draghy", he was still recorded as organist in the queen dowager's chapel 1, and quite possibly not till after 1695, when a "Mr. Baptist", as he was often called, appeared in a list of teachers in a project for the establishment of "Royal Academies".2 Benefit concerts for "Baptist" — almost certainly him — were given in York Buildings in 1698 and 1701. In Feb. 1697 a birthday Ode, probably for Princess Anne, by "Signior Baptist", was given there.3

Add footnotes:
1 *See* E. Chamberlayne, 'The Present State of England', 18th ed. 1694.
2 *See* Michael Tilmouth's article 'The Royal Academies of 1695' (M. & L., XXXVIII, 1957, p. 326).
3 'London Gazette', 22 Feb. 1697.

ii   **DRAGONETTI**
Par. 3, l. 4 *should read*:
the great master in Vienna, where he also met Beethoven, with whom he played in 1799. In 1808 and 1809

ll. 9 -10 *should read*:
pianoforte. There he renewed acquaintance with Beethoven and also made that of Sechter, whom he

765   ii   **DRESDEN**
BIBL., l. 4. FURSTENAU *should read*:
FÜRSTENAU

Add to BIBL.:
ENGLÄNDER, RICHARD, 'Die Dresdner Instrumentalmusik in der Zeit der Wiener Klassik' (Uppsala & Wiesbaden, 1956).
HOFMANN, ERNA HEDWIG, 'Capella sanctae crucis: der Dresdner Kreuzchor in Geschichte und Gegenwart' (Berlin, 1956).

DRESDEN, Sem
Par. 1, l. 2 *should read*:
1881 ; d. The Hague, 30 July 1957).

766   i   Par. 2, l. 16 *should read*:
the libretto. A posthumous opera, 'François Villon', orchestrated from a vocal score by Jan Mul, was produced at the Holland Festival in the Municipal Theatre of Amsterdam on 15 July 1958.   H. A., adds.

767   i   **DRESSLER**
Par. 2, l. 10 *should read*:
were republished by Eitner in 'Publikationen der Gesellschaft für Musikforschung', Vol. XXVIII.

See also Beethoven (vars. for pf.) *should read*:
See also Chorwerk, Vol. 28 (modern reprint of motets).

Add after **DREULETTE**:
DREW, David (*b*. London, 19 Sept. 1930). English musicologist. He was educated at Harrow and Peterhouse, Cambridge (1950–1953), where he took a mixed degree in History and English Literature. He studied the pianoforte, the oboe and composition while still at school, but is otherwise largely self-taught in music. In 1955–56 he lectured at Dartington Summer School of Music, where he also held a class in film music with Roman Vlad, and in 1956–57 he was lecturer for the Extra-Mural Department of Birmingham University.
Drew made his mark very early as a penetrating critic of modern music. His most important articles, all published in 'The Score', are:
'Messiaen: a Provisional Study.' (Dec. 1954, Sept. & Dec. 1955).
'Leonard Bernstein: "Wonderful Town"' (June 1955).
'Roberto Gerhard: the Musical Character' (Sept. 1956; with a catalogue).
'Stravinsky's Revisions' (June 1957).
His other publications include: 'American Chamber Music' (Pelican Book 'Chamber Music', ed. by Alec Robertson) and the very extended and important study of 'Modern French Music' (in 'European Music in the 20th Century', ed. by Howard Hartog). A book of his own on the life and work of Kurt Weill, which is also, by implication, a cultural history of Germany between the two world wars, is (1958) in preparation.   E. B.

ii   **DREYER, J. M.**
l. 1. Dates *should read*:
(*b*. Röttingen, 24 June 1746; *d*. Ellwangen, 22 Mar. 1824).

769   ii   **DROZDOWSKI**
Par. 1, l. 2. Cracow, 1857; *should read*:
Cracow, 2 Feb. 1857;

772   ii   **DRUM**
Add after Par. 2:
Among the curiosities composed for kettledrums is a 'Concertstück' by Julius Tausch for six timpani (tuned F, B♭, c, d, e♭ and f)

and orchestra, written about 1878, consisting of a March and Polonaise, and containing a cadenza. An outstanding later composer remarkable for his subtle treatment of the kettledrums is Sibelius (*see* Bibl. article by Ralph Wood). A recent work for three kettledrums alone is a Sonata in four movements by Daniel Jones.

776   *Add at end, before* BIBL. :

(*PLATES* 33, Vol. IV, p. 496, No. 6 ; 35, Vol. IV, p. 504, No. 1 ; 49, Vol. VI, p. 622.)

Add to BIBL. :

SHIVAS, ANDREW A., ' The Art of Timpanist and Drummer ', ' Student's Music Library ' (London, 1927).
WOOD, RALPH W., ' Sibelius's Use of Percussion ' (M. & L., XXIII, 1942, p. 10).

782   ii   **Dryden**
              Add to l. 7 :
Draghi (G. B., Cecilia Ode).

784   i   **Dsida**
              l. 1. **Jenö** *should read* :
Jenó

791   ii   **DU CAURROY**
              Add to See also :
Maîtres Musiciens, Vol. 17 (modern ed. of ' Mélanges ').

792   ii   **DUET**
              Par. 3, ll. 3-4 *should read* :
Carlton and Thomas Tomkins for two players at one virginal.¹ The earliest printed works of which

795   i   **DUFAY**
              See also. l. 1 *should read* :
See also Amer. Inst. Musicol., C.M.M., 1 (modern ed. of complete works). Chanson (mus. ex.). Chorwerk, Vol. 49 (modern reprint of hymns). Faburden (mus. ex.).

       ii   *Add before* **DUFRESNE** :

DUFOURCQ, Norbert (*b*. Saint-Jean de Braye, Loiret, 21 Sept. 1904).
French organist and musicologist. His father, Albert Dufourcq, was hon. Professor of Medieval History at Bordeaux, where his son was educated at the Lycée. Later he studied at the Collège Stanislas, the Lycée Henri IV and the Sorbonne in Paris. He worked for the degrees of Bachelier ès Lettres-Philosophie in 1920–21 and Licencié ès Lettres (history and geography) in 1922–24. His musical studies were pursued under Amédée Gastoué from 1913 to 1920 and afterwards under André Marchal and Marie Rose Hublé. In 1923 he was appointed organist of the Church of Saint-Merry in Paris, in 1927 he became one of the founders and Secretary of the Association des Amis de l'Orgue and in 1928 Secretary of the Larousse Dictionaries (History, Fine Arts and Music

sections). He took the degree of Docteur ès Lettres in 1935 with the first work mentioned below. In addition to other distinguished educational posts he has held that of Professor of Musical History at the Paris Conservatoire. He is a council member of the Société Française de Musicologie and a member of its publications board, as well as a member of the Commission des Monuments Historiques (for the organs in France).

Dufourcq is a frequent and learned contributor to various musical periodicals, and among his numerous published works the following are outstanding :
' Esquisse d'une histoire de l'orgue en France du XIIIᵉ à la fin du XVIIIᵉ siècle ' (Paris, 1935).
' Documents inédits relatifs à l'orgue français ', 2 vols. (Paris, 1934–35).
' Trois Siècles de musique d'orgue ' (Paris, 1936).
' Les Grandes Formes de la musique d'orgue ' (Paris, 1937).
' La Musique d'orgue française de Jehan Titelouze à Jehan Alain ' (Paris, 1941 ; 2nd ed. 1949).
' Les Cliquot : facteurs d'orgue du roy ' (Paris, 1942).
' Le Grand-Orgue et les organistes de Saint-Merry de Paris : pour un tricentenaire, 1647–1947 ' (Paris, 1947).
' Jean-Sébastien Bach : génie latin, génie allemand ? ' (Paris, 1947 ; 2nd ed. 1949).
' L'Orgue ' (Collection ' Que sais-je ? ') (Paris, 1948).
' Jean-Sébastien Bach : le maître de l'orgue ' (Paris, 1948).
' Le Clavecin ' (Collection ' Que sais-je ? ') (Paris, 1949).
' La Musique française ' (Paris, 1949).
' Nicolas Lebègue : étude biographique ' (Paris, 1954).

In 1957 appeared under his direction an important work on Lalande (Delalande) by four pupils of the late André Tessier and based on papers left by him : ' Notes et références pour servir à une histoire de Michel-Richard Delalande . . . précédées de documents inédits et suivies du catalogue thématique. . . .'
Dufourcq is also the editor of ' La Musique des origines à nos jours ' (Paris, 3rd ed., 1950), of the quarterly ' L'Orgue ' and of several collections.   E. B.

800   i   **DULCIMER**
              Add at end, before See also :
(*PLATE* 69, Vol. VIII, p. 146 [iv], p. 6.)

              DULCKEN
              Par. 1, l. 2. 20 Mar. *should read* :
29 Mar.

801   i   **DULICHIUS**
              Add at end :
See also Denkmäler (2), Vols. 31 & 41 (modern ed. of ' Centuriae ').

       ii   **Dumas, jun.**
              l. 4 *should read* :
opera). Sauguet (' Dame aux camélias ', ballet). Traviata (Verdi, opera). Verdi (do.). Vlad

              Dumas, A., sen.
              Add to l. 1 :
Berlioz (song).

802 i DUMKA

Cancel article and replace by:

DUMKA (plur. **Dumki** or **Dumky**). A word occurring in all Slavonic languages in different forms, derived from the verbs *dumać*, *dumat'* or *dumaty*, describing a sullen or meditative mood. It assumed a special significance in Ukrainian (Ruthenian) folklore, where it connoted meditations on heroic deeds of the past, describing events remembered by the peasantry. The word *dumki* or *dumky* (*i.e.* little *dumas*) was already in use in the 17th century, either as the title of songs, mainly of folk origin, or of poems, or even of collections of short meditations in verse.

It was probably K. Kurpiński who first introduced it to the musical vocabulary by publishing the 'Dumka włościan Jabłonny' ('Dumka of the Jabłonna Peasants') set to words by J. D. Minasowicz, in the Warsaw 'Musical Weekly' in 1821. When in 1849 Moniuszko wrote a song entitled 'Kozak' ('Cossack') he added the subtitle of *dumka*, and this has remained one of the most popular pieces of the kind in Poland. It was published at Wilno in 1850, in Warsaw in 1852, in Paris (in French as 'Cosaque') in 1862, in Berlin (in Polish, German and French) in 1865 and in St. Petersburg (in Russian) in 1870. Later it reappeared in hundreds of different editions and arrangements for duet, men's quartet, partsongs, etc. Moniuszko also wrote, before 1852, a 'Dumka' ('Nie śpię nie jem'='I neither sleep nor eat') and another ('Przychodź miły'='Do come, beloved'), published at Wilno in 1852 and 1858 respectively, as well as other songs of the same kind, though not so entitled. In 1877 Albert Sowiński published in Warsaw a collection entitled 'Starodawne dumy i śpiewy' ('Ancient Dumas and Songs').

Dvořák's 'Dumka' for pianoforte (translated 'Elegy' instead of 'Meditation' or 'Rêverie') was composed in 1876 and his 'Dumky' Trio (Op. 90) in 1891; it is thus impossible to maintain the assertion that it was he who introduced the species to music or the word to musical terminology.   C. R. H.

DUMP

ll. 1-4 should read:

DUMP. A piece of music generally thought, probably by association with the word in the sense of a fit of melancholy, to be expressive of sadness: but Shakespeare ('Romeo', IV, iv) has "doleful and merry dumps". The name occurs mostly with sets of variations, the earliest known example being 'My Lady Carey's Dompe' of the early 16th century (B.M., MS Royal, App. 58). In 17th- and 18th-century books of instrumental music it is also occasionally met

802 ii *Signature should read*:

F. K., rev. G. R. (iii).

Add at end:

BIBL.—WARD, J. M., 'Dolfull Dumps' (Journ. Amer. Musicol. Soc., Vol. IV, 1951, p. 111).

DUNAYEVSKY

Par. 1, l. 2 should read:

Poltava, 30 Jan. 1900; *d.* Moscow, 25 July 1955).

807 i DUNIECKI

Cancel Par. 2 (list of works) and replace by:

'Korylla' (lib. by P. Duniecki), prod. Leopol, 18 May 1859.
'Paziowie królowej Marysieńki' ('The Pages of Queen Mary') (lib. by P. Duniecki), prod. Leopol, 16 Dec. 1864.
'Pokusa' ('Temptation') (own lib.), prod. Cracow, 24 Apr. 1866.
'Doctor Pandolfo' (own lib.) (1866).
'Odaliski' ('The Odalisques') (lib. by P. Duniecki), prod. Cracow, 9 June 1866.
'Zemsta Stasi' ('Stasia's Revenge') (1867).
'Loczki panny Proci' ('Miss Procia's Locks') (1867).
'Igor' (1867-70), unfinished.

ii DUNKLEY

Par. 1, l. 2 should read:

don, 16 July 1869; *d.* Waldwick, New Jersey, 5 Jan. 1956).

808 i *l. 6 should read*:

music and songs. He claimed to be the discoverer of the "pitch-controlled voice".

DUNN, Geoffrey

Par. 2, l. 5 should read:

1928, Associate in 1932 and Fellow in 1942. During his

ii *Par. 2, l. 15 should read*:

professor. He is responsible for numerous admirable translations of foreign operas broadcast by the B.B.C.

Dunsany
Add after See:

Dello Joio ('Ruby', opera).

809 i DUNSTABLE

Add after Par. 2 (2nd stanza of poem):

The examination of a great quantity of early documents in the Public Record Office and elsewhere has convinced John Harvey (*see* BIBL.) that Dunstable came of a distinguished family of skinners and landowners, who lived in the Walbrook district of London, where the composer was buried.

According to Richard Greene (*see* BIBL.), who gives detailed evidence,

John Dunstable, "clerk", became a canon of Hereford Cathedral and prebendary of Putson Minor on

April 28, 1419, and . . . resigned both the canonry and the prebend before (and presumably not long before) May 28, 1440. . . . He was therefore in receipt of an income from the diocese of Hereford during two decades which must have included many of his productive years. . . . his status as canon and prebendary of Hereford need not have interfered with the foreign travel implied by his being in service of the Duke of Bedford and by the predominantly continental sources of his extant works. By no means all the canons of Hereford were required to be in residence. . . .

809   i   Par. 3, ll. 2-5 *should read*:

the height of his foreign renown in 1437, when Le Franc's verses were written; but Wooldridge's guess of " *c.* 1390 " [3] for the date of his birth is hardly justifiable in the light of Greene's information quoted above. Jules Combarieu [4] gives 1370, but

810   ii   *Add to* BIBL.:

GREENE, RICHARD L., 'John Dunstable: a Quincentenary Supplement' (M.Q., XL, July 1954, p. 360).
HARVEY, JOHN, 'Gothic England' (London, 1947).
TROWELL, BRIAN, 'Some English Contemporaries of Dunstable' (Proc. Roy. Mus. Ass., Vol. LXXXI, 1954-55).

Add to See also, l. 1:

Musica Britannica, Vol. 8 (modern ed. of works).

811   i   **DUPARC, Elisabeth**
             Par. 2, l. 2.   Francesina ". *should read*:

Francescina ".

Par. 3, l. 4 *should read*:

which the *Francesina* [sic] performed several dances to the

Par. 4, l. 23 *should read*:

throat of the Francesina [sic] ". In 1744 and 1745

812   i   **DU PLESSIS**
             Transfer article to p. 802, *place after*
             DU MONT.

Par. 2, l. 11 *should read*:

composition at the R.A.M. in London. He returned to South Africa in 1954 to become lecturer in music at the University of Cape Town, later at the University of Stellenbosch.

ii   Par. 3. *Add after* l. 3:
Symphony, Op. 14 (1953–54).

Add after l. 4:
String Quartet, Op. 13 (1950–53).
Trio for vn., cello & pf., Op. 20 (1958).

Add after l. 6:
Sonata for pf. duet, Op. 10 (1953).
3 pf. Duets, Op. 16 (1955).
7 Preludes for pf., Op. 18 (1956).
' Fantasy on an 11th-Century Organum ' for 2 pfs., Op. 19 (1956).

I

812   ii   *Add after* l. 8:
' Five Invocations ' for tenor & pf. (poems by Webster and Fletcher), Op. 12 (1953).
' Three Sonnets from the Portuguese ' for mezzo-soprano & pf. (E. B. Browning), Op. 15 (1954).

814   ii   **DUPRÉ**
             Par. 6, l. 7 *should read*:

Fontainebleau. In 1954 he succeeded Delvincourt as director of the Paris Conservatoire.

815   ii   ORGAN MUSIC
             Op. 29 *should read*:
29. ' Le Chemin de la Croix ' (after Claudel).

Add after Op. 47:
48. ' Six Antiennes pour le temps de Noël.'

816   ii   **DUPUIS, Albert**
             Par. 2, ll. 6-7 *should read*:

Cantorum in Paris and took the second Belgian Prix de Rome in 1899 with ' Les Cloches nu-

819   ii   **DURANTE**
             Par. 2, l. 7 *should read*:

between those dates, except that he was admitted to membership of the Congregazione e Accademia di Santa Cecilia in Rome in 1718 and must have been living there at the time. There are persistent

820   ii   Par. 4, l. 4.   Bologna *should read*:
Venice

821   i   Par. 1, l. 4.   Marchesi's *should read*:
Marchese's

Add at end:

BIBL.—AUERBACH, JOHANNA MARIA, ' Die Messen des Francesco Durante . . .: ein Beitrag zur Geschichte der neapolitanischen Kirchenmusik ' (Munich, 1954).
See also Classici Musica Italiana, Vol. 11 (modern ed.). Fitzwilliam Music (do.).

ii   **DURCHKOMPONIERT**
      l. 5 *should read*:

rendered by " continuously set " or " on-running ".[1] It designates

Add footnote:
[1] Maurice J. E. Brown uses this term in his book on Schubert (1958). It deserves to gain general currency.

823   i   **DURÓN**
             Par. 3, l. 17 *should read*:

mens of his work are printed by Eslava (' O vos omnes '), Pedrell

824   ii   **DUŠEK, F. X.**
             Add at end:
See also Musica Antiqua Bohemica, Vol. 8 (modern ed. of 8 pf. sonatas).

824   ii   **DUŠEK, Josepha**
Par. 1, l. 2.   1754 *should read*:

1753

825   i   ll. 16-17 *should read*:

year, but was to be dedicated to Countess Josephine Clary, though it was published without dedication. Fétis's statement that Josepha Dušek

828   i   **DUSSEK**
PIANOFORTE CONCERTOS
Op. 20. *Delete* (MS in Brussels Conservatoire)

829   i   *Add at end, before See also*:

BIBL.—BLOM, ERIC, 'The Prophecies of Dussek' in 'Classics: Major and Minor' (London, 1958).
TRUSCOTT, HAROLD, 'Dussek and the Concerto' (M. Rev., XVI, 1955, p. 27).

Add to See also, l. 3:
Musica Antiqua Bohemica, Vol. 21 (modern ed. of 'Leçons progressives', Op. 16).

DUSTMANN
Par. 1, l. 2 *should read*:

Meyer) (*b.* Aachen, 22 Aug. 1831 ; *d.* Berlin, 2 Mar. 1899).

ii   **DUTILLEUX**
Par. 1, l. 1 *should read*:

Sonata (1948), the ballets 'La Belle Époque' and 'Salmacis', the former

l. 5 *should read*:

Brontë), a 'Symphonie de danses' for orchestra, chamber music and songs.

838   ii   **DVOŘÁK**
Par. 3, l. 17 *should read*:

generation of Czech musicians.
A collected edition of Dvořák's works was begun in Prague in 1954.   O. Š.

839   i   *Add to* BIBL.:
BOESE, HELMUT, 'Zwei Urmusikanten: Smetana, Dvořák' (Zürich, 1955).

—	7 Interludes for small orch.	For dramatic performances at the Czech Provisional Theatre.

CLAPHAM, JOHN, 'Dvořák and the Impact of America' (M. Rev., XV, 1954, p. 203).
'Dvořák and the Philharmonic Society' (M. & L., XXXIX, 1958, p. 123).
'Dvořák's First Cello Concerto' (M. & L., XXXVII, 1956, p. 350).
'The Evolution of Dvořák's Symphony "From the New World"' (M.Q., XLIV, Apr. 1958, p. 167).

ii   *Add to* BIBL.:
HOŘEJŠ, ANTONÍN, 'Antonín Dvořák: the Composer's Life in Pictures' (Prague, 1955).
KVĚT, J. M., 'Mládí Antonína Dvořáka' (Prague, 1943).

NEWMARCH, ROSA, 'The Letters of Dvořák to Hans Richter' (Mus. T., LXXIII, July-Sept. 1932).

839   ii   BIBL., l. 9. ŠIRP *should read*:

SIRP

ll. 10 & 12. Antonin *should read*:
Antonín

Add after l. 14 (3rd work by Šourek):
'Antonín Dvořák: his Life and Works', in English (Prague, 1952).
'The Chamber Music of Antonín Dvořák' (Prague, 1956).
'The Orchestral Works of Antonín Dvořák' (Prague, 1956).

l. 15 *should read*:
to his Friends, in Czech) (Prague, 1941) ; Eng. trans., 'Antonín Dvořák: Letters and Reminiscences' (London, 1954).

CATALOGUE
OPERAS
Col. 2, ll. 4-5 *should read*:
'Tvrdé palice' ('The Stubborn Lovers' [2]).

Add footnote:
[2] The English title given in the new Collected Edition of Dvořák's works.

l. 1. Olomouc, Czech The- *should read*:
Olomouc, Municipal The-

l. 3. *Op.* 14 *should read*:
$\begin{cases} 2 \\ 14 \end{cases}$

ll. 3 & 4. Year of Composition *should read*:
1871 ; new setting 1874 (rev.

ll. 3, 6, 8 & 11. Czech Theatre *should read*:
Czech Provisional Theatre

l. 8. — 'Vanda.' Zákrejs *should read*:
25. 'Vanda.' F. Zákrejs

l. 13. Prague, Czech Theatre *should read*:
Prague, New Czech Theatre

INCIDENTAL MUSIC
ll. 1-2. 5 Feb. *should read*:
3 Feb.

Add before l. 1 :
1867.

CHORAL WORKS WITH ORCHESTRA
l. 1. *Op.* 30 *should read*:
$\begin{cases} 4 \\ 30 \end{cases}$

Delete l. 3 ('Song of the Czechs').

840   —   l. 1. *Op.* 58 *should read*:
$\begin{cases} 28 \\ 58 \end{cases}$

Jacopone da Todi. *should read*:
? Jacopone da Todi.

840 — CHORAL WORKS WITH ORCHES-
            TRA
            1877. *should read*:
1876–77.

            l. 3. *Op.* 79 *should read*:
{ 52
{ 79
            Mar. 1879. *should read*:
16 Mar. 1879.

            l. 4. voices. *should read*:
voices, arr. for mixed voices, 1887.

            l. 7. *Add First Performance*:
Plzeň, 14 Apr. 1886.

            l. 9. 1886. *should read*:
1885–86.

            l. 18. 1893. *should read*:
1892–93.

            l. 19. tata, with tenor & bass solo. *should
            read*:
tata, with alto, tenor & bass solo.

            l. 20. 20 May *should read*:
29 May.
            CHORAL WORK WITH PIANO-
            FORTE
            ll. 3 & 4 *should read*:
2. The Magic Well.
3. The Maiden in the Forest.

            UNACCOMPANIED CHORAL
            WORKS
            ll. 4 & 5. Traditional. *should read*:
Traditional Moravian.

            l. 6. Heyduk, Czech & Mora- *should
            read*:
Heyduk & Mora-

    Add before Op. 27 :

    8 | 'The Song of a Czech.' | F. J. Kamenický. | Male Voices. | 1877.

            ORCHESTRAL WORKS
            Add before l. 1 :

| 53 | Polka, B♭ ma., and Galop, E ma., for small orch. | | — | 1861–62. |

            l. 5 — *should read*:
Part of string Quartet in E mi. in 1 movement.

    Add after l. 5 :

| — | 'May Night', Nocturne (string parts only preserved). | | — | 1872. |

841 — *Add before Op.* 60 :

| 25 | Overture to 'Vanda'. | | — | 1879. |
| — | Waltz (publ. in pianoforte version only). | | — | 1879. |

    Add after Op. 59 :

| 64 | Overture to 'Dimitrij'. | 1st overture, later replaced in the opera. | 1882. |

            Op. 60. — *should read*:
Op. 58.
            Op. 70. 1885 *should read*:
1884–85.

| 75a | 'Drobnosti', Terzetto. | 2 vns. & viola. | 1887. |

            Op. 72. 1886 *should read*:
1886–87.
            Op. 93. 1892 *should read*:
1891–92.
            Op. 95. 1893 *should read*:
1891–93.
            Op. 110. 'The Wild Dove' *should read*:
'The Turtle Dove'

841 — SOLO INSTRUMENT AND OR-
            CHESTRA
            l. 1. ? *should read*:
Ludvig Peer.

            l. 2. ? *should read*:
Josef Markus.
            l. 2. 1876. *should read*:
1887.
            (*Transfer* l. 2 *to stand after Op.* 53.)

            l. 5. 1880. *should read*:
1879–80.
            l. 6. 1893. *should read*:
1891.
            l. 9. 1895. *should read*:
1894–95.

            CHAMBER MUSIC
            l. 3. later for voice & *should read*:
orig. for voice &

            l. 3. 1865. *should read*:
1887.
            (*Transfer* ll. 3–4 *to* p. 842, *to stand after Op.*
            81.)

            l. 5. 1870. *should read*:
1870–71.
            (*Transfer* l. 5 *to stand after Op.* 10.)

            l. 6. 1870. *should read*:
1869 or 1870.

            l. 8. A ma. (unpublished). *should read*:
A ma. (orig. *Op.* 5, unpublished).

            Op. 51. 1879. *should read*:
1878–79.

842 — *Op.* 65, Vn., viola & cello *should read*:
Vn., cello & pf.

            Op. 74. 'Terzetto.' *should read*:
'Terzetto', C ma.

            After Op. 81 *and* 'Evening Songs' *transferred
            from above insert*:

            Op. 90. 1891. *should read*:
1890–91.

            VIOLIN AND PIANOFORTE
            Op. 11. With orch. *should read*:
With orch. (arr. of Andantino from string Quartet in
F mi.)
            Op. 75. — *should read*:
'Drobnosti' (*see* Chamber Music).

842 — VIOLONCELLO AND PIANOFORTE
Insert before l. 1 :

| — | Sonata, F mi. (cello part only preserved). | | — | 1871. |

PIANOFORTE SOLO
Op. 53. ' Polka ', B♭ ma. 1862. *should read* :

| | — | | ' Polka ', E ma. | | 1860. | |

Insert after Op. 36 :

| | 41 | | ' Scottish Dances.' | | 1877. | |

843 — *Delete* ' Allegro scherzando ' *after Op.* 85.

PIANOFORTE DUETS
Delete Op. 41.

Op. 72, l. 8. 15. A mi. *should read* :
15. C. ma.

Add after PIANOFORTE DUETS :

846   i   **DYBECK**
BIBL. l. 8 *should read* :
(' Arv ', 1948–49).

ii   *Add after* **DYGAS** :
DYES, John.   *See* TYES, JOHN.

ORGAN MUSIC

| | — | | 4 Preludes and Fugues (unpublished). | | 1858–59. | |

844 — SONGS
Add before Op. 2 :

| — | | 2 Songs (unpublished). | | Adolf Heyduk. | | 1865. | |

Op. 83. 1888 *should read* :
1865 (rev. 1888).

(*Transfer Op.* 83 *to stand between Op.* 2 & *Op.* 5.)

Op. 2, l. 1. 83 and ' Cypresses ' *should read* :
83 and ' Cypresses ' [1]

Op. 6. 1. Once fell a maid asleep. *should read* :
The Maiden and the Grass.

Op. 7. 6 Songs : *should read* :
6 Songs (formerly Op. 17) :

Op. 7. 1873. *should read* :
1872.

Op. 3. *Add at end* :
4. May the Lord delight.

Op. 31. Nos. 4-8 *should be* :
Nos. 5-9.

Add after Op. 31 :

| 19b | Sacred Songs for contralto or baritone :
1. Ave Maria.
2. Ave Maris Stella. | Liturgical. | 1877. |

Op. 99. 4. God is my shepherd. *should read* :
4. The Lord is my shepherd.

10. Sing a joyful song. *should read* :
10. O sing unto the Lord.

Add footnote :

847   i   **DYGON**
Par. 2, l. 4 *should read* :
Royal Library at the B.M. A most elaborate manuscript treatise on proportions by him is in the library of Trinity College, Cambridge.
H. C. C., rev.

ii   *Add after* **DYLAN** :
DYLETSKY, Nikolay Pavlovich (*b.* Kiev, *c.* 1630 : *d.* Moscow, *c.* 1690).
Russian theorist and composer. He studied music in Warsaw, probably under Jacek Różycki, and then moved to Vilno, where he published, in Polish, a treatise on music, ' Gramatyka muzyczna ' in 1675. Later he went to Smolensk and he finally settled in Moscow, where he was chorus master at the Orthodox Chapel as well as teacher of composition and singing. At Smolensk he published his book in 1677, in Russian this time, and it was reissued in Moscow in 1679 and 1681. In it he mentions contemporary Polish composers whom he had met in Warsaw and Vilno.
C. R. H.

[1] It is not satisfactory to list ' Cypresses ' only under *Op.* 2, Songs, and *Op.* 83, 8 Love Songs, because there were 18 in the set composed in 1865. The *Op.* 2 songs are Nos. 1, 5, 11 and 13 of the original set ; *Op.* 83 consists of Nos. 8, 3, 9, 6, 17, 14, 2 and 4. The ' Evening Songs ' for stg. 4tet are Nos. 2, 3, 4, 6, 7, 8, 12, 14, 17 and 18. Nos. 10, 15 and 16 have not been published in any form. The complete set of songs is as follows :

1. Go forth my song, delay not.
2. When thy sweet glances on me fall.
3. Death reigns in many a human breast.
4. Thou only, dear one.
5. 'Twas wondrous sweet that dream of ours.
6. I know that on my love to thee.
7. O charming golden rose.
8. Never will love lead us.
9. I wander oft past yonder house.
10. Doubts often torment me.
11. Nought to my heart can bring relief.
12. I gaze on the leaf so dear.
13. Rest in the valley.
14. In deepest forest glade I stand.
15. My soul into melancholy plunges.
16. There stands the ancient cliff.
17. Nature lies peaceful.
18. You ask why my songs surge forth.

845 — VOCAL DUETS
Op. 19 (*and a new line after it*) *should read* :

| 19a | Sacred Duet (with organ), ' O Sanctissima '. | Liturgical. | Contralto & baritone. | 1879. |
| — | ' Child's Song ' (unpublished). | S. Backora. | 2 voices unaccomp. | 1889. |

849   i   DYSON
CHORAL WORKS
Add at end :

Cantata ' Agincourt ', on lines from Shakespeare's ' Henry V ' and on the ' Hymn after Agincourt ' (1956).

850   ii   EAGLES
Entry should read :

EAGLES (Eccles), Solomon (*b.* ?,

Transfer from ECCLES (1), p. 877, col. i, ll. 2-9 and col. ii, pars. 1-3 and par. 4, ll. 1-5.

Then continue :

tious words. He returned to London, where he died and was buried at Spitalfields. He is known to have been a composer, but nothing remains of his work, the music previously attributed to him being by Solomon Eccles, very probably his son.   w. h. h., rev.

851   i   EAR-TRAINING
Footnote, l. 4. solfège should read :
solfège

852   ii   *Footnote, l. 1. solfège should read :*
solfège

857   ii   *Add to* Bibl. :
Taylor, Eric, ' A Method of Aural Training ', 3 Parts (Oxford, 1955–56).

See also should read :
See also Solfége. Teaching of Music.

872   i   EASTON, Florence
Par. 1, l. 2 *should read :*

Middlesbrough-on-Tees, 24 Oct. 1884 ; *d.* New York, 13 Aug. 1955).

873   i   EBERHARD VON FRESINGEN
Name *should read :*

EBERHARD VON FREISING

Par. 2, l. 3 *should read :*

larum ' and ' Regula ad fundendas nolas, id

l. 5 *should read :*

duced in Gerbert, II, 282. The manuscript is now in the Munich State Library. A modern edition of ' Regula . . .' is in J. Smits van Waesberghe's ' Cymbala ' (Amer. Inst. Musicol., 1951).   e. v. d. s., adds.

EBERL
Par. 1, l. 1.   1766 *should read :*
1765

874   ii   EBERLIN
Add at end :
See also Denkmäler (3), Vol. 28 (modern ed. of ' Blutschwitzende Jesus ').

876   i   ECCARD
Par. 2, l. 5 *should read :*

Musikwerke ', Vol. XXV (1897), which also includes sacred songs. He notes

877   i   ECCLES
Par. 2 *should read :*

(1) **Solomon Eccles (Eagles)** (*b.* ? ; *d.* ?), violinist and composer, very probably son of Solomon Eagles (or Eccles), the Quaker fanatic, musician and shoemaker [1], since it was the custom of the time to name the eldest son after the father and music ran in the family. He is mentioned as one of the court violinists in 1685, but the name Eagles occurs in the list of violinists who played in the masque ' Calisto ' given at Whitehall in 1674, and this may have been a solitary appearance before he settled down to serious study. At the time of his appointment in 1685 he attempted to find a post for his son Henry (3), whose name appears on a warrant in that year ; but as the boy was not sufficiently experienced, he had to wait until 1689, when both he and his father were appointed private musicians to William and Mary. Solomon was constantly in demand at court functions involving music and was often given a special allowance to cover the expenses of riding daily to Windsor when the royal family was in residence there. He was still in service under Nicholas Staggins as one of the violinists of the royal household in 1700 and probably died during the next decade or thereabouts.

Add footnote :
[1] *See* Eagles.

ii   *Cancel Pars. 1-3 and Par. 4, ll. 1-5.*

ll. 6-13 *should read :*

He contributed music to Playford's ' The Division Violin ' (1684) and to Aphra Behn's ' The City Heiress ' and Otway's ' Venice Preserved ', both produced at the Dorset Gardens Theatre in 1682.[2]   d. w. s.

(2) **John Eccles**
l. 1.   1668 [2] ; *should read :*
1668 [3] ;

l. 20.   ' Theatre Music ' [3] *should read :*
' Theatre Music ' [4]

Footnotes 1-3 become 2-4.

878   ii   (3) **Henry Eccles**
ll. 4-5 *should read :*

ability and a member of the Royal Band from the accession of William and Mary in 1689 to 1710. Conceiving himself neglected in

879   i   **(4) Thomas Eccles**
     l. 2. *d. ?) should read* :
d. ?, c. 1745)

880   i   **ECKARDT**
         Par. 1, l. 2 *should read* :
burg, 21 Jan. 1735 ; *d.* Paris, 24 July 1809).

     ii   **ECKHARDT-GRAMATTÉ**
         Par. 1, l. 2. Sophie *should read* :
Sonia

881   i   *Add at end* :
In 1954 she settled in Winnipeg, Canada.

         ECONOMIDIS
         Par. 1, l. 2 *should read* :
23 Oct. 1889 ; *d.* Athens, 10 Dec. 1957).

882   i   **ÉCOSSAISE**
         Par. 3 *should read* :
has an up-beat.[1]

         Add after this :
Böhme [2] remarks :

In its present form the polka resembles the well-known écossaise-waltz (*Schottisch*), except that the steps are more sharply marked and the dancer draws up the foot, setting it down again audibly, almost stamping.

In an anonymous ' Ball-Room Instructor ' published in London in 1849 we read (p. 24) :

This dance [the Schotische] has its origin from the Polka. It is danced in couples, and its position is identical with the valse.

         Add footnotes :

[1] Franz Böhme, ' Geschichte des Tanzes in Deutschland ' (Leipzig, 1886), Vol. II, No. 257, which bears the title of ' Polka (Russische Polka, Doppelpolka) ' and is described as " 1842 bekannt, um 1860 sehr beliebt ".
[2] *Op. cit.*

884   ii   **EDINBURGH**
         Footnote should read :
See GLASGOW, Vol. III, p. 659, ii.

     i   *Add after* Par. 5 :
Mention must be made of Edinburgh's great newspaper, ' The Scotsman ', for the considerable space it devotes to music criticism and articles on music written by Christopher Grier, one of the outstanding musical journalists in Great Britain.

885   ii   **EDINBURGH FESTIVAL**
         Par. 1, l. 12 *should read* :
associated with the Festival from the first. The first director was Rudolf Bing, who, on taking up his appointment at the New York Metropolitan Opera in 1950, was succeeded by Ian Hunter, Robert Noel Ponsonby and Lord Harewood.

886   i   *Add after* **Edison** :

EDITING. An editor is required to prepare for publication or performance a musical text of which the state is such that to present it merely as it stands is insufficient or misleading. The care given by recent and present-day composers to the details of their notation, and the ease with which their intentions can be discovered from it, should make the intervention of an editor almost unnecessary, faithful transcription and routine proof-correcting being virtually all that is needed to secure that their work is adequately presented, in so far as notation is able to present it at all. But until perhaps a century ago these conditions did not obtain, and the editor has much necessary work to do on behalf of classical music. In the case of pre-classical music — that is to say music of the baroque and earlier periods — his work is further increased by an actual difference in the composers' attitude towards notation.

It is the modern habit to trust as little as possible to the initiative of performers, and as much as possible to the written text, in which we incorporate not only the pitch and rhythm of the notes but also their expression, so far as signs and verbal instructions can convey it. We can see the beginnings of this procedure in a few exceptional baroque composers, such as Couperin and J. S. Bach ; but it was still the usual preference in their time to trust not as little but as much as possible to the performer's initiative, in the deliberate conviction that a more flexible and spontaneous effect was to be gained in this way. This advantage was generally felt to outweigh the disadvantage of suffering from vain or incompetent performers whose power to impose their own inflated notions on the music is at least curtailed by our modern insistence on playing what is put in front of us (with the now quite minor exception of concerto cadenzas). The truth, however, is that no notation can tie down the tempo or the expression, as opposed to the notes, beyond a certain point and that, even if it could, the result would be an intolerable rigidity. Initiative in the performer is always a primary element of interpretation, but not always to the same extent.

It follows from these facts that the proper functions of an editor will vary within wide extremes. It is important for him to have a clear view of what these functions are, because of the damage he can do to the music if he misunderstands them :

(1) In every instance it is his business to set out clearly what the composer wrote, or if for good reasons he does not do so, to make reasonably clear what is original and what editorial. This may be done exactly by a variety of typographical devices, or explained

more generally in a preface, or even sufficiently implied by the obvious purpose of the edition, though a plain statement is always better and can do no harm.

(2) There are probably no good reasons for altering (as opposed to supplementing) what the composer wrote in the case of recent and present-day music — it is difficult to say how recent, but a century at the most should be the limit. In the case of earlier music there is the excellent reason that what the composer wrote was often not what he intended, and, broadly speaking, the earlier the music the greater this divergence between notation and intention.

The divergence may apply to the notes themselves [1], to the expression [2] or to both (and this is commonest). Since the conventions which guided the original performers and alone made the system workable have, on the whole, been lost, an editor who is merely a faithful transcriber may be an unwitting deceiver. He may not deceive scholars who are as expert as himself, but he will certainly deceive the normal performer.

(3) He may, therefore, decide to serve primarily his fellow-experts with a scholar's edition. In that event, he has the duty to collate all available sources, both manuscript and printed, using on them the ingenuity of a detective and the integrity of a judge. His difficulties will range from slight to insuperable, his results from obvious to unavoidably controversial. His methods should be those which have long been established in the fine art of literary editing, but which have been disastrously neglected in musical editing until lately, and still are in far too many instances, from lack of the necessary understanding and, in the best sense of the word, academic discipline.

(4) He may, alternatively, decide to serve primarily the practising musician with a performing edition. Provided that it is clear by statement or implication what he is doing, he has no need to preserve intact what the composer wrote, but on the contrary the duty to amplify or modify it (sometimes it will be possible just to supplement it) with his own suggestions as to what the composer intended. He can only do this by way of an approximate example, since the original was by definition left free to the performer's trained initiative, but if he knows his work the result should at least come nearer to what might have occurred under the original conditions than the normal modern performer has otherwise much chance of producing. Further legitimate and useful supplementary matter in a performing edition may include fingerings, which composers of

[1] *See* NOTATION, MUSICA FICTA, THOROUGH-BASS, ORNAMENTATION, ORNAMENTS.
[2] *See* EXPRESSION, DOTTED NOTES, INÉGALES, TEMPO, RHYTHM.

any period do not normally provide, and additional marks of phrasing and expression where even a recent composer has not provided enough of these. But this latter is a dangerous field where many editors, even of recent music and still more of early music, have gone to a most damaging excess. In general, anachronism is the performing editor's worst enemy. There are other incongruities of style to be avoided, but anachronism is the most probable and treacherous.

(5) There have, finally, been successful instances of a scholar's and a performer's edition skilfully and ingeniously combined, but they are very much the exception, and the usual result of such compromise editions being to confuse the performer without really giving the scholar the full and reliable information he requires, they are better avoided.

R. D.

BIBL.—DART, THURSTON, ' The Interpretation of Music ' (London, 1954).
EMERY, WALTER, ' Editions and Musicians ' (London, 1957).
STEVENS, DENIS, ' Problems of Editing and Publishing Old Music ' (Congress Report of the International Musicological Society, New York, 1961).

889   i   **EFFREM**
Par. 1, l. 1 *should read*:

EFFREM, Muzio (Mutio) (*b*. Bari, ? ; *d*. ?).

Par. 2, l. 3 *should read*:

was for twenty-two years in

EGENOLF
Add at end:

BIBL.—BRIDGMAN, NAN, ' Christian Egenolf, imprimeur de musique ' (' Annales musicologiques ', III, p. 77).

ii   **EGGE**
Par. 1, l. 1. Granskerad, *should read*:

Granshered,

Par. 2, ll. 6-12 *should read*:

Society in succession to Arne Eggen. His works include 2 Symphonies (1945 and 1947), 2 pianoforte Concertos, a violin Concerto, Sonatas for violin and pianoforte and for pianoforte solo (' Draumkvede-Sonate '), choral works, pianoforte pieces (' Fantasi i halling ') and songs.

Egge is regarded as one of the leading Norwegian composers of his generation. In his early works particularly the influence of Norwegian folk music is to be found, and his early style employs diatonic melodies built on extended scales, with a texture that is usually polyphonic and dissonant. In his later works he uses for the most part the normal scales and a technique of complex tonalities.   J. H. (ii), adds. O. G.

889   ii   **EGGEN**
Par. 1, l. 2. *should read* :
1881 ;   *d.* Drammhen, 26 Oct. 1955).

Par. 2, l. 9 *should read* :
opera ' Olav Liljekrans ' (after an early play by Ibsen). An opera on

891   i   *Add after* Par. 2:
Egk devised the idea and wrote the libretto for Boris Blacher's ' Abstrakte Oper ' (1953).

Add to BIBL. :
WÖRNER, KARL, ' Egk and Orff ' (M. Rev., XIV, 1953, pp. 186.

CATALOGUE :
OPERAS
ll. 5-6 *should read* :
' Columbus ' (libretto by the composer, revision of radio opera of 1933), prod. Frankfort o/M., 13 Jan. 1942.

l. 8 *should read* :
mayor encanto amor ' (1948), prod. Berlin, 18 Dec. 1948.

Add after ' Circe ' :
' Irische Legende ', libretto by the composer on Yeats's story ' The Countess Kathleen O'Shea ', prod. Salzburg Festival, 17 Aug. 1955.

Add at end :
' Der Revisor ', libretto on Gogol's comedy, prod. Schwetzingen, 9 May 1957.

BALLETS
Add at end :
' Die chinesische Nachtigall ', after Hans Andersen.

895   i   **EGYPTIAN MUSIC**
Par. 2, ll. 27-28 *should read* :
this reign. Verdi's ' Aida ' was commissioned for its inauguration (1871), but the house was actually opened with Meyerbeer's ' Huguenots ', ' Aida ' being produced on 24 Dec. Strange as

897   i   *Add to* BIBL., HICKMANN, after l. 13, ' Cahiers d'histoire . . .' :
' Le Problème de la notation musicale dans l'Égypte ancienne ' (Cairo, 1955).
' Musique et vie musicale sous les Pharaons ', 3 vols. (Paris, 1956).
' Terminologie musicale de l'Égypte ancienne ' (Cairo, 1955).
' 45 Siècles de musique dans l'Égypte ancienne, à travers la sculpture, la peinture, l'instrument ' (Paris, 1956).

899   i   **Eichendorff**
Add before Brahms :
Berg (Alban, song).

l. 13 *should read* :
2 choral works ; 2 song cycles with orch. ; poems for voice & orch. ; 8 songs with

900   i   **EICHNER**
Add at end :
See also Sondheimer Ed., Vol. 15 (modern ed. of vn. & pf. sonatas).

900   ii   **EINEM**
Add after l. 2. :
' Ballade ' for 40th Anniversary of Cleveland Orchestra (1958).

901   i   **EINSTEIN**
Par. 4, l. 10 *should read* :
York & London, 1947). A volume of ' Essays in Music ' was published posthumously in New York in 1956.   H. C. C. & E. B.

903   i   **EISTEDDFOD**
Par. 2, l. 36. 15,000 *should read* :
150,000

EITNER
Par. 1, l. 2. Tamplin *should read* :
Templin

    ii   Par. 1, l. 14. biblio- *should read* :
bio-biblio-

904   ii   **ELDERING**
Par. 1, l. 2. June 1943 *should read* :
17 June 1943

905   i   Par. 1, l. 2 *should read* :
Musik at Cologne. He was killed in an airraid on that city.

908   ii   **ELECTROPHONIC INSTRUMENTS**
Add to BIBL. :
DOUGLAS, ALAN, ' The Electrical Production of Music ' (London, 1957).
' The Electronic [sic] Musical Instrument Manual : Guide to Theory and Design' (New York, Toronto & London, 1954).

Add before **ELEGY** :

ELECTROPHONIC (or **ELECTRONIC**) **MUSIC.** A development dating from the late 1940s and cultivated mainly in Germany at present. It has been particularly encouraged by the Cologne branch of the North-West German Radio, which provided facilities for experimental work, and its leading exponents are Dr. Herbert Eimert and Dr. Werner Meyer-Eppler. In this music the sounds are actually produced by electrophonic instruments : there are no performers and no microphonic recordings of external sounds, nor is there any generally accepted system of musical notation. The sounds produced electrophonically are recorded on magnetophone tapes and may then be rearranged, altered or distorted as in concrete music. Unlike earlier electrophonic instruments, those used here do not attempt to imitate the sound of normal musical instruments ; their aim is to create entirely new sound-structures that can range from the simple to the extremely complicated. These methods clearly widen the potential range of musical expression, but at present electrophonic music is still at an experimental stage and cannot be said to have produced any results of genuine artistic value. However, it has attracted the attention of some of the young German composers, including Karlheinz Stockhausen, and its future development will be watched with interest. Public demonstrations of electrophonic music were first given at the Darmstadt International Summer Schools of 1951–52 and at the Cologne New Music Festival of 1953.

In New York Edgar Varèse has experimented along similar lines for some years, but the results of his researches have not yet been heard in Europe.   H. S. (ii).

BIBL.—EIMERT, HERBERT & STOCKHAUSEN, KARLHEINZ, ' Die Reihe, No. 1 : Electronic Music ' (London, Vienna & Zürich, 1958).

See also Concrete Music.

912   i   **ELGAR**
            Par. 1, l. 3.   Richter's direction
            should read :

the composer's direction

920   ii   *Add to* BIBL. :

CHAMBERS, HENRY A. (ed.), ' Edward Elgar : Centenary Sketches ' (London, 1957).
ELGAR, EDWARD, ' Letters of Edward Elgar and Other Writings ', ed. by Percy M. Young (London, 1956).
McVEAGH, DIANA, ' Edward Elgar : his Life and Music ' (London, 1955).
MITCHELL, DONALD, ' Some Thoughts on Elgar (1857–1934) ' (M. & L., XXXVIII, 1957, p. 113).
YOUNG, PERCY M., ' Elgar, O.M. : a Study of a Musician ' (London, 1955).

CATALOGUE
WORKS FOR THE STAGE
Col. 2, l. 26 *should read* :
3 songs for baritone from ' The Starlight Express ' : ' To the Children ',

Col. 4, l. 4 *should read* :
MS.²

Add footnote :
² A pianoforte Suite of six pieces arranged by Albert W. Ketèlbey was published in 1916.

924   —   ORCHESTRAL WORKS
            ll. 23-30 *should read* :

7	' Sevillana.'	?	1884.	Worcester Philharmonic Soc., 1 May 1884.	W. C. Stockley.
10	3 Pieces for small orch.	1881.	1889.	New Brighton, 16 July 1899.	Lady Mary Lygon.
	1. Mazurka.		MS.	Stockley's concert, Birmingham, 13 Dec. 1883.	
	2. Sérénade mauresque.		MS.		
	3. Contrasts (Gavotte, A.D. 1700–1900).		1899.		

925   —   *Op.* 39, l. 11.   24 Aug. *should read* :
4 Sept.
            l. 13.   30 Sept. *should read* :
20 Sept.

926   —   CHAMBER MUSIC
            Op. 6.   for flute, 2 oboes, *should read*
for 2 flutes, oboe,

927   —   CARILLON
            Op. 54 *should read* :
—

928   i   **ELIAS SALOMONIS**
            Name *should read* :

ELIAS SALOMO(NIS)

        ii   l. 2 *should read* :
lar music of his time, but is concerned mainly with combating the decline of plainsong.
                                        D. H. B., adds.

929   i   **Eliot, T. S.**
            ll. 5-6 *should read* :
Men ', trumpet & orch.).   Pizzetti (' Murder in the Cathedral ', opera).   Porter (Q., ' Sweeney Agonistes ', incid. m.).   Rawsthorne (' Practical Cats ', voice & orch.).   Shaw (M., ' Rock ', choral

931   i   **ELKIN, Robert**
            Par. 2, ll. 6-7 *should read* :
was chairman of the Music Publishers' Association, and since 1947 he has

            Par. 3, l. 4.   Philharmonic Orchestra *should read* :
Philharmonic Society

932   ii   **ELLING**
            Par. 1, l. 1.   **Catherinus** *should read* :

Catharinus

934   ii   *Add after* **Elmenhorst** :
            ELMO, Cloe (*b.* Lecce, 9 Apr. 1910).
Italian mezzo-soprano singer.   She studied with Edwige Ghibaudo at the Accademia di Santa Cecilia in Rome.   In 1932 she entered for an international singing contest in Vienna and won first place with her singing of Beethoven's ' Ah Perfido ! ' and an aria from ' La Wally ' ;   further study with Rinolfi and Pedrini led to her début as Santuzza at Cagliari.   She followed this with appearances as Orfeo in Rome, and from 1936 to 1943 she was leading mezzo-soprano at La Scala, Milan, singing such parts as Mistress Quickly, Ulrica, Azucena, the Princess in ' Adriana Lecouvreur '.   After the war she was engaged for the

Metropolitan, New York, and while in America was chosen by Toscanini to sing Mistress Quickly in his broadcast performance and recording of ' Falstaff '. She has also sung in Bach under Klemperer and Molinari. While not possessing the classical line and schooled vocalism of Stignani, she has a naturally beautiful voice and a dynamic stage personality.   H. D. R.

937   i   **ELWELL,** List of Works
l. 7 *should read :*
Pastorale ' for voice & orch. (1947).

ELWES
Par. 2, ll. 5-6 *should read :*
(1889) Lady Winefride Fielding, daughter of the Earl of Denbigh (*d.* 1959) and served in the Diplo-

941   ii   *Add after* **EMERY, George :**
EMERY, Walter (Henry James) (*b.* Tilshead, Wiltshire, 14 June 1909).
English organist and musicologist. He studied with various musicians at home and with Percy Fry, then organist of St. Thomas, Salisbury. In 1928 he obtained an organ scholarship to the R.A.M. in London and remained there until 1934 as a pupil of Marchant and Sowerbutts ; during his last year there he taught paper-work as a sub-professor. In 1931–39 he was organist at St. Giles, Cripplegate, and in 1937 he joined the staff of Novello & Co. During the second world war he served in the R.A.M.C. in 1941–46.
From 1938 Emery published numerous scholarly articles in Mus. T., M. & L., M. Rev., ' The Organ ' and other periodicals and made himself known by degrees as a first-rate specialist in the work of Bach and the problems of its performance, although his interest in music generally has remained far-reaching. His publications in book-form include ' The St. Matthew Passion : its Preparation and Performance ' (with Sir Adrian Boult) (London, 1949) ; ' Bach's Ornaments ' (London, 1953), a practical as well as learned work of great importance ; several booklets in the series ' Notes on Bach's Organ Works ', which are textual and historical commentaries on the new Novello edition of those works, in which he collaborates with John Dykes Bower. Emery also contributed a chapter on organ music of 1700–50 to the N.O.H.M. and edited Part ii of Bach's ' Clavierübung ' for the Neue Bach Ausgabe.   E. B.

944   i   **ENCORE**
ll. 6-7 *should read :*
in 1712, when Steele referred in ' The Spectator ' (No. 314). A song, ' The Bath

944   i   **ENESCO**
Par. 1, l. 2 *should read :*
Dorohoiŭ, 19 Aug. 1881 ; *d.* Paris, 4 May 1955).

ii   *Add to* Bibl. :
Enesco, Georges & Gavoty, Bernard, ' Les Souvenirs de Georges Enesco ' (Paris, 1955).

946   ii   **ENGLEBERT OF ADMONT**
Par. 1, l. 2.   (*b.* ? ; *should read :*
(*b.* Volkersdorf, *c.* 1250 ;

Par. 2, ll. 3-4 *should read :*
He was Abbot of the Benedictine monastery of Admont from 1297 to 1327, but ended his days as a simple monk.

ll. 6-7 *should read :*
' Scriptores . . .', is an almost purely speculative work.

947   i   **ENGLISH FINGERING**
l. 1 *should read :*
See Continental Fingering.   Fingering

ENGLISH FOLK DANCE AND SONG SOCIETY
Par. 1, l. 2.   1932 *should read :*
1931

950   i   **ENGLISH MUSICIANS ABROAD**
Par. 2, l. 21 *should read :*
reached Rome by 1585, at which time he was singing bass in the choir of the English College there ; and perhaps also

ii   *Add at end :*
Bibl.—Mueller, Paul Eduard, ' The Influence and Activities of English Musicians on the Continent during the late Sixteenth and Early Seventeenth Centuries ' (Ann Arbor, Mich., 1954).

951   i   **ENGLISH OPERA GROUP**
l. 20 *should read :*
musical functions abroad, notably the Venice Festival of 1955, at which the first world performance of Britten's ' The Turn of the Screw ' was given.

Add new paragraph :
The home base, so to speak, of the English Opera Group is Aldeburgh, Britten's home in Suffolk, where it takes part in the annual festival, held on a modest scale but with much care for perfection in performance. Yet although it seems admirably at home there, it has long proved itself capable of going out into the world and taking an artistic place of importance anywhere.

952   i   **"ENGLISH" SUITES**
Add at end:
See also Dieupart.

953   i   **ENGRAVING**
(c. 1620)   Par. 4, ll. 1-2. (c. 1606–1610) should read:

    ii   *Add at top of col.:*
Locke, Matthew, 'Melothesia', 1673.

Add at end:

BIBL.—HIND, A. M., 'Engraving in England in the Sixteenth and Seventeenth Centuries', Part II (Cambridge, 1955).
HUMPHRIES, CHARLES & SMITH, WILLIAM C., 'Music Publishing in the British Isles from the Earliest Times to the Middle of the Nineteenth Century' (London, 1954).

955   i   **"ENIGMA" VARIATIONS**
Var. XIII *should read:*

Var. XIII. * * * = Lady Mary Lygon (later Lady Mary Trefusis).

956   ii   **ENTFÜHRUNG AUS DEM SERAIL**
Footnote 2, l. 5 should read:
though the Turkish setting is similar. Bickerstaffe's 'The Sultan, or A Peep into the Seraglio' is somewhat nearer Bretzner's play, and although the latter cannot be called a German adaptation of it, two of Bickerstaffe's characters are certainly the prototypes of two in Mozart's opera: "Osmyn, chief of the Eunuchs" and "Roxalana, an English Slave". The latter has all Blonde's impudence and independence, which so much impresses the Sultan that he marries her and dismisses the ladies of the harem. Osmyn, of course, has not the amorous propensities of Stephanie's Osmin, does not make love to her, but merely bullies her, much as in the opera. There are no lovers, master and servant, like Belmonte and Pedrillo, and there is no elopement.

Add to Footnote 2:
There is, however, another possible source, which may have served Bickerstaffe also: a pasticcio with words by Favart, 'Soliman second, ou Les Trois Sultanes' (Paris, 1761), also known as 'Roxelane', in its turn based on Marmontel. The alternative title suggests a direct connection with Bickerstaffe, all of whose stage works appeared between 1760 and 1771. 'Soliman' was used by J. M. Kraus for a Swedish opera in 1789 and by Süssmayr for a German one in 1799.

957   i   **ENTREMET**
l. 2 *should read:*

brief entertainment, usually a series of tableaux with dances accompanied by all kinds of vocal and instrumental music, per-

    ii   l. 2 *should read:*

and 15th centuries. It was the forerunner of the later interludes and masques.

                   G. R. (iii).

959   i   **EQUALI**
Par. 2, ll. 1-3 *should read:*

Beethoven's Equali, written in 1812, are the most famous specimens of the type. They were sung, in an arrangement for men's chorus, at the composer's funeral. The first

and third were set to liturgical words, 'Miserere' and 'Amplius', the second to words specially written for the occasion by Grillparzer: 'Du, dem nie im Leben'.[1] They are still

959   i   *Add footnote:*
[1] These arrangements are shown in the appendix to Seyfried's 'Beethoven Studies', in the English (2nd) edition (1853), translated by Pierson, pp. 56, 61 & 70.

960   ii   **ERBACH**
Add at end:
See also Denkmäler (2) II, Vol. 4 (ii) (modern ed.).

ERDMANN
Par. 1, l. 2 *should read:*

Latvia, 5 Mar. 1896; d. Hamburg, 21 June 1958).

966   i   **ERLANGER**
Par. 2, ll. 9-10 *should read:*

orchestra (1921). Later works were a Requiem for solo voices, chorus and orchestra, and the ballet 'Les Cent Baisers', produced at Covent Garden in 1935.

ERLEBACH
Add at end:
See also Denkmäler (2), Vols. 46-47 (modern ed. of 'Harmonische Freude').

ERLKÖNIG
End should read:

translated "Elfenkönig"—king of the elves.[2] Goethe's poem was set to music by a vast number of other composers (see BIBL.).

                   E. B.

BIBL.—TAPPERT, WILHELM, '70 Erlkönig-Kompositionen' (Berlin, 1906).

967   ii   **ERSHOV**
Dates *should read:*

(b. Maly Nesvetay, Don district, 20 Nov. 1867; d. Tashkent, 21 Nov. 1943).

968   i   *Add after* **Erskine, John:**

ERSKINE, Thomas Alexander. See KELLIE, EARL OF.

969   i   **ESCRIBANO**
Par. 1, l. 2 *should read:*

d. Rome, 7 Oct. 1557).[1]

            Par. 2, l. 3. *For* 1507 *read:*
1503
       Add footnote:
[1] *See* J. M. Llorens Cisteró, 'Juan Escribano, cantor pontifico y compositor' ('Anuario Musical', XII, 1957).

970   ii   **ESLAVA**
l. 6. Patino *should read:*
Patiño

971 ii **ESPLÁ**
Par. 1, l. 1. 1889 *should read*:
1886 ¹).

Add footnote:
¹ According to the official birth certificate.

974 ii **ESSIPOV**
Name *should read*:
ESSIPOVA, Anna Nikolayevna

975 ii **ESTHER**
l. 6. 29 Aug. *should read*:
? 29 Aug.

l. 9. 2 May 1732 *should read*:
20 Apr. 1732

976 ii **ETLER**
Add at end:

In 1958 he was one of ten composers commissioned to write a work for the celebration of the fortieth anniversary of the Cleveland Symphony Orchestra, his contribution being a Concerto in One Movement.

978 ii **Euripides**
Par. 1, l. 3 *should read*:

m.). Gadsby (do.). Handel ('Admeto'). Holst (choruses). Koechlin

979 i Par. 5, l. 3 *should read*:

(incid. m.). Koreshchenko (do.). Palmer (R., chorus). Thomson (V., incid. m.).

980 ii **EVANS, D. E.**
Par. 1, l. 1. Newcastle-Emlyn
should read:
Newcastle Emlyn

l. 2. Cardiganshire *should read*:
Carmarthenshire

981 i *Add before* **EVANS, Harry**:

EVANS, (Llewellyn) Geraint (*b.* Pontypridd, Glamorgan, 16 Feb. 1922).
Welsh baritone singer. After leaving school he embarked on a business career, but at the age of seventeen began to study singing at Cardiff and took part in a number of amateur performances, including Mendelssohn's ' Elijah ', in which he sang the title-part. His studies were interrupted by the war, during which he served in the R.A.F. At Hamburg he worked under Trevor Harvey for the British Forces Network, arranging programmes and singing. He was heard by the bass Theo Hermann, who was so impressed with his voice that he gave him singing lessons.
Evans also studied later with Fernando Carpi at Geneva and with Walter Hyde at the G.S.M. in London. He joined the Covent Garden company in 1948, making his début

as the Nightwatchman in ' The Mastersingers '. In his second season he sang Figaro (Mozart) and gradually built up a large repertory, including Escamillo, Schaunard, Lescaut, Papageno, Marcello, Balstrode (' Peter Grimes ') and Sharpless. Three parts in works by Britten and Walton were created by him at Covent Garden: Mr. Flint (' Billy Budd '), Mountjoy (' Gloriana ') and Antenor (' Troilus and Cressida ').
He has taken part in the Glyndebourne Festivals since 1950 appearing as Guglielmo (' Così '), Masetto, Papageno, Leporello, Abbata (Busoni's ' Arlecchino ') and the Music Master (' Ariadne auf Naxos '). In 1957 he achieved two great personal successes, at Covent Garden with his Beckmesser, a complete musical and dramatic portrait of the small-minded, mean and jealous town-clerk unspoilt by buffoonery; and at Glyndebourne with his Falstaff, which a discerning critic considered " worthy to be remembered in the historic sequence of famous Falstaffs ". In 1959 he sang an authoritative Enrico at Covent Garden in ' Lucia di Lammermoor ' and then took over Gobbi's part of Posa in ' Don Carlos '.
Although Covent Garden did not rush him into opportunities, he has been one of the Royal Opera's most successful products. His voice, while not over-large, is fully adequate to a full-sized theatre and has been carefully trained. He brings to his parts an authority and virility rare among British-born singers and has developed an acting technique that enables him to present a great variety of characters with originality and consistency.

H. D. R.

983 ii *Add before* **EXIMENO**:
EXCESTRE, William (*b.* ?; *d.* ?).
English 14th–15th-century singer and composer. He was active during the reign of Henry V, of whose Chapel Royal he was a member. In 1393 he was first listed as a clerk of the Chapel Royal. In the following year he was granted a prebend in St. Stephen's, Westminster. He is thus one of the senior members of that group of composers who contributed to the ' Old Hall Manuscript ', and the comparatively archaic style of his music confirms his position in this group. Three compositions, a ' Gloria ', ' Credo ' and ' Sanctus ', have been preserved: all are three-part works.
Both ' Gloria ' and ' Credo ' are in balladeMass style, (I, 55; II, 158) and rely for their contrasts mainly on duet sections which alternate with the three-part texture assigned to a tenor voice and two instruments. The vocal part of the ' Gloria ' is freely based on Gloria 5 of the Sarum Kyriale. The ' Sanctus ' (III, 90) is based on a non-liturgical *cantus*

firmus found among a group of monophonic pieces in mensural notation written on the flyleaves of a Sarum Gradual (B.M., Lansdowne MS 462). It is in *conductus* style, and neither the intonation of the ' Sanctus ' nor the ' Benedictus ' has been set in harmony. The use of perfect prolation throughout is yet another indication of the relatively early style of this music.   D. W. S.

BIBL.—BORREN, CHARLES VAN DEN, ' Études sur le XVᵉ siècle musical ' (Antwerp, 1941).
BUKOFZER, MANFRED, ' Studies in Medieval and Renaissance Music ' (New York, 1950).
RAMSBOTHAM, ALEXANDER, ed., ' The Old Hall Manuscript ', Vols. I-III (London, 1933–38).

986   i   **EXPRESSION**
         Par. 1, l. 5. *adagio should read* :
largo

994   i   *Add before* **Eyck, Robert van** :

EYCK, Jacob van (*b.* ?, *c.* 1590; *d.* Utrecht, 26 Mar. 1657).
Dutch recorder and carillon player, organist and composer. His mother belonged to the noble family of Bax, and he thus bore the title of Jonkheer. Nothing is known of his life, except that he was blind, before his appointment as carillonist at the Cathedral of Utrecht in 1624. He complained that his salary of 400 guilders was insufficient, since he needed special assistance owing to his blindness, and it was raised to 500 guilders in 1628. From 1632 he received another 80 guilders for playing the carillon at St. John's Church as well, and later 20 more for occasionally diverting the promenaders in the churchyard with the recorder, for which he published, probably in 1646, two books of pieces, ' Der Fluyten Lust-hof ', dedicated to Constantijn Huygens. Two other works, ' Euterpe ' and ' Der Goden Fluythemel ' are lost.

Book I of ' Der Fluyten Lust-hof ', containing variations on psalm-tunes, folksongs and dances, has been republished under the editorship of Gerrit Vellekoop (Amsterdam, 1957).   E. B.

994   ii   **EYE MUSIC**
         Par. 6, l. 7. in 1425 or so *should read* :
in 1360 or so

Add after **FACKELTANZ**:

FACY (Facey, Facie, Facio), Hugh (*b.*
? Exeter, ?; *d.* ?).
English 17th-century composer. He was
probably the son or a relation of Anthony
Facy, who as a " 46 years old vicar choral of
good name and fame " was ordained deacon
on 23 Dec. 1604 and priest on 24 Feb. 1605
at Exeter Cathedral (Register of Ordination
157?–1667). Another relation may have
been Lewis (Ludovicus) Facy, chorister, who
was admitted there to a Secondary's place on
11 June 1614.
Very little is known about Hugh Facy. He
was a Secondary at Exeter Cathedral at a
time when Edward Gibbons was responsible
for teaching music to the choristers and
secondaries. There are a few entries in the
Chapter Act Book referring to him:

1 Mar. 1618: They consented that Hugh Facey
should sometimes play on the Organs at Service time;
6 Nov. 1619: They gave leave to Hugh Facey to
be absent from the service of the Quire for one whole
year next ensuing without prejudice unto him in rega-d
to his Secondaries place in this Church and to receave
his stipend due to that place in the mean time.

A year later he was granted leave again
for another year. It is not known what
happened to him afterwards. He probably
had Roman Catholic sympathies, for he used
a Latin text in his Magnificat and set the
plainsong ' Ave maris stella ' for the organ.
An interesting feature of the Magnificat,
which is probably in holograph, are the
expression marks *suaviter* and *fortiter*.
The following works by Facy are known:

' Magnificat A 4 voc. and Bassus Continuus ', MS (B.M.,
RCM 1181 [5 parts], *cantus* imperfect).
4 Fancies for strings in 3 parts, one of them called
"ecco" (Sibley Lib., Eastman School of Music,
Rochester Univ., N.Y., *altus* part missing).
2 Solos for Bass Viol (Henry Watson Lib., Manchester,
m. 832. V. u. 51).
Organ pieces (N.Y., Drexel 5611): Voluntary.
' Ave maris stella.'
9 Virginal pieces (N.Y., Drexel 5611).
3 Virginal pieces (B.M. Add. MS 36,661; two of them
in Drexel 5611).
Virginal piece, ' An Almayn ' (N.Y., Drexel 5612).

s. J.

BIBL.—JEANS, SUSI, ' Musical Life at Exeter Cathedral '
(' The Organist's Quarterly Record ', July 1958).

BIBL. l. 4 *should read*:
in ' Musica d' oggi ', Jan. 1925.

Par. 2, l. 1 *should read*:
French soprano singer. She was the
daughter of a tailor and received vocal

Add footnote:
[1] Larousse has 1812, but Bouvet (*see* Bibl.) quotes the
birth certificate.

ii **FALCONIERI**
Footnote 3. M. Bertolotti, *should read*:
A. Bertolotti,

servizio della casa Farnese ' (' Archivio storico per le
provincie parmensi ', new series, Vol. XXII *bis*, ' In
onore del Presidente Marrotti ', 1922).

Falke
See Foerster *should read*:
See Berg (Alban, 2 songs). Foerster

After war service in the R.A.F. he was
appointed Head of the British Council in
Italy. From 1950 to 1960 he was Professor of
Singing at Cornell University, U.S.A., but
revisited England and the Commonwealth at
various times to give concerts and to adjudi-
cate. In the autumn of 1960 he succeeded
Sir Ernest Bullock as Director of the R.C.M.

Eng. trans. by Jean Wagstaff (London, 1954).

PAHLEN, KURT, ' Manuel de Falla und die Musik in
Spanien ' (Freiburg i/B., 1953).

14   ii   **FAMITSIN**
Par. 1, ll. 1-2 *should read*:

FAMINTSIN¹, Alexander Sergeyevich
(*b.* Kaluga district, 5 Nov. 1841 ; *d.* Ligovo
nr. St.

l. 17.   Dombra *should read*:
Domra

Par. 3, l. 1.   Famitsin *should read*:
Famintsin

Add footnote :
¹ This, not Famitsin, is the correct form of the name.

16   i   **FANFARE**
Par. 3, l. 27 *should read*:

beth ' and his film scores for ' Henry V ',
' Hamlet ' and ' Richard III '.   Walton also
wrote a fanfare for the coronation of Queen
Elizabeth II in 1953.

19   ii   **FANTASY (1)**
Par. 1, l. 6 *should read*:

panions are unfortunately lost, and a splendid
six-part fantasy only recently discovered,
rather vocal in style but admirably effective.

21   ii   *Add to* BIBL. :
ARNOLD, CECILY & JOHNSON, MARSHALL, ' The English
Fantasy Suite ' (Proc. Roy. Mus. Ass., LXXXII,
1955-56).

25   i   **FARINELLI**
BIBL., l. 11.   HÄBOCK *should read*:
HABÖCK

33   ii   **FARRANT, Daniel**
Par. 2, l. 4 *should read*:

from 1607 to 1641, when his name occurs in
the accounts for the last time.

Par. 2, l. 9 *should read*:

the lute and bandora.   A ' Pavan ' of his may
be seen in Christ Church MS. 423-8.   He
married a daughter, Katherine, of the elder
Nicholas Lanier.   E. H. F., adds.

35   i   **FARRENC (1)**
Par. 2, l. 1 *should read*:

He published a full score of Beethoven's
' Fidelio ' in 1826, more than twenty years
before it appeared in either Austria or Germany.   He took an important part in the
second

37   ii   **FASOLO, ? and FASOLO, G. B.**
l. 1 (of **FASOLO, ?**) *should read*:

FASOLO, Giovanni Battista (*b.* Asti, ? ;
d. ?).

Par. 2, l. 2 *should read*:

His talent, as a young man, to judge from
his two principal

37   ii   Par. 2, l. 10.   ' Gazetta *should read* :
' Gazzetta

Par. 3, ll. 11-14 *should read* :
picciosi.

*Delete rest of this paragraph, also name
and dates (Par. 4) following.*

Par. 5, l. 1 *should read*:
He had become a

38   i   Par. 1, ll. 2-3 *should read*:

reale near Palermo.   In these late years he
became a more serious composer and published two important works : an ' Annuale '
(Venice, 1645) containing.

l. 15 *should read*:

18-21).   He died some time after 1660.
                              N. F. (ii).

Fauchois
l. 1.   *Add after See* :
Bondeville (' Madame Bovary ', opera).

FAUGUES
Delete Par. 2 *and replace by* :

    French 15th-century composer.   Tinctoris
and an anonymous Spanish writer list him
among the contemporaries of Okeghem,
Busnois, Regis and Caron, the immediate
disciples of Dunstable, Dufay and Binchois.
His name also appears in the motet ' Omnium
bonorum plena ' by Compère, which gives a
similar list of composers.   All his surviving
works are Masses, but only two have been
published, namely a ' L'Homme armé ' Mass
and one on the chanson ' Le Serviteur '.   The
others include a ' Missa super Basse Danse '
and a Mass entitled ' Je suis en la mer '.
The ' L'Homme armé ' Mass is for 3 voices
and seems relatively early, though it is
technically mature.   Certain passages are in
fact for 4 voices, but these are all presented
by canon at the fifth between *altus* and *tenor*.
The composition employs the method of
repeating certain sections in order to obtain
unity, and the later version of the same Mass
in a Sistine Chapel manuscript takes this
procedure even farther.   Evidence that the
Mass on ' Le Serviteur ' is also by Faugues, as
Tinctoris maintains, though the often unreliable Trent codices give the name of Okeghem, is provided by the use of the same
technique there.   The parody technique is
also quite developed here, for not only does the
composer draw on all three voices of the
chanson for his material, but he also paraphrases the *superius* and employs all three
voices of the chanson simultaneously.
    The ' Missa L'Homme armé ' is published
in ' Monumenta polyphoniae liturgicae
Sanctae Ecclesiae Romanae ', 1948, Series

I, Fasc. 4; the 'Missa Le Serviteur' in D.T.Ö., XIX, I, 1912. In 1960 the Complete Works of Faugues, edited with an Introduction and facsimiles by George C. Schuetze, were published by the Institute of Medieval Music, Brooklyn, N.Y.   G. R. (iii).

See also O. J. Gombosi, 'Jacob Obrecht' (1925).

38 ii FAURÉ
Par. 1, ll. 2-4 *should read*:

M. de Saubiac, deputy for Ariège, visited Foix in 1854, he heard Gabriel play the pianoforte and was so impressed with the child's talent that he persuaded his father to send him to Niedermeyer's school in Paris. On 6 July the elder Fauré, having convinced himself that his son's gifts were developing more and more promisingly, wrote to Saubiac [3], asking him to recommend the boy to Niedermeyer, who agreed not only to

Add footnote:

[3] This letter makes it clear that it was not Niedermeyer who visited the Faurés at Foix, as has been repeatedly stated.

39 — Heading *should read*:
FAURÉ: 1871–1896

40 — Heading *should read*:
FAURÉ: Last Years — The Music

41 — Heading *should read*:
FAURÉ: The Music

42 — Heading *should read*:
FAURÉ: Bibliography — Works

i BIBL., l. 23. 1929). *should read*:

1929); rev. ed. with 'Réflexions sur la confiance fauréenne' & 'Notes sur l'interprétation des œuvres' (Paris, 1957).

ii *See also*. l. 6 *should read*:

947-48 (mus. ex.); p. 953 (do.).

43-44 — Headings *should read*:
FAURÉ: Works

44 — CATALOGUE
Add to PIANOFORTE DUET:

| | Quadrille on Themes from Wagner's 'Ring' (with Messager). |

45 — Heading *should read*:
FAURÉ: Works

47 i FAURE, Jean-Baptiste
Par. 2, l. 28 *should read*:

two books of songs, the most popular of which was 'Les Rameaux', and 'La Voix et

47 ii *Add after* FAUXBOURDON:
FAVARETTO, Giorgio (*b.* Venice, 2 Mar. 1902).
Italian pianist. He studied at the Venice Conservatory "B. Marcello", composition with M. Agostini and pianoforte with Gino Tagliapietro, and took a diploma at the Naples Conservatory. He has devoted himself especially to chamber music, appearing with the most noted instrumentalists and vocal soloists; and he is one of the accompanists most in demand, particularly for programmes of romantic *Lieder* and modern songs. He founded the association "Un' ora di musica" at Milan. In 1942 he was appointed director of the chamber music section of the Radio in Rome. He is a very busy teacher of vocal interpretation, both privately and at the Accademia Musicale Chigiana at Siena.   G. M. G.

48 i FAVART (1)
See also. l. 7 *should read*:
Duni (E. R., 6 libs.). Entführung aus dem Serail (? source of lib.). Francœur (parody in 'Pirame').

ii l. 3 *should read*:
Hiller (J. A., 3 *Singspiele*). Kraus (J. M., 'Soliman der II'). Libretto. Monsigny (3

50 i FAYRFAX
Par. 1, l. 3 *should read*:
St. Albans, 24 Oct. 1521).

52 i l. 9. r seo *should read*:
roseo

53 i Par. 1, l. 2. example above. *should read*:
example on p. 51.

54 i *Add at end*:
The Complete Works of Fayrfax, edited by Edwin B. Warren, are being issued by the American Institute of Musicology.

Add to BIBL.:
EDWIN B. WARREN, 'The Life and Works of Robert Fayrfax' ('Musica Disciplina', XI, 1957, p. 152). 'The Masses of Robert Fayrfax' ('Musica Disciplina', XII, 1958, p. 145).

| | | | | c. 1888. |

55 i *Add before* FEDERICI:
FÉDÉRATION INTERNATIONALE DES JEUNESSES MUSICALES. *See* JEUNESSES MUSICALES.

Add after FEDELTÀ PREMIATA:
Federici, Camillo (Giovanni Battista Viassolo). *See* Rossini ('Elisabetta', opera).

55   ii   *Add before* **FEDRA**:

FEDOROV, Vladimir (Mikhailovich)
(*b.* Tchernigov, 5 Aug. 1901).
French musicologist, librarian and composer of Russian birth. Son of a well-known
politician and minister under the tsarist
régime, he studied at schools in St. Petersburg, Moscow, Odessa and Novorosyisk and at
the University of Rostov-on-Don. After the
family's emigration to Turkey and France he
continued his studies at the Paris Sorbonne
and Conservatoire, completing them at the
Conservatories of Leipzig and Dresden. His
teachers were V. Zavadsky for pianoforte,
Wolff, Neumann, Gédalge and Vidal for
harmony, counterpoint and fugue, and André
Pirro for musicology. He worked with the last
on a thesis concerning the music of the Mass
in the 15th century. As librarian he was at
the Sorbonne from 1933 to 1943, at the Bibliothèque de Documentation Internationale Contemporaine from 1943 to 1946 and at the
Bibliothèque Nationale (Music Dept.) from
1946 onwards. Since 1950 he has been active
in organizing the International Association of
Music Libraries, of which he was general
secretary from 1950 to 1955 and vice-president
from 1955 onwards. He is chief editor of the
' Fontes Artis Musicae ' (1954–) and has been
secretary of the Commission Internationale
Mixte of the International Repertoire of
Musical Sources since 1951. In 1957 he became a member of the council of the International Musicological Society. An imposing
number of articles published in the most
various periodicals and encyclopedias includes
valuable studies of Russian music and contributions on medieval music and musical
librarianship. A volume of gramophone
records of 13th-century music was published
by the Lyre-Bird Press under his direction.
His compositions include pianoforte music,
some songs on texts by Michelangelo, a pianoforte Concerto, ' Suite luxembourgeoise ' for
chamber orchestra and ' Quatre Haïku japo-
nais ' for voice and wind quartet.

G. R. (iii).

56   i   **FEINBERG**
Par. 2, l. 7 *should read*:

remained in manuscript, include 2 pianoforte concertos, 6 pianoforte

59   i   **FELSZTYŃSKI**
Footnote 3, l. 2 *should read*:
in ' Monumenta Musices Sacrae in Polonia ', Vol. II
(Poznań,

61   ii   **FENNEY**
Par. 1, l. 2 *should read*:

May 1891 ; *d.* Epsom, *c.* July 1957).

K

64   i   **FERGUSON,** CATALOGUE
Add to ORCHESTRAL WORKS:
16. ' Overture for an Occasion ' (1953).

Add after this:
BRASS BAND
15. 2 Fanfares for 4 trumpets & 3 trombs. (1952).

PIANOFORTE AND ORCHESTRA
should read:
PIANOFORTE AND STRING ORCHESTRA

ii   SONGS
2. 3 Medieval Carols *should read*:
3. 3 Medieval Carols.

65   i   **FERNÁNDEZ DE CASTIL-
LEJA**
Add at end:
See also Eslava (modern reprints).

FERNÂNDEZ, O. L.
Cancel Pars. 2 *and* 3 *and* signature
(*not* BIBL.) *and transfer* Pars. 2
and 3 of **LORENZO FER-
NÂNDEZ** *from* Vol. V, p. 399.

Add to BIBL. :
FRANÇA, ENRICO NOGUIERA, ' Lorenzo Fernândez, compositor brasileiro ' (Rio de Janeiro, 1950).

68   i   **FERRABOSCO (3)**
Par. 1, l. 3 *should read*:
until his death. He married a daughter,
Ellen, of the elder Nicholas Lanier.

Par. 2, ll. 7-9 *should read*:
and contrapuntal mastery; and several
pavans, two of which, the ' Four-note Pavan '
and the ' Dovehouse Pavan ', both in five
parts, rank

See also, l. 2. (mus. cr.) *should read*:
(mus. ex.).

Par. 4, l. 4 *should read*:
fantasies in four and six parts, the best of
which display

l. 8 *should read*:
in five parts, two of which, the ' Four-note

70   ii   **FERRARI, C.**
Par. 1, l. 2. 1780 *should read*:
1790

FERRARI, D.
Par. 2, l. 1 *should read*:
Italian violinist and composer, brother of the
preceding. He was a

72   i   **Ferretti, Jacopo**
Add after See:
Bellini (' Il fù ed il sarà ', lib.).

72   i   *Add before* **FERRI**:
FERRETTI, (Dom) Paolo (*b.* Subiaco, 3 Dec. 1866; *d.* Bologna, 23 May 1938). Italian musical scholar. He studied theology in Rome and after teaching at a monastery near Parma he became abbot of the Benedictine monastery of San Giovanni there. He was on the committee of the Società Santa Cecilia and in 1911 became President of the Pontifical Institute. He was an authority on the rhythmic treatment of Gregorian plainsong and published important works on the subject, including ' Principi teorici e pratici del canto gregoriano ' (1906) and ' Il cursus metrico e il ritmo delle melodie del canto gregoriano ' (1913).   E. B.

73   i   **FERRIER, Kathleen**
Add at end:
BIBL.—' Kathleen Ferrier : a Memorial ', ed. by Neville Cardus (London, 1954).
RIGBY, CHARLES, ' Kathleen Ferrier : a Biography ' (London, 1956).

ii   **FERROUD**
Add at end:
BIBL.—ROSTAND, CLAUDE, ' L'Œuvre de Pierre-Octave Ferroud ' (Paris, 1958).

74   ii   **FESTA, Costanzo**
Par. 3, l. 3 *should read*:
menta Polyph. Italica, Vol. II), and a collected edition of the Hymns, transcribed by Glen Haydon, was published in 1958 by the Pontifical Institute of Sacred Music, Rome.

77   i   **FÉTIS (2)**
Par. 1, l. 2. Bougives *should read*:
Bouvigne

78   ii   **FEVIN, A.**
Add at end:
See also Eslava (modern reprints). Maîtres Musiciens, Vol. 9 (modern ed. of Mass).

FÉVRIER
Par. 1, l. 1. 1875). *should read*:
1875; *d.* Paris, 8 July 1957).

79   ii   **FIBICH**
Par. 1, l. 1. Šeboriče *should read*:
Šerbořice

82   —   **CATALOGUE**
OPERAS
Col. 5, l. 1. Czech Theatre *should read*:
Provisional Theatre

l. 3. Czech Theatre *should read*:
New Czech Theatre

ll. 5, 7, 9, 11 and 13. Czech Theatre *should read*:
National Theatre

83   i   **FICHER**
Par. 1, l. 1. 2 Jan. *should read*:
14 Jan.

83   ii   l. 1 *should read*:
phony (1932); 3 symphonies, a violin Concerto, 3 string quartets,

FICKENSCHER
Par. 1, l. 2 *should read*:
Illinois, 9 Mar. 1871; *d.* San Francisco, 15 Apr. 1954).

FICKER
Par. 1, l. 2 *should read*:
1886; *d.* Igls, Tyrol, 2 Aug. 1954).

84   ii   *Add before* **FIEDEL**:
FIDO(E) (Fidow), John (*b.* ?, *c.* 1575; *d.* ? Worcester, *c.* 1640).
English organist and composer. He was organist of Hereford Cathedral from 1593 until he was expelled for using abusive language to the vicars-choral in Feb. 1595. He then went as master of the choristers to Worcester Cathedral, where he remained until Oct. 1596, and the following January he was summoned back to Hereford to be organist and to hold a deacon's stall ; but he remained there only until Oct. 1597. He was minor canon at Worcester from 1611 and assistant organist from 1625, presumably holding both appointments until his death. The bass part of his anthem ' Hear me, O Lord ' appears in a number of sources, including R.C.M. 1051, and the complete work (less organ part) is in the Peterhouse part-books. The bass parts of two other anthems, ' Deliver me from mine enemies ', and ' I call with my whole heart ', are at Gloucester Cathedral.   W. K. F.
BIBL.—ATKINS, IVOR, ' The Early Occupants of the Office of Organist and Master of the Choristers of the Cathedral Church, . . . Worcester ' (Worcestershire Hist. Soc., 1918).

87   ii   **FIELD**
Add to BIBL. :
BLOM, ERIC, ' John Field ' in ' Classics : Major and Minor ' (London, 1958).

89   i   **FIGNER, M. I.**
Par. 1, ll. 1-2. Dates *should read*:
(*b.* Florence, 4 Mar. 1859; *d.* Paris, 8 July 1952).

Par. 2, l. 1 *should read*:
Italo-Russian soprano

Par. 3, ll. 1-3 *should read*:
Medea Mei went to Russia with Figner in 1887 and made her début in that country on 8 May of that year at the Imperial Opera of St. Petersburg in the part of Valentine in ' The Huguenots'. She married Figner in St. Petersburg on 20 Feb. 1889, having been received into the Greek Orthodox Church a few days earlier. The pair soon became

89   i   *Add at end:*

BIBL.—FIGNER, MEDEA IVANOVNA, ' My Reminiscences [in Russian] ' (St. Petersburg, 1912).

ii   **FIGNER, N. N.**
Par. 1, ll. 1-2.   Dates *should read:*
(*b.* Kazan, 10 Feb. 1857; *d.* Kiev, 13 Dec. 1919).

96   ii   **FILM MUSIC**
Par. 3, ll. 14-16 *should read:*

quired by the action of the film. Nothing like the intensity of a full symphony orchestra, playing *forte,* can be

107   ii   Par. 2, l. 13.   Hermann *should read:*
Herrmann

108   i   Par. 3, l. 8.   Hermann *should read:*
Herrmann

110   i   *Add to* BIBL.:

McCARTY, CLIFFORD, ' Film Composers in America : a Checklist of the Work ' (Glendale, Cal., 1953).
MANVELL, ROGER & HUNTLEY, JOHN, ' The Technique of Film Music ' (London & New York, 1957).

FILOSOFO DI CAMPAGNA
l. 2.   *See* GOLDONI. *should read:*
See GALUPPI.

FILTZ
Par. 1, l. 1 *should read:*

FILTZ, Anton (Antonín Fils) (*b.* ?, *c.* 1730; *d.* Mannheim,

Par. 2, ll. 1-2 *should read:*

Bohemian violoncellist and composer. He was a pupil of Johann

ii   *Add at end:*

See also Musica Antiqua Bohemica, Vol. 18 (modern ed. of Concerto for fl. & pf.). Sondheimer Ed., Vol. 23 (modern ed. of Symphony).

111   i   **FINCK, Heinrich**
Par. 2, l. 3.   Warsaw *should read:*
Cracow

ll. 8-12 *should read:*

(f. 146) in 1482.[3]
In maturer years Finck returned to Poland and became *musicus regius* under Jan Olbracht (1492), Aleksander (1501) and Sigismond I (1506). Soon after he went to

112   ii   *Add at end:*

See also Chorwerk, Vols. 9, 21, 32 (modern reprints). Publikationen G.M.F., Vol. 7 (modern ed.).

114   i   **FINCK, Hermann**
Par. 4, l. 5 *should read:*
aus und machs nit lang . . .'.

114   i   *Add at end:*

A modern facsimile reprint of ' Practica musica ' is to be published in ' Documenta Musicologica ', Vol. 12.   C. S.

BIBL.—MATZDORF, PAUL, ' Die " Practica Musica " Hermann Fincks ' (Frankfort o/M. & Cassel, 1957).
See also Publikationen G.M.F., Vol. 7 (modern ed.).

ii   **FINE, Irving**
Par. 1, l. 2.   1915). *should read:*
1914).

Add after **FINÉ:**

FINGER CYMBALS. Tiny cymbals emitting no particular tuned note, and clipped to the fingers of the player. These cymbals, usually found in pairs, are of great antiquity, but have been revived for performances of ancient and medieval music.

118   ii   **FINGERING**
Par. 1, l. 3.   early 17th cent.) *should read:*
early 18th cent.)

127   i   Par. 1, l. 17.   J. G. Walther *should read:*
J. J. Walther

134   i   **FINK, Christian**
Par. 1, l. 2.   1822 *should read:*
1831

Par. 2, l. 1 *should read:*

German organist and composer. He was educated at the Stuttgart Orphans' Seminary in 1846–49 and studied

FINK, G. W.
Par. 1, l. 2.   Halle *should read:*
Leipzig [1]
Add footnote:
[1] Fétis had Halle, and this has been repeated by many dictionaries.

135   ii   **FINZI**
Par. 1.   1901). *should read:*
1901 ; *d.* Oxford, 27 Sept. 1956).

136   i   *Add at bottom:*

BIBL.—FERGUSON, HOWARD, ' Gerald Finzi (1901–56) ' (M. & L., XXXVIII, 1957, p. 129).

ii   CATALOGUE
l. 3.   *Op. should read:*
Op.[1]

CHORUS AND ORCHESTRA
Add after Op. 30:

39. ' In Terra Pax ' (Robert Bridges & St. Luke), Christmas Scene for soprano, baritone, chorus & orch. (1956).

UNACCOMPANIED CHORUS
Add after Op. 33:

34. ' Muses and Graces ' (Ursula Wood), unison song.
37. ' White-flowring Days ' (Edmund Blunden), S.C.T.B., in ' A Garland for the Queen ' (1953).

136 ii CHORUS AND ORGAN
Add after Op. 27:
36. ' Magnificat ' (posthumous).

VOICES WITH PIANOFORTE
l. 1. 5 Two-part Songs *should read*:
5 Two-part & 5 Unison Songs

ORCHESTRAL WORKS
Add after Op. 11:
20. ' The Fall of the Leaf ', elegy (posthumous).
25. Prelude for stgs. (posthumous).

SOLO INSTRUMENT AND OR-
CHESTRA
Add after Op. 6:
10. ' Eclogue ' for pf. & stgs. (posthumous).

Add after Op. 31:
38. ' Grand Fantasia and Toccata ' for pf. (1954).
40. Concerto for cello (1956).

Add after CHAMBER MUSIC:
VOCAL CHAMBER MUSIC
2. 2 Songs (Thomas Hardy) for baritone & stg. 4tet
    1. By Footpath and Stile.
    2. The Oxen.

VIOLIN AND PIANOFORTE
22. ' Elegy ' (posthumous).

Add footnote:
[1] The opus numbers 3 and 4 have remained un-
assigned. Dates are those of publication.

137 i *Add before Op.* 14:
13. ' Oh fair to see ', 6 songs (various poets) for high
    voice (posth.)
    1. Oh fair to see (Christina Rossetti).
    2. As I lay under the early sun (Edward Shanks).
    3. Only the wanderer (Ivor Gurney).
    4. To joy (Edmund Blunden).
    5. Harvest (Blunden).
    6. Since we loved (Robert Bridges).

Add after Op. 18:
19. ' Till Earth outwears ', 7 songs (Hardy) for high
    voice (posth.)
    1. Let me enjoy the earth.
    2. In years defaced.
    3. The Market Girl.
    4. I look into my glass.
    5. It never looks like summer.
    6. Let a lunar eclipse.
    7. Life laughs onwards.

Add after Op. 28:
— ' To a Poet ', 6 songs (var. poets) for low voice
    (posth.)
    1. On parent knees (attrib. to Sir William
       Jones).
    2. The Birthright (Walter De la Mare).
    3. Intrada (Thomas Traherne).
    4. Ode on the Rejection of St. Cecilia (George
       Barker).
    5. Time on Castle Hill (F. L. Lucas).
    6. To a poet a thousand years hence (J. E.
       Flecker).
— ' I said to Love ', 6 songs (Hardy) for low voice
    (posth.)
    1. I need not go.
    2. At Middle-Field Gate in February.
    3. Two Lips.
    4. In five-score summers.
    5. For life I had never cared greatly.
    6. I said to Love.

FIOCCO (1)
Par. 1, l. 2. Nov. *should read*:
Sept.[1]

l. 9. four *should read*:
three

137 i Par. 1, l. 16. twelve *should read*:
eleven

Add footnote:
[1] Thus in the registers of Sainte-Gudule; " Nov."
in the accounts of the royal chapel is a mistake.

ii FIOCCO (2)
l. 2 *should read*:
15 Dec.] 1686 ; *d.* Brussels, [buried 30 Mar.]
1746),

FIOCCO (3)
Par. 1, l. 2 *should read*:
20 Jan. 1703 ; *d.* Brussels, 22 June 1741),
seventh child

l. 13 *should read*:
brother, but resigned in July 1731 and on 29
July was appointed

l. 15 *should read*:
where he arrived on 3 Sept.   He also became

138 i Par. 2, l. 2. plair *should read*:
plaire

Add at end:
See also Monumenta Mus. Belg., Vol. 3 (reprint of
harpsichord works).

141 i FIPPLE FLUTE
Add at end, before See also:
(*PLATE* 21, Vol. III, p. 176, Nos. 3-5.)

142 ii FISCHER, Edwin
Par. 1. *Add at end*:
d. Zürich, 24 Jan. 1960).

144 i FISCHER, J. C. (F.)
Add to See also:
Denkmäler (2), Vol. 10 (modern ed. of ' Journal du
printemps ').

FISCHER, J. Caspar
Transfer See also at end to col. ii, at end of
J. Christian FISCHER.

145 i FISCHER, Kurt von
Par. 2, l. 8 *should read*:
there.   In 1957 he was appointed Professor
and director of the Musikwissenschaftliches
Seminar in the University of Zürich, having
acted as visiting lecturer at Basel University
in 1956–57.

Add at end:
' Studien zur italienischen Musik des Trecento und
frühen Quattrocento ' (with full catalogue of
sources of secular music) (Berne, 1956).
' Die Variation ' (' Das Musikwerk ' series) (Cologne,
1956).
' Zu J. Wolfs Übertragung des Squarcialupi-Kodex '
(' Musikforschung ', 1956, No. 1).
' Zur Theorie der Variation des 18. und beginnenden
19. Jahrhunderts ' (' Festschrift Schmidt-Görg ',
Bonn, 1957).
' Der Codex Reina (Paris, B.N., n.a. 6771) ' (' Musica
Disciplina ', XI, 1957).

146　i　**FISCHER, Wilhelm**
Add at end:
Bibl.—' Festschrift Wilhelm Fischer ' (Innsbruck, 1956).

147　ii　**FISTOULARI**
Par. 1, l. 2 *should read*:
Kiev, 20 Aug. 1907).

Last line *should read*:
daughter Anna in 1942; the marriage was dissolved in 1956.

148　i　**FITELBERG, G.**
Par. 3, l. 10 *should read*:
ducting in Portugal and America (Buenos Aires, 1940–41, U.S.A., 1942–45). In 1945–1946

149　ii　*Add before* **FLACCOMIO**:
FJELDSTAD, Øivin (*b.* Oslo, 2 May 1903).
Norwegian violinist and conductor. He studied the violin with G. Lange in Oslo (1913–23) and conducting with W. Davissohn at Leipzig (1928). Since 1935 he has been associated with the Norwegian State Broadcasting Company. In 1954 he conducted in the U.S.A. He is a noted interpreter of modern music and also a well-known conductor of classical and romantic music. He conducted the Oslo Philharmonic Orchestra at the I.S.C.M. concerts in Oslo in 1953.
O. G.

150　i　**FLACKTON**
Par. 1, l. 3. 5 Jan. 1793). *should read*:
5 Jan. 1798).

Par. 3, l. 1. Possibly John Flackton, William's brother, *should read*:
John Flackton, no doubt William's brother,

ii　**FLAGSTAD**
Par. 2, l. 22 *should read*:
she toured in Australia. She returned to Norway in 1941.

151　i　*Add at end, before signature*:
In 1958 Kirsten Flagstad was appointed director of the National Opera at Oslo.

Flaischlen
See Gál *should read*:
See Berg (Alban, song). Gál

Flaubert
l. 1. *Add after See*:
Bondeville (' Madame Bovary ', opera).

ii　**FLECHA (ii)**
Par. 1, l. 2 *should read*:
gona, 1530; *d.* Solsona, Lérida, 20 Feb. 1604).

151　ii　*Delete signature at end and add*:
Six *ensaladas* by the elder Flecha from his nephew's collection published in Prague in 1581 were reprinted by Anglès in a modern transcription, with an introductory study, at Barcelona in 1954.　　　J. B. T., adds.

152　i　**Flecker**
l. 4 *should read*:
Delius (' Hassan ', incid. m.). Finzi (song). Holland (T., 3 songs).

153　i　*Add before* **FLEISCHMANN, Friedrich**:
FLEISCHMANN, Aloys (Georg) (*b.* Munich, 13 Apr. 1910).
Irish educationist, conductor and composer of German birth. He took the degrees of B.Mus. (1931) and M.A. (1932) at University College, Cork, and attended postgraduate courses in 1932–34 at the Munich State Academy of Music, where he studied composition under Joseph Haas, and at Munich University. Returning to Cork, he was appointed Professor of Music at University College in 1934, a post he still holds (1958). He founded both the Cork Symphony Orchestra (1934), of which he is conductor, and the Cork Orchestral Society (1938), which organizes a series of concerts during the season and has brought to Cork orchestras such as the London Philharmonic, Hallé, Philharmonia and Vienna Philharmonic. He is Chairman of the Munster branch of the Music Teachers' Association of Ireland and takes an active part in the organization of the annual Festival of Cork.
Fleischmann is the editor of ' Music in Ireland ', published by the Cork University Press in 1952, and a contributor to a number of periodicals and encyclopedias. As a composer he has had three ballets produced at the Cork Opera House; they are among the works listed below:
Chinese Ballet, ' The Golden Bell of Ko ' (1948).
Ballet, ' An Cóitín Dearg ' (1951).
Ballet, ' Macha Ruadh ' (1954).
' Clare's Dragoons ' for baritone, war pipes, chorus & orch. (commissioned by Radio Eireann for the Thomas Davis and Young Ireland Centenary, 1945).
Choral Suite, ' The Three Sea Captains ' (1956).
Choral Dance Suite, ' The Planting Stick ', for chorus & small orch. (1957).
Overture, ' The Four Masters ', for orch. (commissioned for the Tercentenary of the Four Masters, 1944).
' Elizabeth McDermott Roe ', Lament for stgs. (1955).
3 Songs for tenor & orch. (1942).
Song Cycle, ' The Fountain of Magic ', for high voice & orch. (1945).
Quintet for stgs. & pf. (1939).
Suite for pf. (1935).　　　　　　　　D. O's.

FLEISHER
Par. 1, l. 2 *should read*:
11 July 1877; *d.* Philadelphia, 9 Jan. 1959).

154   i   **FLESCH**
Add to Bibl. :

Flesch, Carl, 'Memoirs', trans. by Hans Keller (London, 1957).

ii   **Fletcher, J.**
l. 3 *should read* :

Davies (H. W., 2 Pastorals, voc. chamber m.). Du Plessis (songs). Glanville-

160   i   **FLORENCE, E.**
Par. 1, l. 3 *should read* :

12 Dec. 1873 ; *d.* London, 1 Nov. 1928).

161   ii   **FLORIMO**
Par. 4, l. 8.   (1885) *should read* :
(1882)

ll. 11-13 *should read* :

Napoli ' (2 vols., Naples, 1869–71), enlarged into 4 vols. as ' La scuola musicale di Napoli ' (1880–84) ; ' Cenno storico sul collegio di musica di S. Pietro a Majella in Napoli ' (Naples, 1873) ;

162   i   Par. 2, l. 2 *should read* :

is chiefly known, ' La scuola musicale . . .', is

163   ii   **FLOTOW**
Add to Bibl. :

" Rosa, S.", ' Friedrich von Flotows Leben ' (Leipzig, 1892). (Biography by his widow.)

165   i   *Add before* **Fluchère** :

FLOYD, Carlisle (*b.* Latta, South Carolina, 12 June 1926).
American composer. The son of the Rev. Carlisle Sessions Floyd, a Methodist clergyman, he spent his early youth in various parishes in the southern part of South Carolina. At the age of ten he began to play the pianoforte on his own initiative, and his mother, herself a pianist, then engaged a teacher for him. Music continued to be one of his interests while he attended high school at North, S.C., where he graduated in 1943.
Winning a scholarship at Converse College, Spartanburg, S.C., he studied there for two years with Ernest Bacon and then followed his teacher to Syracuse University, Syracuse, N.Y., where he received his bachelor's degree in 1946. At twenty-one he joined the faculty of the University of Florida School of Music at Tallahassee, with which he has been associated ever since. He took a year's leave in 1949 to study for a master's degree at Syracuse, where his one-act opera or musical play, ' Slow Dusk ', was first performed that spring.
Floyd has written the librettos for all his operas. The second, ' Fugitives ', was performed at Florida State University in 1951, but he then withdrew it. ' Susannah ', first

staged at the University on 24 Feb. 1955, was given its first metropolitan performance by the New York City Opera Company on 27 Sept. 1956, winning praise which soon brought Floyd to national attention. The City Opera continued ' Susannah ' in its repertory during the next two years and produced it at the World's Fair in Brussels between 24 and 29 June 1958. Including performances by other American opera companies and university and college workshops, it had been given more than fifty times by the end of 1958. His fourth opera, ' Wuthering Heights ', based on Emily Brontë's novel, was commissioned by the Santa Fé (N.M.) Opera, which first produced it there on 16 July 1958.
Floyd has written several non-operatic works, including a pianoforte Sonata, a Theme and Variations and ' Lost Eden ' for 2 pianofortes and a ' Nocturne ' for soprano and orchestra, but he is best known so far by ' Susannah ', which reveals a distinct if not yet fully developed talent for dramatic expression in music and the projection of definite emotional atmospheres. With a setting in a Tennessee mountain valley, the score often conveys a convincing national and regional flavour without drawing upon folk music.
One of the reviews of the première of ' Wuthering Heights ' noted certain drawbacks, such as a difficult vocal line and sometimes dense orchestration, but also found the work to be often moving and powerful, with thematic interest and vocally beautiful episodes. Floyd revised the work for a spring production by the New York City Opera in 1959.
In the autumn of 1958, after two years' absence, Floyd returned to the University of Florida to hold courses in opera composition and libretto writing.   F. D. P.

166   i   **FLUGELHORN**
Add at end :
(*PLATE* 14, Vol. II, p. 446, Nos. 7 & 8.)

167   i   **FLUTE**
Par. 2, ll. 2-3 *should read* :
Some modern composers demand a whole tone higher than this, an extension quite

Par. 6, ll. 1-2 *should read* :
The flute is generally regarded as the least imperfect of all woodwind instruments. It has more-

ii   Par. 2, l. 14 *should read* :
chestrated passage. Its lower notes, however, can be played more softly than the corresponding and equivalent notes on the flute. Beethoven was among the

176   ii   *Add to* BIBL. :
GIRARD, A., 'Histoire et richesse de la flûte' (Paris, 1953).

181   i   **FOIDART, C. M.**
Par. 1, l. 2 *should read*:

8 Nov. 1902 ; *d.* Tucson, Arizona, 9 Jan. 1959).

Par. 3, ll. 12-13 *should read*:

viola at the Brussels Conservatoire. In 1950 he joined the Paganini Quartet in the U.S.A. In Britain he was known as a B.B.C. broadcaster.   A. L. C.

193   ii   **FOLK MUSIC (Austrian)**
Add at end:
'Jahrbuch des oesterreichischen Volksliedwerkes ', ed. by Leopold Nowak, Leopold Schmidt & Raimund Zoder (Vienna, 1952, in progress).

208   i   **FOLK MUSIC (Bulgarian)**
After Ex. 13, ll. 6-7 *should read*:
one-eighth. They have not the same rapidity as the hemiolic measures ($\int$ = 120-252 as against $\int^{\mathbb{N}}$ = 240-

213   ii   **FOLK MUSIC (Canadian)**
Add to BIBL. (FRENCH-CANADIAN) :
HARCOURT, MARGUERITE & D'HARCOURT, RAOUL, ' Chansons folkloriques françaises au Canada : leur langue musicale ' (Quebec & Paris, 1956).

215   i   **FOLK MUSIC (Cuban)**
1st musical example :
Add tie between the last two D's.

2nd musical example, stave 3, bar 3 :
Add tie between 2nd and 3rd G ; add triplet figure *3* above group of last three notes.

223   i   **FOLK MUSIC (Czech)**
          BIBL., l. 12. Ustni *should read*:
Ústni
       ii   l. 7. ULEHLA *should read*:
ÚLEHLA

231   ii   **FOLK MUSIC (English)**
Par. 2, l. 9 *should read*:
records of English traditional singers. It is true that many recordings have in recent years been taken by the B.B.C., but by no means all the singers concerned had retained the traditional style. The

236   ii   *Add to* BIBL. (FOLKSONG COLLECTIONS) :
DEAN-SMITH, MARGARET, ' A Guide to English Folk Song Collections 1822-1952, with an Index to their Contents, Historical Annotations and an Introduction ' (Liverpool, 1954).

237   i   BIBLIOGRAPHY
          Par. 1, *titles* LLOYD, PEARCE *and* REICHEN-BACH *should be transferred to the section* BOOKS AND ARTICLES *below.*

237   i   (BOOKS AND ARTICLES)
          l. 4 *should read*:
clusions ' (London, 1907 ; 3rd ed. 1954).
          Section FOLK DANCE COLLECTIONS, l. 7, *should be transferred above* l. 4 (as 2nd title ALFORD & GALLOP).

239   i   **FOLK MUSIC (Finnish)**
          Add to BIBL. :
ALA-KÖNNI, ERKKI, ' Die Polski-Tänze in Finnland : eine ethno-musikologische Untersuchung ' (Helsingfors, 1956).

248   i   **FOLK MUSIC (French)**
          Ex. 6 : *Heading and 1st line of text should read* :
ENTRE (*not* ETRE)
Entre (*not* Etre)

250   i   Par. 1, l. 15. fisherman's *should read* :
fishermen's

267   ii   **FOLK MUSIC (German)**
          Add to BIBL. (TREATISES) :
SALMEN, WALTER, ' Das Erbe des ostdeutschen Volksgesanges : Geschichte und Verzeichnis seiner Quellen und Sammlungen ' (Würzburg, 1956).

272   ii   **FOLK MUSIC (Greek)**
          Transfer 3rd musical example, b), to stand immediately below the 1st Example 11*a*), *and move Example* 12 *below* Par. 1, l. 12.

279   i   **FOLK MUSIC (Hungarian)**
          Footnote 2, l. 2 *should read*:
telvételek ', ed. Dénes Bartha (Budapest, 1937).

285   ii   BIBL. ll. 5-6 *should read*:
' Aranyi János népdalgyüteménye ' (' The Folksong Collection of J. A.'), ed. Z. Kodály & Á. Gyulai

286   i   BIBL., BARTHA, l. 9. H. der P.'s *should read*:
H. de P.'s

299   i   **FOLK MUSIC (Irish)**
          Entry 1909-36. *Transfer to stand after* 1908 *below.*

299-304   **FOLK MUSIC (Italian)**
          Replace present article by the following :
Italian.[1]   INTRODUCTION.—Ethnomusicology in Italy is a very young science, and not until quite recently has it been possible to

[1] The entry by Professor Alfredo Bonaccorsi in the 5th edition was published as a most valuable study of the influence of folk music on the work of Italian composers, and as such it retains its interest ; but it was in a sense an interim study and does not give what is really required of a section of the FOLK MUSIC article in Grove, *i.e.* a consideration of the present-day state of Italian folk music, its many regional varieties and its approach by modern research. This had not been attempted systematically at the time that Grove V was being prepared for publication. The present article by Professor Diego Carpitella, which, like other sections of the FOLK MUSIC entry, deals with folk dances and instruments as well as folksongs, is the first important and up-to-date study of the kind to be published in any work of reference.

consider folk music from a scholarly and modern point of view. For instance, the collecting of material by a method of direct inquiry — that is to say, on the spot — was first systematically carried out by Favara, who worked in Sicily at the end of the 19th and in the earliest years of the 20th century. The sound-recording of folksongs, on the other hand, dates no farther back than 1948, when a Centro Nazionale Studi di Musica Popolare was founded under the auspices of the Accademia di Santa Cecilia in Rome and of Radiotelevisione Italiana. The Archives of this Centre possess to-day some 5000 Italian folksongs, recorded on magnetic tape.

The long delay in the study of ethnomusicology in Italy was due to numerous and complex historical and cultural reasons: to a predominantly literary tradition in the study of folksong, which caused the musical text to be too often regarded as merely complementary instead of equally essential; to the fact that collections of popular songs, from the early 19th century until the present day, never made a clear distinction between what was fundamentally folk (predominantly peasant) and merely popular music (predominantly urban and artisan); to a tendency in Italian history to work on folk music within regional boundaries and thus to impede a nation-wide view and circulation; to the prevalent popularity of opera all through the 19th century; and not least to the great importance of a cultivated art of music in Italy, which tended to obscure research in the field of folk music.

The present state of study permits us to assert that what is basically folk music remained for centuries completely out of touch with art music in Italy, while on the other hand " popular " music was influenced by cultivated music in different ways and at various times (as for instance the *canzonette* of the 17th and 18th centuries or the *canzoni*, *romanze* and patriotic hymns of the 19th, which were influenced by operatic music); and in its turn art music adopted such popular elements as had already become more or less stylized (the work of Handel, A. Scarlatti, Frescobaldi, etc., Orazio Vecchi, Alessandro Striggio, the *laudi spirituali*, the Neapolitan *opera buffa*, etc., and in our century the music of Sinigaglia, Casella, Respighi, Pizzetti and others).

STRUCTURE AND CLASSIFICATION. — The study of " basic " Italian folk music to-day is indebted exclusively to original material discovered in the course of recent research.

The most conservative regions in the matter of folk music are those of the Centre and the South (Umbria, Tuscany, the Abruzzi and Molise, Lazio, Apulia, Lucania and Calabria) and the insular ones (Sicily and Sardinia).

As regards scalic structure, the most ancient basis of Italian folk music is modal; and modality is found not only in the southern and insular but also in the northern regions. This modality is not due to the influence of old religious music, unlike which folk music has retained it indefinitely. These ancient characteristics of the scale are to be traced above all in the *ninne-nanne* (lullabies), in many labour songs and in funeral lamentations (in which pentatonic scales sometimes appear). Where there is no trace of modality, examples of the natural scale are frequently found, uninfluenced by the tempered scale, which appears only in recent folk music indebted to cultivated music.

Ex. 1.—NINNA-NANNA
(Cinquefrondi, Calabria)

Bearing in mind the antiquity of modal and natural scales, the elementary and repetitive structure of the songs and the nature of vocalization (which in the early examples is usually high and forced), we arrive at a first great divison in Italian folk music: an ancient style and a modern style. This sub-division concerns the musical side only and has nothing to do with the words of the songs. Cases of non-synchronization between words and music are in fact very frequent: we thus often find songs the words of which are recent and literate while the music has remained archaic; and again there are recent tunes to fairly ancient words (especially in epic-lyrical songs).

Apart from the classification into ancient and modern styles, another is attempted to-day which orders folksongs according to the occasions on which they are sung, or the function which a song once served or still serves in the community. According to this kind of classification we find the following sub-divisions:

I. Lullabies (*see* Ex. 1), children's games, love songs, dances, funeral lamentations:

Ex. 2.—LAMENTO FUNEBRE (Ferrandina, Lucania) [1]

O   cic-cil-le mie o bel-le!

II. Seasonal and ritualistic songs (Christmas, New Year, Epiphany, Easter, Carnival, May).

III. Labour and occupational songs (carriers, miners, sulphur-workers, shepherds, fishermen, farmers, etc.):

Ex. 3.—CANTO DI PORTATORI (Positano, Campania)

Ex. 4.—CANTO DI LAVORO (Sicily) [2]

E va-iu a li ci-mi ci-mi di li can-ni

E va-iu cug-ghiennu li branchi e li bru-ni

IV. Recreation songs (*stornelli, ottave rime, epic-lyrical canzoni*, narrative songs):

Ex. 5.—STORNELLO (rustic type) [3]

A - mo rea-mo - re____ tu

sta-i al-la mo-re-a e i a-glie so - le

Ex. 6.—STORNELLO (artisan type)

Lento
Pe- schi fio-ren-ti __ ho canzo-na - to

dician-no-ve a - man-ti ho can-zo-na-to

di-cian-no ve a-man ti __ e se can-zo-no

Allegro
voi sa-ran-no ven-ti col - go la

ro - sa e la-scio star la fo-glia ho tan-ta

vo-glia di far con te l'a - mor

POLYPHONIC FORMS.—The antiquity of many specimens of Italian folk music may also be deduced from some "primitive" forms of polyphony. In many cases there is a transition from elementary to more complex forms, which however does not imply a change from an ancient to a modern style in the course of time. The tradition which

[1] E. De Martino, ' Morte e pianto rituale nel mondo antico ' (including notes on and musical transcriptions of the ' Lamento Lucano ' by Diego Carpitella, pp. 98-99) (Turin, 1958).

[2] A. Favara, ' Corpus di musiche popolari siciliane ', ed. by O. Tiby (Accademia di Scienze Lettere e Arti di Palermo, 1957), p. 24.

[3] L. Colacicchi, ' Canti popolari di Ciociaria ' in ' Atti del III° Congresso Nazionale di Arti e Tradizioni Popolari ' (Rome, 1936), p. 316.

asserts that central, southern and insular
Italian song is purely monodic while that of
the northern regions is in parts is shown by
recent evidence to be not altogether acceptable.
The fact is that the early style shows two
different modes of polyphonic organization;
and as regards the choral development in the
North, this is a comparatively recent phenomenon, due in part to the establishment of
choral groups singing "popular" music.
Among the most interesting examples of elementary polyphony are the *canti a vatoccu*
found in the Marshes and in Umbria. *A
vatoccu* means "bell-like". The outstanding
feature of these songs, in its different variants,
is a rudimentary "imitation" between two
voices, one male, the other female (a kind of
catch); and from the harmonic point of view
their characteristics are the confinement of
the melody within a diminished fourth and
a conspicuous clash of sevenths in the final
cadence:

Ex. 7.—CANTO A VATOCCU (Marshes) [1]

Other examples of "elementary" polyphony occur in the lamentations for Good
Friday, intoned in Sicily during processions.
Peculiar to these lamentations, especially in
the matter of intonation and vocal colour,
are certain characteristics of Arabic provenance. A high solo voice intones a verse, on
the final cadence of which other voices enter
contrapuntally, exclusively male and supported by a pedal bass:

Ex. 8.—LAMINTARI (Recalmuto, Sicily) [2]

[1] G. Ginobili, ' Canti popolareschi piceni ' (Macerata,
1955), p. ii.
[2] Favara, *op. cit.*, Vol. II, p. 397.

Similarly primitive are the *canti di battipali*
(piledrivers) of Venice. These are songs still
to be heard to-day, though more and more
rarely, accompanying the piledriving in the
lagoon. The song supports the rhythm of the
labour: a man, often the oldest, is in command while the others, one at a time, strike
the post. The end of the song coincides with
the stroke. The words of these songs, especially in the past, were in *ottava rima* and often
contained references to the crusades; nowadays they are concerned with love and with
historical facts, interspersed with incitements
to work.

More complex forms are to be found in
southern Italy (*e.g.* for three voices), with
short contrapuntal snatches supported either
by the bagpipe or by a small organ. The
species in which this polyphony deploys itself
in natural intonation are *serenate* and *stornelli*.
But the most interesting and complex forms
in Italian folk music are unquestionably those
represented by the choruses of Sardinian
shepherds and Ligurian mariners, all of
which remain in the ancient style. Sardinian
folk music has always retained its very particular features in Italian popular music,
especially a homogeneity due to historical
reasons, among which geographical isolation
is by no means the least important.

From the archaeological point of view it
is important to point out that the most ancient
Sardinian remains go back to the neolithic
age, like the famous conical structures known
as *nuraghi*. There are also frequent harkings
back to the Phoenician civilization of the
Mediterranean; and the most recent historico-
sociological research has retraced the historical course of some pastoral communities of
the north-eastern region of the island —
the Barbagia — which are perhaps among the
most ancient in Europe. The most famous
Sardinian choruses are precisely the *sos
tenores* of the Barbagia. The shepherds habitu-
ally assemble four singers, who engage in a

poetico-musical dialogue. The first of them, called *Sa boghe*, taking up a rigid position

lables such as " ba-ri-llà ", " bim-bo-rò " or " bim-ba-rà ":

Ex. 9.—Su Tenore (Sardinia) [1]

apart from the others, standing or seated, begins to sing one verse in a voice alternating between high and low, and develops a song pronouncing each syllable in a continually tremulous and sobbing tone — a declamatory syllabic *rubato*. At the end of this exposition, the length of which depends on the words, their significance and their emotional stimulus, this singer falls silent, and on his last note the other three voices enter, known respectively as *Su bassu* (with a raucous, cavernous, metallic sound), *Sa mesa boghe* and *Sa contra*. These voices between them are approximately a third and a fifth, and a fourth and a sixth apart in pitch: approximately, because the Sardinian songs frequently show an uncertainty of intonation and contain " blue " notes, apart from numerous clashes of seconds which give them a peculiar character of asperity and angularity. The three voices do not repeat all the words proposed by the solo voice, but derive their rhythmic shapes from the scansion of certain traditional syl-

When this rhythmic incident is concluded, the solo voice resumes the song, only to be again interrupted by the other three voices, and so on. The vocal delivery of the *sos tenores* is distinguished by naturalistic imitations showing an affinity with noises of the animal world (bleatings, lowings, etc.), by the calls the shepherds use for their flocks (howls, whistles, vocal distortions) and by the compass of the songs (strangled or sobbing voice, frequent *portamenti*). These choral songs, which may be for as many as four or five voices — when they take the name of *tasgia* — also accompany the *ballo tondo*, which is in fact among the most ancient round-dances of the Mediterranean and related to, for instance, the Catalan *sardana* and the *kolo* of the Balkans.

Other most important examples of Italian folk polyphony are those of the Ligurian *trallalero*, still sung to-day, especially among the wharfingers of the Genoese port. It is

[1] G. Fara, 'L' anima musicale d' Italia' (Rome, 1920), App. of music, No. 73.

not yet possible to determine the origin of
these songs precisely, nor to tell whether they
were sung in early times by marine sail-
makers.   The performers are usually seven,
the part of the uppermost being so high that
it seems to call for a woman's voice.   All
these voices together form a polyphonic fabric
of very elaborately vocalized parts.   The words
are as a rule quite short, but the music, owing
to its highly ornate character, may go on
indefinitely.   Some aspects of intonation and
of polyphonic design relate the *trallalero* to the
Sardinian choral songs.

which the others respond.   The words are a
compound of invocation, incitement to work
and imprecation, and they have an erotic
undertone.   The style derives from North
Africa : the most important tunny fisheries of
the Mediterranean are in fact on the north
coast of Africa, in Sicily, Sardinia and Calabria.   To which must be added that some of
the occupational terms of tunny-fishing have
an Arabic origin (the head of the team, for
instance, is called *rais*).

INSTRUMENTS.[1]—The Italian folk instruments, like the folksongs, are to be divided

Ex. 10.—TRALLALERO (Genoa, Liguria)

Still to be considered among the elementary
polyphonic forms are some " repartee songs "
for two voices or one solo voice and chorus.
The former include the *canti alla stesa* (extension), *canti all' altalena* (see-saw) and *canzoni
alla boara* (cowherd) of central and northern
Italy (Molise, Lazio, Umbria, Romagna) ;
the latter, *i.e.* the songs for a single voice and
chorus, include some *stornelli da lavoro* (labour)
of central Italy (Lazio, Umbria) and above all
the antiphonal songs which the Sicilian
mariners perform while catching tunny-fish.
These songs are intoned during the culminat-
ing period of the catch, when the fish are har-
pooned in the " death chamber " formed by
the boats arranged in a square.   At that
moment the head of the team starts a song to

into ancient and modern specimens.   Among
the ancient instruments to be enumerated are
*castagnole, triangolo, fistola, lira, launeddas, pifferi,
tamburelli, zampogna* [2], *ocarina, brogna, cupa-cupa,
scacciapensieri, chitarra battente* and *tamburo*;
among the modern ones *chitarra* and *organetto*.
   It is clear that, like the instruments, the
voice (and thus a great deal of the ancient
style) succeeds in retaining its original
characteristics.   One of the most important
of the ancient instruments is undoubtedly the
zampogna, the bagpipe which is to be regarded

[1] No attempt is made here to translate the names of
the instruments, for many of which there is in fact no
equivalent in English ; but they can be identified from
the accompanying illustrations.
[2] For another illustration *see PLATE* 2, BAGPIPES,
Vol. I, p. 352.

as the typical instrument of the South (Molise, Abruzzi, Campania, Lucania, Lazio, Calabria), especially among the shepherd communities. The songs accompanied by the *zampogna* are *stornelli*, serenades, pastorals and tarantellas, as well as some ritual songs such as the *maggio* of Molise (*e.g.* 'La Pagliara', which is not unlike 'Green George': a man covered in a cone made of grass goes about the country, and the women throw water on his back from the windows in the belief that this will ensure the water supply):

its name: some say it comes from *lionasci* (*i.e.* the oleander, which is the tree from which it is said to have been originally made); others decide for *lianu* (*i.e. canto fermo*, the single note emitted by the *tumbu*); or again — and this is the most plausible interpretation — from a union of *lau* (the laurel from which the ancient aulos was constructed) with *cannas* (reed), producing *canneddas* (little reed). The *cunzertu* (*i.e.* the ensemble) may be managed in various ways, eliciting higher or lower notes and, according to Fara, sad or merry sounds

Ex. 11.—LA PAGLIARA (Fossalto, Molise) [1]

But the earliest of all the Italian folk instruments may be said to be the Sardinian *launeddas* [2], which up to the present have been most closely studied by Fara. Evidence for this instrument in the Mediterranean area has been found among the statuettes, *nuraghide*, of the neolithic age. It has three reeds of different lengths: the longest, which produces a single low note, is the *tumbu*; the medium-sized reed, called *mancosa*, gives the middle register and is bound to the *tumbu* with a short cord; the smallest, called *mancosedda*, produces the highest notes. The player holds the *tumbu* and the *mancosa* in his left hand and the *mancosedda* in the right. The instrument has great polyphonic possibilities. There are various notions concerning the derivation of

that seem to imitate the human voice of the Sardinian peasantry and various characters: *mediana-pipia* (child, girl-baby), *fiuda* (widow), *mongia* (nun); or allude to musical matters: *fiorassiu* (ornamentation), *organu* (organ), *contrappuntu* (counterpoint). In the *cabissa* (*i.e.* the mouthpiece) there is a single-beating reed called *limbatta* or *linguazza*, with two characteristic features: a free end turned downwards and a small piece of wax fixed to that end. This reed is extremely adaptable, capable of producing quarter-tones and allowing for perfect accord with the voices, which in Sardinian music abound in intervals smaller than a semitone ("blue" notes, etc.). One of the difficulties in playing this instrument is that of breath-control, since the three reeds of the mouthpieces have all to be kept in the mouth at the same time.

Instruments such as the violin, guitar, mandoline, small organ and, most recently, the clarinet and the *fisarmonica*, generally

[1] A. M. Cirese, 'La pagliara maie maie' in 'Molise', special number of 'La Lapa' (Rome), Vol. III, Nos. 1-2, 1955, pp. 33-36.
[2] G. Fara, 'Su uno strumento musicale sardo' in Riv. Mus. It., Vol. XX, 1913, pp. 763-91; Vol. XXI, 1914, pp. 13-51.

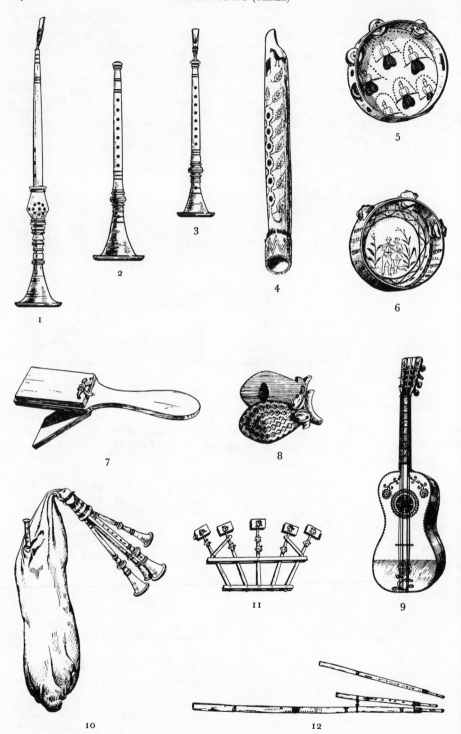

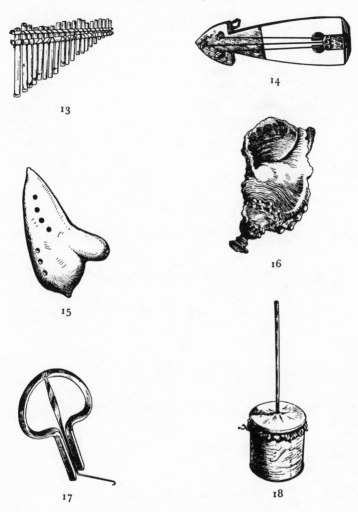

KEY TO ILLUSTRATIONS

No.
1. LAZIO—*Piffero* of turned wood, with mouthpiece (maximum length *c.* 2′ 6″).
2. LAZIO—*Piffero* without mouthpiece (max. length *c.* 1′ 8″).
3. LAZIO—*Piffero* with mouthpiece (max. length *c.* 1′ 5″).
4. SICILY—*Zufolo* of cane with coloured incisions in red and blue, made and used by shepherds (max. length *c.* 11½″)
5. MARSHES—*Cembalo Loreto*, timbrel of wood and skin, with painted figures in colour and with metal jingles (max. diameter *c.* 1′ 5″, height *c.* 3½″).
6. SICILY—*Tammuredda*, women's timbrel, with painted figures in red and blue on parchment and jingles of lath. (max. diameter *c.* 1′ 4½″, height *c.* 3¾″).
7. SARDINIA—*Ciocca-Ciocca, macetere* made of three pieces of wood (max. length *c.* 8″).
8. TUSCANY (S. Marcello Pistoiese)—Castanets of carved wood with leather handles and two metal jingles (max. height *c.* 2¾″).
9. CALABRIA (Cosenza)—Guitar with 8 strings, decorated with roses in red and blue (max. length *c.* 1′ 6″; body *c.* 9″).
10. CALABRIA—Bagpipe (*zampogna*) (max. length: pipes *c.* 2′ 1½″, skin bag *c.* 2′ 9″, mouthpiece *c.* 4″).
11. CAMPANIA—Tricheballacche, Neapolitan instrument with 5 wooden hammers, the central one fixed, the others movable, with appliances of lath ("festa di Piedigrotta") (length of the longer strut 1′ 9½″, the shorter 1′ 3″).
12. SARDINIA—*Launeddas* (length of the largest pipe [in 2 parts] *c.* 2′ 11″).
13. CAMPANIA (Caserta)—*Fistola* of cane (length of the braces *c.* 1′ ¾″, of the longest pipe *c.* 9″, of the shortest *c.* 2½″).
14. CALABRIA (Catanzaro)—3-stringed Lyre with twine strings (max. length *c.* 1′ 5″, width of base *c.* 4½″).
15. LUCANIA—*Ocarina* of terracotta (max. length *c.* 7½″).
16. SICILY—*Bragna* made of a shell (max. length *c.* 8″).
17. CAMPANIA—*Pu-ti-pù* (Jew's Harp).
18. CAMPANIA—*Scacciapensieri*.

accompany such folksongs as have suffered a
certain amount of stylization. The most recent
appearances of these instruments have subjected the melodic structure of the songs to
the tempered scale and often robbed the vocal
style of its original characteristics. Nevertheless, not long ago cases of instrumental acclimatization have been found in which the modern
instruments have adapted themselves to the
archaic style, as in the case of the guitar with
some *stornelli* and dances of the peasants and
mariners of southern Italy or in that of the
shepherds' songs in Sardinia and Gargano.
This is also the case with the *organetto*, which
in some localities compensates for the loss of
the *zampogna* and imitates it:

instrumental acclimatization, in the sense that
some modern instruments (guitar, small organ)
have assimilated in performance some stylistic
features of the past. Moreover, in many of
these ancient dances it is possible to retrace
choreographic elements (by way of literary and
pictorial documents) and the occasion of their
use as well as the music (*see* Exs. 13 and 14).

In Apulia we still find examples of the
pizzica very different from the well-known
stylized and popularized *tarantella*, of which
the *pizzica* is the ancient sung and danced
form. It takes its name from the sting of the
tarantula, the poisonous spider, which was to
be healed only by means of this dance.
We find the same contemporaneousness of

Ex. 12.—SCURA MAIE (Abruzzi)

DANCES.—The criterion of subdivision into
ancient and modern also applies to folk and
popular dances. The dances which to-day
may be considered both ancient and popular
are the *saltarello*, distributed particularly
through the central regions (some evidence
for it is found as early as the mural paintings
in the Etruscan caves of Tarquinia, 5th
century B.C.); the *tarantella* (mentioned long
before the Christian era by Strabo, Galen,
Pliny and Aristotle), which in general represents the folk dance of the South (the Apulian
pizzica, the Sicilian *fasola*); the *trescone*
(spread widely over the central and northern
regions (for which we have medieval literary
evidence); the Sardinian *ballo tondo* (round-
dance) with its extremely ancient ritual origins.
As a rule these dances, as well as being sung,
are accompanied by instruments of equal
antiquity (*zampogna, launeddas, tamburello*),
although here again we note a process of

choreographic, folk-lore and musical elements
in the Sardinian round-dances, whether they
are accompanied by voices or by the *launeddas*.
It may be said, however, that the greater part
of Italian folk dances is in the modern style.
One of the most revealing examples is found
in Sicily, where the musical style of the dances
(*e.g.* the *fasola*, accompanied on the *friscalettu*)
differs strikingly from the ancient vocal style.

Italy possesses some hundreds of popular
dances in the modern style (*e.g. bergamasca,
castellana, controdanza, gagliarda, giga, girometta,
monferrina, pavanella, perigurdin, piva, polesana,
ruggero*, etc.). To render any historical account
of these dances is a complicated business. The
names of many of them, in fact, date from the
Renaissance or earlier, and they were popular
at one time; but it was during the Renaissance
and through a process of stylization that they
found their way into the cultivated and
courtly suite. Later, stylized by that time,

they spread and became popular, keeping their names but having often lost their original character. In time these dances changed their choreography and their music, so that what is a popular *padovana* or *giga* to-day may often resemble a mazurka or a polka of the 19th century. One of the most interesting cases of the kind is that of the *furlana*, which in the course of time and of successive stylizations has come down to us in forms that go no farther back than the 19th century, while its original characteristics, both choreographic and musical, are still to be found in the *resiana*, which is a popular dance of the Slavonic community of Carnia (Friuli) (*see* Ex. 15, p. 146).

Ex. 13.—LA PIZZICA (Taranto, Apulia) [1]

*) Words not recoverable

[1] D. Carpitella, *Ritmi e melodie di danze popolari in Italia* (Rome, 1956), Ex. 5.

L

Ex. 14.—SALTARELLO (Frosinone, Lazio) [1]

The Renaissance origins of "popular" Italian dances in the modern style may also be retraced through the figure dances that still exist: *e.g. ballo dei bastoni, danza della spada, ballo del fazzoletto* (stick, sword and kerchief dances), *moresca* (Morris dance), *laccio d' amore, l' Amanti nova*, etc.[2]

MODERN STYLE.—Apart from the classification into ancient and modern styles, recent studies in Italian folk music have shown that

Ex. 15.—RESIANA (S. Giorgia di Resia, Carnia) [3]

*) | = Loud stamping
|| = Louder stamping

[1] L. Colacicchi, *op. cit.*, p. 308.
[2] B. M. Galanti, 'La danza della spada in Italia' (Rome, 1942); A. G. Bragaglia, 'Danze popolari italiane' (Rome, 1950).   [3] D. Carpitella, *op. cit.*, words not recoverable.

the folk-musical materials often present contra-
dictions in their apparent unity, in the sense
that between the literary text, the music and
the song's occasion there is not always a strict
identity of time and form. Among the most
interesting examples revealing this fact are
the famous *maggi* (May songs) so widely
distributed in central Italy (Tuscany, Umbria).
They are scenic songs sung by peasants during
the month of May, and their literary text may
be chivalrous poetry (Ariosto, Tasso), poems
by Dante (*e.g.* the episode of Pia de' Tolomei),
classical poetry (Virgil, Ovid) or heroic-
comic words (*e.g.* by Guerino il Meschino), or
even chronicles of current events or love
poetry (*maggi a serenata*). Although they have
lost their ritual function, these songs derive
from the sung *rappresentazioni* and their forms
are discoverable already in the 15th and 16th
centuries; they have even been considered to
be popular components of Italian opera by
reason of their formal structure: introduction
(choral or instrumental), recitative (for men's
voices), ritornello or *sviolinata* (interlude).
From the folk-lore point of view, however,
there is no identity between the elements
constituting the *maggi*. The ritual occasion has
lost its original significance and has become
a dramatic abstraction; the recitative has
retained its ancient rustic style; the ritornello
or interlude is often a 19th-century dance
(mazurka, polka); the choral introduction has
analogies with the post-Renaissance *canzone*:

Ex. 16.—Maggio [1]

[1] D. Carpitella, *op. cit.*
[2] D. Carpitella, *op. cit.*, Ex. 21.

A similar discontinuity is to be seen in the
ottave rime, which, be they peasant or artisan
cultivations, have a traditional, ancient musical style while the words may be either ancient
(chivalrous poems, Dantesque lyrics, Latin
classics, etc.) or modern (chronicles or love
poems). The *ottave rime* are means of improvisation spread over central Italy (Tuscany,
Umbria, Lazio), the region where the dialect
became the standard Italian and thus favoured
the circulation of cultured texts among the
uncultured classes:

Ex. 17.—Ottava Rima (Lazio) [3]

[3] G. Nataletti, 'I poeti a braccio della campagna
romana' in 'Atti del IIIo Congresso Nazionale di Arti e
Tradizioni Popolari' (Rome, 1936), p. 391.

The same kind of discontinuity, again, is to be found in the songs attached to the old dramatic *rappresentazioni* of ritualistic origin, such as the ' Sega della Vecchia ' in Umbria, an age-old ceremony ushering in the spring, held in mid-Lent, at which an oak is sawn in order to deliver the tree from the spirit of evil. But the songs in these performances especially Piedmont, rooted in Celtic romance. The words of these songs, difficult as it is to deal with the problem of dating them, certainly go back to the Renaissance and even the Middle Ages. Here are some of their titles : ' Donna lombarda ' (which according to some authorities derives from the 6th-century story of Rosamunda and Alboino) :

Ex. 19.—DONNA LOMBARDA (Baiardo, Liguria)

are in a recent style, both the opening and closing ones of praying and dismissal, and those to the rhythm of which the oak is sawn :

Ex. 18.—LA VECCHIA
(Pontefelcino, Umbria)

One of the most interesting cases of divergencies between the literary and the musical texts is unquestionably that of the epic-lyrical and the narrative *canzoni*. They are among the most important patrimonies of Italian folk music. The fountainhead of this form is considered to be northern Italy and

' Cecilia ' (the story of a woman who, to save her husband's life, yields her honour to a cruel and ungrateful hangman [? early 16th century]) ; ' Un' eroina ' (the theme of the ballad ' Lady Isabel and the Elf-King ') ; ' Il marito giustiziere ' (same subject as the Portuguese romance ' Bernal Francez ') ; ' La donna rapita ' or ' Scibilia Nobili ' (which according to some goes back to the Middle Ages, 13th and 14th centuries, and thus to the age of barbarous piracies) ; ' La pesca dell' anello ' (believed to be connected with the legend of Cola-Pesce of the time of Ferdinand II, King of Sicily) :

Ex. 20.—LA PESCA DELL' ANELLO
(Piedmont) [1]

[1] C. Nigra, ' Canti popolari del Piemonte ' (Turin, 1957 ; new ed. of the first of 1888), p. 417.

'Il pellegrino di Roma' (which has some incidents in common with the Anglo-Scottish 'Lord Ingram and Chiel Wyet'); 'La finta monacella'; 'L'amante confessore'; 'La prova' (similar to the Portuguese 'Bella Infanta', the Spanish 'Caballero de lejas tierras' and the German 'Liebesprobe'); 'La bevanda sonnifera' (which has its roots in the 'Dolopathos' of the 12th century); the 'Amata morta'; 'Il convegno notturno'; 'Il cognato traditore'; 'Verde Oliva' (one of the epic-lyrical songs most widely spread over southern Italy, dealing with a custom of the past which ordained that an ill-married girl should make a vow of chastity for the first night, or three nights, after marriage), which was followed by numerous other narrative songs.

From the musical point of view these epic-lyrical and narrative songs are seen to belong largely to the modern style, and it must also be borne in mind that this repertory assumed, especially from the 16th century onwards, the artisan character of Italian folk music. Nevertheless, it is possible even to-day to find the earliest examples of the modern style in Liguria (Ex. 19), Piedmont and Lombardy, and there is no doubt that among these

recent tunes, and it is in this form that the repertory in question spread itself all over Italy towards the end of the 19th and in the early 20th century.

Other examples of modern stylization are the present-day *villotte* of Friuli, which have nothing in common with the 15th- and 16th-century *villotte*, nor with any of the ancient peasant songs sung in Friuli and Carnia until about forty years ago. The earliest examples of this type are distinguished by their modal scales and more especially their melodic movement by fourths, which is typical of the Slavonic-Friulian zone (Ex. 29):

Ex. 21.—VILLOTTA ANTICA [1]

The modern *villotte*, on the other hand, are the outcome of recent 19th-century stylizations, as may be clearly seen from the harmonization and the choral lay-out of an artisan type:

Ex. 22.—VILLOTTA MODERNA

particular songs are to be found the most interesting specimens of folk and popular music of the 16th, 17th and 18th centuries. It is especially in the 19th century that these literary texts became adapted to the most

The same stylization was also undergone by the alpine songs, among which it is particularly

[1] E. Adaiewski de Schoultz, 'Anciennes Mélodies et chansons populaires d'Italie' in Riv. Mus. It., Vol. XVI, 1909.

difficult to-day to find original forms.

The same discontinuity between musical and literary texts is again found in folk and popular religious music, which has traditional religious words in Italian: Songs for the Nativity, for Epiphany, for Easter, prayer-songs, etc., adapted to tunes both ancient and modern. If we except a few Sicilian examples (Ex. 8) and some Sardinian ones of the type of *Su Tenore* (Ex. 10), Italian religious folk music usually belongs to the modern style, which, however, does not exclude ancient elements, as for example the modal character of many passages in 'Il pianto delle zitelle', a *sacra rappresentazione* cultivated in Lazio, or more precisely at Ciociaria (a region in which folksongs have a modal substratum quite free from ecclesiastical influence; a "Miserere" in this *rappresentazione* in particular has affinities with a Tuscan *maggio* song, as has been clearly demonstrated):

Ex. 23.—MISERERE (Vallepietra, Lazio) [1]

The various aspects the modern style has assumed in the course of time, and the social stratum, peasant or artisan, in which a particular patrimony of folk music has taken root, have given rise to the question of "popular" Italian music, in which folk and cultivated elements become involved by turns. One of the most interesting examples in that respect is the Neapolitan *canzonetta*, the history of which can be traced back to the 15th and 16th centuries, where already an urban and artisan character, distinct from country aspects, is to be discerned:

Ex. 25.—GRIDO DI VENDITORE
(Naples, Campania) [3]

This Neapolitan song, although retaining some characteristic folk features, in the course of the centuries soon underwent cultural influence of various kinds which partially transformed it. Caravaglios has recently thrown light on the relationships between the street-cries of ambulant vendors and some traditional Neapolitan songs (*e.g.* the cry of an ice-cream man and the song 'Pepparella'):

Ex. 26.—PEPPARELLA (Naples, Campania) [4]

In Italy there is a large repertory of regional folksongs which during the 19th century showed a strong tendency to absorb national and patriotic ideologies under the influence of cultivated music and opera in particular. There is ample documentation for this in the collections of "popular" songs published by Ricordi up to the end of the first half of the 19th century.

Ex. 24.—LA CANZONE DI S. GIUSEPPE
(Fermo, Marshes) [2]

[1] L. Colacicchi, 'Il "Pianto delle Zitelle"' in 'Lares', Vol. VII, 1936, p. 105.
[2] G. Ginobili, *op. cit.*, p. 1.

[3] G. Caravaglios, 'Il contenuto poetico ed il contenuto musicale nei gridi dei venditori ambulanti napoletani' in 'Atti dell' Accademia Pontaniana' (Naples, 1932), Vol. LXII.
[4] V. De Meglio, 'Eco di Napoli' (Milan, 1930–31, new ed.).

ETHNICAL ISLANDS.—Of great importance in recent research of Italian folk music has been the study of the peculiarities of various ethnical islands distributed over various parts of the peninsula. Of especial importance among them are the Albanian communities in Calabria, Lucania (Pallagorio, Carfizzi, San Costantino Albanese, etc.), Sicily (Piana dei Greci), and the Slavonic-Albanian pockets of Molise (Ururi, Portocannone, Campomarino, Montecilfone, Acquaviva, Collecroce, Montemitro, San Felice del Molise).[1] The Albanian communities settled all along the eastern coast of Italy migrated to the peninsula towards the second half of the 15th century, under the pressure of the Turks in the Balkans. It was then that they established villages in low-lying parts of the coast, hardly penetrating inland, to serve as outposts of defence in case of invasion. But it was the Albanians in Calabria, Lucania and Sicily above all who preserved the traditional songs (funeral lamentations and lullabies) and the ritual songs, as for instance those sung at wedding ceremonies. In Calabria there are songs and dances for the preparations of the bridal bed, the clothing of the bride and for the processions accompanying her. The funeral lamentations too persist particularly in Calabria, some being pentatonic:

Ex. 27.—LAMENTO FUNEBRE
(Castroregio, Calabria)

The persistence of traditional customs and dresses in the Albanian communities is also due to the almost complete preservation of their original language. They often know Albanian, through daily and familiar use, and Italian, especially through connections with the state and with commerce, but are unfamiliar with the dialect of the region in which they live; and they have in fact their own tradition of popular poetry:

Ex. 28.—KAREGINA: NUPTIAL DANCE [2]
(S. Costantino Albanese, Lucania)

What is more, for the Albanians both of Calabria and of Sicily the Catholic Church, while following the accepted liturgy, gives oriental rhythms to its music. On the other hand the Slavonic community of Molise has suffered a certain discontinuity and decadence in its musical patrimony, in spite of the fact that in the past it gave rise to interesting processes of acclimatization.

The Slavs of Carnia, however, whose stabilization in Friuli antedates that of the other Albanian Slavs in Italy, keep their patrimony intact, having the advantage of their particular geographical situation. Its most carefully preserved music, which is

---

[1] A. M. Cirese, op. cit., pp. 55-58.

[2] D. Carpitella, op. cit., Ex. 9.

also bilingual, are the wedding songs and
dances:

Ex. 29.—Canto di Nozze (S. Giorgio di Resia, Carnia)

and the labour songs. Many of the dances
still existing, like the *resiaskin* or *resiana*, were
originally ritual fire dances, and their instrumental performance, by a violin and a kind
of viola da gamba, clearly reveals the Balkan
influence.

Of the Albanians of Calabria and Lucania
it must also be said that the process of decay
in the archaic patrimony was hastened by
the intervention of modern instruments like
the guitar and the small organ; yet even
in the most recent popular music it is possible
to trace modes of performance which are
ethnically ancient.

A chapter of its own is suggested by the
folksong of the Upper Adige, of an alpine type
and clearly influenced by Tyrolese elements.
It must be pointed out that in this zone
organized choral songs are widely disseminated, which means that they are to be described as popular rather than folk music
proper. As for the songs of the Val d' Aosta,
in Piedmont, the most typical are peasant
songs in a French patois (*lingua patuà*); they
are of an alpine-popular type sung as
organized choruses.

Also within the framework of recent research and the specialist study of ethnical
islands is the music of the Jewish communities in Italy, resident chiefly in the cities.
This particularly interesting subject has
recently been treated by Levi, who emphasizes
the importance of the links between oriental
and western Jewish music and has found
affinities between Hebrew liturgy and some
Italian folksongs, such as the Piedmontese
' La crava ', which is a paraphrase of the
Hebrew ' Chad Gadià ' (*see* Ex. 30).

Conclusion.—Although the still too recent
scientific inquiries into Italian folk music
have so far (summer 1958) limited a thorough
analysis of structural and morphological
elements, it has been possible by this time to

determine some fundamental characteristics:
(*a*) the greatest antiquity of songs linked in
the past with magic and religious rituals
(lullabies, laments, some of the labour songs);
(*b*) the fundamentally modal nature of early
songs free from the influence of religious or
cultivated music; (*c*) a broad division into
an ancient and a modern style — the rustic
folk music belonging to the former while the
latter comprises " popular " and artisan
music (the origins of this style reaching back
to the late Middle Ages and including epic-
lyrical-narrative songs, religious folksongs,

Ex. 30.—La Crava (Piedmont) [1]

E   la   cra-va c'a la   Pa- stü-
-ra-va c'a l'à   rutt al   butt   Ah ca bun
vin c'a je-ra 'nt'al   me   butt   l'è la
cra - va c'à l'à   rutt   al   butt

canzonette, etc.); (*d*) the complete independence of archaic folk music of any cultural
influence whatever; (*e*) the utter difference
between rustic folk music and " popular "
artisan music, due to a conspicuous rupture in
the relationship between town and country,
where the backward state of the country is
seen in opposition to the great civic and
courtly developments, particularly during the

[1] L. Levi, ' Canti tradizionali e tradizioni liturgiche
giudeo-italiane ' in ' La Rassegna Mensile di Israel '
(Venice), Vol. XXIII, No. 9, pp. 403-11; No. 10, pp.
435-45.

Renaissance (whence came the cultivated music of Italy); (f) the vital survival of the music of ethnical islands (Albanian, Slavonic, Greek and Jewish) with various characteristics of acclimatization.

BIBLIOGRAPHY.—The bibliography of Italian folk music still suffers from some uncertainties in methodical research: the distinction between folk and "popular" music is not clearly made; the ancient and modern styles are not well differentiated, even in broad outlines; there had been until fairly recently a lack of experience in the methods of direct research and sound-recording; and insufficient recognition of the discrepancies, both in time and in form, of the musical, folklore and literary components of the material. For all that, it is possible to list some publications which already represent a valid classification of the enormous Italian folk music treasury.

In this respect, the first bibliographical summary of value is that drawn up by F. Liuzzi and P. Toschi for the " Dossiers de la coopération intellectuelle ", ' Musique et chanson populaires ' (Paris, 1934), where the chapter devoted to Italian folk music (pp. 90-143) is thus subdivided: Libraries; Cultural Associations; Specialists; Cinematographic documentaries. The strictly biographical part is arranged as follows: (1) Study of the music, Italian folksong and dance; (2) General Collections; (3) Regional Collections. This volume was followed by a supplement, again published by the Institut de la Coopération Intellectuelle, ' Folklore musical ' (Paris, 1939), by the same two editors (pp. 320-27), which contains addenda to the bibliography and the general and regional collections.

Of no small importance, still as summary material, is the bibliography by C. Caravaglios in his large volume ' Il folklore musicale in Italia ' (Naples, 1936, pp. 257-467). In this publication are found very many useful references, among others to all the collections published by the house of Ricordi from the middle of the 19th century to the present day; but it must be used with caution because of the haphazard way in which the material is presented, the strictly musical publications not being distinguished from the general and the literary ones.

Another bibliographical list to be mentioned is that by F. B. Pratella in ' Primo documentario per la storia dell' etnofonia in Italia ' (Udine, 1941, pp. 13-39), the chief defect of which is the lack of any differentiation between folk and popular music.

The most recent bibliographical contribution is that by G. Nataletti, ' Il folklore musicale in Italia dal 1918 ad oggi ' (Rome, 1948), in which the list is limited to the most

modern works and the problems of sound-recording and of commercial records are considered.

The following list of works is limited to publications where general or specialized studies give some indication of the most modern problems raised by Italian folk music:

BARBI, M., ' Poesia e musica popolare ' in ' Atti del IIIº Congresso Nazionale delle Arti e Tradizioni Popolari ' (Rome, 1936).
BONACCORSI, A., ' Il folklore musicale in Toscana ' (Florence, 1956).
' Il teatro delle campagne toscane: Il Bruscello ' in ' Musica d' Oggi ', 1934; ' Il maggio ' in Riv. Mus. It., 1930; ' La Zinganetta ' in ' Lares ', 1935.
' La musica popolare ' (Florence, 1943).
CARAVAGLIOS, C., ' I canti delle trincee ' (Rome, 1930).
' Il contenuto poetico ed il contenuto musicale nei gridi dei venditori ambulanti napoletani ' in ' Atti dell' Accademia Pontaniana ', Vol. LXII (Naples, 1932).
' Il folklore musicale in Italia ' (Naples, 1936).
' La ricerca folklorica in Italia ': I. ' Sulla raccolta e sulla trascrizione dei componimenti musicali popolari ' (Rome, 1932).
' Le origini della canzone napoletana ' (Naples, 1921).
' Per la fonocineteca italiana di Stato ' (Naples, 1934).
CARPITELLA, D., ' Gli studi sul folklore musicale in Italia ' in ' Società ', VIII, No. 3, 1952.
' Musica popolare e musica di consumo ' (Rome, 1955).
' Problemi attuali della musica popolare in Italia ' in ' Ricordiana ', II, No. 9, 1956.
' Prospettive e problemi nuovi degli studi di musica popolare in Italia ' in ' Atti del VIº Congresso Nazionale delle Tradizioni Popolari ', 1956.
' Ritmi e melodie di danze popolari in Italia ' (Rome, 1956).
' Una spedizione etnologica in Lucania ' in ' Società ', VIII, No. 4, 1952.
' Catalogo delle registrazioni sonore di canti popolari italiani delle varie regioni, depositati nell' Archivio del Centro Nazionale Studi di Musica Popolare ' (Accademia di S. Cecilia — Radiotelevisione Italiana), Jan. 1954; Supp., June 1954 (unfinished).
' Catalogo delle registrazioni sonore di danze popolari italiane effettuate fino al 30 aprile 1958, e depositate nell' Archivio del Centro Nazionale Studi di Musica Popolare.'
COCCHIARA, G., ' L' anima del popolo italiano nei suoi canti ' (Milan, 1929), with an appendix of folk music compiled by and commented on the F. B. Pratella.
COLACICCHI, L., ' Canti popolari di Ciociaria ' in ' Atti del IIIº Congresso Nazionale di Arti e Tradizioni Popolari ' (Rome, 1936).
' Il pianto delle zitelle ' in ' Lares ', VII, 1936.
FARA, G., ' Appunti di etnofonia comparata ' in Riv. Mus. It., XXIX, 1922.
' Bricicche di etnofonia marchigiana ' in ' Musica d' Oggi ', 1925, 1929, 1932.
' Canto del popolo e musica dotta ' in Riv. Mus. It., XXXVII, 1930.
' Etnofonia e canzone popolare ' in ' La nuova musica ' (Florence, 1917).
' Etnofonia pugliese ' in ' Japigia ', VI, 1935.
' Genesi e prime forme della polifonia ' in Riv. Mus. It., XXXIII, 1926.
' L' anima musicale italiana ' (Rome, 1920).
' Musica popolare sarda ' (Turin, 1909).
' Saggio di geografia etnofonica ' (Catania, 1930).
' Studi etnofonici ' in ' La critica musicale ' (Florence, 1919-22).
' Su uno strumento musicale sardo ' in Riv. Mus. It., XX, 1913; XXI, 1914.
FAVARA, A., ' Corpus di musiche popolari siciliane ', ed. by O. Tiby, 2 vols. (Palermo & Milan, 1957).
GABRIEL, GAVINO, ' Canti di Sardegna ' (Milan, 1923).
' Canti e cantatori della Gallura ' in Riv. Mus. It., XVII, 1910.
' Laofonografia ' in ' Atti del IIIº Congresso Nazionale di Arti e Tradizioni Popolari ' (Rome, 1936).
' Voci e canne d' armonia in Sardegna ' (Rome, 1954).

'Il Centro Nazionale Studi di Musical Popolare e gli studj etnomusicologici in Italia dal 1948 al 1958' (Rome, 1958).
LIUZZI, F. & NATALETTI, G., Della raccolta dei canti popolari' in 'Atti del IIIº Congresso Nazionale di Arti e Tradizioni Popolari' (Rome, 1936).
LOMAX, A., 'Nuova ipotesi sul canto folkloristico italiano nel quadro della musica popolare' in 'Nuovi Argomenti', Nos. 17-18, Rome, 1955–56.
NATALETTI, G., 'I poeti a braccio della campagna romana' in 'Atti del IIIº Congresso Nazionale di Arti e Tradizioni Popolari' (Rome, 1936).
'Improvvisatori ed improvvisazioni' in 'Musica d' Oggi', 1935.
'La musica a spirale' in 'Quadrivio' (Rome, 1933).
'Otto canti popolari della campagna romana' in 'Lares', 1934.
'Su una orazione in dialetto siciliano e su alcuni canti della campagna romana' in 'Rassegna Dorica' (Rome, 1934).
'Voci della vecchia Roma' in 'Folklore italiano' (Naples, 1930).
NATALETTI, G. & ANZELLOTTI, A., 'Per la storia critica della musica del popolo' in 'Lares', IV, 1934.
NIGRA, C., 'Canti popolari del Piemonte' (Turin, 1888; new ed. 1957).
PRATELLA, F. B., 'Etnofonia di Romagna' (Udine, 1938).
'Primo documentario per la storia dell' etnofonia in Italia' (Udine, 1941).
'Saggi di comparazione etnofonica' (Rome, 1943).
'Saggio di gridi, canzoni, cori a danze del popolo italiano' (Bologna, 1919).
'Variazioni ed evoluzione della poesia e della musica popolare' in 'Musica d' Oggi', XIII, 1913.
SANTOLI, V., 'Canto popolare' (article in 'Enciclopedia Italiana Treccani').
'Cinque canti popolari della Raccolta Barbi' (Bologna, 1938).
'I canti popolari italiani: ricerche e questioni' (Florence, 1940).
TORREFRANCA, F., 'Problemi del dopoguerra musicale' in 'La critica musicale' (Florence, 1918).
TOSCHI, P., 'Fenomenologia del canto popolare' (Rome, 1947).
'Problemi cronologici della musica e della poesia sarda' (Bari, 1958).

DISCOGRAPHY.—HENNIG, W., 'Folk Music from Italy' (Ethnic Folkways Library, p. 520).
LOMAX, A. & CARPITELLA, D., 'Northern and Central Italy' and 'Southern Italy and Islands', ed. for 'The Columbia World Library of Folk and Primitive Music' (Columbia, KL. 5173-74).
'Music and Song of Italy' (Tradition Records, TLP 1030).

D. C.

308   ii   FOLK MUSIC (Jewish)
Phono G.-K. 1569 at head of 1st musical example should read:
Phono G.-K. 1509

313   ii   Add to BIBL., Israeli Folksong:
LINDER, SVEN, 'Palästinische Volksgesänge', Vol. I, ed. by Heimer Ringgren (Uppsala, 1952).

Add before Latvian:
Lappish. See SAMISH.

317   i   FOLK MUSIC (Mexican)
Add to BIBL., before l. 1:
'Revue Musicale', No. 237, 1956 ('La Musique au Mexique').

320   —   FOLK MUSIC (Netherlandish)
Heading of 1st musical example, BOSSN, should read:
BOSSU

331   ii   FOLK MUSIC (Polish)
Par. 1, l. 2 should read:
The Hayduck, a lively dance,

333   i   Par. 5, l. 8.   zajaczek should read:
żajaczek

336   i   Par. 4, l. 2.   gesle should read:
gesle

337   i   Par. 1, l. 2.   gesliki should read:
gesliki

340   i   FOLK MUSIC (Portuguese)
Par. 2, l. 17 should read:
a fair example:

Foi me acci-fa ao Porto San-to As ce-a-ras ama-re-lu>.

(Present ex. goes to p. 341.)

ii   1st musical example should read:

(Present ex. goes to p. 341.)

2nd musical example should read:

(Present ex. goes to p. 341.)

341   i   Par. 2, l. 19 should read:
surprises of the latest investigations. The following example, a pilgrimage song from Monsanto (Beira-Baixa), is very interesting for its " exotic " flavour:

SANTA CRUZ

Ai, oh di-vi - na San-ta Cruz 'A tua por - ta che- guei. Ai, tan-tos an - jos me a com- pa-nhem Co-mo de— pas-sa-das dei.

341   i   Par. 3, l. 12 *should read*:

mind reminiscences of Oriental music. Here is a beautiful example of modal song : an old Christmas carol from Évora (Alentejo) :

NATAL

Par. 4, l. 7 *should read*:

occasionally.   As an example of this spontaneous polyphony, here is a midsummer song from Ribeiro-do-Cávado (Minho) :

SÃO JOÃO

The present author himself was

ii   Par. 1, l. 8 *should read*:

liturgical melodies.   The following, a nocturnal prayer for the souls of the departed, collected by the present contributor at S. Miguel d'Acha (Beira-Baixa), illustrates this rhythmic freedom, clearly indebted to plainsong :

ENCOMENDAÇÃO DAS ALMAS

342   i   BIBL., COLLECTIONS, l. 11.   canções
should read:
canções

343-346   **FOLK MUSIC (Russian)**
Replace present article by the following :

Russian.   1. OUTLINE HISTORY OF FOLK-SONG.   (1) *Pagan Russia.*—Russian music is intimately connected with the culture of the pagan Slavs.   Slavic tribes from the most ancient times have inhabited the Eastern and South-eastern regions of Europe and also part of the North-eastern territory stretching from the shores of the Baltic to the upper Volga. Remote descendants of the Slavs have dwelt in the forest-steppe area for the last several thousand years creating an individual and developed culture, traces of which have been unearthed by archeological investigation and preserved among the people in the form of mythological beliefs.   The Slavic nations are also connected with the Scythians described by Herodotus.   The Slavs were essentially an agricultural people who worshipped the sun and earth.   The main sources of information regarding the customs of the Slavs, apart from folksong and archeological research, are a number of Byzantine and Arabian writers, including among the latter Ibn-Fadlan, who describes in great detail the music and funeral rites of the Volga Bulgars, c. A.D. 992, and the Arabian geographer Omar Ibn-Dasta (also 10th century).

Many of the rites and rituals have remained in folksong to the present day. The extraordinary persistence of the pagan customs was a continual source of anxiety to the Church which saw in them a threat to its own existence. Worship of *Rod* (" fate " or " destiny ") lasted long into the 16th century when it was accompanied by various diversions in the form of dancing, singing and rejoicing. Another element — fire — long retained an important place in the songs of the Slavs, being the manifestation of the sun, the source of all life. The name for fire was *Svarozhich* (derived from Old Indic *svar*, " light ", " sun ", " sky "). In an attempt to gain the confidence of the populace, the Church took over many pagan rites and attributes, giving them new names. Thus, the prophet Elijah became the reincarnation of Perun, god of Thunder; John the Baptist was identified with the deity Kupala; and churches were frequently built on the former sites of heathen temples and shrines. Bells, which since the most ancient times have been used as an obligatory accompaniment of prayers and religious ceremonies to frighten away evil spirits, were employed to mark the hours and periods of the day. They were also sounded at funeral rites and their use for this purpose survives to the present day in Shamanism and the religious cults of many non-Christian and semi-barbaric tribes. It is interesting to note that the word *pop* which, with the advent of Christianity, was employed to mean priest, originally implied " a male singer ". As the ancient Slavs were primarily an agricultural people, their whole life centred on the seasonal year, and their music took the form of songs expressing the desire for prosperity and fertility, ritual songs, or songs relating to human emotions and catastrophes. One of the characteristic features of the majority of the ancient ceremonial songs is the repetition of certain formulae and incantations. The tunes are of the simplest design and nature and follow closely the rhythm of the words. The melody would probably be varied with each verse. The following incantation is a plea for rain:

Ex.1

Quickly

Do-shchi-ku, do-shchi-ku, zva-ri me-ni
v ze-le - nó- mu

bor-shchi-ku   tai po-stav   na go-ri
gor-shchi-ku   shchob ne i - li   ko-ma-ri

The ritual songs can be divided into three categories: (1) funeral lamentations; (2) wedding songs; and (3) songs of the celebra-

tions of the successive play of the sun-cycle (calendar songs).

The funeral lament is probably one of the oldest forms of literature and Elsa Mahler, in her valuable contribution, ' Altrussische Volkslieder', records that in remote districts of Pskov, it is still alive. According to Vernadsky [1], to whom much of this section is indebted,

the funeral rites were accompanied throughout by dirges, and all women in a clan, or community, were expected to take part. There was usually at least one woman weeper endowed with an exceptionally good memory and high musical abilities, and in a large community there might be quite a number. These were recognized adepts of the craft. As they aged they trained the ablest girls of the younger generation. In that way the tradition was kept alive in some localities in North Russia down to the 20th century. The wailing rites began at the moment of death. Special laments were chanted when the coffin was lowered into the grave, at the return of the funeral, and on entering the house. Additional wailing rites were performed at the grave for at least forty days. There were different forms of dirge for particular occasions. Thus, there were widow's laments for her deceased husband and *vice versa*, children's laments for their parents and parents' laments at the loss of a child. The weeping for the wife was in most cases performed not by the husband but by a female relative. Special dirges were chanted at the grave exhorting the deceased to return to life. Some laments liken man's death to the sunset or the sleep of a tree in winter. When the family arrived home after the burial, a memorial banquet was served, a place being laid for the deceased at the table. The women weepers would chant further dirges, turning in the direction of the cemetery. In some of the North-Russian laments, the daughter addresses her deceased parent and offers him (or her) a drink. When a prominent leader or hero died, memorial services assumed a tribal, or national character. In many cases, the lament for the dead hero provided the nucleus for an epic poem. In that case the funeral dirge would become the source of an epos, though epic poems were often written during the hero's lifetime. It is a remarkable fact that not only the women but the men engaged in these lamentations, and evidence of this is preserved in the old Russian chronicles. The dead remained as guardians of their descendants and could be supplicated in time of anxiety or jubilation.

The funeral melodies are characterized by a strong declamatory opening. Their vocal span is usually rather limited — a third or a fifth. The melodic line consists of variations of a few basic formulae closely following the pattern of the verse. The melodies of the lamentations are especially free. The rhythm follows that of the words. Between each line would probably be inserted a wail or cry:

Ex.2

A-kh (i) mi - la- i   ti moi,

a - ti   ra-z (i) ya-sen   so - kol!

A-kh (i) da - le-ko li   ti,

akh, so-b(i) ral-sya —— srya-dil -   (sya)

[1] ' The Origins of Russia ' (Oxford, 1959).

The second great group of ritual songs is connected with the marriage ceremonies. The majority of Russian folk-rites were accompanied by some form of dramatic action, and even as late as the nineteenth century, the cycle of the old Russian wedding amounted to a play in which not only the bride and bridegroom and family participated, but the whole village, each man and woman having to perform an individual part. Characteristically, Russian peasants, even in recent years, when referring to a wedding used the expression " to play a wedding " (*igrat svadbu*). The wedding ritual consisted of several acts beginning with the coming of the bridegroom's kinsmen to the fiancée's father, usually at night, as the old convention demanded. The performance lasted for several days, taking place in each of the relatives' homes in turn. A variety of songs was an essential feature of the ceremonies, special songs being considered proper for each day and each stage of the occasion. In the early stages, the fiancée was expected to lament the loss of her girlhood freedom, as well as the parting with her parents. At the betrothal, the women of the family lamented over her, bewailing her impending departure to " the land of strangers ". If the fiancée were an orphan, she expressed her grief at the thought that she had no parent to bid her God-speed, but she asked the departed parent to bestow a blessing on her nevertheless. It is interesting to note that Stravinsky's ' Les Noces ' (' Svadebka ') is remarkably faithful both in its use of authentic melodies and its depiction of ritual customs (*see* Example 10, *below*).

The third important category of ritual songs is that associated with the yearly cycle. The sun was considered the source of life on earth. The yearly course of the sun, through the four seasons, was understood as a cosmic drama — the death and the re-birth of the Sun-god. The day of the winter solstice was celebrated as the birth of the god. After Russia's conversion to Christianity (in A.D. 988), this festival merged with the Nativity. In the Russian and Ukrainian customs associated with Christmas, as well as in Russian and Ukrainian carols, many pre-Christian traits were preserved. " Carol " in Russian (and Ukrainian) is *kolyada*. This term derives from the Latin word *calendae* which penetrated into Russia through Byzantium. The word was substituted in the Middle Ages for the original Slavic term *kolo* (" wheel " or " round dance "). The main theme of the *kolyadi* (plural of *kolyada*) is prayer for a good harvest the next summer. There are remnants of ancient magical incantations in the *kolyadi* as well as hints of the sacrifices to the Sun-god in ancient times. Here is an example of a *kolyada* :

Ex. 3

Moderato

1. Oi dva brat-chi - ka si - no ko-si - lo,
2. Se-stri-tsya Ga - lya is - ti no-si - la,

.oi dva brat-chi - ka, si - no ko-si - lo.
se-stri-tsya Ga - lya is - ti no-si - la.

The next solar festival was that of the vernal equinox. Some of the customs connected with it survived in Russian habits of the so-called " Butter-week " (*maslyanitsa*), which is the last week before Lent. The special dish in the fare of the Butter-week is the pancake (*blini*) and the round shape of a *blin* symbolizes the sundisk. In old Russia, the Butter-week was the proper time for various entertainments, such as boxing, wrestling and tobogganing. Companies of itinerant actors and musicians (*skomorokhi*) performed short plays, some of them remnants of the old sacred drama of heathen times. An outgrowth of these shows was the puppet-theatre (*Petrushka*). The vernal equinox signified the approaching spring thaw. With this, the tale of the melting of the Snow-maiden (' Snegurochka ') was associated. This too was a time for rejoicing and was accompanied by appropriate songs such as the following. It will be observed that it is pentatonic and probably of great antiquity :

Ex. 4

Moderato

Oi -li zhe. - ves - na

ve - snya - nich - ka,

gdë tvo - ya — doch - ka —

pa - nya - no - chka?

The time of the thaw is the period of the rapid rise of the sun's ardency and the re-awakening of the forces of life. " Ardent " (*yari*) is the special epithet of the sun at this stage of its course. According to Vernadsky,

in Russian folk lore, the creative virility of the sun was personified in the image of the god Yarilo. Yarilo was the god of spring. It is likely that, for the old Slavs, the new year began on the day of the vernal equinox. In Kievite Russia, the new year began on 1 March. It was only in the Mongol period that the Byzantine date for the beginning of the new year (1 September) was introduced in Russia. Peter the Great moved it to 1 January to comply with Western habits. Yarilo was in full power between the vernal equinox and the summer solstice. There were two ancient festivals around the summer solstice, one preceding it (the so-called *Semik*), and the other following it (the so-called *Kupala*). Semik was celebrated in the forests and on the shores of lakes and rivers. Water, water nymphs (*rusalki*) and trees (especially the birch and linden) played an important rôle in the festivities. It was dedicated to the souls of the dead, but actually was mainly a festival of youth and of pre-matrimonial love. The Kupala festival took place on the day of St. John the Baptist (24 June) and was dedicated to Yarilo. A huge bonfire was built at these festivals, often on the bank of a river or a lake. A large wooden wheel was kindled at the top of a hill and set in motion to roll downhill. Men, women and maidens danced and sang round the bonfire and jumped over it. This was done because of the belief in the purifying function of the fire. Two effigies, one male and one female, were made of straw. The male was called Yarilo, the female Kupala. These figures were burned together. The rolling of the fire-wheel at the Kupala-festival symbolized the impending turn of the sun after the solstice and the shorter days to come. This meant the waning of Yarilo's power and indeed, a few days after the Kupala-festival, the rite of Yarilo's burial would take place.

Special rites were performed at the time of the harvest, the culmination of the festival being the sounding of a single note on a horn. The illustration below of a harvesting song comes from the district of Bryansk:

Ex. 5

Zhi - tĕ, __ zhi - tĕ, zhe-i mo-lo - di - ĕ, __

ser-pĭ zo-lo-tï- (ĕ) Ob-zhi-na-em sya __

ve-cher-kom, kho-lo - dkom, a le-sor-h-kom k dvo (ru)

The cult of certain plants and animals was also associated with sun-worship, the birch tree, in particular, being especially venerated. Of the animals, the horse, the deer, the bull or cow, and the goat were those most closely connected with sun-worship. In a description of the Kolyada festivities in Muscovy in 1648, it is said that the participants in the ritual wore the *skomorokhi* masks and garments and led along with them a " devilish mare " (a horse being the symbol of the sun, and consequently, representative of pagan customs). In Russian folklore, the golden horse (or a horse with a golden mane or golden tail) is symbolic of the sun. The deer likewise was a sun-animal, while the deer with golden antlers is a favourite character in Slavic folklore. Both in Russian and Serbian folksongs, the golden antlers represent the sun's radiance. Similarly, the white bull (or a white cow) is likened in Slavic folklore to the Sun or to Daylight, whereas the black bull or cow personifies Night.

The names of Veles-Volos often occur in folksongs. This twin deity was akin to the Greek Apollo, god of poetry and music as well as of flocks. According to an old tradition,

Veles is also the Holy Spirit, the connection between spirit and music being identical with that of the Greek πνεῦμα. Other deities to whom reference is frequently made are Perun, the god of Thunder and War, to whom the oak was sacred. In Russian folklore, he sometimes appears as a beneficent deity. In the spring he comes with thunder and lightning and fertilizes the earth with showers. He then chases the clouds away to let the sun shine. Another common name in folklore is that of Lada, ancient Slavic goddess of love and spring, and her sons Dido and Lel.

Among the outstanding features of the melodies of the calendar songs may be noted the limitedness of the melodic range, the repetition of basic phrases (especially characteristic of Russian folksong), and the presence of occasional melismata. The songs are, for the most part, slow in tempo. A peculiarity is that often, at the conclusion of the song, the melody will break off in the middle of a word, the last syllable of which is not sung, but is rhythmically scanned (cf. Examples 4 and 5).

From the above, it will be appreciated that, in many cases, the folksongs are our sole guide to the customs and rituals of a comparatively unknown period of Russian history. The fact that so many distinct references have been handed down in the course of over a thousand years, though the significance of much is doubtless unappreciated by the majority of their exponents, attests to a truly remarkable conservatism, and it is understandable that, in face of such stubborn resistance, the Church should have waged unceasing war on the resilient symbols of paganism and the ubiquitous powers of darkness.

During the Middle Ages, the Slavs divided into three distinct branches: the Western Slavs, from whom descended the Czechs, the Poles and the tribes along the River Elbe; the Southern Slavs, who became the Bulgars, the Serbs and the Croats; and the Eastern Slavs who split up into a number of peoples between the Dnepr and the Dnestr. It is they who are the founders of Kiev.

(2) *The Kiev Period.*—The official adoption of Christianity by Prince Vladimir had far-reaching effects on the political life of Russia, if its impetus on the musical life of the people was infinitesimally gradual. Apart from establishing ties with Byzantium, the Greeks, the Southern Slavs and the countries of the West, it succeeded in achieving the unity of the Russian state. Under wise government, culture flourished in the form of music, literature, art, handicraft and the applied sciences. Russian literature had existed for a considerable period, but apart from the rise of ecclesiastical writings, such as ' The Ipatyevsky

Chronicle', the early 11th century onwards was outstanding in its wealth of folk creation, the chief form of which was the ballad. Among the most famous epics may be mentioned the 'Slovo o polku Igoreva' ('The Epic of Igor's Host'), c. 1187. Such was the vitality of the folk tradition that monastic chroniclers did not hesitate to introduce examples of folklore and folk idiom (in the form of proverbs, rustic expressions, etc.) into their work. The period was essentially one of assimilation and the Kiev churches are an excellent illustration of the grafting of foreign art (in this case, Byzantine) on to the native traditions, a pattern which repeats itself constantly throughout Russian history.

From the very first, the ecclesiastical authorities battled against the pagan customs embodied in the folksongs, folk instruments and the popular festivals, which nevertheless continued to flourish. Christianity, though first the property of the nobility, was gradually accepted by the people by way of a compromise: viz., the pagan customs were linked with the Christian, leading to a dual belief which has remained to the present day. (This duality is excellently described by Gogol in his story ('Christmas Eve'.)

The flowering of folk music in Kievite Russia is marked by the appearance of the heroic ballads which have been preserved to the present in the form of epic songs and *bïliny*, reflecting the social and historical events of the 10th to 14th centuries. The term *bïlina* comprises a vast group of epic (narrative) songs and ballads and was introduced into literary usage in the 1830's. In Northern Russia, the epic ballads are popularly called *stárini*. The *bïliny* of the so-called "Kiev cycle", have come down to us in later transcriptions (not earlier than the 17th to 18th centuries), and although Russian folk art has remained remarkably consistent over the course of years, the original characteristics and individuality of many of the *bïliny* have undoubtedly suffered in the process. The main theme of the Kiev cycle is patriotism, heroism, the struggle for national unity and freedom. In depth of content, construction and formal beauty, the *bïliny* occupy a distinctive place in world literature. The fact that many of the creators were drawn from the people shows remarkable emancipation for a feudalistic régime. The heroes of a number of *bïliny* were the people themselves as, for example, the knight-ploughman Mikula Selyaninovich, and his peasant-son Ilya Muromets. The *bïliny* reflected historical events, and the names of many of the characters were based on fact. This, however, did not prevent the introduction of fantastic elements. Thus, the leader of the Polovtsian hordes, Khan Tugor, was transformed into the dragon Tugarin Zmeëvich who flew with wings and breathed fire.

Among the outstanding performers of the songs and ballads appears the figure of Bayan, the legendary creator of the brilliant 'Slovo o polku Igoreva'. His name has remained in Russian literature as the epitome of the gifted folk musician, creating and performing his work, accompanying himself on the *gusli* (*see* Section (2) *below*).

A great part in Russian musical history is played by the *skomorokhi* (clowns and buffoons) who contributed, to a certain degree, the comic elements of the ballads, but these will receive separate consideration (*see* Section (3) *below*).

At a later period, the *bïliny* divided into two distinct traditions (the so-called "Northern", and the "South-Russian"), which differ both in their manner of performance and in their melodic structure. In the northern districts, the epic ballads (*stárini*) are performed by a ballad-singer (*pevets-skazitel*) in an individual declamatory manner. The melodies, for the most part, are of a solemn, peaceful, majestic nature, their range being seldom more than an octave. The final syllables of each verse are often rhythmically prolonged to give to the melody an imposing grandeur:

Ex. 6

The South-Russian and Central-Russian *bïliny*, on the other hand, are performed by a chorus and are notable for their greater melodiousness. The example below is almost entirely free of semitones, which is not typical of the *stárini*:

Ex.7

.1. Chto ne be - la - ya be - re - za
2. To___ sïn pe - red ma - ter - yu

k zem - le klo - nit - sya___
pre - klo - nya - et - sya___

Ne shel - ko - va - ya tra - va
Kla - nyal - sya Dob - ri - niush - ka

pri - klo - nya - et - sya.___
rod - noi ma - tush - ke.___

The significance of the Russian *biliny* was very great. The ballads were an unwritten record of Kievite Russia at the time of its greatest fame and achievement. Later they were to bear witness to the crippling struggle against the Tartar invasion.

During the 11th to 12th centuries, Kievite Russia was subject to continual incursions by nomadic raiders. With the passage of time, new centres of culture and commerce began to arise, although the calendar songs, the heroic ballads and the ancient customs continued unchanged. A further unity was provided by the Russian language which was universally understood (throughout Russia). The literature of the time is permeated with folk idioms, expressions, proverbs and sayings. The influence of the folk spirit is also discernible in the growth of Russian ecclesiastical chant which began to assimilate local features. In the 13th century, Russia was overrun by the Tartar hordes led by the formidable Khan Batu, and the central and southern regions became subject to the Tartar yoke.

(3) *The Novgorod Period.*—Veliki Novgorod (Great Novgorod) suffered less from the Tartar invasions than elsewhere and consequently played a great part in the salvation of Russia's culture. This was due partly to its geographical location and its close relationship with Kiev. Kievite architects had been responsible for many of Novgorod's buildings and churches; Novgorod cathedral shared the same name as that of Kiev — St. Sofia, and there was continual communication between the two cities. With the collapse of Kiev, Novgorod, thanks to its position on the river Volga, became the great centre of trade, in every sense the heir of Kiev's legacy. Although prime place of importance was taken by the boyars (the Russian noblemen), this later fell to the rich merchantmen.

Our best source of knowledge of Novgorod and its institutions is the folksong literature. The territories comprising the former province of Novgorod were vast, and one of these districts (called Zavolochye) has been especially fertile in yielding genuine folksongs dating from that period.

The northern music is characterized by distinctive intonations often of a modal character. The tonal melodies, so typical of the central and southern regions, are conspicuously absent in the majority of northern songs. Especially characteristic is the presence of the tritone — the augmented fourth and diminished fifth — and also certain tritonic features such as fragments of a tone-semitone scale and passages of diminished triads. The sound of the melodies is quite different from those of central and southern Russia:

Ex.8

Ai, pol - no li, so - -

- - olnï - shko.

Ex.9

Sve-tla-ya Grid-nya,Sve-tlaya,Gridnya,

da Va - si - lie - va.

The music entwines round a single root with smooth melismata of sound to one syllable.

Ex.10

I - no du - -

- nu - - li___

ye - - - - - t (ï) - rï

The main categories of songs to be found in Novgorod are the epic ballads, the funeral lamentations, the slow *khorovods*, the Christmas carols, the majestic wedding songs and the comic songs of the *skomorokhi*. Of the calendar songs, the most common are the *svyatochnië* (new year) songs which are also termed " *vinogradya* ". An interesting feature of many of the carols is their epic character, which sometimes is directly connected with *biliny* literature (as, for example, one *kolyadka* whose subject is Ilya Muromets and the falcon-boat).

The principal form to flourish in Novgorod was the *bilina*. The new epic ballads (*epicheskië skazi*), like those of Kiev, realistically mirrored the everyday life of Novgorod with its street vendors and entertainments, its feasts in honour of visiting merchants and the persistent rivalry between different communities. As befitted a great trading city, the Novgorod heroes, both in fiction and reality, sailed far and wide, even visiting Venice. The main figures of the Novgorod *biliny* are Sadko, the *gusli*-player (who in some versions appears as a *skomorokh*), and the reckless Vasilii Buslaev. The names of both heroes occur in a 12th-century chronicle. Sadko, with some justification, has been termed the Russian Orpheus.

(4) *The Muscovite Period* (15th to 17th centuries).—During the 14th century, the Muscovite princes gradually began to recover their strength. The battle of Kulikovo in 1380 was decisive in showing that a united Russia could resist the might of the Golden Horde. These events were faithfully recorded in the epic ballads. The 15th century saw the formation of a central state in Russia. In course of time, power became concentrated in Moscow and the phrase " Moskva belokammennaya " (lit. " Moscow built of white Stone ") became renowned in folksong as a symbol of Russia's unity, the successor to the ancient realm of Kiev. As the period of Muscovite Russia was a time of artistic advancement and enterprise, it was not surprising that music too should enjoy a sudden impetus. One of the newest forms of creation was the " historical song " (*istoricheskaya pesnya*). This term was coined by folklore investigators to signify songs and ballads describing the destiny of Russia, historical personages and events. In the north, the majority of the oldest historical songs dealing with the events of the 16th and 17th centuries, like the *biliny*, were termed *stárini*, and were frequently sung by ballad singers to the same melodies as the *biliny* of the Kiev and Novgorod cycles, or to melodies similar to them. The following is an historical song dealing with the capture of Kazan :

M

Ex.11

In central and southern Russia, the historical songs are sometimes popularly called *protyazhnië* (protracted) or *doselnië*. Stylistically, they are close to the so-called " protracted lyrical song " (*protyazhnaya liricheskaya pesnya*). From the poetical point of view, the historical songs differ from the *biliny* in their more accurate description of historical events. The fantastic element and the threefold repetition common in the *biliny* are rarely encountered. The majority of historical songs are associated with the reign of Ivan the Terrible (1533–84). Another genre is the " protracted lyrical song " which expresses the spiritual experiences of the Russian people. In Muscovite Russia, the traditional form of wedding continued to exist on the basis of the various nuptial rites preserved from the days of the pagan Slavs. Here are the melodies of a laudatory lyrical song, and a comic marriage song (Exs. 12 and 13) :

Ex.12

Variants of the marriage songs were widespread over Muscovite Russia, both among the peasants and mercantile classes. The period also saw the removal of the *khorovod* (round dance) from the calendar Spring cycle and its establishment as an independent vocal

Ex.13

Very Quickly

U na-she-vo Sva - ta so-lo-men-na kha - ta,

REFRAIN Tutti

ti do-li - na, ti do-li - na, ti do-li-nush-ka mo-ya.

2. Dro v(ï) ni po - le - na,
Po ne - ve - stu e - kha - li,
Pi - va boch-ku pro - li - li,

grya - zi po ko - le - no,
v o - go - rod za - e - kha - li,
vsiu ka - pu - stu po - li - li.

REFRAIN

Ti do-li - na, ti-do-li - na, ti do-li-nush-ka mo-ya.

Ex.14

Not very quickly

Uzh vï go-rï, vi-mo-i go-rï Vo-ro-byë

Tutti

vo - ro-byë ___ vski - ë.

2. Vo - ro-byë - vski - ë.

Tutti

E - - - - -

- oi, da nu, che - vo zhe vï ___ go-rï,

go-rï, vï, vï spo-ro ___

vï spo-ro ___ di - li.

gory of songs is connected with revolutionary outbursts of which Stepan Razin became a popular figure on account of his daring exploits on the River Volga in 1670–71. Stylistically, the songs continue in the vein of the " protracted historical song ":

Ex.15

Protractedly

Female Voices

Tune

Male Voices

Ai ___ na rech-kë Ka-

tam zhi ___

mi - shin - kë tam ___ zhi ___

Tutti V Ai ___

li - liu-di, o - ni vo - (ë)

li - liu-di, o - ni vo - (ë)

genre. During the 16th to 17th centuries, and even the 18th, many new *khorovody* came into being, reflecting the various aspects of Russian life. The 15th to 16th centuries saw the formation of a Russian vocal (and cultural-artistic) style, one which differs considerably from that of Kiev. Its stylistic peculiarity lies in the greater melodic range and an increase in ornament (*see* Ex. 14)

A characteristic feature of the folksong culture of the period (during the 15th and 16th centuries) is the so-called *podgolosnaya polifoniya* or " under-voice polyphony ", but this will receive separate discussion (*see* (6), p. 166).

The 17th century was the turning point in Russia's development. The results of new reforms, the opening up of her economy and territorial expansion, the gradual influx of foreign blood and new ideas, all had far-reaching effects. The sharp contrasts are reflected in folk music which during the 17th century experiences great changes affecting not only its themes but its genres and aims of musical and poetic expression. A large cate-

Another type of song which first appears about this time is that of protest against the unbearable weight of family existence (especially the tyranny of elderly relatives) which stifles one's independence. Lyrical song also reaches a high level of development in the 17th century. Characteristic of this genre is the wide, expressive melody and its great rhythmic freedom:

Ex.16

The " lyrical protracted song " is undoubtedly one of the most beautiful and individual forms of Russian folk music. Mention must also be made of the satirical songs which ridicule established laws and conventions. Often their inspiration was drawn (like that of the lyrical songs) from the domestic environment, but it was also directed against any form of covetousness or oppression. The turn of the century was marked by the entry of serf musicians into the homes of the nobility as exponents of folk art, a movement which in the course of less than a century was to lead to the development of Russian national opera in the hands of Fomin, Pashkevich and Matinsky.

(5) *The Russia of Peter's Reforms.*—In the 18th century, musicians and amateurs began to take a practical interest in folksong by wandering round from village to village noting down folksong texts and transcribing the melodies. The era also marked the appearance of a number of new folksong genres. These were the military recruiting and marching songs. In the towns and cities appeared the *gorodskaya pesnya* or town song. The 18th century was a time of great unrest in Russia and many of the songs, rather in the spirit of the *bïliny*, look back to periods of former prosperity and to the popular heroes such as Razin and Pugachev.

Among the new genres must be mentioned the military recruit songs (*rekrutskïë pesni*), which came into being with Peter the Great's enforcement of compulsory military service. The main ideas underlying them are compassion for the peasant deprived of labour, and grief at separation from family and friends. Together with the recruit songs are the military campaign or marching songs (*pokhodnïë pesni*). These have served as the prototypes for military songs up to our own era, the essential features being a strong rhythm and words in praise of the valour and achievements of the Russian generals. In a sense they continue the traditions of the historical song. The third new genre was the town song and vocal lyric. These were very varied in subject matter and in many cases dealt with social problems.

The 18th century also marks the appearance of the first folksong anthologies. Whereas only the texts of a few individual songs have come down to us from the 17th century, whole volumes of folksongs were published, or written in manuscript, in the 18th. Interest in folksong was widespread and the leading writers and poets turned to it as the most important source of Russian poetry and literary language. The names of the first collectors of folksong are unknown, but in the second half of the 18th century, three collections are outstanding, namely, those of Trutovsky, Prach and Kirsha Danilov.

Trutovsky and Prach were both members

of literary circles, and in consequence took their folksongs mostly from the town sphere. The anthologies provided an endless source of material for composers in the 18th and 19th centuries.

Trutovsky's collection consisted of four parts which appeared over the course of twenty years (vol. I — 1776; vol. II — 1778; vol. III — 1779; vol. IV — 1795). Each volume contained twenty songs which were written in two-parts on two separate staves. In performance, it was left to the discretion of the accompanist to fill in the harmony, the lower part serving as an " unfigured bass ". Whereas the anonymous collections of the early 18th century were written in simple three-part harmony, the two upper voices being in thirds and sixths, Trutovsky's arrangements were more elaborate, but were obviously written with an instrument in mind (probably the *gusli* with which he used to accompany himself). Trutovsky's anthology is valuable in that it gives a vivid representation of the songs of the time, including historical, humorous, satiric, dance, military, Ukrainian and lyrical town songs. Of particular interest are the songs of the peasant rebellions which otherwise are preserved only in isolated manuscripts (being seldom printed as a result of censorship). The town song usually took the form either of sentimental ballads or lively dances, a good illustration being the following which is typical of Trutovsky's manner of arrangement:

Ex.17

Allegro

Akh,po mo-stu,mo-stu, po ka-li-no-vu mo-stu,

akh,shel tu-ta de-tin-ka, u-da-loi mo-lo-dets.

Of even greater popularity was the Lvov-Prach collection which also served as a source of material for Russian composers. The anthology is in two volumes, consisting of 100 and 150 songs, which appeared in 1790 and 1806 respectively. Many of the songs arranged by Prach were borrowed from Trutovsky, but Prach is superior in that he tried to give his work scientific significance. The Lvov-Prach collection is divided into six groups: historical, dance, wedding, *khorovody*, ritual and Ukrainian songs. Although his accompani-

ments are more elaborate than those of Trutovsky, he makes little or no attempt to make them conform to the modal and melodic structure of authentic folksong.

Kirsha Danilov's collection, which was compiled in Western Siberia in the middle of the 18th century, remained in manuscript for a considerable length of time, but was eventually published in 1804 under the title 'Drevnië rossiiskïe stikhotvoreniya' ('Ancient Russian Verses'). The identity of Kirsha Danilov is unknown, but it seems likely that he was a member of the services. The choice of some of the songs is very unusual for the time and in a sense supplements the work of Trutovsky and Prach who worked mostly in the town sphere. Danilov's collection consists of historical songs, *biliny*, accounts of military engagements, and a number of humorous (army) ballads. The tunes appear to have been written down exactly as they were performed, but as they are all in the key of D major, it seems that originally they were instrumental rather than vocal. Many of the songs are written to the same melody, for like the composers of the ancient *biliny*, Danilov knew more texts than tunes.

The first half of the 19th century saw the flourishing of the town song and the town 'romance'. The song developed in a manner analogous to the growth of the towns themselves and had great influence on the creation of the early Russian song writers.

The Napoleonic Wars produced a number of new soldiers' songs — heroic, marching, humorous and satiric. The protracted military songs eulogizing the Russian generals are sometimes of an epic grandeur, whilst the lively soldiers' songs, usually in a steady marching rhythm (in the following case seeming to mock Napoleon and his army), are of a very different character:

Ex.18

Allegro

Chto ne pïl— vpo - le pï -

- lit, ne dub-ra - vu-shka shu -

- mit, Fran-tsuz sar-mi-ei va-lit, nam ne-

- vzgo-do-iu gro - zit.

Also common were the recruit song and the revolutionary song. The latter not infrequently supplied new words to familiar tunes. About this time, the Ukrainian and gypsy songs began to achieve popularity in the towns, the gypsy performers, in particular, being great favourites on account of their full-blooded, impassioned renderings of folksongs. Their manner of performance had considerable effect both on literature and the early contemporaries of Glinka, viz. Dargomïzhsky, Varlamov, Gurilev, Alabiev and Verstovsky. Gypsy choirs often employed guitars and *banduras*. Later on in the century, the gypsy music deteriorated and in the course of time became little better than cheap music-hall entertainment.

The 19th century was marked by an increased interest in folksong, and the literature of the period shows strong differences of opinion as to the manner of its treatment and transcription. Whereas the 18th century collected folk music naïvely, the 19th century subjected it to critical analysis.

In the 1830's, a number of new folksong collections began to appear which share an equal place with Prach in importance. The compilers of these anthologies were two composers, Kashin and Rupin. The latter's anthology was published from 1831 to 1833. Rupin's method of treatment was to decorate the folksong with all kinds of embellishments fashionable at the time. Sometimes he arranged the folksong in variation form so that it somewhat resembled an operatic aria. Another method, favoured at the beginning of the 19th century, especially by Kashin, was to make concert arrangements of folksongs in which a slow protracted song would be contrasted with a rapid dance, both being developed in the form of brilliant variations.

Kashin's collection (1833–34) was of great importance as he determined to evolve a

selection far-reaching in its scope. It was divided into three sections (protracted, semi-protracted and dance songs) and contained the most representative songs from the town sphere including the protracted ballads, ritual songs, *khorovody*, recruit and soldiers' songs and song-' romances '. Kashin's method of arranging the songs was equally enterprising. He discarded the simple three-part harmony, used in other collections, and surrounded the melodies with imaginative accompaniments. In the case of the dance songs, he subtly underlined the rhythms. Of particular interest are his song-romances in 3-4 time. These were often sung to a guitar accompaniment.

The folksong traditions of the early 19th century were perpetuated by the song-writers Varlamov and Gurilev. They excelled in the art of variations. In the slow protracted songs, the variations were of a melodic character, the melody being embellished, the harmony unchanging; in the dance songs, the melody remained unaltered whilst the accompaniment was subjected to ingenious development. In the course of time (in the first decade of the 19th century), composers had so assimilated folk music that they were able to write convincingly in the folk idiom.

The second half of the 19th century saw the concrete application of Russian folksong in the works of the Russian nationalists. The increasing awareness of folksong and its properties is exemplified by the work of the Imperial Geographical Society, who in 1884 appointed T. I. Filippov head of a commission to study and collect folksongs from different regions of Russia. Many of these were incorporated and harmonized in the collections of Rimsky-Korsakov, Lyapunov, Lyadov, etc. Other important collectors and arrangers of folksong are Balakirev, Melgunov, Prokunin, Lopatin, Sokalsky, Lineva, Vilboa, etc. Folksongs in different variants often re-occur in these collections. Tchaikovsky, for example, borrowed a number of songs from Vilboa's anthology in his first volume of folksongs, and from Balakirev in his second. Rimsky-Korsakov likewise appropriated melodies from earlier collections such as Prach, Stakhovich, Vilboa, etc., besides writing down tunes sung by his friends.

Folksongs continued to be created and even in 1939, Elsa Mahler found folk traditions flourishing in remote districts with unabated vigour. The Second World War saw the reappearance of many familiar melodies with new words, together with the *chastushki* (popular songs, sometimes of a satirical or humorous nature). The Russian government does much to foster folk music by encouraging folk orchestras and bringing ballad singers to festivals from all over the Soviet Union.

(6) *Folk Music and the 'Podgolosnaya' Polyphony.*—The question of Russian folk polyphony has long proved a stumbling block in academic discussion, but thanks to the researches of Russian musicologists, outstanding among whom is the late A. D. Kastalsky, the position has now been clarified. The first printed collections of folk music did not appear until 1776, and the actual study of them began in about the middle of the 19th century. But during this comparatively short period, the views on Russian folksong underwent a series of modifications, which were first exhibited in the methods of harmonization. These are well known through the collections of Balakirev, Rimsky-Korsakov and Lyadov. In their collections, the songs are provided with piano accompaniments based on the harmony which created the fame of the Russian national school. The 20th century, however, tends to regard the efforts of the Russian nationalists to a certain extent as obsolete and stamped with the impress of the theories of their day rather than permeated with the essential quality of the Russian harmony and folk melos. The first Russian musicologist to attempt to transcribe scientifically the folk polyphony was V. P. Prokunin who included four polyphonic songs in his collection of 1871–72. His efforts were continued by Melgunov in his two volumes 1879–85, but the final word in the matter has perhaps been given by Kastalsky in his detailed analysis ' Osobennosti narodno-muzikalnoi sistemï ' (' Peculiarities of the Russian Folkmusical System ').

One of the outstanding peculiarities of Russian folksong is the employment of the natural major and minor scales, both in their pure form and with certain characteristic modifications. These modifications take the following forms: the natural minor scale is often varied by the use of the flattened supertonic (probably a result of oriental influence):

Ex.19

together with the sharpened submediant:

Ex.20

While the natural major scale often employs a sharpened subdominant:

Ex.21

and a flattened submediant (which, though rarely found in authentic folksongs, is common in the works of the nationalists).

Since the Russian folksong is based mainly on the natural major and minor scales, it is not surprising that the latter often include a flattened seventh in place of a leading note. In Kastalsky's opinion, this is analogous to the flattened supertonic of the relative minor scale.

Putting together all the divergencies from the generally accepted major and minor scales which are most often encountered in Russian folk music, the following combination, representing both a major and a minor scale, is obtained:

Ex.22

The flattened sixth in the major and the enharmonic sharpened seventh in the relative minor, together with the occasional appearance of the augmented second, further increase the possible combinations.

It is obvious that the folk harmony is not determined by the academic forms of the West. Furthermore, the harmony employed by the nationalists in the 19th century differs considerably from the true folk polyphony. The following example illustrates a folk melody as harmonized (*a*) by Mussorgsky (in *Khovanshchina*) and (*b*) in the folk harmonization (from Melgunov's collection).

Ex.23

Mussorgsky has harmonized the melody in the harmonic minor, whereas in the folk version it is sung in the natural minor. The opening and the middle and final cadences are in unison. The bass, as is usual in Russian folk harmonization, is distinguished by mobility. The dominant triad of the European harmonization is here replaced by a triad constructed on the flattened seventh.

It should be pointed out that Russian folk music in no way derives from the ecclesiastical modes, although they share certain common features.

It is known that the Russian *podgolosnaya* (underpart) polyphony was in existence during the 15th to 16th centuries, though whether it existed before that date is by no means certain. In style, it offers a parallel to the crude polyphony of certain primitive peoples, although it has its own laws. Russian polyphony owes its origin to the temporary breaking away of the second, third and other parts from the unison of the principal tune, to intervals harmonizing with the melody. Thus the original form of any polyphony must be regarded as consisting of variants of the fundamental melody, sung simultaneously with it (*cf.* Examples 15 and 16). Gradually developing more and more freedom and boldness they end by supplying an independent polyphony, the theoretical basis of which consists in the observance of a difference of intervals between the singer of the principal melody and the other voices. This results sometimes in consecutive seconds, fourths, fifths, sevenths and ninths.

Polyphony occurs not only in the historical but in the humorous, *khorovod*, dance and wedding songs. However, it is in the " protracted historical song " (and also the slow *khorovod*) that the Russian folk polyphony may be heard to the best advantage. A characteristic feature is that folk polyphony varies from region to region. According to Professor Gippius, this has occurred as the result of particular historical conditions of development in different Russian districts.

As a final word on folksong, it should be pointed out that as folk music is essentially an oral tradition, the melodies, as they appear in folksong anthologies, only hold true for the first verse, each subsequent verse being varied in accordance with the metrical requirements. In the case of folk polyphony, where the element of extemporization plays an important part, much rests on the question of spontaneous ingenuity. The Russians have long been renowned for their choral singing and it is impossible to write down on paper the remarkable effects which are often achieved. It is also of importance to note that polyphony is not found in the town song genres. When removed from its native habitat, folksong has a habit of losing its originality.

2. RUSSIAN FOLK INSTRUMENTAL MUSIC.— Russian folk instrumental music in the majority of cases is directly connected with folksong. Only in the instance of military instruments, hunting fanfares (which are frequently described in the ancient Russian writings), shepherds' calls, etc., is the music distinct from folksong. The ancient chronicles attest to the fact that the Eastern Slavs possessed both string, wind and percussion instruments including *gusli*, *trubi*, *roga*, *dudki*, *sopeli*, *svireli*, *sipovochka* and later, in the 16th to 17th centuries, the *gudok* and *domra*. Among the percussion instruments surviving to the present day may be mentioned the *lozhki* (lit. spoons [1]) which take the place of the Spanish and Italian castanets. These often have several rows of little bells fastened to them.

The favourite stringed instrument of the Eastern Slavs was the *gusli* and descriptions of performance on this are commonplace in folksong and *biliny* literature. Drawings and paintings of *guslis* are found in many representations of the art of ancient Russia (miniatures, frescoes, etc.). The other common bowed instrument, though later than the *gusli* in origin, was the *gudok*. Research suggests that this first appeared in Russia between the 14th and 15th centuries together with a number of other instruments of Eastern origin such as the *domra*, *surni*, etc. The name " gudok " first appears in literature in the 17th century. The terms " gudenië ", " gudebnië sosudi ", found in early literature, are misleading as they were used in relation to most instruments. A parallel with the term " organizing ", etc., in the West is immediately apparent. The *gudok* survived in folk music up to the 19th century. According to various accounts, the melody was played on the highest string, and accompanied on the two lower strings which were tuned a fifth below. The third type of stringed instrument included the *domra* and the *balalaika*. Some sources claim that the *domra* was borrowed from Asiatic peoples and was a Russified form of the Arabian *tunbúr*. The *domra* is played with a plectrum, while the *balalaika* is played with the fingers. The *domra* has three strings and was probably adopted by the *skomorokhi* during the period of Mongol dominion. Instruments of a similar nature (and even name, such as *dumbra*, *domr*, etc.) are still found among the present inhabitants of Central Asia. The *balalaika* (which usually has only two strings) first appears in the eighteenth century and is distinguished by its triangular body. It probably acquired this shape on account of its being simpler and easier to make in large numbers. The

The spoon was a Shamanistic symbol.

balalaika even at the present time, is still one of the most widespread and favourite instruments of the Russian people and is used in accompanying both song and dance. Imitation of the *balalaika* is found in numerous works of the Russian nationalists including Glinka's ' Kamarinskaya ', Balakirev's ' Overture on Three Russian Themes ', Serov's ' Vrazhya Sila ', to mention only a few.

Ex.24

E-shche gdë zhe e - to vi - da - no,

E - shche gdë zhe e - to slï - kha - no.

The Russian wind instruments are equally varied. Among them may be mentioned the pipes (*roga*), the trumpets (*trubi*), embouchure pipes or horns (*rozhki*), and many instruments of the flute type such as the *dudka*, the *svirel*, the *sipovichki* and lastly the reed instrument, the *zhaleika*.

The *zhaleika* is an instrument of the clarinet family made of cane or wood and possessing a single vibrating tongue or reed. Shepherd *zhaleikas* sometimes have a bell of natural cow horn, as a result of which they are often confused with the *rozhok* — an embouchure instrument. The *zhaleika* is either single or double, the former consisting of two tubes with equally spaced finger holes, the latter with unevenly spaced openings which thus makes possible playing in two parts. The *zhaleika* is used primarily as a solo instrument on which protracted (*protyazhnïe*) as well as dance melodies are performed, in addition to pastoral music. Sometimes the *zhaleika* is used to accompany choral ensembles, joining the choir *podgolosï* at the end of the solo introduction. Imitation of the *zhaleika* is also commonplace in the writing of the Russian nationalists (*see* Rimsky-Korsakov's *Snegurochka* in particular).

The *volinka* is another tongue-instrument of the clarinet type, consisting of a bag made of goat or calf's skin with two or three tubes. One or more of these gives out a continuous bass drone, while the player plays the tune on the other pipe. Polyphonic playing is possible.

Of the instruments of the flute type, of great interest is the many stemmed *svirel*

which is of great antiquity, being known historically as the syrinx or " pan-pipes ". Such pipes were discovered in the sixties of the last century in the province of Kursk, under the name *kuvichki*. The Kursk *kuvichki* consist of five (sometimes three) cane whistles or pipes which are graduated in length and have their ends stopped. They are not fastened together. The player arranges them according to their notes (there is approximately a tone difference between them) and holding them in front of the lips blows into them moving the *kuvichki* rapidly from one corner of the mouth to the other, in tune with a dance song played (for example) on several *dudki* (the general term for any kind of wind instrument). Performing on the *kuvichki* is considered to be a difficult task and demands much practice. It is interesting to note that only women play it. *Kuvichki* are used both as solo and ensemble instruments.

The Russian folk embouchure instruments comprise various forms of shepherds' pipes and trumpets. Among this category may be mentioned the natural aurochs [1] horns formerly in great use among the Eastern Slavs. A splendid example of an aurochs horn with a silver mounting was discovered in a Chernigov *kurgan* (tumulus) in the last century. Reference to performance on the aurochs horn is often met with in songs in *bïliny*. Such was the persistence of the tradition that when the aurochs species became extinct, horns were made of wood, but still preserving the ancient form. Even to-day, in remote districts, shepherds' horns shaped like natural horns, but made of wood bound with birch bark, are encountered. It is interesting to note that apart from their use in the hunt and in military music, trumpets and horns were employed in various ritual ceremonies, as for example in the so-called " obsequies of Kostroma " (the departure of Summer — *see* Section (1) *above*). Their employment is referred to in a number of wedding songs.

Among the embouchure instruments surviving to the present day, of particular importance are the shepherds' pipes (*rozhki*). The more primitive (without finger-holes) give only the natural harmonic series and are used mainly for the purpose of signals. The pipes of a more elaborate nature are used as musical instruments (*see* Ex. 25).

The *rozhki* are both solo and ensemble instruments. In the latter case, they are of different size and vary from 30 centimetres to a metre in length. The small pipe is called a *vizgunok*. The bass pipe is roughly twice the size of the treble and sounds an octave lower. Two *vizgunki* and a bass pipe are often used in combination, but usually an ensemble consists of half a dozen pipes or more. One of

[1] The European bison.

the most celebrated pipe ensembles was that of N. V. Kondratyev, from the province of Kursk, which gave performances at the end of the 19th and the early 20th century in a number of Russian towns. It also travelled abroad.

Ex.25

Ex.26 ♩=168

The Russian instrumental folk polyphony is almost identical with that of the choral. The performance begins with an introduction on a solo pipe followed by the rest of the instruments which develop and elaborate the original tune (*see* Ex. 26).

Folk instrumental ensembles are sometimes mixed, thus, the *khorovody* (round-dances) of the province of Kursk are accompanied by a large ensemble of *dudki* and *kuvichki*. In 1937, a group of research workers from the Moscow State Conservatory wrote down a number of songs (mostly dances) which were performed by a mixed ensemble. This consisted of four sets of *kuvichki* (both 5-stemmed and 3-stemmed) played by women, two *zhaleikas*, and a violin.

The most common instrument of the present era is the accordion. Originally introduced into the province of Tula in the fifties of the last century, it was soon adopted by the people. The accordion plays an important rôle both as a solo and accompanying instrument, and is used especially in the performance of the *chastushka*.

3. THE *SKOMOROKHI*.—The origin of the *skomorokhi* (clowns and buffoons) in Russia is uncertain, but some scholars hold that they were descended from the Roman and Byzantine theatres and circuses thus making them first cousins of the Medieval European *jongleurs*. Their connection with the old pagan rites and the development of the puppet theatre has already been mentioned above.

References to the rôle played by the *skomorokhi* in Kievite Russia are numberless and are to be found even within the walls of their principal oppressor — the Church. The skill of the *skomorokh* was diverse. He was not only a singer and performer, an actor and a clown, but a dancer, acrobat, conjurer, juggler and animal impersonator (primarily of bears). Being essentially a man of intelligence, he was called upon to take part in both Christian and non-Christian celebrations (especially weddings and banquets), as a result of his comprehensive knowledge of folksongs and folk ritual. The exuberance of the *skomorokhi* was incompatible with ecclesiastical dogma, however, and the Church subjected them to endless persecution. The principal instruments of the *skomorokhi* were the *gusli*, *dudki* and the *gudok*. The *domra* was introduced during the Novgorod period and remained their property for centuries. The main repertoire of the *skomorokhi* consisted of humorous songs and ballads (called variously *skomoroshini*, *nebilitsi*, *peregudki*, etc.) as well as

the *biliny* ballads. The *skomorokhi* ballads of
the Novgorod period usually have short verses
of about 8-12 syllables with two, three or four
stresses. The melodies are essentially simple,
of rhythmic clarity and a rapid tempo. Many
are of a dance-like nature. In some of the
biliny, the *skomorokhi* themselves take part.
The following ballad describes the manner
in which they help a rich Novgorod merchant
prove his wife's infidelity, though the whole
is couched in a vein of social satire:

Ex.28 PATTER

"Ba-ba, tï, ba-ba,go-su-da-rï-nya v lap-tyakh,ku
-da tï po-shla - to?"   "Na   tor -
- zhi-shchë,moi ba-tiush-ka, na tor - zhi - shchë."

Ex.27

Lively

V stol - nom   No - vo-go - ro - de,

bï - lo v u - li - tse vo lu - rye - vskoï,

v slo-bo-de bï - lo Te - re - ntye - vskoi,

a   i   zhil   bïl bo - ga - tï - gost,

a po i - me - ni Te - ren - ti - shche.

U ne - vo dvor na tse - loi   ver - ste,

a kru-gom dvo - ra zhe-lez - nï - tïn.

The *skomorokhi* in Novgorod enjoyed legal
rights (a privilege denied them elsewhere)
and had their own hostelries and settlements.

Another aspect of the *skomorokhi* art, apart
from the *biliny*, is revealed by the next example.
The song is a comic dialogue between a
country priest and an old woman who is trying
to celebrate the memory of her deceased
husband but has forgotten his name. The
music is a mixture of parody on ecclesiastical
chant and patter-recitative. The satirical
dialogue is rounded off with a lively dance
song of the *Kamarinskaya* type in which the
old woman tries to show what kind of song
her *skomorokh*-husband sang during his lifetime. Doubtless the performance would be
accompanied by vivid gesture (*see* Ex. 28).

The later history of the *skomorokhi* is a sad
one. One of their great patrons was Ivan the
Terrible who invited hundreds of them from
Novgorod to Moscow. During this period,
it became the general practice to make music
collectively, groups of *domras*, or violin and
gudok being a favourite combination.

In the 17th century, the age-old struggle
between the priests and the *skomorokhi* came
to a head. In the year 1649, in Moscow,
their instruments were collected and destroyed
and they were obliged to seek safety in the
remote districts of Northern Russia and
Siberia. From then on, the *skomorokhi*
throughout Russia virtually disappear from
ecclesiastical and civic records. Modern research, however, has discovered isolated
settlements still in existence preserving, often
in a remarkably pure form, the ballads and
music of previous centuries which have long
disappeared elsewhere. The *skomorokhi* were
undoubtedly guilty of licentiousness and
crime, but they provided a lively impetus to
the everyday life of both noble and peasant.
Their vigour did much to preserve the musical
heritage of ancient Russia.

FOLKSONG COLLECTIONS

AGRENEVA-SLAVYANSKAYA, ' Opisaniĕ russkoi krestyan-
    skoi svadbi ' (St. Petersburg, 1889).
ALBRECHT, E. K., ' Sbornik soldatskikh, kazatskikh i
    matrosskikh pesen ' (St. Petersburg, 1886).
BALAKIREV, M., ' Sbornik russkikh narodnikh pesen '
    (St. Petersburg, 1886).
' 35 pesen russkovo naroda ' (St. Petersburg, 1900).
BELYAĔV, V., ' Ranneĕ russkoĕ mnogogolosiĕ. Separa-
    tum e libro memoriali cui titulus " Studia
    memoriae Belae Bartók sacra " ' (' Academia ',
    Budapest).
CHULKOV, M. D., ' Sobraniĕ raznikh pesen ' (1770).
DANILOV, KIRSHA, ' Drevniĕ rossiiskiĕ stikhotvoreniya '
    (St. Petersburg, 1804).
DÜTSCH, G. O., ' Pesni russkovo naroda. Sobrani v
    guberniyakh Arkhangelskoi i Olonetskoi v 1886
    godu G. O. Dutschem i F. M. Istominom ' (1894).
FILIPPOV & RIMSKY-KORSAKOV, ' 40 narodnikh pesen,
    sobrannikh T. I. Filippova i garmonizovannikh
    N. A. Rimskim-Korsakovim ' (1882).
GRIGORYEV, A., ' Arkhangelskiĕ biliny i istoricheskiĕ
    pesni '.
GURILEV, A. L., ' Izbranniĕ narodniĕ russkiĕ pesni '
    (1849).
HILFERDING, A., ' Onezhskiĕ biliny '. Edition of the
    Academy of Science of the U.S.S.R. (Moscow-
    Leningrad, 1938).
ISTOMIN & LYAPUNOV, ' Pesni russkovo naroda (sobrani
    v guberniyakh Vologodskoy, Vyatskoy i Kostrom-
    skoy v 1893 godu) ' (St. Petersburg, 1899).
KASHIN, D., ' Russkiĕ narodniĕ pesni ' (1833–34).
LINEVA, E., ' Velikorusskiĕ pesni v narodnoi garmoni-
    zatsii ' (Vol. I, St. Petersburg, 1904 ; Vol. II, 1909).
LYADOV, A. (Collection taken from that of Imperial
    Geographical Society).
LYAPUNOV, S. M., ' 35 pesen russkovo naroda '.

MELGUNOV, I. N., 'Russkië pesni neprosredstvenno s golosov naroda zapisannië' (two volumes, 1879–85).
PALCHIKOV, N. E., 'Krestyanskië pesni, zapisannië v s. Nikolaëvke menzelinskovo uëzda Ufimskoi gubernii' (1888).
PRACH, I., 'Sobranië russkikh narodnikh pesen s ikh golosami, polozhennikh na muziku I. Prachem' (Vol. I, 1790; Vol. II, 1806).
PROKUNIN, V. P., 'Russkië narodnië pesni dlya odnovo golosa' (two volumes, 1872–73, ed. Tchaikovsky).
PROKUNIN & LOPATIN, 'Sbornik russkikh narodnikh liricheskikh pesen. Opit sistematicheskovo svoda so storoni bitovovo i khudozhestvennovo ikh soderzhaniya.' Two volumes.
RIBNIKOV, P. N., 'Pesni . . . Narodnië biliny, stàrini i pobivalshchini' (issued in four vols., 1861–67; 2nd ed. 1909–10 in three vols., ed. Gruzinsky).
RIMSKY-KORSAKOV, A. N., 'Sbornik 100 pesen' (1877).
RUPIN, I. A., 'Sbornik russkikh pesen' (1831–33)
SAKHAROV, I. R., 'Pesni russkovo naroda' (five vols., 1838–39).
STAKHOVICH, M. A., 'Sobranië russkikh narodnikh pesen.' Tekst i melodii sobral i muziku aranzhiroval dlya fortepiano i semistrunnoi gitari Mikhaïl Stakhovich' (four vols., 1851–54).
TCHAIKOVSKY, P. I., 'Sbornik narodnikh pesen v perelozhenii dlya fortepiano v 4 ruki' (1868–69).
TRUTOVSKY, V. F., 'Sbornik russkikh prostikh pesen s notami' (Vol. I, 1776; Vol. II, 1778; Vol. III, 1779; Vol. IV, 1795).
VARLAMOV, A. E., 'Russkii pevets'.
VILBOA, K. P., '100 russkikh pesen', ed. A. Grigoryev (2nd ed. 1894).
'Russkië romansi i narodnië pesni' (1874, 2nd ed. 1889).

BIBLIOGRAPHY

In a subject so vast as Russian folk music, it is impossible to list all the available sources. Useful bibliographies are given in Olkhovsky's 'Music under the Soviets', Vernadsky's 'The Origins of Russia', and Kaiëv's 'Russkaya Literatura'. Numerous articles on folk music are also to be found in the journals 'Sovetskaya muzika' and 'Sovetskaya etnografiya'.
AZADOVSKII, M. K., 'Istoriya russkoi folkloristiki' (Moscow, 1958).
BESSARABOFF, N., 'Ancient European Musical Instruments' (Harvard University Press, 1941).
'Bolshaya sovetskaya entsiklopedia' (2nd ed., Moscow, 1949–).
BUGOSLAVSKY, S. E. & SHISHOV, I. P., 'Russkaya narodnaya pesnya' (Moscow, 1936).
DANILOV, KIRSHA, 'Drevnië rossiiskië stikhotvoreniya', ed. Evgenyev & Putilov (Moscow–Leningrad, 1958).
FINAGIN, A. V., 'Russkaya narodnaya pesnya' (Leningrad, 1932).
FINDEISEN, N. F., 'Ocherki po istorii muziki v Rossii' (Moscow–Leningrad, 1928–29).
GARBUZOV, N. A., 'Drevnerusskoë narodnoë mnogogolosië' (Moscow–Leningrad, 1948).
GINZBURG, S. L., ed., 'Istoriya russkoi muziki v notnikh obraztsakh' (Moscow–Leningrad, 1940–49).
GIPPIUS, E. V., 'Intonatsionnië elementi russkoi chastushki' ('Sovetskii folklor', Moscow, April–May, 1936).
GRUBER, R. I., 'Istoriya muzikalnoi kulturi' (Vol. I, Moscow–Leningrad, 1941; Vol. II, Moscow, 1953).
KAIËV, A. A., 'Russkaya literatura' (Moscow, 1958).
KASTALSKY, A. D., 'Osobennosti narodno-russkoi muzikalnoi sistemi' (Moscow–Leningrad, 1923).
KELDISH, I. V., 'Istoriya russkoi muziki' (Moscow, 1947–48).
LIVANOVA, T., 'Russkaya muzikalnaya kultura XVIII veka' (Moscow, 1952).
MAHLER, E., 'Altrussische Volkslieder aus dem Pečoryland' (Basel, 1951).
MITAWA, L., 'Das russische Volkslied' ('Die Musik', Vol. IV, 4).
NESTYEV, I. V., 'Russkaya sovetskaya pesnya' (Moscow, 1951).
NOVOSELSKY, A., 'Ocherki po istorii russkikh narodnikh muzikalnikh instrumentov' (Moscow, 1931).
OLKHOVSKY, A. V., 'Music under the Soviets' (London, 1955).
ORLOV, G. P., 'Muzikalnaya literatura: bibliograficheskii ukazatel knizhnoi i zhurnalnoi literaturi muzike na russkom yazike' (Leningrad, 1936).

'Polnoë sobranië russkikh letopisei', published by the Russian Archaeographical Commission (1841–1921).
RALSTON, W. R. S., 'The Songs of the Russian People as Illustrative of Slavonic Mythology and Russian Social Life' (London, 1872).
SEAMAN, G. R., 'Russian Folk-song Anthologies in the Eighteenth Century' (M. & L., XL, No. 3, 1959).
SEROV, A. N., 'Russkaya narodnaya pesnya kak predmet nauki' (Moscow, 1952).
SIDELNIKOV, V. M., 'Russkoë narodnoë tvorchestvo i estrada: populyarni ocherk' (Moscow, 1950).
SOKALSKY, P. P., 'Russkaya narodnaya muzika, velikorusskaya i malorusskaya v eë stroenii melodicheskom i ritmicheskom i otlichiya eë ot osnov sovremennoi garmonicheskoi muziki' (Kharkov, 1888).
SWAN, A. J., 'The Nature of the Russian Folk-song' (M.Q., XXIX, 1949).
TUMANINA, N. V., 'Istoriya russkoi muziki' (Vol. I, Moscow, 1957; Vol. II, 1958).
VERNADSKY, G., 'The Origins of Russia' (Oxford, 1959).
VERTKOV, K. A., 'Russkaya rogovaya muzika' (Leningrad, 1948).
VINCENT, J., 'The Diatonic Modes in Modern Music' (California, 1951).

346　　i　　*Add before* **Scottish:**

Samish. The Arctic people known as Sames — previously Lapps or Finns — have been living in the north of Norway, Sweden, Finland and Russia for some 2000 years. They make their living by the breeding of reindeer. They number about 32,000 and 21,000 of them have their homes in Norway (Finnmarken). Of the Norwegian Sames only 1200 are still nomadic; the others support themselves by fishing. Linguistically they belong to the Finno-Ugrian race, their language being divided into several dialects, and their speech borrows many Norwegian words. Samish folk music is exclusively vocal; there is no evidence that it ever used instruments, with the exception of the sorcerer's drum, which in pagan times was used during heathen sacrifices. The melodies of the Sames consist of short themes with indefinite conclusions, and they may thus be repeated endlessly. They have no tonality and are frequently pentatonic. The name for the songs is *joyk* (? *jouik*), and they are sometimes descriptive in character. The old pagan sacrificial rock, for instance, which is shaped like an eagle's beak, seems to be described by means of abrupt intervals:

KÅBDESBAKKE

Noted by K. Tirén

A - rᵉ - na-si vuoi-dov　　a - lå　a - rus-
- lå　a - lå　　a - lå　*etc.*

("I offer to the eagle . . .")

But as a rule the *joyk* interprets the feelings of the singer as he perceives nature, other people, and so on. Thus the *joyk* which describes the cuckoo does not imitate the falling third sung by the bird. Unfortunately the stock of extant melodies that remains from ancient times was collected and taken down no longer than fifty years ago. The missionaries who converted the Sames to Christianity about 1700 prohibited not only the old sacrificial songs, but also the secular *joyk* without any pagan words. Explorers of the 18th century therefore concluded that the Sames had no music, as they never heard them sing. But since about 1900 scholars have been greatly interested in the *joyk* of the Sames, and the melodies that have been found are of great importance. Here are two specimens:

Noted by R. Graff

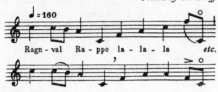

Ragn - val   Ra - ppe   la - la - la   *etc.*

To HAVELBA (*Clangula hyemalis*) [1]

Noted by R. Graff

Agn ã - gã agn ã - gã ã agn-gã ã agn-gã

N.B.—Notes marked o, if performed thus ![note] by the singer have no fixed pitch for the lower note ![note].

To the Same song is a vital force, no less. He will sing the old songs only for a listener he trusts, who can speak his language and is willing to lead his kind of life. Many tourists nowadays travel in Finnmark and some bring their tape recorders with them in the hope of recording a Samic *joyk*, but most of the tunes collected in this way are utterly worthless, elements of old song being mixed with quite recent material, and what is sung to tourists is often borrowed from Norwegian and Swedish melodies. The original *joyk* can be studied only with the aid of the existing scientific material.   O. M. S.

BIBL.—EMSHEIMER, E., 'Lappischer Kultgesang' (in 'Kongress-Bericht Lüneburg', 1950).
GRAFF, R., 'Music of Norwegian Lappland' (in 'Journal of the International Folk Music Council', 1954).

―――――――――――――
[1] An Arctic bird.

LAUNIS, A., 'Lappische Juoigosmelodien' (Helsingfors, 1908, 824 numbers).
TIRÉN, K., 'Die lappische Volksmusik' (Stockholm, 1942, 563 numbers).

353   ii   **FOLK MUSIC (Scottish)**
Signature M. L. (ii) *should read*:
M. L.

361   ii   **FOLK MUSIC (Siovak)**
BIBL. 2. *Printed*, l. 5. Mušik *should read*:
Mušík

368   i   **FOLK MUSIC (South American)**
Add to BIBL. :
ARETZ-THIELE, ISABEL, 'El folklore musical argentino' (Buenos Aires, 1952).
LEKIS, LISA, 'Folk Dances of Latin America' (New York, 1958).
LÓPEZ FLORES, JOAQUÍN, 'Danzas tradicionales argentinas', 2nd ed. (Buenos Aires, 1954).

387   i   **FOLK MUSIC (Turkish)**
Signature A. A. S. *should read*:
A. A. S. (ii).

398   i   **FOLK MUSIC (U.S.A.)**
BIBL. *should read*:
GREENWAY, JOHN, 'American Folk Songs of Protest' (Philadelphia & Oxford, 1953).
See also footnotes.

422   i   **FOLK MUSIC**
Add to GENERAL BIBLIOGRAPHY:
CHAMBERS, G. B., 'Folksong-Plainsong' (London, 1956).
'Folk Songs of Europe', ed. by Maud Karpeles for the International Folk Music Council (International Folk Song Series) (London, 1956).
KARPELES, MAUD, 'The Collecting of Folk Music and other Ethnomusicological Material: a Manual for Field Workers' (London, 1958).

ii   **FOMIN**
Par. 2. *Cut from* l. 2 *to the end* (*incl. See also*) *and substitute*:

studied music at the St. Petersburg Academy of Arts from 1776, at first under Buini, from 1777 under Raupach, who died in Dec. 1778, and finally under Sartori, leaving in 1782. He then went to Bologna, where he was a pupil of Martini and after the latter's death in 1784 of Mattei. His life after his return to St. Petersburg in 1786 is obscure apart from the productions of his stage works, and even these have been much confused by historians. It is obvious that he could have had nothing to do, at the age of eleven, with 'Aniuta' (libretto by Mikhail Vassilevich Popov), which has been called "the first opera by a Russian composer", produced at the Tsarskoye Selo Palace on 6 Sept. 1772, but was in fact a pasticcio with music by Piccinni, Grétry, Martín y Soler and others. Nor was 'Miller, Wizard, Cheat and Marriage-

Broker', produced in Moscow on 31 Jan. 1779, by him.[1]

Fomin seems to have held some post, certainly after the accession of Paul I in 1796, at the State Theatre, perhaps as coach at first and as conductor later on. The first work for the stage known to be his own is the ballet-opera 'Boyeslav, the Hero of Nov-gorod' (libretto partly by Catherine II), produced at the Hermitage on 8 Dec. 1786. Later productions, all in St. Petersburg, were 'Coachmen at the Posting-Stage', a one-act opera (13 Jan. 1787); the folk scene 'The Evening Party' (1788); 'The Americans' (composed 1788, produced 19 Feb. 1800); 'Witch, Fortune-Teller and Marriage-Broker' (1791); and the melodrama 'Orpheus and Eurydice' (13 Jan. 1792). Two more operas were given after his death: 'Clorinda and Milo' (17 Nov. 1800) and 'The Golden Apple' (1803).   E. B.

[1] The composer is now known to have been an obscure violinist named Sokolovsky. It is possible that Fomin wrote an overture and a few numbers for a later performance of this piece, which remained popular in Russia until well into the 19th century; and very likely it has also been confused with his own 'Witch, Fortune-Teller and Marriage-Broker'.

423   ii   **Fontane**
              l. 2 *should read*:

mouth', song). Grimm (F.-K., songs). Loewe (2 songs). Radó (song).

FONTANELLI
Par. 2, l. 21 *should read*:

back to Venosa, Gesualdo [4] and Naples, where

Add footnote:

[4] Gesualdo was also the name of the place where the composer had a castle.

424   i   *Add before* **FOOTE**:

FONTEYNS, ? (*b.* ? ; *d.* ?, ? 1447).
English composer. One composition ascribed to " Fonteyns " is found in the 'Old Hall Manuscript' (I, 159), and although this one work is assimilated into the *œuvre* of Pierre Fontaine by Marix (*see* Bibl., p. 235) it is not definite that the two composers should be merged into one. Fontaine was a native of Rouen, according to Marix; but Bukofzer (*see* Bibl., p. 91) notes that in view of the links between the 'Old Hall Manuscript' and the Fountains Fragment, the name " Fonteyns " may refer to Fountains Abbey, the possible training-ground of this composer.
On the other hand, the visits of the English Chapel Royal to France and Burgundy, and the fact that music by French and Italian composers is contained in the 'Old Hall Manuscript' make it possible that one work by Fontaine (who died about 1447 and was thus a contemporary of Power and Dunstable) was brought back to England and copied into

that source. The work in question is a *conductus* setting of the antiphon 'Regali ex progenie', with the plainsong in the middle voice. It was sung at Lauds at the feast of the Conception of the B.V.M.   D. W. S.

BIBL.—BUKOFZER, MANFRED, 'Studies in Medieval and Renaissance Music' (New York, 1950).
MARIX, JEANNE, 'Histoire de la musique et des musiciens de la cour de Bourgogne sous le règne de Philippe le Bon' (Strasbourg, 1939).
RAMSBOTHAM, ALEXANDER, ed., 'The Old Hall Manuscript', Vol. I (London, 1933).

424   ii   **FOOTE**
              Par. 1, l. 1 *should read*:

gardening. His eightieth birthday was celebrated with a performance of the 'Night Piece' by the Boston Symphony Orchestra.

427   i   **FORD, Ernest**
              Par. 1, l. 2. London, June *should read*:

London, 2 June

428   i   **FOREST**
              Par. 1, l. 1 *should read*:

FOREST, John (*b.* ? ; *d.* Wells, 1446).

Par. 2, l. 1 *should read*:

English composer. He seems

Add before See also:

This composer may be identified with the John Forrest who held various prebends at Lincoln from 1394 onwards, at Lichfield and York between 1415 and 1419 (during which time he was Archdeacon of Surrey) and eventually became Dean of Wells Cathedral in 1425. He held this office until his death in 1446; his will is preserved in Somerset House (P.C.C. 30 Luffenham).   D. W. S.

BIBL.—HARVEY, JOHN, 'Gothic England' (London, 1947).

       ii   **FORKEL**
              Par. 2, l. 20. Literatur *should read*:

Litteratur

445   i   **FORM**
              Add to BIBL. :

NESTLER, GERHARD, 'Die Form in der Musik: eine europäische Musikgeschichte' (Zürich, 1954).

447   ii   **FORQUERAY (3)**
              l. 2 *should read*:

1681 ; *d.* Montfort l'Amaury, 30 May 1757), prob. brother of the

FORQUERAY (4)
ll. 1-2 *should read*:

(4) Jean Baptiste (Antoine) Forqueray
(*b.* Paris, 3 Apr. 1699 ; *d.* Paris, 15 Aug. 1782), viola da gamba

448   i   *Add before* **FORSELL** :
FORREST, John.   *See* Forest.

ii   **FORSELL**
l. 1.   haftroligt *should read* :
haft roligt

449   i   **FÖRSTER**
Par. 2, ll. 5-10 *should read* :

working under him as an accountant on Count Vetter's estate. He afterwards served in the Prussian army, where he was oboist in Fouqué's regiment, and in 1768 he became a pupil of the organist Franz Pausewang at Mittelwalde. After some unsettled years, which took him to Prague for a time, he settled in Vienna some time between 1776 and 1779 in order to cultivate music thoroughly. There he soon became one of the most valued teachers of thorough-bass and composition. In 1802

Par. 3, l. 6 *should read* :
went to him for lessons in quartet writing.[1]

l. 11.   peared [1] *should read* :
peared.[2]

Add footnote :
[1] This has been repeatedly asserted on no other evidence than Beethoven's remark to Förster's son that he had often recommended his father to pupils as his early teacher. That Beethoven knew the elder Förster and his work well, however, is established, and if Beethoven did speak of him as his teacher, he presumably meant what he said.

Footnote 1 becomes 2.

ii   *Add at top of col.* :
The following is a list of Förster's compositions, so far as they are known, according to a thematic list in D.T.Ö., XXXV, i, 67 :

3 Sonatas for clavier, with vn. & cello (1760–64).
14 Pieces for stg. 4tet, ' La Nina ' (1764–70).[1]
6 Sonatas for clavier, with vn. (1770–74).
3 Divertimenti for clavier, with 2 vns. & cello (1786–74).
3 Divertimenti for clavier, with vn. & cello (c. 1771).
Divertimento for clavier, with vn., viola & cello (1771).
8 Sonatas for clavier, with 2 vns. & cello (1774).[2]
Sonata for clavier, with vn. (c. 1775).
Divertimento for 2 vns. & cello (c. 1776).
' Rondo alla polacca ' for pf. & orch. (1780).
3 Duets for flute (or vn.) & pf., Op. 5 (1792).
6 String Quartets, Op. 7 (1794).
2 Pf. Quartets, Op. 8 (1794).
Sextet for flute, bassoon, vn., viola, cello & pf., Op. 9 (1795).
2 Pf. Quartets, Op. 10 (1796).
2 Pf. Quartets, Op. 11 (1796).
' Notturno concertante ' for orch. (1799).
6 String Quartets, Op. 16 (1799).
3 Pf. Trios, Op. 18 (1800).
13 String Quartets (1801).
Octet for oboe, clar., bassoon, vn., viola, cello, d. bass & pf. (1802).
String Quintet, C mi., Op. 19 (1802).[3]
String Quintet, A mi., Op. 20 (1802).
6 String Quartets, Op. 21 (1803).
String Quintet, E♭ ma., Op. 26 (1804).
18 String Quartets (1805).

[1] First violin parts lost.
[2] Three of these probably identical with the Divertimenti of 1764–74.
[3] All the string quintets are for 2 violins, 2 violas and cello.

4 Sonatas for vn. & pf. (1808).
' Fantaisie et sonate ' for stg. 5tet, arr. of a pf. Fantasy, Op 25, of 1803.

449   ii   **FORSTER, Georg**
Par. 1, l. 1.   Amberg, *should read* :
Annaberg,

450   —   *Add at end:*
See also Chorwerk, Vol. 63 (modern reprint of songs). Denkmäler (5) I, Vol. 20 (modern ed.). Publikationen G.M.F., Vol. 33 (modern ed.).

ii   **Fort**
l. 3 (2 vocal duets) *should read* :
(2 choruses, 2 vocal duets).

451   i   **FORTI**
Par. 1, l. 5 *should read* :
Pizarro in the revival of ' Fidelio ' in 1814, taking the part over from Vogl, who had been taken ill,

452   i   **FORTNER, CATALOGUE**
Add to OPERAS :
' Der Wald ', after Federico García Lorca, prod. Essen, 18 Dec. 1954 (incorporated into ' Die Bluthochzeit ').

Add after l. 2 :
' Die Bluthochzeit ' (lib. after Lorca) (1956), prod. Cologne, 8 June 1957.

Add at end :
' Corrila ', lib. after Gérard de Nerval, prod. Berlin, 1958.

453   i   **FÖRTSCH**
Add to BIBL. :
Weidemann, Clara, ' Leben und Wirken des Johann Philipp Förtsch ' (Cassel & Basel, 1955).

454   i   **FOSS, Hubert**
Par. 1, l. 11 *should read* :
1927 ; Vol. II, 1934 ; Vol. III, 1951). In 1946 he published ' The Concert-Goer's Handbook '. His

455   i   **FOSTER, Arnold**
Par. 3, l. 2 *should read* :
apart from this ballet, ' Lord Bateman ', a ballad opera on folk tunes (1948–56), ' Three Festive Carols ' for chorus and orchestra (1946) ; ' The Fairy Isle ', a

456   i   **FOSTER, Stephen**
Par. 1, ll. 1-2.   Pittsburg *should read* :
Pittsburgh
Par. 2, l. 7.   the lattice *should read* :
thy lattice

ii   *Add to* BIBL. :
Fuld, James J., ' A Pictorial Bibliography of the First Editions of Stephen C. Foster ' (Philadelphia, 1957). Hodges, F., ' Stephen Foster, Democrat ' (Pittsburgh, 1946).

458   i   **Fouqué**
l. 1.   *See* Hoffmann *should read*:
See Henze ('Ondine', ballet).   Hoffmann

459   i   **FOURESTIER**
l. 6 *should read*:
there. In 1947–48 he was guest conductor at the Metropolitan Opera in New York. His wife is a pupil and ardent admirer

462   i   **FRANÇAIX,** CATALOGUE
OPERAS
l. 8 *should read*:
Gérard de Nerval) (1945), prod. Bordeaux, 7 May 1950.

BALLETS
l. 4 *should read*:
Hans Andersen) (1935), prod. Paris, Opéra, 15 June 1936.

463   i   **FRANCESCO DA MILANO**
Par. 2, l. 9 *should read*:
by him, and over 70 fantasies have been traced (1954).   E. V. D. S., adds.

FRANCESINA, LA. *should read*:
FRANCESCINA, LA.

Move up this entry to stand before
FRANCESCO DA MILANO.

ii   *Add after* **Francheville**:

FRANCHOIS, Jean (*b.* Gembloux, ?; *d.* ?).
French 14th–15th-century composer. He was *chapelain* to the Dukes of Burgundy early in the 15th century, in the service of Philippe le Hardi in 1404, and remained a member of the chapel on the accession of Jean sans Peur. As a forerunner of Dufay he is as important as his more prolific contemporaries, Arnold and Hugo de Lantins. His style to some extent bridges the gulf between strict isorhythmic features of the 14th century and freely-used imitative passages that were to become increasingly significant in the development of the Franco-Netherlandish school.
Nine of his works are extant, and two more have been ascribed to him on stylistic grounds. A paired 'Gloria' and 'Credo' transmitted by manuscript sources at Bologna, Oxford, Cambrai, Aosta and Munich demonstrate the great favour in which his work was held. A similar pair is to be found in the Trent Manuscripts, with concordances in the choirbooks at Munich and Aosta. Recently Dr. Laurence Feininger has attributed to Franchois another 'Gloria — Credo' pair which is preserved, without any indication of the composer's name, at Bologna (Bibl. Martini, Q 15). This same manuscript contains a fine motet for two altos and instrumental group, 'Ave virgo, lux Maria'. The motet proper, which is isorhythmic, is preceded by a three-part

prelude marked "trumpetta introitus", and the melodic leaps of the individual lines also bear out the possibility of performance on brass instruments. The tenor of the motet can be identified as 'Sancta Maria succurre miseris', which indicates that the work was written specially for Vespers on the Feast of the Nativity of the B.V.M. Besides these liturgical works, three chansons and one instrumental piece survive, the latter in the Buxheim Organ Book. There are modern editions of most of Franchois's surviving music by Feininger, Ficker and Van den Borren.   D. W. S.

BIBLIOGRAPHY
BESSELER, HEINRICH, 'Bourdon und Fauxbourdon' (Leipzig, 1950).
'Die Entstehung der Posaune' ('Acta Musicologica', XXII, 1950).
BORREN, CHARLES VAN DEN, 'Études sur le XVᵉ siècle musical' (Antwerp, 1941).
'Pièces polyphoniques profanes de provenance liégeoise' (Brussels, 1950).
'Polyphonia Sacra' (Burnham, 1932).
FEININGER, LAURENCE (ed.), 'Documenta polyphoniae liturgicae Sanctae Ecclesiae Romanae', Ser. I, No. 11.
FICKER, RUDOLF VON (ed.), 'Denkmäler der Tonkunst in Österreich', Vol. 76.
MARIX, JEANNE, 'Histoire de la musique et des musiciens de la cour de Bourgogne sous le règne de Philippe le Bon' (Strasbourg, 1939).
REESE, GUSTAVE, 'Music in the Renaissance' (New York, 1954).
VAN, GUILLAUME DE, 'An Inventory of the Manuscript Bologna, Q 15 (*Olim* 37)' ('Musica Disciplina', II, 1948).
WOLF, JOHANNES, 'Geschichte der Mensural-Notation' (Leipzig, 1904).

464   i   *Add before* **FRANCIS**:
FRANCI, Carlo (*b.* Buenos Aires, 18 July 1927).
Italian composer and conductor. He studied composition under Petrassi and conducting under Previtali in Rome. He is active as an orchestral conductor in Italy and abroad, and is director of the Radio Eireann Symphony Orchestra in Dublin. His 'Primo concerto' was the winning work in the International Composers' Competition held under the patronage of Queen Elisabeth of Belgium, and his one-act opera 'L'imperatore' was produced at the Teatro delle Novità at Bergamo in the autumn of 1958. Among other works to be noted are the third Concerto and 'Musica per archi e timpani'.
G. M. G.

ii   **Francis of Assisi**
l. 3.   Donastia *should read*:
Donostia

473   ii   **FRANCK, César**
Add to BIBL.:
KUNEL, MAURICE, 'César Franck inconnu . . . d'après des documents inédits' (Brussels, 1958).

475   —   CATALOGUE
SONGS
Col. 4, l. 3.   Mme Louise Boutet *should read*:
Jules Leter.

476 — CATALOGUE
SONGS
l. 12 *should be* l. 2 *and read*:

| 'Aimer.' | Joseph Méry. | 1842–43. | Mme Louise Boutet de Monvel. |

i **FRANCK, J. W.**
Dates *should read*:
(*b*. Unterschwaningen, [bapt. 17] June 1644; *d*. ? London, ?).

Par. 2, ll. 1-4 *should read*:
German composer. It is not known where he received his musical education,

477 ii l. 6 *should read*:
See also Böhm (collab.). Denkmäler (5) II (modern ed. of ' Drey Töchter Cecrops ').

FRANCK, Melchior
See also should read:
See also Chorwerk, Vols. 24, 38, 53 (modern reprints). Quodlibet.

481 i **FRANCUS DE INSULA**
l. 5 *should read*:
Oxford manuscript. His extant work is published in Vol. II of ' Early Fifteenth-Century Music ', edited by Gilbert Reaney (Amer. Inst. of Musicology, 1958). E. D. (ii).

487 ii **FRASER, John**
Par. 1, l. 2. *c*. 1804 *should read*: *c*. 1794.

Add at end, before See also:
BIBL.—FRASER, JAMES ROY, ' Memoir of John Fraser, Newfield, Johnstone ' (Paisley, 1879).

488 ii **FRAZZI**
Par. 1, l. 2. 1 Jan. 1888). *should read*:
1 Aug. 1888).

489 i **FREDDI**
Entry should read:
FREDDI, Amadio (*b*. Padua, *c*. 1575; *d*. ?).
Italian composer. He was a singer at the Cappella S. Antonio at Padua in 1594 and *maestro di cappella* there in 1606. From 1615 to 1626 he was at Treviso Cathedral as *maestro*, in 1632 at Vicenza and in 1634 at Padua again. He composed church music and madrigals published at Venice in 1601, 1605, 1614, etc. E. V. D. S., adds.

490 i **FREDERICK II**
Add to BIBL.:
YORKE-LONG, ALAN, ' Music at Court : four Eighteenth-Century Studies ' (London, 1954).

491 i **FREITAS BRANCO**
Par. 1, l. 2 *should read*:
Oct. 1890; *d*. Lisbon, 27 Nov. 1955).

491 ii Par. 2, l. 2 *should read*:
newspapers and reviews, and to the last he held

494 ii **FRESCOBALDI**
Add to BIBL. :
MACHABEY, ARMAND, ' Girolamo Frescobaldi Ferrarensis ' (Paris, 1952).
REDLICH, H. F., ' Girolamo Frescobaldi ' (M. Rev., XIV, 1953, p. 282).

See also should read:
See also Classici Musica Italiana, Vol. 12 (modern ed. of sonatas). Ruggiero (use of ground).

497 ii *Add after* **FRICHOT** :
FRICK, Gottlob (*b*. Olbronn, Württemberg, 28 July 1906).
German bass singer. He studied at the Stuttgart High School for Music and obtained his first engagement at the Landestheater, Stuttgart, from 1927 to 1931. Engagements followed at Coburg, Freiburg and Königsberg, and then, in 1941, he became a member of the Dresden State Opera, remaining there for ten years. While at Dresden he sang Favart in the local première of Kienzl's ' Der Kuhreigen ', Caliban in the world première of Sutermeister's ' Die Zauberinsel ', the Carpenter in Haas's ' Die Hochzeit des Jobs ', as well as such parts as Rocco, Falstaff (Nicolai), Pogner, Gremin (' Eugene Onegin '), the Peasant in Orff's ' Die Kluge ' and Tomasso in ' Tiefland '. In 1945 he was made a *Kammersänger* and in 1947 he went to the Berlin State Opera, singing the bass parts in the Wagnerian repertory. Appearances at the Scala, Milan, and the Liceo, Barcelona, followed, and in 1951 he made his London début at Covent Garden in the ' Ring ', singing Fafner, Hunding and Hagen. The following year he sang Sarastro, Caspar and Pogner with the Hamburg State Opera at the Edinburgh Festival, and since 1953 has been a member of both the Munich and Vienna State Operas.
Gottlob Frick has a large, dark-coloured voice, which sounds just as rich in the lower reaches as at the top. In fact he is one of the few large-voiced " black " German basses now singing, and is admirably suited to the part of Hagen, which he sang with much success when he returned to Covent Garden in the summer of 1957. His deeply felt and sensitively sung Gurnemanz in 1959 was judged the equal of Ludwig Weber's.

H. D. R.

498 i **FRICKER**
Footnote should read:
[1] Jean Racine, the poet, is said to be among his ancestors, but this has not been substantiated.

499   ii   CATALOGUE
            CHORAL WORKS
            Add after l. 2 :
27. ' Musick's Empire ' (Andrew Marvell) for chorus
    & small orch.
29. ' A Vision of Judgment ' (Cynewulf) for soprano,
    tenor, chorus and orch.

            ORCHESTRAL WORKS
            Add at end:
32. Comedy Overture.
36. Symphony No. 3 (1960).

            SOLO INSTRUMENTS AND OR-
            CHESTRA
            Add at end:
33. Toccata for pf. and Orchestra.

            CHAMBER MUSIC
            Add at end:
30. Octet for flute, clarinet, horn, bassoon and stgs.
34. Serenade for flute, clarinet, bass clarinet, harp, viola
    and cello.
35. Trio for flute, oboe and pf.

500   i   PIANOFORTE SOLO
            Add at end:
31. Variations for pf.

                  l. 9.   2. *should read* :
12.

            FRID
            Par. 1, l. 1.   1904 *should read* :
25 Jan. 1904).

501   i   **FRIDERICI, D.**
            Add at end:
See also Denkmäler (5), II (modern ed.).

            FRIDERICI-JAKOWICKA
            Par. 2, l. 24.   sonnanbula *should
            read* :
sonnambula

      ii   **FRIEBERT**
            Par. 1, l. 1.   (*b.* ? ; *should read* :
(*b.* ?, 1723 ;

502   ii   *Add to* BIBL. :
BAUER, H., ' Joseph Friebert ' (Munich, 1952).

503   i   **FRIEDLÄNDER, Max**
            Add to BIBL. :
DENT, E. J., ' Max Friedländer ' (M.M.R., June 1934).

504   ii   **FRIGEL**
            BIBL., l. 2.   sekraterare *should read* :
sekreteare
            l. 3.   Tra *should read* :
Två

506   i   **FROBERGER**
            Par. 1, ll. 2-3 *should read* :
gart ², 18 May 1616 ; *d.* Héricourt nr. Mont-
béliard [Mömpelgard], 7 May 1667).

      ii   Par. 5, l. 12 *should read* :
organ works was published in the D.T.Ö.,
Vols. IV, VI and X,

N

507   i   **FRÖHLICH (3)**
            l. 2 *should read* :
1797 ;   *d.* Vienna, 30 June 1879), contralto
singer,

            FRÖHLICH (4)
            l. 2.   1808 *should read* :
1803

            Add before **Froissart** :

FROIDEBISE, Pierre (Jean Marie) (*b.*
Ohey, Namur, 15 May 1914).
Belgian composer.   He studied at the Conservatoire Royal of Brussels with Jean Absil
and became a private pupil of Paul Gilson
for composition.   After a sojourn in Paris,
where he studied the organ with Tournemire,
he was appointed professor of harmony at
the Royal Conservatory of Liège.   He is also
choirmaster of the Grand Séminaire there.
His compositions include works for orchestra,
a few cantatas, chamber, pianoforte and organ
music and songs.   Among the last ' Amer-
cœur ', 3 Japanese poems for voice and orchestra, are outstanding.   He reached the
general public with music for 2 films, ' Visite
à Picasso ' and ' Lumière des hommes '.
                                          A. L. C.

            **FROM BOHEMIA'S FIELDS
            AND GROVES**
            l. 2 *should read* :
GROVES.   *See* SMETANA (' Má Vlast ').

            FROMM
            l. 1 *should read* :
FROMM, Andreas (*b.* Pänitz, Brandenburg, 1621 ; *d.* Strahov, Prague, 1683).

            l. 2 *should read* :
German composer.   He was

      ii   Par. 1, l. 5.   Leitmeritz *should
            read* :
Litoměřice

508   ii   **FROTTOLA**
            Add to BIBL. :
DISERTORI, BENVENUTO, ' La frottola nella storia della
    musica ' (Cremona, 1954).

510   i   **FRY, W. H.**
            Par. 1, l. 2.   1815 *should read* :
1813

      ii   *Add to* BIBL. (2nd work by Upton) :
' William Henry Fry, American Journalist and Com-
    poser-Critic ' (New York, 1954).

            FRYER
            Par. 1, l. 2 *should read* :
21 May 1877 ; *d.* London, 7 Feb. 1957).

512   ii   *Add after* **FUENTES**:

FUGA, Sandro (*b.* Mogliano Veneto [Treviso], 26 Nov. 1906).
Italian pianist and composer. He studied at the Conservatory " G. Verdi " at Turin, where he took a diploma in 1928. From 1932 onwards he has been professor of the pianoforte there. His compositions include numerous works of every kind : among the most significant may be named the ' Divertimento ' for pianoforte and orchestra, the Sonata for violoncello and pianoforte, 3 string Quartets, 3 ' Concerti sacri ' scored respectively for chorus and orchestra, for baritone, chorus and orchestra, and for orchestra alone, the ' Concertino ' for trumpet and orchestra, the violoncello Concerto and the 4 impressions for orchestra and speaker, ' Ultime lettere da Stalingrado ', which obtained the Marzotto prize. For the stage he has written the one-act *lauda drammatica* ' La croce deserta ' (Bergamo, 1950) and the one-act *commedia eroicomica* ' Otto Schnaffs ' (Turin, 1950).   G. M. G.

FUGUE
Add to page headings :

514 —
: Subjects

515 —
: Subjects — Answers

516 —
: Answers

517 —
: Counter-Subjects — Exposition — Middle Section

518 —
: Middle Section

519 —
: Stretto — Climax and Coda

520 —
: Chorale Fugue

521   i   BIBL. (MODERN WORKS), l. 1. (DENT, EDWARD J.) *should read*:
DENT, EDWARD J.

l. 2 *should read*:
(Cambridge, 1941 ; new ed. 1958).

Add:

BARFORD, PHILIP T., ' The Idea of Fugue ' (M. Rev., XV, 1954, p. 173).
DICKINSON, A. E. F., ' Bach's Fugal Works : with an Account of Fugue before and after Bach ' (London, 1956).
GHISLANZONI, ALBERTO, ' Storia della fuga ' (Milan, 1952).

MANN, ALFRED, ' The Study of Fugue ' (New Brunswick, N.J., 1958).
TOVEY, DONALD F., Article on ' Fugue ' in ' Encyclopaedia Britannica ' (var. eds.).

521   ii   *Add top of col.* :

FUHRMANN, Christa. *See* LANDON, H. C. ROBBINS.

FULEIHAN
Par. 1, l. 2.   1901 *should read*:
1900

526   i   **FURMEDGE**
Par. 1, l. 2 *should read*:
1898 ; *d.* London, Oct. 1956).

       ii   **FURTWÄNGLER**
Par. 1, l. 2 *should read*:
25 Jan. 1886 ; *d.* nr. Baden-Baden, 30 Nov. 1954).

527   ii   Par. 1, l. 2 *should read*:
musical posts. An invitation to conduct the Chicago Symphony Orchestra was cancelled owing to local protests. There was some reluctance in

Add to BIBL. :

FURTWÄNGLER, WILHELM, ' Gespräche über Musik ' (Zürich, 1948) ; Eng. trans. by L. J. Lawrence, ' Concerning Music ' (London, 1953).
' Vermächtnis (Nachgelassene Schriften) ' (Wiesbaden, 1956).
RIESS, CURT, ' Furtwängler : Musik und Politik ' (Berne, 1953) ; Eng. trans. by Margaret Goldsmith (London, 1955).
' Wilhelm Furtwängler im Urteil seiner Zeit ', ed. by Martin Hürlimann (Zürich & Freiburg i/B., 1955).

528   ii   **FUX**
BIBL., l. 11. LEISS *should read*:
LIESS

After l. 15 *add*:
' Fuxiana ' (Vienna, 1958).

530   ii   *Add before* **GABBRIELLI**:

GABARAIN, Marina de (*b.* San Sebastián, ?).
Spanish contralto singer. She began to study music at home as a child and had her first systematic vocal training under Ricci in Italy. Later she studied with Pierre Bernac in Paris, at the R.C.M. and with Elena Gerhardt in London, then with Lotte Leonard in Paris and finally with Ricci again. She sang Carmen with the Carl Rosa company to gain operatic experience and also studied acting with Irene Worth. In 1952 she made a brilliant success at Glyndebourne in Rossini's ' Cenerentola ' and two years later appeared there as Baba the Turk in Stravinsky's 'Rake's Progress '. She has also sung at orchestral concerts in Britain, Switzerland and elsewhere.   E. B.

532   i   GABRIELI, Andrea
Par. 2, l. 1.   In July 1566 *should read*:

In July 1564

ll. 13-17 *should read*:
Gabrieli was succeeded at his death by Bell' Haver. His nephew and chief disciple, Giovanni Gabrieli, had for some time acted as a deputy for Merulo at the first organ and had been appointed second organist in 1585, when Andrea

Par. 3, ll. 12-17 *should read*:
his life Hans Leo Hassler became his pupil for a year.

533   ii   MODERN REPRINTS
l. 4, Vol. I *should read*:
Vols. I & II

534   i   GABRIELI, Giovanni
Par. 1, l. 2.   21 Aug. *should read*:
12 Aug.

Par. 2, ll. 17-20 *should read*:
second organist in 1584, a post which he held until his death. Bell' Haver was first organist in 1586–88 and Guami in 1588–91.

Par. 3, ll. 14-16 *should read*:
care of the latter's foreign disciple Gregor Aichinger, who studied with Giovanni in approximately

535   i   *Add after* Par. 1 :
The American Institute of Musicology has undertaken the publication of a collected edition, ' Opera Omnia ', the first volume of which, edited by Denis Arnold, appeared in 1956.

Add to BIBL. :
ARNOLD, DENIS, ' Ceremonial Music in Venice at the Time of the Gabrielis ' (Proc. Roy. Mus. Ass., Vol. LXXXII, 1955–56).

536   ii   *Add to See also*:
Chorwerk, Vol. 10 (modern reprint of 3 motets).

537   ii   GABUSSI, G. C.
Par. 1, l. 1.   Bologna, ? ;   *should read*:
Bologna, *c.* 1555 [1] ;

l. 2 *should read*:
d. Milan, 12 Sept. 1611).

Add footnote :
[1] A letter from Costanzo Porta to Cardinal Borromeo, quoted in Garbelotti's book on Porta and dated 1582, refers to Gabussi as " un giovanetto di 27 anni ".

537   ii   Par. 2, l. 1 *should read*:
Italian composer.   He was a

540   i   GADSKI
Par. 2, l. 10.   1896 *should read*:
1895

ii   GADZHIBEKOV
Par. 1, l. 2 *should read*:
Karabi, Azerbaijan, 17 Sept. 1885 ; *d.* Baku, 23 Nov. 1948).

541   ii   GAFORI
Par. 3, l. 3 *should read*:
1934.   Modern facsimile reprints of A, C and H are to be published in ' Documenta Musicologica ', Vols. 13-15.   W. B. S., adds.

545   i   GAGLIANO
See also. l. 3 *should read*:
collab. in ' Sposalizio '). Publikationen G.M.F., Vol. 9 (modern ed. of ' Dafne ').

546   i   GAITA
Add to line :
(*PLATE* 2, Vol. I, p. 352, No. 8.)

ii   GÁL
Par. 1, l. 1.   Brno *should read*:
Brunn nr. Vienna

Par. 2, l. 6 *should read*:
took a degree in philosophy.   In 1913 he published an excellent study on Beethoven's early style, ' Die Stileigentümlichkeiten des jungen Beethoven ', in Vol. IV of S.M.W.   In 1919 he

Par. 3, l. 13 *should read*:
him lecturer at the University, a post he held until 1957, when he was succeeded by Hans Redlich.   In 1958 Gál received the Austrian State Prize for Music.

547   ii   CATALOGUE
PIANOFORTE MUSIC
Add after Op. 7 :
24. Suite (1926).

SONGS
Op. 33.   3 Songs *should read*:
5 Songs

548   i   *Insert after* GALATÉE :
GALEAZZI, Francesco.   *See* GALLEAZZI.

ii   GALILEI
Add at end :
See also Istituzioni, Vol. 4 (modern reprint).

549 i GALINDO
BALLETS
l. 3. Ferúa *should read*:
Feria

ii *Add after* **GALINDO** :

GALIOT, Johannes (*b.* ? ; *d.* ?).
French 14th-century composer. The four
3-part compositions attributed to him all
appear in the important Chantilly MS 1047.
One of these, ' En attendant esperance ', is
probably by Jacobus de Sentluch, known as
Jacomi at the court of John I of Aragon, since
his name appears at the head of the piece in
the Modena Codex M. 5. 24, and even in
Chantilly the name appears after the second
strophe of text. Moreover, this particular
ballade features all the special note-forms so
beloved by Jacomi. The mistake was quite
natural, since another ballade by Galiot is
called ' En attendant souffrir ' and a rondeau
' En attendant d'amer '.

Probably the most complicated work by
Galiot is the ballade ' Le Sault perilleux ',
which opens the third fascicle of the Chantilly
MS and is adorned with an illustration of
clerics singing from manuscripts. It employs
red notes frequently, and not only has the
mensuration signs C and ☉, but also ☉ and
☉ with the special meanings of four notes
against three and nine against eight respectively. The concluding section with syncopations and duplets in prevailing 6-8 time is
typical. Syncopation seems to have interested
Galiot particularly, as it did many men
writing about this time, *c.* 1380. Here is a
typical example from ' En attendant souffrir ' :

Although the *cantus* is relatively complicated,
the lower parts are simpler, particularly the
tenor, which must keep the other parts together. ' En attendant d'amer ' is an isorhythmic rondeau, *i.e.* it is divided into two
halves identical rhythmically. Syncopation is
even more prevalent than in ' En attendant
souffrir ', and, though the *tenor* remains simple,
the *contratenor* joins in with hemiola cross-
rhythms (3-4 against the normal 6-8).

' En attendant souffrir ' and ' En attendant
esperance ' are in W. Apel's ' French Secular
Music of the Late Fourteenth Century ' (1950).
G. R. (iii).

GALLEAZZI
Add at end :
See also Vivaldi (collab. in ' Odio vinto ').

550 i GALLENBERG
Par. 4, l. 10. 1816 *should read* :
1836

553 i GALLIARD
Add after Par. 2 :
The following is an example of a typical
galliard :

'The Earl of Salisbury's Galliard'
(Wm.Byrd, 'Parthenia')

554 i GALLICO
Par. 1, l. 2 *should read* :
1868 ; *d.* New York, 6 July 1955).

GALLICULUS
Add at end :
See also Chorwerk, Vol. 44 (modern reprint of Easter
Mass).

ii **GALLO, R.**
Par. 2, l. 4 *should read* :
added a third part. This, the only known
work of his, appeared in 1958 in Vol. II of
' Early Fifteenth-Century Music ', edited by
Gilbert Reaney and published by the American Institute of Musicology.   E. D. (ii).

555 i Galloway
Transfer to Col. ii, above **GALLUS.**

557 ii GALUPPI
LIBRETTOS BY GOLDONI
l. 8. calamità *should read* :
calamita

558 ii *Add to See also* :
Classici Musica Italiana, Vol. 13 (modern ed. of ' Filosofo
di campagna ').

560 ii *Add before* GANDO :

GANDINO, Adolfo (*b.* Bra, Piedmont, 29
July 1878 ; *d.* Bologna, 7 June 1940).
Italian composer. He was a son of the
famous Latinist Giovanni Battista Gandino
and became a pupil of Martucci. Grown up
in a home frequented by such literary figures

as Carducci, Pascoli, Panzacchi, D' Ovidio and others, he at first came under such powerful literary influences that he himself came to cultivate literature as well as music; and these two cultural currents became so intimately fused as to produce the happiest results in the field of music.

Among Gandino's most important compositions are the operas ' Trilby ' (after Nodier's story), ' Jaufré Rudel ', ' Imelda de' Lambertazzi ' : ' Himnus in Romam ' for chorus and orchestra; symphonic and chamber music; pianoforte works and a large number of songs, many of them to poems by Giovanni Pascoli.

E. B.

560   ii   *Add after* **GANDO** :

GANEVAL, Émilienne. *See* MACHABEY.

563   i   HEADING
GARAUDE *should read* :
GARAUDÉ

GARBUSOVA
Par. 1, l. 2.   1909). *should read* :
1906).

ii   **GARCIA (1)**
Par. 1, l. 2.   2 June *should read* :
9 June

566   i   **GARDANO (5)**
See also should read :
See also Florilège, Vol. 8 (modern ed. of duos by Antonio). Trionfo di Dori (publ. of).

568   ii   **GARDNER, John**
Add after Par. 2 :

Gardner's most ambitious work is the full-scale opera ' The Moon and Sixpence ', based on Somerset Maugham's novel, which was produced at Sadler's Wells Theatre on 24 May 1957. A pianoforte Concerto was first heard at the Cheltenham Festival the same year.

571   i   **GASCOGNE**
Add at end :
See also Maitres Musiciens, Vol. 5 (modern ed. of chansons).

GASPARINI
Par. 2, l. 5.   *maestro di cappella* *should read* :
maestro di coro

574   i   **GAST**
Add to BIBL. :
' Nietzsche : Lettres à Peter Gast ', trans. by Louise Servicen, 2 vols. (Monaco, 1957).

i-ii   **" GASTEIN " SYMPHONY**
ll. 4-5 *should read* :
Austrian watering-place of Gastein in Aug. and Sept. 1825. No

574   ii   **GASTOLDI**
Par. 2, l. 4 *should read* :
of ' Balletti a cinque voci, con li suoi versi per cantare, suonare et ballare '

l. 12 *should read* :
gallant be ', the latter the madrigal ' Tutti venite armati '. Two others, ' Viver lieto voglio '

577   i   **GAUBERT**
Par. 1, l. 1.   4 July *should read* :
3 July

l. 2.   10 July *should read* :
8 July

580   i   **GAULTIER (3)**
Add to See also :
Publications Soc. Franç., Vol. 7 (facsimile of ' Rhétorique ').

ii   **Gautier, Théophile**
l. 3.   (2 songs). *should read* :
(3 songs).

581   ii   **GAVAZZENI**
Add at end :
BIBL.—' Gavazzeni, Gianandrea : quaderno del musicista (1940–1950) ' (Bergamo, 1952).

582   i   **GAVINIÈS**
Par. 1, l. 2.   22 Sept. *should read* :
8 Sept.

586   ii   *Add before* **Gebler** :

GEBHARD, Heinrich (*b.* Sobernheim, Rhineland, 25 July 1878).
American pianist and composer of German birth. The family emigrated to the U.S.A. when he was eight. He had already been taught music by a military bandmaster. He studied the pianoforte with Clayton Johns at Boston until he was seventeen and then went to Vienna to finish his training under Leschetizky and to study composition with Heuberger. After his return to the U.S.A. he appeared for many years as a concert pianist. In 1951 he was appointed to conduct the Master Class in pianoforte playing in the Faculty of Fine Arts of Boston University, and he retired in 1957.

Gebhard's compositions include a cantata, ' Amar and Maja ', for women's chorus and pianoforte, a Fantasy for pianoforte and orchestra, a ' Divertissement ' for pianoforte and chamber orchestra, a string Quartet and a violin and pianoforte Sonata. His book, ' The Art of Pedalling ', was published in 1959.

E. B.

587   i   **GÉDALGE**
Par. 1, l. 1.   name *should read* :
GEDALGE 1

Par. 3, l. 1 *should read* :
Gedalge's works include

Add footnote :
1 Sometimes spelt Gédalge, but the weight of evidence is against the accent. It occurs mainly on works published outside France.

GEERES
l. 1.   *d.* ?). *should read* :
d. Durham, [buried 4] Mar. 1642).

Par. 2, ll. 1-4 *should read* :
English composer. Almost nothing is known of his life except that his son John was baptized at Durham on 30 Sept. 1632. His name appears in the Treasurer's Accounts of Durham Cathedral during the years 1632–1636 as that of a lay clerk ; but as many of the account books of that period are missing it is likely that he held this post for a longer time. This impression is strengthened by the appearance of his name among those whose stipends were increased in 1632–34. In the latter year he is described as "Baccalaureus in Musica". Three anthems of his are preserved in a manuscript dated from Durham Cathedral, 1664 (B.M. Add. MS 30,478).

Signature should read :
W. K. F.

588   i   **Geibel**
Add before Brahms :
Berg (Alban, song).

590   ii   **GELINEK**
Footnote 2, l. 1 should read :
2 Letter G is not used in Czech, except for adopted words and names, but he was generally

Gellert
l. 1.   Refs. *should read* :
See Bach (C. P. E., 54 'Geistliche Oden', 11 other songs).
Delete Bach (J. S., 32).

GEMELLUM
l. 1 *should read* :
GEMELLUM. *See* GYMEL.

Cancel ll. 2-5.

591   i   *Cancel* ll. 1-4.

592   ii   **GEMINIANI**
l. 9.   (Op. 5) (London). *should read* :
(Opp. 3 & 5) (London).

593   i   **GENERALI**
Par. 1, ll. 1-2 *should read* :
GENERALI, Pietro 1 (*b.* Masserano, 23 Oct. 1773 2 ; *d.* Novara, 3 Nov. 1832).

Add footnote :
1 The real surname was Mercandetti.

Footnote 1 becomes 2.

Par. 2, l. 5.   twenty *should read* :
twenty-nine

594   ii   **GENET**
Add to BIBL. :
RIGSBY, LEE, ' Elzéar Genet, A Renaissance Composer ' ('Studies in Music History and Theory', Tallahassee, 1955).

596   i   **GENZMER**
Par. 1, l. 2.   2 Feb. *should read* :
9 Feb.

ii   **GEORGIADES**
Par. 2, l. 14 *should read* :
University in 1949. In 1955 he was appointed to a professorship at the University of Munich. His literary works,

598   ii   **GERBER, Rudolf**
Par. 1, l. 2 *should read* :
15 Apr. 1899 ; *d.* Göttingen, 6 May 1957).

600   i   **GERHARD**
Par. 3, l. 14.   on his personal *should read* :
or his personal

601   ii   *Add at end* :
BIBL.—' The Score ', special issue for 60th birthday, No. 17. Sept. 1956.

Gerhardt
l. 1 *should read* :
Gerhardt, Paul. *See* Buxtehude (cantata based on song by G.). Chorale. Ebeling (J. G.
Add to BIBL. :
IHLEMFELD, KURT, ' Huldigung für Paul Gerhardt ' (Berlin, 1956).

602   i-ii   **GERL, Franz Xaver** and **Thaddäus**
Delete present articles and replace by :
GERL, Franz Xaver (*b.* Andorf, 30 Nov. 1764 ; *d.* Mannheim, 9 Mar. 1827).
German bass singer and composer. He joined Schikaneder's theatrical company as actor and singer in or before 1788 and from 1789 to 1793 sang first bass parts at the Theater auf der Wieden (the "Freihaus" theatre) in Vienna ; he also supplied music for some of the operas performed there, often in collaboration with Schack (who sang tenor parts), *e.g.* Schikaneder's ' Die zween Anton,

oder Der dumme Gärtner aus dem Gebirge' (1789, with many sequels), Gieseke's 'Don Quixote', 'Wienerzeitung' and 'Schlaraffenland' (1790–92). 'Der Stein der Weisen' (1790) contains music by Gerl, Schack, Henneberg and Mozart. Mozart wrote the air with double-bass *obbligato* 'Per questa bella mano' (K. 612, 8 Mar. 1791) "für Herrn Görl und Pichelberger" and on 30 Sept. of that year Gerl was the first Sarastro in Mozart's 'Zauberflöte', while his wife Barbara, born Reisinger (*b.* Pressburg, 1775; *d.* Mannheim, 25 May 1806), was the first Papagena. About 1795 Gerl left Vienna for Brünn (Brno), where he wrote music for Kotzebue's 'Die Spanier in Peru' and another operetta, 'Graf Balberone, oder Die Maskerade' (1796), which was afterwards, under different titles, performed in Vienna and Hamburg. This operetta (words by Franzky, from Goldoni's 'Contessina') was announced for performance in Vienna (9 Dec. 1797, as 'Die Maskerade, oder Liebe macht alle Stände gleich') as by "the former member of this theatre". From May 1802 until shortly before his death Gerl sang bass parts at the Mannheim Nationaltheater.

A. L., rev.

See also Mozart (concert aria written for). Schack (collab. in 2 operas).

GERL, Judas Thaddäus (*b.* Straubing, 28 Oct. 1774; *d.* Bayreuth, 13 Apr. 1844).
German bass singer and composer, brother of the preceding. He was a boy singer in the Salzburg choir under Leopold Mozart and, according to Gerber, became known as a composer of some flute concertos about 1782. Gerl's wife, Franziska, born Costeletzky, whom he married on 15 Mar. 1804, was a singer. Nothing further seems to be known about his musical activities. According to Komorzynski he died as bailiff of an estate (" Schlossverwalter ") at Bayreuth.

A. L., rev.

605 ii **GERMANI**
Par. 1, l. 1. Rome, 1906). *should read*:

Rome, 5 Apr. 1906).

Par. 2, l. 13 *should read*:
the Curtis Institute of Philadelphia in 1936. He returned to Italy before 1948 and became organist of St. Peter's in Rome.

GERNSHEIM
Par. 1, l. 2. 11 Sept. *should read*:
10 Sept.

606 ii **GÉROLD**
Par. 1, l. 2 *should read*:
Oct. 1866; *d.* Allenwiller, Alsace, 16 Feb. 1956).

607 i **GERSHWIN**
Par. 1, l. 2. 25 Sept. *should read*:
26 Sept.

ii *Add to* BIBL.:

ARMITAGE, MERLE, 'George Gershwin: Man and Legend' (New York, 1958).
EWEN, DAVID, 'A Journey to Greatness: the Life and Music of George Gershwin' (New York, 1956).
GOLDBERG, ISAAC, 'George Gershwin: Study in American Music', new ed. supplement by Edith Garson (New York, 1958).

608 i **GERSTBERGER**
Par. 1, l. 2 *should read*:
Neisse, Silesia, 12 Feb. 1892; *d.* Bremen, 30 Oct. 1955).

ii **GERSTENBERG**
Par. 2, l. 12 *should read*:
High School for Music and Theatre there. After a period as Professor at Tübingen he was appointed to a similar post at Heidelberg in 1957, in succession to Thrasybulos Georgiades.

GERSTER, Etelka
Par. 3, l. 1 *should read*:
During the seasons of 1878–83 Gerster sang in opera

609 ii *Add before* **GERTSEM**:
GERTLER, André (*b.* Budapest, 26 July 1907).
Hungarian violinist. He settled in Belgium about 1939 and became professor of chamber music at the Brussels Conservatoire in 1940. In 1947 he was appointed professor of the violin there. His distinction as a teacher is matched by his reputation as a concert performer, and he excels especially in the interpretation of modern music, including that of Bartók. He has appeared in various countries, including Great Britain, and in 1955 he was engaged by William Glock to hold a holiday course at the Summer School of Music at Dartington Hall, Totnes. A. L. C.

610 i **GERVAISE**
Add at end:
See also Maitres Musiciens, Vol. 23 (modern ed. of dances).

GERVASIUS DE ANGLIA
Delete whole entry and replace by:
GERVASE, John } *See* JERVAYS,
GERVASIUS DE ANGLIA } JOHN.

619 i **GESUALDO**
Par. 1, l. 3. took place in *should read*:
took place on 16 Oct.

620 ii *Add at end:*

See also Classici Musica Italiana, Vol. 14 (modern ed. of madrigals). Istituzioni, Vol. 5 (modern ed. of sacred music).

GEVAERT
Par. 1, l. 2. Oudenarde *should read:*
Audenarde

621 ii GEYER
Par. 1, l. 1. 1888). *should read:*
1888; *d.* Zürich, 11 Dec. 1956).

622 i GHEDINI
OPERAS
l. 4. (T. Pinelli) *should read:*
(Tullio Pinelli)

l. 7 *should read:*
Milan, 21 Feb. 1948.

ii *Add to* SOLO INSTRUMENTS AND ORCHESTRA:
' Musica da concerto ' for viola (1954).
' Concerto Basiliensis ' for vn.

625 i *Add after* **GHISELLE :**
GHISI, Federico (*b.* Shanghai, 25 Feb. 1901).
Italian musicologist and composer. He studied composition in Milan and later at the Turin Conservatory under Ghedini, at the same time developing his interest in early Italian music, especially that of the Ars Nova, the sixteenth century in Florence and the Roman baroque period. Apart from his courses in musical history at the University of Florence, Ghisi has lectured in many European cities, and his command of English has in recent years taken him farther afield in Britain and America. His wide diversity of musical interests is reflected in his compositions as well as in his scholarly work, and since 1938 he has written operas, ballet music, choral works, orchestral and chamber music and songs. Most important among these are the ' Cantata da camera ' for soprano, flute, viola and harp (1938) ; ' Sinfonia italiana ' for orchestra (1939) ; ' Tre canzoni strumentali ' for piano and string orchestra (1946) ; ' Air varié sur l'octave de Héro et Léandre ' for soprano, harpsichord and piano (1950) ; ' Fantasia allegra ' for orch. (1951) ; ' Il passatempo ' ballet (1952) ; ' Marco Polo's Chinese Stories ', scenic pantomimes for voices and instruments (1956) ; ' Sant' Alessio ', sacred scenes for chorus and orchestra (1957) ; ' Pyramus and Thisbe ', opera in 1 act (1943) ; two television operas on stories by O. Henry — ' The Gift of the Magi ' (1959) ; ' The Cop and the Anthem ' (1960).

PUBLICATIONS
' I canti carnaschialeschi nelle fonti musicali del XV e XVI secolo ' (Florence, 1937).

' Le feste musicali della Firenze medicea (1480-1589) ' (Florence, 1939).
' Italian Ars Nova Music' ('Musica Disciplina', I, 1946).
' A Second Sienese Fragment of the Italian Ars Nova ' ('Musica Disciplina', II, 1948).
' Ballet Entertainments in Pitti Palace, Florence, 1608-1625 ' (M.Q., XXXV, 1949).
' The Oratorios of Giacomo Carissimi in Hamburg Staats-Bibliothek ' (Kongress-Bericht Lüneburg, 1950).
' Strambotti e laude nel travestimento spirituale della poesia musicale del quattrocento ' ('Collectanea historiae musicae', I, 1953).
' Un Aspect inédit des intermèdes de 1589 à la cour médicéenne" ('Les Fêtes de la Renaissance', 1956).
' La Réforme mélodramatique en Italie' ('Histoire de la musique — Encyclopédie La Pléiade', 1960).
D. W. S.

626 i GIACOMELLI
Par. 1, l. 2. Parma, 24 Jan. *should read:*
Loreto, 25 Jan.

627 ii GIANNETTINI
Par. 1, l. 3. *c.* 12 July *should read:*
12 July

GIANNINI, V.
Par. 2, l. 4. Leitz *should read:*
Letz

l. 9. ' Lucidia ' *should read:*
' Lucedia '

l. 10 *should read:*
at Munich on 20 Oct. 1934 and ' The Scarlet Letter ',

629 i GIAZOTTO
l. 17 *should read:*
la vita nell' opera ' (Milan, 1948). In 1958 he was appointed Professor of Musical History at the University of Florence, the chair vacated by the death of Fausto Torrefranca.

630 i GIBBONS (2)
Add after Par. 1 :
On 21 Mar. 1612 the Dean and Chapter of Exeter Cathedral granted Gibbons the rectories and tithes of sheaves of corn of Gwennep and St. Issey, alias Eglosruk, for the term of the lives of his three children. Both the rectories were in Cornwall (Chapel Act Book, 1607-28, D. & C., Exeter MS 3553). On 12 Oct. 1626 he bought a large estate from Dr. William Peterson, one of the resident Canons and later Dean of Exeter Cathedral. The property, called Aishley Park, was part of an estate named Middlehill, near Tiverton, and comprised about 1000 acres (Calendar of Devon Deeds, 1604-1763).
There are numerous references to Edward Gibbons and his activities in the Chapter Act Book, in the account books of the Cathedral and of the College of Vicars Choral at Exeter. In addition to his stipend of £20 a year for instructing the secondaries and choristers in instrumental music, he received quarterly

payments of 25s., which were his share in the organist's salary together with 33s. 4d. in respect of his house rent. His stipend and diet money from the College of Vicars Choral amounted to £16 a year, and while he was Custos of the College he received a fee of 6s. 8d. for the same period. He was reimbursed for the choristers' gowns and candles each quarter and had to collect the salaries for the secondaries and choristers. Owing to gaps in the account books from 1645 to 1660, it is not known for how long Gibbons stayed at Exeter Cathedral, but according to the extraordinary accounts he received his usual payment of £7 : 6 : 8 for stipend, house rent and choristers' candles at Christmas 1645, a year after he signed the ordinary account book for the last time. According to a note in the account book of the College of Vicars Choral wages, although due to Gibbons and others in 1645, were paid in May 1647.

On 17 July 1650 Ross Swanton, Gibbons's grandson (*nepos ex filia*), was granted letters of administration for the purpose of disposing of his chattels and property, and settling his debts. It would thus appear that Edward Gibbons died earlier the same year (Somerset House, P.C.C.).　　　　　　　　　s. J.

630　i　Par. 2, ll. 2-4 *should read*:

vives. At Ely is an anthem, ' How doth the city ' (Sc. 18, 300), and in the British Museum an organ prelude (probably to the same), ' How hath the city sate solitary ' (B.M., Harley, 7340/194). A three-part anthem, ' Awake

Add after Par. 2 :

BIBL.—JEANS, SUSI, ' The Musical Life at Exeter Cathedral ' (' The Organist's Quarterly Record ', July 1958).

633　i　GIBBONS (5)
Add to BIBL.:

DART, THURSTON, ' The Printed Fantasies of Orlando Gibbons ' M. & L., XXXVII, 1956, p. 342).
PALMER, WILLIAM, ' Gibbons's Verse Anthems ' (M. & L., XXXV, 1954, p. 107).

635　i　GIBBONS (6)
See also. l. 2 *should read*:

(collab. in ' Cupid and Death '). Musica Britannica, Vol. 2 (modern ed. of ' Cupid and Death ').

637　i　*Add after* GIBERT :

GIBSON, Alexander (*b.* Motherwell, Lanarkshire, 11 Feb. 1926).
Scottish conductor. He studied at Glasgow in 1943-44, at the R.C.M. in London from 1948 to 1952, where he took the A.R.C.M. (he also holds the L.R.A.M. and A.R.C.O.), and he attended finishing courses at the Salzburg Mozarteum in 1951 and the Siena Accademia Chigiana in 1952. During those two years he was already coach and assistant conductor at the Sadler's Wells Opera in

London. After a period as assistant conductor of the B.B.C. Scottish Orchestra at Glasgow in 1952-54, he returned to Sadler's Wells, where he did admirable work as principal conductor in 1954-57 and as Musical Director in 1957-59; but he returned to Scotland in Sept. 1959 as chief conductor and Musical Director of the Scottish National Orchestra. He has also been guest conductor at the Royal Opera, Covent Garden, in 1957-58, has conducted the principal British orchestras in concerts and broadcasts, toured in Scandinavia, Italy, France and Austria, and conducted a concert of British Music at the Brussels World Fair in 1958. He has been in charge of many first performances for the B.B.C. as well as that of John Gardner's opera ' The Moon and Sixpence ' at Sadler's Wells in 1957.　　　　　　　　　E. B.

637　ii　Gide
　　　l. 1 *should read*:

See Auric (' Symphonie pastorale ', film). Cras (trans. of Tagore). Honegger

　　　l. 3 *should read*:

for orch.). Milhaud (' Saul ', incid. m.; ' Retour de l'enfant prodigue ',

GIEBUROWSKI
Par. 1, l. 2 *should read*:

6 Feb. 1876 ; *d.* Warsaw, 17 Sept. 1943).
　　　　　　　　　●

638　i　GIESEKING
Par. 1, l. 2 *should read*:

Lyons, 5 Nov. 1895 ; *d.* London, 26 Oct. 1956).

　　ii　*Add after* l. 3 :

Gieseking died after an operation in London while on a visit to fulfil a professional engagement.

639　i　GIGLI
Par. 1, l. 2 *should read*:

1890; *d.* Rome, 30 Nov. 1957).

Add to BIBL.:

GIGLI, BENIAMINO, ' Memoirs ', trans. by Darina Silone (London, 1957).

640　i　GIGOUT
Add to BIBL.:

DUFOURCQ, NORBERT, ' La Musique d'orgue française ' (Paris, 1949).

641　i　GILCHRIST
Par. 1, l. 2.　1863). *should read*:

1863 ; *d.* nr. Lancaster, 24 July 1954).

　　ii　*Add before* GILES :

GILELS, Emil (*b.* Odessa, 19 Oct. 1916).
Russian pianist. He studied first at Odessa under B. Reingbald and afterwards in Moscow under H. Neuhaus. In 1933 he won the

first prize at the first All-Union Executant Musicians' Contest; in 1936 the second prize at the International Competition in Vienna; in 1938 the first at the International Ysaÿe Competition in Brussels. During the second world war he performed for troops, etc. in the U.S.S.R., visiting Leningrad during the blockade of the city. He was awarded the Stalin Prize in 1946. In 1948 he took part in the Prague Spring Festival. The Moscow Conservatory appointed him professor in 1951. He was given the title of People's Artist in 1954 and in 1956 he made a concert tour in the U.S.A.   s. c. r.

645   ii   GINASTERA
Delete entry and substitute:

GINASTERA, Alberto (Evaristo) (*b.* Buenos Aires, 11 Apr. 1916).
Argentine composer. He studied at the Conservatorio Williams and the National Conservatory in Buenos Aires, at the latter under José André. He followed the lead of Alberto Williams in cultivating a national musical idiom, but he developed a more advanced style.
Ginastera's works include the following:

1. Ballet ' Panambí ' (1937), prod. Teatro Colón, Buenos Aires, 1940.
2. Ballet ' Estancia ' (1941), prod. Teatro Colón, Buenos Aires, 1952.
3. Lamentations of the Prophet Jeremiah, 3 motets for unaccomp. chorus (1946).
4. ' Overture to the " Creole " Faust ' for orch., based on the poem ' Fausto ' by Estanislao del Campo (1943).
5. ' Sinfonia elegiaca ' for orch. (1944).
6. ' Pampeana No. 3 ' for orch. (1953).
7. ' Variaciones concertantes ' for chamber orch. (1953).
8. ' Impressions of the Puna ' for flute & stg. 4tet. (1934).
9. ' Songs of Tucumán ' for voice, flute, vn., harp & drums (1938).
10. String Quartet No. 1 (1948).
11. ' Pampeana No. 1 ', rhapsody for vn. & pf. (1947).
12. ' Pampeana No. 2 ', rhapsody for cello & pf. (1950).
13. 3 Argentine Dances for pf. (1937).
14. 3 Pieces for pf. (1940)
    1. Cuyana.
    2. Norteña.
    3. Criolla.
15. 12 American Preludes for pf. (1944).
16. Suite ' Danzas criollas ' for pf. (1946).
17. Sonata for pf. (1952).
18. ' Toccata, Villancico and Fugue ' for organ (1947).
19. ' Dos canciones ' for voice & pf. (1938).
20. 5 Argentine Popular Songs for voice & pf. (1943).
                                        n. f., adds.

Bibl.—Chase, Gilbert, ' Alberto Ginastera: Argentine Composer ' (M.Q., XLIII, Oct. 1957, p. 339). ' Alberto Ginastera — Portrait of an Argentine Composer ' (' Tempo ', No. 44, 1957).

GINES PÉREZ
Add at end:
See also Hispaniae Schola, Vol. 5 (modern reprint).

648   ii   Giorgione
Transfer to stand after **GIORGI, Teresa.**

648   ii   GIORNOVICHI
Par. 1, l. 1 *should read:*
GIORNOVICHI (Giornovicchi), Giovanni Mane (also

l. 3 *should read:*
d. St. Petersburg, 23 [2] Nov. 1804).

Add footnote:
[2] The St. Petersburg ' Messager du Nord ' gives 11 Nov. (old style).

649   ii   GIOVANNI DA CASCIA
Par. 2, ll. 3-6 *should read:*
della Scala, at Verona. He is one of the members of the first generation of *trecento* secular polyphonists. He composed madrigals, caccie, ballate, etc.   e. v. d. s., rev.

651   i   *Add before* GIRAFFE:
GIPSY MUSIC. *See* Gypsy Music.

653   ii   *Add before* GIULIO CESARE:
GIULINI, Carlo Maria (*b.* Barletta, 9 May 1914).
Italian conductor. He studied composition and the viola at the Accademia di Santa Cecilia in Rome, where he also took his conducting course. In 1946 he was appointed Musical Director of Radio Italiana, and among the operas he conducted for the radio were Scarlatti's ' Il trionfo dell' onore ', Malipiero's ' L' allegra brigata ', Bizet's ' Don Procopio ' and Verdi's ' Due Foscari ', as well as the more popular works in the repertory. In 1949 and 1950 he directed orchestral concerts at the Venice Festival; in 1951 he conducted a concert performance of Verdi's ' Attila ' and in 1952 Galuppi's ' La diavolessa '. At the Florence Festival he has also been responsible for a number of unfamiliar works, including Cavalli's ' Didone ' (1952), Weber's ' Euryanthe ' (1954) and Donizetti's ' Don Sebastiano ' (1955). In 1953 Giulini made his first appearance at the Milan Scala, and in the ensuing seasons he has conducted many operas there, including several in which he collaborated with Luchino Visconti, the producer and designer, and also with Maria Callas, the soprano (' Alceste ', ' La Traviata ', etc.). His direction of the Scala production of ' L'Italiana in Algeri ' with Giulietta Simionato at the Holland Festival in 1955 caused a sensation; so brilliantly was it executed that the first act finale was encored.
Giulini visited Great Britain for the first time in 1955 to conduct the Glyndebourne production of ' Falstaff ' at Edinburgh. His great success in Britain, however, was the Covent Garden centenary production of Verdi's ' Don Carlos ' in 1958, when once again he enjoyed the collaboration of Visconti.

The care with which the work was prepared, the fine ensemble achieved between stage and pit, and the excellent playing drawn from the orchestra completely vindicated Italian grand opera. There is little doubt that Giulini must rank as the finest Italian opera conductor of the day. In the concert-hall he is no less successful. His warm romantic Brahms, his crystal-clear Mozart and Haydn, and exciting interpretations of the moderns, leave no doubt that he is one of the outstanding musicians of to-day.   H. D. R.

655   i   **GIZZIELLO**
Par. 5, ll. 9-10 *should read*:

engaged both him and Caffarelli to sing in a setting of Metastasio's ' Achille in Sciro '. Caffarelli

657   i   **GLAREAN(US)**
Par. 1, l. 23 *should read*:

schaft für Musikforschung, Vols. XVI-XVIII), with the examples

661   i   **GLAZUNOV**
Par. 4, ll. 1-2 *should read*:

In Soviet Russia Glazunov's music is regarded

ii   Par. 1, ll. 1-4 *should read*:

as a model of Russian " classicism ", though to outsiders it would seem precisely what is now condemned there as " formal " and " bourgeois ", if by these terms is meant

ll. 8-10 *should read*:

nically slick. Many critics outside the U.S.S.R. now take that view of it. They do not deny that

662   i   CATALOGUE
Par. 1 (ORCHESTRAL WORKS)
Add after Op. 69 :
73. ' Ouverture solennelle.'

SOLO INSTRUMENT AND OR-CHESTRA
Delete Op. 73.

664   ii   **GLETLE**
Par. 1, l. 2.   Switzerland, ?;
should read:

Switzerland, 1626;

Add at end:

Bibl.—Schanzlin, Hans Peter, ' Johann Melchior Gletles Motetten ' (Berne, 1954).

GLIÈRE
Par. 1, l. 2 *should read*:

Kiev, 11 Jan. 1875; *d.* Moscow, 23 June 1956).

666   i   **GLINKA**
Par. 4, l. 3 *should read*:

Fräulein Klammer. In 1816 he went to St. Petersburg and on 14 Feb. 1818 he entered the Blagorodnyi Pension,

ii   Par. 1, ll. 1-2 *should read*:

an aristocratic private school there, from which he graduated in 1822. During this period he

667   ii   Par. 2, l. 1. Little Russia *should read*:
the Ukraine

668   ii   Par. 1, ll. 8-11 *should read*:

been sung, he is said to have caught a cold, but it is not true that he died suddenly in spite of not appearing seriously indisposed even two days before his death. The fact is that the autopsy revealed an enlargement of the liver which left scarcely room for the stomach, and that he could not take nourish-ment for three weeks. He died, literally of starvation, at 5 a.m. on 15 Feb.

669   i   *Add to* Bibl.:
Dippel, Paul Gerhardt, ' Klingende Einkehr : Michail Glinka und Berlin ' (Berlin, 1953).

ii   *Add below heading* INCIDENTAL MUSIC:
Music for the play ' The Moldavian Gypsy ' (1836).[2]

Add footnote :
[2] Discovered in the archives of the Leningrad Con-servatory. The play was produced in St. Petersburg on 8 April 1836.

671   i   **GLIŃSKI**
Par. 4, l. 5. Purcellina *should read*:
Purcelliana

672   i   **GLOCK**
Par. 2, l. 13 *should read*:

Bryanston, Dorset (later removed to Darting-ton Hall, Totnes, Devonshire), of which he is director,

ll. 19-20 *should read*:

Glock adjudicated at Canadian music festivals in

ll. 24-25 *should read*:

a short life of Schubert, reissued in a volume of the Penguin series (1935). In 1959 he suc-ceeded R. J. F. Howgill as Controller of Music for the B.B.C.   E. B.

See also should read:
See also Summer School of Music.

ii   **GLOGAUER LIEDERBUCH**
l. 4 *should read*:
canons. *See* Song, p. 919.

Add at end :
See also Denkmäler (5) I, Vols. 4 & 8 (modern ed.).

673   i   **GLOSA**
l. 2 *should read* :
ORNAMENTS, C.

675   i   **GLUCK**
Par. 2, l. 25.   Tein *should read* :
Tyn

682   i   Page heading *should read* :
GLUCK : Bibliography — Works

BIBL. l. 18 *should read* :
(London, 1936); German ed., 'Gluck: sein Leben, seine Werke' (Zürich & Stuttgart, 1954).

Add to BIBL. :
HASTINGS, MARGARET, 'Gluck's " Alceste " ' (M. & L., XXXVI, 1955, p. 39).

683   —   ITALIAN OPERAS
Col. 1, l. 1.   e d' Ebe.' *should read* :
e d' Ebe.'[1]

         l. 10.   vestale '). *should read* :
vestale ').[2]

Col. 3, ll. 30-31 *should read* :
(Composed 1765[3], not performed[4]).

FRENCH OPERAS
Col. 2, l. 13.   L. H. Dancourt. *should read* :
L. H. Dancourt, after Lesage.

Add footnotes :
[1] Modern edition, *see* DENKMÄLER (2) II, Vol. 14.
[2] Modern edition, *see* DENKMÄLER (3), Vol. 44.

Footnotes 1 & 2 *become* 3 & 4.

Add after ' Orphée et Eurydice ' :

'L'Arbre enchanté' (2nd version, *see* 1759).	Altered by Moline, with Jean Joseph Vadé.	Versailles, 27 Feb. 1775.

684   —   BALLETS
Col. 1, l. 3.   ' Don Juan.' *should read* :
' Don Juan.'[1]

Add footnote :
[1] Modern edition, *see* DENKMÄLER (3), Vol. 30.

    i   *Add before* **GLÜCKLICHE HAND** :
GLUCK SOCIETY. A society for the promotion of Gluck's works was launched in Germany under the name of Gluckgesellschaft, and it began publication (Verlag der Gluckgesellschaft) with the opera ' La Rencontre imprévue ' under the German title of ' Die Pilger von Mecca ', edited by Max Arend, with the original French text under the German translation. Publication ceased thereafter and the society came to an end for lack of support.   E. B.

685   ii   **GLYNDEBOURNE**
Par. 3, l. 3 *should read* :
ductor-in-chief. This fell to Vittorio Gui. Mr. Christie was made a Companion of Honour in 1954.
In 1956, for the Mozart bicentenary,

Glyndebourne returned to the exclusive cultivation of that master, with his six greatest operas in the programmes, two in new productions.

685   ii   **GLYNNE**
Par. 1, l. 1.   Swansea, 1907). *should read* :
Swansea, 24 Jan. 1906).

686   i   Par. 1, l. 12 *should read* :
any trace of buffoonery. He is equally admirable as King Dodon in ' The Golden Weathercock ' and as Kecal in ' The Bartered Bride '. Glynne's voice is a

GNECCHI
Par. 1, l. 2 *should read* :
1876 ; *d.* Milan, 5 Feb. 1954).

ii   **GNESSIN**
Par. 1, l. 2 *should read* :
Rostov-on-Don, 2 Feb. 1883 ; *d.* Moscow, 6 May 1957).

688   i   *Add after* **GOBIATUS** :

GOBLE, Robert (*b.* Thursley, Surrey, 30 Oct. 1903).
English musical instrument maker. He is the son of a wheelwright, with further generations of woodworking ancestors behind that. He was educated locally. As a boy of fourteen he met Arnold Dolmetsch and was drawn to the revival of early musical instruments under that pioneer. He entered the Dolmetsch workshops in 1925 and contributed especially to the manufacture of hand-turned recorders. The same year he married the harpsichordist and gambist Elizabeth Brown, then a scholar at the Dolmetsch Foundation. In 1937 he set up his own business, specializing in recorders, harpsichords and clavichords. In 1947 he moved to his present larger premises at Headington Quarry, Oxford, where he employs a number of workmen including his elder son, Andrea, a talented recipient of the family gift of craftsmanship.

Goble's recorders gained an excellent reputation, but have at present been discontinued owing to heavy demands on working-time. Goble now concentrates on harpsichords, spinets and clavichords. Examples of his large harpsichords are now in the hands of the B.B.C. and other broadcasting organizations, a number of universities in the old world and the new, and several performers of distinction. Among the many possible and legitimate ideals of harpsichord making he prefers, like his master, a true chamber instrument in which contrast between the different registers is not carried to extremes at the expense of the total blend of sound; but his instruments have their own distinctive quality and rank with the best produced in modern times.

R. D.

690   i   **GOD SAVE THE QUEEN**
      Add to BIBL.:

DART, THURSTON, 'Maurice Greene and the National Anthem' (M. & L., XXXVII, July 1956, p. 205).

   Add before See also (2nd work by Scholes):
' " God save the Queen " : the History and Romance of the World's First National Anthem ' (Oxford, 1954).

693   ii   **GOEDICKE**
      Par. 1, l. 2.   1877). *should read*:
1877; *d.* Moscow, July 1957).

694   i   **GOEHLER**
      Par. 1, l. 2 *should read*:
29 June 1874: *d.* Lübeck, 4 Mar. 1954).

695   i   **Goethe**
      Par. 1, l. 1.   Beecke *should read*:
Beecke

      ll. 2-3 *should read*:
Gläser (F.). Kerpen. Kienlen. Reichardt (J. F.). Schubert. Stolze.

      ' Faust ', l. 9. *Delete* Ginastera (overture).

      ii   Poems. l. 3 *should read*:
canons). Berg (Alban, 3 songs). Berger, W. (' Gesang der Geister ', chorus).

      Poems. l. 8 *should read*:
opera). Cornelius (chorus). Dallapiccola (song from ' Westöstlicher Divan ' for voice & 3 clars.). Dieren (songs). Dukas

      Par. 5, l. 14 *should read*:
work). Grimm (F.-K., songs). Groot (3 songs with orch., 7 with pf.). Hallnäs

      l. 40 *should read*:
works). Taneyev (song). Tomašek (songs). Trunk (5 partsongs). Valen

696   i   *Add to* BIBL.:

COTTI, JÜRG, ' Die Musik in Goethes " Faust " ' (Winterthur, 1957).
MACKWORTH-YOUNG, G., ' Goethe's " Prometheus " ' (Proc. Roy. Mus. Ass., Vol. LXXVIII, 1951–52).

      BIBL. ll. 25-26 *should read*:

STERNFELD, FREDERICK W., ' Goethe and Music : a List of Parodies ; and Goethe's Relationship to Music : a List of References ' (New York, 1954). ' Musical Springs of Goethe's Poetry ' (M.Q., XXXV, 1949, p. 511).
TAPPERT, WILHELM, ' 70 Erlkönig-Kompositionen ' (Berlin, 1906).

      ii   *Add after* **GOETZ**:

GOEYVAERTS, Karel (August) (*b.* Antwerp, 8 June 1923).
Belgian musicologist and composer. He studied at the Conservatories of Antwerp

and Paris, later under Milhaud and Messiaen in Paris and became professor of musical history at the Musical Academy of Antwerp. In 1949 he won the Prix Lily Boulanger and in 1950 the Prix Halphen, both for composition. As a composer he followed what he has himself called the " traditional " twelve-note technique up to 1950, and his works in that manner include two violin Concertos as well as ' Music for Contralto, Violin and Pianoforte '. His later works, to which he began to give opus numbers, are based on a single fundamental idea on which he erects musical structures showing it in a great variety of different aspects.

Works by Goeyvaerts have been performed at the I.S.C.M. festivals of 1950 and 1953, at the first Unesco concert in Paris in 1950, at the Festival of Darmstadt, the Bayerischer Rundfunk, etc.

His later works are:

Instrumental:
No. I for 2 pianofortes.
No. II for 13 instruments.
No. III for strings and percussion sounds.
No. VI with 180 sound-objects.

Electrophonic:
No. IV with death sounds.
Composition No. V.
Composition No. VII.

A. L. C.

697   i   **GOFF**
      Add after Par. 5, *before signature*:
Goff was created O.B.E. in the 1959 New Year's Honours.

      Gogol
      ll. 2-3 *should read*:
operas). Dzerzhinsky (' Poem of the Dnieper ', for pf.). Egk (' Revisor ', opera). Glazunov (memorial prelude for orch.). Glinka

      ii   *Add before* **Gold**:

GOLACHOWSKI, Stanisław (*b.* Cieszyn, 1907; *d.* Łódź, 19 Jan. 1951).
Polish musicologist. He studied under Jachimecki at Cracow University, obtaining the degree of Master of Philosophy (Music) with a dissertation on ' Antoni Stolpe (1851–1872) '. Deeply interested in acoustics, he studied this subject for many years and published the results in 1949 in what became a standard handbook for professional musicians and students as well as for the general public. He also published several essays and a book on as well as the letters of Karol Szymanowski.

C. R. H.

698   i   **GOLDBERG, Szymon**
      Par. 1, l. 2.   1909). *should read*:
1 June 1909).

698   i   **GOLDEN COCKEREL**
should read:
GOLDEN WEATHERCOCK

ii   *Add before* **GOLDING**:
GOLDER, Robert (*b.*?; *d.*?).
English 16th-century organist and composer. He is probably the Robert Golder who trained choristers for a drapers' pageant in London in 1541, was *conduct* at St. Lawrence, Jewry, there in 1547 and of St. Mary-at-Hill in 1550. He was organist at Windsor about 1560–63. A 4-voice setting of ' In nomine ' by " Mr. Golder " is in the Baldwin Book (RM. 24. d. 2).   H. B. (ii).

GOLDMAN
Par. 1, l. 2 *should read*:
Kentucky, 1 Jan. 1878; *d*. New York, 21 Feb. 1956).

Par. 2, ll. 17-18 *should read*:
largest parks, where for thirty years at least Goldman never missed a concert of this series. The

700   ii   **GOLDMARK, Rubin**
Par. 3, l. 6 *should read*:
orchestra; a pianoforte Quintet (Paderewski Prize, 1909), a pianoforte Trio,

701   i   **Goldoni**
ll. 3-4. *Add*:
Calamita de' cuori (Galuppi, opera).

l. 18. Jeppesen (opera). *should read*:
Jeppesen (' Rosaura ', opera).

GOLDOVSKY
Par. 1, l. 1.   Moscow, 1908).
should read:
Moscow, 7 June 1908).

702   ii   **GOLDSCHMIDT, Hugo**
Par. 2, l. 7. zu *should read*:
zur
        l. 8. (1904). *should read*:
(1901 & 1904).

        l. 11. ' Geschichte . . . 1915). *should read*:
' Die Musikästhetik des 18. Jahrhunderts und ihre Beziehungen zu seinem Kunstschaffen ' (1915).

703   i   **GOLESTAN**
Par. 1, l. 2 *should read*:
26 May 1875; *d*. Paris, 22 Apr. 1956).

704   ii   *Add before* **GOLUBEV**:
GOLTZ, Christel (*b*. Dortmund, 8 July, ?).
German soprano singer. She comes of a professional family, her parents being successful circus acrobats who toured under the auspices of Barnum & Bailey. She started her career as a dancer, studying at Munich with Anna Orenelli; but discovering she had a voice, she took singing lessons from F. Leeb at Munich and before she was twenty was singing in operetta at the Deutsches Theater. In 1935 she became a member of the chorus of the small opera-house at Fürth, where she sang her first leading part, Agathe in ' Freischütz '. There followed a season at Plauen, where she added Santuzza, Eva and Octavian to her repertory; and she was then engaged for the Dresden State Opera by Karl Böhm for the 1936–37 season, remaining a member of the company until the end of the 1949–50 season. While at Dresden she sang the title-part in Orff's ' Antigonae ' and in virtually the whole soprano repertory, Italian as well as German.

In 1947 Goltz was heard in Berlin at both the State Opera and Städtische Oper; she then began to appear in Vienna and Munich, where she was heard as Elektra, Salome, Alceste, the Countess in Strauss's ' Capriccio ', Leonore in ' Fidelio ' and Tosca. In 1951 she made her Covent Garden début as Salome, and the following year she was chosen by Kleiber to sing Marie in ' Wozzeck ' there, a part she has also sung at Salzburg, Vienna and Buenos Aires. At Salzburg she created the title-part in Liebermann's ' Penelope ' in 1954 and later that year made her New York début at the Metropolitan as Salome. During the 1957–58 season she sang her first Isolde and at that time had a repertory of nearly 120 operas.

Goltz has a clear, brilliant voice, three octaves in range, but not inherently beautiful. Like that of many of her German colleagues, her acting is intense, and she prepares her parts with enormous care. She is married to Theodor Schenk, a pupil of Hindemith and formerly a horn player in the Dresden orchestra.   H. D. R.

706   i   **GOMBERT**
Add at end:
See also Amer. Inst. Musicol. (C.M.M.), Vol. 6 (modern ed. of complete works). Collectio O.M.B., Vols. 8 & 12 (modern ed.).

GOMBOSI
Par. 1, l. 2 *should read*:
Oct. 1902; *d*. Natick, Mass., 17 Feb. 1955).

711   ii   **GOODSON**
Par. 1, l. 2 *should read*:
Herts., 18 June 1872; *d*. London, 14 Apr. 1958).

712   ii   **GOOSSENS (2)**
l. 2 *should read*:
28 Jan. 1867; *d*. London, 31 July 1958), violinist and conductor, son of

712   ii   **GOOSSENS (3)**
l. 1 *should read*:

(3) (Sir) Eugene Goossens (iii) (*b.*
London, 26

713   ii   Par. 3, l. 3 *should read*:

the Legion of Honour, and he was knighted
in 1955.

714   ii   Last line. Words *should read*:
Works

715   i   l. before *See also*. Words *should read*:
Works

716   ii   **GORCZYCKI**
Par. 3, l. 13 *should read*:

He died less than four months later.

717   i   *Add at end*:

See also Monumenta Mus. Sac. Pol., Vol. 2 (modern
reprints).

Add before **Gordon, John B.**:

GORDON, James (Charles Gérard;
bapt. **Carel Gerhard)** (*b.* Cape Town, 22
May 1791; *d.* ? Lausanne, *c.* 1845).
Swiss flautist and flute maker of Dutch and
Scottish descent. He was the son of an officer
who in 1777 went into the service of the Dutch
East India Company at the Cape of Good
Hope, and of a French-Swiss mother. The
father committed suicide in 1795 and the
mother returned to Switzerland soon after,
settling at Lausanne. James, married in 1812,
became a soldier and joined the Swiss Guards
of Charles X in Paris in 1814. He narrowly
escaped with his life when the Guards were
butchered outside the Louvre in the 1830
Revolution. According to Welch (*see* Bibl.)
he received a pension, and he returned to
Switzerland. The same authority says that
while in Paris he learnt much about flute
making from Buffet; but he was not a pupil
for flute playing of Drouet, as many writers
assert, but of Tulou, who probably gave him
finishing lessons, as he had almost certainly
played the instrument before he went to
Paris. He became insane in Switzerland and
had eventually to be confined in an asylum,
where he remained until his death but for a
lucid interval in 1839. It is not precisely
known when he died, but he was dead by 1847.
There is no evidence for the statement often
made that he took his own life.
Gordon began to make improvements in
the construction of the flute in 1826, but it is
uncertain whether Boehm had anticipated his
modifications of the instrument or merely
carried them to the success which was to con-
nect his name with them. Welch deals at
some length with the controversies over
priority.   P. R. K.

BIBL.—KIRBY, PERCIVAL R., 'Captain Gordon, the
    Flute Maker' (M. & L., XXXVIII, 1957, p. 250).
ROCKSTRO, R. S., 'A Treatise on . . . . the Flute' (Lon-
    don, 1890).
WELCH, C., 'History of the Boehm Flute' (London,
    1896).
See also Boehm (Theobald). Flute.

717   ii   **GORDON, William**
Delete whole article.

718   i   **GORGIA**
l. 2 *should read*:

ORNAMENTS, C.

722   i   **GOSSEC**
See also should read:

See also Marseillaise (accomp. for). Sondheimer Ed.,
Vol. 42 (modern ed. of Symphony). Symphony, p. 219.

ii   **GOSTLING**
Add at end, before signature:

He seems to have been on reasonably intimate terms also with Blow, whom he appointed "his lawful attorney" on 19 July
1691. It appears that he was summoned to
Windsor, and that his attendance was spread
over the years 1683–84; his admission to the
king's "private music" is recorded in the
autumn of 1685, an appointment which was
renewed, together with one to the "vocal
music" in July 1689 and Mar. 1697. It
would appear that the exercise of his
ecclesiastical functions was interspersed with
employment as a musician, when he would be
prevented from performing his ecclesiastical
duties.
His son, William, who was baptized in
Canterbury Cathedral on 30 Jan. 1696, and
died in that city on 9 Mar. 1777, spent
most of his life in the district after leaving
Cambridge in 1720, and held a minor canonry
at the Cathedral from 1727 until his death. He
died intestate, administration being granted
to his daughter Hester a month after his
decease. His interest for the musician lies in
the part-books of church music which once
formed part of his library. The so-called
"Barnard" MS books (RCM 1045–51) have
his book-plates, as have a set of eight books
to be dated after 1670 now in the library of
York Minster. The *medius decani* book of this
latter set, of which the title, according to the
tenor decani book, is: 'A Book of Services
for a Quire', contains a reference to a collection made at Lincoln, and therefore in all
probability William inherited these books
from his father, as perhaps he did the others
also, since there seems to be no evidence that
he was particularly interested in music. The
haphazard way in which the music is set out
in these books suggests that they were not
intended for use in actual performance, as
the "Barnard" books may well have been.
The countertenor, tenor and bass books of

the set made up from both editions of Day's 'Certaine Notes' (1560–65) now in the British Museum have the name " W. Gostling " written in them. According to DNB, his library was sold in 1778, but it appears that there is no record of the sale at the British Museum.

722   ii   *Signature should read*:

J. A. F.-M., adds. W. H. C. & W. K. F.

BIBL.—COCK, F. W., 'A Note on the Rev. Wm. Gostling' ('Archaeologia Cantiana', XLVII, 1935, p. 1).

723   ii   **GOTTSCHALK**
Add to BIBL.:

LOGGINS, VERNON, 'Where the Words end: the Life of Louis Moreau Gottschalk' (Baton Rouge, Louisiana 1958).

727   i   **GOUDIMEL**
See also should read:

See also Maîtres Musiciens, Vols. 2, 4 & 6 (modern reprint of Psalms). Monuments Mus. Franç., Vol. 9 (modern reprint of Masses). Riv. Mus. It., VI, p. 495.

729   i   **GOUNOD**
Par. 1, l. 2.   18 June *should read*:

17 June

733   ii   **GOUNOD**
CHAMBER MUSIC
ll. 8-9 *should be* ll. 6-7.

(1885)   l. 9.   (1888) *should read*:

735   i   *Add before* **GOUTER**:

GOÛT POLONAIS (Fr.; Ger. *Polnischer Geschmack* or *nach Art der Polen*). A musical term introduced at the beginning of the 18th century to define the characteristic features of the Polish style in music and dances.

C. R. H.

738   i   **Gozzi**
l. 7 *should read*:

incid. m. or opera). Hartmann (3, 'Ravnen', opera). Henze ('König Hirsch', opera).

l. 10. *Add*:

Liuzzi ('Augellin bel verde', puppet opera).

Grabbe
See Borek should read:

See Berg (Alban, song). Borek

GRABBE, Johann
Add at end:

See also Chorwerk, Vol. 35 (reprint of madrigal).

GRABNER
Par. 3, l. 7 *should read*:

a 'Perkeo Suite' for wind. He also wrote a Concerto for organ and strings, a

ii   **GRABOWIECKI**
Add at end:

See also Polonaise (Vol. VI, p. 845): the wordless musical examples in B♭ ma.

741   i   *Add before* **GRADUAL**:

GRADSTEIN, Alfred (*b.* Częstochowa, 30 Oct. 1904; *d.* Warsaw, 29 Sept. 1954). Polish composer. He began his musical studies under Statkowski at the Warsaw Conservatory and continued them under Marx in Vienna. For nearly eighteen years he lived in France, but he returned to his native country after the second world war. In 1948 he was appointed secretary-general of the Union of Polish Composers in Warsaw.

Gradstein's works include a pianoforte Concerto, a Sonatina for violin and pianoforte and 'Hommage à Chopin' consisting of 12 studies for pianoforte dedicated to Chopin's memory. For his cantata 'Słowo o Stalinie' ('Word about Stalin'), set to a poem by W. Broniewski, he was awarded a State Prize of the third class in 1952. He also wrote numerous popular songs for the masses.

C. R. H.

GRADUAL
See also. l. 2 *should read*:

Music. Paléographie Mus. (for modern reprints).

742   i   **GRAENER**
Par. 2, l. 3.   Stein Conservatory
should read:

Stern Conservatory

Par. 3, l. 1 *should read*:

His best-known opera, 'Friedemann Bach',

CATALOGUE
OPERAS
l. 15 *should read*:

drama), prod. Berlin, 14 Mar. 1935.

Add at end:

'Schwanhild' (lib. by T. von O. Anthes), prod. Cologne, 4 Jan. 1942.

CHORAL WORKS
Add at end:

99. 'Marien-Kantate' for solo voices, chorus & orch.

ii   ORCHESTRAL WORKS
Add at end:

82. 'Comedietta.'
88. 'Die Flöte von Sanssouci', suite for chamber orch.
96. 'Sinfonia breve.'
107. 'Turmwächterlied.'
110. 'Wiener Sinfonie.'

743   i   **GRAF, Max**
Par. 1.   1873). *should read*:

1873; *d.* Vienna, 23 June 1958).

744   i   **GRAHAM**
Par. 2, l. 27 *should read*:

adapted to their appropriate Melodies'. A sonnet in honour of Beethoven by George Graham was erroneously attributed to the Scottish poet James Graham (1765–1811) by Thayer (Vol. II, p. 209).

W. H. H., adds.

745 ii **GRAM**
Par. 1, l. 2 *should read* :
1881 ; *d.* Copenhagen, 4 Feb. 1956).

753 ii **GRAMOPHONE**
Par. 2, ll. 28-31 *should read* :
adumbrated in the latter part of this article.
It is now established at 38 Russell Square,
London W.C.1. In 1956 it began to publish
a quarterly ' Bulletin '.   D. S.-T.

754 i Par. 1, l. 4 *should read* :
output of records into a single volume. A first Supplement was appended to the original edition.
Supplements 1952 II & III, 1953 & 1957.

l. 28 *should read* :
Record Year ', Vols. I & II (London, 1952-53). ' The
Record Guide ' (rev. ed.) (1955) ; ' The Record Guide
Supplement ' (1956). Guides to the

Add to BIBL. (GUIDES, etc.) :
GELATT, ROLAND, ' The Fabulous Phonograph : from
Tinfoil to High Fidelity ' (Philadelphia, 1955;
London, 1956).
GREEN, IRVING & RADCLIFFE, JAMES R., ' The High
Fidelity Handbook ' (New York, 1955).
JOHNSON, WILLIAM WARD, ' The Gramophone Book : a
Complete Guide for all Lovers of Recorded Music '
(London, 1954).
KOLODIN, IRVING, ' The Guide to Long-Playing Records :
Orchestral Music ' (New York, 1955).
MARCH, I., GREENFIELD, E. & STEVENS, D., ' The
Stereo Record Guide ' (London, 1960).
MILLER, PHILIP L., ' The Guide to Long-Playing
Records : Vocal Music ' (New York, 1955).
RAMSEY, FREDERIC, ' A Guide to Longplay Records '
(New York, 1954).
SCHONBERG, HAROLD C., ' The Guide to Long-Playing
Records : Instrumental Music ' (New York, 1955).
WILSON, PERCY, ' The Gramophone Handbook ' (Lon-
don, 1957).

Add to BIBL. (MISC.) :
CANDÉ, ROLAND DE, ' Ouverture pour une discothèque '
(Paris, 1956).

755 ii **GRANADOS**
Add to BIBL. :
FERNÁNDEZ-CID, ANTONIO, ' Granados (Obertura) '
(Madrid, 1956).

756 ii SONGS
Delete ll. 7-10 *and substitute* :
5-7. La maja dolorosa, 3 songs
Oh muerte cruel.
Ay majo de mi vida.
De aqual majo amante.
8. El mirar de la maja.
9. Amor y odio.
10. Callejeo.
11. Las curratacas modestas (duet).
12. El majo olvidado.

757 ii **GRANDI**
Par. 1, l. 1. **Alessandro** *should
read* :
Alessandro (1)

758 i Page heading *should read* :
GRANDI (Alessandro)

o

758 ii *Add to* BIBL. :
ARNOLD, DENIS, ' Alessandro Grandi, Disciple of Monteverdi ' (M.Q., XLIII, 1957, p. 171).

Add at end :
See also Chorwerk, Vol. 40 (modern reprint of concert motets).

Add before **GRANDI, Margherita** :
GRANDI, Alessandro (2) (*b.* prob.
Sicily, ? ; *d.* ?).
Italian 17th-century composer, possibly
related to the preceding. He is known by
several books of church music published at
Bologna from about 1680. These works,
although formerly thought to be reprints of
the earlier Grandi's music, are written in a
late 17th-century style, and it seems probable
that this composer was one of a group working
in the church of San Petronio at Bologna.
D. M. A.

762 i **GRAUN (3)**
l. 2. 1704 *should read* :
1701

763 ii BIBL., l. 6. MENNICKE, K. *should read* :
MENNICKE, C.

764 ii **GRAUPNER, Christoph**
Add at end :
See also Mitteldeutsches Musikarchiv, I, Vol. 2
(modern ed. of 8 Partitas).

766 ii **GRAZIANI, Francesco**
Par. 1. Dates *should read* :
(*b.* Fermo, 26 Apr. 1828 ; *d.* Grottazzolina
nr. Fermo, 30 June 1901)

769 ii **GRECHANINOV**
Par. 1, l. 2 *should read* :
vich (*b.* Moscow, 25 Oct. 1864 ; *d.* New
York, 3 Jan. 1956).

783 i **GREENE, Eric**
Par. 1, l. 2. 1903). *should read* :
8 Feb. 1903).

785 i **GREENE, Maurice**
Add to BIBL. :
DART, THURSTON, ' Maurice Greene and the National
Anthem ' (M. & L., XXXVII, July 1956, p. 205).

786 i **GREGOIR**
Par. 2, l. 9. Biberich *should read* :
Biebrich

788 i **GREGORIAN MUSIC**
Add to BIBL. :
APEL, WILLI, ' Gregorian Chant ' (London, 1958).
JOHNER, DOMINICUS, ' Wort und Ton im Choral : ein
Beitrag zur Aesthetik des gregorianischen Gesanges '
(Leipzig, 1953).

See also should read :
See also Notation. Plainsong. Solesmes.

789   ii   **GREITER**
Add to BIBL. :

LOWINSKY, EDWARD E., 'Matthaeus Greiter's "Fortuna"': an Experiment in Chromaticism and in Musical Iconography' (M.Q., XLII & XLIII, 1956–57).

795   —   **GRÉTRY,** CATALOGUE
Col. 2, l. 7 *should read* :
after Voltaire's ' L'Ingénu '.

797   i   **GRÉTRY, A. D. L.**
Par. 1, l. 3 *should read* :
Paris, 25 Aug. 1790).

798   i   **GREVILLIUS**
Par. 1, l. 13.   Konstföreningen *should read* :

Konsertföreningen

ii   **GRIEG**
Par. 3, l. 16 *should read* :
father, Alexander Greig [1], was of

ll. 18-20 *should read* :
between 1760 and 1770, engaged in the lobster-exporting

l. 25 *should read* :
English Consul.[2]

Add footnote :
[1] The spelling " Grieg " was adopted to conform with Norwegian pronunciation.
Footnote 1 *becomes* 2.

804   ii   BIBL., l. 26. nordische *should read* :
nordländische

805   i   *Add to* BIBL. :
SCHJELDERUP-EBBE, DAG, 'A Study of Grieg's Harmony' (Oslo, 1953).

806   —   CATALOGUE
PIANOFORTE SOLO
Col. 2, l. 10. Aelfedans *should read* :
Elversdans

809   —   SONGS
Op. 33, No. 3, Col. 2.   Saarede *should read* :
Særde

No. 4, Col. 2.   Tytteberet *should read* :
Tyteberet

Op. 39, No. 3, Col. 2.   Liden *should read* :
I Liden

810   —   *Op.* 44, No. 4, Col. 2.   Ingebjorg *should read* :
Ingebjørg

811   ii   *Add before* **GRIESBACH** :
GRIER, Christopher.   *See* EDINBURGH, Vol. II, p. 885, i.

812   i   **GRIESINGER**
Par. 1, l. 1.   (*b.* ? ; *d. should read* :
b. Leonberg nr. Stuttgart, 8 Jan. 1769 ; *d.*

812   i   Par. 1, l. 2 *should read* :
Vienna, 9 Apr. 1845).

Par. 2, ll. 1 and 2 *should read* :
German author.   He studied theology at Tübingen and in 1791 went to French Switzerland as a teacher.   In 1797 he moved to Leipzig, where some translations from the French made by him brought him into touch with the publisher Gottfried Christoph Härtel. In 1799 he became tutor to the son of Count Schönfeld, Saxon ambassador to the Austrian court, and moved to Vienna, where he became acquainted with Haydn and Beethoven.   In 1804 he acquired Saxon citizenship and became secretary to the Saxon legation.   After a year at Dresden in 1813–14 he returned to Vienna.   He was ennobled in 1819, became privy councillor to the legation in 1828 and *chargé d'affaires* in 1831.

Griesinger knew Haydn well during the last years of the latter's life and claims to report directly from his lips, often in his very words, in a little work he wrote on that master : ' Biographische Notizen über

ll. 6-12 *should read* :
kopf & Härtel of Leipzig in 1810.   It was

ii   *Cancel* Par. 2.

Signature should read :
G., rev.

814   i   **GRIGNY**
Add to BIBL. :
DUFOURCQ, NORBERT, 'La Musique d'orgue française ' (Paris, 1949).

Grillparzer
l. 2 *should read* :
opera project ; words for vocal arr. of ' Equali ' for B.'s funeral).   Braunfels (' Traum ein Leben ',

l. 6 *should read* :
(K., ' Melusine ', lib.).   Mahler (? ' Argonauten ', opera). Mederitsch (pf. teacher).

ii   *Add before* **GRIMALDI** :

GRIMACE, ? (*b.* ? ; *c.* ?).
French 14th-century composer.   He has left five compositions, of which three are ballades and the other two a virelai and a rondeau.   Apart from the virelai and one ballade, which are in four parts, they were all originally for three voices.   The ballade ' Dedens mon cuer ' is incomplete, since half the *tenor* and all the *contratenor* are missing. Grimace follows closely in the footsteps of Guillaume de Machaut, and, unlike many composers who flourished after 1380, he is not preoccupied with rhythmic and notational complexities.   The bitextual ballade ' Se Zephirus — Se Jupiter ' with an accompanying *tenor* brings to mind Machaut's ' Quand

Theseus — Ne quier veoir', partly because of the descending melodic line in *cantus* I and the motifs 𝅘𝅥𝅮𝅘𝅥𝅮𝅘𝅥𝅮 and 𝅘𝅥𝅮𝅘𝅥𝅮𝅘𝅥𝅮. The 4-part ballade in 3-4 time has a *triplum*, whose chief function seems to be to increase the excitement with scurrying quavers or hocket passages. The fanfare-like opening of the *tenor* is a feature of Grimace's work, and it is particularly apparent in the virelai ' Alarme, alarme '. The *tenor* and *contratenor* are very clearly paired together, and the *contratenor* is not without syncopations. Imitation of the alarm signal is frequent in the first half of the composition, which is full of life, though it is only a battle of love. ' Dedens mon cuer ' has much in common with the bitextual composition, though the rhythm is perhaps more flexible and there is a charming imitative passage at the end of both halves of the composition.

' Alarme, alarme ' is published in W. Apel's ' French Secular Music of the Late Fourteenth Century ' (1950).

G. R. (iii).

814   ii   *Add after* **Grimani** :

GRIMM, Friedrich-Karl (*b.* Chemnitz 9 Jan. 1902).

German pianist, conductor and composer. He studied at Leipzig and Berlin, under Stephan Krehl for composition, Alfred Szendrei for orchestration, Robert Teichmüller, Max von Pauer and James Kwast for pianoforte and Hermann Abert and Theodor Kroyer for musicology. Later on he took a finishing course in conducting with Clemens Krauss at Salzburg. In 1926–29 he gave concerts of classical music and works of his own in Germany, and in 1929–30 he lived in London, where he gave a concert of his own chamber compositions at the Grotrian Hall. He became artistic assistant to Paul Graener and his successor as head of the master class in composition at the Stern Conservatory in Berlin in 1932. He was a member of the jury for the Section of German composers in 1937–1944 and began to write music for films about that time.

The following are among Grimm's principal compositions :

FILM MUSIC
Symphonic scores for 10 documentaries.

ORCHESTRAL WORKS
Symph. poem ' Lucrezia Borgia '.
Symph. poem ' Judith '.
' Nocturnes.'
Scherzo for stgs.
Habanera and Castilian Dance.

CHAMBER MUSIC
Trio Sonata for clar., bassoon & pf.
String Quartet.
Quintet for pf. & stgs.
Chamber Music for voice, vn. & pf.

ONE INSTRUMENT AND PIANOFORTE
' Jungle Book ' Suite for cello (after Kipling).
Sonata for cello.
Sonata for viola.
Sonata for oboe.
Sonata for clar.
Sonata for bassoon.
' Serenata ' for Eng. horn.

PIANOFORTE MUSIC
Sonata.
Concert Studies.
Studies for the left hand.
' Nocturnes ' (incl. ' Early Morning in Hyde Park ').
Hungarian Dances.
Spanish Dances.
Preludes.
Concert Paraphrase on Lehár's ' Count of Luxemburg '.

SONGS
' Songs of the Sea ' (words by Rainer Maria Rilke, Theodor Storm, Oscar Wilde, Theodor Fontane & others).
Goethe Songs.
Rilke Songs.
' Songs of Sensibility.'   E. B.

815   i   **Grimmelshausen**
l. 1 *should read* :

Grimmelshausen, Hans Jakob von. *See* David (J. N., motet). Gál (' Nacht–

816   ii   **GRISWOLD**
Par. 1, l. 2.   25 Feb. *should read* :
26 Feb.

817   i   *Add after* **GROBSTIMME** :

GROCHEO, Johannes de (*b.* ? ; *d.* ?).

13th–14th-century musical theorist of uncertain nationality. He must have lived in Paris about 1300. Since he speaks of sermons written by himself, he was doubtless a priest. His treatise ' De musica ' is to be found in two 14th-century manuscripts in London and Darmstadt, of which the London copy is probably the earlier and more reliable one. Both the Wolf and Rohloff editions are, however, taken from the Darmstadt manuscript.

The unique character of Grocheo's treatise is due to its empirical method and untraditional outlook. For instance, number symbolism is regarded with scepticism, except where other explanations fail, and Boethius, *the* authority of medieval musical theorists, is rejected out of hand. Boethius's almost universally accepted classification of music into cosmic, human (of the body) and instrumental does not appeal for once. Heavenly bodies do not make music, whatever the ancients thought, and who ever heard of human complexion sounding, even if the parts of the body are in harmony among each other ? Grocheo admits that music varies according to countries, uses, languages, etc., and so takes Paris as his basis, since all the liberal arts are studied most closely there. He feels that music can best be considered as either *simplex* or *composita*, whereby he seems to make a distinction between popular and learned elements, including the division monody: polyphony. *Musica ecclesiastica* is said to be made up of both simple and composite music. His descriptions of secular music are of interest, because theorists are rarely concerned with it. Different genres are attributed to different social layers, *e.g.* the *chanson de geste* to the old, the labourers and the lower classes, to help them to put up with their sufferings during leisure hours; and the *cantus coronatus* to kings and nobles, to give them courage and liberality. Nevertheless some of these distinctions must be viewed with scepticism, since *cantus coronatus* is more likely to refer to the crowning of poets at festivals than to kings. Similarly, although Grocheo says the *cantus coronatus* consists of seven stanzas, the modern edition reveals only five stanzas and a three-line *envoi*.

Other forms discussed are the *ductia*, *stantipes* and *rondeau*. The *rondeau* is apparently sung slowly. *Ductia* and *stantipes* are for dancing, and are obviously primarily instrumental, though these textless melodies may be sung. The *stantipes*, evidently a latinization of *estampie*, is distinguished from its partner the *ductia* by its greater length, though both consist of a number of double versicles with *ouvert* and *clos* endings. Of the polyphonic forms Grocheo describes the two-part pure organum, the motet and the hocket. Conductus is considered as coming under the same heading as organum, except that it is not based on a precomposed plainsong but generally on an entirely new melodic *cantus firmus*.

The section on church music is relatively extended, but there is little new material in it. Grocheo considers that the mode of a piece is not defined merely by the note that ends a piece of plainsong, but also by the notes that begin it and those that appear at important points in the middle. The Kyrie and Sanctus are both considered as slow pieces, and the Kyrie consists of nothing but perfect longs, like the *cantus coronatus*. A hint that *lectio, epistola* and *evangelium* at least are not measured like other music is provided by Grocheo's statement that these forms are governed by the rules of accent and grammar and are not the concern of the musician.   G. R. (iii).

BIBL.—ROHLOFF, E., 'Der Musiktraktat des Joh. de Grocheo' (Leipzig, 1943).
'Studien zum Musiktraktat des Joh. de Grocheo' (Leipzig, 1930).
WOLF, JOHANNES, 'Die Musiklehre des Johannes de Grocheo' (S.I.M., I, 1899, pp. 15-130).

819 ii **GROSSVATER-TANZ**
Par. 1, ll. 3-4 *should read*:
dance which was greatly in vogue at weddings. It was long supposed to date from the 17th century, but is now known to be by Karl Gottlieb Hering (1765-1853). Spohr had to intro-

820 i ll. 4-5 *should read*:
it is used by Schumann in his 'Carnaval' to represent the

l. 7 *should read*:
Davidsbündler'. He had already used it (section in triple time only) in

ii **Groth**
Add to BIBL. :
BRAHMS, JOHANNES & GROTH, KLAUS, 'Briefe der Freundschaft' (Heide, n.d.)

826 ii **GROVÉ**
Par. 4, ll. 6-7 *should read*:
churches in South Africa. He taught for a time at the S.A. College of Music in Capetown, but in the mid-1950s left for the U.S.A., where after further studies with Piston and Copland he became lecturer on music at the Peabody Conservatory of Baltimore.

Par. 6. *Add after* l. 2 :
'Sinfonia concertante' for orch. (1956).
Tower Music for brass insts. (1954).
Symphony for wind insts. (1958).

Add after l. 5 :
Quintet for flute, oboe, viola, bass clar. & harp (1952)
Trio for woodwind (1952).
Quartet for stgs. & harp (1954).
String Quartet (1955).
Quartet for woodwind (1956).

Add after l. 8 :
Sonata for flute & pf. (1955).

827 i **GROVEN**
Replace Pars. 2-4 *by* :
Norwegian composer and folk-music collector. Keenly interested in folk music from childhood, he became a noted performer on the Hardanger fiddle and collected a large number of folk tunes. He has for years experimented with acoustical problems and has constructed an organ with considerably purer tuning than the instrument ordinarily in use. He was folk-music adviser to the Norwegian State Radio in 1932-45.
Groven is a prolific composer in a diatonic modal style. Among his works are 2 Symphonies, a pianoforte Concerto, choral works with orchestra ('Mot Ballade', 1933) and a number of tuneful songs.   O. G.

GROVES, Charles
Par. 2, l. 29 *should read*:
remuneration. Groves received the order of O.B.E. in 1958.   E. B.

830 i **GRUENBERG**
Par. 5, l. 4. 1945 *should read*:
1944

831   i   *Add before* **Grun**:

GRÜMMER, Elisabeth (*b.* Niedergentz, Alsace-Lorraine, 31 Mar. 1911).
German soprano singer. After the world war of 1914–18 she moved with her parents from Alsace-Lorraine to Thuringia. She studied for the stage at Meiningen and appeared as a professional actress for three years at Aachen, where she married the leader of the orchestra. Until then she had no idea of becoming a singer, although blessed with a beautiful natural voice. She was then persuaded to study singing and after six years made her début at Aachen as the First Flower Maiden in ' Parsifal ', following it with a successful Octavian. She was engaged as first lyric soprano at Duisburg and then went to Prague. When the German theatres closed in 1944, she worked for a time as a post-office sorter, while her husband was in a factory. In 1946 she went to Berlin to join the company of the Städtische Oper, where she was heard as Agathe, Desdemona, Eva, Pamina and Ellen Orford in the first Berlin performance of ' Peter Grimes '. Her Eva was so successful that she was asked to repeat it in Eastern Berlin and Dresden, and then in London under Beecham in 1951, and at Bayreuth in 1957 and 1958. In 1952 she appeared with the Hamburg company at Edinburgh as Agathe, Pamina and Octavian, and since 1953 has sung regularly at Vienna and Salzburg. She now divides her time equally between Vienna, Hamburg and Berlin, and also finds time for *Lieder* recitals and oratorio appearances. Her beautiful voice, aristocratic style and innate musicianship specially suit her to Mozartian parts : and her Countess, Donna Anna, Pamina and Ilia are greatly admired.   H. D. R.

GRÜNEBAUM
Par. 1, l. 2. 1872). *should read*:
2 Jan. 1872 ; *d.* Chipstead, Surrey, 5 Apr. 1954).

   ii   Par. 2, l. 1.   Grunebaum *should read*:
Grünebaum

Gruppe
Add at end of line:
Strauss (R., song).

835   i   **GUARNERI**
Add to BIBL.:
PETHERICK, HORACE, ' Joseph Guarnerius ' (London, 1906).
PICCOLELLIS, A., ' Liutai antichi e moderni ' (Florence, 1886).

Add before **GUARNERI, Camargo**
GUARNIERI, Antonio (*b.* Venice, 2 Feb. 1883 ; *d.* Milan, 26 Oct. 1952).

Italian conductor. He studied the violoncello, the pianoforte and counterpoint at the Conservatory " B. Marcello " in Venice, continuing later with the study of composition under Enrico Bossi. At a very early age he began to tour as a concert cellist in Italy and abroad, and he joined the Martucci Quartet. As a conductor he first came out in 1901, beginning a career that was to become exceptionally brilliant. He conducted opera and concerts in the most important European centres. In 1913 he was nominated director of Italian opera in Vienna, but soon abandoned this post owing to dissensions with the manager of the theatre. He was a favourite with the public as conductor of the outstanding opera of the repertory, but was especially appreciated as an interpreter of Wagner, to the knowledge of whom he contributed a great deal even in the less important places. He composed vocal chamber music and ' Impressioni di Spagna ' for orchestra.
      G. M. G.

835   i   **GUARNIERI, (M.) C.**
     Par. 1, l. 2.   Tieté *should read*:
Tietê

836   i   **GÜDEN**
     Delete whole article:
See GUEDEN.

   ii   **GUDENIAN**
     Add at end:
BIBL.—KAFA, KOYOUN (HAIG GUDENIAN), ' The Call of the Ancient East ' (Ann Arbor, Mich., 1957).

Add after **GUÉBAUR**:

GUEDEN, Hilde (*b.* Vienna, 15 Sept. 1917).
Austrian soprano singer. The daughter of Austrian and Hungarian parents, she entered the Vienna Conservatory to study dancing and the pianoforte. Soon vocal studies took first place, and her voice teacher was Mme Wetzelsberger. When only seventeen she sang in Robert Stolz's operetta ' Servus, Servus ' in Vienna, and then was engaged for the Zürich Municipal Theatre for the 1940–1941 season, making her début as Cherubino. In 1941 she was engaged by Clemens Krauss for the Munich State Opera, where she remained for two seasons, during which she was heard by Strauss, who suggested that she should study the part of Sophie, which she sang both in German and then in Italian in Rome under Serafin. From 1942 until 1945 her career was interrupted by the war, but in 1946 she joined the Vienna State Opera. Her London début was at Covent Garden with the Vienna Company in 1947, when she was heard as Zerlina and Cherubino. In 1950 she was made Austrian *Kammersängerin*,

the youngest singer ever to be awarded this title. The same year she became a member of the Metropolitan Opera, New York, where she has appeared regularly ever since in the German, French and Italian repertory, and as Anne Trulove in the American première of ' The Rake's Progress '. She has appeared at the Edinburgh and Salzburg Festivals, and in 1954 at the latter festival sang Zerbinetta for the first time in ' Ariadne auf Naxos ', displaying a newly acquired coloratura technique. This, added to her fresh, charming voice and youthful personality, gained her a triumph. She scored another success as Aminta in the revival of Strauss's ' Die schweigsame Frau ' at Salzburg in 1959.

Hilde Gueden is an amazingly versatile artist. She is gifted with great intelligence, and this, coupled with her sure vocal technique, makes her a much sought-after artist for modern works. She has sung in Weill's ' Mahagonny ' at Venice, Britten's ' Lucretia ' and Blacher's ' Romeo und Julia ' at Salzburg. She is also particularly suited to Viennese operetta, and undertakes parts in Johann Strauss and Lehár with as much care and preparation as the more serious works in the repertory.   H. D. R.

837   i   *Add after* **Guérin, Eugénie de** :
Guérin, Louis. *See* Berlioz (song).

839   i   **GUERRERO, F.**
Par. 2, l. 3 *should read* :

scribed by Daza and Mudarra. A collected edition was begun by the Consejo Superior di Investigaciones Científicas at Barcelona in 1955.

Add at end :
See also Eslava (modern reprints). Hispaniae Schola, Vols. 2 & 6 (modern reprints).

ii   *Add after* **GUESDRON** :

GUEST, Douglas (Albert) (*b*. Mortomley, Yorkshire, 9 May 1916).
English organist, conductor and composer. He attended Reading School in 1930–33, studied at the R.C.M. in London in 1933–35 and went to Cambridge in the latter year as Organ Scholar of King's College and Stewart of Rannoch Scholar in Music, taking the M.A. and the Mus. B. He is also an A.R.C.O. On leaving Cambridge in 1939 he went on active war service as a Major in the Royal Artillery, serving until 1945 and being mentioned in despatches. From 1945 to 1950 he was Director of Music at Uppingham School and from 1950 to 1957 Organist and Master of the Choristers of Salisbury Cathedral as well as Director of Music of St. Mary's School, Calne. In 1957 he was appointed Organist and Master of the Choristers of

Worcester Cathedral and thus became one of the conductors of the Three Choirs Festival.

Guest has done exceptionally fine work for the B.B.C., broadcasting both with the Salisbury choir, which he brought to a remarkable level of excellence, and as an independent choral-orchestral conductor. During his time at Salisbury he also conducted many concerts with the Bournemouth Symphony Orchestra and elsewhere in the provinces, as well as various choirs and orchestras in London in performances of Purcell, Bach, Telemann, etc. He is also a festival adjudicator, examiner to the Associated Board and Chairman of the Governing Council of the National Youth Orchestra of Great Britain. As a composer he has so far (1957) published a ' Missa brevis ' for unaccompanied chorus.   E. B.

842   i   *Add after* **Guidiccioni** :
GUIDO (*b*. ? ; *d*. ?).
French 14th-century composer. His technique dates the three 3-part compositions preserved in MS Chantilly 1047 as belonging to the last third of the century. The text of the ballade ' Or voit tout en aventure ' laments that modern composers do not follow Philippe de Vitry's moderation, though Guido employs new note-forms in his own lively but not over-elaborate piece. In the rondeau ' Dieux gart ', Guido says : " God save the man who will sing this ", and the *cantus* is full of syncopations, while the *tenor* thrives on tritones. The isorhythmic rondeau ' Robin, muse, muse, muse ' suggests performance on the bagpipe.

' Dieux gart ' is published in Johannes Wolf's ' Geschichte der Mensural-Notation ', II-III (1904).   G. R. (iii).

843   i   **GUIDO D' AREZZO**
Par. 4, l. 4 *should read* :

1880), and again by J. Smits van Waesberghe in 1955 as Vol. IV of ' Corpus Scriptorum de Musica ' published by the American Institute of Musicology. This scholar has also edited the commentaries and other works, such as the ' Metrologus ' and the ' Liber argumentatorum ' (The Hague, 1957).   W. H. F., rev.

Add to BIBL. :
OESCH, HANS, ' Guido von Arezzo : Biographisches und Theoretisches unter besonderer Berücksichtigung der sogenannten odonischen Traktate ' (Berne, 1954).
SMITS VAN WAESBERGHE, J., ' De musicopaedagogico et theoretico Guidone Aretino eiusque vita et moribus ' (Florence, 1953).
(Ed.), ' Guidonis Aretini Micrologus ' (Amsterdam, 1955).

See also. l. 1 *should read* :
See also Accidentals. Aribon. Amer. Inst. Musicol. (C.S.M.), Vol. 4 (modern ed. of ' Micrologus '). Gamut. Hexachord.

847 i **GUITAR**
Par. 2, l. 16. and 45 *should read*:
and 40

848 ii Par. 3, l. 2. (*b*. 1890) *should read*:
(*b* 1893)

849 i *Add to* BIBL. :

BONE, PHILIP J., 'The Guitar and Mandolin: Biographies of Celebrated Players and Composers' (London, 1954).
BREAM, JULIAN, 'How to write for the Guitar' ('The Score', No. 19, Mar. 1957).

Add at end, before See also :

(*PLATE* 42, Vol. V, p. 432, No. 6; *PLATE* 68, Vol. VIII, p. 146 (iii), Nos. 2, 3 & 5.)

850 i **GUMPELTZHAIMER**
Add at end:
See also Denkmäler (2) II, Vol. 10 (ii) (modern ed.).

GUNDISALVUS
Par. 2, l. 20. Aristote *should read*:
Lambertus

ii Par. 1, l. 1 *should read*:
(*c*. 1270) and the anonymous compilers of the 'Quatuor principalia musicae'.

Add to BIBL. :

PIETZSCH, G., 'Die Klassifikation der Musik von Boethius bis Ugolino von Orvieto' (Halle, 1932).

851 i **GUNDRY**
Par. 2, l. 6 *should read*:
1948. There are also some unpublished poems.

852 i **GUNSBOURG**
Par. 1, l. 2 *should read*:
Dec. 1859; *d*. Monte Carlo, 31 May 1955).

854 i **GURLITT, M.**
Par. 1, l. 13 *should read*:
had been neglected there in his absence. In 1955 the Emperor of Japan bestowed an order on him for his contribution to Japanese cultural life.

854 i ORCHESTRAL WORKS
Add at end:
Reconstruction of Schumann's 'Carnaval' for full orch. for the 100th anniversary of his death (1956). Japanese Court Music, arr. for orch.

856 i **GURNEY**
Add at end:
See also Finzi (song to poem by G.).

ii *Add before* Gusev :
GURVIN, Olav (*b*. Tysnes, 24 Dec. 1893). Norwegian musicologist. He studied at Heidelberg, Berlin and the University of Oslo, where he took the Ph.D. in 1938 with a study of Fartein Valen's style ('Frå tonalitet til atonalitet'). He has been active as a choral conductor and from 1945 as music critic in Oslo.

In 1947 Gurvin became Associate Professor of Music at Oslo University and in 1957 Professor. He has also been director of the Norwegian Institute for Folk Music Research since 1951. In collaboration with Ø. Anker he edited the collected works of Nordraak, and among his own publications are the articles 'Photography as an Aid in Folk-Music Research' ('Norveg', 1953) and 'Some Comments on Tonality in Contemporary Music' ('Norsk Musikkgranskning', 1953–55). He is the editor of the great folk-music work 'Norwegian Folk Music' which began publication in 1958. D. S.-E.

857 i **GUY-ROPARTZ**
Par. 1, l. 2 *should read*:
Lanloup [1], Côtes-du-Nord, 15 June 1864; *d*. Lanloup, 22 Nov. 1955).

Add footnote :
[1] Not Guingamp, as some dictionaries have it: this was the name of his estate at Lanloup.

858 i **GUYOT**
Add at end:
See also Collectio O.M.B., Vol. 12 (modern ed.).

863 ii **GYROWETZ**
Par. 1, l. 1 *should read*:
GYROWETZ, Adalbert (Vojcĕch Jírovec) (*b*.

864 ii *See also*. l. 2 *should read*:
leithner (2, libs.). Symphony, p. 219. Verdi ('Giorno di regno',

VOL. IV

in London with the British Symphony Orchestra under Sir Adrian Boult. In

27 ii **HALLSTRÖM**
BIBL., l. 2. arhundradet *should read*:
århundradet

Halm, August
Delete name; whole entry should be under **Halm, Friedrich.**

28 i **HALVORSEN**
Par. 3, l. 7 *should read*:
wegian Festival Overture ', ' Suite ancienne ' and 2 Norwegian

l. 13. the last exponents *should read*:
the exponents

ii *Add at end, before signature*:
Halvorsen's most popular piece is the march ' Entry of the Boyars ' for orchestra.

HAM
l. 1. Dates *should read*:
(*b.* Bath, 7 June 1858; *d.* Brighton, 4 Feb. 1940).

29 ii **HAMBOURG (1)**
l. 2 *should read*:
May 1879; *d.* London, 26 Aug. 1960), pianist. He was a favourite pupil

HAMBOURG (3)
l. 2 *should read*:
Jan. 1885; *d.* Toronto, 24 Nov. 1954), violoncellist, brother of the pre-

30 i **HAMBURG**
Par. 1, ll. 14-15 *should read*:
Opera, in 1678. Johann Theile (1646–1724) taught at Hamburg. Mattheson, at one

l. 24. 1702 *should read*:
1720

31 i Par. 5, ll. 8-9. Hussmann *should read*:
Husmann

Add to BIBL.:
WOLFF, HELLMUTH CHRISTIAN, ' Die Barockoper in Hamburg ', 2 vols. (Wolfenbüttel, 1957).

HAMEL, F.
Par. 1, l. 2 *should read*:
Paris, 19 Feb. 1903; *d.* Cassel, 9 Dec. 1957).

33 i **HAMILTON, Iain,** List of Works:
Add before BALLET:
OPERA
Op.
33. ' Rondo ', *opera buffa* in 1 act.

BALLET
Entry should read:
14. ' Clerk Saunders ' (1951).

33 i *Add below* BALLET:
CHORAL WORKS
20. 4 Border Songs for unaccomp. chorus.
21. ' The Fray of Suport ' for unaccomp. chorus.
23. 5 Madrigals for unaccomp. chorus.

Add to ORCHESTRAL WORKS:
17. Overture to Ben Jonson's ' Bartholomew Fair '.
19. Symph. Variations.
24. Themes for stg. orch.
32. Scottish Dances.

Add below SOLO INSTRUMENTS AND ORCHESTRA:
15. Vn. Concerto.

Add below CHAMBER MUSIC:
25. Trio for vn., cello & pf.
26. ' Christmas Suite ' for 2 fl. & pf.
27a. ' Songs of Summer ' for soprano, clar. & pf.
28. Octet for stgs.
31. ' Serenata ' for clar. & vn.

Add below SOLO WIND INSTRUMENT AND PIANOFORTE:
18. ' Divertimento ' for clar.
22. Clar. Sonata.

Add below PIANOFORTE SOLO:
16. 4 Pieces for children.
30. 3 Pieces.
SONGS
27b. ' Songs of Summer ' for soprano & pf.

VOCAL QUARTET
29. Cantata for 4tet & pf.
BIBL.—MILNER, ANTHONY, ' Some Observations on the Music of Iain Hamilton ' (Mus. T., July 1956).

35 i **HAMMERSCHLAG**
Par. 1, l. 12, *add*:
Two books of old keyboard music edited by him were published posthumously in 1954, containing pieces by Bach, Bakfark, Couperin, Farnaby, Muffat, Purcell and others.

36 i **HAMMERSCHMIDT**
Add at end:
See also Denkmäler (2), Vol 40 (modern ed. of works). (3), Vol. 8 (modern ed. of ' Dialoghi ').

37 ii **HANDEL**
Par. 1, l. 2. **Friedrich**) *should read*:
Friederich)

40 ii Par. 3, l. 14 *should read*:
a river excursion of the king for which

l. 25 *should read*:
present the evidence against a connection between the music and a reconciliation is strong. Prof.

41 i Par. 2, l. 23 *should read*:
with J. S. Bach, which he seems to have made no effort to bring about.

46 i Par. 4, l. 2 *should read*:
England at that date, except at St. Paul's Cathedral. Handel's concertos are

49   i   *Add to* BIBL. :

DEAN, WINTON, ' The Dramatic Element in Handel's Oratorios ' (Proc. Roy. Mus. Ass., Vol. LXXIX, 1952–53).
' Handel's Dramatic Oratorios and Masques ' (Oxford, 1959).
DEUTSCH, OTTO ERICH, ' Handel : a Documentary Biography ' (London, 1955).
LARSEN, JENS PETER, ' Handel's Messiah : Origins — Composition — Sources ' (London, 1957).
MYERS, ROBERT MANSON, ' Handel, Dryden & Milton : Being a Series of Observations on the Poems of Dryden and Milton, as Alter'd and Adapted by Mr. Handel. To which are added, authentick texts of several of Mr. Handel's Oratorio's ' (London, 1956).
SERAUKY, WALTER, ' Georg Friedrich Händel : sein Leben — sein Werk ', Vol. III : ' Von Händels innerer Neuorientierung bis zum Abschluss des " Samson " (1738–43) ' (Cassel & Basel, 1956).
SHAW, WATKINS, ' John Matthews's Manuscript of " Messiah " ', M. & L., XXXIX, 1958, p. 101.

     ii   l. 20 *should read* :

' Händel Jahrbuch ', ed. by Max Schneider & Rudolf Steglich (Leipzig,

50   —   CATALOGUE
           OPERAS
           Col. 2, l. 3.   Feustking. *should read* :
Feustking.[2]

         l. 17 *should read* :
Nicola Francesco Haym, ? adapted from a libretto by Girolamo Frigimelica Roberti.

         Add footnote :
[2] The libretto of Keiser's ' Octavia '.

51   Col. 1, l. 6.   ' Alessandro.' [1] *should read* :
' Alessandro. ' [2]

         Col. 2, l. 5 *should read* :
Antonio Salvi [1], adapted by Haym.

         l. 12 *should read* :
da Alceste '.[3]

         l. 16.   Salvi's ' Adelaide ', *should read* :
Salvi's ' Berengario ',

         l. 30 *should read* :
with alterations, ? adapted by Francis Colman, sen.

         l. 32 *should read* :
furioso '.[4]

         l. 41 *should read* :
Niccolò Minato, with alterations.[5]

         Col. 3, l. 34.   1 May 1739.[2] *should read* :
1 May 1739.

         PASTICCIOS [3] *should read* :
PASTICCIOS [7]

         Add footnotes :
[1] Original set by Perti (1710) ; but Dent (' Handel : a Symposium ', London, 1954) suggests Stefano Ghigi's libretto of ' Flavio Berturido ', set by Pollarolo (1706) as a more probable source, the characters being almost wholly identical.

         Footnote 1 becomes 2.

[3] Derived from Euripides, prod. Venice, 1660, set by Zioni.
[4] The story adapted by Shakespeare for ' Much Ado about Nothing '.
[5] Minato's original libretto was that of Cavalli's ' Xerse ' (1654).

         Footnotes 2 & 3 become 6 & 7.

52   —   CATALOGUE
           SECULAR CHORAL WORKS
           Col. 3, l. 4.   6 Feb. 1714. *should read* :
6 Feb. 1713.

53   —   ORATORIOS
           Col. 3, l. 4.   2 May 1732. *should read* :
20 Apr. 1732.

55   —   CANTATAS FOR VARIOUS VOICES
           l. 25.   gnuola.) *should read* :
gnuola.) [3]

         end. Add footnote :
[3] The autograph of an air from this, " Dizente mis ozos ", in an altered version, was sold at Sotheby's in London, Apr. 1954. *See* p. 56, footnote 2, for three other songs in the same set.

56   —   *Add to Footnote 2* :
A manuscript collection of harpsichord pieces by Handel and others, sold by auction at Sotheby's in London, Apr. 1954, includes four songs in the composer's hand, the Spanish song mentioned on p. 55, footnote 3 ; No. 1 of the 7 French songs, with a different bass ; a French chanson, ' Quand on suit l'amoureuse loix ', not otherwise known ; and an " Air en Langue Allemande ", ' Der Mund spricht zwar gezwungen Nein ,' unidentified elsewhere.

61   ii   **HANDEL SOCIETY (1)**
           ll. 22-23 *should read* :
1848 until 1858, when the number of volumes reached sixteen.   G.

63   i   **HANDSCHIN**
           Par. 1, l. 2 *should read* :
Apr. 1886 ; d. Basel, 25 Nov. 1955).

     ii   *Add at end* :
BIBL.—HANDSCHIN, JACQUES, ' Aufsätze und Bibliographie : Gedenkschrift ' (Berne & Stuttgart, 1957).

HANKE
           Par. 1, l. 2.   d. ?). *should read* :
d. Flensburg, 10 June 1803).

64   ii   **HANNIKAINEN (2)**
           l. 2 *should read* :
Jyväskylä, 19 Oct. 1892 ; d. Helsingfors, 25 July 1955), pianist and com-

66   ii   **HANSLICK**
           Par. 5, l. 3.   English (1891) *should read* :
(English, 1891 & 1957)

         Par. 5, ll. 14-15 *should read* :
' Aus dem Tagebuche eines Musikers ' (1892).
' Aus meinem Leben ' (1894).

67   i   BIBL. *Add after* l. 8 :
' The Beautiful in Music ', trans. by Gustav Cohen, ed. by Mirros Weitz (New York, 1957).

HANSON
           Par. 4, l. 4.   Augustata *should read* :
Augustana

67   ii   CATALOGUE
          ORCHESTRAL WORKS
          Add at end:
' Mosaics ' in passacaglia form, for 40th Anniversary of
Cleveland Orchestra (1958).

69   i   **HARASZTI**
          Par. 1, l. 3 *should read*:
1885; d. Paris, 27 Dec. 1958).

     ii   **Hardy**
          l. 4. Finzi (30 songs) *should read*:
Finzi (2 songs with stg. 4tet; 43 songs with pf.)

          l. 12 *should read*:
Williams (incid. m. for do., dramatic version; song).

71   i   *Add before* **HARMAN, Carter**:

HARMAN, Alec (Richard Alexander)
(*b.* Gooty, Madras Province, India, 19 Nov.
1917).
English musicologist. He was educated at
Sidcot School, Winscombe, Somerset (1928–
1936) and studied music at the R.C.M. in
London in 1937–40 and 1942–43, taking the
A.R.C.M. and G.R.S.M. diplomas in 1943,
when he was appointed Director of Music at
Durham School, a post he retained until 1949,
when he took the B. Mus. (Dunelm). He was
then appointed Lecturer in Music by the
Durham Colleges of the University of Durham.
In 1945–50 he was also a member of the
Durham County Music Committee. Apart
from his lecturing, he has done a good deal of
broadcasting to schools.
Among Harman's publications the first
was an admirable edition of Morley's ' Plain
and Easy Introduction of Practical Music '
(London, 1952). He has also edited Marenzio's madrigals included in the ' Musica
Transalpina ' of 1588 and 1597 (London,
1955). As an author he contributes scholarly
articles to various musical periodicals and

published the first two volumes of ' Man and
his Music ': Vol. I, ' Medieval and Early
Renaissance Music ' (London, 1958) and Vol.
II, ' Late Renaissance and Baroque Music '
(London, 1959). He is also a contributor to
M.G.G.   E. B.

72   i   *Add*:

HARMONIC ANALYSIS.—The purpose
of this article is to list and describe as shortly
as possible the chords used in " traditional "
harmony. Particulars of their provenance and
use must be sought in some text-book on the
subject.
The tables given below will, it is hoped, give
some idea of the normal harmonic vocabulary
from *c.* 1700 to 1900. They cover the triads,
sevenths, augmented sixths and augmented
fifths, diatonic and chromatic, in the major
and minor keys. Ninths have not been included in these lists, since their appearance as
complete chords, with the ninth as an essential
(as opposed to a decorative) note, is rare.
Elevenths and thirteenths have also been
omitted; in essential and complete form they
are even rarer than ninths. The whole
matter of fundamental basses generating
ninths, elevenths and thirteenths is contrary
to the present writer's view of harmonic
theory [1], though the addition of a minor ninth
to the dominant, tonic chromatic and supertonic chromatic sevenths is used, possibly
illogically, as a convenient method of classifying
the diminished-seventh chords.
The two forms of minor scale (harmonic and
melodic) have been regarded as a single entity
for the purpose of chord formation, and the
chords brought about by the use of these two
forms are considered to be diatonic. This
procedure is open to objection, but has been
adopted for the sake of simplicity.
          [1] *See* article on HARMONY.

DIATONIC CHORDS IN THE MAJOR KEY

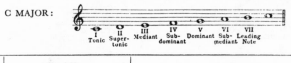

Degree of Scale	Chord Name and Character	" Root " Position and Inversions			
I	Tonic Triad (Major Common Chord)	Root Position	1st Inversion 6 3	2nd Inversion 6 4	
	Tonic Seventh (Major 7th)	Root Position 7	1st Inversion 6 5	2nd Inversion 6 4 3	3rd Inversion 6 4 2

Degree of Scale	Chord Name and Character	" Root " Position and Inversions
II	Supertonic Triad (Minor Common Chord)	Root Position 1st Inversion 6 3 2nd Inversion 6 4
	Supertonic Seventh (Minor 7th)	Root Position 7 1st Inversion 6 5 2nd Inversion 6 4 3 3rd Inversion 6 4 2
		* often called " Added Sixth on Subdominant "
III	Mediant Triad (Minor Common Chord)	Root Position 1st Inversion 6 3 2nd Inversion 6 4
	Mediant Seventh (Minor 7th)	Root Position 7 1st Inversion 6 5 2nd Inversion 6 4 3 3rd Inversion 6 4 2
IV	Subdominant Triad (Major Common Chord)	Root Position 1st Inversion 6 3 2nd Inversion 6 4
	Subdominant Seventh (Major 7th)	Root Position 1st Inversion 6 5 2nd Inversion 6 4 3 3rd Inversion 6 4 2
V	Dominant Triad (Major Common Chord)	Root Position 1st Inversion 6 3 2nd Inversion 6 4
	Dominant Seventh (Minor 7th)	Root Position 7 1st Inversion 6 5 2nd Inversion 6 4 3 3rd Inversion 6 4 2
VI	Submediant Triad (Minor Common Chord)	Root Position 1st Inversion 6 3 2nd Inversion 6 4
	Submediant Seventh (Minor 7th)	Root Position 7 1st Inversion 6 5 2nd Inversion 6 4 3 3rd Inversion 6 4 2

Degree of Scale	Chord Name and Character	"Root" Position and Inversions
VII	Leading Note Triad (Diminished Triad)	Root Position · 1st Inversion 6 3 · 2nd Inversion 6 4
	Leading Note Seventh (Minor 7th)	Root Position 7 · 1st Inversion 6 5 · 2nd Inversion 6 4 3 · 3rd Inversion 6 4 2

CHROMATIC CHORDS IN THE MAJOR KEY

Degree of Scale	Chord Name and Character	"Root" Position and Inversions
I	Tonic Chromatic Seventh (Minor 7th)	Root Position ♭7 · 1st Inversion 6 ♭5 · 2nd Inversion 6 4 ♭3 · 3rd Inversion 4 2
♭II	Major Triad on Flat Super-tonic (known in its first inversion as "Neapolitan Sixth")	Root Position ♭5 · 1st Inversion Neapolitan 6th ♭6 ♭3 · 2nd Inversion 6 ♭4
	Augmented Sixths on Flat Supertonic "Italian"	Root Position ♯6 · 1st Inversion ♭6 ♯4 · 2nd Inversion ♭5 ♭3
	Augmented Sixth on Flat Supertonic "German"	Root Position ♯6 ♭5 · 1st Inversion ♭6 ♯4 ♭3 · 2nd Inversion ♭4 ♯2 · 3rd Inversion ♭7 ♭3
	Augmented Sixth on Flat Supertonic "French"	Root Position ♯6 4 3 · 1st Inversion ♭6 ♯4 2 · 2nd Inversion 7 ♯3 · 3rd Inversion 6 5 ♭3
II	Supertonic Chromatic Triad (Major Common Chord)	Root Position ♯3 · 1st Inversion 6 3 · 2nd Inversion ♯6 4
	Supertonic Chromatic Seventh (Minor 7th)	Root Position 7 ♯3 · 1st Inversion 6 5 · 2nd Inversion ♯6 4 3 · 3rd Inversion 6 ♯4 2

Degree of Scale	Chord Name and Character	"Root" Position and Inversions
II (contd.)	Supertonic Diminished Triad	
	Supertonic Diminished Triad with added minor 7th	
IV	Subdominant Minor Triad (Minor Common Chord)	
♭VI	Major Triad on Flat Submediant (Major Common Chord)	
	Augmented Sixth on Flat Submediant "Italian"	
	Augmented Sixth on Flat Submediant "German"	
	Augmented Sixth on Flat Submediant "French"	
VI	Major Triad on Submediant (Major Common Chord)	
	Minor Seventh added to Major Triad on Submediant	

DIATONIC CHORDS IN THE MINOR KEY

C MINOR :

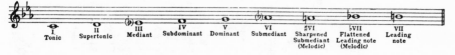

Degree of Scale	Chord Name and Character	" Root " Position and Inversions
I	Tonic Triad (Minor Common Chord)	Root Position · 1st Inversion 6 3 · 2nd Inversion 6 4
	Tonic Seventh (Minor 7th)	Root Position 7 · 1st Inversion 6 5 · 2nd Inversion 6 4 3 · 3rd Inversion ✓6 4 2
	(Occasionally a major 7th may be added to the tonic minor triad.)	
II	Supertonic Diminished Triad	Root Position · 1st Inversion 6 ·3 · 2nd Inversion 6 4
	Supertonic Seventh (Minor 7th)	Root Position 7 · 1st Inversion 6 5 · 2nd Inversion 6 4 3 · 3rd Inversion 6 4 2
	(1st inversion also known as added 6th on Subdominant.)	
	Supertonic Minor Triad (Minor Common Chord, derived from Melodic Minor Scale)	Root Position ♯5 · 1st Inversion 6 ♯3 · 2nd Inversion 6 4
	Supertonic Minor Triad with added Minor Seventh (Melodic Scale)	Root Position 7 ♯5 · 1st Inversion 6 5 ♯3 · 2nd Inversion 6 4 3 · 3rd Inversion ♯4 4 2
III	Mediant Triad (Augmented Triad)	Root Position ♯5 · 1st Inversion 6 ♯3 · 2nd Inversion 6 4
	Mediant Seventh (Major 7th added to the Augmented Triad)	Root Position 7 ♯5 · 1st Inversion 6 5 ♯3 · 2nd Inversion 6 4 3 · 3rd Inversion ♯6 4 2

Degree of Scale	Chord Name and Character	" Root " Position and Inversions
III (contd.)	Mediant Triad (Major Common Chord) (Melodic Scale)	
	Mediant Seventh (Major 7th added to above) (Melodic Scale)	
IV	Subdominant Minor Triad (Minor Common Chord)	
	Subdominant Seventh (Minor 7th)	
	Subdominant Major Triad (Major Common Chord) (Melodic Scale)	
	Subdominant Major Triad with Minor Seventh added (Melodic Scale)	
V	Dominant Triad (Major Common Chord)	
	Dominant Seventh (Minor 7th)	
	Dominant Minor Triad (Minor Common Chord) (Melodic Scale)	
	Dominant Minor Triad with Minor Seventh (Melodic Scale)	

Degree of Scale	Chord Name and Character	"Root" Position and Inversions
♭ VI	Submediant Triad (Major Common Chord)	Root Position 1st Inversion 6 2nd Inversion 6 4
	Submediant Seventh (Major 7th)	Root Position 7 1st Inversion 6 5 2nd Inversion 6 4 3 3rd Inversion 6 4 2
♯ VI	Major Submediant Diminished Triad (Melodic Scale)	Root Position 1st Inversion ♯6 2nd Inversion 6 ♯4
	Major Submediant Diminished Triad with Minor Seventh (Melodic Scale)	Root Position 7 1st Inversion ♯6 5 2nd Inversion 6 ♯4 3 3rd Inversion 6 ♯2
♭ VII	Major Triad on Flat Leading-note (Melodic Scale)	Root Position 1st Inversion 6 2nd Inversion 6 4
	Major Triad on Flat Leading-note with Minor Seventh added (Melodic Scale)	Root Position 7 1st Inversion 6 5 2nd Inversion 6 4 3 3rd Inversion 6 4 2
♯ VII	Leading-note Triad (Diminished Triad)	Root Position 1st Inversion (♯)6 2nd Inversion 6 (♯)4
	Leading-note Diminished Seventh (See Diminished 7th)	Root Position (♭)7 1st Inversion ♯6 5 2nd Inversion 6 ♯4 3 3rd Inversion 6 ♯2

CHROMATIC CHORDS IN THE MINOR KEY

I	Tonic Chromatic Seventh (Tonic Major Triad with minor 7th added)	Root Position 7 ♯3 1st Inversion 6 5 2nd Inversion ♯6 4 3 3rd Inversion 6 ♯2

P

Degree of Scale	Chord Name and Character	" Root " Position and Inversions
♭ II	Major Triad on Flat Supertonic (1st inversion known as " Neapolitan 6th ")	
	Augmented Sixth on Flat Supertonic " Italian "	
	Augmented Sixth on Flat Supertonic " German "	
	Augmented Sixth on Flat Supertonic " French "	
II	Supertonic Chromatic Triad (Major Common Chord)	
	Supertonic Chromatic Seventh (Minor 7th added to Supertonic Chromatic Chord)	
♭ VI	Augmented Sixth on (Flat) Submediant " Italian "	
	Augmented Sixth on (Flat) Submediant " German "	
	Augmented Sixth on (Flat) Submediant " French "	

DIMINISHED-SEVENTH CHORDS

Every major and minor key has within its bounds of diatonic or chromatic harmony three distinct diminished sevenths. They are : (1) the dominant minor ninth with the root omitted, (2) the tonic chromatic ninth and (3) the supertonic chromatic ninth similarly treated. By inverting these chords and altering their spelling where necessary a diminished seventh is available (either in "root position" or "inversion" which produces the same effect in equal temperament, since every interval of the chord is a minor third) on every diatonic or chromatic degree of the scale. These three series of diminished seventh are, by the aid of enharmonic adjustment, common to all keys. The following examples will show the provenance of the diminished seventh on every step of the chromatic scale.

C major or minor

Dominant

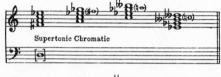

Supertonic Chromatic

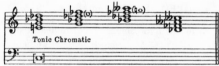

Tonic Chromatic

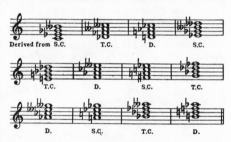

Another example will show how any diminished seventh may belong to any key (major or minor) by enharmonic change :

1. C (supertonic chromatic)   G (dominant)
   D (tonic chromatic)
2. Bb (dominant)   Eb (supertonic chromatic)
   F (tonic chromatic)
3. E (dominant)   A (supertonic chromatic)
   B (tonic chromatic)
4. C# (dominant)   F# (supertonic chromatic)
   G# (tonic chromatic)

AUGMENTED-FIFTH CHORDS

The substitution of an augmented fifth for the perfect fifth in the tonic, subdominant, dominant and supertonic chromatic chords of the major key (or, in the case of the minor key, tonic major, subdominant major, dominant and supertonic chromatic), gives, by use of inversions, all the augmented fifth chords on the pianoforte. Like diminished sevenths these are available on any degree of the chromatic scale, and each is common to every key, major or minor :

C major or minor

For the sake of completeness mention may be made of some rarer chromatic chords not included in the lists given above (inversions are not shown, but are available).

On the flattened second degree of the scale a chromatic minor triad is possible, in both major and minor modes. This very rare and remote chord may be found occasionally in the works of 19th-century composers, for example at the end of the slow movement of Schubert's C major Quintet :

C major or minor

Two chromatic chords, on the *mediant* and *flattened mediant* of the major key may be noticed :

C major

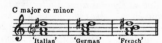

The first, a major triad with or without a seventh added, occurs sporadically in the classical and romantic periods ; the second, a major triad on the flattened mediant, is a very telling later usage.

The possibility of *augmented-sixth chords on the subdominant* must not be overlooked. They have been used by composers of the late 19th and early 20th centuries such as Grieg, Brahms and Elgar :

C major or minor

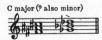

'Italian'   'German'   'French'

On the *sharpened fourth (or flattened fifth) degree* of the scale a major common chord is, very exceptionally, found. The best-known example occurs in the first bar of the slow movement of Dvořák's "New World" Symphony :

C major (? also minor)

On the *Dominant* three chromatic chords make occasional appearances as real chromatic harmony; they are (1) a minor triad (with the possible addition of a seventh) and (2) a diminished triad (and seventh) in the major key: in the minor key this diminished triad (3) is also found:

Though these chords are not part of the harmonic vocabulary of the classical period, they are used very effectively by Grieg, Dvořák and Debussy.

The flat submediant in both modes can sustain a minor triad. This very striking chromatic harmony belongs to the vocabulary of the 20th century rather than to the classical age:

On the flat seventh degree of both modes the possible chromatic chords are as follows:

(1) The major triad on the flat seventh of the major key is a chord of modal origin and tendency. In modern times it has been used with a seventh, major or minor, added.

(2) The minor triad with or without a minor seventh appears in works by composers such as Rimsky-Korsakov.

(3) In the minor key the minor triad on (*b*) VII possesses, like (1), a strongly modal character.

Two chords on the (raised) leading-note bring this brief survey to an end. These are a major triad and possible seventh in the major key, and a minor triad in the minor key.

The first of these is a most effective remote chromatic chord. Its use may be well seen in the slow movement of Dvořák's cello Concerto. The second, equally striking, is well illustrated in the last movement of the same composer's D minor Symphony.   H. K. A.

89 i **HARMONY**
Add to BIBL.:

JACOBS, ROBERT L., 'Harmony for the Listener: an Unconventional Textbook' (Oxford, 1958).
SCHENKER, HEINRICH, 'Harmony', ed. by Oswald Jonas, trans. by Elisabeth Mann Borgese (Chicago & Cambridge, 1954).
SCHOENBERG, ARNOLD, 'Structural Functions of Harmony' (London, 1954).

93 ii **HARP**
BIBL. Last line *should read*:

ZINGEL, HANS JOACHIM, 'Die Harfe als Symbol und allegorisches Attribut' ('Musikforschung', Vol. X, 1957, p. 39).
'Harfe und Harfenspiel' (Halle, 1932).

Add at end:

(*PLATE* 31, Vol. IV, p. 488; *PLATE* 32, Vol. IV, p. 492; *PLATE* 70, Vol. VIII, p. 146 (v), Nos. 1, 2 & 5; *PLATE* 71, Vol. VIII, p. 186, Nos. 1, 4 & 6.)

94 i **HARP LUTE**
Par. 2, l. 2. *PLATE* 67 *should read*:

PLATE 68

Par. 3, l. 2. *PLATE* 67 *should read*:

PLATE 68

Par. 5, l. 17. *PLATE* 69 *should read*:

PLATE 70

95 i *Add before* **HARPER, Thomas**:

HARPER, Heather (*b*. Belfast, 8 May 1930).

British soprano singer. She studied at the Trinity College of Music in London in 1949–1953 and took the F.T.C.L. for pianoforte. In Dec. 1954 she made her début as Lady Macbeth in the Oxford University Opera Club's production of Verdi's 'Macbeth'. She also sang with the English Opera Group at Glyndebourne and has appeared with the Welsh National Opera Company and the New Opera Company. Her appearances in opera on television are both visually and aurally very successful, and have shown her vocal versatility in equally admirable performances of dramatic and florid singing ('Traviata') and lyrical work (Mimi in 'Bohème'). Her stage performance as Belinda in Purcell's 'Dido and Aeneas' at Ingestre Hall in 1958 was outstanding for sensitivity, skill and style.

Heather Harper is equally many-sided and successful in concert work. Her song recitals show intelligence and refinement in choice and delivery. In oratorio, ranging from Bach to Honegger, she has made a striking impression, in Spain as well as in the British Isles, where she has appeared at several festivals. The voice is not very powerful, but wide-ranging, flexible and beautiful in quality, and it is always at the service of a keen musical understanding and feeling.   E. B.

HARPSICHORD
Par. 1, l. 5 *should read*:

cordio; Pol. *klawesyn*; Port. *cravo*).

102   ii   BIBL., l. 33. *Cancel heading* PERFORMANCE *and transfer 8 titles below it to* p. 110, BIBL. *for* **HARPSICHORD PLAYING.**

Add to BIBL.:

BOALCH, DONALD, 'Makers of the Harpsichord and Clavichord: 1440 to 1840' (London & Cardiff, 1956).

RUSSELL, RAYMOND, 'The Harpsichord since 1800' (Proc. Roy. Mus. Ass., Vol. LXXXII, 1955–56).

SCHULZE, RICHARD, 'How to Build a Baroque Harpsichord' (New York, 1954).

Add at end:

(*PLATE* 23, Vol. IV, Frontispiece; *PLATE* 39, Vol. IV, p. 736 (iii).)

110   ii   **HARPSICHORD PLAYING**
BIBL. *Transfer 8 titles under* PERFORMANCE *from* p. 102, col. ii.

Add to BIBL.:

HARICH-SCHNEIDER, ETA, 'The Harpsichord: an Introduction to Technique, Style and Historical Sources' (London, 1958).

111   i   *Add before* **HARRINGTON:**
HARRIET COHEN INTERNATIONAL AWARDS. *See* COHEN, HARRIET.

114   i   **HARRISON, May**
l. 2 *should read:*

India, ?; *d.* South Nutfield, Surrey, 8 June 1959), violinist. At the age of ten she won

115   i   **HARRISON, Arthur**
Par. 2, ll. 6–7 *should read:*

Downpatrick (1914), York (1916, 1931), Manchester (1916, 1934, 1956), Gloucester (1920), Oxford (1922, 1930),

Par. 3, l. 13 *should read:*

Aberdeenshire. This instrument was presented by the owner to the Temple Church, London, in 1954. Harrison's most ambitious work,

116   i   **HARRISON, Julius**
Par. 2, ll. 19–21 *should read:*

chorus and orchestra, begun in 1951, an even more broadly planned and impressive work, was produced at the Worcester Festival of 1957.

CATALOGUE
CHURCH MUSIC
Add at end:

Requiem Mass for 4 solo voices, chorus & orch.

ii   **HARRISON, Lou**
Par. 7. *Add at bottom:*

'Scene from William Morris' for flute, vn., viola, cello, harp & pf. (1955).

117   ii   **HARSÁNYI**
Par. 1, l. 2 *should read:*

June 1898; *d.* Paris, 19 Sept. 1954).

118   ii   BALLETS.
l. 6. 1945 *should read:*
1946.

122   ii   **HART HOUSE QUARTET**
ll. 17–20 *should read:*

viola, and Boris Hambourg, cello. In 1936 de Kresz decided to return to his

l. 26 *should read:*

was replaced by Adolf Koldolfsky. The Quartet was discontinued in 1946.

123   ii   **Harte**
l. 2. Weinberger *should read:*
Spelman

l. 3 *should read:*

casts of Pokerflat', opera). Weinberger (do.).

HARTEVELD
Par. 1, ll. 1–2 *should read:*

HARTEVELD, Wilhelm (*b.* Stockholm, 1862; *d.* Stockholm, 1927).

124   i   **HARTMAN**
Par. 2, l. 13 *should read:*

chestra. He conducted the Hamburg N.W.D.R. Orchestra and the Vienna Radio Orchestra in 1955 and was for two seasons assistant to Igor Markevich for the Summer Academy master classes at the Mozarteum of Salzburg.

HARTMANN (1)
ll. 22–24 *should read:*

høgen Mast", but this was an older tune by D. L. Rogert and merely

125   i   **HARTMANN, T. A.**
Par. 1, l. 2 *should read:*

(**de**) (*b.* Moscow, 21 Sept. 1886; *d.* Princeton, N.J., 26 Mar. 1956).

128   ii   **HASLINGER (2)**
ll. 16–21 *should read:*

cantata 'Der glorreiche Augenblick' (Op. 136), the Fugue for string quintet (Op. 137) and the 'Leonore' Overture No. 1 (Op. 138); Spohr's Symphonies 4

129   i   **HASPRES**
Par. 1, l. 12 *should read:*

Dufay. His extant work is published in Vol. II of 'Early Fifteenth-Century Music', edited by Gilbert Reaney (Amer. Inst. of Musicology, 1958).   E. D. (ii).

i   **HASSE**
Par. 2, ll. 24–25 *should read:*

the purpose of serious study. He repaired to Naples about 1724 and became a pupil of

129   i   Par. 2, ll. 29-30 *should read* :
In 1725 he received the

    ii   Par. 1, l. 14.   1730 five more
                should read :
1730 six more

131   i   CATALOGUE
          OPERAS
          l. 3 *should read* :
' Tigrane ' (Francesco Silvani), Naples, 4 Nov. 1729.

> *Transfer this title to stand after* ' Ulderica '
> *6 lines below.*

    ii   INTERMEZZI
          l. 2 *should read* :
e Balanzone '), Naples, 4 Nov. 1729 (with his ' Tigrane ').

> *Transfer this title (3 lines) to stand after* ' La
> fantesca ' *13 lines below.*

          l. 12.   (Andrea Belmuro) *should read* :
(Bernardo Saddumene)

          INCIDENTAL MUSIC
          l. 1.   Marchesi's *should read* :
Marchese's

132   ii   *See also.* l. 3 *should read* :
ode for).   Denkmäler (2), Vol. 20 (modern ed. of
Conversione di Sant' Agostino ').   Höpken (new
setting of ' Bevitore ' lib.).

134   i   HASSLER (2)
          See also. l. 2 *should read* :
Chorale.   Chorwerk, Vol. 14 (modern reprint of chro-
matic motet).   Denkmäler (2), Vol. 2 (modern ed. of
' Cantiones ') ;   Vol. 7 (modern ed. of Masses) ;   Second
Series, Vols. 4-5 & 11 (modern ed. of works).   Publi-
kationen G.M.F., Vol. 15 (modern ed. of ' Lustgarten').

135   i   HATTON, John
          Add at end :
BIBL.—CARR, J. ARTHUR, ' Hatton and Best of Liver-
    pool ' (' Liverpool Libraries, Museums and Arts
    Committee Bulletin ', Vol. I, No. 2, Oct. 1951).

          Add after **Hatton** :

HAUBENSTOCK-RAMATI, Roman (*b.*
Cracow, 27 Feb. 1919).
Polish composer. He went to school at
Cracow, studied musical theory and composition under Malawski and Koffler, and
musicology at the Universities of Cracow and
Lwów in 1937–40. In 1948–50 he was
Musical Director of Radio Cracow and editor
of the periodical ' Ruch Muzyczny '. From
1950 to 1957 he lived in Israel, where he was
the founder and first director of the Central
Library of Music and professor at the Israeli
Academy of Music. In 1957 he worked at
the Studio des Recherches de Musique Concrète in Paris, but on becoming music adviser
to Universal Edition he removed to Vienna,
where he now lives (1959).
After comparatively orthodox beginnings,
Haubenstock-Ramati affiliated himself artistically to the group of composers representing

the latest tendencies, including *musique concrète*, to which he contributed ' Amen de
verre ', ' Chanson populaire ', ' Passacaille '
and ' Exergue pour une symphonie ' (all
produced by Radio-Télévision Française,
1957). Works performed at I.S.C.M. Festivals have been ' Blessings ' for voice and 9
instruments (Donaueschingen, 1954), ' Pocket-
size Concerto ' (do., 1956), ' Recitativo ed
aria ' for harpsichord and orchestra (Zürich,
1957) and ' Symphonies de timbres ' (Darmstadt, 1957). Other works are ' Ricercari '
for string trio (1952), ' Chants et prismes '
(1958), ' Ständchen sur le nom de Heinrich
Strobel ' for orchestra (1958), ' Sequences '
for violin and orchestra (1958), ' Interpola-
tions ' for flute (1959) and ' La Chapelle ' for
orchestra (1959).   E. B.

135   i   HAUER
          Par. 1, l. 2 *should read* :
Neustadt, 19 Mar. 1883 ;   *d.* Vienna, 22 Sept.
1959).

136   ii   CHORAL WORKS
          l. 9.   — Cantata *should read* :
67. Cantata

137   ii   HAUK
          Par. 1, ll. 1-2 *should read* :
HAUK, Minnie (Mignon Hauck) (*b.* New
York, 16 Nov. 1851 ;   *d.* Triebschen, Lake of
Lucerne, 6 Feb.

140   ii   HAUSSMANN
          Par. 1 and Par. 2, l. 1 *should read* :
HAUSSMANN, Valentin (*b.* Nuremberg,
c. 1590 ;   *d.* ?).
German composer. He

141   i   HAVERGAL
          Par. 3, l. 13.   (published 1847).
          should read :
(published 18   ).

          l. 16.   In 1849 *should read* :
In 1847

142   i   *Add before* **Hawkesworth** :

HAWKES & SON. *See* LONDON, Vol. V,
p. 383, ii.

144   ii   HAY, E. N.
          Par. 1, l. 2 *should read* :
19 Apr. 1889 ;   *d.* Port Stewart, Londonderry,
10 Sept.

157   i   HAYDN
          Par. 1, l. 6 *should read* :
opportunity offered, is said to have usually
chosen one of

157 ii Par. 2, ll. 11-14 *should read*:

find Dragonetti and Brigitta Banti, whom the famous double-bass player had accompanied to London in 1794. That fine singer and good-natured artist struck up a lasting friendship, and it was for her that he composed

160 i Par. 3, l. 12. till 1806. *should read*: till 1804.

ii Par. 1, ll. 3-4. 1300 ducats *should read*:
500 florins

165 i BIBL. GRIESINGER, l. 2, *should read*:

Haydn' (Leipzig, 1810; modern ed. by Franz Grasberger, Vienna, 1954).

HOPKINSON & OLDMAN entry *should read*:

HOPKINSON, CECIL & OLDMAN, C. B., 'Haydn's Settings of Scottish Songs in the Collections of Napier and Whyte' and 'Thomson's Collection of National Song, with special reference to Haydn and Beethoven: Addenda and Corrigenda' ('Edinburgh Bibliographical Society Transactions', Vol. III, Part ii, Edinburgh, 1954).
Thomson's Col- . . . etc.

Add to BIBL. :

HOBOKEN, ANTHONY VAN, 'Joseph Haydn: Thematisch-bibliographisches Werkverzeichnis', Vol. I: Instrumental Works (Mainz & London, 1957).
LANDON, C. H. ROBBINS, 'The Original Versions of Haydn's First "Salomon" Symphonies' (M. Rev., XV, 1954, p. 1).
'The Symphonies of Joseph Haydn' (London, 1955).
LARSEN, 'Haydn', article in Sohlman's 'Musiklexikon', Vol. II (Stockholm, 1950).

166 — CATALOGUE OF WORKS
Add at end of note under heading:
For much of the information contained in this list the compiler is indebted to J. P. Larsen's article in Sohlman's 'Musiklexikon' (*see* Bibl.).

OPERAS
Col. 1, l. 3. Nespoli *should read*:
di Napoli

Col. 2, l. 14 *should read*:
'La Rencontre imprévue', based on Lesage.

167 — Col. 4, ll. 7-8. *Delete* Added to in 1805.

GERMAN PUPPET OPERAS
Delete l. 3.

INCIDENTAL MUSIC
Col. 4, ll. 11-14. *Delete sentence* Music reported . . . 1939 war.

CHURCH MUSIC: (a) MASSES.
Col. 7, l. 2. Lost. *should read*:
Hitherto regarded as lost, but discovered by H. C. Robbins Landon at the Monastery of Göttweig in 1957.

168 — Col. 4, ll. 18-19 *should read*:
'Missa Sti. Bernardi de

Col. 5, ll. 12-13 *should read*:
pets, drums, flute, 2 oboes, 2 clarinets, 2 bassoons, 2 horns, 2 vns.

Col. 5, l. 20. trumpet *should read*:
2 trumpets

Col. 5, ll. 27-28 *should read*:
trumpets, drums,

168 — Col. 5, ll. 33-34 *should read*:
oboes, 2 bassoons, 2 horns, 2 trumpets, drums &

Col. 7. *Delete ll.* 20-27.

(b) MISCELLANEOUS
Col. 3, l. 2 *should read*:
2 vns., 2 oboes, 2 trumpets, drums,

169 — Col. 3, l. 18 *should read*:
2 oboes, 2 trumpets, drums &

Col. 5, l. 1. An old copy *should read*:
The autograph

170 — CHORAL WORKS WITH ORCHESTRA
Col. 4, ll. 8-10 *should read*:
c. 1770.

171 — Col. 5, l. 25 *should read*:
as a *quartetto*.

Delete ll. 26-28.

SOLO CANTATAS, ARIAS, ETC.
Col. 2. *Delete l.* 8.

172 — Col. 6, l. 9 *should read*:
writing. Autograph MS score by Elssler at Göttweig.

ORCHESTRAL WORKS
(a) SYMPHONIES
Col. 3, l. 2 *should read*
2 oboes, 2 horns & stgs.

l. 26 *should read*:
2 oboes, 2 horns & stgs.

l. 27 *should read*:
2 oboes, 2 horns ad lib. & stgs.

l. 38. 2 flutes *should read*:
2 oboes

173 — Col. 3, l. 10 *should read*:
2 oboes, 2 horns, drums & stgs.

l. 15 *should read*:
2 oboes, 2 horns (or trumpets), drums & stgs.

l. 19 *should read*:
2 oboes, bassoon *obbligato*, 2 horns & stgs.

l. 23 *should read*:
2 oboes, 2 bassoons *obbligato*, 2 horns & stgs.

l. 33 *should read*:
2 oboes, 2 horns, 2 trumpets, drums & stgs.

35 *should read*:
2 oboes, bassoon *obbligato*, 2 horns & stgs.

l. 41 *should read*:
2 oboes, 2 bassoons *obbligato*, 2 horns

Col. 4, Symphony 60. 1775? *should read*:
1774.

Col. 5, Symphony 57. *Add remark*:
Autograph and early MSS lack trumpets and drums.

Col. 5, Symphony 63. *Add remark*:
One authentic version includes trumpets and drums.

174　—　Col. 3, l. 4 *should read*:
horns & stgs.

ll. 13-14 *should read*:
Flute, bassoon *obbligato*, 2 oboes, 4 horns, solo vn., solo cello & stgs.

l. 16 *should read*:
2 horns, 2 trumpets, drums & stgs.

Symphony 88, l. 2 *should read*:
2 horns, 2 trumpets, drums & stgs.

Symphony 90, l. 2 *should read*:
2 horns, 2 trumpets, drums & stgs.

Symphony 96, col. 2 *should read*:
D ma.[1]
Add footnote:
[1] Long known by the nickname of 'The Miracle', which however properly belongs to No. 102 (*see* MIRACLE).

175　—　Symphony 102, col. 2 *should read*:
B♭ ma., 'The Miracle'.[1]

Add footnote:
[1] This nickname was for long wrongly attached to No. 96 (*see* MIRACLE).

(*b*) OVERTURES
Col. 3, l. 20 *should read*:
2 horns, 2 trumpets, drums & stgs.

l. 21 *should read*:
2 oboes, 2 horns, 2 trumpets, drums & stgs.

176　—　Col. 5. *Delete remark.*

(*d*) MARCHES
Col. 4, l. 4. 1777 ? *should read*:
1777.
Col. 5, ll. 25-26 *should read*:
From 'Il mondo della luna' (1777). Autograph score in Berlin State Lib.

177　—　*Footnote should read*:
[1] Complete list in Breitkopf Catalogue of 1787, complete set of MSS at Zittau.

179　—　CONCERTOS
(*a*) CLAVIER OR ORGAN CONCERTOS
Col. 3, l. 1. 2 horns *should read*:
2 trumpets
Col. 5, ll. 7-8 *should read*:
logue, 1763, as for 2 oboes, 2 trumpets (*clarini*), 2 vns., viola & bass.

(*b*) MISCELLANEOUS
Col. 5, ll. 5-6. *Delete remark.*

180　—　Col. 1. *Add at end*:
Concerto for horn.

Col. 2. *Add at end*:
D ma.
Col. 4. *Add at end*:
c. 1770 (?).
Col. 5, l. 16. ? lost. *should read*:
Lost (only in Entwurf Catalogue).

ll. 17-20 *should read*:
Breitkopf Catalogue, 1781, authenticity not confirmed.

Last section, Col. 5 (*Date*):
Add after l. 3, *following* ? before 1765.:
Lost (only in Entwurf Catalogue).

181　—　CHAMBER MUSIC
(*a*) STRING QUARTETS
Col. 4, Quartets 63-68. *Delete* (1792 ?)

182　—　Col. 3, l. 1 *should read*:
Authenticity questioned; almost certainly not genuine.

Delete l. 2.

188　—　SONATAS FOR PIANOFORTE
Col. 3, l. 7 *should read*:
c. 1766.
l. 8 *should read*:
c. 1766.

191　—　VOCAL DUETS
Col. 5, l. 1. 1800. *should read*:
1796.
l. 2 *should read*:
? 1796.

Col. 6. *Transfer remark* The autograph . . . text, 1796. *to preceding work.*

206　ii　**HAYDN, M.**
Par. 1, l. 4 *should read*:
Empress Maria Theresa, consort of Francis II, hearing of his losses,

207　ii　**HAYDN ORCHESTRA**
Par. 1. *Add at end*:

The tenth anniversary was commemorated by a concert at the Royal Festival Hall, where already in 1951, at the Festival of Britain, a Haydn series was performed including most of the works played during Haydn's first visit to London 160 years earlier. About this time the orchestra began to make gramophone records, an activity in which it has since been notably successful. It also broadcasts regularly on the Third Programme and Home Service, and has appeared on television. By 1959 the orchestra had played at least half of Haydn's 104 symphonies, many of them for the first time in living memory.

Add at end:
See also Newstone.

208　i　**HAYDON**
Par. 3, ll. 17-18 *should read*:
been translated, and 'Introduction to Musicology' (1941). He translated Jeppesen's 'Counterpoint: the Polyphonic Vocal Style of the 16th Century' (1939). As a

HAYES (1)
Par. 1, l. 2. 1705 [1]; *should read*:
1707 [1]
Footnote should read:
[1] Baptized at the Church of St. John the Baptist, Gloucester, 26 Jan. 1708.

213　i　**HEARING**
Entry should read:
HEARING. *See* ACOUSTICS. DIPLACUSIS.

213 ii **Hebbel**
l. 3. song). *should read*:
2 songs).

l. 6 *should read*:
3 duets). Ettinger (' Judith ', opera). Holmboe (' Requiem '). Jirák (5 songs).

214 i **HEBREW MUSIC**
Signature P. G. (ii) *should read*:
P. G.

ii **HECKEL, J. A. and W.**
ll. 1-4 *should read*:
HECKEL, Johann Adam (*b*. Adorf [Vogtland], 14 July 1812; *d*. Biebrich, 13 Apr. 1877).
HECKEL, Wilhelm (*b*. Biebrich, 25 Jan. 1856; *d*. Biebrich, 13 Jan. 1909).

216 i **HECKELPHONE**
Add at end:
(*PLATE* 46, Vol. VI, p. 160, No. 10.)

217 i **HEDMONDT**
Par. 1, ll. 1-2. **Christian Emmanuel** *should read*:
Emmanuel Christian

Par. 2, l. 16 *should read*:
in Edinburgh, where for many years he was producer for the Edinburgh Opera Company and as a veteran sang in his own production of Stanford's ' Shamus O'Brien '.
E. B. & S. D.

219 ii **Heine**
l. 3 *should read*:
Beliczay (2 songs). Berg (Alban, song). Berners (' Lieder-Album '). Borodin

l. 5 *should read*:
(Frank, 3 songs). Bruckner (solo 4tet). Chevreuille (' Atta Troll ', chamber opera). Chopin (ac-

l. 7 *should read*:
Criticism, p. 524. Cui (' William Ratcliff ', opera). Dallapiccola (cantata ' An Mathilde ').

l. 22 *should read*:
(3 songs). Mendelssohn (5 partsongs, 7 songs, 3 duets). Meyerbeer (' C'est elle ', song).

220 i l. 6. p. 602 *should read*:
p. 604

l. 14 *should read*:
Vesque von Püttlingen (146 songs). Wagner (R., ' Fliegende Holländer ', opera; ' Deux

Add at end:
BIBL.—BECKER, HEINZ, ' Der Fall Heine-Meyerbeer: neue Dokumente revidieren ein Geschichtsurteil ' (Berlin, 1958).

223 i *Add after* **HEISE**:
HEISS, Hermann (*b*. Darmstadt, 29 Dec. 1897).
German composer. Self-taught in music as a child, he began to write down his improvisations at the age of thirteen and, after service in the first world war, he studied briefly under Sekles and others. By 1923 he had decided to turn to twelve-note composition, and he collaborated with Hauer in the book ' Die Zwölftontechnik ' (1926). In 1932 he attended Schoenberg's master course in Berlin, but he developed a system of his own going beyond those of both Schoenberg and Hauer, which he calls *peritonale Tonbewegungslehre*. Heiss taught music for five years at a free school, but in 1933 was forced by the Hitler rule to retire owing to his " undesirable " tendencies. From 1946 he has taught at the International Holiday Courses at Darmstadt-Kranichstein and as a visiting professor at various German music schools and universities. In 1953 he was given a master class for composition at the Darmstadt Academy of Music and in 1955 a studio for electronic music at Kranichstein.

All but a few of the works written by Heiss before and during the second world war suffered destruction at that period : those that survived are a Chaconne for pianoforte (1932), 2 Concertini for 2 violins and strings (1942), a pianoforte Concerto (1944) and some chamber music. Later works include an opera, 3 ballets, a cantata ' Winternacht ' (1952), ' Sinfonia atematica ' (1950) and ' Sinfonia giocosa ' for orchestra, ' Konfigurationen ' for orchestra (after Paul Klee), ' Duo-Konzert ' for violin, pianoforte and orchestra (1948), Concerto for flute and chamber orchestra (1953–54) a string Trio (1953), pianoforte and organ works, electronic music, and songs, including ' Expression K ' to words by Franz Kafka.
E. B.

224 i **HEKKING (5)**
l. 2. 1879), *should read*:
1879; *d*. Paris, 5 June 1942),

ii **HELDER**
Dates *should read*:
(*b*. Gotha, 1585; *d*. Remstedt nr. Gotha, 28 Oct. 1635).

Par. 2, l. 1 *should read*:
German composer. He

226 ii **HELLENDAAL**
Add at end:
See also Vereniging, Vol. 41 (reprint of 4 cello sonatas).

226 ii **HELLER, Stephen**
Par. 1, l. 2 *should read*:
May ? 1813 or 1814 [4]; *d.* Paris, 14 Jan. 1888).

Add footnote:
[4] In a letter to Schumann dated 15 May 1836 Heller says this is his twenty-third birthday. But in his memoirs (S.I.M., Oct. 1911) he complains: " Les malheureux artistes, ci-devant enfants prodiges, ne savent jamais au juste leur âge. L'affiche de concert est leur extrait baptistaire . . . . Voici un acte officiel rédigé par mon père : ' Aujour d'hui, lundi, le 13 décembre 1829 . . . le jeune pianiste Stephen, âgé de 11 ans ' (j'en avais 13) ". Thus, if his father was right, the year of his birth would have been 1818, and if he was wrong, 1816.

Par. 2, l. 19 *should read*:
too expensive, and Anton Halm, who had been a successful pianist and teacher in Vienna since 1815, was

230 i **Hellman**
l. 1. ' Little Foxes ' *should read*:
' Regina '

232 i **HELMONT**
Add at end:
See also Monumenta Mus. Belg., Vol. 6 (modern ed of keyboard music).

236 ii **HEMING, Percy**
Par. 1, l. 2 *should read*:
1887 ; *d.* London, 11 Jan. 1956).

237 ii **HEMPEL**
Par. 1, l. 2 *should read*:
1885 ; *d.* Berlin, 7 Oct. 1955).

238 i l. 18. *leggiero should read*:
leggero

239 i **HEMSI**
Par. 1, l. 2 *should read*:
Turkey, 23 Dec. 1896).

Par. 2, l. 12. ' Coplas Sefaradies '
should read:
' Coplas Sefardies '

240 ii **HENNEBERG, C. F.**
Name *should read*:
HENNERBERG

Transfer article to p. 241, *to stand before* **HENNIUS**

Par. 2, l. 9. Henneberg *should read*:
Hennerberg

Par. 3, l. 5. ' Brevsammlinger *should read*:
' Brevsammlingar

241 i l. 1. Henneberg *should read*:
Hennerberg

243 ii **HENSEL, Heinrich**
Par. 1, l. 2. 1878 *should read*:
1874

244 i **HENSELT**
Par. 1, l. 2. 12 May *should read*:
9 May

245 ii **HENZE**
Par. 1, l. 3 *should read*:
logical level. A ballet ' Ondine ' commissioned by the Royal Ballet, was produced in London, at Covent Garden, on 27 Oct. 1958.

List of Works
l. 4. Provost's *should read*:
Prévost's

Add after l. 5 :
' König Hirsch ', opera (libretto by Heinz von Cramer, on Gozzi's play ' Il re cervo '), prod. Berlin 23 Sept. 1956.

Add after ' Rosa Silber ' (l. 9) :
' Maratona di danza ', ballet, prod. Berlin, 24 Sept. 1957.

Insert after l. 9 :
' Ondine ', ballet after La Motte Fouqué (1956), prod. London, Covent Garden Theatre, 27 Oct. 1958.

Add after Pf. Concerto :
' Ode an den Westwind ' (after Shelley) for cello & orch. (1953).

246 i **HER FOSTER-DAUGHTER**
l. 9 *should read*:
1924, 1st in Britain, London, Covent Garden Theatre (in English), 10 Dec. 1956.

247 ii **HERBECK**
Par. 3, l. 1 *should read*:
It was Herbeck who in 1865 brought to light a mass of Schubert manuscripts that included the hitherto unknown B minor Symphony. He possessed several orders, including

HERBERIGS
Par. 2, l. 4 *should read*:
comic opera, ' Le Mariage de Rosine ' (after Beaumarchais), was

List of Works
Add after l. 7 :
' Antoine et Cléopâtre ', symph. poem after Shakespeare (1949).
' De Vrolijke Vrouwtjes van Windsor ', symph. poem after Shakespeare (1950).

l. 8 *should read*:
2 Suites for brass insts. (1946).

l. 9 *should read*:
2 Pf. Concertos (1933 & 1953).

Herbert, (Sir) Alan (Patrick)
l. 4. (F., ' Red Pen ', lib.). *should read*:
(G., ' Red Pen ', lib.).

248   i   **HERBERT, Victor**
Par. 2, l. 13.   Wizard of the Mill '
should read :
Wizard of the Nile '

249   i   **HERBST**
Add at end :
See also Denkmäler (5) II (modern ed. of vocal concertos).

HERING
Par. 1, l. 2.   1766 *should read* :
1765
ii   l. 7 *should read* :

various instruments. The 'Grossvater-Tanz' quoted by Schumann in 'Papillons' and 'Carnaval' is by him, a fact that has been forgotten. The dance was so frequently used as the final *Kehraus* at balls in Germany and Austria during the 19th century without any mention of the composer's name that it has long been accepted as a traditional tune of unknown provenance.
         E. V. D. S., adds.

ii   **HERMANNUS CONTRACTUS**
Par. 2, ll. 3-6 *should read* :

Vehringen. In 1020 he became a pupil at the monastery of Reichenau², which played an important part in the evolution of music, and later he became a Benedictine monk there. His surname is not

ll. 10-11 *should read* :

lived. His chronicle from the birth of Christ to 1054 contains important musico-

Add footnote :
² Not St. Gall, as asserted by Trithemius and repeated by many authorities after him.

250   ii   **HERNRIED**
Par. 1, l. 2 *should read* :
1883 ; *d.* Detroit, 3 Sept. 1951).

252   ii   **HÉROLD**
Par. 4, l. 2.   'Le' *should read* :
' La '

254   i   BIBL. l. 3.   'F. Hérold' *should read* :
' F. [the son Ferdinand] Hérold ' (Paris, 1882).

256   i   **HERMANN, Hugo**
CATALOGUE, Op. 76 *should read* :
76. Concerto for harpsichord & chamber orch.

257   i   **HERTEL, J. W.**
Add at end :
BIBL.—HERTEL, JOHANN WILHELM, 'Autobiographie', ed. by Erich Schenk ('Wiener musikwissenschaftliche Beiträge', Vol. 3) (Graz, Vienna & Cologne, 1957).

257   ii   **HERTZ, Michał**
Par. 1, l. 1.   (*b.* ?, 1844 ; *should read* :
(*b.* Warsaw, 28 Sept. 1844 ;

259   ii   **Herwegh**
Add to l. 2 :
Wagner, pp. 103 & 105.

261   i   **HERZOG, J. G.**
Par. 1, ll. 2-3.   Dates *should read* :
(*b.* Hummendorf nr. Kronach, 5 Aug. 1822 ; *d.* Munich, 3 Feb. 1909).

ii   **HESDIN**
Add at end :
See also Maîtres Musiciens, Vol. 5 (modern ed. of chansons).

264   ii   **HESSENBERG**, CATALOGUE ORCHESTRAL WORKS
Add after l. 5 :
' Intrada und Variationen über ein Thema von Jakob Regnart ' (1956).

265   ii   **HEUCKEROTH**
Par. 1, l. 2 *should read* :
rinus (*b.* Amsterdam, 17 Apr. 1853 ; *d.* Amsterdam, 19 Mar. 1936).

267   ii   **HEWITT**
Par. 1, l. 35.   Odhecton *should read* :
Odhecaton

269   ii   **HEXACHORD**
See also should read :
See also Accidentals. Gamut. Notation (p. 113). Solmization,

270   i   **HEYDEN (1)**
l. 1 *should read* :
(1) Sebald Heyden (*b.* Bruck nr. Erlangen, 8 Dec. 1499 ;

l. 3 *should read* :
at the Spitalschule of Nuremberg in 1519

ii   BIBL., l. 1.   KOSAL *should read* :
KOSEL

HEYDINGHAM
Delete entire entry.

276   i   **HIDALGO**
Add at end :
See also Publicacions Catalunya, Vol. 11 (modern ed. of ' Celos . . .').

277   ii   **HILL, Alfred**
Par. 2, l. 11 *should read* :
at the Sydney Conservatory. In 1947 he became president of the Composers' Society of Australia. He was also

277   ii   **HILL & SON**
      Par. 1, ll. 6-7, Par. 2, l. 3 and Par.
      3, l. 1.   Elliott *should read*:

Elliot

284   ii   **HILSBERG, A.**
      Par. 2, l. 18 *should read*:

a series of its summer concerts. He is now
(1956) conductor of the New Orleans Symphony Orchestra.

      HILSBERG, I.
      Par. 1, l. 2.   1907 *should read*:
1894

285   i   **HILTON, John (ii)**
      Par. 1, l. 2 *should read*:

d. London, [prob. 21] Mar. 1657).

288   i   **HINDEMITH**
      Par. 3, l. 17 *should read*:

characteristic.

Add new paragraph after this:

After the 1939-45 war Hindemith, who
was then in the U.S.A., refused the invitation
to become director of the Berlin High School
for Music, but he soon afterwards went to
live in Europe again.   E. E., adds.

289   i   *Add to* BIBL. :

BRINER, ANDREAS, 'Eine Bekenntnisoper Paul Hindemiths ["Die Harmonie der Welt"]' (Schw. M.Z., Jan. & Feb. 1959).
CAZDEN, NORMAN, 'Hindemith and Nature' (M. Rev., XV, 1954, p. 288).
HYMANSON, WILLIAM, 'Hindemith's Variations' (M. Rev., XIII, 1952, p. 14).
'Paul Hindemith: Zeugnis in Bildern', introduced by Heinrich Strobel (Mainz, 1955).
STEPHAN, RUDOLF, 'Hindemith's "Marienlieder"' (M. Rev., Vol. XV, 1954, p. 275).
WESTPHAL, ELISABETH, 'Paul Hindemith: eine Bibliographie . . . seit 1922 . . .' (Cologne, 1957).

—   CATALOGUE
      OPERAS
      Col. 4, l. 7 *should read*:

sion, Zürich, 20 June 1952.

                    l. 8.   17 July *should read*:
15 July

      Add at end:

| — | | 'Harmonie der Welt', 5 acts. | Composer, inspired by Johann Kepler's speculations. | Munich, 11 Aug. 1957. |

      ii   BALLETS
      l. 2 *should read*:

Krell) (1923).

      CHORAL WORKS WITH ORCHESTRA
      Entries should read:

—   'Das Unaufhörliche', oratorio for solo voices, chorus, boys' chorus & orch. (Gottfried Benn) (1931).
—   'When Lilacs Last in the Dooryard Bloomed', an American Requiem (Walt Whitman) for solo voices, chorus & orch. (1946).

—   'Apparebit repentina dies', for chorus & brass (1947).
—   'Cantique de l'espérance' (Claudel), for mezzo-soprano, chorus & 2 orchs. (1952).

289   ii   CHORAL WORKS WITH PIANO-FORTE
      l. 3 *should read*:

mixed chorus (1940).

      UNACCOMPANIED CHORAL WORKS
      Add under heading:

33. 6 Songs on Old Texts for mixed voices (1923)
      1. Vom Hausregiment.
      2. Frauenklage.
      3. Art lässt nicht von Art.
      4. Der Liebe Schrein.
      5. Heimliches Glück.
      6. Landsknechtstrinklied.
43. No. 2. 'Lieder für Singkreise' (1927).

290   i   *Add at top of column*:

—   3 Choruses for men's voices (1939)
      1. Das verfluchte Geld (traditional).
      2. Nun, da der Tag (Nietzsche).
      3. Die Stiefmutter (traditional).
—   6 Chansons for mixed voices (Rainer Maria Rilke) (1939)
      1. La Biche.
      2. Un Cygne.
      3. Puisque tout passe.
      4. Printemps.
      5. En hiver.
      6. Verger.
—   'Der Tod' (Hölderlin) (1939).
—   'Erster Schnee' (Gottfried Keller) (1939).
—   Variations on an Old Dance Song (1939).
—   'The Demon of the Gibbet' (FitzJames O'Brien) (1949).

      ORCHESTRAL WORKS
      l. 4.   (1927). *should read*:
(1926).

      l. 20.   (1931). *should read*:
(1930).

      l. 24.   (1941). *should read*:
(1940).

      l. 25.   (1944). *should read*:
(1943).

      Add after this:

—   Symphonic Metamorphoses on a Theme by Weber (1943).
—   'Hérodiade' (based on a poem by Stéphane Mallarmé) for chamber orch. (1944).
—   'Sinfonia serena' (1946).
—   'Sinfonietta', E ma. (1950).
—   Symphony 'Harmonie der Welt' (1951).

      MILITARY BAND
—   Symphony, B♭ ma. (1951).

      SOLO INSTRUMENTS
      l. 8.   (1930). *should read*:
(1928).

      l. 11.   (1931). *should read*:
(1930).

      l. 18.   (1946). *should read*:
(1945).

      Add at end of this section:

—   Clar. Concerto (1947).
—   Concerto for trumpet, bassoon & orch. (1949).
—   Concerto for woodwind, harp & orch. (1949).
—   Horn Concerto (1949).

      CHAMBER MUSIC
      l. 9.   (1924). *should read*:
(1923).

290   ii   CHAMBER MUSIC
           l. 1. (1924). *should read*:
(1923).
           Add after Op. 47 :
— 2 Canonic Duets for vns. (1929).

           l. 19. (1934). *should read*:
(1936).
           l. 21. (1944). *should read*:
(1946).
           Add at end of this section :
— Septet for wind insts. (1948).
— Sonata for 4 horns (1952).

           UNACCOMPANIED VIOLIN
           Delete — Sonata, E ma. (1935).

           VIOLIN AND PIANOFORTE
           Cancel 3 lines and replace by :
11. No. 1. Sonata, E♭ ma. (1918).
    No. 2. Sonata, D ma. (1918).
— Sonata, C ma. (1928).
— Sonata, E ma. (1935).

           UNACCOMPANIED VIOLA
           l. 1. (1923). *should read*:
(1919).
           l. 2. (1923). *should read*:
(1922).

           VIOLA AND PIANOFORTE
           l. 1. (1922). *should read*:
(1919).
           l. 2. (1929). *should read*:
(1923).

           VIOLONCELLO AND PIANOFORTE
           Cancel 3 lines and replace by :
8. 3 Pieces (1917).
11. No. 3. Sonata, A mi. (1919).
— 3 Easy Pieces (1938).
— Sonata (1948).

           DOUBLE BASS AND PIANOFORTE
— Sonata (1949).

           WIND INSTRUMENTS AND PIANO-
           FORTE
           ll. 1-9. Dates *should read*:
(1936). (1938). (1938). (1939); (1939). (1939). (1941).
(1941). (1942).

291   i   PIANOFORTE SOLO
           l. 3. (1928). *should read*:
(1922).
           l. 11. (1930). *should read*:
(1929).
           l. 13. (1943). *should read*:
(1942).

           HARP MUSIC
           (1940). *should read*:
(1939).

           SONGS FOR VOICE AND PIANO-
           FORTE
           l. 18. (1924). *should read*:
(1922-23).
           Add after this :
— 3 Motets for soprano (1941-44)
    1. Cum natus esset.
    2. Nuptiae factae sunt.
    3. Pastores loquebantur.

           l. 19. (1944). *should read*:
(1942-44).
           l. 31. (1945). *should read*:
(1942).
           Add at end, before See also :
           LITERARY WORKS
' Unterweisung im Tonsatz '
    Part i : ' Theoretischer Teil ' (1937).
    Part ii : ' Übungsbuch für den zweistimmigen Satz '
           (1939).
' A Concentrated Course in Traditional Harmony '
    (1943).

' Elementary Training for Musicians ' (1946).
' Harmonieübungen für Fortgeschrittene ' (1949).
' A Composer's World : Horizons and Limitations '
    (1952).
' Johann Sebastian Bach : ein verpflichtendes Erbe '
    (1952).

291   ii   **HINGSTON**
           Par. 2, l. 3 *should read* :

the musicians to Charles I. His name occurs
in a list of members of the choir of York
Minster dated 24 July 1618.[4] Afterwards he

           Add footnote :
    [4] Included in a part-book still at York (*see* Fellowes,
' Tudor Church Music ', App. p. 12).

292   i   **HINNER**
           Par. 2, l. 4.   1755 *should read* :
1775

293   i   **HIPKINS**
           Par. 3, l. 4 *should read* :
Rare, and Unique ' (1888)[1], with a beautiful

           Footnote 1. Smaller edition *should read* :
Enlarged edition

295   ii   **HIRZEL-LANGENHAN**
           Par. 2, l. 8. Scholl Berg *should read* :
Schloss Berg

           HISLOP
           Par. 1, l. 2.   1887). *should read* :
1884).

299   ii   **HISTORIES**
           Add after L. Bourgnès :
J. Reiss, ' Historya muzyki ' (Warsaw, 1921).

           l. 42 *should read* :
2 vols. (1929-30) ; rev., 3 vols. (1933-37).

300   i   *Add after* T. M. Finney (l. 31) :
Della Corte, A. & Pannain, G., ' Storia della
    musica ', 3 vols. (1935, 2nd ed. 1942).

           l. 33 *should read* :
H. Leichtentritt, ' Music, History and Ideas '

           l. 39 *should read* :
Fr. Abbiati, ' Storia della musica ', 5 vols.
    (1939-46).

           Add at end of section :
Westrup, J. A. (ed.) ' New Oxford History of
    Music ' (1954–   ).

304   i   *Add before* (vi) *Spain* :
           (vi) *Poland*
F. Bylicki, ' Die Musik der Polen ' (Vienna,
    1892).
J. M. Chomiński & Z. Lissa (eds.), ' Historia
    muzyki powszechnej ' (Vol. I) (Cracow,
    1956).

M. Gliński (ed.), 'Muzka polska', a monograph (Warsaw, 1927).
Z. Jachimecki, 'Historya muzyki polskiej' (Cracow, 1920).
'Muzyka polska w rozwoju historycznym', 2 vols. (Cracow, 1949–51).
M. Karasowski, 'Rys historyczny opery polskiej' (Warsaw, 1859).
K. Michałowski, 'Opery polskie' (Cracow, 1954).
H. Opieński, 'La Musique polonaise' (Paris, 1918).
A. Poliński, 'Historya muzyki polskiej' (Lwów, 1907).
J. Prosnak, 'Kultura muzyczna Warszawy XVIII w.' (Cracow, 1956).
J. Reiss, 'Najpiękniejsza ze wszystkich jest muzyka polska' (Cracow, 1946).
T. Strumiłło, 'Szkice z polskiego życia muzycznego XIX w.' (Cracow, 1954).
'Zródła i początki romantyzmu w muzyce polskiej' (Cracow, 1956).
J. Sulikowski, 'Polish Music', a pamphlet, (London, 1944).
Z. M. Szweykowski, 'Kultura muzyczna XVI-wiecznej Polski' (Cracow, 1957).

304 ii (vi) *Spain should read*:
(vii) *Spain*

306 ii *Add at end*:
BIBL.—WESTRUP, J. A., 'An Introduction to Musical History' (London, 1955).

308 ii **HOBOKEN**
Add at end, before signature:
In 1957 appeared the first of two volumes of the great work of van Hoboken's life, the catalogue of all the extant or known works by Haydn. It contains the instrumental works and is to be followed by a second volume devoted to the vocal music and containing various appendices. This is a book comparable in value only to Köchel's Mozart catalogue. Its full title is 'Joseph Haydn: Thematisch-bibliographisches Werkverzeichnis'.

309 ii **HOCKET**
Par. 1, l. 1. (*d.* 1374) *should read*:
(*d.* 1377)

310 i *Add before* **HODEMONT**:
HODDINOTT, Alun (*b.* Bargoed, Glamorgan, 11 Aug. 1929).
Welsh composer and musical scholar. He attended Gomerton Grammar School in 1941–46 and the University College of South Wales in 1946–51, taking the B. Mus. degree there. In 1951 he was appointed lecturer in music at the Cardiff College of Music and Drama. As a composer he studied with the Glamorgan Scholarship, which he held during

the whole of his period at the University College, and in 1953 he obtained the Walford Davies Prize for composition. In 1956 the B.B.C. commissioned a Septet from Hoddinott for the tenth anniversary of the Third Programme. This is his Op. 10 and is scored for clarinet, horn, bassoon, violin, viola, cello and pianoforte. His earlier compositions are the following:
Op.
1. String Trio (1949).
2. 2 Songs for bass (1950).
3. Clarinet Concerto (1950).
4. *a.* 'Lullaby' for voice & pf. (1950).
   b. 'Fugal Overture' for orch. (1952).
5. 'Nocturne' for orch. (1952).
6. Quartet for clar., vn., viola & cello (1953–54).
7. Symphony (1954–55).
8. Oboe Concerto (1955).
9. 'Nocturne' for pf. (1956).   E. B.

313 i **HOFFMAN, Jan**
Par. 2, ll. 12-13 *should read*:
of Music at Cracow. In 1949 and 1955 he was a member of the jury of the 4th and 5th Chopin International

314 ii **HOFFMANN, E. T. A.**
Add to BIBL.:
EHINGER, HANS, 'E. T. A. Hoffmann als Musiker und Musikschriftsteller' (Olten & Cologne, 1954).
PIANA, THEO, 'E. T. A. Hoffmann: ein Lebensbild' (Berlin, 1953).

316 i **HOFFMEISTER, F. A.**
Add at end:
See also Sondheimer Ed., Vol. 33 (modern ed. of Symphony).

ii **HOFHAIMER**
Par. 4, ll. 8-9 *should read*:
unsurpassed. A number of his organ compositions are preserved. In a manuscript of

317 i *Add to* BIBL.:
WESSELY, OTHMAR, 'Neue Hofhaimeriana' (Vienna, 1955).

318 i **HOFMANN**
Par. 1, l. 2 *should read*:
Kazimierz) (*b.* Cracow, 20 Jan. 1876; *d.* Los Angeles, 16 Feb. 1957).

ii **Hofmannsthal**
Par. 2, l. 3. *Add before* Elektra:
Berg (Alban, 2 songs).

Add to BIBL.:
HAMMELMAN, H. A., 'Hugo von Hofmannsthal' (New Haven, Conn., 1957).

320 i **HOLBROOKE**
Par. 1, l. 2 *should read*:
Croydon, Surrey, 5 July 1878; *d.* London, 5 Aug. 1958).

322   i   **HOLDER, William**
Par. 2, l. 13.   1731 *should read*:
1701

ii   **Hölderlin**
l. 1 *should read*:
60 pf. pieces, 6 sets of songs).   Hindemith (chorus).
Kornauth (choruses).

l. 3 *should read*:
('Antigonae' & 'Oedipus', operas).   Pfitzner (song).
Redlich (trilogy

Add at end;
BIBL.—'Hölderlin-Jahrbuch, 1953' (Tübingen, 1953),
incl. 3 articles on musical settings.
KELLETAT, ALFRED, 'Bibliographie der Vertonungen
Hölderlins' (Stuttgart, 1953).

325   i   **HOLLANDER, C. J.**
Add at end:
See also Chorwerk, Vol. 30 (modern reprint of motet).
Collectio O.M.B., Vols. 1, 4–6, 9 (modern ed.).

HOLLÄNDER, Victor
Par. 1, l. 3.   24 Dec. *should read*:
24 Oct.

ii   **HÖLLER**
Par. 2, l. 17 *should read*:
position at the Munich High School, of which
he was elected president in 1954.

326   i   ORCHESTRAL WORKS
Add after l. 7:
— Fugue for stgs. (1948).

l. 8 *should read*:
40. Symphony, C♯ mi. (1950).

327   ii   **HOLMBOE,** CATALOGUE OF
WORKS
Replace as follows:

Op.   OPERAS
23. 'Fanden og Borgmesteren' ('The Devil and the
Mayor') (lib. by Walther Kolbenhoff) (1940).
42. 'Lave og Jon' (lib. by Lis Torbjørnsen) (1946).

BALLET
32. 'Den galsindede Tyrk' ('The Ill-tempered Turk')
(scen. by Aksel Salto) (1943).

CHORAL WORKS
— 'Requiem' (Friedrich Hebbel) for boys' voices &
chamber orch. (1931).
13. Psalm LXII for boys' voices (1937).
29. Symphony No. 4 ('Sinfonia sacra') for chorus &
orch. (1941).
54. 5 Latin Songs for unaccomp. chorus (1952).
59. 3 Latin Songs for unaccomp. chorus (1952).
60. 2 Latin Songs for unaccomp. chorus (1953).
61. 4 Latin Songs for unaccomp. chorus (1953).
Also occasional cantatas and partsongs.

ORCHESTRAL WORKS
— Concerto for chamber orch. (1931).
— 'Divertimento' No. 2 for stgs. (1933).
1. Suite No. 1 for chamber orch. (1935).
4. Symphony No. 1 for chamber orch. (1935).
6. Suite No. 2 for chamber orch. (1936).
11. Suite No. 3 for chamber orch. (1936).
15. Symphony No. 2 (1938).
25. Symphony No. 3 ('Sinfonia rustica') (1941).
28. Symph. Overture (1941).
35. Symphony No. 5 (1944).

38. 'Sinfonia concertante' (Chamber Concerto No. 8)
for chamber orch. (1945).
40. Chamber Concerto No. 10 for woodwind, brass &
perc. (1946).
43. Symphony No. 6 (1947).
50. Symphony No. 7 (1950).
53. Chamber Symphony (1951).
56. Symphony No. 8 (1951–52).

SOLO INSTRUMENTS AND
CHAMBER ORCHESTRA
— 'Divertimento' No. 1 for flute, oboe, clar. & stgs.
(1931).
5. 'Rhapsody' for flute (1935).
14. Concerto for vn. (1938).
17. Chamber Concerto No. 1 for pf., stgs. & timp. (1939).
20. Chamber Concerto No. 2 for flute, vn., celesta,
stgs. & perc. (1940).
21. Chamber Concerto No. 3 for clar., 2 horns, 2
trumpets & stgs. (1940).
22. 'Concertino' for vn., viola & stgs. (1940).
24. 'Concertino' for vn. & stgs. (1940).
30. Chamber Concerto No. 4 for vn., cello & pf. (1942).
31. Chamber Concerto No. 5 for viola. (1943).
33. Chamber Concerto No. 6 for vn. (1943).
37. Chamber Concerto No. 7 for oboe (1944).
39. Chamber Concerto No. 9 for vn. & viola. (1946).
44. Chamber Concerto No. 11 for 2 horns, trumpet &
stgs. (1948).
52. Chamber Concerto No. 12 for trombone (1950).

SOLO VOICES AND ORCHESTRA
62. 'Traet' for 4 voices & chamber orch. (1953).

CHAMBER MUSIC
3. 'Serenade' for flute, clar., vn., viola & cello (1936).
8. 'Rhapsodic Interlude' for vn., clar. & pf. (1938).
9. Quartet for flute, vn., cello & pf. (1936).
10. Quintet for flute, oboe, clar., vn. & viola (1936).
18. 'Serenade' for flute, vn., cello & pf. (1940).
19. 'Notturno' for flute, oboe, clar., horn & bassoon
(1940).
26. String Quartet No. 1 (1941).
46. String Quartet No. 2 (1949).
47. String Quartet No. 3 (1949).
48. String Quartet No. 4 (1949).
51. 'Isometric' for 2 vns. & pf. (1950).
55. 'Primavera' for flute, vn., cello & pf. (1951).
63. String Quartet No. 5 (1953–54).
64. Trio for vn., cello & pf. (1954).

VIOLIN AND PIANOFORTE
2. Sonata No. 1 (1935).
16. Sonata No. 2 (1939).
Also pianoforte works and songs.

331   i   **HOLST**
Par. 2, l. 11 *should read*:
James Allen's Girls' School, Dulwich, where
he continued to teach until 1920, and the

333   ii   *Add to* BIBL.:
CANTRICK, ROBERT, '"Hammersmith" and the Two
Worlds of Gustav Holst' (M. & L., XXXVII, July
1956, p. 211).

338   —   List of Works
Col. 3, l. 1.   rans. *should read*:
trans.

339   i   **HOLTER**
Par. 1, l. 1.   Gansdal, *should read*:
Gausdal,

l. 2.   25 Jan. *should read*:
27 Jan.

339   i   Par. 2, l. 4 *should read*:

Christiania.   His works include an opera, 'Donna Julia ', a Symphony in F major, an orchestral

l. 6 *should read*:

choral music.   He was chairman of the Norwegian Music Association for a quarter of a century.

Hölty
l. 2 *should read*:

Bach (C. P. E., 2 songs).   Beethoven (song).   Brahms (5 songs, 1 duet).   Cornelius

ii   **HOLZ**
Par. 2, ll. 12-15 *should read*:

Beethoven.[2]   On the other hand it would be unjust to suggest that drink was not his only failing, merely on the strength of another letter of Beethoven's [3], in which describes him as a " Monsieur terrible amoureux " : Holz was about to be married in the autumn of 1826.

340   ii   **HOLZBAUER**
Add at end:

See also Denkmäler (2), Vols. 8–9 (modern ed. of ' Günther ').

341   ii   **Homer**
l. 12 *should read*:

(' Vaart van Ulysses ', cantata.   Margaritis (epic symphony ' Ulysses and Nausicaa ').   Michaelides (' Ulysses ',

342   i   **HOMILIUS**
Par. 1, l. 2.   *d.* Leipzig, *should read*:

d. Dresden,

344   i   **HONEGGER**
Par. 1, l. 2 *should read*:

Mar. 1892 : *d.* Paris, 27 Nov. 1955).

345   ii   Par. 1, l. 12 *should read*:

same name.   He married the pianist and composer Andrée

BIBL., l. 14.   (Zürich, 1933). *should read*:
(Zürich, 1954).

Add to BIBL. :

GAUTHIER, ANDRÉ, ' Arthur Honegger ' Lyons, 1957).
LANDOWSKI, MARCEL, ' Honegger ' (' Solfége ' series) (Paris, 1957).
MATTER, JEAN, ' Honegger, ou La Quête de joie ' (Lausanne & Paris, 1956).
REICH, WILLI, (ed.), ' Arthur Honegger : Nachklang : Schriften, Photos, Dokumente ' (Zürich, 1957).

—   CATALOGUE
OPERAS
Col. 4, l. 14 *should read*:

Parisiens, 20 Feb. 1938.

345   —   BALLETS
Col. 1, ll. 15-16 *should read*:

pnin & Harsányi), also known as ' L'Homme à la peau de léopard '.

347   i   SONGS
l. 21.   Souvenir *should read*:
Souvenirs

HONEGGER, Henri
Par. 1, l. 1.   Geneva, 1904). *should read*:

Geneva, 10 June 1904).

355   i   **Hopkins**
l. 2.   *Add before* Maconchy :

Kirchner (L., song).

ii   *Add before* **Hoppenot** :
HOPPELTANZ. *See* SALTARELLO.

363   ii   **HORN**
Par. 1, ll. 1-2 *should read*:

The term *cuivré* is generally understood to mean " stopped and played

371   ii   Par. 5, l. 3.   Dec. 1887), *should read*:

Mar. 1887 [3]),

Add footnote:

[3] According to an obituary in ' Le Ménestrel ' for 17 Apr. 1887 (not 25 Dec.).

372   ii   *Delete* * *before* :

Lewy, Eduard Constantin.
Lewy, Joseph Rudolph.

378   i   *Add before* **HORN, C. E.** :

HORN, Camillo (*b.* Reichenberg [Liberec], 29 Dec. 1860 ; *d.* Vienna, 3 Sept. 1941).
Austrian composer.   He was a pupil of Bruckner in Vienna, later worked there as critic and conductor, and became professor at the Musical Academy.   His works consist mainly of choruses (unaccompanied and with orchestra), chamber and pianoforte music, songs and duets.   They include :

Op.
10. ' Thusnelda ' (Klopstock) for voice & orch.
33. ' Albumblatt ' and ' Fantasie ' for pf. left hand.
40. Symphony, F mi.
50. Stg. Quintet.
58. Sonata for horn & pf.   E. B.

383   i   Page heading *should read*:
HORSZOWSKI

HORST
Par. 2, l. 3.   ' Choros ' *should read*:
' Chorus '

HORSZOWSKI
Par. 1, l. 2 *should read*:

23 June 1892).

384 i **HORWUD**
Par. 1, l. 1 *should read* :
HORWUD, (?) William (*b.* ? ; *d.* ?).

Par. 2, ll. 11-16 *should read* :
that referred to above. He was master of the
Fraternity of St. Nicholas in London in 1464.

ii *Add after* **HOSTINSKÝ** :
HOTCHKIS, John (Percy) (*b.* Taunton,
22 Nov. 1916).
English composer and conductor. He was
educated at Sherborne (1930–34) and at
Selwyn College, Cambridge, where he was
organ scholar and a pupil of Edward J. Dent,
Henry Moule and C. B. Rootham. His first
ambition was to become a cathedral organist,
but this gave way to a strong interest in music
for theatre, radio and television, and from
1948 onwards he composed music for all three
media and in a relatively short time achieved
a remarkable degree of success. Well over
100 radio productions featured his incidental
music, ranging from Greek tragedies to
modern English, French and American plays,
by way of mystery plays, Shakespeare,
Restoration drama, and plays by Plautus,
Molière, Tchekov, Strindberg and Sheridan.
Hotchkiss has also provided musical scores for
television productions (including Orwell's
' 1984 ' and a yearly Christmas play for
children) as well as for many theatrical productions in London and New York.
In 1957 and 1958 he wrote the music for
' Son et Lumière ' at Greenwich, and continued to provide scores for film and radio
use, most of which he conducted himself.
His other works include an Overture (1947),
a Fantasia for oboe and orchestra (1948), a
song cycle to texts by James Joyce (1947),
a setting of Psalm 23 (1949) and ' The Bell
Song ' for soloists, chorus and organ (1950).
                                          D. W. S.

385 i **HOTHBY**
Par. 3, ll. 5-6 *should read* :
script is itself a copy of one at Ferrara, said to
have been made by Padre

l. 9 *should read* :
positions by Hothby. It is now available as
Faenza 117 (*see* D. Plamenac, ' Keyboard
Music of the 14th Century in the Codex
Faenza 117 ' in Journ. Amer. Musicol. Soc.,
IV, 1951).

Signature should read :
                                    A. H.-H., adds.

ii **HOTTETERRE**
(1) **Jean.** l. 2 *should read* :
c. 1690 [1]).

385 ii (2) **Nicolas.** l. 2 *should read* :
10 May 1694), son of the preceding.

(4) **Louis.** l. 6 *should read* :
Pierre Chédeville. He was probably the
author of the ' Traité de flûte ' (1707) long
attributed to Jacques (6).

(5) **Nicolas,** l. 6. La Barre [1]
     should read :
La Barre [2]

Add footnote :
[1] According to Mauger (*see* Bibl.) he witnessed a
marriage on 16 Oct. 1689, having already witnessed
that of his son Nicolas on 20 Aug. 1685 ; the date 1678
previously given for his death is therefore wrong.

Footnote 1 becomes 2.

386 i (6) **Jacques.** l. 17 *should read* :
pupils. Jacques was long thought to be the
author of a ' Traité

l. 20 *should read* :
1760, but Mauger (*see* Bibl.) attributes it to
Louis (4).

Add to BIBL. :
MAUGER, N., ' Les Hotteterre : nouvelles recherches '
(Paris, 1912).

ii **HOVHANESS**
Par. 1, l. 1. Summerville *should
read* :
Somerville

388 ii *Add before* **HOWELL** :
HOWE, John (1) (*b.* ? York, ? ; *d.* London,
1519).
HOWE, John (2) (*b.* ? London, ? ; *d.*
London, 1571).
English organ builders, father and son.
Their business was the first of its kind of any
importance in England. They were so powerful that they virtually drove all other organ
builders out of business, and the hitherto
flourishing guild of organ builders became
extinct in 1531, when the younger Howe
received permission to become a member of
the Skinners Company.
The Howes' workshops were at Walbrook,
" at the sign of the Organe Pype ". During
their lives there were over a hundred churches
in the City of London alone ; some records
for about a quarter of these survive, and only
two of them fail to mention the Howes, who
carried out minor repairs and tuning under a
covenant which seems to have been at the
rate of 1s. a year per organ.
The first mention of the family comes from
York, where repairs were made to the Minster
organs in 1485, and it is possible that the
family came from there. Apart from work
done in the City, the Howes are known to

have built and repaired organs in other parts of London, such as Lambeth, Westminster and Wandsworth; also at Bletchingley, York, Coventry and Sheffield.   H. B. (ii).

BIBL.—SUMNER, W. L., ' The Organ ', 2nd ed. London, (1955).

390   i   HOWELLS
Par. 2, l. 7 *should read*:

Oxford. He received the C.B.E. in 1953 and was appointed Professor of Music in London University in succession to Stanley Marchant, whose post had been temporarily filled by George Oldroyd and Henry Coates.

ii   HOWELLS, CATALOGUE
CHURCH MUSIC
Add at end:
— Introit, ' Behold, O God our defender ' (Coronation 1953).

391   i   PIANOFORTE MUSIC
Add at end:
— ' Cobbler's Hornpipe ' (1926).
— ' A Sailor Tune ' (1930).

ii   HOWES
At end of Par. 6 (list of books) *add*:
' The Music of Ralph Vaughan Williams ' (1954).

l. 5. ' Mankind and Music ' (1948) *should read*:
' Man, Mind and Music ' (1948).

393   ii   HRISTIĆ
Par. 1. Belgrade, 1885). *should read*:

Belgrade, 19 June 1885; *d.* Belgrade, 27 Aug. 1958).

395   i   HUBER, Kurt
Par. 1, l. 2. *d.* Munich, *should read*:
d. Berlin,

ii   Par. 1, l. 12 *should read*:
arrested at Munich and beheaded in Berlin. His works include:

HUBERMAN
Par. 1, ll. 1-2. Places of birth and death *should read*:

Częstochowa nr. Warsaw; Nant-sur-Corsier, Switzerland

Par. 3, ll. 5-8 *should read*:

given in Vienna on 12 Jan. 1895. He made a sensation and attracted the favourable notice of the capricious Viennese public; and a later concert, on 29 Jan. 1896, was attended by

396   i   HUBERT
Par. 1, l. 2. 9 Mar. *should read*:
19 Mar.

396   i   HUBERTY
Par. 1, l. 2 *should read*:

Belgium, 2 Feb. 1879; *d.* Ostend, 10 Mar. 1955).

Par. 2, l. 11. In 1916 he became *should read*:

In 1915 he became

ii   HUCBALD
Add to BIBL. :
WEAKLAND, REMBERT, ' Hucbald as Musician and Theorist ' (M.Q., XLII, Jan. 1956, p. 66).

397   ii   HUDSON, Robert
Par. 1, l. 2 *should read*:
1739; *d.* Eton, 19 June 1815).

Par. 2, l. 5 *should read*:

Mildred, Bread Street. On 22 Nov. of the same year he was ap-

399   i   HUELGAS CODEX
Par. 3, l. 5 *should read*:

ció musical ' (' Publicacions Catalunya ', Vol. VI).

ii   HUGHES
Par. 2, ll. 11-12 *should read*:

at Pershore Abbey, and in 1926 was transferred to Nashdom Abbey in Buckinghamshire, of which

BOOKS
l. 13 *should read*:
Cambridge ' (Cambridge, 1955).

l. 15 *should read*:
Oxford, 1955).

Add at end:
' Septuagesima; Reminiscences of the Plainsong and Medieval Music Society, and of other things, personal and musical ' (London, 1959).

400   ii   *Add before* HUGHES, Herbert

HUGHES, Gervase (Alfred Booth) (*b.* Birmingham, 1 Sept. 1905).
English composer, conductor and author. He was educated at Malvern College and Corpus Christi College, Oxford, where he took the B.A. and B. Mus. degrees in 1927, proceeding to M.A. in 1949. He studied music under F. H. Shera at Malvern, Ernest Walker at Oxford, also, among others, with Thomas Wood and Armstrong Gibbs. In 1926–29 he was on the musical staff of the British National Opera Company and conducted ' Carmen ', ' Faust ' and ' Samson and Delilah '; but he was able to accept other engagements during that period, such as the conducting of a provincial tour of Oscar Straus's ' The Last Waltz '. In 1929–30 he

arranged and subsequently conducted Handel's ' Julius Caesar ' for the London Opera Festival. In 1933 he gave up music as a profession, but he still finds time for composition and other musical activities, such as studies which led to the writing of ' The Music of Arthur Sullivan ', a comprehensive and detailed work based on close research and showing keen critical insight, which was ready for publication in 1959.

Hughes's compositions include an opera, ' Imogen's Choice '; Scenes from Shakepeare's ' Twelfth Night ' (unfinished opera); the operettas ' Castle Creevey ' (which was produced and published), ' Penelope ' and ' Venetian Fantasy '; ' Symphonic Suite ' in A minor and ' Overture for a Musical Comedy ' for orchestra; Trio for oboe, bassoon and pianoforte; a few pianoforte pieces; about 20 songs.   E. B.

404 ii *Add before* HUMBY :

Humblot, Pierre. *See* Milhaud (' Juanita ', incid. m.).

405 ii HUMFREY
LIST OF ANTHEMS
By the waters . . .
  l. 2. 1176. *should read* :
1176; R.C.M. 1067.

    *Haste Thee . . .
  l. 3. 1034. *should read* :
1034; R.C.M. 1068.

    Have mercy . . .
  Delete ll. 1-4 *and substitute* :
*Have mercy upon me, O God. B.M. Add. 30932.
Have mercy upon me, O God (Boyce). B.M. Add. 17784 (bass part), 17840, 33235, Harl. 7338; Ch. Ch. Oxon. 621; R.C.M. 1068.

    Hear, O Heavens
  l. 3. 1034. *should read* :
1034; R.C.M. 1052.

    Lift up . . .
  l. 2. graph). *should read* :
graph); R.C.M. 1060.

406 i *Like as . . .
  l. 4. 1034. *should read* :
1034; R.C.M. 1060, 1068.

    *Lord, teach us . . .
  l. 3. 1029. *should read* :
1029; R.C.M., 1060, 1067, 1068.

    *O give thanks.
  l. 3. Univ. *should read* :
Univ.; R.C.M. 1060.

    *O Lord . . .
  l. 3. 1034. *should read* :
1034; R.C.M. 1060.

    *O praise . . .
  l. 3. Univ. *should read* :
Univ.; B.M. Add. 38648; R.C.M. 1060.

    *Rejoice . . .
  l. 2. 33235; *should read* :
34203;

406 i LIST OF ANTHEMS
    *Thou art . . .
  l. 3. 1176. *should read* :
1176; B.M. Add. 38648; R.C.M. 1059, 1068.

405-6   *Add new titles* :

*Almighty God, who madest thy blessed Son. Birmingham Univ. Barber Inst. MS 5001.
Hear my prayer, O God. B.M. Egerton MS 2960.
O praise God in his holiness. Durham Cath. MSS (organ part only).

ii HUMMEL, J. N.
  Footnote 2, l. 1 *should read* :
² Beethoven had gone to Vienna in Nov. 1792 and

407 i Par. 1, l. 2 *should read* :
performed (1807). Schindler reported, untrustworthily as usual, that on this occasion some

    l. 8 *should read* :
faded away. Actually, in a note of early Dec. 1813 Beethoven addressed Hummel as " allerliebster Hummel " and concluded " stehe ich dir mit Leib und Seel zu dienst ".

In 1810 Hummel succeeded in securing a

    Par. 4, l. 4 *should read* :
and the teacher of Hiller, Henselt and

408 i *Add to* BIBL. :
MEYER, W., ' Johann Nepomuk Hummel als Klavierkomponist ' (Kiel, 1922).
SPORCK, G., ' L'Interprétation des sonates de Johann Nepomuk Hummel ' (Paris, 1933).

411 ii HUMPERDINCK
  Add to BIBL. :
THAMM, EBERHARD, ' Der Bestand der lyrischen Werke Engelbert Humperdincks ' (Mainz, 1951).

412 i HUMPHRIES, J. S. & John
  Add at end :

Hawkins assumed that these were one and the same person, and he seems to have been right, although Moffat, who edited a Humphries sonata as No. 13 of his ' Old English Violin Music ', disputed this. The fact that the J. S. sonatas are called " opera prima " and John's concertos Opp. 2 and 3 suggests a single composer; besides, there is a set of solo sonatas by John Humphries, without opus number, and these two sets of sonatas have prefaces in a similar style and contain works similarly organized.

ii HUNGARIAN STRING QUARTET
  Par. 1, l. 3 *should read* :
four artists, now dissolved :

    Par. 3, l. 6 *should read* :
for violinists. Végh afterwards formed a quartet of his own.

413   i   **HUNT, Arabella**
          Par. 2, l. 15 and
       ii   Par. 1, l. 1 *should read*:
Congreve (not from his ode) subjoined. An
ode on her death, by

          l. 4 *should read*:
J. S. Kusser. A copy of the original edition
is in the Chetham Library, Manchester.

414   ii   **HUNTER**
          Par. 2, l. 14 *should read*:
praised by ' Blackwood '. Poems by her were
used for Beethoven's settings of 12 Scottish
Songs of 1815 (No. 12) and 26 Welsh Songs
of 1817 (Nos. 5, 9-11 & 17).[1] She was also

          l. 23 *should read*:
that distinction.   G., adds.

          Add footnote:
[1] For titles *see* BEETHOVEN, pp. 592-93.

415   i   **HURDY-GURDY**
          Par. 1, ll. 4-5 *should read*:
Drehleier, Radleier; Lat. *organistrum*). This
has now a place only among

          Footnote 2.   1784 *should read*:
1874

416   ii   **HURLEBUSCH**
          Add to See also:
Vereniging, Vol. 32 (reprint of clavier works).

417   i   **HURLSTONE**
          Par. 1, l. 1.   **William (Yeates)**
          should read:

William (Martin Yeates)

       ii   CATALOGUE
          ORCHESTRAL WORKS
          Add at end:
Five Dances.

          CHAMBER MUSIC
          l. 2 *should read*:
Quartet, E mi., for vn., viola, cello & pf., Op. 43.

          PIANOFORTE MUSIC
          l. 2 *should read*:
' Five Easy Waltzes ', Op. 1.

418   i   *Add after* **Hus**:
HUSA, Karel (*b.* Prague, 7 Aug. 1921).
Czech composer. He studied composition
and conducting at the Prague Conservatory,
and in 1946 went to Paris to continue his
studies with Honegger at the École Normale
de Musique, with Nadia Boulanger and
briefly with Milhaud. His Divertimento for
strings was performed there by the I.S.C.M.
in 1949, and he has been represented at
various European festivals, beginning with

" Spring in Prague " (string Quartet No. 1)
and following with I.S.C.M. in Brussels, 1950,
Darmstadt, 1951–52 and 1954, Donaueschingen, 1953, and Frankfort o/M., 1954. He left
his native country for political reasons and
settled in the U.S.A., where his pianoforte
Concertino was first performed at Boston in
1950. In 1954 he joined the Music Department of Cornell University.

Husa's works also include a Symphony, a
' Sinfonietta ' and ' Fresque ' for orchestra;
a ' Portrait ' for strings; 2 string Quartets,
a Trio for viola, clarinet and cello; and a
Sonata and Sonatina for pianoforte.   E. B.

HÜSCH, Gerhard (*b.* Hanover, 2 Feb.
1901).
German baritone singer. He studied with
Hans Enge and made his début at Bremen in
1924. Engagements followed at Cologne from
1927 to 1930 and in Berlin from 1930 until
1942, first at the Städtische Oper then at the
State Opera. He first came to Covent Garden
in 1930 as Falke in Bruno Walter's ' Fledermaus ' production, and was then heard as
Papageno the following year, and again in
1938 under Beecham. At Bayreuth in 1930
and 1931 he sang an outstanding Wolfram
in ' Tannhäuser '.

Hüsch possessed a lyric baritone voice
capable of softness and sweetness in Italian
opera, and of sonorous warmth and metallic
timbre in German. He had a great feeling
for words, and his performances of Schubert's
song cycles were regarded as models of style
and examples of the finest *Lieder* singing.
Apart from a few post-war appearances, he
has devoted himself in recent years to
teaching.   H. D. R.

420   ii   *Add before* **HUYGENS**:
HUYBRECHTS, Albert (*b.* Dinant, 12
Feb. 1899; *d.* Brussels, 21 Feb. 1938).
Belgian composer. He was a great-nephew
of François Servais, and there was thus a
musical strain in his family.[1] He studied at
the Brussels Conservatoire under P. Marchand,
L. Du Bois, Joseph Jongen and Ernest Closson.
In 1926 he gained two American prizes: the
Coolidge Prize at Washington for his violin
and piano Sonata and the Ojai Valley Prize
in California for his string Quartet. His work
showed great originality and enterprise, but
his premature death arrested the full development of his genius.

Huybrecht's works include incidental music
for the ' Agamemnon ' of Aeschylus; ' Chant
d'angoisse ' and ' Sérénade ' for orchestra;
' Divertissement ' for brass and percussion;
Concertino and ' Chant funèbre ' for cello

[1] He may even have been descended from Liszt (*see*
footnote, Vol. VII, p. 719).

and orchestra; two string Quartets, Trio for flute, viola and pianoforte, Sonata for violin and pianoforte, etc.   A. L. C.

421   ii   **HUYGENS**
See also. l. 3 *should read:*
written for). Vereniging, Vol. 11 (reprint of ' Pathodia ').

433   i   **HYMN**
Add to BIBL. :
JULIAN, JOHN, ' A Dictionary of Hymnology . . . the Origin and History of Christian Hymns of all Ages and Nations ', 2 vols., new reprint (New York, 1957).
McCUTCHAN, ROBERT GUY, ' Hymn-Tune Names: their Source and Significance ' (Nashville, 1957).
ROUTLEY, ERIK, ' The Music of Christian Hymnody: a Study of the Development of the Hymn Tune since the Reformation, with special Reference to English Protestantism ' (London, 1957).

435   ii   **IBERT,** CATALOGUE
OPERA
Title of last item *should read:*
' Les Petites Cardinal '

BALLETS
l. 11 *should read:*
prod. Paris, Opéra, 30 Apr. 1934.

Add after this:
' Les Amours de Jupiter ', prod. Paris, 9 Mar. 1946.

l. 13 *should read:*
vantes's ' Don Quixote ', scen. by E. de Gramont, prod. Paris, 5 May 1950.

INCIDENTAL MUSIC
Add after l. 4 :
' Donogoo ', play by Jules Romains (1930).

FILM MUSIC
l. 1. after Cervantes. *should read:*
after Cervantes.[1]

Add footnote:
[1] Originally commissioned from Ravel, but left unfinished by him except for the 3 songs ' Don Quichotte à Dulcinée '.

ORCHESTRAL WORKS
l. 5. ' Scherzo féerique ' (1925). *should read:*
' Féerique ', scherzo (1925).

Delete l. 6 (' Jeux ').

ll. 7-8 *should read:*
Symph. Suite ' Paris ', from the incidental music to ' Donogoo ' (1932).

Delete l. 10 ' Capriccio '

436   i   SOLO INSTRUMENT AND OR-CHESTRA
l. 5. (1951). *should read:*
(1948).

ii   **IBKOWSKI**
BIBL. CHYBIŃSKY *should read:*
CHYBIŃSKI

438   ii   **Ibsen**
l. 2. *Add before* Borgstrøm :
Berg (Alban, song).

438   ii   **Ibsen**
l. 4 *should read:*
orch.; ' Paa Vidderne ', voice & orch.; 1 song). Egge (' Olav Liljekrans ', opera). Egk

444   ii   **IN NOMINE**
Par. 4, l. 13 *should read:*
the harmony, carry on fuges, and interspers discords,

Footnote. p. 68). *should read:*
p. 69).

447   i   *Add to* BIBL. :
REESE, GUSTAVE, ' The Origin of the English *In nomine* ' (Journ. Amer. Musicol. Soc., II, 1949, p. 7).

IN QUESTA TOMBA OSCURA
Par. 1, ll. 10-11. Reichardt, Cherubini, Asioli, *should read:*
Reichardt [1], Cherubini [1], Asioli [1],

Add footnote:
[1] Not in the original edition.

448   ii   **INCIDENTAL MUSIC**
Par. 3, ll. 17-18 *should read:*
ments. By Shakespeare's time the dumbshow was beginning to be obsolete [2]; his use of it in ' Ham-

Par. 4, l. 1 *should read:*
In 1576–77 the first public theatres, The Theatre and The Curtain, were built in

Add footnote:
[2] F. A. Foster, ' Dumbshew in Elizabethan Drama ', mentions it as being used by Webster in ' The White Devil ' (*c.* 1612) and Goffe in ' The Raging Turk ' (*c.* 1618).

449   i   Par. 1, l. 1 *should read:*
dores, theorboes; *Bagpipes* [1]; *Harp* [2]; *Whistling Bird-Pots* [3]; *Organ.* This imposing list

ll. 16-21 *should read:*
IV, iii. *Woodwind:* a woodwind consort of treble, alto and tenor cornetts, with a serpent for bass, played act-tunes at Blackfriars with "organs", in Marston's ' Sophonisba '[4], where musical directions are given in unusually full details. *Hautboys:* used in consorts of 4 sizes,

l. 31. wry-neck'd pipe "
should read:
wry-neck'd fife "

ll. 36-38 *should read:*
' A Mad World, My Masters ', where the Blackfriars organ is used satirically to show off the stupid artistic pretensions of upstarts. Apart from such gratuitous

Par. 2, l. 3 *should read:*
in Arend van Buchell's copy of de Witt's sketch of ' The Swan ' (*c.* 1596) almost

449   i   Par. 2, ll. 8-9 *should read*:

be found about 1640 (Killigrew's ' Parson's Wedding ', published in 1664 but performed probably before 1642 [5]). Frequent use was made of " music

Add footnotes :

[1] Shirley's ' Hyde Park '.
[2] ' The Valiant Welshman ' by " R. A." ? (Armin).
[3] Fletcher's ' The Pilgrim ' and ' The Prophetess ' and Shirley's ' Hyde Park '.
[4] But there is no evidence that this kind of consort was usual. From the instruments we know the theatres to have possessed and the musicians associated with the theatres we gather that consorts such as Morley and Rosseter wrote their music for were usual. (*See* Thurston Dart, ' Morley's Consort Lessons, 1598 ', Proc. Roy. Mus. Ass., Vol. LXXIV, 1947-48.)
[5] G. Bentley, ' The Jacobean and Caroline Stage ', Vol. I, p. 123.

ii   Par. 2, ll. 2-3 *should read*:

Rose and Blackfriar's Theatres about 1600 and continued until the closing of the theatres in 1642. It was a regular feature especially at the private theatres. There might also be actual dancing, as well as

Par. 4, l. 1 *should read*:

It was common for a play to end with a dance, a song or some kind of ceremonial

Par. 5, l. 4 *should read*:

ascent of an angel into heaven ; it was due to old superstitious associations of music with the supernatural, and no doubt it

Par. 7, l. 5 *should read*:

has ten, fourteen and nineteen songs in the 1608, 1630 and 1638 editions respectively'. Unaccompanied vocal

455   i   **INCORPORATED SOCIETY OF MUSICIANS**
Delete Par. 2.

Par. 3, ll. 5-6 *should read*:

had been formerly. Its main objects were codified as follows : The Promotion of the Art of Music, and the Maintenance of the honour and interests of the Musical Profession. The present Secretary is Denis H. R. Brearley.

Par. 4, ll. 2-5 *should read*:

musicians. Candidates for full membership must be solely engaged in the practice of music as a profession; other qualified persons may be elected as Associates. There are 50 local

INDIA
Par. 1, l. 1.   (*b.* Palermo *should read*:

(*b.* ? Palermo

l. 2 *should read*:

1582; *d.* ? Modena, [before 19 Apr.] 1629).

455   i   Par. 2, ll. 2-3 *should read*:

Palermitan family, but it is possible that he spent his childhood at Naples, and he may even have been born there. It is not known where and with whom he studied music. In 1608 he was at

ll. 9-10 *should read*:

musicians, and probably Naples. Until 1611 he seems to have had no settled home, but in this year

ii   Par. 2, ll. 17-19 *should read*:

of sacred music, and in the following year he seems to have been living again at Modena, where he may have died.

Par. 3, l. 15.   editors *should read*:
publishers

Add to BIBL. :

FORTUNE, NIGEL, ' Italian Secular Monody from 1600 to 1635 : an Introductory Survey' (M.Q., XXXIX, 1953, p. 171).
' Sigismondo d'India : an Introduction to his Life and Works ' (Proc. Roy. Mus. Ass., Vol. LXXXI, 1954-55, p. 29).

3 further works by MOMPELLIO :

' " Opere recitative, Balletti et Inventioni " di Sigismondo d' India per la corte di Savoia' (' Collectanea Historiae Musicae ', II, 1957, p. 291).
' Sigismondo d' India e il suo primo libro di " Musiche da cantar solo " ' (' Collectanea Historiae Musicae ', I, 1953, p. 113).
' Sigismondo d'India : musicista palermitano ' (Milan, 1957).

460   ii   **INDIAN MUSIC**
Add to BIBL. :

GOSVAMI, O., ' The Story of Indian Music : its Growth and Synthesis ' (Bombay, 1957).

467   i   **INDY**
Par. 1, l. 2.   1 Dec. *should read*:
2 Dec.

472   i   Par. 1, l. 2 *should read*:

production at the Opéra on 9 June 1920, the

473   ii   *Add to* BIBL. :

BLOM, ERIC, ' Vincent d'Indy's " Enigma " [' Tableaux de voyage ']', in ' Classics : Major and Minor ' (London, 1958).

474   —   ORCHESTRAL WORKS
Col. 5, l. 21 *should read*:
1906.

Footnote 1 *should read*:

[1] 1st performed Eden Theatre, Paris, under Lamoureux, 25 Feb. 1886.

475   —   SOLO INSTRUMENTS AND ORCHESTRA
Op. 89. Col. ii *should read*:

' Concert ' for flute, cello, pf. & stgs.

478   i   **INÉGALES**
Par. 4, l. 6.   2nd musical example, the semiquaver rest *should be* a demisemiquaver rest.

484   i   **INFLECTION**
3rd musical example words: plentitudine
should read:
plenitudine

ii   **INGEGNERI**
Add at end:
See also Istituzioni, Vol. 6 (modern ed. of madrigals).

INGENHOVEN
Par. 1, l. 2. 1876). *should read:*
1876; *d.* Hoenderloo, 20 May 1951).

485   ii   **INSANGUINE**
Par. 1, ll. 1-2 *should read:*
INSANGUINE, Giacomo (Antonio Francesco Paolo Michele) [1] (*b.* Monopoli, Bari, 22 Mar. 1728; *d.* Naples, 1 Feb. 1795).

Par. 3, l. 5.   'Didona *should read:*
'Didone

504   ii   **INSTRUMENTS**
Add to Bibl.:
Baines, Anthony, 'Woodwind Instruments and their History' (London, 1957).
Valentin, Erich, 'Handbuch der Instrumentenkunde' (Ratisbon, 1954).

505   —   Table
l. 38. Bersaglieri Horn *should read:*
Bersag(lieri) Horn

508   —   Table
69   Col. 2, l. 10. (*Plate*) 6 *should read:*

511   i   **INSTRUMENTS, COLLECTIONS OF**
Add after Liverpool:
Llandudno: W. Barrow   K

514   i   **SWEDEN**
Skara, C *should read:*
G

SWITZERLAND
Add below Lucerne:
Triebschen (Wagner Villa)   G

515   ii   **(D) AFRICA**
l. 2.   Public Museum *should read:*
South African Museum

Add after l. 3:
Johannesburg — Africana Museum, Public Library (Prof. Percival R. Kirby's collection of over 500 Bushman, Hottentot and Bantu instruments).   E

517   ii   **INTERNATIONAL FOLK MUSIC COUNCIL**
Par. 2, l. 8.   Montreal in Aug. 1950. *should read:*
Basel in 1948.

517   ii   Par. 2.   *Add at end:*

An important development of the Council's work has been the co-operation with radio organizations in all parts of the world and the appointment of a special radio committee. To the publications have been added an 'International Catalogue of Recorded Folk Music' and 'Folk Songs of Europe', an anthology of nearly 200 folksongs from 30 European countries.

An international conference has been held each year since the first at Basel in 1948 (not Montreal in 1950, as previously stated). Two were held in the Americas, in the U.S.A. and Brazil, and the others in Europe. International Festivals are normally held every three years.   M. K. (ii).

519   i   **INTERNATIONAL SOCIETY FOR CONTEMPORARY MUSIC**
Par. 2.   *Add to list:*
1955.   Baden-Baden.
1956.   Stockholm.
1957.   Zürich.
1958.   Strasbourg.
1959.   Rome and Naples.
1960.   Cologne.

ii   **INTERNATIONAL SOCIETY FOR MUSICOLOGY**
Add at end, before signature:

Further Congresses were held at Oxford (1955) and Cologne (1958).

An important series of facsimile reprints of old theoretical treatises, 'Documenta Musicologica', is published by the Bärenreiter-Verlag under the auspices of the I.S.M.

525   i   **INTRADA**
Add at end:
Bibl.—Reimann, Margarete, 'Materialien zu einer Definition der Intrada' ('Musikforschung', 1957, No. 3).

527   ii   **INVITATORIUM**
Par. 1, ll. 4-5 *should read:*

which is sung in conjunction with the 94th Psalm (Latin numbering: English 95), 'O come let us sing', at the beginning

Par. 2, l. 2 *should read:*

applied to the Psalm itself, especially by

Add before **IONIAN MODE**:

IOMMELLI, Niccolò. *See* Jommelli.[1]

Add footnote:

[1] There is no letter J (consonant) in Italian; what looks like it is merely a calligraphic long I (vowel). This has dropped out of use except as an initial, as in this instance.

537   ii   **IRELAND**
Par. 4, l. 4.   Rosetti *should read:*
Rossetti

544 — CATALOGUE
Col. 1, l. 3 *should read*:
' Tutto è sciolto.'

548 ii **ISAAC**
Add to BIBL.:
CUYLER, LOUISE, ' The Sequences of Isaac's "Choralis Constantinus" ' (Journ. Amer. Musicol. Soc., III, 1950, p. 3).
' Choralis Constantinus III ' (Univ. of Michigan Publications, Fine Arts, Vol. II, 1950).
' Five Polyphonic Masses by Heinrich Isaac' (Ann Arbor, 1956).

Add at end:
See also Chorwerk, Vols. 7, 60 (modern reprints).

549 ii *Add before* **ISABEAU**:
ISAACS, Leonard (*b.* Manchester, 3 Jan. 1909).
English pianist and musical administrator, son of Edward Isaacs (*see above*). He was educated at Manchester Grammar School from 1921 to 1924 and studied at the R.C.M. in London from 1925 to 1930, his principal teachers being Herbert Fryer, Gordon Jacob and Malcolm Sargent. Subsequently he pursued his studies under Alfred Cortot in Paris and under Egon Petri in Berlin, and on returning to London took the degree of B.Mus. at London University. After five years of wide experience in the musical profession he joined the Music Department of the B.B.C., where he rapidly gained a reputation as a shrewd judge of music and musical talent, and as an organizer of uncommon ability. He was European Music Supervisor from 1941 to 1948 (with several years of war service intervening) and later became Music Programme Organizer (1948–50), Third Programme Music Organizer (1950–54) and is now Chief Assistant (Choral and Orchestral Music). There is no doubt that the musical content of Third Programme broadcasts reached its highest peak of excellence during his four-year regime, and he personally supervised the preparation and production of such notable and diverse series as ' Early Christian Chant ', in collaboration with Egon Wellesz, and ' Arnold Schoenberg ', with Michael Tippett.
Isaacs has adjudicated at many musical festivals and in this capacity has toured Canada more than once. He has published both original compositions and arrangements, and among the latter his version of Bach's ' Art of Fugue ' (London, 1950) stands out by reason of its sensitive use of the contrasting colours of a chamber ensemble and its eminent practicability.   D. W. S.

ISAMITT
Par. 1, l. 2. 1887). *should read*:
1885).

551 i **ISOLA DISABITATA**
l. 2 *should read*:
GOLDONI. HAYDN. METASTASIO.

554 ii **ISOZ**
Par. 1, l. 2. 1878). *should read*:
1878; *d.* Rákoskeresztur nr. Budapest, 6 June 1956).

557 ii **ISSERLIS**
Par. 1, l. 1. Kizhinev *should read*:
Kishinev

560 i **IVES**
Par. 1, l. 2. New York, May *should read*:
New York, 19 May

Par 4, ll. 3-4 *should read*:
No. 3 was first performed at a concert sponsored by the League of Composers in New York, on 5 Apr. 1946. This work

ii CATALOGUE
Last line *should read*:
Also 114 songs, organ pieces, &c.

Add at end:
BIBL.—COWELL, HENRY & SIDNEY, ' Charles Ives and his Music ' (New York & Oxford, 1955).

562 i **IVOGÜN**
Par. 2, l. 8. Erl *should read*:
Erb.

ll. 9-11 *should read*:
After her retirement from the stage

> (*The information that Maria Ivogün retired from the stage owing to failing eyesight and subsequent blindness appeared in the 5th edition owing to a false rumour which circulated shortly before its publication. It is happily untrue.*)

565 i **JACHINO**
Par. 1, l. 2. 1889). *should read*:
1887).

568 ii **JACOB,** CATALOGUE:
ARRANGEMENTS FOR ORCHESTRA
l. 7. E ma. *should read*:
E♭ ma.

569 i *Add after* **JACOB POLAK**:
JACOBELLI, Giovanni Battista (*b.* ?; *d.* ?).
Italian 17th-century ecclesiastic, singer and composer. He was engaged as tenor at the royal chapel in Warsaw and was also confessor to the queen. In 1650 he was made a

canon in the bishopric of Varmia. One of his canons was published in ' Cribrum musicum ' (Xenia Apollinea), published by Marco Scacchi at Venice in 1643. No other works of his are known.   G. R. H.

JACOBI, Erwin R. (Reuben) (b. Strasbourg, 21 Sept. 1909).

German musicologist. He was educated at the Goethe Gymnasium at Frankfort o/M. and studied domestic economy at the Technical High Schools of Munich and Charlottenburg, where he took a diploma. In 1934 he emigrated to Israel, where he devoted himself to agriculture and colonization, and later to administration and industry. But he returned to Europe, settling in Switzerland and decided to change over to a musical career. He had learnt the pianoforte and the violin as a child and was much influenced by Albert Schweitzer, with whom his family was on friendly terms. His further studies included the harpsichord with Wanda Landowska, theory with Hindemith and musicology with Curt Sachs and A.-E. Cherbuliez. He has been active in Switzerland as a performer and teacher since 1952, and in 1959 he was appointed lecturer in music at Zürich University.

Jacobi's book, ' Die Entwicklung der Musiktheorie in England nach der Zeit von Jean-Philippe Rameau ' (Strasbourg, 1957–60), was partly translated in the Yale ' Journal of Music Theory ' as ' Harmonic Theory in England after the Time of Rameau ' (Nov. 1957). Other important writings include ' Augustus Frederic Christopher Kollmann als Theoretiker ' (A.M.W., 1956, III-IV, pp. 263-70), articles on the Swiss theorist Jean-Adam Serre, on Schweitzer, &c. As an editor he has produced modern editions, based on the original text, of C. P. E. Bach's Concerto in E♭ for harpsichord, fortepiano and orchestra and of Rameau's ' Pièces de clavecin ', and these were followed in 1959 by Rameau's ' Pièces de clavecin ', Tartini's ' Traité des agréments ', Turk's ' Klavierschule ' and Boismortier's ' Quatre Suites de pièces de clavecin '.   E. B.

572   i   *Add after* **JACOBUS DE LEODIO** :

JACOMI (Jacob de Senleches [Sentluch], Jacopinus Selesses) (b. ? ; d. ?).

French 14th-century composer. He became a minstrel of John I of Aragon (1350–95), a keen musician and himself a composer. Jacomi's real name must have been Jacobus de Sentluch, though the manuscript sources preserve his name in a corrupt manner. Jacomi was the name given to him at the court of Barcelona. He may be either Jacomi

Capeta, a celebrated bagpipe player; or Jacomi lo Bègue. Jacomi is mentioned from the year 1372 and Jacomi Capeta served John and his successor Martin I till 1404. Jacomi lo Bègue was apparently dismissed in 1379 after the arrival of new singers from Avignon, and then a post was sought for him at the court of Castile. It seems likely therefore that this was the man who wrote the *ballade* for the death of Eleanor of Aragon, Queen of Castile, in 1382. Other (or the same) Jacomis served count Pere d'Urgell in 1381 and the Duke of Montblanc in 1391. Of the six compositions preserved, two are *virelais* and the rest *ballades*, with the possible exception of ' La harpe de melodie ', which has the form of the Italian *caccia* musically. The two *virelais* may be earlier works, since the text of a very complex *ballade* refers to the composer's previous habit of composing *virelais*. All the *ballades* are most complex works rhythmically and notationally, though none of them is for more than three voices. Typical is ' La harpe de melodie ', which employs black, red and white notes, though only the red notes seem to have the usual values. In other works extended syncopations and unusual note-values produce the effect of a written-out rubato.

The complete works, except ' La harpe de melodie ', are available in W. Apel's ' French Secular Music of the Late Fourteenth Century ' (1950) ; biographies in H. Anglès, ' El music Jacomi . . .' in ' Homenatge a A. Rubió i Lluch ', I (1936).   G. R. (iii)

JACOPO DA BOLOGNA (b. Bologna, ? ; d. ?).

Italian 14th-century composer and theorist. He is said to have been a great virtuoso on the Gothic harp, which, as we know from evidence in Boccaccio, was often used in a consort of voices and instruments early in the 14th century. He was a musician at the court of Luchino Visconti at Milan, and after his patron's death in 1349 he is next heard of as being in the service of Mastino II Della Scala, who died in 1351. Some time before that he had taught Francesco Landini, then in his early twenties.

Jacopo was one of the first composers to give the Italian Ars Nova its impulse: breaking away from the traditional Ars Antiqua, he and Giovanni da Cascia developed this new school of polyphonic music, of the second phase of which Landini became the great representative.

Thirty-six of Jacopo's compositions have survived, 30 of which are madrigals (unconnected with the 16th-century madrigal apart from the name), the others being two motets in praise of Luchino, *caccie* and a *lauda*. The madrigals are in two or three parts, of which the upper parts are often in canon and always melismatic, with the lowest (tenor) part as a supporting bass. The words of one of the 2-part madrigals, ' Non al suo amante ', are by Petrarch.

Jacopo was a theorist as well as a great composer. His treatise, ' L' arte del biscanto misurato secondo al maestro Jacopo da Bologna ' is preserved in the Biblioteca Medicea-Laurenziana at Florence; it has been reprinted in Italian, with a German translation by Johannes Wolf in ' Theodor Kroyer-Festschrift '. It is concerned mainly with notation. The original sources of his music are at Florence, in the same library and the Biblioteca Nazionale Centrale; the Biblioteca Universitaria at Padua; the Biblioteca Comunale at Faenza; the B.M. and the Bibliothèque Nationale in Paris.   M. W.

BIBL.—MARROCCO, W. THOMAS, 'The Music of Jacopo da Bologna ' (Berkeley & Los Angeles, 1954).
PLAMENAC, DRAGAN, ' Another Paduan Fragment of Trecento Music ' (Journ. Amer. Musicol. Soc., VIII, 1955, p. 165).

572   ii   **JACOTIN**
Add at end:

See also Maîtres Musiciens, Vol. 5 (modern ed. of chansons).

JACQUES DE LIÈGE
Par. 2, ll. 4-5 *should read:*

Pierre de La Croix. According to Bragard (*see* Bibl.) the ' Speculum musicae '

l. 8 *should read:*

1330, at an abbey in that town. The author suggests that those who wish to know his name should string together the initial letters of the seven chapters, which spell IACOBUS.

Add to BIBL.:

BRAGARD, ROGER, ' Le Speculum Musicae du Compilateur Jacques de Liège ' (' Musica Disciplina ', VII, 1953; VIII, 1954).

Delete GROSSMANN *entry*.

See also should read:

See also Corp. Script. Mus., Vol. III (modern ed. of ' Speculum ', 7 vols.). Muris (Johannes de).

573   i   **JACQUES**
Par. 1, l. 1. **Reginald** *should read:*

(Thomas) Reginald

Par. 2, ll. 1-2 *should read:*

English conductor, organist, educationist and broadcaster. He was educated at the

Par. 3, ll. 20-23 *should read:*

in choir-training and kindred topics. In 1936 he formed a small orchestra under his own name, and this has

573   ii   Par. 2, ll. 20-21 *should read:*
with both old and modern works. He was created C.B.E. in 1954.

578   i   **Jammes**
l. 3.   27 songs; *should read:*
33 songs;

JANÁČEK
Par. 1, l. 2.   *d.* Prague, *should read:*
d. Morava-Ostrava,

581   i   Par. 5, l. 10 *should read:*
' Její Pastorkyna ' (' Jenufa ') is still considered the com-

582   i   BIBL. l. 5 *should read:*
Czech version by A. Fuchs (Prague, 1924). Revised German version (Vienna & London, 1956).

Add to BIBL. (2nd work by HOLLAENDER) :

' The Music of Leoš Janáček: its Origin in Folklore ' (M.Q., XLI, p. 171, 1955).

ii   ll. 24-26 *should read:*

SEDA, JAROSLAV, ' Leos Janacek ' (Prague, 1954). Trans. by Margot Milner & Vilém Fried (Prague, 1956).
ŠTĚDROŇ, BOHUMÍR : ' Janáček ve vzopímkách a dopisech' (' J. in Recollections and Letters ') (Prague, 1946). Ger. trans. by I. Schwarz-Tunovský, ' Leoš Janáček in Briefen und Erinnerungen ' (Prague, 1955).

CATALOGUE
OPERAS
Col. 1, l. 14.   stol ' *should read:*
století '

585   i   **JANISSARY MUSIC**
Par. 1, l. 18.   (*d.* 1735) *should read:*
(*d.* 1733)

ii   **JANITSCH**
Par. 2, l. 3. 1773 *should read:*
1733

587   i   **JANNEQUIN**
Add to See also:

Collectio O.M.B., Vol. XII (modern ed.). Florilège, Vols. 1 & 3 (modern ed. of chansons). Maîtres Musiciens, Vols. 5 & 7 (do.).

593   i   **JAPANESE MUSIC**
Add to BIBL. :

HARICH-SCHNEIDER, ETA, ' The Present Condition of Japanese Court Music ' (M.Q., XXXIX, 1953, p. 49).
' Revue Musicale ', No. 235, 1956 (' La Musique au Japon ').

595   i   **JARECKI, Henryk**
Par. 1, l. 2.   1864 *should read:*
1846

597   JÄRNEFELT, Armas
Par. 1, l. 2 *should read*:
puri [Viborg], 14 Aug. 1869; *d.* Stockholm, 23 June 1958).

ii   **JARNOWICK**
Par. 2, ll. 1-2.   grandson *should read*:
son

l. 10 *should read*:
de la Porte Saint-Martin in 1819), at

598   ii   JAUBERT
Par. 1, l. 2.   ?, June *should read*:
Sarre, 19 June

Par. 2, l. 5 *should read*:
law for music in 1923.   He became in Paris musical

l. 7 *should read*:
some forty scores.   The best-known film for which he wrote music was 'Carnet de bal' (1938).

l. 11 *should read*:
(1937), 'Concerto a due' for violin, cello and strings; 'Intermède' for string orchestra,

604   ii   JAZZ
Add to BIBL. :
BERENDT, JOACHIM ERNST, 'Das Jazz Buch: Entwick-lung und Bedeutung der Jazzmusik' (Frankfurt o/M., 1953).
'Variationen über Jazz' (Munich, 1956).
FEATHER, LEONARD, 'The Encyclopedia of Jazz' (New York, 1955).
MERRIAM, ALAN P., 'A Bibliography of Jazz' (Phila-delphia, 1954).

605   i   *Add to* BIBL.:
MORGAN, ALUN & HORRICKS, RAYMOND, 'Modern Jazz: a Survey of Developments since 1939' (London, 1956).
PANASSIÉ, HUGUES & GAUTIER, MADELEINE, 'Diction-naire du jazz' (Paris, 1954).
PANASSIÉ, HUGUES & GAUTIER, MADELEINE, 'Guide to Jazz', ed. by A. A. Gurwitsch (London & Boston, Mass., 1956).
STEARNS, MARSHALL W., 'The Story of Jazz' (New York & Oxford, 1956).
TESTONI, G. C., 'Enciclopedia del jazz' (Milan, 1953).
ULANOV, BARRY, 'A Handbook of Jazz' (New York, 1957).

606   ii   JEEP
Par. 1, l. 2 *should read*:
1582; *d.* Hanau, 19 Nov. 1644).

Par. 2, l. 2 *should read*:
in 1609.   From 1610 he was *Kapellmeister* to

l. 4 *should read*:
remained until 1633, when he became cathe-dral organist at Frankfort o/M.   In 1640 he removed to Hanau, where he was appointed *Kapellmeister* in 1642.   He composed a book of

606   ii   Par. 2, l. 6 *should read*:
appearing in many editions, the latest by Hans Joachim Moser.   E. v. d. s., rev.

607   ii   JEFFRIES, Matthew
Par. 2, ll. 3-6 *should read*:
1593 [2], and referred to by him as an "eminent musician".   He was elected vicar-choral at Wells Cathedral on 28 Dec. 1579, and a pay-ment to him as master of the choristers is noted in the Communar's book for 1587–88. He was elected Receiver-General of the vicars in 1585, and the existing registers' last record of his name is as Senior in 1593.   He is said to have been related to George Jeffries.   He supplicated for the degree of B.Mus. at Oxford on 25 Feb. 1594, his exercise being a "choral hymn in six parts".[3]   The words of an

Signature should read:
J. M. (ii), adds. W. K. F.

JEFFRIES, Stephen
Par. 2, l. 5.   scandal [3] *should read*:
scandal [4]

Add footnote:
[3] *See* Clark, 'Register of the University of Oxford', II, 1, p. 146.

Footnote 3 *becomes* 4.

607   ii⎫   JELICH
608   i⎭   *Delete whole entry and replace by*:
JELIĆ, Vinko [1] (*b.* Rijeka [Fiume], 1596; *d.* ?).
Croatian lutenist, tenor singer and com-poser.   In 1606 he became a chorister in the court chapel of the Archduke Ferdinand at Graz under Matteo Ferrabosco, who gave him musical instruction.   His brother Peter also went there, but died in 1609, when Vinko returned to his birthplace until the autumn of 1610, when he went back to Graz and for the next five years attended in turn the "Gym-nasium" and the University.   He played in the archduke's orchestra and in 1616 began to study theology.   The following year he went to Alsace to join the establishment of the Archduke Leopold at Zabern, where he was ordained priest in 1618.   But although ap-pointed vicar of the collegiate church of St. Mary there, he took an active share in the musical activities of the court.   The Thirty Years' War drove Leopold from Zabern, but Jelić remained there and is last heard of in 1636, when the town fell into the hands of France.
Three works by Jelić were printed in his

[1] Originally Jeličić and known in German-speaking countries as Vincenz Jelich, under which name he was previously entered in this Dictionary.

lifetime: 'Parnassia militia', Op. 1 (Strasbourg, 1622), containing 22 *concerti spirituali* for 1-4 voices and organ continuo, 2 more with 2 violins and 4 *ricercari* for cornett and trombone; 'Arion primus', Op. 2 (Strasbourg, 1628), containing 33 similar vocal works and one for contralto, 3 trombones and organ; 'Arion secundus', Op. 3 (Strasbourg, 1628), containing Vesper Psalms for 4 voices and organ continuo, a Magnificat, a 'Salve Regina' and 8 Psalm tunes for violins or cornetts with trombones or bassoons. A modern edition of Op. 1 appeared at Zagreb in 1957.   E. B.

608   ii   **JEMNITZ**
             Par. 1, l. 2.   1899 *should read*:
1890

609   ii   CATALOGUE:
             ORGAN MUSIC
             ll. 2-3 *should read*:
42(?). Sonata " per pedale d' organo " (unfinished, lost).

610   i   **JENA SYMPHONY**
            l. 23 *should read*:
composer's grandfather Louis". In 1957, however, H. C. Robbins Landon, in the course of researches made at the monastery of Göttweig, was able to establish that the work is by Friedrich Witt (1771-1837).

                                    w. m., adds.

                Add to Bibl. :

H. C. Robbins Landon, ' The " Jena " Symphony ' (M. Rev., XVIII, 1957).

612   ii   *Add after* Jensen, Johannes :

JENSEN, Ludvig (Paul) Irgens (*b*. Oslo, 13 Apr. 1894).
Norwegian composer. He studied philology and the pianoforte, but was mainly self-taught as a composer. In 1928 he aroused interest by winning a prize in the Nordic section of the Schubert centenary competition with his ' Passacaglia ' for orchestra.
Jensen's style, which is to some extent influenced by Norwegian folk music, is diatonic and modal in character. Among his major works are a dramatic symphony, 'Heimferd ', for solo voices, chorus and orchestra (also performed as an opera), a Symphony in D minor (1943), ' Tema med variasjoner ' for orchestra, and orchestral suite ' Partita sinfonia ' and many songs.   o. g.

613   ii   **JEPPESEN**
             l. 6 *should read*:
works are an opera, ' Rosaura ', to a libretto of his own based on a play by Goldoni, produced in Copenhagen on 20 Sept. 1950, a

614   ii   *Add before* **JERVIS-READ**:
JERVAYS, John (*b*. ? ; *d*. ?).
English 14th–15th-century singer and composer. A 3-part ' Gloria ' by him occurs in the ' Old Hall Manuscript ' and at Bologna (Bibl. Martini, Q 15). He may have been the John Jervays (or Gervase) who was granted a prebend in Bayeux Cathedral in 1422, and ejected two years later on the grounds that he held this office unlawfully. Like many English composers of his day, he was only a visitor to the Continent, not a resident there. Thus he was ineligible to accept appointments in a French diocese.
The ' Gloria ' (I, 114), which bears the ascription ' Gervasius de Anglia ' in the Bologna source, is in ballade-Mass style, for alto voice and two instruments. It is followed immediately in the Bologna manuscript by a ' Credo ' of Dunstable and ' Sanctus ' and ' Agnus Dei ' of Benet, all four serving as a composite Mass cycle.   d. w. s.

Bibl.—Besseler, Heinrich, ' Bourdon und Fauxbourdon ' (Leipzig, 1950).
Ramsbotham, Alexander, ed., ' The Old Hall Manuscript ', Vol. I (London, 1933).
Trowell, Brian, ' Some English Contemporaries of Dunstable ' (Proc. Roy. Mus. Ass., Vol. LXXXI, 1954-55).

615   i   *Add before* **JEUX**:
JEUNESSES MUSICALES. An international organization founded in 1946 whose full official name is La Fédération Internationale des Jeunesses Musicales (F.I.J.M.). Its membership at present (1957) includes 19 countries in Europe, the Americas and Africa. At the 11th Congress held in Madrid in 1956 it was decided to establish a Press Bureau at Munich, whose task it should be to make the activities of the organization more widely known and to distribute periodical circulars in several languages. The aims of F.I.J.M. are summarized as follows in the first of these news-sheets :

. . . to spread among the young a knowledge of and taste for good music and the arts in general by giving greater scope within the movement to initiative and work among themselves, regardless of any political, racial, religious or linguistic considerations.

At each congress, held in some important centre, the international orchestra of F.I.J.M. performs under the direction of a well-known resident conductor.
At the Madrid congress of 1956 Joachim Lieben of Vienna was re-elected president. The secretary is Dr. Marcel Cuvelier (Brussels), the founder of F.I.J.M. Pierre Pillet (Geneva) is treasurer, and other officers are Klaus Bieringer (Munich), Humphrey Burton (London), Jacques Longchampt (Paris), Norbert Stelmes (Luxemburg) and Max Vredenburg (Amsterdam). The officers are all capable of re-election.

The 12th congress was arranged to take place in Vienna in Apr. 1957; further, a transatlantic exchange was planned between young Belgian and Canadian musicians for 1956–57 and Dutch and Uruguayan musicians for 1957–58, each group to give 60 concerts in various places of their respective countries. The 13th congress will be held in Brussels during the International Exhibition of 1958.

The publishing-house of Schott at Mainz has undertaken to publish a collection of works by young composers, to be chosen by an international jury, under the collective title of 'Jeunes Compositeurs Internationaux'.

E. B.

629   ii   **JEWISH MUSIC**
Musical example 2.   Serape expugnava-runt *should read*:
Saepe expugnaverunt

Confitemini
Mus. ex. 3.   Confitamini *should read*:

de Egypto
Mus. ex. (2).   ex Egypto *should read*:

636   i   *Add to* BIBL. (General):
BERL, HEINRICH, 'Das Judentum in der Musik' (Stuttgart, 1926).
BROD, MAX, 'Die Musik Israels' (Tel Aviv, 1951).
GALPIN, F. W., 'The Music of the Sumerians and their Successors' (Cambridge, 1937).
RABINOVITCH, ISRAEL, 'Of Jewish Music' (Montreal, 1952).
ROTHMÜLLER, AARON MARKO, 'The Music of the Jews: an Historical Appreciation' (London & New York, 1954).
SENDREY, ALFRED, 'Bibliography of Jewish Music' (New York, 1951).

ii   *Signature should read*:
E. W. (iii).

637   ii   **JEWS IN MUSIC**
Signature P. G. (ii). *should read*:
P. G.

Add to BIBL.:
ROTHMÜLLER, AARON MARKO, 'The Music of the Jews: an Historical Appreciation' (London & New York, 1954).

JEŽEK
Par. 1, l. 2.   1 Jan. 1942 *should read*:
31 Dec. 1941

642   i   **JIRÁNEK**
Par. 1, l. 1.   Ledce *should read*:
Ledec (of which Ledce is the Czech locative).

JIROVEC *should read*:
JÍROVEC

Add after **JÍROVEC**:
JO. DE ALTE CURIE.   *See* ACOURT.

643   ii   **JOACHIM**
Add before See also:
The Newberry Library of Chicago, according to its Bulletin, Vol. IV, No. 6, acquired in 1957 some 400 letters to and from Joachim dating from 1874 to 1900 and including a good deal of correspondence with Philipp Spitta and Heinrich and Elisabeth von Herzogenberg.

644   ii   *Add after* **Jodelle**:
JOHANNES AFFLIGEMENSIS.   *See* COTTON, JOHN.

JOHANSEN
Par. 1, l. 1.   Vefsen, *should read*:
Vefsn,

Par. 2, ll. 8-9.   'Norsk Intelligensedblad' *should read*:
'Norske Intelligenssedler'

Par. 3, ll. 1-6 *should read*:
Among Johansen's compositions are large-scale choral works ('Voluspå', 'Draumkvedet', etc.), the University cantata 'Ignis ardens', orchestral music ('Pan', 'Symphonic Fantasy', etc.), chamber music and a large number of pianoforte pieces and songs. His style is influenced by Norwegian folk music and impressionism.

In 1934 Johansen published a biography and

645   i   **JOHN IV**
Add at end:
BIBL.—BRANCO, LUÍS FREITAS, 'D. João IV, músico' (Lisbon, 1956).

ii   **JOHN BROWN'S BODY**
Par. 4.   *Insert between* ll. 2 *and* 3:
entitled 'The Battle-Hymn of the Republic',

646   i   *Add before* **JOHN OF DAMASCUS**:
JOHN OF AFFLIGEM.   *See* COTTON, JOHN.

Add after **JOHN OF FORNSETE**:
JOHNER, (Dom) Franz (*b.* Waldsee, Württemberg, 1 Dec. 1874; *d.* Beuron, 6 Jan. 1955).
German musical scholar. He studied theology, philosophy and music in Prague, at Seckau, at the Benedictine monastery of Beuron and at Cucujaes in Portugal, and music also under Joseph Haas at Stuttgart. He taught Gregorian plainsong at Beuron and at the Cologne High School for music, was ordained priest in 1898 and became professor in 1930. His expert knowledge of

Gregorian plainsong has produced the following works, among others:

'Neue Schule des gregorianischen Choralgesanges' (1906 and later eds., also Eng., Fr. & It.).
'Cantus ecclesiastici' (1909 and later).
'Der gregorianische Choral' (1924, also Danish).

E. B.

646   ii   JOHNSON, Edward
Par. 1, l. 2 *should read*:

22 Aug. 1878; *d.* Guelph, Ont., 20 Apr. 1959).

647   i   Par. 3, l. 13 *should read*:
vocal and interpretative efficiency. He was succeeded by Rudolf Bing in 1950. Through-

649   i   JOHNSON, Robert (1)
CATALOGUE:
CHURCH MUSIC
Judei   l. 1.   judei *should read*:

l. 6 *should read*:
'[Dum transisset] Sabbatum', 4 v., B.M. Add. 17802-5

ll. 20-21 *should read*:
'[Dum transisset] Sabbatum', 5 v., B.M. Add. 11586. Christ Church, 984-88 (in Burney, 1935, pp. 795, 814).

Transfer this entry to stand below l. 7 *above.*

651   i   JOHNSTONE
Par. 2, l. 8 *should read*:

composed in 1949. In 1953 the Corporation of Manchester commissioned him to write an orchestral work for the City Charter Centenary Festival. This was 'The Oak and the Ash', and it was performed that year in Manchester by the Hallé Orchestra.

652   ii   JOLIVET
Add at end:
BIBL.—'La Vérité de Jeanne', oratorio, libretto and commentary (Rev. Mus., No. 237, 1957).

655   i   JOMMELLI
Add to See also, l. 1:
Classici Musica Italiana, Vol. 15 (extracts from 'Passione di Gesù Cristo').

ii   JONAS
Par. 2, l. 6 *should read*:
forte and musical theory. He taught at the

l. 9 *should read*:
Institute, founded by him) from 1935 to 1938. Until Dec.

657   i   JONES
Par. 1, l. 16 *should read*:
mobilization he returned to live at Swansea. The University of Wales made him a Doctor of Music in 1951. On the foundation of the Guild for the Promotion of Welsh Music in 1954 Jones was elected President.

657   ii   Par. 3, l. 12 *should read*:
of Britain. No. 4 (Aug. 1954) was commissioned by the National Eisteddfod Council and dedicated to Dylan Thomas.

CATALOGUE
Add under heading:
RADIO MUSIC
Songs for Dylan Thomas's 'Under Milk Wood'.

658   i   Add after l. 11:
Symphony No. 4 (1954).

JONES Edward (2)
Par. 1. Dates *should read*:
(*b.* Llanderfel, Merionethshire, 29 Mar. 1752; *d.* London, 18 Apr. 1824 [1]).

Add footnote:
[1] The days of both his birth and death were Easter Sundays.

662   i   JONGEN, Joseph
Par. 1, l. 1. Sept. *should read*:
Dec.[1]

l. 2.   13 July *should read*:
12 July

Add footnote:
[1] According to an official pamphlet issued by the Centre Belge de Documentation Musicale.

663   i   JONGEN, Léon
Par. 1, l. 1.   1885 *should read*:
1884

664   ii   Jonson
See. Add to l. 1:
Antheil ('Volpone', opera).

Add to l. 9:
Hamilton (I., 'Bartholomew Fair', overture).

l. 12.   2 masques). *should read*:
4 masques).

Add to l. 15:
Palmer (R., chorus).

665   i   JONSSON
GÖSTA   BIBL., l. 1.   GÖSTAX *should read*:

JORDA
Par. 2, l. 11 *should read*:
made a number of recordings. In 1954 he was appointed conductor of the San Francisco Symphony Orchestra. He has ap-

ii   JOSEFFY
Par. 4, l. 6 *should read*:
and his orchestra. He was appointed pianoforte professor at the New York National Conservatory of Music in 1888 and was there when Dvořák became director in 1892, succeeding him in that post in 1895. With advancing years his

669 ii JOSQUIN DES PRÉS
Add to BIBL. :

SARTORI, CLAUDIO, 'Josquin des Prés, cantore del duomo di Milano (1459–1472)' ('Annales Musicologiques', IV, 1956, p. 55).

See also. l. 2 *should read* :

J.). Chorwerk, Vols. 1, 3, 20, 23, 30, 33, 42, 54, 57, 64 (modern reprints). Collectio O.M.B., Vols. 6-8 & 12 (modern ed.). Köler (Mass on motet by J.). La Hèle (masses on

l. 4 *should read* :

cambiata (use of, exx.). Publikationen G.M.F., Vol. 5 (modern ed.). Song, p. 922 (mus. ex.). Vereniging, Vol. 44 (reprint of motet).

671 ii JOUBERT
Par. 1, l. 15 *should read* :

at the University of Hull.

Delete Par. 3 *(Catalogue) and replace by* :
OPERA
Op.
17. ' In the Drought ', 1 act (lib. by Adolph Wood. Afrikaans trans. by Anton Hartman).

RADIO OPERA
11. ' Antigone ' (lib. by Rachel Trickett).

BALLET
4. ' Vlei Legend ' (1952).

CHORAL WORKS
7a. Carol.
7b. Anthem.
8. ' Te Deum ' for double chorus & orch. (1948).
12. ' The Burghers of Calais ', cantata for solo voices, chorus and small orch.
14. Carol ' There is no rose '.
16. Anthem ' Great Lord of Lords '.
18. ' To Pan ', partsong for S.S.A. & Pf.
19. ' Libera plebem ', motet for S.A.A.T.B.B. unaccomp.
22. ' Incantation ' for S.A.T.B. unaccomp.
27. ' Welcome, Yule ', carol for S.A.T.B. unaccomp.
29. ' Solus ad victimam ', motet for unaccomp. chorus.

ORCHESTRAL WORKS
3. Overture (1951).
9. Symphonic Prelude (1948).
20. Symphony.
28. ' A North Country Overture.'

SOLO INSTRUMENT AND ORCHESTRA
13. Vn. Concerto.
25. Pf. Concerto.

CHAMBER MUSIC
1. String Quartet (1950).
10. Miniature String Quartet.

VIOLA AND PIANOFORTE
6. Sonata (1952).

PIANOFORTE MUSIC
2. ' Divertimento ' for pf. duet (1950).
21. Dance Suite.
24. Sonata.

ORGAN
15. Prelude on the ' Old Hundredth '.

HARP
23. Suite.

SONGS
5. 5 Songs for tenor (1951).
26. 4 Songs for tenor.

BIBL., l. 1. Ommegangen ' *should read* :
Ommegang '

672 ii Joyce
ll. 1-2 *should read* :

Joyce, James. *See* Antheil (song). Barber (S., songs). Bate (songs). Bax (song). Bliss (song). Bridge (Frank, song). Citkowitz (song cycle). Dallapiccola (poem for voice and chamber orch.).

l. 6. Moeran (9 songs). *should read* :
Moeran (10 songs).

676 i JUNGBAUER
Par. 1, l. 3 *should read* :

nr. Ingolstadt, 25 Mar. 1823).

JUON
Par. 2, ll. 1-4 *should read* :

Russian composer of Swiss descent. His family came from the Grisons and his father was an insurance official in Moscow, where he went to a German school. In 1888 he joined

l. 6. Hrimaly *should read* :
Hřímalÿ

677 i JUROVSKÝ
Par. 1, l. 1. Ulmanka *should read* :

Ulanka

683 i JUXON
Par. 1, l. 1 *should read* :

JUXON, William (or ? **George)** [1] (*b.* ? ; *d.* Canterbury,

Footnote. ll. 1-3 *should read* :

[1] The date of his death makes the conjecture that he may have been the same person as Archbishop Juxon, Laud's successor, an impossible one.

ii l. 4 *should read* :

is in B.M. Add. 30478-9 and also in the Peter-

684 i KABALEVSKY
Par. 2, ll. 6-9 *should read* :

entered the Skriabin Music School in 1919, a *technicum* with whose director, V. Selivanov, he studied the pianoforte. He studied composition at the same time with Vassilenko and Catoire. On leaving this school in 1925 he was

ii *Add to* BIBL. :

DANILEVICH, L., ' Dmitry Kabalevsky ' (Moscow, 1954).

CATALOGUE :
SOLO INSTRUMENT AND OR-CHESTRA
Add at end :

Pf. Concerto No 3 (1952).

CHAMBER MUSIC
ll. 1-2 *should read* :

String Quartet No. 1, A mi., Op. 4 (1929).
String Quartet No. 2 (1946).

685 i PIANOFORTE MUSIC
l. 2 *should read*:
Sonata No. 1, Op. 6 (1929).

ll. 6-8 *should read*:
24 Preludes (1943–44).
Sonata No. 2 (1945).
Sonata No. 3 (1946).

688 ii **Kafka**
l. 1 Henze *should read*:
Heiss (songs). Henze

689 ii **Kaiser**
l. 2. Casal y Chapí *should read*:
Casal Chapí

690 ii **KALCHER**
Par. 1, l. 2 *should read*:
sing, Bavaria, 15 May 1764; *d.* Munich, 2
Feb. 1827).

691 ii **KALISCHER**
Par. 2, l. 1. profound *should read*:
prolific but uncritical

693 ii **KÁLMÁN**
Add at end:
BIBL.—OESTERREICHER, RUDOLF, 'Emmerich Kálmán:
der Weg eines Komponisten' (Zürich, 1954).

697 i **KAMINSKI**
Par. 1, l. 3. 14 June *should read*:
21 June

ii *Add to* BIBL.:
SAMSON, INGRID, 'Das Vokalschaffen von Heinrich
Kaminski, mit Ausnahme der Opern' (Frankfurt
o/M., 1956).

CATALOGUE
OPERAS
l. 5 *should read*:
music-drama for narrator and orch., completed
1946, prod. Göttingen, 29 Jan. 1950.

698 ii *Add after* **KANIA**:
KANN, Hans (*b.* Vienna, 14 Feb. 1927).
Austrian pianist and composer. He studied
the pianoforte with August Göllner, Otto
Schulhof and Friedrich Wührer, and composition with Josef Lechthaler and the Schoenberg pupil Pollnaur. In 1945 he began his
concert activities with recitals in Austria and
Germany, and he has since appeared at
numerous orchestral concerts under distinguished conductors. In 1955 he gave the
first performance of Wagner-Régeny's Piano
Concerto at the Vienna Festival. He holds
diplomas and medals of the international
pianists' competitions at Geneva, Bolzano,
Munich and Vienna. He has also broadcast
frequently and made gramophone records.
In 1950–52 Kann taught at the Vienna
Academy and in 1954 he was appointed professor of the pianoforte at the University of

the State Academy of Japan in Tokyo, in
succession to Leonid Kreutzer. His compositions include a string Trio, Music on
Flemish Folksongs for recorder and pianoforte, Sonatina, 'Klavierstück' and 'Tanz-
stück' for pianoforte, 2 pieces for two pianofortes and songs. E. B.

699 ii **KAPP**
Par. 1, l. 2 *should read*:
works and letters. His augmented edition of
Emerich Kastner's 'Beethovens sämtliche
Briefe' (1923) is also valuable. His other
studies include:

Add to books at end:
'200 Jahre Staatsoper im Bild' (1942).

700 i **KAPRÁL**
Par. 3, l. 4 *should read*:
celona, 20 Apr. 1936.

ii **KARAJAN**
Par. 2, l. 19 *should read*:
which he has also toured abroad. In 1955 he
visited the U.S.A. and succeeded Furtwängler
as conductor of the Berlin Philharmonic
Orchestra. In 1956 he became artistic
director of the Vienna State Opera.

707 i **KASHIN**
Par. 1, l. 2 *should read*:
c. 1769 [1]; *d.* Moscow, 22 Dec. 1841).

Par. 2, ll. 1-2 *should read*:
Russian composer. He was a serf owned
by one Bibikov, but was liberated in 1799.
He became a pupil of Sarti in Bessarabia in
1788 and composed three operas: 'Natalia',

Add footnote:
[1] Kashin is known to have given a concert in 1790
and to have been at least twenty at that time.

ii **KASKI**
Par. 1, l. 2 *should read*:
Pielisjärvi, 21 June 1885; *d.* Helsingfors, 19
Sept. 1957).

KASSERN
Par. 1, l. 2 *should read*:
19 Mar. 1904; *d.* New York, 2 May 1957).

708 i **KASTALSKY**
Par. 2, l. 5. 1900. *should read*:
1910.

ii *Add after* **KASTALSKY**:
KASTNER, Emerich (*b.* Vienna, 29 Mar.
1847; *d.* Vienna, 5 Dec. 1916).
Austrian musical author and editor. He
published a 'Richard Wagner Katalog'

(Offenbach, 1878) and started an annual 'Richard Wagner Kalender' in 1881, of which, however, only three issues were published (until 1883). 'Bühnenfestspiele zu Bayreuth' and 'Wagneriana' appeared in Vienna in 1884 and 1885. He became editor of the 'Wiener musikalische Zeitung' in 1885 (continued as 'Wiener musikalische Chronik' from 1887). Ironically enough, in view of its title, his 'Neuestes und vollständigstes Tonkünstler und Opernlexikon', begun in 1889, was not destined ever to be completed. An appendix to Nottebohm's Beethoven Catalogue, 'Biblioteca Beethoveniana', was brought up to date by Theodor von Frimmel in 1925.

Kastner edited 'Beethovens sämtliche Briefe' (Leipzig, 1911, enlarged edition by Julius Kapp, 1923) and, with Kapp, 'Richard Wagner; gesammelte Briefe' (Leipzig, 1914).

E. B.

709 i **KASTNER, J. G.**
Treatises, No. 16 *should read*:
'La Harpe d'Éole. . . .'

ii **KASTNER, M. S.**
Par. 2, ll. 1-2 *should read*:

British-born musicologist, pianist and harpsichord player of Alsatian origin. He studied music at Amster-

Par. 3, l. 15 *should read*:

and composers. In 1958 appeared under his editorship modern facsimile reprints of Juan Bermudo's 'Declaración de instrumentos musicales' (1555) and Francisco Salinas's 'De musica libri septem' (1577) in the 'Documenta Musicologica' series of the International Society for Musicology. His edition of the keyboard works of Coelho began (in 1959) the series 'Portugaliae Musica'.

710 ii **KAUFFMANN, Paul**
Par. 1, l. 1. Dates *should read*:
(*b.* Nuremberg, [bapt. 29 Oct.] 1568; *d.* Nuremberg, [buried 9] Oct. 1632).

Par. 2, l. 1 *should read*:
German music publisher.

712 ii **KAYSER, Isfrid**
Par. 1, l. 1. Dates *should read*:
(*b.* Türkheim o/Wertach, 13 Mar. 1712; *d.* Kloster Marchtal nr. Ehingen, 1 Mar. 1771).

Par. 2, l. 1 *should read*:
German composer. He was a

KAYSER, P. C.
Par. 1, l. 2. Zürich *should read*:
Oberstrass nr. Zürich

R

713 i **KAZANLY**
Par. 1, l. 2. 15 Aug. *should read*:
5 Aug.

ii **KAZURO**
Par. 1, l. 2 *should read*:
Wilno, 1 Aug. 1882).

714 ii **Keats**
l. 3. Britten ('Serenade' for *should read*:
Britten ('Nocturne', No. 7; 'Serenade' for

KEEL
Par. 1, l. 1. 1871). *should read*:
1871; *d.* London, Aug. 1954).

715 ii **KEILBERTH**
Par. 2, l. 19 *should read*:
European countries. In 1958 he succeeded Ferenc Fricsay as conductor-in-chief of the Munich State Opera.   K. W. B.

717 ii **KEISER**
See also, l. 3 *should read*:
(collabs.). Handel, p. 50 ('Nero', adapt. of lib.). Hasse (engaged for Hamburg Opera).

718 i **Keller, Gottfried**
l. 4 *should read*:
and Juliet', opera). Hegar (partsong). Hindemith (chorus). Křenek (3

ii **KELLER**
Par. 1, ll. 3-6 *should read*:
reviewer for 'The Music Review'. In 1949 he became joint editor of the periodical 'Music Survey', founded in 1947, in succession to C. H. Stepan. He became a

Add at end:
In 1959 he joined the B.B.C. Music Division.

719 i **KELLEY**
Par. 2, l. 16. (1915) *should read*:
(1894)

Par. 4, l. 8. (1922); *should read*:
(1919);

l. 9. (1922); *should read*:
(1913);

KELLIE
Par. 2, l. 2 *should read*:
He was a pupil of Stamitz at Mannheim about 1750, and his six trio

l. 5 *should read*:
heim school.

He was still abroad, as Viscount Fenton, when his father died on 3 Apr. 1756 and he succeeded to the title. After his return to

Scotland he spent most of his life in Edinburgh. He was a member of the Musical Society of Edinburgh and in 1772 is described as its Deputy Governor.

According to W. B. Howie there is a record by Boswell saying that on 26 Oct. 1764 a " concerto " by Kellie was played at Cassel as an overture to Molière's ' Tartuffe '.

Lord Kellie also wrote sym-

719   i   Par. 2, l. 6.   minuets, *should read*: minuets[2],

Add footnote:

[2] The minuets are in fact second movements of the overtures.

ii   Par. 1, ll. 4-6 *should read*:

General) Reid, who seems to have formed the Society of the Temple of Apollo.

Kellie remained a bachelor. Drink and high living caused a great deterioration in his health and fortune. In 1769 his estate, apart from Kellie Castle, was sold. He died on his return journey home after a visit to the Continent (? Spa) for a cure. Robert

KELLNER, J. C.
Par. 2, l. 9.   freude ' [2] *should read*:

freude ' [3]

Footnote 2 becomes 3.

KELLNER, Johann Peter
Par. 1, l. 3 *should read*:

roda, 19 Apr. 1772).

720   ii   *Add after* KELLY, Cuthbert:

KELLY, Earl of.   *See* KELLIE.

721   i   KELLY, Michael
Par. 3, l. 2.   Finaroli *should read*:

Fenaroli

722   i   KELSEY
Par. 1, l. 2 *should read*:

July 1891 ; *d.* Cardiff, 16 Dec. 1958).

ii   KELWAY, Thomas
Par. 1, l. 2.   1749 *should read*:

1744 [3]

Add footnote:

[3] Not 1749, a date wrongly inscribed on the memorial at Chichester Cathedral when it was recut in 1846. The correct date is given by C. E. Welch in ' Two Cathedral Organists' (' Chichester Papers ', No. 8) ; *see also* article on Thomas Kelway by W. D. Peckham (' Sussex Notes and Queries ', Feb. 1749).

723   ii   *Add before* KEMPERS :

KEMPE, Rudolf (*b.* Niederpoyritz nr. Dresden, 14 June 1910).

German conductor. He studied in the Orchestral School of the Dresden State Orches-

tra and graduated from it as first oboist and coach in the Leipzig Gewandhaus Orchestra in 1929. He remained there until 1936, when he began to be active as a conductor at Leipzig. Having afterwards held conductorships at Chemnitz and Weimar, he became Musical Director-in-chief of the Dresden State Orchestra in 1949, and in 1952-54 he held a similar post at the Bavarian State Opera in Munich.

Kempe is now so widely known and successful that he no longer holds a permanent appointment but pursues a brilliant career with casual engagements. These have included, since 1954, operatic performances at the Komische Oper and State Opera in Berlin, the Vienna State Opera, the London Royal Opera at Covent Garden, the Gran Teatro at Barcelona, the Metropolitan Opera in New York and the Salzburg Festivals. He has also fulfilled concert engagements at the Edinburgh and Holland Festivals, at Dresden, Leipzig, Berlin, Munich, Buenos Aires, Venice, Trieste, Vienna, Milan, London, New York and some smaller German towns as well as in Australia. He has conducted broadcast concerts from Leipzig, Dresden, Berlin, Munich, Frankfort, Cologne, London and Rome.

E. B.

BIBL.—JÄCKEL, HILDEGARD & SCHMIEDEL, GOTTFRIED, ' Bildnis des schaffenden Künstlers : ein Dirigent bei der Arbeit ' (Leipzig, 1955).

726   i   KENNEDY, Marjorie
Par. 1, l. 16 *should read*:

her memoirs, ' A Life of Song ', in 1928.

Par. 2, l. 7 *should read*:

' Hebridean Song and the Laws of Interpretation.'

727   ii   KEPLER
Add at end:

See also Hindemith (' Harmonie der Welt ', opera & symphony).

728   i   KERLE
Add at end:

See also Denkmäler (2) II, Vol. 26 (modern ed.).

729   i   KERLL
l. 6.   XLIX *should read*:

XXV

l. 7.   LIX *should read*:

XXX

KERPEN
Par. 1, l. 2 *should read*:

(*b.* Engers, 23 Mar. 1749; *d.* Heilbronn, 31 Dec. 1802).

Par. 2, l. 1 *should read*:

German amateur composer.

729   i   **KERR, Grainger**
Par. 1, l. 2 *should read*:
Dundee, 12 Oct. 1864; *d.* London, 24 Feb. 1955).

ii   **KERR, Harrison**
Par. 1, l. 2.   1899). *should read*:
1897).

731   i   **KETTLE-DRUM** *should read*:
KETTLE-DRUM. *See* DRUM. (*PLATES* 32, Vol. IV, p. 492, No. 4; 49, Vol. VI, p. 622, No. 1.)

KEUCHENTHAL
Par. 1.   Dates *should read*:
(*b.* Ellrich am Harz, 1522; *d.* St. Andreasberg, 1583).

Par. 2, l. 1 *should read*:
German clergyman and musi-

KEUSSLER
Par. 1, l. 2.   Niederwalthe *should read*:
Niederwartha

735   ii   **KEY BUGLE**
See also should read:
See also Military Calls. Ophicleide. *PLATE* 14, Vol. II, p. 446, No. 6.

747   ii   **KHACHATURIAN**
CATALOGUE:
Add to BALLETS:
'Spartacus' (1954).

748   i   *Add to See also*:
Makarova (wife).

KHANDOSHKIN
Par. 1, l. 1.   **Evastafievich** *should read*:
Evstafievich

l. 2 *should read*:
(*b.* ?, *c.* 1747; *d.* St. Petersburg, 16 Mar. 1804).

Par. 2, l. 3 *should read*:
in Russia. Little is known of his biography

l. 5 *should read*:
was a pupil of Tito Porta at Tartini's school at Padua. He returned to Russia in 1762, played in the court orchestra and became its leader in 1773. His compositions

749   i   **KIEL**
Par. 1, l. 2.   14 Sept. *should read*:
13 Sept.

749   ii   **KIENLEN**
Par. 1, l. 2 *should read*:
[bapt. 14] Dec. 1783; *d.* Dessau, 7 Dec. 1829).

750   ii   **KIENZL**
Add before See also:
BIBL.—SITTNER, HANS (ed.), 'Wilhelm Kienzls "Lebenswanderung" im Auszug' (Zürich, 1953).

751   i   **KIESEWETTER**
Par. 2, ll. 2-4 *should read*:
Ambros, the musical historian. He made friends in Vienna with Beethoven, who had settled there in 1792, but in 1794 was appointed to the Military Chancellery and sent to the headquarters at Schwetzingen on the Rhine. He was occupied with the army until 1801, when he returned to Vienna. He became an

ii   **KILADZE**
Par. 1 *should read*:
KILADZE, Grigory Varfolomeyevich
(*b.* Batum, 28 Oct. 1902).

l. 2.   Batum, 1905). *should read*:
Batum, 3 Dec. 1903).

752   ii   **KILPINEN**
Par. 1, l. 2 *should read*:
fors, 4 Feb. 1892; *d.* Helsingfors, 2 Mar. 1959).

753   ii   **KINDERMANN**
Par. 2, l. 22.   XXI *should read*:
XXI-XXIV

754   i   **KINDLER**
Par. 2, ll. 11-12 *should read*:
organized and conducted the National Symphony Orchestra at Washington until his death. His sister Frieda, a pianist, was married

KING, A. H.
Par. 2, ll. 9-17 *should read*:
where he had been Superintendent of the Music Room since Nov. 1944, and became the Editor of the annual volume of accessions of music. In 1948 he was appointed Hon. Secretary of the 'British Union Catalogue of Early Music', and he continued to serve as Secretary after the change of the Council into a registered company after the publication of the Catalogue in Sept. 1957.

Add new paragraph after this:
In 1951 King was elected Vice-President of the International Association of Music

Libraries, and in 1955 he became its President, holding this office until 1959. From 1951 onwards he served as Chairman of the Executive Committee of the British Institute of Recorded Sound.

754   i   Pars. 4 & 5 *should read*:

A number of articles containing important new information on Mozart were reissued in book-form in 1955 under the title of ' Mozart in Retrospect: Studies in Criticism and Bibliography '; a second edition appeared in 1956, and a German translation of the first chapter was published as ' Mozart in Spiegel der Geschichte: 1756–1956 ' (Cassel, 1956: No. 9 of ' Musikwissenschaftliche Arbeiten '). An edition of Alfred Einstein's ' Short History of Music ' with 224 illustrations selected by King appeared in 1953. Among his articles the following may be mentioned:

' The Music of the British Museum, 1753–1953 ' (Proc. Roy. Mus. Ass., Session 79, 1953).
' Some Notes on the Armonica ' (M.M.R., Mar.-Apr. 1956).
' The Music Information Services of the British Museum ' (' Journal of Documentation ', Mar. 1957).
' William Barclay Squire, 1855–1955, Music Librarian ' (' The Library ', Mar. 1957).

755   ii   **KING STEPHEN**
          ll. 14-17 *should read*:

missioned to compose it. He provided an overture for each as well as 8 numbers for ' Die Ruinen ' and 9 for ' King Stephen '. The pieces were

757   i   **KING'S THEATRE**
          Par. 1, ll. 1-2 *should read*:

Love ' (7 Mar. 1706) spoken plays only were produced at the new house until it became

759   ii   **KINSKY**
          Par. 1, l. 2 *should read*:

Prussia, 29 Sept. 1882; *d.* Berlin, 7 Apr. 1951).

760   i   BOOKS
          After l. 7 *add*:

' Das Werk Beethovens: thematisch-bibliographisches Verzeichnis ' (posth., ed. by Hans Halm) (Berlin, 1955).

Kipling
l. 7. *Add*:

Grimm (F.-K., ' Jungle-Book ' suite, cello & pf.).

KIPNIS
          Par. 1, l. 2 *should read*:
13 Feb. 1891).

ii   **KIRBY**
          Par. 2, l. 20 *should read*:

in primitive music. He retired as Professor Emeritus in Dec. 1952 to pursue musical

and historical research. In 1954 he became President of the South African Association for the Advancement of Science.

760   ii   Par. 3, l. 6.   Old Cape Shanty
          should read:

Old Capstan Shanty.

Par. 5. *Add at bottom*:

' The Musical Instruments of the Native Races of South Africa ' (Oxford, 1934; 2nd ed. Johannesburg, 1953).

761   i   *Add at end*:

' A Source Book of the Wreck of the Grosvenor East Indiaman ' (Cape Town, 1953).
' Andrew Smith and Natal ' (Cape Town, 1956).

762   i   **KIRCHGESSNER**
          Footnote. l. 3 *should read*:

belong to the spring or early summer of 1791, and he assigns it the number 617a.

ii   *Add after* **KIRCHMANN**:

KIRCHNER, Leon (*b.* Brooklyn, N.Y., 24 Jan. 1919).

American composer of German and Russian descent. The family moved to Los Angeles when he was nine years of age. He began to compose early and studied the pianoforte. He became a pupil of Toch for composition and later, giving up medical studies, of Schoenberg. In 1938–39 he studied at the University of California at Berkeley, where he came under the very different influence of Bloch, but he returned to Los Angeles and prepared himself for academic honours under Albert Elkus and Edward Strickland. After a course under Sessions in New York, he joined the Army Signal Corps in 1943. On being discharged in 1946 he took the B.A. and was appointed University lecturer at Berkeley. In 1954 he was appointed Professor of Music at Oakland, California.

Kirchner has been described by Aaron Copland as belonging to the " Bartók-Berg axis " in music, but his earlier works also showed other influences, such as that of Mahler. The following is a list of his works up to 1955:

' Dawn ' (García Lorca) for chorus & organ (1943–46).
' Sinfonia ' for orch. (1951).
' Toccata ' for stgs., wind & perc. (1955).
Piece for pf. & orch. (1946).
Pf. Concerto (1953).
String Quartet (1949).
Trio for vn., cello & pf. (1954).
Duo for vn. & pf. (1947).
' Sonata concertante ' for vn. & pf. (1952).
Pf. Sonata (1948).
' Little Suite ' for pf. (1949).
Songs for soprano & pf.
     Letter (S. Alexander) (1943).
     The Times are Nightfall (Gerard Manley Hopkins) (1943).
     Of Obedience (Walt Whitman) (1950).
     The Runner (Whitman) (1950).

E. B.

BIBL.—RINGER, ALEXANDER L., ' Leon Kirchner ' (M.Q., XLIII, 1957, p. 1).

768 i **KISIELEWSKI**
Par. 1, l. 1.   Warsaw, 1911). *should read*:
Warsaw, 1911 ; *d.* Warsaw, 20 June 1955).

769 i **KISTNER (2)**
l. 1.   Leipzig, 1805 ; *should read*:
Leipzig, ? ;

771 ii **KITTEL, Kaspar**
Par. 1.   Dates *should read*:
(*b.* Lauenstein, 1603 ; *d.* Dresden, 9 Oct. 1639).

Par. 2, l. 1 *should read*:
German composer.   He was

ll. 6-7 *should read*:
inspector of instruments.¹   A follower

Add footnote :
¹ It was not he, but Christoph Kittel, who became
court organist at Dresden until 1669, when he was
succeeded by another Kaspar Kittel.

772 i **KJELLSTRÖM**
Par. 1, l. 2.   5 Feb. 1951). *should read* :
5 Dec. 1950).

773 i **KJERULF**
Add at end :
BIBL.—GRINDE, NILS, ' En Halfdan Kjerulf-biografi '
(' Norsk Musikkgranskning ', 1954–55).

774 ii *Add before* **KLEBER**
KLEBE, Giselher (*b.* Mannheim, 28 June
1925).
German composer.   He studied with Josef
Rufer and Boris Blacher.   His work first
attracted attention beyond Germany in 1954,
when a Rhapsody for orchestra won a prize
at the International Festival in Rome in Apr.
and his violin Sonata, Op. 14, was broadcast
by the B.B.C.'s Third Programme in Oct.
His enterprise in the use of unusual musical
media is shown by a ' Szene ' for 4 solo violins,
tutti violins and pianoforte duet, and by two
works for speaker, chorus and orchestra,
' Römische Elegien ' and ' Die Zwitschermaschine ', the latter inspired by drawings by
Paul Klee.   This work received its first performance at the Donaueschingen Festival of
1955.   Other works include a Double Concerto for violin, cello and orchestra, and a
4-act opera, ' Die Räuber ', based on Schiller's
play, which was produced at the new Cologne
opera-house during a week of modern German
works in 1957.   E. B.

775 i **KLECKI**
Par. 3, l. 8 *should read* :
Orchestra, and in 1958 he succeeded Walter
Hendl as Musical Director of the Dallas
(Texas) Symphony Orchestra.

775 i **KLECZYŃSKI (1)**
Par. 1, l. 1.   *b.*?, 1756; *should read* :
b. ?, 14 June 1756;

ii *Add before* **KLEEBERG** :
Klee, Paul. *See* Klebe (' Zwitschermaschine '). Heiss
(' Konfigurationen ' for orch.).

776 i **KLEIBER**
Par. 1, l. 1.   1890). *should read* :
1890 ; *d.* Zürich, 27 Jan. 1956).

ii *Add at end* :
BIBL.—RUSSELL, JOHN, ' Erich Kleiber : a Memoir '
(London, 1957).

777 ii **KLEINKNECHT**
(**1**). l. 1 *should read* :

(**1**) **Hans Conrad Kleinknecht** (*b.* ?,
1630 ; *d.* ?, 1705),

(**2**). ll. 1-2 *should read* :

(**2**) **Johann Kleinknecht** (*b.* Ulm, 7 Dec.
1676 ; *d.* Ulm, 4 June 1751), *Konzertmeister*,
? son of the preceding.

778 i **Kleist, Ewald von**
l. 1.   Refs. *should read* :
See Bach (C. P. E., 2 songs).   Schubert (part-

780 i **KLENAU,** CATALOGUE
OPERAS
Delete l. 11 *and substitute* :
' Elisabeth von England ' (Cassel, 29 Mar. 1939).¹

Footnote. ll. 1-2 *should read* :
¹ Given at the Berlin State Opera in 1940, the title
changed to ' Die Königin ' for performance in Germany
during

781 ii **" KLENOVSKY "**
ll. 6-8 *should read* :
novsky ".   Wood probably adopted it from
the Russian word *klen*—maple wood in order

783 i **KLINDWORTH**
Par. 3, ll. 6-7 *should read* :
Berlin, which in 1893 merged with the Schar-
wenka Conservatory, the two becoming the
Konservatorium der Musik Klindworth-
Scharwenka.   He taught there until 1897
and retired to Potsdam in 1898, devoting
himself to

ii **KLINGENSTEIN**
Par. 1, l. 1.   Dates *should read* :
(*b.* ? Peiting nr. Schongau, 1545 ; *d.* Augsburg, 1 Mar.

784 i **KLÖFFLER**
Par. 1, l. 2 *should read* :
(*b.* Cassel, 20 Apr. 1725 ; *d.* Burgsteinfurt nr.
Münster, [buried 21] Feb. 1790).

784   i   **Klopstock**
l. 1. Refs. *should read*:
See Bach (C. P. E., 4 songs). Dalberg ('Evas Klagen',

l. 3. *Add*:
Horn (C., 'Thusnelda', voc. scene).

785   i   **KLOTZ**
(3). ll. 1-2 *should read*:
(3) **Sebastian Klotz** (*b*. Mittenwald, 18
Jan. 1696; *d*. Mittenwald, 20 Jan. 1775), son
of the preceding. He sur-

(4). ll. 1-2 *should read*:
(4) **Johann Carl Klotz** (*b*. Mittenwald, 29
Jan. 1709; *d*. Mittenwald, 25 May 1769),
brother of the preceding. He
Delete last 2 lines (The relationships
. . . obscure.)

(5). ll. 1-2 *should read*:
(5) **Georg Klotz** (*b*. Mittenwald, 1723;
d. Mittenwald, 1 Nov. 1797), son of (3),
represents the stage of the art

(6). ll. 1-2 *should read*:
(6) **Michael Klotz** (*b*. Mittenwald, 25
Sept. 1749; *d*. Mittenwald, 19 Jan. 1814),
son of (4).

(7). ll. 1-2 *should read*:
(7) **Carl Klotz** (*b*. Mittenwald, 5 Nov.
1726; *d*. Mittenwald, ?), son of (5).

(8). ll. 1-2 *should read*:
(8) **Egidius Klotz (ii)** (*b*. Mittenwald, 1
Sept. 1733; *d*. Mittenwald, 8 Aug. 1805),
son of (3).

ii   **KNAB**
Par. 1, l. 2 *should read*:
conia, 19 Feb. 1881; *d*. Wörishofen, 24 June
1951).

788   ii   **KNIGHT, Robert**
Delete entire entry.

KNIGHT, Thomas
Par. 1, ll. 2-3 *should read*:
poser, once referred to in error as Robert, with
the result that a fictitious composer came into
being. Nothing is known of his birth,

ll. 8-13 *should read*:
mained there until at least 1549. John Day
included

ll. 19-end *should read*:
house) and a Kyrie and two motets occur in
B.M. Add. MSS 17802-5.

792   i   **KOBRZA**
Cancel entry.

KOBZA
Entry should read:
KOBZA, KOBSA.   *See* BAGPIPE (POLAND).
'UD.

ii   **KOCH,** List of Works
l. 11. 'Archipelag' *should read*:
Arkipelag'

793   i   **KOCH, H. C.**
Par. 1, l. 2.   12 Mar. *should read*:
19 Mar.

ii   **KOCHAŃSKI, Wacław**
Par. 1. Dates *should read*:
(*b*. Kamieniec, Podolia, 2 Mar. 1878; *d*.
Warsaw, 5 June 1939).

794   ii   **KOCZALSKI**
Par. 1, l. 2.   3 Jan. 1885 *should read*:
3 Jan. 1884

KOCŽWARA
Par. 2, ll. 1-3 *should read*:
Bohemian musician. He lived at Bath
between 1775 and 1777, as may be gathered
from his six string Quartets, Op. 3, dedicated
to Lady Craven, " to be had of the author at
Bath and at Welcker's Music Shop, No. 9,
opposite the Opera House Hay-Market, London "; for Welcker was at that address during
those two years only.[2] Later on Koczwara
settled in London, where he published a set
of six songs

l. 11.   Martin's.[2] *should read*:
Martin's.[3]

Add footnote:
[2] Information from Mr. A. Hyatt King, Superintendent of the Music Room, British Museum.

Footnote 2 becomes 3.

805   ii   **KŒCHLIN**
Par. 1, l. 2 *should read*:
1867; *d*. Le Canadel, Var, 31 Dec. 1950).

814   i   **KOHAULT**
Par. 1, ll. 1-2. Dates *should read*:
(*b*. Žatek, 4 May 1738; *d*. Paris, 1793).

815   ii   *Add before* **Kolář**:
KOŁACZKOWSKI, Jerzy (*b*. Złoczów,
S.E. Poland, 23 Sept. 1907).
Polish conductor and chorus master. He
completed his musical education under

Koffler and Adam Sołtys at the Lwów Conservatory. In 1933 he was appointed conductor of two Polish choral societies, 'Echo-Macierz' and 'Lutnia' at Lwów, the post he held until 1939. He also conducted symphony concerts. In 1937 he became Head of Music Dept. at the Lwów Radio. During the second world war he found himself with the Polish Armed Forces in Scotland, and it was there that in 1940 he founded the 'Polish Army Choir'[1] with which he gave nearly 450 concerts. He appeared as a guest conductor with the London Philharmonic and London Symphony Orchestras as well as with the Liverpool Symphony Orchestra. He also made several recordings in London.

In 1946 he returned to his native country to take the post of the Assistant Director of Music Department of the 'Polskie Radio' in Warsaw. In 1948 he founded the Polish Radio Choir which he conducted for several years. Now he is Programme Organizer of the Folk Music and Choral sections of the Polish Radio in Warsaw.

C. R. H.

[1] See 'Polish Army Choir', Vol. VI. pp. 838-39.

815   ii   **KOLB**
Par. 1, l. 1. Köstlarn should read:
Kösslarn

l. 2. 1703; should read:
[bapt. 29 Jan.] 1703;

816   ii   **KÖLER**
Par. 1, ll. 1-2. Dates should read:
(b. Zwickau, c. 1532; d. Zwickau, 25 July 1565).

Par. 2, ll. 1-7 should read:

German composer. He entered the University of Ingolstadt in 1551 as a " pauper ", having finished his schooling at the Latin school of his native town. After a year or two in Bohemia, where he apparently held some non-musical employment and married a local girl, he was cantor at Joachimsthal in 1556-57 and then at Altenburg, when in 1563 he was called to be Kapellmeister to the Duke Johann Albrecht I of Mecklenburg at Schwerin. The town council of Zwickau called him back home to become cantor of St. Mary's, the principal church. But he held the post only for barely four months, dying of some unknown cause in his early thirties.

817   i   Add at end:

BIBL.—EISMANN, GEORG, 'David Köler: ein protestantischer Komponist des 16. Jahrhunderts' (Berlin, 1958).

817   ii   **KOLLMANN (1)**
Par. 1, l. 1 should read:

(1) August Friedrich (Christoph) Kollmann (b.

l. 2.   c. 1756; should read:
21 Mar. 1756;

Par. 2, l. 6. 'Essay on Practical Harmony' should read:
'An Essay on Musical Harmony'

l. 10. 'New should read:
'A New

818   i   Par. 1, ll. 4-10 should read:

Seventh'. He also proposed (1799) an edition of Bach's 'Well-tempered Clavier'.[1] A curiosity of his, and a piece of programme music quite in the taste of the time, is an orchestral symphony on a shipwreck that took place on 6 Jan. 1786 off the Dorset coast at Seacombe. An arrangement of this appeared ten years later with the following title[2]:

THE SHIPWRECK OR LOSS OF THE HALSEWELL EAST INDIA-MAN being a grand instrumental piece adapted to the pianoforte with an accompaniment for a violin and violoncello, composed, arranged and humbly dedicated to his Excellency Baron Lenthe by

A. F. KOLLMANN
Corri, Dussek and Co. 1796.

Add footnotes:

[1] A manuscript copy of Part I in the University Library at St. Andrews bears the following inscription: THIS COPY OF THESE SPLENDID FUGUES AND PRELUDES WAS THE FIRST COPY WHICH CAME INTO ENGLAND FOR THE EXPRESS USE OF AUG. FRED. CHRIST. KOLLMANN, AND TRANSCRIBED IN GERMANY BY HIS DESIRE. AND FROM THIS COPY WHICH WAS LENT TO THE LATE MR SAMUEL WESLEY AND FROM WHICH HE (MR S. WESLEY AND THE LATE MR HORN) ED. THE PUBLICATION OF THE 24 PRELUDES AND FUGUES BY SEB. BACH BEARING WESLEY AND HORN'S NAME.
[2] Copy in the B.M., press-mark g. 161 (5).

Signature should read:
G., adds. s. G. (ii).

Add after **KÖLN**:

KOLNEDER, Walter (b. Wels, Upper Austria, 1 July 1910).

Austrian musicologist and violist. He studied at the Salzburg Mozarteum and with Wilhelm Fischer (musicology) in Vienna, where he also interested himself in folk music research. He taught at the Graz Conservatory in 1936-39 and at the High School for Musical Education there from the same year to 1945. In 1947-53 he was leader of the violas in the Municipal Orchestra, Innsbruck. In 1953 he became director of the Conservatory of Luxemburg, a post he still retained when he was appointed lecturer in music at the University of Saarbrücken, where he took his doctor's degree that year, his dissertation being 'Antonio Vivaldi: neue Studien zur

Biographie und Stilistik seiner Werke'. 'Aufführungspraxis bei Vivaldi' was published in 1955. He has also written numerous articles on this master, who is his chief speciality, others being Austrian folk music and Bartók. Kolneder has edited much 17th- and 18th-century music apart from Vivaldi, including M.-A. Charpentier, Stradella, Albinoni, Torelli, Telemann, Leopold Mozart, etc. He is the contributor of two chapters on 18th-century music to the N.O.H.M., on orchestral music and the solo concerto.

E. B.

818   ii   **KONDRACKI**
Par. 1, l. 2.   4 Oct. *should read*:
5 Sept.

820   i   **KONING**
Par. 1, l. 2 *should read*:
d. Amsterdam, between 9 Dec. 1717 and 28 Feb. 1718).

ii   **KONJOVIC**
Date *should read*:
(b. Sombor, Serbia, 6 May 1882).

821   ii   **KOPILOV**
Par. 1, l. 2 *should read*:
(b. St. Petersburg, 14 July 1854; d. Strelna nr. St. Petersburg,

823   ii   *Add before* **KORESHCHENKO**:
KOREAN TEMPLE BLOCKS. Nontonal percussion instruments made of hollow wood, originally used in light and dance music but occasionally found in modern orchestral scores.

824   ii   **KORNAUTH**
Par. 2, l. 10 *should read*:
Guido Adler. In 1910 he visited the U.S.A. In 1916 he became coach at

l. 16 *should read*:
abroad. In

l. 26.   1913 *should read*:
1912

List of Works
ORCHESTRAL WORKS
Op. 20 & 35 *should read*:
20. 'Orchestersuite.'
35. Symph. Suite No. 2.

825   i   **KORNGOLD**
Par. 1, l 2.   1897). *should read*:
1897; d. Hollywood, 29 Nov. 1957).

Par. 2, l. 4.   eleven *should read*:
thirteen

825   i   Par. 2, l. 6 *should read*:
the Vienna Court Opera. It was orchestrated by Zemlinsky from a pianoforte Suite. Two pianoforte

ii   List of Works
PANTOMIME
l. 2.   1908 *should read*:
4 Oct. 1910.

PIANOFORTE AND ORCHESTRA
Entry should read:
SOLO INSTRUMENT AND ORCHESTRA
17. Pf. Concerto, C♯ ma.
35. Vn. Concerto.

KOROLEWICZ-WAYDOWA
Par. 1, l. 2 *should read*:
Warsaw, 1875; d. Warsaw, 20 June 1955).

829   ii   **KOSSENKO**
Par. 1, l. 2.   1896; *should read*:
23 Nov. 1896;

830   ii   **KOVAL**
Par. 1 *should read*:
KOVAL, Marian Victorovich (b. Pristan Voznessenya nr. Olonets, 17 Aug. 1907).

832   i   **KOZELUCH**
Par. 1, l. 1.   **Leopold** *should read*:
Leopold (Antonín)

ii   *Add at end*:
BIBL.—WEINMANN, ALEXANDER, 'Verzeichnis der Verlagswerke des musikalischen Magazins Leopold Koželuh' (Vienna, 1950).

KOŽELUH
Par. 2, l. 9.   12 Mar. *should read*:
2 Mar.

BIBL.   1944 *should read*:
1946

Add at end:
See also Musica Antiqua Bohemica, Vol. 15 (modern ed. of stg. 4tet).

KOZINA
Par. 1, l. 2 *should read*:
venia, 4 June 1907).

833   ii   **KRAF**
Par. 1. Dates *should read*:
(b. Neustadt, c. 1590; d. Altdorf-Weingarten 15 Mar. 1662).

Par. 2, l. 1 *should read*:
German organist and com-

834   ii   **KRAFT (3)**, l. 2.   d. ?), *should read*:
d. Stuttgart, 4 Dec. 1874),

835   i   **KRAIŃSKI**
Par. 1. Dates *should read* :
(*b.* ?, 1556; *d.* Łaszczów, 21 Jan. 1618).

ii   **KRAMM**
Par. 1, l. 2 *should read* :
1890; *d.* Oslo, 27 Apr. 1958).

Par. 2, l. 1 *should read* :
Norwegian conductor, violinist and pianist
of German origin.

l. 21 *should read* :
Radio, which office he retained, with the
exception of the years 1940–45, until 1957.
                                    M. K. W.
KRANZ
Par. 1, l. 2 *should read* :
6 Apr. 1752; *d.* Stuttgart, 20 Feb. 1810).

836   i   **Krasnahorská**
l. 4 *should read* :
lib.). Secret (Smetana, lib.). Smetana (4 libs.).

Kraszewski
l. 1. **Jósef** *should read* :
Józef
See Paderewski *should read* :
See Malawski (' Stara baśń ', incid. m.). Paderewski

l. 2. Różicki *should read* :
Różycki

ii   **KRATZER (3)**
l. 2. Warsaw, 1890 *should read* :
Warsaw, 15 Nov. 1890

837   i   **KRAUS, J. M.**
Par. 1, l. 2 *should read* :
den II, eller De tre Sultaninnorna ' (after
Favart).[1] This had

l. 18 *should read* :
Stockholm.
A Symphony in C minor of 1783 is re-
printed in Vol. II of ' Monumenta Musicae
Svecicae ' (1959).   K. D.

Add footnote :
[1] For the complicated history of the libretto *see*
ENTFÜHRUNG AUS DEM SERAIL.

Add to BIBL. :
DALE, KATHLEEN, ' The " Swedish Mozart " ' (' Listen-
er ', 15 Sept. 1955).
' Verzeichnis der musikalischen Werke von Jos. Kraus '
(A.M.W., 1925).

BIBL., l. 8. " Aventyraren " *should read* :
" Äfventyraren "

KRAUS, Lambert
Par. 1, l. 1. Pfreund, *should read* :
Pfreimd,

837   i   Par. 1, l. 2. ? ; *should read* :
[bapt. 27] Sept. 1729;

KRAUS, Lili
Par. 1. 1908 *should read* :
3 Apr. 1905

ii   *Add before* **KRAUSE** :
KRAUS, Otakar (*b.* Prague, 10 Dec. 1909).
British (naturalized) baritone singer of
Czech birth. He studied in Prague with
Konrad Wallerstein and in Milan with
Fernando Carpi. He made his début at Brno
as Amonasro in 1935 and after an engagement at the Bratislava Opera in 1936–39 he
settled in England. During the war years he
was heard in Mussorgsky's ' Sorochintsy Fair '
at the Savoy and Adelphi Theatres in London,
and afterwards with the Carl Rosa Opera as
Valentine, Silvio, Germont, Sharpless, Scarpia,
Dapertutto and Dr. Miracle. In 1946 he
joined the English Opera Group and created
the part of Tarquinius in Britten's ' The Rape
of Lucretia ' at Glyndebourne in 1946; he
also sang Lockit in ' The Beggar's Opera '
(Britten version) and the Vicar in ' Albert
Herring '. For the 1950–51 season he was a
member of the Netherlands Opera in
Amsterdam.

In 1951 he was engaged by Covent Garden
to appear in the ' Ring ' as Alberich, and this
led to a permanent engagement by the Royal
Opera, which is still (1960) in force. His
parts there have included Diomede in Walton's
' Troilus and Cressida ' and King Fisher in
Tippett's ' The Midsummer Marriage ', both
of which he created. His exceptionally wide
range of parts have further included Caspar,
Pizarro, Kurwenal, Klingsor, the Doctor in
' Wozzeck ', Jokanaan, Orestes, Scarpia,
Renato, Amonasro, Rigoletto and Rangoni.
At the Venice Festival of 1951 he created
Nick Shadow in Stravinsky's ' The Rake's
Progress ', repeating the part at La Scala,
Milan, and at Glyndebourne in 1958.

Kraus also sang Alberich under Kleiber
in Rome (1952–53), under Karajan in Vienna
(1959), and under Kempe at Bayreuth (1960).
He took part in the 1952 season at Rio, singing
Pizarro, the Flying Dutchman and Kurwenal.
His partly Italian training makes him a
smoother singer in the Wagnerian parts than
many German artists; but he shines especially
as an extremely versatile and accomplished
singing actor. He is always a vital and
striking stage figure, and a master of make-up.
                                    H. D. R.

KRAUSE
Par. 1, l. 2 *should read* :
zig, Silesia, [bapt. 17] Apr. 1719; *d.* Berlin,
4 May 1770).

838   i   **KRAUSS, Clemens**
      Add to BIBL. :
GREGOR, JOSEPH, ' Clemens Krauss: eine musikalische
    Sendung ' (Vienna & Zürich, 1953).
PANDER, OSCAR VON, ' Clemens Krauss in München '
    (Munich, 1955).

      KREBS, J. L.
      Par. 1, l. 3 *should read* :
1 Jan. 1780).

842   i   **KREISSLE VON HELLBORN**
          Par. 1, l. 2.   1812 ; *should read* :
19 Jan. 1822 ;

847   —   **KŘENEK,** CATALOGUE
          OPERAS
          Col. 3, l. 12.   ? *should read* :
Composer.

          Col. 5.   *Add to last line* (' Dark Waters ') :
Los Angeles, Bovard Auditorium, 2 May 1951.

          Add at end :
| — | ' The Belfry ', 1 act. | Composer, based on | 1906. | Chicago, Mar. 1957. |
| | | Herman Melville. | | |

      ii   ORCHESTRAL WORKS
           l. 22 *should read* :
' Symphonic Elegy ' for stgs. in memory of Anton
    Webern (1946).

           Add at end :
11 Short Pieces (1954).

           SOLO INSTRUMENTS AND OR-
           CHESTRA
           Op. 29 *should read* :
29. Vn. Concerto No. 1 (1924).

           Add at end :
— Concerto for harp (1951).
— Cello Concerto (1953).
— Vn. Concerto No. 2 (1953).

848   i   PIANOFORTE MUSIC
          Add at end :
— 20 Miniatures (1940).

      ii   BOOKS, etc.
           Add after l. 19 :
Ockeghem ' (New York, 1953).

      KRESS, Jakob
      Par. 1, ll. 1-2.   *c.* 1736). *should
      read* :
1730).

849   i   **KRESS, J. A.**
          Par. 1, ll. 1-2. Dates *should read* :
(*b.* ?, 1644 ; *d.* Stuttgart, 23 July 1684).

      ii   **KRETZSCHMAR**
           Par. 1, l. 3.   12 May *should read* :
10 May

850   i   **KREUSSER**
          Par. 1, l. 2 *should read* :
feld, 31 Dec. 1743 ; *d.* Frankfort o/M., 3
Nov. 1810).

852   i   **KREUTZER SONATA**
          ll. 6-11 *should read* :
Rodolphe Kreutzer, whom Beethoven had
met in 1798. The composer first played the
work in public with the mulatto violinist
George Bridgetower, with whom he afterwards quarrelled, and who would no doubt
otherwise have been the dedicatee. The last
movement was origin-

855   i   **KRIEGK**
          Par. 1 *should read* :
      KRIEGK, Johann Jacob (*b.* Meiningen,
23 June 1750 ; *d.* Meiningen, 24 Dec. 1814).

859   ii   **KRUMPHOLZ**
           Par. 1, l. 2 *should read* :
Budenice nr. Zlonice, 8 May 1742 ; *d.* Paris,
19 Feb.

860   ii   **KRUSEMAN**
           Par. 1, l. 2 *should read* :
dam, 17 Nov. 1887 ; *d.* The Hague, 31 Jan.
1955).

           Par. 2, ll. 32-34 *should read* :
these is a large ' Geïllustreerd Muzieklexicon ',
edited in collaboration with G. Keller and
issued in 1932, with a supplement, edited with
Henri Zagwijn, issued in 1949.   An attractive
but small

861   ii   **KUBA**
           Par. 1, l. 2 *should read* :
16 Apr. 1863 ; *d.* Prague, 30 Nov. 1956).

863   i   **KUBELÍK**
          Par. 3, l. 5 *should read* :
Symphony Orchestra.   In 1955, back in
London again, he became Musical Director
of the Royal Opera at Covent Garden.   He
is also a gifted

868   i   **KUHNAU**
          Add to See also :
Denkmäler (2), Vol. IV (modern ed. of clavier works).

      ii   **KULENKAMPFF**
           Par. 1, l. 2.   Schaffhausen, Oct.
           should read :
Zürich, 5 Oct.

869   ii   *Add before* **KUNDERA** :
           KUNC, Zinka.   *See* MILANOV.

872   i   **KUNTZEN (3)**
          l. 8.   Keerlighed *should read* :
Kærlighed

873   ii   **KURTH**
Par. 1, l. 2.   2 Apr. *should read*:
2 Aug.

875   i   **KÜRZINGER, I. F. X.**
Par. 1, l. 2 *should read*:
Rosenheim, Bavaria, 30 Jan. 1724; *d.* Würzburg, 12 Aug.

KÜRZINGER, P. I.
Par. 1, ll. 1-2.   Dates *should read*:
(*b.* Mergentheim, 28 Apr. 1750; *d.* Vienna, ? after 1820).

877   i   **KUSSER**
Add to See also:
Denkmäler (5) II (modern ed. of extracts from 'Erindo ').

ii   **KUTCHER**
Par. 2, ll. 7-8 *should read*:
Kutcher String Quartet with Peter Tas, Raymond Jeremy and Douglas Cameron.   Tas

was later succeeded in turn by Frederick Grinke and Max Salpeter.

879   i   **KVAPIL**
Par. 1, l. 2 *should read*:
Moravia, 21 Apr. 1892; *d.* Brno, 18 Feb. 1958).

881   ii   **KYRIE**
Par. 3, ll. 9-11 *should read*:
adapted this to the Kyrie of the present Prayer Book, and his adaptation is in frequent use.   The ninefold Kyrie is now very generally used in place of the Responses to the Commandments.   The Kyrie provided by Marbeck for a

Signature should read:
w. s. r., adds. w. h. f., rev.

Cancel footnote.

VOL. V

12   ii   **L'AFFILARD**
Entry should read:

L'AFFILARD, Michel.   *See* AFFILARD.

Cancel article.

13   i   **La Fontaine**
l. 3 *should read:*

& pf.).   Colasse ('Astrée', lib.).   Couperin (4, song).
Cox (H., 3 songs).

15   ii   **LA GUERRE**
Add at end:

See also Lyrebird Press (modern ed. of harpsichord
pieces & 'Céphale et Procris').

17   i   **LA HÈLE**
Par. 1, ll. 2-3 *should read:*

Antwerp, 1547; *d.* Madrid, 19 Feb. 1587).

18   ii   *Add before* **LAJARTE**:

LAISSEZ VIBRER. A term used to direct
percussion instrumentalists and harpists to
allow the instrument or string to vibrate until
the sound has died away. It is frequently
used also to cancel the indication 'sec'.

24   i   **LALANDE, Michel**
Par. 1, l. 1 *should read:*

LALANDE, Michel-Richard de [1]   (*b.*
Paris,

Add footnote:

[1] The spelling "Delalande" appears in several signatures of his own, but on a bass viol that belonged to him,
now in the possession of Thurston Dart, he signed himself "Monsieur Richard, Sieur de Lalande", as though
his Christian name had been Michel, his surname
Richard, and he called himself the Squire of Lalande,
or perhaps even of the Lande. The truth is, of course,
the French people, like English, had no consistent spelling for their names and signed themselves in various
ways as fancy dictated at the moment; and whatever
French practice may be for future treatment of this composer's name in works of reference, catalogues and so
on, English-speaking readers will always be much more
likely to look for him under letter L than letter D, not
to mention letter R.
In his preface to 'Notes et références' (*see* Bibl.)
Norbert Dufourcq says the name was always spelt
"Delalande" by the composer and his family, and
reproduces the signature in facsimile. He adds that he
could find no evidence for the assertion sometimes made
that the prefix "de" was due to the composer's having
been ennobled by the king.

l. 2.   Dec. *should read:*
15 Dec.

25   i   *Add to* BIBL.:

DUFOURCQ, NORBERT (ed.), 'Notes et références pour
servir à une histoire de Michel-Richard Delalande
. . . établies d'après les papiers d'André Tessier,
précédées de documents inédits et suivies du catalogue thématique de l'œuvre, publiées par . . .
Marcelle Benoit, Marie Bert, Sylvie Spycket &
Odile Vivier' (Paris, 1957).

Add to See also:

Lyrebird Press (modern ed. of 'Symphonies').

25   ii   **LALEWICZ**
Par. 2, l. 1 *should read:*

Argentine (naturalized) pianist of Polish
origin: He was a

ll. 12-13 *should read:*

in Buenos Aires. Among his pupils were
Artur Rodziński, Mieczysław Münz, Zyg-
munt Dygat,

31   ii   **LAMBERT**
Par. 4, l. 23 *should read:*

performances at the pianoforte. He had a
special affection for Puccini's work and conducted his 'Manon Lescaut' at Covent
Garden in 1937 and 'Turandot' in 1939;
the latter work also in later revivals in a lavish
new production.

Par. 6, l. 5 *should read:*

Roseingrave, among others. In 1946 he made
an arrangement of Purcell's 'Fairy Queen'
for Covent Garden, and this was revived there
in 1951. His critical

33   i   **LAMBERT, Lucien**
Par 1, l. 1. Jan. *should read:*
5 Jan.

35   ii   *Add after* **LAMM**:

LAMMERS, Gerda (*b.* Berlin, ?).
German soprano singer. She studied at
the Berlin High School for Music under Lula
Mysz-Gmeiner and also with Margret Schwed-
ler-Lohmann. The first fifteen years of her
career were spent in concert and *Lieder* singing, and she gained a great reputation as an
interpreter of Bach. It was not until 1955
that she turned to the opera stage, and in the
summer of that year she sang Ortlinde at
Bayreuth. She was engaged for the Cassel
Opera the same autumn, making her début
in the difficult part of Marie in 'Wozzeck'
and following it with the title-part of Elektra.
During the next four seasons at Cassel she
sang Senta, Penthesilea in Schoeck's opera of
that name, Alceste, the "Sängerin" in
Hindemith's 'Cardillac', Santuzza, the title
part in 'Medea', Isolde, and Donna Anna.
In Nov. 1957, when she happened to be in
London to sing at a private concert, Christel
Goltz, who had been engaged to sing Elektra
at Covent Garden, fell ill; Lammers was
rushed to the opera-house for an audition and
made her English stage début before an
audience most of whom had never heard of
her. Her success was phenomenal, and the
ovation which greeted her at the close of the
evening was one of the greatest in the history
of the house. She sang Elektra's fiendishly
difficult music as if she were embarking on
a *Lieder* programme, never forcing her voice

or making an unpleasant sound. Her acting had a simplicity and dignity that was most moving. Lammers was re-engaged to sing the same part during the theatre's centenary celebrations in May 1958 and a few weeks later was heard as Dido in Purcell's ' Dido and Aeneas ' at Ingestre Hall. She sang Kundry in ' Parsifal ' at Covent Garden in 1959. Despite her great operatic triumph she still regards the concert platform as her main musical activity.   H. D. R.

39   i   **LAMPUGNANI**
Par. 3, ll. 5-7 *should read*:

gran Tamerlano ' there, and that the ' Rossane ' witnessed by

41   ii   **LANDI**
Add to BIBL. :

FORTUNE, NIGEL, ' Italian Secular Monody from 1600 to 1635 : an Introductory Survey ' (M.Q., XXXIX, 1953, p. 171).

LANDINI
Add to BIBL. :

NOLTHENIUS, HÉLÈNE, ' Renaissance in Mei : Florentijns leven rond Francesco Landini ' (Utrecht & Antwerp, 1956).

See also should read :
See also Song, p. 916.

42   i   *Add before* **Landor** :
LANDON, H. C. (Howard Chandler) Robbins (*b.* Boston, Mass., 6 Mar. 1926). American musicologist. He studied musical history with Alfred J. Swan and composition with Harl MacDonald at Swarthmore College, and afterwards musicology with Karl Geiringer at Boston University, where he took the B.Mus. in 1947. In that year he founded the Haydn Society, which however remained inactive until 1949, and he was its General Secretary until 1951, when the Research Office in Vienna, where he went to live, was discontinued. He is an editor of the new collected editions of Haydn's and Mozart's works, and a member of the Zentralinstitut für Mozartforschung of Salzburg. He is engaged (1956), with Professor Jan La Rue, on a thematic and source catalogue of all symphonies and related works written between 1750 and 1800.
Landon's first book was ' The Symphonies of Joseph Haydn ' (London, 1955), a large and very important work of reference which he was anxious to publish in England. The second was ' The Mozart Companion ' (London, 1956), edited by him and Donald Mitchell. He has contributed to M. Rev. (on Haydn), to the ' American Record Guide ' (on Bruckner) and, writing in German as well as in English, to the ' Oesterreichische Musik-

zeitschrift ' and ' Das Mozart-Buch ' (Olten, 1956). He is also the editor of many scholarly editions of music, including much Haydn and a new reconstruction of Mozart's unfinished C minor Mass. In 1957, at the monastery of Göttweig, he discovered the composer of the " Jena " Symphony, wrongly attributed to Beethoven.   E. B.
See also Jena Symphony.

42   ii   **LANDOWSKA**
Par. 1, l. 2 *should read* :
1879 ; *d.* Lakeville, Conn., 16 Aug. 1959).

43   ii   Par. 2, l. 5 *should read* :
champêtre '. Among later works stimulated by her is Frank Martin's Concerto. Her campaign for the re-

45   ii   **LANG, P. H.**
Par. 2, l. 4 *should read* :
at the Universities of Heidelberg and Paris and at Cornell

46   i   *Add at end* :
In 1955 Lang entered on a new phase of his career by accepting the post of Music Critic to the New York Herald Tribune. His reviews and weekly essays are distinguished by a penetrating yet lively style based on vast erudition and the solid rock of musical scholarship. As adviser to the publishing house of W. W. Norton he has been largely responsible for building up one of the world's finest catalogues of books on music. As President of the International Society for Musicology (1955-58) he did much to broaden the scope and aims of the Society and to maintain the high standard of its congresses. He is a Fellow of the American Academy of Arts and Sciences, and D.Mus. (*h.c.*) of Temple University and N.E. Conservatory.

48   i   **LANGE, F. C.**
Par. 2, l. 8 *should read* :
Arts et Traditions Populaires (Paris). In 1958 he returned to Uruguay as Director of the Instituto Interamericano de Musicología at Montevideo.

50-51   **LANIER**
Add at end :
LANIER(E).[1] English family of musicians of French descent.
An examination of the wills of the family has made it possible to construct a vast family tree which, though showing more than fifty descendants from Nicholas (2) before 1660, is far from complete. Much has been clarified,

[1] Also Laneare, Laneer, Laneir, Lanière, Lannear, Lanyer, etc.

although two puzzles remain: the relationship of the first Nicholas (2) to the first John (1) — possibly brothers — and of a Nicholas who was buried in London, at St. Martin-in-the-Fields in 1646. Most authorities (following Vertue) have assumed that it was he and not Nicholas (4) who produced the two books of etchings supposedly dated 1636 and 1638, since the title-plate of the first mentions that it was done "a l'età sua giovanile di sessanta otto". On examination, however, 1636 appears to be a misreading for 1656, in which year Nicholas (4) actually was sixty-eight (the second book is in fact undated). It is he, of course, who is much more likely to have carried out the engraving, and it is fairly certain that he owned some of the originals. But the question remains who that other Nicholas was. A return of recusants at Westminster dated 23 Dec. 1628 seems to provide the answer, for it includes one "Nicholas Laneere, a cook, in St. Martin's".

John (1) was as unreproductive as Nicholas (2) was the reverse, for only a single daughter survived him, whereas Nicholas was the father of at least eleven children: six sons (John [3], Alfonso [5], Andrea [6], Clement [7], Innocent [8] and Jerome [9]), all of whom served in the royal band, and five daughters, two of whom made musical marriages — Katherine to Daniel Farrant and Ellen to Alfonso Ferrabosco (iii). Of the next generation, John (3) had seven children surviving to maturity, including Nicholas (4), John (10) and Judith, the wife of Edward Norgate. Clement (7) had nine children and Jerome (9) eleven, one of whom, William (13), served in the royal music. Andrea (6) had eight children; a son, Thomas (12), was in the royal band, as was Henry (11), the son of Alfonso (5).

(1) **John (Jean) Lanier(e)** (or **Lanière**) (b. Rouen, ?; d. London, 29 Nov. 1572). He settled in London in 1561, perhaps having come from France with his brother Nicholas (2). In the return of aliens for Nov. 1571 he is described as a "Frenchman and musician, his wife and ij children hathe byn here tenne yeares and are of the French Churche". The return for May of the same year calls him "John Lanyarde, denizein and musicion to the Quene's Maᵗⁱᵉ . . .", so that he is obviously the sackbut player who served the queen from 1563 to 1572. He had property in Crutched Friars.

(2) **Nicholas Lanier(e)** (or **Lanière**) (b. Rouen, ?; d. Greenwich, 1612 [1]), brother? of the preceding. It was he who founded the English branch of the family. While the Earl of Hertford was in Paris in 1561, "Nicholas Laigner, late of the company to the late French King Henry . . . a good player on

[1] Between 28 Jan. and 1 July.

the flute and also on the cornet . . . sober, honest . . . born at Rouen", was engaged to serve both as a messenger and as a replacement for Petit Guillaume, one of the queen's flute players lately dead. Confirmation of his service under Henri II is to be found in lists of "chantres et autres joueurs d'instruments" of the French king's chamber, which include Nicolas Lasnier for the years 1559 and 1560.[2]

Lanier settled in London and lodged for several years with another French musician, Guillaume de Vache, and later owned property at East Greenwich. The return of aliens for 1567 mentions both him and de Vache as "musicons, servauntes to the quenes maᵗⁱᵉ" and says that Nicholas had been resident for five years. It was probably he who caused John (1) to join him in England, for he took up his place in the queen's band in 1561. He served in it until his death in 1612.

(3) **John Lanier(e)** (b. ?; d. 1616 [3]), sackbut player, son of the preceding. He lived at Camberwell and had other property at Shudy Camps, Cambridgeshire, not at Greenwich as had hitherto been supposed. He was sackbut player in the royal band from 1582 until the time of his death. He was probably the John Lannyer who, on 12 Oct. 1585, was married, at Holy Trinity, Minories, to the daughter of Mark Antony Galliardello, another court musician, where his son Nicholas (4) was christened nearly three years later.

(4) **Nicholas Lanier(e)** (b. London, [bapt. 10 Sept.] 1588; d. London, Feb. 1666), singer, composer and painter, son of the preceding. There is no reason to suppose, as has been done hitherto, that he played the flute in the royal band in 1604 — that was more likely his grandfather Nicholas (2) — nor that he was in the service of Prince Henry, but he may be the "Laniere" alluded to by Herrick in a poem to Henry Lawes. In 1613 he wrote and sang the song 'Bring away this sacred tree' in Campion's masque for the marriage of Robert Carr, Earl of Somerset, and Lady Frances Howard.

Lanier composed the music for Ben Jonson's masque 'Lovers made Men' given at Lord Haye's house on 22 Feb. 1617, and in it he is described as introducing the "stylo recitativo", apparently for the first time in England. He sang in the piece and painted the scenery. He also provided music for the same poet's masques 'The Vision of Delight'

[2] Archives Nationales, KK 129 f. 46 v, and Bibl. Nat. Dupuy 852 f. 23 v. I am indebted to M. François Lesure for this information, although he doubts whether the family came from Rouen. In any case, there was a family of instrumentalists named Lagnier living in Paris at this time.

[3] Between 21 Nov. and 21 Dec.

(1617), 'Gypsies Metamorphosed'[1] (1621) and 'Masque of Augurs' (1622). As Master of the King's Musick after 1626 he must have been concerned with the production of many more, but he is not known to have composed any masque music after 1622. This appointment, at a salary of £200 a year, is dated 11 July 1626. But before that, in 1625, his knowledge of the art of painting was turned to account, for he was sent to Italy by Charles I and the Duke of Buckingham to buy pictures. He set out in June for Genoa and Venice, where he stayed with the agent Daniel Nys. He was in England by Oct. 1627, and later in that year he travelled by way of Brussels, Basel and Venice to Mantua, where he and Nys between them bought part of the late duke's collection of pictures and statuary. The total purchase cost about £35,000 but the king did not settle the debt for several years. When Charles's own collection was sold after his execution Lanier paid more than £500 for certain items, including his own portrait by Van Dyck. He had also acquired for the king a 'St. Peter' by Guido Reni and exchanged pictures with that artist. Some of the pictures from Mantua are still in the royal collection at Hampton Court, but the rest were dispersed and are now at the National Gallery, the Louvre, the Belvedere, the Prado, the Uffizi and elsewhere, about half of them or a little more being probably still traceable. There were also hundreds of prints bearing Lanier's mark (a small star), of which 34 are at Windsor, but many were stolen or have otherwise disappeared.

On 6 Feb. 1629 Lanier was arrested, with his brother John (10) and uncles Andrea (6), Clement (7) and Jerome (9), for disorderly behaviour in the street. The affair caused a considerable stir, and an angry exchange of letters between the City and court ensued. In 1630 Lanier set Herrick's poem on the birth of Prince Charles to music.

In 1646 he was at Antwerp, The Hague and Utrecht: "old, unhappye in a manner in exile, plundered not only of his fortune, but of all his musicall papers, nay, almost of his witts and vertue", as he described himself in a letter to Constantijn Huygens. He was also in France at one stage, and William Sanderson in 'Graphice' (1658) says that "Laniere in Paris, by a cunning way of tempering his colours with Chimney Soote, the Painting becomes duskish, and seems ancient; which done, he roules up and thereby it crackls, and so mistaken for an old Principall, it being well copied from a good hand".

In 1656 Lanier published a book of etchings (most of them by Lukas Vostermann) from drawings by Parmegiano that had been in the Earl of Arundel's collection: 'Proue

prime fatti a l'aqua forte da N: Lanier a l'età sua giovanile di sessanta otto Anni 1656'. A similar set from drawings by Parmagiano and Giulio Romano is entitled 'Maschere delineato di Julio Romano ex Coll[ne] NLanier', but bears no date. Six portraits (including sketches) of him are known or suspected, including those by Van Dyck (painted at Genoa and said to have been the cause of the king's inviting that artist to England, where he stayed with Lanier's brother-in-law Edward Norgate) and Rembrandt.

Several songs and dialogues by him are in the B.M. (Add. MSS 11608, 29396; Eg. MS 2013). A cantata, 'Hero and Leander', is in B.M. (Add. MS 14399, 33236). Songs are also to be found in B.M. Add. MSS 10337, 22100, 34160; Lambeth MS 1041; New York Public Library Drexel MSS 4041, 4275; Bodl. Lib. MS Don. C. 57; Ch. Ch. MSS 17, 18; Edinburgh Univ. Lib. MS Dc. 1.69; Advocates' Lib., Edinburgh, MSS 5.2.14, 5.2.17; Anderson Lib., Glasgow Univ. MS R. d. 58-61; Fitz. 'John Bull MS' 52. D; Magdalene Coll., Cambridge, Pepys MS 2803; Trinity Coll., Dublin, MS F. 5.13. All these are 17th-century sources and for the most part independent of the songs which Playford issued from 1652 onwards. These are given in Day & Murrie's 'English Song-Books 1651-1702' (1940).

Lanier is generally credited with having introduced *stile recitativo* into Jonson's masques of 1617. In the absence of music this claim must be accepted only with the knowledge that it was not made until 1640, nor ever independently substantiated; and it is unlikely that *stile recitativo* meant the same to Ben Jonson as it did to Davenant and a later generation of musicians. But Lanier was obviously an innovator, for his song in Campian's masque (1613), "Bring away this sacred tree", is one of the earliest declamatory ayres, a type which the Lawes brothers, Wilson, Coleman and Lanier himself developed between 1620 and 1660. This song was printed by Parry in O.H.M., Vol. III (2nd ed., 1938, p. 201), but erroneously assigned to Davenant's masque 'Luminalia' (1637), a mistake inherited from J. Stafford Smith's 'Musica Antiqua' (1812), where it is also printed. By dating the song a quarter of a century too late Parry somewhat reduced its significance. In the voice-part syllabic quantities were exaggerated so that strong (or long) syllables received three, four, six or eight times the length of short syllables (usually quavers). The accompaniment was chordal, anticipating a true continuo realization, though not as yet figured in the bass. The effect was of a heroic declamation, almost completely unmelodic, though strongly

---

[1] With Robert Johnson.

tonal and peculiarly suited to the sumptuous baroqueries of Inigo Jones. Nor was it surprising that the necessity of being heard in a large masquing hall above a considerable orchestra caused the intimate style of the lute-song proper to suffer an eclipse.

On his return from Italy Lanier composed his cantata ' Hero and Leander '[1], which was very different from his declamatory ayres and much closer to the recitative style of Monteverdi. It was surely inspired by Italian models. The narrative is set in *recitativo secco*, while the various moods of Hero's soliloquy — her agonies and near-delirium in expectation of Leander and final grief at his death — are expressed with amazing force. There is a variety in the declamation and a boldness in harmonic treatment that make Henry Lawes's ' Ariadne ' lament a feeble imitation. One other formal innovation which Lanier may have imported was the strophically varied aria over a ground-bass: he set Carew's ' No more shall meades be decked with flowers ' in this way.

It is evident that much of Lanier's output has not survived; indeed he implies as much in the letter quoted above. Even so, he is undoubtedly one of the most important songwriters following Dowland. He was the composer of the first English ' opera ', ' Lovers made Men ' (1617), for although it may not have been in recitative, the music was continuous throughout. His artistic taste brought to England some of the world's greatest works of art, now sadly dispersed and destroyed. He was, as Roger North said, an " ingenious virtuoso ".

(5) Alfonso Lanier (*b.* ? ; *d.* London, 1613), son of (2). He served as recorder player in the royal music from 1594 to his death, but he must also have held an army commission, for he is referred to as Captain Alfonso Lanier and was awarded a " grant of the office of weighing of hay and straw brought to London and Westminster, for 20 years " in 1604. On his death the patent devolved upon his widow Emelia (herself the authoress of a book of poems, ' Salve Deus Rex Judeorum ' [1611]). But she, in rather an unbusinesslike fashion, made it over to her brother-in-law, Innocent, and was poorly compensated in return. As late as 1636 she petitioned the then holder, Clement, for compensation, but without receiving satisfaction.

(6) Andrea Lanier (*b.* ? ; *d.* Greenwich, [buried 2 Nov.] 1660), wind player, brother of the preceding, son of (2). He succeeded to his father's place as one of the flutes in the royal music in 1612, which he held for the rest of his life; but he seems to have played

the cornett as well and was in receipt of payments from about 1603. From June 1626 onwards he was paid extra to keep and teach two boys the flute and cornett, and in 1633 his brother Alfonso's son Andrea was added to his charge. In 1640 his two original pupils were replaced by another nephew, William (13), and his own son Thomas (12), who received his father's place in 1660. Andrea was buried at Greenwich.

(7) Clement Lanier (*b.* ? ; *d.* London, 1661), wind player, brother of the preceding, son of (2). He played the sackbut, cornett and recorder in the king's band from 1604 onwards. The hay-weighing monopoly which had been assigned to Alfonso was given to Clement in 1636, with compensation to be paid to Alfonso's widow Emelia. This he seems to have been extremely loth to do, and some litigation on this and other matters respecting his office followed. According to Vertue he bought £98 worth of goods and pictures at the sale of Charles I's estate.

(8) Innocent Lanier (*b.* ? ; *d.* London, 1625), flautist, brother of the preceding, son of (2). He played the flute in the royal band from 1592 to his death. He does not appear to have married, and his character seems rather sour. At the death of his brother Alfonso he persuaded the widow, Emelia, to make over the hay-weighing office to him, so that he might obtain a new grant for a further twenty-one years and share half the profit with her. He received the grant in 1616, but all he paid Emelia was £8. In 1619, together with Hugh Lydiard and his brother-in-law Alfonso Ferrabosco, he was granted a licence " to cleanse the Thames of flats and shelves, with grant of fines . . . for annoyances in the river, of permission to sell sand and gravel they dig out, and of an allowance of 1[d]. a ton of strangers' goods imported and exported ". This must have been a very profitable monopoly, yet there were many complaints of its bad management, and he proved " an ill partner " to his associates. There was also trouble over his property at Lewisham. After his death letters of administration were granted to his brother Clement.

(9) Jerome Lanier (*b.* ? ; *d.* Greenwich, 1657), wind player, brother of the preceding, son of (2). He served as a cornett, sackbut and hautboy player in the royal band from 1603 to 1642. Like several of his brothers he seems to have profited from a patent, this time for the transport of lampreys, and like Clement and Nicholas (4) he was an art connoisseur. He paid at least £239 for goods and pictures at the sale of Charles I's collection and housed them in his place at Greenwich, where in 1652 John Evelyn was invited to see them :

---

[1] Manfred Bukofzer printed a short section of this in ' Music in the Baroque Era ' (1948), p. 183.

2 Aug. . . . I went to see *Jer: Laniers* rare Collection of Pictures, especially those of *Julio Romanos*, which

S

surely had been the Kings . . . there were also excellent things by *Polydore, Guido, Raphael, Tintoret* &c.

Richard Symonds tells how, when Charles I acquired part of the Mantua collection,

quick silver was got in amongst them and made them all black. Mr Hieronomo Laniere told me that to cleanse them first he tryd fasting spittle. then he mixt it wth warm milk. & those would not do. at last he cleansed them with Aqua Vita alone. being warm'd & that took of all the spotts & Blackness. & he says twill take of Old Varnishes.

Jerome was buried at Greenwich.

(10) John Lanier (*b.* ? ; *d.* London, 1650), son of John (3). He served as musician for the lutes and voices in the king's band from 1625 to 1642. He sang the part of Irene in Shirley's 'Triumph of Peace' (1634) and is mentioned in Richard Lovelace's 'Lucasta' (1649) as having set some of the songs. But neither these nor any others appear to have survived. He was buried at St. Giles-in-the-Fields.

(11) Henry Lanier (*b.* ? ; *d.* London, 1633), flautist, cousin of the preceding, son of Alfonso (5). He was appointed flute player in the royal music in the place of Nicholas Guy in 1629. In the year of his death his son Andrea was put under his uncle Andrea (6) to be trained in music, but nothing is heard of him again.

(12) Thomas Lanier (*b.* London, [bapt. 23 June] 1633 ; *d.* ?, *c.* 1686), wind player and lutenist, cousin of the preceding, son of Andrea (6). He served as flute and cornett player in the royal band from 1643 to 1668 and from then on as one of the lutes until 1686. His father trained him in music, and at the Restoration he petitioned the king " for the continuance of the three places of music in which in 1643 the late king joined him with his father ". Between 1661 and 1662 three accusations were filed against him for debt and in the next two years he was in court three times, twice as defendant and once as plaintiff. In 1660 " Thomas Lanier, of the Inner Temple " petitioned the king for the receivership of Suffolk, Cambridgeshire, Leicestershire and Warwickshire, or some other county, on the strength of his family's long and loyal service, but although he did so several times, he does not seem to have been successful. An attorney was appointed for him in 1686 and he probably died soon after, since his name disappears from the records after that date. He was the father of General Sir John Lanier, Governor of Jersey.

(13) William Lanier (*b.* London, [bapt. 21 Sept.] 1618 ; *d.* ?, *c.* 1661), sackbut player, cousin of the preceding, son of Jerome (9). There is a " grant of a musicians place for the sackbuts to Jerome and Wm. Laniere, his son " dated 28 Jan. 1626, at which time he was not yet eight. His cousin Thomas also held a place from his tenth year. Probably

these places were reserved for them until they had reached the required standard, for regular payments to William did not begin until 1641, when he succeeded to John Adson's place. He may have died before the Restoration, or as late as 1661, when John Singleton took his place as from 3 June.   I. S.

BIBLIOGRAPHY

Cust, L. ' The Lanier Family ' (' Miscellanea Genealogica et Heraldica ', VI, Fifth series, 1926–28, pp. 375-83).
' Foreign Artists of the Reformed Religion Working in London, 1560–1660 ' (Proc. of the Huguenot Soc. of London, VII, 1903, pp. 78-80).
Emslie, McD. ' Nicholas Lanier's Innovations in English Song ' (M. & L., XLI, 1960, pp. 13-27).
Glück, G. ' Some Portraits of Musicians by Van Dyck ' (' The Burlington Magazine ', LXIX, 1936, pp. 148-153).
de Hevesy, A. ' Rembrandt and Nicholas Lanier ' (*ibid.* pp. 152-54).
Luzio, A. ' La Galleria dei Gonzaga venduta all' Inghiltera nel 1627–1628 ', 1913, pp. 137-67.
Noel Sainsbury, W. ' Original Unpublished Papers relating to Sir Peter Paul Rubens ', 1859, pp. 320-40.
Spink, I. ' Lanier in Italy ' (M. & L., XL, 1959, pp. 242-52).
Stuart-Wortley, C. ' Portraits by Van Dyck ' (Old Master Drawings, 1937, pp. 26-27).

51   i   LANIER (4)

A detailed list of 56 of the pictures bought in Italy by Nicholas Lanier, the whereabouts of which have been ascertained, was published in M. & L., XL, July 1959, at the end of Ian Spink's article ' Lanier in Italy '.

     ii   *Add before* **LANKVELD** :

LANIGAN, John (*b.* Melbourne, 7 Jan. 1921).

Australian tenor singer. He was educated at St. Thomas's College, Clifton Hill, Melbourne, and after studying singing he was the prize-winner in the " Sun Aria " Competition there in 1945. In 1948 he went to Milan to continue his studies there for a year. He joined the Royal Opera, Covent Garden, in London in 1951 as a leading tenor and made an immediate success, especially in lyrical parts. His Tamino in ' The Magic Flute ' was outstandingly good, sung with beautifully mellow tone and fine phrasing. In 1955 he appeared in the production of Tippett's ' Midsummer Marriage '.   E. B.

52   ii   LANNER
BIBL.   Last item *should read* :
Weinmann, Alexander, ' Verzeichnis der in Druck erschienenen Werke von Joseph Lanner ', Vienna, 1948).

53   i   LANTINS, A. de
     Add at end :
Bibl.—*See* Lantins, H. de.

LANTINS, H. de
     Add to Bibl. (2nd work by Borren) :
' Pièces polyphoniques profanes de provenance liégeoise (XVe siècle) ' (Brussels, 1950). Contains complete secular works by A. and H. de Lantins.

53 ii **LAPICIDA**
  Par. 1, l. 1. (*b.* ?; *d.* ?). *should*
  read:
(*b.* ?, *c.* 1450; *d.* Vienna, 19 Nov. 1547).

55 ii *Add after* **LAROCHE**:
LARSEN, Jens Peter (*b.* Copenhagen,
14 June 1902).
Danish musicologist. He studied under Th.
Laub and at Copenhagen University, taking
the M.A. in 1928 and the degree of Ph.D.
(musicology) in 1939. He began to teach
musical theory at the University in 1928,
advanced to the post of lecturer in music in
1939, to that of Professor of Musicology in
1945, and in 1949 became head of the Institute
for Musicology in the University. At the
same time he was organist at Vangede Church
near Copenhagen from 1930 to 1945, and
since 1933 he has been teacher of music in
the University Training-College for Clergymen.
Larsen is a member of the Music Council
and of the board of the Musikhistorisk
Museum in Copenhagen, as well as chairman
of the Danish Society of Musicology founded
in 1954. In 1954-55 he was chairman of the
Committee of the Copenhagen Music and
Ballet Festival and in 1949-54 general editor
of the collected edition of Haydn's works
published by the Haydn Society of Boston,
U.S.A. From 1955 he acted in the same
capacity for the edition prepared by the
Haydn Institute of Cologne, and he was a
vice-chairman of the board of that Institute,
but resigned in 1957.
In order to give it wide currency his important book ' Die Haydn-Überlieferung '
(Copenhagen, 1939) was published in German, and for the same reason ' Handel's
Messiah ' (London, New York & Copenhagen,
1956) appeared in English. Larsen's work as
one of the most notable Haydn scholars also
resulted in his publication of ' Drei Haydn
Kataloge ' (Copenhagen, 1941), a facsimile
reproduction of Haydn's own *Entwurf* Catalogue, the Kees Catalogue and the Catalogue
drawn up by Haydn's copyist Elssler. A
book on C. E. F. Weyse's songs appeared in
Danish (' Weyses sange ', Copenhagen, 1942).
Danish church music has also occupied
Larsen's attention. He published a hymn-
book with Mogens Wöldike (' Den danske
koralbog ', Copenhagen, 1954), wrote the
article ' Messetoner ' in ' Dansk kirkesang '
for 1935 and the musical part of ' Forslag til
en dansk højmesseliturgi ' in the same periodical for 1943. He contributed the important
article on Haydn to Sohlman's Swedish
' Musiklexikon ' (Stockholm, 1950), and
' Mozart's Symphonies ' to ' The Mozart
Companion ' edited by H. C. Robbins Landon
and Donald Mitchell (London, 1956). ' Haydn

und das kleine Quartbuch ' was a series of
articles forming part of a polemic with A.
Sandberger in ' Acta musicologica ' for 1935-
1937. Numerous smaller articles of his have
appeared, mainly in Danish periodicals (*e.g.*
' Litaniet i den danske kirke ' [1949]), and
he has also brought out various editions of
music.   E. B.

55 ii **LARSÉN-TODSEN**
  Par. 2, ll. 18-20 *should read*:
in London at Covent Garden, and Brünnhilde
in 1927 and 1930, and at Bayreuth in 1927-31.
She sang as

LARSON
Add at end:
BIBL.—OSBORNSON, H., ' Einar Larson ' (' Musikrevy ',
  1954, No. 4).

56 i **LARSSON**
  Add to BIBL.:
WALLNER, BO, BLOMSTEDT, HERBERT & LONDBERG,
  FOLKE, ' Lars-Erik Larsson och hans concertinor '
  (Stockholm, 1957).

Add before **LA RUE**:

La RUE, (Adrian) Jan (Pieters) (*b.* Kisa-
ran, Sumatra, 31 July 1918).
American musicologist. He studied at
Harvard (1940) and Princeton (1942) Universities, and took the Ph.D. degree at Harvard
in 1952. In 1942-43, and again in 1946-47,
he was Instructor in Music at Wellesley College, where in 1947 he advanced to the post
of Assistant Professor and in 1949 to that of
Associate Professor. The same year he was
elected Chairman of the Music Department.
He is General Editor and Director of the
Wellesley Edition and was Secretary of the
American Musicological Society in 1954-55.
In the latter year he went to Vienna in order
to do research work, especially on the symphony in the 18th century, the result being a
thematic catalogue of nearly 6000 symphonies
dated from *c.* 1740 to *c.* 1810, compiled in
collaboration with H. C. Robbins Landon,
which is still (1956) in manuscript. In 1957
he became Professor at New York University
in succession to Curt Sachs.
LaRue's early studies were devoted to
music of the Far East, and its results appeared
in two articles: ' Native Music on Okinawa '
(M.Q., Apr. 1946) and ' The Okinawan Notation System ' (Journ. Amer. Musicol. Soc.,
spring 1951). In 1955 he contributed an
essay on ' Bifocal Tonality: an Explanation
for Ambiguous Baroque Cadences ' to ' Essays
in Music ', a Harvard University volume
dedicated to Archibald T. Davison. He has
also published studies on the symphony and
on watermarks in music paper as a dating
resource. He is a contributor to the N.O.H.M.

on the symphony and concerto, and he wrote an essay on the phrase structure in Haydn's symphonies for the *Festschrift* for Otto Kinkeldey. An article on 'British Music Paper: 1770–1820' in M.M.R., Sept.-Oct. 1957 contains valuable new research material. He edited the Report of the Eighth Congress of the International Musicological Society (New York, 1961).   E. B.

56   ii   **LA RUE, Pierre de**
          Add to BIBL. :

ROBYNS, JOSEF, 'Pierre de La Rue: een biobibliographische studie' (Brussels, 1954).
TIRABASSI, A., 'Liber Missarum Pierre de La Rue' (Malines, 1941). Contains 7 Masses in full score.

          Add at end :

See also Chorwerk, Vol. 11 (modern reprints of Requiem and motet). Maîtres Musiciens, Vol. 8 (modern ed. of Mass).

57   i   *Add before* **LAS INFANTAS**
LAS HUELGAS CODEX. *See* HUELGAS CODEX.

      ii   **LAS INFANTAS**
          Add at end :
See also Eslava (modern reprint).

69   i   **LASSUS**
          Par. 1, l. 2.   'Sdgenosi *should read* :
'Sdegnosi

71   i   *Add to* BIBL. :

BOETTICHER, WOLFGANG, 'Orlando di Lasso und seine Zeit 1532–1594', Vol. I : 'Monographie' (Cassel & Basel, 1958).

82   i   *See also,* ll. 1-2 *should read* :

See also Chorwerk, Vols. 13, 34, 37, 41, 48 (modern reprints). Collectio O.M.B., Vols. 7, 8, 10, 12 (modern ed.). Cornett (tune with diminutions, mus. ex.). Dehn (motets scored by). Florilège, Vol. 2 (modern ed. of chansons). La Hèle (masses on motets

          ll. 4-5 *should read* :
(ex. of). Maîtres Musiciens, Vol. 1 (modern ed. of 'Meslanges'). Paciotti (Mass ? on motet by L.). Troiano ('Cortigiana innamorata', lib.).

84   ii   **LAUB**
          Par. 1, l. 2.   18 Mar. *should read* :
17 Mar.

          Par. 2, l. 1.   Austrian *should read* :
Czech

86   i   **LAUDI SPIRITUALI**
          Add to BIBL. :
LIUZZI, FERNANDO, 'La lauda e i primordi della melodia italiana', 2 vols. (Rome, 1935).

87   ii   **LAURI-VOLPI**
          Par. 1, l. 1.   Rome *should read* :
Lanuvio

          l. 2.   1894 *should read* :
1892

87   ii   Par. 2, l. 8 *should read* :
in Rome in 1920 and sang the Duke in 'Rigoletto' under Toscanini at the Milan Scala in 1922, but after some successes in

          l. 12 *should read* :
letto' on 26 Jan. 1923.   Before he left that

          l. 15 *should read* :
Covent Garden Opera in London (1925 and 1936), where he

88   ii   Heading *should read* :
LAVALLÉE

          LAVALEE
          Par. 1, l. 1.   Surname *should read* :
LAVALLÉE

          Par. 2, l. 4 *should read* :
where he studied in 1873-75.

          ll. 14-16 *should read* :
Association (U.S.A.).   But he had settled at Boston, Mass., by 1881, and he remained there to the end of his life.

          Par. 3, ll. 5-9 *should read* :
national anthem by French-Canadians, the words of which were written by Judge Routhier.   It

89   i   Par. 1, ll. 1-2.   Boston in 1881
          should read :
Springfield, Ill., on 25 Mar. 1882.

          Add at end, before See also :
BIBL.—LAPIERRE, E., 'Calixa Lavallée: musicien national du Canada' (Montreal, 1937).

92   i   Heading *should read* :
LAVROVSKAYA

          LAVROVSKA
          Par. 1, ll. 1-2 *should read* :
LAVROVSKAYA, Elizaveta Andreyevna
b. Kashin, Tver, 12 Oct. 1845 ; d. Petrograd, 4 Feb. 1919).

          Par. 2, l. 14.   Zereteyev *should read* :
Tsertelev

93   i   **LAWES (2)**
          Par. 1, ll. 5-7 *should read* :
sworn an epistler of the Chapel Royal.   In

94   i   **LAWES (4)**
          Par. 1, l. 6 *should read* :
musicians in ordinary to Charles I and on 3 Nov. 1626 one of the Gentlemen of the Chapel Royal.   In 1633

94   i   Par. 1.   *Add after* l. 10:

He also contributed the greater part of the instrumental and vocal music for Davenant's ' Britannia Triumphans ' in 1638 and set the Song of the Goddesses in Shirley's ' Triumph of Beauty ' about 1644.[4]

Add footnote:
[4] According to Murray Lefkowitz (*see* Bibl.).

     ii   BIBL., l. 2.   1923 *should read*:
1933

     Add to BIBL.:

LEFKOWITZ, MURRAY, ' William Lawes ', in ' Studies in the History of Music ', ed. by Egon Wellesz, Vol. III (London, 1959).

95   i   **LAWRENCE, Marjorie**
         Par. 2, l. 1 *should read*:

In 1941 Marjorie Lawrence was

     ii   **LAWROWSKA**
          Entry should read:
     LAWROWSKA. *See* LAVROVSKAYA.

     LAY
     Delete last sentence and add at end:
BIBL.—REANEY, GILBERT, ' The *Lais* of Guillaume de Machaut and their Background ' (Proc. Roy. Mus. Ass., Vol. LXXXII, 1955–56).

96   ii   **LAZARO VALVASENSI**
          Par. 2, l. 7.   Stravangante " *should read*:
Stravagante "

     l. 15.   some early examples *should read*:
some examples

98   i   **LEADER**
         Par. 3, l. 2.   generally *should read*:
occasionally

     l. 3 *should read*:

as the " leader ", but this has not been generally accepted as a technical term : it is only a literary circumlocution.   H. C. G.

     LE BÈGUE
     Par. 1, l. 2.   *c.* 1630 *should read*:
1631

     ii   *Add at end*:
BIBL.—DUFOURCQ, NORBERT, ' Nicolas Lebègue (1631–1702) ' (Paris, 1955).

99   i   **LEBERTOUL**
         Par. 1, l. 2 *should read*:

by Dannemann. His extant work is published in Vol. II of ' Early Fifteenth-Century Music ', edited by Gilbert Reaney (Amer. Inst. of Musicology, 1958).   E. D. (ii).

101   i   **LECHNER**
          Delete Par. 4.

      ii   *Delete* Par. 1.

      After Par. 2 *and before signature add*:

A collected edition, edited by Konrad Ameln, was started by the Bärenreiter-Verlag in 1954. Its contents are planned as follows :
1. ' Motectae sacrae 4, 5 & 6 vocum ' (1575).
2. ' Newe teutsche Lieder ' for 3 voices (1576–77).
3. ' Newe teutsche Lieder ' for 4 & 5 voices (1577).
4. ' SVM canticum quod vulgo Magnificat inscribitur, 4 vocum ' (1578).
5. ' Newe teutsche Lieder / Erstlich durch . . . Jacobum Regnart / . . . mit 5 Stimmen ' (1579).
6. ' Sacrum cantionum 5 & 6 vocum, liber secundus ' (1581).
7. ' Newe teutsche Lieder / mit 5 vnd 4 Stimmen ' (1582).
8. ' Liber Missarum 6 & 5 vocum ' (1592).
9. ' Neue lustige teutsche Lieder ' for 4 voices (1586).
10. ' Septem Psalmi poenitentiales 6 vocibus compositi ' (1587).
11. ' Neue geistliche vnd weltliche teutsche Lider ' for 4 & 5 voices (1589).
12. ' Figuralpassion nach dem Evangelisten Johannes ' for 4 voices (1593).
13. ' Newe gaistliche vnd welltliche teutsche Gesanng, sampt zwayen lateinischen ' for 4 & 5 voices (1606).
14.–15. Occasional Works (1575–1604).

102   i   **LECLAIR**
          Footnote 3, l. 1.   Slominsky *should read*:
Slonimsky

      ii   **LECLAIR (1)**
           Add to See also:
Publikationen G.M.F., Vol. 31 (modern ed. of 12 Sonatas and a Trio).

104   i   **Leconte de Lisle**
          Add to See, l. 7:
Servais (' Iôn ', opera).

      ii   **LECUONA**
           Par. 2, l. 2 *should read*:
and began to compose at an early age. He studied at the Havana Conservatory until 1911 and later

      l. 4 *should read*:
successful, toured extensively with it and wrote a great number of popular

105   ii   *Add before* **LEEDS** :
           Lee, Sophia. *See* Rossini (' Elisabetta ', opera).

108   ii   **LEEDS**
           Add at end:

CRITICISM.—' The Yorkshire Post ', the most important newspaper in its region, must be mentioned for the tradition it has long upheld of devoting a good deal of space to music criticism and articles on music. Work of fine quality was done for music as well as for the fine arts by Herbert Thompson during his forty years' association with that paper (1886–1936), and A. H. Ashworth continued to serve the two arts until 1940. The present music critic is Ernest Bradbury.

H. T. & A. H. A., adds.

109   i   LEFEBVRE, C. É.
Par. 1, l. 2. *d. Paris, should read:*

d. Aix-les-Bains,

110   ii   LE FLEM
Par. 3, l. 10 *should read:*

for 'Les Paralytiques volent'. A one-act opera, 'La Magicienne de la mer', to a libretto by José Bruyr, was produced by the Opéra-Comique on 29 Oct. 1954.

LE FLEMING
Add after Le Fleming's works include:

INCIDENTAL MUSIC

'Your Trumpets, Angels', Festival of Britain play by K. M. Baxter (1951).

CHURCH MUSIC

Festival Evensong for Liverpool Cathedral.

STRING ORCHESTRA *should read:*
ORCHESTRA

Suite in G ma. for stgs.
Suite, 'London River' (1956).

Add after PIANOFORTE DUET:
SONGS

'A Quiet Company', cycle (from Walter De la Mare's 'Ding Dong Bell').

Le Fort
l. 2 *should read:*

hymns). Poulenc ('Dialogues des Carmélites', opera).

112   ii   LEGEND OF THE INVISIBLE CITY
l. 3. неьидимомь *should read:*

невидимом

l. 4. Китежь *should read:*

Китежѣ

Февроніе *should read:*

Февроніи

LEGEND OF TSAR SALTAN
l. 2. Скаска *should read:*

Сказка

113   ii   LEGRANT, G.
Par. 2, l. 14 *should read:*

lived. His extant work is published in Vol. II of 'Early Fifteenth-Century Music', edited by Gilbert Reaney (Amer. Inst. of Musicology, 1958).   E. D. (ii).

113   ii   LEGRANT, J.
Par. 2, l. 5 *should read:*

Trent 87 & 90). His extant work is published in Vol. II of 'Early Fifteenth-Century Music', edited by Gilbert Reaney (Amer. Inst. of Musicology, 1958).   E. V. D. S.

114   i   LEGRENZI
Add at end:

BIBL.—FOGACCIA, PIETRO, 'Giovanni Legrenzi' (Bergamo & Rome, 1954).

115   i   LEHÁR
Add to BIBL.:

'Katalog der Bühnenwerke von Franz Lehár' (Vienna, 1955).

LE HEURTEUR
Add at end:

See also Florilège, Vol. 8 (modern ed. of duos).

116   i   LEHMANN, Liza
Par. 3, l. 16 *should read:*

produced in London on 28 Dec. 1915. She also

LEHMANN, Lotte
Par. 1, l. 2. 2 July 1885 *should read:*

22 Feb. 1888

Par. 2, l. 8. In 1913 *should read:*
On 2 June 1914

l. 10. Sophie *should read:*

Oktavian

118   i   LEICHTENTRITT
l. 12 *should read:*

University. His works in English include 'Music, History and Ideas' (1938), 'Musical Form' (1951) and 'Music of the Western Nations' (1957).   H. C. C. adds.

LEIDER
Par. 2, l. 16 *should read:*

favourable criticism. She appeared there each summer season until 1938, her non-Wagnerian parts being Donna Anna, Gluck's Armide, Leonora in 'Trovatore' and the Marschallin in 'Rosenkavalier', but was not equally successful in all these parts. She may be reckoned

ll. 26-31 *should read:*

years. She also appeared with success in Chicago and New York, and at the Vienna State Opera and other leading continental theatres. She lives in Berlin (1956), where she teaches.

118   ii   **LEIGH, Adele**
Par. 2, l. 20 *should read*:
broadcast a number of times. In 1953–54 she sang Pamina in Holland under Krips, and in 1955 she created the part of Bella in Tippett's ' Midsummer Marriage ' at Covent Garden.

119   i   *Add before* **LEIGHTON (Sir) William**:
LEIGHTON, Kenneth (*b.* Wakefield, 2 Oct. 1929).
English composer. He was educated at Queen Elizabeth Grammar School in his native town and at Queen's College, Oxford, where he took the B.A. (Classics) in 1950 and the B. Mus. in 1951. Having won the Mendelssohn Scholarship in 1951, he went to Rome to study under Petrassi. Other awards obtained by him were the Royal Philharmonic Prize in 1950 and 1951, the George Butterworth Award in 1951 and the Busoni Prize, which he won at Bolzano in 1956 with his ' Fantasia contrappuntistica' among 87 competitors from 24 different countries. He was professor of harmony, etc., at the Royal Naval School in 1952–53, Gregory Fellow in Music at Leeds University in 1953–56, and in the latter year he was appointed lecturer in composition at Edinburgh University.
The following is a list of Leighton's compositions up to 1956:

CHORAL WORKS
3 Carols for soprano & S.A.T.B.
' A Christmas Carol ' for baritone, chorus, stgs. & pf. or organ.
Suite ' The Birds ' for soprano, tenor, chorus, stgs. & pf.

ORCHESTRAL WORKS
Overture ' Primavera Romana'.
Symphony for stgs.
Passacaglia, Chorale and Fugue.

SOLO INSTRUMENTS AND ORCHESTRA
Pf. Concerto (1951).
Vn. Concerto (1952).
Concerto for oboe & stgs. (1953).
Concerto for 2 pfs., timp. & stgs.
Cello Concerto (1955–56).
Concerto for viola, harp, timp. & stgs.

CHAMBER MUSIC
String Quartet (1956).

VIOLIN AND PIANOFORTE
Sonata No. 1 (1951).
Sonata No. 2 (1956).

VIOLA AND PIANOFORTE
Fantasy on the name of BACH (1955).

VIOLONCELLO AND PIANOFORTE
' Elegy ' (1953).

PIANOFORTE SOLO
2 Sonatinas (1949).
Sonata No. 1 (1950).
5 Studies (1952).
Variations, Op. 30 (1955).
Sonata No. 2 (1954).

Sonata No. 3 (1954).
' Fantasia contrappuntistica ' (1956).

TWO PIANOFORTES
Scherzo (1953).

E. B.

120   i   **LEIPZIG**
Par. 2, l. 21 *should read*:
great organ writers ancient and modern.[1]
The
ll. 38–41 *should read*:
as organist. The magnificent organ
l. 47 *should read*:
cantor in the mid-1930s, but he resigned in the 1950s after refusing to perform a work by Shostakovich at the suggestion of the local authorities.

Add footnote:
[1] For the 14th-century graduals used at the Church *see* Denkmäler (4), Vols. V & VII.

121   i   Par. 2, l. 13 *should read*:
is Johannes Arpe, its opera director Heinrich Voigt and its musical director Helmut Seydel-

Add to Par. 4, in order of dates:
1943. Orff, ' Catulli Carmina '.
1953. Alan Bush, ' Wat Tyler '.

ii   **LEITMOTIV**
Par. 1, l. 3.   Hans von Wolzogen
should read:
W. Jähns [1]

Add footnote:
[1] Preface to his catalogue of Weber's works (1871).

122   i   2nd musical example. Bar 1, rhythm *should read*:
E♭ crotchet, B♭ minim, 2nd B♭ and G quavers.

ii   *Add at end, before* BIBL. :
The term can now be shown not to have been invented by Heinrich von Wolzogen, who wrote explanatory booklets on Wagner's operas in 1876. Hanslick used it in an account of ' Die Meistersinger ' written for the Vienna performance in 1870. He speaks of the " so-called *Gedächtnis-* or *Leitmotive*", which seems to suggest that the final form was not yet firmly established. Ernest Newman (' Life of Wagner ', Vol. III) has shown that Wagner himself used the term *Hauptmotiv* in 1867. *Motiv* by itself can, of course, be traced much farther back, being used by Hanslick as early as 1854.   S. D.

LE JEUNE
Par. 1, ll. 2-3 *should read*:
Valenciennes, 1528; *d.* Paris, [buried 26] Sept. 1600 [1]).

Footnote should read:
[1] *See* ' Musica Disciplina ', 1949.

124　*Add to See also:*

Florilège, Vol. 6 (modern ed. of chansons). Amer. Inst. Musicol. (Misc.), Vol. 1 (modern ed. of airs, 1608). Maîtres Musiciens, Vols. 11-14, 16 & 20-22 (modern reprints). Monuments Mus. Franç., Vols. 1 & 8 (modern ed. of ' Octonaires ', etc.).

ii　**LEJEUNE**
　　l. 18.　Gilbert *should read*:
Gilibert

125　ii　**LELEU, Jean**
　　　　Add at end:

See also Chorwerk, Vol. 15 (modern reprint of secular choruses). Collectio O.M.B., Vol. 12 (modern ed.).

126　ii　**LE MAISTRE**
　　　　Add at end:

See also Chorwerk, Vol. 30 (modern reprint of motet). Collectio O.M.B., Vol. 8 (modern ed.).

127　ii　**LEMMENS**
　　　　Par. 1, l. 1 *should read*:

LEMMENS, Nicolas Jacques (Niklaas Jaak) (*b.* Zoerle-

128　i　*Add before* **LEMOINE**:

LEMNITZ, Tiana (*b.* Metz, 26 Oct. 1897). German soprano singer. She was educated at Metz, where she spent four years at the Music School, studying with Dr. Hoch, followed by three further years with Antoni Kohmann. She made her début at Aachen in 1922, where she remained for seven years. From 1929 to 1933 she was leading lyric soprano at Hanover and then, after one year as a guest artist at Dresden, she joined the Berlin State Opera in 1934, remaining there until her retirement in 1957. While in Berlin she sang lyric and lyric-dramatic parts in the German, Italian, French and Russian repertories. Her parts ranged from Mimì and Micaela to Aida and Desdemona; from Pamina and Mařenka to Sieglinde and Octavian, and from Tatiana and Halka to Eurydice and Elsa. Later in her career she sang the Marschallin, Milada in Smetana's ' Dalibor ', Jenufa and Nastassia in Tchaikovsky's ' The Enchantress '.

Lemnitz made her Covent Garden début on the opening night of the 1936 season as Eva and immediately established herself as one of the most sensitive and finished artists to have come out of Germany. Her Octavian was considered one of the best ever seen; and when two years later she sang her deeply touching Pamina, in which her exquisite *pianissimo* was employed to the full, she was hailed as the finest interpreter of the part since Claire Dux. In that same season she also sang Sieglinde and Elsa, as well as repeating her Octavian and Eva. Apart from her London appearances before the second world war and two appearances at the Teatro

Colón of Buenos Aires, Lemnitz's career was mostly confined to central Europe, and she appeared in Poland, Rumania, Austria, Switzerland, etc. as a guest artist. As a *Lieder* singer she was no less distinguished than as an opera singer, and it was in a concert of Brahms and Wolf and the Wagner Wesendonk songs that she bade farewell to the Berlin public on 7 April 1957.　　　　H. D. R.

128　ii　**LEMOYNE, J. B.**
　　　　Par. 2, l. 11.　(1872) *should read*:
(1782)

131　i　**LENZ, Heinrich**
　　　　Par. 1, l. 1 *should read*:

LENZ, Heinrich (Gerhard) von (*b.* Cologne, 1764 ;

　　　　Par. 2, l. 10 *should read*:

dissolution of that institution in 1831 ; but he remained in Warsaw to the end of his life, teaching privately.

133　ii　**LEO, Leonardo**
　　　　Add to Bibl.:

Leo, V., ' Leonardo Leo e sua epoca musicale ' (Brindisi, 1894).
Schlitzer, Franco (ed.), ' Tommaso Traetta, Leonardo Leo, Vincenzo Bellini : notizie e documenti ' (Siena, 1952).

134　ii　l. 6.　Marchesi *should read*:
Marchese

135　ii　*See also.*　ll. 3-4 *should read*:

sofferenza '). Fitzwilliam Music (reprints of sacred works). Logroscino (aria contrib. to ' Demetrio '; new setting of ' Amor vuol sofferenza '). Sondheimer Ed., Vols. 46 & 47 (modern ed. of symphonies).

138　ii　**LÉONIN**
　　　　Par. 1, l. 2.　duplus *should read*:
duplum

　　　　Par. 3, l. 1.　Léonin's free organal melodies *should read*:

Léonin's melodies

　　　　Add to Bibl.:

Waite, William G., ' The Rhythm of the Twelfth-Century Polyphony : its Theory and Practice ' (New Haven, Conn. & Oxford, 1954).[4]

　　　　Add footnote:

[4] This work contains the complete works of Léonin.

LEONOVA
Par. 1, l. 2.　Petersburg, 1896).
should read:
Petersburg, 6 Feb. 1896).

140　ii　**LEOPOLITA**
　　　　Add at end:

See also Monumenta Mus. Sac. Pol., Vol. 3 (modern ed. of ' Missa Paschalis ').

141   ii   **L'ÉPINE**
l. 1.   Signoar F. Margarit a *should read*:
Signora F. Margarita

142   i   **Lermontov**
l. 1.   Yurevich *should read*:
Yurievich

l. 7.   Medtner (1 song). *should read*:
Medtner (2 songs).

143   i   **LE ROY, Adrien**
Add to BIBL.:
LESURE, FRANÇOIS & THIBAULT, GENEVIÈVE, 'Bibliographie des éditions d'Adrien Le Roy et Robert Ballard (1551–1598) ' (Paris, 1955).

ii   **LERT**
Par. 1, l. 2 *should read*:
Vienna, 12 May 1883; *d.* Baltimore, 30 Jan. 1955).

144   i   **Le Sage**
ll. 2–3 *should read*:
boiteux ', chamber opera). Gluck, ' Isle de Merlin ' & ' Rencontre imprévue ', operas). Haydn (' Krumme Teufel ' & ' Incontro improviso ', operas). Philidor

ii   **LESCHETIZKY**
Par. 3, l. 12. Donnimirska *should read*:
Donimirska

145   i   *Add to* BIBL.:
WOODHOUSE, GEORGE, ' How Leschetizky Taught ' (M. & L., XXXV, 1954, p. 220).

146   ii   **Lessing**
l. 1.   Refs. *should read*:
See Bach (C. P. E., 4 songs). Beethoven (song).

LESSON
Par. 3, l. 5. (London, 1611) *should read*:
(London, 1599)

147   i   **L'ESTOCART**
Par. 2, l. 6 *should read*:
Expert's collection). A modern facsimile reprint of the complete ' Cent-cinquante Pseaumes de David ' appears in ' Documenta Musicologica ', Series I, Vol. vii.
E. v. d. s., adds.

Add at end:
See also Monuments Mus. Franç., Vol. 10 (modern reprint of ' Octonaires ').

148   ii   **LESUEUR**
Par. 3, l. 11. Boaz '. *should read*:
Booz '.

150   i   *Add before* **LESZCZYŃSKI**:
LESURE, François (*b.* Paris, 23 May 1923).
French musicologist and librarian. He studied at the École des Chartes (*archiviste-*

paléographe) and at the Sorbonne, the Paris Conservatoire and the École des Hautes Études. Occupied since 1950 as a librarian in the Music Department of the Bibliothèque Nationale, Lesure began about the same time to publish many articles, particularly on the 16th-century French chanson and on 16th-and 17th-century instruments. More recently he has also been occupied with Mozart research. He is a member of the editorial board and secretary for the ' Annales Musicologiques '. Again acting as secretary, he has proved an indefatigable organizer of the ' Repertoire of Musical Sources ', a complete catalogue of all musical manuscripts and prints before 1800, sponsored by the International Association of Music Libraries and UNESCO. His books include the ' Bibliographie des éditions d'Adrien Le Roy et Robert Ballard ', with the collaboration of G. Thibault (Paris, 1955); ' Musicians and Poets of the French Renaissance ' (New York, 1955); ' Mozart en France ' (Paris, 1956). In addition he collaborated with D. P. Walker in editing Claude Le Jeune's Airs (1608) and he has edited a volume of 16th-century French chansons transcribed by a number of specialists. His articles for various encyclopedias are of great value.   G. R. (iii).

150   i   *Add after* **LESZCZYŃSKI**:
LESZETYCKI, Teodor. *See* LESCHETIZKY, THEODOR.

151   i   **Leuven**
l. 2.   *Add*:
Berlioz (song).

LEVA
Par. 1, l. 2.   *d.* ?). *should read*:
d. Naples, 28 July 1955).

154   ii   **LEVIDIS**
Par. 2, l. 8 *should read*:
remained there for twenty-nine years, returning after spending the years 1939–47 in Greece. Many

155   ii   **LEWIS, Anthony**
Par. 4, ll. 13–14 *should read*:
a *cappella* (1938), an ' Elegy and Capriccio ' for trumpet and orchestra (1947) and ' A Tribute of Praise ' (words from the Psalms) for unaccompanied chorus (1953), performed at the Worcester Festivals of 1954 and 1957.

Lewis, Cecil Day
Add after See:
Bliss (' Song of Welcome ', cantata; ' Elegiac Sonnet ' for tenor, stg. 4tet & pf.).

156   i   **LEWIS, Richard**
Par. 2, l. 37 *should read*:
difficult works. In 1954 he created the part
of Troilus in Walton's 'Troilus and Cressida'
at Covent Garden, and in 1955 that of Jack
in Tippett's 'Midsummer Marriage'.

157   i   **Li Tai-Po**
l. 4 *should read*:
Lambert (C., 8 songs with insts.). Mahler ('Lied von
der Erde'). Roussel (song).

160   ii   **LIBERTH**
Par. 1, l. 1. Name *should read*:
LIBERT(H)

Par. 2. *Add at end*:
His extant work is published in Vol. II of
'Early Fifteenth-Century Music', edited by
Gilbert Reaney (Amer. Inst. of Musicology,
1958).

162   i   **LIBRARIES**
Par. 3, ll. 32-34 *should read*:
bibliography. Director: Dr. L. Nowak.

163   i   Par. 4, ll. 9-11 *should read*:
1938). The library was purchased by the
University of Michigan in July 1954, but the
Belgian government expressed a wish that it
should remain in Belgium.

183   i   Par. 3, ll. 1-2 *should read*:
(i) The Kidson Collection, the library of
the late Frank

l. 7 *should read*:
Index of Airs, in 57 vols.

ii   Par. 3, ll. 8-10 *should read*:
tions. City Librarian: F. G. B. Hut-

189   i   Par. 3, l. 16 *should read*:
rowers in the country, through the national
Central Library and regional bureaux, and
full use may be

l. 31 *should read*:
Council was gathered with Dr. Eric Blom,
C.B.E., as

ii   Par. 1, ll. 27-28 *should read*:
(over 36,000 items of music and musical
literature and over 5,000 gramophone records,
now on permanent loan to the Institute of
Recorded Sound).

l. 41 *should read*:
Great Britain and other

ii   Par. 1, l. 45 *should read*:
Librarian, Miss Joan Pemberton.

190   i   *Add after Par. 2*:
t. Dulwich College. The library contains
a collection of 12 MS volumes in the hand of
John Reading, who was organist of the College in 1696–98. The MSS were compiled
after Reading left Dulwich and were given
and dedicated to the College by him. Nine
of the MS volumes (LXXXV-XCII and Mus.
MS III) contain music from Italian and
English operas as well as cantatas by Galliard
and Pepusch. Orchestral parts and harpsichord scores of all these works are complete.
The remaining three MS volumes include
among others 'Divine Harmonie' (1717), a
collection of anthems by Purcell, Blow,
Weldon, Humfrey, Croft and Reading, lessons
for the harpsichord ('The Ladys Entertainment'), chant-tunes and many organ
voluntaries. Librarian: W. S. Wright.

u. Plainsong and Mediaeval Music Society.
The Society's Library, now kept in the Music
Library, Senate House (University of London)
has been gradually built up since the 1890's
and includes all the liturgical and musical
books formerly belonging to the Rev. Thomas
Helmore. A catalogue was published in 1928.
Librarian: Jeremy Noble.

195   i   York.
Delete entry and substitute:

YORK. The Minster Library contains
well over 400 musical works. In addition to
those mentioned in Vol. V. p. 195, the following should be singled out: 11 books of anthems, etc., in score, mainly of the 17th
century; 4 part-books of fantasies by Jenkins,
Ward and Tomkins; several autograph MSS
of the works of Walmisley (Services, an Overture, 'Victoria') and Stanford (Service in
B flat); 2 valuable part-books containing
services by Byrd, Parsons, etc., one of which
(the Dunnington-Jefferson MS) is described
fully in the Appendix to the Tudor Church
Music series; 13 motets for voices and continuo by Carissimi; 12 Concerti by Albinoni.
Among the printed books there are over sixty
volumes of 18th-century editions of full and
vocal scores of Handel's works as well as many
early volumes of music by Byrd, Dering,
Monteverdi, Tallis, etc., and a copy of the
1597 edition of Morley's 'Plaine and Easie
Introduction to Practicall Musicke'. A
fuller account appeared in 'The Musical
Times' of Feb. 1958 and a comprehensive
card-index is in course of preparation. Canon-
Residentiary, Chancellor and Librarian:
R. E. Cant.

ii   Par. 4, l. 1. Gaemeente *should read*:
Gemeente

197 i Par. 7, l. 2. Malatestina *should read*:
Malatestiana

Par. 10 (CORTONA), ll. 7-9 *should read*:
For a reproduction of this MS *see* Fernando Liuzzi, ' La lauda e i primordi della melodia italiana ' (Rome, 1935). There are also two

ii Par. 3 (FLORENCE), ll. 2-3. Magliabechiana *should read*:
Magliabecchiana

198 i Par. 2, l. 1 *should read*:
e. Biblioteca Marucelliana. An important collection of opera librettos and some

199 ii PADUA. ll. 1-2 *should read*:
PADUA. *a*. Biblioteca Civica, annexed to the Museo e gli Antichi Archivi del Comune ; this possesses a

201 ii VENICE. *c*. l. 1. Querini-Stampaglia. *should read*:
Querini-Stampalia.

202 i POLAND. Par. 1, l. 2. Chybińsky *should read*:
Chybiński

ii Par. 5, l. 2. Prokopiezwicz *should read*:
Prokopiewicz

l. 3. ' Przeglad Bibliotecznyg ' *should read*:
' Przegląd Biblioteczny '

204 ii SWEDEN. Par. 4, l. 2. Akadamien *should read*:
Akademien

205 i Par. 1, ll. 22-23 *should read*:
in ' Nordisk Tidskrift för Bok- och Biblioteksväsen ' (1927).

Par. 4, l. 7 *should read*:
Buxtehude, also Handel concertos and works by Italian composers. *See* M.f.M. (1889) ; ' La Biblio-

Par. 5, l. 15. STRÄNGNÄS *should read*:
STRÄNGNÄS

l. 16. VASTERÅS *should read*:
VÄSTERÅS

l. 17. VÄXJÖ *should read*:
VÄXSJÖ

207 i Par. 4, l. 12. disks *should read*:
discs

208 i Par. 1, l. 3. Kondelka *should read*:
Koudelka

211 i *Add after* Par. 4:
EVANSTON, ILLINOIS. Northwestern University Music School Library has a large collection of books, scores and records.

213 i Par. 1, l. 37. disks *should read*:
discs

216 i Par. 4, l. 5. disks *should read*:
discs

218 ii Par. 3, l. 13. disks *should read*:
discs

220 i Par. 2, l. 7. disks *should read*:
discs

221 i Par. 8, l. 1. SAO PAULO *should read*:
SÃO PAULO

222 ii *Add to* BIBL.:
ALBRECHT, OTTO E., ' A Census of Autograph Musical Manuscripts of European Composers in American Libraries ' (Philadelphia, 1953).

230 i **LIBRETTO**
Par. 3, ll. 28-29 *should read*:
Arnold Bennett (2 works by Goossens), Ronald Duncan (Britten's ' Rape of Lucretia '), J. B. Priestley (Bliss's ' The Olympians '), E. M. Forster (Britten's ' Billy Budd ') and Christopher Hassall (Walton's ' Troilus and Cressida ') have written librettos.

ii *Add to* BIBL.:
DELLA CORTE, ANDREA, ' Il libretto e il melodramma ' (Turin, 1951).

Delete author's name in l. 1 (' La " poesia per)

231 i **LICETTE**
Par. 2, l. 15 *should read*:
tinued to appear as prima donna. She sang at Covent Garden in several international seasons during the years 1919-29.

ii **Lichnowsky**
l. 5 *should read*:
(2) Count Moritz Lichnowsky (*b*. 1771 ; *d*. 17 Mar. 1837),
Add after l. 8:
(4) Countess Henriette Lichnowsky (*d. c.* 1830), sister of (1) and (2).

233 i **LIDÓN**
Par. 1, l. 2. 13 Feb. *should read*:
11 Feb.

233 i Par. 2, l. 14 *should read*:
' Glauca y Coriolano ' (performed Madrid,

Add at end:
See also Eslava (modern reprint of ' Ave maris stella ').

ii **LIE**
Par. 2, ll. 10-12 *should read*:
ducting posts at Bergen and Christiania.

Par. 3, l. 3. ' Orientalisk *should read*:
' Orientalsk

LIEBERMANN
Par. 1, l. 1. Zürich, 1910). *should read*:
Zürich, 14 Sept. 1910).

Par. 2, l. 13 *should read*:
qualities of sound. His operas have recently been successful, at any rate as experiments. In ' Penelope ', for example, he attempted a new approach on the basis of a problematic libretto, working on opposed levels of antiquity and modernity kept respectively in a serial and picturesque and parodistic idiom. His melodic style is realistically expressive, his harmony often somewhat monotonously uniform and his orchestration brilliantly effective. His orchestral works

List of Works
Add after l. 1 :
Opera ' Penelope ' (lib. by Strobel), prod. Salzburg Festival, 17 Aug. 1954.
Opera ' School for Wives ' (lib. by Elizabeth Montagu, on Molière's ' L'École des femmes '), prod. Louisville, U.S.A., 3 Dec. 1955; German adaptation as ' Die Schule der Frauen ' by Heinrich Strobel, prod. Salzburg Festival, 17 Aug. 1957.

Add after l. 3 :
Concerto for jazz band and orch. (1954).

235 ii **Liliencron**
See Brahms *should read*:
See Berg (Alban, song). Brahms

238 ii *Add before* **Lincoln** :
LINCKE, Paul (Carl Emil) (*b*. Berlin, 7 Nov. 1866; *d*. Klausthal-Zellerfeld, 4 Sept. 1946).
German conductor and composer. He studied at the Music School of Wittenberg and became conductor at the Parodie Theater in Berlin in 1900. For the next dozen years he worked there and at other operetta theatres in Berlin, and also toured with the Apollo Theater. He wrote a number of operettas, some of which were very successful ; also music for revues, farces and burlesques. In 1920 he founded a publishing house, the Apollo Verlag. His first operetta was ' Ein Abenteuer im Harem ' and his last ' Ein

Liebestraum ' (Hamburg, 1940) ; among those between were ' Spree-Amazone ', ' Venus auf Erden ', ' Frau Luna ', ' Fräulein Loreley', ' Lysistrata ' (after Aristophanes [1902] [1]), ' Casanova ' (1914) and ' Prinzess Rosine '.

E. B.

[1] A song from this, ' Glühwürmchen ', became immensely popular. A few notes from it appear on a postage stamp issue in 1956 to commemorate the tenth anniversary of Lincke's death.

241 i **LIND**
BIBL., l. 11. Anteckningar *should read*:
Anteckningar

l. 22. Sanfundet för Musikförskning *should read*:
Samfundet för Musikforskning

l. 27. handraåsdagen *should read*:
hundraårsdagen

Add to BIBL. :
BULMAN, JOAN, ' Jenny Lind : a Biography ' (London, 1956).

ii **LINDBERG, Oskar**
Par. 1, l. 2 *should read*:
23 Feb. 1887 ; *d*. Stockholm, 10 Apr. 1955).

LINDBLAD
Par. 1, l. 1. Skeninga *should read*:
Skänninge

ll. 2-3. 28 Aug. *should read*:
23 Aug.

242 i BIBL., l. 1. främsti *should read*:
främst i

243 ii **LINDEMAN (1)**
Add at end:
BIBL.—HERNES, ASBJORN, ' Ole Andreas Lindeman og hans tid ' (Oslo, 1956).

250 ii **LIONCOURT**
Par. 2, l. 2. d'Indy at the *should read*:
d'Indy, his uncle by marriage at the

251 — Page Heading *should stand in centre and read*:
LIPIŃSKI

252 i Heading *should read*:
LIPKOVSKAYA

LIPKOVSKA
Par. 1, l. 1 *should read*:
LIPKOVSKAYA, Lydia (*b*. Babino, Bessarabia, 10 May 1884; *d*. Beirut, 22 Jan. 1955).

Par. 2, l. 22 *should read*:
Manon Lescaut and Juliette.

Lipkovskaya fled from Russia in 1919, reappeared in Europe and America in 1920 and afterwards lived in Paris and in her native

Bessarabia, now part of Rumania. In 1941–1943 she sang in opera at Odessa, then under Rumanian occupation, and also acted in plays. In 1945 she returned to Paris, where she taught at the Russian Conservatory, and her last years were spent at Beirut, where she taught at a music school and was partly supported by the Tolstoy Foundation of New York. H. K., adds.

252 i *Add before* **Lipparini**:

LIPP, Wilma (*b.* Vienna, 26 Apr. 1925). Austrian soprano singer. She was originally intended for a business career and went to a commercial school in Vienna, but she herself was intent on making singing her career. She studied voice with Friedl Sindl and dramatic art with Anna Bahr-Mildenburg and Alfred Jerger. When she was seventeen she sang at a concert conducted by Josef Marx, and a year later she made her operatic début as Rosina in ' Il barbiere di Siviglia '. In 1945 she was engaged by Josef Krips for the Vienna State Opera, of which company she has remained a member ever since, being made *Kammersängerin* in 1955. In Vienna she has been heard in German and Italian parts, including Queen of Night, Blondchen, Constanze, Zerbinetta, Sophie, the Italian Singer in ' Capriccio ' (which she also sang at the work's first Salzburg performance in 1950), Lady Harriet in ' Martha ', Violetta, Gilda, Adina and Adele in ' Fledermaus '. She has appeared as a guest artist all over Germany and Italy. She made her Covent Garden début in 1950 as Gilda and has also sung Queen of Night, Violetta and Olympia with the Covent Garden Company. During the 1957–58 season she extended her repertory from coloratura to lyric parts, and was heard in Vienna as Pamina and Mimì, and as Mařenka at the Bregenz Festival. In August 1960 she sang Eva in ' Meistersinger ' at the Munich Festival.

Wilma Lipp possesses a pure limpid voice and an assured coloratura technique. Although she has appeared in Italian opera a good deal, her typical Viennese voice and training tend to make her interpretations of such parts as Gilda and Violetta rather pallid and un-Italian, though they remain beautifully sung. In Mozart and Strauss, however, she is one of the few singers of the present time who can sing correctly the exacting music of the high Mozart and Strauss parts. H. D. R.

253 ii **LIRA DA BRACCIO**
Add at end:

(*PLATE* 67, Vol. VIII, p. 146 (ii), No. 5.)

LIRA DA GAMBA
Add at end:

(*PLATE* 67, Vol. VIII, p. 146 (ii), No. 4.)

254 i **LISSENKO**
Par. 1, l. 1. **Vitalevich** *should read*:

Vitalievich

Par. 1, l. 2. Grinsky, *should read*:

Grilky,

255 i OPERETTAS
l. 1. ' Chronomortsy ' *should read*:
' Chernomortsy '

ii **LISTOV**
Par. 1, l. 1. (*b.* ?, 1900). *should read*:

b. Odessa, 19 Aug. 1900).

256 i **LISZT**
Par. 3, l. 2 *should read*:
ances in public at Sopron (Oct.) and Poszony (Pressburg) (26 Nov.) with

ii Par. 1, l. 3 *should read*:

went to Vienna in 1821, where his father placed him under Carl Czerny[1] and where he made his first

Add footnote:

[1] In his MS Reminiscences Czerny says this was in 1819 and that Liszt was about eight years of age, but it is clear that his memory played him false and that the boy was in his tenth year. The performance on 1 Dec. 1822 took place after some eighteen months' teaching.

Footnotes 1–3 become 2–4.

l. 9 *should read*:
(according to tradition) Beethoven was present and at the end publicly

262 ii BIBL. ll. 7–11 *should read*:
BOISSIER, C., ' Liszt pédagogue: leçons de piano données par Liszt à Mlle V. Boissier à Paris en 1832 ' (Paris, 1928); German trans., ' Franz Liszt als Lehrer ' (Dresden, 1930).

HARASZTI *entries should read*:
HARASZTI, EMIL, ' Deux Agents secrets de causes ennemies: Wagner et Liszt ' (' Revue d'Histoire Diplomatique ', July-Dec. 1952).
' Die Autorschaft der literarischen Werke Franz Liszts ' (' Ungarische Jahrbücher ', Vol. XXI, Nos. 1–3).
' Genèse des Préludes de Liszt ' (R. de M., 1953).
' Le Problème Liszt ' (' Acta Musicologica ', Dec. 1937).
' Les Origines de l'orchestration de Franz Liszt ' (R. de M., Dec. 1952).

HERVEY *entry should read*:
HERVEY, ARTHUR, ' F. Liszt ' (London, n.d.).

Add to BIBL.:
BECKETT, WALTER, ' Liszt ' (' Master Musicians ') (London, 1956).
HALDANE, CHARLOTTE, ' The Galley Slaves of Love: the Story of Marie d'Agoult and Franz Liszt ' (London, 1957).

263 i l. 3. BLANDIRE *should read*:
BLANDINE

263   ii   SITWELL (London, 1934). *should read*: (London, 1934; rev. 1955).

264   —   CATALOGUE
Col. 2, l. 2.   Paroles de Mrs. *should read*: Paroles de MM.

266   —   Col. 3, l. 12 *should read*:
and MSS, L.M. Aut. of an 1865 version, John Vallier, London. Perf. Weimar, 17

271   —   Col. 4, ll. 12-13 *should read*:
Set up by Haslinger but not pub. ; copy L.M. ; pub. 1953, Zenemükiadó Vállalat, Budapest.

281   —   Col. 3, ll. 20-22 *should read*:
May 1866. Aut. Otto Haas, London.

282   —   No. **205**, col. 2, l. 2.   Magyar arcképek' *should read*:
Magyar történelmi arcképek'

l. 4 *should read*:
2. Josef Eötvös.

l. 5 *should read*:
3. Michael Vörösmarty.

l. 6 *should read*:
4. Ladislaus Teleky.

l. 7 *should read*:
5. Franz Deák.

Col. 3.   *Cancel present entry and substitute*:
1884. 4 is the ' Trauermarsch ' from **206**; 6 and 7 are slightly different versions of **195** and **194**. Aut. H.N.M.

Col. 4.   1-5 unpublished. *should read*:
1956, Zenemükiado Vállalat, Budapest.

No. **215**, col. 2, l. 27.   ' Trois Valses oubliées.' *should read*:
' Quatre Valses oubliées.'

Col. 3, ll. 29-30 *should read*:
1881, 1882, 1883, 1885. Aut. of 2 Sotheby, London, 1954; of 3 in Paris Conservatoire; of 4 in Library of Congress, Washington.

Col. 4, l. 28 *should read*:
1, 1881 ; 2 and 3, Bote & Bock; 4, Theodore Presser Co, Bryn Mawr, Pennsylvania.

Col. 6.   *Add after* l. 14 :
(1-3 only)

Add after **216** :
Col. 1 :

216a

Col. 2 :
' Bagatelle ohne Tonart.'   ' Bagatelle sans tonalité.'

Col. 3 :
1885, originally intended to be the 4th Mephisto Waltz (but *cf.* **696**). Aut. L.M.

Col. 4 :
1956, Zenemükiado Vállalat, Budapest.

283   —   No. **224**, col. 3.   *Cancel present entry and substitute* :
1881-82. Auts. B.M. & H.N.M. MS., L.M. For pf. 4 hands, **617**.

283   —   No. **224**, col. 4, l. 12 *should read* :
tions, Vol. I). 1955, version with some additional passages, Zenemükiado Vállalat, Budapest.

285   —   Col. 3.   *Add at end* (No. **245**) :
Aut. Davis & Orioli, London.

301   —   Col. 2, l. 1.   Bulow *should read* :
Bülow

302   —   Col. 3, l. 3 *should read* :
1869. MS, L.M.

314   —   Col. 2, l. 10 *should read* :
4me Valse oubliée ', **215**.

Col. 4, l. 64 *should read* :
L. d'A., Corr. II, 211, 1842. Lost.

315   i   WORKS BY OTHER COMPOSERS
l. 2.   verscehen *should read* :
versehen

316   i   **LISZT SOCIETY**
l. 25 *should read* :
previously unpublished. The contents of Vol. 4 are : ' Galop ' in A mi., ' Valses oubliées ' Nos. 2 & 3, ' Valse mélancolique ' (original version) and ' Valse de concert sur deux motifs de Lucia et Parisina '. The address of the

317   i   **LITERES**
Par. 1, l. 1 *should read* :
LITERES (CARRIÓN), Antonio (*b.* Artá, Majorca [1], *c.*

Par. 2, l. 1 *should read* :
Spanish organist, violoncellist and composer. He was composer and cellist under Charles II, Philip V and Ferdinand VI. The

Add Par. 4 *before signature* :
Literes had two musical sons : José Literes Sánchez (*d.* 26 Sept. 1746) and Antonio Literes Montalbo (*d.* 2 Dec. 1768), biographical details of whom have been almost inextricably confused with those of their father. Solar Quintes (*see* BIBL.) has more or less disentangled the facts.

Add at end :
BIBL.—SOLAR QUINTES, N. A., ' Antonio Literes Carrión y sus hijos ' (' Anuario Musical ', Vol. V, Barcelona, 1950).

Add footnote :
[1] According to Solar Quintes (*see* Bibl.), who has also established the fact that the date of death sometimes given as " after 1752 " refers to his son Antonio Literes Montalbo.

Footnote 1 *becomes* 2.

ii   **LITOLFF**
See also, l. 3.   ' Robiespierre ' *should read* :
' Robespierre '

333 ii **LITURGICAL MUSIC-DRAMA**
MS H. 304 *Footnote 4.* MS 304 *should read:*

342 ii *Delete Par. 1 and substitute:*

THE DUTCH EASTER PLAY.—About 1947 a previously unknown version of the Easter Sepulchre drama, of considerable proportions and unique arrangement, was discovered in the Royal Library at The Hague, actually in two separate manuscripts, which differ only in slight detail regarding text and music. They are registered as (1) MS 76. F. 3 and (2) MS 71. J. 70.

The version has been made the subject of a monograph, ' A Dutch Easter Play ', in ' Musica Disciplina ', Vol. VII, 1953, by Jos. Smits van Waesberghe, and it is clear from his transcription of the texts and music, and his commentary thereon, that an important version has come to light, a *Ludus Paschalis* of the same large dimensions as the four already known (Klosterneuburg, MS 574; Munich, MS lat. 4660a; Tours, MS 927 — all of the 13th century; and Saint-Quentin, MS 86 of the 14th century), and definitely tidier in its construction than any of them. Dr. van Waesberghe refers to the joint version as "The Dutch Easter Play", to MS 76. F. 3 as " MS A " — " The Maestricht Easter Play " —and to MS 71. J. 70 as " MS B " — " The Egmond Easter Play ", after the probable places of their origins.

MS A, which has suffered the fate of many another medieval manuscript in having been used in the binding of a later liturgical book and suffering thereby, dates from the late 12th or early 13th century. The musical notation is very clear — heavy German neumes (*Hufnägel*) on four lines. It is clearly established that the manuscript must have belonged to the Church of Our Lady at Maastricht.

MS B is contained in a *hymnarium*, which by internal evidence has been traced back to the Benedictine Abbey of St. Adelbert at Egmond, founded *c.* 950. The actual manuscript is of the 15th century, but there is no doubt that it represents the copying of an earlier one.

Dr. van Waesberghe, arguing from the evidence of the texts, supposes a Norman-French origin for the play and, in the opinion of the present writer, that view is supported by the evidence of the music, except that there seems to be one small borrowing from German sources, mentioned below. Except for one or two short passages the melodies are all recognizable, and many of them show the same characteristics as are found in the settings of similar texts in what may be termed a family group of basically French plays, of varying dimensions. Some of these are: the brief 12th-century Norman-Sicilian version now at Madrid (MS 132), the 12th-century Ripoll version at Vich (MS 111), the 13th-century ' Fleury Play ' (Orleans, MS 201) and the lengthy, ill-arranged, carelessly copied 13th-century *Ludus Paschalis* from Tours (MS 927). Various textual items in the Dutch play are precisely detailed, often enough in one or another (or in several) of the French versions, but there is enough variation in the musical settings to make it probable that all manuscripts, including the Dutch, have drawn material from an older, still unrecovered source.

One curious feature in the Dutch play is the use of the phrase " Rabboni, quod dicitur : Magister ", addressed by Mary Magdalene to Christ. The French dramas that use the dialogue at all reduce the speech to the single word, " Rabboni ! ", no doubt realizing that the second part of the phrase (". . . that is to say, ' Master ' ") is merely a biblical gloss. It is strange to find the skilful arranger of the Dutch play falling into this ineptitude, which belongs indeed to the *Zehnsilbenspiel* group of German plays, from which the Dutch play has also borrowed the musical setting of the words.

The great virtue of the Dutch play lies in the fact that it is a unique and most skilful selection and rearrangement of established material, a great improvement on the other four surviving examples of the *Ludus Paschalis* type. A successful innovation is the incorporation into the frame of the *Visitatio Sepulchri* of the *Peregrinus* happenings, as related in St. Luke xxiv. 13-32, elsewhere always a separate drama. The arranger introduces Cleophas and his companion after the conclusion of the Christ-Magdalene scene. It is these two disciples who sing the lyrical first part of the sequence *Victimae Paschali*, and it is they, instead of Peter and John, who meet and question Mary Magdalene (" Dic nobis, Maria, quid vidisti in via ? "). Then they encounter the Stranger, and a shortened form of the *Peregrinus* is given (without the scene at the table) to the usual music.

The " Quem quaeritis " dialogue section as here treated, though using the familiar texts, is part of the time set to definitely unfamiliar music, not to be found elsewhere.

Lastly, a unique and very satisfactory finish to the drama is achieved by the transfer of established sentences like " Cito euntes, dicite discipulis . . ." (" Go quickly, say to the disciples . . .") and " Eamus nunciate mirum . . ." (" Let us go to announce the wonder . . .") from their usual position after the " Quem quaeritis " dialogue to the final moments, when before the concluding antiphon " Surrexit Dominus de sepulchro . . ."

the grave-clothes are displayed to the congregation.

Altogether the Dutch Easter Play represents a valuable addition to the list of recovered Easter Sepulchre dramas, and is one that, owing to its skilful construction, could be revived in actual performance.

343   i   *Add to* BIBL. :

BOWLES, EDMUND A., ' The Role of Musical Instruments in Medieval Sacred Drama ' (M.Q., XLV, 1959, p. 67).
KAFF, LUDWIG, ' Mittelalterliche Oster- und Passionsspiele aus Oberösterreich im Spiegel musikwissenschaftlicher Betrachtung ' (Linz, 1956).
KRIEG, EDUARD, ' Das lateinische Osterspiel von Tours ' (Würzburg, 1956).

LITUUS
Par. 1, l. 8.   Vol. I, No. 1 *should read* :

Vol. I, p. 1004, No. 1

344   i   LITVINNE
        Par. 2, l. 27.   1901. *should read* :
1908.

Add before LIVERATI :

LIUZZI, Fernando (*b*. Senigallia, 19 Dec. 1884 ; *d*. Florence, 6 Oct. 1940).
Italian musicologist and composer. He studied under Fano at first and later at Munich under Reger and Mottl. On his return to Italy he was appointed professor of harmony at the Conservatory of Parma and later at that of Florence, also professor of musical history at the University of Rome. He distinguished himself by doing excellent work on behalf of old Italian music, both by performances of such things as Orazio Vecchi's ' Amfiparnaso ' and the ' Oedipus Rex ' of Sophocles with Andrea Gabrieli's music, and by an edition of *laudi*, with an extensive study : ' La lauda e i primordi della melodia italiana ' (Rome, 1935). His other writings include studies of Italian musicians written in French in order to make them more widely known and a volume of critical essays entitled ' Estetica della musica '.

Liuzzi's compositions include a puppet opera, ' L' augellin bel verde ' (after Gozzi) ; incidental music for Pirandello's ' Scamandro ' ; the oratorios ' La Passione ', ' Laudi francescane ' and ' Le vergini savie e le vergini folle ' ; Neapolitan impressions ' Gaiola e Marechiaro ' for orchestra ; a Sonata and two pieces for violin and pianoforte ; organ music ; 5 sets of songs including Italian, Greek and Serbian folksongs, &c.

E. B.

345   i   LIVERPOOL
        Par. 2, l. 2 *should read* :

Philharmonic Society, founded in 1840, now Royal Liverpool Philharmonic Society, began

346   ii   LIVIETTA E TRACOLLO
        Entry should read :

LIVIETTA E TRACOLLO   (Pergolesi).
See CONTADINA ASTUTA.

Add after Livy :

LJUNGBERG, Göta (Albertina) (*b*. Sundsvall, 4 Oct. 1893 ; *d*. Lidingö nr. Stockholm, 28 June 1955).
Swedish soprano singer. She studied at the Stockholm Conservatory and with Filippi, Ferguson, Vanzo and Bachner. She was also a pupil of Gillis Bratt at the Royal Opera School of Stockholm and later of Mme Cahier in Stockholm. She made her stage début in 1918 at the Royal Opera in Stockholm, to which she was attached in 1918–26. She sang as a guest at the Berlin State Opera in 1922 and 1926 and then began to appear at the chief opera-houses of Europe. Although not exceptionally impressive as a singer, she won considerable success by her beauty and her dramatic talent. As Salome in Strauss's opera she was remarkable as a dancer as well as a singer and actress. In London, at Covent Garden, she appeared in that part and also as Sieglinde in the late 1920s, and she was chosen for the title-part of Goossens's ' Judith ' for the production of that work in 1929.

Göta Ljungberg made her début in the U.S.A. at the New York Metropolitan Opera in Jan. 1932, as Sieglinde, and in Dec. of that year she appeared as Chrysothemis in the first performance at the Metropolitan of Strauss's ' Elektra '. She created the part of Lady Marigold Sandys in the world première of Howard Hanson's ' Merry Mount ' in Feb. 1934. She sang at many concerts and gave recitals both in the U.S.A. and in South America.   K. D.

LLANGOLLEN FOLK MUSIC FESTIVAL. *See* EISTEDDFOD (International).

347   i   LLEWELLYN
        l. 2 *should read* :

' Hugh the Drover '. In 1950 he joined the Carl Rosa Opera and in 1951 he created the title-part of George Lloyd's ' John Socman '. To his qualities as a

        ii   LLOYD, C. H., List of Works
            CHORAL WORKS
            l. 13. Leaner's Harvest *should read* :
Gleaners' Harvest

        LLOYD, David
        Par. 2, l. 7 *should read* :

sion as Macduff in Verdi's ' Macbeth ' in 1938 and also sang Ottavio in ' Don Giovanni ', and he appeared at

349   ii   **LLOYD, Ll. S.**
Par. 1, l. 2 *should read*:
Cheadle Hulme, Cheshire, 20 Apr. 1876; *d.* Birmingham, 14 Aug. 1956).

351   ii   **LOBO, Alfonso**
Add at end:
See also Eslava (modern reprints).

352   ii   **LOCATELLI**
Add to See also:
Classici Musica Italiana, Vol. 16 (modern ed.). Vereniging, Vol. 31 (modern ed. of 2 sonatas).

353   i   **LOCKE**
Par. 4, l. 6 *should read*:
coronation.³ This is thought to stand alone

ll. 19-20 *should read*:
which, it has been said, he received the appointment of Composer in Ordinary to the King; but the fact is that he already held this in 1660.

Add footnote:
³ For full details *see* Eric Halfpenny's article, ' The " Entertainment " of Charles II ' in M. & L., XXXVIII, Jan. 1957.
Footnote 3 becomes 4.

ii   Par. 4, ll. 4-7 *should read*:
graph manuscript.⁵ Soon afterwards, having, according to A.

Add footnote:
⁵ Rimbault, in his edition of Roger North's ' Memoires ', tried in a footnote to identify " Psalmes to musick in parts for the use of some vertuoso ladyes in the city " with a set of MS anthems now in the British Museum; but these are for men's voices, and no work by Locke answering to North's description is known.

353   ii   Par. 5, l. 14 *should read*:
editorial care of Boyce, with Locke named

355   i   Par. 4, l. 2 *should read*:
in 1663. MS (19th-century copy) at Boston, U.S.A., Public Library.

ii   INSTRUMENTAL MUSIC
l. 6. 1678-79) *should read*:
1663)
Add after l. 7:
' Melothesia ' (Carr, London, 1673).

Add to See also:
Musica Britannica, Vol. 2 (modern ed. of ' Cupid and Death ').

359   ii   **LOEILLET**
Delete Pars. 1-3 *and substitute*:
Family of distinguished Flemish musicians whose biographical details have become greatly confused. Distinction between the three commonest names appearing on 18th-century title pages (" Jean Baptiste Loeillet de Gant ", " Mr. John Loeillet ", " Jacob Jean Baptiste Loeillet ") have to be deduced principally from dates of publication of their works and internal musical evidence. The main confusions surround (2), (3) and (4) in the following list, (3) and (4) having frequently been considered to have been one and the same man.

In John's will, dated 1 Sept. 1729, he refers to his brothers Pierre at Ghent and Jacob at Munich. Noé is mentioned as being at Bordeaux and his uncle's son was to receive the very best of his harpsichords. It is therefore clear that John was Jean Baptiste, son of J. B. François. The few contemporary English records carefully distinguish between John

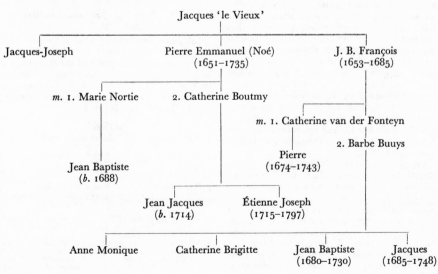

Jacques ' le Vieux '

Jacques-Joseph   Pierre Emmanuel (Noé)   J. B. François
(1651-1735)   (1653-1685)

m. 1. Marie Nortie   2. Catherine Boutmy

m. 1. Catherine van der Fonteyn

2. Barbe Buuys

Pierre
(1674-1743)

Jean Baptiste
(*b.* 1688)

Jean Jacques   Étienne Joseph
(*b.* 1714)   (1715-1797)

Anne Monique   Catherine Brigitte   Jean Baptiste   Jacques
(1680-1730)   (1685-1748)

and the composer who called himself " Jean Baptiste Loeillet de Gant " on his title-pages. Hawkins called John " a relation as it is supposed of J. B. Loeillet de Gant " and clearly thought them different men. A catalogue of Walsh's publications dated 1741 separates the works appearing under the two names. All John's works, with the exception of that by Daniel Wright, were published by Walsh in London. All J. B.'s appeared first with Roger in Amsterdam, though they were later pirated by Walsh. It seems inconceivable that Walsh would have published J. B.'s works under that name when John was known to him personally, had one man written both sets. Fétis assumed that John came to London via France, though there is no evidence to suggest a visit, and the only Loeillet works printed in France were those by Jacques in 1728. J. B.'s dedications to members of the French nobility presume that their author was at some time resident in France; yet John was clearly living in London at the time those dedications were made. Walsh would not have consciously duplicated Op. 1, 2, 3 and 4 had the London Loeillet been the author of both sets. From the dates of publication it seems likely that there were two men, and Bergmans says there was a Loeillet at the court of the Archbishop of Lyons, one of the dedicatees of J. B.'s sonata volumes. If John remained in London why were several volumes printed in Amsterdam with French dedications ? If he visited France regularly why did Walsh keep the two names separate, since " de Gant " is in itself a distinguishing factor ? Internal evidence shows differences, though only slight, between the styles of the sonatas attributed to the two men. John has a gift for melodic extension, for a richer harmony and ternary forms, whilst J. B. is less adept at counterpoint, prefers a less disjunct bass and the relative minor for slow movements. Jacques is altogether less conservative, and the concertos (influenced by dall' Abaco who was then living in south Germany) may thus be attributed to him.

(1) **Étienne Joseph** (b. Mâcon, 1715; d. Ghent, 1797), third son of (7) by his second wife, Catherine Boutmy. He was attached to the Chapelle Royale and the cathedral of SS. Michel and Gudule in Brussels as violinist and organist.

(2) **Jacques** (also called **Jacob Jean-Baptiste**) (b. Ghent, 7 July 1685; d. Ghent, 28 Nov. 1746), posthumous son of (5) by his second wife, Barbe Buuys.

He was oboist to the city of Ghent in 1702, a post he continued to hold, though paying a deputy, until 1736. It is supposed that he joined the service of the Elector Max Emmanuel of Bavaria when the latter was in the Low Countries, for Jacques is mentioned as being in his service at Munich in 1726. The following year he visited Versailles and, after two remarkable concerts in which he played various instruments and delighted the court with his mimicry, was appointed " Hautbois de la Chambre du Roi ". It is presumed that he travelled between Munich and Paris, as John's will of 1729 mentions him in Munich, and he finally returned to Ghent in 1746; his widow was granted a pension by the King of France. His application for publication in Parish was seconded by Montéclair.

WORKS

1. VI Sonates à deux Flûtes Traversières . . . sans Basse. Op. 4. Paris : Boivin 1728.
2. VI Sonates pour une Flûte Traversière . . . avec Basse. Op. 5. Paris : Boivin 1728.
   (Both these works are entitled " Par Jacob Jean Baptiste Loeillet de Gand ".)
3. Concerto in E♭ for Oboe and Strings.
4. Concerto in D for Flute and Strings.
   (Both works exist in MSS at the University of Rostock.)

359 ii **(3) Jean Baptiste Loeillet** should read :

(3) Jean Baptiste Loeillet (called **John**).

360 ii *Delete* CATALOGUE OF WORKS *and substitute* :

WORKS

1. Sonatas for Variety of Instruments. . . . Op. 1. Walsh & Hare, 1722.
2. XII Sonatas in Three parts. . . . Op. 2. Walsh & Hare, 1725.
3. XII Solos Six for a Common Flute. . . . Op. 3. Walsh & Hare, 1729.
4. Lessons for the Harpsichord or Spinet. . . . Daniel Wright, 1709-15.
5. Six Suits of Lessons for the Harpsichord. . . . Walsh & Hare, 1723.
   (All these works are by " Mr. John Loeillet ", except that by Wright where the composer is called " Mr. Baptist Lully ". All the Walsh publications were later reissued by him.)

Delete **(4) Jacques Loeillet** *and substitute* :

(4) Jean Baptiste (b. Ghent, 1688; d. ?), son of (7) by his first wife, Marie Mortier. He was at the archiepiscopal court at Lyons, and is presumed to have spent most of his life in France. All his works were published at Amsterdam by Roger under the imprint " Jean Baptiste Loeillet de Gant ".

WORKS

1. XII Sonates à une Flûte et Basse. Roger No. 85, Op. 1. 1705 (ded. to M. de St. Suplix).
2. XII Sonates . . . etc. Roger No. 346, Op. 2. 1715 (ded. to Conte de Matignon).
3. XII Sonates . . . etc. Roger No. 365, Op. 3. 1715 (ded. to Duchesse de Valentinois).
4. XII Sonates . . . etc. Roger No. 401, Op. 4. 1715 (ded. to François de Neuville, archb. of Lyons).
5. VI Sonates . . . etc. Roger No. 427, Op. 5, No. 1. 1720.
6. VI Sonates à deux Flûtes . . . sans Basse. Roger No. 428, Op. 5, No. 2. 1720. (All Op. 5 is ded. to Conte de Toulouse.)
7. Six Sonatas of Two parts Fitted & Contriv'd for Two Flutes. . . . Walsh No. 57. 1730.
   (With the exception of No. 7 attributed to " Mr. Loeillet of Gant ", all are composed by " Jean

Baptiste Loeillet de Gant ". Nos. 1-4 were reprinted by Walsh under the same name, with the exception of the first reprint of No. 1 which was by "Jean Luly of Gant". The dates of Walsh's reprints are 1712, 1715, 1718, 1725. No. 5 was reprinted by Walsh in 1728. No. 7 is a reissue by Walsh of various sonatas appearing in the earlier volumes.)

(5) **Jean Baptiste François** (*b.* Ghent, 1653; *d.* Ghent, 1685), brother of (7), a barber-surgeon and " bourgeois " of the city of Ghent.

(6) **Pierre** (*b.* Ghent, 1674; *d.* Ghent, 1743), fiirst son of (5) by his first wife, Catherine van der Fonteyn. Oboist and dancing-master at Ghent. Succeeded (7) as violinist in cathedral of St. Bavon.

(7) **Pierre Emmanuel** (called **Noé**) (*b.* ?; *d.* Ghent, 1735), violinist, dancing-master and concert director in Ghent, and from 1715 to 1730 at Bordeaux.

BIBLIOGRAPHY

BERGMANS, P., ' Une Famille de musiciens belges du XVIIIe siècle : les Loeillet ' (Brussels, 1928).
' Monumenta Musicae Belgicae ', I (Brussels, 1932).
CLOSSON, E., Preface to 18 Sonatas by Loeillet (ed. Béon) (Paris, 1912).
PRIESTMAN, B., ' Catalogue thématique des œuvres de Jean-Baptiste, John, and Jacques Loeillet ' (Rev. Belge de Musicologie, VI, 1953, p. 219).
VAN DEN BORREN, C., ' La Musique en Belgique ' (Brussels, 1950).
VERMEIRE-ROOS, ' De Loeillets, een voornaam geslacht van Musici te Gent ' (' Miscellanea Musicologica Floris van der Mueren ', 1950).   B. P.

363   ii   **LOEWENBERG**
Par. 3, ll. 12-15 *should read*:
history of the English theatre and compiled ' The Theatre of the British Isles, excluding London : a Bibliography ', published by the Society for Theatre Research in 1950. He further worked, at an office

366   ii   **LOHET**
Add to footnote :
Twenty of these fugues have been republished, transcribed and edited by Katarzyna Swaryczewska, in a supplement to the Polish quarterly ' Muzyka ', Vol. II, 1957, No. 3.

367   i   **LÖHLEIN**
Par. 1, l. 2 *should read*:
o/Heide, Coburg, [bapt. 16 July] 1725 ; *d.* Danzig, 16 Dec.

Par. 2, l. 6.   1760 *should read*:
1758
l. 8 *should read*:
1763 he entered the University of Leipzig, where he remained as violinist and
l. 10.   1779 *should read*:
1781

368   i   **LOMAKIN**
Par. 1, l. 1.   (*b.* ?, *should read*:
(*b.* St. Petersburg,

368   i   *Add after* **LOMAKIN**
LOMBARD MANNER. *See* SCOTCH SNAP.

381   i   **LONDON**
Par. 2, l. 37.   (1611) *should read*:
(1612 or early 1613)

ii   Par. 3, ll. 19-21.   *Cancel and substitute as follows* :
But Richard Carr took over active control in 1684, on the retirement of John, who had since 1683 carried on alone another business he had founded in 1679 in partnership with Anne Godbid. Henry's connection with Carr does not seem to have lasted long ; at any rate he conducted the business in his own name from 1696.

382   i   Par. 1.   *Cancel* ll. 1-2.
l. 3.   *Cancel* (1700).
Par. 2, l. 10.   1736 *should read*:
1735
l. 12 *should read*:
John Cullen, at work *c.* 1702 to 1713.
Par. 3, l. 13.   his son William *should read*:
his son or grandson William
l. 17.   1768, died in 1780 *should read*:
1767, died about Jan. 1776
l. 18.   *c.* 1783 *should read*:
in June 1784
Par. 4, l. 6.   (1730–35) *should read*:
(1732–36)
l. 7.   (1740–72) *should read*:
(*c.* 1740–*c.* 1762)
l. 10 *should read*:
and subsequently nine of his operas;
l. 14 *should read*:
3rd ed. 1744, and ' Calliope ', 2nd ed. 1746).
Cancel ll. 15-16.

ii   Par. 1.   *Cancel* ll. 1-2.
Par. 2, l. 18.   1726 *should read*:
1762

384   i   Par. 4, l. 3 *should read*:
from Dallam in Lancashire late in the 16th

385   ii   Par. 2, l. 11.   1880 *should read*:
1800

386   ii   Par. 1, l. 21 *should read*:

orchestral instruments. Hawkes & Son, now amalgamated with that firm, are equally important makers of military band instruments. Of the four principal

387   ii   *Add after* **LONDON CHORAL SOCIETY**:

LONDON COLLEGE OF MUSIC. This music school was founded in 1887 and incorporated in 1939 as an educational institution without share capital or any other commercial attribute. It is controlled by its Corporation acting through an Executive Council. Its present Director (1958) is Dr. Reginald Hunt, D.Mus. (London), F.R.C.O., F.L.C.M. In addition to being a teaching institution, catering both for the full-time professional student and the part-time amateur student, it is also a recognized examining body.

The College building is centrally situated in Great Marlborough Street, near Oxford Circus. Its accommodation includes 30 studios and practice rooms, reference library and concert-hall. The latter contains a three-manual modern organ. For the convenience of its numerous part-time evening students the College remains open until 8.30 P.M. on weekdays.

Players and singers may join the choir and/ or orchestra, though not otherwise enrolled as students. Besides the College orchestra, which gives regular concerts, there is a training orchestra which prepares instrumentalists for membership of the main body.

Examinations for diplomas in music and in speech are held at the College and at certain approved centres at home and abroad three times a year. Examinations for certificates in 8 grades (and in 3 introductory grades) are similarly held throughout the British Isles and overseas. College scholarships and local exhibitions are awarded annually.

As a teaching institution the College provides for the full-time students three main courses:

(1) The ordinary Professional Course for students intending to become performers — three years' duration.
(2) The Graduate Course for intending teachers — three years leading to the Graduate Diploma, which may be followed by a year's teacher training at the University of London Institute of Education.
(3) The School Music Course for intending teachers — two years leading to the School Music Diploma, which may be followed by a year's teacher training at a training college.

These courses and the following diplomas are recognized by the Ministry of Education:

(1) The Graduate Diploma — G.L.C.M. — as a graduate equivalent qualification.
(2) The School Music (Licentiateship) Diploma — L.L.C.M. in School Music — accepted for qualified teacher status.

(3) The Teacher's Diploma in a (Practical) Musical Subject — L.L.C.M. (T.D.).

The last diploma, unlike the preceding diplomas, may be taken externally.

Other diplomas comprise:

(1) Speech — L.L.C.M. (T.D.).
(2) Practical Music —A.L.C.M., L.L.C.M., F.L.C.M. (Performers).
(3) Theory and Speech — A.Mus.L.C.M. and L.Mus.L.C.M.
(4) Composition — F.L.C.M.   W. L. S.

388   i   *Add after* **LONDON MADRIGAL GROUP**:

LONDON MOTET AND MADRIGAL CLUB. An association formed in 1942 on the initiative of Henry Lawley by a group of enthusiasts who had been attending a madrigal course at a summer school of music. Its objects are (*a*) the cultivation of the art of singing motets, madrigals and other similar music, and (*b*) the encouragement of the formation of madrigal groups anywhere in Britain and, to that end, to afford opportunities of conducting group singing. Meetings are held monthly, and there is also an annual re-union meeting for old members. The membership is about fifty and the President is David Willcocks. The conductors have been Franck Odell, Robert Hasberry and (at present [1958]) Michael Pope.   E. B.

389   ii   **LONDON STRING QUARTET**
Add at end, before signature:

In 1955 the New London Quartet adopted the name of London String Quartet. At present (1960) the players are Erich Gruenberg, John Tunnel, Keith Cummings and Douglas Cameron.

390   i   **LONDON SYMPHONY ORCHESTRA**
Par. 2, l. 11 *should read*:

take part in the Three Choirs Festival since 1920.

Par. 4, l. 1.   1945 *should read*:
1948

Add at end:

BIBL.—FOSS, HUBERT & GOODWIN, NOEL, 'London Symphony: Portrait of an Orchestra' (London, 1954).

391   i   **LONG, Kathleen**
l. 8 *should read*:

France as in her own country. She was created C.B.E. in the Birthday Honours of 1957.

ii   **Longfellow**
l. 21 *should read*:

'Arsenal', cantata). Spelman ('Courtship of Miles Standish', opera). Stanford ('Spanish Student',

392　ii　**LONGO, Achille**
Par. 1, l. 2 *should read*:
1900; *d.* Naples, 28 May 1954).

393　i　*Add after* **LOON**:
LOOSE, Emmy (*b.* Oustí nad Labem
[Aussig], 22 Jan. 1920).
Czech soprano singer. She studied singing,
pianoforte and musical theory in Prague, and
made her first stage appearance, while still a
student, as one of the Pages in 'Lohengrin'.
Her first professional engagement was with
the Hanover Opera where she made her début
as Blondchen in Mozart's 'Entführung' in
1940. The following year she sang Aennchen
in 'Freischütz' as a guest artist in Vienna.
As a result she was invited to join the State
Opera for the 1942–43 season, and she has
been a member of the company ever since.
She has been particularly outstanding as a
soubrette, and her Papagena, Susanna,
Despina, Zerlina, Blondchen and Adele in
'Fledermaus' are especially distinguished.
In addition she has been heard as Sophie,
Anne Trulove ('The Rake's Progress'),
Musetta, Gilda and Norina. She made her
London début at Covent Garden with the
Vienna State Opera in 1947 and has sung as
a guest artist with the resident company on a
number of occasions since. Being primarily
a Mozart singer, she is in great demand at the
various summer festivals and has been heard
at Aix-en-Provence, Glyndebourne, Florence
and Salzburg. Although her vocalism is not
perfect, and the voice itself has not the pure
quality of some of her Viennese colleagues,
Loose's sparkling stage personality and
infectious spirits help to enliven any performance in which she participates.

H. D. R.

ii　**LOPATNIKOV**
Par. 2, l. 20 *should read*:
in Germany and in the U.S.A. In 1944 he
became an American citizen and in 1945
professor of composition at the Carnegie
Institute in Philadelphia. His output

394　i　Par. 2, l. 18 *should read*:
(Op. 22), 'Sinfonietta' (Op. 27) and 'Concertino' for orchestra (1945).

395　i　**LOPES GRAÇA**
Add before CATALOGUE:
BIBL.—HENRIQUES, MÁRIO VENTURA, 'Fernando Lopes
Graça na música portuguesa contemporánea'
(Sacavém, 1956).

396　ii　**Lorca**
ll. 5–6 *should read*:
(2 puppet plays). Fortner ('Wald', opera; 'Bluthochzeit', incid. m. & opera). Milhaud ('House of
Bernarda Alba', do.). Nono (App., 'Romance de la
guardia civil española'). Revueltas

397　i　**LORENZ**
Par. 2, l. 11 *should read*:
singing Walther in 'Die Meistersinger' and
Lohengrin to the Elsa of Maria Je-

ll. 15–16 *should read*:
1933 to 1942, and in 1952, he sang Tristan
and Siegfried at the Bayreuth festival performances. In London he appeared at Covent
Garden in 1934 and 1937. His first

ll. 23–24 *should read*:
and Rome, where he sang Wagner in Italian.
He is especially famous

399　i　**LORENZO FERNÂNDEZ**
Par. 1 *should read*:
LORENZO FERNÂNDEZ, Oscar. *See*
FERNÂNDEZ, OSCAR LORENZO.

Transfer Pars. 2 *and* 3 *to* Vol. III,
p. 65.

400　i　**LORTZING**
Par. 1, l. 23. Mathisson *should
read*:
Matthisson

403　i　*Add to* BIBL.:
SANDERS, ERNEST, '"Oberon" and "Zar und Zimmermann"' (M.Q., XL, 1954, p. 521).

ii　**LOS ANGELES**
Par. 1, l. 1 *should read*:
LOS ANGELES, Victoria (real name
Victoria Gamez Cima) (*b.* Barcelona,

405　i　**LOTHAR**
Par. 2, l. 19 *should read*:
forte pieces; songs, etc. A magic opera,
'Rappelkopf', based on a play by Ferdinand
Raimund, was written for the celebrations of
the 800th anniversary of Munich held in the
summer of 1958.　　　E. B.

Loti
l. 5 *should read*:
('Ramuntcho', incid. m.). Rawsthorne ('Madame
Chrysanthème', ballet). Taylor (Deems, 'Ramuntcho',
opera).

406　ii　**LOTTI**
See also. l. 2 *should read*:
plagiarism from). Denkmäler (2), Vol. LX (modern
ed. of Masses). Fux (overture to 'Costantino').

407　i　**LOUIS FERDINAND**
Par. 3, l. 11. Hummel *should read*:
Friedrich Himmel

408　i　**LOULIÉ**
Par. 2, l. 5. Poris *should read*:
Paris

408   ii   *Add before* **LOURIÉ**:

LOURER (Fr.). A violinist's term for an effect of bowing also known as *portato* in Italian, but with no English equivalent. A series of two or more notes are played in one bow. The movement of the bow is neither fully continuous (as in the slur) nor wholly interrupted (as in *staccato*), nor again does the bow spring from the string (as in *spiccato*). The bow is slowed down but not stopped between each note, its pressure on the string being lightened; as it resumes speed again, it is given additional pressure on the string. The result is a variety of throbbing or pulsation which cannot be exactly reproduced on instruments other than bowed strings.

The sound does not quite cease between the notes, which are nevertheless separated by an emphasis not strongly marked yet somehow peculiarly significant. The effect is emotional and has therefore to be used with restraint, but on the right occasion it is one of the most telling available. A very typical and beautiful use is made of it in the variations of Beethoven's C♯ minor Quartet, at the *adagio, ma non troppo e semplice*, where all four instruments are played homophonically in this technique.

The family of viols is equally capable of the *lourer*, and since the technique is one of the most legitimate and natural on any bowed string instrument, it must be assumed to be of indefinite antiquity. In the 17th century the use of various techniques of taking several more or less separated notes in one bow can be demonstrated from the contemporary treatises. In Leopold Mozart's 'Violinschule' of 1756 two passages occur which appear to describe the *lourer*, though it is also possible that something nearer to a normal *staccato* of several notes to one bow is intended (Augsburg, 1756, VI, 11, and VII, 17; trans. E. Knocker, London, 1948, pp. 110 & 119).

The normal notation is 𝅘𝅥𝅮𝅘𝅥𝅮𝅘𝅥𝅮𝅘𝅥𝅮𝅘𝅥𝅮𝅘𝅥𝅮, etc., or for a crisper variety showing more separation between notes 𝅘𝅥𝅮𝅘𝅥𝅮𝅘𝅥𝅮𝅘𝅥𝅮𝅘𝅥𝅮𝅘𝅥𝅮, etc., Leopold Mozart gives 𝅘𝅥𝅮𝅘𝅥𝅮𝅘𝅥𝅮.   R. D.

LOURIÉ
Par. 6, l. 1 *should read*:

Lourié settled in the U.S.A. in 1941. His more recent works show a deepen-

Add before **LOUYS**:

Louvet de Couvret, Jean-Baptiste. *See* Luigini ('Faublas', opera).

409   i   **Lovelace**
l. 1. *See* Parry *should read*:
See Lanier (10, songs in 'Lucasta'). Parry

411   i   **LOWE**
Par. 2, ll. 2-6 *should read*:

parts in Handel's oratorios: Philistine Man and Israelite Officer in 'Samson' (1743), Joshua (1748), Jonathan in 'Alexander Balus' (1748), Zadok in 'Solomon' (1749), First Elder in 'Susanna' (1749), Septimus in 'Theodora' (1750) and Attendant on Pleasure in 'The Choice of Hercules' (1751). He sang under Handel in five seasons (1743 and 1748–51) and appeared also in 'Messiah', 'Alexander's Feast', 'L'Allegro', 'Judas Maccabæus', 'Hercules' and 'Esther'. He sang at Ruckholt House, Essex, in Oct. 1743 (in 'Alexander's Feast') and again in May and June 1744; between these dates he was at Dublin, where he sang in the first performance of Arne's oratorio 'The Death of Abel' at the Theatre Royal in Smock Alley on 18 Feb. 1744. In 1745

l. 8 *should read*:

hall Gardens, on 27 May 1749 he appeared in the first performance of Handel's Foundling Hospital Anthem, and in 1763 he became lessee

412   i   *Add after* **LOWLAND**:
Lowndes, Marie Adelaide Belloc. *See* Belloc Lowndes.

LUALDI
Par. 1, l. 2. 1887 *should read*:
1885

ii   List of Works
l. 4 *should read*:
'La figlia del re' (after the 'Antigone' of Sophocles), prod. Turin, Teatro Regio, 18 Mar.

Add after 'Samnium':
Divertimento for orch.

413   i   **LÜBECK, Louis**
l. 1. Hague, 1838; *should read*:
Hague, 14 Feb. 1838;

LÜBECK (2)
(1) Vincenz Lübeck
Par. 2, l. 2 *should read*:
tatas, 6 preludes and fugues for organ and

414   i   **LUBIN**
Par. 1, ll. 5-8 *should read*:
This, as well as Isolde, she also sang in London, at Covent Garden, in 1939, after appearing there with the Paris Opéra company in 1937.

ii   **LUCAS, Clarence**
Par. 3, l. 1 *should read*:

In 1893 Lucas received the B. Mus. degree from Toronto University and took up his residence

415 i Par. 1, ll. 1-3 *should read*:

operas, only two of which appear to have been produced, 'The Money Spider' and 'Peggy Machree' (England, 1904; U.S.A., 1907). He also composed four oratorios and

418 i **LUCIA, F. de**
Par. 2, ll. 14-15 *should read*:

in 1892, when, again under Harris's management, he appeared at Covent Garden in the first performances there of Mascagni's 'Cavalleria rusticana' and 'L'amico Fritz', and again in 1893, when he was

LUCIANI
Par. 1, l. 2-3 *should read*:

viva delle Fonti, Bari, 9 June 1884; d. Acquaviva, 7 Dec. 1950).

419 ii **LUDFORD**
Par 1, l. 1 *should read*:

LUDFORD, Nicholas (b. ?, c. 1485; d. London, c. 1557).

Par. 2, ll. 1-7 *should read*:

English composer. In 1521 he was admitted to the Fraternity of St. Nicholas (the City of London Guild of Parish Clerks) and spent many years as a member of the musical establishment of the Royal Free Chapel of St. Stephen's, Westminster. On 3 July 1538 he was

Add at end:

BIBL.—BAILLIE, HUGH, 'Nicholas Ludford' (M.Q., XLIV, Apr. 1958, p. 196).
BERGSAGEL, J. D., 'An Introduction to Ludford' ('Musica Disciplina', XIV, 1960, p. 105).

LUDIKAR
Par. 2, l. 13. 1923-35 *should read*:
1926-32

420 i *Add after* **LUDOVIC**:

Ludwig, Emil. *See* Zeisl ('Return of Ulysses', incid. m.).

Add after **LUDWIG, Joseph**:

LUDWIG, Leopold (b. Witkowitz, Moravia, 12 Jan. 1908).
Austrian conductor. After studying the pianoforte under Emil Paur at the Vienna Conservatory he began his career as conductor at several opera-houses in southern Germany and at Brno. In 1936 he became musical director of the Oldenburg State Opera and at the same time fulfilled regular guest engagements at the Berlin State Opera. In 1939 he went to Vienna as first conductor of the State Opera and in 1943 to Berlin in the same capacity at the Deutsches Opernhaus. After the second world war he conducted regularly at both the Municipal and the State Operas there. In 1950 he was appointed musical director of the Hamburg State Opera, with which he appeared at the

Edinburgh Festival in 1952. He is also active as conductor of symphony concerts and has visited many European musical centres, such as Vienna, Paris, Amsterdam, Naples and Milan (Teatro alla Scala).   K. W. B.

i-ii **LUGG, John**
Delete article and replace by:

LUGGE (Lugg, Luge), John (b. ? Exeter, c. 1587; d. ? Exeter, ?).
English composer and organist. He was a vicar choral at Exeter Cathedral. Owing to gaps in the Cathedral records his exact dates of birth and death are not known. He was most probably the son of Thomas Lugge, one of the vicars choral of Exeter Cathedral, who married Grace Odham on 28 Sept. 1586, and who later for reasons of his unruly behaviour was deprived of his vicar's place.[1] It may be assumed that John Lugge was born sometime in 1587; if so, he would not yet have been sixteen years of age when on 19 Mar. 1603 he signed the pay-book of the Cathedral as "organiste". The appointment of very young organists was not unusual in those days; Matthew Godwin, one of Lugge's gifted predecessors at the Cathedral, was also appointed at fifteen.

For his services as organist Lugge received from the Dean and Chapter a salary of £10 per annum, which from 1608 onwards he had to share with Edward Gibbons, the newly appointed "Informator Chorustarum". On Midsummer Day 1605, Lugge became a vicar choral and received as such a salary of £10 per annum from the Custos and College of Vicars Choral, as well as free board and lodgings. He must have married about the same time, because in 1606 a daughter Mary was born to him and his wife Rebecca. Altogether the Lugges had six children and lived in a house in the Old Kallenderhay close to the Cathedral.

Lugge's leanings towards Roman Catholicism got him into serious trouble in 1618. His brother Peter, who had been brought up in Lisbon, was deeply involved in religious and political intrigue. A compromising letter written on 9 Dec. 1617[2] from him to John was intercepted and led to John's examination by Bishop William Cotton of Exeter. It is difficult to know how far Lugge was involved in this matter, but the bishop in his report dated 24 Jan. 1618 to Sir Thomas Lake, the Secretary of State, defends Lugge. He describes him as a young man without settled views in religion,

who doth with tears hereafter avow never to hover about this candle, least like a fly he be singed, and though I fear, and by conference do suspect that he has eaten a little bit, or mumbled a piece of this forbidden fruit, yet I verily believe he hath spit it all out again.

[1] Consistory Court Records 181, Castle Museum, Exeter.   [2] P.R.O., SPDS James I, Vol. 1495.

With the report of Lugge's examination the bishop sent a protestation in which Lugge declares his innocence, and a certificate of the vicars choral affirming it.[1] Three years later, on 19 Nov. 1621, Lugge was suspected again and his house was searched, but nothing of importance was found.[2]

There are numerous references to John Lugge in the records of Exeter Cathedral. He held his organist's appointment for at least forty-two years until, in 1645, the musical activities at the Cathedral were interrupted by the Civil War. Besides his salaries, he received occasional *ex-gratia* payments and fees for minor organ repairs which he undertook himself. In 1644 his wife died and in 1646 he transferred the lease of his house in the Old Kallenderhay to his daughter Mary. According to an entry in the accounts of the College of Vicars Choral he seems to have received a payment as late as 1647. It is not known when and where he died.

Lugge's reputation as a composer must have been considerable in his own times. His anthem 'Behold how good and joyful' had been included in Thomas Myriell's 'Tristitiae remedium' (1616) ; a further six anthems (words only) appear in a collection of anthem texts (B.M. MS Harley 4241) together with anthems of the great Elizabethan and Jacobean composers. Of his Service in D major Burney wrote : " the modulation and counterpoint of his Service is excellent in the Old Cathedral Style and deserves to be still in use " (B.M. Add. MS 11587). His organ pieces at Christ Church Library, Oxford, are in autograph and form a very important collection containing the principal forms of organ compositions of the period. Some of the vocal works, signed " Lugge " (without Christian name) and previously attributed to Robert Lugge (no doubt as a result of the entry in 'Fasti Oxon.'), must be ascribed to John. It is most unlikely that Robert Lugge, who " went beyond the seas " when eighteen years old, left any works of importance behind.

CATALOGUE OF WORKS

VOCAL

Service in D ma. (a 4). B.M. Harley MS 7340, f. 46 (score). Ely Cath. MS 18, p. 27 (score). (Te D., Jub., Ky., Creed, Magnificat, N. Dim.)
Service in D mi. (a 4). Ch. Ch. Oxford MS 437, f. 36v. (organ part). (Te D., Jub., Ky., Creed, Magnificat, N. Dim.)
Short Service in A ma. (a 4). B.M. Add. MSS 17792-17794, 17796. (4 part-books, Cantus, Altus, Tenor, Bassus.) (Venite, Te D., Magnificat, N. Dim.)
Short Service in C ma. (a 4). Oxford Ch. Ch. MS 6 (organ part). (Te D., Bdtus., Ky., Creed, Magnificat, N. Dim.)
Litany. Organ part only printed in J. Jebb, 'The Choral Responses and Litanies of the United Church of England and Ireland' (1847–57), Vol. II, p. 212.

[1] P.R.O., SPDS James I, Vol. 95.
[2] P.R.O., SPDS James I, Vol. 123.

'Behold how good and joyful ', verse anthem (a 5). B.M. Harley MS 7339, f. 149 (score). Peterhouse (part-books, Cantoris countertenor missing).
' It is a good thing to give thanks ', full anthem (a 5). B.M. Add. MSS 29372-76 (part-books, I-IV f. 83v.; V, f. 70v.). B.M. Harley MS 4142, f. 2 (words only).
' Let my complaint ', verse anthem for tenor and bass. Peterhouse. Oxford Ch. Ch. MS 437 (organ part only). B.M. Harley MS 4142, f. 14v. (words only).
' I am the Resurrection ', full anthem. Oxford Ch. Ch. MS 437, f. 5v. (organ part only). B.M. Harley MS 4142, f. 11 (words only).
' Keep, we beseech Thee ', full anthem. B.M. Harley MS 4142, f. 12 (words only).
' Not every one that saith ', full anthem. B.M. Harley MS 4142, f. 16 (words only).
' Stir up, we beseech Thee ', full anthem. B.M. Harley MS 4142, f. 25v. (words only).
' To drive away ', catch. R.C.M. MS II, c. 15 (2), f. 39. Printed in John Hilton's ' Catch that Catch can ' (London, editions 1658 and 1663), p. 112.

KEYBOARD WORKS

Miserere, Christ qui lux. Oxford Ch. Ch. MS 49, pp. 202-42.
Gloria tibi Trinitas (six settings). Oxford Ch. Ch. MS 49, pp. 202-42.
In Nomine. Oxford Ch. Ch. MS 49, pp. 202-42.
Ut re, mi, fa, so, la. Oxford Ch. Ch. MS 49, pp. 202-42.
3 Voluntaries for double organ. Oxford Ch. Ch. MS 49, pp. 202-42.
2 Toys. Paris Conservatoire MS Res. 1186, ff. 112, 122.
Jigg. Oxford Ch. Ch. MS 431, f. 5.

There are modern editions, by Susi Jeans and John Steele, of ' Three Voluntaries for a Double Organ ' (Novello, London) and ' Two Toys and a Jigg ' (Schott, Mainz).

s. J.

421   ii   **LUGG, Robert**
Delete whole entry and replace by :

LUGGE (Lugg, Luge), Robert (b. Exeter, 6 Nov. 1620 ; d. ?).

English organist and (?) composer, son of the preceding. He was appointed organist of St. John's College, Oxford, when only fifteen years of age, and graduated B. Mus. in 1638. On 13 Feb. 1639 Archbishop Laud ordered in the Court of High Commission that he should be sent back to his father at Exeter, to be well looked after.[1] Soon after that trial he " went beyond the seas and exchanged his religion for that of Rome ".[2] His somewhat unstable character was very well described in a letter from his father to the Vice-Chancellor of Oxford University.[3] Some vocal music listed under John Lugge above has been conjecturally attributed to Robert, but is much more likely to be by his father.

s. J.

[1] P.R.O., SPDS Charles I, Vol. XXV.
[2] Wood, Fasti Oxon.
[3] St. John's Coll. Muniments, LX, 32.

422   i   **LUIGINI**
l. 1. *After opéra-comique add* :

(after Louvet de Couvret)

Footnote 2, l. 1. Slominsky *should read* :
Slonimsky

425   ii   **LULLY**
BIBL., l. 7.   texte de livret *should read* :
texte du livret

Add to BIBL. :
CUDWORTH, C. L., ' " Baptist's Vein " — French Orchestral Music and its Influence, from 1650 to 1750' (Proc. Roy. Mus. Ass., Vol. LXXXIII, 1956–1957).

427   i   *See also. Add to* l. 12 :
Publikationen G.M.F., Vol. 13 (modern ed. of 'Armide ').

428   ii   **LUND, Signe**
Par. 1 l. 2 *should read* :
1868 ; *d.* Oslo, 6 Apr. 1950).

429   i   **Lunel**
l. 2 *should read* :
Milhaud (6 libs. ; 'Barba Garibo ', spectacle ; cantata ; 8 songs). Sauguet

430   i   *Add before* **LUPIS** :
LUPI, Roberto (*b.* Milan, 28 Nov. 1908). Italian composer and conductor. He studied at the Milan Conservatory, where he took a diploma in composition in 1934. He now teaches harmony and counterpoint at the Conservatory of Florence. In 1936 he published his first essays in the new resources of harmony and counterpoint (*armonia di gravitazione*) which he subsequently established more firmly on a theoretical basis. He is also interested in early Italian music, which he has published in modern editions and performed at his concerts. His interpretations of lute music must be especially mentioned.
As a composer Lupi has produced the *sacra rappresentazione* ' La danza di Salomé ' (Perugia, 1952), the *mistero melodrammatico* ' La nuova Euridice' (Bergamo, 1957), symphonic choral music ('Sacra Symphonia', 'Orpheus', etc.), vocal and instrumental chamber music, music for the harp, etc. He began his career as an orchestral conductor in 1937 by winning the national competition for young conductors. He has conducted all the chief Italian and some foreign orchestras.
G. M. G.

431   ii   **LUR**
Par. 1, l. 5 *should read* :
peat bogs of Denmark and Sweden, as well as near Stavanger, on the west coast of Norway, nineteen

432   ii   **LUSSAN**
Par. 1, l. 2.   1863 *should read* :
1862

439   ii   **LUTE**
Add at end :
(*PLATES* 32, Vol. IV, p. 492, No. 6 ; 40, Vol. V, Frontispiece, No. 3 ; 42, Vol. V p. 432, No. 3 ; 71, Vol. VIII, p. 186, No. 8.)

444   ii   **LUTE MUSIC**
Add to BIBL. :
DART, THURSTON, ' Lord Herbert of Cherbury's Lute-Book' (M. & L., XXXVIII, 1957, p. 136).
JACQUOT, JEAN, (ed.) ' Le Luth et sa musique ' (Paris, 1959).

445   i   *Add to* BIBL. :
LUMSDEN, DAVID, ' English Lute Music, 1540–1620 : an Introduction' (Proc. Roy. Mus. Ass., Vol. LXXXIII, 1956–57).
SPENCER, ROBERT, ' The Weld Lute Book' ('The Lute Society Journal', I, 1958, p. 121).

     ii   *Add at end* :
See also Luthistes Espagnols (for modern reprints).

447   ii   **LUTHER**
Add to BIBL. :
BURBA, KLAUS, ' Die Christologie in Luthers Liedern ' (Gütersloh, 1956).

448   i   **LUTINA**
Add at end of line :
(*PLATES* 32, Vol. IV, p. 492, No. 2 ; 40, Vol. V, Frontispiece, No. 6 ; 42, Vol. V, p. 432, No. 1.)

     ii   **LUTYENS,** CATALOGUE
ORCHESTRAL WORKS
Add at end :
' Son et lumière ' at Cardiff Castle (1958).

449   i   *Add before* PIANOFORTE MUSIC :
CLARINET AND PIANOFORTE
' Valediction ' in memory of Dylan Thomas (1953).

450   i   **LUYTHON**
Par. 2, l. 32.   3 July *should read* :
4 July

     ii   BIBL., l. 6.   1907 *should read* :
1917

Add to BIBL. :
WATELET, J., ' Charles Guillet, Giovanni [de] Macque, Carolus Luython : werken voor orgel . . .' (' Monumenta Musicae Belgicae ', Vol. IV, Antwerp, 1938).[3]

Add footnote :
[3] Contains Luython's complete organ music and a preface by Anny Piscaer.

LUZZASCHI
Par. 2, l. 6.   Van der Straeten [3]
should read :
Van der Straeten [4]

Footnote 3 becomes 4.

451   i   **LVOV**
Par. 1, l. 2.   1798 ; *should read* :
1799 [1] ;

Add footnote :
[1] According to ' Notes upon a Musical Journey in Germany in 1844 ' by Wiktor Każyński, who was Lvov's secretary.

451 i Par. 3, ll. 1-3 *should read*:

Lvov composed the following instrumental works:

Variations, D mi., for vn. with stg. 4tet, ded. to Lipiński (1835).
Fantasy No. 1 for vn. & orch. (1838).
' Les Mélodies de F. Schubert avec accomp. de violon obligé ' (1838).
Fantasy No. 2, on Russian airs for vn., orch. & chorus (1839).
' Concert dans le mode d'une scène dramatique ' for vn. & orch. (1840).
' Le Duel: Divertissement pour violon et violoncelle (concertants) ' for vn. & orch., ded. to Meyerbeer (1842).

 ii **LYNE**
  Par. 1, l. 1. Slater, Mo., 1891 ;
  should read:

Slater, Missouri, 28 Mar. 1887 ;

456 i *Add before* **LYRE-GUITAR**:

(*PLATE* 71, Vol. VIII, p. 186, No. 5.)

LYREBIRD PRESS, THE (Éditions de l'Oiseau-Lyre). A publishing venture organized and financed by Mrs. Louise B. M. Hanson Dyer in 1932 and established in France. The catalogue comprises three distinct sections: (1) limited editions, luxuriously produced and costly; (2) unlimited editions, mainly of extracts and separate works on a small scale issued at very moderate prices; (3) gramophone records of rare music not otherwise obtainable in this form and including the first long-playing records to be issued in France.

The following limited editions have so far appeared:

François Couperin, Complete Works: general editor, Maurice Cauchie:
Vol.
1. Œuvres didactiques, ed. by Paul Brunold.
2-5. Pièces de clavecin, ed. by Maurice Cauchie.
6. Pièces d'orgue, ed. by Paul Brunold.
7-10. Musique de chambre, ed. by Amédée Gastoué & André Schaeffner.
11-12. Musique vocale, ed. by Paul Brunold & André Tessier.
Louis Couperin, Complete Works, ed. by Paul Brunold.
' Le Grand Orgue de l'Église de Saint-Gervais de Paris ' by Paul Brunold.
Annibale Padovano, 13 Ricercari for organ, ed. by N. Pierront & J. P. Hennebains.
' The Catalogue of the Manuscripts at St. Michael's College, Tenbury ', by Edmund H. Fellowes.
' Trésor de musique byzantine ', 2 vols., ed. by Egon Wellesz.
13 Books of Motets published by Pierre Attaignant, 1534-35, ed. by A. Smijers.
Polyphonic Music of the 13th Century (Montpellier MS. H. 196), 4 vols., ed. by Yvonne Rokseth.
Polyphonic Music of the 14th Century, ed. by L. Schrade.
Charles Dieupart, Works, 2 vols., ed. by Paul Brunold.
John Blow, 2 Sonatas for 2 violins, viola da gamba and bass, ed. by W. Gillies Whittaker.
The Musicians of the Court of Burgundy (Reign of Philippe le Bon, 15th Century), ed. by J. Marix.
Henry Purcell, 12 Sonatas, ed. by W. Gillies Whittaker.
' Colindes ', Christmas Song of Rumania, ed. by M. Humbert-Lavergne.
John Blow, ' Venus and Adonis ', opera, ed. by Anthony Lewis, with drawings by Marie Laurencin.
William Byrd, Keyboard Music, ed. by Stephen Tuttle.
Guillaume Landré, Trio for violin, cello & pianoforte.
M. Sutherland, Sonata for violin & pianoforte.

The unlimited editions are partly extracts from the limited editions; others include the following:

OLD MUSIC

6 13th-century Motets, transcribed by Yvonne Rokseth.
' Les Monuments de l'Ars Nova ', 6 books.
Clérambault, Louis-Nicolas, 14 Pièces de clavecin.
Couperin, François-Gervais, ' La Chaumière ' for voice & continuo.
La Guerre, Élisabeth Jacquet de, 12 Pièces de clavecin.
' Céphale et Procris ' for voice, flute & continuo.
Lalande, Michel de, ' Sinfonies pour les soupers du roi ', arr. by Roger Désormière.
Playford's ' The Dancing Master ':
 6 Dances arr. for pf. by Imogen Holst.
 5 Pieces arr. for pipes by Arthur Benjamin.
Rameau, Jean-Philippe, ' Les Paladins ', 2nd suite for small orch., arr. by Roger Désormière.

MODERN MUSIC

Barraud, Henri, Trio for oboe, clar. & bassoon.
Bate, Stanley, Sonata for flute & pf.
Glanville-Hicks, Peggy, Choral Suite for women's voices, oboe and stgs.
 4 Songs for voice & pf.
Holst, Imogen, 6 Scottish Folksongs for voice & pf.
Ikonomov, Boyan, Trio for oboe, clar. & bassoon.
 String Quartet No. 2.
Koechlin, Charles, ' L'Ancienne Maison de campagne ', suite for pf.
 Sonatina No. 1 for organ.
 Choral in F mi. for organ.
 Septet for wind insts.
 2 Sonatas for clar. & pf.
Landré, Guillaume, Suite for stgs. & pf.
Milhaud, Darius, ' Suite d'après Corrette ' for oboe, clar. & bassoon.
Sauguet, Henri, ' La Voyante ', cantata for soprano & chamber orch.   E. B.

458 i **McARDEN**
  Par. 1, l. 1 *should read*:

McARDEN, Joy (Jo Ijzenman) (*b.* Diemerburg nr. Amsterdam, 16 Jan. 1893 ;

  Par. 2, l. 2 *should read*:

Emma Calvé, Roberto Tamanti, Mme Charles Cahier and

  l. 4 *should read*:

début in Copenhagen in 1920 and later sang at opera-

 ii Par. 1, l. 2 *should read*:

Hague, etc. She toured in Australia in 1928–1930 and established a music school at Melbourne. She was an extremely versatile

  ll. 9-10 *should read*:

performances of vocal works by Ravel. Her first husband was the French author J. C. Demarquette. Having married a second time and settled in Birmingham, she taught

459 i **MACBETH, A.**
  Par. 1, l. 1. **Allen** *should read*:
Allan

461 ii Page Heading, MACDIARMID
  should read:

McDONALD

461   ii   **McDONALD, Harl**
Par. 1, l. 2 *should read*:
Colorado, 27 July 1899; *d.* Princeton, N.J., 30 Mar. 1955).

462   i   List of Works
Add after Suite ' From Childhood ':
Vn. Concerto (1945).

   ii   *Add after* **MACDONALD**:
MACDOWELL COLONY, THE.
and transfer article from p. 465, col. ii.

MACDOWELL
Par. 3, l. 12 *should read*:
the Frankfurt Conservatory and the composition class

Add after Par. 3:
In 1884 MacDowell married the American pianist Marian Griswold Nevins, who had been his pupil at Darmstadt. She was a great help to him and after his illness and death did much to promote his work. She survived him for nearly half a century, dying at Los Angeles on 23 Aug. 1956, at the age of ninety-eight.

463   ii   BIBL., l. 10. LAURENCE *should read*:
LAWRENCE

465   ii   **MACDOWELL MEMORIAL ASSOCIATION** *should read*:
MACDOWELL COLONY, THE.

Transfer article to p. 462, col. ii.

Par. 3, ll. 4-6 *should read*:
intercourse.   H. E. K.

469   i   **MACFARREN**
BIBL., l. 1. ' Sir George Macfarren '
should read:
' George Alexander Macfarren: his Life, Works and Influence '

470   i   *Add after* **Mácha**:
MACHABEY, Armand (*b.* Pont-de-Roide, Doubs, 7 May 1886).
French musicologist and composer. He took the degree of Docteur ès Lettres at Paris University with a dissertation entitled ' Histoire et évolution des formes en Occident jusqu'au XVᵉ siècle ' in 1928, the examiner being André Pirro. This was reissued in a revised version, brought up to date, as ' Genèse de la tonalité occidentale ' in 1955. The following are Machabey's books on music :
' Anton Bruckner ' (1946).
' Précis Manuel d'histoire de la musique ' (2nd ed., 1947).
' Maurice Ravel ' (1947).

' Traité de la critique musicale ' (1947).
' Le Bel canto ' (1948).
' Portraits de trente jeunes musiciens français ' (1949).
' La Notation musicale ' (1952).
' Gerolamo Frescobaldi ' (1952).
' Guillaume de Machault : la vie et l'œuvre musicale ', 2 vols. (1955).

He also published, in 1951, the ' Diffinitorium ' by Tinctoris in a modern edition of the original text with a French translation and transcribed Machaut's 4-part Mass (1948). He has contributed to many musical encyclopedias and to French and foreign musical periodicals, and is one of the directors of the ' Larousse de la Musique '. As a composer he produced 14 Dances for small orchestra, 6 Pieces for violin and pianoforte and ' 4 Préludes brefs ' for pianoforte.

Mme Machabey (Émilienne Ganeval) is a coach at the Paris Conservatoire and a composer with a Sonatina for violin and pianoforte, various pianoforte pieces and songs to her credit.   E. B.

472   ii   **MACHAUT**
Add to BIBL. :
LEVARIE, SIEGMUND, ' Guillaume de Machaut ' (New York, 1954).
MACHABEY, ARMAND, ' Guillaume de Machault : la vie et l'œuvre musicale ', 2 vols. (Paris, 1955).
REANEY, GILBERT, ' The Lais of Guillaume de Machaut and their Background ' (Proc. Roy. Mus. Ass., Vol. LXXXII, 1955–56).

See also. Add to l. 1 :
Amer. Inst. Musicol. (C.M.M.), Vol. 2 (modern ed. of Mass). Denkmäler (4), Vols. I & III (modern ed.).

473   i   **MACISZEWSKI**
Par. 1, l. 2 *should read*:
21 May 1927).

477   i   **MACKENZIE,** CATALOGUE
ORCHESTRAL WORKS
Op. 22 *should read*:
21.

478   ii   **McKIE**
Par 2, l. 3 *should read*:
having won the Clarke Scholarship at the

479   i   ll. 2-6 *should read*:
1941, while serving in the R.A.F., he was appointed Organist and Master of the Choristers at Westminster Abbey, eventually taking up this post in 1946. He officiated at the Coronation of Queen Elizabeth II on 2 June 1953, as Director of Music, and subsequently received the honour of knighthood.   H. C. C.

481   i   **MACMILLAN**
Par. 3, l. 6 *should read*:
succession to A. S. Vogt (resigned 1942), and in 1931 he was

l. 8 *should read*:
Orchestra (resigned 1956). Within four years he built up the

481   i   Par. 3, l. 15 *should read*:

Canada. He was Dean of the Faculty of Music in the University of Toronto until 1952 and is Chairman of the Canadian Music Council, President of the Composers' Authors' and Publishers' Association of Canada and (since 1942) conductor of the Toronto Mendelssohn Choir.

483   i   **MACONCHY**, CATALOGUE
CHORAL WORKS
Add at end:
6 Settings of W. B. Yeats for soprano & women's chorus (1951).

ORCHESTRAL WORKS
Add at end:
' Nocturne ' (1950–51).
Symphony for double stg. orch. (1953).
Overture ' Proud Thames ' (1953).

SOLO AND ORCHESTRA
Add at end:
Concertino for pf. & stgs. (1949).
Concertino for bassoon & stgs. (1952).

CHAMBER MUSIC
Add at end:
String Quartet No. 6 (1950).
Duo (Theme and Variations) for vn. & cello (1951).
String Quartet No. 7 (1957).

ii   SOLO INSTRUMENTS
Add at end:
4 Pieces for unaccomp. double bass (1954).

McPHEE
Par. 6, l. 10 *should read*:

plays. His two books, ' A House in Bali ' (1946) and

484   i   List of Works
l. 5 *should read*:
' Tabuh-Tabuhan', on Balinese themes, for orch. (1936).

486   i   *Add after* **MACURA**:

McVEAGH, Diana (Mary) (*b*. Songei Siput, Malaya, 6 Sept. 1926).
English musicologist. She was educated at Malvern Girls' College and musically at the R.C.M. in London in 1944–47, taking the A.R.C.M. and G.R.S.M. diplomas, and winning the Colles Prize. Between 1947 and 1950 she was on the music staff in London of Godolphin and Latymer School, Hammersmith, and lectured on music both for the Workers' Educational Association and the London County Council. In 1951 she was appointed Tutorial Class Lecturer for London University. Since her marriage she has also been engaged in part-time musical journalism. As an author she began as a contributor to ' Music & Letters ' and other journals, and her first book was an important biographical and critical work on Elgar, published in 1955. After the death of Gerald

Finzi in 1956 she was invited to write a monograph on that composer. Critical insight combines with a graceful and forthright style in making Diana McVeagh a writer on music with a distinctive personality.   E. B.

486   i   *Add after* **Madariaga**:

MADEIRA, Jean (Browning) (*b*. Centralia, Illinois, 14 Nov. 1924).
American mezzo-soprano singer. Her mother, of Anglo-Irish descent, was a pianoforte teacher and her father, of Indian descent, the superintendent of a coal mine on the banks of the Mississippi. When she was five she began studying the pianoforte with her mother and at fifteen played the Beethoven C minor Concerto with the St. Louis Symphony Orchestra under Vladimir Golschmann. Generous citizens of St. Louis helped to finance a trip for her to New York, where she entered for a scholarship at the Juilliard School; there the pianist Olga Samaroff heard her sing, and suggested that she should enter the school's vocal department and not its instrumental one. As Jean Browning she sang with the Summer Opera at Chautauqua and then with Fortuno Gallo's touring San Carlo company; her parts at this time included Ulrica, Delilah, Amneris, Azucena, Carmen, Maddalena and Lola. In the summer of 1948 she went to London to understudy Marie Powers in Menotti's ' The Medium '.
In 1947 Jean Browning had married Francis Madeira, conductor of the Rhode Island Philharmonic Orchestra, and as Jean Browning Madeira she made her début at the Metropolitan, New York, in the autumn of 1948 as the First Norn in ' Götterdämmerung '. During the next six years she sang more important parts in New York, including Suzuki, Erda, La Cieca, Amneris, Preziosilla, Azucena and Ulrica. In the summer of 1954 she sang Carmen at Puerto Rico and in the autumn of the same year Delilah at the Royal Opera of Stockholm. This was the beginning of Madeira's European career. Appearances followed in 1955 at Munich (Carmen), London (Erda) and Bayreuth; she sang Orfeo in Brussels (under Monteux), Carmen in Vienna and Amneris during the reopening celebrations of the Vienna State Opera. In 1956 she appeared as Klytemnestra at the Salzburg Festival and in 1957 as Carmen at Aix-en-Provence. She is now on joint contract with the Metropolitan and the Vienna State Opera, and sang Carmen and Delilah in Buenos Aires in 1958.
Madeira's voice is an excellent one, rich and dark in timbre. This, coupled with a fine stage presence and dramatic intelligence, makes her a compelling figure on the stage.
H. D. R.

486   i   *Add before* **MADETOJA** :

MADERNA, Bruno (*b.* Venice, 1920).
Italian conductor and composer. He
studied under Hermann Scherchen and has
made his way as a highly gifted conductor in
Italy, France, Germany, Spain and Switzerland. As a composer he has been particularly
successful at the Darmstadt Holiday Courses,
where in 1949 his Fantasy and Fugue on
B.A.C.H. for two pianofortes was produced,
in 1950 his ' Composizione in tre tempi '
for chamber orchestra and in 1952 his ' Musica
per due dimensioni '. Later works are a
Serenade for 11 instruments and a string
Quartet (1955).   E. B.

499   ii   **MADRIGAL SOCIETY**
           Par. 3, l. 12.   Sir G. Ouseley
           should read :

Sir Frederick G. Ouseley

500   ii   Par. 2, l. 2 *should read* :

filled by J. G. Craufurd. The Society's
library, which includes valuable 17th-century
manuscripts and printed books, is housed in
the British Museum.   J. G. C.

Add to BIBL. :

CRAUFURD, J. G., ' The Madrigal Society ' (Proc. Roy.
Mus. Ass., Vol. LXXXII, 1955–56).

501   ii   **Maeterlinck**
           l. 3 *should read* :
Bleue (Dukas).   Baeyens ('Blue Bird ', incid. m.).
Boulanger (L., ' Princesse Maleine ',

502   ii   **MAGANINI**
           Par. 3, l. 13 *should read* :

Orchestral Fancy ' (first performed 1931);
opera ' Tennessee's Partner ' (first performed
1942).

503   i   **MAGGINI**
          Par. 1. Dates *should read* :

(*b.* Botticino Sera nr. Brescia, [bapt. 25 Aug.]
1580 ; *d.* Brescia, 1630 [1]).

Add footnote :
[1] According to the plaque fixed in 1907 to the house
where he was born he died during the pestilence of 1630.

511   ii   **MAHLER**
           Par. 1, l. 1 *should read* :

Kaliště, 7 July 1860 [2];

Add footnote :
[2] Mahler's parents later on said the date was 1 July,
but the birth certificate, according to a photostat kindly
supplied by M. Nicolas Slonimsky, leaves no doubt that
7 July is correct.

512   i   Par. 1, l. 1.   Theodor Krenn
          should read :
Franz Krenn

512   i   Par. 1, l. 9 *should read* :

position, ' Das klagende Lied ', first conceived as an opera.

      ii   Par. 1, l. 13 *should read* :

Lane. The same year he also conducted at
Covent Garden. It was during these years
that his
      l. 15.   In 1895 *should read* :
About 1895

513   i   Par. 1, ll. 12-16 *should read* :

kovsky's ' Queen of Spades '. In 1910 he
returned once more to Europe, broken in
health, and after a few concerts of his own
works at Munich (first performance of the
eighth Symphony), Paris and Amsterdam
(the last-named, both

      ll. 20-21 *should read* :

Willem Mengelberg), he went to America
for the last time. There he conducted another
series of concerts until his final collapse on 21
Feb. 1911, from which he never recovered.
He returned to Europe gravely ill in Apr. and
died in Vienna in his fifty-first year on 18 May.

515   i   Par. 3, l. 8.   über Feld *should read* :
übers Feld

516   i   Par. 2, l. 7 *should read* :

lished in 1924 and a concert edition in full
score of two middle movements in 1951, by
an anonymous editor ; the score of the first
movement

      ii   BIBL.   l. 49 *should read* :

James Galston (London, 1937). New ed., trans.
supervised by Lotte Walter Lindt (London, 1958).

Add to BIBL. :

MITCHELL, DONALD, ' Gustav Mahler : the Early Years '
    (London, 1958)
REDLICH, HANS, ' Bruckner and Mahler ' (' Master
    Musicians ' series) (London, 1955).
' Gustav Mahler : eine Erkenntnis ' (Nuremberg,
    1929).

CATALOGUE
OPERAS
Col. 1, ll. 1-2 *should read* :
' Herzog Ernst von Schwaben.'
' Die Argonauten.'
' Rübezahl.'

Col. 2, ll. 1-2 *should read* :
Josef Steiner (? after Uhland).
Composer (? after Grillparzer).
Composer, on a popular legend.

Col. 3, ll. 1-2 *should read* :
? 1877–78, unfinished, lost.
? 1880, prelude only, lost.
1883, first act only, lost.

SYMPHONIC WORKS
Col. 3, l. 1 *should read* :
1st (operatic) version (*Märchenspiel*), in 3 parts, 1880 ;
    2nd version, in 2 parts, 1888 ; 3rd version (rev. and
    re-scored), 1896–98, publ. 1898.

517 —   SYMPHONIC WORKS
1896.   Symphony No. 3, col. 4 *should read*:

Symphony No. 5, col. 1 *should read*:
Symphony No. 5, C minor.

Col. 4 *should read*:
Publ. 1901, repeatedly rev., last rev. (1910) not yet publ.

Symphony No. 6, col. 4 *should read*:
1905.

Symphony No. 7, D ma. *should read*:
Symphony No. 7, E. mi.

Symphony No. 9, col. 1 *should read*:
Symphony No. 9, D ma.-Db ma.

Col. 4 *should read*:
1910.

Col. 3, l. 12 *should read*:
Chinese poems (Li Tai-Po, etc.) trans. from Hans

Col. 1, l. 10. (unfinished). *should read*:
(unfinished, 1910).

Col. 4, l. 10:
Delete 1910.

SONGS
l. 1, col. 3. 1882. *should read*:
Vol. I, *c.* 1883 ; Vols. II-III, *c.* 1888–92.

l. 2, col. 3. 1883. *should read*:
Comp. 1883–85 ; rev. & publ. 1897.

l. 3, col. 3. 1888. *should read*:
Comp. 1888–99 ; publ. 1905.

l. 35, col. 1 *should read*:
5 Songs to Poems by Rückert (with orch.)

l. 4, col. 3. 1902. *should read*:
Comp. 1901–4 ; publ. 1905.

l. 47, col. 1 *should read*:
' Revelge ' (with orch.).

l. 6, col. 3. last years. *should read*:
Comp. *c.* 1899, publ. 1905.

l. 48, col. 1 *should read*:
' Der Tambourg'sell ' (with orch.).

l. 7, col. 3. last years. *should read*:
Comp. 1899, publ. 1905.

*Add at end of Catalogue, below the
rule*:
A number of fragmentary, lost and doubtful
early works are listed in Donald Mitchell's
' Gustav Mahler : the Early Years ' (*see* BIBL.),
pp. 116-20.

521   i   *Add before* **MAINE** :
MAINARDI, Enrico (*b.* Milan, 19 May
1897).
Italian violoncellist. He studied under
Giuseppe Magrini at the Milan Conservatory
and subsequently under Hugo Becker in
Berlin. He first appeared as a concert artist
in 1910. After teaching in Berlin he became
in 1932 professor of the higher violoncello

class at the Accademia di Santa Cecilia in
Rome. He has composed works for chamber
music (cello and pianoforte, solo cello, trio)
and for orchestra, edited classical works for
the cello and also appeared as conductor.

           G. M. G.

521   ii   **MAINE**
      Par. 2, l. 7 *should read*:
also be named. Nearly twenty years after
his retirement from the profession of music
critic, in 1957, he published a book of essays,
' Twang with Our Music '. His novels and
biographies

MAINZER
      Par. 1, l. 1.   Trier, 1801 [2] *should
      read*:
Trier, 21 Oct. 1800 [2]

      Footnote 2.   Cancel l. 1.

522   ii   **MAITRES MUSICIENS** *should
      read*:
MAÎTRES MUSICIENS

526   i   **MAKAROVA**
      Par. 2, l. 9 *should read*:
servatory. She is the wife of Aram Khachaturian.

     ii   **MAKLAKIEWICZ**
      Par. 1, l. 2.   1899). *should read*:
1899 ; d. Warsaw, 8 Feb. 1954).

      Par. 2, l. 22 *should read*:
State Music Prize. In 1947 he became
director of the Cracow Conservatory.

      Par. 7, l. 8.   ' Grunwald ' *should read*:
' Grünewald '

527   i   **MAŁACHOWSKI**
      Par. 2, l. 1.   16th–17th-century
      should read:
17th-century

      l. 4.   (1622) *should read*:
(1662)

MALAWSKI
      Par. 1.   Dates *should read*:
(*b.* Przemyśl, 4 July 1904 ; d. Cracow, 26
Dec. 1957).

      Par. 2, ll. 9-10 *should read*:
given in Amsterdam in June 1948. In 1949
he won two prizes for his ' Symphonic
Studies ' and ' Toccata and Fugue in the Form

of Variations ', written in 1948 and 1949
respectively. He received the State Award
(2nd grade) for his pedagogic and creative
activity during the past decade in 1955.
Malawski's compositions include:

527   i   CATALOGUE
             Add before CHORAL WORK :

             INCIDENTAL MUSIC
' Burza ' (' The Tempest') (Shakespeare), radio version
    (1937) ; 2 stage versions (1938 & 1940).
' Stara Baśń ' (' The Ancient Tale ') (J. I. Kraszewski)
    (1949).
' Sen nocy letniej ' (' A Midsummer Night's Dream ')
    (Shakespeare) (1954).
' Legenda o miłości ' (' Legend of Love ') (N. Hikmet)
    (1955).

             CHORAL WORK *should read* :
             CHORAL WORKS

             Add below Cantata :
' Wyspa gorgon ' ('Island of Gorgons ') (Miciński)
    (1939).
' Wierchy ' (' The Peaks ') (J. Mazur) (1939).
' Mała suita ' (' Little Suite ') for unaccompanied
    chorus (1952).

        ii   ORCHESTRAL WORKS
             l. 3. (1938). *should read* :
(1937).

             l. 4 *should read* :
Symphony No. 1 (1938–44).

             Add after l. 5 :
' Suita popularna ' (1952).
Symphony No. 2 (1956).
' Hungaria ' (Nov.-Dec. 1956).

             PIANOFORTE AND ORCHESTRA
             l. 1. Studies.' *should read* :
Studies ' (1948).

             Add (l. 2) :
Toccata and Fugue in the Form of Variations (1949).

             CHAMBER MUSIC
             Add below heading :
String Quartet No. 1 (1926).
Sextet for stgs. (1935).

             Add after l. 1 :
Trio for vn., cello & pf. (1953).

             VIOLIN AND PIANOFORTE
             Add below l. 2 :
' Mazurka ' (1951).
' Andante and Allegro ' (1951).
' Siciliana e rondo ' on a theme by Janiewicz (1951).

             PIANOFORTE MUSIC
             Add below l. 2 :
' Tryptyk goralski ' (' Highland Triptych ') (1950).
    Also music for films, recitations with wind sextet and
songs.   C. R. H.

MALBECQ
Add at end :

His extant work is published in Vol. II of
' Early Fifteenth-Century Music ', edited by
Gilbert Reaney (Amer. Inst. of Musicology,
1958).

528   ii   MALCOLM
            Par. 1, l. 2 *should read* :

1687 ; *d.* Queen Anne's County, Maryland,
June 1763 [1]).

            Par. 2, l. 1 *should read* :

Scottish scientist, clergyman and author.
He was a

            Add footnote :
[1] The ' Maryland Gazette ' of 30 June said " a few
days ago ".

529   i   *Add at end, before* BIBL. :

Some time in or before 1740, when he was
a school teacher in New York, Malcolm went
to America, where he remained until his
death. He was rector of St. Michael's Church
at Marblehead near Boston in 1740–49, then
of St. Mary's at Annapolis, Maryland, and
from 1754 of St. Paul's at Queen Anne's
County, in the same state.   E. B.

Add before MAŁCUŻYŃSKI :

MALCOLM, George (John) (*b.* London,
28 Feb. 1917).
English harpsichordist, pianist and conductor. He began his musical studies at the
R.C.M. in London at the age of seven, combining these with a general education at Wimble-
don Jesuit College. In 1934 he went up to
Oxford (Balliol College) and read for degrees
in classics and music, afterwards returning to
the R.C.M. where he had previously been one
of Herbert Fryer's most brilliant pupils. After
war service he was appointed Master of the
Cathedral Music at Westminster Cathedral,
and rapidly brought the choir to a high
degree of perfection, adding to the repertory
many works by early and modern composers.
He composed, in 1959, a ' Missa ad Praesepe '
for use at the Cathedral, and in the same year
Benjamin Britten wrote a ' Missa Brevis ' for
Malcolm and his choirboys.
    As a performer Malcolm has always pre-
ferred the piano and harpsichord to the organ,
and it is as a harpsichord player that he has
achieved his widest renown. His records of
Bach, Scarlatti and Purcell are models of
musical sensitivity and stylistic judgment, and
as a continuo player he is almost unrivalled.
He reserves his piano playing mainly for
chamber music, in which he has joined with
such artists as Dennis Brain, Campoli and
Manoug Parikian. As a choral conductor he
is uncompromising in his demand for a bright,
keen tone that is completely opposed to the
prevalent ' cathedral hoot', and he has
proved time and time again that his method
is as suitable for classical polyphony as for
the most complex modern score. Besides
a few original compositions, Malcolm has
contributed chapters on ' The Purcell

Realizations' and 'Dido and Aeneas' to the symposium on Benjamin Britten, edited by Keller and Mitchell. In 1959 Malcolm left Westminster Cathedral in order to devote more time to solo-playing and conducting.

D. W. S.

529 ii Malczewski:
l. 2 *should read:*

opera). Rzepko (A., do., incid. m.). Sołtys (M., 'Ukrainian Tale', opera). Statkowski

530 ii MALEINGREAU
Par. 1, l. 2 *should read:*

23 Nov. 1887; *d.* Brussels, 1956).

532 i MALIBRAN
Par. 2, l. 2 *should read:*

was the daughter of Manuel Garcia, the elder. When

534 i MALINOWSKI
Par. 1, l. 2. 1943 *should read:*

1944

535 ii MALIPIERO
BIBL., ll. 31-32. *Cancel* 'Rassegna Musicale' *entry.*

536 — CATALOGUE
OPERAS
Add at end of table:

'Il festino', 1 act.	Gherardo de Rossi.	Bergamo, Oct. 1954.
'Donna Urraca', 1 act.	Comedy on Prosper Mérimée's story.	Bergamo, Oct. 1954.
'Il figliuol prodigo', 5 scenes.	From a play by Pierozzo Castellan de Castellani.	Florence, Teatro della Pergola, 14 May 1957.

537 ii MALIPIERO, R.
Add at end:

BIBL.—SARTORI, CLAUDIO, 'Riccardo Malipiero' (Milan, 1957).

545 ii MANCHICOURT
Add at end:

See also Collectio O.M.B., Vol. 12 (modern ed.).

547 i MANDIKIAN
Par. 3, l. 9 *should read:*

opera 'Incognita'. In 1953–54 she sang at Covent Garden and in the latter year she joined the English Opera Group.

548 ii MANDOLINE
Add to BIBL.:

BONE, PHILLIP J., 'The Guitar and Mandolin: Biographies of Celebrated Players and Composers' (London, 1954).

549 i MANDORE
Add at end:

(*PLATE* 32, Vol. IV, p. 492, No. 2.)

ii *Add after* **MANFREDINA:**

MANFREDINI, Francesco (*b.* Pistoia, 1688; *d.* ?, 1748).
Italian violinist and composer. He was appointed solo violinist to the church of San

Petronio at Bologna, where he was elected a member of the Accademia Filarmonica. In 1711 he became *maestro di cappella* to Antonio I, Prince of Monaco. He wrote oratorios and instrumental works, the latter including Op. 1, 12 Trio Sonatas (1704); Op. 2, 12 'Sinfonie da chiesa' (1709); Op. 3, 12 Concertos (*concerti grossi*) for 2 solo violins, strings and continuo (1718) dedicated to the prince.

552 i Mann
l. 3 *should read:*

opera-ballet). Margaritis (story 'The Prodigy' inspired by).

ii MANN, William
Par. 3, l. 8 *should read:*

(London, 1950). This was to have been followed by

Add at end:

In 1960 he was appointed Music Critic of 'The Times' in succession to Frank Howes.

553 ii MANNES
Par. 3, l. 9 *should read:*

at the Metropolitan Museum of Art, resigning in 1947. He

554 ii MANNHEIM SCHOOL
Add to See also:

Denkmäler (2) II, Vols. XV-XVI (modern ed. of chamber music).

555 ii MANOJLOVIC *should read:*
MANOJLOVIĆ

Par. 1, l. 2 *should read:*

Serbia, 3 Dec. 1890; *d.* Belgrade, 2 Oct. 1949).

556 ii MANZIARLY
Par. 1, l. 2. 1900 *should read:*

1899

Manzoni
l. 5 *should read:*

Promessi sposi (Ponchielli, opera). Rossini ('Bianca e Faliero', opera). Verdi (Requiem

559 i MARAGLIANO MORI
Par. 1, l. 2. Piacenza, *should read:*

Pavia,

ii MARAIS
Par. 1, l. 1. 31 Mar. *should read:*

31 May

559   ii   Par. 2, l. 14.   à son 2 violes *should read*:

à une et à deux violes

Par. 3, l. 5.   rue de La Harpe *should read*:

rue Bertin Poirée

560   i   Par. 3, l. 3.   dauphiness *should read*:

dauphin

ll. 13-14 *should read*:

the music. One of his daughters, Marguerite Pélagie, married the composer Nicolas Bernier.

563   ii   **MARBECK**
Add to BIBL. :
FELLOWES, E. H., 'The Office of the Holy Communion as set by John Merbecke' (London, 1949).

564   ii   **MARCELLO, B.**
Par. 1, l. 12 *should read*:
187-97, supplemented in Q.-L. A modern reprint of 'Il teatro alla moda', edited by Andrea d'Angeli, was published by Ricordi of Milan in 1956.

BIBL., l. 2.   (Milan, 1940) *should read*:
(Milan, 1946)

Add to See also, l. 1 :
Classici Musica Italiana, Vol. 17 (modern ed. of cantatas).

567   ii   **MARCHAL**
Par. 3, l. 12.   *Add*:
On 24 Mar. 1954 he took part, with Ralph Downes, in the opening of the Royal Festival Hall organ in London.

570   i   *Add* **Marchese** *entry from* p. 571 *before*
MARCHESE VILLANO.

571   i   **Marchesi, Annibale** *should read*:
Marchese, Annibale

Transfer entry to p. 570, Col. 1.

MARCHESI
Par. 1, l. 2 *should read*:
Milan, 8 Aug. 1754; *d.* Milan, 14 Dec. 1829).

572   ii   **MARCHETTUS OF PADUA**
Add before See also :
BIBL.—PIRROTTA, NINO, 'Marchettus de Padua and the Italian Ars Nova' ('Musica Disciplina', IX, 1955).
SARTORI, CLAUDIO, 'La notazione italiana del trecento. . . .' (Florence, 1938).[2]

Add footnote :
[2] Includes an important discussion of the relationship between Beldemandis and Marchettus.

U

573   i   **MARCOUX**
Par. 1, l. 1 *should read* :
MARCOUX, Vanni (actually **Jean Émile Diogène**) (*b.* Turin, 12 June

l. 2.   1879). *should read* :
1877).

574   i   *Add before* **MAREK** :
MARÉCHAL, Samuel. *See* MARESCHALL.

576   ii   **MARENZIO**
Add to BIBL. :
ENGEL, HANS, 'Luca Marenzio' (in Italian) (Florence, 1956).

Add to See also, l. 1 :
Denkmäler (4), Vols. IV & VI (complete modern ed.).

577   i   **MARESCHALL**
Par. 1, l. 2.   May 1554 *should read* :
22 May 1554

Add at end :
BIBL.   KENDALL, R., 'The Life and Works of Samuel Mareschall' (M.Q., XXX, Jan. 1944).

ii   *Add before* **MARGHERITA D'ANJOU** :
MARGARITIS, Loris (*b.* Aegion, 15 Aug. 1895 ; *d.* Athens, 27 Sept. 1953).
Greek pianist and composer. He appeared as an infant prodigy pianist and composer at the age of six. Thomas Mann's short story, 'The Prodigy' (1903), was inspired by one of his early recitals at Munich. He studied in Berlin under Bernhard Stavenhagen and at Munich under Felix Mottl. Appointed pianoforte professor at the Salonica Conservatory in 1915, he became Assistant Director in 1936. He was also a visiting professor at the Mozarteum in Salzburg from 1928 to his death.
Margaritis's compositions include an opera, 'John Capodistrias' (produced in Vienna in 1931), the Epic Symphony 'Ulysses and Nausicaa' (after Homer), many works for pianoforte, including a Suite and a Sonatina, and several songs.   S. M.

578   i   **MARIA ANTONIA WALPURGIS**
Add to BIBL. :
YORKE-LONG, ALAN, 'Music at Court: four Eighteenth-Century Studies' (London, 1954).

i-ii **MARIANI**
Delete whole entry (*except* BIBL. *and* Ref.) *and replace by* :
MARIANI, Angelo (Maurizio Gaspare) (*b.* Ravenna, 11 Oct. 1821 [1]; *d.* Genoa, 13 June 1873).
[1] Mariani himself, in a manuscript autobiography, in a letter to Francesco Regli and in notes on the backs of various documents, insisted, quite wrongly, that he was born in 1824.

Italian conductor and composer. He began to study the violin at the age of eleven under Pietro Casalini and continued under Giovanni Nostini, Casalini's successor at the Accademia Filarmonica of Ravenna. At fifteen he played the violin at concerts in various towns of the Romagna. He studied harmony and composition first with a nobleman and priest, Girolamo Roberti, and then with a monk named Levrini, from Rimini, a pupil of Mattei, at the monastery of Sant' Apollinare at Ravenna.

In 1843 Mariani became conductor of a brass band at Sant' Agata Feltria, where he taught himself to play various wind instruments and composed much music. In the same year, during an opera season at Macerata, where he played the viola in the orchestra, he wrote two overtures (*sinfonie*) which were performed with success. He was called to Faenza in 1844, as teacher and orchestral conductor to the Accademia Filarmonica. He continued to compose freely, and one of his overtures brought him a letter from Rossini, who had had it copied for performance by the pupils of the Liceo Filarmonico at Bologna. His contract at Faenza expired at the end of May 1844; after directing, as *maestro concertatore*, a short season of opera at Trento in June, he spent some months at Bologna, studying counterpoint under Marchesi. Later in the year he was engaged at the theatre at Messina, for the long Sicilian season of autumn and Carnival 1844–45.

It is often stated that Mariani made his début as operatic conductor at Messina, but he had already done that at Trento, and in his autobiography he says that the orchestra at Messina refused to play under him. He wrote works for the brass band of the Royal Orphanage and for the Accademia Filarmonica of Messina, and directed their concerts. After a month at Naples in Apr. 1845, he returned to Bologna until Sept., when he directed a short season at a new theatre at Bagnacavallo. Then in Nov. he returned to Messina, where he again encountered the hostility of the opera orchestra and the favours of the amateur musicians. It is not clear exactly what he did do at the Messina theatre — perhaps played as a member of the orchestra. He left before the end of the season.

In May 1846 Mariani went to Milan, and he himself dated the real beginning of his career as a conductor from that time. He was engaged first at the Teatro Re and then at the Teatro Carcano. In the autumn he was at Stradella, for the opening of another new theatre, and then, in the Carnival season 1846–47, at Vicenza. Describing the course of his career in his autobiography, it is at this point that he states that he believes he

was the first in Italy to abolish the old custom of dividing the direction of the orchestra between a *maestro concertatore* (at the *cembalo*) and a violin-conductor. Possibly an earlier attempt to introduce this reforming measure had led to the trouble at Messina. In the spring of 1847 he was back at Milan, at the Teatro Carcano, and again at Vicenza in Sept., when he conducted Pacini's music for a performance of Sophocles' 'Oedipus Rex', with mammoth chorus and orchestra, in the Teatro Olimpico, as part of the festivities attending the ninth congress of Italian scientists. As a result he was appointed conductor at the Court Theatre in Copenhagen and left Italy at the beginning of Nov. The season in Copenhagen was interrupted by the death of King Christian VIII. A Requiem Mass written by Mariani for the king was performed twice. After news arrived of the revolution at Milan in Mar. 1848 Mariani returned to Italy and enrolled in the volunteers, but it is doubtful whether he saw any fighting; after the failure of the revolution he took an engagement in Constantinople, where he remained for over two years as conductor of the Italian theatre. He composed a new Turkish National Anthem and two so-called dramatic cantatas, 'Matilde' and 'La fidanzata del guerriero', which are probably fragments of an unfinished opera.

Mariani returned to Italy in Dec. 1851, to conduct opera in a new theatre at Messina, where he stayed until Apr. 1852, when he went to Naples. There he heard that a conductor was being looked for at Genoa. He was engaged for the Teatro Carlo Felice, and although he intended to stay only two months, his appointment was made permanent at the end of the season and he signed a contract for nine years on 1 July. The greater part of the rest of his life was spent at Genoa.

The resources of the Teatro Carlo Felice were limited, but under Mariani's direction the performances reached a high standard. He himself always chafed under the restrictions of his appointment at Genoa; he received offers of employment in Paris, Madrid, Cairo, Naples and elsewhere, but a strange irresolution prevented him from taking advantage of them. His appointment, however, allowed him to conduct the autumn seasons of opera at the Teatro Comunale, Bologna, in 1860–61, 1864–65 and 1867–72, and it was there that he achieved his greatest triumphs.

Mariani exercised an extraordinary personal fascination on all those who were under his direction. No matter who was the composer, he always threw himself heart and soul into the music he conducted at the moment. He was celebrated for his performances of the operas of Meyerbeer and Verdi. The twin peaks of his career were the first production of

'Don Carlos' in Italy, at the Teatro Comunale, Bologna, on 27 Oct. 1867, and that of 'Lohengrin' at the same theatre on 1 Nov. 1871 — the first performance of any of Wagner's operas in Italy. Between those two dates occured the great tragedy of his emotional life, the breach in his long friendship with Verdi and his abandonment by the singer Teresa Stolz, to whom he had been engaged, for reasons that have been endlessly disputed and are not clear yet. In 1872 Mariani introduced 'Tannhäuser to Italy at Bologna, with much less success than 'Lohengrin' had achieved in the previous year. He was already desperately ill; he died of cancer, in appalling circumstances, in the attic of the Palazzo Sauli, the house rented by Verdi at Genoa.

Besides the works already named, Mariani composed many songs, published in volumes with picturesque titles: 'Liete e tristi rimembranze', 'La rosa felsinea', 'Il Trovatore nella Liguria', 'Care memorie della Liguria', 'Eco della riviera di Genova', 'Il colle di Carignano', etc.

F. W. (ii).

579   i   **MARIÉS DE LA TOUR D'EIFFEL, LES.** *should read*: **MARIÉS DE LA TOUR EIFFEL, LES.**

MARIMBA *and* MARIMBA GONGS

Delete both articles and replace by:

MARIMBA. A percussion instrument utilizing the combination of a tuned wooden bar and a resonator tuned in unison, giving a musical sound of definite pitch when the bar is struck with a mallet. Every note of the scale has a bar and resonator, the latter being necessary to amplify the weak sounds of the bars and to produce the instrument's characteristic tone-quality.

The bars are graduated in size, giving a triangular shape to the keyboard. Each one is tuned by cutting out a curve on the underside between the two node-points until the pitch falls to the desired frequency. The bars are supported on cords passing through holes drilled at the node-points to allow them to vibrate freely. Pegs mounted on the framework support the cords at points between the bars. The performer plays the marimba standing.

In primitive marimbas the resonators are hollow gourds, bamboo tubes or even wooden boxes. In any case the resonators are graduated in size, tuned and lined with their open ends under the centres of the bars they serve, but not touching them. The tuned bar and resonator is an invention of the savage mind; consequently the marimba has been found chiefly among primitive peoples in tropical regions where hardwood is abundant. It is particularly associated with Africa, whence the name of the instrument comes.

The marimba has existed in crude forms since ancient times, with a variety of names. Often blocks of stone were used for sounding-elements. However, the word marimba now applies only to the wooden-bar instrument with resonators and a great range of notes including the bass, and must therefore be distinguished from the xylophone.

The development and perfection of the marimba occurred in the New World. It had existed among the primitives of Central America, and some improvements were introduced by imported Africans. Sebastián Hurtado, seeing possibilities in the instrument, made the prototype of the modern marimba in 1894. It had a keyboard of $5\frac{1}{2}$ octaves, the bars being arranged for the first time in two rows and in the same order as the keys of the pianoforte. The resonators were flaring wooden boxes with pointed ends. Near the lower end of each resonator was a small hole covered by a cured intestinal membrane from cows or pigs, held in place by a ring of pliable wax allowing adjustment of its tension. This vibrated sympathetically with the bars, greatly increasing the resonators' response, making low bass notes possible and imparting a reed-like tone to the instrument. This is the distinguishing feature of the Central American marimba.

Hurtado's sons became virtuosi and helped to popularize the new marimba with their famous Hurtado Brothers' Royal Marimba Band of Guatemala. To-day the finest marimbas of Central America have a compass at the most of seven octaves (C,—c^v) and are often ten feet long, though smaller sizes are also used. When played in ensemble, each manned by several musicians with their graded rubber-tipped mallets, the effect is orchestral. Sustained tone can be produced as well as detached, and a great range of dynamics is possible.

In the U.S.A. manufacture of marimbas began about 1910. Much research on the acoustics involved was done in the factories of J. C. Deagan and U. G. Leedy, and the following decade saw fine marimbas, bass marimbas, xylophones and metal-bar percussion instruments offered to the public. Stopped metal tubes, graduated in length like organ pipes, served as resonators, which, for very deep notes were made U-shaped; and the vibrating membrane feature was used in some models.

The manufactured marimba has an organ-like tone, especially when the low notes are rolled, and with four-mallet playing, using soft yarn-wound rubber mallets. The treble section is more percussive, however. Percy Grainger, who until recently was the only prominent musician aware of the new instruments, included the marimba in some of his works.

About 1920 the manufacturers arbitrarily discontinued notes on all bar-percussion instruments lower than c, one octave below middle C, seriously limiting the possibilities of the marimba. To-day the standard size is four octaves, c—c''''. Improved tuning methods eliminate harsh overtones from the rosewood bars, and the marimba is now a recognized orchestral instrument, boasts of many virtuosi and has reached the concert stage. It has superseded the xylophone because of its greater range and superior tone-quality.

Clair Omar Musser, virtuoso and composer, is largely responsible for the current recognition of the marimba, having campaigned on its behalf for many years. His 100-piece marimba band (with specially made bass marimbas) gave a memorable concert at Carnegie Hall, New York, in 1935. Paul Creston's ' Concertino ' for marimba and orchestra demonstrates the possibilities of the instrument. It is prominent in Charles M. Loeffler's ' Evocation ', and Milhaud has written a marimba Concerto. Recently the International Guild of Bar-Percussionists has been founded to advance the cause of the marimba and allied instruments.   F. K. M.

BIBL.—NADEL, SIEGFRIED, ' Marimba-Musik ' (Vienna & Leipzig, 1931).

580   ii   **MARINUZZI, G. (i)**
Par. 2, l. 17 *should read*:
by assassination. In 1934 he appeared at Covent Garden in London. He was conductor-in-chief of the Rome Opera in 1928–34 and of the Milan Scala in 1934–45.

581   ii   **MARIOTTE**
Par. 1, l. 2. Paris, 22 Dec. *should read*:
Izieux [Loire], 30 Nov.

582   i   Par. 1, ll. 8-9 *should read*:
Leconte. ' Nele Dooryn ', to a libretto by Camille Mauclair, was produced on 17 Oct. 1940, at the Paris Opéra-Comique, and on 17 Feb. 1935 the same theatre

ii   **MARKEVICH**
Add at end, before signature :
Markevich is the permanent conductor of the Lamoureux Orchestra in Paris and also conducts the Philharmonic Orchestra of Havana and is musical director of the Orchestre Symphonique at Montreal. In 1957 he was decorated by the Legion of Honour.

583   i   **MARMONTEL, A.**
Par. 1, l. 2.   1907 *should read*:
1908

MARMONTEL, J. F.
Par. 3, l. 4 *should read*:
Dibdin (1, ' Shepherdess of the Alps '). Entführung aus dem Serail (? source of lib.). Frischmuth

ii   Marot
l. 2 *should read*:
L., trans. of Psalms). Delvincourt (4 songs). Françaix (epigram for chorus &

584   i   **MARQUÉS PUIG**
Par. 1, l. 2.   1897). *should read*:
16 Sept. 1897).

ii   **MARRIAGE, THE**
l. 1.   (' Женитба ') *should read*:
(' Женитьба ')

MARROCCO
Par. 3.   *Add at end*:
' The Music of Jacopo da Bologna ' (Berkeley, Cal., 1954) is a complete edition of that master's extant works.

585   ii   **MARSCHNER**
BIBL., l. 3.   ' Die Operas H. *should read*:
' Die Opern H.

Add to BIBL. :
KÖHLOR, VOLKMAR, ' Heinrich Marschner's Bühnenwerke und Verzeichnis der bis zu Marschners Tod 1861 im Druck erschienenen Werke des Komponisten ' (Göttingen, 1955).

588   ii   **MARSH, John**
Par. 2, l. 2 *should read*:
that he was one of the few English composers of the

ll. 4-5 *should read*:
symphonies. He was able to do this

589   ii   *Add after* **MARSHALL** :
MARSICK, Armand (b. Liège, 20 Sept. 1877 ; d. Brussels, 30 Apr. 1959).
Belgian violinist, conductor and composer. He first learnt the violin from his father, Louis Marsick, and then studied under Heynberg, Dupuis and Radoux at the Liège Conservatory. Having become leader of the theatre orchestra at Nancy, he studied composition there with Guy-Ropartz. In 1898 he went to Paris as leader of the Colonne Orchestra and studied further under Lenepveu and d'Indy. He was director of the Conservatory of Athens in 1908–21 and of that of Bilbao in 1922–27, when he returned to

Belgium to become professor of harmony at the Conservatory of Liège, where he founded the Société des Concerts Symphoniques, which he conducted till 1939.

The following are among Marsick's principal compositions:

OPERAS
'La Jane', 1 act (1903).
'Lara', 3 acts (lib. by C. Kloster after Byron) (1913).
'L'Anneau nuptial', 3 acts (Ugo Fleres) (1920).

ORCHESTRAL WORKS
Symph. poem 'La Source' (1908).
Suite 'Scènes de montagnes' (1910).
Suite 'Tableaux grecs' (1912).
'Tableaux de voyage' (1939).
Quartet for horns (1950), Sonata for vn. & pf. (1900), inst. pieces with pf., pf. works & songs.   E. B.

591   ii   **MARTENOT**
Par. 1, l. 10 *should read*:

scores. Olivier Messiaen has been particularly assiduous in using Ondes Martenot.

Add after **MARTHA**:

MARTIN. The French name for a baritone voice of exceptional range. It was first made familiar on the Parisian operatic stage by a singer of this type, Jean Blaise Martin (1768–1837). A modern instance of its use is the part of Ramiro in Ravel's 'L'Heure espagnole'.   E. B.

593   ii   **MARTIN, Frank**
Add at end, before BIBL.:

'Der Sturm' is Martin's first opera, properly speaking, but it is linked up with earlier scenic works, especially 'Le Vin herbé', which shows operatic traits just as the opera shows oratorio-like features. Martin himself declared that he did not wish to make an " opera " out of Shakespeare's 'Tempest', but rather a work in the nature of Monteverdi's 'Tasso' (? 'Combattimento'), Lully's 'Armide' or Debussy's 'Pelléas', in which poetry is sung instead of being spoken. He therefore called the work a " magic comedy by Shakespeare, set to music by F. Martin ". In this work he contrasts different levels of the dramatic action by means of different stylistic elements. While Ariel's share is represented by the magically suave sounds of a small choir, Caliban and the comic characters are given dodecaphonic music and the aristocrats a light and refined style often imbued with jazz elements.

Add to BIBL.:
Article on 'Der Sturm' in 'Blätter der Wiener Staatsoper', June 1956.

594   i   BIBL. ll. 3-4 *should read*:
MARTIN, FRANK. 'Responsabilité du compositeur' ('Polyphonie', 1948, No. 2), with biographical notes and a catalogue of works.

594   i   CATALOGUE
Add before BALLETS
OPERA
'Der Sturm' (lib. A. W. von Schlegel's trans. of Shakespeare's 'Tempest'), prod. Vienna, State Opera, 17 June 1956.

595   i   **MARTÍN Y SOLER**
Par. 1, l. 3.   1806 *should read*:
1806 [3]

Add footnote:
[3] The registry of death of the Catholic parish of St. Catherine at St. Petersburg has been found (*see* R. Aloys Mooser, 'Annales de la musique et des musiciens en Russie', Vol. II, p. 459) ; it gives this date for his death and 5 Feb. for that of the funeral.

ii   Par. 1, l. 12.   anima ".[3] *should read*:
anima ".[4]

List of Works
OPERAS
Col. 3, l. 4.   1781.[4] *should read*:
1781.[5]

Footnotes 3 & 4 become 4 & 5.

596   —   Col. 3, l. 18.   1791. *should read*:
1795.

l. 20.   spesi *should read*:
sposi

ii   **MARTINENGO, Gabriele**
Par. 2, l. 5 *should read*:
named being successful. In 1560 Martinengo was recommended to the cathedral of Udine by Willaert. At that time he was *maestro di cappella* at the cathedral of Zara, and the cathedral chapter were reluctant to let him go, so that he was unable to take up the appointment until the following year. He remained at Udine until 1567, when he was succeeded by Ippolito Camatera.[1]
Martinengo's known

Add footnote:
[1] An interesting letter giving his terms of appointment at Udine may be found in Vale, 'La cappella musicale del duomo di Udine' ('Note d' Archivio', VIII [1930], p. 204 ff.).

MARTINENGO, G. C.
Par. 2, ll. 1-2 *should read*:
Italian composer, son of the preceding. He was appointed *maestro di cappella* of the cathedral at Udine in 1600, but left that post when he was made successor to

599   ii   **MARTINI, G. B.**
See also. l. 3 *should read*:
Classici Musica Italiana, Vol. 18 (modern ed. of sonatas). Eximeno (controversy with). Fitzwilliam Music (reprint of sacred works). Mattei (pupil & friend). Mitteldeutsches Musikarchiv, I, Vol. 5 (modern ed. of 6 sonatas).

600   i   **MARTINŮ**
          Par. 1, l. 2 *should read*:

Bohemia, 8 Dec. 1890 ; *d.* Liestal, Switzerland,
28 Aug. 1959).

601   i   Par. 1, l. 4 *should read*:

works in Paris in Feb. 1946. He, however,
retained the American citizenship he had
acquired and the Prague appointment proved
transitory. In 1957 he was resident composer
at the American Academy in Rome.

BIBL.   *Delete* ll. 1-2 [1]

Add footnote :

[1] Šafránek lists Copland's book in his Bibliography,
but although he seems to have used it for general
information, the only reference to Martinů he makes in
connection with it is that it does not mention him.

WORKS [1] *should read*:
WORKS [2]

Footnote 1 *becomes* 2.

OPERAS
Title of second opera should read :
' Les Larmes du couteau '

ii   ORCHESTRAL WORKS
     Add at end :
Symph. Prelude ' The Rock ', for 40th Anniversary of
     Cleveland Orchestra (1958).

602   i   *Add after* l. 23 :
Trio, D mi., for vn., cello & pf., 1953.

603   ii   **MARTUCCI, P.**
           Transfer BIBL. *to* **MARTUCCI,**
           G. *above.*

Marvell
ll. 2-3 *should read* :
voc. chamber m.).   Fricker (' Musick's Empire ', choral
work).   White (F., ' Nymph's Complaint ', voc.
chamber m.).

604   i   **MARX, A. B.**
          Par. 1, l. 2.   25 *should read* :
26

605   i   **MARX, Joseph**
          Par. 3, l. 1 *should read* :

Marx's compositions include motets, a Hölderlin cantata and various other choral

607   i   **MASCAGNI**
          Par. 2, l. 5.   Sonzongo *should*
          read :
Sonzogno

ii   Par. 3, l. 10 *should read* :
letta ' (text by G. Forzano, on Ouida's ' Two
Little Wooden Shoes '), produced at

608   **MASCHERONI**
        Par. 1, l. 1 *should read* :

MASCHERONI, Edoardo (Antonio) (*b.*
Milan, 4

        l. 2.   1857 *should read* :
1852

610   i   **MASON, Lowell**
          Par. 1, l. 2.   24 Jan. *should read* :
8 Jan.

611   ii   **MASON, Colin**
           Par. 2, ll. 8-9 *should read* :
" Master Musicians " series. This work has,
however, been abandoned for the time being.
In

MASON, George
Par. 2, ll. 2-3 *should read* :

is known to have been in the service of Francis
Clifford, Earl of Cumberland, in 1611[1], and
probably continuously up to 1617, when on
6 Aug. James I was entertained on his progress at Brougham Castle. Only the songs of
this entertainment were printed and published
by John Earsden in 1618, with the following
title :

Par. 4 *should read* :

These songs comprise the most complete
surviving music for any Stuart masque before
' Cupid and Death ' (1653) ; but unfortunately the text has been lost. Henry Clifford (son of the Earl) devised it, and Thomas
Campion may have been consulted in some
capacity. In Nichols's ' Progresses . . . of
King James ', Vol. III (1828, p. 392), a
letter from the Earl to his son is printed, part
of which reads :

Sonn, I have till now expected your lettres, according
to your promis at your departure ; so did George
Minson [Mason] your directions touching the musick,
whereupon he mought the better have writt to Dr.
Campion. He is now gone to my Lord President's
[at York], and will be ready to do as he heares from
you. For my own opinion, albeit I will not dislyke your
devise, I fynde plainly, upon better consideration, the
charge for that Entertainment will grow very great,
besyde the musick . . .

Little else is known for certain of Mason's
life. J. E. West in his ' Cathedral Organists '
(1921, p. 127) says that he was organist of
Trinity College, Cambridge, from 1612 to
1629, but this has not been verified in a search
of the college records, which are incomplete
for this period.[2] However, it is unlikely that
West invented the name, and the inclusion
of the words of a verse anthem by George
Mason (Psalm XLIII, ' Judge me, O God ')

[1] W. Woodfill, ' Musicians in English Society ' (1953),
p. 257.
[2] Thanks are due to Mr. H. M. Adams, the librarian,
for undertaking this investigation.

in Clifford's 'Divine Services and Anthems'
(1664, p. 281) supports the view that at some
time in his career he was organist or choirmaster of an important church. It is interesting to note that among incomplete viol
parts of 8 pavans by " Mr. Mason " in B.M.
Add. MSS 30826-8 is an anonymous piece
called 'Trinitye Colledge Pavan'. Anthony
Wood, in his manuscript notes on musicians [3],
states that Mason graduated Bachelor of
Music at Cambridge in 1601, and although
there is no direct confirmation of this, someone unknown was admitted to this degree in
that year.[4] Of course, in all this it is quite
possible that two musicians of the same name
are being confused.

J. Stafford Smith printed the 'Ayres'
(1618) in his 'Musica Antiqua' (1812, pp.
150-65) without, it should be noted, transcribing the lute tablature — hence his
accompaniments are not to be trusted.

　　　　　　　　　　　　　　I. S.

³ Bodl. MS Wood, D. 19 (4), f. 89 v.
⁴ C. F. Abdy Williams, 'Degrees in Music' (1893),
p. 124.

611　ii　**MASON, John (i)**
Cancel whole entry.

MASON, John (ii)
Entry should read:

MASON, John (*b.* ? Chichester, ?; *d.*
? Hereford, ?).
English 15th–16th-century composer. He
is described as " of Chichester " in the Peterhouse partbooks at Cambridge, which contain
four 5-part motets, all of which lack the tenor
part. He was admitted clerk of Magdalen
College, Oxford, in 1508, graduated B.Mus.
on 12 Feb. 1509 and was in the same year
appointed

612　i　*Par. 1, l. 7 should read:*

May 1545. He is mentioned by Morley, as
" Sir John Mason " in

616　ii　**MASQUE**
Footnote. l. 3 should read:
and by the B.B.C., have been given of late years. The
work is published in 'Musica Britannica' (Vol. 2).

617　i　*Add to* BIBL. :
CUTTS, JOHN P., 'Jacobean Masque and Stage Music'
　　(M. & L., XXXV, 1954, p. 185).

　　　　BIBL., l. 13. Johnsonian *should read:*
Jonsonian

624　—　**MASSENET,** CATALOGUE
　　　　OPERAS
　　　　Add after l. 8 of col. 1 :

| 'La Navarraise.' | Jules Claretie & Henri Cain. | London, Covent Garden Theatre, 20 June 1894. |

625　ii　**MASSON**
　　　　Par. 1, l. 1. Cette, *should read:*
Sète,

　　　　l. 2. 1882). *should read:*
1882; *d.* Paris, 27 Jan. 1954).

628　i　*Add before* **MATHEW** :
MATHEUS DE SANCTO JOHANNE
(Mayhuet de Joan) (*b.* ? ; *d.* ?).
French 14th-century composer. The name
" Mayhuet " (Chantilly, Musée Condé MS
1047) and its variant, " Mayshuet " ('Old
Hall Manuscript'), is an anagram of " Math-
yeu " or " Mathyeus "; other composers in
the former source appear under anagrams or
reversed names, such as Trebor and S.
Uciredor. Six works by Matheus have been
preserved, the sources additional to the two
just mentioned being Modena (Bibl. Estense,
MS M.5.24, olim lat. 568) and Ivrea (Bibl.
Capitolare).

Among the five secular works are three
ballades, 'Sans vous ne puis', 'Inclite flos
Gebennensis' and 'Sience n'a nul annemi';
and two rondeaux, 'Je chante ung chant'
and 'Fortune faulce, parverse', the former
being isorhythmic. His most ambitious work
seems to be a paraliturgical motet, 'Arae
post libamina / Nunc surgunt in populo' ('Old
Hall', III, 150), which is for two voices and
three instruments. The five-part texture of
this isorhythmic motet gives rise to frequent
diatonic discords which lend the music a
certain piquancy, by no means unsuitable to
the literary texts. The uppermost voice begins with the " Benedicamus Domino " trope
'Arae post libamina', but ends on a narrative note, the verse-form changing to prose
for an account of how " a skilled and famous
Frenchman wrote this piece in French but
recast it in Latin, a language more agreeable
to the English ". Both texts inveigh against
vainglorious musicians and singers, apparently
as numerous in the 14th century as in any
other.　　　　　　　　　　　D. W. S.

BIBL.—BUKOFZER, MANFRED, 'Studies in Medieval and
　　Renaissance Music' (New York, 1950).
RAMSBOTHAM, ALEXANDER, ed., 'The Old Hall Manu-
　　script' (London, 1938).
REANEY, GILBERT, 'The Manuscript Chantilly, Musée
　　Condé 1047' ('Musica Disciplina', VIII, 1954).

629　i　**MATHIS DER MALER**
　　　　l. 6 *should read:*

1952. 1st in U.S.A., Boston University, 17
Feb. 1956.

MATINSKY
Par. 2, ll. 5-6 *should read:*
of an opera, 'The Renaissance', and in

630   ii   **MÁTRAY**, CATALOGUE OF
WORKS
MUSIC
Add after l. 2 :

Incidental music for István Balog's ' Czerni Gyuró vagy
Belgrád megvétele a Serviusok által ' (' Gyuró
Czerni, or The Capture of Belgrade by the Ser-
bians') (1812–13).

631   ii   **MATTEIS, Nicholas**
Delete entry and substitute:

MATTEIS, Nicholas (*b.* ? ; *d.* Shrewsbury,
1749).
Italian violinist, son of the following. He
was one of his father's finest pupils, and served
as violinist of the Imperial Chapel at Vienna
from 1717 to 1724. In Prague, he wrote
ballet music for an opera by Fux, who had
been commissioned to supply music for the
coronation festivities of Charles VII. Matteis returned to England in 1737, settling in
Shrewsbury, where he taught languages and
violin-playing.   D. W. S.

BIBL. (*Transfer from* **Matteis, Nicola**).

MATTEIS, Nicola
Par. 9, l. 2 *should read*:

and it is now excessively rare.[3]

Add at end:
BIBL.—TILMOUTH, MICHAEL, ' Nicola Matteis ' (M.Q.,
XLVI, 1960, p. 22).

Add footnote :
[3] An Italian edition, ' Le false consonanze della
musica ', was published in London about 1685.

Transfer BIBL. *to* **Matteis, Nicholas.**

632   i   *Add before* **MATTERS** :

MATTEO DA PERUGIA (*b.* Perugia, ? ;
d. ?).
Italian 14th–15th-century composer. He
was a singer at Milan Cathedral from 1402 to
1407 and again from 1414 to at least 1416.
One report says he died in 1418, but, if this
is based on fact, the documents are now
destroyed by fire and cannot confirm it. It
seems likely that between 1407 and 1414
Matteo was first in the service of his patron
Pietro Filargo, Archbishop of Milan, who
later became Pope Alexander V, and then
perhaps in that of his successor, John XXIII.
Before 1407 Matteo was the only singer to
be called " biscantator ", though during his
absence, after a period without such a musician, Ambrogio da Pessano was appointed
(1411). After Matteo's return both men
worked together till 1416. Since Matteo
wrote no church music with words in more
than one or two parts, it is tempting to suggest that the duet music at least was written
between 1414 and 1416. He left a large body
of compositions compared with most writers

of the time, for at least thirty pieces bear his
name, and six more are very probably his
work. Of the first thirty, twenty-two are
written to French texts and the rest consist of
six Mass movements and two Italian *ballate*.
The number of Mass movements is sub-
stantially increased by five of the six anonymous compositions, the other piece being a
motet. In addition, Matteo wrote a number
of additional parts for works by other composers, including a *contratenor* for Grenon's
' Je ne requier ' and one for Ciconia's
' Lizadra donna '.
Apart from a motet built over an Agnus
Dei, all the Mass pieces are Glorias or Credos.
They are very varied in form and may be for
three or four performers. One Gloria is in
cantilena or song style with a free upper texted
voice over two textless accompanying parts,
another is built like a *caccia* throughout, another is in strict isorhythmic motet style and,
of course, the device of musical rhyme may
crop up in any of these. Most of the pieces
are less complicated than the most elaborate
secular songs, but one of the Glorias has a
most ornate top part :

The two Italian pieces are not very interesting musically. ' Già da rete d' amor ' lies
very low in what would now be called F minor,
while ' Sera quel zorno mai ' is rather overfull
of syncopations and rapid florid passages.
Like the Italian *ballate*, nearly all the French
pieces are in three parts, though three rondeaux and one virelai are in only two parts.
Only one of the 2-part rondeaux, however,
has text in both voices. Altogether there are
four ballades, seven virelais, ten rondeaux and
a canon. Of the ballades, ' Le greygnour
bien ' is a *tour de force* in rhythmic and mensural
complexities. The facsimile (Apel, Pl. I)
reveals widespread use of red notes, white
notes, hollow red notes, half-white and half-
black ligatures, though the degree to which
syncopation is employed, not to mention the
simultaneous combination of different men-
surations, can be seen only from the transcription. It would be wrong to imagine that the
majority of Matteo's songs are of this type.
' Pres du soloil ' is a relatively simple ballade
with a charming melody and straightforward
accompaniment, and the same is true of the
virelai ' Helas, avril '. Most attractive of all,
perhaps, is the virelai ' Belle sans per ' written

in the old *modus* measure with imperfect time and prolation:

'Andray soulet' is a 3-part canon at the unison, in which the text explains that each voice must enter when the first (and then the second) reach bottom D. The combination of the three voices is harmonically most satisfying.

Matteo da Perugia has been too long considered as a composer who was primarily interested in notation. The recent publication of his Mass pieces and his varied secular output reveal a composer of talent with a very happy vein of melody, which admittedly can be obscured by rhythmic preoccupations. An attempt to render the notation of his time more precise by new note-forms is in itself deserving of praise rather than condemnation. W. Apel has reprinted 22 French pieces in 'French Secular Music of the Late Fourteenth Century' (1950); the complete works, with the exception of 9 French pieces, are published in G. Cesari & F. Fano, 'La cappella musicale del duomo di Milano', I (1956).

G. R. (iii).

BIBL.—PIRROTTA, N., 'Il Codice Estense Lat. 568 . . .' in 'Atti della Reale Accademia di Scienze, Lettere a Arti di Palermo', Series IV, Vol. V, Part ii.
SARTORI, C., 'Matteo da Perugia e Bertrand Feragut . . .' ('Acta Musicologica', XXVIII, 1956).

632 ii **MATTERS**
l. 2 *should read*:
Progress' and in 1953 that of Cecil in Britten's 'Gloriana' at Covent Garden.

634 i **MATTHESON**
Add after Par. 1, *before signature*:
A modern facsimile reprint of 'Der vollkommene Capellmeister' appeared in 'Documenta Musicologica', Series I, Vol. v, and 'Das neu-eröffnete Orchester' is to be published in the same edition, Vol. 17.

634 i *Add to* BIBL.:
MATTHESON, JOHANN, 'Grosse Generalbass-Schule' (1731), ed. by W. Fortner (Mainz, 1956). 'Der vollkommene Capellmeister', facsimile reprint ed. by Margarete Reimann (Cassel & Basel, 1954).

See also. Add to l. 3:
Mitteldeutsches Musikarchiv, I, Vol. 1 (modern ed. of clavier music).

ii **MATTHEWS, Thomas**
Par. 2, l. 14. *Add after* Covent Garden:
He left this in 1952 to become leader of the London Symphony Orchestra until 1954, when he became leader of the Scottish Orchestra.

Matthisson
l. 2 *should read*:
songs, incl. 'Adelaide', & canon). Lortzing (choral hymn). Schröter (1, songs).

635 i **MATZENAUER**
Par. 2, ll. 24-25 *should read*:
correctly judged. She sang at Bayreuth in 1911, but her European career practically

l. 34 *should read*:
again heard in England, and she gave her farewell performance in New York on 12 Feb. 1931. She was the re-

Mauclair
l. 2 *should read*:
(3 songs). Mariotte ('Nele Dooryn', lib.). Schmitt (F., song).

636 i **MAUDUIT**
Add to See also:
Florilège, Vol. 7 (modern ed. of psalms). Maîtres Musiciens, Vol. 10 (modern ed. of chansonnettes).

ii **Maugham**
l. 1. *See* Goossens *should read*:
See Gardner ('Moon and Sixpence', opera). Goossens

637 i **MAURER**
Par. 1, l. 2. 25 Oct. *should read*:
6 Nov.

Par. 2, ll. 14 and 19. Vsovologsky *should read*:
Vsevolozhsky

ii **MAXWELL-LYTE**
Par. 1, l. 2 *should read*:
Apr. 1908; d. nr. Grenoble, Aug. 1955).

638 i Par. 1, l. 13 *should read*:
Flow to give concerts to the Fleet. She was killed, together with her sister, the actress Meg Maxwell-Lyte, in a motoring accident.

638   ii   **MAY, Florence**
Dates *should read*:
(*b*. London, 6 Feb. 1845; *d*. London, 29 June 1923).

639   i   *Add before* **MAYER, Wilhelm**
MAYER-SERRA, Otto (*b*. Barcelona, 12 July 1904).
Spanish musicologist. His father was German and his mother Catalan. He studied first in France and later in Germany under Hermann Abert, Curt Sachs, Johannes Wolf and Erich von Hornbostel. In 1933 he returned to Spain and became music critic of the Barcelona weekly ' Mirador ', published in Catalan. In 1936 he was appointed chief of the Music Division of the Propaganda Ministry in the Catalan Government, and he served in the Loyalist Army in 1938–39. But although at that time he wrote in Catalan, he is equally capable of doing so in Castilian, which he used after his emigration to Mexico in 1940. He has made a career there as teacher and author of books on music, which include ' El romanticismo musical ' (1940), ' Panorama de la música mexicana ' (1941), ' Panorama de la música hispano-americana ' (1944) and ' Música y músicos de Latino-América ', 2 vols. (1947), all published in Mexico City, as is the ' Enciclopedia de la música ' edited by him (1943).   N. S.

Add before **Maykov**:
MAYHUET. *See* MATHEUS DE SANCTO JOHANNE.

640   i   **MAYR, Richard**
l. 2 *should read*:
parts. He appeared at Covent Garden until 1931 and was a member of the Metropolitan Opera in New York in 1929–30.

ii   **Mayrhofer**
Add at end:
BIBL.—' The Schubert-Mayrhofer Songs ', with English translations by E. G. Porter (London, 1954).

641   i   *Add before* **MAZAS**:
MAYSHUET. *See* MATHEUS DE SANCTO JOHANNE.

MAZAS
Par. 1, l. 2 *should read*:
23 Sept. 1782; *d*. Bordeaux, 26 Aug. 1849).

MAZELLIER
Par. 1, l. 2 *should read*:
1879; *d*. Paris, Feb. 1959).

641   ii   **MAZÉR**
Add to BIBL. :
JOHANSSON, CARL, ' Något om Mazérs Musiksamling i Kungliga Musikaliska Akademiens Bibliotek ' (S.T.M., 1951).

644   i   **MAZZOCCHI, V.**
BIBL.   *Cancel* SALZA *entry*.

MAZZOLENI
Par. 3, l. 8 *should read*:
direction, since 1945, the latter organization has made

l. 11 *should read*:
Canadian composers. He received the hon. Mus. Doc. degree from the University of Rochester, N.Y., in 1949.

Par. 4, ll. 2–3 *should read*:
as a guest conductor, as with the Concerts Symphoniques at Montreal, and he was associate conductor of the Toronto Symphony Orchestra in 1942–48. His com-

647   i   **MECHANICAL VIRGINAL**
Add at end:
BIBL.—PROTZ, A., ' Mechanische Musikinstrumente ' (Cassel, 1939).

648   ii   **MEDITERRANEAN MUSIC**
Signature P. G. (ii) *should read*:
P. G.

MEDTNER
Par. 2, l. 8 *should read*:
forte lessons with his uncle, Theodore Goedicke. He advanced very rapidly and in

l. 11. Sapellnikov *should read*:
Sapelnikov

650   ii   *Add to* BIBL. :
HOLT, RICHARD (ed. by), ' Nicholas Medtner (1879–1951): a Tribute to his Art and Personality ' (London, 1956).
PINSONNEAULT, BERNARD, ' Nicolas Medtner ' (in French) (Montreal, 1956).

652   i   Tutchev, 12 *entries should read*:
Tuchev

ii   l. 3. Tutchev *should read*:
Tuchev

653   i   **MEFISTOFELE**
l. 1. 4 acts, with an *should read*:
4 acts, with a prologue and an

ll. 3–4 *should read*:
based on Goethe's ' Faust '. Original version, in 5 acts, produced Milan, Teatro alla Scala, 5 Mar. 1868; revised version produced Bologna, 4 Oct. 1875. 1st perf.

659   ii   **MEL**
IX, 4   Bibl., l. 3.   IX, ev. 4 *should read*:

MELANI (1)
Footnote 5, l. 3 should read:
Vatican Library (Biblioteca Chigiana) in Rome.

660   i   **MELBA**
      Par. 1, l. 3.   1859; *should read*:
1861 [1];

   Add footnote:

[1] This is an almost unique case of a singer's birth being recorded as too early, but 1859, usually given, has been proved wrong. According to Nicolas Slonimsky, who has procured copies of her birth, marriage and death certificates, she was married on 22 Dec. 1882, at the age of 21 and died on 23 Feb. 1931, at the age of 69.

662   i   **MELCHIOR**
      Par. 2, l. 1 *should read*:

American tenor singer of Danish birth. After studying at the

      ll. 14-17 *should read*:

the Metropolitan Opera, New York, to which he was attached from 1928 to 1950. He sang frequently elsewhere in the U.S.A. during the second world war, but not again in England since. He appeared at Bayreuth between 1924 and 1931.

      Par. 4, l. 8 *should read*:

valier of the Legion of Honour. He became an American citizen in 1947 and is hon.

665   i   **MELLERS,** List of Works
      OPERAS
      l. 3 (George Moore) *should read*:
(George Moor)

   ii   **MELNIKOV**
      Par. 1, l. 2 *should read*:

Moscow, 4 Mar. 1832; *d*. St. Petersburg, 8 July 1906).

      Par. 2, l. 13.   in Sept. 1867 *should read*:

on 6 Oct. 1867

666   ii   **MELODRAMA**
      Add at end:

Bibl.—Veen, J. van der, 'Le Mélodrame musical de Rousseau au romantisme' (The Hague & London, 1955).

669   i   **MELODY**
      Add to Bibl. :
Edwards, Arthur C., 'The Art of Melody' (New York, 1956).
Waesberghe, J. S. van, 'A Textbook of Melody' (Rome, 1955).

   ii   **MELSA**
      Par. 1, l. 1.   Warsaw, Aug. *should read*:
Warsaw, 14 Aug.

669   ii   **Melville**
      l. 4 *should read*:
'Moby Dick', cantata). Křenek ('Belfry', opera; 'Cantata for War-

673   i   **MENASCE**
      Par. 1, l. 2 *should read*:
19 Aug. 1905; *d*. Gstaad, 28 Jan. 1960).

      Par. 2, ll. 1-2.   Austrian birth.
      should read:
Franco-Egyptian and German descent.

677   i   **MENDELSSOHN**
      Footnote 2.   ll. 3-4 *should read*:
had seemed probable that these volumes had been destroyed during the second world war, but they have been photographed and studied since.

679   ii   Par. 3, l. 15.   single achievement.
      should read:
single achievement.[11]

      Add footnote:

[11] For the cuts made by Mendelssohn in Bach's work *see* R. Sterndale Bennett, 'Three Abridged Versions of Bach's St. Matthew Passion' (M. & L., XXXVII, 1956, p. 336).

687   ii   *Last line*.   1841 *should read*:
1840

690   ii   Par. 2, l. 15.   subscription *should read*:
private

693   ii   Par. 2, l. 3 *should read*:
But excuse me if I should not be able to come, for I have

699   ii   *Add to* Bibl. :
Erskine, J., 'Song without Words: the Story of Felix Mendelssohn' (New York, 1941).

708   i   **MÉNÉTRANDISE**
      l. 12.   Grande   Mxnxtrxndxsx
      should read:
Grande et Ancienne Mxnxtrxndxsx.

      MENGELBERG, Kurt
      Par. 1, l. 2 *should read*:
feld, 1 Feb. 1892; *d*. Monte Carlo, 13 Oct. 1959).

710   ii   **MENNIN**
      Par. 2.   *Add after* l. 8 (Fantasia):
Concerto for pf. & orch., for 40th Anniversary of Cleveland Orchestra (1958).

      Add at end:

He has written three more Symphonies, No. 6 being finished in 1957.

      MENOTTI
      Par. 2, l. 1.   American composer of Italian birth. *should read*:
Italian composer.

711 i Par. 1, l. 8 *should read*:

later opera is ' The Consul ' (prod. Philadelphia, 1 Mar. 1950). This too

Par. 2, l. 5 *should read*:

on 21 Feb. 1952. In 1954 followed the three-act opera ' The Saint of Bleecker Street ', produced at the Broadway Theatre in New York on 27 Dec.

Add at end:

In 1958 followed a madrigal opera, ' The Unicorn, the Gorgon and the Manticore, or The Three Sundays of a Poet ', based on a Bestiary, a work very different from Menotti's earlier operas, partly inspired by Orazio Vecchi's ' Amfiparnaso ' and partly exploring new ways of combining orchestral and choral music with mime and ballet. On the other hand, the work produced in the American Theatre at the Brussels World Fair on 20 Aug. 1958, ' Maria Golovin ', reverted to the manner of the earlier work, which it showed in its full maturity.

Par. 3, l. 7 *should read*:

heim Fellowship in 1946. Although he has lived so long in the U.S.A., he has retained his Italian citizenship.

Add at end:
See also Barber (S., lib. of ' Vanessa ').

712 i **MENUHIN**
Add at end:

In recent years Menuhin has added numerous important modern works to his repertoire (Bartók's Solo Sonata is dedicated to him) and has also revived unknown music from the past, such as the early violin Concerto of Mendelssohn, which he has edited and published. He is an admirer of Eastern music, and has often spoken about its structure and aesthetic importance with authority and eloquence. As an indefatigable organizer, leader and violinist, he has devoted considerable time to music festivals at Bath and Gstaad, which bear the imprint of his catholic tastes and unmistakable artistic personality. Violin in hand, he directs the Bath Festival Orchestra in true 18th-century style, and has achieved notable success in his performances of the Bach Brandenburg Concertos and Orchestral Suites.

BIBL.—MAGIDOFF, ROBERT, ' Yehudi Menuhin: the Story of the Man and the Musician ' (Garden City, N.Y., 1955).

MERIAN
Par. 1, l. 2. Basel, Nov. *should read*:

Basel, 15 Nov.

715 ii **MERIKANTO, Aarre**
Par. 1, l. 2 *should read*:

July 1893; *d.* Helsingfors, 28 Sept. 1958).

716 i **Mérimée**
l. 5 *should read*:

adopted). Mackenzie (' Colomba ', opera). Malipiero (' Donna Urraca ', opera). Pacini

718 ii **MERSENNE**
Par. 1, l. 15 *should read*:

' De la nature des sons ' (1635). A modern facsimile edition of the ' Harmonie universelle ', with an English translation by Roger E. Chapman, was published by Martinus Nijhoff at The Hague in 1957. Another facsimile of ' Harmonie universelle ' is to appear in ' Documenta Musicologica ', Vol. 18.

719 i **MERULA**
Par. 5, l. 4 *should read*:

voices, ' Nominativo, hic, haec, hoc '. He also wrote organ music, including a ' Sonata cromatica ', reprinted in Vol. 3 of Torchi's ' L' arte musicale in Italia '.

720 i **MERULO, Claudio**
BIBL., l. 2. (Milan, 1931) *should read*:
(Milan, 1859; new ed. 1931).

Add to BIBL.:
PIDOUX, P., ' Claudio Merulo, Canzonen 1592 ' (Cassel, 1941). A complete modern edition.

MERULO, G. A.
Add signature:
E. V. D. S.

721 ii **MESSAGER**
See also. l. 1 *should read*:

See also Fauré (collab. in Quadrille from Wagner's ' Ring ', pf. duet). Leroux (X., collab. in ' Montagne enchantée ', incid.

724 ii **MESSIAEN**
Add to BIBL.:
DREW, DAVID, ' Messiaen: a Provisional Study ' (' The Score ', Dec. 1954, Sept. & Dec. 1955).
ROSTAND, CLAUDE, ' Messiaen et ses trois styles ' (Schw. Mz., IV, Apr. 1957, p. 133).

CATALOGUE
CHAMBER MUSIC
l. 3. ' Le Mort *should read*:
' La Mort

725 i **MESSIAH**
Add at end, before See also:
BIBL.—*see* HANDEL.

726 ii **Metastasio**
BIBL. l. 1 *should read*:
BURNEY, CHARLES, ' Memoirs of the Letters and Writings of the Abate Metastasio ', 3 vols.

727 i BIBL.
  ' Demetrio ', l. 4 *should read*:
(2 settings). Paisiello. Pérez (D.). Pescetti. Piccinni.
Rossini (' Demetrio e Polibio ', altered).

  ' Ezio ', ll. 1-2. by Auletta. *See also*
    Bertoni. *should read*:
by Porpora. *See also* Auletta. Bertoni.

  l. 4 *should read*:
sions). Lampugnani. Leo. Scarlatti (6).

  ii ' Semiramide riconosciuta ', l. 2. Vinci.
      should read:
Vinci.[1]

  Add footnote :
[1] This may have been preceded by Porpora's setting,
Venice, Carnival (*i.e.* after 25 Dec.) 1728.

729 ii **MEULEMANS**
    Par. 2. *Cancel* ll. 8-11 *and replace by* :
The catalogue of Meulemans's compositions, which is enormous, includes the
following works :

OPERAS
' Vikings ', 3 acts (lib. by E. Buskens) (1919).
' Adriaen Brouwer ', 3 acts (F. de Witt-Huberts) (1926).
' Egmont ', 3 acts (J. van Rooy) (1944).

INCIDENTAL MUSIC
Vondel's ' Jozef im Dothan ' (1927).
c. 24 other plays.

SACRED MUSIC
8 Masses.
3 ' Te Deum '.

ORCHESTRAL WORKS
14 Symphonies.
4 Symphonic Sketches (1940).
Symphonic Triptych (1951).
Concerto for orch. (1953).

SOLO INSTRUMENTS AND ORCHESTRA
Pf. Concerto (1941).
' Concertino ' for pf. (1942).
Variations for pf. (1945).
3 vn. Concertos.
Viola Concerto.
2 cello Concertos.

CHAMBER MUSIC
5 string Quartets.
Quintet for 2 vns., viola, cello & pf.
2 wind Quintets.

ORGAN MUSIC
Sonata (1915).
2 Symphonies (1949).
Numerous pf. works and songs.   E. B.

730 i *Delete whole par.*

  Add before **Mey** :

MEXICAN MUSIC. *See* FOLK MUSIC,
Vol. III, p. 314.

  ii *Add before* **MEYER, Gregor** :

MEYER, Ernst Hermann (*b.* Berlin, 8
Dec. 1905).
German musicologist and composer. He
studied with Hindemith and Butting at the
Berlin High School for Music and also took
private lessons in composition under Hanns
Eisler and others. In 1927-30 he studied at

the Universities of Berlin and Heidelberg,
devoting himself to musicology at the latter
and taking the Ph.D. degree. He lived in
London in 1933-48, where he studied old
English music, taught musical appreciation at
the W.E.A., gave historical concerts and was
conductor of the London Co-operative Choirs.
He also examined at Cambridge University
and acted as composer, technician and editor
for films. In 1948 he returned to Germany
and was appointed Professor of Music Sociology at the University of Berlin (Humboldt
University). He became a member of the
Deutsche Akademie der Künste in 1950, took
the National Prize of D.D.R. in 1950 and
1952, and the International Prize for composition at Bucharest in 1953.
The following are Meyer's chief works :

BOOKS
' Die mehrstimmige Spielmusik des 17. Jahrhunderts
  in Nord- und Mitteleuropa ' (Cassel, 1934).
' English Chamber Music ' (London, 1946) (also in
  German & Russian).
' Musik im Zeitgeschehen ' (Berlin, 1952) (also in
  English, Russian, Chinese, Bulgarian & Rumanian).
' Aufsätze über Musik ' (Berlin, 1957).

COMPOSITIONS
Ballet and incidental music, music for 43 films, radio
  plays and television.
' Mansfelder Oratorium ' (1950).
7 Cantatas for solo voices, chorus & orch. (1951-58).
9 ' Landschaftsbilder aus Deutschland ' for unaccom-
  panied women's voices (1954).
Partsongs, accompanied and unaccompanied.
Symphony for stgs. (1946).
Trio for oboe, flute & harp (1935).
Quintet for clar. & stgs. (1944).
Suite for 2 trumpets, 2 pfs. & perc. (1944, rev. 1957).
Trio for vn., cello & pf. (1948).
Stg. Quartet No. 1 (1956).
Stg. Quartet No. 2 (1957).
Ode ' Now Voyager ' (Walt Whitman) for baritone &
  stgs. (1946, new version 1955).
Sonata for vn. & pf. (1929).
Theme, 15 Variations, Chaconne and Fugue for pf.
  (1935).
' From a Little Girl's Diary ' for pf. (1956).
' Eine Folge von 4 Klavierstücken ' for pf. (1947, 1956).
Numerous Songs.

Articles on 16th- and 17th-century music
and on musical sociology were contributed by
Meyer to M. & L., ' The Listener ', Mus. T.
and many other English, German, French,
Czech and Russian periodicals. He has written two chapters for the N.O.H.M. and a
study of early Dutch music (' Tijdschrift ',
1938-39).   E. B.

735 ii **MEYERBEER**
    Add to BIBL. :
BECKER, HEINZ, ' Der Fall Heine-Meyerbeer : neue
Dokumente revidieren ein Geschichtsurteil ' (Ber-
lin, 1958).

736 i CATALOGUE
    SONGS
    l. 7 *should read* :
voix '. A manuscript has recently been discovered
of a setting of ' C'est elle ' " (paroles de Heine) ",
dated 8 Mar. 1838. The poem is the well-known
' Die Rose, die Lilie ' in ' Dichterliebe '. Meyerbeer set the French words and the German original
is shown below them.

736   ii   **MEZZA**
          Add at end:

As a qualification of tempo, MEZZO MOVI-
MENTO (half speed) is occasionally found.

737   i   **MI**
          See also. Solmization. *should read:*
Solmization; the note E.

738   i   **MIASKOVSKY,** List of Sym-
          phonies
E ma.   No. 20. F ma. *should read:*

          No. 22. (1941). *should read:*
B mi. (' Symphony-Ballade ') (1941), prod. Tiflis, 12
Jan. 1942.

          No. 23. (1941) *should read:*
A mi. (1941)

          No. 24. (1943) *should read:*
F mi. (1943)

          No. 25. (1946) *should read:*
Db ma. (1946)

          No. 26 *should read:*
(Op. 79), C ma.

          No. 27. (Op. 87). *should read:*
(Op. 85), C mi., prod. Moscow, 9 Dec. 1950.

739   i   **MIČA**
          Par. 3, l. 4 *should read:*

now attributed to a cousin, Ján Adam
František Miča, of the next genera-

      ii   *Add to See also:*
Musica Antiqua Bohemica, Vol. 19 (modern ed. of
' Concertino notturno ' [by J. A. F. Miča]).

740   i   **MICHAELIDES**
          Par. 2, l. 13. the Executive Board
          should read:
the Board of Adjudicators

          Par. 3, ll. 1-3 *should read:*
Michaelides was a member of the Adjudicators' Board at the International Musical
Eisteddfod of Llangollen in 1949, 1951–53,
1957 and 1958.

          l. 10 *should read:*
Basel (Sept. 1948) and Venice (Sept. 1949).
On 8 Apr. 1957 he was appointed Director of
the State Conservatory of Salonica.

      ii   **MICHEAU**
          Par. 2, l. 6 *should read:*
the Teatro alla Scala at Milan, London
(Covent Garden, 1937), the Colón

741   i   **Michelangelo**
          l. 3 *should read:*
(7 choruses; poem for voice & chamber orch.). Frottola
(poems set). Gade (N. V.,

742   ii   **Miciński**
          l. 1. *See* Różicki *should read:*
See Malawski (Cantata & ' Wyspa gorgon ', choral
works). Różicki

          Mickiewicz
          l. 11 *should read:*
Szeluto (' Pan Tadeusz ', opera). Szopski (' Lilie ',
opera). Szymanowska (mother-in-

          l. 14 *should read:*
Wydżga (' Pan Tadeusz ', opera). Zeleński (' Konrad
Wallenrod ', do.).

744   i   **Middleton**
          l. 1. *Add after See:*
Britten (' Nocturne ', No. 4).

          MIDGLEY, Walter
          Par. 1, l. 2 *should read:*
shire, 13 Sept. 1914).

      ii   *Add after* **MIDLAND INSTI-
          TUTE SCHOOL:**

MIDSUMMER   MARRIAGE,   THE.
Opera in 3 acts by Michael Tippett. Libretto
by the Composer. Produced London, Covent
Garden Theatre, 27 Jan. 1955.

747   i   **MIGOT**
          Par. 1, l. 1. **George** *should read:*
Georges

      ii   *Footnote should read:*
      [1] The same work as ' Contes de fées '.

748   i   *Add after* VIOLONCELLO AND PIANO-
          FORTE:
          SOLO FLUTE
'Ève et le serpent.'

750   i   **MIHALOVICI**
          Par. 2, l. 1. opera *should read:*
operas

          l. 2 *should read:*
' L'Intransigeant Pluton ', ' Phaedra ' (Stuttgart, 1951) and ' Die Heimkehr ' (Düsseldorf,
1954); the ballets ' Kara-

752   ii   **MILAN**
          Par. 2, l. 11. Cannobiane. *should
          read:*
Canobbiana.

753   i   Par. 3, l. 12 *should read:*
temple of our age. Dr. Antonio Ghirin-
ghelli and Victor de Sabata became directors
in 1955.

          Par. 4, l. 5 *should read:*
important exhibits. In 1955 further structural alterations were completed, and a smaller
theatre, La Piccola Scala, was opened in 1956.

754 i *Add to* BIBL. :

FANO, FABIO, ' La ˙cappella musicale del duomo di Milano : le origini e il primo maestro di cappella, Matteo da Perugia ' (Milan, 1956).
SARTORI, CLAUDIO, ' Organs, Organ-Builders and Organists in Milan, 1450–1476 ; New and Unpublished Documents ' (M.Q., XLIII, 1957, p. 57).

755 i **MILAN, Luis**
Add at end :

See also Denkmäler (4), Vol. II (modern ed. of ' Libro . . . de vihuela . . .').

ii Page Heading, MILANUZII *should read* :

MILANUZZI

Add before **MILANUZZI** :

MILANOV, Zinka (*b.* Zagreb, 17 May 1906).
Yugoslav soprano singer. She was known under her maiden name of Kunc until 1937, when she married Predrag Milanov, a Yugoslav actor. She came of a musical family. Her brother was a talented child pianist and composed some two dozen songs for his sister's early recitals. At the age of four she started to study singing, and when she was eight sang Carmen at a home performance of that opera. When she was twelve her voice began to change from mezzo to soprano, and two years later she became a student at the Royal Music Academy of Zagreb. The following year she made her first concert appearance and was heard by the famous Milka Ternina, who was so impressed by the young soprano that she offered to coach her. Three years of study with Ternina followed, and in Oct. 1927 she made her début as Leonora in ' Trovatore ' at Ljubljana. From 1928 to 1935 she was leading soprano at Zagreb National Theatre, and in eight years sang more than 350 performances, all in Croatian, including Manon Lescaut, Minnie (' La fanciulla del West '), Giorgetta, Rachel (' La Juive '), Fidelio, Fiora (' L' amore dei tre re '), Elsa, Sieglinde, and the Marschallin. She made a few guest appearances in Germany (Dresden), Austria (Graz) and Czechoslovakia (Prague, Brno and Bratislava), then in 1936 she was engaged for the German Theatre in Prague.
The turning-point in Milanov's career came in 1937, when she was invited to sing in the Verdi Requiem under Toscanini at Salzburg. This was immediately followed by a contract for the Metropolitan Opera in New York, where she made her début as Leonora in ' Trovatore ' on 17 Dec. 1937. Apart from a short break covering the 1948 and 1949 seasons she has remained a member of the Metropolitan ever since, and been heard widely in America with the Chicago and San Francisco Operas, and in South America at the Teatro Colón, Buenos Aires. She has

made few appearances, however, in Europe during the last twenty years, being heard only once at the Scala, Milan (1949–50), and twice at Covent Garden, when she sang Tosca (1956 and 1957) and Leonora in ' Trovatore ' (1957).

H. D. R.

755 ii **MILANUZII**
Par. 1, l. 1. Name *should read* :

MILANUZZI

Par. 2 and throughout article. Name *should read* :
Milanuzzi

756 i **MILDER-HAUPTMANN**
Par. 2, l. 3. *Add after first sentence* :
She studied at first with Tull, then with Haydn's protégé Sigismund Neukomm.

Add at end :
In 1814 she sang Leonora 22 times in Vienna, after which the opera was not heard there again until 1822.

ii Par 1, 7 *lines from end. For* Thayer *read* :
Schindler

757 i **MILFORD, R.**
Par. 1, l. 2 *should read* :
ford, 22 Jan. 1903; *d.* Lyme Regis, 29 Dec. 1959).

761 i **MILHAUD**
BIBL. 1. 6 *should read* :
catalogue chronologique complet ' (Paris, 1949 ; Supplement [works dating from Nov. 1949 to Apr. 1956], 1956).

ii *Add to* BIBL. :
MASON, COLIN, ' The Chamber Music of Milhaud ' (M.Q., XLIII, July 1957, p. 326).

CATALOGUE
OPERAS
Col. 1, l. 19 *should read* :
' David ', 5 acts.

Col. 3, l. 11 *should read* :
1952–53.

Col. 4. *After* l. 15 *add* (' Bolivar ') :
Paris, Opéra, 12 May 1950.

l. 17. 1954. *should read* :
1 June 1954 (concert performance) ; 1st stage performance, Milan, Teatro alla Scala, 2 Jan. 1955.

BALLETS
Add at end :
Col. 1 :
' Vendanges.'

Col. 2 :
P. de Rothschild.

Col. 3 :
1952.

761 — CATALOGUE
INCIDENTAL MUSIC
Col. 1, l. 2. ' L'Orestie ' should read :
' L'Orestie d'Aeschyle '

762 — Add at end :
Col. 1 :
' The Winter's Tale.'
' Christophe Colomb.'
' Saul.'
' Protée ' (new version).
' Juanito.'

Col. 2 :
Shakespeare, trans. C. A. Puget.
Claudel, adapt. Jean Louis Barrault.
André Gide.
Claudel.
Pierre Humblot.

Col. 3 :
1950.
1952.
1954.
1955.
1955.

Col. 4 :
Paris, Comédie-Française, 1950.
Paris, Théâtre Marigny, 1 Oct. 1953.
Toulon, Citadelle, 2 July 1954.
Paris, Comédie-Française, Feb. 1955.
Paris, Théâtre des Capucines, Jan. 1956.

i SPECTACLE WITH FIREWORKS
should read :
SPECTACLES

l. 1 should read :
' Fête de la musique ' (words by Paul Claudel), with
fireworks, Paris Exhibition (1939).

Add at end :
' Barba Garibo ' (scen. by Armand Lunel) (1949–50),
prod. Menton, 19 Feb. 1950.

ii FILM MUSIC
Add at end :
' Gauguin ', by Alain Resnais (1950).
' La Vie commence demain ', by Nicole Vedrès (1950).
' Ils étaient tous des volontaires ', documentary for the
10th anniversary of the Liberation (1954).

RADIO MUSIC
Add at end :
' Le Repos du septième jour ', by Claudel (1950).
' Samael ', by André Spite (1953).
' Le Dibbouk ', by Anski (1953).
' Étude poétique ', montage musical, by C. Roy (1954).

763 i CHORAL WORKS
Add at end :
' Cantate des Proverbes ' (biblical) for women's voices,
harp, oboe & cello (1951).
' Les Miracles de la foi ' (Book of Daniel) for tenor,
reciter, choir & orch. (1951).
Cantata ' Le Château du feu ' (Jean Cassou) for chorus
& orch. (1954).
3 Psalms of David (Latin words) for unaccomp. chorus
(1954).
' Service pour la veille du Sabbat ' (liturgical) for
children's chorus & organ (1955).
' Deux Poèmes de Louise de Vilmorin ' for unaccomp.
chorus (1955)
1. Fado (fantaisie).
2. L'Alphabet des aveux.

ii ORCHESTRAL WORKS
Add at end :
Symphony No. 5 (1953).
' Suite campagnarde ' (1953).
' Suite méditerranéenne ' (1953).

' Pensée amicale ' for stgs., for Pierre Monteux's 80th
birthday (1955).
Symphony No. 6 (1955).
Symphony No. 7 (1955).
' La Couronne de Marguerites ', for Marguerite Long's
jubilee (1956).

763 ii MILITARY BAND MUSIC
Add at end :
' West Point Suite ' (1951).

SOLO INSTRUMENTS AND OR-
CHESTRA
Add at end :
' Suite Opus 300 ' for 2 pfs. (1950).
' Concertino d'automne ' for 2 pfs. & 8 insts. (1951).
' Concertino d'été ' for viola & small orch. (1951).
' Suite concertante ' for pf. (based on the Concerto for
marimba & vibraphone) (1952).
Concerto for harp (1953).
' Concerto d'hiver ' for trombone & stgs. (1953).
' Suite cisalpine sur des airs populaires piémontais ' for
cello (1954).
Viola Concerto No. 2 (1954–55).
Pf. Concerto No. 5 (1955).

764 i CHAMBER MUSIC
Add at end :
String Quartet No. 16 (1950).
String Quartet No. 17 (1950).
String Quartet No. 18 (1950–51).
Quintet for stgs. & pf. (1951).
Quintet for 2 vns., va., cello & double bass (1952).
Sonatina for vn. & cello (1953).
Quintet for 2 vns., 2 vas. & cello (1953).
Quintet for 2 vns., va. & 2 cellos (1956).

ii WIND INSTRUMENT AND PIANO-
FORTE
Add at end :
' Caprice ' for clar. (1954).
' Danse ' for alto saxophone (1954).
' Églogue ' for flute (1954).
Sonatina for oboe (1954).
' Duo concertant ' for clar. (1956).

PIANOFORTE SOLO
Add after l. 58 :
' Accueil amical : pièces enfantines ' (1944 & 1947).

Add at end :
' Jeu ' (1950).
' Le Candelabre à sept branches ' (1951)
1. Premier jour de l'an.
2. Jour de pénitence.
3. Fête des cabanes.
4. La Résistance des Macchabées.
5. Fête de la reine Esther.
6. Fête de la Pâque.
7. Fête de la Pentecôte.
' Hymne de la glorification ' (1953–54).
Sonatina (1956).

765 i TWO PIANOFORTES
Add at end :
' Divertissements ' (1953)
1. La Française.
2. L'Espagnole.
3. L'Italienne.
4. La Provençale.

ORGAN MUSIC
Add at end :
' Petite Suite ' (1955).

766 i SONGS
Add at end :
' Les Temps faciles ' (Marsan) (1950).
' Petites Légendes ' (Maurice Carême) (1952)
Set I :
1. Sortilèges.
2. Les Feuilles.
3. L'Amoureux.

4. La Prière.
5. La Dormeuse.
6. La Peine.
   Set II :
1. La Chance.
2. Le Lièvre et le blé.
3. La Bise.
4. Destinée.
5. Le Beau Navire.
6. Le Charme.
' Fontaines et sources ' (Francis Jammes) (1956)
1. La Fontaine de Lestapis.
2. Fontaine sainte.
3. La Source qui filtre.
4. La Grande Cascade.
5. Source au pied de Maubec.
6. Source.

766   ii   VOCAL QUARTETS
           Add at end :
' Deux Poèmes de Louise de Vilmorin ' (1955)
1. Fado (fantaisie).
2. L'Alphabet des aveux.

768   ii   **MILITARY BAND**
           Par. 2, l. 10.   movements *should
           read* :
motion

770   i   Par. 1, l. 6.   " flutes in B " *should
           read* :
" flutes in B♭ "

771   i   *Footnote*, l. 1. E♭ *should read* :
B♭,

773   i   *Add to* Bibl. (2nd work by Farmer) :
' History of the Royal Artillery Band : 1762–1953 '
(London, 1954).

775   ii   **MILITARY CALLS**
           Par. 5, l. 3 *should read* :
extant is to be found in a Copenhagen manuscript of the late 16th century, and the next
in date is the second book of

779   i   Bibl.—Farmer, ' Handel's Kettledrums '
           (London, 1949). *should read* :
(London, 1950).

      ii   **MILLAR**
           Add to Bibl. :
Patrick, M., ' Four Centuries of Scottish Psalmody '
(London, 1949).

MILLER, Edward
Par. 1, l. 1.   Norwich, 1731 ;
           should read :
Norwich, 30 Oct. 1735 ;

Add before **MILLERAN** :
MILLER, Władysław (i) (*b.* ? ; *d.* ?).
Polish 19th-century bass singer. He studied
under Quattrini in Warsaw and later became
a leading singer (*buffo*) at the Opera there.
He often appeared abroad, especially in Italy,
Spain and Portugal, admired for his voice and
acting. The title of Court Singer to the King of
Portugal was conferred on him.   C. R. H.

x

MILLER, Władysław (ii) (*b.* Monte
Albano, Italy, 1862 ; *d.* Warsaw, 2 July 1929).
Polish composer, son of the preceding. He
composed, to librettos of his own, the following
opérettes-bouffes : ' Oaza ' (in Italian) ; ' Miłość
nieszczęsna ' (' An Unfortunate Love ') ;
' Król migdałowy ' (' The Almond King ')
(*c.* 1890) ; ' Kwiat paproci ' (' Fern Flower ')
(*c.* 1895) ; ' Murzyn Vidal ' (' The Negro
Vidal '), prod. at Leopol in 1898.   C. R. H.

782   i   **MILNER**
           Par. 1, l. 2.   *b.* London *should
           read* :
b. Bristol

           Delete Par. 3 *and replace by* :
Milner's compositions up to 1959 are the
following [1] :
Op.
1. ' Salutatio Angelica ' for contralto, chorus &
   chamber orch. (1951).
2. ' Improperia ' for double chorus, stgs. & organ
   (1949).
3. Mass for unaccomp. chorus (1952).
4. Quartet for oboe & stgs. (1953).
5. ' The Song of Akhenaten ' for soprano & chamber
   orch. (1954).
6. No. 1.   ' Rondo saltato ' for organ (1955).
   No. 2.   Psalm CXXVIII, ' Blessed are all they '
   for unaccomp. chorus (1955).
7. ' The City of Desolation ' for soprano, chorus &
   orch. (1955).
— Vespers for congregational use (1955).
— Compline for congregational use (1956).
8. ' St. Francis ', triptych for tenor, chorus & orch.
   (1957).
9. ' The Harrowing of Hell ' for unaccomp. chorus,
   with tenor & bass solos (1956).
10. ' Benedic, anima mea, Dominum ' for unaccomp.
    double chorus (1955).
11. ' Our Lady's Hours ', song cycle for soprano & pf.
    (1957).
12. ' Cast wide the folding doorways of the East ' for
    unaccomp. chorus (1957).[2]
13. No. 1.   ' I have surely built thee a house ' for
    chorus & organ (1958).
    No. 2.   Festival Anthem for St. Cecilia for chorus
    & organ (1958).
14. Variations for orch. (1959).   E. B.

Bibl.—Jacobs, Arthur, ' The Music of Anthony
Milner ' (Mus. T., Sept. 1958, p. 482).
Stevens, Denis, ' Milner's " St. Francis " ' (M.Q.,
XLIV, 1958, p. 240).

[1] The dates are generally those of first performances.
[2] For Vaughan Williams's 85th birthday concert.

      ii   **MILOJEVIC**
           Par. 1, l. 1.   15 Oct. *should read* :
27 Oct.

           l. 2.   Belgrade, 1946 *should read* :
Belgrade, 16 June 1946

784   ii   **MINGOTTI (2)**
           Par. 2, l. 8.   1764 *should read* :
1767

785   i   Bibl. l. 2 *should read* :
unternehmungen : 1732 bis 1856 ' (Leipzig, 1915) ;
sequel, ' A. und P. Mingotti ' (Dresden, 1917).

789   i   **MINUET**
BIBL. l. 4 *should read*:
p. 162, and in 'Classics: Major and Minor' (London, 1958).

Add to BIBL. :
GOLDMANN, HELMUT, 'Das Menuett in der deutschen Musikgeschichte des 17. und 18. Jahrhunderts' (Nuremberg, 1956).

790   i   **"MIRACLE" SYMPHONY**
ll. 3-4 *should read*:

102, in B♭ major, written for Salomon's concerts in London in 1794-95 [1], and first performed at the King's Theatre on 5 Feb. 1795. The name is due to an

Add footnote :
[1] This nickname had long been attached to the wrong work: Symphony No. 96, in D major. The mistake was discovered by H. C. Robbins Landon and noted in his book, 'The Symphonies of Joseph Haydn' (London, 1955), p. 534.

MIRECKI
Par. 3, l. 4 *should read*:

forzati' in Lisbon on 7 Mar. 1826. It was performed at Florence in 1831, in which year he settled at Genoa as a

Par. 4, l. 2 *should read*:

fluenced by the Italian masters. During his sojourn in Italy he wrote another opera, 'Cornelio Bentivoglio', which was produced at Milan on 18 Mar. 1844. Besides

   ii   *Add after* **MIRITU** :

MIRLITON (Fr.). A toy instrument consisting of a simple cylindrical pipe with a hole for a mouthpiece pierced at the side, one end stopped and the other covered with light parchment or onion skin. It is not played, strictly speaking, but sung into, and a reedy tone not unlike that of the oboe is produced. The instrument resembles the eunuch flute, but is even more primitive. It was known as Kazoo in England. The 'Danse des mirlitons' in Tchaikovsky's 'Nutcracker' ballet makes no attempt to imitate the sound of this instrument.   E. B.

MIRROR CANON or FUGUE
ll. 3-4 *should read*:

pair of parts, are so devised as to appear upside down as well as right side

l. 6 *should read*:

a thing reflected in a looking-glass held at an angle below the object reflected.

791   i   **MISSA**
Par. 2, l. 3. he took the Prix de Rome *should read*:

he received honourable mention for the Prix de Rome

791   ii   **MISSA SOLEMNIS**
Par. 3, l. 1 *should read*:
The first performance took place at St. Petersburg on 6 Apr. 1824, and the first performance in Western Europe followed in Vienna.

792   i   **MITCHELL, Donald**
Par. 3, ll. 12-14 *should read*:

A large-scale book on Mahler's life and works, at which he had been at work for several years, eventually grew to such proportions that a volume on the composer's early years was published separately, to begin with. Mitchell's published writings include the following :

Par. 4. Heading *should read*:
BOOKS

Add after l. 3 :
'Gustav Mahler: the Early Years' (London, 1958).

793   i   **MITROPOULOS**
Par. 1, l. 2 *should read* :

Mar. 1896 ; *d*. Milan, 2 Nov. 1960).

   ii   Par. 4, ll. 22-23 *should read* :

permanent conductor. In 1951 he appeared at the Edinburgh Festival. He conducted opera at the Milan Scala in 1952 and the New York Metropolitan Opera in 1954-55.

Par. 5 *should read* :

Mitropoulos became an American citizen in 1946 and received the honorary degree of Ph.D. from Harvard University. In 1958 he was succeeded by Leonard Bernstein as conductor-in-chief of the New York Philharmonic Orchestra.

794   i   *Add after* **MITSUKURI** :

MITTELDEUTSCHES MUSIKARCHIV. A collection of old music published at Wiesbaden by the Musicological Seminary of the Friedrich Schiller University of Jena.

SERIES I : CLAVIER MUSIC
1. Johann Mattheson, 'Die wohlklingende Fingersprache', Fugues and Suite movements.
2. Johann Christoph Graupner, 8 Partitas.
3-4. Giovanni Benedetto Platti, 12 Sonatas.
5. Giovanni Battista Martini, 6 Sonatas.
6. Johann Gottfried Müthel, 3 Sonatas.
7. Müthel, 2 Ariosi with 12 Variations.

SERIES II : CHAMBER MUSIC
1. Johann Christoph Pepusch, 3 Trio-Sonatas for violin, oboe and bass.

795   ii   **MOBERG, C. A.**
Par. 2, l. 5 *should read*:

musical journals. He published 'Från Kyrka- och Hovmusik till offentlig Konsert' (1942), 'Die liturgi-

797   ii   **MODENA**
Add to BIBL.:
RONCAGLIA, GINO, 'La cappella musicale del duomo di Modena' (Florence, 1957).

805   i   **MODINHA**
Add before See also:
BIBL.—SIQUEIRA, BAPTISTA, 'Modinhas do passado: investigaçzes folclóricas' (Rio de Janeiro, 1955).

Add before **MODULATION**:

MÖDL, Martha (*b*. Nuremberg, 22 Mar. 1912).
German soprano singer. She studied at the Conservatory of her native town, financing her studies by working as a secretary in a business house. In her early years her voice was a mezzo-soprano, and accordingly she made her début as Azucena at Remscheid in 1944. She was engaged by the Düsseldorf Opera from 1945 to 1949, singing Dorabella, Octavian, the Composer in 'Ariadne auf Naxos', Clytemnestra, Eboli, Carmen and Marie in 'Wozzeck'. In 1949 she became a member of the Hamburg State Opera and soon found her voice changing to a dramatic soprano. During 1950–51 she appeared as Lady Macbeth in Berlin, and then added Kundry, Venus, Isolde and the 'Walküre' Brünnhilde to her repertory. It was as Kundry that she was heard in the first post-war Bayreuth Festival in 1951, and she has sung there every summer since, where her Kundry, Isolde, Brünnhilde, Sieglinde and Gutrune have become an outstanding feature of the Wieland and Wolfgang Wagner productions. She acknowledges her success as a Wagnerian artist to the careful coaching and musical inspiration of Wagner's grandsons.
Mödl's first appearance in England was in the 1949–50 season, when she sang Carmen at Covent Garden. She was heard with the Hamburg Company at Edinburgh in 1952, as Leonore in 'Fidelio' and as Octavian, and with the Stuttgart Opera at the Royal Festival Hall, London, in 1955 as Isolde and at Edinburgh in 1958 in the same part. She was chosen to sing Leonore in 'Fidelio' at the reopening of the Vienna State Opera in 1955 and sang Brünnhilde at Covent Garden in 1959. She makes regular guest appearances at the leading German opera-houses, the Scala, Milan, and the Metropolitan, New York.
Martha Mödl's whole approach to her art typifies the new ideas of operatic interpretation current in post-war Germany. These stress the importance of acting before singing and encourage an intensity in portraying the emotions that is rare on the operatic stage. This has an invigorating effect on the audience, but it also has its dangers, for after a series of performances such as those at Bayreuth,

the voice is apt to tire more quickly than is the case with more restrained singers. This results in a period of vocal uncertainty, which is apt to happen in the case of Mödl. Her voice, with its warm and beautiful lower register, an inheritance from her mezzo-soprano days, is, however, always at the service of this highly individual and intelligent singer.   H. D. R.

814   ii   **MOERAN**
Add to BIBL.:
EVANS, EDWIN, 'Moeran's Symphony in G minor' (Mus. T., Feb. 1938).

CATALOGUE
ORCHESTRAL WORKS
Cancel Suite, 'Farrago' (1932).

815   i   SONGS
Add after 'Blue-eyed Spring':
'Tilly' (contributed to 'Joyce Book', 1932).

818   i   **MOHAMMEDAN MUSIC**
Par. 2, l. 4.   (*masha'id*) *should read*:
(*nasha'id*)

MOHAUPT
Par. 1, l. 2 *should read*:
1904; *d.* Reichenau, Austria, 3 July 1957).

ii   Par. 1, l. 2 *should read*:
York, remaining in the U.S.A. until 1955, when he returned to Europe.

Par. 2, l. 6.   a Concerto, *should read*:
a Concerto for orchestra,

l. 10 *should read*:
Concerto, etc. A later opera, 'Der grüne Kakadu', was accepted by the Hamburg Opera for production during the 1957–58 season, and another, in one act, 'Zwillings-komödie' (on Plautus, the source of Shakespeare's 'Comedy of Errors'), was produced at Carlsruhe in 1957.   E. B.

819   i   **MOJSISOVICS**
Par. 1, l. 2 *should read*:
10 May 1877; *d.* Graz, 10 Mar. 1953).

ii   **MOKRANJAC**
Par. 1, l. 2 *should read*:
bia, 9 Jan. 1856; *d.* Skoplje, 29 Sept. 1914).

820   i   Page Heading, MOKRUSSOV *should read*:
MOKROUSSOV

MOKRUSSOV
Par. 1, l. 1 *should read*:
MOKROUSSOV, Boris Andreyevich (*b.* Nizhny-Nov-

820   ii   **Molière**
           l. 19 *should read*:
opera).   Kellie ('Tartuffe', concerto used as overture).
Kosa (do., opera).   Kraus (J. M., 'Am-

l. 21 *should read*:
opera).   Lavergne ('Princesse d'Élide', do.).   Liebermann ('School for Wives', do.).   Listov

821   i   *Add before* **MOLINARO**:
MOLINARI-PRADELLI, Francesco (*b.*
Bologna, 4 July 1911).
Italian conductor.   He attended Bernardino Molinari's course of orchestral conducting
at the Accademia di Santa Cecilia in Rome.
From 1938 he has conducted opera and concerts in the principal musical centres in Italy
and abroad.   G. M. G.

824   ii   **MOLTER**
           Par. 3, ll. 15-16.   Two clarinet
           concertos *should read*:
Four clarinet concertos

825   i   Par. 1, l. 2 *should read*:
nique.   They are republished in 'Das Erbe
deutscher Musik', Vol. XLI, edited by Heinz
Becker.   A. L., adds.

           Mombelli
           l. 1.   **Vigano** *should read*:
Viganò

           Mombert, A. *should read*:
Mombert, Alfred.

826   i   Page Heading, MONASTERO Y
           AGUEROS *should read*:
MONASTERIO Y AGUEROS

           MONASTERO Y AGUEROS
           Par. 1, l. 1.   **MONASTERO**
           should read:
MONASTERIO

      ii   **MONCAYO**
           Par. 1, l. 2 *should read*:
June 1912; *d.* Mexico City, 16 June 1958).

827   ii   **MONDONVILLE**
           Add to See also:
Publications Soc. Franç., Vol. 9 (modern ed. of
'Pièces de clavecin en sonates ').

830   —   **MONIUSZKO,** CATALOGUE
           OPERAS
           Col. 4, l. 8.   26 Sept. *should read*:
28 Sept.

      i   SONGS
           l. 2.   270 songs, published *should read*:
270 songs, 140 of them published

830   ii   **MONK, E. G.**
           Par. 1, l. 3 *should read*:
Oxford, 3 Jan. 1900).

831   ii   **MONK, W. H.**
           ll. 3-4.   one of the musical editors
           of *should read*:
musical editor of

835   ii   **MONSIGNY**
           Add to BIBL.:
DRUILHE, PAULE, 'Monsigny: sa vie et son œuvre
(Paris, 1955).

           CATALOGUE
           Col. 2, l. 7 *should read*:
Sedaine (after Robert Dodsley's play 'The King and
the Miller of Mansfield ').

836   ii   **MONTAGU-NATHAN**
           Par. 1, l. 2.   1877). *should read*:
1877; *d.* London, 15 Nov. 1958).

           Par. 2, l. 24 *should read*:
tions in London, notably the Camargo Ballet
Society, and at Henley-on-Thames,

837   i   List of Books
           Add at end:
'Mlle Camargo' (London, 1932).

838   ii   **MONTE**
           Par. 3, ll. 2-3.   thirty-eight *should
           read*:
forty-eight

839   —   MASSES
           Col. 1, l. 19 *should read*:
'Sine nomine.' [1]

      i   *Add at end*:
See also Collectio O.M.B., Vol. 6 (modern ed.).
Vereniging, Vol. 38 (do. of Mass).

           *Delete footnote (also ref. to it at head of page)
           and substitute*:
[1] Based on Palestrina's madrigal 'Vestina i colli '.

      ii   **MONTELLA**
           Add at end:
See also Istituzioni, Vol. 5 (modern reprint).

840   i   **MONTEMEZZI**
           Par. 1, ll. 2-3.   Vigasio nr. Verona,
           should read:
Vigasio,

      ii   ll. 6-8 *should read*:
are the one-act opera ' L' incantesimo ', broadcast in 1943 under his direction and produced
in the arena at Verona on 9 Aug. 1952, and
the symphonic poem ' Italia

845   i   **MONTEVERDI**
Add to BIBL., Section A. :

PANNAIN, G., ' Studi monteverdiani ' (Rass. Mus., Vol. XX, No. 1-2, 1958).
SARTORI, CLAUDIO, ' Monteverdi ' (Brescia, 1953).

Add to BIBL., Section B :

ABERT, ANNA AMALIE, ' Claudio Monteverdi und das musikalische Drama ' (Lippstadt, 1953).
OSTHOFF, WOLFGANG, ' Das dramatische Spätwerk Claudio Monteverdis ' (Heidelberg, 1954).

847 —   CATALOGUE
          OPERAS AND BALLETS
          Col. 5, l. 4. Benvenuto *should read* :
Benvenuti

848 —   RELIGIOUS MUSIC
          Col. 1, l. 23. ' Sanctissimi Virginis *should read* :
' Sanctissimae Virgini

Col. 5. *Add after* l. 6 :
D. W. Stevens, London, 1961.

849 —   Col. 1. *Add after* l. 8 (Domine . . .) :
Exulta filio Sion.
Exultent Caeli.

Col. 2. *Add after* l. 13 (do.) :
S. solo & cont.
A.T.B. *soli*, S.S.A.T.B. *ripieni*, insts. *ad lib.* & cont.

Col. 3. *Add after* l. 9 (do.) :
Calvi (' Quarta raccolta de sacri canti ', Venice, 1629).
Calvi, 1629.

Delete Footnote 1 *and substitute* :
' Da capella ' implies the absence of instrumental doubling of the upper parts. The usual *basso continuo* for organ is present.

Delete Footnote 5 *and substitute* :
Of the above items 5 are motets, and not part of Vespers : ' Nigra sum ', ' Pulchra es ', ' Duo Seraphim ', ' Audi coelum ', ' Sonata sopra Sancta Maria '.

850 —   2nd entry in col. *First Issue* :
Transfer to col. *Modern Editions*

856 —   Col. 1, l. 10. ' Gira il nemico ' and following four titles should be numbered i-v.

857 —   *See also should read* :
See also Arcadelt (influence). Arte Musicale in Italia (modern ed.). Artusi (criticism). Classici Musica Italiana, Vol. 19 (modern ed. of ' Combattimento '). Istituzioni, Vol. 6) do. of ' Sacrae cantiunculae ' & canzonets). Opera. . . . etc.

859   ii   *Add before* **MONTRE** :

MONTPELLIER MANUSCRIPT.   *See*
LYREBIRD PRESS (modern ed.).

860   ii   **MONUMENTA MUSICAE BELGICAE,** List
          l. 8. vom Helmont *should read* :
van Helmont

861   ii   *Add before* **MONUMENTA MUSICES SACRAE IN POLONIA** :

MONUMENTA MUSICAE SVECICAE.
A series devoted to the publication of Swedish music of the past published by the Svenska Samfundet för Musikforskning under the auspices of the Kungl. Musikaliska Akademien, and published by Almqvist & Wiksell of Stockholm. Publication began late in 1958, in which year only one volume appeared, containing the ' Assaggi à violino solo ' by Johan Helmich Roman (*c.* 1740). It contains three plates of facsimile reproduction of the manuscript and an introduction and notes in English and German. Later volumes are sometimes to contain Swedish texts with translations into one or the other of these two languages.

Vol. II, published in the spring of 1959, contained the Symphony in C minor by Joseph Martin Kraus (1783). Later volumes will continue with works by Roman and Kraus, and include string quartets by J. Wikmansson, an anonymous early 17th-century St. John Passion, works by Vincenzo Albrici (Master of Queen Christina's music), H. P. Johnsen's ' 24 Oden ' (1754) and works by members of the Düben family, including the elder Gustaf Düben's ' Odae Sveticae ' (1674).   E. B.

864   ii   *Add before* **MOOR, Karel** :
Moor, George. *See* Mellers (' Trial of Jewelled Peacock ', puppet masque).

MOOR
Par. 1, l. 2 *should read* :
1873 ; *d.* Prague, 30 Mar. 1945).

865   ii   **Moore, George**
          ll. 2-3 *should read* :
incid. m.). Jacob (G. ' Esther Waters ', film). O'Neil

MOORE, Gerald
Add at end :
Moore published a second book, ' Singer and Accompanist : the Performance of Fifty Songs ', in 1953 and was created C.B.E. in 1954.

866   i   *Add before* **Moore, T. Sturge** :
Moore, Marianne. *See* Rubbra (songs).

MOORE, Thomas (2)
Par. 1, l. 2 *should read* :
1779 ; *d.* Devizes, 25 Feb. 1852).

877   i   **MOOSER, Aloys**
          Par. 1, l. 1.   Fribourg, 1770 ;
          should read :
Niederhelfenschwyl, 27 June 1770 ;

877   i   Par. 1, l. 2.   1829). *should read*: 1839).

MOOSER, R. A.
Par. 3, l. 1.   comique en *should read*: comique français en

l. 2 *should read*:
(Geneva, 1932, new ed. 1954).

l. 11.   (1948–52). *should read*: (1948–51).

Add at end:
' Aspects de la musique contemporaine, 1953–1957 ' (Geneva, 1957).

878   i   **MORALES**
Par. 3, l. 6 *should read*:

ducats. His next notable appointment, after two years at Plasencia, was

882   ii   *Add to* BIBL.:
' Anuario Musical ', Vol. VIII (Barcelona, 1953), issue largely devoted to Morales.

885   i   *Add to See also*:
Eslava (modern reprints). Hispaniae Schola, Vol. 1 (do.).

    ii   **MORALES, O.**
Par. 1, l. 2 *should read*:
Almería, 13 Oct. 1874; d. Tällberg, 29 Apr. 1957).

886   ii   **MORALT (3)**
l. 2.   1874 *should read*: 1847

889   ii   *Add before* **MOREIRA**:
MORECOCKE, Robert (b. ?; d. London, 1582).
English 16th-century composer. He was *conduct* of St. Michael's Church, Cornhill, in London in 1547–49 and a Gentleman of the Chapel Royal at the time of Edward VI until his death. A 3-part ' Gloria laus ' of his is in the Baldwin Manuscript (B.M., R.M. 24. d. 2)
H. B. (ii).

891   ii   **MORGAN, ?**
Par. 4, l. 5 *should read*:
and harpsichord. Some pieces of his are also included in George Bingham's ' Airs anglois ', published by Estienne Roger of Amsterdam.

Morgenstern
Add at end:
Zeisl (' Moon Pictures ', voice & orch.).

892   ii   **Mörike**
Add to BIBL.:
KUNZ, WILTRUD, ' Musik in Eduard Mörikes Leben und Schaffen ' (Munich, 1951).

See Brahms should read:
See Berg (Alban, song). Brahms

893   i   **MORINI**
Par. 1, l. 1 *should read*:
MORINI, Erica (Erika) (b. Vienna, 5 Jan. 1905).

Add after **MORISCA**
MORISON, Elsie (Jean) (b. Ballarat, Victoria, 15 Aug. 1924).
Australian soprano singer. She took the three years' diploma course at the Melbourne Conservatorium of Music in 1943–45 and obtained the L.R.S.M. After a further course of study at the R.C.M. in London in 1947–48 she joined the Sadler's Wells Opera, where she remained until 1950. In 1953 she was engaged by the Royal Opera, Covent Garden, and in 1953–56 was engaged each season by the Glyndebourne Opera. In May 1957 she visited Australia to sing Mimi in ' La Bohème ' and Mařenka in ' The Bartered Bride ' with the Elizabethan Opera Company. She received the Portuguese Order of Public Education in 1955.

Apart from opera, Elsie Morison has also distinguished herself as a concert artist as well as in broadcasts and gramophone recordings. She has appeared as an oratorio singer in Denmark, Holland and France as well as in the British Isles. She is distinguished by a clear and limpid voice, sensitive phrasing and considerable versatility in acting. A peculiarly touching quality lends great charm to her interpretations of such diverse parts as Pamina, Mimi, Antonia in ' Tales of Hoffmann ' and Anne in Stravinsky's ' The Rake's Progress ', in which last part she appeared both in the B.B.C.'s broadcast performance and in the Glyndebourne production.

E. B.

    ii   **MORITZ**
Add at end:
See also Denkmäler (5), II (modern ed.).

894   ii   **MORLACCHI**
Par. 1, l. 9. Repuin *should read*: Repin

895   i   Par. 1, l. 1 *should read*:
bruck, where he died. His remains were transferred to Perugia on 26 Sept. 1951. He left an unfinished

MORLAYE
Add after Par. 2:
Very little is known of Morlaye's career, except that he was settled in Paris by 1541, married and describing himself as a merchant, but giving lessons in lute and viol playing. In 1545 he became associated with one Michel de Castellas for the sale of lutes and strings.

There is a modern edition of ' Psaumes de Pierre Certon réduits pour chant et luth par Guillaume Morlaye ', edited by Richard de Morcourt (Paris, 1957).
E. v. d. s., adds.

895   i   **MORLEY**
Par. 1, l. 2.   ? 1603). *should read*:
Oct. 1602).

897   i   Par. 4, ll. 12-21 *should read*:
pendio della musica ' (1588). In his defence it has been argued that in these examples both Tigrini and Morley were simply showing the best way of making formal closes; and as the best are not unlimited in number, it was not surprising if, in a crowd of others, the same examples sometimes occurred in different textbooks. But the modern edition of 1952 (*see* Bibl.) proves conclusively that Morley did in fact appropriate many of Tigrini's cadences.

ii   Par. 2, l. 6. John Harman *should read*:
R. Alec Harman

R. Alec   BIBL., l. 6. John *should read*:

Add to BIBL. :
BECK, SYDNEY (ed.), ' The First Book of Consort Lessons ' (New York, 1959).
UHLER, JOHN EARLE, ' Morley's Canzonets for Three Voices ' (with facsimile of the 1624 German ed.) (Baton Rouge, Louisiana, 1957).

901   i   **Morris**
l. 2 *should read*:
for the right ', song). Harrison (Lou, ' Scene from W. M.'). Hart (F., 3 songs). Holst (4

902   ii   **MORTARI**
Par. 2, ll. 3-4 *should read*:
act operas ' L' allegra piazzetta ', produced in Rome in 1945, and ' La figlia del diavolo ' (Milan, Scala, Mar. 1954); the ' Trittico ' for

903   ii   **MORTELMANS, Lodewijk**
Par. 1, l. 2.   26 June *should read*:
24 June

905   i   **MOSCHELES**
Par. 4, l. 7.   1865 *should read*:
1866

906   ii   **MOSER, H. J.**
Par. 2, l. 9.   ' Die Musik- *should read*:
' Die Musiker-

907   i   Par. 1, l. 6 *should read*:
the Nazi régime. In 1947 he settled at Weimar.

907   i   BOOKS
l. 9 *should read*:
' Musiklexikon ' (Leipzig, 1932–35; rev. 1943).

ii   **MÖSER, Karl**
Par. 1, l. 4 *should read*:
ducted the first Berlin performance of Beethoven's

910   ii   **MOSS**
Par. 2, l. 6 *should read*:
were published (copies in the Paris Bibl. Nat. and the Rowe

911   i   **MOSSOLOV**
Add at end of ORCHESTRAL WORKS:
Symphony No. 5 (1947).

Add at end of SOLO INSTRUMENTS AND ORCHESTRA:
Vn. Concerto (1946).

912   i   **MOSZKOWSKI**
Par. 2, ll. 3-4:
place in its time, though it was afterwards almost wholly forgotten until broadcasting gave it a renewed lease of life in its programmes of entertaining music. The more serious works on

915   ii   **MOTET**
See also. l. 2 *should read*:
Faburden. Isorhythm. Lyrebird Press (modern ed. of 13th-cent. motets). Organum. Trope.

919   i   **MOURET**
Par. 2, l. 15.   14 Nov. *should read*:
14 Sept.

ii   **MOUTH ORGAN**
Par. 2, l. 12 *should read*:
tell from instruments still in use. But the mouth organ, under the name of harmonica (under the head of ARMONICA it will be seen that this creates confusion) has recently taken a new lease of life, thanks mainly to its chief artistic exponent, Larry Adler, for whom Vaughan Williams and other serious composers have written concert works.

920   ii   **MOUTON**
ll. 1-2 *should read*:
MOUTON, Charles (*b. ?; d. ?*).
French 17th–18th-century lutenist. He was a pupil of Gaultier

921   ii   **MOUTON**
Add to BIBL. :
KAST, APUL, ' Studien zu den Messen des Jean Mouton ' (Frankfort o/M., 1955).

See also should read:
See also Collectio O.M.B., Vol. 8 (modern ed.). Maîtres Musiciens, Vol. 9 (do. of Mass). Paix (parody mass on motet).

923   ii   **MOZART (1)**
           BIBL. l. 13 *should read*:
biography of his son (1919). A facsimile of the 'Violin-schule' was published by Breitkopf & Härtel of Leipzig in 1956.

935   ii   **MOZART (3)**
           Footnote 3, l. 8.   Stahremberg *should read*:
Starhemberg

943   i   Par. 3, ll. 4-5 *should read*:
acquaintance at Verona. The portrait has generally been ascribed to one of several painters of that name, but is now known to be by Saverio Dalla Rosa, from whom it was commissioned by the receiver-general, Pietro Luggiati.

956   i   BIBL., I. CHIEF SOURCES. l. 52 *should read*:
1919-21, revised ed., 1923-24; new ed. rev. by Anna Amalie Abert, 3 vols., 1956). (Issued as a

      ii   II. SUPPLEMENTARY LITERATURE. l. 14
           should read:
'Mozart' (London, 1935; German trans., Zürich, 1954).
           Add to BIBL. :
BLOM, ERIC, ' The Literary Ancestry and the Music of "Figaro"' in 'Classics: Major and Minor' (London, 1958).
' The Music of "Così fan tutte"' (*ibid.*).
DALCHOW, JOHANNES, 'Mozarts Krankheiten, 1756-63' (Bergisch Gladbach, 1955).
DELLA CORTE, ANDREA, ' Tutto il teatro di Mozart' (Turin, 1957).
FELLERER, KARL GUSTAV, 'Mozarts Kirchenmusik' (Salzburg, 1955).
GOLDSCHMITT, ADOLF, 'Mozart: Genius und Mensch', ed. by Pogge von Ranken (Hamburg, 1955).
GREITHER, ALOIS, ' Die sieben grossen Opern Mozarts: Versuch über das Verhältnis der Texte zur Musik' (Heidelberg, 1956).

957   i   BIBL. l. 13 *should read*:
2nd ed., rev. 1944), Eng. trans., 'Mozart's Don Juan', by Eric Earnshaw Smith (London, 1957).

           Add to BIBL. :
HOCQUARD, JEAN-VICTOR, 'La Pensée de Mozart' (Paris, 1958).
HUGHES, SPIKE, ' Famous Mozart Operas: an Analytical Guide for the Opera-Goer and Armchair Listener' (London, 1957).
JACOB, HEINRICH EDUARD, 'Mozart, oder Geist, Musik und Schicksal' (Frankfurt o/M., 1955).

           (2nd work by KING) :
' Mozart in Retrospect' (Oxford, 1955).

           Add to BIBL. :
KOMORZYNSKI, EGON, 'Mozart: Sendung und Schicksal' (Vienna, 1955).
LANDON, H. C. R. & MITCHELL, D., ' The Mozart Companion' (London, 1956).
' L'Année Mozart en France: livre d'or du bicentenaire' (Rev. Mus., No. 231, 1956).
NETTL, P., ' Mozart and Masonry' (New York, 1957).

           NIEMETSCHEK. l. 5 *should read*:
E. Rychnovský, Prague, 1905). Eng. trans., ' Life of Mozart', by Helen Mautner (London, 1956).

           Add to BIBL. :
NOVELLO, V. & M., ' A Mozart Pilgrimage: being the Travel Diaries of Vincent and Mary Novello in the Year 1829', transcribed and compiled by Nerina Medici di Marignano, ed. by Rosemary Hughes (London, 1955).

      ii   l. 12.   ROUCHE *should read*:
ROUCHÉ

957   ii   *Add to* BIBL. :
SCHENK, ERICH, 'Wolfgang Amadeus Mozart: eine Biographie' (Zürich, 1955).
SCHNEIDER, OTTO, 'Mozart in Wirklichkeit' (Vienna, 1955).
SLONIMSKY, NICOLAS, ' The Weather at Mozart's Funeral' (M.Q., XLVI, 1960, p. 12).
SZABOLCSI, BENCE, ' Exoticisms in Mozart' (M. & L., XXXVII, 1956, p. 323).
VERCHALY, ANDRÉ (ed.), ' Influences étrangères dans l'œuvre de W. A. Mozart' (Paris, 1958).

959   —   CATALOGUE
           DRAMATIC WORKS
           Col. 4, l. 8.   after Bretzner. *should read*:
after Bretzner.[2]

           Add footnote :
[2] For earlier sources *see* ENTFÜHRUNG AUS DEM SERAIL.

980   —   Col. 5, l. 8 *should read*:
After 29 Apr.[1] 1784 (for Regina

           PIANOFORTE SOLO
           Col. 3, l. 27.   de Séville '.[1] *should read*:
de Séville '.[2]

981   —   *Add* footnote :
[1] Performed on that day with the pianoforte part incomplete.

           Footnote 1 *becomes* 2.

983   ii   **MOZART (4)**
           Add at end, before See also :
BIBL.—BERGER, LUDWIG, ' Die unverhoffte Lebensreise der Constanze Mozart: aus den verlorenen Aufzeichnungen des . . . G. N. von Nissen' (Tübingen, 1955).

           MOZART (5)
           l. 16 *should read*:
teaching music. It was he who suggested a plan for the establishment of a choral society at Lwów. Thanks to his energy, his artistry and, of course, the fame of his name, the Towarzystwo Muzyczne came into being. It gave a number of concerts and musical *soirées*, but lapsed soon after Mozart's departure from the town in 1840.
Both as pianist and com-

           Add at end :
BIBL.—GEIRINGER, KARL, ' W. A. Mozart the Younger' (M.Q., Oct. 1941).
HUMMEL, WALTER, ' W. A. Mozarts Söhne' (Cassel & Basel, 1956).

984   i   **MOZART AND SALIERI**
           l. 2. Салъери *should read*:
Сальери

           MOZART OPERA COMPANY
           l. 9. owes *should read*:
owed

           ll. 26-29 *should read*:
permanent basis; but unfortunately the organization collapsed after its first venture.

984   ii   **MRAVINA**
Par. 1, ll. 1-2 *should read*:

MRAVINA [1], **Evgenia Konstantinovna**
(*b.* ?, 1864; *d.* Yalta, 25 Oct. 1914).

Add footnote:
[1] Actually Mravinskaya.

985   i   **MUDARRA**
Par. 1, l. 1 *should read*:

MUDARRA, Alonso de (*b.* ?, *c.* 1508; *d.*
Seville, 1 Apr. 1580).

Par. 2, l. 1 *should read*:

Spanish lutenist. He is said

Par. 4, l. 13 *should read*:

XV y XVI '). There is a modern edition of
' Tres libros ' by Emilio Pujol (Barcelona,
1946).

MUDD, John
Delete entry and replace by:
MUDD, John (*b.* ?; *d.* London, [buried
26 July] 1639).
English organist. He was at Peterborough
Cathedral from 1583 to 1630, and his place
there seems to have been taken by Thomas
Mudd (ii) in 1631-32. He was a vicar choral
and epistoler. In 1629 he was awarded £4
as " benevolence money ". He must have
died in London, not at Peterborough, as
previously stated, since he was buried there at
St. Giles's Church, Cripplegate. He may
have been a composer, but no works of his
can be traced.

MUDD, Thomas
Delete article and replace by:
MUDD, Thomas (i) (*b.* London, *c.* 1560;
d. ?).
English composer and organist. His name
was included in F. Meres's list of England's
sixteen " excellent Musitians " (' Palladia
Tamia ', 1598), where he is described as
" sometimes fellow of Pembrook hal in Cambridge ". He attended St. Paul's in London
and went to Cambridge in 1578 with one of
the sizarships for the sons of London mercers.
Mudd was the author of a lost comedy in
which he " had censured and too saucily
reflected on " the Mayor of Cambridge,
whereupon he was committed to the tolbooth
by the vice-chancellor on 23 Feb. 1582 and
made to stay there for three days. He then
apologized to the mayor and was granted
pardon. He became a Fellow of Pembroke
Hall and continued so until as late as 1590.
A 5-part ' In Nomine ' for voices or instruments by him is at the British Museum (B.M.
Add. MS 31390, f. 117 [1]).

[1] Not 177, as in Grove V.

MUDD, Thomas (ii) (*b.*; *d.* ? Durham,
? 1 Aug. 1667).
English 17th-century organist and composer. It was probably he, not Thomas (i),
who took John Mudd's place at Peterborough
Cathedral from 1631 to 1632. He is mentioned again early in 1661 in the Chapter Act
Books of Exeter Cathedral. Various payments
by the Dean and Chapter to him are recorded,
but he does not seem to have held a post there.
On 6 Apr. 1661 he received some money from
them to cover his expenses for a journey to
London. At the same time it was ordered
that the house in which he lived should not
be disposed of without the Dean's consent.
He travelled to Lincoln and served for a short
time as organist of the cathedral in 1662, but
his bibulous tendencies appear to have upset
the authorities, and he soon returned to Exeter.
On 5 Mar. 1664 Mudd was nominated one of
the organists at Exeter Cathedral. He also
had to sing in the choir and received a salary
of £20 a year — " as long as he behaves himself (*quam diu se bene gesserit*) ". He also received £4 for his clothes and charges. Considering the condition on which he was
employed, he seems to have been identical
with Mudd, the unruly organist of Lincoln
Cathedral, whose bad behaviour and drunken
habits are described in two letters from the
precentor to the Dean of Lincoln, dated 14
and 16 Mar. 1663. Both contain requests for
a new and more civil organist.
Mudd did not stay long at Exeter Cathedral.
Regular payments to him are recorded in the
Extraordinary Solutions Account (D. & C.,
Exeter 3787) from 14 Mar. 1664 to 15 Mar.
1665. On the latter date he received some
extra money : " Item paid more for Mr.
Mudd by way of Augmentacion this quarter
in full of all demands £3 15s.". It is not
known why he left, but on 25 Mar. 1665
Theodore Colby was admitted as organist,
and Mudd is not mentioned any more.
Most of the anthems listed by " Mudd "
are by this Thomas Mudd. There are keyboard pieces, ' A lesson of Voluntarie of 3
parts ' and ' The Answer to ye former lesson ',
in the Paris Bibliothèque Nationale (Rés.
1186).   s. j.

985   ii   **MUDGE**
Paragraphs 1 and 2 *should read*:

MUDGE, Richard (*b.* Bideford, 1718; *d.*
Great Packington nr. Birmingham, 3 Apr.
1763).
English composer. He was the son of the
Rev. Zachariah Mudge, vicar of Plymouth.
In 1735 he entered Pembroke College, Oxford,
as a Rouse exhibitioner, taking the B.A. in
1738 and the M.A. in 1741, in which year he
was ordained curate of

986   i   Par. 1 *should read*:
Great Packington near Birmingham. The living was the gift of the Earl of Aylesford, who also presented him with the living of Little Packington and, in 1756, of Bedworth near Nuneaton, where, however, he is not known to have ever resided or officiated.

Par. 2, ll. 1-2 *should read*:
The only work published, in the 1750s, under the name of Mudge consists of six concertos for two solo

Add at end:
BIBL.—FLINT, S. R., ' Mudge Memoirs' (privately printed, 1883).

987   ii   **MUFFAT, Georg**
Par. 1, l. 1.   Schlettstadt, *c.* 1645;
should read:
Megève, [bapt. 1 June] 1653;

Par. 2, ll. 3-4 *should read*:
years in Paris, was appointed organist at Molsheim on 31 Mar. 1671, became organist to the

988   i   **MUGNONE**
Par. 2, l. 4.   Vesi *should read*:
Cesi

991   i   **MÜLLER-BLATTAU**
Par. 1, l. 2.   28 May *should read*:
21 May

992   i   **MÜLLER-HERMANN**
Par. 1, l. 2 *should read*:
Vienna, 15 Jan. 1878; *d.* Vienna, 19 Apr. 1941).

993   i   *Add before* **MÜLLER, Paul**:
MÜLLER, Maria (*b.* Litoměřice, 29 Jan. 1898; *d.* Bayreuth, 13 Mar. 1958).
Czech soprano singer. She studied in Vienna with the Danish tenor Erik Schmedes and made her début as Elsa at Linz in 1919. Engagements followed at the German Theatre in Prague and at Munich, and in 1925 she was engaged for the Metropolitan Opera, New York, where she made her début as Sieglinde. She remained a member of the Metropolitan until the end of the 1934-35 season, singing leading parts in a number of American premières, including Maria in Montemezzi's ' Giovanni Gallurese' (1925), the title-part in Alfano's ' Madonna Imperia ' (1928), Mariola in Pizzetti's ' Fra Gherardo ' (1929) and Dorota in ' Schwanda ' (1931). She was also heard as Donna Elvira, Agathe, Mařjenka, Octavian, Aida, Cio-Cio-San and the lighter Wagnerian repertory. She sang in Berlin, both at the Städtische Oper under

Bruno Walter, where she was first heard as Euryanthe in 1926, and later at the State Opera, where she remained until 1943. After the second world war she sang again at the Städtische Oper as Elisabeth, Sieglinde and Ariadne, but was not in good health and retired shortly afterwards to go and live at Bayreuth, her spiritual home. There she sang regularly from 1930 until 1939 (Senta, Eva, Elisabeth, Elsa, Sieglinde) ; while at Salzburg she appeared in 1931 (Eurydice), 1933 (Rezia) and 1934 (Donna Elvira). Her Covent Garden début was as Eva in 1934 under Beecham, and she sang Sieglinde in the 1937 ' Ring' cycles under Furtwängler. Other parts in her large repertory were Helen in Strauss's ' Aegyptische Helena ', Jenufa, Iphigenia in Gluck's ' Iphigénie en Tauride ', Djula in Gotovac's ' Ero the Joker ', Pamina, Tosca and Marguerite.

Maria Müller possessed a warm, vibrant voice. She sang Elsa and Elisabeth with a rare purity of tone, and her Sieglinde, while not quite so womanly as Lotte Lehmann's, was a moving creation, reaching great heights in the ecstatic outburst in the last act.

H. D. R.

996   ii   **MULLINER BOOK**
Add at end:
Among new identifications and concordances that have come to light in recent years are the following : No. 0, ' O ye happy dames', is in fact complete, and appears under the title of ' My hart ys lenid on the lande' in B.M. Stowe 389, f. 120; No. 10, ' Fansye' (Newman), exists in two versions in the March lute book; No. 83, ' O ye tender babes' (Tallis), is a setting of a prose text in William Lily's ' Introduction of the Eyght Partes of Speche' (1542) ; No. 112 is a keyboard reduction of ' When that the fifty day was come' from Tye's ' Acts of the Apostles'; No. 116, ' A Pavyon' (Newman), is also well known from other sources, such as William Ballet's lute book and the Dowland lute book in the Folger Library, Washington.
Of the music for cittern and gittern, No. viii is a setting of ' Chi passa per la strada '; No. 8 is two separate pieces, the first ending at bar 10, the second, a Pavane on the *passamezzo antico*, beginning at bar 11.

D. W. S.

Add to Bibl.:
LOWINSKY, E., ' English Organ Music of the Renaissance' (M.Q., XXXIX, 1953).
STEVENS, D. W., ' A Musical Admonition to Tudor Schoolboys ' (M. & L., XXXVIII, 1957).
WARD, J., ' Les Sources de la musique pour le clavier en Angleterre ' (' La Musique instrumentale de la Renaissance ', Paris, 1955).

1000   i   **MÜNCH, Charles**
Add at end:
BIBL.—MÜNCH, CHARLES, ' I am a Conductor ', trans. by Leonard Burkat (New York & London, 1955).

1001   ii   **MUNDY**
Par. 2, l. 4 *should read* :

there for at least the next twelve months. In 1547 he was *conduct* of St. Martin Vintry and in 1548-58 parish clerk at St. Mary-at-Hill. He

1002   ii   **MUNICH**
Par. 2, ll. 7-10 *should read* :

been built in 1901 as a theatre large enough for the production of Wagner's works after the manner of Bayreuth and, it appears, with the object of outrivalling Bayreuth by holding Wagner festivals earlier in the year. This was defeated, however, by the fact that a contract made by Wagner with Ludwig II covered performances at the Royal Court Theatre alone. Karl Zeiss took over the management of the Staatstheater, but he died in 1923.

Par. 4, ll. 15-18 *should read* :

Opera in 1954 was Georg Hartmann and its musical director Georg Solti, but the former is now (1956) replaced by Rudolf Hartmann, Solti being succeeded by Rudolf Kempe and he in turn by Knappertsbusch (1954). In 1956 the appointment of Ferenc Fricsay was announced, but he resigned in 1958 before his contract had expired and was succeeded by Joseph Keilberth.

1005   ii   *Add before* **MURCIANA** :

MURATORE, Lucien (*b.* Marseilles, 29 Aug. 1876; *d.* Paris, 16 July 1954).
French tenor singer. He studied singing and bassoon at the Marseilles Conservatory and became an actor for a short time, but made further studies in opera at the Paris Conservatoire and made his début at the Opéra-Comique on 2 Dec. 1902. In 1905 he first appeared at the Opéra in Gluck's 'Armide'. Massenet wrote parts in 'Ariane', 'Bacchus' and 'Roma' for him. In 1913 he made his first appearance in the U.S.A., at Boston, and then joined the Chicago Opera. Having served briefly in the French army early in the 1914–18 war, he returned to the U.S.A. and also sang at the Teatro Colón in Buenos Aires for the first time in 1917. He was twice married to opera singers, first to Marguerite Bériza and in 1913 to Lina Cavalieri, from whom he was divorced in 1927. His experience as an actor served him well in the interpretation of various tenor parts as convincing characters.   E. B.

Add after **MURCIANA** :

MURDER IN THE CATHEDRAL. Opera by Pizzetti. *See* ASSASSINIO NELLA CATTEDRALE.

1005   ii   *Add before* **MURIS** :
Murillo, Bartolomé Esteban. *See* Vlach-Vrutický (symph. poem on picture).

MURIS
Par. 2, l. 1 *should read* :

Welsh, English, French or (?) Swiss 14th-century philosopher,

1006   i   *After l. 19, insert new paragraph* :

One of the strongest pieces of evidence in favour of his having come from Britain is in John Aleyn's extraordinary motet called ' Sub Arthuro plebs ', which celebrates the glories of English musicians of the 14th century in an aggressively nationalistic fashion. J. de Muris is one of the many insular musicians here mentioned, and since most of them have had their names latinized, it is reasonable to suppose that " Muris " may stand for " of walls ", or in the spelling of the time " walis ", which in turn may mean " Wales ".

1008   i   *Signature should read* :
J. F. R. S., adds. R. T. D.

1009   i   **MURKY BASS**
Cancel entry and replace by :

MURKY BASS. An accompaniment in broken bass octaves played on keyboard instruments. The term was previously described as English in this Dictionary and elsewhere and its application to broken octaves as " obscure " ; but although it is certainly used in English musical terminology, as also in German (with variants such as *murcky* and *murzky*) and in French as *mourqui*, it is now known to be of Polish origin. Broken octaves were played by Polish folk instruments, the *basetla* and the *basy*, and it appears that German musicians happened to hear their music at a small village named Murcki [1] in Polish Silesia, and that a " murky bass " was thus a bass as heard at Murcki.[2]   E. B.

Add footnotes :
[1] Pronounced " moortsky " in Polish, but the " ck " sound in German being similar to that of plain " k ", the letter C was dropped under the misapprehension that it was superfluous (*cf.* Klecki=Kletzki, Vol. IV, p. 775).
[2] For further details *see* an article by Czesław Raymund Halski in M. & L., XXXIX, Jan. 1958.

1013   i   *Add after* **MUSICA ANTIQUA (2)** :

MUSICA ANTIQUA BOHEMICA. A collection of music by old Bohemian composers published in Prague under State control. The following volumes have been published up to 1956 :

3. Bohuslav Černohorský, Organ Pieces.
4. Jan Hugo Voříšek (Worzischek), Pf. Sonata, Op. 20.
7. Václav Pichl, Prelude and 6 fugues for solo vn., Op. 41.
8. František Xaver Dušek, 8 pf. Sonatas.

9. Jan Zach, Sonata for 2 vns. & cello.
10. Jiří Benda, Concerto, G mi., for pf. & stgs.
11. Czech Classics, Selection of compositions for vn. & pf.
12. Czech Classics, Organ pieces by composers of the 18th & early 19th centuries.
14. Czech Classics, Pf. works.
15. Leopold Antonín Koželuh (Kozeluch), Stg. Quartet, B♭ ma., Op. 31 No. 1.
16. Antonín Vranický (Wranitzky), Concerto, B♭ ma., for vn. & pf.
17. Czech Sonatinas for pf.
18. Antonín Fils (Filtz), Concerto, D ma., for flute. & pf.
19. Jan Adam František Míča, ' Concertino notturno ', E♭ ma., for chamber orch.
20. Czech Classics, Pf. works.
21. Jan Ladislav Dusík (Dussek), 12 Leçons progressives for pf., Op. 16.

1013   ii   **MUSICA BRITANNICA**
Add at end :

Later volumes are :

8. John Dunstable, Complete Works, ed. by Manfred Bukofzer.
9. Jacobean Consort Music, ed. by Thurston Dart and William Coates.
10.-12. ' The Eton Choirbook ', ed. by F. Ll. Harrison.
13. William Boyce, Selected Overtures, ed. by Gerald Finzi.
14. John Bull, Keyboard Music, Vol. I, ed. by John Steele & Francis Cameron.
15. ' Music of Scotland : 1500–1900 ', ed. by Kenneth Elliott, with song-texts ed. by Helena Mennie Shire.
16. Stephen Storace, ' No Song No Supper ', ed. by Roger Fiske.

1018   i   **MUSICAL BOX**
Add to BIBL. :

CHAPUIS, ALFRED, ' Histoire de la boîte à musique et de la musique mécanique ' (Lausanne, 1955).

MUSICAL CLOCKS
Add at end :

BIBL.—BUCHNER, ALEXANDER, ' Česke Automatofony ' (Prague, 1957). (Summary in English.)
See also Hassler (2, manufacture).

MUSICAL GLASSES
Add after ARMONICA :

(*PLATE* 35, Vol. IV, p. 504, No. 5.)

1019   i   **MUSICIANS' BENEVOLENT FUND**
Par. 1, l. 1.   and Frank Howes.
should read :

, Frank Howes and Sir Steuart Wilson.

1020   ii   **MUSICIANS' UNION**
Par. 1, ll. 3-5 *should read* :

this is situated at 29 Catherine Place, S.W. 1 (London branch, 23 Sicilian Avenue, W.C. 1), and its general secretary is Hardie Ratcliffe. It has branches

1027   ii   **MUSICOLOGY**
Add to BIBL. :

FELLERER, K. G., ' Einführung in die Musikwissenschaft ', 2nd ed. (Hamburg, 1956).
HAYDON, GLEN, ' Introduction to Musicology ' (New York, 1941, 2nd ed. 1947).
HUSMANN, HEINRICH, ' Einführung in die Musikwissenschaft ' (Heidelberg, 1958).
MENDEL, ARTHUR, SACHS, CURT & PRATT, CARROLL C., ' Some Aspects of Musicology : three Essays ' (New York, 1957).

1029   ii   *Add after* MUSIN :

MUSIQUE CONCRÈTE. *See* CONCRETE MUSIC.

1030   i   **Musset**
l. 15 *should read* :
opera ; 3 songs). Puccini (' Edgar ', opera). Rasse (' Déidamia ', opera). Rey

1038   i   **MUSSORGSKY**
Add to BIBL. :

CALVOCORESSI, M. D., ' Modest Mussorgsky : his Life and Works ' (London, 1956).

1042   ii   **MUTATION**
Par. 1, l. 1. fourteen and sixteen
should read :
thirteen and sixteen

1046   ii   **MUZIO**
Par. 1, l. 1 *should read* :

MUZIO, Claudia [3] (*b.* Pavia, 7 Feb. 1889 ; *d.*

Add footnote :
[3] The name is Claudina Muzzio in the birth certificate.

Par. 2, l. 15 *should read* :

Covent Garden in 1914, she sang

l. 18 *should read* :

the Metropolitan she created the part of Giorgetta in the

l. 19. ' It tabarro ' *should read* :

' Il tabarro '

l. 21. 4 Dec. *should read* :

14 Dec.

l. 25 *should read* :

Chicago. She was with the Rome Opera 1928–35. She also sang frequently in South

1047   i   *Add after* MYERS :

MYNERS, John (*b.* ? ; *d.* London, 2 July 1615).
English musician. He was in the service of Thomas Sackville, first Earl of Dorset, and later among the musicians of Prince Henry, at whose funeral he played. The Sackville Papers [1] give details of some payments made to him by the Earl's household : 3 Oct. 1607 : " Paid to John Miners one of your lordship's

[1] Kent Archives Office, Maidstone, U 269, A1/1.

musicians in discharge of his bill for strings bought for your lordship's viols and violins 19s."; 3 Mar. 1608: "Paid to John Miners in discharge of a bill for viol strings of sundry sorts by him bought and provided 43s.".

On 28 Mar. 1615 Myners was sworn in as a Gentleman of the Chapel Royal, but as there was no place vacant at the time, he went to Exeter and became one of the vicars choral of the Cathedral. On 24 Apr. next, however, Thomas Sampson, Clerk of the Check in the Chapel Royal, was drowned, and Myners took up his appointment on 4 June 1615, only to die himself less than a month later.

There is an entry on the account book of the College of Vicars Choral at Exeter of a payment of £4 made to him for the midsummer quarter very shortly before he left. A copy of his resignation of his place there is entered in the Cheque Book of the Chapel Royal.[2] It reads as follows:

RESIGNATION.
The Copye of Jo. Myners resignacion of his place in the Church of Exon; to our Lord the Deane of his Majestes Chappell.

[2] Edward Rimbault, 'The Old Cheque Book or Book of Remembrance of the Chapel Royal' (Camden Record Society, New Series, Vol. III).

"Wheras I, John Myners, by especiall favor of you good Lordship, and the general consent of the Gentlemen of the Chappell, was sworne in ordinarie to the next place that should fall of what part soever, since which tyme, at the earnest request of some friendes of mine (beinge as then there was no place voyd in the Chappell), I went to Exeter, and ther was made a member of that body, but presently after I was certified of the death of Mr Sampson, whenupon I came to your Lordshipp about it, and your Lordshipp hath offered it me freely, the which then unadvisedly I refused, but Your Lordshipp more favouringe me (then I deserved) would not take that my first deniall, but gave me longer tyme to consider therof afterwards " . . . (he promises to forget all rights and interests in Exeter and if he betakes himself again to Exeter, " will loose all hope, benefitts, which belonge by my place in the Chappell ").

4th of June 1615.

         Jo: MYNERS
         Witnesses heerof

         ANTH. HARRISON Substitute
         Jo: HEWLETT
                       s. J.

1047   i   **MYRIELL**
         Par. 2, l. 7.   Fétis Library, *should read*:

Royal Library,

1048   ii   **MYSZ-GMEINER**
         Par. 1, l. 2.   *d.* ? *should read*:

d. Schwerin

---

873   ii   **KURTH**
         Par. 1, l. 2.   2 Apr. *should read*:
2 Aug.

875   i   **KÜRZINGER, I. F. X.**
         Par. 1, l. 2 *should read*:
Rosenheim, Bavaria, 30 Jan. 1724; *d.* Würzburg, 12 Aug.

         KÜRZINGER, P. I.
         Par. 1, ll. 1-2.   Dates *should read*:
(*b.* Mergentheim, 28 Apr. 1750; *d.* Vienna, ? after 1820).

877   i   **KUSSER**
         Add to See also:
Denkmäler (5) II (modern ed. of extracts from ' Erindo ').

         ii   **KUTCHER**
         Par. 2, ll. 7-8 *should read*:
Kutcher String Quartet with Peter Tas, Raymond Jeremy and Douglas Cameron. Tas

was later succeeded in turn by Frederick Grinke and Max Salpeter.

879   i   **KVAPIL**
         Par. 1, l. 2 *should read*:
Moravia, 21 Apr. 1892; *d.* Brno, 18 Feb. 1958).

881   ii   **KYRIE**
         Par. 3, ll. 9-11 *should read*:
adapted this to the Kyrie of the present Prayer Book, and his adaptation is in frequent use. The ninefold Kyrie is now very generally used in place of the Responses to the Commandments. The Kyrie provided by Marbeck for a

         Signature should read:
W. S. R., adds. W. H. F., rev.

         Cancel footnote.

VOL. VI

Page Col.

2   i   *Add before* **NACHBAUR**:
NACAIRES (Fr.).   *See* NAKERS.

ii   *Add before* **NACHTGALL**:
NACHTANZ.   *See* SALTARELLO.

4   i   **NAICH**
Add to BIBL.:

QUITIN, JOSÉ, ' A propos des Hubert Naich de Liège et d'un tableau de la Galleria Pitti à Florence ' (Revue Belge de Musicol., XI, 1957, p. 134).
SINDONA, ENIO, ' È Hubert Naich e non Jacob Hobrecht il compagno cantore del Verdelot nel quadro della Galleria Pitti ' (Acta Musicol., XXIX, 1957, p. 1).

NAÏL
See LARA. *should read*:
See DE LARA.

Add before **Nairn**:
NAÏLA (' La Source '), ballet.   *See* DELIBES, Vol. II, p. 651, footnote 3.

ii   **NAKERS**
Par. 1, ll. 5-6 *should read*:
the back of an attendant.   (*See* PLATES 31, Vol. IV, p. 488, No. 4; 32, Vol. IV, p. 492, No. 4; 35, Vol. IV, p. 504, No. 1.)

5   i   **NALSON**
Par. 1, ll. 1-2 *should read*:
NALSON, Valentine (*b*. London, 1682; *d*. York, 1722).

Add at end:
A manuscript at York Minster (M/83) mentions that he was a son of J. Nalson, the pamphleteer, and was educated at Huntingdon and St. John's College, Cambridge. He was ordained deacon in 1706, appointed minor canon in 1708 and vicar of St. Martin's, Coney Street, York, in 1710.

7   i   **NAPIER**
ll. 14-15 *should read*:
songs, the first volume with accompaniments for pianoforte, violin and violoncello, the second with pianoforte and violin, and the third with figured bass only.   This proved so success-

9   i   **NAPOLEÃO**
Par. 1.   Dates *should read*:
(*b*. Oporto, 6 Mar. 1843; *d*. Rio de Janeiro, 12 May 1925).

Page Col.

9   ii   **NAPOLI**
Par. 2, ll. 13-14 *should read*:
and was produced there in 1953.   Other operas by Napoli include ' Miseria è nobiltà ' (Naples, 1945), ' Un curioso accidente ' (Bergamo, 1950) and ' I peccatori ' (Naples, 1954).

10   i   **NÁPRAVNÍK**, List of Works
l. 1.   ' Nizhegorodcy ' *should read*:
' Nizhegorodtsy '

Nizhegorod *should read*:
Nizhny-Novgorod

12   ii   **NASH**
Par. 1.   London, 1896 *should read*:
London, 14 June 1896

13   i   **NAT**
Par. 1, l. 2 *should read*:
1890; *d*. Paris, 1 Sept. 1956).

18   ii   **NATIONAL ANTHEMS**
DENMARK.
l. 4.   D. L. Rogart *should read*:
D. L. Rogert

20   ii   GUATEMALA.
l. 4.   Rafael Álvarez *should read*:
Rafael Álvarez Oraile.

21   i   *Delete par.* HOLKAR'S DOMINIONS.

ICELAND.
l. 2.   Jochumsen *should read*:
Jochumsson

ii   INDORE *should read*:
INDORE. ' Prabho prarth ana parisa amuchi ': (*followed by musical example and three lines of* HOLKAR'S DOMINIONS).

24   i   NEW ZEALAND.
Musical example *should read*:

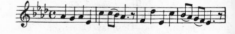

ll. 5-6 *should read*:
Bracken, were set to music by John J. Woods in 1876.   New

318

24 i New Zealand
ll. 8-15 *should read*:

other than 'God save the King', but 'God defend New Zealand' is now regarded as the Dominion's national song, while 'God save the Queen' continues to be used as the national anthem. A setting of the same words by R. A. Horne, published in 1923, gained some currency, but in 1940 the New Zealand Government officially adopted the setting by Woods.

25 ii Poland
Replace par. after musical quotation:

Known under two names, 'Poland has not perished yet' and 'Mazurka of Dąbrowski'. The words were written by Józef Wybicki (1747–1822), a young Polish legionary, who was a poet and set the words to a folk tune, which he first sang in that form at a gathering of Polish army officers at Reggio in July 1797. The assertion that the music was composed by Count Michał Kleofas Ogiński (1765–1833), who did write a march for the Polish legions in Italy, has been proved erroneous. The song soon became very popular in Poland. According to an eye-witness, it was sung by all the people gathered in the streets of Poznań when General Dąbrowski entered that city on 6 Nov. 1806. It was authorized by the new Polish republican government as its national anthem in 1927, the Ministry of Education settling the official version of both words and tune. In 1948 the Ministry of Culture and Arts established a slightly altered version, harmonized by K. Sikorski.

26 i Russia.
l. 1. Susa *should read*:
Soyuza

ii l. 2. died in 1915 *should read*:
died in 1932

27 ii Spain.
l. 6 *should read*:
also the 'Himno de Riego':

l. 8 *should read*:
composed by Huerta *c.* 1860, based on a tune from a sonata by Mateo Albéniz. Party songs play an

28 ii United States.
ll. 23-24 *should read*:
Smith's version was first sung at Boston on 4 July 1831. 'Hail Columbia!' is another, said to

l. 30 *should read*:
must also be mentioned, although it hardly comes within this category:

29 ii *Add to* Bibl.:
Shaw, Martin & Coleman, Henry, 'National Anthems of the World' (London, 1960).

32 i *Add before* NAU:
NATURALE. An Italian term signifying cancellation of a previous instruction, e.g. *sul ponticello, sul tasto, sec.*

35 i NAUMANN (1)
Add to See also:
Sondheimer Ed., Vols. 7, 16, 17, 30, 31 (modern ed. of var. works).

NAUMANN (3)
ll. 1-2. Dates *should read*:
(*b.* Freiburg i/B., 15 Aug. 1832; *d.* Jena, 15 Dec. 1910).

36 i NAVARRA
Par. 2, l. 10 *should read*:
appeared several times with the London Symphony Orchestra and then at the Cheltenham Festival of

ii NAVARRO, Juan (i)
Transfer signature J. B. T. *below list of MSS.*

40 i NEATE, Charles
Par. 3, l. 6. five *should read*:
three

41 i NECHAYEV
Par. 1, l. 2 *should read*:
Moscow, 28 Sept. 1895; *d.* Moscow, 5 June 1956).

43 ii NEEFE
Bibl. l. 9 *should read*:
1915 (edited by A. Einstein). Paul Nettl's 'Forgotten Musicians' (New York, 1951) draws on it.

45 i NEGRI, Gino
Add at end:
Bibl.—Mila, Massimo, 'A Scandalous Musician' ('The Score', No. 15, Mar. 1956).

ii NEIDHART VON REUENTAL
Add to Bibl.:
Hatto, A. T. & Taylor, R. J., 'The Songs of Neidhart von Reuental' (Manchester, 1958).

47 i NEJEDLÝ (3)
l. 2. 1 Jan. 1945 *should read*:
30 Dec. 1944

ii *Add after* Nekrassov:
NELSON. Opera in 5 acts by Berkeley. Libretto by Alan Pryce-Jones. Produced London, Sadler's Wells Theatre, 22 Sept. 1954.

49 ii *Add before* NEPOMUCENO:
NEOFORENSIS. *See* Nowotarski.

51 ii **Nerval**
l. 3 *should read*:
(Berlioz). Desmarquez (songs). Fortner ('Corrila', opera). Françaix ('Main de

52 i **Nestroy**
l. 2. *Add at end*:
Sutermeister ('Titus Feuerfuchs', opera).

53 i *Add before* **NEUE SACHLICH-KEIT**:

NEUE MUSIKGESELLSCHAFT. *See* SCHERCHEN.

Add before **NEUKOMM**:

NEUGER, Konrad (*b.* Cracow, 1892; *d.* Chicago, 15 Apr. 1948).
Polish conductor and chorus master. He studied first at Cracow and later in Vienna and Munich. His career as conductor was begun at the Volksoper in Vienna, but after one season he moved to a new post as conductor at the Munich State Opera, and later to a similar one at Leipzig. In 1931 he went to the U.S.A., where for the first two years he acted as chorus master at the Philadelphia Opera, going afterwards in the same capacity to the Metropolitan Opera in New York. In 1939 he was appointed Director of the Opera (Hull House) at Chicago. In May 1947 he was attacked by paralysis, and he died eleven months later. C. R. H.

55 ii **NEVADA, Mignon**
Par. 1, l. 2. 1890 *should read*:
1886

56 i ll. 3-4 *should read*:
London on 3 Oct. 1910 as Ophelia in Thomas's 'Hamlet' (Beecham season, with Camillieri as conductor). She was then frequently engaged in

NEVEU
Par. 1, l. 1. Paris, 1919 *should read*:
Paris, 11 Aug. 1919

58 ii **NEW YORK**
ll. 9-12. *Cut* Smaller auditoriums . . . increasing frequency, *and substitute*:
The Carnegie Recital Hall and Carl Fischer Hall (260 seats) are among the most frequently used smaller auditoriums.

63 i Par. 1, ll. 3-4. Mitropoulos was 1950-51 *should read*:
Mitropoulos has been the sole regular conductor until 1958, when Leonard Bernstein succeeded him.

63 Par. 5, ll. 11-15. *Cut* The present schedule . . . years of age., *and substitute*:
His successors were Boris Buketoff, a young American, in 1950 and Wilfred Pelletier in 1953. The present schedule includes a regular series of five Saturday mornings and a series of three concerts for children under nine years of age.

Par. 7, l. 1. The seasons are eight weeks *should read*:
The seasons are six weeks

64 i Par. 4, ll. 16-22. *Cut* The current autumn . . . spring and summer, *and substitute*:
After Toscanini's retirement in Apr. 1954 the orchestra was divided into smaller groups for other broadcasts. During its last years its autumn and winter seasons have consisted of from twenty-two to twenty-four weekly broadcasts under Toscanini and others.

ii Par. 2, ll. 3-5. *Cut* the highest rate . . . artistic *and substitute*:
the highest rate for a seat is $3.60 — is provided by the New York City Opera Company. László Halasz was its first artistic

l. 6 *should read*:
director, and he was succeeded by Joseph Rosenstock in 1951. It began its career at the New York

Par. 3, l. 1 *should read*:
In their repertory both Halasz and Rosenstock have shown con-

l. 11 *should read*:
Grant Still's 'Troubled Island'. Other productions were the first world performance of David Tamkin's 'The Dybbuk' (Oct. 1951), Wolf-Ferrari's 'I quattro rusteghi' (Oct. 1951), Berg's 'Wozzeck' (Apr. 1952) and Bartók's 'Bluebeard's Castle' (Oct. 1952).

Par. 4. *Cut paragraph and substitute*:
Joseph Rosenstock, who succeeded Halasz in Dec. 1951, continued a progressive policy until Dec. 1955, when he left for Japan. Opera has also been provided in recent years by Fortune Gallo's touring San Carlo Opera in short spring seasons and, at Brooklyn, by Alfredo Salmaggi's Popular Price Opera Company. On television several performances are given annually by the N.B.C. Television Opera Theatre.

67 ii Par. 2, ll. 4-7. 1936. Its . . . are devoted to *should read*:
1936. Its regular seasons consisted of sixteen concerts each season at the Town Hall on

Sunday afternoons at 5.30. The programmes, usually limited to ninety minutes, were devoted to

67   ii   Par. 2, ll. 12-15. Friends have . . . devoted to compre- *should read* :

Friends had no permanent performing group, but engaged their artists according to the demands of each season's programmes. In these much attention was devoted to compre-

Par. 3. *Cut whole paragraph and substitute* :

The New Friends' series came to an end in 1953, but were succeeded in the 1953-54 season by the Concert Society of New York, which has a similar schedule and similar comprehensive policy of programme-making. More diversity, however, has replaced the New Friends' concentration upon a given composer or composers each season.

69   ii   Par. 3, ll. 12-17. munity funds. Julius . . . . (1919-47). *should read* :

munity funds. Robert Ward is the director of the Music School Settlement, which has 1000 pupils a year. His predecessors include Thomas Tapper (1907-9), David Mannes (1910-15), Arthur Farwell (1915-19), Melzar Chaffee (1919-47) and Julius Rudel (1947-52).

Par. 4, l. 11. Gregory Mason, now professor emeritus, 1919- *should read* :

Gregory Mason, 1919-

l. 14. music in May . . . orchestral *should read* :

music in May 1945; this, up to 1950, included an orchestral

l. 18. produces *should read* :

produced

70   i   Par. 7, ll. 2-3. 1883-1939 ' (Oxford, 1939), *should read* :

1883-1950 ' (New York, 1953),

72   i   Par. 2. *Cut whole paragraph and substitute* :

Johnson retired after the 1949-50 season. His successor, Rudolf Bing, had been active in Great Britain as general manager of the Glyndebourne Opera and director of the Edinburgh Festival. Among the features of his first four seasons were a smaller repertory, a change in the long-standing subscription system which permits more repetitions of each opera and completely new productions of fourteen more or less familiar works. Stravinsky's ' The Rake's Progress ', which had its

American première on 14 Feb. 1953, was the only new opera offered during the period. A campaign for $1,500,000 was launched early in 1953.

72   i   *Add to* BIBL. :

KOLODIN, IRVING, ' The Story of the Metropolitan Opera, 1883-1950 : a Candid History ' (New York, 1953).

74   i   **NEWMAN**
Par. 1, l. 2 *should read* :

1868 ; *d.* Tadworth, 7 July 1959).

Add before See also :

BIBL.—' Fanfare for Ernest Newman ', ed. by Herbert van Thal (London, 1955).

75   ii   **NEWSTONE**
Delete entry and substitute :

NEWSTONE, Harry (*b.* Winnipeg, 21 June 1921).

British conductor. He was born in Canada of Russian parents who took British nationality, and the family settled in London in 1927. Although intended to become an architect, he developed a strong desire to devote himself to music, and after studying alone for a time he was accepted by Herbert Howells as a pupil for harmony, counterpoint, composition and general musicianship. In 1945 a Government Award enabled him to attend a full-time course at the G.S.M., where he studied conducting under Edric Cundell and Aylmer Buesst as well as the pianoforte, viola, flute and horn. He gained the A.G.S.M. Diploma in conducting and later also took the L.R.A.M. During the springs of 1954 and 1956, with a scholarship from the Italian Government and the British Council, he took the finishing course in conducting under Fernando Previtali at the Accademia di Santa Cecilia in Rome, and was awarded the diploma.

In 1949 Newstone founded the Haydn Orchestra in London, primarily to remedy the neglect of so much of Haydn's music, but also to give high-class performances of music of all periods. He revised the text of all Haydn's symphonies written for London from the earliest sources for a broadcast series commemorating the 150th anniversary of the composer's death in 1959. In 1955 he was invited to conduct the Berlin Mozart Orchestra and in 1956 he conducted the Danish State Radio Orchestra in Copenhagen. He was so successful as to be invited again by both capitals, and he has also made recordings with the Hamburg Pro Arte and Chamber Orchestras.   E. B.

See also Haydn Orchestra.

76   ii   **NEZERITIS**
Par. 1, l. 1. 1 Dec. *should read* :

30 Nov.

77　ii　**NICHOLLS**
Par. 1, l. 2 *should read*:
Cheltenham, 14 July 1877; *d.* London, 21 Sept. 1959).

79　i　**NICHOLSON**
Par. 1, l. 19 *should read*:
hurst (later at Canterbury and now at Addington Palace, Croydon), Nicholson's

81　i　**NICOLAI, Philipp**
Add at end, before signature:
Two cantatas by Buxtehude are based on songs by Nicolai.

83　i　**NIDECKI**
Par. 2, l. 10 *should read*:
Zauberspiele) performed there at the time. During his stay in the Austrian capital he also wrote nine German operettas, produced there between 1831 and 1837.

85　i　**NIEDT**
Par. 2, l. 28 *should read*:
thorough-bass upon it. Modern facsimile reprints of the three parts of ' Musicalische Handleitung ' are to appear in ' Documenta Musicologica ', Vols. 20-22.

J. R. M., adds.

86　ii　**NIELSEN, Carl**
Add to BIBL.:
' Carl Nielsens brev ', selected & edited by Irmelin Eggert Møller & Torben Meyer (Copenhagen, 1954).

88　i　**NIELSEN, Flora**
Par. 2, l. 1 *should read*:
Canadian mezzo-soprano (formerly soprano) singer. Her real name is Sybil Crawley. She was educated

l. 5 *should read*:
also in Hamburg and Vienna. She sang under her own name for

l. 10 *should read*:
season at Sadler's Wells, where she appeared as Lady Macbeth in Collingwood's ' Macbeth ' (1934). On changing to a mezzo-soprano she appeared as Brangäne at Covent Garden in 1938, and finally she settled

ii　**NIELSEN, Hans**
Add at end:
See also Chorwerk, Vol. 35 (modern reprint of Italian madrigals).

90　i　**NIETZSCHE**
Par. 2, ll. 21-22 *should read*:
He also regarded the works of Peter Gast, an amateur composer like himself, as being southern, so much so that

90　ii　*See also.* l. 6 *should read*:
work). Gast (praise of). Hindemith (chorus). Ingen hoven (symph. fantasy on

Add to BIBL.:
' Nietzsche: Lettres à Peter Gast ', trans. by Louise Servicen, 2 vols. (Monaco, 1957).

91　ii　**" NIGGER QUARTET "**
l. 4 *should read*:
tunes. The nickname being considered somewhat offensive, the work is now referred to by gramophone companies as the " American " Quartet.

93　i　**NIKISCH**
Par. 2, l. 12. 1913) *should read*:
1913 and 1914)

ii　**NIKOLAIDI**
l. 2 *should read*:
work. In 1951 she became a member of the Metropolitan Opera in New York.

Add after **NIKOROWICZ**:
NILSSON, Birgit (*b.* Karup, South Sweden, 17 May 1922).
Swedish soprano singer. She is the daughter of a farming family and was born in the country. When she was seventeen she was heard by a singing-teacher who advised her to study. Her parents did not approve of this suggestion and so she was sent to a school of domestic science. Eventually she was able to persuade her parents to change their minds, and in 1941 she began her vocal studies at the Royal Academy in Stockholm; when she applied for a vacancy there she was awarded first place out of forty-seven applicants. She spent three years in the solo class and then a further two in the opera class, her teacher being Joseph Hislop. In 1946–47 she sang Agathe at the Royal Opera, Stockholm, and the following year she leapt to fame when she was chosen to sing Lady Macbeth under Fritz Busch. Between 1947 and 1951 she was singing regularly at Stockholm as the Marschallin, Sieglinde, Donna Anna, Venus, Senta, Aida, Tosca and Lisa in ' The Queen of Spades '.
Nilsson's first important appearance outside Sweden was at Glyndebourne in 1951 as Electra in ' Idomeneo ', but she made only a slight impression, and it took another four years before her international reputation was established. During the 1954–55 season she sang the ' Götterdämmerung ' Brünnhilde for the first time in Stockholm, and also Isolde and Salome. The same season she made her Munich début as Brünnhilde in the complete ' Ring ', and she has been heard there

regularly since, especially in the summer festivals. Her American début was at San Francisco in 1956 as Brünnhilde, and in 1957 she sang the same part in Chicago, returning there in 1958 as Isolde and Turandot. She was chosen to sing Isolde at Bayreuth in the new production by Wolfgang Wagner in 1957. Her first Covent Garden appearance was as Brünnhilde in the autumn ' Ring ' in 1957, when she was hailed as the finest Wagnerian soprano since Flagstad. She confirmed the impressions she had created when she sang Isolde at Covent Garden in June 1958, producing a stream of beautiful tone such as had not been heard in an Isolde since the Flagstad of the 1930s. Nilsson's voice is even throughout its range, pure in sound and perfect in intonation, with a free, ringing top. Her phrasing and conception of Brünnhilde and Isolde have shown great artistic strides forward in the last few years, and vocally she is the supreme Wagnerian soprano of the day.

H. D. R.

94 ii **NIN-CULMELL**
Par. 2, l. 1 *should read*:

Cuban pianist, conductor and composer. He first

Par. 3, ll. 7-8 *should read*:

school at Middlebury College. In 1943 he served in the Cuban army. In 1946 he became conductor of the Berkshire Community Orchestra at Williamstown (Mass.). His compositions include, apart from the Quintet, a pianoforte Concerto (1946), ' Three

96 ii **NOBLE, Dennis**
Par. 2, l. 10 *should read*:

Covent Garden, where he appeared from 1924 and returned in the first post-war season of 1947, singing Escamillo and Lescaut. He has been perhaps most fre-

Add before **NOBLE, T. T.** :

NOBLE, (John) Jeremy (*b.* London, 27 Mar. 1930).
English critic and musicologist. He was educated at Aldenham School (1943–47) and at Worcester College, Oxford (1949–53), where he read Greats. He pursued his musical studies privately and developed an interest in early English music which soon led to wider fields of scholarship including transcription, criticism and bibliography. An unusually catholic taste in music enabled him to serve as Librarian to the Plainsong and Mediaeval Music Society, and to contribute chapters to ' La Musique instrumentale de la Renaissance ' (Paris, 1955) and ' The Decca Book

of Ballet ' (London, 1958). His activities as a broadcaster have ranged widely and some of his finest work has appeared in the form of series of programmes devoted to Venetian composers of the 16th and 17th centuries and to such composers as Cipriano de Rore and Josquin des Prés. He has written reviews and critical notices for numerous London journals and periodicals, and visited America in 1958–59, where he lectured on English music. In October 1960 he joined the musical staff of the London ' Times '.

D. W. S.

97 i **Nobre**
l. 1 *should read* :
Nobre, António. *See* Lopes Graça (2 choruses,

ii **NOCTURNE**
Add at end :
BIBL.—JANKÉLÉVITCH, VLADIMIR, ' Le Nocturne : Fauré, Chopin et la nuit ; Satie et le matin ' (Paris, 1957).

Nodier
l. 1. *Add after See* :
Gandino (' Trilby ', opera).

101 i *Add after* **NONNENGEIGE** :
NONO, Luigi (*b.* Venice, 29 Jan. 1924).
Italian composer. He studied conducting with Hermann Scherchen and composition with Bruno Maderna. He is devoted to twelve-note composition and made his first appearance, at the Darmstadt Holiday Courses of 1950, with orchestral Variations on a note-series by Schoenberg. The following year, at the same place, Scherchen produced his ' Polifonica-monodia-ritmica ' for orchestra, and in 1952 Maderna conducted the cantata ' España en el corazón '. This work was afterwards heard at Hamburg, Cologne and Baden-Baden. Altogether Nono's success has so far (1957) been confined mainly to Germany. To a commission to write a work for performance at Donaueschingen in 1953 he responded with ' Due espressioni ' for orchestra. In 1955 he composed ' Canti per tredici ' for 13 instruments, and in the following year ' Romance de la guardia civil española ' (Part III of an ' Epitaph for García Lorca ') was broadcast for the first time.

In 1957 ' La terra e la compagna ', a setting of poems by Cesare Pavese for soprano, tenor, chorus and instruments, was broadcast by the Munich Radio. Another choral work, ' La terra promessa ' (Giuseppe Ungaretti), for 2 sopranos, chorus and percussion, was produced at the Kranichstein holiday course in Sept. 1958.

E. B.

ii **NOORDT (1)**
Add at end :
See also Vereniging, Vol. 19 (reprint of Tablature Book).

101   ii   **NORCOM(B)E (3)**
Par. 1, ll. 2-4 *should read* :

violist. He was in the service of the Archduke Albert in Brussels in 1602 and was still there in 1641 and 1647. The records exist for the years 1612–18 of payments made to him by the court amounting to an average of 250 florins *per tercio*.[1] Nothing more is known of him.

Add footnote :

[1] Chambre des Comptes MSS Nos. 1837-38, Archives Générales du Royaume, Brussels.

102   ii   **NORDICA**
l. 12 *should read* :

del Festival. In 1898, 1899, 1902 and 1906 she

103   ii   **NORDRAAK**
Add to BIBL. :

GURVIN, OLAV, ' Rikard Nordraak og den nasjonale föresetnadene for han i kunstmusikken ' (' Syn og Segn ', 1942).

104   i   *Add before* **NORFOLK** :

NORÉNA, (Kaja) Eidé (*b.* Horten, 26 Apr. 1884).

Norwegian soprano singer. Her maiden name was Kaja Andrea Karoline Eide Hansen. She studied singing with Ellen Gulbranson in Christiania and Raimund von Zur Mühlen in London. After her operatic début as Amor in Gluck's ' Orfeo ' at Oslo in 1907 she sang at the National Theatre in Oslo from 1908 to 1918. An engagement at the Royal Stockholm Opera followed, but the soprano's international career began late, and it was not until 1924 that she was heard outside Scandinavia. This was at the Scala, Milan, where she sang Gilda under Toscanini. She was then engaged for the 1924 Covent Garden season as Gilda and Violetta, and was a fairly regular visitor to London in the 1920s and 1930s, singing, in addition to those two parts, Mimì, Liù, Micaela and Desdemona, the last in 1937 with Martinelli and Tibbett under Beecham being considered one of the most beautiful and distinguished performances of the part ever to have been heard in London.

Noréna joined the Metropolitan Opera, New York, in 1933, remaining there until 1938; she was also heard in Paris, Monte Carlo, Vichy and Amsterdam. At this last city in 1932 she sang in a production of ' Tales of Hoffmann ' sponsored by the Wagner Society, under Pierre Monteux, appearing as Olympia, Giulietta and Antonia, and scoring a great personal triumph. Her parts further included Juliette, Nedda, Marguerite, the Queen of Shemakhan and Mathilde in ' Guillaume Tell '. Noréna had a beautiful and perfectly trained soprano voice. She was a trifle cool in temperament, but sang with impeccable taste and could on occasions be profoundly moving.

H. D. R.

104   i   *Add before* **NORLIND** :

NORGATE, Edward (*b.* Cambridge, ? ; *d.* London, [buried 23 Dec.] 1650).

English heraldic artist and instrument maker. He was born some time before 1587 as the son of Robert Norgate, Master of Corpus Christi College, Cambridge, after whose death in that year his mother married Nicholas Felton, later Bishop of Ely. He was brought up by Felton, but instead of going to the University, he went to London, where he served the king in numerous capacities.

His non-musical appointments included that of Blue Mantle Pursuivant (1616) and Windsor Herald (1633), and for most of his life he was engaged in writing and illuminating royal patents, diplomatic correspondence, etc. He travelled a good deal : to Brussels as an agent for the purpose of buying pictures for the queen's cabinet at Greenwich and to Italy on a similar errand for the Earl of Arundel. His first wife, Judith Lanier (sister of Nicholas Lanier who was likewise an art connoisseur), must have died before 1619, for in that year he married his second wife, Ursula Brighouse.[1]

Norgate was granted the office of tuner of the king's virginals, organs, etc., on 25 Nov. 1611 conjointly with Andrea Bassano. Payments were made to him up to 1641 for building a new organ at Richmond (£120 in 1639) and making repairs and alterations to all the other organs and virginals in the royal palaces : St. James (1631-7), Whitehall (1629, -31, -2, -9, -41), Hampton Court (1629, -31, -7, -9, -41) and Greenwich (1631, -2, -41). During this period he held the place alone, and after the restoration his son Arthur was granted a patent in the same office (9 June 1660), although for some reason he held this only until 2 July 1660, when John Hingeston was appointed.

In May 1632 a warrant for an allowance of 15s. a day was made to Norgate towards " the diet and lodging of Signior Antonio Van Dike and his servants, to begin from the 1st April last " for the duration of Van Dyck's stay.

He was also a fine organist, as we learn from a letter from Sir William Swann (an amateur musician living in Holland) to Constantijn Huygens :

. . . yesterday wee have bin in our devotions . . . in the presence of one Mr Northget, a great lover of musike and a verre good organist . . . he is one of the kings servants, clarke of the signet office, and one of his

[1] For further details concerned with these aspects of his career see the D.N.B. article.

May^{tes} heraults, and verre well knowen to Mr. Laynier, of whose arrivall wee heere doe long to heare . . .
[Utr:cht, 25 Mar. 1646]
I. S.

104   i   **NORLIND**
Par. 1, l. 2.   Stockholm *should read*:
Uppsala

105   ii   **NORTH, Roger**
Add to BIBL. :

BURTON, MARTIN C., ' Mr. Prencourt and Roger North on Teaching Music ' (M.Q., XLIV, Jan. 1958, p. 32).
WILSON, JOHN, ' Roger North on Music ' (London, 1959).

108   ii   **NOTARI**
Par. 1, l. 2 *should read*:
(*b*. Padua, 14 Jan. 1566 ; *d*. London, Dec. 1663).

Par. 2, ll. 1-3 *should read*:

Italian singer, lutenist and composer. He became a citizen of Venice, where he was a member of the Accademia degli Sprovisti, but went to live in England some time before 1611, when he was a musician in the household of Prince Henry. His ' Prime

Add after Par. 2 :

The contents of ' Prime musiche nuove ' are shown in Ian Spink's article (*see* Bibl.), which also gives further details of Notari's career in England.
According to Hind (*see* Bibl.) the only known copy of the portrait frontispiece to Notari's book is in the Fitzwilliam Museum at Cambridge ; it takes the form of a bust enclosed in an oval frame, with two verses in his praise by colleagues in the Venetian academy to which he belonged. It is reproduced in Hind's book, Vol. II, pp. 323-24.

Add after signature :

BIBL.—HIND, ARTHUR M., ' Engraving in England in the Sixteenth and Seventeenth Centuries ', 2 vols. (Cambridge, 1955).
SPINK, IAN, ' Angelo Notari and his " Prime musiche nuove " ' (M.M.R., Sept.–Oct. 1957).

122   ii   **NOTATION**
Par. 1, l. 5.   <u>17</u> *should read* :
|—<u>17</u>—|

123   ii   *Add to* BIBL. :

PARRISH, CARL, ' The Notation of Medieval Music ' (New York, 1957 ; London, 1958).
WINTERNITZ, EMANUEL, ' Musical Autographs from Monteverdi to Hindemith ', 2 vols. (Princeton & London, 1956).

126   i   **NOTKER**
See also. p. 111 *should read* :
p. 114

127   i   **NOTRE-DAME SCHOOL**
Par. 2, l. 10 *should read* :

usually interspersed their " free " melismas with

Par. 3, l. 20 *should read* :

the points of concord depends largely on

ll. 24-28 *should read* :

monic sense as we understand it. Despite the increasing frequency of thirds in

128   i   *Add at end* :

BIBLIOGRAPHY

ANGLÈS, HIGINI, ' El Còdex musical de Las Huelgas ' (Barcelona, 1931).
' La música a Catalunya fins al segle XIII ' (Barcelona, 1935).
APEL, WILLI, ' From St. Martial to Notre-Dame ' (Jour. Amer. Mus. Soc., II, 1949, p. 145).
' The Notation of Polyphonic Music ' (Cambridge, Mass., 1949).
AUBRY, PIERRE, ' Cent Motets du XIIIe siècle ' (Paris, 1908).
BAXTER, J. H., ' An old St. Andrews Music Book ' (London, 1931).
BESSELER, HEINRICH, ' Die Musik des Mittelalters und der Renaissance ' (Potsdam, 1931).
' Studien zur Musik des Mittelalters. II : Die Motette von Franko von Köln bis Philippe von Vitry ' (A.M.W., VIII, 1927, p. 137).
COUSSEMAKER, EDMOND DE, ' Histoire de l'harmonie au moyen-âge ' (Paris, 1852).
' Scriptorum de musica ' (Paris, 1864-76).
DITTMER, LUTHER, ' A Central Source of Notre-Dame Polyphony ' (Brooklyn, 1959).
' Facsimile Reproduction of the Manuscript Wolfenbüttel 1099 ' (Brooklyn, 1960).
FELLERER, KARL GUSTAV, ' Zur Kirchenmusikpflege im 13. Jahrhundert ' (' Kirchenmusikalisches Jahrbuch ', XXVIII, 1933, p. 7).
FICKER, RUDOLF VON, ' Polyphonic Music of the Gothic Period ' (M.Q., XV, 1929, p. 483).
' Probleme der modalen Notation ' (Acta Musicol., XVIII, 1946, p. 2).
GENNRICH, FRIEDRICH, ' Perotins Beata Viscera Mariae Virginis und die " Modaltheorie " ' (' Musikforschung ', I, 1948, p. 225).
' Rhythmik der Ars Antiqua ' (Darmstadt, 1954).
' Perotinus Magnus : Das Organum " Alleluia Nativitas " und seine Sippe ' (Darmstadt, 1955).
' Musica sine Littera ' (Darmstadt, 1956).
GERBERT, MARTIN, ' Scriptores ecclesiastici de musica sacra potissimum ' (St. Blasien, 1784).
GÉROLD, THÉODORE, ' Histoire de la musique des origines à la fin du XIVe siècle ' (Paris, 1936).
GRÖNINGER, EDUARD, ' Repertoire-Untersuchungen zum mehrstimmigen Notre-Dame Conductus ' (Regensburg, 1939).
HANDSCHIN, JACQUES, ' Was brachte die Notre-Dame-Schule Neues ? ' (Z.M.W., VI, 1924, p. 545).
' Notizen über die Notre-Dame-Conductus ' (' Bericht über den musikwissenschaftlichen Kongress der deutschen Musikgesellschaft in Leipzig ') (Leipzig, 1926).
' Zur Notre-Dame-Rhythmik ' (Z.M.W., VII, 1925, p. 386).
' Zur Geschichte von Notre-Dame ' (Acta Musicol., IV, 1932, pp. 5, 49).
HUSMANN, HEINRICH, ' Die dreistimmigen Organa der Notre-Dame-Schule, mit besonderer Berücksichtigung der Handschriften Wolfenbüttel und Montpellier ' (Leipzig, 1935).
' Die Offiziumsorgana der Notre Dame-Zeit ' (J.M.P., XLII, 1936, p. 31).
' Die drei- und vierstimmigen Notre-Dame-Organa ' (Leipzig, 1940).
KUHLMANN, GEORG, ' Die zweistimmigen französischen Motetten des Codex Montpellier ' (Würzburg, 1938).
LUDWIG, FRIEDRICH, ' Die liturgischen Organa Leonins und Perotins ' (' Riemann-Festschrift ') (Leipzig, 1909).

'Die mehrstimmige Musik des 11. und 12. Jahrhunderts' ('Bericht über den III. Kongress der Internationalen Musikgesellschaft') (Leipzig, 1910).
'Repertorium organorum recentioris et motetorum vetustissimi stili' (Halle, 1910).
'Über den Entstehungsort der grossen "Notre-Dame-Handschriften"' ('Festschrift für Guido Adler') (Vienna, 1930).
'Perotinus Magnus' (A.M.W., III, 1921, p. 361).
MICHALITSCHKE, ANTON MARIA, 'Die Theorie des Modus' (Regensburg, 1923).
REESE, GUSTAVE, 'Music in the Middle Ages' (New York, 1940).
ROKSETH, YVONNE, 'Le Contrepoint double vers 1248' ('Mélanges de musicologie offerts à M. Lionel de la Laurencie') (Paris, 1933).
'Polyphonies du XIIIe siècle' (Paris, 1939).
ROSENTHAL, ALBI, 'Le Manuscrit de La Clayette retrouvé' ('Annales Musicologiques', I, 1953, p. 105).
SCHMIDT, HELMUT, 'Zur Melodiebildung Leonins und Perotins' (Z.M.W., XIV, 1931, p. 129).
SCHNEIDER, MARIUS, 'Zur Satztechnik der Notre-Dame-Schule' (Z.M.W., XIV, 1931, p. 398).
SCHRADE, LEO, 'Political Compositions in French Music of the 12th and 13th Centuries: The Coronation of French Kings' ('Annales Musicologiques', I, 1953, p. 9).
TISCHLER, HANS, 'New Historical Aspects of the Parisian Organa' ('Speculum', XXV, 1950, p. 21).
'The Evolution of Form in the Earliest Motets' (Acta Musicol., XXXI, 1959, p. 86).
WOLF, JOHANNES, 'Geschichte der Mensuralnotation von 1250–1460' (Leipzig, 1904).
'Handbuch der Notationskunde' (Leipzig, 1913–19).

130   ii   **NOVAIS**
Par. 1, ll. 1-2 *should read*:

NOVAES, Guiomar (*b*. São Paulo, 28 Feb. 1895).

136   ii   **NOVELLO (3)**
Add at end:

BIBL.—MACKENZIE-GRIEVE, AVERIL, 'Clara Novello: 1818–1908' (London, 1955).

138   i   *Add after* **NOVOTNÝ**:

NOWAK, Leopold (*b*. Vienna, 17 Aug. 1904).
Austrian musicologist. At the age of nine he became a choirboy under Dominik Joseph Peterlini and while still at school was taught the pianoforte and the organ by Louis Dité. He studied at Vienna University in 1923–27, took the Ph.D. degree, studied counterpoint with Franz Schmitt and assisted Robert Lach at the Musikwissenschaftliches Institut in 1928–39. In 1932 he was appointed lecturer in musical history at the University and in 1939 Professor. After the second world war, in 1946, he succeeded Robert Haas as director of the music section of the Austrian National Library. This appointment involved his collaboration in the new edition of Bruckner's works, and he is also an editorial member of the D.T.Ö. In 1955 the cross of a Commander of the Order of St. Gregory was bestowed on him.
Nowak has written numerous learned articles, especially on church music, and in 1932 he published 'Grundzüge einer Geschichte des Basso ostinato in der abendländischen Musik'.   E. B.

141   ii   **NYSTROEM,** List of Works
l. 13 *should read*:
No. 3, 'Sinfonia concertante', with solo cello (1945).

Delete l. 21.

142   ii   *Add before* **Obata**:
OAKER, John. *See* OKEOVER.

155   ii   **OBOE**
Add after Par. 2:

Since the publication of Grove V the author of this article has been fortunate in making contact with two professional oboists whose technique was formed many years ago on the original Barret system instrument. While they do not deny the occasional advantage of an alternative control over the half-hole plate, both are of the opinion that the primary use of the extra thumb touch is to prevent a "change-over" of the automatic octave keys which would otherwise occur when the left ring finger is raised in playing f″, f♯″ and g″.
P. B.

158-9   Page Headings. Makes *should read*:
Makers

160   i   *Add after* Par. 1:
The technique employed by makers of the curved *cor anglais* and basset horns in the 18th and early 19th centuries has been subject to much speculation and controversy among organologists. Musical writers have repeatedly asserted that these tubes were formed either by bending under the influence of heat and moisture or glueing and binding together two curved shells hollowed out of plank wood, as in the case of the cornetti and serpents. The recognized instability of such heat-formed articles as chair backs or the crooks of walking sticks seems to invalidate the first suggestion, while known museum examples show that the second method seems to have been excessively rare. Indeed, among the many specimens he has investigated, the present writer has come across only one instrument showing this construction. This is a wide-bore tenor of the type for which Bessaraboff has reserved the designation " oboe da caccia ", and it seems very doubtful if the " plank " method was ever applied to the true *cor anglais* with a narrow bore. There is, in fact, a very good and practical reason against it.
If we look at almost any contemporary picture of a player on the curved cornett we see that the instrument was held with the plane of curvature across the body, in a more or less horizontal position, and that the finger-holes were bored perpendicular to this plane, *i.e.* through the component shells. On the other hand, the playing position of the bent *cor anglais* requires the holes to be placed

along the actual curvature of the tube, just where the seam between the shells must naturally occur in the " plank " construction. This is obviously an unsatisfactory arrangement where a glued join is involved or where undercutting of the holes might be required. There is also the objection that, in playing, the glued join on the inner curvature of the tube would lie just where condensed moisture tends most to collect.

Since the section of this Dictionary dealing with the curved *cor anglais* (Vol. VI, p. 159 ff.) went into print an opportunity has occurred for fresh research in this matter, and the techniques of the 18th- and 19th-century instrument makers are now fully understood. It may be indeed that evidence has been available for over sixty years and has lain unrecognized for lack of adequate description. In the catalogue of the César Snoeck collection, published at Ghent in 1894, there is a rather obscure entry which reads as follows :

962 *Vieille taille de hautbois.* En arc du cercle, à deux clefs. Instrument de transition entre la taille de hautbois et le cor Anglais. Deux de ses parties sont recouvertes de cuir ; la troisième l'a été également ; cette partie dénudée, met sous les yeux le moyen qu'employaient les facteurs au 17me siècle pour produire des tubes courbés.

Unfortunately this instrument does not figure in Sachs's list of 1145 specimens from the Snoeck collection transferred in 1902 to the Berlin Hochschule, nor among the 436 Flemish examples presented to the Brussels Conservatoire in 1908, and its fate is unknown. We are therefore without information as to the method of construction Snoeck mentions ; neither have we his reasons for assigning the instrument to the 17th century.

Towards the end of the 19th century certain French *cor anglais* were made with the upper section alone quite gently curved. In these the top joint was built up of five or six separate pieces permanently united by tenons. Circumferential seams are clearly visible on the outside, and sometimes on the inside of the tube also, if examined with the aid of a small surgical inspection lamp. It may therefore be reasonably supposed that the same method of building up was used to form the earlier and more strongly curved instruments. These are, however, invariably covered with a skin of leather (often beautifully tooled and polished), so that although many of them do show internal seams, the exterior ones must be taken on trust.

The recent acquisition of a fine early Italian *cor anglais* in much the same state as Snoeck's example stimulated the author to re-investigate the whole matter. The instrument in question had suffered much from damp, and on both curved joints the covering was loose and partly destroyed. In the process of restoration the leather was turned back and it then became evident that the exterior seams did not pass completely round the tube. Internally, however, the instrument showed the same transverse joins as in other similar specimens. The method of construction was now quite clear. The tube had been turned and bored in the usual manner, and then a series of transverse wedges had been cut out of it. The apex of each wedge removed penetrated quite half the thickness of the tube wall, leaving the various sections connected by a strip of wood thin enough to bend without too much strain and allowing the gaps to be closed and cemented. The process was that used by joiners who will notch the back of a moulding before applying it to a curved surface. Moreover, before the wedges were sawn out a flat had been planed on the tube which, after bending, formed a bed along the inner curvature to which a wooden " splint " had been glued and pinned. The resulting structure was completely rigid :

The evidence afforded by a single specimen, however convincing in itself, could not, of course, be regarded as of general application ; as many typical instruments as possible were therefore examined in detail. Since all these were leather-covered and none, as collector's pieces, could be denuded for investigation, it was decided to try X-ray photography. After some experiment a suitable method was worked out which gave good differentiation on the plates between wood, leather and metal. The results were extremely interesting. Of the specimens X-rayed the great majority revealed the " notching " technique ; a few proved to be built up out of detached sections ; none showed any evidence of a join running along the length of the tube. The methods of retaining the curvature, however, and of anchoring the sections together showed considerable variety. The majority of 18th-century specimens were provided with the glued and pinned wooden splint as described above. An early 19th-century German *cor* showed a metal splint screwed to all the sections, but not sunk below the surface. Another 18th-century example, by the well-known Florentine maker Bimboni, represented a particularly interesting type. In this case the tube had certainly been notched and bent, but the curve was maintained not by a splint but by a series of wooden keys each shaped like two keystones joined at their narrow ends and inset across the seams. These prevented the sections from separating by literally " dovetailing " them together :

A Triébert *cor* of *c.* 1850 with apparently no remarkable features either inside or out proved to have both joints built up of several quite separate sections simply butted together without the use of tenons. Instead each junction was bridged by three or four narrow wooden keys sunk deep in the wall of the tube and retained by wooden pegs. This would seem to be less strong mechanically than any of the older constructions, but in fact this instrument shows no sign of weakness or instability :

Finally one of the gently curved French joints of the late 19th century tenoned type was X-rayed for comparison, and another interesting feature came to light. It was found that the tenons uniting the various parts had not been turned down from the wood of the sections themselves, but were in fact separate short tubes cemented into sockets and further retained by wooden pegs :

It will have been seen that the often quoted idea that the bores of bent wooden instruments must necessarily, by reason of their construction, be less accurate or highly finished than those of straight ones is quite fallacious. In fact they were undoubtedly produced by exactly the same tools and methods. It is true that such bores formed a sequence of obtuse angles and not true curves, which indeed could only be produced by the " plank " method, but the approximation, especially in the later examples, was really surprisingly close, as the X-ray photographs have demonstrated.   P. B.

169   i   *Add before* BIBL. :

(*PLATE* 34, Vol. IV, p. 500, No. 1.)

Add to BIBL. :

BATE, PHILIP, ' The Oboe : an Outline of its History, Development and Construction ' (London, 1956).
ROTHWELL, EVELYN, ' Oboe Technique ' (Oxford, 1953). Also Footnotes.

ii   *Add after* **OBOE (2)**

OBOUKHOV, Nicolay. *See* OBUKHOV.

OBOUSSIER
Par. 1, l. 2 *should read* :

1900 ; *d.* Zürich, 10 June 1957).

Par. 2.   *Add at end* :

His death was caused by murder : he was found stabbed in his flat.

OBRECHT
Par. 1, ll. 1-2.   *c.* 1453 ; *should read* :

22 Nov.[2] 1452 ;

Add footnote :

[2] The day and month are given in an article by Bain Murray, ' New Light on Jacob Obrecht's Development ' (M.Q., Oct. 1957). The year 1452 is more probable than 1453, as he entered the University in 1470 (Aug.).

170   ii   *Add to* BIBL. :

KYRIAZIS, MARIA, ' Die Cantusfirmus Technik in den Messen Obrechts ' (Berne, 1952).
MURRAY, BAIN, ' New Light on Jacob Obrecht's Development : a Biographical Study ' (M.Q., XLIII, Oct. 1957, p. 500).
' Jacob Obrecht's Connection with the Church of Our Lady in Antwerp ' (' Revue Belge de Musicologie ', XI, 1957, p. 125).

Add to See also :

Vereniging, Vols. 9, 18, 44, etc. (modern reprints).

OBUKHOV
Par. 1, l. 2 *should read* :

1892 ; *d.* Paris, 13 June 1954).

173   i   *Add after* **OCHSENKUHN**:
OCHSENMENUETTE, DIE. *See* Ox
Minuet.

ii   *Add before* **OCTAVINA**:

OCTAVIN (Ger. **Oktavin**). A wood-wind single-reed conically-bored instrument. Its invention has been usually attributed to Julius Jehring (1824–1905), a bassoon-maker in Adorf, Vogtland, Germany. In fact, Oskar Adler, wood-wind maker in Markneukirchen, and Hermann Jordan of the same town were granted a Patent in 1893 (Deutsches Reich Patentschrift Nr. 83005 of 27 Sept. 1893 and Deutsches Reich Gebrauchsmuster Nr. 22115, Klasse 51, of 11 October 1893). The same patentees took out a British Patent for the instrument shortly after (Brit. Pat. Nr. 20598 of 31 Oct. 1893). The instrument is only 40 cm. in height and is made of rosewood (palisander), resembling the butt-joint of a bassoon. To the wider bore is fitted a small metal bell, turned outwards at a right-angle. To the narrower bore an ebonite joint is added, terminating in a clarinet-type beak-mouthpiece. Fourteen keys and three rings are fingered, much as a simple-system oboe. The Patent specification claims that any player of clarinet, oboe, bassoon or flute can easily acquire the technique of the instrument. Originally the octavin was made in C and B♭ with compass from a to f''' (or g to e♭'''). Other models occur: one with a straight single tube, while a bass, descending to G, is mentioned by W. Altenburg ('Die Klarinette', Heilbronn, 1904). Despite the pretentious claims of the maker, the octavin has attained no popularity in Europe, though it is said to have done so in America. Few musicians know of its existence and even musical dictionaries are silent in regard to it. The tone somewhat resembles that of the soprano saxophone but is less pleasant, and it has been said that the octavin " appears to incorporate the more undesirable features of the saxophone and clarinet without any of their virtues ".
Illustration : A. Carse, ' Musical Wind Instruments ', Plate IX E. Fingering Chart by Zimmermann, Leipzig.   L. G. L.

174   i   **ODAK**
Par. 1. l. 7. in Prague *should read*:
at Geneva

ii   **ODO**
Par. 1, l. 1. Tours, *should read*:
Cluny,

175   i   Par. 1, l. 11. Beaune *should read*:
Baume

175   ii   **O'DWYER**
Par. 1. Dates *should read*:
(*b*. Bristol, 27 Jan. 1862 : *d*. Dublin, 6 Jan. 1949).

Par. 2, ll. 5-6 *should read*:
first opera to a libretto in Irish, ' Eithne ', on 3 Aug. 1909, and in 1914 was appointed lecturer in

176   i   **OEGLIN**
Par. 2, l. 21. IX *should read*:
VIII

Add at end, before signature:
A facsimile reprint of the 1512 ' Liederbuch ' is to be published in ' Documenta Musicologica ', Vol. 23.

ii   **OFFENBACH**
Par. 1, l. 3 *should read*:
5 Oct. 1880 [1]).

Add footnote:
[1] During the night of 4-5 Oct., according to a report in ' Le Temps ' of 6 Oct. a few minutes before 3.30 a.m.

177   ii   Bibl. *Add after* l. 12 (2nd title under Offenbach) :
' Orpheus in America : Offenbach's Diary of his Journey to the New World ', trans. by Landor Mac-Clintock (Bloomington, Ind., 1957).

179   —   CATALOGUE
OPERETTAS
Col. 2, l. 55 *should read*:
& Arnold Mortier, after Jules Verne.

181   ii   **OHMS**
Par. 1, l. 1. **Elizabeth** *should read*:
Elisabeth

Par. 2, ll. 7-12 *should read*:
of the Bavarian State Opera at Munich, and sang two parts (1926–29) at La Scala, Milan, under Toscanini. She also appeared at Covent Garden,

182   i   **OISEAU-LYRE**
Lyre-bird Press *should read*:
Lyrebird Press.

After this add:
OISTRAKH, David Feodorovich (*b*. Odessa, 30 Sept. 1908).
Russian violinist. He studied under Stoliarsky at the Conservatory of his native town and made his début as a concert artist at the age of nineteen. He obtained the first prize in a national competition in 1935 and in 1937 won the first international prize for violinists in Brussels. The Stalin prize was awarded to him in 1942. He made his name in Russia

as the country's outstanding violinist, both as a virtuoso and as an interpreter, and he has also been exceptionally successful abroad, as at the Prague Festival of 1946 and in London in 1954. He not only gives superlative performances of the violin classics, but has also introduced a number of important new works for his instrument by modern Russian composers, such as Miaskovsky, Prokofiev and Khachaturian.   E. B.

OISTRAKH, Igor Davidovich (b. Odessa, 1931).

Russian violinist, son of the preceding. He studied under his father at the Moscow Conservatory. In 1952 he won the first prize at the Wieniawski International Competition at Poznań. Although he doubtless owed some of his first successes partly to his famous name, he soon proved to be an artist of outstanding quality in his own right. He has toured widely in the U.S.S.R. and abroad, visiting Great Britain in 1953 and 1957.   s. c. r.

182   i   **OKAR**
Entry should read:
OKAR, John.   *See* OKEOVER.

183   i   **OKEGHEM**
Par. 5, l. 4.   progress. *should read*: progress.[4]
Add to BIBL. :
KŘENEK, ERNST, 'Johannes Okeghem' (New York, 1953).
(2nd work by Plamenac):
    'A Postscript to Volume II of the Collected Works of Johannes Ockeghem ' (Jour. Amer. Musicol. Soc., III, 1950, p. 33).
    Add at end :
    See also Chorwerk, Vol. 4 (modern reprint of ' Missa Mi-Mi ').
    Add footnote :
[4] For a first volume under the same editorship *see also* DENKMÄLER (4), Vol. I.   A second, revised edition was published by the American Musicological Society in 1959.

ii   **OKELAND**
l. 2 *should read* :
for the burial of Henry VIII in that year.[4] He remained through the reign of Edward VI. In 1533-35 he was organist of St. Mary-at-Hill. He
l. 6 *should read* :
(1560). A 4-part Kyrie by him is in B.M. Add.

OKER
Delete entire article and replace by the following :
OKEOVER (Oaker [5]**), John** (b. ? Staffordshire, ? ; d. Wells, 1663).
English organist viol-player (?) and com-

poser. The family of Okeover, of which he is probably a member, has its seat in Staffordshire, where it can be traced back to the eleventh century.[6] The fact that he gave some books towards the refurnishing of the vicar's library at Wells seems to suggest that he was in better financial circumstances than at least some of his fellows. He was admitted vicar-choral and organist at Wells Cathedral on probation on 16 Feb. 1620; the fabric accounts for that year, however, show a payment to " Mr. Brown, the organist ". Okeover was admitted perpetual vicar-choral at the termination of his period of probation and became master of the choristers on 1 June 1625. The existing registers show him to have been at this period a frequent attender at meetings of the vicars, of whom he became Receiver in 1627 and Senior in 1628. His adherence to the Book of Common Prayer is shown by his substitution of the Magnificat and Nunc Dimittis for the customary anthems.

Okeover graduated B.Mus. at Oxford in 1630. His name appears in the Cathedral accounts at Gloucester as that of the master of the choristers in 1639-41, apparently after a year's vacancy, but he remained in close touch with Wells until Dec. 1642 at least. His name appears in the Communar's paper book as having received payment in 1641-42, and the Puritan Survey for 1649 shows that he was occupying a house in the Vicars' Close at Wells at that time. An undated deed of about 1662 strongly suggests that he was resident at Wells throughout the Commonwealth; this refers to his " long and tedious sickness ". It seems that he died at Wells before the winter of 1663, for the Communar's book shows that the full organist's stipend for the year 1663-64 was paid to one John Browne, and that in 1665 a sum was paid " to Mrs. Oaker for her son John Oaker, one of the choristers ". This is signed " Mary Oker ", whereas one would expect the elder John to have signed had he been in a position to do so.[7]

Some songs by Okeover (under Oker) are mentioned in Q.-L. Presumably these are the three-part fancies contained in Bodl. MSS Mus. Sch. d. 245-7, which are described thus on p. 94 of d. 245. The same source also contains two " duos " by him. Perhaps these are the " several ayrees of 2 and three parts for the violin, viol and base viol " which Wood believed to be extant.[8]   B.M. Add. MSS 17786-91 and 17792-6 contain a number of pavans and fancies by Okeover. Four anthems are attributed to him. R.C.M. 1045-51 contain all four parts of " Grant we beseech thee ", a setting of the Collect for the 21st Sunday after Trinity, and there is at Gloucester an organ score of an anthem, ' Hear my prayer, O good Lord '. In addition, R.C.M. 1051 contains the *bassus cantoris* parts of two others: 'God shall send forth his mercy' and 'The King shall rejoice'.

W. K. F.

Footnote 5 should read:

[5] This was the abbreviation by which John Okeover was usually referred to; that the latter form is correct is attested by the fact that it was the form he adopted almost invariably in signing his name. But it is also found as Okar and Ockeover as well as Oaker.

Footnote 6 should read:

[6] *See* Burke's 'Landed Gentry', 1952, pp. 1919-20.

Add footnote:

[7] For much of this information reference may be made to Hist. MSS Com., 'Calendar of the Manuscripts of the Dean and Chapter of Wells', Vol. II, 1914.

[8] Fasti I, col. 468.

184   i   **OLCZEWSKA**
Par. 2, ll. 8-10 *should read:*

sang as a guest artist at the Vienna Opera, where her success was so great that she held a permanent place there from 1924 to 1930.

ll. 15-17 *should read:*

Brangäne, Herodias and Waltraute. She took part in the German seasons there each year until 1933, and added to her reputation by a

l. 28 *should read:*

failure. She also appeared at the New York Metropolitan Opera and in Chicago.

186   ii   *Add before* **OLDYS**:

OLDROYD, George (*b*. Healey, Yorkshire, 1 Dec. 1886; *d*. London, 26 Feb. 1951). English musical scholar, conductor, composer and teacher. He studied theory and organ with Eaglefield Hull and the violin with Johann Rasch and Frank Arnold, and took the D. Mus. degree in 1917. He was for a time organist at the English Church in Paris. Having settled in London, he became organist successively of St. Alban's Church, Holborn, and St. Michael's, Croydon. He also became professor at the Trinity College of Music and conductor of the Croydon Bach Society. On the death of Stanley Marchant in 1949 he was appointed King Edward VII Professor of Music at London University. He received the honorary doctorate from the Archbishop of Canterbury (D. Mus. Cantuar). As a composer Oldroyd devoted himself mainly to church music, his most important work being a 'Stabat Mater', and to secular choral music, including a number of part-songs. His book, 'The Technique and Spirit of Fugue: an Historical Study' (Oxford, 1948), is a scholarly and valuable work.

E. B.

187   ii   *Add after* **Oliva**:

OLIVER, ? (*b*. ?; *d*. ?).
English 14th-15th-century composer. He is represented by four works in the 'Old Hall Manuscript'. All are for three voices and in *conductus* style, which may indicate some measure of seniority in the group of composers whose music has been transmitted by this source. The 'Credo' (II, 22) offers additional evidence of an earlier style in its use of major prolation, which is unrelieved except for a section in perfect time at 'Crucifixus'. The two settings of 'Sanctus' (III, 81; III, 86) employ a freely decorated *cantus firmus* in the treble part, the chants being Sarum 2 and 5 respectively. Similarly constructed, but using Sarum 6 is the 'Agnus Dei' (III, 141), which changes its metre for each of the three invocations, ending with a final tripla at 'pacem'. To judge by the r style, these pieces favour a date as early as the last decade of the 14th century. D. W. S.

BIBL.—BUKOFZER, MANFRED, 'Studies in Medieval and Renaissance Music' (New York, 1950).
RAMSBOTHAM, ALEXANDER, 'The Old Hall Manuscript', Vols. II & III (London, 1935 & 1938).

188   i   **OLLONE**
Par. 1, l. 2 *should read*:
1875; *d*. Paris, 15 May, 1959).

ii   Par. 1, l. 7.   1923 *should read*:
1922

l. 8.   George *should read*:
Georges

Add after **OLMEDA**:

OLOFF, Efraim (*b*. nr. Warsaw, 1685; *d*. Toruń, 1735).
German-Polish theologian and musician. He was the son of a Protestant pastor and succeeded his father as minister of the Evangelical Church of the Holy Trinity at Toruń. He wrote a most valuable book, 'Polnische Lieder-Geschichte', which was published after his death at Gdansk (Danzig) in 1744 and has been reissued several times since.

C. R. H.

OLSEN
Par. 1, l. 2.   10 Nov. *should read*:
9 Nov.

Par. 2, ll. 9-10.   Fust Lendermann *should read*:
Just Lindeman

189   i   Par. 2, ll. 8-9 *should read*:
by four grand operas: 'Stig Hvide', 'Stallo', 'Klippeøerne' and 'Lajla', the librettos of which he wrote

189   i   Par. 2, ll. 11-14 *should read*:

(1908). He wrote one oratorio, 'Nidaros', a fairy comedy, 'Svein Uræd', and four large-scale cantatas, 'Ludvig Holberg', 'Griffenfelt', 'Broderbud' and 'Tourist Cantata'.

Add before OLSSON:

OLSEN, (Carl Gustav) Sparre (*b.* Stavanger, 25 Apr. 1903). Norwegian composer. He studied with Fartein Valen, Percy Grainger and at the High School for Music in Berlin. He has been active as music critic and choral conductor at Bergen (1935-39). His compositions include incidental music for the play 'Ane på Torp', works for chorus and orchestra (*e.g.* 'Ver Sanctum'), a Symphony in one movement (1939) and many other orchestral works ('Musikk for orkester', 'Nidarosdomen'), and numerous pianoforte pieces and songs which achieved popularity in Norway.   D. S.-E.

190   i   **ONDŘÍČEK (3)**
Par. 1, l. 2 *should read*:

Apr. 1857; *d.* Milan, 12 Apr. 1922), violinist,

191   i   **ONDŘÍČEK (5)**
l. 2 *should read*:

1882; *d.* Boston, Mass., 30 Dec. 1958), violinist and teacher, brother of the

ONEGIN
Par. 1, l. 1 *should read*:

ONEGIN (Hoffmann), (Elisabeth Elfriede Emilie) Sigrid (*b.* Stockholm, 1 June

l. 2.   1891; *should read*:
1889;

ii   l. 1.   1912 *should read*:
1913

ll. 2-3 *should read*:

Eugene Onegin (1883-1919; actually Lvov, a great-nephew of Lvov who had adopted the name of Pushkin's poem and Tchaikovsky's opera), and in 1920 to a German doctor, Fritz Penzoldt. She was

BIBL. *should read*:

PENZOLDT, F., 'Sigrid Onegin: Leben und Werk' (Magdeburg, 1939; 3rd ed., Neustadt, 1953).

193   ii   **ONSLOW**
Par. 1, l. 3.   1853). *should read*:
1853 [1]).

Add footnote:

[1] Not 1852, as given in many other dictionaries, following an error in 'Le Ménestrel' (1863).

198   ii   **OPERA**
Par. 3, 2 ll. from end.   1606 *should read*:
1607

199   i   Par. 3, ll. 2-28 and
     ii   Par. 1, ll. 1-2 *should read*:

importance took place in 1607 at Mantua. Claudio Monteverdi, *maestro di cappella* to the reigning duke, Vincenzo Gonzaga, produced there his first opera, on the subject of Orpheus and Eurydice, dramatized by a poet now known to have been the younger Alessandro Striggio, not, as had previously been supposed, Poliziano. It was entitled 'La favola d' Orfeo' to distinguish it from Peri's 'Euridice'. The following year Rinuccini prepared for the festival organized on the occasion of the marriage of Francesco Gonzaga with Margherita, Infanta of Savoy, the librettos of two operas, entitled 'Dafne' and 'Arianna', the first of which was set to music by Marco da Gagliano and the second by Monteverdi. Both were written in the *stile rappresentativo* and both were deservedly successful, though not in an equal degree. After the first performance of 'Dafne' we hear of it no more; but 'Arianna' produced an extraordinary effect upon the audience, more especially in the scene in which the forsaken Ariadne bewails the departure of her faithless lover.

Monteverdi was a man of astonishing genius, already famous for the boldness of his innovations in the style of the madrigal. 'La favola d' Orfeo' was in many respects immeasurably superior to any opera that had preceded it.

220   ii   Musical examples. Man töre
            should read:
Man töte

            Par. 2, l. 8.   and 'Der Friedenstag' *should read*:
and 'Friedenstag'

224   i   Par. 4, l. 3.   'Re Enza' *should read*:
'Re Enzo'

227   i   Par. 2, l. 6.   all the characters
            should read:
some of the characters

            Par. 3, ll. 12-13.   'The City of Kitezh' *should read*:
'The Invisible City of Kitezh'

            l. 13.   'The Golden Cockerel' *should read*:
'The Golden Weathercock'

231   i   *Add to* BIBL. (EARLY OPERA):

WOLFF, HELLMUTH CHRISTIAN, 'Die Barockoper in Hamburg', 2 vols. (Wolfenbüttel, 1957).

231　i　*Add to* BIBL. (HISTORY AND AESTHETICS) :
ARUNDELL, DENNIS, ' The [English] Critic at the Opera '
(London, 1957).
KERMAN, JOSEPH, ' Opera as Drama ' (New York, 1956).

ii　BIBL.　l. 37 *should read* :
(Cambridge, 1934 ; 2nd ed., rev., Geneva, 1955).

232　i　BIBL. (RUSSIAN OPERA). ll. 3-5 *should read* :
MOOSER, R. A., ' Annales de la musique et des musiciens
en Russie au XVIIIᵉ siècle ', 3 vols. (Geneva,
1948–51).
' L'Opéra comique français en Russie au XVIIIᵉ
siècle ' (Geneva, 1932, new ed. 1954).

ii　*Add to* BIBL. (PERFORMANCE) :
SKRAUP, SIEGMUND, ' Die Oper als lebendiges Theater '
(Berlin, 1956).

SYNOPSES AND GUIDES
l. 13 *should read* :
1922 ; rev. by the Earl of Harewood, 1954).

Add (2nd work by Newman) :
' More Opera Nights ' (London, 1954).

OPERAS
l. 4. the year 1600 *should read* :
the year 1597

233　i　*Add at top* :
1597 Peri, ' Dafne ', Florence.

ii　1723, Hasse, ' Tigrane ', Naples, *transfer
to* 1729.

234　i　1734, l. 4. ' Livietta e Tracollo ' *should
read* :
' La contadina astuta '

1743, Lampugnani, ' Rossane ', London,
transfer to 1746.

235　i　1781. *Add at end* :
Hopkinson, ' The Temple of Minerva ', Philadelphia.

237　ii　1845. *Add at end* :
Fry, ' Leonora ', Philadelphia.

238　i　1864. *Add at end* :
Fry, ' Notre-Dame de Paris ', Philadelphia.

240　i　1912. *Add at end* :
Damrosch, ' The Dove of Peace ', Philadelphia.

1917. *Add at end* :
Hadley, ' Azora ', Chicago.

1918. *Add at end* :
Hadley, ' Bianca ', New York.

241　i　1934. *Add at end* :
Thomson, ' Four Saints in Three Acts ', Hartford, Conn.

1937. *Add at end* :
Blitzstein, ' The Cradle will Rock ', New York.
Damrosch, ' The Man without a Country ', New York.

1939. *Insert after* Sauguet :
Frazzi, ' Re Lear ', Bologna.

1940. *Insert after* Villa-Lobos :
Sutermeister, ' Romeo und Julia ', Dresden.

241　ii　1941. *Insert before* Blitzstein :
Malipiero, ' Ecuba ', Rome.

1942. *Insert before* Strauss :
Egk, ' Columbus ', Frankfort o/M.
Malipiero, ' I capricci di Callot ', Rome.

Add at end :
Thomson, ' Salomon and Balkis ', New York.

Insert after 1942 :
1943 Malipiero, ' La vita è sogno ', Naples.
Orff, ' Die Kluge ', Frankfort o/M.
Orff, ' Catulli Carmina ', Leipzig.

1944. *Insert after* Bentzon :
Haas, ' Die Hochzeit des Jobs ', Dresden.
Sauguet, ' La Gageure imprévue ', Paris.

1948. *Insert after* Kodály :
Martin, ' Le Vin herbé ', Salzburg.

Insert after Atterberg :
Hartmann (K. A.), ' Des Simplicius Simplicissimus
Jugend ', Cologne.

1949. *Insert after* Pizzetti :
Henze, ' Das Wundertheater ', Berlin.
Petrassi, ' Il Cordovano ', Milan.

1950, Menotti, New York. *should read* :
Philadelphia.

1951. *Insert after* Vaughan Williams :
Křenek, ' Dark Waters ', Los Angeles.

1952. *Insert before* Strauss :
Henze, ' Boulevard Solitude ', Hanover.
Liebermann, ' Leonore 40/45 ', Basel.
Frazzi, ' Don Chisciotte ', Florence.
Castelnuovo-Tedesco, ' Aucassin et Nicolette ', Florence.

1953. *Insert before* Britten :
Pizzetti, ' Cagliostro ', Milan.
Martinů, ' The Marriage ', New York (television).
Orff, ' Trionfo d' Afrodite ', Milan.
Antheil, ' Volpone ', Los Angeles.

Insert after Einem :
Bush, ' Wat Tyler ', Leipzig.

Add at end :
1954 Mortari, ' La figlia del diavolo ', Milan.
Copland, ' The Tender Land ', New York.
Lualdi, ' Il diavolo nel campanile ', Florence.
Liebermann, ' Penelope ', Salzburg.
Britten, ' The Turn of the Screw ', Venice.
Berkeley, ' Nelson ', London.
Delvincourt, ' La Femme à barbe ', Paris.
Walton, ' Troilus and Cressida ', London.
Pizzetti, ' La figlia di Jorio ', Naples.
Fortner, ' Der Wald ', Essen.
Menotti, ' The Saint of Bleecker Street ', New
York.
1955 Milhaud, ' David ', Milan.
Tippett, ' The Midsummer Marriage ', London.
Barraud, ' Numance ', Paris.
Egk, ' Irische Legende ', Salzburg.
Schibler, ' Die Füsse im Feuer ', Zürich.
1956 Martin, ' Der Sturm ', Vienna.
R. Malipiero, ' La donna è mobile ', Milan.
1957 Fortner, ' Die Bluthochzeit ', Cologne.
Hindemith, ' Die Harmonie der Welt ', Munich.
Schoenberg, ' Moses and Aaron ', Zürich.
Poulenc, ' Dialogues des Carmélites ', Milan.
Glukh, ' Denis Davydov ', Leningrad.

1958 Barber, ' Vanessa ', New York.
   Pizzetti, ' Assassinio nella cattedrale ', Milan.
1959 Blomdahl, ' Aniara ', Stockholm.
   Orff, ' Oedipus ', Stuttgart.
   Henze, ' König Hirsch ', Darmstadt.
   Klebe, ' Die tödlichen Wünsche ', Düsseldorf.
1960 Britten, ' A Midsummer Night's Dream ', Alde-
   burgh.

241   ii   *Add before* **OPERNBALL** :

OPERETTA (Ital., little opera, small opera). The term, although Italian, has become universal in a number of variants (*opérette* in French, *Operette* in German, etc.), but is used in the Italian form in English. It denotes opera, or more strictly speaking, comic opera, not necessarily on a small scale as to size, but light in character both in its subject and its music. The element of comedy invariably predominates, but it has room for sentiment (*e.g.* Johann Strauss, jun.), for parody (*e.g.* Offenbach) and for satire (*e.g.* Sullivan). These three composers represent its best period (*c.* 1850–1900) in the three countries in which, thanks to them, the type flourished most artistically: Austria, France and England, in each case mainly in the capitals, Vienna, Paris and London, which remained its chief centres. As *opéra-bouffe* (which indeed was Offenbach's name for it already) it continued most abundantly and attractively in Paris (Audran, Lecocq, Hervé, Messager) ; in London it had some graceful representatives (Sidney Jones, Lionel Monckton, Howard Talbot) and in Vienna some most successful ones towards the end of its best period (Lehár, Leo Fall, Oscar Straus). New York caught up with it just in time to produce some engaging examples (Gershwin, Jerome Kern), but by their time — the early 20th century — it had begun to degenerate into " musical comedy " (Amer. " musicals "), in which plots had become stereotyped and often sentimental, both humour and music were sadly enfeebled, and artistic pretensions were upheld only by increasingly lavish and not often correspondingly tasteful productions which failed to sustain the vitality of operetta as musical species of art.   E. B.

BIBL.—KELLER, O., ' Die Operette in ihrer geschichtlichen Entwicklung ' (Leipzig, 1925).
MACKINLAY, M. STERLING, ' Light Opera ' (London, 1926).
OSTER, LOUIS, ' Les Opérettes du répertoire courant contenant l'analyse de 101 opérettes de 43 compositeurs ' (Paris, 1953).

OPHIBARITON
Add to See RUSSIAN BASSOON :

(*PLATE* 59, Vol. VII, p. 712, No. 8.)

242   i   **OPHICLEIDE**
         Par. 3, l. 11. Vol. II, No. 5 *should read* :

Vol. II, p. 446, No. 5

247   i   **OPIEŃSKI**
         OPERAS
         l. 3 *should read* :
         Poznań, 27 Apr. 1923.

         l. 6 *should read* :
         epilogue, libretto by the Composer, prod. Poznań, 21 Dec. 1927.

      ii   **OPUS**
         Par. 1, l. 7 *should read* :
         but was not used by that master, though to a small extent and erratically by his publishers, nor fully

249   ii   **ORATORIO**
         Par. 2, l. 1.   Giovanni Carissimi *should read* :
         Giacomo Carissimi

250   i   Par. 3, l. 1.   illustrious disciple *should read* :
         illustrious follower

255   i   Par. 2, ll. 40-45 *should read* :
         listeners. Porpora's ' Santa Eugenia ', with its twenty changes of scene in the first act and seventeen in the second, and its three comic characters singing in the Neapolitan dialect, is a *dramma sacro* written for the Naples stage in 1721 ; it is similar to Pergolesi's ' Conversione di San Guglielmo ' mentioned above, and in spite of certain relics of

262   i   *Add to* BIBL. :
         MASSENKEIL, GÜNTHER, ' Die oratorische Kunst in den lateinischen Historien und Oratorien Giacomo Carissimis ' (Mainz, 1952).

278   i   **ORCHESTRATION**
         Add to BIBL. :
         PARROTT, IAN, ' Method in Orchestration ' (' Student's Music Library ' series) (London, 1957).
         PISTON, WALTER, ' Orchestration ' (New York, 1955).
         READ, GARDNER, ' Thesaurus of Orchestral Devices ' (London, 1953).

      ii   **ORD**
         Par. 3, l. 20 *should read* :
         and use. In 1958 the order of C.B.E. was bestowed on him.   H. C. C. (adds.).

279   ii   **ORDA-WDOWCZAK**
         Par. 2, ll. 11-12.   the first prize *should read* :
         a diploma.

         l. 22 *should read* :
         woman and domiciled in London, where he has appeared at the Sadler's Wells Opera.

282   i   **ORFF**
         Add to BIBL. :
         HELM, EVERETT, ' Carl Orff ' (M.Q., XLI, 1955, p. 285).

KIEKERT, INGEBORG, ' Die musikalische Form in den Werken Carl Orff's ' (Ratisbon, 1957).
LIESS, ANDREAS, ' Carl Orff: Idee und Werk ' (Zürich, 1955).
WÖRNER, KARL, ' Egk and Orff ' (M. Rev., XIV, 1953, p. 186).

282   i   OPERAS
            l. 15 *should read*:

teatro mágico ', prod. Munich, 20 Oct. 1953.

Add at end:

' Oedipus ', Sophocles, trans. Hölderlin, prod. Stuttgart, May 1959.

298   i   **ORGAN**
            Par. 7, l. 17.   Henry Loosemore
            should read:

John Loosemore

315   ii   Fig. 24.   Under illustration *should read*:

Fig. 24 [1]

Add footnote:

[1] For further illustrations *see* TUNING, Vol. VIII, pp. 593-94.

324   i   Par. 2, l. 1.   In 1901 *should read*:

In 1930

335   ii   *Add at end*:

(*PLATES* 33, Vol. IV, p. 496, No. 1; 43, Vol. VI, Frontispiece; 47, Vol. VI, p. 288, Nos. 2 & 3.)

336   ii   BIBL. (CONTINENTAL WORKS)
            l. 44 *should read*:

1938; 4th ed., Cassel & Basel, 1953).

345   ii   **ORGAN PLAYING**
            Par. 3, l. 9.   the exception of C ♯
            should read:

the exception of G♯

350   i   **ORGAN STOPS**
            Add after Par. 4:

BAARPIJP.—A Dutch word not synonymous with the German *Bärpfeife*, being derived from the Dutch *baar*—peasant. It is a Gemshorn (*i.e.* tapered flute) stop. There is an 8-ft. example in the organ in the church of St. Bavo, Haarlem (Muller).

            Par. 5, l. 1.   BARPFEIFE *should read*:

BÄRPFEIFE

            l. 4 *should read*:

16th- and 17th-century organs.

            Delete ll. 5-6.

351   ii   *Add after* Par. 4:

COPULA.—An 8-ft. flute stop specified by Mozart in his Church Sonatas K. 244 and 245.

" Copula " is always a coupler, *i.e.* a mechanical device, but *Koppel*, *Coppel* or *Copel*, though they may mean a coupler, are more generally stops of baroque and rococo organs (1620–1780). The stop was spindle-shaped and had a small orifice at the top. Its tone was neutral but not uninteresting. It was used for blending with other tones, *e.g.* as a basis for building tonal pyramids with mutation stops, to support the tone of slow gambas, etc., and binding other raw tones together. Mozart no doubt used it in his church sonatas for organ and strings because it blends admirably with string tone.

358   i   *Add after* Par 5:

Originally the word " sesquialtera " meant " one to one-and-a-half " or a 2: 3 ratio, or " one and a smaller one ". But later it was often corrupted into " sexquialtera " to stress the interval of a sixth between the nazard and the tierce.

360   ii   *Add to* BIBL.:

GEER, EZRA HAROLD, ' Organ Registration in Theory and Practice ' (Glen Rock, N.J., 1957).

361   i   **ORGANISTRUM**
            Add to See HURDY-GURDY.:

(*PLATE* 48, Vol. VI, p. 538, No. 3.)

362   ii   **ORGENI**
            Par. 1, l. 2.   St. Jorgen *should*
            read:

St. Jörgen

            l. 3 *should read*:

Hungary, 17 Dec. 1841; *d.* Vienna, 15 Mar. 1926).

            Par. 2, l. 1 *should read*:

Austrian soprano singer. Her father was an Austrian officer stationed in Hungary at the time of her birth. She was a pupil

383   ii   **ORNAMENTATION**
            Add to BIBL.:

ALDRICH, PUTNAM, ' Bach's Ornamentation ' (New York, 1950).

384   i   BIBL. l. 4 *should read*:

1907; 2nd ed. 1953).

            Add to BIBL.:

GEORGII, WALTER, ' Die Verzierungen in der Musik: Theorie und Praxis ' (Zürich & Freiburg i/B., 1957).
SCHMITZ, HANS-PETER, ' Die Kunst der Verzierung im 18. Jahrhundert ' (Cassel & Basel, 1955).

387   ii   **ORNAMENTS**
            Par. 3, ll. 1-2 *should read*:

Grassineau's signs in his ' Dictionary ' of 1740 give the same, cribbed from Prelleur; his terms (by then perhaps

416   ii   Par. 5, l. 6 *should read*:

other languages (Ital. *passaggio, gorgia, minuta*; Span.

433   i   Par. 3, l. 12 *should read*:

shows it (at second hand) as a mordent; Geminiani (' Art of

436   i   Musical examples, stave 6 *should read*:

439   ii   l. 23.   Glosa, D *should read*:
C

         l. 24.   Gorgia, D *should read*:
C

448   ii   Bibl., l. 48.   (Bologna, 1773) *should read*: (Bologna, 1723)

449   i   **ORNITHOPARCUS**
        Par. 2, l. 13 *should read*:

by John Dowland (London, 1606). A modern facsimile reprint is to be published in ' Documenta Musicologica ', Vol. 24.

        ORNSTEIN
        Par. 4, l. 6.   Paul Rosenfeld *should read*:
David Ewen

Add to Bibl. :

Ewen, David, ' Ornstein ', in ' Composers of Today ' (New York, 1934).
Martens, F. H., ' Leo Ornstein: The Man, His Ideas, His Work ' (New York, 1917).

450   i   **ORPHARION**
        Add to See also:

(*PLATE* 69, Vol. VIII, p. 146 (iv), No. 3.)

453   i   **ORR, Robin**
        Par. 2, l. 13 *should read*:

took his Mus. B. in 1932, his M.A. in 1938 and his Mus. D. in 1950.

        Par. 3, l. 5 *should read*:

St. John's College, Cambridge, from which he resigned in 1951. During the

        l. 10 *should read*:

College. From 1950 to 1956 he taught at the R.C.M. in London, and at present occupies the Chair of Music in the University of Glasgow.

453   i   *Delete* Par. 4 *and*
    ii   Par. 1, *and replace by*:

CATALOGUE OF WORKS

INCIDENTAL MUSIC

' Oedipus at Colonus ' (Sophocles) for men's voices & orch. (1950).

RADIO INCIDENTAL MUSIC

The ' Winter's Tale ' (Shakespeare) for chamber orch. (1947).
' Deirdre of the Sorrows ' (Synge) for full orch. (1951).

CHORAL WORKS

' They shall put their trust in the Lord ' for S.A.T.B. (1946).
Festival Te Deum for chorus & orch. or organ (1950).
' Bessie Bell ', Scots song for S.A.T.B. (1951).
Te Deum and Jubilate, C ma., for chorus & organ (1953).
' I was glad ' for S.A.T.B. (1955).
' Spring Cantata ' for mezzo-sop., chorus, stgs., pf. & percussion (1955).
' Colin's Cattle ', Scots song for S.A.T.B.

ORCHESTRAL WORKS

Overture ' The Prospect of Whitby ' (1948).
Italian Overture for woodwind, harpsichord & stgs. (1953).
Rhapsody for stg. orch. (1956).

MUSIC FOR BRASS

2 Fanfares for 4 natural E♭ trumpets (1949).

CHAMBER MUSIC

3 ' Songs of Innocence ' (William Blake) for voice & stg. 4tet (1929).
Prelude and Fugue for stg. 4tet (1934, rev. 1946).
3 Latin Psalms for voice & stg. 4tet (1939).
Serenade for stg. trio (1948).
4 ' Romantic Songs ' (Medieval Latin and Helen Waddell) for tenor, oboe & stg. 4tet (1949).
3 ' Pastorals ' (Mary Webb) for soprano, flute, viola & pf. (1951).
Duo for vn. & cello (1953).

ONE INSTRUMENT AND PIANOFORTE

Sonatina for cello & pf. (1938, rev. 1948).
Sonatina for vn. & pf. (1941).
Sonata for viola & pf. (1947).
' Sicilienne and Chaconne ' for viola & pf. (1949).
Serenade for horn & pf. (1951).
Sonata for violin & clavier (1956).

ORGAN MUSIC

' Toccata alla marcia ' (1937, rev. 1947).
Three Preludes on Scottish Psalm Tunes (1958).

SONGS

3 Chinese Songs (trans. Arthur Waley) (1943).
' A Lament ' & ' Drinking Song ' (Helen Waddell, from the Chinese) (1945).
' Hot Cake ' (Arthur Waley, from the Chinese) (1947).
' Cupid enchain'd' (17th cent.), unaccomp. (1951).
' My true love hath my heart ' (Philip Sidney) (1952).
7 Scots Songs, arranged (1954).

455   i   **ORTIZ, Diego**
        See also. l. 1 *should read*:

See also Divisions. Eslava (modern reprints). Narváez. Ruggiero (treatment of

456   i   **OSBORN**
        Par. 1, l. 1.   1905). *should read*:

1905; *d.* Basel, 8 June 1955).

460   ii   *Add after* **Ostrovsky**:

OSTROWSKI, Feliks (*b.* Kraśnik nr. Lublin, 3 Jan. 1802; *d.* Warsaw, 14 Nov. 1860).

Polish pianist and composer. He studied with the Abbé Lubaczewski at Kraśnik and later under Würfel at the Warsaw Conservatory. Many of his unpublished pianoforte compositions are lost, among them a ' Grande Sonate ' as well as mazurkas and nocturnes; but some works published in his lifetime and in manuscript have survived. They include 3 Polonaises and an ' Adagio and Rondo ' for pianoforte.

Of Ostrowski's five children his daughter Teodozja (married name Sewenar) (1852–1905) became an opera singer in Warsaw, and his fourth son, Józef (1858–1905), a composer of many ' Romances ' for pianoforte and songs.   C. R. H.

462   i   **OTAÑO Y EGUINO**
Par. 1, l. 2.   1880). *should read*:

1880; *d.* San Sebastián, 29 Apr. 1957).

463   ii   **OTHMAYR**
Par. 1, l. 3.   7 Feb. *should read*:
4 Feb.

Par. 2, l. 6.   Heilbronn. *should read*:

Heilsbronn.[1]

l. 15.   songs [1] *should read*:
songs [2]

Add footnote:
[1] Moser, in his ' Musiklexikon ', expressly says " nicht Heilbronn ! ".

Footnote 1 *becomes* 2.

Add at end, before BIBL.:
See also Denkmäler (5) I, Vol. 16 (modern ed. of ' Symbola ').

464   i   **OTT**
Add at end:
See also Publikationen G.M.F., Vols. 1-4 (modern reprint of ' Liederbuch ').

467   i   **Ouida**
l. 2 *should read*:
(' Mosharózsa ', opera). Mascagni (' Lodoletta ,' opera). Missa (' Muguette ', opera).

472   i   **Owen, Wilfred**
l. 1.   *Add at end*:
Britten (' Nocturne ', No. 6).

473   i   **OXFORD**
Add after Par. 3:

The Oxford Harmonic Society, conducted by G. A. Thewlis, M.A., is the second-largest choral society in the city and has done much to give unfamiliar and new works a hearing.

z

474   ii   Par. 4, l. 15.   (1949) *should read*:
1949 (spring). ' Much Ado About Nothing ' (Stanford).
1949 (autumn). ' Iphigenia in Tauris ' (Gluck).

Add at end of paragraph:
1954. ' Macbeth ' (Verdi).
1955. ' The Fair Maid of Perth ' (Bizet).
1956. ' The Secret ' (Smetana).
1957. ' Ernani ' (Verdi).
1958.{' Oedipus Rex ' (Stravinsky), in Latin.
     {' L'Enfant et les sortilèges ' (Ravel), in French.

Add at end, before See also:
BIBL.—CARPENTER, NAN COOKE, ' The Study of Music at the University of Oxford in the Renaissance (1450–1600) ' (M.Q., XLI, 1955, p. 191).

475   i   **OXFORD UNIVERSITY PRESS**
Par. 1, l. 1.   15 *should read*:
House. In 1947 plans for ' The New Oxford History of Music ', to be published in ten Volumes under the general editorship of Professor J. A. Westrup, began to materialize and by 1959 Vols. I and II had appeared.

ii   *Add before* **Ozaneaux**:
OYSTRAKH, David Feodorovich.   *See* OISTRAKH.

OZIMIŃSKI
Par. 1, l. 2 *should read*:
1877; *d.* Warsaw, 1945).

477   ii   **PACCHIONI**
Add at end:
BIBL.—RONCAGLIA, GINO, ' La cappella musicale del duomo di Modena ' (Florence, 1957).

479   i   **PACHELBEL, Johann**
Add to BIBL.:
EGGEBRECHT, H. H., ' Johann Pachelbel als Vokalkomponist ' (Trossingen, 1954).

481   ii   **PADBRUÉ, Cornelis**
Par. 2.   *Add after* l. 11:
He also wrote music for Vondel's ' Kruisbergh '.

Add at end:
See also Vereniging, Vol. 42 (reprint of ' Kruisbergh ')

PADBRUÉ, David
l. 1 *should read*:
PADBRUÉ (Pabbruwe [1]), David P. (*b.* ? ; *d.* ?).

Add footnote:
[1] As spelt by his present-day descendants in Holland.

483   ii   **PADEREWSKI**
Par. 3, l. 11.   LL.D. *should read*:
D.C.L.

484   i   *Add to* BIBL.:
KELLOGG, CHARLOTTE, ' Paderewski ' (New York, 1956).

489   i   *Add after* **PAESIELLO** :

PAGANI, Alfonso (*b.* ? ; *d.* ?, *c.* 1629). Italian violinist and composer. He went to Poland in 1604 and became a member of the royal chapel at Cracow and later in Warsaw. His 8-part motet ' Confirmatum est cor virginis ' was published in Lilius's collection ' Melodiae sacrae ' at Cracow in 1604. No other works of his are known.

C. R. H.

493   ii   **PAGANINI**
Add to BIBL. :
COURCY, GERALDINE I. C. DE, ' Paganini, the Genoese ' (Norman, Oklahoma, 1957).

494   i   CATALOGUE
Op. 14, ll. 1-2.   ' Barccaba ' *should read* :
' Barucabà '

495   ii   **PAINE**
Par. 2, l. 3.   Hermann Kretschmar
should read :

Hermann Kotzschmar

497   i   **PAISIBLE, L. H.**
Par. 1, l. 2 *should read* :

d. St. Petersburg, 30 Mar. 1782 [3]).

Par. 2, l. 11 *should read* :

Petersburg, where he arrived in Oct. 1778, where he settled for the rest of his life and where

l. 14 *should read* :

Catherine. The story goes that owing to the intrigues

l. 17 *should read* :

were frustrated ; but Lolli had left Russia in 1777, before Paisible's arrival, and on his return in 1780 the latter had had plenty of time to establish himself. He does not, however, seem to have succeeded. Two public concerts which

Add footnote :
[3] Documentary evidence for this date is given by Mooser, ' Annales de la musique . . . en Russie au XVIIIᵉ siècle '.

BIBL.   l. 1 *should read* :

BIBL.—MOOSER, ALOYS, ' Annales de la musique et des musiciens en Russie au XVIIIᵉ siècle ' (Geneva, 1950, Vol. II, pp. 274-78).
' Les Infortunes et la fin tragique

PAISIELLO
Par. 1, l. 2 *should read* :

Taranto, 9 May [4] 1740 ; *d.* Naples, 5 June 1816).
Add footnote :
[4] According to the certificate of baptism quoted by Della Corte (*see* Bibl.).

ii   Par. 1, l. 11.   Contumacci *should read* :

Cotumacci

498   i   Par. 1, l. 1 *should read* :

some of his best music. The libretto, based on Voltaire's ' Candide ', was by Giovanni Battista Casti, and its subject is the adventurer Baron Theodor Neuhoff, who was king of Corsica for a few months in 1736. Mozart was present at the first performance of the opera at the Vienna Burg Theatre on 23 Aug. 1784. After Paisiello's return to

499   ii   *See also.* l. 4 *should read* :

Tulipano '). Cimarosa (rivalry). Classici Musica Italiana, Vol. 20 (extracts from ' Nina '). Dussek J. L., vars.

501   ii   **PALAU**
Add to BIBL. :
LEÓN TELLO, FRANCISCO JOSÉ, ' La obra pianística de Manuel Palau ' (Valencia, 1956).

502   i   HEADING, PÁLENICEK *should read* :
PÁLENÍČEK

PALÉOGRAPHIE MUSICALE
Add after Vol. XV :
XVI. ' L'Antiphonaire du Mont-Renaud ', facsimiles 185-92.

504   ii   **PALERMO**
Add to BIBL. :
TIBY, OTTAVIO, ' Il Real Teatro carolino e l' ottocento musicale palermitano ' (Florence, 1957).

PALESTER
Par. 3, l. 5 *should read* :
Concertino (written for the Warsaw I.S.C.M. Festival, but not performed) ;

508   ii   **PALESTRINA**
Par. 2, l. 2.   1570 *should read* :
1571

512   i   Par. 2, l. 5.   19th century *should read* :
17th century

Par. 3, l. 14.   Murcelli *should read* :
Marcelli

515   —   CATALOGUE
Col. 1, l. 5 *should read* :
Aeterna Christi Munera.

l. 32 *should read* :
Illumina oculos meos.[5]

l. 55 *should read* :
Missa secunda.

Col. 2, l. 31 (Hodie) *should read* :
S.A.T.B., S.A.T.B.

l. 47 (Missa secunda) *should read* :
S.A.T.T.B.

Col. 3, l. 8.   (re-edition 1596) *should read* :
1596.

515 — CATALOGUE
1593–94.

Col. 3, l. 17. 1594. *should read*:

1593–94.

l. 18. 1594. *should read*:

1595.

ll. 28–30 *should read*:

1593–94.

l. 32. 1594. *should read*:

1590.

l. 37. 1509. *should read*:

1593–94.

l. 39. 1594. *should read*:

1582.

l. 45 (Missa secunda) *should read*:

Delete (*see* Primi toni).

Add the following in alphabetical order :

Beate Marie Virg. I.	*a* 5.
Beate Marie Virg. II.	*a* 5.
Beate Marie Virg. III.	*a* 5.
Benedicta es.	*a* 6.
Christus resurgens.	*a* 4.
Dominicalis (authenticity disputed).	*a* 5.
In duplicibus minoribus, I.	*a* 5.
In duplicibus minoribus, II.	*a* 5.
In festis Apostolorum, I.	*a* 5.
In semiduplicibus maioribus, I.	*a* 5.
In semiduplicibus maioribus, II.	*a* 5.
Missa quinta toni.	*a* 6.

MS.		
MS.		
MS.		
MS.		
MS.		
1592.		
MS.		
MS.		
MS.		
MS.		
MS.		
1600.		

Footnote 5. In the 1595 edition this Mass
was given *should read*:

⁵ This Mass was also given

516 — Col. 1, l. 15 *should read*:
Primi toni.

l. 34. Sine titulo (Missa). *should read*:
Sine titulo (Io mi son giovinetta).

Delete (Missa secunda)

1591.

Col. 3, l. 13. 1554 *should read*:

1593–94.

l. 15. 1594 *should read*:

1590.

l. 26. (re-edition 1596). *should read*:

MS.

Between ll. 27 & 28 *insert* :

Add the following MASSES *in alphabetical order* :

Quando lieta speravi.	*a* 5.
Sine nomine (a voci mutate).	*a* 4.

525   i   *See also.* ll. 1-2 *should read*:

See also Arcadelt (influence). Classici Musica Italiana, Vol. 21 (modern ed. of canzonets & madrigals). Colombani (ded. of Psalms). Denkmäler (1), Vol. I (modern ed. of motets). Guidetti (collab. in ' Directorium chori ').

529   i   **PALM**
      Par. 2, l. 13. sätta *should read*:
satta

530   i   **PALMER, Henry**
      Par. 1.   d. ?) *should read*:
d. ? Durham, ?).

530   i   Par. 2, l. 1 *should read*:

English 16th–17th-century composer. He became a lay clerk at Durham Cathedral between 1617 and 1628. On 7 May 1628 a Chapter Act (partially reproduced in Nicholson, ' Quires and Places ', p. 46) decreed that he or " such others as . . . shalbe thought meete from tyme to tyme " should have charge of the choristers in place of Richard Hutchinson. In 1631 his stipend was increased by £6 per annum, and it would thus seem that his service had been found satisfactory. He was still at Durham in 1636, and was described as a " lay singingman " on 14 Apr. 1638, when the burial of his son was recorded.

l. 2 *should read*:

Some of Palmer's work was included in the Durham choir-

Signature should read:

J. M. (ii), adds. W. K. F.

PALMER, Robert (ii)
Add at bottom of col. :

' The Trojan Women ' (Euripides) for women's chorus, wind & perc. (1955).
' Slow, slow, fresh fount ' (Ben Jonson) for unaccomp. chorus (1953).
Symphony No. 1 (1953).

ii   List of Works
     l. 3 *should read*:

' K. 19 ', symph. elegy for orch. (1945).

1600.		
MS.		

ll. 11 to end *should read*:

String Quartet No. 2 (1943–47).
String Quartet No. 3 (1954).
Chamber Concerto for vn., oboe & stg. 4tet (1949).
Quartet for stgs. & pf. (1947).
Quintet for stgs. & pf. (1950).
Quintet for wind insts. (1951).
Quintet for clar., stgs. & pf. (1952).
Sonata for vn. & pf. (1942).
Sonata for viola & pf. (1951).
Pf. Sonata No. 1 (1938-46).
3 Preludes for pf. (1941).
Pf. Sonata No. 2 (1942-48).
Sonata for pf. duet (1952).
Sonata for 2 pfs. (1944).
2 Songs (Walt Whitman) (1940).

Add at end :

BIBL.—AUSTIN, WILLIAM, ' The Music of Robert Palmer ' (M.Q., XLII, Jan. 1956, p. 35).

534　i　**PANDERO**
l. 1. Heyse's *should read*:
Geibel's

PANDIATONI(CI)SM
Par. 5, l. 4. A.B.D.F., etc. *should read*:
G.B.D.F., etc.

ii　*Add before* **PANDOURA**:

PANDORA (Bandora, Bandore). In western Europe the name denotes a bass instrument of the guitar family, with wire strings. The neck is fretted in semitones, the belly and back are flat, and the outline of the body is scalloped. Very few specimens of the instrument are known to have survived; an illustration of Canon Galpin's 17th-century example will be found on PLATE 69 (Vol. VIII, following p. 146). The earliest reference to the instrument appears to be in the stage directions for Gascoigne's tragedy of 'Jocasta' (1566), and it does not seem to have outlived the 17th century. The earliest tuning, used in Barley's 'New Booke of Tabliture' (1596) and Morley's 'Consort Lessons' (1599), is C, D, G, c, e, a, all courses consisting of a pair of unison strings. Later a seventh pair was added, tuned to G,.

Its function in music-making was primarily to provide a richly sonorous continuo part, either as an accompaniment to the voice (Barley) or as part of a broken consort (Morley), and many musicians seem to have considered it superior to the harpsichord for this purpose. Pepys mentions its use for continuo playing as late as 1662 — " musique (with a bandore for the base) did give me a levett " — and it was a standard instrument in many English town bands and theatrical companies of the 17th century. About one hundred solos for the pandora occur in English lute manuscripts of the period 1540 to 1620. There is little or no evidence for its use on the continent of Europe, despite its mention in the preface of Agazzari's 'Del suonare il basso . . .' (1607) in a list of continuo instruments and its inclusion by Praetorius in his 'Syntagma' (1619). Giustiniani, writing in 1628, used the name to refer to a kind of theorbo-lute,

with many strings added in the bass and at the top, and, between these, others of brass or silver; so that because of the great range and the number of strings, you can play any perfect composition exquisitely, with an advantage over other instruments in the tremolo and in playing softly and loudly.

He named the Piccinino brothers as particularly expert on the instrument; it may have been the same as the English pandora, but it is more likely to have been a kind of archcittern.[1]

Some account of the oriental instrument

[1] *See* CITTERN.

from which the pandora ultimately derived will be found elsewhere.[2] A possible medieval ancestor is shown on PLATE 22 (Vol. III, facing p. 848). Panofsky's book (*see* Bibl.) enables one to hear some of the overtones that the instrument's name must have sounded in the ears of contemporary society.

R. T. D.

BIBL.—DART, T., 'The Cittern and its English Music' (' Galpin Society Journal ', I, pp. 46-63).
FORTUNE, N., 'Giustiniani on Instruments' (*ibid.*, V, pp. 48-54).
LUMSDEN, D., 'The Sources of English Lute Music (1540–1620) ', (*ibid.*, VI, pp. 20-21: English lute manuscripts containing bandora music are listed).
PANOFSKY, D. & E., 'Pandora's Box: the Changing Aspects of a Mythical Symbol' (London, 1956).

(*PLATES* 22, Vol. III, p. 848, No. 3; 69, Vol. VIII, p. 146 (iv), No. 2.)

[2] *See* PERSIAN MUSIC. TAMBURA.

536　i　**PANDURINA**
Add at end of line:
(*PLATE* 42, Vol. V, p. 432, No. 2.)

ii　**PANIZZA**
Par. 1, l. 7.　(nine consecutive
should read:
(eight consecutive

l. 12 *should read*:
Toscanini, of the Scala Theatre in Milan. He was chief conductor at the New York Metropolitan Opera in 1934–42, succeeding Tullio Serafin, but returned to the Scala for 1946–48.

538　ii　**PANPIPES**
Add at end:
See also Illustration, p. 282; PLATE 48.

542　i　**PANUFNIK**
Par. 2, l. 20 *should read*:
(Paris). In 1954 he settled in England with his British-born wife.

Add at end of Par. 2 :
In 1957 he succeeded Rudolf Schwarz as conductor and musical director of the City of Birmingham Orchestra.

PANUFNIK, Tomasz
Par. 1, l. 2 *should read*:
1874; *d.* Warsaw, 18 Sept. 1951).

ii　**PANZÉRA**
Par. 1, l. 2.　Geneva, *should read*:
Hyères[1],
Par. 2, l. 1.　Swiss baritone *should read*:
French or Swiss baritone

Add footnote :
[1] Geneva, according to some sources.

543   **PAPANDOPULO**
        Par. 1, l. 1.   Zagreb, *should read* :
Honef o/Rhine,

545   ii   **PARADISI**
            Add at end :
See also Classici Musica Italiana, Vol. 22 (modern ed.
of sonatas).

553   ii   **PARIS**
            Add to BIBL. :
LEJEUNE, ANDRÉ & WOLF, STÉPHANIE, 'Les Quinzes
   Salles de l'Opéra de Paris, 1669–1955' (Paris,
   1955).

555   i   **PARKER, Horatio**
           Par. 1, l. 3.   Cederhurst *should*
                read :
Cedarhurst

556   ii   **PARKER**
            List of Works
            Op. 16 *should read* :
16. ' Normannenzug ' for unaccomp. chorus.[1]

            Op. 69 *should read* :
69. ' The Norsemen's Raid ' for men's chorus & organ.[2]

            Add footnotes :
[1] Identical with Op. 69 (English edition).
[2] Identical with Op. 16 (German edition).

559   i   **PARMET**
           Par. 2, l. 19 *should read* :
Sibelius's symphonies. A work containing
close analyses of these appeared in Swedish
at Helsingfors in 1955, entitled ' Sibelius
Symfonier : en studie i musikförståelse '.

561   i   **PARROTT**
           Par. 3.   *Add after* l. 11 :
Solemn Overture to Shakespeare's ' Romeo
and Juliet ' ;

            Add at end :
BIBL.—REDLICH, H. F., 'A New Welsh Folk Opera'
   (M. & L., XXXVII, 1956, p. 101).

568   i   *Add before* **Parsons, Theophile** :

PARSONS, Robert (*b.* ? Exeter, ? ; *d.*
Exeter, 1676).
English composer. He is unconnected with
the preceding, of whom there are no working
records at Exeter, although he was born
there. He became a lay vicar and priest
vicar of Exeter Cathedral in 1619. The
Chapter Act Book for 1607–28 (D. and C.
Exeter MS 3553, f. 83v.) records on 19 June,
after his nomination :

Mr. Lugge on behalf of the Custos and College of
Vicars came and affirmed that the answer of the Vicars
touching Robert Parsons was that the Major parte of
the vicars were against him, and thought him not fitt
for a Countertenor. Afterwards the said President and
Chapter decreed the said Parsons to be installed. . . .

He seems to have been able to leave his duties
for considerable periods.   An entry on 4 Nov.
1620 (*ibid.*, f. 92) says :

Item they gave leave to Robert Parsons to be absent
from the Service of the Quire between this and Christmas next in regard of his business in Lawe this term in
London.

And again on 29 Jan. 1628 (*ibid.*, 1622–30,
f. 100) : " Leave granted to Mr. Parson for
6 months business ".   Perhaps he was liti-
ginous and quarrelsome : the following note
of 1622 indicates a difference with Edward
Gibbons : " It. payed for beer when Mr.
Parsons reconsiled himself to Mr. Gibbons ".
Parsons also became rector of St. Martin's
Church, Exeter, and Custos of the College of
Vicars Choral.
Much of the music composed by this
Robert Parsons has been wrongly ascribed to
his elder namesake.   Probably all the verse
anthems are by him.   S. J.

568   ii   **PARSONS (i)**
            Par. 1, l. 18 *should read* :
work. The tenor part of an anthem, ' Remem-
ber not, O Lord ', ascribed to him, is in the
Gloucester part-books.
                        E. B., adds. W. K. F.
            Add to BIBL. :
FORD, WYN K., ' Concerning William Parsons ' (M. &
   L., XXXVII, 1956, p. 333).

571   ii   **PARTHENIA INVIOLATA**
            Add at end :
BIBL.—BRENNECKE, ERNEST, ' " Parthenia Inviolata " ' :
   the Second Book of Keyboard Music printed in
   England ' (Mus. T., LXXV, 1934, p. 701).

572   ii   **PASCHE**
            Par. 2, l. 11 *should read* :
of Richard III's enemies.   In 1513 he was a
member of the Fraternity of St. Nicholas in
London ; in 1517 the Bede Roll of the
Fraternity records the death of his wife
Embryth.   In 1515 a " Mr. Passhe of London " had the " over syght " of the new
organs of Kingston-on-Thames parish church,
and this was probably the composer.   He
was clerk of St. Peter West Cheap in 1528.
Nothing more is

573   i   **Pascoli**
           l. 1.   *See* Pannain *should read* :
See Gandino (songs).   Pannain

574   ii   *Add after* **PASPY** :
PASQUA, Giuseppe (*b.* ? ; *d.* ?).
Italian 18th-century composer.   He went
to Poland and was engaged at the theatre of
the Primate of Poland in Warsaw between
1769 and 1775.   He produced there an
opérette-bouffe, ' A qui mieux ' (1769) and
wrote a cantata, ' Per pace signata ' (1775).
                        C. R. II.

575   i   PASQUINI
Par. 2, l. 14 *should read* :

Queen Christina of Sweden, for whose Rome
Academy of 1687 he wrote music which was
conducted by Corelli.   He was also in the

577   ii   *Add before* PASSHE :
PASSET, ? (*b.* ? Tours, ? ; *d.* ?).
French 15th-century composer.   His biography is unknown, but the Oxford manuscript (Bodl. Can. misc. 213) bears, added to
his name, the words " de tornaco " (of Tours),
albeit in a later hand.   He has left two compositions, both Rondeaux.   The first, ' Se vous
scaviés ', occurs in a Strasbourg manuscript
under the name Cesaris, but the much more
authoritative Bologna manuscript as well as
the style confirm the attribution to Passet.   The
second, ' Si me fault faire departie ', is slightly
damaged because it occurs at the bottom of
the last page of the Oxford manuscript, but
it is interesting since its text obviously accounts
for its position in the codex.   Both works are
three-voice compositions with text in the
cantus only, which is supported by the usual
accompanying *tenor* and *contratenor*.   The first
piece is published with the complete works of
Cesaris in Vol. I of ' Early Fifteenth-Century
Music ', edited by Gilbert Reaney (Amer.
Inst. of Musicology, 1955) and the second in
Vol. II of the same series (1959).

                                             G. R. (iii).

586   ii   PASSION MUSIC
Add to BIBL. :

FISCHER, KURT VON, ' Zur Geschichte der Passions-
komposition des 16. Jahrhunderts in Italien '
(A.f.M., XI, 3, p. 189).

587   i   *Add to* BIBL. :
SMALLMAN, BASIL, ' The Background of Passion Music :
J. S. Bach and his Predecessors ' (London, 1957).

594   ii   PATZAK
Par. 3, l. 17 *should read* :

after the second world war (1946), and he
appeared on the stage there, at Covent
Garden, several times from 1947.   He is also

596   ii   PAULLET
Par. 2, l. 4 *should read* :

Dannemann.   His extant work is published
in Vol. II of ' Early Fifteenth-Century Music ',
edited by Gilbert Reaney (Amer. Inst. of
Musicology, 1959).   E. D. (ii).

597   i   PAULSON, List of Works
l. 11.   ostgötarapsodi *should read* :
östgötarapsodi

**601   i   Page Heading, PAVESI, *should
read* :**
PAVESE

601   *Add before* PAVESI :
Pavese, Cesare.   *See* Nono (' Terra e compagna ').

ii   PAVESI
Add at end :

On 1 Dec. 1810 the Teatro San Carlo at
Naples produced ' Odoardo e Cristina ',
to a libretto by Giovanni Schmidt, based on
Scribe, which was adapted by Tottola and
Aldobrandini in 1819, renamed ' Eduardo e
Cristina ', for a pasticcio by Rossini.

604   i   PEARSALL
Add to BIBL. :
HUNT, EDGAR, ' Robert Lucas Pearsall ' (Proc. Roy.
Mus. Ass., Vol. LXXXII, 1955–56).

609   ii   PEDERSØN
Add at end :
See also Chorwerk, Vol. 35 (reprint of Italian madri-
gal).

611   ii   PEDROTTI
Par. 1, l. 2.   1892 *should read* :
1893

613   i   PEERSON
Par. 6, l. 6.   Verstegan the elder.
should read :
Verstegan (*c.* 1550–1640).

ii   *Add before* CATALOGUE :
BIBL.—WAILES, MARYLIN, ' Martin Peerson ' (Proc.
Roy. Mus. Ass., Vol. LXXX, 1953–54).

614   ii   PEETERS
Par. 2, l. 14 *should read* :

Concertos for organ and orchestra (Op. 52)
and for pianoforte and orchestra (Op. 74) ;

l. 17 *should read* :

organ ; chamber music including a Trio for
woodwind, a Suite for 4 trombones and a
' Lay ' for violin, cello and pianoforte ; a
Suite for orchestra and many pianoforte

l. 20 *should read* :

grégorien ' and ' Ars organi ', a complete
technical and aesthetic organ method in 3
parts and 4 languages.
                                      H. A. & A. L. C.

615   ii   PELEMANS
Par. 4.   *Add before* l. 1 :

Chamber opera ' La Rose de Bakawali ' (lib. by A.
Lepage).
Chamber opera ' Le Combat de la vierge et du diable '
(lib. by J. Weterings) (1949).
Opera ' De Mannen van Smeerop ' (lib. by P. S. M.
Kröjer) (1952).

l. 1 *should read* :

Ballet ' Miles Gloriosus ' (1945).

615 ii List of Works
l. 8 *should read:*
Oratorio ' Floris en Blancefloer '.

Add after l. 8 :
7 Symphonies.

Add after l. 9 :
Concerto for orch.
3 Concertinos for chamber orch.

l. 11 *should read:*
2 pf. Concertos.

616 i l. 1 *should read:*
Concerto for harpsichord & orch.

l. 2 *should read:*
5 String Quartets.

l. 7 *should read:*
16 Sonatas for pf.

ii **PELLETIER**
l. 13. ' Golden Cockerel ' *should read:*
' Golden Weathercock '

ll. 16-17 *should read:*
became one of the guest conductors of the Concerts Symphoniques at Montreal. He left the Metropolitan in 1950, but continues to reside in New York.

Add before **PELOPE:**
PELLICCIA, Arrigo (*b.* Viareggio, 20 Feb. 1912).
Italian violinist. He began to learn the violin under his father's guidance and later took a diploma at the Bologna Conservatory (1928). He then attended finishing courses in violin playing at the Accademia di Santa Cecilia in Rome (Arrigo Serato) and in Berlin (Carl Flesch). He began his career as concert artist in 1931, playing in the most important cities of Italy and abroad, both as soloist and in chamber-music groups, among others the Trio Santoliquido-Pelliccia-Amfitheatrof. Since 1939 he has held a violin professorship at the Conservatorio di San Pietro a Maiella at Naples. G. M. G.

617 i **PEÑALOSA, Francisco**
Add at end:
See also Eslava (modern reprints).

ii *Add after* **PENNA:**
PENNARD, ? (*b.* ? ; *d.* ?).
English 14th–15th-century composer. His paired ' Gloria ' and ' Credo ' have been transmitted by the ' Old Hall Manuscript ', and a related source from Fountains Abbey in Yorkshire (B.M. Add MS 40011 B). Pennard is named as the composer of the ' Credo ' in ' Old Hall ' (II, 241) remarkable for containing the longest single isorhythmic period

in the entire repertory of this manuscript. It is a 4-part work, for two alto voices and four instruments. Except for the " Amen ", which is a brilliant hocket, the altos alternate in singing the text of the ' Credo '; the voice not singing, however, was probably expected to play the instrumental part. It is significant that exactly one perfect breve rest is used to separate the vocal from the instrumental passages throughout the composition. This would presumably allow just enough time for the singer to change from voice to instrument and back again. The instrumental sections, but not the vocal ones, have an isorhythmic pattern of their own : thus each voice is alternately free and isorhythmic.

This technique of isorhythmic alternation is sufficiently rare to allow the ascription of an anonymous ' Gloria ' (Fountains Fragment, f.9) which also makes extensive use of it, to Pennard. Manfred Bukofzer has pointed out that the *cantus firmus* of this ' Gloria ' is the verse " Tibi laus, tibi gloria, tibi gratiarum actio " of the antiphon ' O beata et benedicta ', sung at Lauds on the feast of Holy Trinity. Since the ' Credo ' too is built on an antiphon from the same feast, ' Te iure laudant ', there is a liturgical as well as a stylistic link, and Pennard may well be the composer of the anonymous ' Gloria '. Both works display a mature technique as well as an inventive mind, and it is a matter for regret that other liturgical pieces by Pennard have not come down to us. D. W. S.

BIBL.—BESSELER, HEINRICH, ' Bourdon und Fauxbourdon ' (Leipzig, 1950).
BUKOFZER, MANFRED, ' Studies in Medieval and Renaissance Music ' (New York, 1950).
RAMSBOTHAM, ALEXANDER, ed., ' The Old Hall Manuscript ', Vol. II (London, 1935).

620 i **PEPPING**
Add before CHURCH MUSIC:
CHORAL WORKS WITH ORCHESTRA
' Te Deum ' for solo voices, chorus & orch. (1956).

621 ii **PEPUSCH**
See also. l. 2 *should read:*
Opera. Mitteldeutsches Musikarchiv, II, Vol. 1 (modern ed. of trio-sonatas). Polly. Thomyris (pasticcio).

622 i **PERAGALLO**
Par. 2, l. 20 *should read:*
pianoforte and orchestra (1949). In Mar. 1954 the Teatro alla Scala at Milan produced his opera ' La gita in campagna ' (libretto by Alberto Moravia).

623 i **PERCUSSION BANDS**
l. 7 *should read:*
reading and conducting. During the last quarter of a century the percussion band movement has made great progress in both primary and secondary schools, and recent

experiments with this kind of musical activity
in special schools for abnormal children and
even in mental hospitals have been found to
have salutary results.   E. B.

623   i   *Add to* Bibl. :

Moore, Stephen S., ' Guide to Percussion Playing '
(London, 1923).

ii   **PEREIRA-SALAS**
Par. 2, l. 6 *should read* :

at the Berkeley Campus of California University (1933–34),

624   i   **PEREZ CASAS**
Par. 1, l. 2 *should read* :

24 Jan. 1873 ; *d.* Madrid, 15 Jan. 1956).

PEREZ, Davide
Par. 1, l. 2.   *c.* 1779). *should read* :
30 Oct. 1778).

ii   Par. 1, l. 7, Par. 2 and Par. 3, l. 1
should read :

in 1779, after his death.

In 1780 Perez's nephew undertook to transport his uncle's manuscripts and other property
to his mother, the composer's sister, at Naples.
On 2 June he embarked on a Swedish ship,
which was soon afterwards attacked by
pirates. The nephew escaped the general
massacre by hiding in the hold among the
cargo ; the ship was scuttled and ran ashore
at Albufeira. The composer's possessions,
which were considerable, were all lost.
Perez's compositions can scarcely be called

Add at end :

Bibl.—Soares, Ernesto, ' David Perez, subsidios para
a biografia do celebre maestro ' (Lisbon, 1935).

628   ii   **PERGOLESI**
Par. 3, l. 1 *should read* :

In the following winter (1731–32) Pergolesi's first

629   ii   Par. 1, l. 13.   Franceso *should
read* :
Francesco

631   i   Par. 2, ll. 12–15 *should read* :

style. An Italianized German, Hasse, was a
very successful composer of inter-

632   —   CATALOGUE
OPERAS AND INTERMEZZI
Col. 4, l. 2.   winter 1731. *should read* :
winter 1731–32.

l. 4.   winter 1731. *should read* :
winter 1731–32.

633   i   List (*b*), l. 4.   Sainte-Gudule). *should read* :
Conservatoire).

633   i   List (*b*), l. 8.   Sainte-Gudule). *should read* :
Conservatoire).

l. 15.   Sainte-Gudule). *should read* :
Conservatoire).

l. 41.   Sainte-Gudule). *should read* :
Conservatoire).

634   i   *See also.* l. 4 *should read* :

attrib. to P.). Classici Musica Italiana, Vol. 23
(extracts from operas). Cooke (B., adds to ' Stabat
Mater '). Fitzwilliam Music (reprint of sacred works).

636   i   **PERI**
Add to Bibl. :

Pirrotta, Nino, ' Temperaments and Tendencies in the
Florentine Camerata ' (M.Q., XL, 1954, p. 169).
' Tragédie et comédie dans la Camerata fiorentina '
in ' Musique et poésie au XVIᵉ siècle ' (Paris,
1954), pp. 287–97.

Footnote 2, l. 3.   p. 55. *should read* :

p. 55, and N. Fortune, ' A Florentine Manuscript and
its Place in Italian Song ' (' Acta Musicologica ', Vol.
XXIII, 1951, pp. 128 & 132).

See also. l. 1 *should read* :

See also Accompaniment, p. 27. Arte Musicale in
Italia (for modern ed.). Classici Musica Italiana, Vol.
24 (extracts from ' Euridice '). Gagliano (M., collab.

ii   **PÉRIER**
Par. 1, l. 2 *should read* :

1869 ; *d.* Paris, 3 Nov. 1954).

Par. 2, l. 11. left in 1900, *should
read* :

left about 1920,

637   i   **PERINELLO**
Par. 1, l. 2 *should read* :

1877 ; *d.* Rome, 6 Jan. 1942).

PERIODICALS
Par. 2, l. 1.   Hofmeister, F. A.
should read :

Hofmeister, Friedrich

638   i   Par. 1, l. 6 *should read* :

identical with that of No. 12 above.

Par. 2, l. 7 *should read* :

all be published in No. 14 above.

ii   *International.   Add after* No. 6 :

7. ' Bulletin du Centre de Documentation
de Musique Internationale.' Ed. Pierre
Capdevielle & others. Paris, 1951–   .

Argentine
Line under heading should read :

(The place of publication in each case except for No. 11
is Buenos Aires)

Add after No. 6 :

6a. ' Revista de música.' 1927–   .

638 ii *Add after* No. 9:

10. 'Mundo musical: revista mensual illustrada.' 1938– .

11. 'Revista de estudios musicales.' Mendoza, Universidad Nacional de Cujo. 1949–.

Austria. No. 1, l. 3 *should read:*
1770–73.[1]

Add footnote:

[1] A course of composition published in weekly parts, not a periodical in the normal sense of the term.

639 i No. 14, l. 2. 1852–62. *should read:*
1852–60.

640 i *Add after* No. 67:

68. 'Olympia: Journal der musikalischen Wettkämpfe.' Ed. H. Ortner. Salzburg, 1950– .

Belgium, No. 7. 'La Guide musicale' *should read:*

'Le Guide musical'

641 i *Britain.* No. 20, l. 6 *should read:*

McNaught; Martin Cooper, 1953–56; Harold Rutland, 1957–60; Robin Hull, 1960; Andrew Porter, 1960–

643 i No. 118, l. 2 *should read:*

1905–7. (The same as No. 25.)

ii No. 154, l. 2 *should read:*

Strangways; Eric Blom; Richard Capell; Eric Blom; J. A. Westrup

645 ii No. 237, l. 2 *should read:*

1950–53; Harold Rosenthal, 1953– .

646 i *Canada. Cancel whole section and replace by:*

Canada

1. 'Le Passe-Temps.' Montreal, 1895–1933.
2. 'L'Art musical.' Montreal, 1897–?
3. 'The Conservatory Bi-Monthly.' Toronto, 1902.
4. 'Musical Canada.' Toronto, 1906–33.
5. 'The Violin.' Toronto, 1906.
6. 'The Canadian Journal of Music.' Toronto, 1914–19.
7. 'Le Canada musical.' Montreal, 1917–1924.
8. 'La Musique.' Quebec, 1913–3?.
9. 'Musi-Canada.' Montreal, 1922– .
10. 'La Lyre.' Montreal, 1924–3?.
11. 'The Toronto Conservatory Quarterly.' Toronto, 192?– .
12. 'Western Music News.' Vancouver, ?1934–?
13. 'La Revue Saint-Grégoire.' Quebec, 193?– .
14. 'Le Diapason.' Montreal, 1944– .

15. 'Le Passe-Temps' (New). Montreal, 194?– .
16. 'Musique et Musiciens.' Montreal, 1952– .

646 ii *Czechoslovakia,* No. 15, l. 3. 1920–23. *should read:*
1920–36.

647 i *Denmark. Add after* No. 26:

27. 'Nordisk Musikkultur.' Ed. Sigurd Berg & K. Lange. Copenhagen, 1952– .

650 i *France.* No. 140 *should read:*

140. 'Contrepoints.' Ed. Fred Goldbeck. 1946– .

Add after No. 140:

141. 'Polyphonie.' Ed. Albert Richard. 1947– .
142. 'Musique contemporaine.' Ed. Tsveta-Maneva. 1951– .

Germany, No. 9, l. 3. 1768–69 *should read:*
1766–70

654 ii *Germany.* No. 206, l. 5 *should read:*

1918-28. (The same title was used for No. 266a, *see* p. 656).

656 ii *Add after* No. 266:

266a. 'Archiv für Musikwissenschaft.' Ed. Willibald Gurlitt. Trossingen, 1944– .

659 i *Italy,* No. 1, l. 2. de musica *should read:*

di musica

No. 2, l. 2 *should read:*

logna, 1823–24.[1]

No. 4, l. 1. Gazetta *should read:*
Gazzetta

No. 5, l. 1. Gazetta *should read:*
Gazzetta

l. 2. 1845–1902 *should read:*
1842–48; 1850–62; 1866–1902.

l. 3. 1903–5. *should read:*
1903–5.[2]

Add footnotes:

[1] Catalogued in the Biblioteca Nazionale, Florence, as "Supplemento alla 'Gazzetta di Bologna'".
[2] This began independently in 1902.

Italy, No. 11. Milan 1863–? *should read:*

Milan, 1853–?

No. 11 *becomes* No. 7.

Nos. 7, 8, 8a, 9, 9a & 10 *become* Nos. 8, 9, 9a, 10, 10a & 11.

659　ii　No. 30, ll. 1-2 *should read*:

30. ' Rivista musicale italiana.' Turin, 1894–

No. 37, l. 1 *should read*:

37. ' Musica d' oggi.' Milan,

660　i　*Add after* No. 53 :

54. ' Musica : rivista internazionale.' Rome, 1946– .
55. ' L' Editore di musica.' Milan, 1948– .
56. ' Bollettino dell' Accademia Musicale Chigiana.'. Siena, 1948– .
57. ' La Scala : rivista dell' Opera.' Ed. Franco Abbiati. Milan, 1948– .
58. ' Musica d' oggi ', new series. Milan, 1958– .

661　i　*Poland*
No. 2.　Pamixtnik *should read*:
Pamiętnik.

No. 5.　kościetny *should read*:
kościelny

No. 8.　Posen *should read*:
Poznań

No. 10.　*Add at end of* l. 2 :

After its revival in 1928 it was edited by Chybiński and Sikorski until 1933; it was revived again after the second world war (edited by a committee) in 1948, and its last issue appeared as No. 29-30 in June 1950.

No. 13.　1935–39 ? *should read*:
1935–36 (2 issues only).

No. 15.　Wiadomosci slaskie *should read*:
Wiadomości śląskie

Add:

16. ' Ruch muzyczny ', edited by a Committee (and published by P.W.M. at Cracow), began to appear as a fortnightly in August 1945. In 1947 it became a monthly, changing simultaneously its size to a bigger one. It ceased to appear after 1949, transformed into a new musical periodical, the ' Muzyka '.
17. ' Muzyka ', a monthly, edited by a Committee, began to appear in April 1950 (No. 1). In 1952 it became bi-monthly, and in the latter form appeared in print for the last time in January–February 1956.
18. ' Muzyka ' — a quarterly, first published in April 1956.
19. ' Studia muzykologiczne ', a half-annual musicological publication, edited by an Editorial Committee, began to appear in 1953.

20. ' Ruch muzyczny', edited by a Committee (and published by P.W.M. at Cracow, began to appear as a fortnightly in May 1957. It is not a continuation of the periodical mentioned above under 16, and has nothing in common with it but name (which was first introduced by Józef Sikorski a hundred years ago).
21. ' Rocznik Chopinowski ', an annnal publication, edited by a Committee, it is published by P.W.M. at Cracow, No. 1 appeared in Sept. 1956. (All the articles are exclusively connected either with Chopin's music or with the interpretation of his works.)

661　i　*Russia*, No. 6, l. 2.　1922–25. *should read*:
1822–25.

662　ii　*Spain. Add after* No. 20 :

21. ' Música : revista trimestral de los conservatorios españoles.' Madrid, 1951– .

663　i　*Sweden. Add at end* :

24. ' Musik och Skola.' Ed. Torsten Erséus. Borås, 1958– .

664　i　*U.S.A.*, No. 15a, l. 4.　1907– . *should read*:
1907-57.

No. 25, l. 2 *should read*:
Thomas Tapper ; P. Kempf. Boston, 1896– .

ii　No. 66, l. 2 *should read*:
letin.' New York, 1936–48. (Continued by No. 76.)

665　i　No. 76, l. 2 *should read*:
Society.' Boston, 1948– . (Continuation of No. 66.)

Add after No. 75 :

75a. ' Musicology.' Ed. E. C. Stone. Middlebury, Vermont, 1946– .

668　ii　Par. 5, ll. 9-10 *should read*:
Ménestrel ', which flourished intermittently from 1833 to 1939. For many years it gave a

670　ii　Par. 2, l. 2.　Gazetta *should read*:
Gazzetta

ll. 33-34.　Bolletino *should read*:
Bollettino

l. 37.　Bolletino *should read*:
Bollettino

671　i　Par. 1, l. 11 *should read*:
Gazeta ' (1894–1917) held the field as the

671 i   Par. 1, ll. 13-15 *should read*:
and research. 'Muzikalny Sovremennik' (1915-17) was a magazine making propaganda for modernism, published irregularly.

672 i   Para. 3, l. 6. (1950–) *should read*:
(1949–)

ii **PERLE, George**
l. 1. (*b.* ?, *should read*:
(*b.* Bayonne, New Jersey,

Par. 2, ll. 6-7 *should read*:
University. Having studied composi-

l. 10 *should read*:
and Gustave Reese at New York University, and had private lessons in composition from Křenek.

673 ii   *Add before* **PERNET**:
PERNEL, Orrea (*b.* St. Mary's Platt, Kent, 9 July 1906).
English violinist. She was educated privately by her father, the architect, sculptor and jeweller Henry Wilson, and was given a basic training in jewelry; but she studied the violin from the age of six, beginning at Venice, continuing under Adila Fachiri in London and Édouard Nadaud at the Paris Conservatoire, taking a first prize there in 1924. She toured widely in Europe, appearing at the I.S.C.M. Festival of 1935 in Prague, visiting Finland the same year and again in 1953, and making a first American tour in 1937, when she played with the Boston Symphony Orchestra under Kussevitsky. She eventually settled in the U.S.A., first as a member of the Music Faculty of Smith College, Northampton, Mass. (1943-44) and afterwards of Bennington College, where she formed a string quartet. In 1950 and 1953 she appeared at the Prades Festival organized by Casals, and in the latter year she reappeared in London.   E. B.

PEROSI
Par. 1, l. 2 *should read*:
20 Dec. 1872; *d.* Rome, 12 Oct. 1956).

674 ii   *Add to* BIBL.
GLIŃSKI, MATEUSZ, 'Lorenzo Perosi' (Milan, 1953).

PÉROTIN
Par. 4, l. 10. troubadour *should read*:
rhythmic

675 i   Par. 1, ll. 5-10 *should read*:
duced, and the use of motivic imitation and voice-exchange is noteworthy.

675 ii   Par. 3, l. 3. not liturgical *should read*:
usually not liturgical

ll. 6-9 *should read*:
the tenor being instrumental. All the voices except the tenor use a note-against-note technique in almost identical rhythms, the text appearing under the two or three upper parts.
Add to BIBL. :
WAITE, WILLIAM G., 'The Rhythm of Twelfth-Century Polyphony' (Yale, 1954).

680 ii   **PERSIAN MUSIC**
Par. 3, l. 6. d e-. *should read*:
d-e.

683 ii   **PERTI**
Par. 1, l. 1. *b.* Bologna, *should read*:
b. Crevalcore nr. Bologna,

684 ii   *Add at end*:
BIBL.—GIEGLING, F., 'G. A. Perti' ('Die Musik-Forschung', 1955).
See also Fitzwilliam Music (reprint of 'Adoramus').

PERTILE
Par. 2, l. 38 *should read*:
of suiting every requirement. He sang at Covent Garden, London, in 1927-29 and 1931. In 1940 he

689 i   **Petrarch**
l. 4 *should read*:
Granados ('Petrarca', opera). Hook (songs). Jacopo da Bologna (madrigal). Kienlen

689 ii   **PETRASSI**
Add to BIBL. :
WEISSMANN, JOHN S., 'Goffredo Petrassi' (Milan, 1957).

690 i   CATALOGUE
Add to ORCHESTRAL WORKS :
Concerto No. 4, for stgs.
Concerto No. 5.

Add before CHAMBER MUSIC :
VOICE AND ORCHESTRA
'Quattro inni sacri' (1950, orig. with organ, *see* Church Music).

ii **PETRELLA**
Par. 4, l. 3. Giovanni II *should read*:
Giovanna II

692 ii   **PETRIDIS**
OPERA
l. 1. 'Zefyra' *should read*:
'Zemfyra'

l. 2. (1923-45) *should read*:
(1923-25).

693 i Petronius
l. 2 *should read*:
'Satyricon', overture). Reutter (H., 'Witwe von Ephesus', opera).

PETROV
Par. 1, l. 2. 1807 *should read*:
1806
l. 3. 14 Mar. *should read*:
11 Mar.

ii PETRUCCI
Par. 1, l. 2. *d.* Venice, *should read*:
d. Fossombrone,

694 — LIST OF PUBLICATIONS
No. 35 *should read*:
35 Strambotti .... Libro quarto. 31 July 1507 (=20)

No. 36 *should read*:
36 Frottole Libro tertio. 26 Nov. 1507 (=19)

No. 39. 1508 *should read*:
1508 ³
No. 42 *should read*:
42 Frottole Libro secondo. 29 Jan. 1508 (=18)

No. 53 *should read*:
53 Missarum Josquin Liber secundus. 11 Apr. 1515 (=23)
Add footnote:
³ This book is lost.

695 i *Add at end*:
See also Denkmäler (4), Vol. 8 (modern ed. of frottole).

696 ii PETZ
Add at end:
See also Denkmäler (2) II, Vols. 27-28 (modern ed.).

697 i PETZOLD
Add at end:
See also Denkmäler (2), Vol. 63 (modern ed. of tower music).

PEUERL
Par. 1. (*b.* ?; *d.* ?). *should read*:
(*b.* ?, *c.* 1570; *d.* ?).

Par. 2, l. 1 *should read*:
Austrian organ builder,

698 i PEVERNAGE
Add at end:
See also Collectio O.M.B., Vol. 8 (modern ed.).

699 ii PFITZNER
Add to BIBL. :
PFITZNER, HANS, 'Reden, Schriften, Briefe', ed. by Walter Abendroth (Berlin, 1955).

700 i CATALOGUE
ORCHESTRA WORKS
Add after Op. 46 :
54. 'Krakauer Begrüssung' (1945, MS).

CHAMBER MUSIC
l. 3 *should read*:
23. Quintet, C ma., for 2 vns., viola, cello & pf. (1908).

711 ii PHILIPP
Par. 1, l. 2. 1863). *should read*:
1863; *d.* Paris, 21 Feb. 1958).

712 i-ii PHILIPS, Peter
Par. 1, ll. 1-2 *should read*:
PHILIPS, Peter ¹ (*b.* ?, 1561; *d.* Brussels, 1628 ²).

Cancel remainder of page and replace by:

English composer and organist. He was born somewhere in England, but lived in the Netherlands at the end of the 16th and in the early 17th centuries, and is thus claimed by Belgian authorities as belonging virtually to the Netherlands school.

Philips may have been a Londoner born, and it is probable that he was brought up there as a chorister at St. Paul's Cathedral. A Catholic almoner of the cathedral, Sebastian Westcote, in his will dated 3 Apr. 1582 ³, left a bequest to " Peter Phillippes likewise remaining with me ", which suggests that he was living at Westcote's almonry house as a former pupil and perhaps as an assistant. Westcote died before 14 Apr. 1582, when his will was proved ⁴, and Philips, apparently homeless and feeling insecure as a Catholic, left England early in Aug. for Italy. On 18 Aug. he was received at the English College of Douai, but before long went on to Rome, where in Oct. he received hospitality for twelve days at the English College. He then entered the service of Cardinal Alessandro Farnese, remaining for three years, and at the same time acted as organist at the English College, where Felice Anerio was *maestro di cappella*. About Sept. 1585 Philips entered the service of Lord Thomas Paget, who had come to Rome and with whom he visited Spain, France and the Netherlands. After a visit to Genoa they left for Spain in Oct. 1585. They travelled there until Sept. 1586, then in France until early 1587, when they settled in Paris until June 1588, with a visit to Brussels about Mar. of that year. Next they stayed at Antwerp until about Feb. 1589, when they returned to Brussels, where Paget died early in 1590.

After his patron's death Philips went to live

¹ The new and more precise information that can now be given on Philips has been extracted from an article by A. G. Petti, ' Peter Philips, Composer and Organist : 1561–1628 ', published in the periodical ' Recusant History ', Vol. IV, No. 2, Apr. 1957.
² In the fifth and earlier editions Philips's death was given as " between 1633 and 1640 ", on the alleged ground that the date 1628 given by Dr. John Southcote's notebook (publ. by the Catholic Record Society, I, 133) was out of the question, since editions of works by Philips published in 1630 and 1633 showed no indication that they were posthumous — a negative proof at best and now shown to have no validity.
³ *See* Mus. Ant., IV, 189.
⁴ Prerogative Court of Canterbury, 14 Tirwhite.

at Antwerp, where he taught the virginals and married a woman about whom nothing is known and whose early death may have occurred at any time between about 1597 and 1606. In 1591 was published at Antwerp his collection of madrigals entitled 'Melodia Olympica di eccellentissimi musici', dedicated to " Sig. Giulio Balbani[1], patrono mio osservantissimo ", and dated Antwerp, 1 Dec. 1590. Other editions of the ' Melodia Olympica' appeared at Antwerp in 1594 and 1611. This work, which contains 67 madrigals by Italian and Netherlands composers, including 4 by Philips, was followed in 1596 by ' Il primo libro de' madrigali a sei voci ', printed at Antwerp by Phalèse and dedicated (Antwerp, 8 Jan. 1596) to Signor Alessandro di Giunta ; a second edition was issued in 1604. In 1598 he published at Phalèse's press in Antwerp a volume of eight-part madrigals, on the title-page of which he appears for the first time described as organist of the Archduke Albert and Archduchess Isabella. This work is dedicated from Antwerp on 24 Sept. 1598 to Sir William Stanley (1548–1630), the Catholic adventurer, who is described as " Collonello d' un Regimento Inglesi & Walloni mio Sig. osseruandiss." The work was reprinted in 1599 and again in 1615. In 1603 there appeared a second book of madrigals for six voices (Antwerp, Phalèse), dedicated from Antwerp, 10 Nov. 1603, to the archduke and archduchess ; a second edition was issued in 1615.

Some time, probably early in 1593, Philips went to Amsterdam to hear and make the acquaintance of Sweelinck, of whom he thought very highly. On his way back to Antwerp he was taken ill at Middelburgh and while there was accused by one Roger Walton of having attempted to kill Elizabeth I and also of having taken part with Lord Paget in burning the queen in effigy in Paris in 1588. He was taken to The Hague for trial in Sept. 1593 and, after lengthy examination, which involved the waiting for evidence from England, released towards the end of the year. He was back at Antwerp by Christmas.

In 1597 Philips left Antwerp for Brussels to enter the service of the Archduke Albert, who had become Governor-General of the Low Countries in 1596. A document of 4 Aug. 1597 first mentions his residence there. He remained organist of the royal chapel until his death, and after Albert's marriage to Isabella of Spain in 1599 was described as " Organist to their Serene Highnesses the Archduke Albert and Isabella ". On 9 Mar. 1610 he was appointed to a canonry in the collegiate church of Saint-Vincent at

Soignies ; but this, like the later chaplaincy at Tirlemont and the canonry at Béthune, does not seem to have involved residence, for he appears to have remained continually in Brussels.

In 1611 Philips and some of his colleagues in the chapel were invited to Mechlin to examine a new organ in the church of Saint-Rombaud, and in Dec. of that year he played at the funeral of the Archduchess Maria of Austria. The court accounts of 1612–18 give his name at the head of the organists and his salary as 305 florins per tercio, which was more than the others received. On 12 Mar. 1622 he walked at the head of the funeral procession commemorating the Archduke Albert, who had died in 1621. Philips's portrait, which is certainly taken from life (as notified in the letterpress), appeared in Jacques Francquart's ' Pompa funebris . . . Alberti Pii . . . veris imaginibus expressa ' (Brussels, 1623).[2] In 1624 he is mentioned as " Pietro Filippini " in a report on the restoration of the organ of the court chapel, according to which he approved of the work done by Mathieu Langhedul.

After the appearance of his six-part madrigals Philips seems to have devoted himself entirely to sacred music, and it is probable that it was in order to be qualified for the canonry of Soignies that he took holy orders. His first published collection of sacred music, the ' Cantiones sacrae ' for five voices, was

[2] It may be seen in the 4th ed. of this Dictionary.

713 i Par. 1, l. 1 *should read*:

published by Phalèse at Antwerp in 1612, with an extra edition in 1617. It

Par. 3, ll. 28-29 *should read*:

he once more appears as canon at Soignies, probably because this was the title by which he was generally known, and it was also accorded him after his death, when in 1633 the

714 i Par. 3, l. 3 *should read*:

century, Philips was, as we have seen, personally

715 i *Add at end of* MADRIGALS :

Edited by Elizabeth Cole from Francis Tregian's Madrigal Anthology (B.M. MS Eg. 3665) (1955) :
4. ' The Nightingale ' (S.S.A.T.B.).
5. ' O false deceit ' (S.S.A.T.B.).

Add at end of MOTETS :

Edited by R. R. Terry (Novello) :
9. ' Cantantibus organis ' (S.S.A.T.B.).
10. ' Gaudent in coelis ' (S.S.A.T.B.).
11. ' Ne reminiscaris Domine ' (S.S.A.T.B.).
12. ' Surgens Jesus ' (S.S.A.T.B.).
13. ' Viae Syon lugent ' (S.S.A.T.B.).
Edited by H. B. Collins (Chester) :
14. ' Alma Redemptoris ' (S.S.A.T.B.).
15. ' Ave Regina ' (S.S.A.T.B.).
16. ' Elegi abjectus esse ' (S.S.A.T.B.).
17. ' O virum mirabillem ' (S.S.A.T.B.).
18. ' Regina coeli ' (S.S.A.T.B.).

[1] The Balbani were a noble family of Lucca, a branch of which was settled at Bruges at the end of the 16th century.

715   i   **PHILLIPPS**
Par. 1, l. 2.   Avon, 1833;   *should
read*:
Avon, 26 Oct. 1833;

718   i   *Add before* **PHILOSOPHER**:
PHILOMUSICA OF LONDON. A string
orchestra specializing mainly in authentic
performances of Renaissance and baroque
music, although representative works of the
classical and romantic periods and music by
living composers also receive attention.
E. B.

719   i   **PHINOT**
Add at end:
See also Collectio O.M.B., Vols. 8 & 9 (modern ed.).

ii   **PHRASE**
Add at end:
BIBL.—BLOM, ERIC, 'Phrase-Lengths' in 'Classics:
Major and Minor' (London, 1958).

723   ii   **PHYSHARMONICA**
Add at end:
Two youths from Germany played on "the
Phys-harmonica, an instrument unknown as
yet in this country", at the dinner of the
Royal Society of Musicians on 21 Apr.
1825.[1]

> [1] *See* 'Musical Magazine', 1825, p. 205.

Signature should read:
A. J. H., adds.

744   i   **PIANOFORTE**
Add to BIBL.:
HIRT, FRANZ JOSEF, 'Meisterwerke des Klavierbaus:
Geschichte der Saitenklaviere von 1440 bis 1880'
(Olten, 1955).

751   i   **PIANOFORTE PLAYING**
Add to BIBL.:
AGUETTANT, LOUIS, 'La Musique de piano des origines
à Ravel' (Paris, 1954).
DALE, KATHLEEN, 'Nineteenth-Century Piano Music:
a Handbook for Pianists' (Oxford, 1954).
GEORGII, WALTER, 'Klaviermusik: Geschichte der
Musik zu 2 und 4 Händen von den Anfängen bis
zur Gegenwart' (Zürich & Freiburg i/B., 1956).
HOPE, ERIC, 'A Handbook of Piano Playing' (London,
1955).
LOESSER, ARTHUR, 'Men, Women and Pianos: a Social
History' (New York, 1954).
MERRICK, FRANK, 'Practising the Piano' (London,
1958).

753   ii   *Add after* **Picasso**:
PICCAVER, Alfred (*b.* Long Sutton,
Lincolnshire, 25 Feb. 1884; *d.* Vienna, 23
Sept. 1958).
British tenor singer. He was brought up
n New York, whither his parents had emigrated when he was one and a half. He
remained there until his late teens, working
as an electrical engineer in the laboratories of
Edison. While in New York he sang in a
church choir and also studied voice as a part-
time pupil at the Metropolitan school, singing in student performances of 'Roméo et
Juliette', 'Der Freischütz' and 'Rigoletto'.
In 1907 he was sent to Europe for health
reasons and accompanied some friends to
Austria who were trying to obtain operatic
engagements. As a joke it was suggested
that he should also give an audition, and as
a result he found himself engaged for the
Prague Opera, where he made his début as
Romeo in 1907. He then began to study
seriously, with Rosario in Milan and then
with Prohaska-Neumann in Prague.
In 1910, while appearing as a guest artist
in Vienna, Piccaver was offered a contract
for the Court Opera, and he remained a
member of the Vienna company until 1937.
During the first world war he tried to leave
Austria through Rumania, but was turned
back at the frontier and escorted back to
Vienna. He was not interned, however, but
allowed to continue his career at the Opera.
While in Vienna he sang in the first Austrian
performances of 'La fanciulla del West' and
'Il tabarro', being personally coached by
Puccini. His parts included Andrea Chénier,
Radamès, Lohengrin, Walther, Faust, Des
Grieux, Don José, Canio, Tamino, Don
Ottavio, Werther, Riccardo, Florestan and
Lensky. He sang with the Chicago Opera
from 1923 to 1925 and at Covent Garden
1924, when he was heard as Cavaradossi and
the Duke in 'Rigoletto'.
Alfred Piccaver was gifted with a large,
robust voice, and on more than one occasion
was compared with Caruso. He retired from
opera when still at the height of his powers
in 1937 and came to live in London, where he
remained until 1955. He returned to Vienna
for the re-opening of the State Opera and was
an honoured guest. He remained there as a
teacher.   H. D. R.

753   ii   **PICCINNI, Niccolò**
Par. 1, l. 1.   Bari, Naples, 16
should read:
Bari, 16

757   ii   **PICCIONI**
Par. 2, l. 3.   in the house of
Desiosi *should read*:
of the Accademia dei Desiosi

l. 6.   Monte Fiaschone *should
read*:
Montefiaschone

760   i   **PICHL**
Add at end:
See also Musica Antiqua Bohemica, Vol. 7 (modern
ed. of Prelude & Fugue for solo vn., Op. 41).

762   i   **PIERNÉ,** CATALOGUE
          OPERAS
          l. 20 *should read*:
'Sophie Arnould', prod. Paris, Opéra-Comique, 21
    Feb. 1927.

          BALLETS
          l. 1.   Colliers *should read*:
Collier

765   ii   **PIFFARO**
           Add at end:
BIBL.—GELLER, HANS, 'I Piffari: musizierende Hirten
    in Rom' (Leipzig, 1954).

768   i   **PIJPER**
          Add to BIBL.:
RINGER, ALEXANDER L., 'Willem Pijper and the
    "Netherlands School" of the 20th Century' (M.Q.,
    XLI, 1955, p. 427).

      ii   CATALOGUE
           OPERAS
           l. 1.   (1933, revised 1934) *should read*:
(1932, rev. 1934).

           l. 2.   1939–46) *should read*:
1939–42).

           CHORAL WORKS
           Add after l. 5:
'Deux Ballades de Paul Fort' for female chorus & pf.
    (1921, orchestrated for chamber orch. 1934)
    1. La Fille morte dans ses amours.
    2. Le Marchand de sable.

           Delate l. 7.

           VOICE AND ORCHESTRA
           Add after l. 1:
    1. Pantomime.
    2. Sur l'herbe.
    3. Cortège.
'Hymne' (P. C. Boutens) for bass (1941–43).

           PIANOFORTE SOLO
           l. 3 *should read*:
Sonatina No. 2 (1925).
Sonatina No. 3 (1926).

769   i   **PILKINGTON (1)**
          Par. 1.   Dates *should read*:
(*b.* ?, *c.* 1562; *d.* Chester, 1638)

774   i   **PINZA**
          Par. 1, l. 2 *should read*:
May 1892; *d.* Stamford, Connecticut, 9 May
1957).

          Par. 2, l. 10.   1919 *should read*:
1920

          l. 13 *should read*:
Scala of Milan (1921–24), where one of his
parts was

774   i   Par. 2, l. 24 *should read*:
American opera companies and in Europe
(Covent Garden, London, 1930, 1934–36,
1939).

          l. 27 *should read*:
between 1934 and 1939.

775   i   **PIPE AND TABOR**
          Par. 1, ll. 4-5 *should read*:
simultaneously by one person. (*See PLATES*
21, Vol. III, p. 176, No. 2; 34, Vol. IV, p.
500, No. 2; 60, Vol. VII, p. 746, No. 10.)

776   ii   *Add after* **Piper, John**:
           Piper, Mifanwy.   *See* Britten ('Turn of the Screw'
lib.).

781   ii   Page Heading, PESENDEL *should
           read*:
PISENDEL

           PISENDEL
           Par. 2, l. 4.   Corelli, *should read*:
Torelli,

782   i   **PISK**
          Par. 3, ll. 4-5 *should read*:
professor to the University of Texas at Austin
in the summers of 1945, 1947 and 1951–52,
and he eventually settled there as Professor
of Musicology. He has

783   ii   **PISTON**
           Add to BIBL.:
AUSTIN, WILLIAM, 'Walter Piston's Fourth Symphony'
    (M. Rev., XVI, 1955, p. 120).

806   i   **PIXIS (3)**
          l. 2.   1788; *should read*:
10 Feb. 1788;

808   ii   **PIZZETTI**
           Add to BIBL.:
GAGAZZENI, G., 'Altri studi pizzettiani' (Bergamo,
    1956).

           BIBL.   l. 15 *should read*:
'Ildebrando Pizzetti' (Turin, 1934, new ed. 1955;
    Eng. trans. by

809   —   Heading *should read*:
PIZZETTI: Works

           CATALOGUE
           OPERAS
           Add at end:

'Cagliostro.'	Composer.	Milan, Teatro alla Scala, 24 Jan. 1953.
'La figlia d' Jorio.'	d' Annunzio, adapted by the Composer.	Naples, Teatro San Carlo, 4 Dec. 1954.
'Assassinio nella cattedrale', 2 acts.	Composer, based on T. S. Eliot's 'Murder in the Cathedral'.	1957.	Milan, Teatro alla Scala, 1 Mar. 1958.

811 i **PLAICHINGER**

Par. 2, ll. 19–20 *should read*:

Venus and Elisabeth in ' Tannhäuser ' and as Elektra. She afterwards became a teacher at

821 i **PLAINSONG**

Add to BIBL. :

APEL, WILLI, ' Gregorian Chant ' (London, 1958).
MURRAY, DOM GREGORY, ' Gregorian Rhythm in the Gregorian Centuries : the Literary Evidence ' (Bath, 1957).
' Plainsong Rhythm : the Editorial Methods of Solesmes ' (Bath, 1957).
VOLLAERTS, J. W. A., ' Rhythmic Proportions in Early Medieval Ecclesiastical Chant ' (Leiden, 1958).

ii **PLAINSONG AND MEDIAE-VAL MUSIC SOCIETY**

Par. 1, l. 8 *should read*:

Denis Stevens.

Add at end of List :

' The Play of Daniel ', edited with an English translation by W. L. Smoldon.

PLAINSONG NOTATION

Delete entry and substitute :

PLAINSONG NOTATION. The subject is treated in detail elsewhere[2], but this article introduces a tabulated list of plainsong symbols, with their names and their interpretation in modern staff notation.

All the special group-symbols used in plainsong notation are built up from a very small vocabulary of basic elements ; and while in theory a limitless number of different combinations of these basic elements is possible, in practice the early teachers and composers of plainsong found that they needed to use only a few of them. At a very early stage in their history these commonly recurring group-symbols were each assigned a special name in order to make them easier to teach, to remember and to understand, and these names were evidently selected on the grounds of their aptness as descriptions of the symbols in question. By long tradition, deriving ultimately from the testimony of his disciple John the Deacon, this was part of the self-imposed task of the pious, ingenious and wise St. Gregory it would certainly seem that most of these names were developed and first used in the Roman song-school founded and directed by him, though a few may have been added at some later stage in the resplendent history of plainsong — the only form of music practised by mankind that can claim some two thousand years of continuous and inspiring life.

The codified system of plainsong neumes and names used in Rome was disseminated throughout the Christian world by such missionaries as St. Augustine and his forty

² (*See* NOTATION, pp. 111-16.)

companions, who went to Canterbury in 597 bearing a copy of the Roman Antiphoner ; St. Chrodegang, bishop of Metz during the reign of king Pépin, who went to Rome in 753 and established a song-school on Roman lines upon his return to Metz ; Simeon of Rome, who founded a song-school at Rouen a few years later ; and the quasi-legendary singers Theodore and Benedict, despatched from Rome in 787 to Metz and Soissons at the request of the Emperor Charlemagne. The chauvinistic and unreliable 11th-century historian of the monastery of St. Gall, Ekkehard, who seems to have been jealous of the renown of the song-school at Metz, sought to establish the superiority of the tradition at his own monastery by fabricating an account of how these two monks were called " Peter " and " the Roman ", and how Peter reached Metz safely while " the Roman " fell ill and was nursed back to health at St. Gall, imparting to the community in gratitude the secrets of the Roman school and bequeathing them his copy of the Gradual with its neumes — a story that is still repeated in most histories of music.

Some traces of the special techniques used for teaching plainsong at Metz (and presumably, therefore, in Rome) are to be found in the theoretical writings of Theoger, Bishop of Metz, whom Du Cange lists as the earliest authority for many of the special names for neumes (*see* his ' Glossarium ', art. ' Heptaphthonga '). Relics of others, perhaps, are comprised in the system of Romanic letters in use at St. Gall, too confidently ascribed by the eager Ekkehard to " the Roman ". It would seem that the teaching-methods of the Roman song-school may have fallen into two halves, the one concerned with notation pure and simple, the other with interpretation ; and that each of the missionary monks was specially expert in one technique. But the true history of so remote a period is almost impossible to recover — many essential documents must have been destroyed in the tragic fire at the learned Gerbert's monastery of St. Blaise in 1768 — and the suggestions put forward here can be no more than hypothetical.

Most plainsong theorists of the last two centuries have been concerned with the history of the neumes rather than of their names, and the only adequate explanation of the whole subject in English appears to be in Helmore's lucid little book on plainsong, first published in the 1870s. This may be supplemented by the outlines given in ' Plainsong for Schools ' and ' A Grammar of Plainsong ', prepared by the Benedictine nuns of Stanbrook. In the accompanying table an attempt has been made to show not only the essential structure of the system but also how the

Name	Meaning	Other Names	Neume		Transcription
			Early	Current	
Virga	a rod, twig		⌐⌐⌐	⌐	♪
bivirga	. . . .		⌐⌐ ⫽		
trivirga	. . . .		⌐⌐⌐ ⫽⫽		
Punctum	a dot, point		. ●	■	♪
bipunctum	. . . .		⁚		
tripunctum :					
gradicus	. . . .		⁚⁚		
trigon	. . . .		⁚⁚		
subpunctum	. . . .		⁚⁚⁚		
Apostropha	an apostrophe		'		
bistropha, strophicus	. . . .		⁾⁾	ᴀᴀ	♫
tristropha, strophicus	. . . .		⁾⁾⁾	ᴀᴀᴀ	♫♩
Clivis	a descent . .	flexa (" bent ") .	∩	ᴘᴀ	♫
flexa strophica	. . . .		∩,		
flexa resupina	. . . .		ξ		
Pes	a foot . .	podatus ("footed")	✓	ᴀ	♫
pes flexus	. . . .		✓		
pes flexus resupinus	. . . .		✓		
pes stratus	. . . .		✓		
pes sinuosus	. . . .		✓		
pes flexus strophicus	. . . .		✓		
Scandicus	a climber . .		✓	ᴀ ᴀ	♫♫
Salicus	a vaulter . .		✓	ᴀ	♫♫
Climacus	a skip down . .		✓	ᴘ	♫♫
Porrectus (=flexa resupina)	stretched . .		∼	◢	♫♩
Torculus	twisted bracelet .		✓	ᴀᴘ	♫♩
Quilisma	a tremolo . .		∿	ᴡ	♪
Pressus (=bistropha, more or less)	pressed . .		⁾⁾	ᴀᴘ	♩
Epiphonus	an " over-sound ".	etaphonus, gnoma, plica ascendens .	∪	ᴊ	♫
Cephalicus	headed . .	sinuosa, tramea, plica descendens	∩	ᴘ	♫
Gutturalis	throaty		∿		
Ancus	bent arm . .		∫		
Oriscus	companion note .		⁾		

2 A

various names and symbols could be modified; the plainsong reforms and simplifica-
tions initiated by the Benedictines of Solesmes
have resulted in the elimination of certain
terms included in the table.   R. T. D.

BIBLIOGRAPHY
GAJARD, DOM AUGUSTIN, 'Notions sur la rythmique
    grégorienne' (Paris, 1944).
GERBERT (ed.) 'De cantu et musica sacra. . . .' (1774).
    'Scriptores . . . de musica sacra' (1784).
HELMORE, REV. J. T., 'Plain-song' (London, c.
    1875).
ROBERTSON, A., 'The Interpretation of Plainchant'
    (London, 1937).
SCHUBIGER, ANSELM, 'Die Sängerschule S. Gallens'
    (Einsiedeln, 1858).
SUÑOL, DOM GREGORY, 'Introducció a la paleografía
    musical gregoriana' (Monserrat, 1925).

823   ii   **PLANTÉ**
           BIBL., l. 1. COMETTANT should read:
COMETTANT

824   ii   **PLATO**
           Add before See also:
BIBL.—AHLVERS, ARTHUR, 'Zahl und Klang bei
    Platon' (Berne & Stuttgart, 1952).

Plautus
l. 3 should read:
Martini (G. B., 'Trinummus', do.). Mohaupt ('Zwillingskomödie', opera). Ranki ('Trinummus', incid.
m.).

828   i   **PLAYFORD**
          Add to BIBL.:
DEAN-SMITH, MARGARET, 'English Tunes Common
    to Playford's "Dancing Master", the Keyboard
    Books and Traditional Songs and Dances' (Proc.
    Roy. Mus. Ass., Vol. LXXIX, 1952–53).
PLAYFORD, JOHN, 'The English Dancing Master',
    facsimile Reprint with an Introduction, Biblio-
    graphy and Notes by Margaret Dean-Smith
    (London, 1957).

Add at end:

See also Lyrebird Press (modern arrangements from
'The Dancing Master').

829   i   **PLEYEL**
          Par. 3, l. 1 should read:

Pleyel settled in Paris about 1795, but
found him-

832   i   **POCHON**
          l. 1. Dates should read:

(b. Yverdon, 30 July 1878; d. Lutry nr.
Lausanne, 26 Feb. 1959).

Par. 2, ll. 9-10 should read:

In 1941 he became director of the Lausanne
Conservatory, a post from which he resigned
in 1957.   W. W. C., adds.

836   i   Add after **POKORNY, Beate**:

POKORNY, Franz Xaver (b. Bohemia,
1729; d. ?).
Bohemian violinist and composer. He
studied under Joseph Riepel at Ratisbon and
about 1752 entered the service of the Count

of Oettingen-Wallerstein, who in 1754 sent
him to Mannheim for a short time to study
further under Holzbauer. A report he sent
from there, dated "Monheim", 4 Feb. 1754,
shows by its very erratic spelling that he must
have learnt German only by ear. He left
Wallerstein on 22 Mar. 1770 to enter the
court chapel of the Prince of Thurn and Taxis,
where he seems to have remained until his
death.
Pokorny composed some 50 symphonies,
more than 100 pianoforte concertos and
other works. Two clarinet concertos are
republished in 'Das Erbe deutscher [!]
Musik', Vol. XLI, edited by Heinz Becker.
                                          E. B.

836   i   **POKRASS**
          l. 1. Kiev, 1889 should read:

Kiev, 7 Nov. 1899

      ii   **POLACCO**
           (d. New York 2 May 1960).
           Par. 2, ll. 13-14 should read:

at San Francisco. In 1911 he directed a production in English of Puccini's 'Girl of

POLDINI
Par. 1. 1869). should read:
1869; d. Vevey, 29 June 1957).

837   i   **POLDOWSKI**
          Par. 1, l. 3. 1880; should read:
1879[1];
          Par. 2, ll. 5-11 should read:

music from an early age by a Miss Ellis, and
in 1892 she entered the Brussels Conservatoire, where she took a first prize for solfége
two years later and studied composition under
Gevaert. She also had private pianoforte
lessons from Pierre-Jean Storck and later
from Michael Hambourg in London, where
she continued composition studies with Percy
Pitt. After her marriage to Sir

          l. 13. Gédalge should read:
Gedalge
          Add footnote:
[1] According to the Registre de l'état civil d'Ixelles;
not 1880.

841   i   **POLLAK**
          Par. 2, l. 17 should read:
part again at Glyndebourne. Her versatility
is shown by her command of two very different parts in 'Figaro': she sang Marcellina
there in 1956, while at Covent Garden she
has sung Cherubino on numerous occasions.

847   i   **POLONIA**
          Par. 2, l. 4. 'Bogurodzika' should
          read:
'Bogurodzica'

848　i　**POLSKA**
Par. 3, l. 4.　Åhlström *should read*:
Ahlström

851　i　**POLYPHONY**
Par. 2, ll. 24-25 *should read*:
of John Dunstable (*d.* 1453), which are now
available complete in Vol. VIII of ' Musica
Britannica ' (for he was

868　i　**PONCHIELLI**
Par. 1, l. 3 *should read*:
16 Jan. 1886).

　　ii　**PONIATOWSKI**
Par. 2, l. 3.　(1714-95) *should read*:
(1764-95)

873　i　**POPOV**
Par. 1, l. 1.　**Gabriel** *should read*:
Gavryil

　　ii　**POPPER**
Par. 1, l. 1.　9 Dec. *should read*:
16 June 1

Add footnote:
1 Not 9 Dec., as in Riemann and elsewhere.

876　i　**PORPORA**
Par. 1, l. 2 *should read*:
17 Aug. 1686 1; *d.* Naples, 3 Mar. 1768 2).

Par. 2, l. 3.　1686 *should read*:
1696

l. 7 *should read*:
of his father (who died in 1717), he became
a charity

Add footnotes:
1 According to the birth certificate, communicated
by Ulisse Prota-Giurleo.
2 Also attested by Prota-Giurleo, who has found a
certificate (Libr. VI Mort., fol. 122 t) in the parish of
Arcivescovado at Naples.

　　ii　Par. 4, ll. 12-14 *should read*:
Naples on 28 Aug. 1720, the empress's birthday, repeated in Vienna the same year on
her name-day, and at Naples in 1722, again

877　i　Par. 2, ll. 13-14 *should read*:
oratorio, or *dramma sacro*, ' Il trionfo della
divina giustizia ', first performed at Naples
in 1716, was given at the ducal court of Milan,

878　ii　Par. 2, l. 4.　1847 *should read*:
1747

879　i　Par. 3, l. 15 *should read*:
in Feb. 1766, but it has now been shown that
the death occurred on 3 Mar. 1768. A
subscription was got up

879　ii　*Add to* BIBL. :
PROTA-GIURLEO, U., ' Per una esatta biografia di Nicolo
Porpora ' (' La Scala ', Jan. 1957).

Add at end:
See also Classici Musica Italiana, Vol. 25 (modern ed.
of sonatas).

880　—　CATALOGUE
OPERAS
Col. 3, l. 3.　June 1713. *should read*
24 June 1713.

ll. 20-21.　Rome . . . 1727. *should read*:
Milan, Teatro Ducale, 26 Dec. 1726.

l. 22.　autumn 1727. *should read*:
autumn 1728.

Col. 4, l. 24 *should read*:
A few arias R.C.M.; libretto in Biblioteca di Brera,
Milan.

881　—　SERENATAS
Add before l. 1 :

"una composizione drammatica." | ? | Naples, 15 Nov.
1711.1 |　　　|

Add after l. 1 :
" una serenata." | ? | Naples, Oct. 1715.2 |　　　|

ORATORIOS
Col. 3, l. 3 *should read*:
Naples, Chiesa di S. Luigi di Palazzo, *Sabato Santo*, 1716.

Cancel Milan, Ducal Court, Lent 1725.
and move up whole line above ' Il martirio
di Santa Eugenia.'

Add footnotes:
1 In the palace of the Prince of Hesse-Darmstadt.
2 On the birthday of the viceroy, Count Daun.

882　ii　**PORTA**
Par. 1, l. 1.　*c.* 1530 *should read*:
1529

884　i　*Add to* BIBL. :
GARBELOTTO, ' Il Padre Costanzo Porta da Cremona '
(Rome, 1955).

　　ii　*Add after* **PORTATIVE ORGAN** :
PORTATO (It.).　*See* LOURER.

PORTER, Quincy
Par. 3, l. 5 *should read*:
Elizabeth Sprague Coolidge medal in 1943.
In 1954 he took the Pulitzer Prize with his
Concerto for two pianofortes.

885　i　*Add after* l. 4 :
Concerto for 2 pfs. & orch. (1954).

886　i　**ROPTRAIT** *should read* :
PORTRAIT

888　i　**POSITIVE ORGAN**
Add at end:
BIBL.—QUOIKA, RUDOLF, ' Das Positiv in Geschichte
und Gegenwart ' (Cassel & Basel, 1957).

889 ii **POST HORN**
Par. 1, l. 15. Vol. I, No. 9 *should read*:

Vol. 1, p. 1004, No. 9

892 i **POSTAGE STAMPS**
Par. 3, l. 8. Some bars of *should read*:

Some words of

893 ii *Add at end*:

NEW ISSUES SINCE 1950 [1]

AUSTRIA:
1951. Lanner, 150th Anniversary. Portrait.
    Kienzl, 10th Anniversary of death. Portrait.
1952. Schrammel, Centenary. Portrait.
1953. Wolf, 50th Anniversary of death. Portrait.
    150th Anniversary of Linz National Theatre.
    View of building.
1954. 2nd International Congress of Catholic Church
    Music. Good picture of organ in St. Florian
    Church.
1955. Reopening of Vienna State Opera. View of
    building.
1956. Mozart Bicentenary. Portrait. (Special post-
    mark used at Salzburg.)
1958. 3rd Austrian Choral Festival, Vienna. Portrait
    of Walther von der Vogelweide.
1959. Haydn, 150th Anniversary of death. Portrait.

BELGIAN COLONIES: CONGO, RUANDA-URUNDI
1956. Mozart Bicentenary. 2 stamps for each colony,
    designs as (b) and (c) below.

BELGIUM:
1956. Mozart Bicentenary. 3 stamps, showing (a)
    Palace of Charles of Lorraine (where Mozart
    played in 1763), (b) portrait as a child, (c)
    portrait of Queen Elizabeth of the Belgians
    and opening bars of Allegro for piano in C
    (K. 9A), composed in Belgium in 1763.
1958. Day of the Postal Museum. Post horn and
    Postilions' badges.
    Eugène Ysaye, Centenary of birth. Portrait.

BRAZIL:
1952. H. Oswald, Centenary. Portrait.
1958. 150th Anniversary of Brazilian Marine Corps.
    Bugler.
1959. Bicentenary of Carmelite Order in Diamantina.
    Design shows church organ.

BULGARIA:
1953. 2 stamps: girl singer accompanied by accor-
    dion, and folk dancers.
1957 (sic). Cultural Anniversaries. Portrait of Mo-
    zart.
1958. Cultural Celebrities. Portrait of Glinka.

CANADA:
1957. 14th U.P.U. Congress, Ottawa. 2 designs
    with prominent post horn.

COLOMBIA:
1958. Air Express Stamp. Design incorporates post
    horn.

CUBA:
1956. Hubert de Blanck, Centenary of birth. Portrait.
1957. Youth Recreation. One design shows ballet
    dancer.
1958. Set of 4 stamps with portraits of composers:
    N. R. Espadero, I. Cervantes, J. White, B.
    de Salas.

CZECHOSLOVAKIA:
1950. Fibich, Centenary. Portrait.
1951. Prague Musical Festival set. Portraits of
    Dvořák and Smetana.
1952. Prague Musical Festival set. Portrait (some-
    what fanciful) of Beethoven.
    Ševčík, Centenary. Portrait.

1953. Slavík, 120th Anniversary of death. Portrait.
    Janáček, 25th Anniversary of death. Portrait.
    70th Anniversary of National Theatre. Portrait
    of Emmy Destinn.
1954. Czech Musicians: portraits of Dvořák, Janáček
    and Smetana.
    Czechoslovak-Russian friendship. Group of
    girl folk-dancers.
1955. International Music Festival, Prague. 2 stamps,
    showing "Music" (female figure) with
    violin and lyre.
    First National Spartacist Games. Folk dancers.
1956. "Pražské Jaro" (Spring Festival), 6 stamps:
    portraits of Mozart, Mysliveček, Benda and
    the Dušek couple; views of the Bertramka
    and the Tyl Theatre.
1957. International Music Festival Jubilee. Portraits
    of J. B. Foerster, J. V. Stamic (Stamitz), F.
    Laub, F. Ondříček, V. Novák and J. Suk.
    Junior Philatelic Exhibition, Pardubice. Young
    collector blowing post horn.
1959. Cultural Anniversaries. Portrait of František
    Benda.

DENMARK:
1959. Ballet and Music Festival. Dancer in Bournon-
    ville's 'La Sylphide'.

EGYPT:
1958. 35th Anniversary of Death of Sayed Darwick
    (composer). Portrait.

FINLAND:
1957. Death of Sibelius. Portrait.
1958. 400th Anniversary of Founding of Pori (Björne-
    borg). Military side-drummers.

FORMOSA:
1959. Tenth World Scout Jamboree. 3 stamps show
    Scout bugler.

FRANCE:
1951. d'Indy, Centenary. Portrait.
1952. Saint-Saëns. Portrait.
1953. Rameau. Portrait.
1956. Ravel. Portrait.
    Lully, Rousseau and Chopin. Portraits.
1957. Victor Schœlcher. Portrait.
    Lully, 270th Anniversary of death.
    Mozart. Portrait.

FRENCH EMPIRE (LAOS):
1953. Good picture of a native orchestra in action.
1957. Set of 6 native musicians, playing flute, pipes,
    xylophone, bells, violin and drums.

FRENCH EMPIRE (POLYNESIA):
1958. Native girl playing (?) guitar.

FRENCH EMPIRE (WEST AFRICA):
1958. Native musician with primitive string instru-
    ment.

GERMANY (FEDERAL REPUBLIC):
1956. Mozart Bicentenary. Spinet and 5 bars from
    Minuet of piano Sonata in E♭ (K. 282).
    Schumann Centenary. Silhouette portrait and
    music.

GERMANY (W. BERLIN):
1950. 2 stamps celebrating Berlin Philharmonic
    Orchestra (one shows a modern harp, the
    other a painting of " Singing Angels ").
1951. Lortzing, Centenary. Portrait.
1952. Beethoven, 125th Anniversary of death. Death
    Mask.
    Zelter. Portrait (one of a set of famous
    Germans).
1954 Richard Strauss, ? 90th Anniversary of birth
    or 5th of death. Portrait (conducting).
1955. Furtwängler Commemoration. Portrait (con-
    ducting).
1956. Paul Lincke (operetta composer and conductor
    at Folies-Bergère!), 10th anniversary of
    death. Portrait and musical autograph.
1957. Postillion in costume with horn.

GERMANY (RUSSIAN ZONE):
1950. Bach, Bicentenary. Set of 4, including a
    portrait and various executants.
1952. Beethoven, 125th Anniversary of death. 2
    Portraits.
    Handel Festival at Halle. 3 Portraits: Handel,
    Lortzing and Weber (a palpable non sequitur).

---

[1] Some of these are mentioned in the article, but a
tabulated list will be found useful.

1953. Schubert, 125th Anniversary of death. Portrait. View of Berlin State Opera House, with portrait of its architect, G. W. von Knobelsdorff.
1954. Second German Youth Assembly. Folk dancers.
1955. View of Deutsche Staatsoper (one of a series of historic buildings).
1956. Mozart Bicentenary. 2 stamps with different portraits.
Schumann Centenary. 2 stamps with portrait superimposed on opening bars of Schubert's (!) song 'Wanderers Nachtlied'. (These were hastily withdrawn.) As last, but redrawn with different music.
1957. Postillion of 1563 blowing horn. "National Prize" Composers. Portraits of Günther Ramin and Hermann Abendroth.
1958. Communist Postal Conference, Moscow. 2 stamps with post horn design.
10th Anniversary of "Pioneer" Organisation. One stamp shows bugler.
1959. Mendelssohn, 150th Anniversary of birth. 2 designs: Concert Hall at Leipzig and opening theme of Italian Symphony.
Handel, Bicentenary of death. 2 stamps: statue, oboe and arms of Halle, and portrait by Hudson.
Postal Ministers' Conference. 2 stamps with post horn design.

GHANA:
1959. 2nd Anniversary of Independence. One design shows talking drums and elephant-horn player.

GREECE:
1957. Portrait of K. Mantzaros (composer).
1959. Ancient Greek Coins. One design shows Apollo and lyre.
Ancient Greek Theatre. One design shows flute, drum and lyre.

GUATEMALA:
1953. Centenary of National Anthem. Portraits of its composer (R. Álvarez Oraile) and author (J. J. Palma).
1959 (sic). Centenary of National Anthem. Above stamp overprinted " 1858 1958 Centenario " in five different colours.

HOLLAND:
1954. Pijper. Portrait.

HUNGARY:
1952. Attractive view of Bolshoi Theatre, Moscow.
1953. Set of portraits of composers: Bartók, Bihari, Erkel, Goldmark, Kodály, Liszt and Mosonyi.
1955. Bartók, 10th Anniversary of death. 3 portrait stamps.
" XXVIII Bélyegnap, 1955, X. 16, MABÉOSZ ".[1]
1956. Hungarian-Polish Philatelic Exhibition. Portraits of Chopin and Liszt.
1957. Hungarian Red Cross Fund. One design shows post horn.
1958. Air stamps. One design shows airliner over Budapest Opera House.
1959. Postal Ministers' Conference. Post horn design.

INDONESIA:
1954. Child Welfare. Various designs of children playing native instruments.

IRELAND:
1952. Thomas Moore, Centenary of death. 2 portrait stamps. (The only British musician of any kind to appear on a stamp.)

ISRAEL:
1955. Jewish New Year. 4 stamps with musicians playing timbrel and cymbals, ram's horn, " tuba " and harp.
1956. Jewish New Year. 3 stamps with musicians playing lyre, cymbals and double oboe.

---

[1] The inscription means " 27th Postage Stamp Day, 16 Oct. 1955 " and MABÉOSZ seems to be an abbreviation of MAgyar BÉlyeg OSZtály=Hungarian Stamp Department. The picture is the lid of a grand piano, with the opening bars of ' Evening with the Szeklers [Transylvanians] ' from Bartók's Ten Easy Pieces for pianoforte, behind a bunch of flowers.

ITALY:
1950. Guido d' Arezzo, 900th Anniversary. Portrait.
1951. Verdi, 50th Anniversary of death. 3 Portraits against quasi-musical backgrounds, including a very fine stack of organ pipes.
1952. Bellini, 150th Anniversary. Portrait.
1953. Corelli, 300th Anniversary. Portrait.
1954. Catalani, Centenary of birth. Portrait.
1958. Puccini, Centenary of birth. Scene from ' La Bohème ' (Rodolfo's Attic).
Leoncavallo, Centenary of birth. Scene from ' I Pagliacci ' (Prologue).
Tenth Anniversary of " Premio Italia ". One design (radio mast and grand piano) representing " Music ".

ITALIAN SOMALILAND:
1959. Opening of Constituent Assembly. One design shows police bugler.

JAPAN:
1955. " Girl playing a glass flute ", painting by Utamaro.

LEBANON:
1956. Baalbek International Drama Festival. One design shows double bass, masks and columns.

LIBERIA:
1957. Inauguration of Antoinette Tubman Child Welfare Organisation. One stamp shows National Anthem and choristers.

LUXEMBURG:
1948. Edmond de La Fontaine. Set of 4 charity stamps with portrait.
1950. J. A. Zinnen. Portrait ⎫ a set of 4 charity stamps
1951. L. Menager. Portrait ⎬ in each case.
1954. National Theatre Fund. One design shows prize sheep and big drum.

MEXICO:
1954. Centenary of National Anthem. Design includes music.

MONACO:
1955. Albert Schweitzer, 80th birthday. 4 stamps, including portrait, views of Lambaréné, &c.

NEW ZEALAND:
1958. Health Stamps. One design shows Boys' Brigade bugler.

NORTH KOREA:
1956. 10th Anniversary of Young Pioneers. Boy bugler and girl drummer.

PERSIA:
1958. Parcel Post Stamps. Post horn design.
1100th Anniversary of birth of Rudaki (poet and musician). 2 designs, one showing Rudaki playing lyre.

POLAND:
1951. Polish Music Festival. Portraits of Chopin and Moniuszko.
1952. 2nd Wieniawski International Violin Competition. Portrait of Wieniawski.
1954. 5th International Chopin Festival, Warsaw. Portrait of Chopin and grand piano.
1955. As last, 2nd issue. 2 stamps showing bust of Chopin.
1957. 3rd Wieniawski International Violin Competition. Portrait of Wieniawski.
1958. Famous Poles. Portrait of Moniuszko.

PORTUGUESE COLONIES: ANGOLA
1957. Set showing native types, including Andulo flute player and various dancers.

RUMANIA:
1953. C. Porumbescu, Centenary. Portrait.
1954. View of " Musical theatre, Bucharest " (? opera house).
1956. Cultural Anniversaries. Portrait of Mozart.
Enesco, 75th Anniversary of birth. 2 portraits, one as a child with violin.
1957. 80th Anniversary of War of Independence. N. Grigorescu's painting ' The Trumpeter ' (a primitive military instrument).
Postage Due. Set of 6 stamps showing post horn.
1958. Cultural Celebrities. Portrait of Glinka.
Tenth Anniversary of Education Reform. Boy bugler.
1959. Cultural Anniversaries. Portrait of Handel.

RUSSIA:
1950. 30th Anniversary of Azerbaijan S.S.R. View of Baku Opera House.
1951. Alabiev. Portrait.
Kalinnikov. Portrait.
175th Anniversary of Bolshoi Theatre, Moscow. Two views, one with portraits of Glinka, Mussorgsky, Borodin, Tchaikovsky and Rimsky-Korsakov.
1954. Tercentenary of Reunion with Ukraine. View of State Opera House, Kiev.
Glinka, 150th Anniversary of birth. 2 stamps, portrait, and view of Glinka as a young man playing piano to friends.
A. Rubinstein, 125th Anniversary of birth. Portrait.
1955. Liadov, Centenary of birth. Portrait.
1956. Cultural Anniversaries. Portrait of Mozart.
1957. Glinka, Centenary of death. 2 stamps, portrait and scene from opera 'Ivan Susanin'.
Balakirev, 120th Anniversary of birth. Portrait.
Set of Moscow views, including one of Bolshoi Theatre.
V. V. Stassov (critic), 50th Anniversary of death (in 1906 !). 2 portrait stamps.
50th Anniversary of death of Grieg. Portrait.
1958. Tchaikovsky International Music Competition, Moscow. 3 stamps: portrait scene from 'Swan Lake' ballet, pianist and violinist.
"Pioneers" Day. One stamp shows bugler.
Rimsky-Korsakov, 50th Anniversary of death. Portrait.
Rudaki, 1100th Anniversary of birth. Portrait.
1959. Haydn, 150th Anniversary of death. Portrait.
Cultural Celebrities. Statue of Tchaikovsky.

SARAWAK:
1957. One design shows Kayan dancing.

SOUTH WEST AFRICA:
1954. Ovambo woman blowing kudu horn.

SPANISH COLONIES: IFNI, SPANISH GUINEA, SPANISH SAHARA
1953. 3 sets with native musicians playing divers rude instruments.
1956. Native drummer (Ifni only).

SWITZERLAND:
1954. Youth Fund and Centenary of death of Father Zwyssig, composer of "Swiss Hymn". One stamp shows opening bars of hymn against mountain background.
1955. Publicity Issue. One design shows alphorn-player; another includes post horn.

TURKEY:
1957. Bergama Fair. Folk dancing.

YUGOSLAVIA:
1954. Cultural Anniversaries. Portrait of V. Lisinski.
1957. Yugoslav Folklore. Set of 6 stamps, some showing present-day musicians and dancers.
Cultural Anniversaries. Portrait of Stevan Mokranjac.

896　ii　**POUEIGH**
Par. 3, l. 16. d'aujour-d'hui (1921), *should read*:
d'aujourd'hui (1911),

897　ii　**POUGIN**
Par. 3, ll. 2-3 *should read*:
of Verdi', was published serially in 'Le Ménestrel' and for the first time in book-form in Italian in 1881, with additions by "Folchetto" (Jacopo Caponi) and illustra-tions by A. Formis. Pougin later produced a revision in French of his own and Folchetto's versions, and this was translated into English

898　i　**POUISHNOV**
Par. 1, l. 1 *should read*:
POUISHNOV (Пышнов [1]), Lev (*b.* Od-essa, 11 Oct. 1891 ; *d.* London, 28 May 1959).

898　i　*Add at end*:
She died in London on 19 June 1959.

Footnote. l. 4 *should read*:
here adopted. The nearest sound in a western language to the Russian letter (ы) is "ui" in French, as in *puis*.

ii　**POULENC**
Par. 3, l. 1. 1920–21 *should read*:
1920–25

l. 11 *should read*:
produced at Florence and at the Paris Opéra-Comique in 1947.

899　ii　Par. 1, l. 11 *should read*:
of its charm.
The University of Oxford conferred an honorary doctorate on Poulenc in 1958.
R. H. M.

Add after Par. 1 :
BIBL.—HELL, HENRI, 'Francis Poulenc : musicien fran-çais' (Paris, 1958).

CATALOGUE
OPERA *should read*:
OPERAS

l. 2 *should read*:
Apollinaire) (1944), prod. Florence, Teatro Verdi, 22 Apr. 1947 ; Paris, Opéra-Comique, 3 June 1947.

Add at end of OPERAS
'Dialogues des Carmélites' (lib. on Georges Bernanos's film version of Gertrud von Le Fort's novel 'Last on the Scaffold'), prod. Milan, Teatro alla Scala, 26 Jan. 1957.

FILM MUSIC
l. 2. Langueurs *should read*:
Langeais

l. 3. Voyage *should read*:
Voyageur

900　ii　SONGS
l. 40 *should read*:
'Tel jour telle nuit' (Éluard) (1937)

903　i　**POWER**
Par. 4, ll. 8-9 *should read*:
treatise [4] preserved in a manuscript tran-scribed about 1450 by John Wylde,

904　i　**PRAEGER**
Par. 2, l. 3 *should read*:
Praeger (1784–1854), violinist, composer and *Kapellmeister.*

ii　*Add after* **PRAENESTINUS** :
PRAEPOSITUS BRIXIENSIS (*b.* ? ; *d.* ?).
Italian 15th-century composer. He flour-ished early in the century. In the Oxford MS Canonici misc. 213 are preserved 4 *ballate,* two for 3 voices with text in the top voice only

and two for 2 voices with text in both voices. French influence is particularly evident in the 3-part works in 6-8 time and the presence of a French text in a 2-part work in a manuscript at Bologna.   G. R. (iii).

905   i   **PRAETORIUS (3)**
    Add at end:
See also Chorwerk, Vol. 14 (modern reprint of chromatic motet).

907   i   **PRAETORIUS (4)**
    Add at end, before signature:
A facsimile reprint of Vols. I–III of the 'Syntagma' is published in 'Documenta Musicologica', Series I, Vol. xiv (orig. Vol. II), Vol. xv (Vol. III) and Vol. xxvi (Vol. I).

    Add at end:
See also Chorwerk, Vol. 51 (modern reprint of songs). Publikationen G.M.F., Vol. 12 (reprint of 'Syntagma', Vol. II).

913   ii   **PRATELLA**
    Par. 1, l. 2 *should read*:
Romagna, 1 Feb. 1880; *d.* Ravenna, 18 May 1955).

917   ii   *Add before* **PRÉS**:
PREPARED PIANO. *See* CAGE, JOHN.

919   ii   *Add before* **Prévost**:
PREVITALI, Fernando (*b.* Adria, 16 Feb. 1907).
Italian conductor. He studied at the Conservatory " G. Verdi " at Turin, his subjects being the violoncello, the organ and composition (with Franco Alfano). He began his career as a conductor as assistant to Vittorio Gui with the Orchestra Sinfonia of Florence (1928–36), and in 1935–53 he was director of the symphony orchestra of the Roman Radio. In 1953 he was appointed artistic director of the Accademia Nazionale di Santa Cecilia in Rome and permanent conductor of the orchestra attached to that institution. He has conducted the most important orchestras in Italy and many abroad, excelling especially in the interpretation of music by living composers. He has himself composed orchestral music, the ballet 'Allucinazioni' (Rome, 1945) and instrumental and vocal chamber music. He succeeded Bernardino Molinari as head of the finishing course in orchestral conducting at the Accademia di Santa Cecilia and has published a ' Guida allo studio della direzione orchestrale ' (1951).   G. M. G.

920   ii   *Add after* **PRIEST VICAR**:
PRIESTLEY, Edmund (*b.* Wibsey, Bradford, 12 Apr. 1889; *d.* Wibsey, 2 Nov. 1957). English musical educationist. He was trained as a teacher at Leeds University in

1907–10 and took the degrees of M.Ed. and B.Sc. there. He taught in an elementary school at Bradford in 1910–12, then as mathematics and music master at Grange Hill High School, Bradford, in 1912–30. During this period he was also part-time lecturer in further education. He was awarded the L.R.A.M. diploma and gained a considerable reputation as a vocalist and choral conductor. In 1930 he was appointed organizing inspector in further education and in 1933 adviser in music under the Bradford Education Committee. Four years later he accepted the newly created post of adviser in music to the West Riding Authority, which he held until his retirement in 1951. From 1938 he took a leading part in establishing recorder playing in schools and youth clubs, and he fostered the growth of non-competitive schools' musical festivals in the West Riding of Yorkshire. In 1942 he introduced a comprehensive plan of instrumental concerts for schools, suitable for a large county area. A chamber orchestra was engaged to give two concerts a day on three days of each week of the school year in secondary schools and training-colleges. A permanent string quartet was later engaged by the Authority to give further concerts in schools and training-colleges. Priestley was a founder-member and first president of the Music Advisers' National Association and an Honorary Life Vice-President of the Schools' Music Association. In 1951 he was awarded the M.B.E. for national service to music.

Among Priestley's publications the following are the most important:
' A Music Guide for Schools ' and ' My Music Guides ' (in collaboration with J. H. Grayson).
' A School Recorder Book ' (in collaboration with F. Fowler).
' The Organisation of a Non-Competitive Music Festival.'   S. S. M.

927   i   **PRIMITIVE MUSIC**
    Add to BIBL. :
NETTL, BRUNO, ' Music in Primitive Culture ' (Cambridge, Mass., & Oxford, 1956).
SCHNEIDER, MARIUS, ' Primitive Music ', in N.O.H.M. (Oxford, 1957).

    ii   **PRIMROSE**
    Par. 1, l. 2. 1904 *should read*:
1903

934   ii   **PRINTING**
    Add at beginning of BIBL. :
HOPKINSON, CECIL, ' A Dictionary of Parisian Music Publishers, 1700–1950 ' (London, 1954).
HUMPHRIES, CHARLES & SMITH, WILLIAM C., ' Music Publishing in the British Isles, from the Earliest Times to the Middle of the Nineteenth Century ' (London, 1954).

935   i   **PRISE DE TROIE**
    l. 2. LES TROYENS. *should read*:
TROYENS, LES.

935   i   *Add after* **PRITCHARD, J. M.** :

PRITCHARD, Thomas Cuthbertson Leithead (*b.* Glasgow, 11 Mar. 1885); *d.* Glasgow, April 1960).
Scottish organist, writer and musical educationist. He was educated at Glasgow University, where he gained an M.A. in mathematics and natural philosophy, and at Edinburgh University, where his studies with Sir Donald Tovey resulted in a double Mus.D. as composer and historian. Pritchard was well known as an organist, and did much to improve church music in Scotland by his lectures and his exemplary work at Belhaven Church, Glasgow. In 1911 he joined the staff of the Royal Scottish Academy of Music and for 21 years was Supervisor of Music in schools. He was joint editor of the ' Revised Church Hymnary ' and musical editor of ' The Scottish Psalters ' (1929). His writings on music, which include numerous articles in English and Scottish journals, are marked by their literary style and accuracy. He had long cultivated a special interest in the music of Schubert, and contributed a notable chapter on ' The Schubert Idiom ' to a symposium on the composer edited by Gerald Abraham.

D. W. S.

936   ii   **PRIX DE ROME**
1921. J. de Sauville de Lapresle *should read* :
Jacques de La Presle

937   i   **PRO ARTE STRING QUAR-TET**
Add at end of Par. 4 :
The Quartet gave performances for a whole week at Cambridge each year from 1932 to 1938.

117 | ' Story about a Real Man. '

938   ii   **PROD'HOMME**
Par. 1, l. 2 *should read* :
Gabriel) (*b.* Paris, 28 Nov. 1871 ; *d.* Paris, 18 June 1956).

940   i   **PRODIGY**
Add at end :
See also Bethune, T. G. (" Blind Tom ").

941   ii   **PROGRAMME MUSIC**
See also should read :
See also Biber (Mystery Sonatas). Kuhnau (Biblical Sonatas). Mundy (J., " Weather " Fantasy).

944   i   **PROGRAMME NOTES**
Add to BIBL. :
BIANCOLLI, LOUIS & MANN, WILLIAM S. (ed.), ' The Analytical Concert Guide ' (London, 1957).

944   ii   **PROKOFIEV**
Par. 1, l. 3.   4 Mar. *should read* :
5 Mar.

945   i   Par. 1, l. 18 *should read* :
awarded to pianists, paying a short visit to London to meet Diaghilev. In 1916 he conducted

Par. 2, ll. 1-3 *should read* :
In the autumn of 1918 he went through Siberia to Japan, thence to San Francisco and New York, and he settled for a time in the U.S.A. In 1920 he paid prolonged visits to Paris and London.

l. 5.   ' The Love of *should read* :
' The Love for

Par. 3, ll. 1-7 *should read* :
In Jan. 1927 Prokofiev paid a visit to Russia and took out Soviet citizenship papers, but he continued for some five years to visit western Europe frequently and did not finally settle down in his native country again until 1932. In 1928 the Dostoyevsky opera,

946   i   Par. 3, l. 7. Love of *should read* :
Love for

CATALOGUE OF WORKS
should read :
CATALOGUE OF WORKS [1]

OPERAS
Col. 2, l. 3.   ' The Love of Three Oranges.' *should read* :
' The Love for Three Oranges.'

Col. 5.   *Add to Op.* 37 :
Venice, Teatro La Fenice, Sept. 1955.

Add to table :
| 1948. |

Add footnote :
[1] Opp. 101, 107-9 and 126-29, being suites from the ballets Opp. 64, 87 and 118, are not listed here.

ii   *Add to* BALLETS :
118. ' Stone Flower.'

Add to FILM MUSIC :
96. ' Lermontov ' (1941).
116. ' Ivan the Terrible ', after Pushkin.

CHORAL WORKS
l. 1.   ' Ivan and the Wave ' *should read* :
' Swan and the Wave '

Op. 7 *should read* :
7. 2 Choruses for women's voices (Balmont) (1910)
1. The White Swan.
2. The Wave.

Op. 85.   ' Toast to Stalin ' *should read* :
' Toast for Stalin's Birthday '

Add :
104. Russian Folksongs.
121. Soldiers' Marching-Song.

946   ii   CHORAL WORKS
           l. 16 *should read*:
124. Oratorio ' On Guard for Peace ' (1950).

947   i   ORCHESTRAL WORKS
          Op. 43 *should read*:
43. ' Divertissements ' (1925-26).

          Op. 57 *should read*:
57. ' Symphonic Song ' (1933).

          Add:
112. Revised version of Symphony No. 4.
120. 2 Waltzes.
122. Suite ' Winter Holiday '.
123. ' Summer Night ', suite based on the opera Op. 86.
130. ' Meeting of the Volga and the Don.'
131. Symphony No. 7.

          SOLO   INSTRUMENT   AND   OR-
          CHESTRA
          Op. 16.   (1914) *should read*:
(1913)

          Op. 26.   (1917) *should read*:
(1921)

          Op. 55.   G mi. *should read*:
G ma.

          Op. 58 *should read*:
58. Cello Concerto No. 1 (1935-38).

          Add:
125. Cello Concerto No. 2 (1950–52).[2]
132. ' Concertino ' for cello.

          CHAMBER MUSIC
          Add before Op. 34:
— Scherzo for 4 bassoons (1916).[3]

          Op. 92.   Kabaldine *should read*:
Kabardin

          Add after CHAMBER MUSIC:
          UNACCOMPANIED VIOLIN
115. Sonata.

          VIOLONCELLO AND PIANOFORTE
          Add:
119. Sonata.

          Add footnotes:

[2] Edited from sketches by Rostropovich, to whom the
work was to be dedicated.
[3] An arrangement of the pianoforte piece Op. 12
No. 9.

     ii   PIANOFORTE MUSIC
          Op. 96. l. 1 *should read*:
96a. 3 Pieces (1942).

          l. 2 *should read*:
1. Waltz from ' War and Peace ' opera.

          l. 3 *should read*:
2. Contredanse from ' Lermontov ' film.

          Add:
103. Sonata No. 9, C ma.

          Add at end:
          VOCAL DUET
106. 2 Duets for tenor and bass.

949   ii   *Add after* **PROPHETESS**:
PROPORTIO. *See* Saltarello.

950   ii   *Add before* **PROPOSTA**:
PROPORZ. *See* Saltarello.

953   ii   *Add before* **PSALMODY**:
**PSALM-TUNE PRELUDE AND INTER-
LUDE.** A unique collection of Psalm-Tune
Preludes and Interludes, composed by John
Reading, is kept at Dulwich College Library
(Mus. MSS I & II). The manuscripts are
in autograph and contain 24 psalm-tune preludes and interludes. The preludes are
modelled on the German type of chorale
prelude, written in three or four parts with
the highly ornamented and broken-up tune
in the treble. The interludes are very short,
usually in two-part writing, and inserted
between the sections of the psalm-tune.

The collection is entitled ' The Psalms Set
full for the Organ or Harpsichord, as they
were Plaid in Churches and Chappels, withe
the Manner of giving them out, as allso with
Great Variety of interludes, Set and Composed by John Reading '. It is not dated but
was probably composed during the first half
of the 18th century.

There are two different settings for most
of the psalm-tunes, which are the following:

York Psalm Tune.
St. David's Psalm Tune.
St. Mary Hackney's Psalm Tune.
London Psalm Tune.
Windsor Psalm Tune.
Canterbury Psalm Tune.
Martyrs Psalm Tune.
Southwell Psalm Tune.
The 100 Psalm Tune Proper.
The 81 Psalm Tune Proper.
The 113 Psalm Tune Proper.
The 119 Psalm Tune Proper.
The 148 Psalm Tune Proper.

                                        S. J.

969   ii   **PSALTER, METRICAL:
           ENGLISH**
           Par. 4, ll. 4-6 *should read*:
work was brought out by Thomas Harper. It
reached a second edition in 1650. The enthusiasm of earlier days

983   ii   **PSALTER, METRICAL:
           SCOTTISH**
           Add to Bibl.:
Pritchard, T. C. L., ' Scottish Psalmody ' (M. & L.,
     XXXI, 1950, p. 73).
' Scottish Psalmody ' (M. Rev., XI, 1950, p. 54).
' The Scottish Metrical Psalter ' (' The Scottish
     Historical Review ', XXX, 1951, p. 55).

984   i   **PSALTERY**
          Add at end:
(*PLATES* 32, Vol. IV, p. 492, No. 5 ; 48,
Vol. VI, p. 538.)

986   i   **PUBLIKATIONEN ÄLTERER
          MUSIC**
          l. 2. Denkmaler *should read*:
Denkmäler

990   i   **PUCCINI**
Add to Bibl. :

Carner, Mosco, ' Puccini : a Critical Biography ' (London, 1958).
Fraccaroli, Arnaldo, ' Giacomo Puccini si confida e racconta ' (Milan, 1957).
Gadda Conti, Piero, ' Vita e melodie di Giacomo Puccini ' (Milan, 1955).
Greenfield, Edward, ' Puccini : Keeper of the Seal ' (London, 1958).
Sartori, Claudio, ' Puccini ' (Milan, 1958).

CATALOGUE
OPERAS
(' Madama Butterfly '), col. 1.   *Add before* l. 9 :
(Revised version.)

Col. 3.   *Add before* l. 16 :
Brescia, 28 May 1904.

993   i   **PUJOL, Joan**
Add at end :
See also Publicacions Catalunya, Vols. 3 & 7 (modern ed.).

994   i   *Add after* **PULITI** :
PULITI-SANTOLIQUIDO, Ornella (*b.* Florence, 4 Nov. 1906).
Italian pianist. She studied with Attilio Brugnoli at the Conservatory of Florence and later with Casella in Rome and Cortot in Paris. She is a professor of the pianoforte at the Accademia di Santa Cecilia in Rome and formed a trio with the violinist Pellicia and the cellist Amfitheatrof which has made many concert tours in Italy and abroad, where, however, she is also highly appreciated as a soloist.   G. M. G.

997   i   **PURCELL (4)**
l. 1.   *c.* 1659 ; *should read* :
1659 ;
l. 10 *should read* :
between 21 Nov. 1658 and 20 Nov. 1659 ; but this is narrowed to between June 1659 and 20 Nov. of that year by the title-page of his ' Sonatas of III Parts ', published in June 1683, which states " aetat. suae 24 ". The

1001   ii   *Add after* Par. 7 :
Te Deum and Jubilate for St. Cecilia's Day (1697).

1002   ii   *Delete* Par. 3 (vii).

1010   ii   *Add to* Bibl. :
Ravenzwaaij, G. van, ' Purcell ' (Haarlem & Antwerp, 1954).
Sietz, Reinhold, ' Henry Purcell : Zeit, Leben, Werk ' (Leipzig, 1955).

Cancel ll. 25-26.

ll. 28-30 *should read* :
Mus. Ass., Vol. XLII, 1935-36).
' Purcell ' (' Master Musicians ' series) (London, 1937).

1014   —   *Footnote* 4. l. 2 *should read* :
Lewis (publ. in ' The Score ', No. 4, Jan. 1951).

1019   i   *See also.* l. 6 *should read* :
Guide ', orch. vars.). Chorwerk, Vol. 17 (modern reprint of 5 anthems). Clarke (J. i, choral song on death

l. 11 *should read* :
vars. on theme for stgs.). Lyrebird Press (modern ed. of 22 sonatas). Masque. Moeschinger (vars.

1021   ii   **PURCELL SOCIETY**
Add after 26. ' King Arthur ' :
27. Miscellaneous Odes and Cantatas. ' From hardy climes ' ; ' Celestial Music ' ; ' Great Parent, hail ' ; ' Hark, Damon, hark ' ; ' Hark how the wild musicians sing ' ; ' If ever I more riches did desire ' ; ' In a deep vision's intellectual scene ' ; ' We reap all the pleasures ' (fragment), ed. by Dennis Arundell, Arnold Goldsbrough & Anthony Lewis. 1957.

Delete par. beginning The following volumes . . . *and replace by* :
All the above volumes, except 2, 24 and 27, are out of print, but are to be gradually reissued with such revision as may be necessary. The edition is to be completed with the following four volumes :
28. Sacred Music, Part iv (Anthems).
29. Sacred Music, Part v (Anthems).
30. Sacred Music, Part vi (Songs and Vocal Ensemble Music).
31. Fantasias and Miscellaneous Instrumental Music.

1022   ii   **PURFLING**
Cancel See also Violin Making. *at end.*

1023   i   **PUSCHMANN**
Par. 1, l. 1.   **Adam Zacharias** *should read* :
Adam [1]

Par. 2, l. 5.   (1574) *should read* :
(1571)

Add footnote :
[1] Not Adam Zacharias, as previously given : Zacharias Puschmann, cantor at Görlitz, was Adam's brother.

Pushkin
See also, l. 15. Cockerel *should read* :
Weathercock

l. 26. (32 songs) *should read* :
(34 songs)

l. 31. ' Dubiovsky ' *should read* :
' Dubrovsky '

l. 38. Cockerel *should read* :
Weathercock

1024   i   **PYAMOUR**
Add at end :
He is described as " one of the clerks of the Chapel Royal " in 1419, when Henry V granted him a corrody at the convent of Luffield, Northants. The boys whom he was commissioned to impress into royal service in the following year were taken to Normandy, and Pyamour, who was then Master of the Children of the Chapel, probably stayed on the Continent and travelled with the king.

In 1427 he was among members of the Duke of Bedford's chapel. The corrody at Luffield was re-assigned in July 1431, by which time he was referred to as deceased.   D. W. S.

BIBL.—HARVEY, JOHN, 'Gothic England' (London, 1947).

1024   i   *Add after* **PYAMOUR** :

PYCARD, ? (*b.* ? ; *d.* ?).

English 14th–15th-century singer and composer. His music is found in only one source, the 'Old Hall Manuscript', but the six complete works there preserved show that his technique was advanced for its time and that he favoured the use of canon and even double canon in his liturgical settings of Mass sections.

Of the four settings of 'Gloria' three are canonic, the fourth being so rich in imitative passages that it often sounds as if strict canon were being used. The 'Gloria' I, 76 has its text shared by two altos and a tenor, with a supporting instrumental part. The second alto is in canon with the tenor, a perfect fourth above, throughout the work ; generally the progressions are smoothly contrived, though the harmony becomes more adventurous as the work reaches its close. In the second setting (I, 84) there is canon at the unison between tenor and contratenor, both purely instrumental parts. In case two instruments were not available, Pycard provided a *solus tenor* part, which produces a conflate of the tenor and contratenor, unfortunately destroying the canon in the process. There is, however, a hidden canon between two upper voices : one only is written out, but it has two verbal texts underlaid, forming a canon at the unison, *comes* following *dux* at precisely the same interval as in the lower parts. The composition is thus for three alto voices and two instruments (one only in case of need).

Similarly scored is the third setting (I, 119), although here no *solus tenor* is provided since the lower parts are complex and interdependent to an unusual degree. The third alto begins as if in canon with the first, but this decoy soon gives way to the regular canonic part in the second alto. There is a brilliant hocket at "cum Sancto Spiritu" which continues almost to the end of the "Amen". The last 'Gloria', which uses the Marian trope "Spiritus et alme orphanorum paraclite", reflects the technique of the Italian *caccia* in its upper voices, both altos. *Alius tenor* is a free instrumental part, but like contratenor and tenor it is isorhythmic. The latter parts are not really a double addition to the texture, since they alternate throughout except when overlapping at a unison. This means that the *solus tenor* is, for once, not a new melody, and besides preserving the plainsong it retains the structure of the isorhythm. The source of the plainsong is the last strophe (" Johannes Jesu care ") of the Sequence "Johannes Jesu Christo multum dilecte" for the feast of St. John Evangelist. From the point of view of texture this music is in four parts, though it appears to be in five ; quite the opposite of I, 84, which is actually in five real parts, though it appears to be in four.

The first 'Credo', for two altos and two instruments, is unfortunately imperfect at certain points owing to the removal of an initial letter on the previous page. There is enough of the second alto part to show that four-part sections alternated throughout with duets between one voice and one instrument. There is little if any imitation, though this device figures largely in the other 'Credo' (II, 135), also in four parts — two altos and two instruments — without ever becoming strict canon. Here the text is shared between the two singers, who are presumably expected to play the instrumental interludes as well. An anonymous 'Credo' (II, 101) is attributed to Pycard, on stylistic grounds, by Manfred Bukofzer.   D. W. S.

BIBL.—BESSELER, HEINRICH, 'Bourdon und Fauxbourdon' (Leipzig, 1950).
BUKOFZER, MANFRED, 'Studies in Medieval and Renaissance Music' (New York, 1950).
RAMSBOTHAM, ALEXANDER, ed., 'The Old Hall Manuscript', Vols. I–III (London, 1933–38).
STRUNK, OLIVER, 'The Music of the Old Hall Manuscript : Postscript' (in BUKOFZER, *op. cit.*).

1026   i   **PYNE (5)**
       Par. 1, l. 1.   1908 *should read* :
1928

1029   i   **QUAGLIATI**
       Par. 1, ll. 7–16 *should read* :

monody. The music is, unfortunately, rather monotonous. The more ambitious 'La sfera armoniosa' is likewise uninventive, though more appealing in the lighter pieces than the more serious ones. It is a collection of monodies and concerted vocal music, some of it written for the marriage of Nicolò Ludovisi, nephew of Pope Gregory XV, and Isabella Gesualda, Carlo Gesualdo's sister. The prevailing style is that commonly found in Roman secular music of this time, which means that it cannot compare with the finest Florentine and Venetian music in the same style, by composers like Caccini, Benedetti, Saracini and d' India. Quagliati makes extensive use of *concertato* instruments ; this is one of the more interesting aspects of the volume.

Footnote 2. l. 1 should read :

² This work and 'La sfera armoniosa' have been edited by V. Gotwals and P. Keppler as 'Smith College Archives', Vol. XIII (Northampton, Mass., 1957). On the text *see* U. Rolandi in 'Rassegna Dorica', Nov.

1030   i   **QUANTZ**
          Par. 3, l. 15 *should read*:

appeared in London a short and inaccurate
abstract of Quantz's remarks about embellishments and cadenzas entitled ' Easy

          Footnote 3. l. 2, *should read*:
appeared at Leipzig in 1906 and 1926. A facsimile of
the third German edition appeared at Cassel in 1953,
' Documenta Musicologica ' (Series I, Vol. i). The
work is much more

          ii   BIBL. l. 5 *should read*:
Kahl (Cologne & Crefeld, 1948). Extracts in Paul
Nettl, ' Forgotten Musicians ' (New York, 1951).

1031   ii   **QUARTET**
           Par. 2, l. 9. Bloch, 2 ; *should read*:
Bloch, 4 ;

1032   i   *Add after* **QUASI** :
Quasimodo, Salvatore. *See* Turchi (2 poems for
voice & pf.).

       ii   **QUATTRINI**
           Par. 1, l. 2 *should read*:
1822 ; *d.* Warsaw, 10 Apr. 1893).

       Add after **QUAVER** :
QUAYLE, Leo (Gordon) (*b.* Pretoria, 11
Dec. 1918).
South African conductor, pianist and composer. He first studied with his father and
then with Isadore Epstein. From the age
of twelve he conducted his own orchestra at
Pretoria. In 1936 he was awarded an overseas scholarship enabling him to study at the
R.C.M. in London under Herbert Fryer
(pianoforte), Constant Lambert (conducting)
and Gordon Jacob (composition). He was
awarded the Hopkinson gold medal for pianoforte playing in 1946, after six years of war
service. In 1951 he became musical director
of the Welsh National Opera Company, and
he was chorus master for the 1953 Glyndebourne season. In 1954 he was appointed
chief conductor of the Sadler's Wells Opera,
a post he held until 1957. He has also been
guest conductor with leading British and

South African orchestras and has frequently
conducted on radio and television.
   In 1958 Quayle returned to South Africa
to become senior lecturer in music at Stellenbosch University and, later in the year, Professor of Music at the University of Bloem-
fontein. His compositions include a ballet,
' La Fenêtre ' (1949), a Trio for violin, cello
and pianoforte (1943), a song cycle (Myles
Bourke) for baritone and orchestra (1945)
and 3 Songs for soprano and pianoforte (1941).
                                         G. F. S.

1033   ii   *Add before* **QUEMPAS** :
           QUELDRYK, ? (*b.* ? ; *d.* ?).
English 14th–15th-century singer and composer. He may possibly have received his
early training at Fountains Abbey, where
there was a strong polyphonic tradition. An
estate at Fountains was known as Queldrike,
and the composer may have taken his name
from it, as John did from Dunstable. Two
works by Queldryk are to be found in the
' Old Hall Manuscript ' : a ' Gloria ' and a
' Credo '. The ' Gloria ' (I, 109) is for two
altos and two instruments, the voices alternating in singing the troped text. A similar
scheme of alternation is found in the ' Credo '
(II, 232) for two altos and one instrument.
Both works are isorhythmic, and both employ
a tenor not founded on plainsong, though the
two *taleae* repeated in diminution may indicate that the composer wrote the works to
a set plan. Since the scheme of alternation
as well as the isorhythmic structure is common
to both works, they may conceivably constitute a Mass pair.   D. W. S.
BIBL.—BUKOFZER, MANFRED, ' Studies in Medieval and
   Renaissance Music ' (New York, 1950).
RAMSBOTHAM, ALEXANDER, ed., ' The Old Hall Manuscript ', Vols. I & II (London, 1933 & 1935).

1037   ii   **QUINTON**
           l. 2 *should read*:
VIOL. (*PLATE* 66, Vol. VIII, p. 146 (i),
No. 6.)

1040   i   **QUODLIBET**
           Add after See also :
Ensalada.

VOL. VII

27 ii *Add to* BIBL. :
BERTENSSON, S. & LEYDA, J., 'Sergei Rachmaninov'
(New York, 1956).
SWAN, ALFRED & KATHERINE, 'Rakhmaninov: Personal
Reminiscences' (M.Q., Jan.-Apr. 1944).

28 — CATALOGUE
OPERAS
Vladimir   Col. 3, l. 1. Vassily *should read* :

CHORAL WORKS
l. 11 *should read* :
chorus & orch. (ded. to Morosov) (1902).

l. 16 *should read* :
orch. (ded. to Willem Mengelberg and the Amsterdam
Concertgebouw Orchestra) (1913).

l. 19. (*c.* 1930) *should read* :
(ded. to Leopold Stokowski) (*c.* 1930).

ORCHESTRAL WORKS
l. 1. (after Lermontov) (1893). *should
read* :
(after Lermontov) (ded. to N. Rimsky-Korsakov) (1893)

l. 3 (1895). *should read* :
(1895).[1]

l. 6 *should read* :
Böcklin's picture (ded. to N. Struve) (1909).

Add after l. 6 :
44. Symphony No. 3 (1936).
45. Symphony, D mi., 1st movement (publ. posth.).
— 'Three Symphonic Dances' (1941).

PIANOFORTE AND ORCHESTRA
l. 6. G mi. (1927). *should read* :
G mi. (ded. to N. Medtner) (1927).

l. 7 *should read* :
43. Rhapsody on a Theme by Paganini (1934).

Add footnote :
[1] Score destroyed by the composer but reconstructed
from parts by Soviet musicians and performed in
Moscow on 17 Oct. 1945.

CHAMBER MUSIC
Add at end :
— 4 Movements of 2 string Quartets (publ. posth.).

VIOLIN AND PIANOFORTE
l. 1 *should read* :
6. 2 Pieces (ded. to Jules Conus) (1893).

VIOLONCELLO AND PIANOFORTE
l. 1 *should read* :
2. 2 Pieces (ded. to A. Brandukov) (1893).

l. 4. C mi. *should read* :
G mi.

ii PIANOFORTE SOLO
l. 26 *should read* :
' Polka by V.R.'[2]

Add footnote :
[2] On a theme by his father, Vassily Rakhmaninov.

SONGS
l. 5. (?). *should read* :
(1893).

29 i SONGS
Op. 14 No. 11, *Op.* 26 Nos. 2 & 11, *Op.* 34
Nos. 9 & 10. (Tyuchev) *should read* :
(Tuchev)
Add at end :
See also Symphony, p. 244.

30 i **RALF, Torsten**
Par. 1, l. 2 *should read* :
Jan. 1901 ; *d.* Stockholm, 27 Apr. 1954).

ll. 14-15 *should read* :
the Metropolitan, New York, in 1945-48 ; in
Buenos Aires in 1945, and at Covent

ii **RAMANN, Lina**
Par. 3, ll. 18-21 *should read* :
volumes in 1882. The over-enthusiasm
exhibited by this work is pardonable, and it
was done with care, minuteness and intelligence, so far as the author's personal bias and
outside interference would allow. But that
interference, which came from the Princess
Sayn Wittgenstein, and through her from
Liszt himself, so seriously distorted many
biographical facts, especially those connected with the relationship between Liszt
and the Comtesse d'Agoult, that it can no
longer be taken seriously as a source

31 i l. 1 *should read* :
of information. Lina Ramann

RAMEAU
Par. 1, l. 1. Date *should read* :
(*b.* Dijon, 25 Sept.[1]

Add footnote :
[1] This is the date of his baptism, but the plaque on
his house at Dijon says " né le 25 septembre 1683 ".

37 ii *Add to* BIBL. :
BERTHIER, PAUL, ' Réflexions sur l'art et la vie de Jean-
Philippe Rameau ' (Paris, 1957).
GIRDLESTONE, CUTHBERT, ' Jean-Philippe Rameau : his
Life and Work ' (London, 1957).
TIÉNOT, YVONNE, ' J.-Ph. Rameau : esquisse biogra-
phique ' (Paris & Brussels, 1954).

39 ii CATALOGUE
HARPSICHORD MUSIC
l. 12 *should read* :
' Pièces de clavecin ' (1724 & 1731 [2]).

l. 13. *Delete* Menuet en rondeau,
C ma.

l. 35. D ma.[2] *should read* :
D ma.[3]

l. 37 *should read* :
' Nouvelles Suites de pièces de clavecin ' (*c.* 1728).[4]

Footnote 2 *becomes* 3.

Add footnotes :
[2] Republished and slightly revised by Rameau. The
full title reads : ' Pièces de clavecin : avec une méthode
pour la méchanique des doigts avec une table pour
les agréments '.
[4] The original titles add '. . . avec des remarques
sur les différents genres de musique '.

40 i HARPSICHORD MUSIC
l. 10. G mi. *should read*:
G mi. (1747).

l. 11. concert ' *should read*:
concerts '

l. 12. composer): *should read*:
composer, 1741):

See also. l. 7 *should read*:
ballet). Lyrebird Press (arr. of suite from ' Les Paladins '). Tambourin (mus. ex.). Variations, p. 680.
Zil-

RAMIN
Par. 1, l. 2 *should read*:
1898; d. Leipzig, 27 Feb. 1956).

41 ii **RAMSEY, Robert**
Par. 2, l. 3. 4 pieces *should read*:
5 pieces

Par. 4, ANTHEMS. *Add after* l. 2 :
How are ye mightye falne. ECG.

Cancel ll. 11-12.

Add at end, before signature:
MADRIGALS
Long ago my hart I gave. ECG.
Sleep fleshlye birth. ECG.

42 i *Add before* **RANDALL, John** :

RANDALL, Greenwood (*b.* Exeter, ? ; *d.* ?).
English 16th–17th-century composer. He was probably the son of William Randall (i). He became a vicar choral at Exeter Cathedral. On 21 Apr. 1610 he was appointed to teach the choristers under Edward Gibbons's supervision. On 10 Feb. 1615 he married Katharine Dunne, a widow, and after her death, on 4 May 1626, Mary, daughter of Edward Gibbons. His name was frequently mentioned in the cathedral records and account books. He received regular payments for " firing for the choristers " and occasional payments for books, paper and pricking music. His name is still mentioned in the last accounts (1644–1645) kept by the Dean and Chapter during the Civil War.
A Morning and Evening Service by Greenwood Randall exists, bass part only (B.M., Add. 17784, p. 132) and there is an organ part (MS Mus. A 2, p. 226) and bass part (MS Mus. C 18, p. 4) at the Durham Cathedral Library. s. J.

Add after **RANDALL, Peter** :

RANDALL (Randal, Randoll), William
(*b.* ? ; *d.* Exeter, ? 1604).
English organist and composer, probably father of Greenwood Randall. A Gentleman of the Chapel Royal, he was one of the sixteen " excellent Musitians " of England named by Meres in his ' Palladis Tamia ' (1598). His name also occurs in a list compiled by Anthony Wood and dated 1695 (Bodl. MS Wood D 19 [4]). Before entering the Chapel Royal Randall was a lay vicar at Exeter Cathedral, where he signed on 7 Oct. 1578 a subscription list of the vicars (MS ' The Case of Robert Withers ', 1607–11, Exeter Cath. Lib.). According to an entry in the Cheque Book of the Chapel Royal, he was sworn in as an epistler of the Chapel on 15 Feb. 1584 and signed himself in the same book as " Organist " on 26 July 1592. The Cheque Book contains further entries about him and a number of his signatures.
On 25 May Elizabeth I, in a letter to the Dean and Chapter and the College of Vicars Choral at Exeter, ordered that William Randall should be restored to his old vicar's place with the annual stipend of £10 and a house, " quyetly to enjoy the same in such a manner as he was wont to doe before his preferment to our service " (P.R.O., State Papers Domestic). He was restored to the place, and the following item appeared in the accounts of the College of Vicars Choral (Accounts of the Custos of Kallenderhay, 1586–1607, Exeter Cath. Lib.) :

Item payed out the 21st day of October 1601 unto one Wm Randall, gent of her Maties Chappell by commons consent, in regards of her Maties Letter of commendacion for a Vicars room among us, which, the sayd Randall has procured, of free gifte the priest Vicars bestowed upon him the some of 33s. 4d.

Randall continued to keep his place at the Chapel Royal, where in 1603 he is still mentioned as one of the Gentlemen who received an allowance of mourning livery for the queen's funeral (Lafontaine, ' The King's Musick '). He is mentioned again among those attending the coronation of James I (Cheque Book of Chapel Royal). It appears that he died before 1 Mar. 1604, on which day Edmund Hooper was sworn into his place *ibid.*).
The following works by William Randall have been traced :

CONSORT OF VIOLS
' In Nomine ' (Bodl. Lib., D 212-6).

ANTHEMS
' Give sentence with me ', 6 v. (B.M. Add. MSS 17792-96: 5 part-books only, *Cantus, Altus, Tenor, Quintus, Bassus*).
' O Father deare ' (B.M. Harley 6346, words only).
' If the Lord Himselfe ' (B.M. Harley 6346, words only)

VIRGINAL PIECES
' Johnsons Medley by Mr. Randall ' (Fitzw., MS 52 D. 25).
' Dowland's Lacrimae sett by Mr. Randall ' (*ibid.*).
' Mr. Newmans Pauane By Mr. Randall ' (*ibid.*).
s. J.

42 i **RANDALL, William**
Par. 2, ll. 1-2 *should read*:
English music seller and publisher, son or grandson of Peter Randall. At

46 ii **RANKL**
Par. 3, ll. 3-4 *should read*:
4 symphonies (one with 3 women's voices)
and a number of choruses and songs.

49 i **RAPHAEL**
Par. 5, l. 1 *should read*:
Raphael takes a special interest in the use of
the saxophone, which, for example, plays an
important part in his Op. 66 for orchestra.
He is principally an instrumental

ii ORCHESTRAL WORKS
Add before Op. 67 :
66. Ballet Suite ' Jabonah '.

SOLO INSTRUMENTS AND OR-
CHESTRA
Add after — Organ Concerto :
71. Concertino for alto saxophone.

CHAMBER MUSIC
74. ' Divertimento ' for alto saxophone & cello.

50 ii **RASELIUS**
Add at end :
See also Denkmäler (2) II, Vols. 29-30 (modern ed.
of ' Cantiones sacrae ').

51 i **RASI**
Par. 2, l. 21 *should read*:
examples of the rather sweet, lyrical and un-
dramatic style of Caccini's songs. He wrote
many of

Add to BIBL. :
FORTUNE, NIGEL, ' Italian Secular Monody from 1600 to
1635: an Introductory Survey ' (M.Q., XXXIX,
1953, p. 171).
MACCLINTOCK, CAROL, ' The Monodies of Francesco
Rasi ' (abstract in Journ. Amer. Musicol. Soc.,
Vol. IX, 1956 p. 242).

ii **RASSE**
Par. 1, l. 2 *should read*:
27 Jan. 1873 ; *d.* Brussels, 4 Jan. 1955).

Par. 3, l. 1. *Add after* ' Déidamia ' :
, based on Alfred de Musset's ' La Coupe et
les lèvres ',

Rasumovsky
Par. 1, l. 2. *d.* ?). *should read* :
d. ?, 1836).

52 i **RATCLIFF**
Refs. *should read* :
See ANDREAE. CUI. DOPPER. HEINE.
MASCAGNI. WILLIAM RATCLIFF.

RATHAUS
Par. 1, l. 2 *should read* :
1895 ; *d.* New York, 21 Nov. 1954).

52 i Par. 2, ll. 8-11 *should read* :
where he lived as a composer and teacher.
From 1938 he was domiciled in America and
lived in New

ii *Add at end* :
BIBL.—SCHWARZ, BORIS, ' Karol Rathaus ' (M.Q., XLI,
1955, p. 481).

Add before **RAUCH** :
RAUCEA, Dario (*b.* Syracuse, 1914).
Italian pianist. He began to study music
at the age of ten and attracted the attention
of Casella, who taught him. He also studied
the pianoforte under Baiardi in Rome and
later with Weingarten, Edwin Fischer and
Sauer in Vienna. He has toured extensively
and with outstanding success, visiting South
Africa and England in 1954.   E. B.

53 ii **RAUTAWAARA**
Par. 2, l. 12. 1934-39 *should read* :
1934-38

60 i **RAVEL**
Par. 1, l. 6. Obukov *should read* :
Obukhov

ii *Add to* BIBL. :
ACKERE, JULES VAN, ' Maurice Ravel ' (Brussels, 1957).
ONNEN, FRANK, ' Maurice Ravel ' (Stockholm, 1946).
PERLEMUTER, VLADO & JOURDAN-MORHANGE, HÉLÈNE,
    ' Ravel d'après Ravel ', 2nd ed. (Lausanne, 1953).
SEROFF, VICTOR I., ' Maurice Ravel ' (New York, 1953).
' Ravel ' (' Solfége ' series) (Paris, 1956).
' Ravel au miroir de ses lettres ', ed. by Marcelle Gerar
    & René Chalupt (Paris, 1956).

61 — CATALOGUE
ORCHESTRAL WORKS
Col. 4, l. 2. Paris, 1890. *should read* :
Paris, 1899.

SOLO INSTRUMENTS AND OR-
CHESTRA
Col. 4, l. 2. Paris, *should read* :
Vienna,

63 i *Add after* **Ravenscroft, Edward**
RAVENSCROFT, John (i) (*b.*? London,? ;
d. ? London, *c.* 1708).
English composer. He seems to have been
a pupil of Corelli in Rome, where he published in 1695 a set of twelve church sonatas,
Op. 1, under the name of " Giovanni Ravenscroft, alias Rederi Inglese ". They were reprinted the same year and under the same
name by E. Roger of Amsterdam. A manuscript copy of this work, which does not
mention his name, calls the composer " Inglese
allievo d' Arcangelo Corelli ". His style
greatly resembles Corelli's, which no doubt
assisted Le Cène of Paris when, some forty
years later, he reissued nine of these sonatas
as that master's Op. 7, which caused Hawkins,
in his History (Vol. IV, pp. 311 & 318) to
accuse Ravenscroft of passing off sonatas by

Corelli. Two editions of Ravenscroft's Op. 2, six 'Sonatas or Chamber Aires for Two Violins and a Thorough Bass', appeared in London in or about 1708, one of which, published by Isaac Vaillant, has "Vivit post Funera Virtus" on its cover while the other mentions "the late Mr. Ravenscroft".   E. B.

BIBL.—NEWMAN, WILLIAM S., 'Giovanni Ravenscroft, John Ravenscroft and Corelli' (M. & L., XXXVIII, Oct. 1957).

63   i   **RAVENSCROFT, John**
Par. 1, l. 1 *should read*:

RAVENSCROFT, John (ii ¹) (*b*. London, ?;

Par. 2, l. 1 *should read*:

English violinist. He was

ll. 8-10 *should read*:

Master'.   W. H. H.

Add footnote:

¹ This article formerly included information appertaining to John Ravenscroft (i), who is now given a detailed entry for the first time.

66   ii   **RAWSTHORNE, List of Works**
Add above CHORAL WORK:
BALLET
'Madame Chrysanthème' (after Pierre Loti), prod. London, Covent Garden Theatre, 1 Apr. 1955.

SOLO INSTRUMENT AND ORCHESTRA
l. 5 *should read*:
Vn. Concerto No. 1 (1947) (an earlier version of this work was

Add at end:
Vn. Concerto No. 2 (1956).

Add before CHAMBER MUSIC:
VOICE AND ORCHESTRA
Practical Cats' (T. S. Eliot), for voice & small orch. (1954).

Add to BIBL.:
AVERY, KENNETH, 'Alan Rawsthorne' (M.M.R., Feb. 1948).

67   i   **RAYGADA PEÑAFIEL**
Par. 1, l. 2 *should read*:
3 Feb. 1898; *d*. Lima, 8 Feb. 1953).

Par. 2. *Delete* l. 14.

69   i   **READING**
Add at end:
John Reading (iii) collected, transcribed and arranged an enormous amount of music written by his contemporaries. He presented Dulwich College with 12 volumes of his manuscript music, written in his own hand. They were all compiled after he left Dulwich College (two of them are dated 1716 and 1717), and they are now kept at the Library there. Nine of the manuscript volumes (Mus. MS

III and Vols. LXXXV-XCII) contain music from operas (mostly Italian but some English), cantatas by Galliard, Hayden and Pepusch as well as some music by Purcell. Harpsichord scores and orchestral parts of these works are complete. A number of pages are missing from the remaining three volumes (Mus. MSS I, II and IV), which contain mostly keyboard music, a great deal of this being transcriptions and arrangements from operas. Mus. MS I contains 'Divine Harmonie or Choice Collection of Anthems Composed by Several Masters, Collected in the Year 1717 by John Reading, Organist'. Among these anthems which he arranged here as "Solos", are anthems by Blow, Purcell, Croft, P. Humfrey and Weldon as well as John Reading's own anthem 'Unto thee, O Lord'. Of great interest are the two collections of psalm-tune preludes and interludes in Mus. MSS I and II, which he composed. The large collection of harpsichord music in Mus. MS II is called 'Mr Readings's great book of Lessons for the Harpsichord. The Ladys Entertainment. Being a Choice Collection of the Most Celebrated Airs and favourit songs out of all Operas set and composed into lessons for the Harpsichord by John Reading, organist of St. John's Hackney.' All three manuscripts (Mus. MSS I, II and IV) contain collections of organ voluntaries, though often the same pieces. Composers represented in these collections are Blow, J. C. Kerll, J. Barratt, Croft, Stanley, Green, Handel, J. James, Froud Sedo and John Reading, who contributed nine voluntaries for the organ.   S. J.

69   i   *Add after* REALIZATION:
REANEY, Gilbert (*b*. Sheffield, 11 Jan. 1924).
English musicologist. He studied at Sheffield University in 1942-43, and at the R.A.M. in London, where he took the L.R.A.M. as solo pianist in 1946. He studied at the Sorbonne in 1950-52, was Research Fellow in Medieval Music at Reading University in 1953-56 and in the latter year was appointed lecturer on the same subject at the University of Birmingham. In 1960 he went as Visiting Professor to Hamburg and then to Los Angeles (University of California).
Apart from his University lecturing, Reaney has arranged programmes and delivered talks for the B.B.C. on the Third Programme and Overseas services, and read papers at numerous musical congresses, including Bamberg (1953), Oxford (1955), Liège (1955) and Hamburg (1956). He is the editor of 'Early Fifteenth-Century Music', published by the American Institute of Musicology (in two volumes) and he has contributed articles to

'Musica Disciplina', 'Acta Musicologica', M. & L., Mus. T., the 'Revue Belge de Musicologie', etc., contributed to M.G.G., 'Larousse de la musique', Grove and a chapter to the N.O.H.M.   E. B.

69   ii   **REBAB**
l. 5.   Vol. VII *should read*:
Vol. VIII

REBEC
Par. 2, ll. 13-14 *should read*:
a bridge and sound-post (*see PLATE* 66, Vol. VIII, p. 146 (i), No. 3). The player

70   i   *Add at end*:
(*PLATES* 32, Vol. IV, p. 492, No. 7; 40, Vol. V, Frontispiece, No. 5.)

73   i   **RECITATIVE**
Add to BIBL.:
WESTRUP, J. A., 'The Nature of Recitative', Proc. Brit. Acad., Vol. XLII (offprint, Oxford, 1957).

78   ii   **RECORDER**
Add at end, before BIBL.:
(*PLATES* 21, Vol. III, p. 176; Nos. 10-12; 32, Vol. IV, p. 492, No. 3; 48, Vol. VI, p. 538.)
Add to BIBL.:
DOLMETSCH, CARL, 'Recorder and German Flute during the 17th and 18th Centuries' (Proc. Roy. Mus. Ass., Vol. LXXXIII, 1956-57).
PETER, HILDEMARIE, 'The Recorder: its Traditions and its Tasks', trans. by Stanley Godman (Berlin-Lichterfelde, 1958).

83   i   **REDLICH**
Par. 2, l. 14. Kauden *should read*:
Kauder

Par. 4, l. 15 *should read*:
from 1943 to 1955 and lecturer for the Extra-Mural

ii   Par. 1, l. 2 *should read*:
pean Music'. In 1955 he was appointed lecturer in the History of Music at Edinburgh University.

Par. 3, l, 1.   (1919. *should read*:
(1929).
Add to BOOKS:
Wagner, 'Parsifal' (1951).
'Bruckner and Mahler' ('Master Musicians' series) (London, 1955).
'Alban Berg: the Man and his Music' (London, 1957).
'Alban Berg: Versuch einer Würdigung' (Vienna, 1957).

86   i   **REED, William Leonard**
Add at end:
In 1952-53 he visited India, Pakistan and Ceylon, and in 1955 toured the Far East, Africa and Europe with the musical play 'The Vanishing Island'. He toured America in 1958 with another play, 'The Crowning Experience' and continued to add to his list of compositions.

87   ii   **REESE, Gustave**
Par. 1, l. 2 *should read*:
sity and was later appointed a resident Pro-

l. 8 *should read*:
from 1940 to 1945. Subsequently he became head of the corresponding department in the firm of Carl Fischer, Inc. In 1935 he founded the

Par. 2, l. 10 *should read*:
has since appeared in several further editions. 'Music of the Renaissance', a sequel to the previous book and more than twice its size, appeared in 1954 (second edition in 1959) and is the finest and most comprehensive study of this period in any language.

88   ii   **REEVES, Sims**
Footnote 1.   l. 1 *should read*:
¹ According to the certificate of baptism dated 25 Oct. 1818, which calls 26 Sept. his "alleged date of birth".

89   ii   **REFICE**
Par. 1, l. 2 *should read*:
Feb. 1883; d. Rio de Janeiro, 11 Sept. 1954).

90   i   Par. 2, ll. 2-4 *should read*:
not exclusively church music, include the oratorios 'Maria Maddalena' and 'Il martirio di Sant' Agnese', and the operas 'Cecilia' (Rome, 1934) and 'Margherita da Cortona' (Milan, Scala, 1938), masses, motets, a Requiem, a 'Stabat Mater', sacred cantatas, symphonic poems

REFORMATION SYMPHONY
l. 6 *should read*:
the Crystal Palace on 30 Nov. 1867. The work quotes the Dresden Amen and the Lutheran chorale 'Ein' feste Burg'.
G., adds.

ii   **REGAL**
Par. 1, l. 18. Vol. VI, No. 3 *should read*:
Vol. VI, p. 288, No. 3

Par. 2, l. 22 *should read*:
VI, p. 288, No. 1).

95   i   **REGER**
Add to BIBL.:
EBERHARD, OTTO, 'Max Reger: Sinnbild einer Epoche' (Wiesbaden, 1957).

(2nd work by REGER, MAX):
'Briefe zwischen der Arbeit', ed. by Ottmar Schreiber (Bonn, 1956).

STEIN, l. 5. (Leipzig, 1933, etc.). *should read*:
(Leipzig, 1954).

WEHMEYER, GRETE, 'Max Reger als Liederkomponist: ein Beitrag zum Problem der Wort-Ton-Beziehung' (Ratisbon, 1955).

97   ii   *Add at end of* PIANOFORTE SOLO:
— Arrangements of Bach's Preludes and Fugues in
E♭, D, E mi., and of Toccata and Fugue in D mi.

Add at end of PIANOFORTE DUET:
— Arrangements of Bach's Fantasia in G, Fantasia
and Fugue in G mi., Passacaglia in C mi., Preludes and Fugues in A mi., D and G, Toccatas
and Fugues in D mi. and E.

102   i   **REGISTRATION**
Par. 2, ll. 3-5 *should read*:

D minor arranged from a work by Vivaldi by
J. S. Bach (*c.* 1715), who added

104   ii   **REGNART (2)**
Add at end:
See also Maîtres Musiciens, Vol. 15 (modern ed. of
chansons).

105   i   **REGNART (3)**
See also should read:
See also Chorwerk, Vol. 30 (modern reprint of
motets). Hessenberg (Intrada & Vars. on theme by
R.). Vaet (memorial motet for R.).

ii   **REHBERG**
Par. 1, l. 2 *should read*:
1900; *d.* Zürich, 22 Oct. 1957).

106   ii   **REICH**
Par. 2, ll. 12-13 *should read*:
periodical 'Modern Music'. His book on
the same composer, 'Alban

REICHA
Par. 1, l. 1 *should read*:

REICHA (Rejcha), Antoine (Antonín)
(*b.* Prague,

108   i   **REICHARDT, J. F.**
Par. 1, l. 3. 26 June *should read*:
27 June

110   i   *See also*. l. 3 *should read*:
Song, p. 936.

REICHARDT, Louise
Add at end:
BIBL.—BRANDT, M. G. W., 'Leben der Luise Reichardt'
(Carlsruhe, 1858).

115   ii   **REINER, Fritz**
l. 8 *should read*:

Orchestra. From 1938 he conducted the
Pittsburgh Symphony Orchestra until 1948,
when he was appointed to the Metropolitan
Opera in New York, where he remained till
1953. He visited London to conduct the

l. 10 *should read*:

hardt's concert on 27 May 1924, and he conducted at Covent Garden there in 1936 and
1937.

117   ii   **REINKEN**
Add at end:
See also Vereniging, Vols. 13 & 14 (modern reprints).

120   ii   **REIZENSTEIN,** CATALOGUE
VIOLIN AND PIANOFORTE
Add at end:
'Fantasia concertante' (1957).

122   ii   **Rembrandt**
l. 3 *should read*:
inspiration of 'Golgotha'). Vlach-Vrutický (symph.
poem on picture).

124   ii   **RENIÉ**
Par. 1, l. 1. 1875). *should read*:
1875; *d.* Paris, 1 Mar. 1956).

127   i   **RESCUE OPERA**
l. 21 *should read*:
Journées' (1800).

Add new paragraph:

Morgan Longyear (*see* BIBL.) mentions the
above as typical examples and adds: Mon-
signy's 'Le Déserteur' (1769—the first),
Grétry's 'Richard, Cœur de Lion' (1784),
'Le Comte d'Albert' (1786) and 'Raoul
Barbe-Bleue' (1789), Dalayrac's 'Raoul,
Sire de Créqui' (1789), Méhul's 'Euphro-
syne' (1790), Cherubini's 'Lodoïska' (1791),
Lesueurs's 'La Caverne' (1793) and
Boieldieu's 'Beniowsky' (1800).   E. B.

Add before See also:
BIBL.—LONGYEAR, R. MORGAN, 'Notes on the Rescue
Opera' (M.Q., XLV, 1959, p. 49).

128   i   **RESINARIUS**
Add at end:
A modern reprint, edited by Inge-Maria
Schröder, was published by the Bärenreiter-
Verlag in 1955.
See also Chorwerk, Vol. 47 (modern reprint of St.
John Passion).

Page Heading, RESOLUTION
should read:
RESNIK

Add before **RESOLUTION**:
RESNIK, Regina (*b.* New York, 30 Aug.
1921).
American mezzo-soprano singer. She was
of Ukrainian parentage. She studied at the
Hunter College in New York, where she
sang all the female parts in the productions
of Gilbert and Sullivan operettas. She then
went to Rosalie Miller to study singing and
was introduced by her teacher to Fritz Busch,
who engaged her to sing Lady Macbeth with
the New Opera Company in New York in
1942 — she was just under twenty and a

soprano. In 1943 she entered for the Metropolitan Auditions of the Air and reached the finals, but her Lady Macbeth had led to her being offered a contract in Mexico City to sing Senta and the 'Fidelio' Leonore under Kleiber, and so she was unable to compete in the finals that year; but in 1944 she was the only woman finalist and received a Metropolitan contract for the 1944–45 season.

Resnik made her début there in December 1944 as Leonora in 'Il Trovatore'. During the next ten years she sang soprano parts at the Metropolitan, including Ellen Orford in the New York première of Britten's 'Peter Grimes', Susanna in 'Khovanshchina', Alice in 'Falstaff' under Beecham, Rosalinde in 'Fledermaus', Leonore in 'Fidelio' under Walter, Tosca, Santuzza, Donna Anna and Elvira, Gutrune and Sieglinde. This last part she sang at Bayreuth in 1953. During the next two years she sang Carmen, Venus and Eboli, and in 1955 decided to make a complete break with the soprano repertory. During the next three years she sang more and more mezzo roles at the Metropolitan, including Amneris, Marina in 'Boris Godunov', Laura in 'Gioconda', Herodias in 'Salome' and the Countess in the world première of Samuel Barber's 'Vanessa'. She appeared as Lucretia in Britten's 'The Rape of Lucretia' at Stratford in Canada in 1957 (she had sung the Female Chorus in the first American performance of the same opera at Chicago in 1947). In the autumn of 1957 she made her Covent Garden début as Carmen and was hailed as one of the best interpreters of the part in recent years. She returned to sing a striking Amneris in the summer of 1958 and opened the 1958–59 season singing Marina in Russian in 'Boris Godunov'.

Resnik has a warm, vibrant voice, and having sung soprano parts, she has a firm and strong high register, which does not exhibit any sense of strain, as is often the case with mezzo-sopranos. Her acting is full of subtle details, and fine musicianship and keen intelligence are apparent in all her work.

H. D. R.

128   i   *Add after* **RESOLUTION** :

RESON, Johannes (*b.* ? ; *d.* ?).

French 14th–15th-century composer. He has left seven compositions, of which two are Rondeaux and five sacred works. The first Rondeau is in fact a simple two-voice refrain, though there are different texts in each voice. Nevertheless the first two phrases employ voice exchange, which binds both voices together. The three-part Rondeau belongs to the conventional northern French song-type exemplified in the works of Malbecque. Instrumental interludes are frequent. Reson's

other works consist of a 'Kyrie', a 'Gloria', a 'Salve Regina' and 2 'Ave, verum'. All are for three voices except the second, two-voice 'Ave, verum'. The 'Kyrie' is in polyphonic song-style in prevailing 6-8 time, but the 'Gloria' is in duple rhythm throughout, and even syncopation is extremely restricted. In one manuscript the 'Salve Regina' has text in *tenor* as well as *cantus*, showing Italian influence, which is also visible in the first 'Ave, verum'. Nevertheless the musical conception of this work is reminiscent of Cesaris's Rondeau 'Je ris, je chante'. The two-part 'Ave, verum' is similar to certain late *trecento* secular works and *laude* with its basic note-against-note movement, though there are occasional short melismas employing triplets.

The general impression of Reson's output is that he began by writing songs in his native language and probably went to Italy where he wrote sacred compositions for liturgical use which are to some extent coloured by their environment. His extant work is published in Vol. II of 'Early Fifteenth-Century Music', edited by Gilbert Reaney (Amer. Inst. of Musicology, 1960).

G. R. (iii).

128   i   **RESPIGHI**
Par. 2, ll. 21–23 *should read* :

himself by taking a composer's diploma in 1901. The following year he visited Berlin and met Max Bruch, with whom he had intended to study. But according to the biographical notes published by his widow (*see* BIBL.) he merely showed Bruch some of his work and, feeling artistically out of touch with him, gave up the idea of becoming his pupil. A pianoforte Concerto of his

129   i   *Add to* BIBL. :
RESPIGHI, ELSA (ed.), 'Ottorino Respighi: dati biografici ordinati da Elsa Respighi' (Milan, 1955).

—   CATALOGUE
OPERAS
Col. 3, l. 3.   1907–9 *should read* :
1912–13.

l. 4.   1907–9 *should read* :
1916–21.

ii   SOLO AND ORCHESTRA
l. 3.   sentiviva ' *should read* :
sensitiva '

132   ii   **RESZKE (1)**
Par. 3, ll. 11–12 *should read* :

side, without losing sight of vocal purity. It is not true that he sang Wagnerian parts only in Italian. He sang for

133   i   **RESZKE (2)**
l. 2.   1855 *should read* :
1853

133   i   Par. 2, ll. 21-24 *should read*:

stofele of Boito, and, most important of all, some of the important Wagnerian parts, including Hans Sachs, King Mark and Hagen; but it is not true that either he or his brother sang Wagner only in Italian. From 1890, for

ii   **RESZKE (3)**
ll. 17-18 *should read*:

marriage to Baron Leopold Kronenberg, one of the founders of the Warsaw Philharmonia.
A. C., rev.

RETHBERG
Par. 2, l. 6 *should read*:

there in 1934, 1935, 1936 and 1939). There was

l. 9 *should read*:

ägyptische Helena' (Dresden, 1928). She retired from the operatic stage in 1942 and lives in the U S.A.

134   i   **RETI**
Par. 1, l. 2 *should read*:

slavia], 27 Nov. 1885; d. Monclair, N.J., 7 Feb. 1957).

135   i   **REUBKE**
Add at end:

BIBL.—GRACE, HARVEY, 'Reubke's Organ Sonata' ('Musical Opinion', XXXVIII, No. 449, Feb. 1915).

ii   **REUTTER, Georg**
Par. 2, ll. 10-12 *should read*:

Some of his instrumental music has been published in D.T.Ö., XIII, ii, but it is now known that only a Fugue and a Toccata are his, the rest being by Strungk. On 8 Jan. 1695 he was knighted in

137   i   **REUTTER, Hermann,** List of Works
OPERAS
Add after l. 11:
— 'Die Witwe von Ephesus' (lib. by Ludwig Andersen, after Petronius), prod. Cologne, 23 June 1954.
— 'Die Brücke von San Luis Rey' (lib. by the composer on Thornton Wilder's novel), prod. Essen, 18 Dec. 1954.

ii   **REUTTER, J. A. K. G.**
Par. 2, ll. 7-8. Prodieri's *should read*:
Predieri's

138   ii   **REVESZ, Geza** *should read*:
RÉVÉSZ, Géza

139   i   **REVUELTAS**
Add to BIBL. :

CONTRERAS, GUILLERMO, 'Silvestre Revueltas: genio atormentado' (Mexico, 1954).

145   i   **RHAPSODY**
Add at end:
BIBL.—JANKÉLÉVITCH, VLADIMIR, 'La Rapsodie: verve et improvisation musicale' (Paris, 1955).

ii   **RHAU**
Par. 2, l. 14 *should read*:

chorales to him.
A modern facsimile reprint of another theoretical work, 'Enchiridion utriusque Musicae practicae I', is published in 'Documenta Musicologica', Series I, Vol. i.
E. V. d. s., adds.

See also should read:
See also Agricola (M.). Denkmäler (5) I, Vols. 21 & 25 (modern ed.).

148   ii   **RHEINBERGER,**
CATALOGUE
ORGAN MUSIC
Op. 119. E♭ ma. should read:
E♭ mi.

149   ii   **RHODES**
Par. 1, l. 2 *should read*:

Staffordshire, 15 Sept. 1889; d. London, 27 Feb. 1956).

150   i   **RHYTHM**
Add to BIBL. :
ELSTON, ARNOLD, 'Some Rhythmic Practices in Contemporary Music' (M.Q., XLII, 1956, p. 318).
WILLEMS, EDGAR, 'Le Rythme musical: étude psychologique' (Paris, 1954).

151   i   **RIADIS**
Par. 1, l. 1.   1890; *should read*:
1885;
Par. 2, l. 12.   1915 *should read*:
1916

152   i   **RIBAUPIERRE**
Par. 1, l. 2 *should read*:

Canton Vaud, 29 May 1893; d. Rochester, N.Y., 17 Jan. 1955).

153   ii   **RICCI**
Par. 2, ll. 2-3 *should read*:

nothing. In 1844 he married Lidia Stolz, who had an identical twin sister, Francesca. He lived with both, and Lidia had a daughter, Adelaide, who in

l. 5 *should read*:

but died soon after, and Francesca a son, Luigi, who settled in

155   ii   **RICHAFORT**
Add at end:
See also Collectio O.M.B., Vol. 12 (modern ed.).

156   i   **RICHARDSON, A. M.**
Par. 1, l. 2.   Essex, June *should read*:
Essex, 1 June

158   ii   RICHTER, F. X.
Add at end:
See also Sondheimer Ed., Vol. 25 (modern ed. of Symphony).

RICHTER, Hans
Par. 2, l. 2. *Kapellmeister should read:*
chapel master

159   i   Par. 3, l. 18 *should read:*
less regularly. But he was associated with the London Symphony Orchestra, founded in 1904, whose first concert he conducted on 9 June of that year.

Par. 4, l. 6. 1904 *should read:*
1903

l. 11. (1909) *should read:*
(1908)

ii   *Add before* **RICIMERO**:
RICHTER, Sviatoslav (*b.* ?, 1914).
Russian pianist. He first studied under his father, a pianist and organist. In 1933–37 he worked as accompanist at the Opera and Ballet Theatre of Odessa, but in 1942–47 he underwent a serious course of study under H. Neuhaus at the Moscow Conservatory. While still there, in 1945, he won the first prize in the third All-Union Executant Musicians' Contest. He won the Stalin Prize (1st class) in 1949. Richter has toured widely and appeared at the Prague Spring Festival of 1956. He played the part of Liszt in the Soviet film 'The Composer Glinka'.   S. C. R.

160   ii   ŘÍDKÝ
Par. 1, l. 2 *should read:*
1897; *d.* Prague, 14 Aug. 1956).

161   ii   RIEGEL (1)
Add at end:
See also Sondheimer Ed., Vols. 5, 12, 14, 18, 50–52 (modern ed. of var. works).

163   i   RIEGGER, List of Works
ORGAN AND ORCHESTRA *should read:*
SOLO INSTRUMENT AND ORCHESTRA

Next lines should read:
Fantasy and Fugue for organ (1930).
Variations for pf.

167   i   RIETI
Par. 2, l. 2. 1940 *should read:*
1939

ii   List of Works
Add before CHORAL WORK:
BALLETS
'Night Shadow' (1941).
'Waltz Academy' (1944).
'Oedipus' (1944).

171   i   RIISAGER
Par. 2, l. 20 *should read:*
'Niels Ebbesen' (1945). A burlesque opera in one act, 'Susanne', to a libretto by Mogens Lorentzen, was produced in Copenhagen on 7 Jan. 1950.

Rilke
l. 2. Berg (Alban, song). *should read:*
Berg (Alban, 3 songs).

ll. 5–6 *should read:*
Gilse (choral song cycle). Grimm (F.-K., songs). Haller ('Verkündigung', cantata). Hindemith (6 French chansons for chorus; 'Marienleben', song cycle;

ii   Rimbaud
l. 2 *should read:*
Bondeville ('Triptyche'). Britten ('Illuminations', voice & orch.). Delage ('Bateau ivre', orch.). Hindemith

RIMBAULT
Par. 5, ll. 6–10 *should read:*
He lectured on music at the Collegiate

172   ii   RIMSKY-KORSAKOV, Andrey
Par. 4, ll. 4–5 *should read:*
his biography of his father, in five fascicles, the last of which appeared posthumously in 1946, and his

RIMSKY-KORSAKOV, Nikolay
Par. 1, l. 3. St. Petersburg *should read:*
Liubensk nr. St. Petersburg,

174   ii   Par. 1, l. 16. Cockerel *should read:*
Weathercock

175   ii   *Add to* BIBL.:
RIMSKY-KORSAKOV, ANDREY, Biography in Russian, 5 fascicles (Leningrad, 1946).

176 —   CATALOGUE
OPERAS
Col. i, l. 5. Cockerel *should read:*
Weathercock

178   ii   *See also. Add to* l. 6:
Symphony, p. 235.

182   i   RIPIENO (1)
l. 1. Ital., "replenished" *should read:*
Ital., "filling", "stuffing", "replenished"

RIPLEY
Par. 1, l. 2 *should read:*
9 July 1908; *d.* Chichester, 21 Dec. 1955).

183   i   **RIST**
Add after Par. 3:

Buxtehude based four cantatas on songs by
Rist and used words by him for an aria in
the cantata ' Gott fähret auf mit Jauchzen '.
E. V. D. S., adds.

184   ii   **RITTER, Frédéric**
Par. 1, l. 2. 22 July *should read*:
4 July

187   i   **RIVOLI, Ludwika**
Dates *should read*:

(*b.* Warsaw, 1814; *d.* Lwów, 1878).

RIVOLI, Paulina
Par. 1, l. 1. Warsaw, 1817 *should read*:

Warsaw, 22 July 1817

190   i   **ROBERTSON, James**
Par. 2, l. 22 *should read*:

conductor at Sadler's Wells Theatre in London, which he left in 1954 to take up an
appointment in New Zealand.

ROBERTSON, Rae
Par. 1, l. 2 *should read*:

ness-shire, 29 Nov. 1893; *d.* Los Angeles, 4
Nov. 1956).

197   ii   **RODOLPHE**
Add at end:
See also Denkmäler (2), Vols. 43-44 (modern ed. of
ballets).

200   i   **RODZINSKI**
Par. 1, l. 2 *should read*:

2 Jan. 1894; *d.* Boston, Mass., 27 Nov. 1958).

ii   ll. 6-7 *should read*:

harmonic-Symphony, a post he filled until
1947, when he resigned before the end of the
season, owing to differences with the management, and

l. 9 *should read*:

Chicago Symphony Orchestra. This too
ended in disagreement in 1948, since when
Rodzinski has lived in Latin America and in
Europe.

201   ii   **ROGER-DUCASSE**
Par. 1, l. 2. 1873). *should read*:

1873; *d.* Taillan nr. Bordeaux, 20 July 1954).

204   i   **ROGERS, Bernard**
SOLO INSTRUMENTS AND OR-
CHESTRA
Add at end:
' Portrait ' for vn.

205   ii   *Add after* **ROGNONE-TAEGIO**:
ROGNONI, Luigi (*b.* Milan, 27 Aug.
1913).
Italian musical historian and critic. He
studied philosophy at Milan University and
music under the guidance of Casella. He
has contributed to newspapers and musical
periodicals, especially on modern music, the
spread of which he promotes by means of
concerts and lectures. He has published a
book on ' L' espressionismo germanico e la
dodecafonia' (1954), another on Rossini (1956)
and others. Since 1958 he has been lecturer
on the history of music at the University of
Palermo.   G. M. G.

ROGOWSKI
Par. 1, l. 2. 1881). *should read*:

1881 ; *d.* Dubrovnik, 14 Mar. 1954).

207   ii   **ROGUSKI**
Par. 1, l. 1. Warsaw, 1839 ;
should read:

Warsaw, 12 May 1839 ;

l. 2 *should read*:

Warsaw, 5 Apr. 1921).

209   ii   **ROIHA**
Par. 1, l. 2 *should read*:

[Viborg], 12 May 1904 ; *d.* Helsingfors, 1956).

211   ii   **ROLLA, Alessandro**
Par. 2, l. 13 *should read*:

in 1807 a professor at the newly opened Milan
Conservatory.

212   i   **ROLLAND**
Par. 5, l. 5. 1916. *should read*:

1915.

ii   *Add to* BIBL. :
' Jean-Christophe et Armel: correspondance entre
Romain Rolland et Jean Bodin ' (Lyons, 1955).

ROLLE
Par. 1, l. 2. 1718 ; *should read*:

1716 ;

213   ii   **Romain,** l. 1. name *should read*:
Romains

l. 2 *should read*:
Trouhadec ', incid. m.). Ibert ('Donogoo ', do.).

214   i   **ROMAN**
Par. 3, l. 9. ' Assaggio ' *should
read*:

' Assaggi '

214 ii Par. 1, l. 2 *should read*:

for piano. The ' Assaggi à violino solo ' form the first volume of the ' Monumenta Musicae Svecicae ' (1958). K. D.

Add to BIBL. :

BERGTSSON, INGMAR, ' J. H. Roman och hans instrumentalmusik ' (Uppsala, 1955).

(3rd work by ÅKE VRETBLAD) :
' Johan Helmich Romans Bibliotek ' (S.T.M., 1953).

215 ii **ROMANTIC**
Add to BIBL. :

CHANTAVOINE, JEAN & GAUDEFROY DEMONBYNES, JEAN, ' Le Romantisme dans la musique européenne ' (Paris, 1955).
GUICHARD, LÉON, ' La Musique et les lettres au temps du romantisme ' (Paris, 1955).
MELLERS, WILFRID, ' Romanticism and the 20th Century ' (' Man and his Music ', Vol. IV) (London, 1957).

220 ii **ROME**
ll. 17-18 *should read*:

of several operas by Mascagni and Puccini's ' Tosca '. The

222 ii **RONCAGLIA**
Par. 2, ll. 1-2 *should read*:

forte with Padre Alessandro, violin with Giuseppe Ferrari and Zelmira Barbi, and composition with Sinigaglia, but decided to

ll. 14-16 *should read*:

settecento ' (Milan, 1934), ' La cappella musicale del duomo di Modena ' (Florence, 1957), and two of varied studies : ' Invito alla musica ' (Milan, 1947, 4th ed. 1958) and ' Invito all' opera ' (Milan, 1949, 2nd ed. 1954). G. M. G., adds.

224 ii **Ronsard**
l. 2 *should read*:

Cour. Berkeley (4 sonnets for 2 tenors & pf.). Bertrand (A. de, chansons). Bizet

l. 13. Richefort *should read*:
Richafort

225 i **RONTANI**
Add to BIBL. :

FORTUNE, NIGEL, ' A Florentine Manuscript and its Place in Italian Song ' (' Acta Musicologica ', Vol. XXIII, 1951, p. 124).

229 ii **RORE**
Add after Par. 1 :

A modern facsimile reprint of Rore's madrigals is to be published in ' Documenta Musicologica ', Vol. 29.

See also. l. 1 *should read*:

See also Arcadelt (influence on). Chorwerk, Vol. 54. Collectio O.M.B., Vols. 7 & 12 (modern ed.). La Hèle (Mass on

231 i *Add before* **Roscommon** :

ROSBAUD, Hans (*b.* Graz, 22 July 1895). German conductor of Austrian birth. Having finished his studies at the Conservatory of Frankfort o/M. he took over the directorship of the Mainz School of Music in 1929 ; but he left in 1930 on being appointed conductor-in-chief and head of the music department of Radio Frankfort. After a short stay at Münster as musical director to that city he spent the years of the second world war at Strasbourg in the same capacity. In 1945 he went to Munich to direct the Philharmonic Orchestra. In 1948 he was appointed principal conductor of the Südwest-Funk symphony orchestra at Baden-Baden, which under his direction became, after complete reorganization, one of Germany's finest. While continuing his activities there he has been conducting the concerts of the Zürich Tonhalle orchestra since 1952. For a number of years he has taken a prominent part in the music festivals of Aix-en-Provence. He has many first performances of important present-day works to his credit. In Mar. 1954 he performed the astonishing feat of deputizing for Hans Schmidt-Isserstedt at short notice in the Hamburg broadcast performance of Schoenberg's ' Moses und Aaron '. K. W. B.

ii **ROSÉ**
Par. 2, l. 7. Buxhaum *should read*:
Buxbaum

Add before **ROSE ET COLAS** :

ROSE, Bernard (William George) (*b.* Little Hallingbury, Hertfordshire, 9 May 1915).
English organist, musicologist and composer. He was educated at Salisbury Cathedral School in 1925–31, studied at the R.C.M. in London from 1933 to 1935, when he went to St. Catharine's College, Cambridge, as organ scholar, staying until 1939, and taking the Mus.B. and M.A. degrees. He was also John Stewart of Rannoch Scholar in Sacred Music there. Later he took the D.Mus. degree at Oxford, where he became organist and conductor of the Eglesfield Musical Society at Queen's College, and was Supernumerary Fellow from 1949, Official Fellow from 1954 and University Lecturer from 1955. In 1957, however, he became Fellow, organist and instructor in music at Magdalen College.
Rose's works include a ' Te Deum, Benedictus and Jubilate ' and a ' Magnificat and Nunc Dimittis ', both for treble voices and organ, and he has arranged five Chorale Preludes by Bach for string orchestra. As an editor he has brought out church music by Dunstable, Byttering, Tomkins and Palestrina. E. B.

235   i   **ROSENBERG,** CATALOGUE:
OPERAS
l. 2. Kungadöttrarna *should read*:
Konungadöttrarna

(1937).   l. 4.   (1939) *should read*:

ORCHESTRAL WORKS
l. 15. Berglagsbilder *should read*:
Bergslagsbilder

Add after this:
Symphony No. 6 (1953).

      ii   CHAMBER MUSIC
           l. 1.   4 string *should read*:
5 string

      Add to BIBL.:
DALE, KATHLEEN, 'Hilding Rosenberg' ('Listener',
   10 Nov. 1949).

236   i   **ROSENMÜLLER**
          Par. 1, l. 1.   Pelsnitz, *should read*:
Ölsnitz,

237   ii   *Add before* **ROSENTHAL, Moriz**:
ROSENTHAL, Harold (David) (*b.* London, 30 Sept. 1917).
English musical editor and author. He was educated at the City of London School and attended University College in London from 1936 to 1940, when he took the B.A. In 1945-46 he took a course at the Institute of Education in the University of London, taking the Diploma of Education. He studied music privately. After Army service he took up a teaching-career, but in 1950 became archivist at the Royal Opera, Covent Garden, until 1956, and was assistant editor of the magazine 'Opera', founded by Lord Harewood, in 1950-53. In the latter year he became editor, with John Warrack as assistant editor.
Rosenthal has been busy as lecturer, broadcaster and writer on opera and operatic subjects since 1950. His publications include the 'Opera Annuals' from 1954 onwards, 'Sopranos of Today' (London, 1956) and 'Two Centuries of Opera at Covent Garden' (London, 1958). He is collaborating with John Warrack in a 'Concise Oxford Dictionary of Opera', to be ready for publication about 1960.   E. B.

239   ii   **ROSSELLI**
           Par. 2, l. 10 *should read*:
collective volumes. Rosselli is the composer of an 'Adoramus te, Christe' often attributed to Palestrina.   E. V. D. S., adds.

240   i   **Rossetti, Christiana**
          l. 3 *should read*:
Elgar (song). Finzi (song). Hart (F.,

241   i   **ROSSI, G. G.**
          Par. 1, l. 2.   Fidanza *should read*:
Fidenza

          Par. 2, ll. 12-13 *should read*:
(Borgo San Donnino, 1871).[1] An overture (*sinfonia*), 'Saul', won a prize of the Milan Società del Quartetto in 1878, and

242   i   *Add before* **ROSSI, Luigi**:
ROSSI-LEMENI, Nicola (*b.* Constantinople, 6 Nov. 1920).
Italo-Russian bass singer. Born of an Italian father who was a colonel in the Italian army and a Russian mother, Zenia Lemeni Macedon, teacher of singing at the Odessa Conservatory, he began to study music at thirteen. He was inspired by the records he heard of Shaliapin and was for the most part self-taught, using gramophone records as models. During the second world war he served in the Italian army and in 1946 was ready to make his début as Varlaam in 'Boris Godunov' at La Fenice, Venice. Appearances followed at Verona and in the autumn season at La Scala, and he scored his first great personal success as Philip in 'Don Carlos' at Trieste in 1946. In 1947 he sang Alvise at Verona in the performance of 'La Gioconda' that introduced Callas to Italy, and the conductor Serafin helped the young bass in the formative years of his career. He married Serafin's daughter in 1949 when he was appearing at the Colón, Buenos Aires. After further successes, including his first appearance in the title-part of 'Boris Godunov' in Rome, he returned to La Scala for the 1950-51 season, and he has sung there in most seasons since as Oroveso, Basilio, Mefistofele, Philip, Henry VIII ('Anna Bolena') and Thomas à Beckett in Pizzetti's 'L'assassinio nella cattedrale', which he created there in 1958. He made his American début at San Francisco in 1951, when his Boris was hailed as "the finest since Shaliapin", and has also sung at the Metropolitan, New York. He sang Boris at Covent Garden in 1953 and Don Giovanni at the Stoll Theatre in 1957. In the same year, having divorced his first wife, he married the soprano Virginia Zeani.
Rossi-Lemeni's repertory further includes the title-parts in Bloch's 'Macbeth', Gruenberg's 'Emperor Jones' and 'Guglielmo Tell', as well as Archibaldo in 'L'amore dei tre re' and Khovansky in 'Khovanshchina'. In recent years his voice, which was originally a large sonorous instrument, appears to have suffered some diminution in power and compass, probably owing to the fact that he received no formal vocal training. His histrionic powers, however, appear completely undiminished.   H. D. R.

242   i   **ROSSI, Luigi**
Par. 1, l. 2.   1598 *should read*:
1597

243   i   *Add to* BIBL.:
GHISLANZONI, ALBERTO, 'Luigi Rossi (Aloysius de Rubeis): biografia e analisi delle composizioni' (Milan & Rome, 1954).

Add before **ROSSI, M. A.**:

ROSSI, Mario (*b.* Rome, 29 Mar. 1902). Italian conductor. He studied composition under Setaccioli and Respighi at the Conservatorio di Santa Cecilia in Rome. From 1926 to 1935 he was assistant to Bernardino Molinari as conductor of the orchestra attached to that institution, and in 1936–43 permanent conductor of the symphony orchestra of the Ente del Teatro Comunale of Florence (Maggio Musicale Fiorentino). Since 1946 he has been conductor of the orchestra of the Turin Radio. He has conducted concerts and opera in the chief Italian cities and abroad.   G. M. G.

ROSSI, M. A.
Par. 1, l. 2 *should read*:
1600; *d.*? Faenza, *c.* 1670).

Add at end:
See also Classici Musica Italiana, Vol. 26 (modern ed.).

245   i   **ROSSINI**
Par. 2, ll. 9-12 *should read*:
he destroyed it. The same fate probably attended a Mass written at the instance of an amateur of the double bass; but some pieces for double bass and strings composed for the same purpose have survived and are published by the Rossini Foundation in ' Quaderni Rossiniani ' (Pesaro, 1954).

ii   Par. 2, l. 1 *should read*:

There is a tradition, which long maintained itself, that the year 1813 began with a joke. It is now known to be false, but the story is here told for what it is worth. According to it Rossini had

l. 18. pertito *should read*:
pentito

l. 36. rivedro *should read*:
rivedrò

246   ii   Par. 1, ll. 4-5 *should read*:
innovator who had dared to use a subject already treated by their old favourite, although Sterbini and the composer had been very careful to produce a new libretto. Rossini, moreover,

247   ii   Par. 3, l. 9 *should read*:
some time, for the revolt of 20 July 1820 of

248   i   Par. 2, ll. 22-24 *should read*:
wedding took place at the parish church of Castenaso, some six miles from Bologna and near Isabella's villa, on 16 Mar. 1822.[1] Rossini has been accused of

Add footnote:
[1] Not, as previously stated, at the chapel of the archbishop's palace, nor was the ceremony performed by Cardinal Opizzoni.

250   ii   Par. 2, ll. 43-44 *should read*:
only six numbers (1 and 5-9) and the others were supplied by Tadolini.[1] The work was

Add footnote:
[1] There is a vocal score published by Aulagnier in which Nos. 2-4 and 10 in the standard Novello edition do not appear, and Nos. 2-7 and 13 are different and must therefore be Tadolini's contribution.

251   i   Par. 3, ll. 8-10 *should read*:
pleted the work by composing the four movements (now 2-4 and 10) originally added by Tadolini (then numbered 2-7 and 13). The work was produced at the Salle

253   i   BIBL. AZZEVEDO *should read*:
AZEVEDO

l. 7. (Turin, 1941). *should read*:
(Turin, 1941; 3rd ed. Milan, 1954: ' Rossini: con l' aggiunta di esperienze rossiniane ').

l. 18. ' Bolletino *should read*:
' Bollettino

l. 37. Giaocchino *should read*:
Gioacchino

ii   *Delete* ll. 1-2 (*they are* RADICIOTTI's *work below*).

Add to BIBL.:
GUI, VITTORIO, ' Rossini's " Barber of Seville " and its Overture ' (M. Rev., XV, 1954, p. 89).

POUGIN. l. 1 *should read*:
POUGIN, A., ' Rossini: notes, impressions, souvenirs, commen-

ROGNONI, LUIGI, ' Rossini: con un' appendice comprendente lettere, documenti, testimonianze' (Modena, 1956).
SCHLITZER, FRANCO (ed.), ' Rossiniana: contributo all' epistolario de G. Rossini ' (Siena, 1956).

Entry STENDHAL, *cancel* ll. 4-5 *and substitute*:
' Life of Rossini.' English translation by Richard N. Coe (London, 1956).

254   —   CATALOGUE
OPERAS

Col. 1, l. 20 *should read*:
La gazzetta, ossia Il matrimonio per concorso.

l. 32. Edoardo *should read*:
Eduardo

Col. 2, l. 1 *should read*:
Vincenzino Viganò Mombelli, alteration of Metastasio's ' Demetrio '.

l. 14 *should read*:
Giovanni Schmidt, on a play by Camillo Federici derived from Sophia Lee's novel ' The Recess

254 — OPERAS
Col. 2, l. 37 *should read*:
after Scribe.[1]

l. 41 *should read*:
Felice Romani, after Manzoni's tragedy ' Il conte di Carmagnola '.

Add footnote:
[1] Originally set as ' Odoardo e Cristina ' by Pavesi in 1810. The libretto was then by Schmidt alone; Tottola and Aldobrandini made alterations for Rossini.

255 — l. 2 of last par. in table *should read*:
13 Apr. 1830), ' Andremo a Parigi ' (from ' Il viaggio a Reims ', Paris, 26 Oct. 1859) and ' Un curioso accidente ' (Paris, 27 Nov. 1859) were produced without Rossini's collaboration.

i RELIGIOUS WORKS
Add after l. 1 :
' Laudamus ' for voice & orch. (? 1808).
' Qui tollis ' and ' Qui sedes ' for voice with horn *obbligato* (? 1808).

Add after l. 5 :
' Quoniam ' for bass & orch. (1832).

l. 6 *should read*:
' Stabat Mater ' (orig. with Giovanni Tadolini, 1832 ; completed 1839).

Add after l. 9 :
O Salutaris ' for 4 voices (1857).

Add after l. 10 :
' Chant de Requiem ' for contralto & pf. (1864).

Delete ll. 11-12 *and substitute* :
' Ave Maria ' for 4 voices (?).
' Cantemus Domino ' for 8 voices (?).

CANTATAS & HYMNS
l. 5. agli Italiani ' *should read*:
dell' indipendenza '

Add after l. 6 :
' Edipo a Coloneo ', incid. music for Giusti's trans. of Sophocles (1815-16).

l. 9. ' Igea ' *should read*:
' Partenope e Igea '

Delete ll. 10-11.

Add before l. 12 :
Cantata for Francis I of Austria (1819).

Delete l. 18, ' Il ritorno '.

Delete l. 23, ' I pastori '.

l. 24. words by ? (1827) *should read*:
words by ?, for the baptism of the banker Aguado's son (1827).

Add after l. 26 :
Chorus for the Tasso tercentenary (1844).

l. 27. ' Inno popolare ' *should read*:
Hymn and Cantata

l. 28. ' Inno nazionale ', *should read*:
Chorus for the Civic Guard of Bologna,

l. 33 *should read*:
' National Hymn ' (' God save the Queen ') for the Birmingham Festival (1867).

255 i ORCHESTRAL WORKS
Add after l. 8 :
Serenade (1829).

ii MISCELLANEOUS VOCAL MUSIC
Add after l. 5 :
' Ahi qual destin ', aria for tenor & chorus (1824).

l. 8. ' Addio a Parigi ' *should read*:
' Addio di Rossini ai Parigini '

Add after l. 9 :
' L' armonica cetra del Nume ', vocal 4tet with chorus (1830).
Arietta with pf. accomp. (1833).

Add after l. 10 :
' Deux Nocturnes ' (1836)
  1. Adieu à l'Italie.
  2. Le Départ.

Delete l. 11 *and substitute* :
' Nizza ', song (1844).

Delete ll. 17-21 *and substitute* :
' Racconto di Francesca da Rimini nella Divina Commedia ' (Dante) (?).
' Animale parlanti del giorno ', canon for 4 sopranos (1858).
' Laus Deo ', scherzo musicale (1861).
' Bolero ' for 2 voices (1863).

CHAMBER MUSIC
Add before l. 1 :
6 Sonatas for 2 vns., cello & double bass (1804).

Add after l. 1 :
6 Quartets for flute, clar., horn & bassoon (1808-9).

INSTRUMENTAL PIECES
Add after l. 2 :
12 Waltzes for 2 flutes (1827).

Add after INSTRUMENTAL PIECES :
PIANOFORTE MUSIC
Waltz in E mi. (1823).
' Il congresso di Verona ' for 4 hands (1823).
' Trois Marches militaires ' for 4 hands (1823)
' La reggia del Nettuno ' for 4 hands (1823).
' L'Âme au Purgatoire ' (1832).

MISCELLANEOUS *should read*:
PÉCHÉS DE VIEILLESSE

l. 1 *should read*:
Miscellaneous compositions for pf., etc.

Add after l. 6 :
ALBUM PER CANTO ITALIANO
  1. ' I gondolieri ', quartet.
  2. ' La lontananza ' for tenor.
  3. ' Tirana alla spagnola rossinizzata ' for soprano.
  4. ' L' ultimo ricordo ' for tenor.
  5. ' La fioraia fiorentina ' for soprano.
  6. ' Le gitane ' for soprano & contralto.
  7. ' Ave Maria ' (on 2 notes) for contralto.
  8.-10. ' La regata veneziana '
      (a) Anzoletta avanti la regata.
      (b) Anzoletta co passa la regata.
      (c) Anzoletta dopo la regata.
  11. ' Il fanciullo smarrito ' for tenor.
  12. ' La passeggiata ', quartet.

ALBUM FRANÇAIS
  1. ' Toast pour le nouvel an ' for S.S.A.A.T.T.B.B.
  2. ' Roméo ', *romanza* for tenor.
  3. ' La Grande Coquette (Ariette Pompadour) ' for mezzo-soprano.
  4. ' Un Sou ', *complainte* for tenor & baritone.

5. ' Zora ' (Émile Deschamps) for mezzo-soprano.
6. La Nuit de Noël ' for bass & chorus.
7. ' Le Dodo des enfants ' for mezzo-soprano.
8. ' Le lazzarone ', *chansonnette de cabaret* for baritone.
9. ' Les Adieux à la vie ' (on one note) for mezzo-soprano.
10. ' Soupir et sourire ', *élegie* for soprano & tenor.
11. ' L'Orpheline du Tyrol ' for soprano.
12. ' Chœur des chasseurs démocrates ' for men's voices, gong & drums.

MORCEAUX RÉSERVÉS

1. ' Chant funèbre à Meyerbeer ' for chorus & snare-drum.
2. ' L' esule ' for tenor.
3. ' Les Amants de Séville ', tirana for contralto & tenor.
4. ' Ave Maria ' for soprano & organ.
5. ' L'Amour à Pékin ' (on a Chinese scale) for tenor.
6. ' Le Chant des Titans ' for chorus, harmonium & bassoon.
7. ' La Prière ' for 8 men's voices.
8. ' Au chevet d'un mourant ', elegy for soprano.
9. ' Le Sylvain ' for mezzo-soprano.
10. ' Cantemus ', *imitazione* for 8 voices.[1]
11. ' Ariette à l'ancienne ' (Jean-Jacques Rousseau) for mezzo-soprano.
12. ' Le Départ ', *tirolese* for 4 women's voices.

QUATRE HORS D'ŒUVRES ET QUATRE MENDIANTS POUR PIANO [2]

(a) LES HORS D'ŒUVRES

1. ' Les Radis.'
2. ' Les Anchois (thème et variations).'
3. ' Les Cornichons (introduction — thème et variations).'
4. ' Le Beurre (thème et variations).'

(b) LES MENDIANTS

1. ' Les Figues sèches.'
2. ' Les Amandes.'
3. ' Les Noisettes.'
4. ' Les Raisins.'

ALBUM DE CHAUMIÈRE
(for Pianoforte)

1. ' Gymnastique d'écartement.'
2. ' Prélude fugassé.'
3. ' Petite Polka chinoise.'
4. ' Petite Valse de boudoir.'
5. ' Prélude inoffensif.'
6. ' Petite Valse " L'Huile de ricin ".'
7. ' Un Profond Sommeil — Un réveil en sursaut.'
8. ' Plein-chant chinois ', scherzo.
9. ' Un Cauchemar.'
10. ' Valse boiteuse.'
11. ' Une Pensée à Florence.'
12. ' Marche.'

ALBUM POUR LES ENFANTS ADOLESCENTS
(for Pianoforte)

1. ' Première Communion ', *andante religioso.*
2. ' Thème naïf et variations.'
3. ' Saltarello à l'italienne.'
4. ' Prélude moresque.'
5. ' Valse lugubre.'
6. ' Impromptu anodin.'
7. ' L'Innocence italienne (suite de La Candeur française.'
8. ' Prélude convulsif.'
9. ' La Lagune de Venise à l'expiration de l'année 1861! ' [3]
10. ' Ouf, les petits pois.'
11. ' Une Sautée.'
12. ' Hachis romantique.'

---

[1] Remark at the end : " Voilà du temps perdu! "
[2] An album of piano pieces containing this and the four following sections, headed : ' UN PEU DE TOUT. Recueil de 56 morceaux sémicomiques. . . . Je dédie ces péchés de vieillesse aux pianistes de la quatrième classe à laquelle j'ai l'honneur d'appartenir.'
[3] Remark at the end : " L'ombre de Radetzky ! ! ! — Arrivée de S.M. ! ! ! — La lagune baissante d'une tierce."

ALBUM DES ENFANTS DÉGOURDIS
(for Pianoforte)

1. ' Mon Prélude hygiénique du matin.'
2. ' Prélude baroque.'
3. ' Memento homo.'
4. ' Assez de memento : dansons.'
5. ' La Pésarèse.'
6. ' Valse torturée.'
7. ' Une Caresse à ma femme.'
8. ' Barcarole.'
9. ' Un Petit Train de plaisir (comico-imitatif).'
10. ' Fausse Couche de polka-mazurka.'
11. ' Étude asthmatique.'
12. ' Un Enterrement en carneval.'

ALBUM DE CHÂTEAU

1. ' Spécimen de l'ancien régime.'
2. ' Prélude pétulant-rococo.'
3. ' Un Regret — Un espoir.'
4. ' Boléro tartare.'
5. ' Prélude prétentieux.'
6. ' Spécimen de mon temps.'
7. ' Valse antidansante.'
8. ' Prélude semi-pastoral.'
9. ' Tarantelle pur sang (avec traversée de la procession).'
10. ' Un Rêve.'
11. ' Prélude soi-disant dramatique.'
12. ' Spécimen de l'avenir.'

ALBUM POUR PIANO, VIOLON, VIOLONCELLE, HARMONIUM ET COR

1. ' Mélodie candide ' for pf.
2. ' La Savoie aimante ' for pf.
3. ' Chansonnette ' for pf.
4. ' Un Mot à Paganini ', elegy for vn.
5. ' Impromptu tarentellisé ' for pf.
6. ' Échantillon du chant de Noël à l'italienne ' for harmonium.
7. ' Marche et réminiscences pour mon dernier voyage ' for pf.[4]
8. ' Prélude, thème et variations ' for horn & pf.[5]
9. ' Prélude italien ' for pf.
10. ' Une Larme — thème et variations ' for cello.
11. ' Échantillon de blague mélodique (sur les noirs de la main droite) ' for pf.
12. ' Petite fanfare à quatre mains.'

MISCELLANÉE POUR PIANO

1. ' Prélude blagueur de bon train-train.'
2. ' Des Tritons, s'il vous plaît (montée-descente).'
3. ' Une Petite Pensée.'
4. ' Une Bagatelle'.
5. ' Une Bagatelle (in nomine patris) — mélodie italienne.'
6. ' Petit Caprice (style Offenbach).'

MISCELLANÉE DE MUSIQUE VOCALE

1. ' Ariette villageoise ' (Jean-Jacques Rousseau) for mezzo-soprano.
2. ' Chanson du bébé ' for mezzo-soprano.
3. ' Amour sans espoir (tiranne à l'espagnole rossinisée) ' for soprano.
4. ' Requiem (à ma belle-mère) ' for soprano.
5. ' O salutaris Hostia de campagne ' for contralto.
6. ' L'Aragonaise ' for soprano.
7. ' Arietta all' antica ' (Metastasio) for soprano.
8. ' Il candore in fuga ', *fugato* for 5 voices.
9. ' Mottetto ' for 4 voices.
10. ' Grande scena " Giovanna d' Arco " ' for soprano.

QUELQUES RIENS POUR ALBUM

24 pieces without title, except Nos. 12, ' Danse sibérienne ', 15, ' Petite Galette allemande ', 16, ' Douces Réminiscences ' and 24, ' Un Rien sur le mode enharmonique ' ; No. 3 is dedicated to Panseron, No. 16 to Carafa ; Nos. 22 and 23 are themes with variations.

MUSIQUE ANODINE

A Prelude followed by 6 settings for various voices with pf. of Metastasio's " Mi lagnerò tacendo ".

---

[4] The reminiscences are from 8 of his operas.
[5] Including a variation " pour les paresseux ".

256   i   **RÖSSLER**
Par. 1, ll. 2-3. Niemeš, 26 Oct.
1746 *should read*:
? Litoměřice, ? 1750 [1]

Par. 2, l. 20 *should read*:
ii, edited by Oskar Kaul; further orchestral works and chamber music is in Vol. XXV.

Add at end:
See also Symphony, p. 212.

Add footnote:
[1] Oskar Kaul (Z.M.W., Vol. XVI, 1934, p. 248) thinks the Niemeš, 26 Oct. 1746, hitherto accepted, refers to another person of the same name.

Add after **RÖSSLER**:
ROSSO, P(etro). *See* Rubeus.

ii   *Add after* **ROSTH**:
ROSTROPOVICH, Mstislav Leopoldovich (*b.* Baku, 23 Mar. 1927).
Russian violoncellist. His parents were both teachers at the Baku Conservatory: his mother a pianist and his father, L. V. Rostropovich, under whom he first studied, a cellist. In 1937–41 he attended the Music School of the Sverdlov District in Moscow and in 1939–1941 (until war-time evacuation) the Music School of the Moscow Conservatory, where he studied composition under Y. O. Messner. In 1943–46 he attended the Conservatory itself as a pupil of S. M. Kozolupov for the cello and of Shebalin for composition; and he remained there as a post-graduate until 1948. He also studied for a time with Casals at Prades. He then became assistant professor, in 1953 lecturer and in 1957 professor.
Rostropovich began to make regular concert appearances in 1942, after evacuation to Chkalov in the Urals. At the Moscow Conservatory he advanced from the second-year course straight to the fifth-year, which he completed with honours. In 1947 and 1949 he won first prizes in music competitions of the World Festivals of Democratic Youth in Prague and Budapest. He has since toured in more than a dozen European countries, including Great Britain, as well as in the U.S.A. and Canada. In 1955 he was awarded the title of " Honoured Artist of the R.S.F.S.R.".

S. C. R.

ROSWÆNGE, Helge (*b.* Copenhagen, 29 Aug. 1897).
Danish tenor singer. He studied physics, chemistry and mathematics, and only later turned to singing after he had completed his technical education. His wife was a singer, and together they gave a concert at Schwerin; this was so successful that he was engaged at Neu-Strelitz, where he made his début as

Don José in 1922. Engagements followed at Altenburg, Basel, Cologne (1927–30) and the Berlin State Opera, where he has been leading tenor since 1930, being especially distinguished in the Italian repertory — Manrico, Riccardo, Radamès, Calaf, Cavaradossi, etc. He first sang at the Salzburg Festival in 1933, when he was heard as Tamino, Huon in ' Oberon ' and in the Verdi Requiem. In 1937 he sang Tamino, the Requiem and Florestan there under Toscanini, and appeared in the latter part at Covent Garden the following year. He sang Parsifal at Bayreuth in 1934 and 1936, but otherwise has eschewed the Wagnerian repertory.
During the years after the second world war Roswænge divided his time between Berlin and Vienna, and at an age when many tenors display decreasing vocal powers, his voice shows no sign of age. It is warm and sonorous, even throughout its scale, and brilliant and lustrous in its top register. He is an impressive singer on the stage, and his appearances in Vienna are invariably greeted with long ovations from his faithful and admiring public.

H. D. R.

257   i   **ROTA**
Par. 2, l. 17 *should read*:
renascence in music. In 1939 he became professor of harmony at the Liceo Musicale of Bari.

Par. 5, l. 9. ' I dua *should read*:
' I due

258   i   **ROTHMÜLLER**
Par. 3, l. 6.   1947 *should read*:
1948

262   ii   **ROUSSEAU, J.-J.**
See also. l. 8 *should read*:
(vars. on theme for orch.). Rossini (2 songs [' Péchés de vieillesse ']).

ROUSSEAU, M. S.
Par. 1, l. 2.   1882). *should read*:
1882 ; *d.* Paris, 11 June 1955).

265   i   **ROUSSEL**
Add to Bibl.:
Pincherle, Marc, ' Albert Roussel ' (Geneva, 1957).

267   i   **ROVESCIO**
Musical example, stave 3, bar 4, bass, third note, D *should read*:
C♯

268   i   *Add after* **Rowlandson**:
ROWLARD (Rowland), ? John (*b.* ? ; *d.* ?, *c.* 1455).
English singer and composer. He may possibly be the John Rowland who witnessed

two deeds mentioned in the Windsor archives for 1454. No further trace of this name is subsequently found. Only one work by Rowlard has been preserved, a 'Gloria' found in the 'Old Hall Manuscript' and also (anonymously) in the Fountains Fragment (B.M. Add. MS 40011 B). It is for alto and two instruments and contains ingenious hocket passages and bold harmonic clashes, besides quoting the music of "propter magnam gloriam" in the middle of the "Amen".   D. W. S.

BIBL.—BUKOFZER, MANFRED, 'Studies in Medieval and Renaissance Music' (New York, 1950). RAMSBOTHAM, ALEXANDER, ed., 'The Old Hall Manuscript' Vols. I-III (London, 1933-38).

268   i   **ROWLEY**
Par. 1, l. 2.   1892). *should read*:
1892; *d*. London, 11 Jan. 1958).

Par. 2, l. 9 *should read*:
(1927) for the music to a mimed ballet. He was vice-chairman of the T.C.L. at the time of his death, which occurred suddenly after a collapse on a tennis court.

ii   **ROY (3)**
ll. 12-14 *should read*:
he taught at St. Lawrence College at Montreal and became cathedral organist and regimental bandmaster at Quebec. He contributed to

272   i   **ROYAL ALBERT HALL**
Add to BIBL.:
CLARK, RONALD W., 'The Royal Albert Hall' (London, 1958).

273   ii   **ROYAL CHORAL SOCIETY**
Par. 2, l. 7 *should read*:
chief instrumentalists. In recent years the Society has engaged existing London orchestras.

277   i   **ROYAL FESTIVAL HALL**
l. 18 *should read*:
conductors on Wednesdays and Sundays, and the Season of the Arts that year included daily concerts given with the support of the Arts Council of Great Britain.

278   ii   **ROYAL MILITARY SCHOOL**
Add at end:
1953. Major David McBain, A.R.C.M.

280   i   **ROYAL MUSICAL ASSOCIATION**
Par. 2, l. 5 *should read*:
was appointed Secretary, a position he held until his retirement on 1 Jan. 1957, when he was succeeded by Dr. Nigel Fortune. Since the founda-

280   i   Par. 3, l. 6 *should read*:
writing is about 450. An index of

l. 8 *should read*:
was published in 1949. Publications for which the Association is wholly or partly responsible are 'Musica Britannica', the publications of the Purcell Society and 'Music & Letters'.   R. E., adds.

284   ii   **ROYAL PHIL. SOC.**
After l. 13 *add*·
1954. Igor Stravinsky.
1957. Bruno Walter.
1959. Sir Malcolm Sargent.

Add before **ROYAL SOCIETY OF MUSICIANS**:
ROYAL SCHOOL OF CHURCH MUSIC.
and transfer article **SCHOOL OF ENGLISH CHURCH MUSIC** *from* pp. 525-26.

285   ii   **ROZHOK**
Add:
(*PLATE* 15, Vol. II, p. 447, No. 7.)

287   ii   **RÓŻYCKI**
Par. 1, l. 2.   1884 *should read*:
1883

291   i   **RUBBRA**
Par. 2, ll. 15-17 *should read*:
the Faculty of Music at Oxford University. In 1948 he was received into the

292   i   Par. 2, ll. 13-14 *should read*:
the lyrical impulse. Examples of this are the Fantasia for violin and orchestra, which

ll. 16-17 *should read*:
the main material of the movement from it, and the 'Sinfonia

ii   *Add to* BIBL.:
PAYNE, ELSIE, 'Some Aspects of Rubbra's Style' (M. Rev., XVI, 1955, p. 198).

293   i   CATALOGUE
Add after l. 5 (*Op.* 71):
78. 'Song of the Soul' for chorus, stgs., harp & kettledrums (1953).

UNACCOMPANIED CHORUS
l. 1 *should read*:
— 'Virgin's Cradle Hymn' (anon.) (1922).

l. 10. 60 *should read*:
58.

Add at end:
81. Carol, 'Star of the Mystic East' for S.A.T.B. (1952).
82. 'Salutation' for S.A.T.B. (1953).
84. Scottish Nursery Song, 'Dance to your Daddie', arr. for S.A.T.B. (1954).
90. Portuguese Folksong, 'Mary Mother', arr. for S.S.A.T.B. (1956).
94. 'Gloria' for double choir (1957).

293   i   ORCHESTRAL WORKS
Add at end:

80. Symphony No. 6 (1954).
88. Symphony No. 7 (1956).

SOLO INSTRUMENT AND OR-
CHESTRA
Op. 75. (1952). *should read:*
(1951).

Add at end:

85. Pf. Concerto, G ma. (1955).
89. Improvisation for vn. (1955).

VOICE AND ORCHESTRA
Add at end:

83. ' Ode to the Queen ' (1953).

CHAMBER MUSIC
l. 5. (1947). *should read:*
(1948).

l. 7. (1951). *should read:*
(1950).

l. 8 *should read:*

73. String Quartet No. 2, E♭ ma. (1951).

Add at end:

86. Fantasy on a Theme by Machaut for recorder, stg.
4tet & harpsichord (1955).

VOCAL CHAMBER MUSIC
Add after Op. 3 :

5. Song, ' O my deir hert ' (anon.) for voice and stg.
4tet (1922).

Add at end:

92. Cantata pastorale for soprano, recorder, cello &
harpsichord (1956).

VIOLIN AND PIANOFORTE
Delete Op. 74.

ii   ORGAN MUSIC
Add at end:

79. ' Meditation ' (1953).

RECORDER AND HARPSICHORD
Title should read:

67. ' Meditationi sopra " Cœurs désolés " ' (1949).

SONGS
Op. 14 *should read:*

14. ' The Night ' (Hilaire Belloc) (1925).

Op. 20. (Murdock *should read:*
(Murdoch

Add at end:

87. Two Sonnets by William Alabaster for low voice,
viola & pf. (1955).
91. ' No Swan so fine ' (Marianne Moore) (1956).

294   i   **Rubens**
l. 2 *should read:*

Blockx (overture). Vlach-Vrutický (symph. poem on
picture).

RUBEUS
Cancel entry and replace by :

RUBEUS, Petrus (*b.* ? ; *d.* ?).
Italian 14th–15th-century composer. He
was the teacher of Georgius Anselmi, who
dedicated his musical treatise to him. They
had apparently discussed the subject-matter
of this work in the baths at Corsena in 1433,
and as Anselmi died in 1443, it seems likely
that Rubeus was at least middle-aged by 1433.

Two motets of his are at Bologna (Liceo
musicale 37) and two *ballate* at Oxford (Bodl.
Can. misc. 213). He is called P. Rosso in the
Oxford manuscript : Rubeus was no doubt
simply the latinized form of this.

                              G. R. (iii).

(Retain Bibliography.)

294   ii   **RUBINI**
Par. 1, l. 2.   1795 *should read:*
1794

295   i   *Add at end:*

BIBL.—TRAINI, C., ' Giovanni Battista Rubini'
(Romano, 1954).

ii   **RUBINSTEIN (1)**
Par. 2, ll. 1-2 *should read:*

(1) Anton Grigorievich Rubinstein (*b.*
Vykhvatinets, Volhynia, 28 Nov. 1829 ; *d.*

297   —   Heading *should read:*
RUBINSTEIN : (A.) Works ; (N. G.)

i   CATALOGUE
CHAMBER MUSIC
Op. 85, A ma. *should read:*
A mi.

PIANOFORTE SOLO
Add after Op. 7 :

8. ' Voix intérieures '
    1. Volkslied.
    2. Rêverie.
    3. Impromptu.

Op. 12. E ma. *should read:*
E mi.

ii   *Add after Op.* 44 :

45*b*. ' Barcarolle ', A mi.

Op. 82. 6 pieces. *should read:*
7 pieces.

Op. 118 *should read:*

118. ' Souvenir de Dresde ', 6 pieces.

SONGS
Delete Op. 8.

Add after Op. 64 :
72. 6 Songs to German poems.

RUBINSTEIN (2)
l. 1.   **Grigorevich** *should read :*

Grigorievich

l. 2.   2 June *should read :*
14 June

298   i   **RUBINSTEIN, Artur**
Par. 2, l. 20 *should read:*

covering remote countries. He became an
American citizen in 1946.

Par. 3, l. 17 *should read:*

class pianists of to-day. He formed a trio
with Heifetz as violinist and Feuermann as
cellist, the latter's place being taken after his
death by Piatigorsky.

Page 305 Add to Table:

No.	No. 4th Edition	Date	Shape	Size	General Description	Former Owners	Present Owner
2a	Andreas Ruckers 43 (wrongly ascribed to him).	1583.	Oblong.	ft. in. ft. in. 3 8 × 1 4	Single keyboard; 3½ oct., chromatic, C—a''; black naturals. Painted case. Outside of lid a landscape with fantastic beasts in the manner of Bosch or Brueghel; inside landscape with a hunt and an inn, "De Swan", on the right. A decorative border round the sides of the case, different in front, running on behind the keyboard, where there are two medallions, one of Catherine de' Medici dated 1581, the other the reverse of one some 20 years older of Diane de Poitiers. The H.R. rose in the soundboard and the initials H.R. on the inside of the flap, showing upright when let down.	Collection Strauss, Paris.	André Meyer, Paris.

Page 310 Add in order:

No.	No. 4th Edition	Date	Shape	Size	General Description	Former Owners	Present Owner
1a	43	1617.	Bentside.	7 6 × 3 0	18th-cent. English casework.	Robert Hass, Los Angeles.	Robert Johnson, Los Angeles.
Page 311							
2a	—	1618.	Bentside.	—	Compass G_1—c''', bass short octave; white naturals. Grained case, decorated with patterned paper. J. R. rose (type 1).		
Page 313							
10a	—	1628.	Bentside.	7 4 × 2 7	4½ octaves, A—d''', chromatic; black naturals. Painted case. The date 1628 on the soundboard has at some time been altered to read 1728. Inscription above keys modern replacement, as is the rose.		
Page 315							
20a	—	1640.	Bentside.	—	2 keyboards. Painted case. I. R. rose. Date 1640 on soundboard.	Acquired in 1640 from the maker by the family who still own it.	Dieter, Graf Landsberg-Velen, Schloss Ahaus, Westphalia.
Page 318							
9a	—	1617.	Oblong.	—	A. R. rose. Inscribed on jackrail ANDREAS RUCKERS ME FECIT ANTWERPIAE 1617. 4½ octaves, C—f''', chromatic. In modern times a second string for each note has been added.	—	Deutsches Museum, Munich.
13a	—	1622.	Bentside.	—	2 keyboards. Painted case with patterned paper. Inscribed above keys ANDREAS RUCKERS ME FECIT ANTWERPIAE.	—	Museum für Kunsthandwerk, Frankfort o/M.
Page 319							
18a	—	1633.	Bentside.	—	5 octaves; black naturals.	Duca Ernesto del Balzo.	Naples Conservatory.
Page 320							
22a	—	1639.	Bentside.	—	Compass nearly 4 octaves, C—b'', 8+8, orig. 8+4. Much restored.	—	Musée Charlier, Brussels.

305 — **RUCKERS**
Correct Table as follows :
in 1579,
No. 1, col. 6, l. 2.   in 1575, *should read* :

No. 4, col. 6, l. 5 *should read* :
ME FECIT ANTWERPIAE. Date 1590 on soundboard.

306 — No. 6, col. 6, l. 5.   (C—a''') *should read* :
(C—a'')

No. 7, col. 6, l. 5.   RUCKERS REFECIT
should read :
RUCKERS ME FECIT

307 — After No. 13, col. 1.   — *should read* :
13a

308 — No. 19, col. 3.   — *should read* :
1658.

Col. 6, ll. 6-7 *should read* :
PIAE. The date 1658 is on the soundboard.

Col. 7.   — *should read* :
Dr. Hanns Neupert, Bamberg.
Mrs. Bizallion.

Col. 8 *should read* :
Raymond Russell.

315 — *Before* No. 22, col. 6, l. 2.   rose (type 3)
should read :
rose (type 2).

No. 23, col. 6, ll. 5-6.   roses (types 2 and
4). *should read* :
roses (types 1 and 2).

322 — *Delete entry of 4th Edition, No. 43.*

325 i **Rückert**
l. 1.   *See* Brahms *should read* :

See Berg (Alban, 2 songs).   Brahms

326 i **RUDNEV**
Par. 1, l. 2 *should read* :
1 Mar. 1878 ; *d.* Helsingfors, 31 July 1958).

ii *Add before* **RUDOLPH** :
RUDOLF, Max (*b.* Frankfort-am-Main,
15 June 1902).
American conductor. He began playing
the piano at the age of seven and later studied
several other instruments and composition.
He attended the University of Frankfort and
graduated from the Hoch Conservatory of
Music, becoming increasingly interested in
symphonic conducting. His interest in opera
was limited. However, as is customary in
Germany, he chose the quickest way to gain
experience and skill in conducting by joining
an opera company. At the age of twenty-five
he held a leading position in Darmstadt and
two years later, in 1929, he left Germany to
conduct opera in Prague. He remained there
until 1935, also appearing as a symphonic conductor. Rudolf left Prague in 1935 and spent
the following five years in Gothenburg, where

2 C

he became a guest conductor of the Gothenburg Orchestra and conductor of the Oratorio
Society. He left in 1940 for the United States
of America, and became a citizen in 1946.
Rudolf joined the Metropolitan Opera's
musical staff in 1945, and in 1950 was
appointed artistic administrator. During his
years with the Metropolitan, Rudolf has conducted fourteen different operas, including
the world première of Bernard Rogers' ' The
Warrior '. In recent years he has appeared
with the Cleveland, Rochester, Dallas,
Houston, San Antonio, Minneapolis and New
York Philharmonic Orchestras, and has made
several recordings.   D. W. S.

328 i **Ruffini**
l. 2 *should read* :
lib.).   Donizetti (' Don Pasquale ', lib.)

RUFFO, Titta *should read* :

RUFFO, Titta [1]

Add footnote :
[1] The family name was Titta. His father named him
Ruffo after a dog accidentally killed a few days before
his birth : hence the name is actually Ruffo Titta.

ii ll. 1-2 *should read* :
of Mussolini's rule out of Italy, in Switzerland
and Paris. He returned in 1937, was arrested
in Rome on 16 Oct., but soon released, and
settled at Florence.

329 i **(5) Vincenzo Ruggieri** (relationship uncertain) *should read* :
(son of Francesco).

ii **RUGGLES**
ORCHESTRAL WORKS.   *Delete* l. 1.
Add at end :
' Organum ' (1945).

Add after CHAMBER MUSIC :
PIANOFORTE MUSIC
' Evocations ' (1937-45).

Add to BIBL. :
HARRISON, LOU, ' Carl Ruggles ' (' The Score ', June
1955).

330 ii **RUMFORD**
Par. 1, l. 2 *should read* :
London, 2 Sept. 1870 ; *d.* North Stoke,
Oxford, 9 Mar. 1957).

331 ii **RUMMEL (7)**
l. 2.   Bordeaux, May *should read* :
Bordeaux, 2 May

333 i *Add before* **RUSSELL, William** :
RUSSELL John (*b.* Stanhope, Durham,
2 Oct. 1914).
English conductor. He studied with
Howells, Alcock and Kathleen Long at the

R.C.M. in London and in 1949 became Music
Adviser to the Reading Education Committee,
devoting his spare time to the conducting of
the Reading and Newbury amateur orchestras
and choral societies, with whom he gave
exceptionally good performances. To an outstanding talent he thus added much valuable
experience. His London début followed early
in 1954, with the Boyd Neel Orchestra at a
Victoria and Albert Museum concert, and on
8 July of that year he made an important
venture of his own by conducting a concert of
works by Finzi at the Royal Festival Hall,
preferring thus to confirm a quickly growing
reputation in the eyes of serious musicians to
courting popularity with a programme of
safe successes.   E. B.

333   ii   **RUSSIAN BASSOON**
             See also should read:
      See also *PLATE* 59, Vol. VII, p. 712, No. 10. Serpent.

336   i   **RUSSIAN CHURCH MUSIC**
            Add to BIBL.:
SWAN, ALFRED J., 'Russian Liturgical Music and its
      Relation to Twentieth-Century Ideals' (M. & L.,
      XXXIX, 1958, p. 265).

337   ii   **RUSSLAN AND LUDMILA**
             l. 1. ' Руслань *should read:*
' Руслан

338   i   **(RUST) 1**
            Add to See also:
Denkmäler (5) II (modern ed. of works for clavier and
strings).

           RUST (2)
           l. 12.   milian Brentano. *should*
           read:
miliane Brentano.

339   i   **Adolf Ruthart**
            Par. 1, l. 2 *should read:*
1849; *d.* Leipzig, 12 Sept. 1934), pianist and
editor,

340   i   **RUTINI, G. M.**
            Add at end:
See also Classici Musica Italiana, Vol. 27 (modern ed.
of sonatas).

           Add after **RUTKOWSKI, Antoni:**
RUTKOWSKI, Bronisław (*b.* Komaje
nr. Wilno, 27 Feb. 1898).
   Polish organist and pedagogue. He completed his general education at St. Petersburg.
He also studied there at the State Conservatory under J. Handschin (organ), V. Kalafaty
(harmony) and J. Wihtols (counterpoint) in
1916–19. He continued his studies under
Surzyński (organ), Rytel and Statkowski
(theory) and Melcer (conducting) at the
Warsaw Conservatory and completed them
with distinction in 1924. He then went to

Paris and studied organ playing with Vierne.
On returning to Warsaw, he became co-
founder and chairman of an Association for
Lovers of Old Music (1927–39), founder of
the Society for publishing Polish Music (1928)
and Director of Summer Music Schools (1927–
1939). He was also editor-in-chief of two
Polish musical periodicals, ' Muzyka polska '
and ' Gazeta muzyczna ', and after the war
of ' Ruch muzyczny '. In 1946 he began
teaching at the Conservatory in Warsaw, and
was appointed Principal of the State Higher
School of Music in Cracow in 1954.
   He has written many musical programmes
for the radio, and numerous articles and
essays on music have appeared in Polish newspapers. His editions of early music include
sacred works by Polish composers of the 17th
and 18th centuries, and his two collections of
songs for schools have achieved wide circulation. As an organist he has appeared in
Poland and abroad, and his concert tours have
taken him to Austria, Hungary, Germany,
Russia and Italy. Several decorations have
been bestowed on him: the Order of Polonia
Restituta, the Gold Cross of Merit and a
military Order of Virtuti Militari. He has
also been awarded the Gold Medal of the city
of Cracow.   C. R. H.
   RUTLAND, Harold (Fred) (*b.* London,
21 Aug. 1900).
   English pianist, critic and author. He was
educated at Wilson's Grammar School (1910–
1916) and began his serious musical studies at
the Guildhall School of Music (1914–18), after
which he went up to Cambridge as organ
scholar of Queen's College. He was Stewart
of Rannoch Scholar in Sacred Music and
graduated B.A. and Mus.B., but at the same
time continued to concentrate on the piano.
Before leaving Cambridge he began a course
of study at the R.C.M. in London, where his
principal teachers were Herbert Fryer, Charles
Wood, Adrian Boult and Arthur Bliss.
   Rutland's professional career began as an
organist and choirmaster, but he soon began
to give piano recitals in London and in the
provinces, besides acting as a deputy teacher
of the piano at the R.C.M. His published
compositions include a song and several piano
pieces, and among works still in manuscript are
a piano Sonatina and 12 settings of poems by
A. E. Housman. From 1940 to 1956 he was
on the staff of the B.B.C., and contributed
informal but informative weekly notes on
musical broadcasts to ' The Radio Times '.
In 1957 he became a lecturer and examiner
at the T.C.M., and in the same year took over
the editorship of ' The Musical Times ', continuing until 1960, when he relinquished this
post in order to undertake a lengthy examining
tour throughout the Commonwealth.
                                        D. W. S.

340   ii   **RUTZ**
Par. 1, l. 6 *should read*:

Mozarteum at Salzburg. Later he became director of the Music Section of the Oester-reichischer Rundfunk and in Apr. 1957, director of the opera and symphony sections of the Westdeutscher Rundfunk at Cologne. He has written

341   i   *Add before* **RYBA**:

RYB, Eugeniusz (*b.* Warsaw, 29 June 1859; *d.* Russia, ?)
Polish composer. He was a pupil of Kątski, Roguski and Żeleński in Warsaw, and continued his studies in St. Petersburg under Auer, Johansen and Rimsky-Korsakov. He wrote an opera 'Branka' ('The Raped Maiden') which was produced in Polish at Kiev. Other works of his include a Symphony in F mi. ; 2 orchestral Suites; a string Quartet in F ma.; several pieces for unaccompanied chorus, songs and 11 Mazurkas for pianoforte. He also wrote a theoretical pamphlet, 'The Resolution of Dissonances'.

                         C. R. H.

342   i   **RYELANDT**
Par. 2, ll. 8-9 *should read*:

tures, symph. poem 'Gethsemani'; 4 stg. quartets; 2 pf. trios; 7 vn. and pf. sonatas; 11 sonatas and 6

Add after **Ryley:**

RYSANEK, Louise (*b.* Vienna, 12 Nov. 1926).
Austrian soprano singer. She studied singing at the Vienna Conservatory with Alfred Jerger. In 1948 she was heard at a concert in Vienna, singing arias from 'Alceste' and 'Un ballo in maschera', and in 1949 she was engaged for the Innsbruck Opera, where she made her début as Agathe in 'Der Freischütz'. At Innsbruck she met the baritone Rudolf Grossmann, with whom she continued her vocal studies and whom she later married. From 1950 to 1952 she was at Saarbrücken, where she extended her repertory, singing Arabella, Donna Anna and Donna Elvira, Desdemona, Tosca, Senta, Sieglinde and Leonora in 'La forza del destino'. In 1951 she sang Sieglinde at the first post-war Bayreuth Festival and the following year joined the Munich State Opera. At Munich she soon established herself as one of the most promising singers of the post-war period. Her rich, opulent voice, with its thrilling upper register and her dramatic temperament, have been heard to advantage in the revivals of 'Die Frau ohne Schatten', in which she sings the Empress, 'Die Aegyptische Helena' (title-part), Chryso-

themis, Danae in Strauss's 'Die Liebe der Danae', Lady Macbeth, Turandot, Sieglinde and Tosca.
Rysanek was first heard in London during the Munich State Opera's season in Sept. 1953, when she sang Danae. During the next two seasons she appeared in London as Chrysothemis and Sieglinde. Her Sieglinde has been hailed as the most womanly since Lotte Lehmann and her singing in Strauss's 'Aegyptische Helena' and 'Frau ohne Schatten' can hardly have been equalled. She is just as successful in Italian opera, and as Lady Macbeth, Amelia and Turandot, which she sang during her first season in America at San Francisco in 1957, she created a sensation. She returned to San Francisco in 1958 to sing Leonora in 'La forza del destino' and Elisabeth in 'Tannhäuser', and made her Chicago début as Aida. She returned to Bayreuth in 1958 to sing Elsa in the new production of 'Lohengrin', and Senta in 1959. She made her New York début in the same year.

                         H. D. R.

342   ii   **RYWACKA**
Par. 1, l. 2.   (*b.* ? ; *should read*:

(*b.* ?, 1817;

Add after **RYWACKA**:

RZEPKO, Adolf (*b.* Prague, 1828; *d.* Warsaw, 31 Mar. 1892).
Polish oboist and composer of Bohemian origin. He was a pupil of Tomašek and Weber. After completing his studies in 1843 he moved to Warsaw, where he remained until his death, teaching, conducting choirs and playing first oboe in the Opera orchestra. He composed several Masses for chorus with organ or orchestra, incidental music for Malczewski's 'Maria' and numerous miniatures for pianoforte which he published under the pen-name of R. Adolf.   C. R. H.

RZEPKO, Władysław (*b.* Warsaw, 1854; *d.* Warsaw, 1932).
Polish composer and teacher, son of the preceding. He wrote mainly choral works as well as music for organ and for pianoforte, also published several didactic books on the art of singing and collections of songs. He edited songs by Chopin and Moniuszko.

                         C. R. H.

343   ii   **SABATA**
Par. 2.   *Add after* l. 9:

which he joined in the 1929–30 season, and

l. 19 *should read*:

ninth Symphony and 'Missa solemnis'. He conducted 'Tristan' at Bayreuth in 1939.

347   i   **SACCHETTI**
Cancel BIBL.

348   i   **SACCHINI**
Par. 2, l. 5 *should read*:
'L'isola d' amore', 1776 (produced in Rome in 1766).

l. 14 *should read*:
'Euriso', 1781.[1]

Add footnote:
[1] This is only 'Creso' under a new name. 'The Morning Chronicle' of 25 June 1781 says that "On Saturday last was revived, at the King's Theatre, the serious opera of *Creso*, under the new title of *Éuriso* . . .".

ii   Par. 2, l. 8 *should read*:
which in still life would have been admirable.[2]

Footnote 1 *becomes* 2.

349   i   *Add before See also*:
BIBL.—SCHLITZER, FRANCO, 'Antonio Sacchini: schede e appunti per una sua storia teatrale' (Siena, 1955).

SACHER
Par. 4, l. 14 *should read*:
in various periodicals. He conducted at Glyndebourne in 1945 and 1955–56.

SACHS
Par. 1, l. 1. 1881). *should read*:
1881; *d.* New York, 5 Feb. 1959).

350   i   **Sachs, Hans**
Add to BIBL.:
GEIGER, EUGEN, 'Der Meistergesang des Hans Sachs: literarhistorische Untersuchung' (Berne, 1956).

SACRATI
Par. 2, l. 10 *should read*:
finta pazza', an *opera seria* [1]

Add footnote:
[1] Not to be confused with Monteverdi's 'La finta pazza Licori' (1627), the libretto of which is also by Strozzi.

356   i   **SADLER'S WELLS**
Par. 3, l. 3. transformed *should read*:
transferred

357   ii   **SAEVERUD**
Par. 1, l. 6 *should read*:
at "Det norske teatret", Oslo, in 1948.

CATALOGUE
Delete CHORAL WORK and *Op.* 27.

ORCHESTRAL WORKS
Add after Op. 5:
8. '50 Variazioni piccole.'

Add after Op. 20:
27. Psalm Symphony.

SOLO INSTRUMENT AND OR-CHESTRA
Add after Op. 13:
14. 'Rondo amoroso' for oboe, bassoon & stgs.

Add at end:
37. Vn. Concerto.

357   ii   PIANOFORTE MUSIC
31. 6 Sonatinas. *should read*:
30. 6 Sonatinas.

361   ii   **SAINT-FOIX**
Par. 1, l. 3. 1874). *should read*:
1874; *d.* Aix-en-Provence, 26 May 1954).

362   i   Par. 1, l. 19 *should read*:
three further volumes (1936, 1939 and 1946). It is

365   i   **ST. MICHAEL'S COLLEGE**
Par. 3, l. 2 *should read*:
music library, a catalogue of the manuscripts in which was published by the Lyrebird Press.

ii   **Saint-Pierre**
l. 6 *should read*:
play. Sauguet ('Images à P. et V.', ballet; do.

370   i   **SAINTE-COLOMBE**
Par. 1. *d.* ?). *should read*:
d. ?, *c.* 1700).

Par. 2, l. 1 *should read*:
French bass-viol player. Although a

ii   ll. 1-2 *should read*:
nobleman and therefore an amateur, he became a famous performer. He

ll. 6-9 *should read*:
three viole da gamba. The 'Mercure galant' (Feb. 1678) mentions him as "si célèbre pour la Viole". He must have died before 1701, when Marais published a 'Tombeau' to his memory in the second book of his 'Pièces de viole'. In 'Le Livre commode des addresses [*sic*] de Paris pour 1692' his name heads the list of "Maîtres pour la Violle", but the space left for his address is filled with a row of dots.   E. v. d. s., adds.

373   i   **SALAZAR**
Par. 1, l. 2 *should read*:
1890; *d.* Mexico City, 27 Sept. 1958).

375   ii   **SALE**
Par. 2, l. 7 *should read*:
as such he became well known from 1936 both for his career in

ll. 12-14 *should read*:
of opera and musical comedy. He appeared as tenor at Covent Garden between 1936 and 1952, and after nearly six years in the

376   i   **SALÉZA**
Par. 1, l. 2 *should read*:
Pyrénées, 18 Oct. 1867; *d.* Paris, 26 Nov. 1916).

376 ii **SALIERI**
Par. 1, ll. 19-20 *should read*:
became court *Kapellmeister*. He was also a director of the Opera for a number of years, till

377 i *Footnote 1. Add at end*:
A different version of this anecdote is given in a letter which formed part of a review printed in a Paris newspaper, ' Le Temps ', dated 21 Mar. 1876 :
" Deux semaines avant sa mort, je lui ai montré mon nouveau chœur que vous avez lu chez moi, sous le titre *Jugement dernier*, en me conseillant de laisser plutôt un chant que l'autre de deux que j'avais faits pour le moment où l'on entend la voix de Dieu. Il m'a dit ces précises paroles : ' Je crois que celui-ci est plus à sa place que l'autre, parce qu'il se détache davantage du chant commun des hommes, et que par conséquent il est plus adapté à l'idée que nous pouvons nous former de la majesté divine ; si pourtant vous n'êtes pas persuadé de ma raison, attendez quelques jours, et je vous en donnerai des nouvelles de l'autre monde.' "

ii *Add to* BIBL. :
BROWN, MAURICE J. E., ' Schubert and Salieri ' (M.M.R., Nov.-Dec. 1958).

378 i *See also*. l. 5 *should read*:
vars. on air). Mozart and Salieri (opera). Rey (J.-B., ii, ? ballet m. for ' Tarare '). Rimsky-Korsakov (' Mozart and Salieri ', opera).

379 ii **SALINAS**
Par. 2, l. 12 *should read*:
language.
A modern facsimile reprint of ' De Musica ' is published in ' Documenta Musicologica ', Series I, Vol. xiii.   J. B. T., adds.

SALINIS
Par. 2, l. 1 *should read*:
French or Netherlands 14th-15th-century com-
ll. 3-4 *should read*:
Bologna, Liceo musicale 37, and one of these at Oxford, Bodl. Can. misc. 213. One of them is published
l. 9 *should read*:
mann. Other known works of his are one *ballade* and a 4-part ' Salve Regina ' with the trope ' Virgo mater '.

380 i **SALMHOFER**
Par. 2, l. 24 *should read*:
Vienna State Opera, of which he was director from the conclusion of the second world war until 1955.

381 ii **SALMOND**
Par. 2, l. 42. 1942. *should read*:
1924.

SALÒ
Par. 1, l. 1. Salò, 1540 *should read*:
Salò, [bapt. 20] May 1540

381 ii Par. 2, l. 2 *should read*:
where he settled in 1562 ; but the story of his career rested entirely upon

389 ii **SALZBURG**
Par. 1, l. 19. 48 parts *should read*:
53 parts

394 ii **SAMINSKY**
Par. 1, l. 2 *should read*:
1882 ; *d.* Port Chester, N.Y., 30 June 1959).

395 i **SAMMARCO**
Par. 3, l. 9 *should read*:
Milan, and in 1919 he reappeared at Covent Garden.

396 ii **SAMMARTINI, G. B.**
Add to BIBL. :
MISHKIN, HENRY G., ' The Published Instrumental Works of Giovanni Battista Sammartini : a Bibliographical Reappraisal ' (M.Q., XLV, 1959, p. 361).

See also should read:
See also Classici Musica Italiana, Vol. 28 (modern ed. of sonatas). Gluck (pupil). Jommelli (collab. in cantata ' Reggia dei fati '). Sondheimer Ed., Vols. 13, 37, 38, 49 (modern ed. of var. works). Symphony, p. 210.

397 i **SAMMONS**
Par. 1, l. 2 *should read*:
23 Feb. 1886 ; *d.* Southdean, Sussex, 24 Aug. 1957).

399 ii **Sand**
Add at end:
BIBL.—MARIX-SPIRE, THÉRÈSE, ' Les Romantiques et la musique : le cas George Sand ' (Paris, 1954).

400 i **SANDERS**
Par. 2, l. 4. Brand. *should read*:
Braud.
l. 12. ' L'Agiya ' *should read*:
' L'Ag'ya '
l. 15 *should read*
the Katherine Dunham dance company. The
Par. 3, l. 6. counterpoint *should read*:
music
l. 11 *should read*:
Unitarian hymnal ' Hymns of the Spirit ' (Boston, 1937). In 1938 he became
ll. 13-14 *should read*:
versity, and he is at present (1958) Chairman of the Music Department and Professor of Music at Brooklyn College in New York.

ii CATALOGUE
BALLET
' L'Agiya ' *should read*:
' L'Ag'ya '

400   ii   CHAMBER MUSIC
                l. 3. B ma. *should read*:
B♭ ma.

403   i   *Add after* **Sannazaro** :

SANTA CROCE, Francesco (*b.* Padua, *c.* 1487; *d.* Loreto, ? 1556). Italian composer. The approximate date of his birth is to be deduced from the date of his ordination in 1512; that he was born at Padua is beyond reasonable doubt, since certain documents call him Francesco Patavino. He is first known as a singer in Padua Cathedral in 1511, where he seems to have remained until July 1512, when he was appointed *maestro di cappella* at the convent of St. Francis at Treviso. Documents show that he continued in this post until 1515. In July of this year he was given an increase in stipend, having threatened to leave, but this did not prevent him from departing the following Nov. His career during the next few years is unknown. He reappears in Apr. 1520 as *maestro di cappella* of Treviso Cathedral, where he remained until 1528, when he probably went to a similar post at Chioggia. In 1531 he removed to Udine, which he seems to have left in 1553. He finally returned to his former post at Treviso Cathedral in July 1537 and remained there until 1551. What happened to him after this is not known, but he may be identified with a canon of Loreto Cathedral who died in 1556.

Santa Croce is of some importance as a composer of church music. He is one of the earliest composers to use *cori spezzati*, having probably learned double-choir writing from Fra Ruffino at Padua. There are ten psalm settings for double choir by him preserved in manuscript in Treviso Cathedral, all showing the composer to have been well aware of the possibilities in the writing for separated choirs. Instead of the traditional imitative counterpoint customary in many Italian compositions of the early 16th century, Santa Croce used very homophonic textures and simple harmonies. His music is especially interesting for its use of short phrases, with each choir singing only two or three bars before being interrupted by the other. It was this sort of technique which was to form the basis of Andrea Gabrieli's style, and Santa Croce may well have been known to Willaert, who started the vogue for *cori spezzati*.   D. M. A.

BIBL.—D'ALESSI, G., 'La cappella musicale del duomo di Treviso: 1300–1633' (Treviso, 1954).

See also Cori spezzati.

ii   **SANTA MARÍA**
        Add at end :

See also Hispaniae Schola, Vol. 6 (modern reprint).

407   i   **SANTORO**
                Par. 1, l. 1. Manaus *should read* :
Manaos

ii   *Add after* **SANZ** :

SANZOGNO, Nino (*b.* Venice, 13 Apr. 1911). Italian conductor. He studied the violin under F. de Guarnieri at the Conservatory "B. Marcello" in Venice and composition under M. Agostini, taking a diploma in 1932. He afterwards attended Hermann Scherchen's conducting course in Brussels and G. Francesco Malipiero's finishing course in composition in Venice. He became conductor of the Gruppo Strumentale Italiano, with which he toured in Italy and abroad (1938–39), then permanent conductor of the Teatro La Fenice in Venice and in 1950 conductor of the Teatro alla Scala in Milan, where he is entrusted especially with concert performances and with the repertory of new operas by modern composers. He thus performed for the first time in Italy, among others, 'The Flaming Angel' (Prokofiev), 'Troilus and Cressida' (Walton), 'Dialogues des Carmélites' (Poulenc), 'David' (Milhaud), 'L' allegra brigata' (Malipiero), 'Mathis der Maler' (Hindemith), 'The Cunning Vixen' (Janáček), 'Lady Macbeth of Mtsensk' (Shostakovich), 'Lulu' (Alban Berg) and many others.   G. M. G.

409   ii   **SARACINI**
                Add to BIBL. :
FORTUNE, NIGEL, 'Italian Secular Monody from 1600 to 1635: an Introductory Survey' (M.Q., XXXIX, 1953, p. 171).

SARADIEV *should read* :
SARADZHEV

Par. 1, ll. 2-3 *should read* :
(*b.* Derbent, Daghestan, Caucasus, 8 Oct. 1877; *d.* Erevan, Sept. 1954).

410   i   **SARASATE**
                Par. 2, l. 24 *should read* :
bella of Spain.[1] This instrument was one of

Add to BIBL. :
ALTADILL, JULIO, 'Memorias de Sarasate' (Pamplona, 1908).

Add footnote :
[1] This statement was refuted by Otto Goldschmidt, in 'The Musical Courier' of 28 Oct. 1908: "As executor of the will of Sarasate, I would like to state that the 1724 Stradivarius which he always played in public (and which did not belong to the Spanish Crown and was not presented to him by Queen Isabella) was bequeathed by him to the Paris Conservatory". A detailed story of Sarasate's two Strads is given in a special chapter in the documentary volume, 'Memorias de Sarasate', by Julio Altadill. From this account it follows irrefutably that Sarasate bought his 1724 Stradivarius in 1866, by trading in his other Italian violin and paying 5000 francs extra. The author adds: "Sarasate was disgusted every time he heard this fable. Isabella II never gave this gift to the child violinist. Sarasate acquired his two Strads with the sweat of his brow."

411   i   **SARGENT**
Par. 2, l. 3 *should read*:
conductor-in-chief of the B.B.C. This came
to an end in 1957, when he was succeeded
by Rudolf Schwarz.

ŠÁRKA
Add at end of line:
SMETANA (' Má Vlast ').

413   ii   **SARTI**
Par. 3, l. 10. Ochakhov *should
read*:
Ochakov

416   i   **SASSOLI RUATA**
Par. 1, l. 2. 1887 *should read*:
1886

418   ii   **SATIE**
Add to BIBL.:
SATIE, ERIK, ' Mémoires d'un amnésique ' (Liège, 1953).

420   ii   **SAUGUET,** CATALOGUE
BALLETS
Add at end:
' La Dame aux camélias ' (on the play by Dumas, jun.;
scen. & choreog. by Tatiana Gsovsky), prod. Berlin
Festival, 29 Sept. 1957.

425   i   *Add before* **SAWICKI**:
SAWALLISCH, Wolfgang (*b.* Munich,
26 Aug. 1923).
German conductor. He studied music
privately at Munich during the second world
war with Hans Sachsse and the pianoforte
with Wolfgang Ruoff. In 1946, after a year
at the Munich Conservatory, he successfully
passed his conductor's course and continued
at the same time his other musical studies
with Joseph Haas and Walter Georgi. In
1947 he joined the Augsburg Opera as first
coach. During his second season he was
entrusted with the preparation of several
operas and operettas, and in 1950–51 became
first *Kapellmeister* for operetta, and two years
later for opera. In Sept. 1953 he was
appointed *Generalmusikdirektor* at Aachen,
where he remained until the end of the 1957–
1958 season, when he left for a three years'
appointment at Wiesbaden. It was announced even before his Wiesbaden appointment began that he would become Cologne's
Generalmusikdirektor in September 1960.
In 1957 Sawallisch was invited to conduct
the new production of ' Tristan und Isolde '
at Bayreuth. He then revealed that he was
an operatic conductor of the front rank, but
one who like Wolfgang and Wieland Wagner
had reacted against heavy Teutonism in
Wagner. He accordingly gave a restrained
and somewhat unpoetic reading of the score.
In 1958, however, he had become inclined
to throw caution to the wind.

Sawallisch is undoubtedly one of the most
gifted of the post-war generation of German
conductors. He has refused offers from
Berlin and New York and chose Wiesbaden,
feeling that only in a provincial opera-house
could a conductor work uninterruptedly with
a permanent ensemble, which he prefers to do.
He sees in the operatic world as a whole, with
its galaxy of stars and much-travelled conductors, a grave and menacing danger.
Sawallisch has not only distinguished himself in the opera-house, but has directed
orchestral concerts. In 1952 and 1953 he
took part in the Salzburg summer classes as
Igor Markevitch's assistant. He has directed
concerts with the German radio orchestras
of Munich, Cologne and Frankfort o/M.,
and public concerts in Munich, Berlin, Vienna
and Brussels. His first appearance in London
was not as a conductor, but as the accompanist to Elisabeth Schwarzkopf in a Hugo
Wolf recital in 1957. In 1958 he conducted
the Philharmonia Orchestra in two concerts
at the Royal Festival Hall.   H. D. R.

434   ii   **SAXOPHONE**
Add at end:
BIBL.—PERRIN, MARCEL, ' Le Saxophone : son histoire,
sa technique et son utilisation dans l'orchestre '
(Paris, 1953).
(*See also* footnotes.)

437   i   **SAYVE (1)**
Add at end:
See also Chorwerk, Vol. 51 (modern reprint of
German songs).

441   ii   **SCALE**
Par. 3, l. 4 *should read*:
the 19th century. The well-known passage

Delete Footnote 5.

442   i   *Add par. after first musical example*:
Liszt early showed a special interest in the
whole-tone scale. In a letter, 20 Aug. 1859, to
Julius Schäffer, musical director at Schwerin,
he quotes a harmonized passage from his
Dante Symphony with the whole-tone scale
in contrary motion, starting on G♯, ascending
in the treble and descending in the bass. He
had become interested in the subject through
the speculations of the theorist Karl Friedrich
Weitzmann, who was a friend of his.

443   i   *Add to* BIBL.:
LLOYD, LL. S., ' The History of our Scale ' (M. Rev.,
XIV, 1953, p. 173).
BIBL., l. 10. *Delete* LLOYD, LL. S.

Add before **SCALETTA**:
SCALERO, Rosario (*b.* Moncalieri nr.
Turin, 24 Dec. 1870; *d.* Settimo Vittone nr.
Turin, 25 Dec. 1954).
Italian violinist and composer. He studied

at the Turin Liceo Musicale and later at Leipzig, and was a violin pupil of Wilhelmj. In 1896 he settled at Lyons as violin teacher, but wishing to take up composition, he went to Vienna as a pupil of Mandyczewski. After seven years there he went to Rome as professor of composition at the Accademia Santa Cecilia. In 1924 he took up a teaching-post at the Curtis Institute at Philadelphia, where Menotti, Barber and Lucas Foss were among his pupils. When he was well over seventy he married a young pupil of his and retired to his native country.

Scalero was one of the few Italian composers of his time who did not devote himself to opera. His works include two sets of Motets, Opp. 6 and 7, and other sacred choral compositions; a Suite for string orchestra with solo quartet, Op. 20; Romantic Pieces for pianoforte, Op. 19; numerous violin pieces, etc.   E. B.

452   ii   **SCARLATTI (1)**
Add to BIBL. :
PAULY, REINHARD G., 'Alessandro Scarlatti's " Tigrane " ' (M. & L., XXXV, 1954, p. 339).
RONGA, LUIGI, ' Motivi critici su Alessandro Scarlatti ' (Riv. Mus. It., LVI, 1, 1954).

DENT. l. 4 *should read* :
1905; new edition annotated by Frank Walker, 1960).

CATALOGUE
OPERAS
Col. 1, l. 29. ' Bassanio *should read* :
' Bassiano

453   —   Cols. 1-3, l. 25. 'La vittoria . . .' Sept. 1708. *Delete whole entry.*

454   i   VOCAL SERENADES AND CANTATAS
Add after l. 22 :
' La vittoria della fede ', lib. by Carlo Sigismondo Capece (Rome, Palazzo Zuccari [Queen of Poland's theatre], 12 Sept. 1708).

455   i   *See also.* l. 1 *should read* :
See also Accompaniment. Classici Musica Italiana, Vol. 30 (modern ed. of cantatas). Gasparini (F. dispute

l. 3 *should read* :
(C. F., collab. in ' Genuida '). Publikationen G.M.F., Vol. 14 (modern ed. of ' Rosaura '). Thomyris (pasticcio).

456   ii   **SCARLATTI (5)**
Par. 2, l. 7. (1712), *should read* :
(1712)²,

Add footnote :
² A copy of this work, not holograph, was discovered all but complete (4 pages missing) in the archives of the Convento di San Francesco della Vigna at Venice (*see* Rass. Mus., XXVII, 1957, No. 4).

457   i   Par. 3, ll. 1-9 *should read* :
This Halle newspaper of 1728 includes the following passage, the source of Walther's

statements, in a communication from Rome dated 18 Sept.:

Meanwhile His Majesty the King of Portugal has permitted all the Italian musicians in Lisbon to stay there; indeed, they have in addition taken into their service the celebrated Chapelmaster Scarlatti, who has also already made all arrangements to leave here towards the end of this month; and on His Majesty's orders 2,000 Thaler have already been paid to him for his travelling expenses.

The only

458   ii   *Add to* BIBL. (2nd work by LONGO) :
' Indice tematico delle sonate per clavicembalo di Domenico Scarlatti ' (Milan, 1952).

BIBL., l. 25. 1937). *should read* :
1937; 2nd ed. 1955).

460   i   *See also. Add to* l. 2 :
Classici Musica Italiana, Vol. 31 (modern ed.).

Footnote 2, l. 2. ' Esercizi ' *should read* :
' Essercizi '

ii   Footnote 4, l. 1. izata' *should read* :
ziata'

464   i   *Add after* **SCHAEFFER, Paul** :
SCHAEFFER, Pierre.   *See* CONCRETE MUSIC.

ii   **SCHAEUBLE**
Par. 4, l. 3. ' Dorian Grey ' *should read* :
' Dorian Gray '

466   i   *Add after* **SCHARF** :
SCHARRER, Irene (*b.* London, 2 Feb. 1888).
English pianist. She studied at the R.A.M. in London and with Tobias Matthay, of whose methods she became one of the chief early exponents. At the age of sixteen she gave a recital in London and later she frequently appeared with various British orchestras. She also toured on the Continent and visited the U.S.A. in 1925.   E. B.

467   ii   **SCHECHNER**
Par. 1, l. 2. *d.* ?, 29 *should read* :
d. Munich, 29

468   i   *Add after* **Scheffel** :
Scheffler, Johann. *See* Silesius.

473   i   **SCHEIDT**
Add to See also :
Denkmäler (2), Vol. I (modern ed. of organ works). Vereniging, Vol. 3 (reprint of ' Tabulatura nova ').

474   ii   **SCHEIN**
Par. 4, l. 6 *should read* :
above specified. He also wrote organ works.

Add after See also Chorale. :
Chorwerk, Vols. 12, 14, 36 (modern reprints).

476   ii   **SCHENK, Johann (1)**
Par. 1, l. 2 *should read*:
or **Joan**) (*b.* ?, 1656; *d.* ?, *c.* 1710).

Par. 2, l. 1 *should read*:
German viol da gamba

List of Works
Op. 8 *should read*:
8. 'La ninfa del Reno' (12 sonatas for 2 viole da
gamba).

477   i   *Add at end*:
See also Vereniging, Vol. 28 (reprint of 'Scherzi
musicali').

ii   **SCHENK, Johann (2)**
Add to BIBL.:
NETTL, PAUL, 'Forgotten Musicians' (New York, 1951),
for autobiographical material.

See also. l. 1 *should read*:
See also Denkmäler (3), Vol. 34 (modern ed. of 'Dorf-
barbier'). Diabelli (sequel to do.). Seidel

Footnote 3. June 1793. *should read*:
June 1794.

478   i   **SCHENKER**
Par. 3, ll. 3-5 *should read*:
'Harmonielehre', 1906 (new edition by
Oswald Jonas, English version, Chicago,
1954; German, 1956); Vol. II, 'Kontra-
punkt' (1st part

ii   *Add to* BIBL.:
SCHENKER, HEINRICH, 'Harmony', ed. by Oswald Jonas,
trans. by Elisabeth Mann Borgese (Chicago, 1954).

479   i   **SCHERCHEN**
Par. 3, l. 20 *should read*:
Spanish and Italian. A later book, 'Vom
Wesen der Musik' (Winterthur, 1946), was
translated as 'The Nature of Music' (Chicago,
1950).

Add at end, before signature:
Scherchen has a laboratory at Gravesano,
Switzerland, where he makes extensive
acoustical experiments.

484   ii   **SCHIEDERMAIR**
Par. 1, l. 2 *should read*:
7 Dec. 1876; *d.* Bensberg nr. Cologne, 30
Apr. 1957).

Par. 2. *Add after* l. 16:
He retired in 1945 and was succeeded by
Joseph Schmidt-Görg.

485   ii   **SCHIKANEDER**
Par. 1, l. 2. **Schickeneder** *should
read*:
Schickheneder

485   ii   Par. 1, l. 3 *should read*:
bing, [bapt. 1 Sept.] 1751; *d.* Vienna, 21
Sept. 1812).

Footnote 2. l. 2 *should read*:
Schikaneder; but *see* Dent, 'Mozart's Operas', pp.
234-42.

487   i   **Schiller**
'Jungfrau von Orleans.' ll. 2-3 *should
read*:
(F. S., incid. m.). Rezniček (opera). Schulz (J. P. C.,
do.). Söderman (incid. m.). Tchaikovsky (opera).

Poems. l. 13 *should read*:
(2 songs). Lortzing ('Bürgschaft', song). MacDowell
(partsong). Mascagni ('Ode to

'Räuber.' l. 2 *should read*:
(3, incid. m.). Klebe (opera). Masnadieri (Verdi,
opera). Merca-

Add at end:
BIBL.—KRAFT, GÜNTHER, 'Schiller und die Musik'
(Erfurt, 1955).

ii   **SCHILLINGS**
Par. 1, l. 2.   1943). *should read*:
1933).

490   ii   **SCHIØTZ**
Par. 2, l. 24 *should read*:
he was created a knight. In Sept. 1958 he
took up an appointment in the Voice Faculty
at the Royal Conservatory of Music in the
University of Toronto.   M. K. W.

Add after **SCHIØTZ**:
SCHIPA, Tito (*b.* Lecce, 2 Jan. 1889).
Italian tenor singer. He studied at the
Conservatory of his birthplace, beginning
vocal lessons when he was fifteen. At the age
of twenty-one he studied with Emilio Piccoli
at Milan and finally, in 1910, after seven
years of vocal preparation, made his début at
Vercelli as Alfredo in 'La Traviata'. During
the next three years appearances in the
smaller Italian provinces followed; in 1912–
1913 he was heard at the Dal Verme in Milan
in 'Sonnambula', 'Traviata' and 'Rigoletto' with the young Galli-Curci, and the
following year he was engaged for the Costanzi
in Rome, where he made his début as Ernesto
in 'Don Pasquale'. Engagements followed
in South America, and in Dec. 1915 he
made his Milan Scala début as Vladimir in
'Prince Igor'. After the first world war he
was engaged for the Chicago Opera, where
he returned each year until 1932. In Nov.
1932 he made his début at the Metropolitan, New York, remaining there three
seasons and returning again in 1940. Between
1929 and 1939 he sang regularly at La Scala,
where he was greatly admired in such parts
as Don Ottavio, Nemorino, Werther, Wilhelm
Meister, Almaviva, Elvino and Paolino. He

sang regularly all over Italy, in Spain and South America. His stage career continued until 1954, but he was still singing at concerts in 1957. He never appeared at Covent Garden. Among the parts he created was Ruggero in Puccini's ' La Rondine ' at Monte Carlo in 1917.

Schipa possessed a perfect vocal technique, musicianship, impeccable taste and style. His voice was not naturally large, but he commanded a wide range of tonal colour and was able to shade his notes from a delicate *pianissimo* to a loud *forte*. His *legato* singing was one of his greatest assets. His phrasing was always aristocratic and his enunciation a model. Of him Gigli said : " Though there were many fine tenors singing during the twenties, thirties and forties, who were endowed with greater vocal potential than Schipa, when he sang, we all had to bow down to his greatness ".   H. D. R.

491   ii   **SCHIRMER**
19 Aug.
    Par. 2, l. 11.   20 Aug. *should read* :

492   i   Par. 2, l. 5.   secretary *should read* :
president

    Add at end :

In 1957 he resigned, and was succeeded by Rudolph Tauhert.

    ii   **SCHJELDERUP**
        Par. 5, l. 4.   ' Bruderøvet ' *should read* :
' Bruderovet '

493   i   **Schlaf**
        l. 1.   (Alban, song) *should read* :
(Alban, 2 songs).

        Schlegel, August
        l. 1.   *See* Schubert *should read* :
See Martin (F., ' Sturm ' [Shakespeare], opera). Schubert

    ii   **SCHLESINGER**
        Par. 1, l. 2.   London, 18 *should read* :
London, 16

        Par. 2, l. 9.   Greek, *should read* :
Greece,

497   i   **SCHMID, E. F.**
        Par. 1, l. 8 *should read* :
beuren in Bavaria. He is president of the German Mozart Society. His published works

        SCHMIDL
        Par. 1, l. 2.   Trieste, Oct. *should read* :
Trieste, 7 Oct.

498   i   **SCHMIDT, Franz**
        BIBL.   l. 2 *should read* :
Schaffen ' (Graz & Vienna, 1951).

    Add before **Schmidt, Georg Philipp** :

SCHMIDT-GARRE, Helmut (*b*. Düsseldorf, 23 June 1907).

German musicologist and critic. He studied at the Conservatory of Düsseldorf and the University of Vienna, where he took the Ph.D. degree in 1930. He was a pupil there of Alban Berg (for composition), Egon Wellesz (orchestration) and Rudolf von Ficker (musicology). He made some way as a composer, but in 1950 withdrew all his compositions, having decided to devote all his time to musical literature. Some of his orchestral and chamber music, however, was performed and broadcast in Germany. In 1947 he became music critic of the ' Münchner Merkur ', and he has remained with this paper, and at Munich. He is also a regular contributor to musical periodicals and to Riemann's music lexicon as well as to the general one of Brockhaus.

Schmidt-Garre's publications in book-form are :

' Die drei- und vierstimmigen Organa ' (Cassel, 1933).
' Drei Benedicamus Domino-Organa ' (Mainz, 1934).
' Harmonielehre ' (Munich, 1950).   E. B.

    ii   **SCHMIDT-ISSERSTEDT**
        Signature should read :
K. W. B.

499   i   **SCHMITT**
        Par. 1, l. 2 *should read* :
et-Moselle, 28 Sept. 1870 ;   d. Neuilly-sur-Seine, 17 Aug. 1958).

500   i   *Add to* BIBL. :
HUCHER, YVES, ' Florent Schmitt : l'homme et l'artiste, son époque et son œuvre ' (Paris, 1953).

501   i   PIANOFORTE SOLO
        Add after Op. 42 :
43. ' Humoresques ' (arr. from Pianoforte Duets).

        PIANOFORTE DUET
        Op. 43.   ' Humoresque ' *should read* :
' Humoresques '

    ii   **SCHMITZ, Arnold**
        Par. 2, l. 4.   Beer-Waldbrunn, *should read* :
Beer-Walbrunn,

502   i   **SCHMITZ, Eujen**
        Par. 1, l. 2 *should read* :
12 July 1882 ;   d. Leipzig, 10 July 1959).

503   1   **SCHNABEL, Artur**
BIBL., l. 2. 1933). *should read*:
1933); Eng. trans. (London, 1935).

Add to BIBL. :
SAERCHINGER, CÉSAR, ' Artur Schnabel : a Biography '
(London, 1957).

    ii **SCHNAPPER**
       Par. 3, l. 19 *should read*:
Catalogue of Music (published 1957).

506   i **SCHNEIDER-TRNAVSKÝ**
       Par. 1, l. 2. 1881). *should read*:
1881 ; *d.* Bratislava, 28 May 1958).

    ii **SCHNITGER**
       Signature should read :
W. L. S. (ii).

509   i **SCHOECK**
       Par. 1, l. 2 *should read*:
Schwyz, 1 Sept. 1886; *d.* Zürich, 8 Mar.
1957).

510   ii *Add to* BIBL. :
CORRODI, HANS, ' Othmar Schoeck : Bild eines Schaffens '
(Frauenfeld, 1956).
VOGEL, TRAUGOTT, ' Othmar Schoeck im Wort :
Äusserungen des Komponisten mit einer Auswahl
zeitgenössischer Bekenntnisse ' (St. Gall, 1957).
VOGEL, WERNER, ' Thematisches Verzeichnis der Werke
von Othmar Schoeck ' (Zürich, 1956).

511   i CATALOGUE
       Add to SOLO VOICES AND OR-
       CHESTRA :
70. ' Nachhall ' (poems by Lenau & Claudius) (1954–
1955).

513   ii **SCHOEMAKER**
       Par. 3, l. 1 *should read*:
Opera, ' Swane ' (lib. by E. De Bom) (1933).

       l. 2 *should read*:
Fairy-play ' Arc-en-ciel ' (lib. by M. de Gelderode)
(1937).

       Add after l. 2 :
Opera ' The Toverviool ' (lib. by A. van de Velde)
(1954).
Ballet ' Breughel-Suite ' (1928).
Ballet ' Pan ' (1937).

515   ii **SCHOENBERG**
       Par. 3, ll. 10-11 *should read*:
' Moses and Aron ' and composed the music
of the first two acts. On 30 May 1933 he was

516   i Par. 3, ll. 8-9 *should read*:
Eb major, and though its twelve-note series
is very freely handled, it is definitely dodeca-

    ii Par. 2, ll. 29-30 *should read*:
(1948) and the three choral works which form
his Op. 50.

520   i Par. 3, ll. 1-3 *should read*:
The ' Ode to Napoleon ' is loosely based
on a twelve-note series, which is handled with
great freedom, the music being based through-

    ii Par. 3, ll. 1-2 *should read*:
Schoenberg's last work, apart from the
choruses Op. 50, was

521   ii *Add to* BIBL. :
BURT, FRANCIS, ' An Antithesis [Schoenberg and
Stravinsky] : I. The Technical Aspect ' (' The
Score ', No. 18, Dec. 1956, p. 7).
KELLER, HANS, ' Schoenberg's Comic Opera ' [' Von
heute auf morgen '] ' (' The Score ', No. 23, July
1958).
NEIGHBOUR, OLIVER, ' Schoenberg : a Talk given to
Composers' Concourse ' (' The Score ', No. 16,
June 1956, p. 19).
RUFER, JOSEF, ' Die Komposition mit 12 Tönen ' (Berlin,
1952) ; Eng. trans., ' Composition with 12 Notes '
(London, 1954).
STUCKENSCHMIDT, H. H., ' Stil und Aesthetik Schön-
bergs ' (Schw. Mz., XCVIII, Mar. 1958).

522   ii CATALOGUE
       ORCHESTRAL WORKS
       l. 6. ' Begleitmusik *should read* :
' Begleitungsmusik

523   ii THEORETICAL WRITINGS
       l. 24. (unpubl.) *should read* :
(London & New York, 1954).

       Add before See also :
A complete list of Schoenberg's articles will be found
in Rufer's book (*see* Bibl.).

       SCHÖFFER
       Add at end :
See also Chorwerk, Vol. 29 (modern reprint of 1513
Song Book).

       SCHÖFFLER
       Par. 2, l. 11 *should read* :
Between 1934 and 1939 he regularly ap-

524   i l. 5. new productions *should read* :
modern works

       Add at end :
In 1949 he became a member of the Metropolitan Opera in New York.

       SCHOLES
       Par. 1, l. 2 *should read* :
24 July 1877 ; *d.* Vevey, Switzerland, 31 July
1958).

       Par. 2, l. 11 *should read* :
B.B.C. as music critic and as musical editor of
' The Radio

       l. 15 *should read* :
above Montreux in Switzerland and

       l. 17 *should read* :
of Musical Educationists (1929 and 1931) at
Lausanne.

524   i   Par. 3, ll. 3-5 *should read* :

Music ' is in a class by itself. It is designed to disprove the repeated

Par. 4, l. 2 *should read* :

Oxford in 1908 and in 1943 obtained that of D.Mus. (hon.). In 1934 he took the degree of

Add after l. 5 :

He is also an M.A. of Oxford (1944) and Litt.D. of Leeds (1954). In 1957 the O.B.E. was conferred on him.

ii   List of Works
        l. 14. 3rd ed. 1941 *should read* :
9th ed. 1955

        Delete next title ' God save the King '.

        Add at end, before signature :
' The Oxford Junior Companion to Music ' (1954).
' God save the Queen ! : the History and Romance of
        the World's First National Anthem ' (1954).
' Dr. Burney's Musical Tours in Europe ', 2 vols. (1959).

525   i   *Add before* **SCHÖNBERG** :

SCHOLZE, Johann Sigismund.   *See*
SPERONTES.

SCHOOL   OF   ENGLISH CHURCH MUSIC.

Entry should read :

SCHOOL   OF   ENGLISH   CHURCH MUSIC.   *See* ROYAL SCHOOL OF CHURCH MUSIC.

Transfer article to p. 284.

526   ii   *Add at end, before signature* :

COURSES FOR BOYS. Seven or eight instructional courses for choirboys are held each year during holidays (three times a year) both at headquarters and at public schools in different parts of the country.

Add after **SCHOOLMASTER** :

SCHOOLS' MUSIC ASSOCIATION. An organization formed in 1938 as a result of the outstanding success of the non-competitive schools' music festivals. It exists to foster in schools the study of the art of music by helping teachers, arranging courses, forming a panel of directors and orchestrators of festival music, giving advice on the formation of non-competitive schools' music festivals, building up a library of music, and organizing from time to time national festivals. Dr. Vaughan Williams and Dr. Armstrong Gibbs have both composed works specially for performance at these festivals.

A News Bulletin is circulated each school term to members and affiliated bodies, and Music Forums are held in different centres

from time to time. A successful scheme has been the launching of an annual music course for nuns, which receives widespread support. The President is Sir Adrian Boult.

S. S. M.

SCHOOLS' MUSIC FESTIVALS (Non-Competitive). The scheme for non-competitive schools' music festivals was originated in 1926 by Ulric Brunner, at that time headmaster of St. Mary's School, Bridgnorth. The first festival took place at Bridgnorth on 14 June 1927, when the director was Dr. Geoffrey Shaw.

The scheme received very strong support from the schools, and it soon spread to other areas in Shropshire and then to Worcestershire. Within a few years festivals were being held in Buckinghamshire, Essex and Yorkshire, followed by other counties. By 1938 the movement had become a national one, playing a most important part in raising the standard of the teaching of music in schools. On 6 May that year a joint National Festival took place at the Royal Albert Hall in London. As a result of the outstanding success of this Festival a national body was formed, now known as The Schools' Music Association.

At a non-competitive festival each school is encouraged to enter complete classes from their schools, not picked choirs. They sing two songs of their own choice, or play two instrumental pieces of their own choosing for instrumental classes, and receive a written criticism of their work from the musical director. There are no public criticisms, no marks and no prizes. In this way the class teacher receives the maximum amount of help, and usually this results in a marked raising of the standard of music teaching in the schools taking part. Music reading classes take place privately, the school class taking part, the teacher and director being the only persons present. Later in the day the director meets the teachers and sums up the festival in general terms. He also takes a rehearsal of the massed choirs in a set programme, and the festival concludes with a massed concert.

S. S. M.

BIBL.—PRIESTLEY, EDMUND, ' The Organization of a
        Non-Competitive Music Festival ' (Leeds, 1942).
        See also Brunner. Schools' Music Association.

527   ii   **SCHOTT & SÖHNE**
        Add at end :
See also Jeunesses Musicales (publication for).

529   i   **SCHRADE**
        Par. 1, l. 20 *should read* :

Academy, among other societies. In 1957 he was appointed Professor of Music at the University of Basel in succession to Jacques Handschin, who died in 1955.

531   i   **SCHREKER**
Add after Par. 1, *before signature* :

In Mar. 1958 an Internationale Franz-
Schreker-Gesellschaft was founded in Berlin
to celebrate the composer's eightieth birthday
and to promote a revival of his work and that
of his pupils.

534   ii   **SCHRÖTER (2)**
Add at end :

Bibl.—Wolf, Konrad, 'Johann Samuel Schroeter'
(M.Q., XLIV, July 1958, p. 338).

535   ii   **SCHUBART**
Add to Bibl. :

Thorn, Eduard, ' Genius in Fesseln : Chr. Fr. D.
Schubarts Leben ' (Geislingen-Steige, 1956).

537   i   **SCHUBERT**
Par. 1, l. 9 *should read* :

this region is the district of Himmelpfort-
grund,

Par. 2, ll. 18-19 *should read* :

the Säulengasse in the district of Himmelpfort-
grund. In 1796 he moved into the district

539   ii   *Footnote.* l. 4 *should read* :

mately 5 feet 2 inches. The Austrian foot, however, is
longer than the English, so that Schubert was below the
minimum height of 5 (Austrian) feet

540   ii   ll. 7-8 *should read* :

love. Salieri is said, on very uncertain evidence, to have been present at the performance
and to have acclaimed Schubert as his pupil,
who

ll. 11-14 *should read* :

St. Augustine and the same hubbub of con-
gratulation seethed round the lad ; but the
story that his father presented him with a
new pianoforte on this occasion is almost
certainly untrue. Something took place
during those

541   i   Par. 2, l. 2 *should read* :

the year Schubert set four or five dramatic
works to

l. 25 *should read* :

which however is undated and now considered
more likely to date from 1819.

ll. 44-45 *should read* :

posed in the autumn (the exact date is unknown, but must be before Oct., when Albert
Stadler heard it sung) was ' Erlkönig ', the
song by which

ii   Par. 1, ll. 6-8 *should read* :

Randhartinger is said, on uncertain evidence,
to have sung the ballad to Schubert's accompaniment amid the tremendous enthusiasm

of the students ; it was more likely in some
other connection that Ruzicka justified his

541   ii   Par. 2, ll. 3-6 *should read* :

Schober, who arrived in Vienna in the autumn
of 1815 to study law,

544   i   Par. 1, l. 1 *should read* :

district of Rossau. The family, augmented by

ii   Par. 6, l. 15 *should read* :

(' The Twin Brothers '), the overture of which
is dated Jan. 1819.

545   ii   Par. 2, l. 14 *should read* :

The anecdote that the Overture for pianoforte in F minor

l. 18 *should read* :

and lunch neglected over it " is extremely
questionable. A male-voice

550   i   Par. 1, ll. 3-4 *should read* :

und Estrella ' (composed in Feb. 1823 but
probably revised for this occasion) ; it is the
work, in D major, which

551   i   Par. 6, l. 4 *should read* :

rooms in a house close to Schwind's home.

553   ii   Par. 2, l. 18 *should read* :

the pianoforte. It was possibly in this year
that Schubert wrote

ll. 24-25 *should read* :

have been the lost Symphony of 1825.[1]   In
Oct. the society decided to vote 100

Add footnote :

[1] The letter is undated and cannot therefore be
ascribed to 1826 with certainty. It could even be of 1828,
in which case the score accompanying it would have
been that of the great C major Symphony, which we
know to have been intended for the society.

554   i   Par. 5, l. 25 *should read* :

but became too ill to do so. There is no
reliable evidence for the story that Schubert,
in the

555   ii   Par. 1, l. 6 *should read* :

composed in 1826 and 1827. That the

557   ii   Par. 5, l. 21 *should read* :

them to Schubert.[1]   There follow settings of
six

Add footnote :

[1] The existence of previous settings of Rellstab by
Schubert, unknown to Schindler, together with other
evidence, proves that this story of his is false.

559   ii   Par. 2, l. 17 *should read* :

great C major Symphony, with severe cuts,
at the Leipzig

570 ii *Add to* BIBL.:

BROWN, MAURICE J. E., 'Schubert's Settings of "Salve Regina"' (M. & L., XXXVII, July 1956, p. 234).
'Some Unpublished Schubert Songs and Song Fragments' (M. Rev., XV, 1954, p. 93).

(2nd work by BROWN):
'Schubert: a Critical Biography' (London, 1958).

l. 29 *should read*:

CAPELL, RICHARD, 'Schubert's Songs' (London, 1928): 2nd ed., rev. by Martin Cooper (New York & London, 1957).

(4th work by DEUTSCH):
'Schubert: Memoirs by his Friends', trans. by Rosamond Ley & John Nowell (London, 1958).
GOLDSCHMIDT, HARRY, 'Franz Schubert: ein Lebensbild' (Berlin, 1954).

571 i

HAAS, HERMANN, 'Ueber die Bedeutung der Harmonik in den Liedern Franz Schuberts' (Bonn, 1957).

| 'Die Allmacht.' | Johann Ladislaus von Pyrker. | Mixed voices & pf. | — | 1826. |

ii

SCHMITZ, EUGEN, 'Schuberts Auswirkung auf die deutsche Musik bis zu Hugo Wolf und Bruckner' (Leipzig, 1954).

l. 19 *should read*:
Deutsch (Vienna, 1954).

Add to BIBL.:

VETTER, WALTHER, 'Der Klassiker Schubert', 2 Vols. (Leipzig, 1953).

CATALOGUE:
OPERAS

? 1819   Col. 4, l. 4. ('Adrast'), 1815. *should read*:

Transfer this line below 'Die Zwillingsbrüder'.

Col. 1. *Add after* l. 18:
Sketches for an unnamed opera.

1823.   Col. 4. *Add following this*:

572 — CHURCH MUSIC
Col. 1, l. 7 *should read*:
'Salve Regina', B♭ ma.

Add after l. 22 ('Stabat Mater'), Col. 1:
Requiem (fragment), F mi.

1816.   Col. 3:

Add after l. 27:
'Tantum ergo', D ma.

Chorus.   Col. 2:

1822.   Col. 3:

Add after l. 28:
Mass (fragment), A mi.

Chorus.   Col. 2:

1822.   Col. 3:

572 — CHORAL WORKS WITH PIANOFORTE
Add before l. 1, Col. 1:
'Viel tausend Sterne.'
'Dithyrambe' (fragment).

Col. 2:
?
Schiller.

Col. 3:
?
Mixed voices & pf.

Col. 4:
—

Col. 5:
prob. 1812.
29 Mar. 1813.

573 — *Delete whole line*, Cols. 1-5: 'Grab und Mond'. . . . 1826.

CHORAL WORKS WITH PIANOFORTE
Add after l. 34 (Col. i, 'Coronach'):

574 — UNACCOMPANIED CHORAL WORKS
Add after l. 10, Col. 1:
'Ruhe.'

Col. 2:
? Schubert.

Col. 3:
Male voices.

Col. 4:
—

Col. 5:
c. 1819

Add after l. 20, Col. 1:
'Grab und Mond.'

Col. 2:
Johann Gabriel Seidl.

Col. 3:
Male voices.

Col. 4:
—

Col. 5:
1826.

575 — CHAMBER MUSIC
l. 7, Col. 1 *should read*:
Quartet, C ma, (No. 2).[3]

l. 18, Col. 1 *should read*:
'Grave', C mi.[4]

l. 37 (Trio, B♭ ma.). 1827. *should read*:
1826.

Add footnote:
[3] *Andante* and finale published in 1955 by Maurice J. E. Brown.

Footnote 3 *becomes* 4.

576 — PIANOFORTE SOLO
Add after l. 1, Col. 1:
Fugue, D mi.
Fantasy, C mi.
2 Minuets, C ma., F ma.

Col. 3:
c. 1812.
c. 1812.
c. 1812.

576 — PIANOFORTE SOLO
l. 21, Col. 1 *should read* :
2 Scherzos, B♭ ma, D♭ ma.

Add after l. 28, Col. 1 :
' Cotillon ', E♭ ma.

Col. 3 :
? 1817.

577 — *Add after* l. 1, Col. 1 :
' Ungarische Melodie ', B mi.[1]

Col. 3 :
1824.

Add after l. 16, Col. 1 :
' Allegretto ', C mi. (fragment).

Col. 3 :
? 1827.

Add footnote :
[1] Sketch for the corresponding section of Op. 54.

Footnotes 1-4 *become* 2-5.

PIANOFORTE DUETS
Add after l. 5, Col. 1 :
3 ' Deutsche '.

Col. 3 :
1818 (publ. 1909).

Add after l. 10, Col. 1 :
Overture to ' Alfonso und Estrella '.
Overture to ' Fierrabras '.

Col. 2 :
69
76

Col. 3 :
1823 .
c. 1824.

Col. 4 (upper line) :
Anna Hönig.

Last line *should read* :
Col. 1 :
' Allegro moderato ', C ma., and ' Andante ', A mi.
(probably spurious).

578 — SONGS
Col. 1, 1812. *Add at end* :
' Der Geistertanz ', 2 sketches. | Friedrich Mathisson. |
| C mi., F mi. |

Col. 2, l. 1. Schücking. *should read* :
Clemens August Schücking.

Col. 2, 1813, l. 5. Friedrich Matthisson.
should read :
Matthisson.

Add after 1813 :
' Ich sass an einer Tempelhalle.' | ? | | C ma.

Col. 5, 1814, *Add for* ' An dem jungen
Morgenhimmel ' :
17 Sept.

Apr. for ' Die Betende ' *should read* :
Sept.

Add for ' Don Gayseros ' :
Sept.

20 Nov. for ' Nachtgesang ' *should read* :
30 Nov.

Add for ' Schäfers Klagelied ' (1st v.) :
30 Nov.

579 — SONGS
Col. 5, 1815, July. for ' Abend ' *should read* :
15 July.

Add for ' An Mignon ' :
27 Feb.

Col. 1. ' An Rosa ' (1st version). *should
read* :
' An Rosa ', I.

' An Rosa ' (2nd version) *should read* :
' An Rosa ', II.

Col. 5. *Add for* ' Augenlied ' :
Oct.

Cols. 1-6, *Delete entry* ' Erwartung, Die.',
etc.

580 — Col. 5. *Add for* ' Furcht der Geliebten ' :
12 Sept.

Add for ' Gebet während der Schlacht ' :
12 Mar.

Cols. 1, 2 & 4. *Delete entry* ' Goldschmied-
gesell, Der.', etc.

Col. 5. *Add for* ' Hektors Abschied ' :
19 Oct.

Add for ' Hoffnung ' :
Autumn

Cols. 1, 2, 4, 5 & 7. *Insert after* ' Idens
Schwanenlied ' :
' Jägers Abendlied ' (1st version). | Goethe. | F ma. | 20
June. | 15 June 1807.

Cols. 1, 2 & 4. *Delete entry* ' Liebhaber in
allen Gestalten ', etc.

Col. 5. July for ' Liedler ' *should read* :
June-Dec.

581 — Cols. 1, 2, 4 & 5. *Insert after* ' Meeresstille ' :
' Mein Gruss an den Mai.' | J. G. Kumpf. | B♭ ma. |
15 Oct.

Cols. 4 & 5. *Add for* ' Nachtgesang ' :
E♭ ma. | 19 Oct.

Col. 1. ' Nonne, Die. ' *should read* :
' Nonne, Die ' (2 versions).

Col. 5. *Add for* ' Rastlose Liebe ' :
19 May.

Cols. 1, 2 & 4. *Delete entry* ' Schweizer-
lied ', etc.

Col. 5. *Add for* ' Schwertlied ' :
12 Mar.

Col. 1. ' Sehnsucht der Liebe.' *should read* :
' Sehnsucht der Liebe ' (2 versions).

Col. 5. 8 Apr. *should read* :
8 Apr. & July.

Col. 5. *Add for* ' Sommernacht ' :
14 Sept.

Col. 5. *Add for* ' Trinklied vor der
Schlacht ' :
12 Mar.

Col. 5. *Add for* ' Unendlichen ' :
15 Sept.

582 — Col. 5. *Add for* ' Vaterlandslied ' :
14 Sept.

Cols. 1, 2, 4 & 7, 1816. *Insert after* ' Am
Bach im Frühling ' :
' Am ersten Maimorgen.' | Claudius. | G ma. | (unpubl.).

582 — SONGS
Cols. 1, 2, 4 & 7. *Insert after* ' An Chloen ' :
' An Chloen ' (fragment). | Uz. | G ma. | (unpubl.).

13 Mar.
Col. 5. *Add for* ' Auf den Tod einer Nachtigall ' :

Dec.
Col. 5. *Add for* ' Didone ' :

Col. 5. ' Entfernten, Die.' *should read* :
' Entfernten, Der.'

Cols. 1-6. *Insert after* ' Erntelied ' :
' Erwartung, Die.' | Schiller. | 116. | B♭ ma. | 25 June. | Joseph Hüttenbrenner.

13 Mar.
Col. 5. 13 May. for ' Frühlingslied.' *should read* :

583 — Col. 5. 13 May for ' Knabenzeit ' *should read* :
13 Mar.

584 — Cols. 1, 2, 4 & 7. *Insert after* ' Mädchens Klage ' :
' Mailied.' | Hölty. | G ma. | (unpubl.).

Cols. 1-5. *Insert after* ' An die Musik ' :
' An eine Quelle.' | Claudius. | 109.3. | Feb.

585 — Cols. 1, 2, 4 & 5. *Insert after* ' Ganymed ' :
' Goldschmiedgesell, Der.' | Goethe. | F ma. | May.

Cols. 1, 2, 4 & 7. *Insert after* ' Kampf ' :
' Klage.' | ? | G mi. | (unpubl.).

Cols. 1, 2, 4 & 5. *Insert after* ' Liebe ' :
' Liebhaber in allen Gestalten.' | Goethe. | A ma. | May.

Cols. 1, 2, 4 & 5. *Insert after* ' Schlaflied ' :
' Schweizerlied.' | Goethe. | F ma. | May.

Cols. 1, 2, 3, 4, 6 & 7. *Insert after this* :
' Sehnsucht.' | Mayrhofer. | 8.2. | C ma. | Count Johann Karl Esterházy. | 9 May 1822.

Aug.[2]
Col. 5. Aug. for ' Litanei ' *should read* :

Cols. 1, 2, 4 & 5. *Delete entry* ' Orest auf Tauris ', etc.

Add footnote :
[2] Possibly composed in 1816.

586 — Cols. 1, 2 & 4, 1819. *Insert after* ' Gebüsche ' :
' Götter Griechenlands, Die.' | Schiller. | A mi.

Cols. 1, 2, 4 & 5. *Insert after* ' Wanderer ' :
' Widerschein ' | Schlechta. | B♭ ma. | May.

587 — Col. 5, 1821. *Add for* ' Jüngling an der Quelle ' :
Apr.

C♯ mi. | Mar.
Cols. 4 & 5. *Add for* ' Mahomets Gesang ' :

Jan.
Col. 5. *Add for* ' Unglückliche ' :

Dec.
Col. 5, 1822. *Add for* ' Musensohn ' :

' Ständchen ', " Leise, leise　　　　　?
lass uns singen ". |

587 — SONGS
Cols. 1, 2, 4 & 5. *Delete entry* ' Vergissmeinnicht ', etc.

Cols. 1, 2, 4 & 5. *Delete entry* ' Zürnende Barde ', etc.

588 — Cols. 1, 2, 4 & 5, 1823. *Insert before* ' Viola ' :
' Vergissmeinnicht.' | Schober. | F mi., etc. | May.

Cols. 1, 2, 4 & 5. *Insert after* ' Viola ' :
' Zürnende Barde, Der. ' | Bruchmann. | G mi.-ma. | Feb.

Aug.-Dec.[1]
Col. 5. *Add for* ' Schöne Müllerin ' :

Apr.
Col. 5, 1825. *Add for* ' Blinde Knabe ' :

Add footnote :
[1] According to investigations made by Maurice J. E. Brown.

589 — Cols. 1, 2, 3, 4, 5 & 7. *Insert after* ' Totengräbers Heimweh ' :
' Um Mitternacht.' | Schulze. | 88.3. | B♭ ma. | Dec. | 12 Dec. 1827.

Col. 1, 1826. ' Fischerweise.' *should read* :
' Fischerweise.' [3]

4th version).[4]
Col 1. ' Mignon's Lied ', 4th version).[3] *should read* :

Cols. 1, 2, 3 & 4. *Insert before this* :
' Echo, Das.' | Ignaz Franz Castelli. | 130. | B♭ ma. |

Cols. 1, 2, 3, 4, 5 & 7. *Delete entry* ' Um Mitternacht ', etc.

Footnote 3 becomes 4.

590 — Col. 5, 1827. C mi.-ma. for ' Annot Lyle's Song ' *should read* :
C mi.-ma.[1]

Cols. 1, 2, 4 & 7. *Insert after* ' Fischers Liebesglück ' :
' Fröhliches Scheiden ' (fragment). | Leitner. | F ma. | (unpubl.).

Feb.-Oct.
Col. 5. *Add for* ' Winterreise ' :

Cols. 1, 2, 3, 4, 5 & 7, 1828. *Insert after* ' Auf dem Strom ' :
' Glaube, Hoffnung, Liebe.' | Kuffner. | 97. | E♭ ma. | Aug. | 6 Oct. 1828.

Add footnote :
[1] Possibly composed in 1825.

591 — Cols. 1, 2, 4 & 5. *Delete entry* ' Widerschein ', etc.

Cols. 1 & 2, Undated. *Delete entry* ' Herrn Josph Spaun ', etc.

VOCAL DUET [3]
Heading *should read* :

VOCAL DUETS [3]
Add below this :
Cols. 1, 2, 4, 5 & 7 :
' Linde Lüfte wehen.' | ? | B mi. | Apr. 1821. | 1929.

592 — VOCAL QUARTETS
Add at end :

2 tenors & 2 basses. |　— |　?

592 — UNACCOMPANIED VOCAL TRIOS
        Add at end of 1813:

| 'Totengräberlied.'

        UNACCOMPANIED VOCAL DUETS
        Add at end:
| 'Jägerlied', voices or horns.

See also. l. 22 *should read:*
cert). Smetana (transcription of 'Der Neugierige' for
pf.). Sonata, p. 905. Song, pp. 938-40. Sulzer
(setting of

594 i **SCHUCH**
        Add at end:
BIBL.—SCHUCH, FRIEDRICH VON, 'Richard Strauss,
    Ernst von Schuch und Dresdens Oper' (Leipzig,
    1953).

        SCHUCH-PROSKA
        Par. 1, l. 2.   1853 *should read:*
1850

    ii **SCHULHOFF**
        Par. 1, l. 2.   Wülsburg *should read:*
Wülzburg

595 i *Add before* **SCHULOPER:**
    SCHULLER, Gunter (*b.* New York, 22
    Nov. 1925).
    American horn player and composer. He
    studied music under his father, a violinist in
    the New York Philharmonic Orchestra, and
    later at the Manhattan School of Music. He
    made his début as a performer-composer with
    the Cincinnati Symphony Orchestra in 1945,
    playing his own horn Concerto under the
    direction of Eugene Goossens. The same
    year he joined the orchestra of the New York
    Metropolitan Opera, where he plays first
    horn. Many of his chamber works have
    been heard in New York, and he has been
    represented in the programme of the I.S.C.M.
    His best-known work so far (1957) is a Sym-
    phony for brass, but his 'Dramatic Over-
    ture' was performed with success at Darm-
    stadt in 1954 and his 'Five Pieces for Five
    Horns' were heard in London in 1955.
                                        E. B.

596 ii **SCHULTZ, Helmut**
        Par. 1, l. 2.   *d.* ?, *should read:*
d. Waldburg, 19 Apr.

598 ii **SCHULZE & Sons**
        Par. 3, ll. 15-17 *should read:*
instruments in England at churches at Leeds
(in conjunction with Hill); Hindley, Wigan;
Tyne Dock, South Shields; Armley, Leeds;
Harro-

599 ii **SCHUMAN**
        Add before CATALOGUE:
BIBL.—SCHREIBER, FLORE RHETA & PERSICHETTI,
    VINCENT, 'William Schuman' (New York &
    London, 1954).

2 D

| Hölty. | 1813. |

| Körner. | 1815. |

CATALOGUE:
OPERA
ll. 1-2 *should read:*
'The Mighty Casey', baseball opera, lib. by Jeremy
    Gury (1953), prod. Hartford, Conn., 4 May 1953.

FILM MUSIC
        War documentary *should read:*
War Information documentary

600 i ORCHESTRAL WORKS
        Add at end:
'Credendum' (1955).
'New England Triptych' (1956).

        CHAMBER MUSIC
        Add at end:
String Quartet No. 4.

602 i **SCHUMANN, Clara**
        Add to BIBL.:
QUEDNAU, WERNER, 'Clara Schumann' (Berlin, 1955).

        SCHUMANN, Elisabeth
    ii Par. 1, l. 2.   1885 *should read:*
1888
        Add at end:
BIBL.—PURITZ, ELISABETH, 'The Teaching of Elisabeth
    Schumann' ('The Score', No. 10, Dec. 1945).

603 i **SCHUMANN-HEINK**
        Par. 3, l. 5.   1906 *should read:*
1914
        l. 13 *should read:*
1917 and intermittently in 1925-32.   She
became an American citizen in 1905.

613 ii **SCHUMANN**
        Par. 1, l. 12 *should read:*
Dargomizhsky, though he and Clara attended
a party at which the former was present.   On
2 Apr. they left St.

627 i *Add to* BIBL.:
BRION, MARCEL, 'Schumann et l'âme romantique'
    (Paris, 1954); Eng. trans. by Geoffrey Sainsbury,
    'Schumann and the Romantic Age' (London,
    1956).
EISMANN, GEORG, 'Robert Schumann: ein Quellenwerk
    über sein Leben und Schaffen', 2 vols. (Leipzig,
    1956).
    ii BIBL., l. 38. SCHUMANN, R., *should read:*
SCHUMANN, EUGENIE,
        Add to BIBL.:
REHBERG, PAULA & WALTER, 'Robert Schumann:
    sein Leben und sein Werk' (Zürich, 1954).
VALABREGA, CESARE, 'Roberto Schumann: arte e
    natura, arte e vita, arte e fede' (Rome, 1934; 3rd
    ed. Parma, 1956).

VALENSI, THÉODORE, 'Le Romantisme de Schumann' (Nice, 1953).
YOUNG, PERCY M., 'Tragic Muse: the Life and Works of Robert Schumann' (London, 1957).

630 — CATALOGUE
1834-37.[14] Col. 3, l. 16. 1834.[14] *should read*:

637 — Op. 142, col. 4. 1852 *should read*:
1840

640 ii SCHUPPANZIGH
Par. 1, l. 2. 1776 *should read*:
20 Nov. 1776

641 ii SCHÜRMANN
Par. 3, l. 11. XVII *should read*:
XIX

642 i SCHÜTZ
Par. 1, l. 2. 8 Oct. *should read*:
4 Oct.[2]

Add footnote:
[2] Othmar Wesseley (*see* Bibl.) argues that Schütz, who was certainly baptized on 9 Oct. 1585, was born on 4 Oct., not 8 Oct., the date hitherto usually accepted.

650 — Heading *should read*:
SCHÜTZ: The Music — Bibliography

ii *Add to* BIBL.:
'Festschrift zur Ehrung von Heinrich Schütz', ed. by Günther Kraft (Weimar, 1954).

MOSER. l. 4 *should read*:
1936); 2nd ed., Cassel & Basel, 1954; Eng. translation by C. F. Pfatteicher (St. Louis, 1959).

651 i *Add to* BIBL.:
WESSELEY, OTHMAR, 'Zur Frage nach dem Geburtstag von Heinrich Schütz' ('Anzeiger der phil.-hist. Klasse der Oesterreichischen Akademie der Wissenschaften', 1953, No. 15, and offprint).

652 ii SCHUYT
Add at end:
See also Vereniging, Vol. 45 (reprint of madrigals for 5 v.).

653 ii SCHWARZ
Par. 3, l. 6 *should read*:
George Weldon. He left Birmingham in 1957 to succeed Sir Malcolm Sargent as conductor of the B.B.C. Symphony Orchestra.

654 i SCHWARZKOPF
Par. 1, l. 23 *should read*:
at Venice. She has sung at the Milan Scala since 1948 and in America since 1954.

ii SCHWEITZER, Albert
Par. 2, ll. 10-19 *should read*:
Strasbourg in 1902-12. He began work on his famous book, 'Jean-Sébastien Bach, le

musicien-poète' in 1903, and it was published in Paris in 1905. He entirely rewrote it in German, and this edition was published at Leipzig the same year. Ernest Newman's English translation (Leipzig & London, 1911) was made from the German version.

654 ii *Add after* Par. 2:
If one interest may be said to have absorbed Schweitzer even more than that in Bach, it is his work as a medical missionary in French Equatorial Africa. His first stay there was in 1913-16; he returned in 1924 and has remained ever since but for occasional visits to Europe, where he has given many organ recitals of Bach's work to collect funds for his tropical hospital, which has been of incalculable benefit to the natives in Equatorial Africa.

Par. 3, ll. 4-8 *should read*:
to found. The first five volumes of the Bach edition were finished in 1913 and published in 1916. Schweitzer returned to its completion many years later, after Widor's death, the first of the three additional volumes appearing in New York in 1957.

Par. 4, ll. 1-4 *should read*:
Schweitzer told the story of his career in an autobiographical volume published in German (Leipzig, 1931) and English (London, 1932). It is inevitably incomplete, but so far as it goes shows in a remarkable manner

655 i Par. 1, l. 4 *should read*:
received the Nobel Prize in 1952.

Add after Par. 1:
Unfortunately the autobiography, which does not deal with every aspect of Schweitzer's life even up to its early date, has never been revised or brought up to date. The standard biography, authorized by and collaborated in by him, is that by George Seaver (*see* BIBL.).
H. C. C., rev.

Add to BIBL.:
'Ehrfurcht vor dem Leben: Albert Schweitzer, eine Freundesgabe zu seinem 80. Geburtstag' (Berne, 1955).
FRESCHOTTE, JACQUES, 'Albert Schweitzer: avec des textes inédits' (Paris, 1952).

l. 6 *should read*:
1951; London, 1953).

l. 19. 1933). *should read*:
1932).

l. 21. 1947). *should read*:
1947; rev. ed. 1956).

658 ii *Add before* SCOBEDO:
SCIUTTI, Graziella (*b.* Turin, ?).
Italian soprano singer. She was educated at normal Italian schools and studied lan-

guages. Having attended the Conservatorio Santa Cecilia in Rome, where she was a pupil of Rachele Maragliano-Mori and others, she took a diploma in 1949. At a very early age she began to make her mark in opera at the Teatro alla Scala, Milan, the Teatro San Carlo, Naples, the Teatro Costanzi, Rome, the Teatro Massimo, Palermo and the Teatro La Fenice, Venice, excelling in the light soprano parts of Cimarosa, Paisiello, Donizetti, Rossini, and so on. In 1951 she sang Carolina in Cimarosa's ' Matrimonio segreto ' at the Aix-en-Provence Festival, and in the same part she appeared at the inauguration of the Piccola Scala at Milan on 26 Dec. 1955, where she also sang Despina in ' Così fan tutte ', her fame as a Mozart interpreter having also been confirmed by her appearances as Susanna, Zerlina and Papagena. In 1954 she first appeared in England, at Glyndebourne, where she was a most charming and accomplished Rosina in Rossini's ' Barbiere ', and in 1956 she sang Oscar in Verdi's ' Ballo in maschera ' in London, at Covent Garden, in English. Her other Verdi parts are Gilda in ' Rigoletto ' and Nanetta in ' Falstaff '. She has also sung in operas by living composers, such as Menotti and Sauguet.

Graziella Sciutti has made successful recital appearances with Italian, French and German songs, and has greatly enlarged her range by singing in oratorio : she has been heard in Bach (both the great Passions and the B minor Mass), Handel, Haydn, Mozart and Pergolesi. Modern composers she has interpreted in concert performances include Stravinsky, Milhaud and Petrassi. In 1954 she received the Harriett Cohen International award as the first singer ever to obtain it.   E. B.

660   ii   **SCORDATURA**
Par. 3, l. 11 *should read :*

frequently employs.

Special uses of *scordatura* for different purposes may be classified as follows :

(*a*) For greater brilliance of tone, as in Mozart's ' Sinfonia concertante ' for violin and viola, in E♭ major, where the latter instrument is tuned up half a tone and its part is written in D major.

(*b*) For the downward increase of the range of string instruments : *e.g.* the cello tuned down for the pedal B♭ in the slow movement of Schumann's piano Quintet ; the double basses tuned down to E♭ for the prelude to Wagner's ' Rheingold ' ; the solo viola tuned down to B for the Sancho Panza section in Strauss's ' Don Quixote '.

Footnote 2. l. 2 should read :

posing instrument when all the strings are tuned to a different key.

661   ii   **SCORE**
Par. 1, l. 11 *should read :*

hymn, ' Salve virgo virginum ', for three voices

Insert after signature W. S. R. :

One of the puzzles of musical history which greatly perplexes students, and an explanation of which is very rarely offered by scholars, is the procedure used by old composers of polyphonic music, up to about the end of the 16th century, in writing down their complicated textures of parts. It is obvious that composition of that kind is utterly impossible without some kind of a score showing all the parts simultaneously ; yet no such scores survive, and anyone who thinks about the problem at all is bound to ask why. Here is an explanation, quoted from Thurston Dart's book ' The Interpretation of Music ' (London, 1954) :

Most composers made use of what were called *cartelle* : blank sheets of parchment or paper, incised with a dozen or more sets of stave-lines. A polyphonic composition would be drafted on these in pencil or ink ; a set of parts could then be prepared from this score ; and finally the original text could be erased with a single sweep of a wet rag or sponge, leaving the sheets clean and ready for future use. It is hardly surprising that no specimen of a *cartella* or composing-sheet is known to exist to-day, for they would have been used over and over again until they fell to pieces and were thrown away. But the evidence for their existence survives, even though only in the form of scattered and ambiguous references here and there.   E. B.

BIBL.—LOWINSKY, EDWARD E., ' On the Use of Scores by Sixteenth-Century Musicians ' (Jour. Amer. Musicol. Soc., I, 1948, p. 17).

Par. 2, l. 1 *should read :*

It will be observed that in the examples here reproduced

664   ii   **SCOTCH SNAP**
Par. 2, l. 11 *should read :*

snap. Vivaldi also cultivated it, and it was known in Italy as a Lombard characteristic and in France as *manière lombarde*. But Quantz, in his ' Versuch ', says : " This style began [in Italy] about 1722, but it seems to resemble Scottish music . . .".

J. M. W.

667   ii   **SCOTT, Cyril,** CATALOGUE
CHAMBER MUSIC
Add after l. 2 :

Sextet for 3 vns., viola, cello & pf. (c. 1904).

CHAMBER MUSIC
l. 5 *should read :*

String Quartet No. 1 (1922).

Add after l. 15 :

String Quartet No. 2 (1959).

668   i   PIANOFORTE SOLO, 1912
l. 7. 3 Poems. *should read :*

5 Poems.

Add at end of PIANOFORTE SOLO :

1956
Sonata.

669   i   **SCOTT, F. G.**
Par. 1, l. 2 *should read*:
Roxburghshire, 25 Jan. 1880; *d.* Glasgow,
6 Nov. 1958).

ii   Par. 1, l. 4 *should read*:
1949. In June 1957 the University of Glasgow conferred an honorary doctorate on him for his services to Scottish music as a composer.

671   i   **SCOTT, Marion**
Par. 2, l. 7 *should read*:
'The R.C.M. Magazine'. The hon. A.R.C.M. was bestowed on her shortly before her death. She also took an

Add at end:
BIBL.—DALE, KATHLEEN, 'Memories of Marion Scott' (M. & L., XXXV, 1954, p. 236).

678   i   *Add before* **SCRIBANO**:
SCRIABIN(E). *See* SKRIABIN.

Scribe
Par. 2, l. 23 *should read*:
de Portici (Aubert, lib.). Offenbach (2 libs.). Pavesi (' Odoardo e Cristina ', opera). Prophète

l. 25. Edoardo *should read*:
Eduardo

683   i   *Add after* **SECONDO**:
SECRET, THE ('Tajemství'). Opera in 3 acts by Smetana. Libretto by Eliška Krasnohorská. Produced Prague, New Czech Theatre, 28 Sept. 1878. 1st perf. abroad, Vienna, 27 Mar. 1895. 1st in Britain, Oxford, 5 Dec. 1956.

ii   **SEEFRIED**
Par. 2, l. 24 *should read*:
She also sang the part of the Composer in 'Ariadne auf Naxos' at the

l. 33 *should read*:
the first time at the Salzburg Festival. She has also sung at the Metropolitan Opera in New York.

684   i   **SEEGER**
Par. 2, l. 2. 'Dedra' *should read*:
'Derdra'

685   i   **SEGOVIA**
Par. 1, l. 1. 17 Feb. *should read*:
17 Mar.

687   i   **SEIBER**
(*d.* Cape Town, 24 Sept. 1960.

693   i   *Add after* **SELENECCER**:
SELESSES, Jacopinus. *See* JACOMI.

693   i   **SELLE**
Par. 2, l. 7 *should read*:
composed a Passion according to St. John, a large number of concertos, madri-

See also should read:
See also Chorwerk, Vol. 26 (modern reprint of St. John Passion). Passion Music.

694   i   **SELMER**
Par. 2, l. 5. Festlog *should read*:
Festtog

ii   BIBL. HALFORSEN, l. 3, *should read*:
HALVORSEN

ll. 5-6 *should read*:
GURVIN & ANKER, Dictionary of Music (Oslo, 1949).

l. 9 *should read*:
' Norges musikkhistorie ' (1921), II, 125.

l. 12. Halforsen *should read*:
Halvorsen

699   i   **SENFL**
Add at end:
See also Chorwerk, Vols. 60, 62 (modern reprints of sacred works). Denkmäler (5) I, Vols. 5, 10, 13, 15 & 19 (modern eds.).

ii   **SENILOV**
Par. 1, l. 2. 9 July *should read*:
8 Aug.

700   i   *Add before* **Senn**:
SENLECHES, Jacob de. *See* JACOMI.

Add after **SENSIBLE**:
SENTLUCH, Jacob de. *See* JACOMI.

704   ii   **SERAFIN**
Par. 2, l. 4 *should read*:
Florence. He has also been musical director of the Teatro alla Scala at Milan, which post he resigned in 1947. Italy is indebted to him for the

705   ii   **SERAUKY**
Par. 1, l. 2 *should read*:
1903; *d.* Leipzig, 20 Aug. 1959).

706   i   Par. 1, l. 3 *should read*:
a professorship in 1940. He is at work on a Handel biography of enormous size, of which the third volume appeared first in 1956, the whole being intended to complete Chrysander's work on Handel, and this volume carrying on where Chrysander left off (nearly 1,000 pages covering a period of five years). His earlier works include:

707   i   **SERES**
Par. 2, l. 16 *should read*:

(1553).   In some copies the colophon reads:
" Imprynted at London by Nycolas Hyll, for
Wyllyam Seres ".

708   ii   *Add after* **Sergel**:

SERIAL COMPOSITION. The principle
of twelve-note composition has been found,
both by composers committed to that system
on the model of Schoenberg and by others, to
be applicable music constructed, strictly or
intermittently, on notes grouped into series
consisting of less than the twelve semitones of
the chromatic scale.   A number of distinguished composers have, since about 1955,
done remarkable work on these lines, including Stravinsky, Dallapiccola, Britten, Seiber,
Searle, etc.   E. B.
See also Twelve-Note Music.

709   i   **SERMISY**
Par. 1, l. 1.   **Claude de** *should
read*:
Claude (Claudin) de

710   ii   *Add to* BIBL.:
PARKINSON, JOHN A., ' A Chanson by Claudin de
Sermisy ' (M. & L., XXXIX, 1958, p. 118).

Add at end:
See also Collectio O.M.B., Vol. 12 (modern ed.).
Florilège, Vol. 8 (do. of duos).   Maîtres Musiciens ', Vol.
5 (do. of chansons).

712   ii   **SEROV**
Add to BIBL.:
SEROV, ALEXANDER N., ' Aufsätze zur Musikgeschichte ',
ed. by N. Notowicz, trans. by Felix Loesch (Berlin,
1955).

718   i   **SERPENT FORVEILLE**
Add at end:
(*PLATE* 59, Vol. VII, p. 712, No. 11.)

ii   **SERRANO Y RUIZ**
Par. 2, l. 9.   ' Ganzalo *should read*:
' Gonzalo

Serré
Delete entry and replace by:
SERRE, Jean-Adam (*b.* Geneva, 10 Nov.
1704; *d.* Geneva, 22 Mar. 1788).
Swiss scientist, painter and musical theorist.
He lived in Paris for some years from 1751,
but returned to Geneva.   As a physicist he is
noted for inventions in connection with the
barometer and thermometer, and as a chemist
he was the first to discover a brown enamel
colour derived from platinum.   He was a
well-known miniature painter and accompanied the famous Swiss painter Jean-

Étienne Liotard on his journeys.   As a musical
theorist he was highly esteemed by Burney
and others for his contributions to the dis-
cussions of harmony, and his books, unjustly
forgotten, are still valuable to-day.   The two
most important are ' Essai sur les principes de
l'harmonie ' (Paris, 1753) and ' Observations
sur les principes de l'harmonie' (Geneva,
1763).   Rousseau, in his ' Dictionnaire ',
mentions him for his endeavour to reconcile
the harmonic system of Rameau and Tartini.
E. B.

BIBL.—JACOBI, ERWIN R., ' Jean-Adam Serre, ein
vergessener Schweizer Musiktheoretiker ' (Schw.
Mus. Ztg., Apr. 1958).

718   ii   **SERRES**
Par. 1, l. 2.   Nérondes, *should read*:
Néronde,

719   i   **SERVAIS (2)**
l. 3.   ? son of *should read*:
? son or adopted son of

l. 6.   ' Jon ' *should read*:
' Iôn ' (based on Leconte de Lisle)

720   i   **SERVICE**
Par. 2, ll. 25-26 *should read*:
same set of books contains eight more complete English Communion Services, some
probably adapted from music for the Catholic
rite and some set to original

724   i   **SESSIONS**
Par. 3, l. 12.   In 1945 *should read*:
In 1944

ii   CATALOGUE:
OPERA *should read*:
OPERAS
Add after ' The Trial of Lucullus ':
' Montezuma ' (1947).

725   i   ORGAN MUSIC
' Chorale ' *should read*:
4 Chorales

Add at end:
BIBL.—SCHUBART, M. A., ' Roger Sessions ' (M.Q.,
XXXII, Apr. 1946).

727   ii   **SEVERI**
Add at end:
BIBL.—CELANI, ENRICO, ' I cantori della Cappella
Pontificia nei secoli XVI-XVIII ' (Riv. Mus. It.,
XIV, 19-7, p. 772).
CHILESOTTI, OSCAR, ' Canzonette del seicento con la
chitarra ' (Riv. Mus. It., XVI, 1909, p. 847).

731   ii   **SHACKLOCK**
Par. 3, ll. 3-4 *should read*:
Holland and in 1953 was a guest artist, as
Brangäne, at the Berlin State Opera.

732   i   **Shakespeare**
l. 1 *should read:*
' All's Well that Ends Well.'   *See* Castelnuovo-
Tedesco (opera). Hoérée (incid. m.)

ii   ' Antony and Cleopatra.'   l. 2 *should read:*
incid. m.).   Gurlitt (M., Symphony).   Herberigs
(symph. poem).   Indy (overture).

' Comedy of Errors.'   l. 3 *should read:*
do.).   Krejčí (I., ' Revolt at Ephesus ', opera).   Mohaupt
(' Zwillingskomödie ', do.).   Ponc

' Henry V.'   l. 2 *should read:*
(' Agincourt ', dram. scene).   Dyson (do., cantata).
(?) Eccles (2, incid. m.).

733   i   ' Love's Labour's Lost.'   l. 1 *should read:*
See Arne (1, song).   Bishop (H., incid.

l. 5 *should read:*
(H., do.).   Quilter (song).   Stravinsky (song with flute,
clar. & va.).   Vaughan Williams (song).

' Merchant of Venice.'   l. 4 *should read:*
Castelnuovo-Tedesco (opera, overture & 1 song).
Clarke (H.,

ii   ' Merry Wives of Windsor.'   l. 2 *should
read:*
(opera).   Herberigs (symph. poem).   Kaun (' Sir John
Falstaff ', humoresque

' Midsummer Night's Dream.'   l. 4 *should
read:*
Bishop, (H., incid. m.).   Britten (opera).   Castelnuovo-
Tedesco (overture

l. 10 *should read:*
masque).   Malawski (incid. m.).   Mancinelli (opera).
Mendelssohn (overture,

l. 16 *should read:*
(partsong).   Vreuls (Opera).   Weismann (incid. m.).
Wolf (H., ' Elfenlied ',

' Much Ado.'   l. 6 *should read:*
(do.).   Handel, p. 51 (' Ariodante ' on same subject).
Hatton (do.).   Khrennikov (do.).   Korngold (E.,

' Othello.'   l. 2 *should read:*
Bardi (incid. m.).   Bernard (A., do.).   Blacher (ballet).
Bortkievich

' Richard III.'   l. 5 *should read:*
man (incid. m.).   Volkmann (do.).   Walton (film).

' Romeo and Juliet.'   l. 6, (scenic oratorio).
should read:
(chamber opera).

l. 19 *should read:*
Milhaud (incid. m.).   Morales (M., opera).   Parrott
(Solemn Overture).   Pasquali

734   i   Songs.   l. 7 *should read:*
Stravinsky (song with flute, clar. & va.).   Warlock (2
songs).

Sonnets, l. 1.   *Add after See:*
Britten (' Nocturne ', No. 8).

' Tempest.'   ll. 1-2 *should read:*
See Arne (1, songs).   Arnold (M., incid. m.).   Arundell
(do.).   Asplmayr (do.).   Atterberg (' Stormen ',

734   i   ' Tempest.'   l. 4 *should read:*
Bardi (incid. m.).   Berkeley (do.).   Berlioz (fantasy in
' Lélio ').   Bishop (H., incid. m.).

l. 25 *should read:*
(Shadwell's version).   Malawski (incid. m.).   Martin
(F., ' Sturm ', opera ; 5 Ariel songs for

l. 33 *should read:*
Sibelius (do.).   Smith, J. C. (opera, adpt.).   Stravinsky
(song with flute, clar. & va.).   Stucken

' Twelfth Night.'   l. 7 *should read:*
away ',   4 versions).   Cornyshe (song ' A Robyn '
[Thomas Wyatt] used).   Dale (B., 2 songs).   Davenport

ii   l. 2 *should read:*
partsong).   Hopkins (do.), Hughes (G., scenes from
unfinished opera).   Humperdinck (incid.

' Winter's Tale.'   l. 10 *should read:*
Macfarren (3, overture).   Milhaud (incid. m.).   Moeran
(' When daisies

Add to BIBL.:
LONG, JOHN H., ' Shakespeare's Use of Music ' (Gaines-
ville, Fla., 1955).
MANIFOLD, J. S., ' The Music in English Drama from
Shakespeare to Purcell ' (London, 1956).

735   ii   **Shanks**
See Gibbs *should read:*
See Finzi (song).   Gibbs

739   ii   **SHAPLEIGH**
Par. 1, l. 2.   4 July *should read:*
2 July

742   i   **SHARP, Cecil**
BIBL.   l. 2 *should read:*
' Cecil Sharp ' (Oxford, 1933 ; rev. ed. 1955).

743   i   **SHAW, Bernard**
Par. 1, l. 2.   London *should read:*
Ayot St. Lawrence, Herts.

Par. 2, l. 9 *should read:*
Star ' and ' The World ' between 1888 and

l. 11 *should read:*
" Corno di Bassetto ".   His notices for ' The
World ' were re-

ii   *Add to* BIBL.:
BENTLEY, ERIC (ed.), ' Shaw on Music : a Selection
from the Music Criticism of Bernard Shaw ' (Garden City, N.Y., 1955).

SHAW, Geoffrey
Par. 2, l. 11 *should read:*
schools for teachers, non-competitive and
competitive festivals.

744   i   **SHAW, Martin**
Par. 1, l. 2 *should read:*
Mar. 1875 ; *d.* Southwold, Suffolk, 24 Oct.
1958).

744   ii   Par. 1, l. 3 *should read*:
Chelmsford. He received the O.B.E. in 1955 and was made an hon. Fellow of the R.C.M. in 1958.

750   ii   **SHAWM**
Add before BIBL. :
(*PLATE* 32, Vol. IV, p. 492, No. 9.)

SHCHERBACHEV, A. V.
Par. 1, l. 2 *should read*:
vich (*b.* Manuilovo, Govt. of Poltava, 20 Jan. 1869; *d.* Kiev, 14 Feb. 1916).

751   i   **SHCHERBACHEV, V. V.**
Par. 1, l. 2 *should read*:
vich (*b.* Warsaw, 24 Jan. 1889; *d.* Leningrad, 5 Mar. 1952).

752   i   **SHEBALIN,** CATALOGUE:
FILM MUSIC
Entry should read:
' The Inspector-General ', after Gogol, ' The Composer Glinka ' and others.

   ii   **SHEDLOCK**
Par. 2, l. 12 *should read*:
' Athenæum ' in 1898, following H. F. Frost, who had held the post since 1889. Shedlock retired in 1916. He

755   i   **SHEFFIELD**
Par. 2, l. 9 *should read*:
Musical Society. He was succeeded in 1948

   ii   **Shelley**
l. 1 *should read*:
See Arnell (' Ode to West Wind ', voice & orch.). Backer-Grøndahl (A.,

l. 7 *should read*:
(' Prometheus Unbound ' & songs). Britten (' Nocturne ', No. 1). Bush (A., ' Song

756   i   l. 12. *Add after* Head (song) :
Henze (' Ode to West Wind ', cello & orch.). Hindemith (song). Holland (T., 2 songs). Howells

SHEPHERD, Arthur
Par. 1, l. 2 *should read*:
19 Feb. 1880 ; *d.* Cleveland, 12 Jan. 1958).

758   ii   **SHERA**
Par. 1, l. 2 *should read*:
May 1882 ; *d.* Sheffield, 21 Feb. 1956).

Par. 2, l. 6. 1916–18 *should read*:
1916–26

l. 11 *should read*:
he held until his retirement in 1948. He

759   i   **SHERIDAN**
Par. 1, l. 2 *should read*:
Mayo, 15 Oct. 1889; *d.* Dublin, 16 Apr. 1958).

Par. 2, ll. 11-14 *should read*:
opera in 1919 at Covent Garden in London as

l. 23 *should read*:
at the Milan Scala in 1921–24, and was again engaged

762   i   **Shilovsky**
l. 1. **Konstantin S.** *should read*:
Konstantin Stepanovich.

   ii   **Shirley**
ll. 4. Lawes (4, do.) *should read*:
Lawes (4, do., song from ' Triumph of Beauty ').

763   i   **SHOFAR**
l. 6 *should read*:
p. 1004, No. 3). The instrument, or an imitation of

766   i   **SHOSTAKOVICH**
Par. 2, ll. 3-4 *should read*:
the ballet ' Bright Rivulet ', produced at Leningrad on 4 June 1935. A few weeks later

ll. 9-11 *should read*:
He then composed a fifth Symphony, which was described in the

Par. 3, l. 20 *should read*:
portance.
The University of Oxford conferred an honorary doctorate on Shostakovich in 1958.
                    E. B.

   ii   CATALOGUE:
ORCHESTRAL WORKS
Add at end:'
81. ' Song of the Forests.'
93. Symphony No. 10 (1955).

767   i   SOLO INSTRUMENTS AND ORCHESTRA
Add at end:
99. Vn. Concerto (1956).

CHAMBER MUSIC
Add at end:
73. String Quartet No. 3.
83. String Quartet No. 4.
92. String Quartet No. 5.

ARRANGEMENTS
l. 1 *should read*:
16. ' Tahiti Trot ', arr. for orch. of ' Tea for Two ' by Vincent Youmans (1928).

Shpazkinsky *should read*:
Shpazhinsky

767   ii   *Add before* **SHUDI**:

SHUARD, Amy (*b*. London, 19 July 1924).
English soprano singer. She studied at the Trinity College of Music in London and afterwards in Italy. In 1948 she was engaged as dramatic soprano by the Sadler's Wells Theatre, where she remained until 1955, gaining valuable experience and successfully performing a number of principal parts, such as that of Magda in Menotti's ' The Consul ', in which she shone both as singer and as a highly accomplished dramatic actress. Her singing was somewhat marred at first by a certain shrillness of her high notes in dynamics above *mezzo-forte*, but she gradually subdued this fault and became an increasingly valuable member of the company. In 1955 she went to the Royal Opera at Covent Garden, where she had already appeared as a guest artist as Aida, etc. Her most important and impressive appearances there in 1956 and 1957 were in the title part of Janáček's ' Jenufa ' and as Cassandra in Berlioz's ' Trojans '.
                                  E. B.

772   i   **SIBELIUS**
       Par. 1, l. 2.   1865). *should read*:

1865;   *d*. Järvenpää nr. Helsingfors, 20 Sept. 1957).

775   ii   *Add to* Bibl.:

Parmet, Simon, ' Sibelius ' symfonier: en studie i musikförståelse ' (Stockholm, 1955).

     l. 26 *should read*:

Ringbom, Nils-Erik, ' Sibelius ' (Stockholm, 1948); trans. by G. I. C. de Courcy (Norman, Oklahoma, 1954).
Tawaststjerna, Erik, ' Ton och tolkning: Sibelius-studier ' (Stockholm, 1957).

CATALOGUE:
     l. below heading, (*Except for the opera, unpublished should read*:

(*Except for the opera and the chamber music, unpublished*

780   —   *Add after Op.* 37:
| — | ' Hymn to Thaïs.'

781   —   l. 10.   *Delete* ' Thaïs.' | ? | *c.* 1924. |

782   i   **SIDE DRUM**
       Add to See Drum:

(*PLATE* 49, Vol. VI, p. 622, No. 1.)

Sidney
l. 2 *should read*:

song).   Moeran (choral canzonet).   Orr (R., song). Parry (H., song).

   ii   **SIEGEL, Rudolf**
       Par. 1, l. 1.   1878). *should read*:

1878;   *d*. Munich, 4 Dec. 1948).

783   ii   *Add before* **SIENA**:

SIEMS, Margarethe (*b*. Dresden, 30 Dec. 1879; *d*. Dresden, 13 Apr. 1952).
German soprano singer. She was the daughter of an architect and in her youth studied the pianoforte and violin. When she was fifteen her teacher, Professor Bohn, advised her to take up singing, and she studied with Anna Maria Orgeni, herself a pupil of Pauline Viardot and Marchesi and also the teacher of Erika Wedekind and Edyth Walker. She was engaged to sing in the May Festival in Prague in 1902 with Caruso, Battistini and Bonci, and in the autumn of the same year became a member of the Prague Opera. In 1908 she was engaged for the Dresden Opera as first dramatic coloratura soprano succeeding Irene Abendroth. While at Dresden she created the parts of Chrysothemis in ' Elektra ' (1909) and the Marschallin in ' Rosenkavalier ' (1911), and at Stuttgart, as a guest, she sang the first Zerbinetta in ' Ariadne auf Naxos ' (1912). In 1913 she made her London début at Covent Garden singing the Marschallin in the first London performances of ' Rosenkavalier ' under Beecham. She reappeared in the same part at Drury Lane the following year. She remained with the Dresden company until 1920, when she moved to Berlin, where she took up a teaching appointment at the State Opera. She continued teaching at Dresden and Breslau until after the second world war.
     Siems possessed a most amazing voice and great dramatic versatility. Thus she could sing the coloratura parts in Bellini, Donizetti and Meyerbeer, and the Queen of Night; the heavier Verdi parts like Leonora, Amelia and Aida; and Wagnerian parts like Venus and Elisabeth, both of which she sang on more than one occasion on the same evening — and even Isolde. Strauss considered her the ideal Marschallin, and also found her the ideal interpreter of his *Lieder*.   H. D. R.

| A. Borgström. | 1900. |

784   ii   **SIENA**
       Par. 3, l. 20.   Alessandro Scarlatti
          should read:
Domenico Scarlatti

785   ii   Bibl. l. 20 *should read*:
Gigli, G., ' Diario sanese' (Lucca, 1723).

     l. 32 *should read*:

Ugurgieri Azzolini, I., ' Le pompe sanesi ' (Pistoia, 1649).

Add after **Sienkiewicz**:

SIEPI, Cesare (*b*. Milan, 10 Feb. 1923). Italian bass singer. He studied singing privately and made his début when eighteen as Sparafucile at Schio. His career was interrupted by the war, and he became an active anti-fascist. In Sept. 1943 he had to take refuge in Switzerland. In Aug. 1945 he returned to Italy and resumed his career at the Fenice Theatre, Venice, where he was heard as Zaccaria in ' Nabucco ' during the 1945–46 season. He sang in the first opera season at the rebuilt Milan Scala, and in 1948 was chosen by Toscanini to sing at the Boito celebrations at the Scala, when he was heard as Mefistofele and Simon Mago in ' Nerone '. In the autumn of 1950 he went to Great Britain with the Scala company, singing at Edinburgh in the Verdi Requiem under De Sabata and at Covent Garden as Pistol in ' Falstaff '. In the autumn of 1950 he was engaged by Rudolf Bing as a last-minute replacement at the Metropolitan, making his début on the opening night of the 1950–51 season, which was also the opening night of Bing's régime as General Manager, as King Philip in ' Don Carlos '. He has been a member of the Metropolitan ever since, and has been heard in most of the leading bass parts in the Italian repertory, as well as Mephistopheles in ' Faust ', the title-part in ' Boris Godunov ', which he sings in English, and in Mozartian parts. He can be said to have taken the place of the late Ezio Pinza as the leading Italian *basso-cantante* of the day. Like Pinza, Siepi is a familiar figure at Salzburg, where he has appeared regularly in the title-part of ' Don Giovanni '. He is a strikingly handsome man and displays great exuberance in his acting and singing in Mozart and Rossini. In more serious parts, like Philip in ' Don Carlos ' and Fiesco in ' Simone Boccanegra ', however, he is strangely unsympathetic, and these characterizations often fail to come to life. His singing too, which is always musicianly and beautiful to hear, can sometimes sound dull.

H. D. R.

790   ii   **SIKORSKI, Kazimierz**
Par. 2, l. 21 *should read*:
tory at Łódź and in 1947 director.

791   ii   **SILBERMANN**
Footnote 4.   l. 7 *should read*:
Notices ' (Mus. T., July 1879). Geiringer (' The Bach Family', p. 360), on the other hand, states that the clavier was given to one Grotthaus as a present.

792   ii   *Add to* BIBL. (2nd work by FLADE) :
' Gottfried Silbermann : ein Beitrag zur Geschichte des deutschen Orgel- und Klavierbaus im Zeitalter Bachs ' (Leipzig, 1953).

Silesius
ll. 1–2 *should read*:
Silesius, Angelus (Johann Scheffler). *See* Beck (C., oratorio). Brunner (' Sprüche '). Burkhard (W., 2 choruses). Buxtehude (3 cantatas based on songs by S.). Haas (J.,

793   i   **SILOTI**
Par. 1, ll. 1-2.   10 Oct. *should read* :
9 Oct.

ii   **SILVA, O. da**
Par. 1 *should read* :
(*b*. Paranhos nr. Oporto, 21 Apr. 1870; *d*. Oporto, 6 Mar. 1958).

Par. 2, l. 3 *should read* :
music, etc. In 1932–52 he lived in Brazil and in 1954 in retirement at Lisbon. A piano Quartet and another for

794   ii   **SILVERI**
Par. 2, ll. 1-2 *should read* :
Italian baritone singer. He was a member of the Rome Opera from 1939, singing small bass parts, and he made his début there as a baritone in 1944 in ' La Traviata ', and in the

SIMILÄ
Par. 1   l. 2 *should read* :
borg], 9 Apr. 1898 ; *d*. Lahti, 9 Jan. 1958).

Par. 2   l. 10 *should read* :
nish, 1945). He toured the U.S.A. in Dec. 1957 and on 8 Dec. conducted a Sibelius birthday concert in New York.
A. R., adds.

795   i   *Add after* **SIMILI** :
SIMIONATO, Giulietta (*b*. Forlì, 15 Dec. 1910).
Italian mezzo-soprano singer. She spent her childhood in Sardinia and began her musical studies at Rovigo with Ettore Lucatello. In 1933 she gained the first place in a Bel Canto competition at Florence and during the next few years sang small parts there, at Padua and La Scala, Milan, while at the same time continuing her studies. In 1938 she sang in Pizzetti's ' L' Orsèolo ' at Florence, and during the 1939–40 Scala season was heard as Beppe in ' L' amico Fritz '. During the next few years she sang Cherubino, Rosina (in its original key), Hänsel, Dorabella and Mignon. Since the war, Simionato has sung almost every year at La Scala, and in the summer of 1947 she was chosen by Toscanini to sing Asteria in Boito's ' Nerone '. Other parts at La Scala have included Charlotte in ' Werther ', Jane Seymour in ' Anna Bolena ', Cenerentola, Isabella in ' L' Italiana in Algeri ', Carmen, Princess de Bouillon in ' Adriana Lecouvreur ' and Leonora in ' La Favorita '. She first went to Great Britain in 1947, when she sang Cherubino at the Edinburgh Festival. In 1952 she went to Covent Garden to sing Adalgisa, Amneris and Azucena opposite Callas. In

1954 Bellini's 'I Capuletti ed i Montecchi' was specially revived for her at Palermo, and her repertory further includes Mistress Quickly, Fidalma in 'Il matrimonio segreto' and Fedora. Her American début was at Chicago in 1954, and she has sung there regularly since. She joined the Metropolitan, New York, in 1959 and sings in Vienna, Lisbon and Barcelona.

Simionato is regarded by many as the successor to Conchita Supervia in the Rossini repertory, and to Stignani as a *bel canto* singer in the operas of Bellini, Donizetti and Verdi. Her voice is a coloratura mezzo of agility, with a personal seductive timbre in its lower reaches. In dramatic parts she sings with a strong, even tone and can colour her voice as the mood of the music requires. She has a charming stage presence, and is vivacious and attractive in comedy, and dignified and moving in the more serious parts she undertakes.

H. D. R.

795   i   **SIMMES**
Add at end:

Nothing further is known of him except that he was in the service of Thomas Sackville, 1st Earl of Dorset. There is an entry in the Sackville Papers, which have been removed from Knole to the Kent Archives Office at Maidstone (Catalogue mark U269, A1/1):

17 Mar. 1608: Paid to William Symmes late one of your Lordship's musicians for his wages due to him for 4 months ended this last of January 1607/8 the sum of twenty nobles by warrant of your lordship 6 li. 13s. 4d.

s. j.

ii   *Add after* **SIMMS:**

SIMON, Alicia (*b.* Warsaw, 13 Nov. 1879).
Polish musicologist. She first studied in her native town, later at the University of Berlin under Brückner, Kretzschmar, Johannes Wolf and others, and finally at Zürich University, where she took the Ph.D. degree with a dissertation in German, 'Die polnischen Elemente in der deutschen Musik bis zur Zeit der Wiener Klassiker', which was published there the same year. She returned to Poland and wrote scholarly articles, essays and treatises on music. The dissertation mentioned above is of great importance and has been quoted by many Polish and foreign writers on music.   c. r. h.

796   i   **SIMON BOCCANEGRA**
ll. 12-13. Edward J. Dent *should read:*

Norman Tucker

ii   **SIMONETTI**
Par. 1, l. 2. 1859 *should read:*

1857

796   ii   Par. 2, l. 4 *should read:*
the Rossini Conservatory at Pesaro. In 1872 he entered the Milan Conservatory. Later,

l. 12 *should read:*
Dancla (violin) and Massenet (counterpoint). In 1881 he joined the Pasdeloup orchestra. He

797   ii   **SIMPSON**
Par. 3, ll. 7 & 17. Violist'. *should read:*
Viol'.

798   i   *Add after* Par. 2:
A lithographed facsimile of the second edition of 'The Division Viol' was published in London by J. Curwen & Sons, Ltd., in 1956.

MS COMPOSITIONS
l. 6. Heidelberg, *should read:*
Hamburg,

799   i   **SIMPSON, Robert**
Par. 3, ll. 5-6 *should read:*
(1943), a Fantasia for strings (1944), 2 Symphonies (1951 & 1957); 3 string Quartets (1951–52,

l. 9 *should read:*
for pianoforte. A second Symphony, for small orchestra, followed in 1956, and the first, which was produced in London in June of that year, has been recorded under the auspices of the British Council.

801   ii   **SINGHER**
Par. 1, l. 1 *should read:*
SINGHER, Martial (Jean Paul) (*b.* Oloron-

Par. 2, ll. 14-15 *should read:*
has also sung at the annual Florence Festival and appeared in London, at Covent Garden, in 1937 in the Paris Opéra's performance of Gluck's 'Alceste'. He was

l. 17 *should read:*
Quichotte à Dulcinée'. He joined the Metropolitan Opera in New York in 1949 and married a daughter of Fritz Busch.

814   ii   **SINGING**
Add to Bibl.:
Graves, Richard, 'Singing for Amateurs' (Oxford, 1954).
Kühner, Hans, 'Grosse Sängerinnen der Klassik und Romantik' (Stuttgart, 1954).
Maragliano Mori, Rachele, 'I maestri del bel canto' (Rome, 1953).

Add at end:
See also Bibl. under Voice-Training.

821   i   **SIRMEN**
Footnote. ll. 1-2 *should read*:
¹ This letter — the autograph of which is lost, but of which there is an imperfect manuscript copy at Pirano — was translated into German by J. A. Hiller

822   i   **SIROLA** *should read*:
ŠIROLA

Par. 1, l. 2 *should read*:
1889; *d.* Zagreb, 10 Apr. 1956).

825   i   **SISTRUM**
Add to See also:
PLATE 71, Vol. VIII, p. 186, No. 3.

Sitwell, Edith
l. 1 *should read*:
See Britten (Canticle No. 3 for tenor, horn & pf.). Head (song). Lucas (L.,

826   ii   **SIX**
Add at end:
BIBL.—RAŠIN, VERA, ' " Les Six " and Jean Cocteau ' (M. & L., XXXVIII, 1957, p. 164). ' Revue Musicale ', No. 236, 1956 (' Le Groupe des Six ').

827   ii   Heading, SKALKOTAS *should read*:
SKALKOTTAS

SKALKOTAS *should read*:
SKALKOTTAS

Par. 1, l. 2 *should read*:
8 Mar. 1904; *d.* Athens, 19 Sept. 1949).

828   i   Par. 2, l. 1.   Skalkotas *should read*:
Skalkottas

l. 10 *should read*:
been performed in many countries. A Skalkottas Committee formed after his death has undertaken the task of collecting his manuscripts and editing his works. Important scores of his have already (1958) been published by Universal Edition, in addition to four Dances issued by the French Institute of Athens (1948). First performances of his works have been given in Germany, Britain, France, Israel, the U.S.A., etc., arousing great interest in his music.

Par. 3, l. 2.   Skalkotas *should read*:
Skalkottas

830   i   **SKLAVOS**
Par. 1, l. 1.   Vraila *should read*:
Braila

831   i   **SKRIABIN**
Par. 1, l. 17.   forty-four *should read*:
forty-three

832   ii   CATALOGUE
PIANOFORTE AND ORCHESTRA
(*c.* 1894) *should read*:
(1898)

835   i   **SKROWACZEWSKI**
Add at end:
On 12 May 1956 he won the first prize in an International Competition for Conductors offered by the Accademia Santa Cecilia in Rome.

ii   **SLADEN**
Par. 2, l. 33.   Isolde *should read*:
Brangäne

SLAVENSKI
Par. 1, l. 2 *should read*:
11 May 1896; *d.* Belgrade, 30 Nov. 1955).

838   i   **SLIDE TRUMPET**
Add to line:
(*PLATE* 74, Vol. VIII, p. 562, No. 4.)

ii   **SLOBODSKAYA**
Par. 2, l. 17.   1933 *should read*:
1934
Par. 3, l. 3.   1930 *should read*:
1932

839   i   Par. 1, l. 2.   revival *should read*:
production

847   ii   **SMETANA**
Footnote 2. l. 1 *should read*:
² This is the more remarkable
ll. 7-8 *should read*:
language. Smetana's mother-tongue too was Czech, but he said as late as 1862, in a let .er written in German, that he had to make a study of it to be able to write it with ease and accuracy. But if in his operas the words have
ll. 10-11 *should read*:
not fit with correct Czech prosody, the reason was also that Czech

848   i   BIBL.   l. 5 *should read*:
sech ' (Paris, 1939) ; Eng. trans. by Daphne Rusbridge, ' Letters and Reminiscences ' (London, 1955).

Add to BIBL.:
BOESE, HELMUT, ' Zwei Urmusikanten : Smetana, Dvořák ' (Zürich, 1955).

ii   BIBL., l. 16.   4 vols. *should read*:
7 vols.

Add to BIBL.:
SMETANA, BEDŘICH, ' Letters and Reminiscences ', ed. by František Bartoš, trans. by Daphne Rusbridge (Prague, 1955).
ZICH, OTAKAR, ' Symfonické básně Smetanovy ' (Prague, 1949).

CATALOGUE:
OPERAS
Col. 4.   9 entries Czech Theatre *should read* (*in that order*):
Provisional Theatre
Provisional Theatre
New Town Theatre
National Theatre

Provisional Theatre
Provisional Theatre
New Czech Theatre
New Czech Theatre
National Theatre

849   i   *Add at top of col.* :

INCIDENTAL MUSIC

Overtures for puppet plays, for small orch. :
1. ' Doctor Faust ' (1862).
2. ' Oldřich and Božena ' (1863).
Music for declamation (1869) :
1. ' The Fisherman ' (Goethe).
2. Libuše's Judgment.'

ORCHESTRAL WORKS
Add in order of dates :
Minuet, B♭ ma. (1842).
Galop of the Bayaderes (1842).
Polka ' For Our Maidens ' (1849).
Polka ' The Countrywoman ' (1879).

VIOLIN AND PIANOFORTE
Add below heading :
Fantasy on a Czech Song (1842).

(1880).   l. 3.   (1878). *should read* :

PIANOFORTE MUSIC
Add in order of dates :
Galop, D ma. (1832).
' Louisa Polka ' (1840).
' Dahlia Polka ' (1840).
' Galop di bravura ' (1840).
3 Impromptus (*c.* 1841).
Polka ' From Student Life ' (1842).
2 Quadrilles (1843).
' Duet without Words ' (1843).
Polka ' Souvenir of Plzeň ' (? 1843).
6 Album Leaves (1844–45).
2 Studies (1844–46).
' Pensée fugitive ' (1845).
' Characteristic Variations ' (1846).
Sonata, G mi. (1846).
Polka, E♭ ma. (1846).
' Characteristic Composition ', C♭ ma. (1847).
' Romance ', B♭ ma. (1848).
' Caprice ', G mi. (1848).
6 Album Leaves ', Op. 2 (1849–50).
6 untitled pieces (*c.* 1850).
' Impromptu ', F mi. (*c.* 1850).
' Toccatina ', B♭ ma. (*c.* 1850).
' To Robert Schumann ' (*c.* 1850).
' The Wayfarer's Song ' (*c.* 1850).
' A roaring, hissing and whirring is heard ' (*c.* 1850).
3 Pieces, ' A Treasury of Melodies ' (1850).
Polka, F mi. (1855).
Transcription of Schubert's song ' Der Neugierige ' (1858).
Polka with Introduction, ' Apparition at the Ball ' (1858).
Concert Study, C ma. (1858).
' Betty's Polka ' (1858).
Fantasy on Czech Folksongs (1862).
Andante, F mi. (1880).
' Romance ', G mi. (1881).

Delete l. 8 (' Lístky . . .)

850   ii   **SMIJERS**
Par. 1, l. 2 *should read* :

veer nr. Breda, 19 July 1888 ; *d.* Utrecht, 15 May 1957).

853   i   **SMITH, Cyril**
Add at end, before signature :
While on tour in Russia in 1956 Smith was suddenly stricken with thrombosis, which paralysed his left hand ; but undaunted by this tragedy, he has continued to play works

arranged for three hands with his wife. His experiences are described in a book published in 1958 (*see* BIBL.).

853   i   *Add after signature* :
BIBL.—SMITH, CYRIL, ' Duet for Three Hands, as told by Joyce Egginton ' (London, 1958).

SMITH, D. S.
Par. 1, l. 3.   1940). *should read* :
1949).

ii   **SMITH, Elias**
Par. 1 *should read* :
SMITH, Elias (*b.* ? ; *d.* Gloucester, 1620).

Par. 2, ll. 1-4 *should read* :

English composer. The name is that of a ' singer ' at Gloucester Cathedral in 1594, and of the Master of the Choristers in 1605, who is mentioned in the earliest extant (1610) Treasurer's accounts there. The act books of the cathedral chapter show that on 19 Oct. 1620 Philip Hosier was appointed *organista et choristarum instructor in loco Eliae Smith mortui.* Another Ely Smith was admitted a lay singing-man there on 4 Oct. 1621. He may well have been the son of the deceased organist, and perhaps is to be identified with the Elias Smith who was a minor canon at Durham Cathedral in 1628 and precentor there in 1636. It is possible that it was he who was master of the grammar school in 1640–46 and was buried as precentor on 9 Dec. 1676. In any event, as an

ll. 7-9 *should read* :

Martyr ", is in some of the part-books at Durham, the *tenor cantoris* being found also in B.M. Add. MSS 30478-9, it seems likely that the composer was connected with that cathedral.

Signature should read :
J. M. (ii), adds. W. K. F.

855   i   **SMITH, J. S.**
Par. 1, l. 2.   1750 ; *should read* :
[bapt. 30 Mar.] 1750 ;

Par. 2, l. 3.   1782, *should read* :
1782 (*d.* 1784),

856   ii   *Add* :
SMITH BRINDLE, Reginald (*b.* nr. Preston, Jan. 1917).
English composer. He studied under D. E. Parry-Williams at the Bangor College of the University of Wales and was awarded the Gwynnedon Scholarship and afterwards a University Fellowship which enabled him to continue his studies under Pizzetti at the

Accademia di Santa Cecilia in Rome, where he received a diploma for advanced composition and the Luigi Sturo Prize. He then studied 12-note technique with Dallapiccola at Florence for two years. He has since lived continuously in Italy, writing music for documentary films, conducting British music and acting as music critic. Among his works are a Concerto for string orchestra, a clarinet Concerto and a Quintet for clarinet, violin, viola, cello and pianoforte. The last obtained the Clements Prize of the South Place Concerts in London in 1953.   E. B.

859   ii   **SMITH, W. C.,** List of Works
ll. 18-19 *should read:*
' Music Publishing in the British Isles from the Earliest

ll. 21-22 *should read:*
with Charles Humphries (London, 1954).

860   i   **SMYTH, Edward**
Par. 1, l. 2 *should read:*
Durham, [buried 4] Feb. 1611.

ii   **SMYTH**
Par. 3, ll. 6-7 *should read:*
' Der Wald ' was produced in Berlin on 9 Apr. 1902; it was given at Covent Garden,

863   i   Par. 2, l. 2 *should read:*
graph).¹

Add footnote:
¹ Manuscripts in the British Museum.

ii   **SMYTH, WILLIAM**
l. 2.   *Delete signature.*

Add new paragraph:
It should be noted that there were several musicians named William Smyth (or Smith) who held positions under the Durham Chapter in the first half of the 17th century. There was a chorister in 1609–15, a " scholasticus " in 1614–17 and a minor canon in 1632–36. Another was sub-chanter at York in 1628–47. The solitary bass part at York contains anthems attributed to him, in addition to those mentioned above: ' O Lord which hast taught all the world ' and ' If the Lord himselfe ', the latter of which is elsewhere attributed to Edward Smith. One of the name was rector of St. Mary-le-Bow at Durham and a minor canon of the Cathedral. He was buried in his church on 21 Apr. 1645.¹   J. M. (ii), adds. w. k. f.

¹ A. G. Matthews, ' Walker Revised ' (1948).

SNEL
Par. 3, l. 5.   (1829) *should read:*
(1825)

863   ii   **SNETZLER**
Delete whole article from l. 2 *and replace by:*

(*b.* Schaffhausen, 6 Apr. 1710; *d.* Schaffhausen, 28 Sept. 1785 ¹).
Swiss (anglicized) organ builder. He was the ninth child of Hans Heinrich Schnetzler (*b.* 1668), a miller on the Rhine, who married in 1692 and had eleven children, the last an artist who also went to England and worked at Oxford. Johann settled in London late in 1746 and had premises there in Oxford Road (now Street) and in Greek Street, Soho. His first organ was that built for the Moravian Church in Fetter Lane (1747) and the second was for the Moravian Church at Fulneck, Leeds (1748). He built the organ for Chesterfield Church in 1756 and the same year, with the support of Charles Burney, that of King's Lynn. He retired to live in Bentinck Street, Westminster, and died in Switzerland, during a visit to his home-town of Schaffhausen. His will is in Somerset House.
Snetzler became the leading English organ builder during the second half of the 18th century. Many of his organ cases are still in existence, *e.g.* at Beverley Minster, Painswick (Glos.) and St. Peter's, Nottingham. He exported many organs to the U.S.A.² His business was taken over by Ohrmann, Nutt and Eliot. Thomas Eliot may be regarded as the father of the firm of Hill, Norman & Beard.   w. l. s. (ii).

See also Hill & Son.   Norman & Beard.

¹ Dates and other particulars are found on documents consulted by the present contributor. Earlier articles in this Dictionary were based on Burney's statements, which are entirely erroneous.
² A long list of these, probably not quite complete, is given in W. L. Sumner's ' The Organ ' (London, 1952).

865   i   **SOBINOV**
Par. 1.   Dates *should read:*
(*b.* Yaroslavl, 7 June 1872; *d.* Riga, 14 Oct. 1934).

Par. 2, l. 13.   Shepkin- *should read:*
Shchepkina-

866   ii   **SOCIETÀ DEL QUARTETTO**
l. 2.   GULLÍ *should read:*
GULLÌ.

871   i   Heading SODRE *should read*¹
SÖDERSTRÖM

Add before **SODRE:**
SÖDERSTRÖM, Elisabeth (*b.* Stockholm, 7 May 1927).
Swedish soprano singer. After attending the College of Stockholm she studied at the

Royal Musical Academy and at the Royal Opera School there. In 1950 she was engaged by the Royal Opera of Stockholm, and she has appeared as a guest artist in opera at Salzburg, Glyndebourne, Hamburg, Cologne and elsewhere. Her performance of the Composer in Strauss's 'Ariadne' at Glyndebourne was considered sheer perfection, both vocally and histrionically. She has also appeared as a concert artist in many European cities, and as recitalist she has an interesting repertory of works by the most advanced modern composers.   E. B.

873   ii   *Add before* **SOGNO DI SCIPIONE** :

SOGNANDO (Ital. = dreaming). A term sometimes found in 20th-century scores, *e.g.* Prokofiev's Violin Concerto No. 1, first movement.

873   i   **SOL-FA**
Par. 2, l. 3.   d' Arezzo in Rome
should read :
d' Arezzo at Arezzo

Add after **SOLA** :

SOLAGE, ? (*b.* ? ; *d.* ?).
French 14th-century composer. His ten extant compositions are preserved in the Chantilly MS 1047. All are secular songs in 3- or 4-part polyphony and consist of 7 Ballades, 2 Virelais and 1 Rondeau. In spite of a distinctly more modern approach, Solage follows very closely in the steps of Guillaume de Machaut. His compositions form an intermediate stage between those of Machaut and those of such writers as Trebor, Senleches (Jacomi) and Philippe de Caserta. His harmonies are often daring, as in the triads of 'En l'amoureux vergier', and his melodic-rhythmic motives unify his compositions. His ballades still have three stanzas of poetry like Machaut's, and in two cases they give the acrostic: " Catheline, la roÿne d'amours ". One of these is unified by what may be called a harmonic motive, almost a plagal cadence, and indeed Solage is fond of excursions into distant keys like A♭. The most extraordinary example of this tendency is the Rondeau 'Fumeux, fume', which seems to be generally in F, begins in G and ends its first half in E♭. The most complex work is the ballade dedicated to the art-loving Duc de Berry, in which syncopations abound and diminution is introduced into all three voices in turn without any indication in the notation. Of the Virelais 'Tres gentil cuer' is particularly charming, but even here an interlocking rhythmic motif is introduced

between tenor and contratenor as an element of unity, *e.g.*

Solage's complete works are transcribed in W. Apel's ' French Secular Music of the Late Fourteenth Century ' (1950).
G. R. (iii).
BIBL.—REANEY, GILBERT, 'The Manuscript Chantilly, Musée Condé 1047' ('Musica Disciplina', VIII, 1954).

873   i   **SOLDAT**
Par. 1, l. 2 *should read* :
Graz, 25 Mar. 1863 ; *d.* Graz, 30 Sept. 1955).

ii   **SOLER**
Par. 4, l. 7 *should read* :
celona, 1933 (' Publicacions Catalunya ', Vol. IX). The edition of his 6 Concertos

877   i   **SOLESMES**
Par. 2, l. 8.   239 *should read* :
234.

(XIII)   l. 15.   (XIV) *should read* :
(XIV)   l. 17.   (XV) *should read* :
(XV)   l. 19.   (XVI) *should read* :

Add after this :
The Saint-Renaud Antiphonary (XVI).

ii   *Add to* BIBL. :
BLANC, MAURICE, ' L'Enseignement musical de Solesmes et la prière chrétienne ' (Paris, 1953).

Heading, SOLFÈGE *should read* :
SOLFÉGE ¹

SOLFÈGE *should read* :
SOLFÉGE ¹

Add footnote :
¹ According to Littré this, not *solfège*, is the correct spelling.

879   i   *Add after* **SOLITAIRE** :
Sollogub, Vladimir Alexandrovich. *See* Tchaikovsky (' Undine ', lib. ; song).

882   i   **Sologub, F. K.**
l. 4 *should read* :
See also Sollogub, V. A.

Delete entry **Sologub, V. A.**

882   ii   **SOLOVIEV**
Par. 1, l. 2.   Petrograd, 14 *should
read* :
Petrograd, 27

886   i   **SOMMER**
Par. 1, l. 2.   **Zincken** *should read* :
Zincke

Footnote 1, l. 1.   an anagram *should read* :
a near-anagram

l. 2.   Zincken *should read* :
Zincke

ii   *Add at end* :
BIBL.—VALENTIN, ERICH, ' Hans Sommer ' (Brunswick, 1938).

908   i   **SONATA**
Add to BIBL. :
MELLERS, WILFRID, ' The Sonata Principle ' (' Man and his Music ', Vol. III) (London, 1957).

909   ii   **SONDHEIMER EDITION**
Add at end, before signature :

53. Beck, F., Symphony in G ma. (1760), score and parts.
54. Vinci, Leonardo, Symphony to ' Alessandro nel-l'Indie ' (1729), score and parts.
55. Boccherini, L., Symphony to ' La Clementina ' (1778), score and parts.
56. Tessarini, C., Divertimento in F ma. (1734), score.
57. Haydn, J., Symphony to ' Il distratto ' (1776), score and parts.

Add before **SONG** :

SONDHEIMER, Robert (*b*. Mainz, 6 Feb. 1881).
German musicologist. He was educated at the Mainz " Gymnasium ", studied music at the Conservatory there and at that of Cologne, as well as at the Master School for Composition in Berlin, and attended the Universities of Bonn, Berlin and Basel, taking the degree of Ph.D., his chief subject being the history of music. He was appointed lecturer at the Volkshochschule in Berlin and also acted as music critic for the ' Börsenkurier ' there. His speciality is the early history of the symphony, on which he has written extensively and learnedly, and he has published numerous editions, in score and parts, of works of the Mannheim school and its contemporaries (*see* SONDHEIMER EDITION). His book, ' Die Theorie der Sinfonie im 18. Jahrhundert ' (Leipzig, 1925), was awarded a prize by the University of Basel, and a book in English on Haydn appeared in London in 1951.
Sondheimer took refuge in London during Hitler's rule in Germany, but even before that he had contributed articles on Boccherini, Beck, Stamitz and others to Cobbett's ' Cyclopedia of Chamber Music '. Among his numerous articles in periodicals the following may be mentioned :

' Boccherini ' (Riv. Mus. It., 1920).
' G. B. Sammartini ' (Z.M.W., 1920).
' Die Sinfonien Franz Becks ' (Z.M.W., 1922).
' Gluck in Paris ' (Z.M.W., 1922).
' Die formale Entwicklung der vorklassischen Sinfonie ' (A.M.W., 1922).
' Die Entwicklung des Orchesters in der vorklassischen Sinfonie ' (' Das Orchester ', 1927).
' On Performing Beethoven's Third and Fifth Symphonies ' (M. Rev., 1941).
E. B.

942   ii   **SONG**
Par. 1, l. 6.   Gipfel ' *should read* :
Gipfeln '

950   ii   *Add to* BIBL. :
NOSKE, FRITS, ' La Mélodie française de Berlioz à Duparc : essai de critique historique ' (Amsterdam & Paris, 1954).
STEVENS, DENIS, (ed.) ' A History of Song ' (London, 1960).

956   i   Par. 1, l. 8.   Somerset *should read* :
Dorset

965   ii   **SONNENFELD**
Cancel present article and replace by :

SONNENFELD, Adolf (*b*. Breslau, 1837 ; *d*. Warsaw, 28 May 1914).
Polish composer of German birth. He wrote several operas, *opérettes-bouffes* and vaudevilles for the Polish stage. His two ballets, ' Melusine ' and ' Pan Twardowski ', were produced in Warsaw during the 1860s, as well as his only symphonic poem, ' Albrecht Dürer in Venice '. Two operas, ' Alfred Wielki ' (' Alfred the Great ') and ' Penthesilea ' (1878), remained unperformed, and one, ' Świtezianki ' (' The Mermaids of Świteź '), received only a concert performance (Warsaw, 9 July 1896). A national work, ' Chłopski mecenas ' (' The Peasants' Maecenas '), a music-drama of folk scenes to a libretto by K. J. Szaniawski, was produced in Warsaw on 28 Aug. 1880. The earliest opera to be given there (26 Aug. 1874) was ' Nocleg w Apeninach ' (' A Night in the Apennines '), the libretto of which is by Count Fredro. All the comic pieces were produced in Warsaw between 1876 and 1887, except ' Modniarka warszawska ' (' A Warsaw Milliner '), which came out at Poznań in 1878, and ' Donato ', which remained unperformed. The last stage work was the opera ' Hańdzia ' (libretto based on the elder W. Rapacki's novel ' Hanza '), produced in Warsaw in 1905.
C. R. H.

967   i   **SONORE**
l. 2.   used *should read* :
use

968   i   **SONTAG**
Par. 1, l. 3.   *d*. ?, *should read* :
d. Mexico City,

969   i   **SOPEÑA IBAÑEZ**
Par. 1, ll. 1-2.   Vallodolid *should read* :
Valladolid

ii   **Sophocles**
Par. 2, l. 4 *should read* :
Lualdi ('Figlia del re', opera). Mendelssohn (incid.
m.). Mulè (do.). Oboussier

'Oedipus Coloneus.' l. 4 *should read* :
Rogier (opera). Rossini (incid. m.). Wetz (chorus).
Zingarelli (opera).

'Oedipus Rex.' l. 6 *should read* :
Martin (F., incid. m.). Orff (opera). Pizzetti (symph.
prelude).

970   i   **SORABJI**
Par. 2, l. 1.   Indian composer.
should read :
Parsi composer.

973   i   **SORO**
Par. 1, l. 2 *should read* :
15 July 1884 ; *d.* Santiago de Chile, 2 Dec.
1954).

SOROCHINTSY FAIR
l. 2.   Ярмарка *should read* :
Ярмарка

1004   i   **ŠOUREK**
Par. 1, l. 2 *should read* :
1883 ; *d.* Prague, 15 Feb. 1956).

1005   i   **SOURIS,** CATALOGUE :
Add before ORCHESTRAL WORKS :
CHORAL WORK
'Le Marchand d'images', Walloon songs for solo
voices, chorus & orch. (1944).

VOICE AND ORCHESTRA
Delete this title.

ii   **SOUTER LIEDEKENS**
Add at end :
See also Collectio O.M.B., Vol. 11 (modern ed.).

1010   i   **SOUTH AFRICA**
Par. 2, ll. 6-7 *should read* :
in 1921, the first Professor of Music being
Percival R. Kirby, who was succeeded on
his retirement in 1957 by F. H. Hartmann
of Grahamstown University. In 1923 this
College received its own

Par. 3, ll. 3-5 *should read* :
bosch (Prof. Fismer, succeeded in 1952 by
Prof. G. Z. van der Spuy), Grahamstown
(Prof. F. H. Hartmann, succeeded by Prof.
G. Gruber), Potchefstroom (Prof. J. P. Malan,
succeeded by Prof. M. C. Roode) and Bloem-
fontein (Prof. Roode, succeeded in 1958 by
Prof. Leo Quayle),

1011   i   Par. 1, l. 4 *should read* :
Enrique Jorda, who left in 1954 to become
conductor of the San Francisco Symphony
Orchestra. From time to time distin-

l. 8 *should read* :
recently, Albert Coates. After Jorda's departure the orchestra has been conducted by a
succession of guest conductors, including
Hugo Rignold, Basil Cameron, George
Weldon, Anthony Collins and William van
Otterloo.

Par. 2, l. 8 *should read* :
recently been increased in size, and in 1955
Frits Schuurman became conductor.

ii   Par. 1, ll. 2-5 and Par. 2, ll. 1-6
should read :
of local musical organizations, including,
until 1953, the Johannesburg Symphony
Orchestra, an amateur body of considerable
size. This was disbanded, together with the
Cape Town and Durban municipal orchestras,
which had given weekly symphony concerts
throughout the year. Some of the members
were incorporated in the enlarged, full-sized
Symphony Orchestra of the S.A.B.C. at
Johannesburg (*c.* 80 members), which gave
its first concerts in 1954. Jeremy Shulman,
Edgar Cree and Anton Hartman are the
conductors.

1012   ii   Bibl. *Add after* l. 2 (2nd work by Bouws)
'Suid-Afrikaanse Komponiste van Gister en Vandag'
(Cape Town, 1957).

Add to Bibl. (2nd work by Kirby) :
'The Musical Instruments of the Native Races of
South Africa' (Johannesburg, 1953).

SOUTH AMERICAN MUSIC
Delete entry.

1014   i   **SOUTH PLACE CONCERTS**
Par. 3 (list of prize works)
Add :
1952. No prize.
1953. Reginald Smith Brindle (Quintet for clarinet,
violin, viola, cello & pianoforte).

Delete present l. 1953.

Add :
1954. Raymond Hockley (String Quartet).
1955. No award.
1956. Geoffrey Winters (String Quartet).
1957. Michael E. Rosa (String Quartet).
1958. Ian Spooner (Trio for clarinet, viola and cello).

Par. 4, l. 11 *should read* :
ment, and she died in 1954. She had worked
for the concerts for

1015   i   **SOWERBY**
SOLO INSTRUMENTS AND OR-
CHESTRA
Add under heading :

' Medieval Poem ' for organ (1926).

Add at end :

Concert Piece for organ (1951).
Suite for organ, brass and kettledrums (1953).

1015   ii   ORGAN MUSIC
Replace entry by :

Suite (1933–34).
Meditations on 6 Communion Hymns (1940).
Toccata, C ma. (1940).
' Canon, Chacony and Fugue ' (1948).
' Ballade ' with Eng. horn (1949).

Add at end :

BIBL.—TUTHILL, BURNETT, ' Leo Sowerby ' (M.Q.,
XXIV, 1938, p. 249).

VOL. VIII

Page Col.

1 ii **SPALDING**
Par. 1, l. 2. 1888). *should read*:
1888; d. New York, 26 May 1953).

2 ii **SPEAIGHT**
Par. 1, l. 2. 1868). *should read*:
1868; d. Cheshunt, 20 Nov. 1947).

3 i **SPECHT**
Par. 2, l. 5. Merkur *should read*:
Merker

ii **SPEER, Daniel**
l. 1. Dates *should read*:
(b. Breslau, 2 July 1636; d. Göppingen, Württemberg, 5 Oct. 1707).

4 i **SPELMAN**
Par. 2, l. 9 *should read*:

U.S.A. He was married that year to the writer Leolyn Louise Everett, many of whose poems he set to music. At the entry of the U.S.A. into the first world war he was appointed Assistant Director of Band Musicians' Training in the War Department, under Wallace Goodrich. Soon after the war he and his wife settled at Florence, where they have lived ever since except during the years 1935-47, when they were in New York. They have frequently visited various European musical centres for performances of his works, and Spelman has been closely connected with the Menton Chamber Music Festival. Some of his works have been commissioned, *e.g.* by Andrés Segovia (3 Preludes for guitar), the Vienna Academy Choir, the Stuttgart Chamber Orchestra and the Corelli Orchestra of Rome.

List of Works:
OPERAS, ETC. *should read*:
STAGE WORKS

Add after l. 5 *under this heading*:
The Princess who was bored ', ballet (L. L. Everett).
' The Courtship of Miles Standish ', opera after Longfellow (1943).

Add to CHORAL WORKS:
' Pagan Oratorio.'

ORCHESTRAL WORKS
l. 3 *should read*:
Suite of Tone Poems, ' Saints' Days ' (1925)
1. Sorrento: The Festival of Little St. Anthony.
2. Venice: The Festival of the Redeemer.
3. Siena: The Palio.
4. Assisi: The Great Pardon of St. Francis.

Page Col.

4 i *Add to* ORCHESTRAL WORKS:
' The Outcasts of Poker Flat ', symph. poem after Bret Harte (1928).
' Divertimento ' for chamber orch.
' Sunday Paper ', suite (1946).

Heading VIOLIN AND ORCHESTRA
should read:
SOLO INSTRUMENT AND ORCHESTRA

Add to this section:
Oboe Concerto (1954).

Add to CHAMBER MUSIC:
Rondo for flute & harp.
String Quartet, D ma.
String Quartet, F ma. (1953).

ii **SPENDIAROV**
Par. 1, l. 2. Khakovka *should read*:
Kakhovka

5 i *Add before* SPEYER:

SPERONTES (**Johann Sigismund Scholze**) (b. Lobendau, Silesia, 20 Mar. 1705; d. Leipzig, 12 Feb. 1750).
German composer and poet. Between 1736 and 1745 he published a collection of poems with music, ' Singende Muse an der Pleisse in zweimal 50 Oden ', set mainly to dances of strongly Polish tendencies. It had a wide appeal and has been quoted in many publications ever since. C. R. H.

BIBL.—FRIEDLÄNDER, M., ' Das deutsche Lied im 18. Jahrhundert ' (Stuttgart, 1902). SIMON, A., ' Polnische Elemente in der deutschen Musik ' (Zürich, 1916). SPITTA, P., ' Musikgeschichtliche Aufsätze ' (Leipzig, 1894).

Add after **SPEZIALE**:
SPEZZATO. *See* CORI SPEZZATI.

ii *Add before* SPIES:

SPIERING, Theodore (b. St. Louis, 5 Sept. 1871; d. Munich, 11 Aug. 1925).
American violinist and conductor. After studying with his father, Ernest Spiering, he became a pupil of Schradieck at Cincinnati and in 1892 of Joachim at the Berlin High School for Music. He was in the Chicago Symphony Orchestra in 1892-96, taught at the Conservatory there in 1898-99 and in the latter year established a violin school of his own. The string quartet he founded continued for twelve years to give frequent chamber concerts and to travel. In 1905 he became violin professor at Stern's Conservatory in Berlin and on his return to the U.S.A.

418

leader of the New York Philharmonic Orchestra. During Mahler's last illness in 1911 he took his place as conductor of that orchestra, having gained experience with an orchestra of his own founded in 1902, with which he toured. After an engagement as conductor to the Volksbühne in Berlin (1912–14) he conducted the Women's Orchestra Club at Brooklyn and taught at the New York College of Music (1914–16). He toured much as a soloist, composed some violin studies and pieces, and edited violin music with Rudolf Ganz.   E. B.

6   i   SPILKA
          Par. 1, l. 2.   1877). *should read*:
1887).

7   i   SPINELLI
          Par. 1, l. 2.   1906). *should read*:
1909).

     ii   SPINET
          Add at end:
(*PLATES* 26, Vol. IV, p. 102, No. 1; 37, Vol. IV, p. 736 (i), No. 3.)

12   i   SPISAK
          Par. 2, l. 11.   York. He *should read*:

York. In Dec. 1953 his second Serenade for orchestra obtained the first prize in the Queen Elisabeth of the Belgians Competition at Brussels. He

          ORCHESTRAL WORKS
          l. 1 *should read*:
Serenade No. 1 (1938).

          Last line. *Add*:
Serenade No. 2 (1953).

13   i   SPIVACKE
          Par. 2, l. 10 *should read*:
Le Fèvre, whom he divorced in 1953. In 1929 he went to Berlin and

          l. 12.   *summa cum should read*:
magna cum

17   ii   SPOHR
          BIBL. l. 4 *should read*:
1860–61; modern reprint, ed. by Eugen Schmitz, (Cassel & Basel, 1954).

          Add to BIBL. :
MAYER, DOROTHY M., 'A Forgotten Master: the Life and Times of Louis Spohr' (London, 1959).
SPOHR, LOUIS, 'Briefwechsel mit seiner Frau Dorette', ed. by Folker Göthel (Cassel & Basel, 1957).

19   ii   SPONTINI
          Par. 1, l. 1.   **Gasparo** *should read*:
Gaspare

25   i   SPONTINI
          Add to BIBL. :
BELARDINELLI, ALESSANDRO, 'Documenti spontiniani inediti: raccolti, tradotti e annotati', 2 vols. (Florence, 1955).

     ii   *Add to* BIBL.:
FRAGAPANE, PAOLO, 'Spontini' (Bologna, 1954).
MUELLER VON ASOW, HEDWIG, 'Gaspare Spontinis Briefwechsel mit Wolfgang von Goethe' (Berlin-Charlottenburg, 1957).
SCHLITZER, FRANCO, 'Frammenti biografici di Gaspare Spontini, con lettere inedite' (Siena, 1955).
'"La finta filosofa" di Gaspare Spontini' ('Il Fuidoro', 1957, & offprint).

26   ii   SPRINGDANS
          l. 1 *should read*:
SPRINGDANS (Norw., Riksmaal; *springleik* in Landsmaal). A Norwegian

          SPRINGER
          Par. 1, l. 2 *should read*:
berg, 19 Dec. 1877; *d.* Vienna, 20 Jan. 1954).

27   i   *Add before* **SPRUNG ÜBER DEN SCHATTEN**:
SPRINGLEIK. See SPRINGDANS.

33   ii   STADER
          Par. 1, l. 1.   Budapest, 1915 *should read*:
Budapest, 5 Nov. 1915).

37   i   STAGGINS (4)
          l. 1.   (*b.* ?; *should read*:
(*b.* ?, 1645;

38   i   STAHL
          Par. 1, l. 3 *should read*:
wig-Holstein, 10 Apr. 1872; *d.* Lübeck, 5 July 1954).

43   i   STAMITZ (1)
          Add to BIBL. :
GRADENWITZ, PETER, 'Johann Stamitz als Kirchenkomponist' ('Musikforschung', XI, 1952, p. 2).

          See also. l. 2 *should read*:
(F. M., satire on S.). Mannheim School. Sondheimer Ed., Vols. 2, 10, 27, 28 & 48 (modern eds. of var. works). Symphony, pp. 210-11.

     ii   *Signature* P. G. (ii). *should read*:
P. G.

          STANCHINSKY
          Par. 1, l. 2. Crimea, 1914). *should read*:
Crimea, 6 Oct. 1914).

45   ii   STANFORD
          Par. 2, l. 14. Reinecke at Hamburg *should read*:
Reinecke at Leipzig

49   ii   *Add to* BIBL. :
HOWELLS, HERBERT, ' Charles Villiers Stanford '
(Proc. Roy. Mus. Ass., Vol. LXXIX, 1952–53).

53   —   CATALOGUE
PIANOFORTE SOLO
Add after Op. 170 :
178. 3 Waltzes.
179. 24 Preludes (in all the keys, 2nd set).

56   ii   **STANLEY (ii)**
Add at end, before signature :

The order of Stanley's published works has
now been established.[3] According to the
custom of the time only the instrumental
works were given opus numbers, but gaps
were left open for Opp. 3, 8 and 9, which
clearly belong to the cantatas.
The list is as follows :

Op.
1. ' Eight Solos for a German Flute, Violin or Harpsicord. Printed for . . . ye Author.' 1740.
2. ' Six Concerto's in Seven Parts . . . Printed for
   the Author.' [1742].
[3]. ' Six Cantata's, for a Voice and Instruments.
   Printed for John Stanley.' 1742.
4. ' Six Solos for a German Flute, Violin, or Harpsicord. Printed for John Johnson.' 1745.
5. ' Ten Voluntarys for the Organ or Harpsicord.
   Printed for John Johnson.' [1748].
6. ' Ten Voluntarys for the Organ or Harpsicord.
   Printed for John Johnson.' [1752].
7. ' Ten Voluntarys for the Organ or Harpsichord.
   Printed for John Johnson.' [1754].
[8]. ' Six Cantata's, for a Voice and Instruments.
   Printed for John Stanley.' [1748].
[9]. ' Three Cantatas and Three Songs for a Voice and
   Instruments. Printed for the Author.' [1751].
10. ' Six Concertos for the Organ, Harpsichord, or
   Forte Piano. Printed for the Author.' 1775.

Add footnote :

[3] *See* John Wilson, ' John Stanley : Some Opus
Numbers and Editions ' (M. & L., XXXIX, 1958, p.
359).

57   i   **STANTON**
Par. 3, l. 5 *should read* :

sity. He retired in 1958 and was succeeded
by Willis Grant. Among several compositions
by Stanton

ii   **STARCZEWSKI**
Par. 1, l. 2.   Warsaw, 1946). *should
read* :
Warsaw, 21 Jan. 1946).

59   i   **STARZER**
Par. 1, l. 1.   ?, 1726 ; *should read* :
Vienna, 1726 ;

60   ii   **STATHAM, H. (D.)**
ll. 6–8 *should read* :

works, and as joint conductor of the Norfolk
and Norwich Triennial Festival with Sir
Thomas Beecham in 1936, Sir Malcolm
Sargent in 1947 and 1951, and Sir John
Barbirolli in 1955. In 1943–44 he was engaged by Jay Pomeroy to conduct twelve
concerts with the London Symphony Or-

chestra at the Cambridge Theatre in London.
In 1944 he took this orchestra on a tour of
Wales. In these capacities he has shown

Add at end :

Statham is a Fellow of St. Michael's College, Tenbury, and of the Royal School of
Church Music. His compositions include :

ANTHEMS
' Drop down ye heavens.'
' Christ hath a garden.'
' Praise thou the Lord ' (1955).

TE DEUMS
C ma., D mi. and F ma. (for centenary of St. Michael's
College, 1956).

EVENING CANTICLES
C ma., G ma. for double choir, E mi. (commissioned
by Royal School of Church Music).

COMMUNION SERVICES
E mi., D ma., G mi. (1954).

ORGAN WORKS
' Rhapsody ' (1929).
' Rhapsody on a Ground ' (1954).
' Four Diversions ' (1957).

60   ii   l. 12. *Signature should read* :
H. C. C., adds.

62   i   **STEBER**
Par. 2, l. 26 *should read* :

Opera at the Edinburgh Festival and in 1954
she appeared as Elsa in ' Lohengrin ' at
Bayreuth.

63   ii   **STEFAN**
Par. 2, ll. 16–17 *should read* :

some time spent in Lisbon from 1939 he
settled in the U.S.A. in 1941.

64   i   **STEFANI (1)**
Par. 2 (list of operas)
Add before l. 1 :
' Król w kraju roskosze ' (' King in Cockaigne '), 1787.

Add after l. 3 :
' Polka ', 1807.

l. 6.   1809. *should read* :
1808.

l. 7 *should read* :
' Papyrus ', 1808.

ii   *Add after* **STEFANO, Ghizzolo** :

STEFANO, Giuseppe Di (*b.* Palermo, 24
June 1921).
Italian tenor singer. The son of a professional soldier, he was educated in a Jesuit
seminary at Milan. One of his fellow-
students, an opera enthusiast, hearing him
sing a popular song, was so excited by the
natural beauty of the voice that he suggested
he should take up singing as a career. His
family made many sacrifices to give their son

the musical education he desired, and went to Milan, where the tenor studied for five years with Luigi Montesanto. He made his début on 21 April 1946 at the Teatro Municipale, Reggio Emilia, as Des Grieux in Massenet's 'Manon'. His initial success was phenomenal and led to his being engaged for a series of concerts in Switzerland. On his return to Italy he appeared in most of the provincial houses, and in Mar. 1947 made his Scala début, again as Des Grieux. Appearances in Rome, Naples, Venice and Barcelona followed. Although not originally engaged for the 1947–48 season at the Metropolitan Opera, New York, he made his début there in Feb. 1948 as the Duke in ' Rigoletto '.

At this stage of his career Di Stefano confined himself to the lighter parts in the repertory, such as Wilhelm Meister in ' Mignon ', Elvino in ' Sonnambula ', Fritz in ' L' amico Fritz ' and Nadir in ' Les Pêcheurs de perles '. His singing at this time was notable for its unfailingly beautiful tone and the use of an exquisite *pianissimo*, the voice possessing a rich velvety sound. In the 1953–54 season, however, he began to sing heavier parts; his singing became rougher and less elegant and the voice larger and less beautiful. By the end of the 1956–57 season he had added such parts as Don José, Canio, Turiddu, Radamès, Alvaro in ' La forza del destino ' and Osaka in Mascagni's ' Iris ' to his repertory; and thus, when he went to Edinburgh to make his British début in the summer of 1957, his Nemorino had less of the vocal charm than many people had hoped for. He now appears regularly in Vienna.

H. D. R.

67   ii   **STEFFANI**
Add at end:
See also Denkmäler (2) II, Vol. 6 (ii) (modern ed.).

STEFFKINS
Par. 1, l. 2.   violinists *should read* violists

Par. 2 *should read*:

(1) **Theodore** (or **Dietrich**) **Steffkins** (*b.* ?; *d.* ?, 1674). He went to England in or before 1636, when he succeeded Maurice Webster in the king's band, of which he was still a member in 1641. It is thought that he was at Hamburg during the Commonwealth. After the Restoration his name appears intermittently in court records between 1661 and 1674. He was much admired by his contemporaries, notably John Jenkins and Thomas Salmon. A manuscript suite of his for unaccompanied bass viol is in the New York Public Library (dated 1664), and further music by him is in the Bodleian (MS Mus. Sch. f. 573).

Cancel Par. 3.

67   ii   Par. 4, ll. 1-2 *should read*:
(2) **Frederick Steffkins** (*b.* ?; *d.* ?), son of the preceding. He

Par. 5, l. 1 *should read*:
(3) **Christian Steffkins** (*b.* ?; *d.* ?),

Add to BIBL. :
HUGHES, C. W., ' The Music for Unaccompanied Bass Viol ' (M. & L., XXV, 1944).
PULVER, J., ' A Biographical Dictionary of Old English Music ' (London, 1927).
WESTRUP, J. A., ' Foreign Musicians in Stuart England ' (M.Q., XXVII, 1941).

72   ii   **STEIN, Erwin**
Par. 1.   1885). *should read*:
1885 ; *d.* London, 19 July 1958).

73   i   *Add at end*:
His miscellaneous writings were published in English under the title of ' Orpheus in New Guises ' (London, 1953).

ii   *Add after* **STEIN, Hedwig**
STEIN, Leon (*b.* Chicago, 18 Sept. 1910). American musicologist, conductor and composer. He attended the American Conservatory at Chicago for violin playing under Herbert Butler and the Crane Junior College for theory under Robert Gomer Jones, also studied conducting with Frederick Stock and Hans Lange. He took the Mus.B. (1931), the Mus.M. (1935) and the Ph.D. (1949) at the De Paul University, Chicago, where he is now Chairman of the Department of Theory and Composition and Director of the Graduate Division. In 1946 he was appointed conductor of the Community Symphony Orchestra of Chicago. He contributed a book, ' The Racial Thinking of Richard Wagner ' to the ' Philosophical Library ' series and has written articles for various musical periodicals. His compositions include the following :

OPERA
' The Fisherman's Wife ', 1 act (1953–54).

CHORAL WORK
' The Lord reigneth ' (Psalm XCVII) for tenor, women's chorus & orch. (1953).

ORCHESTRAL WORKS
Prelude and Fugue (1935).
Passacaglia (1936).
' Sinfonietta ' for stgs. (1938).
Symphony No. 1, G ma. (1940).
' Three Hassidic Dances ' (1940–41).
Symphony No. 2, E ma. (1942).
Suite for small orch. (1943).
Triptych on 3 Poems by Walt Whitman (1943).
' A Festive Overture ' (1950).
Symphonic Movement (1950).
Symphony No. 3, A ma. (1950–51).

SOLO INSTRUMENTS AND ORCHESTRA
Vn. Concerto, A ma. (1938–39).
Rhapsody for flute, harp & stgs. (1954).

E. B.

75 i *Add after* **STEKKE**:
STELLA, Antonietta (*b.* Perugia, 15 Mar. 1930).
Italian soprano singer. She studied at the Perugia Conservatory with Aldo Zeetti and Francesco Morlacchi. After winning prizes in the Concorso Nazionale organized by E.N.A.L. at Bologna in 1949 and in the Consorso at Spoleto in 1950, where she appeared as Leonora in 'Il Trovatore', she was engaged for the Rome Opera, where she made her début as Leonora in 'La forza del destino'. She was soon engaged by the leading Italian theatres and also appeared in Germany, Spain, Portugal and Switzerland. Her Covent Garden début took place in the summer of 1955 as Aida, and she joined the New York Metropolitan for the 1956–57 season, where she has been greatly admired in Verdi and Puccini parts, especially as Butterfly, which she sang in the new production of that opera in 1958. She has also sung in South America and Japan, and appears regularly at La Scala and in Vienna. Her repertory also includes Wagnerian parts (Senta, Sieglinde, Elisabeth and Elsa) and parts in modern Italian works ('La fiamma', 'Anea', 'Maria Egiziaca'). Stella possesses an intrinsically beautiful voice, with a flawless upper register and an exquisite *pianissimo*.

H. D. R.

STELLFELD
Par 3, l. 4 *should read*:
the 16th–18th centuries. It was sold to the University of Michigan in 1954. He had a rare series

STENBORG
Par. 2. *Delete* l. 3.

ii Par. 1, l. 1 *should read*:
entered a government office in 1767, and he pursued office work and theatre work concurrently from the age of fifteen. He also studied for a time at the University of Uppsala. From

STENHAMMAR, P. U.
Par. 1, l. 2 *should read*:
valla, 20 Feb. 1829; *d.* Stockholm, 8 Feb. 1875).
Add signature:
K. D.

76 i **STENHAMMAR, W. E.**
Add to BIBL.:
'Wilhelm Stenhammar och kammermusiken' (S.T.M., 1952–53).

77 i **STEPANIAN**
Par. 1, l. 1. **Aro** (*b. should read*:
Aro Leonovich (*b.*

l. 2 *should read*:
Kirovobad], 24 Apr. 1897).

80 ii **STERLING**
l. 21 *should read*:
daughter Jean Sterling MacKinlay. Her son and biographer, Malcolm Sterling MacKinlay (*d.* 1952), was a pianist and his sister's accompanist.

82 i **STERNFELD**
Par. 1, l. 2. (*b. ?*, 25 *should read*:
(*b.* Vienna, 25

Par. 2, l. 18 *should read*:
ship in 1950 and 1951. In 1956 he was appointed lecturer at the University of Oxford and edits the Proceedings of the Royal Musical Association.

ii **STERNICKA-NIEKRASZOWA**
Par. 1, l. 2 *should read*:
(*b. ?*, 20 Sept. 1898; *d.* Warsaw, 27 June 1932).

STEURLEIN
Par. 1, l. 1 *should read*:
STEUERLEIN (Steurlein, Steurlin), Johann (*b.*

Transfer this entry to stand before **STEUERMANN** *above*.

83 ii **STEVENS, Bernard**
List of works:
Add to ORCHESTRAL WORKS:
— Dance Suite (1957).

Add to VIOLIN AND PIANOFORTE:
— Fantasy on a Theme by Dowland (1956).

84 i **STEVENS, Denis**
Par. 2, l. 19 *should read*:
Britannica' (1951).

Delete the rest and add:
From 1950 onwards he made extensive contributions to B.B.C. programmes and produced many series of programmes, dealing with Machaut, Dufay, Dunstable, Tallis, Monteverdi, Torelli, Vivaldi and Telemann. Among radio opera productions were Monteverdi's 'Orfeo', in which hitherto unsolved rhythmical problems were clarified for the first time; and Marc-Antoine Charpentier's 'Médée', a revival which has done much to restore its author to the place he deserves in the history of opera. In 1954 Stevens left the Music Department in order to concentrate on large-scale recording projects for the B.B.C. Transcription Service, including a 'History of British Music' and 'Chapel Royal'. At the same time he began to collaborate with

Douglas Cleverdon of Features Department, and this partnership led to the provision of historically accurate music for ' Aucassin and Nicolette ' and ' Vincenzo ', the latter a tragicomedy by Henry Reed on the subject of Vincenzo Gonzaga.

Stevens's interest in dramatic music led him to provide Elizabethan material for the lyrics in ' As You Like It ' (Mermaid Theatre, 1953), fourteenth- and fifteenth-century music for the York Mystery Plays (1954, 1957) and thirteenth-century motets on St. Thomas of Canterbury for T. S. Eliot's ' Murder in the Cathedral ' (Gloucester, 1955). In 1953 the British Council sent him to eight Italian towns, where he lectured in Italian on the music of John Dunstable, the quincentenary of whose death was then being commemorated. These activities resulted in invitations to Cornell University, Ithaca, N.Y., as Visiting Professor of Music in 1955 and to Columbia University in 1956. He is Secretary of the Plainsong and Mediaeval Music Society, a Fellow of the Society of Antiquaries, and Conductor of the Ambrosian Singers and Players.

Publications include :

BOOKS AND MUSIC

Thomas Tallis: Complete Keyboard Works (London, 1953).
' Altenglische Orgelmusik ' (Cassel, 1954).
' Altenglische Klaviermusik ' (Cassel, 1954).
The Mulliner Book (2nd, revised edition) (London, 1954).
The Concerti Grossi of William Boyce (London 1954–   ).
' In Nomine Stücke ' (Cassel, 1955).
' The Cries of London ', by Orlando Gibbons (London, 1955).
' Thomas Tomkins : 1572–1656 ' (London, 1957).
Robert Carver : Complete Works (1959–   ).
' Tudor Church Music ' (New York, 1955 ; new edition, London, 1960).
' A History of Song ' (London, 1960).

ARTICLES

' The Keyboard Music of Thomas Tallis ' (Mus. T., July 1952).
' Purcell's Art of Fantasia ' (M. & L., Oct. 1952).
' Busoni and Liszt ' (' The Concerto ', Pelican Books, 1952).
' La Musique d'orgue anglaise avant la Réforme ' (Rev. de Musicol., Dec. 1953).
' La Chanson anglaise avant l'école madrigaliste ' (' Musique et Poésie ', 1954).
' A Recently Discovered English Source of the Fourteenth-Century ' (M.Q., Jan. 1955).
' Seventeenth-century Italian Music in the Bodleian Library ' (' Acta Musicologica ', XXVI, 1955).
' Processional Psalms in Faburden ' (' Musica Disciplina ', IX, 1955).
' Further Light on "Fulgens Praeclara" ' (Jour. Amer. Musicol. Soc., IX, 1956, p. 1).
' The Manuscript Edinburgh, National Library of Scotland, Adv. MS. 5. 1. 15 ' (' Musica Disciplina ', XIII, 1959, p. 155).

E. B.

84   ii   Column heading *should read*:
STEVENS (Risë)

STEVENS, Rise *should read* :
STEVENS, Risë

Par. 3, l. 1.   Rise *should read* :
Risë

85   ii   *Add before* **Stevenson, R. L.**

STEVENSON, Robert (*b.* Melrose, New Mexico, 3 July 1916).
American musicologist. He obtained the degrees of B.Litt., Oxon, S.T.B. *c.l.* of Harvard, M.Mus. of Yale and Ph.D. of the University of Rochester, N.Y. His honours include the Juilliard Fellowship (1934–38), Charles Ditson Travelling Fellowship (Yale University, 1939–40), Bearns Prize and Baier Fellowship (Columbia University, 1942 & 1946) and Ford Foundation Faculty Fellowship (1953–54). He served in the U.S. Army in 1943–46, was instructor at Westminster Choir College, Princeton, N.J. in 1946–49, and in 1950 was appointed Assistant Professor of Music at the University of California at Los Angeles. In 1953–54 he did research work in Europe, with headquarters at Queen's College, Oxford, specializing in old Spanish music and visiting Spain for that purpose.

Stevenson has contributed to learned American periodicals, including ' Notes ', M.Q., ' Musica Disciplina ', Journ. Amer. Musicol. Soc., ' Hispanic American Historical Review ', etc., and, apart from several compositions, has published the following books :

' Music in Mexico : a Historical Survey ' (New York, 1952).
' Patterns of Protestant Church Music ' (Durham, 1953).
' Music before the Classic Era ' (London, 1958).
' Spanish Music in the Age of Columbus ' (The Hague, 1959).
' Spanish Cathedral Music in the Golden Age ' (Berkeley and Los Angeles, 1961).
' Shakespeare's Religious Frontier ' (The Hague, 1958).

E. B.

86   ii   Heading, STIASTNY *should read* :
STIASTNÝ

88   i   **Stiehler**
              Add after See :
Strauss (R., song).

89   i   *Add before* **STIMME** :

STILLER, Emil (*b.* Breslau, 17 May 1845 ; *d.* Warsaw, 23 Jan. 1911).
Polish violinist and teacher of German origin. He studied under A. Boerner, Schoen, Damrosch and, finally, under David at Leipzig. In 1870 he went to Warsaw, where he remained until his death. He taught music there and for many years played second violin in the Warsaw String Quartet founded by Barcewicz. He died suddenly of a heart attack.   C. R. H.

94   ii   *Add before* **STOCKHOLM** :

STOCKHAUSEN, Karlheinz (*b.* Mödrath nr. Cologne, 22 Aug. 1928).
German composer. He studied at Cologne under Frank Martin and later in Paris with

Messiaen and Pierre Schaeffer. He was not, however, strongly influenced by any of them, but devoted himself to composition in twelve-note technique. Among his works are 'Kreuzspiel', produced at the Darmstadt Holiday Courses in 1948, 'Spiel für Orchester' (Donaueschingen), 'Schlag-Quartett' for pianoforte and kettle-drums (Munich) and 'Kontra-Punkte No. 1' (Cologne). In Nov. 1956 the Bayrischer Rundfunk at Munich broadcast 'Zeitmass' for flute, oboe, English horn, clarinet and bassoon.

E. B.

96 ii **STOCKMARR**
Par. 1, l. 2. Jan. 1944). *should read*:
2 Feb. 1944).

97 ii **STOJOWSKI**
Par. 1, l. 3. 6 Nov. *should read*:
5 Nov.

98 i **STOKOWSKI**
Par. 1, l. 3 *should read*:
1882 [1]).

Add footnote:

[1] According to a copy of the Birth Certificate supplied to Mr. Nicolas Slonimsky by Somerset House (Registration District Marylebone, Sub-District All Souls).

99 i Par. 1, ll. 12-13 *should read*:

Center in 1942 and conducted throughout the 1942–45 seasons. He was a guest conductor of

l. 22 *should read*:

festivals. From 1955 he has been conductor of the Houston Symphony Orchestra.

Par. 2, l. 19 *should read*:

All of Us' (New York, 1943).

100 i **STOLTZER**
Par. 2, ll. 13-16 *should read*:
wards by the Turks. According to L. Hoffmann-Erbrecht [1], however, an old source confirms that he was drowned, and although the greater part of his works appeared in collections between 1536 and 1544, this does not prove that he was then still alive.

Par. 3, l. 9. voices [1] *should read*:
voices.[2]

Add footnote:
[1] Article in 'Musica', Sept. 1958.

Footnote 1 becomes 2.

MODERN REPRINTS. l. 10 *should read*:
Werke einzelner Meister', Vol. X [ii], Leipzig, 1942).

See also. l. 2 *should read*:
selected Works, ed.). Chorwerk, Vol. 6 (modern reprint of 37th Psalm).

100 i **STOLZ**
Par. 2, l. 1 *should read*:

Czech soprano singer. She studied with Josef Neruda in Prague, then at the Conservatory with Giovanni Batista Gardigiani, left there in Oct. 1851 and later studied under Voytěch Cabouna in Prague. In 1856 she appeared at a concert given by Luigi Ricci's pupils at Trieste, and she did not appear in Italy until 1864, after visits to Tiflis, Odessa, Constantinople, Nice, Granada and other places.

Teresa Stolz lives in musical

ll. 17-23 *should read*:

from 1865 to 1874, when she sang in Verdi's Requiem. She undertook a Russian tour in 1876–77 and retired in the latter year, emerging once more in 1879 to sing in a single charity performance of the Requiem at the Scala. s. h. p., adds.

104 ii **Storm**
l. 2 *should read*:
(song). Grimm (F.–K., songs). Hessenberg (10 songs with chamber m.).

106 i **STRADELLA**
Par. 1, ll. 1-2. Montefestino *should read*:

Monfestino

l. 2. 28 Feb. *should read*:
25 Feb.

Par. 2, l. 6. Montefestino *should read*:
Monfestino

107 ii BIBL. l. 1 *should read*:
BIBL.—CATELANI, ANGELO, 'Delle opere di A. Stradella esistenti nell' Ar-

l. 3. (Modena, 1865). *should read*:
(Modena, 1866).

Add to BIBL.:

ALLAM, EDWARD, 'Alessandro Stradella' (Proc. Roy. Mus. Ass., Vol. LXXX, 1953–54).
GIAZOTTO, REMO, 'La musica a Genova' (Genoa, 1951).
KROHN, ERNST C., 'Some Solo Cantatas of Alessandro Stradella' ('Manuscripta', St. Louis University Library, Vol. II, No. 1, p. 3).

See also. l. 1 *should read*:
See also Fitzwilliam Music (reprint of 'Dove Battista'). Niedermeyer (for the spurious aria 'Pictà,

112 ii **STRADIVARI**
BIBL., l. 27. indagini au *should read*:
indagini su

115 i **STRATTON**
Par. 1, l. 2 *should read*:

don, 18 July 1897; *d.* London, 4 Sept. 1954).

115 ii **STRAUBE**
Add to BIBL. :
STRAUBE, KARL, ' Briefe eines Thomaskantors ', ed. by
W. Gurlitt & H.-O. Hudemann (Stuttgart, 1952).

116 i **STRAUS**
Par. 1, l. 1.   6 Mar. 1870). *should
read* :
6 Apr. 1870 ; *d.* Ischl, 11 Jan. 1954).

118 i **STRAUSS (Family)**
Add to BIBL. :
JACOB, HEINRICH EDUARD, ' Johann Strauss, Vater und
Sohn ' (Hamburg, 1953).
SCHÖNHERR, MAX & REINÖHL, KARL, ' Johann Strauss,
Vater : ein Werkverzeichnis ' (Vienna, Zürich &
London, 1954).
WEINMANN, ALEXANDER, ' Verzeichnis sämtlicher Werke
von Johann Strauss, Vater und Sohn' (Vienna,
1956).

120 i *Add to* BIBL. (2nd work by JACOB) :
' Johann Strauss, Vater und Sohn' (Hamburg, 1953).

122 — Heading *should read* :
STRAUSS : Johann (ii), Works—Josef

123 i Heading *should read*
STRAUSS : Eduard

—	Symphony for wind insts.

—	' Vier letzte Lieder ' [1] for high voice		
	1. Frühling.	Hermann Hesse.	
	2. September.	Hesse.	
	3. Beim Schlafengehen.	Hesse.	
	4. Im Abendrot.	Joseph von Eichendorff.	

126 i **STRAUSS, Richard**
Par. 3, l. 5 *should read* :
Vienna in 1939, but was finished in 1940
under the new title of ' Die Liebe der Danae '.
The

130 ii *Add to* BIBL. :
ERHARDT, OTTO, ' Richard Strauss : Leben, Wirken,
Schaffen ' (Olten & Freiburg i/B., 1953).

131 i BIBL. *Delete* ll. 8-9 (book by MANN).

l. 13 *should read* :
tisches Verzeichnis (Vienna & Wiesbaden, 1955 ff.).

—	3 Songs		
	1. Rote Rosen.	Karl Stiehler.	
	2. Die erwachte Rose.	Friedrich von Sallet.	
	3. Begegnung.	O. F. Gruppe.	

[1] Rediscovered by Otto Albrecht in 1958.

ii BIBL., l. 9. *Add* :
Eng. trans., ' Recollections and Reflections ', by
L. J. Lawrence (London, 1953).

---

131 ii BIBL. l. 22 *should read* :
' Richard Strauss und Wien : eine Wahlverwandtschaft ' (Vienna,

Add to BIBL. :
KRAUSE, ERNST, ' Richard Strauss : Gestalt und Werk '
(Leipzig, 1955).
' Richard Strauss Jahrbuch ', ed. by Willi Schuh (Bonn
& London, 1954 ff.).
' Richard Strauss und Joseph Gregor : Briefwechsel,
1934-49 ', ed. by Roland Tenschert (Salzburg,
1955).
SCHUCH, FRIEDRICH VON, ' Richard Strauss, Ernst von
Schuch und Dresdens Oper ' (Leipzig, 1953).
SCHUH, WILLI & TRENNER, FRANZ (ed.), ' Correspond-
ence : Hans von Bülow and Richard Strauss ',
trans. by Anthony Gishford (London, 1955).
STRAUSS, RICHARD & ZWEIG, STEFAN, ' Briefwechsel ',
ed. by Willi Schuh (Frankfort o/M., 1957).
TRENNER, FRANZ (ed.), ' Richard Strauss : Dokumente
seines Lebens und Schaffens ' (Munich, 1954).

STRAUSS, RICHARD, 2nd work :
' Briefe an die Eltern : 1882-1906 ', ed. by Willi
Schuh (Zürich, 1954).

STRAUSS & HOFMANNSTHAL. l. 2 *should read* :
' Briefwechsel ', ed. by Franz & Alice Strauss
(Berlin,

l. 4 *should read* :
England (London, 1927). Enlarged Ger. ed., by
Willi Schuh (Zürich, 1954).

132 — CATALOGUE:
ORCHESTRAL WORKS
Add after l. 34 (col. 2) :

:	1934.		

133 — VOICE AND ORCHESTRA, ll. 16-20
should read :

	.		1948.

PIANOFORTE SOLO,
Col. 5, l. 7 *should read* :
' Improvisationen und Fuge.' [2]

Add footnote :
[1] Nos. 1, 3 and 2, in that order, were entitled ' Drei
Gesänge ' by Strauss, ' Beim Schlafengehen ' being first
called ' Vor dem Schlafengehen '. ' Im Abendrot '
was a separate song. The publication in the present
form is posthumous.

Footnote 1 *becomes* 2.

134 — SONGS WITH PIANOFORTE, *after*
Op. 15 *cancel* SONGS *and close up vertical
rules.*

SONGS
Add before Op. 17 :

			1883.[1]

135 — l. 12.
Col. 2, Op. 46 No. 1. Obedach *should read* :
Obedach

136 i **STRAVINSKY, F. I.**
Par 1, l. 1.   **Ignatevich** (*b. ?,*
should read:
Ignatievich (*b.* Tchernigov,

l. 2 *should read*:
15 July 1843; *d.* St. Petersburg, 3 Dec. 1902).

137 i **STRAVINSKY**
Par. 1, l. 2.   17 June *should read*:
17 June [1]

Add footnote:
[1] Stravinsky was born on St. Igor's day, 5 June 1882, according to the Julian calendar. That day corresponded

| 'Agon', ballet. | Chor. by Balanchin.

to 17 June 1882, Gregorian style, the difference between the Russian and the western calendars being 12 days in the 19th century; but the difference increased by one day for each century because the old-style calendar had an extra leap-year every hundred years. Thus 5 June O.S. became 18 June N.S. in the 20th century, until 1918, when the Gregorian calendar was adopted by Russia, and Stravinsky accordingly kept his birthday on that date from 1901 onwards. Thus, when he celebrated his 75th anniversary in 1957, his friends, relatives and publishers pointed out that it fell on 18 June, and that 17 June, usually given in works of reference, including the present Dictionary, was wrong; but the fact remains that he was born on the day which then was 5 June in Russia and 17 June in the western world.

Par. 2, l. 21 *should read*:
Korsakov's teaching.[2]

Footnote 1 becomes 2.

139 ii Par. 2, l. 4.   (Venice, 1948) *should*
read:
(New York, 1947)

140 i Par. 3, l. 12.   for fifteen wind
instruments *should read*:
for sixteen instruments

ii Par. 2, l. 10.   Progress' (1951).
should read:
Progress' (1951).[1]

Add footnote:
[1] In 1954 Stravinsky planned an English opera on a libretto by Dylan Thomas, but this remained unwritten on account of the poet's death.

141 ii *Add to* BIBL.:
BURT, FRANCIS, 'An Antithesis [Schoenberg and Stravinsky]: I. The Technical Aspect' ('The Score', No., 18, Dec. 1956, p. 7).
CRAFT, ROBERT, 'A Concert for St. Mark' ('The Score', No. 18, Dec. 1956, p. 35).
'Igor Stravinsky: a Complete Catalogue of his Published Works' (London, 1957).
LINDLAR, HEINRICH, 'Igor Strawinskys sakraler Gesang: Geist und Form der Christkultischen Kompositionen' (Ratisbon, 1957).
'The Score', 75th birthday number, No. 20, Jan. 1957 (contributions by Robert Craft, Henry Boys, Hans Keller, Roger Sessions, Roberto Gerhard, Maurice Perrin, David Drew).

141 ii BIBL., l. 11 from bottom.   *Add*:
Eng. trans., 'The Message of Igor Stravinsky', by Robert Craft & André Marion (London, 1953).

Add to BIBL.:
STRAVINSKY, IGOR, CRAFT, ROBERT, BOULEZ, PIERRE & STOCKHAUSEN, KARLHEINZ, 'Avec Strawinsky' (Monaco, 1958).
STROBEL, HEINRICH, 'Stravinsky: Classic Humanist', trans. by Hans Rosenwald (New York, 1955).
'Igor Strawinsky' (Zürich & Freiburg i/B., 1956).

142 — CATALOGUE
STAGE WORKS
Col. 1, l. 20.   Musagtes *should read*:
Musagetes

Col. 3, l. 23.   1947. *should read*:
New York, 1947.

Add at end:
| Paris, 12 Oct. 1957.

i CHORAL WORKS
l. 5.   *Add below title*:
1. On Saints' Day at Chigisakh.
2. Ovsen.
3. The Pike.
4. Master Portly.

l. 12 *should read*:
Mass for chorus & double wind quintet (1948).

Add at end:
'Canticum sacrum ad honorem Sancti Marci nominis' for tenor, baritone, chorus & orch. (1956).
'J. S. Bach: Canonic Variations on "Vom Himmel hoch da komm' ich her"' for chorus & orch. (1956).
'Threni' (Latin texts from Lamentations of Jeremiah) for 6 solo voices, chorus and orch. (1958).

ORCHESTRAL WORKS
l. 12.   *Add below* orchestrated) (1929):
1. Danse.
2. Excentrique.
3. Cantique.
4. Madrid.

l. 14.   for 16 wind instruments *should read*:
for 16 instruments

l. 17.   *Add after title*:
1. Marche-Introduction.
2. Pas d'action.
3. Thème varié.
4. Pas de deux.

ii l. 1.   *Add after title*:
1. Intrada.
2. Song.
3. Wedding Dance.
4. Cortège.

l. 3.   *Add after title*:
1. Eulogy.
2. Eclogue.
3. Epitaph.

Add at end:
'Greetings Prelude for the 80th Birthday of Pierre Monteux' (1955).

SOLO INSTRUMENT AND ORCHESTRA
Add at end:
Movements for pf. and orch. (1958–59).

VOICE AND ORCHESTRA
Add below title:
1. The Shepherdess.
2. The Faun.
3. The Torrent.

142   ii   CHAMBER MUSIC
           l. 1.   *Add below title:*
1. Akahito.
2. Mazatsumi.
3. Tsaraiuki.

      l. 2.   (' Pleasant Songs ') *should read:*
(' Peasant Songs ')

      l. 2.   *Add below title:*
1. L'Oncle Armand.
2. Le Four.
3. Le Colonel.
4. Le Vieux et le lièvre.

      l. 4.   *Add below title:*
1. Sur le poêle.
2. Intérieur.
3. Dodo.
4. Ce qu'il a le chat.

      Add at end:
3 Songs from William Shakespeare for mezzo-soprano,
   flute, clar. & va. (1953)
1. Musick to heare.
2. Full fadom five.
3. When daisies pied.
' In Memoriam Dylan Thomas ' for tenor, stg. 4tet &
   4 trombs. (1954).
4 Russian Songs for voice, flute, harp & guitar (1954)
1. The Drake.
2. A Russian Spiritual.
3. Geese and Swans.
4. Tilimbom.
Epitaphium for Count Max Egon von Fürstenberg, for
   fl., clar., harp (1959).
' A la mémoire de Raoul Dufy ', for stg. quartet (1959).

143   i   PIANOFORTE MUSIC
          l. 3.   *Add below title:*
1. March.
2. Waltz.
3. Polka.

      l. 4.   *Add below title:*
1. Andante.
2. Española.
3. Balalaika.
4. Napolitana.
5. Galop.

      SONGS
          l. 2 *should read:*
Dew ' (Sergey Gorodetsky) (1907).

      l. 4.   *Add below title:*
1. La Bonne Chanson.
2. Sagesse.

      l. 5.   *Add below title:*
1. The Flower.
2. The Dove.

      l. 6.   *Add below title:*
1. The Magpie.
2. The Rook.
3. Caw, caw, jackdaw.

      l. 7.   *Add below title:*
1. Tilimbom.
2. Chanson de l'ours.
3. Berceuse.

      l. 8.   *Add below title:*
1. Canard.
2. Chanson pour compter.
3. Le moineau est assis.
4. Chant dissident.

STREATFEILD
      Par. 2, l. 12.   1902, *should read:*
1912,

144   ii   *Add after* **STRETTO :**
           STRETTON, Thomas (*b.* ? ; *d.* ?).
           English 16th-century composer.   All that
is known of him is that he instructed choristers
for the London Drapers' Company pageant
in 1541.   A song of his, ' Behold and see how
byrds dothe fly ', for one voice, is preserved in
B.M. Pr. K. 1.e. 1.   H. B. (ii).

146   ii   **STRINASACCHI**
           Par. 2, l. 8.   24 Apr. *should read:*
29 Apr.

148   i   *Add after* **STRISCIANDO :**
          STROBL, Rudolf (*b.* Opawa, Silesia,
1831 ; *d.* Warsaw, 14 May 1915).
          Polish pianist and teacher of German origin.
Having studied in Vienna, he went to Warsaw
at the age of twenty-four and began a career
as private teacher.   In 1866 he joined the
staff of the Conservatory, where he remained
until near the time of his death.   Among his
pupils were Paderewski, Melcer, Śliwiński,
Sygietyński and Ludomir Różycki.
                                        C. R. H.

150   ii   **Strozzi, Giulio**
           l. 3.   *Add:*
Sacrati (' Finta pazza ', lib.).

      STRUCK
           Par. 1, ll. 1-2 *should read:*
      STRUCK, Paul Frederick (*b.* Stralsund,
1776 ; *d.* Germany, 1820).

151   i   **STRUNGK, N. A.**
          Par. 1, l. 2.   Brunswick, Nov.
          should read:
Brunswick, [bapt. 15] Nov.

      ii   Par. 1, ll. 13-16 *should read:*
26 Jan. 1688 Carlo Pallavicino died at
Dresden, and Johann Georg III of Saxony
appointed Strungk chamber organist and
vice-*Kapellmeister* to the Dresden court chapel,
with a salary of 500 thaler.

      Par. 2, ll. 1-3 *should read:*
Pallavicino left an unfinished opera which
Strungk

152   ii   **STUART**
           Par. 2, l. 1 *should read:*
English organist and composer.   He was
organist at Salford and Manchester until
1895, when he settled in London.   He made
a success with

154   i   **STUCKEN**
          Par. 1, l. 3.   18 Aug. *should read:*
16 Aug.

154 ii *Add after* **STUCKEN**:

STUCKENSCHMIDT, Hans Heinz (*b.* Strasbourg, 1 Nov. 1901).

German critic and musicologist. He studied music privately and at the age of twenty began to contribute to newspapers and musical periodicals. In 1923–24 he directed a series of modern concerts at Hamburg, and between 1924 and 1928 he lived by turns in Vienna, Paris and Berlin. In the latter year he moved to Prague, but returned to Berlin in 1929 as music critic to the 'Berliner Zeitung am Mittag'. In 1934 the Nazi rule forbade him to write. He then wrote for German papers in Prague in 1937–41, when another prohibition brought this activity to an end. After military service and inprisonment in 1942–45 he became director of the RIAS studio for new music in Berlin in 1946, music critic of the 'Neue Zeitung' in 1947 and professor of musical history at the Technical University there in 1948. His books 'Arnold Schoenberg' and 'Neue Musik zwischen den beiden Kriegen' were both published in 1951.

E. B.

155 i **STUDER**
   SOLO INSTRUMENTS AND OR-
   CHESTRA. *Add at end*:

'Kleines Konzert' for pf., 2 flutes & stgs. (1953).

157 ii **STURGEON**
   Par 3. *Delete* ll. 8-9, list of works
   and signature, *and substitute*:

Windsor. Of Sturgeon's seven extant works, all of which are in the 'Old Hall Manuscript', only five have been preserved in complete form. There are two settings of 'Gloria' in ballade-Mass style (III, [18]; III, [44]) and one in *conductus* style (I, 11) which may pair with the Credo (II, 51), having stylistic features in common with it, besides similar clefs and mode.

The three-part isorhythmic motet 'Salve mater Domini / Salve templum gratie / it in nomine Domini' (III, 51) has for its tenor the continuation of the plainsong used by Damett in his 'Salvatoris mater pia / Sancte Georgi Deo care / Benedictus Marie filius qui ve'. The letter "n" was omitted in this remarkable sharing of one theme by two composers. Many similarities in the two motets—notably the texts which pray for deliverance in time of war and sickness, the texture (alto and tenor, with one instrument) and the rhythmical similarity between the opening four bars of each can only be attributed to the fact that they were composed for the same occasion. Since both Sturgeon and Damett are known to have accompanied Henry V to France in 1416, these two motets may have been written for performance there. It is significant that no other known works

by either composer make use of isorhythmic technique, then a characteristically French trait. In view of an impending trip to France, they would not unnaturally take pains to write in the French manner as a compliment to their audience.

J. M. (ii), adds R. T. D. and D. W. S.

161 ii **SUCHOŇ**
   Add at end:

BIBL.—ZAVARSKÝ, ERNEST, 'Eugen Suchoň' (Bratislava, 1955).

162 ii *Add before* **SUDROPHONE**:

Sudermann, Hermann. *See* Tarp ('Prinsessen i det Fjerne', opera).

163 ii Heading ṢUFI & DARWISH
   should read:

ṢŪFĪ & DARWĪSH

164 ii **SUGGIA**
   Par. 2, l. 9. Paul Klengel *should*
   read:

Julius Klengel

173 ii **SUK, Váša**
   Par. 1, l. 1. 16 Nov. *should read*:

1 Nov.

181 i **SULLIVAN**
   Par. 2, l. 16 *should read*:

the pace (*see* HEMIOLE).

182 i *Add to* BIBL.:

HUGHES, GERVASE, 'The Music of Arthur Sullivan' (London, 1960).
WILLIAMSON, AUDREY, 'Gilbert and Sullivan Opera: a New Assessment' (London, 1953).

   CATALOGUE
   OPERETTAS,
   Col. 1, l. 12 *should read*:

'The Pirates of Penzance, or The Slave of Duty' [1]

   l. 18. Yeoman *should read*:
Yeoman
   Col. 3, l. 3. 1st published per- *should read*:
1st public per-

   Add footnote:

[1] Gilbert's original sub-title was 'Love and Duty'.

186 ii **SUMER IS ICUMEN IN**
   Footnote 4 should read:

[4] Reproduced in facsimile as a frontispiece to Vol. VII.

187 ii *Add to* BIBL.:

HANDSCHIN, JACQUES, 'The Summer Canon and its Background' ('Musica Disciplina', III, 1949, p. 55; V, 1951, p. 65).
PIRROTTA, NINO, 'On the Problem of "Sumer is Icumen In"' ('Musica Disciplina', II, 1948, p. 205).

187 ii **SUMERIAN MUSIC**
   l. 2. *PLATE* 70 *should read*:

PLATE 71.

188   i   **SUMMER   SCHOOL   OF
MUSIC**
Transfer article Bryanston School
of Music *from Vol. I*, p. 989 *to
before* **SUMSION**.

Par. 1, l. 1 *should read*:
SUMMER SCHOOL OF MUSIC. An

ll. 3-4 *should read*:
courses, which are held each summer, first at
Bryanston School in Dorset and now at
Dartington Hall, Totnes, Devon. It was
founded

l. 9 *should read*:
standards. Thus the Summer School has
included

ii   Par. 2, ll. 1-2 *should read*:
Composition: Malcolm Arnold, Boris Blacher, Nadia
Boulanger, Alan Bush, Paul Hindemith, Bernard
Naylor, Roman Vlad.

l. 5 *should read*:
Conducting: Roger Desormière, Hermann Scherchen.

l. 9 *should read*:
Pianoforte Playing: Maria Donska, Monique Haas,
Dame Myra Hess,

l. 11 *should read*:
String Playing: Georges Enesco, André Gertler, Lionel
Tertis.

l. 12 *should read*:
Singing: Elizabeth Puritz, Elisabeth Schumann.

Par. 6, l. 1 *should read*:
The Summer School was financed in

ll. 4-5 *should read*:
the Earl of Harewood, T. F. Coade and Edric
Cundell as

188   ii   *Add after* **SUNLESS**:

SUÑOL Y BAULENAS, Gregorio María
(*b.* Barcelona, 7 Sept. 1879; *d.* Rome, 26
Oct. 1946).
Spanish musical scholar. He studied at
the Escalonía of Montserrat and at the abbey
of Solesmes. He became prior of the monastery of Montserrat and made a special study
of Gregorian plainsong, being elected president
of the Asociación Gregoriana of Barcelona.
His works include, in Spanish, ' Método com-
pleto del cante gregoriano ' (translated into
French and German) and ' Introducción a
la paleografía musical gregoriana ', and, in
Catalan, ' Els cants dels Romeus '.
                                                    E. B.

192   i   **SUSATO**
Add at end:
See also Vereniging, Vol. 29 (reprint of first music
book).

192   i   Page Heading SUSPENSION
should read:
SUSAY

Add before **SUSPENSION**:
SUSAY, Johannes (*b.* ? ; *d.* ?).
French 14th-century composer. He may
have been the son of Pierre de Suzay, who
was a clerk of the queen's chapel in 1332.
Maistre Jehan de Suzay is cited by the anonymous author of a treatise of 14th-century
versification, and indeed three of his four
compositions are *ballades* on mythological
texts. The other work, a Gloria, comes from
the Avignon circle of composers, but gives
only the surname of the composer.
The Gloria is in A. Gastoué's ' Le Manuscrit . . . d'Apt ' (1936).   G. R. (iii).

193   ii   **SÜSSMAYR**
Footnote 3. l. 1 *should read*:
³ For the complicated history of the libretto *see*
ENTFÜHRUNG AUS DEM SERAIL. Beethoven published
variations on the air '' Tändeln

195   i   **SUTERMEISTER**
OPERAS
Add at end:
' Titus Feuerfuchs ' (lib. by Composer, after Johann
Nestroy's farce ' Der Talisman '), prod. Basel, 14
Apr. 1958.

ii   *Add before* **SUTOR**:
SUTHERLAND, Joan (*b.* Sydney, 7 Nov.
1929).
Australian soprano singer. She studied at
the Sydney Conservatory, where she made
her operatic début in Goossens's ' Judith '
at the age of twenty-one. In 1952 she went
to London, where she joined the company of
the Royal Opera, Covent Garden, making
her first appearance as the First Lady in ' The
Magic Flute '. During the same season she
appeared there as the Countess in ' Figaro ',
Amelia's in Verdi's ' Ballo in maschera ' and
Lady Rich in Britten's ' Gloriana '. Later
parts at Covent Garden were Agathe in
' Freischütz ', Aida, Micaela in ' Carmen ',
Pamina in ' The Magic Flute ' and Eva in
' Meistersinger '. She also created the leading
soprano part in the production of Tippett's
' The Midsummer Marriage ' in Jan. 1955.
She was the first British artist to sing the
Countess in ' Figaro ' at Glyndeborne (1956),
and she has sung the title-part of Weber's
' Euryanthe ' and Vitellia in Mozart's
' Clemenza di Tito ' for the B.B.C. She has
proved her versatility in recent years by
adding operas by Donizetti and Handel to
her repertoire.
Naturally gifted with a voice of fine quality,
Joan Sutherland is an admirably schooled
artist, and although better suited to lyrical

than to heroic parts, she is quite capable of holding her own in such a work as 'Aida' and of developing further in that direction.

E. B.

195   ii   **SUTRO (1)**
Par. 2, l. 2 *should read*:
Sept. 1870; *d*. Baltimore, 11 Jan. 1957).

Add before Suvorov:

SUTTER, J. Toussaint de (*b*. Ghent, 10 Apr. 1889).
Belgian conductor and composer. He studied at the Ghent Conservatory and won the Belgian Prix de Rome in 1919, on his return from service in the first world war. He then made an artistic tour in Italy, France and Germany, and was appointed director of the Conservatoire and conductor of the Kursaal orchestra at Ostend. From 1936 to 1954 he was director of the Ghent Conservatory and conductor of the symphony concerts organized by that institution. He now lives in retirement at Brussels.

De Sutter belongs to the impressionist school of composers, and his work shows a strong Russian influence. His output, which is small, includes the oratorio 'Vlaanderen'; the cantatas 'Ode au Roi chevalier' and 'Chant de fête'; the symphonic poems 'Ivan Tchernovitch', 'Page pour la mort d'un enfant', 'Roland' and 'Tsilla'; Symphonic Variations for orch.; 'Introduction et danse' for violin and orch., 'Lamento' for cello and orch.; 'Triptyque verlainien' for soprano and orch.; chamber music, songs, &c.

A. L. C.

196   ii   **SVEDBOM**
BIBL., l. 5. Rom for halvhundred *should read*:
Rom för halvhundred

197   ii   **SVENDSEN**
Par. 4, *Op*. 11. 'Zorahayde' *should read*:
'Zorahayda'

201   i   **SWARTHOUT**
Par. 1, l. 2. Mo., *should read*:
Missouri,

203   i   **SWEELINCK**
See also. Add after Amsterdam.:
Chorwerk, Vol. 14 (modern reprint of chromatic motet).

See also. l. 2 *should read*:
after S.). Vereniging, Vols. 1, 3, 5-7, 12, 15, 17, & three unnumbered (modern reprints).

ii   **ŚWIERZYŃSKI**
Par. 1, l. 2 *should read*:
Oct. 1868; *d*. Warsaw, 30 June 1957).

204   ii   **SWINSTEAD**
Par. 1, l. 2 *should read*:
25 June 1880; *d*. Southwold, 14 Aug. 1959).

SWOLFS
Par. 1, l. 2 *should read*:
1878; *d*. Brussels, 1955).

205   i   Par. 2, l. 10 *should read*:
Antwerp. In 1948 he became president of the

Add after **SWORD DANCE**:

SWYNFORD, ? (*b*. ?; *d*. ?).
English 14th–15th-century singer and composer. His 'Credo' for two altos, tenor and instrument is preserved in the 'Old Hall Manuscript' (II, 213) and is a skilful example of insular use of isorhythmic technique. That this use is confined to the tenor may possibly indicate reliance on Italian models, though the way in which the liturgical text is telescoped is more typical of English than of continental works. That Swynford was not above punning is shown by the statement of the instrumental tenor for the second time at "secundum scripturas".

D. W. S.

BIBL.—BUKOFZER, MANFRED, 'Studies in Medieval and Renaissance Music' (New York, 1950).
RAMSBOTHAM, ALEXANDER, ed., 'The Old Hall Manuscript', Vol. II (London, 1935).

ii   *Add after* **SYLVIA**:

SYMMES, William. *See* SIMMES.

208   i   **SYMPHONIE FANTASTIQUE**
Add at end:
Berlioz wrote two versions of the programme for this symphony. In the first the poet does not take poison ("opium") until the fourth movement, 'Marche au supplice'; in the later version the whole symphony is supposed to describe scenes produced under narcotic influence (opium not specifically mentioned). Berlioz also, however, expressed the hope that the work should be intelligible if the audience knew only the titles of each movement.

S. D.

210   ii   **SYMPHONY**
Par. 3, l. 10. (1746– *should read*:
(1745–

212   i   Par. 4, l. 1. C. F. Abel (1725– *should read*:
K. F. Abel (1723–

237   ii   Par. 4, l. 5 *should read*:
resurrected and first performed by Weingartner in 1935, since

244 i Par. 6, ll. 2-4 *should read*:
(1895) was withdrawn later, but reconstructed from the parts in 1945. No. 2 (1907) is in the main a gloomy work, suffering

247 i Par. 3, ll. 1-2 *should read*:
It was eight years before the Symphony in D major (1943) followed; the vitality of the

250 ii *Add to* BIBL.:
BORREL, EUGÈNE, ' La Symphonie: formes, écoles et œuvres musicales ' (Paris, 1954).

251 ii **Synge**
l. 3 *should read*:
do. & 'Deirdre of the Sorrows', operas). Orr (R., ' Deirdre ', radio m.). Pedrollo

265 ii **SZELÉNYI**
Par. 1, l. 2 *should read*:
Zólyom, 8 Aug. 1904).

268 i **SZELL**
Par. 1, l. 19 *should read*:
of Europe and also in the U.S.A. In 1946 he became conductor of the Cleveland Orchestra.

SZELUTO
Par. 1, l. 1. ?, 1884 *should read*:
St. Petersburg, 23 July 1884

Par. 2, l. 20 *should read*:
Blows of Destiny', etc. Among several operas, the last, written in 1954 at the age of seventy, is ' Pan Tadeusz ' to a libretto of his own based on Mickiewicz's epic.

269 i **SZENKAR**
Par. 2, l. 23. *After* Moscow. *add*:
In 1939–49 he was in Rio de Janeiro as conductor of the Brazilian Symphony Orchestra, which he founded, and of the Municipal Theatre. On his return to Germany in 1950 he conducted at Mannheim and Cologne, and in 1952 he was appointed director of the Düsseldorf Opera and conductor of the Düsseldorf Symphony Orchestra.

ii **SZERVÁNSKY,** CATALOGUE:
CHORAL WORKS
l. 5. (? 1950) *should read*:
(1949).
Add after ORCHESTRAL WORKS:
CLARINET AND ORCHESTRA
Serenade (1954).

270 ii *Add after* **SZOPSKI**:
SZPANOWSKI, Franciszek (*b.* Warsaw, 30 Mar. 1892).
Polish violinist and composer. He was a pupil of Joachim and later of Kodály. His compositions include 2 violin Concertos, some orchestral pieces and many songs.
C. R. H.

270 ii **SZPINALSKI**
Par. 1, l. 2 *should read*:
Russia, 15 Nov. 1901; *d.* Paris, 12 June 1957).

271 i **SZTOMPKA**
Par. 1. (*b.* ?, 1904). *should read*:
(*b.* Bogusławiec nr. Łuck, 1901).

ii **SZULC (2)**
Par. 1, l. 2. 1875). *should read*:
1875; *d.* Paris, 10 Apr. 1956.

272 ii **SZYMANOWSKA, Maria**
Par. 1, l. 2. *c.* 1790; *should read*:
14 Dec. 1789;

Par. 2, ll. 2-3 *should read*:
first with F. Lessel, a pupil of Haydn, but not with John Field in Moscow, as has been stated (a statement contradicted by herself), although she knew him well and can hardly fail to have been influenced by him. She toured

ll. 8-9 *should read*:
her striking beauty and appearance, overpraised her by placing her

ll. 13-14 *should read*:
nung', is a direct allusion to her. She settled in St. Petersburg in Mar. 1828 as pianist and teacher, and died there of cholera. She had married Theophilus Joseph Szymanowski in 1810; they were divorced in 1820.

288 ii *Add before* **TABOR PIPE**:
TÁBOR. *See* SMETANA (' Má Vlast ').

290 i **TAGLIAPIETRA, Gino**
Par. 1, l. 1. Lubiana *should read*:
Ljubljana

l. 2 *should read*:
May 1887; *d.* Venice, 8 Aug. 1954).

TAGLIAVINI
Par. 1, l. 1. **Ferrucio** *should read*:
Ferruccio

l. 2. 15 Aug. *should read*.
14 Aug.

ii **Tagore**
ll. 1-2. (' Giardiniere ', songs). *should read*:
(' Giardiniere ', songs with orch. & with pf.).

l. 5 *should read*:
nuovo-Tedesco (2 songs). Coke (' Gardener ', song cycle). Cras (' Offrande lyrique ').

291   ii   **TAILLEFERRE**
l. 8 *should read*:

emigrated to the U.S.A. in 1942. On 9 Mar. 1951 the Paris Opéra-Comique produced her opera in three scenes ' Il était un petit navire '.

TAILOUR
Par. 1, l. 1. **Robert** *should read*:
Robert [1]

Add footnote:
[1] For his son *see* TAYLOR, JOHN.

292   ii   **TAKACS**
Par. 3, l. 7. Cincinnatic *should read*:
Cincinnati

294   ii   **TALLIS**
Par. 3, l. 5 *should read*:

earliest known facts about him are that he was *joculator organorum* of Dover Priory in 1532, *conduct* of St. Mary-at-Hill, London, in 1537 and that he held

297   i   Par. 1, ll. 1-3 *should read*:
five-part setting was printed by Barnard. On internal evidence, in spite of

ll. 10-12 *should read*:

ascribed there to Tallis, was almost certainly also in five parts, a countertenor part being clearly missing. In the

298   ii   SERVICES, ETC.
ll. 1-6 *should read*:

Preecs I, *a* 5. Barnard (1641) ; R.C.M. MSS 1045-51 (*c.* 1625) ; Pet. MSS 33, 34, 38, 39 & 2 unnumbered partbooks (*c.* 1635, no tenor) ; Ch. Ch. MSS 1220-24 (*c.* 1660, no sop. & alto 2).
Preces II, *a* 4. Pet. MSS 35, 36, 42, 44 (*c.* 1635).
Responses I, *a* 5. R.C.M. MSS 1045-51 (no alto 2) ; Pet. MSS 33, 34, 38, 39 (no tenor) ; Ch. Ch. MSS 1220-24 (no sop. & alto 2).
Responses II, *a* 5. Barnard ; Pet. MSS 35, 36, 42, 44 44 (no alto 2).

l. 8. Litany *a* 4. *should read*:
Litany *a* 5.[1]

Add footnote:
[1] Although only 4 parts are preserved, it is clear that a fifth (countertenor) is missing.

300   ii   **TAMAGNO**
Par. 1, l. 1. 1851 ; *should read*:
28 Dec. 1850 ;

301   ii   **TAMBOURINE**
Par. 1, ll. 15-16 *should read*:

an illustration is given on *PLATE* 49, Vol. VI, p. 622, No. 3.

303   ii   **TANEYEV, S. I.**
Add to BIBL.:

WEINBERG, JACOB, ' Sergei Ivanovitch Taneiev ' (M.Q., XLIV, Jan. 1958, p. 19).

304   i   CATALOGUE:
ORCHESTRAL WORKS:
l. 5 *should read*:
12. Symphony " No. 1 ", C mi.[2] (1896–97).

ii   SONGS
Op. 17 No. 1. Island *should read*:
Isle

Nos. 2 & 3. (anon.) *should read*:
(Balmont, after Shelley).

No. 6. (anon.) *should read*:
(Ellis, after Stecchetti).

Add at end of SONGS:
— ' The Find ' (Kolomeyetsev, after Goethe).

305   i   **TANGENT**
See also should read:
See also Clavichord. Illustration, Vol. II, p. 337.

ii   **TANGO**
Add at end:
BIBL.—CARELLA, TULIO, ' El tango : mito y escenia ' (Buenos Aires, 1956).

306   i   **TANSMAN,** CATALOGUE:
OPERAS
Add after l. 5:
' Le Serment ' (lib. by Dominique Vincent), prod. Brussels, 11 Mar. 1955.

307   ii   **TAPISSIER**
Add at end:
BIBL.—REANEY, GILBERT, ' Early Fifteenth-Century Music ', Vol. I (New York, 1955).

309   ii   **TARDOS**
Par. 2, l. 8. Bucharest *should read*:
Budapest

311   ii   **TARP**
Add after CATALOGUE OF WORKS:
OPERA
' Prinsessen i det Fjerne ' (on a novel by Hermann Sudermann), prod. Copenhagen, 18 May 1953.

314   ii   **TARTINI**
Par. 2, ll. 15-16 *should read*:

raised some literary controversy on the subject. He failed to come to any clear conclusions, but is generally credited with the discovery of the difference tone.[2]

Par. 3, l. 12 *should read*:
Mainwaring tells us [3], his contemporaries often

Add footnote:
[2] *See* ACOUSTICS, p. 36.

Footnote 2 becomes 3.

315   i   Par. 4, l. 11. (Paris, 1782) *should read*:
(Paris, 1771).

315 i Par. 4, ll. 19-21 *should read*:
(London, 1771, 2nd ed. 1779), French translation ('Journal de Musique', Paris, 1773), German translations in J. A. Hiller's 'Lebensbeschreibungen' (Leipzig, 1784) and by H. L. Rohrmann (Hanover, 1786).[1] The 'Traité des agréments', announced in 'Mercure de France' as published " chez l'auteur " (*i.e.* the translator, P. Denis), was reissued in 1782 by La Chevardière. It is surmised [2] that the translation was made, at the suggestion of Tartini's French pupil Lahoussaye, while the author was still alive, and that he supervised it.

Par. 5, l. 8 *should read*:
The only contemporary portrait, in oils, by an unknown painter, dating from *c.* 1765 to 1768, is in the Bologna Conservatory. All the others are much later. There is one in the gallery of the

Add footnotes:
[1] A modern edition of the 'Traité des agréments', by Erwin R. Jacobi, with text in French, German and English, was published at Celle in 1959.
[2] By Erwin R. Jacobi in his modern edition of the 'Traité' with French, English and German text.

ii Par. 5, l. 3 *should read*:
possesses a portrait in oils of Tartini, which is a copy of the Bologna Conservatory portrait, and there

l. 13 *should read*:
LVI of the 3rd and 4th editions. This is also based on the Bologna Conservatory portrait, and the original of the engraving is in the National Library in Vienna.

See also. l. 1 *should read*:
See also Bowing. Classici Musica Italiana, Vol. 32 (modern ed. of sonatas). Jacob (G., Concertino arr. for clar.).

316 i **TASCHE**
Par. 1, l. 1 *should read*:
TASCHE (Ital., lit. pockets, pouches, bags; sing. of *tasca*). The popular name of a festival

l. 5 *should read*:
republican government. The name is due to the bags in which the votes were collected. The

318 ii **TATE,** List of Works
Add above OPERETTA:
OPERA
'The Lodger' (libretto by David Franklin, on the novel by Mrs. Belloc Lowndes) (1957-58).

Add before ORCHESTRAL WORKS:
CHORAL WORK
Scene from 'The Bacchae' (Euripides), for double choir unaccomp. or with organ, prod. Leeds Festival, 1953.

2 F

318 ii *Add at end of* CHAMBER MUSIC:
Air and Variations for vn., clar. & pf. (1957).

Add at end of VOCAL CHAMBER MUSIC:
'The Lady of Shalott' (Tennyson) for tenor, va., 2 pfs., celesta & perc., for 10th anniversary of B.B.C. Third Programme (1956).

319 i *Add before* SONGS:
VIOLIN AND PIANOFORTE
'Triptych' ('Prelude, Scherzo and Soliloquy') (1954).

TWO PIANOFORTES
Sonatina (1957).
Add before signature:

BIBL.—CARNER, MOSCO, 'The Music of Phyllis Tate' (M. & L., XXXV, 1954, p. 128).

320 i **TAUBER**
Par. 2, l. 2 *should read*:
birth. His real name was Ernst Seiffert. He studied singing with Carl Barnes at

ii l. 15 *should read*:
man version). In 1947 he made his final appearance at Covent Garden, as Don Ottavio, during a visit to the Company of the Vienna State Opera. Tauber's first marriage was

321 ii **TAUSCH, Julius**
Par. 2, l. 6. Reitz's *should read*:
Rietz's

Par. 3, l. 5 *should read*:
pieces, solo and accompanied. A curious work, written about 1878, is a 'Concertstück' for 6 kettledrums and orchestra.[1]
G., adds.

Add footnote:
[1] For details of this *see* DRUM, p. 772.

326 i Page Heading TAYLOR, J. D.
should read:
TAYLOR (John)

Add before **TAYLOR, J. D.**:
TAYLOR, John (*b.* ?; *d.* ?).
English 17th-century instrumentalist and composer. His father, Robert [1], was one of the royal musicians from 1625 to 1637, as well as a London wait from 1620 to 1637. His instruments were " orpheryon and base vyoll and poliphon "; and at his death, John succeeded to his place as a musician for 'viols and voyce' in the King's Music (3 Oct. 1637). He wrote an elegy on the death of " his Friend and Fellow, Mr. William Lawes " in Henry Lawes's 'Choice Psalms' (1648) and several songs, two of which Playford printed in 'Select Musical Ayres and Dialogues' (1652) and 'Catch that Catch Can' (1663),

and subsequently reprinted Manuscripts containing his songs are B.M. Add. MS 29396; New York Public Library, Drexel MSS 4257, and especially 4041, which, since it is primarily a source of pre-Commonwealth play-songs, may indicate that the composer (like John Gamble) was a theatre musician at some time before 1642. He died before the Restoration (1660). An 'Ayre' and 'Sarabande' were included by Playford in 'Court-Ayres' (1655), Nos. 118 and 119, ascribed to John Taylor; there is also some instrumental music by him in Bodl. Lib. MS Mus. Sch. d. 220, and a bass part of an 'Aire, Aire, Almaine and Serrabrand' in Ch. Ch. MS 1022. The same library contains songs and consort music by Robert Taylor (MSS 439 and 725-8).   I. S.

¹ *See* TAILOUR.

326   i   **TAYLOR, J. D.**
Par. 3, l. 7 *should read*:

1937 he wrote a third opera, 'Ramuntcho', to a libretto of his own based on Pierre Loti's novel,

l. 9 *should read*:

Opera Company on 7 Feb. 1942.

343   —   **TCHAIKOVSKY**
Heading *should read*:

TCHAIKOVSKY: Bibliography—Works

LIST OF WORKS:
OPERAS
Col. 3, l. 4. Sologub *should read*:
Sollogub

345   —   ORCHESTRAL WORKS
Col. 5, l. 15. 4 Mar. *should read*:
22 Feb.

346   —   WORKS FOR SOLO INSTRUMENTS
WITH ORCHESTRA
Op. 23, col. 5 *should read*:

Boston, 25 Oct. 1875.

Op. 35, col. 5. New York, 1879. *should read*:

Vienna, 4 Dec. 1881.

349   —   SONGS
Col. 3, l. 59. Sologub *should read*:
V. A. Sollogub

351   i   Tchekhov
l. 3 *should read*:

incid. m.). Bucchi ('Contrabasso', opera). Chailly (2 1-act operas). Ferroud ('Chirurgie', opera). Nottara ('Over

TCHEREPNIN, A. N.
Par. 3, l. 13 *should read*:

Shiao-Yen. In 1949 he was appointed professor of theory at the De Paul University, Chicago.

351   ii   OPERAS
l. 4 *should read*:

Hofmannsthal), prod. Vienna, 17 Mar. 1933.

Add after this:

'The Farmer and the Fairy', prod. Aspen, Colorado, 13 Aug. 1952.

BALLETS
l. 1. 1923). *should read*:
10 Sept. 1923).

l. 2. 1934). *should read*:
19 June 1935).

l. 3. (New York, 1937). *should read*:
(Richmond, Virginia, 10 Oct. 1938).

l. 6. (Paris, 1945). *should read*:
(Paris, 14 Oct. 1945).

Add after this:
'La Femme et son ombre' (Paris, 14 June 1948).

ORCHESTRAL WORKS
l. 5 *should read*:
Symphony No. 1 (1927).

Add at end:
Symphony No. 2 (1952).
Suite (1954).
Symphony No. 3 (1955).

SOLO INSTRUMENTS AND OR-
CHESTRA
l. 6. cello & orch. *should read*:
cello & orch. (1923).

and transfer to stand above l. 1.

354   i   **TE DEUM LAUDAMUS**
Last par. ll. 3-6 *should read*:

phonic music. Palestrina's Mass 'Te Deum', for six voices, is one of the finest examples, and makes extensive use of the melody. Aston, in his Mass 'Te Deum', restricts himself to only one phrase of the hymn, whereas in Taverner's motet 'Ave Dei Patris Filia' the five different phrases serve an effective structural purpose. But the number

369   ii   **TEACHING OF MUSIC**
Add to BIBL.:

FIELDEN, THOMAS, 'Marks and Remarks: Music Examinations and their Problems' (London, 1957). MURSELL, JAMES T., 'Music Education: Principles and Programs' (Morristown, N.J., 1956).

Add before **TEBALDINI**:

TEBALDI, Renata (*b*. Pesaro, 1 Feb. 1922).
Italian soprano singer. She was brought up at Parma, where she studied music with the view to becoming a concert pianist. She developed the habit of singing while she played the pianoforte and her teacher, Professor Passani, was so amazed by the richness and range of her voice that he suggested she should audition to a singing-teacher. Thus, when she was eighteen she entered the Arrigo

Boito Conservatory at Parma, where she became a pupil of Carmen Melis. In 1944, owing to the bombing, she left the Conservatory before obtaining her diploma; and on 23 May the same year she made her début as Elena in Boito's 'Mefistofele' at Rovigo. This was followed by appearances in the Italian provinces. In 1946 she was heard by Toscanini, who had gone to Italy to audition singers for the reopening of the Milan Scala, and she was chosen by him to sing under him at the opening night on 11 May 1946, as soprano soloist in the *preghiera* from Rossini's 'Mosè' and in Verdi's 'Te Deum'. In the first winter opera season at the rebuilt Scala (1946–47) she sang Mimì and Eva. Appearances followed at Venice, Naples, Rome and elsewhere in Italy, and from 1949 until 1954 she sang regularly at La Scala, where her parts included Madeleine de Coigny, Adriana Lecouvreur, Tosca, Desdemona and the title-part in Catalani's 'La Wally'. From 1955 to 1959 she did not appear there, but although it has been said that the great rivalry that exists between her and Callas was the reason, this has been categorically denied by both singers.

Tebaldi is a great favourite at the San Carlo, Naples, and both there and in South America she has been compared with the great Claudia Muzio, especially for her interpretation of Violetta. Tebaldi first sang in London, at Covent Garden, in the autumn of 1950, when she was heard as Desdemona on the opening night of the Scala's London season; she was also heard in the Verdi Requiem. She returned to London in the summer of 1955 to sing Tosca. Her American début was at San Francisco in 1950. She has subsequently sung in Chicago and has been a member of the Metropolitan, New York, since the 1954–55 season. Besides the usual *lirico-spinto* repertory, Tebaldi has sung the title-part in Spontini's 'Olympia' (Florence, 1950), Pamira in Rossini's 'L' assedio di Corinto' (Florence, 1949), Cleopatra in Handel's 'Giulio Cesare' (Naples, 1950) and the title-part in Verdi's 'Giovanna d' Arco' (Naples and Paris, 1950).

Tebaldi's voice is one of the most beautiful to have come out of Italy this century; she does not indulge in the super-abundance of chest-notes so dear to many Italian sopranos, and her *mezza-voce* singing is a pure joy to hear. Early in her career her interpretations lacked dramatic conviction, but more recently there has been evidence of a heightened sense of drama in her interpretations, and the voice, which in the years following her first London appearances began to show some strain and lost a little of its beauty and steadiness, is once again the lovely thing it originally was.

H. D. R.

371 i **TELEMANN**
Par. 3, l. 10 *should read*:
are Vol. XXIX, Concertos, Vol. LVII, Odes and Songs, and Vols.

l. 20 *should read*:
to August Corbet.
A Telemann Society was formed in Germany in 1958.   A. M., adds.

ii   *See also,* l. 2 *should read*:
J. G., 'Gensericus' recast by T.). Denkmäler (5) I, Vol. VI (modern ed. of 'Pimpinone'); Vol. XI (do. of concertos). Reger (vars. for

TELHARMONIUM
l. 2. Thomas Cahill *should read*:
Thaddeus Cahill

374 i **TEMPERAMENTS**
Par. 2, ll. 1-2 *should read*:
A particular illustration of musical intervals is to be found in the

377-80   Headings, Mean Tone *should read*:
Mean-tone

393 ii **Tennyson**
l. 4. Britten ('Sere- *should read*:
Britten ('Nocturne', No. 2; 'Sere-

394 ii **TENOR TUBA**
See also should read:
See also Tuba. Illustration, Vol. VII, p. 428.

395 ii **TENOROON**
See also should read:
See also Bassoon. *PLATE* 15, Vol. II, p. 447, No. 10.

TENSCHERT
Last book-title *should read*:
'Richard Strauss und Wien: eine Wahlverwandtschaft'

396 i **TERNINA**
     Par. 1, l. 2. 1864 *should read*:
1863

402 ii *Add after* **TESTAMENT, LE**:
TESTI, Flavio (*b.* Florence, 1923).
Italian composer. He studied at the Conservatory "G. Verdi" at Turin under Giulio Gedda and Luigi Perrachio, and he took a laureate in letters at Milan University. His most important works include the one-act opera 'Il furore di Oreste' (Bergamo, 1956), 'Crocifissione' for men's chorus, strings, brass and 3 pianofortes (1953), 'Stabat Mater' for soprano, chorus and instruments (1957), Concerto for orchestra and 'Musica da concerto' for violin and orchestra.

G. M. G.

404   ii   **TEYTE**
Par. 1, l. 1.   *? should read*:
17 Apr. 1888

Par. 2, l. 4 *should read*:
in Mozart at the Opéra-Comique, after a
first stage appearance as Zerlina in ' Don
Giovanni ' at Monte Carlo in 1907.

l. 7 *should read*:
et Mélisande ' at that theatre in May 1908.
Debussy also

Par. 2.   *Add at end*:
In 1957 she received the decoration of Chevalier of the French Legion of Honour, and she
was created D.B.E. in 1958.

405   i   **THALBEN-BALL**
Par. 1, ll. 1-4 *should read*:
F.R.C.M. since 1950. He was acting organist
of the Temple Church from 1919 until 1923,
when he was officially appointed, and he
became curator organist of the Royal Albert
Hall in 1930. Since 1949 he has been

THALBERG
Par. 1, ll. 1-2 *should read*:
**THALBERG, Sigismond (Fortuné
François)** (*b*. Pâquis nr. Geneva, 8 Jan.
1812 [1]; *d*. Posilipo, 27 Apr. 1871).

Par. 2, ll. 1-5 *should read*:
German or Austrian pianist and composer.
He was said to be the natural son of Count
Moritz Dietrichstein and Baroness von
Wetzlar, but the birth certificate clearly states
that his parents were Joseph Thalberg and
Fortunée Stein, both of Frankfort. Although
described as " mariés ", the wording rather
suggests that each was married to someone
else. It seems possible that Dietrichstein
induced Joseph Thalberg to assume paternity
and that the mother was a baroness in disguise ;
but the circumstances remain mysterious.
At the age of ten he was sent to Vienna,
intended for a diplomatic career ; he attended

Footnote 1. l. 1 should read:
[1] According to the Archiviste d'État of Geneva
(1955). The date 7 Jan. is given by Fétis, who is followed

l. 5 *should read*:
7 Feb.
Delete l. 6.

407   i   **THATCHER**
Par. 1, l. 2.   1888). *should read*:
1888 ; *d*. Cranleigh, Surrey, 6 May 1957).

ii   **THAYER**
Par. 2, l. 4 from end.   1925 *should
read*:
1917

408   i   *Add after* **THEATRE ORGAN**:
THEBOM, Blanche (*b*. Monessen, Pennsylvania, 19 Sept. 1919).
American mezzo-soprano singer. Her
parents were both born in Sweden, but she is
a native of the U.S.A. She spent her childhood at Canton, Ohio, and the only musical
studies during her youth were directed to the
pianoforte. On a visit to Sweden with her
parents in 1938 she took part in a ship's
concert, and among the passengers was Kosti
Vehanen, Marian Anderson's accompanist ;
he was impressed by what he heard and urged
her to go to New York to study singing.
Sponsored by a local industrialist and his wife,
Thebom went to New York in the spring of
1939 and began her vocal studies. Her chief
teachers were Edyth Walker for voice and
Lothar Wallerstein for stage. In Nov. 1941
she was able to make her début singing in the
Brahms Alto Rhapsody with the Philadelphia
Orchestra under Ormandy. Two years later
she sang with the Minneapolis Orchestra
under Mitropoulos, and gave a New York
recital. This brought her to the attention
of Edward Johnson, who engaged her for
the Metropolitan 1944–45 season, and she
made her début with the company at Philadelphia in Nov. 1944 as Brangäne, her first
appearance on any stage. She followed this
up with Fricka, Erda and Laura in ' La
Gioconda '. During the next ten years she
became the company's leading mezzo-soprano
and besides singing all the Wagnerian
repertory, including Venus in ' Tannhäuser ',
she was heard as Delilah, Amneris, Eboli,
Marina in ' Boris Godunov ' and Marfa in
' Khovanshchina '. She made appearances
in San Francisco, Chicago and elsewhere in
America, and in 1950 she sang Dorabella at
Glyndebourne. In 1957 she was engaged to
sing the part of Dido in the Covent Garden
production of ' The Trojans '. Unfortunately
she was past her vocal best by then ; but
during the 1940s and early 1950s her voice
was rich and warm, and her singing displayed
colour and beauty. Her acting was indifferent, but her strikingly handsome stage
presence was an added asset.   H. D. R.

409   i   **THEILE**
Add at end:
See also Chorwerk, Vol. 16 (modern reprint of Mass).

411   ii   **THEORBO**
Add at end:
PLATE 42, Vol. V, p. 432, No. 4.

418   ii   **THERAPY**
Add to Bibl.:
Pontvik, Aleks, ' Grundgedanken zur psychischen
    Heilwirkung der Musik ' (Zürich, 1948).
' Heilen durch Musik ' (Zürich, 1955).

419   ii   *Add after* **THIBAUD** :
THIBAULT, Geneviève (Comtesse de Chambure) (*b.* Neuilly-sur-Seine, 20 May 1902). French musicologist. She was educated in Paris, though travelling widely, particularly in Italy. At the Sorbonne she gained the *Licence ès lettres* and the *Diplôme d'études supérieures*, following these degrees with the *Diplôme de l'École des Hautes Études*. A capable business-woman, she has nevertheless given her time freely to the advancement of musical research, stimulated like other French musicologists by the teaching of André Pirro. She has built up a fine library of music and books on music, which contains many 16th-century part-books and a most important late 15th-century *chansonnier* (the 'Nivelle de la Chaussée'). To a generation of music students she has played the part of mentor, helping them in their work and giving them free access to her library. Founder of the Société de Musique d'Autrefois, which has given concerts on her fine collection of old instruments, she now publishes in the name of that Society the 'Annales musicologiques', an exemplary year-book devoted to serious studies of medieval and Renaissance music, and she has inaugurated a 'Monuments' series most happily begun with Gombosi's edition of the Capirola Lute-Book.

Mme de Chambure is also a powerful supporter of the French Musicological Society, and since 1955 has been lecturing at the Music Department of the Sorbonne. Her own studies have been particularly concerned with the French chanson from the 15th century onwards. In longer studies she has generally collaborated with other scholars : with E. Droz in 'Poètes et musiciens du XVᵉ siècle' (Paris, 1924) ; with A. Pirro, E. Droz and Y. Rokseth in 'Trois Chansonniers français du XVᵉ siècle' (Paris, 1927) ; with L. Perceau in the 'Bibliographie des poésies de P. de Ronsard mises en musique au XVIᵉ siècle' (Paris, 1941) ; and with F. Lesure in the 'Bibliographie des éditions d'Adrien Le Roy et Robert Ballard' (Paris, 1955). Important shorter articles include essays on some of Ronsard's musicians and bibliographies of 16th-century music printers. The relationships between music and poetry and music and art in the 15th and 16th centuries have also been profitably investigated.

G. R. (iii).

422   ii   **THOINAN**
Par. 1, l. 3 *should read* :
Paris, 26 May 1894).
Delete footnote.

424   ii   **Thomas, Dylan**
Refs. *should read* :
See Jones (D., radio m. for 'Under Milk Wood'; songs; ded. of Symphony No. 4). Stravinsky ('In memoriam D. T.'; planned opera).

426   i   **THOMAS, Kurt**
Par. 2, l. 13 *should read* :
teacher of theory at the Leipzig Conservatory and in 1956 he succeeded Günther Ramin as Cantor of St. Thomas's Church there.

429   ii   **THOMPSON, Oscar**
Par. 2, l. 4 *should read* :
several books on music, the most important being 'Debussy, Man and Artist' (1937) and was editor-in-chief

430   i   **THOMPSON, R.**
     Add to ORCHESTRAL WORKS :
Symphony No. 3 (1949).

436   i   **THORNE**
Par. 1, ll. 1-4 *should read* :
Baldwin, which contains the motet 'Stella coeli exstirpavit'. A 4-part 'In nomine' is in the Bodleian Library (MS Mus. Sch. d. 212-6).

450   ii   **THOROUGH-BASS**
     BIBL. l. 12 *should read* :
1762, and some later eds. ; Eng. trans., London & New York, 1949).

451   ii   **THRANE**
Par. 1, l. 1.   **Valdemar** *should read* :

Waldemar

l. 2.   *d.* Christiania, *should read* :
d. Drammen,

453   ii   **THREE CHOIRS FESTIVAL**
Par. 4, l. 6 *should read* :
negotiating the revival. The London Symphony Orchestra has been regularly engaged to take part ever since. The organists of

454   ii   *Add after* Par. 2 :
In 1950 Meredith Davies succeeded Hull as cathedral organist at Hereford. He is a more than ordinarily fine conductor, and through his influence the Hereford Festival programme of 1955 was strikingly enterprising.

Add to BIBL. :
SHAW, H. WATKINS, 'The Three Choirs Festival' (Worcester & London, 1954).

455   ii   **THURSBY**
Par. 1, ll. 1-2 *should read* :
THURSBY, Emma (Cecilia) (*b.* Brooklyn, N.Y., 21 Feb. 1845; *d.* New York, 4 Feb. 1931).

456   i   THURSFIELD
Par. 1, ll. 1-2 *should read*:
THURSFIELD (born **Reman**), **Anne**
(Loyse) (*b.* New York, 28 Mar. 1885; *d.*
London, 5 June

THURSTON
Par. 1, l. 2.   1901). *should read*:
1901; *d.* London, 12 Dec. 1953).

464   ii   TIBY
Par. 1, l. 1.   1891).   *should read*:
1891; *d.* Palermo, 4 Dec. 1955).

**465   i ** Par. 1, ll. 9-12 *should read*:
He lived at Palermo and was engaged in
editing over a thousand Sicilian folksongs
collected by his father-in-law, Alberto Favara,
to be published in the early 1950s, and he
prepared a modern edition of the *corpus* of the

     ii   Heading, TIE *should read*:
TICHÝ

467   ii   TIESSEN
Add at end:
BIBL.—TIESSEN, HEINZ, ' Selbstzeugnis des Künstlers '
(' Musica ', Apr. 1948).

469   i   TIKHOTSY
Par. 1, l. 1 *should read*:
TIKOTSKY, Evgeny Karlovich (*b.*
St. Petersburg,

Par. 3, l. 1.   Tikhotsy *should read*:
Tikotsky

Par. 5, l. 1.   Tikhotsy *should read*:
Tikotsky

     ii   Par. 1, l. 9.   Bruka *should read*:
Brovka

Par. 3, l. 1.   Tikhotsy *should read*:
Tikotsky

480   i   TIME
Add to BIBL. :
SACHS, CURT, ' Rhythm and Tempo ' (London, 1953).

TIMOTHEUS
Add at end:
This title was often applied to Handel's
' Alexander's Feast ' in 19th-century Germany
and Austria.

481   i   TINCTORIS
Par. 3, ll. 26-28 *should read*:
is undated, but is known to have been printed
by Gerardus de Lisa at Treviso

**481   ii ** Par. 1, l. 1 *should read*:
about 1495. One writer suggests 1492 as the

483   ii   TIPPETT
Add to BIBL. :
DICKINSON, A. E. F., ' Round about " The Midsummer
Marriage " ' (M. & L., XXXVII, 1956, p. 50).
MASON, COLIN, ' Tippett's Piano Concerto ' (' The
Score ', No. 16, June 1956, p. 63).
TIPPETT, M., ' Moving into Aquarius ' (London, 1959).

CATALOGUE:
OPERA
l. 2 *should read*:
(1952), prod. London, Covent Garden Theatre,
27 Jan. 1955.

484   i   CHORAL WORKS
Add at end:
' Crown of the Year ', cantata for girls' voices & var.
insts. (1958).

ORCHESTRAL WORKS
Add at end:
Symphony No. 2 (1958).

PIANOFORTE AND ORCHESTRA
Add at end:
Concerto (1956).

CHAMBER MUSIC
Add at end:
Sonata for 4 horns (1955).

486   i   TITOV (3)
l. 2.   ?, 22 Dec. *should read*:
St. Petersburg, 22 Dec.

TO ANACREON IN HEAVEN
Delete (song by John Stafford
Smith).

See should read:
See SMITH, JOHN STAFFORD ; STAR-
SPANGLED BANNER.

488   i   TOCH
Par. 2, l. 17 *should read*:
book on the subject, ' The Shaping Forces in
Music ', which is published in America.

Par. 3, l. 6.   No. 2, *should read*:
No. 1,

     ii   ORCHESTRAL WORKS
Op. 72 *should read*:
72. Symphony No. 1.

After that add:
— Symphony No. 2.
— Symphony No. 3.

Add at end:
— ' Notturno ' for small orch.

CHAMBER MUSIC
Add at end:
— Stg. Quartet No. 8.
— ' Vanity of Vanities ', cantata for 2 voices & 5 insts.

489   i   *Add at end, after* SONGS :

BOOK

'The Shaping Forces in Music' (New York, 1948).
BIBL.—PISK, P. A., 'Ernst Toch' (M.Q., XXIV, Oct. 1938).

Todi, J. da
l. 1. *Add after See*
Dallapiccola (Christmas Concerto).

493   ii   **TOLLIUS**
Add at end :
See also Vereniging, Vol. 24 (reprint of madrigals).

494   i   **TOMAŠEK**
Par. 1, l. 3.   2 June *should read* :
3 Apr.

495   i   **TOMASI, Henri**
Par. 2, l. 11 *should read* :
generation in France. In 1939, on the out-break of war, he joined the army (Chasseurs Alpins). He was conductor of the Opera at Monte Carlo from 1946 to 1950, and in 1952 he received the Grand Prix de Musique Française.

Delete the rest and replace by :

CATALOGUE OF WORKS

OPERAS

'Don Juan de Mañara' (lib. by O. V. de Milosz) (1952), prod. Munich, 29 Mar. 1956.
'Sampiero Corso' (lib. by Raphael Cuttoli) (1956), prod. Bordeaux, May 1956.

OPERA-BALLET

'Atlantide' (lib. by P. Benoît & F. Didelot) (1954), prod. Mulhouse, 26 Feb. 1954.

BALLETS

'La Grisi' (1935), prod. Paris, Opéra, 7 Oct. 1935.
'La Rosière du village' (1936), prod. Paris, Opéra-Comique, 26 May 1936.
'Les Santons' (1938), prod. Paris, Opéra, 18 Nov. 1938.
'La Féerie cambodgienne' (1952), prod. Marseilles, Opéra, 31 Jan. 1952.
'Les Folies mazarguaises' (1953), prod. Marseilles, Opéra, 5 Oct. 1953.
'Noces de cendre' (1954), prod. Strasbourg, 19 Jan. 1954.

ORCHESTRAL WORKS

'Pièces brèves', suite for small orch. (1929).
'Mélodies corses' (1931).
'Chants de Cyrnos' (1931).
'Vocero', symph. poem (1933).
'Scènes municipales' for small orch. (1933).
'Chanson des sables' (1933).
'Tam-Tam', symph. poem (1933).
'Chants laotiens' (1934).
'Deux Danses cambodgiennes' for small orch. (1934).
'Colomba: tableaux symphoniques' (1936).
'Chants des Geishas' (1936).
'Caravanes, ou Impressions sahariennes' for small orch. (1938).
'Petite Suite médiévale' for small orch. (1938).
'Nuits de Provence', symph. suite (1952).

MILITARY BAND

'France d'outre-mer : marche héroïque' (1940).

SOLO INSTRUMENTS AND ORCHESTRA

'Obsession' for cello (1929).
'Cyrnos' with principal pf. (1929).
'Chant hébraïque' for vn. (1929).
'Capriccio' for vn. (1931).
'Ballade' for saxophone (1939).
'Concert asiatique' for perc. (1939).
Concerto for flute (1947).
Concerto for trumpet (1949).
Concerto for va. (1951).
Concerto for saxophone (1951).
Concerto for horn (1955).

VOICE AND ORCHESTRA

'Chant de la fée des îles' for high voice (1944).

CHAMBER MUSIC

'Concert champêtre' for oboe, clar. & bassoon (1939).
4 Songs (F. Carco, José Heredia) for mezzo-soprano, flute, va. & harp (1941).
Trio for vn., va. & cello (1943).
'Divertimento Corsica' for woodwind trio (1952).
Quintet for wind insts. (1952).

PIANOFORTE MUSIC

'Paysages', 3 pieces (1930).
'Le Coin de Claudinet', 12 easy pieces (1948).

SONGS

2 Songs (Paul Fort) (1933).
2 Songs (Francis Jammes) (1933).
2 Songs (H. Charasson) (1955).

VOCAL DUETS

'Chansons écossaises' for soprano & tenor (1936).
F. R., adds.

495   i   **TOMASINI (1)**
Par. 1, l. 6.   (Eisenstadt) *should read* :
(Pressburg)

ii   **TOMASINI (2)**
l. 2. [Eisenstadt] *should read* :
[Pressburg]

496   i   **TOMKINS (2)**
Par. 6, ll. 3-5 *should read* :
Mary de Lode in the same town. His name appears among those of the minor canons in the earliest extant treasurer's accounts of the Cathedral (1610) and does not disappear from them until 1627. The precentor was elected annually at that period, and Tomkins was first elected to that post on 14 Oct. 1618. He was re-elected for a number of years, but there is no evidence that he had special

TOMKINS
(3) Thomas Tomkins
See also, remove line to end of **(4) Thomas Tomkins,** p. 497, col. ii.

TOMKINS (4). l. 3 *should read* :
[buried 9] June 1656), organist and composer, brother of

497 i **TOMKINS (4)**
Delete Par. 3.

i-ii *Delete Catalogue and replace by* :

CATALOGUE OF WORKS [2]

SERVICES

Title	Contents	Form
First Service.	Venite, Te Deum, Benedictus, Kyrie, Creed, Magnificat, Nunc Dimittis.	Full.
Second Service.	Venite, Te Deum, Jubilate, Kyrie, Creed, Magnificat, Nunc Dimittis.	Full.
Third Service.	Te Deum, Jubilate, Magnificat, Nunc Dimittis.	Verse.
Fourth Service.	Te Deum, Magnificat, Nunc Dimittis.	Verse.
Fifth Service.	Te Deum, Jubilate, Magnificat, Nunc Dimittis.	Verse.

A sixth and seventh Service (verse), Magnificat and Nunc Dimittis only, are incomplete.

PRECES AND PSALMODY

Preces.
Responses.
First Litany.
Second Litany (" Common Litany ").
Psalm XV, ' Lord who shall dwell ', for Ascension.
Psalm XLVII, ' O clap your hands ', for Whitsunday.

Psalm Tunes :
Dunfermline.
Martyrs.
Old 113th.
St. David's.
Windsor.
Worcester.
York.

FULL ANTHEMS

Title	Number of Voices [3]	Occasion
' Almighty and everlasting God.'	4	Ash Wednesday.
' Almighty God the fountain of all wisdom.'	5	Collect after the Offertory.
' Arise O Lord and have mercy.'		
' Arise O Lord God lift up thy hand.'	5	
' Arise O Lord into thy resting place.'	5	
' Awake up my glory.'	3	
' Be strong and of good courage.'	7	Coronation of James I.
' Blessed is he that considereth.'	6	
' Blessed is he whose unrighteousness' (Penitential Psalm II).	3	
' Deal with me O Lord.'	3	
' Dear Lord of Life.'		
' From deepest horror of sad penitence.'	6	
' Give ear unto my words ; My voice shalt thou hear.'	4	
' Glory be to the Father.'	3	
' Grant us, gracious Lord, so to eat.'		Communion.
' Great and marvellous.'	5	
' Have mercy.'	5	
' Have mercy upon me O God ' (Penitential Psalm IV).	3	
' He that hath pity on the poor.'	5	
' Hear my prayer O Lord ' (Penitential Psalm V).	3	
' Hear my prayer O Lord ' (Penitential Psalm VII).	3	
' Holy holy holy Lord God ' (Sanctus with Alleluias).	5	
' I am the resurrection ; I heard a voice from heaven.'	4	Burial Service.
' I have gone astray.'	3	
' It is my well-beloved's voice.'	6	Ded. to Dr. Ailmer.
' Lord enter not into judgment.'	5	
' O be favourable unto Sion.'	4	
' O give thanks unto the Lord.'	4	
' O God the proud are risen up ' (first setting).	8	
' O God the proud are risen up ' (second setting).	8 (?)	
' O God wonderful art thou.'	5	
' O how amiable are thy dwellings.'	4	
' O Israel if thou return.'	6	
' O Lord do away as the night.'	3	
' O Lord God of hosts.'	3	
' O Lord how glorious.'	3	
' O Lord how manifold.'	4	

[2] Taken from Denis Stevens's work on the composer (*see* Bibl.).
[3] It is not possible to specify the voices, since all the anthems are written for a high-pitched organ and voice-parts are accordingly notated at a lower pitch than they would actually sound. Thus what Tomkins would call an anthem for A.T.T.B.B. would now be sung by S.A.T.T.B. or even S.S.A.T.B., depending on the choirmaster and the degree of transposition he wished to make.

Title	Number of Voices	Occasion
' O Lord I have loved.'	5	
' O Lord open thou our lips.'	3	
' O Lord rebuke me not ' (Penitential Psalm I).	3	
' O Lord wipe away my sins.'		
' O praise the Lord all ye heathen.'	12	
' O praise the Lord all ye heathen.'	5	
' O pray for the peace of Jerusalem.'	4	
' O sing unto the Lord.'	7	
' Out of the deep have I called ' (Penitential Psalm VI).	3	
' Praise the Lord O my soul.'	4	
' Put me not to rebuke ' (Penitential Psalm III).	3	
' Remember me O Lord.'	4	
' Sadock the priest.'		Coronation of Charles I.
' Set up thyself O God ' (incomplete).	6	
' The heavens declare the glory.'	4	
' The hills stand about Jerusalem.'	3	
' Then David mourned.'	5	
' Thou healest the broken.'	3	
' Turn thou us.'	4	
' Turn unto the Lord.'	6	Ded. to Nathaniel Tomkins.
' When David heard.'	5	Ded. to Thomas Myriell.
' Who shall ascend the hill of God.'	6	
' Whom have I in heaven.'	3	
' Why art thou so full of heaviness.'	5	
' Withdraw not thou thy mercy.'	5	
' Woe is me.'	6	Ded. to John Tomkins.

VERSE ANTHEMS

Title	Solo voices	Occasion
' Above the stars my Saviour dwells.'	A.	
' Almighty and everlasting God.'	S.S.A.	Purification.
' Almighty and everlasting God.'		St. Thomas.
' Almighty God which hast instructed.'	S.A.A.T.B.	
' Almighty God which hast knit together.'	S.S.A.A.T.T.B.B.	All Saints.
' Almighty God who hast given.'	S.S.A.A.T.B.B.	Christmas.
' Almighty God whose praise.'	S.S.A.T.B.	Holy Innocents.
' Behold I bring you glad tidings ; Glory be to God.'	S.	Christmas.
' Behold it is Christ.'	S.S.B.B.	
' Behold the hour cometh.'	S.S.A.T.B.	
' Blessed be the Lord God of Israel.'	S.A.	
' Christ rising again from the dead.'	S.A.T.B.	Easter.
' Come let us go up.'	S.S.A.A.T.B.	
' Death is swallowed up.'		
' Deliver me from mine enemies.'	S.S.A.T.B.B.	
' Give sentence with me, O God.'	B.B.	
' Glory be to God on high.'	S.S.A.B.	
' God who as at this time.'	S.S.A.T.B.	Whitsunday.
' Hear me when I call.'	S.S.A.	
' Hear my prayer O good Lord.'	A.A.	
' Hear my prayer, O Lord.'	B.	
' I will lift up mine eyes ' (' My help cometh ').	A.A.B.	
' Jesus came when the doors were shut.'		
' Know you not.'		Funeral of Prince Henry.
' Leave O my soul.'	S.S.A.B.	
' Merciful Lord we beseech thee.'	S.A.T.B.	
' My beloved spake.'	S.S.B.	
' My dwelling is above.'		
' My shepherd is the living Lord.'	A.A.	
' Not in the merits ' (' Stripped of my merits ').	S.A.B.	
' O Lord God of hosts.'	S.S.A.A.T.B.B.	
' O Lord grant the King a long life.'	S.A.B.	Coronation of Charles I.
' O Lord let me know mine end.'	A.	
' O Lord thou hast dealt.'	S.S.A.B.	
' O pray for the peace of Jerusalem.'	S.S.A.T.B.	
' O that the salvation.'	S.S.B.B.	
' O think upon thy servant.'		
' Out of the deep.'	S.	
' Praise the Lord O my soul.'	S.S.A.B.	
' Praise the Lord O ye servants.'	T.	
' Sing unto God.'	S.B.	
' Stephen being full of the Holy Ghost.'	S.S.A.A.T.B.B.	
' Sweet Saviour.'		
' The Lord bless us.'		
' The Lord even the most mighty.'	A.	
' Thou art my King, O God.'	B.	
' Turn thou us, O good Lord.'	S.S.A.B.	
' Who can tell how oft he offendeth.'	A.	
' Who is this that cometh.'	S.A.A.T.B.	
' Ye people all.'		

SECULAR VOCAL MUSIC

Title	Number of voices	Dedication
' Adieu, ye city-prisoning towers.'	5	William White.
' Cloris, whenas I woo.'	5	Orlando Gibbons.
' Come, shepherds, sing with me.'	5	Nathaniel Giles.
' Fond men that do so highly prize.'	3	Nicholas Tomkins.
' Fusca, in thy starry eyes.'	5	Phineas Fletcher.
' How great delight.'	3	William Cross.
' Love, cease tormenting.'	3	Thomas Day.
' Music divine.'	6	William Heather (Heyther).
' No more will I thy love.'	3	William Walker.
' O let me die for true love.'	4	John Daniel.
' O let me live for true love.'	4	John Dowland.
' Oft did I marle.'	6	John Ward.
' Our hasty life away doth post.'	3	Thomas Tomkins, sen.
' Oyez! has any found a lad ? '	4	John Coperario.
' Phyllis, now cease to move me.'	5	Henry Molle.
' Phyllis, yet see him dying.'	5	Nicholas Carlton.
' See, see, the shepherd's queen.'	5	John Stevens.
' Sure there is no god of love.'	3	Humphrey Withy.
' The fauns and satyrs tripping.'	5	Elizabeth I.
' To the shady woods.'	5	Robert Chetwode.
' Too much I once lamented.'	5	William Byrd.
' Was ever wretch tormented.'	4	Giles Tomkins.
' Weep no more thou sorry boy.'	4	Peregrine Tomkins.
' When I observe.'	6	Thomas Warwick.
' Yet again, as soon revived.'	4	Robert Tomkins.

CONSORT MUSIC

' Alman ' a 4.
14 Fantasies a 3.
Fantasy a 5.
4 Fantasies a 6.

2 ' In nomine ' a 3.
1 Pavan a 4; 9 Pavans a 5.
Pavan and Galliard a 6.
' Ut re mi ' a 4.

KEYBOARD MUSIC

Title	Date	Title	Date
' A Sad Pavan for these dis-tracted times.'	14 Feb. 1649.	Pavan, A mi. (also for strings).	
' A Short Verse.'		Pavan : Lord Canterbury.	1647.
' A Substantial Verse : main-taining the point.'		Pavan & Galliard : Earl Straf-ford (short version).	29 Sept. 1647.
' Barafostus' Dream.'		Pavan & Galliard : Earl Straf-ford.	2 Oct. 1647.
' Bitts or morcells ' (fragments).		Pavan & Galliard.	Apr. & 1 Oct. 1650.
' Clarifica me pater.'	Sept. 1650.		
' Fancy ', G ma.	9 Sept. 1646.	Pavan & Galliard.	4 & 7 Sept. 1654.
' Fancy ', C ma.	8 July 1647.	Pavan & Galliard : of three parts.	
' Fancy ', G ma.	24 Oct. 1648.	Piece of a Prelude.	9 July 1647.
' Fancy ', A mi.		Prelude, G ma.	
' Fancy : for two to play.'		Prelude, A mi.	
' Fancy : for viols.'		' Robin Hood.'	
' Fortune my foe.'	4 July 1654.	' Robin Hood.'	
' Galliard.'		Short Pavan.	
' Go from my window ' (frag-ment).		' The Hunting Galliard.'	
' Ground ', G ma.		' The Lady Folliot's Galliard.'	
' Ground ', D ma.		' The Perpetual Round.'	7-8 Sept. 1654.
' In nomine ' (version 1).	20-28 Jan. 1647.	' Toy : made at Poole Court.'	
' In nomine ' (version 2).	20 Jan. 1647	' Toy : Mr. Church (also ' Almain ').	
	2 Aug. 1650.	' Ut mi re ', G ma.	
' In nomine ', A mi.	May 1648.	' Ut re mi fal sol la : for a beginner.'	
' In nomine ', A mi.	16 June 1648.	' Ut re mi fa sol la ', G ma. (also for strings).	
' In nomine ', A mi.	27 Oct. 1648.	' Ut re mi fa sol la ', G ma.	
' In nomine ', A mi. (version 1).	Feb. 1650.	' Ut re mi fa sol la ', G ma.	
' In nomine ', D mi. (version 2).	14 Feb. 1650.	' Ut re mi fa sol la ', G ma. (fragment).	
' In nomine ', A mi.	28 June 1652.	' Ut re mi fa sol la ', F ma.	30 June 1654.
' Miserere ', G ma.	15 Sept. 1648.	' Verse, of three parts.'	12 Aug. 1650.
' Miserere ', G ma.	7 Oct. 1648.	[Verse i]	
' Miserere ', G ma.	26 May 1651.	[Verse ii]	
' Miserere ', G ma.	3-4 Feb. 1652.	[Verse iii]	
' Miserere ', G ma.		Voluntary in C.	10 Aug.-10 Sept. 1647.
' Miserere ', G ma.			
' Miserere ', G ma.			
' Miserere ', G ma.			
Offertory.	1637.	Voluntary, A mi.	
' On a Plainsong.'		Voluntary, D mi.	
Pavan, G ma.	10 Sept. 1647.	' What if a day.'	
Pavan, G ma.	14 Sept. 1647.	' Worcester Brawls.'	
Pavan, G ma.	20 Aug. 1650.		

497   ii   *Add at end:*
See also Musica Britannica, Vol. 5 (modern ed. of keyboard works).

Add See also from p. 496, col. i.

(6) Robert Tomkins
Cancel entry and replace by:
(6) John Tomkins (*b.* ? ; *d.* ?), ? son of John (1). He was a chorister of Worcester Cathedral in 1611, according to Atkins, p. 45 (*see* BIBL.).

498   i   **(9) Robert Tomkins**
ll. 3-6 *should read:*

He was a composer and viol player, and was appointed musician for the consort in place of Robert Kyndersley on 28 Mar. 1633. Two years later his salary was confirmed as £40 per annum. In 1641 he is named, together with his brother Giles, as one of the musicians for the lutes, viols and voices, but he must have died before the Restoration, because the earliest available list of the new musical establishment of Charles II (dated 1660) states that Robert's place in the broken consort had been taken by Henry Hawes. Organ parts only of three anthems are found in Batten's organ book, and the texts of these, with six further anthems, occur in the Chapel Royal anthem book (B.M., Harl. 6346). His brother inscribed

(12) Giles Tomkins
l. 11 *should read:*

had six children.   E. H. F., adds. D. W. S.

Add to BIBL.:
ROSE, BERNARD, 'Thomas Tomkins' (Proc. Roy. Mus. Ass., Vol. LXXXII, 1955-56).
STEVENS, DENIS, 'Thomas Tomkins: 1572-1656' (London, 1957).

Add before **Tomlinson:**
TÖMLICH, Antoinette. *See* WOLF, ENDRE.

TOMMASINI
Par. 1, l. 2.   1870; *should read:*
1878;

503   i   **TONALITY**
Add to BIBL.:
MACHABEY, ARMAND, 'Genèse de la tonalité musicale des origines au XVe siècle' (Paris, 1955).
RETI, RUDOLPH, 'Tonality, Atonality, Pantonality: a Study of some Trends in Twentieth-Century Music' (London, 1958).

TONE
l. 6.   German or American *should read:*
German-American

513   i   **TORCHI**
Par. 1, l. 1.   Mondano, *should read:*
Mordano,

514   i   **TORELLI**
Par. 2, ll. 2-3 *should read:*
Bologna from 1686 as leader of the church orchestra of San Petronio, but in 1697 accepted the post of

ll. 5-6 *should read:*
denburg-Ansbach, where he remained until 1699.

515   ii   **TORREFRANCA**
Par. 1, l. 3 *should read:*
1 Feb. 1883; *d.* Rome, 26 Nov. 1955).

516   ii   **TORRI**
Add at end:
See also Denkmäler (2) II, Vols. XIX-XX (modern ed.).

TORRINGTON
Par. 1, l. 2.   Staffs., *should read:*
Worcs.,

517   ii   **TOSCANINI**
Par. 1, l. 2 *should read:*
1867; *d.* New York, 16 Jan. 1957).

518   ii   Par. 2, ll. 3-5 *should read:*
but in the same city the National Broadcasting Company Orchestra was formed for him by Rodzinski, and he conducted its concerts for some years.

519   i   Par. 2, l. 14 *should read:*
Slavonic music, apart from Tchaikovsky, he has given scant attention.

ii   BIBL., *Add after* l. 3:
'Toscanini, visto da un critico' (Turin, 1958).

l. 7.   (Milan, 1951) *should read:*
(Milan, 1951); Eng. trans., 'The Magic Baton: Toscanini's Life for Music' (London, 1957).

Add to BIBL.:
CHOTZINOFF, SAMUEL, 'Toscanini: an Intimate Portrait' (New York, 1956).
MARSH, ROBERT C., 'Toscanini and the Art of Orchestral Performance' (London, 1956).

520   ii   *Add before* **Tóth:**
TOTENBERG, Roman (*b.* Łódź, 1 Jan. 1911).
American violinist of Polish birth. He began his studies at the age of seven in Russia, where his father worked as an architect, and from 1921 continued at the Warsaw Conservatory. In 1925-29 he studied the violin

under Michałowicz and composition under Maliszewski at the Chopin School of Music. In 1929 he won a prize to represent Poland abroad, gave concerts in Czechoslovakia and Latvia, and the same year won a State scholarship to continue his studies under Carl Flesch. In 1932 he made his début in Berlin and between 1933 and 1938 settled in Paris, where he studied under Enesco and Monteux while touring in Europe and the Americas. In 1935–36 he joined Szymanowski in performance of the latter's works in France, England and Scandinavia.

In 1936 Totenberg made his début in the U.S.A., where he settled in 1938 and became an American citizen. He makes transcontinental tours of the U.S.A. with a small orchestra, teaches during the summer months and often visits Europe. His playing is characterized by great clarity, deep feeling and unusual power in bowing.   C. R. H.

525   ii   TOWARZYSTWO WYDAW-NICZE
Add at end:

16. Różycki, J. H., 'Magnificemus in cantico', concerto for 2 sopranos, bass and organ.
17. Pękiel, B., 'Missa pulcherrima' for S.A.T.B. *a cappella.*
18. Podbielski, J., 'Praeludium' for organ or harpsichord.
19. Pękiel, B., 2 Latin Carols for S.A.T.B. *a cappella.*
20. Chybiński, A. E., 36 Dances from the Tablature by Jan de Lublin.
21. Jarzębski, A., 'Chromatica', concerto *a* 3 (2 vns., cello and bass).
22. Polak, J., Preludes, Fantasies and Dances for lute.
23. Długoraj, W., Fantasies and Villanellas for lute.
24. Diomedes Cato, Preludes, Fantasies, Dances and Madrigals for lute.
25. Szarzyński, S. S., 'Ave Regina', antiphon for solo voice, 2 vns., *viola di basso* and continuo.
26. Szarzyński, S. S., 'Ad hymnos ad cantus', motets for A.T.B., 2 vns., *viola alta, viola tenore, viola bassa* and organ.
27. Jarzębski, A., 'Bentrovala', concerto for 2 violins, cello & continuo.
28. Wacław of Szamotuły, 'Pieśni' for S.A.T.B. *a cappella.*
29. Mielczewski, M., 'Canzona a 2' for 2 violins, cello & harpsichord.
30. Pękiel, B., 40 Pieces for the lute.
31. Zieleński, M., 'Domus mea', *communio* for S.A.T.B. with organ.
32. Jarzębski, A., 'Sentinella', concerto for 3 violins & harpsichord.
33. Szadek, T., 'Dies est laetitiae', Mass for T.T.B.B. *a cappella.*
34. Bazylik, C., 'Pieśni' for S.A.T.B. *a cappella.*
35. Leopolita, M., 'Missa paschalis' for S.A.T.B. *cappella.*
36. Zienleński, M., 'Exiit sermo inter fratres' & 'Si consurrexistis cum Christo', *communiones* for baritone & organ.   C. R. H.

526   i   TOY SYMPHONY
Par. 1, l. 13 *should read:*

sort of divertimento (actually called 'Cassatio') in G major—by Leopold Mozart.

ii   TOYE, Francis
Par. 1, ll. 1–3 *should read:*

lished.[1] His two most important books

526   ii   Par. 2, l. 7 *should read:*
in 1946. He was created C.B.E. in 1954.

TOYE, Geoffrey
Par. 2, l. 22 *should read:*
Royal Opera, Covent Garden. An opera to a libretto by A. P. Herbert, 'The Red Pen', was broadcast on 7 Feb. 1927. He produced

Par. 3 *should read:*

Early works composed jointly for Boxford by the brothers Toye were the masques 'The Well in the Wood', 'Day and Night' (performed 31 July 1912) and two others.

Footnote should read:
[1] For four early works *see* TOYE, GEOFFREY.

527   i   TRABACI
Signature should read:
J. R. M., adds F. W. (ii).

Add at end:
See also Istituzioni, Vol. 5 (for Pannain's ed.).

528   ii   TRAETTA
Add to BIBL.:
SARACINO, EMANUELE, 'Tommaso Traetta: cenni biografico-artistici' (Bitonto, 1954).
SCHLITZER, FRANCO (ed.), 'Tommaso Traetta, Leonardo Leo, Vincenzo Bellini: notizie e documenti' (Siena, 1952).

529   ii   *Delete* ORCHESTRAL WORK *and entry below it, and replace by:*

An instrumental divertimento, 'Le quattro stagioni e i dodici mesi dell' anno' ('"for 4 orchestras"—which is very unlikely), mentioned in a letter from Catherine II of Russia dated 21–23 Dec. 1770, is not by Traetta.[4]

See also, l. 2 *should read:*
Denkmäler (2) II, Vols. 14 & 17 (modern ed. of selected works). Raupach (H. F., ballet m. for operas by T.).

Footnote 4 should read:
[4] *See* R.-A. Mooser, 'Annales de la musique . . . en Russie', Vol. II, p. 100.

Traherne
l. 2 *should read:*
voice & orch.; 1 song).

530   i   TRANCHELL, CATALOGUE:
Add before BALLETS:
MUSICAL COMEDY
'Zuleika', after Max Beerbohm's 'Zuleika Dobson', prod. Cambridge, 1955.

537   i   TRAUBEL
Par. 1, l. 2.   16 June 1903).
should read:
20 June 1899).

Par. 2, l. 30 *should read:*

country she had visited was Canada. Later that year she left the Metropolitan after a dispute over her wish to sing at supper clubs, and she made her first appearance at such a club at Chicago on 11 Sept. She has

537   ii   TRAUTONIUM
l. 2 *should read*:

strument invented by Friedrich Trautwein (1888–1957) of

538   ii   *Add before* TREE:

TREBOR, ? Robert (*b.* ? ; *d.* ?). French 14th-century composer. He has been identified with Trebol, a minstrel who was in the service of Martin I of Aragon as late as 1409, but it is not certain that this identification can be maintained. The fact is that the name Trebor is attached to six Ballades in the Chantilly MS 1047, while the anagram Borlet (= Trebol) is at the head of a single Virelai with a folksong in the tenor. It is possible that the scribe made a mistake and wrote " r " for " l ", but it is also possible that Trebor is an inverted form of Robert, for the same manuscript has S. Uciredor for Rodericus. In any case Trebor was connected with the Aragon court, for two Ballades are written for Gaston Phébus, Count of Foix, and two for John I, King of Aragon. Another work refers to a wedding at Avignon, which has been tentatively identified with that of John, Duc de Berry, to Jeanne de Boulogne, sponsored by Gaston Phébus in 1389. Three Roberts may be considered as identical with the composer Trebor, namely Robert Nyot, a singer at the papal court at Avignon in 1394, Robertus de Palato, secretary to John, King of Bohemia, in 1335, and Robertus Dunathoy, expert in grammar and music, and chaplain to Guy de Boulogne, uncle of the future Clement VII, during the years 1362–66. One of Trebor's compositions refers to the coming Sardinian campaign of John I of Aragon, hence may be dated from *c.* 1388. All Trebor's Ballades are for three voices, *i.e. cantus* with text and *tenor* and *contratenor* without. They may be compared with the works of Solage with regard to the use of rhythmic motifs and syncopation. Trebor is perhaps more modern in taking up new note-forms like ♩ and ♪, while he also frequently writes duplets against prevailing triple values.

Trebor's complete works are transcribed in W. Apel, ' French Secular Music of the Late Fourteenth Century ' (1950), which also includes a Virelai by Borlet.

G. R. (iii).

BIBL.—REANEY, GILBERT, ' The Manuscript Chantilly, Musée Condé 1947 ' (' Musica Disciplina ', VIII, 1954).

541   i   TREND
Par. 1, l. 2 *should read*:

Southampton, 17 Dec. 1887; *d.* Cambridge, 20 Apr. 1958).

544   i   TRIANGLE
Add at end

PLATE 49, Vol. VI, p. 622, No. 3.

551   i   *Add before* TROIS FERMIERS:

TROILUS AND CRESSIDA. Opera in 3 acts by Walton. Libretto by Christopher Hassall, based on Chaucer's poem. Produced London, Covent Garden Theatre, 3 Dec. 1954. 1st perf. abroad, San Francisco, 7 Oct. 1955.

559   ii   TROUBADOURS
Add to BIBL.:

FLEMING, JOHN ARNOLD, ' The Troubadours of Provence ' (Glasgow, 1952).
HOEPFFNER, ERNEST, ' Les Troubadours dans leur vie et dans leurs œuvres ' (Paris, 1955).
OLIVIER, JOSEPH, ' Musique et rythme traditionnels des troubadours: le tambourin provençal ' (Saint-Rémy de Provence, 1954).

560   i   TROUTBECK
Par. 3, l. 10 *should read*:

Hymn Book '.

571   i   TRUMPET
Table, l. 2, major sixth *should read*:

minor sixth

     ii   *Add at end*

PLATES 32, Vol. IV, p. 492, No. 8; 34, Vol. IV, p. 500, No. 7.

573   i   TRUMPET MARINE
Par. 4, l. 17 *should read*:

by Praetorius and in Ephraim Chambers's ' Cyclopaedia ' (London, 1728), from which the description was lifted by Grassineau. The triangular

574   i   Par. 3, l. 17.   p. 146 *should read*:
p. 146 (i)

581   ii   Tuchev
ll. 1-2. (13 songs) *should read*:
(15 songs).

585   ii   TUNDER
See also. l. 1 *should read*:

See also Buxtehude (son-in-law). Denkmäler (2), Vol. III (modern ed. of solo cantatas and choral works). Doppio Pedale (early

601   i   TUNSTED
Par. 2, l. 1 *should read*:

Although not certainly by Tunsted, ' De quatuor principalibus ' treats of

TUOTILO
Par. 1. Dates *should read*:

(*b.* ? ; *d.* St. Gall, 27 Apr. 915).

Par. 2, l. 1 *should read*:

? Swiss musical scholar.

601 ii **TURCHI**
Par. 3, l. 10 *should read*:

breve' for string quartet (1947), 'Preludi e fughette' for pianoforte and 'Due poesie di Salvatore Quasimodo' for voice and pianoforte, Five Comments

TURCZYŃSKI
Par. 1, l. 2. 1889). *should read*:
1884; *d.* Lausanne, 27 Dec. 1953).

602 ii *Add before* **Turgenev**:
TURECK, Rosalyn (*b.* Chicago, 14 Dec. 1914).
American pianist. She made her début at the age of nine with two recitals, and at eleven played with the Chicago Symphony Orchestra. In 1928 she won the first prize in the Greater Chicago Piano Playing Tournament among 15,000 children; in 1929 she gave her first two all-Bach recitals in Chicago, the following year she entered the Juilliard Graduate School in New York with a four-years' fellowship, and she graduated there *cum laude* in 1936. The next year she gave her first series of six all-Bach concerts at New York Town Hall, and there and elsewhere in New York she continued these series almost annually from 1944. Her first European tour took place in 1947; it included Scandinavia and London (B.B.C. 3rd programme). Similar tours followed annually in 1953–56, gradually extending to Ireland, Scotland (Edinburgh Festivals 1955–56), France, Holland, Germany, Switzerland and Italy (Venice Biennale 1956). As a teacher she is on the faculties of the Juilliard School and Columbia University in New York.

Rosalyn Tureck specializes, though by no means exclusively, in Bach, whose keyboard works she plays on the pianoforte, anachronistically but with an insight, authority and perfection that amount to a very distinctive and convincing style of her own.

E. B.

605 i **TURINA**
Par. 2, l. 10. Mozskowski *should read*:
Moszkowski

607 i CATALOGUE
PIANOFORTE SOLO
Op. 55. Set II *should read*:
Set I

608 i **TURINI**
Add at end:
See also Classici Musica Italiana, Vol. 33 (modern ed. of sonatas).

TURK
Par. 1, l. 7. Burney *should read*:
two friends

608 ii **TÜRK**
Par. 2, l. 17 *should read*:
(1782) — were popular. A modern facsimile reprint of the 'Clavierschule' is to be published in 'Documenta Musicologica', Vol. 30.

613 ii *Add after* **TURN**:
TURN OF THE SCREW, THE. Opera in 2 acts, with a prologue, by Britten. Libretto by Myfanwy Piper, based on Henry James's story. Produced Venice, Teatro La Fenice, 14 Sept. 1954. 1st perf. in England, London, Sadler's Wells Theatre, 6 Oct. 1954.

TURNER, Eva
Par. 1, l. 2. Mar. 1898). *should read*:
Mar. 1892).

614 i l. 31 *should read*:
arias from Weber's operas. On her retirement from the stage she settled in the U.S.A. She teaches at Norman, Oklahoma.

616 ii **TURSKI**
Par. 1, l. 1. **Żbigniew** *should read*:
Zbigniew

Add after **TUT**
Tutchev, Feodor Ivanovich. *See* Tuchev.

617 i **TUXEN**
Par. 1, l. 1. 1902). *should read*:
1902; *d.* Copenhagen, 28 Aug. 1957).

ii *Add before* **TVISØNGUR**:
TVEITT, (Nils) Geirr (*b.* Kvam, 19 Oct. 1908).
Norwegian pianist and composer. He studied at the Leipzig Conservatory and in Paris and Vienna. As a composer he has been greatly influenced by Norwegian folk music. Among his works are four operas (to his own librettos), music for several ballets ('Baldurs draumar', 'Birgingu'), three symphonies and various other orchestral works ('Hundrad Hardingtonar'), five pianoforte concertos, a violin Concerto, chamber music, *c.* 50 pianoforte sonatas and a large number of songs. D. S.-E.

622 ii **TWELVE-NOTE MUSIC**
Par. 1, l. 1 *should read*:
of the use of the series in canon forms. The first movement of his

623 ii *Add to* BIBL. :

' Die Reihe : Information über serielle Musik ', ed. by Herbert Eimert (Vienna, Zürich & London, 1955, in progress).
JELINEK, HANNS, ' Anleitung zur Zwölftonkomposition ', Vol. I (Vienna, 1954).

After l. 10 *add* (2nd book by Hauer):

' Kardinalsätze zur Zwölftontechnik ' (' Plan ', Oct. 1945).

KELLY, ROBERT, ' Theme and Variations : a Study of Linear Twelve Tone Composition ' (Dubuaue, Iowa, 1958).

l. 14. *Delete author's name*, KŘENEK, ERNST.

Add to BIBL. :

KŘENEK, ERNST, ' Is Twelve-Tone Technique on the Decline? ' (M.Q., XXXIX, Oct. 1953).

624 i

NEIGHBOUR, OLIVER, ' The Evolution of Twelve-Note Music ' (Proc. Roy. Mus. Ass., Vol. LXXXI, 1954–55).

Add 2nd work by Perle :

' The Harmonic Problem in Twelve-Note Music ' (M. Rev., XV, 1954, p. 257).

PFROGNER, HERMANN, ' Die Zwölfordnung der Töne ' (Zürich, 1953).
ROGNONI, LUIGI, ' Espressionismo e dodecafonia ' (Milan, 1954).

l. 12 *should read* :

(Berlin, 1952) ; Eng. trans. as ' Composition with Twelve Notes related only to one another ' by Humphrey Searle (London, 1954).

STADLEN, PETER, ' Serialism Reconsidered ' (' The Score ', No. 22, Feb. 1958).
VLAD, ROMAN, ' Storia della dodecafonia ' (Milan, 1958).

See also should read :

See also Panchromaticism. Serial Composition.

627 ii *Add before* **Tyl** :

TYES, John (*b.* ? ; *d.* ?).
English 14th–15th-century organist and composer. He may be identical with the John Dynes who was organist of Winchester in 1402. Two of his works are to be found in the ' Old Hall Manuscript ' : a ' Gloria ' and a ' Sanctus '. The ' Gloria ' (I, 50) is a three-part isorhythmic composition for two alto voices (which declaim the text in alternation) and one instrument. The four voices required for the ' Sanctus ' (III, 94) are two altos and two tenors, and although the *conductus* principle is used to a certain extent, there is considerable freedom in the individual parts and occasional reduction to three-part texture in faburden style. The *cantus firmus*, in the lowest part, is based on Sarum 5. D. W. S.

BIBL.—BUKOFZER, MANFRED, ' Studies in Medieval and Renaissance Music ' (New York, 1950).
HUGHES, DOM ANSELM, ' Music in the Chapel of Henry VI ' (Proc. Mus. Ass., Vol. LX, 1933).
RAMSBOTHAM, ALEXANDER, ed., ' The Old Hall Manuscript ', Vols. I & III (London, 1933 & 1938).

628 i **Tynan**
ll. 1-2. *Delete* Rubbra (song).

628 i *Add after* **TYPOPHONE**

TYPP, W. (*b.* ? ; *d.* ?).
English 14th–15th-century singer and composer. Seven of his works are preserved in the ' Old Hall Manuscript ' : two settings of ' Credo ', four of ' Sanctus ' and one of ' Agnus Dei '. The first ' Credo ' (II, 44) is a simple *conductus*-style setting, with the plainsong of the first Sarum Credo shared between middle and treble voices. The other (II, 224) is more complex altogether. It is set for alto, tenor and one instrument, which plays the antiphon to the third Psalm at Lauds on Sundays, " Benedicam te Domine in vita mea ", in isorhythmic form. The text is shared between the two voice parts, which are active simultaneously for most of the time.

The four ' Sanctus ' settings are all for three voices, in *conductus* style. The first (III, 4) disperses the plainsong, Sarum 1, throughout all voices ; the second (III, 12) makes use of the same technique, this time with Sarum 2, which threads its way through middle and tenor voices. The last two settings (III, 30 ; III, 38) have the plainsong—Sarum 6 and 10 respectively—in the middle voice. The same clefs are used for the ' Sanctus ' (III, 30) and the ' Agnus Dei ' (III, 122), which again has the plainsong in the middle voice. They might therefore have been sung as a pair. D. W. S.

BIBL.—BUKOFZER, MANFRED, ' Studies in Medieval and Renaissance Music ' (New York, 1950).
RAMSBOTHAM, ALEXANDER, ed., ' The Old Hall Manuscript ', Vols. II & III (London, 1935 & 1938).

629 ii **UCCELLINI**
Par. 1. Dates *should read* :

(*b.* Forlimpopoli, ? 1603 ; *d.* ? Parma, 10 Sept. 1680).

630 i *Add at end* :

BIBL.—RONCAGLIA, GINO, ' La cappella musicale del duomo di Modena ' (Florence, 1957).

632 i *Add after* **Udall** :

UDBYE, Martin Andreas (*b.* Trondhjem, 18 June 1820 ; *d.* Trondhjem, 10 Jan. 1889).
Norwegian organist and composer. He studied at the Leipzig Conservatory under Hauptmann and Becker, and became organist at Trondhjem Hospital Church, previously the Church of Our Lady. His opera, ' Fredkulla ', which is regarded as the first Norwegian opera without spoken dialogue, was about to have its first performance when the Christiania theatre when the building was burnt down in 1877. Among Udbye's works are incidental music for several plays, cantatas and other works for chorus and orchestra (' Aasgaardsreien '), chamber music, etc.

D. S.-E.

632　ii　**UGOLINI**
Par. 1, l. 2. Nassini *should read*:
Nanini

Add before **UHL**:

UHDE, Hermann (*b*. Bremen, 1914).
German bass-baritone singer. He is the
son of a German father and an American
mother. At the age of eighteen he began to
study singing at Bremen and in 1936 he made
his operatic début there in small parts, but
during his two years there quickly advanced
to more important bass parts. In 1938–40 he
was at Freiburg i/B. and in 1940–42 at Munich,
still as a bass. He then decided to undergo
further training as a baritone and went to
the Opera at The Hague, where he appeared
in such parts as Don Juan, Escamillo and
Scarpia. After serving in the German army
during the second world war and being taken
prisoner by the Americans in France, he
returned home in 1947, sang at the Hanover
Opera in 1948 and at Hamburg and the
Vienna State Opera before 1951, when he
rejoined the Munich Opera. Apart from this
standing engagement he frequently makes
guest appearances, as for instance at Salzburg
in Orff's 'Antigone' (1949) and Britten's
'Rape of Lucretia' (1950), at the Bayreuth
Festivals of 1951–53, at Milan, Rome, Naples
and Trieste, and in 1953 in London, at Covent
Garden as Mandryka in Strauss's 'Arabella'
with the Munich company and as Telramund
in 'Lohengrin' in English with the resident
company.　　　　　　　　　　　E. B.

633　i　**Ühland**
l. 10 *should read*:

281; 307-8, songs). Loewe (15 songs). Mahler (?
'Herzog Ernst von Schwaben', opera). Mendelssohn

UILLEANN PIPES
l. 2 *should read*:
Union Pipes. *See* FOLK MUSIC: IRISH, p. 297,
col. ii.

637　i　**UNGER, Hermann**
Par. 1, l. 2 *should read*:
26 Oct. 1886; *d*. Cologne, 31 Dec. 1958).

ii　*Add at end, before signature*:
At the time of his death Unger was head
librarian at the High School of Music of
Cologne, where he had also been acting
Director at various times.

638　ii　**UNION PIPES** *should read*:
UNION PIPES (not **Uilleann Pipes**).
See FOLK MUSIC: IRISH, p. 297, col. ii.

Add reference:
PLATE 2, Vol. I, p. 352, No. 7.

638　ii　**UNIVERSAL EDITION**
Cancel entry and replace by:

UNIVERSAL EDITION. A firm of music
publishers founded in Vienna in 1901. It
rapidly expanded, taking over a large number
of smaller publishing concerns, the most important being that of Josef Aibl of Munich.
It very rapidly reached the front rank of
European publishing houses. Apart from
issuing a very large number of classical
editions, it brought out during the years before
the first world war works by Bruckner, Mahler,
Reger and Richard Strauss.

Under its enterprising director, Emil
Hertzka, Universal Edition was from its
beginning greatly concerned with the younger
generation of composers. It publishes the
works by Berg, Schoenberg and Webern, Bartók and Kodály, Delius and Ethel Smyth, Casella, Janáček, Křenek, Malipiero, Milhaud,
Szymanowski, etc.; also the complete works
by Monteverdi (in 16 volumes) edited by
G. F. Malipiero.

Periodical magazines before the second
world war were 'Der Anbruch' and 'Pult
und Taktstock'. A number of books on
music, such as the 'Urlinie' and other works
by Heinrich Schenker, were also brought out.

During the 1939–45 war activities were
severely limited by the Nazis, but after the
war Universal Edition quickly recovered.
Apart from the Vienna company, sister concerns undertaking their own publishing
activities have been established in London
and Zürich. All three companies are especially interested in pioneer work for modern
music, and they have built up an international catalogue of many of the leading
composers, such as Martin, Martinů, Dallapiccola, Skalkottas, Liebermann, Peragallo,
Einem, Tansman, Boulez, Stockhausen, etc.
Recent developments in serial music are
specially dealt with in the magazine 'Die
Reihe', started in 1955 and published at
irregular intervals, of which an English
version is in preparation. Universal Edition
also publishes the Philharmonia pocket score
containing many classical and contemporary
works. 'The Symphonies of Joseph Haydn'
by H. C. Robbins Landon was published by
the London house in 1955. Since the re-
establishment Universal Edition has been
under the direction of Dr. Alfred A. Kalmus,
Alfred Schlee and Ernst Hartmann.
　　　　　　　　　　　　　　　E. B.

639　ii　**UPPSALA**
See also. l. 2 *should read*:
Libraries (p. 205, for University Library). Moberg.
Svensson. Vallerius.

641　ii　**URIBE HOLGUÍN**
Par. 2, l. 11. sentimento *should read*:
sentimento

642   ii   **URIO**
Par. 2, l. 4 *should read*:
(Bergedorf, 1871), later withdrawn from that series and added as an appendix to his collected Handel edition. It has been examined

646   i   **UTENTHAL**
Add at end:
See also Chorwerk, Vol. 30 (modern reprint of motet).

650   i   **VAET**
Add at end:
See also Chorwerk, Vol. 2 (modern reprint of motets). Collectio O.M.B., Vols 2, 4, 5, & 9 (modern ed.).

Add after **VAGANS**:

VAILLANT, Johannes (*b.* ? ; *d.* ?).
French 14th-century composer and theorist. He kept a music school in Paris. A Jewish treatise on counterpoint has been preserved which apparently originates in Vaillant's teaching *via* a Jewish teacher at the Sorbonne. Five compositions occur in a Chantilly manuscript, one dated Paris, 1369. Three pieces are rondeaux, one a virelai and one a ballade. A rondeau with three different texts sung simultaneously exchanges long stretches of melody between the parts, while an isorhythmic rondeau for only two voices has a text which may have been sung by Vaillant's pupils: 'Pour ce que je ne sai gaires, sui je venus pur aprendre'. The virelai is a typical 14th-century spring song, introducing birdcalls, and it was so popular that sacred texts were set to it and Oswald von Wolkenstein arranged it to suit German taste in a 2-part version with the words 'Der may mit lieber zal'.
The tritextual rondeau and the virelai are transcribed in W. Apel's 'French Secular Music of the Late Fourteenth Century' (1950).   G. R. (iii).

ii   *Add before* **VALCARCEL**:

VALABREGA, Cesare (*b.* Novara, 27 Dec. 1898).
Italian pianist, critic and musicologist. He took the master diploma in pianoforte playing at the Conservatory of Pesaro in 1915 and the *Laurea in Lettere* at Bologna University in 1921. A career as concert pianist, lecturer and critic in Italy and other countries in Europe and beyond brought him the appointments of professor of musical history at the Conservatorio S. Pietro a Maiella at Naples and of lecturer on old Italian music for the Corsi di Alta Cultura at the Università per Stranieri of Perugia. He is also musical commentator for Radio Roma, where by 1956 he had introduced more than seven hundred broadcasts of symphonic and chamber music. In Rome he founded the Associazione Romana

2 G

'Concerti Storici'. He is a contributor to the principal Italian newspapers and reviews, to the 'Enciclopedia Ricordi', the 'Enciclopedia Italiana' and Larousse. In 1957 the Discoteca di Stato began to issue under his editorship a 'Storia della musica italiana' on 40 long-playing records. In 1958 the President of the Italian Republic bestowed on him the silver medal " Ai Benemeriti della Cultura e dell' Arte ". His publications include:
'Schumann: arte e natura; arte e vita; arte e fede' (1934, 3rd ed. 1956).
'Domenico Scarlatti: il suo secolo, la sua opera' (1937, 2nd ed. 1955).
'Il piccolo dizionario musicale per tutti' (1949, 2nd ed. 1952).
'Johann Sebastian Bach' (1950).
'Adolfo Gandino: musicista bolognese' (1950).
'La lirica di camera di Vincenzo Davico' (1953).   E. B.

650   ii   **VALCARCEL**
Par. 1, l. 2.   1943). *should read*: 1942).

651   ii   **VALEN,** CATALOGUE
'Vaagn   CHORAL WORKS
Op. 27. 'Vaan *should read*:

ORCHESTRAL WORKS
Op. 20 *should read*:
20. 'Le Cimetière marin' (after Paul Valéry) (1934).

Op. 21. title *should read*:
'La Isla de la Calmas'

SOPRANO AND ORCHESTRA
chinesische   *Op.* 8. chineisches *should read*:

VALENCIA
Par. 1, l. 2 *should read*:
Nov. 1904; *d.* Cali, 22 July 1952).

655   ii   **VALERIUS**
See also *should read*:
See also Amsterdam. Vereniging, Vol. 2 (reprints from lute-book).

Valéry
l. 5 *should read*:
bas (song). Valen (' Cimetière marin' for orch.).

656   i   **VALLAS**
Par. 1, l. 2 *should read*:
1879; *d.* Lyons, 9 May 1956).

657   i   **VALLERIUS**
Add at end, before BIBL. :
Many Polish musicologists, among them Opieński and Simon, give the name of the author of 'De tactu musico' as Wallerius-Retzelius.   C. R. H.

Add after **VALLET**:

VALLETTI, Cesare (*b.* Rome, 18 Dec. 1922).
Italian tenor singer. After studying privately he made his début at Bari in 1947 as Alfredo in 'La Traviata'. Soon he was

singing all over Italy. In 1950 he visited London with La Scala Company to sing Fenton in ' Falstaff ' and sang at La Scala for the next few years as Nemorino, Almaviva, Filipetto (' Quattro rusteghi '), Lindoro (' L' Italiana in Algeri ') and other *tenore di grazia* parts. Since 1953–54 he has sung regularly at the Metropolitan, New York, where he has been especially admired as Don Ottavio (which he has sung at Salzburg), Des Grieux, Ferrando (' Così fan tutte ') and Ernesto. He returned to Covent Garden in 1953 to sing Alfredo opposite Callas. Valletti does not possess a large voice, but he sings with a style and elegance rare among Italian tenors, and is probably the nearest approach to-day to Tito Schipa.

H. D. R.

667 ii **VAMP-HORN**
ll. 6-10 *should read*:

notices. It was made of tin and varied from 2 ft. to 6 ft. in length. There is a specimen in the Lincoln Museum, formerly in the church at Potter Hanworth (Lincs.). Others are in the following churches:

> Ashurst (Sussex)
> Braybrook (Northants)
> Charing (Kent)
> East Leake (Notts)
> Harrington (Northants)
> Haversham (Bucks)
> Willoughton (Lincs)

It seems likely that vamp-horns were originally used at sea [1], since the extant specimens correspond closely to the model described and illustrated by Sir Samuel Morland in his ' The Tuba-Stentoro-Phonica: an Instrument of Excellent Use as well at Sea, as at Land, invented in the year 1670 and humbly presented to the King's Most Excellent Majesty in 1671 '. Morland had conducted experiments with the king. Using one of his trumpets, he spoke to the king who was standing at one end of the Mall while he was at the other (a distance of 850 yards). The king heard him " clearly and articulately ", and was so impressed that he commanded three of the largest size to be delivered to Deal Castle, where they were used for issuing orders to ships at sea. At Willoughton there is a tradition that the trumpet was " left in the village by an old sea captain ".

A handsome French speaking-trumpet (1738), made by Jacques Vincent and engraved with the arms of Molinier de Puydieu, is in the Victoria and Albert Museum (Room 84) in London. It is essentially the same as an English vamp-horn.

F. W. G., adds. S. G. (ii).

BIBL.—GODMAN, STANLEY, ' Trumpets as Loudspeakers ' (' Country Life ', 11 Dec. 1958).

[1] A. F. Kollmann makes a reference to a speaking-trumpet in his descriptive piece ' The Shipwreck of the Halsewell ' (*see* KOLLMANN [1]).

669 i **VAŇHAL**
Add at end:

See also Sondheimer Ed., Vol. 29 (modern ed. of Symphony).

VANNEO
Par. 2, l. 3 *should read*:

Ascoli. His didactic treatise on music, ' Recanetum de musica aurea ' [1], ranks

Add footnote:

[1] A modern facsimile reprint is to be published in ' Documenta Musicologica ', Vol. 31.

VANZO
Par. 1, l. 2.   17 Dec. *should read*: 13 Dec.

ii **VARÈSE**
Par. 1, l. 1.   **Edgar** *should read*:

Edgard [1]

Add footnote:
[1] Changed from Edgar in 1942.

670 i List of Works:
l. 4. ' Ironisation ' *should read*:
' Ionization '

Add at end:
' Density 21.5 ' for solo flute.

Add to BIBL.:
WILKINSON, MARC, ' An Introduction to the Music of Edgar Varèse ' (' The Score ', No. 19, Mar. 1957, p. 5).

685 ii **VARIATIONS**
Omit repeat signs in 2nd musical example.

687 ii *Add to* BIBL. (2nd work by FISCHER):
' Die Variation ' (' Das Musikwerk ' series) (Cologne, 1956).

VARLAMOV
Par. 1, l. 1.   **Igorovich** *should read*:
Egorovich

l. 3. Oct. 1848). *should read*:
27 Oct. 1848).

688 i **VARNEY, Louis**
Par. 1, l. 1. New Orleans, 1844; *should read*:
New Orleans, 30 May 1844;

689 ii **VASSILENKO**
Par. 1, l. 2 *should read*:
Moscow, 30 Mar. 1872; *d.* Moscow, 11 Mar. 1956).

691 i **VATERLÄNDISCHER KÜNSTLERVEREIN**
Par. 2, ll. 6-7 *should read*:
since Karl Czerny's variation is dated as early as 7 May 1819 and Schubert's contribution to the set Mar. 1821. No fewer than

ii *Footnote 5. l. 3 should read*:
in *op. cit.* (1st ed.), and the article in the 'Beethoven Jahrbuch' for 1908 mentioned in footnote 1, p. 682, shows conclusively that these were two different men.

'The First Nowell', a Nativity play (with Roy Douglas).	Simona Pakenham.	1958.

692 ii **VAUCORBEIL**
Par. 1, l. 19 *should read*:
16 July 1879; but he died before his contract had expired.

695 i **VAUGHAN WILLIAMS**
Par. 1, l. 2. 1872). *should read*:
1872; *d.* London, 26 Aug. 1958).

'The Mayor of Casterbridge.'	

'The Dim Little Island.'	1949.

Par. 2, l. 3. Charterhouse in London *should read*:
Charterhouse School

700 ii *After last line add* (3rd work by Howes):
'The Music of Ralph Vaughan Williams' (Oxford, 1954).

'Epithalamion', cantata founded on the Masque 'The Bridal Day' for baritone, chorus & small orch.	Ursula Wood, after Spenser.	1953.

701 i *Add to* BIBL. (2nd work by Kimmel):
'Vaughan Williams's Melodic Style' (M.Q., Oct. 1941).
PAKENHAM, SIMONA, 'Ralph Vaughan Williams: a Discovery of his Music' (London, 1957).
PAYNE, ELSIE, 'Vaughan Williams and Folksong' (M. Rev., XV, 1954, p. 103).

CATALOGUE
OPERAS
Heading, OPERAS *should read*:
STAGE WORKS

Add at end of this section:

	1958.	London, Drury Lane Theatre, 19 Dec. 1958.

BALLETS
Heading *should read*:
BALLETS AND MASQUES

Col. 1, l. 6. (MS). *should read*:
and singing.

Col. 3, l. 10. — *should read*:
B.B.C. Television, 1953.

INCIDENTAL MUSIC
Add at end:

Dramatic version of Thomas Hardy's novel.	Bristol 1957.

FILM MUSIC
Add at end:

CHORAL WORKS WITH ORCHESTRA
Col. 1, l. 16 *should read*:
'Magnificat' for soprano, contralto, women's

Add at end:

Add before PARTSONGS:

CHORUS AND ORGAN

Title	Words	Voices	Composed or published
'The Pilgrim Pavement.'	Margaret Ridgeley Partridge.	Soprano, S.A.T.B.	
Motet: 'A Vision of Aeroplanes'.	From Ezekiel.	S.A.T.B.	1956.

704 — ORCHESTRAL WORKS
Col. 4, l. 4. London, 1910 *should read*:
Gloucester, Three Choirs Festival, 1910.

705 — *Add at end*:

Symphony No. 8, D mi.	1955–56.		Manchester, 2 May 1956.
Symphony No. 9, E mi.	1957.	Royal Philharmonic Society.	London, 2 Apr. 1958.

SOLO INSTRUMENTS AND ORCHESTRA
Add at end:

Concerto for bass tuba.	1954.	London, 13 June 1954.

706 — *Add before* PIANOFORTE SOLO :

VIOLIN AND PIANOFORTE

Title	Composed
'Romance and Pastorale.' Sonata, A mi.	1952.

708 — SONGS, *top of page* :
alter 9 Housman Songs *as follows* :
'Along the Field', 8 songs for voice & vn.
A. E. Housman. Publ. 1954.
1.
2. } (as before).
3.
4. Good-bye.
5. In the morning.
6. The sigh that heaves the grasses.
7. Fancy's knell.
8. With rue my heart is laden.

711 ii *Add before* VEALE :

VAVAYANNIS, Theodore (*b.* Philiatra, 22 Mar. 1905).
Greek conductor. He studied harmony and counterpoint at the Athens Conservatory under Economidis and Butnikov, and orchestral conducting under Mitropoulos. After conducting at the Royal Theatre in 1935–36 and for the Athens Radio from 1938, he was appointed in 1942 permanent conductor of the Athens State Orchestra, taking over its general directorship after the death of Economidis on 10 Dec. 1957. He has appeared as conductor in Berlin, Geneva, Monte Carlo, Paris, Stuttgart, Washington and other musical centres. S. M.

713 i **VECCHI, Orazio**
Par. 4, l. 2. Eitner in ' Die Oper ' *should read* :
Eitner in ' Publikationen der Gesellschaft für Musikforschung ', Vol. XXX.

ii *Add to* BIBL. :
' Orazio Vecchi : contributi di studio nel 4⁰ centenario de la nascita ' (Accad. di Sc., Lett. e Arti, Modena, 1950).
' Relazione su le manifestazioni che ebbero luogo in Modena negli anni 1949 e 1950 ' (Modena, 1951).
RONCAGLIA, GINO, ' La cappella musicale del duomo di Modena ' (Florence, 1957).
' Il luogo e la data di nascita di Orazio Vecchi ' (Rass. Mus., Apr. 1929).

716 ii **VELUT**
Par. 2, ll. 2-6 *should read* :
Manuscript compositions of his are preserved at Bologna (a Gloria, a Credo and a motet, the last also at Trent) and in the Bodleian Library, Oxford (4 songs and a motet). One of the songs, ' Je voel servir ', has been republished in score by Stainer. His extant work is published in Vol. II of ' Early Fifteenth-Century Music ', edited by Gilbert Reaney (Amer. Inst. of Musicology, 1960).
E. V. D. S., adds.

719 i **VENICE**
Par. 3, l. 18. Marcantonio Cesti *should read* :
Pietro Antonio Cesti

720 i Par. 2, l. 16. Nando Ballo *should read* :
Ferdinando Ballo

Add to BIBL. (2nd work by Worsthorne) :
' Venetian Opera in the Seventeenth Century ' (Oxford, 1954).

721 i **VENTO, I. de**
Add at end :
See also Chorwerk, Vol. 30 (modern reprint of motet).

723 i **VERACINI**
Add at end :
See also Classici Musica Italiana, Vol. 34 (modern ed. of sonatas).

VERBRUGGHEN
Par. 1, l. 2 *should read* :
Brussels, 1 Aug. 1873 ; *d.* Northfield, Minnesota, 12 Nov.

727 i **VERCORE**
Par. 5, l. 7. Hermannus Cú *should read* :
Hermannus Cū

731 ii **VERDI**
Par. 3, l. 4. momentary false relations *should read* :
semitonal clashes

736 i Par. 3, ll. 1-4 *should read* :
The final transference from the Palazzo Orlandi [1] at Busseto to the new home at Sant' Agata took place in the spring of 1851, although the earliest letter actually headed " Sant'

Add footnote :
[1] So called to-day, from its present owners. It was originally the Palazzo Dordoni. Verdi bought it in 1845 from Contardo Cavalli and refers to it in his accounts as " Palazzo ex-Cavalli."

737 — Heading *should read* :
VERDI : ' Traviata '—1853–1855

ii Par. 1, ll. 2-4 *should read* :
had a past : she had had two illegitimate children. It is the tone of

Par. 5, ll. 15-16 *should read* :
occupied the composer's mind since 1843 ; in 1850 he had discussed it with Cammarano ;

739 i Par. 2, ll. 1-3 *should read*:
On 29 Aug. 1859 Verdi and Giuseppina were married by the

ii Par. 1, l. 1. parliament for Busseto. *should read*
parliament for Borgo San Donnino (the modern Fidenza).

Par. 3, l. 7. *vivandière, should read*:
gypsy girl,

740 ii Par. 1, ll. 46-47 *should read*:
the final duet has been considered an un-

ll. 50-52 *should read*:
1866 and appears in the original (French) vocal score. The *marziale* section is rather

742 i Par. 1, l. 38 *should read*:
her confessor, Don Francesco Montebruno:

Par. 6, l. 2 *should read*:
Monsignor Salvatore Magnasco, Archbishop of Genoa from 1871 to 1892, concerns Verdi's atti-

ii Par. 1, l. 5. Collanges *should read*:
Collonges

Par. 2, l. 7 *should read*:
' Stabat Mater' was a good Catholic.[1]

Add footnote:
[1] Since this was written the contributor of this article has discovered that the letters here quoted are pious forgeries. The problems connected with the relations between Verdi and Stolz, as well as the question of Verdi's attitude towards religion, will have to be reconsidered, but for various reasons this cannot be done before this Supplement is due to go to press.

743 i Par. 2, l. 12. of Boito own *should read*:
of Boito's own

744 ii *Add to* BIBL.:
BARBLAN, GUGLIELMO, 'Un prezioso spartito del "Falstaff"' (Milan, 1957).

l. 12 *should read*:
p. 329, and in 'Classics: Major and Minor' (London, 1958).

Add to BIBL. (Cenzato):
(2nd ed., Milan, 1955).

l. 56. rev. 1951). *should read*:
rev. 1951; abridged Eng. trans. by Elisabeth Abbott (London, 1954).

745 i l. 15. (Milan, 1951). *should read*:
(Milan, 1898).

l. 23. 2nd ed. 1951).[1] *should read*:
2nd ed., Milan, 1951).[1]

745 ii BIBL. *Delete* ll. 16-17.

Add to BIBL.:
YBARRA, THOMAS RUSSELL, 'Verdi: Miracle Man of Opera' (New York, 1955).

CATALOGUE
OPERAS
Col. 1, l. 19. 'Araldo' *should read*:
' Aroldo'

Col. 3, l. 3. 5 Aug. *should read*:
5 Sept.

746 — Col. 1, l. 9. 'Araldo' *should read*:
' Aroldo'

l. 17. 1867). *should read*:
1867) (revised version in 4 acts).

Col. 2, ll. 32-33 *should read*:
Italian translation by A. de Lauzières.

i SACRED CHORAL WORKS
l. 3. (1880). *should read*:
(comp. ? 1878–79, perf. 1880).

l. 5. (1889). *should read*:
(comp. 1889, perf. 1895).

l. 6. (1898). *should read*:
(comp. 1896–97, perf. 1898).

l. 7. (1898). *should read*:
(comp. 1895–96, perf. 1898).

l. 8 *should read*:
' Laudi alla Vergine Maria' (Dante), for 4-part women's chorus.

l. 9. (1898). *should read*:
(comp. ?, perf. 1898).

SECULAR CHORAL WORKS
l. 1. Cantata *should read*:
Hymn

l. 2. ' Inno alle nazioni' *should read*:
' Inno delle nazioni'

VOICE AND ORCHESTRA
l. 1. (1880). *should read*:
(comp. ?, perf. 1880).

ii SONGS
l. 6. mistera *should read*:
mistero

Add after l. 8:
' Fiorellin che sorge appena' (Piave) (1850).[2]

ll. 9-11. *footnote refs.* 2-4 *should read*:
3, 4, 5.

l. 12. Signor' (?) (1894).[5] *should read*:
Signor' (1894).[6]

Add footnote:
[2] Published by Giuseppe Stefani in 'Verdi e Trieste' (1951).

Footnotes 2-5 *become* 3-6.

Footnote 5. l. 5 *should read*:
Mar. 1941. The words are a paraphrase of 'Agnus Dei' by Verdi and Boito.

752   i   VERETTI

Bacchelli   Par. 4, l. 1.   Bacchell *should read*:

figliuol   l. 5.   figliol *should read*:

Add at end:
'Divertimento' for clavichord and 6 insts.

753   ii   Verlaine
l. 4 *should read*:
Stravinsky (2 songs). Sutter ('Triptyque verlainien').

VERMONT
Add at end:
See also Maîtres Musiciens, Vol. 5 (modern ed. of chansons).

754   i   VERNE (2)
l. 2 *should read*:
9 Aug. 1868; *d.* London, 12 Apr. 1958), pianist and composer. She took

    ii   **Verne**
l. 2 *should read*:
incid. m.). Offenbach ('Voyage dans la lune' & 'Docteur Ox', operettas).

756   ii   Verstegan, Robert *should read*:
Verstegan, Richard

758   i   VESPERS
Delete signature and add:

One of the most frequently performed settings of the Vespers is that of Monteverdi, from his publication of 1610. Unfortunately the composer has been so misrepresented and the liturgical meaning of the music so distorted that some clarification is desirable.

In its general plan Monteverdi's publication, issued in eight part-books, differs little from those of his contemporaries. It was the custom then to include in any one set of part-books an almost bewildering variety of liturgical forms, a mélange that would have been unthinkable fifty years before. During Palestrina's lifetime, Masses and motets and lamentations usually appeared in separate publications, but Monteverdi's age willingly tolerated collections whose odd assortment of items was nothing if not baroque: Masses rubbed shoulders with psalms, motets with *falsi bordoni*, litanies with instrumental pieces, some of them with secular names and a distinctly secular flavour. But the printer was fair to his public, for he always provided an index and a title-page, from one or both of which it was generally possible to assess the scope of the collection and the resources necessary for performance.

Monteverdi's title-page is no exception;

indeed there are two title-pages, one for the *Bassus Generalis* and the other for the remaining seven vocal and instrumental part-books. The former, which is the more elaborate and explicit of the two, reads as follows:

SANCTISSIMÆ
VIRGINI
MISSA SENIS VOCIBVS
AD ECCLESIARUM CHOROS
Ac Vesperæ Pluribus Decantandæ
CUM NONNVLLIS SACRIS CONCENTIBVS
ad Sacella sive Principum Cubicula
accommodata
OPERA
A CLAUDIO MONTEVERDE
nuper effecta
AC BEATISS. PAVLO V. PONT. MAX.
CONSECRATA

It is perfectly clear that Monteverdi wanted his six-part Mass to occupy the most important position on the title-page. The music for Vespers is then briefly mentioned in one line: "and Vespers to be performed by several [musicians]". At this point, according to countless writers on Monteverdi (not to mention editors of his so-called "Vespers"), the information imparted by the title-page comes to an abrupt end. The phrase "Vesperæ Pluribus Decantandæ" has been understood to refer to the entire contents apart from the Mass. Nobody has explained what Monteverdi (or his publisher Ricciardo Amadino) meant by the next few lines in the title, which are obviously equal if not superior in importance to the phrase about the Vespers: "with some sacred pieces works recently composed by Claudio Monteverdi and intended for princely chapels and apartments".

There would be no point in referring in bold type to music which did not actually exist in the part-books, and since both Monteverdi and Amadino were honourable men and the publication as a whole had been accepted by Pope Paul V, it must be assumed that there really were a few sacred pieces, or motets, quite apart from the Mass and the Vespers. Unfortunately these have never been properly identified, and the result is that the purpose and function of the 14 separate items following the Mass have been either ignored, misinterpreted or misunderstood from the time of Winterfeld onwards. All that Amadino did was to replace the vague and old-fashioned word "motet" by a long and impressive phrase calculated to catch the eye of organists whose Sunday duties may have included the provision of a holy aubade or a sacred serenade. These pieces were spread out among the psalm settings so that even those who had not bothered to read the title-page might have a second chance of grasping and appreciating the unusually varied nature of the collection.

The printed sequence of the fourteen items is as follows (italics show the compositions proper to Vespers) : *Domine ad adjuvandum* ; *Dixit Dominus* ; Nigra sum ; *Laudate pueri* ; Pulchra es ; *Laetatus sum* ; Duo Seraphim ; *Nisi Dominus* ; Audi coelum ; *Lauda Jerusalem* ; Sancta Maria ; *Ave maris stella* ; *Magnificat a 7* ; *Magnificat a 6*. Confusion has recently been worse confounded by attempts to call the pieces for princely chapels and apartments " antiphons ", which they most decidedly are not. Monteverdi never called them antiphons, since he knew full well that antiphons were never set in polyphony, but were always chanted in plainsong before and after each psalm. He also knew that antiphon and psalm, from time immemorial, had shared the same mode or tone, so that the transition from one to the other might be as smooth as possible. The hitherto accepted modern sequence of items results in precisely the opposite effect, as when ' Duo Seraphim ', ending in G major, is followed by the unequivocal F major of ' Nisi Dominus ' ; or when ' Audi coelum ', ending on a chord of D, is followed by the outspoken C major of ' Lauda Jerusalem '.

It may be stated, quite categorically, that the following texts are not antiphons, nor have they any connection with Vespers of the Blessed Virgin : ' Nigra sum ' ; 'Pulchra es ' ; ' Duo Seraphim ' ; ' Audi coelum ' ; ' Sonata sopra Sancta Maria '. By sheer coincidence, one of the five antiphons prescribed for this service begins with the words ' Nigra sum ', but Monteverdi's text is much longer than that of the antiphon, and has clearly been compiled especially as a motet text from various chapters and verses of ' The Song of Solomon '. It could not possibly be an antiphon by any stretch of the imagination. The other items (with the exception of ' Sancta Maria, ora pro nobis ' which is part of the Litany) are compilations of a similar nature, and may even have been put together by Monteverdi.

Placing aside these five works — the four motets and the Litany fragment — as being the " sacred pieces intended for princely chapels and apartments " mentioned on the title-page, we find remaining that portion of the Vespers which composers are permitted to set to music : the response ' Domine ad adjuvandum ', the five appointed psalms, the hymn ' Ave maris stella ', and ' Magnificat ', of which Monteverdi provides two settings just as many of his contemporaries did. One requires only six voices and organ, and was probably intended for First Vespers, while the other (included in this edition) is on a much larger scale as befitted the musical

trappings for Second Vespers, a service of great solemnity and splendour. Musicians of the generation before Monteverdi's would have set only alternate verses of ' Ave maris stella ' and of ' Magnificat ', but his are through-composed because he had at his disposal a colourful palette of instruments and voices to take the place of the old antiphonal contrast of monody and polyphony. Nevertheless something must be added to his music if a performance is to reflect with reasonable accuracy the liturgical forms with which he was dealing.

In the first place, the performance cannot start with a response any more than a conversation can start with a repartee. The intonation of ' Deus in adjutorium meum intende ' must precede the brassy and jubilant response derived from the prelude to ' Orfeo '. This is both easy and obvious. Rather less easy is the problem of what antiphons to use for the five psalms and ' Magnificat '. Normally each antiphon, according to its mode, is followed by a psalm in the corresponding tone ; here we have psalms built on definite and recognizable tones, but no antiphons to match. Here are the six items in question, showing the tones used by Monteverdi by way of cantus firmus, and opposite each the antiphons traditionally sung at Vespers of the B.V.M. :

' Dixit Dominus '
(down a fourth)=4A   3a = *Dum esset rex*
' Laudate pueri ' (at pitch)=8G   4A=*Laeva ejus*
' Laetatus sum '
(up a fourth)=2D   3b = *Nigra sum*
' Nisi Dominus ' (at pitch)=6F   8G=*Jam hiems transiit*
' Lauda Jerusalem '
(at pitch)=3a   4A=*Speciosa facta es*
' Magnificat ' (up a fourth)=1D   8G=*Beatam me dicent*

It will be seen that in no case does the mode of the antiphon agree with the tone of the psalm, the probable reason being that in Monteverdi's time the chapel of Santa Barbara at Mantua was not subject to the full weight of Roman authority and regulations. Many monastic orders and private chapels follow their own variations in the liturgy, and there is no reason to suppose that Mantua was an exception.

By slightly rearranging the pattern and using three of the proper antiphons and three more from Vespers of the Visitation and Nativity of the B.V.M., the modes and tones can be made to agree satisfactorily in the following manner :

' Dixit Dominus '   =4A=*Laeva ejus*
' Laudate pueri '   =8G=*Jam hiems transiit*
' Laetatus sum '   =2D= *Intravit Maria* (Visitation)
' Nisi Dominus '   =6F= *Regali ex progenie* (Nativity)
' Lauda Jerusalem '   =3a = *Dum esset rex*
' Magnificat '   = 1D= *Gloriosae Virginis* (Nativity)

Except on the highest feasts, antiphons are now sung in full only *after* the psalm ; before it they are sung only as far as the first word or so. When the psalms are set elaborately, this partial intonation is not at all satisfactory either from an artistic or liturgical standpoint, and it is therefore advisable to sing the antiphons in full both before and after the psalms.

It is often asked if Monteverdi intended the Vespers to be sung complete and at one sitting. He certainly never envisaged the kind of performances that have become customary in recent years, with psalms and motets reeled off one after the other just as Amadino had printed them. But there are indications in the structure of the music that point to a premeditated plan of performance and orchestration. The eight separate items that are truly part of Vespers show a remarkable symmetry, in that the first two and the last two make use of an instrumental group, while the middle four need only the organ. ' Laudate pueri ' is the first of the middle four, and is clearly marked " a 8 voci soli nel organo ". There are no ritornelli in this psalm or in the three following ones, understood to be accompanied also by the organ alone. Much has been made of references in the ' Syntagma Musicum ' of Praetorius to possible ways of scoring the hymn ' Ave maris stella ', but it cannot be sufficiently stressed that what was thought fashionable in Wolfenbüttel and Venice about 1619 bore little relation to what was practicable in Mantua in 1610. It would, of course, be possible to stage performances of the Vespers in the German, French, Spanish or English styles then current; but these performances would not necessarily throw any light on what happened in Mantua. There, resources were modest but of good quality, and Monteverdi had at his beck and call some of the finest soloists in the whole of Italy. That is why the first three psalms, the hymn and the seven-part ' Magnificat ' contain such a remarkable proportion of solo writing.

w. s. r., rev. w. h. f., adds. d. w. s.

758   ii   **VESQUE VON PÜTTLINGEN**
l. 38 *should read*:

58, besides including two masses, etc. He wrote a vast number of songs, including 146 settings of Heine, and also

760   i   **VETTER**
Par. 3 (BOOKS)
Add at end:

' Mythos, Melos, Musica : ausgewählte Aufsätze zur Musikgeschichte ', Series I (Leipzig, 1957).

ii   **VIADANA**
Par. 2, l. 3. Costanzo Porta
should read:

Ercole Porta

761   i   **VIANA DA MOTA**
Par. 1, l. 2. 1 June *should read*:
31 May

ii   **VIANESI**
Par. 1, l. 3. 11 Nov. *should read*:
4 Nov.

763   i-ii **VIBRAPHONE**
Delete article and replace by:
VIBRAPHONE (VIBRAHARP [1]**).** A percussion instrument whose notes are produced by vibrations of metal bars amplified by a special type of resonator producing a pulsating tone or *vibrato*. It belongs to the bar-percussion family and is therefore played with rubber-tipped or yarn-wound rubber mallets. The vibraphone's appearance is the same as that of the manufactured marimba, and its aluminium-alloy bars are mounted likewise on cords, left free to vibrate. Their tone is of long duration but can be silenced by means of a damper pedal similar in action to that of the pianoforte. The vibraphone has a clear, sweet tone like that of the celesta, but loud playing will add a somewhat twanging quality.

The vibraphone's outstanding feature is the *vibrato*. A shaft extends lengthwise along the upper ends of the tubular resonators, in each of which is a vane attached to the shaft. The vanes are flat metal pieces which, when rotated by the shafts, partially close and open the resonators, throwing them out of tune and in tune periodically, creating a pulsating tone comparable to the tremolo of the pipe organ and regulated by altering the speed of the electric motor turning the shaft. When no *vibrato* is desired the motor is shut off and the vanes rest in a vertical position, leaving the resonators in tune.

Owing to the sustained tone impressive chords can be created by arpeggios. Use of the damper pedal makes four-mallet chord playing effective, and brilliant *staccato* execution in the manner of the xylophone can be had for variety by using hard-headed mallets and allowing the damper pedal partially to stifle the bars. The compass of the vibraphone is three octaves, f–f''' beginning a fifth lower than the celesta. A lower range is possible and desirable, but manufacturers are not generous in this respect.

The vibraphone was developed in the mid-1920s in the U.S.A. It has been used mainly in popular music, but recently found its way into symphonic scores, notably in Ralph Vaughan Williams's seventh (' Sinfonia antartica ') and eighth Symphonies, in Alban Berg's opera ' Lulu ', Francis Chagrin's Prelude and Fugue and Olivier Messiaen's ' Trois Liturgies de la Présence Divine '.

F. K. M.

[1] The name more frequently used in America.

765 ii **VICARS-CHORAL**
Cancel entry and replace by :

Originally the function of the Vicars seems to have been the performance of the liturgy and, more particularly, of its musical requirements, on behalf of the residentiaries in English secular cathedrals. In later times this sense of deputizing seems to have become obscured. The proportion of vicars in holy orders varies with place and time. Very seldom were they all required to be in priest's orders ; at St. Paul's Cathedral, London, all such vicars were " minor canons ", a term not in general use until the establishment of the cathedrals of the new foundation. In general each vicar was in orders appropriate to the prebend to which he was attached — priest, deacon or subdeacon — and therefore to the duties appertaining to his office.

The number of vicars at any cathedral originally equalled the number of canons, since each residentiary appointed his own vicar, whom in earlier times he helped to support and with whom he stood in a personal relationship. Towards the end of the middle ages, however, the vicars formed their own autonomous corporations. Such bodies were not otherwise unknown in cathedrals at this period : at Lincoln a house was given to the " poor clerks " (the younger clerks attending the services) for them to live in together. A little later the bishop, Oliver Sutton (1280–99), founded the vicars' college, although the office had been in existence since the time of St. Hugh (1186–1200). At Chichester, however, this development does not seem to have taken place until the 15th century, and the statutes were codified only in 1534. On the other hand, the statutes of the vicars at Wells date from 1394.

The government of these colleges varied in detail. At Wells an annual election was to be held on St. Matthew's Day to choose two Principals and five Seniors, to be responsible to the Dean and Chapter for the sobriety and efficiency of the college ; at the same time, domestic officers were to be chosen. At least in post-Reformation times little distinction seems to be made in the records between lay and priest vicars. On the other hand, at Lincoln there were two provosts, one for the senior or priest vicars, the other for the junior vicars — vicars in minor orders or, later, lay vicars. At Chichester the annual election was concerned with but one Principal in addition to the domestic officers.

As separate corporations, cathedral vicars administered their own property. A further illustration of their independence is provided by an entry in the registers of the Wells vicars. In 1563 the Master of the Children at the Chapel Royal requested the Principals to allow an older man to remain among them.

The principals declined, saying that they already had a number of inactive vicars in their midst, and that they required newcomers to be younger men. The decision was not unjustified ; the registers show plainly that some vicars were very desultory in their attendance at the meetings of the college, and the minutes of the Dean and Chapter indicate that the vicars did not always carry out their duties satisfactorily. But the Dean and Chapter were always responsible for the admission of vicars, to which the chapter minutes make frequent reference. At Norwich the minor canons, of equivalent status to vicars-choral, were appointed by the Dean and Chapter. At Wells and elsewhere a probationary year was required, at the end of which a candidate was " perpetuated " in his vicarship, subject to examination and reports on his morals and general suitability for the office. There are, however, instances in which the requirement as to probation was waived or relaxed ; in 1487, for example, John Gyles was perpetuated at Wells on the testimony of the vicars, although he could not repeat his psalter, because of weakness (*infirmitatem*). He was instructed, however, to rectify this omission without delay. On the other hand, young vicars were sent to the grammar school when their services were not required otherwise, and some vicars were granted leave of absence to attend a university. It followed that some vicars would enter priest's orders while members of the college, and at Norwich it was not unknown for a minor canon to become precentor.

In addition to their normal duties of singing the choir offices, all of which they were expected to attend, the vicars performed other functions. At York the senior vicar acted as the second succentor (*succentor vicariorum*) and was also responsible for the instruction and correction of the choristers — that is, to act as master of the choristers. At Wells two vicars were commissaries of the Dean and Chapter in 1339, and they regularly filled other minor offices in the establishment by election. At Salisbury the sub-magister of the choristers was a vicar, as also was the organist at many cathedrals in later times, and the medieval master of the choristers at Lincoln.

From the end of the 15th century the numbers of vicars decreased, although their intellectual standing generally was probably higher than that of their predecessors. At Chichester, for instance, the number declined from the normal thirty in 1232 and later, to fourteen and, finally, four in the 16th century. At Chester there seem to have been six minor canons on the establishment towards the close of the 16th century, the same number as obtained in the time of Henry VIII. At Lincoln there were twenty-five vicars in 1501, of whom fifteen were priests. This total was reduced to twelve at the Reformation, and to nine in 1729. At Wells, however, things were not quite so bad. The Charter of Elizabeth I laid down an establishment of between fourteen and twenty vicars. In the period up to the Commonwealth and immediately after the Restoration the number was maintained at twelve, although there were fourteen as late as 1638. Twelve vicars, most of them graduates, were to be found at Hereford in 1634, according to a narrative in B.M. MS Lansdowne 213.

The declining numbers of the vicars were made up by the introduction of lay singing-men, sometimes called " conducts ", who began to appear before the close of the middle ages. In 1548, and possibly earlier, there were three conducts at Chichester, who were later increased to four. At Chester there were six from the time of Henry VIII to the turn of the century. At York there were seven singing-men to four vicars in 1663. At Norwich there were eight each of minor canons and of lay clerks; the latter were sometimes promoted to fill vacancies among their superiors. At Wells there seems to be no clear indication of the number of lay clerks employed, although the survey of the Vicars' Close carried out by the Commonwealth commissioners in 1649 shows clearly the lack of numbers among the vicars, since each vicar is shown as having two or three houses assigned to him. At Exeter, on the other hand, both vicars and lay singing-men alike were enjoined by the Injunctions of 1559 to be in the choir, correctly attired, at a quarter to eight in order to say Morning Prayer, but penalties for vicars only were specified for non-compliance.

Although the vicars' corporations were dissolved by 1936, the name was retained for the lay singing-men of St. Paul's Cathedral, London. Under their bye-laws, issued in 1938 and revised in 1946-47, the maximum age for admission is 35 years, and a period of two years probation is required; retirement is compulsory at the age of 60. Fines for late attendance are imposed, though these may be remitted at the discretion of the Dean and Chapter. However, attendance by authorized deputy is permitted on a limited number of occasions each year.   W. K. F.

BIBLIOGRAPHY

EDWARDS, K., ' The English Secular Cathedrals ' (Manchester, 1949).
MADDISON, A. R., ' A Short Account of the Vicars-Choral, Poor Clerks, Organists and Choristers of Lincoln Cathedral ' (London, 1878).
PECKHAM, W. D., ' The Vicars Choral of Chichester Cathedral ', ' Sussex Archaeological Collections ', Vol. 78.
REYNOLDS, H. E., ' Wells Cathedral ' (Wells, 1881).

766   ii   **VICENTINO**
Par. 1, l. 16 *should read*:
on the harpsichord.
A modern facsimile reprint of ' L' antica musica ' is to be published in ' Documenta Musicologica ', Vol. 32.
               H. P. (ii), adds.

Add after **VICH** :

VICKERS, Jon(athan Stewart) (*b*. Prince Albert, Saskatchewan, Canada, 29 Oct. 1926).

Canadian tenor singer. He studied under George Lambert at the Royal Conservatory of Music, Toronto. After appearing in Canada as Don José and as the Male Chorus in Britten's ' The Rape of Lucretia ' at the 1956 Stratford (Ont.) Festival, he began to sing regularly over the Canadian Radio in Wagner concerts. In the 1956–57 season he sang Florestan in a concert performance of ' Fidelio ' in New York opposite Inge Borkh. He went to London and joined the Covent Garden Opera in the spring of 1957, making his début during the company's provincial tour as King Gustavus (Riccardo) in ' A Masked Ball ', and repeating the part in London. He revealed himself immediately as a fine dramatic tenor, possessing a voice of exciting quality and capable of singing intelligible English. These impressions were strengthened when he sang Don José a week later, and Aeneas in Covent Garden's historic production of ' The Trojans '. During his second London season he added Radamès to his repertory and was then heard in Italian as Don Carlos in the Covent Garden centenary production of Verdi's ' Don Carlo ', holding his own with such eminent foreign artists as Brouwenstijn, Gobbi and Christoff. In the summer of 1958 he became the first British tenor to sing Siegmund at Bayreuth, which part he repeated in London in the autumn. He was next heard as Samson in the stage version of Handel's oratorio staged at Covent Garden, first at the Leeds Festival and then in London, his moving singing of " Total eclipse " being especially notable. He then went to Dallas, Texas, to sing Jason in Cherubini's ' Medea ' opposite Callas. During the first three months of 1959 he sang at the Vienna State Opera (Siegmund, Don José, Radamès and Canio) and in the summer of 1959 sang his first Parsifal in London, afterwards returning to Bayreuth for his second season. In the autumn of 1959 he was due to make his début with the San Francisco Opera and then to join the Metropolitan Opera, New York for the second part of the 1959–60 season.

It is generally agreed that Vickers is the finest British heroic tenor of the present day, both vocally and physically pre-eminently suited for such parts as Tristan, Siegfried and Othello.   H. D. R.

773   **VICTORIA,** CATALOGUE :
       MASSES
       Col. 2, ll. 1 (Alma . . .), 4 (Ave Regina),
       8 (Laetatus), 16 (Pro victoria) & 18 (Salve),
& organ.   add :

775   LITANY
       Col. 2.   Add :
& organ.

       PSALMS
       Col. 2, ll. 1-7.   Add :

}& organ.

       ANTIPHONS OF THE B.V.M.
       Col. 2, ll. 2-3, 6 & 10.   Add :
& organ.

776   SEQUENCES
       Col. 2, ll. 1-3.   Add :
& organ.

       Add at end (under frame) :
See also Hispaniae Schola, Vol. 6 (modern reprint of Faburden).

777   ii   **VIEIRA BRANDÃO**
             Par. 1, l. 2 should read :
quira, 26 Sept. 1911).

778   i   **VIEIRA, Ernesto**
            Par. 1, l. 1.   (b. ?) should read :
(b. Lisbon, 24 May 1848 ; d. Lisbon, 26 Apr. 1915).

            Par. 2, l. 2 should read :
cionario biografico dos musicos portugueses '

       VIELLE
       Add after HURDY GURDY.
PLATES 32, Vol. IV, p. 492 ; 66, Vol. VIII, p. 146 (i), No. 11.

781   i   **VIENNA**
            Footnote should read :
¹ It is not the same as the Theater auf der Wieden where Mozart's ' Zauberflöte ' was produced, which stood some distance away.

788   i   Add to BIBL. :
BAUER, ANTON, ' Opern und Operetten in Wien : Verzeichnis ihrer Erstaufführungen in der Zeit von 1629 bis zur Gegenwart ' (Graz, Cologne & Vienna, 1955).
KRALIK, HEINRICH, ' The Vienna Opera House ', trans. by Michael H. Law (Vienna & London, 1955).
LESSING, ERICH, ' Szene : ein Bildwerk über die Wiener Staatsoper und das Burgtheater ' (Vienna, 1955).
OREL, ALFRED, ' Musikstadt Wien ' (Vienna & Stuttgart, 1953).

789   ii   **VIEUXTEMPS**
             Par. 3, l. 3 should read :
America in 1844. That year he married Josephine Elder, an eminent pianist in Vienna. A large number of composi-

             ll. 9-11 should read :
1845. Shortly after this he accepted an invitation to

791   ii   **VIHUELA**
             Add after Par. 1 (Flemish lute). :
A vihuela de mano, probably the only surviving specimen in the world, is in the Musée Jacquemart-André in Paris.

792   ii   **VILLA-LOBOS**
             Par. 1, l. 2 should read :
5 Mar. 1887 ; d. Rio de Janeiro, 17 Nov. 1959).

797   i   Add to BIBL. :
MARIZ, V., 'Heitor Villa-Lobos' (Rio de Janeiro, 1950).

       ii   **VILLANCICO**
             Add to BIBL. :
POPE, ISABEL, ' El villancico polifónico ', in ' Cancionero de Upsala ' (Mexico City, 1944).

             Add at end :
See also Monumentos de la Música Española, Vols. 5, 8, 9, 10. Publicacions Catalunya, Vol. 12 (modern ed. of 18th-cent. villancicos).

798   i   **VILLANELLA**
            Add to BIBL. :
GALANTI, BIANCA MARIA, ' Le villanelle alla napolitana ' (Florence, 1954).

       ii   **Villon**
             l. 4 should read :
Dieren (ballad with chamber m.). Dresden (opera). Henze (5 madrigals

799   i   **Vilmorin**
            l. 2 should read :
4tets). Manziarly (songs). Milhaud (2 choruses, song, 2 voc. 4tets). Poulenc (12

       ii   Add before **VINCENT** :
       VINAY, Ramón (b. Chillán, Chile, 31 Aug. 1914).
Chilean tenor singer. He was born of French-Italian parents and educated at the local École Normale before being taken to France to complete his education. At school in France he studied the violin, but not singing. Shortly before the war he went to New Mexico to gain experience in one of his father's businesses, and while there was persuaded by a friend to enter for an amateur radio competition for singers. He was heard by a member of the Mexico City Opera and engaged for the company, making his début in the baritone part of Di Luna in ' Il Trovatore '. After singing the baritone repertory

for some time he found that his voice was changing, and a period of further study followed. He made his tenor début also in Mexico, as Don José in ' Carmen '. In 1944 he sang his first Othello and followed this with appearances as Des Grieux in ' Manon Lescaut ', Samson and Cavaradossi. Singing opposite him as Tosca was the American-Indian soprano Mobley Lushanya, whom he married.

In the autumn of 1945 Vinay made his New York début at the City Center as Don José, and this led to an engagement at the Metropolitan Opera, where his first part was again Don José. He has been a member of the Metropolitan ever since. During the 1946–47 season he was called on to sing Othello at short notice when Torsten Ralf fell ill; his performance and its attendant success resulted in his being engaged by Toscanini to sing the same part for a broadcast performance with the N.B.C. Symphony Orchestra, and Vinay coached the part with the great conductor. The success of the New York ' Otello ' opened the doors of La Scala at Milan to him, and he inaugurated the 1947–48 season there as Othello, a part he has sung all over Italy, at Salzburg and Covent Garden, where he was first heard with the Scala Company in 1950. Other Covent Garden appearances have been as Siegmund and Tristan. Vinay's fame as a Wagnerian dates from his first Tristan at San Francisco in 1950, opposite Flagstad. In 1952 he was engaged by Wieland Wagner for Bayreuth, where he sang each year until 1957, being heard as Tristan, Parsifal, Tannhäuser and Siegmund. In 1958 he appeared at the Teatro Colón in Buenos Aires as Othello and Samson under Beecham. Vinay's versatility is such that he has also assumed with great success such parts as Lensky in ' Eugene Onegin ' and Cyrano de Bergerac in Alfano's opera of that name.

Singing so many Othellos has taken toll of Vinay's voice. Originally he sang with ease and a full, splendid tone; but more recently he has exhibited a great strain in his singing, and the voice has lost some of its original volume. His artistry, intelligence and musicianship, however, are always in evidence, and his acting, full of pathos and nobility, is of a standard rare among operatic artists.

H. D. R.

800   ii   *Add before* **VINCENTI**:

VINCENT, John (*b.* Birmingham, Alabama, 17 May 1902).

American composer and conductor. He took a diploma at the New England Conservatory in 1927, studied at the George Peabody College, Nashville, Tennessee and at Harvard University (1933–35). In 1935–37 he at-

tended the École Normale de Musique in Paris and in 1941 took the Ph.D. at Cornell University. He studied composition with Chadwick, Piston, Nadia Boulanger and Roy Harris. From 1930 onwards he held various teaching posts and he is now (1958) Professor of Music at the University of California and Music Director of the Los Angeles Chamber Symphony Orchestra. His book, ' The Diatonic Modes in Modern Music ', was published in 1951 (rev. 1957).

The following are among Vincent's principal compositions:

Ballet, ' Three Jacks ' (1953).
Incidental music for Richard Hubler's Christmas play
 ' Hallow'd Time ' (1954).
' Three Grecian Songs ' for unaccomp. chorus (1951).
' Festival Symphony ', D ma. (1955, rev. 1957).
' Miracle of the Cherry Tree ' for contralto & orch.
String Quartet (1938).
Pf. Quartet (1957).   E. B.

801   i   **VINCI**
          Par. 1, l. 10.   Leo's *should read*:
Vinci's

      ii   **VINCI, L. da**
          Par. 1, ll. 1-2.   Empoli, 1452 *should read*:
Empoli, 15 Apr. 1452

805   i   **VIOL (1)**
          Refs. after Par. 5 *should read*:
          See PLATES 48, Vol. VI, p. 538 ; 66 & 67, Vol. VIII, p. 146 (i & ii).

809   i   **VIOLIN FAMILY**
          Add after Par. 3 :
PLATE 64, Vol. VIII, Frontispiece.

810   ii   Par. x, l. 6.   Scandinavia *should read*:
Norway

811   i   BIBL. ll. 5-6 *should read*:
          (Neuberg, 1864, 1874, out of print) ; trans. by J. Broadhouse (London, n.d.).

      ii   *Delete* ll. 6-7 (HART).
          l. 8 *should read*:
HAWEIS, H. R., ' Old Violins ' (London, 1898 ; Edinburgh,
          l. 11.   (1882–90). *should read*:
(1882).
          Delete ll. 19-20 (' Die Geigen- und . . .').
          l. 23.   1889). *should read*:
1895).
          l. 26.   1894). *should read*:
1920).
          l. 39.   Stradivarius ' *should read*:
Stradivari '
          l. 53 *should read*:
Violin Family ' (London, n.d.).
          ll. 60-61.   6th ed. (Leipzig, 1920). *should read*:
7th ed. (Leipzig, 1927).

812   i   Bibl. l. 7. 1916). *should read*: 1915).

VIOLIN MAKING
l. 11. 1903). *should read*:
1902).

Delete ll. 23-24 (' The Violin Makers . . .).

l. 27. MANGIN *should read*:
MAUGIN

ll. 42-43 *should read*:
SIMOUTRE, N. E., ' Aux amateurs du violon : historique, construction, réparation et conservation de cet instrument ' (Basel, 1883).

l. 49. 1876). *should read*:
1876–78).

l. 53. ' Lutomonographie ' *should read*:
' Luthomonographie '

EARLY HISTORY. l. 6 *should read*:
(Copenhagen, 1915–31) ; Eng. trans. by J. Pulver (London, n.d.).

813   i   **VIOLIN PLAYING**
Par. 4, l. 5. the year of *should read*:
two years after

814   i   Par. 3, l. 17. Early in the 18th *should read*:
Early in the 19th

821   i   BIBL., l. 16. 1740). *should read*:
1751).

l. 34. Violinschulc *should read*:
Violinschule

821   i   *Add to* BIBL. :
KINSEY, HERBERT, ' The Foundations of Violin Playing and Musicianship ' (London, 1954).
MANGEOT, ANDRÉ, ' Violin Technique : Notes for Players and Teachers ' (London, 1954).

824   i   **VIOLONCELLO PLAYING**
Add at end:
The ' Bachiana Brasileira ' No. 1, by Villa-Lobos, is for 8 cellos.
Add to BIBL. :
EISENBERG, MAURICE, ' Cello Playing of Today ' (London, 1957).

VIOTTA
Par. 1, l. 2. 18 Feb. *should read*:
17 Feb.

   ii   **VIOTTI**
Par. 1, ll. 2-3. Vercelli ¹, 12 May 1755 ; *should read*:
Vercelli, 12 May 1755 ¹ ;

Par. 2, ll. 1-5 *should read*:
Italian violinist and composer. His father was a
Delete footnote *and replace by*:
¹ Not 23 May 1753, as previously stated. This was the date of birth of an elder brother, christened Giovanni Battista, who died immediately and after whom the later child was named.

827   ii   *Add to* BIBL. :
GIAZOTTO, REMO, ' Giovan Battista Viotti ' Milan, 1956).

VOL. IX

No.	Title	Composer
1	Johnson's Medley.	[Edward Johnson, set by] Mr. Randall.
2	Dowlands Lacrimae out of my cosin Maryes booke.	[Dowland, set by ?]
3	[coranto.]	Tisdale.
4	[coranto.]	Tisdale.
5	Mr. Newmans pavane.	[Newman, set by] Mr Randall.
6	Pavane.	Mr. Marchunt.
7	Galliard can she excuse : and may serve to Lacrimae.	[Dowland, set by ?]
8	Corrigiter : or ye old hunts upp.	Mr. Birde.
9	Dowlands Lacrimae.	sett by Mr. Randall.
10	Passmezo d'Italie.	?
11	Galliard del Passmezo.	?
12	Susann un iour a .5. voc.	[Lassus, set by ?]
13	Pavane.	Mr. Birde.
14	Passmeass : Pavan.	Mr. Morley.
15	Pavane.	Mr. Morley, sett by Mr. Heybourne.
16	The Galiard to the Pavane before.	Mr. Morley [set by Heybourne ?].
17	Poules Wharf.	?
18	My dezire.	?
19	Pavane.	Mr. Robert Johnson.
20	Mr. John Holmes Paven [or] Robin Smarts Delight.	[John Holmes.]
21	[an incomplete pavan].	

to one Priscilla Bunbury and its contents are as follows:

MS 8), consisting mainly of lute music by members of the 17th-century Anglo-French

No.	Title	Fol. No.	Composer
1	[incomplete]	1 r.	Mr. Gibbons
2	The white Ribbin	1 v.	
3	The freinds Good Night	2 r.	
4	The Celebran	2 v.	
5	A Jigg	3 r.	
6	Put up thy Dagger Jemmy	3 v.	
7	Money is a Gallant thinge	4 r.	
8	Rappaks Jigg	4 v.	
9	The maukin	7 r.	
10	George	7 v.	
11	la holland [aise ?]	7 v.	
12	Mrs. Prissilla Bunburie hir Delight	8 r.	
13	Almaine	8 v.	Mr. Gibbons
14	[no title]	8 v.	Randall Jewett
15	A Maske	9 r.	[Gibbons]
16	Berchen Greene Hollan	9 v.	
17	A french Lesson	9 v.	
18	Swinnertons Almaine	10 v.	
19	A Maske	11 v.	
20	A Coranto	12 r.	
21	The Buildinges	12 v.	
22	Churtons farwell	13 r.	R. Jewett
23	Almaine	13 r.	R. Jewett
24	Grayes Inn Maske	13 v.	
25	The new Rant	14 r.	
26	The parson of the parrish	14 v.	
27	Captaine Owens Delight	15 r.	
28	A horne pipe	15 v.	R. H.
29	The battle by mr bird	17 v.	[Byrd]
30	The buildinge	27 v.	
31	Frogg gall :	28 v.	Robt Hall
32	The pleasing widdow		Robert Hall
33	Mock widdow		Robert Hall
34	My Choyce [is made. etc.]		R. H. F. P. B. M.
35	The Nightingaill		

16 ii Par. 3, l. 26 *should read*: script versions of this composition.[3] If the last

Add footnote:
[2] *See* his article in M. & L., XXXVI, 1955, p. 365).

Footnote 2 becomes 3.

17 ii Par. 3, l. 2, *before* No. 11, *insert*:
No. 8 is by John Bull;

After Par. 3 *insert*:
Another MS belonging to Lord Dalhousie is Lady Jean Campbell's Book (Panmure

school (Gaultier and others), but also including eight pieces of virginal music:

No.	Title
1.	The Bears Daunce.
2.	[jig.]
3.	Almayne.
4.	Almayne.
5.	Almayne.
6.	Almayne.
7.	Ane Air, Orlando [Gibbons?].
8.	Saraband, Orlando [Gibbons?].

17 ii Par. 4, l. 5. *For* named pieces are as follows : *substitute* :

contents are as follows:

No.	Title	Composer
—	fragmentary leaves.	?
1.	Delyt [pavan].	[Edward] Johnson.
2.	Ground.	Kinloch ?
3.	?	?
4.	?	D[uncan] B[urnett].
5.	The Batell of Pavie.	set be williame kinloche.
6.	ane almane on the same.	[Kinloch ?]
7.	?	?
8.	[long] Pavan.	[Kinloch ?]
9.	galliard of ye lang paven.	set be williem Kinloch.
10.	?	?
11.	Sussanna [un jour].	[Lassus, set by ?]
12.	Pasmessour [pavan].	Kinloch.
13.	galliard [to passymeasures].	[Kinloch.]
14.	the quadrant paven.	set be williame Kinloch.
15.	Gaillart [to quadro].	[Kinloch ?]
16.	Gaillart [on a ground].	?
17.	fantassie.	Kinloch.
18.	Passmeasour [pavan.]	Maister Bird.
19.	[its galliard.]	my Pene [-Byrd].
20.	The Quene of Inglonds Lessoune.	?
21.	[The Queen's Good-night.]	?
22.	[coranto.]	?
23.	[galliard.]	?

18　i　Par. 3.　Last line *should read* :
by John M. Ward, has been published as
Vol. 3 of the Wellesley Edition, 1954.

After Par. 3 *add* :
The contents are as follows :

No.	Titles, &c.
—	Some scribbles, and the old class-marks R. 13 and G. 109.
—	Blank.
1.	[passymeasures pavan.]
2.	[its galliard.]
3.	[pavan] qd mastyre taylere.
4.	[its galliard.]
5.	[pavan.]
6.	[its galliard.]
7.	[pavan.]
8.	[its galliard.]
9.	[Milanese pavan.]
10.	[The Queen's Good-night.]
11.	[reprise to a pavan ' d'anvers '.]
12.	[branle simple?]
13.	[Was not good King Solomon.]
14.	[branle courant?]
15.	[alman ' le prince '.]
16.	[its reprise.]
17.	[galliard?]
18.	[branle de bourgogne?]
19.	[alman ' 'S medelijn '.]
20.	[dance ' L'homme armé '.]
21.	[pavan.]
22.	[its galliard.]
23.	[galliard.]
24.	[Like as the lark.]
25.	[The goddess of love.]
26.	[pavan.]
27.	[its galliard.]
28.	[branle courant?]
29.	[branle double?]
30.	[qui passa.]
—	Blank.

19　i　*Add to* BIBL. :

DART, THURSTON, ' New Sources of Virginal Music '
(M. & L., XXXV, 1954, p. 93).
DICKINSON, A. E. F., ' English Virginal Music ' (M. Rev.,
XVI, 1955, p. 13).
COLE, ELIZABETH, ' Seven Problems of the Fitzwilliam
Virginal Book ' (Proc. Roy. Mus. Ass., Vol.
LXXIX, 1952–53).

ii　VISÉE
Par. 1, l. 1.　*c.* 1725). *should read* :
c. 1733).

23　i　VITALI, T. A.
Add at end :

BIBL.—RINALDI, M., ' Sull' autenticità della " Ciaccona " di Tommaso Antonio Vitali ' (Rass. Mus.,
XXIV, 2, 1954).

VITÁŠEK *should read* :
VITÁSEK

24　i　VITRUVIUS
BIBL., l. 6. SONTHEIMER, ' Vitruv *should
read* :
SONDHEIMER, ROBERT, ' Vitruv

25　ii　VITRY
Add to BIBL. :

GASTOUÉ, A., ' Le Manuscrit . . . du Trésor d'Apt '
(Paris, 1946).
GILLES, ANDRÉ, & REANEY, GILBERT, ' A New Source
for the *Ars Nova* of Philippe de Vitry ' (' Musica
Disciplina ', XII, 1958, p. 59).
SCHRADE, LEO, ' Philippe de Vitry : Some New Dis-
coveries ' (M.Q., XLII, 1956, p. 330).

25　ii　VITTADINI
Par. 1, l. 2.　29 Nov. *should read* :
30 Nov.

27　ii　VIVALDI
Par. 2, ll. 2-6 *should read* :

mentions a " magnificent instrumental concert
[at Venice] which lasted nearly two hours,
the music, including the ' Te Deum ', was by
the famous Vivaldi ". French connec-

28　ii　Par. 5, ll. 1-2 *should read* :

Vivaldi's music had long been entirely
forgotten ; the only example in print until
recently was the

l. 8 *should read* :

fore an important musical event, and editions
of vocal works have appeared both in Europe
and in the U.S.A., revised by Alfredo Casella,
Vito Frazzi, Virgilio Mortari and others. A
facsimile of the oratorio ' Juditha triumphans '
has also appeared.

29　ii　*Signature should read* :
O. R. (ii), rev.

BIBL. *Delete* ll. 3-4.

l. 5 *should read* :

ALTMANN, W. ' Thematischer Katalog der gedruckten
Werke

l. 16.　*Delete* LUCIANI, S. A.,

Add to BIBL. :

' Antonio Vivaldi : indice tematico ' (Milan, 1955, in
progress).
BAIGNÈRES, CLAUDE, ' Vivaldi : vie, mort et résurrec-
tion ' (Paris, 1955).
BERRI, PIETRO, ' Indice disconografico vivaldiano '
(Milan, 1953).
BONACORSI, A., ' I concerti di Antonio Vivaldi ' (Riv.
Mus. It., 1932).
KOLNEDER, WALTER, ' Aufführungspraxis bei Vivaldi '
(Leipzig, 1956).

Add, 2nd work by PINCHERLE :

' Vivaldi ' (Paris, 1955 ; Eng. trans. by Christopher
Hatch, ' Vivaldi, Genius of the Baroque ', New
York, 1957, London, 1958).

30　i　BIBL. *Delete* ll. 2-3.

Add to BIBL. :

SALTER, LEWIS S., ' An Index to Ricordi's Edition of
Vivaldi ' (' Notes ', June 1954, pp. 366-74).

31　ii　CATALOGUE
SOLO CONCERTOS
l. 1.　447 Concertos *should read* :

408 Concertos [6]

Add footnote :

[6] 447, previously given, was the number in the
' Inventaire thématique ', Vol. II of Pincherle's work
of 1948 (*see* Bibl.), but the total number he arrives at in
his later book of 1955 is 454 ; this includes, however,
the 46 *Concerti ripieni* listed here separately under
CONCERTI GROSSI and erroneously counted in again
under SOLO CONCERTOS.

31   ii   SOLO CONCERTOS
Op. 3, No. 8. 3 vns. *should read*:
2 vns. & cello.

No. 10. 4 vns. & cello. *should read*:
4 vns.

32   i   Par. 2, l. 5. 20 for 1 cello *should read*:
27 for 1 cello

l. 6. 16 for flute *should read*:
18 for flute

l. 7. 38 for bassoon, 6 for viola d' amore,
should read:
37 for bassoon, 8 for viola d' amore,

SONATAS
l. 1. 73 Sonatas *should read*:
75 Sonatas

ii   *Add at end, before See also*:
ORGAN MUSIC
2 Pieces [2]

Add footnote:
[2] Discovered by G. Francesco Malipiero in a manuscript containing works by Pescetti.

See also. l. 4 *should read*:
Classici Musica Italiana, Vol. 35 (modern ed. of ' Stagioni '). Fesch (use of music by). Sondheimer Ed., Vol.
26 (modern ed. of Concerto).

33   i   *Add after* **VIVO**:
VLACH-VRUTICKÝ, Josef (*b*. Vrutice
Benátecká nr. Lysá nad Labem, 24 Jan. 1897).
Czech composer, teacher and conductor.
He studied at the Prague Conservatory in
1918–24, the last two years in the master class
for composition of Josef Foerster. In 1922 he
began a teaching-career at a school in Prague,
which he continued afterwards in Yugoslavia,
where in 1930 he became lecturer in music at
the University of Dubrovnik and in 1939
professor at the Academy of Music there. He
returned to Prague in 1944, where he held
various important teaching appointments,
and in 1948 he became director of the
Municipal School of Music at Most. He also
made his mark as a writer on music and as
choral and orchestral conductor.
Vlach-Vrutický's compositions include over
a hundred opus numbers, among which the
more important are the following :

Op.
OPERA
20. ' Rychtář z Kozlovic ' (City of Prague Prize, 1934).

BALLET
68. ' Arja.'

CHURCH MUSIC
18. Te Deum for solo voices, chorus, organ & orch.
48. ' Missa jubilaris ' for chorus & orch.
54. ' Hymnus in hon. St. Thomae ' for chorus & orch.
64. ' Cantata scholaris ' for chorus & orch.
76. Improperia for unaccomp. double choir.

2 H

ORCHESTRAL WORKS
19. ' Symphonie poétique ', 3 symph. poems on pictures
by Murillo, Rubens and Rembrandt.
49. Concert Overture.
50. Prelude and Fugue on the Czech chorale ' Svatý
Václave ' (1941).
60. Symphonietta for stgs.
92. ' Diptyques héroïques.'
93a. ' Victoria 1945.'
93b. ' In Memoriam.'
96. Spring Symphony.

CHAMBER MUSIC
10. String Quartet No. 1.
32. String Quartet No. 2.
39. Trio for vn., cello & pf.
59. Prelude and Fugue for viola & cello.
75. String Quartet No. 3.

VIOLIN AND PIANOFORTE
42. Sonata.

SOLO VIOLIN
65. Sonata.
66. Partita.

PIANOFORTE MUSIC
69. ' Sonata concertante.'
Also unaccompanied choruses, pf. and organ
works, and songs.
E. B.

33   ii   **VLAD**
l. 15 *should read*:
mento ' for 11 instruments (1948). Among
more recent works are the cantata ' Le Ciel
est vide ' for chorus and orchestra, a ' Divertimento ' for harpsichord and several instruments and ' Variazioni concertanti ' on 12
notes, from Mozart's ' Don Giovanni '. Vlad
is

VLADIGEROV
Par. 1, l. 1. **Panchu** (*b*. Zürich,
should read:
Pancho (*b*. Schumen,

Add before **VOCAL ASSOCIA-
TION**:
VLTAVA. *See* SMETANA (' Má Vlast ').

35   ii   **VOGEL, J. C.**
Add at end:
BIBL.—BICKEL, AUGUST, ' Johann Christoph Vogel, der
grosse Nürnberger Komponist zwischen Gluck und
Mozart ' (Nuremberg, 1956).

36   i   **VOGEL**
Par. 4, l. 1. ' Wagaus *should read*:
' Wagadus

l. 2. (1930). *should read*:
(1930–47).

List of Works :
Add after ' Madrigaux ':
' Arpiade ' (poems by Hans Arp) for soprano, speaking
chorus & 5 insts. (1954).

36 ii VOGELWEIDE
Add to BIBL. :

KLEIN, K. K., ' Zur Spruchdichtung und Heimatfrage Walthers von der Vogelweide ' (Innsbruck, 1952).
KRALIK, DIETRICH, ' Die Elegie Walthers von der Vogelweide ' (Vienna, 1952).
MAURER, FRIEDRICH (ed.), ' Die Lieder Walthers von der Vogelweiden unter Beifügung erhaltener und erschlossener Melodien ', Vol. I (Tübingen, 1955).

See also Busoni *should read* :
See also Berg (Alban, song). Busoni

37 ii VOGL, J. M.
Par. 1, l. 5 *should read* :

powers. It was possibly due to him and two of his colleagues at the Opera, Saal and Weinmüller, that Beethoven made his third version of ' Fidelio ', for they had chosen a revival of the work for their benefit performance.[1] Vogl sang Pizarro in the first six performances or so, beginning on 23 May 1814, but was succeeded by Forti on 18 July, having been taken ill.

Add footnote :
[1] *See* Thayer's Life of Beethoven, ed. Krehbiel, Vol. I, p. 230.

Add before See also :
BIBL.—LIESS, ANDREAS, ' Johann Michael Vogl : Hofoperist und Schubertsänger ' (Graz & Cologne, 1954).

38 i VOGLER, Carl
Par. 1, l. 2. August *should read* :
Augst

41 i VOGLER, G. J.
Add to BIBL. :

SANNER, L. E., ' Abbé Georg Joseph Vogler som musikteoretiker ' (S.T.M., 1950).

43 i VOGT, A. S.
Par. 1, ll. 1-2. Washington, Ont., *should read* :
Elmira, Ont.,

Par. 2, ll. 11-13 *should read* :

conducting it, with an interruption in 1897–1900, from its foundation until 1917, when he resigned and was succeded by H. A. Fricker. Vogt was principal of the Toronto Conservatory in 1913–26 and dean of the faculty of music in the University in 1919–26.

Par. 3, ll. 11-15 *should read* :

1937, but it soon changed its name to Society for Contemporary Music. Its purpose was to stimulate creative work among young Canadian musicians, and under its auspices many new works were performed ; but it no longer exists.

66 i VOICE-TRAINING
Par. 2, l. 27. *Delete signature.*

Add before BIBL. :

SPECIAL OBSERVATIONS ON THE STROKE OF THE GLOTTIS (*Coup de la glotte*).—In the original article on this subject attention was drawn to the fact that no single feature of the old method of voice-training has been the subject of so much controversy as this much-abused mode of attack. Further exploration of the methods of the old Italian school, and particularly that of launching the sound generally adopted (which, incidentally, Monteverdi called " the stroke of the throat "), have led to the conclusion that the expression " stroke of the glottis " has come to bear a meaning quite different from that given to it by Manuel Garcia (who invented it), by Monteverdi and by all those other teachers of the old school who imparted it without using any special technical term to describe it. It is therefore most desirable that this general misunderstanding, to which the original article itself contributed, should be cleared up once and for all.

It is now generally believed by teachers everywhere that by the term " the stroke of the glottis " Manuel Garcia referred to the technique of launching a vowel sound by preceding it with a kind of glottal consonant. Such a consonant actually exists in Arabic and certain other languages, and it has a symbol assigned to it in the Arabic alphabet. It is the kind of consonant which anyone might use in announcing, for instance, the name " Julia Arden ", *i.e.* where two contiguous and similar vowels are not separated by a consonant. W. A. Aitken described it as " a kind of cough ". It came in for a good deal of condemnation within Garcia's own lifetime, often by teachers who in every other respect revered and supported him.

The misunderstanding arose mainly from the fact that many fine singers of the old school did employ the glottal consonant quite frequently when attacking vowel sounds and appeared to derive benefit from its use. (The example of Dinh Gilly was quoted in the original article.) The trouble was that no one seemed able to conceive any kind of glottal " stroke " other than that of the glottal consonant. Marcel Journet so identified it and recommended its use whenever possible for vowel attacks.

The crucial question, however, is, how Manuel Garcia himself, the inventor of the expression, described it. It must be remembered that whatever it might be, it was not a new feature introduced by him, for he stated unequivocally, quite late in life, that he had added nothing whatever to what he himself had received from his father. The evidence is quite conclusive that the method christened "the stroke of the glottis" was the mode of attack which he received from his father, Manuel del Popolo Garcia, that his father received it from Ansani (which links it with Porpora), and that it can be traced right back to the 16th century.

In an explanatory footnote to Section 10 of his 'Hints on Singing' Manuel Garcia warns his readers that the meaning of the term "stroke of the glottis" has been seriously misrepresented. He goes on to say that it refers to "a physical act of which there should be merely a mental cognizance, not an actual physical sensation. The articulation which gives the precise and clean start to the sound is not *felt* in the throat (*i.e.* the larynx) of the singer." Clearly, then, the term cannot possibly refer to the glottal consonant, which is always so felt. (The word "articulation", in the above context, refers to the articulation of the glottis, so that the vocal cords are fully approximated, occluding the air passage at the centre point of each vibratory arc and transforming all the air into sound.) It would appear, therefore, that the glottal consonant, as employed by so many fine singers, is used as a kind of adjunct to the stroke of the glottis, and that it is this use of it that has caused much of the confusion surrounding the term.

This mode of attack, together with the method of breathing, formed the basis upon which the whole art of *bel canto* was built; it is of the highest importance that every teacher of the art should understand it. To this end it will be necessary to discuss the problem in detail. For *il bel canto* is an art; that is to say, it is built, not upon vocal habit, but upon respiratory and vocal artifice. In the words of Marco da Gagliano (*c.* 1575–1642), written in his preface to Peri's opera 'Dafne', it is "Quella *artifiziosa* maniera di recitare cantando che tutta Italia ammira" ("this *ingenious* method [*i.e.* this method based upon artifice] of uttering words and music that all Italy admires").[1]

In the old Italian school singing was placed into two categories. These were:

(a) *Il canto naturale*, or natural singing. The making of voice by a habitual use of the breath, *i.e.* by breathing out against a closed glottis; (b) *L' arte del canto*, or the art of singing. The making of voice by an unhabitual and very skilful use of the breath.

It is easy to understand that a habitual method of using the breath and the articulative organs will produce what might be called the habitual voice. What is not so immediately apparent to anyone who has gone no farther than *il canto naturale* is that

---

[1] The Italian word "artifiziosa" in this context does not mean the same thing as the modern English word "artificial", which suggests something not natural. The word "artefactual" is therefore suggested as a better translation.

an artefactual method of using these two essentials of voice will produce a second type of voice — the artefactual voice — which differs strongly from the habitual voice, both in tonal characteristic and in the sensations to which it gives rise in the mind of the singer.

The human vocal machine is really an infinitely complex assembly of muscles, tendons, cartilages and bones which extends from the base of the torso to the base of the brain. Indeed, Jenny Lind used to say that a good singer sings with the entire body, including the legs. Now what is often lost sight of to-day is that this machine is not a haphazard assembly of components, any one of which may be used in isolation from the rest. As nature designed it, it is a single, perfectly integrated machine, every single component of which should work in perfect co-ordination with all the others. The singer cannot control or manage it by concentrating his attention upon any particular muscle or group of muscles; he can only interfere with its harmonious inter-action by so doing. His control must be of a kind that can be applied to the instrument as a whole: a control which co-ordinates, and maintains in co-ordinate action, the entire instrument from base to summit, *i.e.* from the pelvic area to the head. There is but one such kind of control, and it is wholly mental. It is not only that the singer's mind is the ultimate governor of the vocal machine; it is the *only* governor capable of maintaining this vastly complex machine in co-ordinate action. The art of singing is a skilful and most unhabitual way of thinking about the vocal process: a mode of thought which results in a certain kind of physical action by the complete machine, rather than a direct stimulation of certain isolated muscles or groups of muscles. We can begin, then, by saying that the stroke of the glottis is wholly a stroke of the mind.

In order to understand what this mode of thought is, and the lines it must follow, it is best to strip the vocal machine down to its simplest elements: to disregard its anatomical complexities and to study it as an essentially simple mechanical device. It is, in fact, a device for transforming a compression of air in the lungs into a special kind of physical movement, *i.e.* the vibrational movement of the vocal cords, just as a steam locomotive is, in essence, a device for transforming a compression of steam in the boiler into a rotatory movement of its wheels. The "boiler" of the vocal "engine" consists of the lungs, the "fuel" being supplied by the respiratory muscles; its "engine" is the larynx and its "funnel", where the used-up air is passed out, consists of the throat and mouth. One of the chief difficulties with which the singer has to cope lies in the fact that this "funnel", through which the exhausted air must pass, is also the channel through which the "end product" of the vibrational movement of the vocal cords — the sound-waves — must also pass in order to reach the ears of the listener. The effect of this unfortunate circumstance is always to establish in the mind of the singer a direct association between the sound and the exhausted air moving through the "funnel", and this mental association is usually reinforced by our habits of conversational speech, so that we tend, quite unthinkingly, to associate flow of breath with flow of voice. As a result of this, part of the energy in the air compression, which should have been transformed into sound-energy, is not so transformed, but is passed out in the form of breath under pressure. The breath is in fact being used wastefully and the larynx does not develop its full efficiency. If all the energy in the lung compression is transformed into sound, then the air passing out through the "funnel" will have no energy and will pass out merely because it is being displaced by the exhaust air which follows it. In the old Italian school this seems to have been well understood, for the classic test of that school for a well-sung note was always that of the taper flame which must not flicker, or the mirror whose surface must remain unclouded, when held close to the open mouth of the singer. When singing a vowel sound in a cold atmosphere, the breath of the singer should be seen to rise straight upwards from the lips; it should not be seen to flow outward from the lips.

Enough has been said to establish the point that in true singing it is the air in the "boiler" and not the air in the "funnel" that must do the job of singing. This means, in practice, that the singer must always sing from the lungs, and not from the mouth or from any locality above the larynx. Manuel Garcia, when summing up the functions of the various organs used in singing, used to tell his pupils that "the lungs are for tone-making". And as the making of the tone is the only part of the vocal process which requires a consciously directed physical activity (the pitch-tensioning of the vocal cords and the movements of the tongue in forming vowels being governed at the subconscious level), it follows that, as has already been said, the active effort of singing should be deliberately placed by the singer upon the lungs.

The vital importance of this technique of "lung-loading" lies in the fact that because the singer cannot possibly feel the physical action of his vocal cords, and consequently cannot know when they are occluding the air passage at the centre point of each vibration, the sensation of a static or

immobilized lung pressure is his only means of telling that they are doing so. When we say that every particle of air used by the glottis is transformed into sound, what we are really saying is that air-pressure energy has been wholly transformed into sound energy, so that the breath possesses no energy whatever after it has passed the glottis, and could not move out of the throat and mouth at all were it not being continuously displaced by the air subsequently used up. This means that when the vocal cords occlude the air passage at the centre point of each vibration, all sensation of moving breath is lost, and the singer feels that, in some strange way, he is singing on a stopped breath. As has already been said, it is his only means of knowing that the glottis is working at maximum efficiency. Moreover — and this is the proper meaning of Manuel Garcia's footnote, quoted at the beginning of this article — the act of breath stoppage is not a direct physical act of the larynx, but a pure act of the will. From the objective point of view taken by Garcia in his writings it is, in fact, a stroke of the glottis, for it is the glottis which, by approximating up to the point of complete occlusion of the air passage, evokes the sensation of a stopped breath; and it does this so precisely and swiftly that the operation may appropriately be called a stroke.[1] From the subjective point of view of the singer, however, it is a pure stroke of the will, the purpose of which is to establish the sensation of breath stoppage, not at the larynx itself, but (seemingly) at the apex of the lungs.

The singer's task, however, does not end with the production of tone from the lungs; he must give his "tone" a pre-selected pitch and a definite vowel-form. Should he then associate his pitch-vowel attack (a) with the locality where the vowel is moulded or (b) with the act of lung-loading that produces it? But it has already been shown that his deliberate and conscious government of the act of loading the lungs is the only means he possesses of exercising control over the full approximation of the vocal cords, so that the instrument attains its maximum efficiency. For this reason it would appear that by adopting course (a) he must inevitably surrender this control to some extent. Furthermore, the three processes with which he must concern himself, i.e. tonal air pressure, pitch-tensioning and vowel moulding, have their only common meeting-point at the larynx: the air pressure extends to the top of the windpipe, the pitch-tensioning occurs at the vocal cords, while the total vowel cavity extends down to the larynx. (The throat cannot be divorced from the mouth

---

[1] This "stroke" or *coup*, however, resembles the *coup d'archet*, or bow-stroke, of the violinist in that it is continuous, not spasmodic.

cavity in forming vowels, since every vowel gesture of the tongue affects its root, which is in the throat.) It is logical to suppose, therefore, that this common meeting-point of the three vocal processes, each of which brings muscular activity into play, is the only point at which a complete co-ordination of the entire musculature of the vocal organ can be established and maintained.

Converting this theoretical proposition into practice, this means that the singer should mentally associate the enunciation of his pitched vowel with the level of the larynx, accompanying his act of enunciation with a deliberate and consciously directed impulse of the mind and will, the purpose of which is to load the lungs with an air pressure appropriate to the pitch and intensity of the note. It is worth emphasizing, however, that this act of attack is purely and wholly an act of the mind and will, and that it must on no account involve the singer in any direct activity of the throat or neck muscles. The breath is not stopped before the attack, as when the glottal consonant is employed; it is (apparently) immobilized *by* that act. The breath is neither pushed through the glottis from below nor drawn through it from above : it is brought to *a state of rest* against the glottis, so that the vocal cords are able to utilize it strictly in accordance with the requirements of pitch and intensity. The term "stroke of the glottis", therefore, as used by Manuel Garcia to define the practice of the historic Italian school of singing, consists of a downward impulse of the mind and will in which the three vocal processes of lung-loading, pitching and vowel-forming are conceived as a single integrated mental process which evokes an instantaneous and co-ordinated response from the entire vocal machine, because the two "subconscious" processes are mentally associated with the consciously directed act of air compression that makes the voice. A vocal attack associated with any point in the head cannot possibly co-ordinate the vocal machine because the three processes have no physical meeting-point in the head.

In view of the somewhat heated atmosphere of controversy which seems to prevail whenever the modern "forward production" theory is called in question, it is advisable to conclude with a few brief observations, the main point being that it is utterly futile. If an argument about vocal method is to serve any useful purpose, there must be some common ground of experience upon which both sides can take their stand, and in this case there is none. That the two different voices exist potentially in every human being is beyond dispute. They are called, in this article, the habitual voice and the artefactual voice. Indeed, the artefactual voice could almost be called a synthetic voice. When a chemical synthesis of two substances is made, the chemist produces, not a mere mixture, but a new substance which had no previous existence. In a very similar way, the exponent of *l' arte del canto* takes "words" and "tone", and produces from them neither "words-plus-tone" nor "tone-plus-words", but something which, in a very real sense, is "word-tone" — a single product which is not at all a mere addition of one product to the other. The question the singing-teacher has to decide, therefore, is which of these two voices will best enable a singer to perform the tasks allotted to him by the composer and to preserve his voice under the stress of a successful professional career. And when it comes to finding an answer to this question, one thing can be said with complete certainty : until a teacher has actually experienced the use of the artefactual voice he can have no grounds for dispute : he can neither argue about it nor refute the testimony of those who practise it, for he can know nothing whatever about it. It is so far removed from the habitual voice that it cannot be understood except by using it, and the futility of this controversy really lies in the fact that the two sides are, in fact, arguing about two different things whose only link is in the word "voice". Moreover, once a teacher has learned to use the artefactual voice, he will no longer wish to argue about it. The present writer knows of no single case where either a teacher or a singer, having learned only the rudiments of true *bel canto*, ever wanted to return to the habitual voice. The sense of assurance, of mastery over one's means and, above all, of physical exhilaration evoked by the use of the artefactual voice is far too keen for anyone to wish to return to the uncertainties and anxieties of "forward production". F. K.

66 i *Add to* BIBL. :

CRANMER, ARTHUR, 'The Art of Singing' ('Student's Music Library') (London, 1957).
GARCIA, MANUEL, 'Hints on Singing' (London, 1894). 'Traité complet de l'art du chant' (Paris, 1847).
GRAVES, RICHARD, 'Singing for Amateurs' (Oxford, 1954).
JOSEPH, B. L., 'Elizabethan Acting' (Oxford, 1951).
KELSEY, FRANKLYN, 'The Foundations of Singing' (London, 1950).
LEVIEN, JOHN MEWBURN, 'Some Notes for Singers' (London, 1940).
LUNN, CHARLES, 'The Philosophy of the Voice' (London, 1824).
NATHAN, ISAAC, 'Musurgia vocalis' (London, 1836).
ROCKSTRO, W. S. & GOLDSCHMIDT, OTTO, 'Jenny Lind, Record and Analysis of the Method of' (London, 1908).
SANTLEY, CHARLES, 'The Art of Singing' (London, 1908).
SCOTT, CHARLES KENNEDY, 'The Fundamentals of Singing' (London, 1954).
TOSI, PIER FRANCESCO, 'Observations on the Florid Song' (London, 1743).
WOOD, HENRY J., 'The Gentle Art of Singing' (Oxford, 1927).
YOUNG, GERALD MACKWORTH, 'What Happens in Singing' (London, 1953).

67   ii   **VOLBACH**
Par. 1, l. 1.   Wippelfürth, *should read*:

Wipperfürth,

ll. 2-3.   6 Dec. 1941 *should read*:
30 Nov. 1940

70   i   **VOLLERTHUN**
Par. 1, l. 2 *should read*:

Danzig, 29 Sept. 1876; *d.* Strausberg, 15 Sept. 1945).

71   i   Voltaire
l. 12 *should read*:

Monsigny ('Belle Arsène', opera).   Paisiello ('Re Teodoro', opera).   Pleyel (1, 'Fée

72   ii   **VOLUNTARY**
Add at end:

THE VOLUNTARY FOR DOUBLE ORGAN.—
A form of English organ composition invented in the early 17th century and devised especially for the " double organ " (a two-manual organ). The development of this form depended largely on the development of the English organ and can be divided into two periods: the first begins soon after 1600, when a second manual was added to some organs, and the second period about 1660, when under the influence of foreign organ-builders mixture and solo stops were added. The last voluntaries for a double organ were written about 1720.

In all voluntaries for double organ it is clearly indicated which of the two manuals should be used. The upper manual was the louder one. It was called " Double ", " Bass ", " Great " or sometimes " upper keys ". The lower manual was softer and possessed fewer stops. It was called " Single ", " Tenor ", " Little ", " Chair " and sometimes " under keys ".

Like the free organ fantasies, the voluntaries for double organ were written in imitative 3- and 4-part counterpoint and consisted of several sections, each built on a new theme. Composers, however, added a new feature to this well-known form by introducing bass solo passages, probably inspired by the current fashion enjoyed by the bass viol. They thus created a new form and all voluntaries for double organ were constructed after the same pattern. At the beginning of each section, both hands always play on the " Single ". When the bass solo begins, it is played by the left hand on the louder " Double ", while the right hand continues on the " Single ". As soon as the bass solo ends, the left hand returns to the " Single ". This happens in every section of the piece. Only the final section is always played by

both hands on the " Double ". The various sections of the composition are held together by ingenious transitions, while the middle section with short themes and fast note-values presents a kind of development, brought to a climax in the final section.

Composers of voluntaries for double organ of the first period were John Lugge, John Hingston and Richard Portman. A ' Fancie for a double Orgaine ' by Orlando Gibbons (Benjamin Cosyn's Virginal Book) cannot be included among this type of organ composition. It seems that Cosyn himself added the indications for use of two manuals and tried to " arrange " Gibbons's " free " fantasy for a double organ. This suspicion is well founded, because the next piece in the same collection, also by Orlando Gibbons, bears signs of further attempts to " arrange ", which after a few bars were given up. Apparently Cosyn was defeated by the unsuitable structure of that piece.

The characteristic feature of the voluntaries for double organ of the second period, *i.e.* after 1660, is the introduction of treble solo passages in addition to the already existing bass solos. These solos were played on the new stops, which were introduced by foreign organ-builders and added to the existing diapason chorus of English organs. Thus bass solos were played on the Sesquialtera and treble solos on the Cornet, sometimes Trumpet, and both accompanied on a soft " Single " or " Chair ".

In the earlier voluntaries of this period composers still adhere to the polyphonic writing and the more compact structure of the typical organ fancy, but by the end of the century there were some important changes in this form of organ composition. The 3- and 4-part imitative part-writing is only found in the first and final section, while the middle sections serve to show off the new solo stops. Moreover, the structure of the voluntary for double organ had loosened up considerably and points to the 18th-century type of organ voluntary, which consists of several completely separate pieces. Two of Christopher Gibbons's voluntaries for double organ exist in a short and a long version (*cf.* B.M. Add. 34695 f. 25b and f. 29b). Several sections for solo stops (Sesquialtera, Cornet and Trumpet) were inserted into the original voluntary, and it is very likely that these additions were made at a later date.

Composers of the second period were Matthew Locke, Christopher Gibbons, John Blow, who was the greatest exponent of this form, John Barret, William Croft and John Reading.   S. J.

BIBL.—JEANS, SUSI, ' Geschichte und Entwicklung des Voluntary for Double Organ in der englischen Orgelmusik des 17. Jahrhunderts ' (' Bericht über

den Internationalen musikwissenschaftlichen Kongress, Hamburg 1956 ', Cassel, 1957).
JEANS & and STEELE, JOHN (eds.), 'Three Voluntaries for Double Organ by John Lugge' (London,1957).

73   i   **Vondel**
ll. 5-6 *should read*:
(chorus). Mengelberg (R., hymn). Meulemans ('Jozef in Dothan', incid. m.). Monnikendam ('Noach', incid. m.). Padbrué (C., music for 'Kruisbergh'). Pijper ('Phaëton', incid. m.). Roos

74   ii   **VOŘÍŠEK**
Par. 1, l. 14.   Sonnleither *should read*:
Sonnleithner

Add at end:
See also Musica Antiqua Bohemica, Vol. 4 (modern ed. of pf. Sonata, Op. 20).

75   i   **VOSS, Charles**
Par. 1, l. 2.   Paris, *should read*:
Verona,
Par. 2, l. 8 *should read*:
sohn. He left Paris in 1860 and settled in Italy.   J. A. F.-M., rev.

ii   **Voss, J. H.**
l. 1.   Refs. *should read*:
See Bach (C. P. E., 5 songs). Brahms (partsong).

76   ii   **VRANKEN (3)**
l. 2 *should read*:
1897; *d.* The Hague, 20 Apr. 1956), organist and composer, son of (1),

77   i   **Vrchlický**
l. 1.   **Frida** *should read*:
Frída

78   i   **VRETBLAD**
Par. 1, l. 2 *should read*:
nås, 5 Apr. 1876; *d.* Stockholm, 15 Jan. 1953).

ii   **VRIESLANDER**
Par. 1, l. 2.   Tegna *should read*:
Tegno

82   i   **VYCPÁLEK**
UNACCOMPANIED CHORAL WORKS
4 lines from end. ' K svaténu Václavu '
should read:
' K svatému Václavu '

ii   *Add at end*:
VYŠEHRAD. *See* SMETANA (' Má Vlast ').
VYVYAN, Jennifer (Bright) (*b.* Broadstairs, Kent, 13 Mar. 1925).
English soprano singer. She was educated at St. Paul's Girls' School in London and Talbot Heath School, Bournemouth. She

studied the pianoforte and singing at the R.A.M. in London from 1941, taking the L.R.A.M. for the former (performance) in 1943 and for the latter (teaching) the next year. In 1945 she also gained the Fred Walker Scholarship for singing, which she studied further with Roy Henderson. To gain stage experience she joined the chorus at Glyndebourne. Before long she appeared with the English Opera Group as Jenny in ' The Beggar's Opera ', Nancy in Britten's ' Albert Herring ' and the Female Chorus in his ' Rape of Lucretia ', including tours abroad. In 1951 she studied under Fernand Carpi with a Boise Travelling Scholarship ; also in Milan and Rome.

Jennifer Vyvyan came fully into her own as an operatic artist in 1952, when she appeared as Constanze in Mozart's ' Seraglio ' at Sadler's Wells, singing with astonishing brilliance, security of intonation and subtlety of phrasing, while the vocal quality was still a little hard. This had mellowed considerably, however, by the time she sang Donna Anna and Fiordiligi at the same theatre, and though her technical assurance in florid singing remained perhaps her outstanding gift, she was soon able to sustain dramatic parts with great success, such as Lady Rich in the production of Britten's ' Gloriana ' in 1953, Electra in ' Idomeneo ' at Glyndebourne and the Governess in Britten's ' The Turn of the Screw ', a part she created in the original production at Venice in 1954 and has since repeated at Florence, in Belgium, Holland, Germany, France and elsewhere. She has also appeared at concerts and in broadcasts in various foreign countries, and in 1956 she appeared in the concert parties in Russia led by Sir Arthur Bliss, in Moscow, Leningrad, Kiev and Kharkov. She became an F.R.A.M. in 1955.   E. B.

84   i   **WACŁAW**
Par. 6, l. 5.   in Polonia ' (Poznań, *should read*:
in Polonia ', Vol. II (Poznań,

ii   **Waddell**
Add at end of l. 3 :
Orr (R., voc. chamber m. & songs).

86   ii   **WAELRAND**
See also should read:
See also Collectio O.M.B., Vol. 1 (modern ed.). Solmization.

88   ii   **WAGENSEIL, G. C.**
Add at end :
See also Sondheimer Ed., Vol. 22 (modern ed. of Symphony).

WAGENSEIL, J. C.
Par. 2, l. 5.   Murner *should read*:
Marner

89   ii   **WAGNER, Johanna**
          Par. 2, ll. 1-2 *should read*:
German soprano singer. She was the
natural daughter of a lieutenant, Bock von
Wülfingen, of Hanover, and was adopted by
Richard Wagner's brother Albert, a

91   i   **WAGNER-RÉGENY**
          Par. 3, l. 16 *should read*:
the 1939-45 war and from 1947 as director of

     ii   PIANOFORTE AND ORCHESTRA
          Add after ' Orchestermusik ':
Concerto (1955).

93   ii   **WAGNER**
          Par. 3, l. 10. Okan's *should read*:
Oken's

94   ii   *Footnote* 5, l. 9. Weinlang *should read*:
Weinbarg

97   ii   Par. 4, l. 9 *should read*:
cedent and became bankrupt. Wagner himself was imprisoned for debt in the Clichy
gaol from 28 Oct. to 17 Nov. 1840. In the
summer

102 ii   Par. 2, ll. 11-12. R. Friegedonk.
          should read:
K. Freigedank.

103 i   Par. 2, l. 2. Herwergh *should read*:
Herwegh

     ii   Par. 1, l. 4. Herwergh *should read*:
Herwegh

105 i   Par. 4, l. 6 *should read*:
distaste for the libretto of ' Les Troyens ',
which Berlioz read to him, and the latter
being

     ii   Par. 2, l. 9. Herwergh *should read*:
Herwegh

121 i   *Add to* BIBL. (ENGLISH):
BARZUN, JACQUES, ' Darwin, Marx, Wagner: Critique
     of a Heritage ', rev. 2nd ed. (New York, 1958).

     BIBL. ll. 5-8 *should read*:
BURRELL, MARY, Richard Wagner: ' his Life and Works
     from 1813 '.

     Add to BIBL. (FRENCH):
DUMESNIL, RENÉ, ' Richard Wagner ' (Paris, 1954).

     ii   *Add to* BIBL. (GERMAN):
KURTH, ERNST, ' Romantische Harmonik und ihre
     Krise in Wagners " Tristan " ' (Berne, 1920;
     Berlin, 1922-23).
LOOS, APUL ARTHUR, ' Richard Wagner: Vollendung
     und Tragik der deutschen Romantik ' (Berne, 1952).
WESTERNHAGEN, CURT VON, ' Richard Wagner: sein
     Werk, sein Wesen, seine Welt ' (Zürich, 1956).

122 ii   *Footnote should read*:
     ¹ A " conjectural reconstruction " of another Quartet
was made by Gerald Abraham in 1945. It is clearly a
first version of what five years later became the ' Siegfried Idyll ' and already contains material used later in
the ' Ring '. The ' Siegfried Idyll ', as Abraham points
out in his preface to the score of the Quartet (which is
in one movement), still bears distinct signs of having
been originally conceived for string quartet.

123 i   CATALOGUE :
          LITERARY WORKS
          l. 10. der letze *should read*:
der letzte

124 ii   *Add after* l. 28 :
          SUPP. VOL. XI
          (Librettos)
' Die Hochzeit ' (1832).
' Die Feen ' (1832-33).
' Das Liebesverbot, oder Die Novize von Palermo '
     (1834).
' Die Bergwerke zu Falun ' (1841-42).
' Die hohe Braut, oder Bianca und Giuseppe ' (1836-42).
' Männerlist grösser als Frauenlist, oder Die glückliche
     Bärenfamilie ' (1837).
' Die Sarazenin ' (1841-43).
' Das Liebesmahl der Apostel ' (1843).
' Friedrich I ' (1846-48).
' Jesus von Nazareth ', sketch (1848).
' Die Sieger ' (1856).
' Tristan und Isolde ', sketches (1854-57).
' Die Meistersinger von Nürnberg ', 3 drafts (1845-61).
' Parzival ', sketches (1857-65).
Venusberg Scene for ' Tannhäuser ', Paris version (1860).

          SUPP. VOL. XII
          (Miscellaneous)
(Each section contains a number of essays, articles,
criticisms, sketches, aphorisms, poems, fragments &c.)
     I. First Essays on Opera (1834-37).
     II. The Paris Period (1840-41).
     III. The Dresden Period (1843-46).
     IV. The Revolution Period (1848-49).
     V. Sketches and Fragments (1849-58).
     VI. The 1860s.
     VII. Concerning Bayreuth (1873-77).
     VIII. Last Writings on Art and Religion.
     IX. Programme Notes.
     X. Poems.
     XI. Appendix.
     XII. Notes and Addenda.

125 i   **WAGNER, Siegfried**
          Par. 2, ll. 7-9 *should read*:
decree was made absolute on 18 July 1870,
and Wagner and Cosima were married on
25 Aug., when Siegfried was more than a year

     ii   BIBL., l. 5. sine Kunst *should read*:
seine Kunst

131 ii   **WALCKER**
          Par. 1, l. 3 *should read*:
time the son (b. Cannstadt, 3 July 1794 ; d.
Ludwigsburg, 2 Oct. 1872) was ready to join
him the firm

          WALDSTEIN
          Par. 1, l. 2. Duchov *should read*:
Duchcov

140 i   **Waley**
          l. 1 *should read*:
Waley, Arthur. *See* ApIvor (song). Britten (6
songs from the Chinese). Copland (song).

          l. 2. Orr (C. W., song). *should read*:
Orr, C. W. (song).

140   ii   **WALKER, Edyth**
          Par. 2, l. 16.   19 Dec. *should read*:
19 Feb.

145   i   **WALLACE, Vincent**
          Par. 1, l. 2.   de Haget nr. *should read*:
de Bagen nr.

Footnote. l. 1 *should read*:
[1] Not Haget, as given by Michel Brenet; in the Letters
ll. 3-4 *should read*:
on 6 Dec. 1865, the place is clearly called Château Bagen.

147   ii   **WALLACE, William**
          Par. 4, l. 5 *should read*:
'Richard Wagner as he lived' (1925) and 'Liszt,

148   ii   **WALLEK-WALEWSKI**
          Par. 1, l. 11.   gęśliczkach *should read*:
gęślizckach

149   i   *Add after* **Waller**:
WALLERIUS-RETZELIUS. *See* VALLERIUS.

153   i   *Add before* **WALTER**:
WALSWORTH, Ivor (*b*. London, 31 Dec. 1909).
English composer. His studies at the R.A.M. included violin, piano, horn, conducting and composition. He gained the Macfarren and Mendelssohn Scholarships, and the A.R.A.M., deciding at an early stage to concentrate on composition, which he studied further in Munich, Budapest and Vienna. One of his early orchestral works, 'Rhapsodic Dance', was performed at the Promenade Concerts in 1932, and although various orchestral works followed, including four Symphonies (I : 1947; II : 1950; III : 1953; IV : 1955), 'Ésion' for pf. & orch., 'Nanquidno' for string orch., and film music, some of his most typical work is to be found in his chamber music, which covers a wide range. He has written a Suite for viola & cello, 'Dialoghi' for violin & cello, Lento ed accelerando ('Leaht, ve yoter mahér') for violin & piano, 2 string Quartets, a piano Trio, a piano Quartet (written for the 10th anniversary concert of the Robert Masters Piano Quartet), Sonatas for piano, violin and piano, flute and piano, recorder and harpsichord, and 'Improvisation' for cello & piano (1960). Among other recent works are a cello Concerto (1959) and a group of electronic compositions, including 'Passacaglia' (1960). Walsworth, who joined the B.B.C. Music Department in 1936, and has been Tran-

scription Music Organizer since 1957, is married to the concert pianist, Joan Davies.
D. W. S.

153   ii   **WALTER, Bruno**
          Par. 2, l. 6.   director of *should read*:
conductor at

Par. 5, l. 2 *should read*:
U.S.A. and in 1941 he appeared as guest conductor at the New York Metropolitan Opera. In 1947-49 he was conductor and musical adviser of the New York Philharmonic-Symphony Orchestra. Since the second world war he has

154   i   *Add to* BIBL.:
MANN, T., 'Bruno Walter on his 70th Birthday' (M.Q., Oct. 1946).

ii   **WALTERSHAUSEN**
          Par. 1, l. 3 *should read*:
1882 ; *d*. Munich, 12 Aug. 1954).

155   ii   **WALTHER**
          Par. 2, ll. 5-8 *should read*:
of its musical history. In 1517-26 he was bass singer in the court choir of Frederick the Wise of Saxony and in the latter year he became municipal cantor at Torgau. In 1548 he was sent

Par. 3, l. 1.   1524 *should read*:
1525

l. 3.   Geystlich *should read*:
Geystliche

l. 4.   for four voices *should read*:
for 3-5 voices

156   i   BIBL.   *Add work by* MICHAELIS *from col. ii.*

See also. l. 2 *should read*:
(earliest Lutheran Passion). Publikationen G.M.F., Vol. 6 (modern ed. of Wittenberg song-book).

ii   **WALTHER, J. G.**
          Par. 1, l. 5 *should read*:
for clavier in 1766.
A modern facsimile reprint of 'Musicalisches Lexicon' is published in 'Documenta Musicologica', Series I, Vol. iii.
G., adds.

BIBL.   *Transfer work by* MICHAELIS *to col. i.*

Add at end:
See also Denkmäler (2), Vol. 26-27 (modern ed. of organ works).

WALTHER, J. J.
See also should read:
See also Beckmann ('Scherzi' for vn. ed.). Denkmäler (5) I, Vol. 17 (modern ed. of do.).

156   ii   **WALTHEW**
Par. 1, l. 3.   6 Dec. *should read*:
14 Nov.

163   i   **WALTON**
Par. 2, ll. 1-2 *should read*:
In 1948 Christopher Hassall, the poet, undertook to write the libretto for an opera

CATALOGUE :
OPERA
l. 1 *should read*:
' Troilus and Cressida ' (lib. by Christopher Hassall, after Chaucer) (1954), prod. London, Covent Garden Theatre, 3 Dec. 1954.

ii   FILM MUSIC
Add at end:
' Richard III ' (Shakespeare) (1954).

' My Lady is a Pretty One ', for voice & stg. 4tet.	Anon., 17th cent.	1929.

' Bethlehem Down.'	Blunt.	1927-30.	1931.	Arnold Dowbiggin.

' The Fairest May.'[1]	Anon. (16th cent.).	1930.	—	Arnold Dowbiggin.

164   —   ORCHESTRAL WORKS
Add at end:

' Johannesburg Festival Overture.'	1955.	City of Johannesburg (for the 70th anniversary).
Partita.	1958.	Cleveland Symphony Orchestra (40th anniversary).

SOLO   INSTRUMENT   WITH   OR-
CHESTRA
Add at end:

Cello Concerto.	1956.	Gregor Piatigorsky.

165   i   **WALTZ**
Par. 1, l. 2.   *valzero should read*:
valzero, or (more usually) *valzer*

169   i   Par. 2, ll. 17-21 *should read*:
waltzes.   Haydn also wrote several sets of orchestral dances, and there are a number

174   i   **WANNING**
Add at end:
See also Vereniging, Vol. 8 (reprint from ' Sententiae ').

176   ii   **WARD, John**
Par. 1, l. 1 *should read*:
WARD, John (*b.* Canterbury, Sept. 1571 [1]; *d.* ?, 1638).

[1] Ward was baptized on 8 Sept. 1571 at St. Mary Magdalene, Canterbury. His will (P.C.C. 99 Lee) is dated 1 Apr. 1636, and was proved by his wife Thomazin (born Clee) on 31 Aug. 1638. These facts are given in an unpublished thesis, at present in the Bodleian Library, by Mr. Christian Strover.

Footnote 1 becomes 2.

178   i   **WARD**
Par. 2, l. 19 *should read*:
and finished his studies.   He taught there and at Columbia University from 1946.

Par. 4, l. 4 *should read*:
' First Harvest ' (1940), ' Jubilation Overture ' (1946) and other orchestral

ii   **WARLICH**
Par. 1, l. 2 *should read*:
burg, 24 May 1877; *d.* New York, 10 Nov. 1939).

181   —   **WARLOCK**, CATALOGUE :
VOCAL CHAMBER MUSIC
Add at end:

1957, in facsimile.	—

182   —   Last line but one of list *should read*:

Add after ' The Fox ' :

Add footnote :
[1] The last song, dated 6 Nov. 1930; unpublished.

183   i   **WARNER**
Par. 1, l. 2 *should read*:
ampton, 4 Jan. 1874; *d.* London, 1 June 1945).

184   i   *Add after* **WARRACK, Guy** :
WARRACK, John (Hamilton) (*b.* London, 9 Feb. 1928).
British musical author and critic, son of the preceding.   He was educated at Winchester College in 1941-46, and after doing national service as a schoolmaster in Greece and Egypt during 1946-48, he entered the R.C.M. in London in 1949, remaining until 1952 and taking the A.R.C.M.   Having made the oboe one of his studies there, he played as a free-lance oboist in the Boyd Neel and Sadler's Wells orchestras between 1951 and 1953, when he joined the Oxford University Press as assistant music editor.   In 1954 he was appointed assistant music critic to ' The Daily Telegraph ' and in 1956 joint editor of the ' Opera ' magazine.   Since 1952 he has

broadcast and contributed articles to various periodicals. His books so far are ' Six Great Composers ', completed for publication in 1958 and, written and compiled in collaboration with Harold Rosenthal, ' The Concise Oxford Dictionary of Opera ', to be published about 1960.   E. B.

184   ii   **WARREN, Leonard**
        Par. 1, l. 2 *should read*:
Apr. 1911 ; *d.* New York, 4 Mar. 1960).

191   ii   *Add before* **Watts, Isaac**:
WATTS, Helen (*b.* Pembrokeshire, Dec. 1927).
   British contralto singer. She learnt the pianoforte as a child, but wished to make a career in psychotherapy. Being too young to begin her training, she entered the R.A.M. in London to spend a year in musical study. There her teachers, Caroline Hatchard and Frederick Jackson, discovered unusual vocal and musicianly gifts in her. She decided to become a concert singer and began to make her way entirely on her own merits and without influence, at first as a member of the B.B.C. chorus. After a difficult beginning with small engagements, and a long-delayed broadcast in a programme of light music in 1953, she made a great impression by her singing of the title-part in Gluck's ' Orpheus ' on the radio, which led to her engagement for two important Bach concerts, broadcast by the Third Programme. In 1955 she recorded solo parts in Handel's ' Sosarme ' and ' Semele ' for Oiseau-Lyre records and in 1958 she made an admirable stage appearance in the Handel Opera Society's production of ' Theodora '.   E. B.

193   i   **Webb, Mary**
        l. 4 *should read*:
Orr (R., voc. chamber m.). Rubbra (song). Williams (Grace, song).

     ii   **WEBB**
        Cancel article and replace by :
WEBB, William (*b.* ? ; *d.* ?).
   English 17th-century composer. The dates 1637 and 1651 are the first and last under which he is mentioned in surviving documents. He became a London Wait in 1637 and was still serving as such in 1645. Playford's list of music teachers in London printed in ' A Musicall Banquet ' (1651) includes him as one " For the Voyce or Viole ". Anthony Wood says that he was a Gentleman of the Chapel Royal and that at the beginning of the rebellion he took a house in Charterhouse Yard, where he taught singing for " maintenance sake ". He died sometime before 1660.
   Although there is a receipt signed by Webb

as a Gentleman of the Chapel Royal dated 1647 (B.M. Add. MS 33965 f. 97), his name does not occur in the " old Cheque Book ". But the title-page of ' Select Ayres and Dialogues ' (1659) refers to him as one of the " Gentlemen and Servants to his late Majesty in his Publick and Private Musick ", so the bulk of the evidence seems to support Wood.
   His style is not so declamatory as Henry Lawes's, and he inclines more to composing partsongs for such convivial collections as Playford's ' Musical Companion ', which, though simple, are among the best of their time. Many of his songs still survive in manuscript, among which the following may be listed: B.M. Add. MSS 10337, 29481, Egerton MS 2013 ; Ch. Ch. MS 87 ; Bodl. Lib. MS Don. C. 57 ; Anderson Library, Glasgow University MS R. d. 58-61 ; New York Public Library, Drexel MS 4257. For the songs printed by Playford (22 in all) *see* Day and Murrie's ' English Song-Books 1651–1702 ' (1940).   I. S.

210   ii   **WEBER**
        Par. 1, ll. 6-7.   29 Apr. 1826.
        should read :
9 Apr. 1826.

218   ii   BIBL., l. 9. (Paris, 1925). *should read* :
(Paris, 1925 ; new ed., 1953).

219   i   BIBL., MOSER. l. 2 *should read* :
Leben und Werk ' (Leipzig, 1941 ; 2nd ed. 1955).

        Add to BIBL. :
GRÜNIGER, FRITZ, ' Carl Maria von Weber : Leben und Werk ' (Freiburg i/B., 1954).

        3rd work by SCHNOOR :
' Weber : Gestalt und Schöpfung ' (Dresden, 1953).

228   i   **WEBERN**
        Add to BIBL. :
CRAFT, ROBERT, ' Anton Webern ' (' The Score ', Sept· 1955).
' Die Reihe ', No. 2. Special Webern number (Vienna, 1955 ; Eng. trans. Bryn Mawr, Penn., 1957).
' Die Reihe 2 : Anton Webern ', No. ed. by Herbert Eimert & Karlheinz Stockhausen, Eng. ed. (London, 1958).
WEBERN, ANTON, ' Dokumente, Bekenntnisse, Erkenntnisse, Analysen ' (Vienna, Zürich and London, 1955).

        ii   *See also.* l. 1 *should read* :
See also Dallapiccola (influence on). Křenek (memorial ' Elegy '). Twelve-Note

        Webster
        l. 3 *should read* :
Du Plessis (songs). Eccles (2, ' Duchess of Malfi ', incid. m.). Milhaud (do.).

229   i   **WECHSELDOMINANTE**
        Add at end :
BIBL.—HAMBURGER, POVL, ' Subdominante und Wechseldominante : eine entwicklungs-geschichtliche Untersuchung ' (Copenhagen & Wiesbaden, 1955).

230   ii **WECKMANN**
Add at end:

See also Denkmäler (2), Vol. 6; (5) II (modern ed.).

231   i **WEELKES**
Par. 1, l. 18 *should read:*

chester, organist ", a post he held from about 1598 to 1601. His name occurs only

l. 22 *should read:*

ist's stipend during this period of office was 13s. 4d. per quarter, probably

Par. 3, l. 4 *should read:*

his supplication for the degree (12 Feb. 1602) men-

ll. 6-14 *should read:*

music. He left a fine autograph on the University Register of Subscription to the Act of Supremacy (July 1602). A few months earlier he had been appointed organist, master of the choristers, lay singing-man and Sherborne clerk at Chichester Cathedral. From the Chapter Records of the Cathedral and various parish registers in the city it appears that he probably arrived at Chichester in the autumn of 1601.

On 20 Feb. 1603 Weelkes married Elizabeth Sandham, daughter of William and Katherine Sandham of the parish of All Saints in the Pallant, Chichester. The baptism of Thomas Weelkes the younger, who later sang in his father's choir, is entered in the Subdeanery Parish Registers on 9 June 1603 and that of their daughter Alice (" Alles ") on 17 Sept. 1606. Their third child, Katherine, does not appear, but the Subdeanery Registers are very defective between 1607 and 1618.

In 1608 appeared Weelkes's ' Ayeres or Phantasticke

l. 21 *should read:*

(edited by Rimbault, 1872), nor in the various other lists of the Gentlemen of the Chapel Royal. He contributed

l. 23 *should read:*

cions ' (1614): ' Most mighty and all-knowing Lord ' a 4,

ll. 27-29 *should read:*

and services which still survive.

The Bishop of Chichester during his visitation to the Cathedral in Jan. 1617 ordered Weelkes's removal from his offices for being " a common drunkard and a notorious swearer and blasphemer " and for spending more time in the " taverne or ale house than in the quire ". Weelkes, however, continued to receive the rather meagre wages of singing-man and organist until his death six years

later, but his loss of income and prestige as master of the choristers and Sherborne clerk must have been disastrous. Little more is known about his remaining years.

231   ii Par. 1, l. 4. *Signature should read:*

G. E. P. A., rev. W. S. C.

232   i Par. 2, ll. 12-16 *should read:*

services is not certain; the direction occurs in contrast to sections marked " Verse " or " Full ". It probably indicates a soloist standing in the centre of the choir.

ii Par. 2, l. 1. ' The Deum ' *should read:*
' Te Deum '

l. 3 *should read:*

ficat and ' Nunc dimittis ' (*ibid.*, fol. 132). The Responses to the Commandments (ed. Rimbault, ' The Choir ', No. 47, 1 July 1864).

Par. 4. ll. 3-6 *should read:*

some inequality. Nothing

ll. 9-21 *should read:*

equally fine are the festive anthems ' Gloria in excelsis . . . Sing, my soul ' and ' Alleluia, I heard a voice '. ' O Lord, arise ', ' When David heard ', ' O Jonathan ' and others show Weelkes's genius for composition in a large number of voices. In contrast to these, some though certainly not all of the verse anthems seem somewhat pedestrian and uninspired. ' Give Ear, O Lord ', ' Give the King Thy Judgments ' and ' If King Manasses ' are especially fine examples of Weelkes's verse anthem style. Several of the full anthems have been printed separately in recent years and a collected edition of the approximately twenty completable anthems is in preparation (1959) for publication.

Par. 6 (instrumental works)
Add at end:

Voluntary and Pavan for virginals (New York Public Library, Drexel MS 5612).

232   ii *Delete list of* ANTHEMS *and replace by the*
233   i *following:*

ANTHEMS

All laud and praise (R.C.M.; Tenb. 791 fol. 74ʳ and fol. 419ᵛ; Ch. Ch. 88, fol. 8).

All people clap your hands (New York Public Library, Drexel MSS 4180-85; BM. Add. MSS 17792-96 and 30933; R.C.M. printed Barnard, MS additions; U. of California).

Alleluia, I heard a voice. Salvation and glory (B.M. Add. MSS 29372-77 and 30478-79; Ch. Ch. 56-60; Durham A.1, C.1, C.2, C.3, C.7, C.11, C.14, C.16, C.17, C.19; R.C.M. 1051; York Minster M-29s; Tenb. 389; Huntington Library, California, HM 461).

An earthly tree (Tenb. 791 fol. 421ᵛ; Ch. Ch. 88 fol. 19).

Behold how good and joyful (listed by Rimbault, Mus. Ant. Soc., 1843).

Behold, O Israel (Tenb. 791 fol. 352ᵛ).

Blessed be the man (Tenb. 791 fol. 415ʳ).

Blessed is he (Tenb. 791 fol. 409ᵛ; Wimborne Minster).

Christ rising. Christ is risen (Tenb. 791 fol. 418ʳ).

Deal bountifully (Tenb. 791 fol. 354ʳ).

Deliver us, O Lord (R.C.M.; probably by William Cox, a canon of Chichester Cathedral and an amateur composer).
Give ear, O lord (Tenb. 791 fol. 54ʳ; B.M. Add. MSS 29372-77).
Give the King Thy judgements. Behold, O God our defender (Tenb. 791 fol. 83ʳ; B.M. Add. MSS 30478-79; R.C.M.; Durham A.2, A.5, C.1, C.2, C.3, C.4, C.5, C.6, C.7, C.9, C.10, C.14, C.16, C.19; York M-29s; Lambeth Palace MS 764 fol. 130ʳ).
Gloria in excelsis. Sing, my soul (B.M. Add. MSS 17786-91; Ch. Ch. 56-60; Tenb. 807-11, 1382 fol. 62ʳ).
Hosanna to the Son (B.M. Add. MSS 17786-91; Tenb. 309, 807-11; Ch. Ch. 56-60).
I lift my heart (R.C.M. 1051).
I love the Lord. The Lord preserveth (Tenb. 791 fol. 424ʳ).
If King Manasses (R.C.M.; Tenb. 791 fol. 64ᵛ; Gloucester Cathedral).
If ye be risen again (Tenb. 791 fol. 430ᵛ).
In Thee, O Lord. Psalm 31 (Tenb. 791 fol. 427ʳ; Wimborne Minster).
In Thee, O Lord. Psalm 71 (Durham A.3, C.2, C.3, C.7, C.11, C.14, C.16, C.19; York M-29s; B.M. Add. MSS 30478-79).
Laboravi (Tenb. 807-11).
Let us lift up our eyes (Clifford, 1664 and B.M. Harley MS 4142 [words only]).
Lord, to Thee I make my moan (Ch. Ch. 56-60; R.C.M.).
Most mighty and all-knowing Lord (Leighton, 1614; B.M. Add. MS 31418; New York PL Drexel MS 4716, and Royal Appendix 63).
O happy he (Leighton, 1614; B.M. Add. MSS 29372-77, 31418; New York PL Drexel MS 4716, and Royal Appendix 63).
O how amiable (Durham A.2, C.2*, C.4, C.5, C.6, C.7, C.10, C.11, C.12, C.15, C.16, C.17, C.27, C.28, C.34; B.M. Add. MSS 30478-79; York Minster M-29s; Peterhouse MSS; University of California).
O Jonathan (B.M. Add. MSS 29366-68, 29372-77, 29427; Ch. Ch. 56-60; Tenb. 1162-67; Huntington Library, California EL 25 A 46-51).
O Lord, arise (B.M. Add. MSS 17786-91, 17792-96; R.C.M.; Tenb. 1382; New York PL Drexel MSS 4180-85).
O Lord God Almighty (Ch. Ch. 1220-24, 1001; St. John's College MS 180 fol. 30ᵛ; Lambeth Palace MS 764 fol. 191ʳ).
O Lord, grant the King (Barnard; B.M. Add. MSS 30478-79, 30078; Harley MS 7339; R.C.M.; Fitzwilliam MS 117; Ely; Ch. Ch. 1001, 1012; St. John's College MS 180, fol. 34ʳ; York Minster Gostling Part Books, bassus decani, p. 146; Lambeth Palace MS 764 fol. 171ᵛ; Gloucester Cathedral).
O Lord, how joyful is the King (B.M. Add. MSS 30478-79; Durham A.5, C.2, C.3, C.7, C.14, C.16, C.19; York Minster M-29s, p. 223).
O Lord, preserve Thee (listed by Rimbault, Mus. Ant. Soc., 1843).
O Lord, rebuke me not (listed by Rimbault, Mus. Ant. Soc., 1843).
O Lord, turn not away (Tenb. 791 fol. 420ʳ).
O mortal man (R.C.M.).
Plead Thou my cause (Tenb. 791 fol. 279ʳ; R.C.M.).
Rejoice in the Lord (mentioned by Bumpus and Foster, organ part only).
Sing unto the Lord (Clifford, 1663 and 1664 [words only]).
Successive course (B.M. Add. MS 30479).
Teach me, O Lord (Wimborne Minster).
The Lord is my shepherd (Wimborne Minster).
Thy mercies great (Clifford, 1664 [words only]).
What joy so true (R.C.M.; Tenb. 791 fol. 423ʳ).
When David heard. O Absalom (B.M., Add. MSS 29366-68, 28372-77, 29427 [Cosyn Virginal Book has different setting?]; Tenb. 807-11, 1162-67; Ch. Ch. 56-60; Bodleian Mus. Sch. MSS f. 20-24; NYPL Drexel MS 4302; Huntington Library, Calif., EL 25, A 46-51).
Why art thou so sad. Still trust in God (Wimborne Minster).
With all our hearts (mentioned by Bumpus and Foster, bass only).
Ye people all (Wimborne Minster; Tenb. 791 fol. 422ʳ).

Note.—Let thy merciful ears, often attributed to Weelkes, is evidently by Mudd.

E. H. F., rev. W. S. C.

233   i   Par. 2, ll. 1-2 *should read*:

The following are Weelkes's published madrigals and other works for several voices [1] (a few more remain in manuscript):

     ii   *Add to* BIBL.:

BRIDGE, FREDERICK, ' Twelve Good Musicians ' (London, 1920).
COLLINS, WALTER S., ' The Anthems of Thomas Weelkes ' (Ph.D. dissertation, University of Michigan, 1960, University Microfilms).
DICKINSON, A. E. F., ' Thomas Weelkes ' (' The Music Masters ', London, 1957).
WELCH, C. E., ' Two Cathedral Organists ' (Chichester, 1957).

234   i   **WEERBECKE**
Par. 2, ll. 8-9 *should read*:

merely Gaspard. But he must not be confused with the Gasparo de Alemania who was *rectore de la*

l. 12 *should read*:

the watch in 1469.² In 1472 and 1474 he is

l. 16 Sforza.² *should read*:

Sforza.³

Add footnote:

² *See* Gustave Reese, ' Music in the Renaissance ', p. 218, note.

Footnote 2 becomes 3.

WEGELIUS
Par. 1, l. 2. 3 Mar. *should read*:
22 Mar.

236   ii   **WEIGL (2)**
OPERAS
l. 2 *should read*:
(1783, for a private puppet theatre).

237   ii   BIBL., l. 4. EISNER-EISENDORF *should read*:
EISNER-EISENHOF

l. 8 *should read*:

NEUMANN, W., ' Joseph Weigl: eine Biographie ' (Cassel, 1955).

240   i   **WEILL**
Add to BIBL.:

BLITZSTEIN, MARK, ' On " Mahagonny " ' (' The Score ', No. 23, July 1958).
BRECHT, BERTOLT, ' Two Essays [I. on ' Mahagonny ']' (' The Score ', No. 23, July 1958).
DREW, DAVID, ' Topicality and the Universal: the Strange Case of Weill's " Die Bürgschaft " ' (M. & L., XXXIX, 1958, p. 242).

     ii   **WEINBERGER**
Par. 1, l. 1. **Jaromir** *should read*:
Jaromír

241   i   Par. 2, l. 12. variations in *should read*:

variations on

241   i   CATALOGUE
          ORCHESTRAL WORKS
          Add at end:
'Song of the High Seas' (1940).
'Lincoln Symphony' (1941).
'Czech Rhapsody' (1941).
'A Bird's Opera' (1941).

ii   l. 5 *should read*:
Sonata, organ pieces, etc.

242   ii   **WEINER,** CATALOGUE
            Op. 10, l. 2. (1903). *should read*:
(1913).

244   ii   **WEINGARTNER,**
            CATALOGUE :
            ARRANGEMENTS FOR ORCHES-
            TRA
            Add at end:
Schubert, unfinished Symphony in E ma.

246   ii   **WEISMANN**
            Add after Par. 3 :
            INCIDENTAL MUSIC
'A Midsummer Night's Dream' (Shakespeare) (1934–
1935).
           Par. 4.   *Add after* l. 1 :
56. Rhapsody.

            Add at end:
110. 'Sinfonietta giocosa.'
111. 'Sinfonietta severa.'
116. 'Sinfonia brevis.'
130. Symphony, B♭ ma.
131. Symphony, B mi.

           Par. 5.   *Add at end*:
128. Cello Concerto, D mi.
138. Pf. Concerto, A mi.
140. Vn. Concerto, E♭ ma.
141. Pf. Concerto, D mi., with stgs. & drums.
145. Vn. Concerto, A mi.

           Delete Op. 37.

           Par. 6.   *Delete Op.* 24, 26, 77 *and substitute*:
14, 24, 42, 66, 84, 85, 102, 133, 147, 154. Stg. Quartets.
26, 49, 61, 77. Trios for vn., cello & pf.
8. Quartet for vn., va., cello & pf.

           Par. 8.   *Delete Op.* 28, 49, 69 *and substitute*:
28, 47, 69, 72a. 79. Sonatas.

            Add after Par. 8 :

            VIOLONCELLO AND PIANOFORTE
9, 73, 137. Sonatas.

            Add before TWO PIANOFORTES :
            PIANOFORTE SOLO
150. 'Der Fugenbaum', 24 Preludes and Fugues.

            Add above signature :

A complete catalogue of Weismann's works
was published by the Julius Weismann Archiv
(Duisburg, 1955).

248   i   **WEISSBERG**
          Par. 1, l. 2 *should read*:
burg, 23 Dec. 1878; *d.* Leningrad, 1 Mar.
1942).

249   ii   **WEITZMANN**
            Par. 2, l. 2.   Henning Klein
            should read:
Henning, Klein

            l. 22 *should read*:
variation, in canon, to the 'Todtentanz'
by Liszt, to whom he had also communicated
his interest in the whole-tone scale.

250   ii   **WELDON**
            Par. 1, l. 1.   1908 *should read*:
5 June 1906

            Par 2, l. 32.   George Schwarz
            should read:
Rudolf Schwarz

254   ii   **WELLESZ**
            Par. 4, l. 4.   a member of *should
            read*:
a Fellow of

           ll. 7-8 *should read*:
the 'New Oxford History of Music'. In 1947
he was

           l. 15 *should read*:
music at Oxford. He was created C.B.E. in
1957.

            Add to BIBL. :
RETI, RUDOLPH, 'Egon Wellesz: Musician and
     Scholar' (M.Q., XLII, 1956, p. 1).

255   —   CATALOGUE
          OPERAS
          Col. 1, l. 6.   — *should read*:
69
          ORCHESTRAL WORKS
          Op. 62. C ma. *should read*:
C mi.
            Add at end:
68. Symphony No. 3, A mi. (1949).
70. Symphony No. 4, G mi.

            CHAMBER MUSIC
            Add at end:
67. Octet for clar., bassoon, horn & stg. 5tet (1948).
73. Suite for woodwind 5tet (1954).

           ii   SONGS
                Op. 63, l. 1 *should read*:
63. 'On Time', 3 songs for baritone (1946–48)

           l. 3 *should read*:
2. On Time (Milton).

256   ii   **WENNERBERG**
            BIBL., l. 3.   HENNEBERG *should read*:
HENNERBERG

258   ii   **WERCKMEISTER**
            Add to BIBL. :
DAMMANN, ROLF, 'Zur Musiklehre des Andreas Werck-
     meister' (A.f.M., XI, 3, p. 206).

259   i   **WERNER, T. W.**
          Par. 1, l. 2 *should read*:
ver, 8 June 1874; *d.* Salzburg, 6 Dec. 1957).

262   ii   **WESLEY, Samuel**
Par. 2, l. 20 *should read* :

laboured assiduously.[6] During 1808 and 1809

l. 24.   1875.[6] *should read* :
1875.[7]

Add footnote :

[6] It is generally supposed that it was G. F. Pinto who introduced Wesley to Bach's music; but *see* KOLLMANN (1), footnote 1.

Footnote 6 *becomes* 7.

264   ii   *Add to* BIBL. :

WESLEY, SAMUEL, ' Letters . . . to Mr. Jacobs . . . relation to . . . the Works of John Sebastian Bach ', ed. by Eliza Wesley, facsimile (London, 1958).

270   ii   **WESTRUP**
Par. 2, l. 5 *should read* :

B.Mus. in 1926, M.A. in 1929 and D.Mus. (*h.c.*) in 1944. He was one

Par. 3, ll. 12-13 *should read* :

returned for a time to schoolmastering, at St. Paul's School, then evacuated to Berkshire.

Par. 4, l. 1 *should read* :

Westrup was appointed lecturer in music at King's College, Newcastle-upon-Tyne, in 1941 and became Barber and Peyton Pro-

Par. 5, ll. 4-8 *should read* :

of the O.H.M. His book on Purcell (1937) combines literary gifts and musical scholarship of the highest quality. He has been working sporadically for many years on an important musico-historical work, ' Music and Society under the Stuarts ', which, however, his many activities have so far prevented him from completing. The

271   i   *Add at end, before signature* :

Westrup has acted as visiting lecturer at several American universities. In 1952 he published a revised edition of Ernest Walker's ' History of Music in England '.

Signature should read :

s. G., adds.

Weterings
l. 2 *should read* :

(2 libs.).   Pelemans (chamber opera).   Sauguet (cantata).

ii   **WETZLER**
Par. 1, l. 2.   8 Oct. *should read* :
8 Sept.

273   ii   **WHINYATES**
Par. 2, l. 27 *should read* :

French Government and in 1952 she received the O.B.E. In 1959 she retired from the

British Council and was succeeded by John Cruft.   E. B.

280   i   **WHITHORNE**
Par. 1, l. 2 *should read* :

Ohio, 6 Sept. 1884;   d. Lyme, Connecticut, 25 Mar. 1958).

281   ii   **Whitman**
l. 24. *Add before* Loeffler :

Kirchner (L., 2 songs).

l. 27 *should read* :
Müller-Hermann (' In Memoriam ', oratorio). Palmer (R., 2 songs). Salm-

l. 33 *should read* :
choral work; 3 songs). Stein (L., Triptych for orch.). Thompson (R., song). Valen

282   ii   **WHYTE, Ian**
(*d.* Glasgow, 27 Mar. 1960).

284   ii   **WIDOR**
Par. 1, l. 2.   24 Feb. 1845 ; *should read* :

21 Feb. 1844;

287   i   **Wieland**
l. 2. Huön *should read* :
Hüon

289   ii   *Add at end* :

WIENIAWSKI INTERNATIONAL COMPETITION FOR COMPOSERS.

A contest established by the Committee of the third Wieniawski International Competition for Violinists in conjunction with the Union of Polish Composers in 1956. The prize-winning work was intended to figure in the programme for that competition, and the conditions were that a work for violin should be produced of 8-12 minutes' duration, of virtuoso standard and not cast in a cyclic form (sonata, sonatina, suite, &c.).

The contestants numbered 128 composers representing 20 countries. No first prize was awarded, the jury considering that none of the works submitted fulfilled all the requirements. The other prizes were as follows :

2nd Prize : Victor Legley (Belgium) : ' Burlesque '.
3rd Prize : Julien François Zbinden (Switzerland) : ' Rhapsody '.
4th Prizes : Mìosław Kabelac (Czechoslovakia) : ' Ballata '.
     Sándor Szokalai (Hungary) : ' Allegro de Concert '.

These works were performed at a public concert held in the Hall of the National Philharmonia in Warsaw on 19 June 1956.
                       C. R. H.

WIENIAWSKI INTERNATIONAL COMPETITION FOR VIOLINISTS.

A contest organized by the Chopin Music School of Warsaw on the initiative of Adam Wieniawski, nephew of Henryk Wieniawski, to celebrate the hundredth anniversary of the composer's birth and to promote interest in violin music. The upper age-limit was 30 at first, but in 1952 it was raised to 32 and, for "fighters for freedom and democracy, inmates of concentration camps and prisoners of war ", to 35.

The competition proceeds by three stages : (1) general elimination ; (2) semi-finals ; (3) finals. The prizes, which originally were unusually high (first prize 25,000 złotys, *i.e.* about £2270, in 1952), have been revised and lowered : the first prize now is 20,000 złotys, which owing to the new rate of exchange amounts to only about £300.

The first competition took place in Warsaw in 1935, 160 violinists representing 23 countries contesting. The prizes were as follows :

1st Prize :   Ginette Neveu (France), aged 16.
2nd Prize : David Oistrakh (U.S.S.R.), aged 27.
3rd Prize : Henry Temianka (England), aged 28.
4th Prize : Bussia Goldstein (U.S.S.R.), aged 13.
5th Prize : Zjerko Spiller (Yugoslavia), aged 27.
6th Prize : Mary Luise Sardo (Italy), aged 24.
7th Prize : Ida Haendel (England), aged 11.
8th Prize : Hubert Anton (Esthonia), aged 22.
9th Prize : Bronisław Gimpel (Poland), aged 24.

After the second world war the second competition took place at Poznań in 1952. 23 violinists representing 7 countries contested.

1st Prize :
  Igor Oistrakh (U.S.S.R.), who also received a silver box for strings owned by Joachim and presented by his granddaughter Irene Joachim.
2nd Prize :
  Wanda Wiłkomirska (Poland).
  Julian Sitkovietsky (U.S.S.R.).
3rd Prizes :
  Blanche Tarjus (France).
  Marine Yashvily (U.S.S.R.).
  Olgar Parkhomienko (U.S.S.R).
4th Prizes :
  Emil Kamilarov (Bulgaria).
  Edward Statkiewicz (Poland).
  Igor Iwanow (Poland).
  Henryk Palulis (Poland).
5th Prize :
  Czaba Bokay (Hungary).

The third competition was held at Poznań in Dec. 1957; 45 violinists representing 15 countries contested. The jury, under the chairmanship of Mme Grażyna Bacewicz, with Yehudi Menuhin as hon. member and David Oistrakh as vice-chairman, consisted of a dozen distinguished musicians, including Gioconda de Vito, Gabriel Bouillon and Max Rostal. The prizes were high : the first amounted to 40,000 złotys (nearly £600), the second to 30,000 złotys, etc.

1st Prize :   Rosa Fajn (U.S.S.R.), aged 28.
2nd Prize : Sidney Harth (U.S.A.), aged 32.
3rd Prize : Mark Komissarov (U.S.S.R.), aged 29.
4th Prize : Agustín Leôn-Ara (Spain), aged 21.
5th Prize : Ayla Erdwan (Turkey), aged 21.
6th Prize : Vladimir Malinin (U.S.S.R.), aged 22.

Some competitors received a consolation prize of 4,000 złotys and all those who passed the second stage of the contest were presented with special souvenir diplomas.

C. R. H.

290   i   **WIERZBIŁŁOWICZ**
Dates *should read* :
(*b.* Warsaw, 8 Jan. 1850 ; *d.* St. Petersburg, 15 Mar. 1911).

Wierzyński
Add at end of line :
Łabuński (F. R., ' Birds ' for sop. & orch.).

292   ii   **WIKMANSON**
BIBL., l. 3.   ' Åminnelstel *should read* :
' Åminnelsatal

295   i   **Wilde**
l. 9 *should read* :
dance). Griffes (song). Grimm (F.-K., songs). Ibert (' Ballad of Reading

296   i   **Wilder, Thornton**
l. 1.   *Add after* See :
Reutter (H., ' Brücke von San Luis Rey ', opera).

301   i   **WILLAERT**
Add to BIBL. :
PISTARINO, GEO, ' Ritratto di Adriano Willaert ' (Riv. Mus. It., LVI, 1, 1954).

See also. l. 2 *should read* :
Amer. Inst. Musicol. (C.M.M.), Vol. 3 (modern ed. of complete works). Chorwerk, Vols. 5, 8, 54, 59 (modern reprints). Collectio O.M.B., Vols. 1 & 2 (modern ed.). Denkmäler (4), Vol. 19 (do.). Merulo (C., meeting with). Vereniging, Vol. 35 (modern ed. of ' Missa super Benedicta ').

WILLAN
Par. 2, l. 6 *should read* :
organist and choirmaster of St. Paul's, which he left for St. Mary Magdalene in 1921.

l. 12 *should read* :
classical plays. From 1920 to 1936 he was Vice-

Par. 3, l. 2 *should read* :
University of Toronto, a post he resigned in 1950 while retaining that of University organist. He is deeply interested

ll. 7-8 *should read* :
several important works, mainly with his own choir, including the war elegy ' Why

ii   Par. 2, ll. 1-3 *should read* :
In 1946 appeared his opera ' Deirdre ' (libretto by John Coulter, after J. M. Synge's ' Deirdre of the Sorrows '), commissioned by the Canadian

303   ii   **WILLIAMS, Alberto**
Add to BIBL. :
' Homenajes a Alberto Williams ' (Buenos Aires, 1942).

305 i **WILLIAMS, C. à B.**
Par. 1, l. 2 *should read*:
Dorchester, 2 July 1890; *d.* Chandler's Ford, Hants, 3 Nov. 1956).

308 i **WILLIAMS, Tom**
Par. 1, ll. 1-2. Llanelly, *should read*:
Carmarthenshire,

309 ii **WILLNER**
Par. 1, l. 2 *should read*:
1881; *d.* London, 7 Apr. 1959).

314 i **WILSON**
Par. 3, l. 4. Dennison *should read*:
Denison

Add at end of Par. 3:
This came to an end in 1955 and from 1957 to 1960 he was Principal of the Birmingham School of Music.

315 ii **WINCKELMANN** *should read*:
WINKELMANN

Par. 3, l. 1 *should read*:
On 26 July 1882 Winkelmann was the

Transfer whole article to p. 318, col. i.

316 i *Add after* **WINDET**:
WINDGASSEN, Wolfgang (*b.* Annemasse, Switzerland, 26 June 1914).
German tenor singer. Although born in Switzerland, he is of German parentage and spent his childhood at Cassel. His father was Fritz Windgassen, leading tenor of the Stuttgart Opera from 1923 to 1944, and his mother was also a singer, the sister of the Dresden soprano Eva van der Osten. When he was nine he heard his first opera, D'Albert's 'Tiefland', in which the leading parts were sung by his father and mother. At fourteen he secured a technical post at the Stuttgart theatre on a voluntary basis, and he studied drama with his father. He entered the local Conservatory, where he studied under Maria Ranzow and then with Alfons Fischer. After serving in the German army from 1937 to 1941 he was able to accept his first engagement at Pforzheim, where he made his début as Alvaro in 'La forza del destino'. When the war ended he was engaged by the Stuttgart Opera, of which company he is still (1958) a member. Singing first the Italian repertory, and parts like Tamino, Max, Hoffmann and Florestan, he began to prepare the Wagnerian repertory, and in the 1950-51 season sang his first Siegmund. In 1951 he

was engaged to sing Parsifal in the Bayreuth Festival, and he has appeared there each year since, singing Siegfried, Lohengrin, Tannhäuser, Walther, Erik and Tristan, and establishing himself as the leading *Heldentenor* in post-war opera. This has lead to engagements all over Europe, and he appears regularly in the Wagnerian seasons at Covent Garden. Besides the parts already mentioned, his repertory also includes Gerard in 'Euryanthe', Rienzi and the Kaiser in 'Die Frau ohne Schatten'.

Windgassen's voice is light by pre-war *Heldentenor* standards, but he knows how to conserve it, and he sings with feeling and great musicality. Few Tristans or Siegfrieds have been able to sing the lyrical portions of their music with as much beauty as Windgassen, and at the same time he knows how to rise to the more dramatic moments in the score.   H. D. R.

318 i **WINKELMANN**
Add article from p. 315 after **WINKEL.**

Add after **WINKLER**:
WINN, Cyril (*b.* London, 26 Dec. 1884). English musical educationist. He was a chorister at St. Paul's Cathedral in London under Charles Macpherson and later Hubert Parry organ Scholar of Exeter College, Oxford, where he took an honours degree in classics. After some years in the teaching service of the L.C.C. he was appointed principal of the Oxford and Bermondsey Day Continuation School. Later he joined the Inspectorate of the Board of Education and succeeded Geoffrey Shaw as Staff Inspector of Music. On retirement he was appointed a lecturer and examiner of Trinity College of Music, of which he is an honorary Fellow.

Winn's name is closely allied with the development of the schools' music non-competitive festivals and he played a leading part in the raising of the standard of music teaching in schools, particularly during what may be termed the revolutionary period of 1930-39. In this respect he has rendered one of the most outstanding services to music.

Winn is known as a composer of songs for schools, two of the best-known being 'The Song of Music Makers' and 'England, Arise', and he has written a number of books, including 'Children Singing', 'Teaching Music' and, in the 'Musical Pilgrim' series, guides to Wagner's 'Mastersingers' and to selected works by Mendelssohn.   S. S. M.

321 i **WIRÉN**
Par. 3. *Add after* l. 17:
Concerto for pf. & orch., Op. 26.

323   i   **WISSMER,** CATALOGUE
STAGE WORKS
Delete l. 2 (' Marion . . .').

Add in its place :
' Capitaine Bruno ', prod. Bordeaux, 4 Mar. 1955.

RADIO MUSIC
Add after l. 2 :
' Marion, ou La Belle au tricorne ', comic opera (1945), prod. Geneva, Radio Suisse Romande, 16 Apr. 1947.

324   ii   **WITT, Friedrich**
Par. 1, l. 2.   1771 *should read* :
8 Nov. 1770

Par. 2, l. 13 *should read* :
band, etc. He is now known to be the composer of the "Jena" Symphony long attributed to Beethoven.   A. L.

Add at end :
See also Jena Symphony.

328   i   **WÓJCIK-KEUPRULIAN**
Par. 1, l. 2.   *d.* Lwów, 1938). *should read* :
d. Lwów, 11 Apr. 1938).

329   i   *Add after* **WOLF, Aaron** :
WOLF, Endre (*b.* Budapest, 6 Nov. 1913). Swedish violinist of Hungarian birth. He studied the violin at the High School for Music in Budapest, at first for a few years with the senior professor, Oscar Studer, a Swiss, and then as a member of the highest class for performers under Jenő Hubay, then director of the institution. He also studied theory and ensemble playing under Leo Weiner. After obtaining his diploma in 1933 he appeared as a recitalist during the following three years, while still continuing to study. In 1936 he accepted the posts of first leader of the Göteborg Symphony Orchestra and leader of the Göteborg String Quartet, taking up his duties in the autumn of that year. He settled in Sweden in 1937, and in 1938 married the pianist Antoinette Tömlich (*b.* Frankfort o/M., 28 June 1906), a pupil of Frida Kwast-Hodapp and M. Mayer-Mahr. Wolf founded his own quartet in 1940, but had to give it up after a few years owing to his extensive concert tours abroad as soloist. He became a Swedish national in 1944.
Since 1945 Wolf has played all over Europe. He gave the first performance in Scandinavia of Walton's violin Concerto, conducted by the composer in Stockholm in 1945, and later of Bartók's unaccompanied violin Sonata. His first appearance in England was in London, at the Royal Albert Hall, with Issy Dobrowen in 1945 ; he played at the Edinburgh Festival in 1954. In the

autumn of that year he was appointed professor of the violin at the Royal Manchester College of Music and became resident in England.   K. D.

329   i   **WOLF, E. W.**
Par. 1, l. 2 *should read* :
nr. Gotha, [bapt. 25 Feb.] 1735 ; *d.* Weimar, Nov. [buried 1 Dec.] 1792).

341   ii   **WOLF**
BIBL., l. 29.   (Vienna & Leipzig, 1941).
should read :
(Vienna & Leipzig, 1941 ; rev. 1953).

Add to BIBL. :
HAMBURGER, PAUL, ' The Interpretation of Picturesque Elements in Wolf's Songs ' (' Tempo ', No. 48, 1958).
LOESER, NORBERT, ' Wolf ' (Haarlem-Antwerp, 1955).

350   i   Heading, OLFF *should read* :
WOLFF

      ii   **WOLFURT**
Par. 1, l. 2 *should read* :
7 Sept. 1880 ; *d.* Munich, 25 Feb. 1957).

Par. 2, l. 18 *should read* :
Municipal Conservatory. In 1945 he settled at Göttingen.

351   i   *Add at end :*
BIBL.—' Zeitschrift für Musik ' (Oct. 1940).

354   ii   **WOOD, Haydn**
Par. 1, l. 2 *should read* :
Mar. 1882 ; *d.* London, 11 Mar. 1959).

358   ii   *Add before* **WOOD, Thomas** :
WOOD, Sinjon. *See* WILLIAMS, CHRISTO-PHER À BECKET.

363   ii   **Wordsworth**
l. 1.   *Add at end :*
Britten (' Nocturne ', No. 5).

364   ii   **WORGAN (2)**
Par. 1, l. 18 *should read* :
Mus. D. On 1 Sept. 1753 he married Sarah Maclean, whom he divorced in June 1768.[2]
He died in his house in Gower Street

WORGAN (3)
Delete ll. 5-6.

367   i   **WORSHIPFUL COMPANY OF MUSICIANS**
Par. 3, l. 3 *should read* :
dated 31 May 1664 [2] :

Add footnote :
[2] Hawkins's date, 13 May 1644, is wrong.

368 ii **WORZISCHEK**
l. 2. Voříšek *should read*:
VOŘÍŠEK

370 i **WOYTOWICZ**
ORCHESTRAL WORKS
Add after l. 5:
Symphony No. 1 (1938).

ii **WRANITZKY, Anton**
Add at end:
See also Musica Antiqua Bohemica, Vol. 16 (modern ed. of Concerto for vn. & pf.).

371 i **WRANITZKY, Paul**
Add to BIBL.:
LaRue, Jan, 'A "Hail & Farewell" Quodlibet Symphony' (M. & L., XXXVII, 1956, p. 250).

374 ii **Wyatt**
Add at end:
BIBL.—MUMFORD, IVY L., 'Musical Settings to the Poems of Sir Thomas Wyatt' (M. & L., XXXVII, 1956, p. 548).
'Sir Thomas Wyatt's Songs: a Trio of Problems in Manuscript Sources' (M. & L., XXXIX, 1958, p. 262).
WARD, JOHN, 'Music for *A Handefull of Pleasant Delites*' (Journal Amer. Musicol. Soc., X, 1957, p. 151).

375 i *Add before* WYK:
WYDŻGA, Jan Tomasz (*b.* Lwów, 1873; *d.* Lwów, 1926).
Polish amateur composer. Besides many songs, he composed two operas: 'Jeńcy' ('Prisoners of War'), to a libretto by Lucjan Rydel, and 'Pan Tadeusz', to a libretto by his daughter Mary based on Mickiewicz's epic. The latter was produced at Lwów on 22 Jan. 1907.   C. R. H.

ii **WYK**
Par. 1, l. 17 *should read*:
Festival in 1951. His song cycle 'Liedere van Liefde en Verlatenheid' was included in the I.S.C.M. programme for the festival held at Haifa in 1954.

CATALOGUE
ORCHESTRAL WORKS
Add at end:
'Aubade' (1955).

PIANOFORTE SOLO
Add at end:
'Night Music' (1955).

SONGS
Add at end:
'Liedere van Liefde en Verlatenheid' (Eugene Marais) for mezzo-soprano & pf. (1953).

Add at end:
BIBL.—FERGUSON, HOWARD, 'Arnold van Wyk: Recently Published Works' ('Tempo', No. 48, 1958).

377 ii **Wyspiański**
Add between ll. 4 *and* 5:
Raczyński (incid. m. for 2 plays).

379 i-ii **XYLOPHONE AND MARIMBA** *and* **XYLORIMBA**
Delete both articles and replace by:

XYLOPHONE. A percussion instrument consisting of a series of hardwood bars graduated in length and tuned to a scale. The name is derived from the Greek ξύλον = wood and φωνή = sound. The bars give a bright, dry sound when struck with hard-headed mallets, but are softer with rubber mallets. Their arrangement follows that of the pianoforte keyboard and, as is the practice with bar-percussion instruments, the bars are held aloft, free to vibrate, on cords passing through their node-points. Formerly strips of felt supported them, slightly deadening the sound.

Unlike the marimba the xylophone is limited to treble notes and traditionally had a compass approximating that of the piccolo. But large xylophones have been made for solo purposes having the compass of the flute plus a higher octave, c'-c''''. These were equipped with resonators for improved tone.

In crude forms the xylophone has been known in Europe for several centuries. The bars rested on ropes of straw, for which reason the German word *Strohfiedel* was applied to the instrument. The bars were in four rows and, like the strings of the cimbalom, were disposed lengthwise to the performer, who stood at the wider end of the instrument. This was the only type of wooden-bar percussion instrument known to civilization when Michael Josef Gusikov (1809-37) became known as a virtuoso. His best xylophone, with the bars properly mounted, had the range of the violin and even without resonators was good enough to attract favourable comment from Chopin, Liszt and Mendelssohn. In fact Mendelssohn accompanied Gusikov at one or more concerts.

The technique of the xylophone allows for brilliant runs, trills and an exhibition of virtuosity. It is applicable to the glockenspiel, marimba and vibraphone, since these instruments have the same arrangement of bars. In the past xylophone solos were rather commonplace, but to-day the marimba has superseded the xylophone outside the orchestra, its extended range encompassing that of the xylophone.

The xylophone appears in many symphonic scores for special effects, as in Saint-Saëns's 'Danse macabre' to imitate the clacking bones of skeletons, an effect for which the modern improved instrument would be less useful. It appears in Mahler's sixth Symphony and often in Puccini's opera 'Turandot'. It is delicately used in Bartók's Concerto for two pianofortes and percussion. Prokofiev and Stravinsky often require it in their orchestrations, but all these composers accept the limitations of the small, traditional xylophone and seem indifferent to the advantages of the improved instrument.

F. K. M.

380   i   *Add before* **YALE UNIVERSITY**:
YAKOVLEV, Leonid Georgievich (*b.* Kherson Govt., 1857; *d.* St. Petersburg, 2 June 1919).
Russian baritone singer. He was the son of a landowner and began his education at the St. Petersburg Classical Gymnasium, concluding it at the Nikolayevsky Cavalry School, becoming a cornet in a Lifeguard regiment and later adjutant to the Governor-General of Kiev. His military career terminated suddenly owing to family financial misfortune, and he was reduced to considering an Inspectorship of Taxes; but this was so distasteful to him that he resolved to exploit what he had hitherto regarded as merely a " drawing-room " talent for music. He decided to take lessons with Riadnov, a well-known provincial operatic artist, at Kiev, who discovered that he possessed a fine operatic voice. In the spring of 1886, on the recommendation of his teacher, he applied for an engagement at the Tiflis Opera, putting forward a repertory of four well-known works of which in fact his knowledge was extremely slight; but on arrival he was invited to undertake at very brief notice the part of Barnaba in Ponchielli's ' Gioconda ', with which, though appearing on the stage for the first time, he scored an immense success. During the ensuing two months he found himself called upon to appear in twenty-one performances, involving eight different parts.

Tchaikovsky, on a visit to Tiflis, spoke so favourably of the young singer to Kondratiev, the producer at the Maryinsky Theatre in St. Petersburg, that he received an invitation to appear there as a guest artist. On 9 April 1887 he took the part of Valentine in ' Faust ' and was immediately engaged and speedily became a public favourite. His voice is described as a lyrico-dramatic baritone, resonant in all registers and full and free in the highest notes, and his delivery as true *bel canto*. His histrionic ability was outstanding, and he devoted much energy to the study of every dramatic aspect of any part. That of Onegin, which he sang 115 times, remained long sacred in the memory of all who heard him. But he was idolized by the public in all the parts he undertook at the Maryinsky, which included Nevers in ' The Huguenots ', Wolfram in ' Tannhäuser ', Yeletsky in ' The Queen of Spades ', Escamillo in ' Carmen ', Griaznoy in ' The Tsar's Bride ', Mizguir in ' The Snow Maiden ' and Rigoletto.

His decline was sad. In 1905 he suffered a severe attack of catarrh, and despite a year's sojourn on the Riviera his voice continued to deteriorate to such an extent as to provoke some severely critical remarks from Rimsky-Korsakov, in whose opera ' Servilia ' he was given the part of Ignatius. Learning that Yakovlev was threatened with penury his friends organized in 1912 a festival commemorating his twenty-fifth year of artistic activity. It was not, however, until 1918, the year before his death, that he was rescued from near-beggary with the offer of the post of producer at the Maryinsky.   M. M.-N.

381   i   **Yeats**
l. 6 *should read*:
Holland (song with orch.).   Dunhill (songs).   Egk (' Irische Legende ', opera).   Elgar

Add before **YODEL**:
YLEWARD, Richard.   *See* AYLWARD.

ii   **YON**
Par. 2, l. 13 *should read*:
St. Peter in Rome. At the time of his death he was organist at St. Patrick's Church, New York. His compositions

382   ii   **YORKSHIRE   SYMPHONY ORCHESTRA**
l. 22 *should read*:
field 3; Halifax 2. In 1954 Maurice Miles was replaced by Nikolay Malko and Norman Del Mar, but the following year the organization unfortunately came to an end for lack of support both on the part of the public in some of the towns and partly of the municipalities.

383   ii   **YOUNG (2)**
Par. 1, ll. 2-4 *should read*:
(2), and this is certainly correct, and Burney is wrong in giving Anthony Young (1) as their father in his ' History '.[1] The three younger

Add footnote:
[1] Confirmed by Cecilia Maria Henslowe, Barthélemon's daughter, in her preface to a selection from her father's oratorio ' Jefte in Masfa '.

387   i   **YRADIER**
Par. 1, l. 1.   Alva *should read*:
Álava

388   i   **YRIARTE**
BIBL.   l. 2 *should read*:
español del melólogo ', 2 vols. (Barcelona, 1949–50).

YSAŸE
Par. 2, l. 5.   Lambert Massart *should read*:
Rodolphe Massart

391   i   **ZABALETA**
          Par. 3, l. 14.   Lecuna *should read*:
Lecuona

392   ii   **ZACCONI**
           Par. 2, l. 9 *should read*:
R.C.M., and a modern facsimile reprint is to
be published in ' Documenta Musicologica ',
Vol. 34.

393   i   **ZACH**
          Add at end:
See also Musica Antiqua Bohemica, Vol. 9 (modern
ed. of Sonata for 2 vns. & cello).

Add before **ZACHAREWITSCH**:

ZACHARA, Antonio (*b.* Teramo, ? ; *d.* ?).
Italian 14th–15th-century composer. He
has left one 2-part madrigal and nine *ballate*,
of which five are for 3 and four for 2 voices.
These works were liked enough for them to
be employed in many cases as parody Mass
movements, not to mention embellished keyboard arrangements. Although Zachara is
confused with Zacharias in the Mass source
under the homonym Zacar, the addition of
the original work-title to Mass movements
proves Zachara to be the composer of three
Gloria-Credo pairs and an additional Credo
(" du Vilage ") and two Glorias, of which
one is marked " Anglicana ". Four of these
works are for 4 voices, the others for 3. The
Credo " du Vilage " or *dominicale* paraphrases
Vatican Credo I, dividing it in migrant style
between the two upper voices. Apart from
his liking for macaronic texts in the secular
works, *e.g.* " Deus deorum Pluto, or 'te
rengrazio ", " Plorans ploravi perche la
fortuna ", " Je suy navrés tan fort. . . . La
nobiltà con tutte le scienze ", Zachara has a
lively fund of melody, a liking for repeated
words and corresponding musical motifs, and
a preference for the French combination of
duple time and triple prolation (= 6-8 time).
The *ballata* ' Un fior gentil ' has an imitative
opening, though in the keyboard version,
which is reduced from three to two voices,
the upper voice ornaments this opening most
attractively without concealing the imitation.
Three *ballate* are published in ' Italian
Ars-Nova Music ' by F. Ghisi in the Supplement to the ' Journal of Renaissance and
Baroque Music ', I (1947), another in
' Musica Disciplina ', IV (1950), p. 151, and
the Credo " du Vilage " in D.T.Ö., XXXI,
p. 16.   G. R. (iii).

Add after **ZACHARIA**:

ZACHARIAS, Nicolaus (*b.* Brindisi, ? ;
d. ?).
Italian 14th–15th-century composer. The
identification with Nicolaus Zacharie and
Magister Zacharias now seems practically

certain, though doubts were expressed on the
subject till recently. Certainly Zacharias is
not, however, to be confused with Antonio
Zachara. In some sources Zacharias is
defined as a papal singer, and the accounts
show he was a member of the papal chapel
from 1420 to 1424 and again in 1434. Moreover, an isorhythmic motet written during
the reign of the Neapolitan Pope John XXIII
(1410–15) suggests that he spent a long time
in the papal service. One can hardly fail to
see the influence of Ciconia's novel *caccia*-
motet ' O felix templum jubila ' in Zacharias's
' Letetur plebs — Pastor qui revelavit ', for
both start in imitation, so that the *motetus*
comes in on the last (ninth) breve of the
triplum entry, while both proudly proclaim
their composer's name at the end of *triplum*
and *motetus*. Ciconia's motet was written for
Stefano Carrara of Padua in 1400. In his
Mass movements Zacharias never goes beyond
three parts, though both of his motets are for
four. One Gloria is for two voices only and
has much in common with his simple two-
part *ballate* with their simultaneous cadences.
Another Gloria *a 3* is Italian in its use of text
in both *cantus* and *tenor* and, like a Gloria by
Matteo da Perugia, has the " Spiritus et
alme " trope. A 3-part Gloria with the usual
text in *cantus* and *tenor*, and the trope " Gloria,
Laus et honor " in the middle voice, is found
in German, Polish and English as well as
Italian manuscripts. The one Credo by
Zacharias is paired with this Gloria in one
Italian manuscript. ' Benche lontan me
trovo ' is a good example of Zacharias's six
2-part and one 3-part *ballate*, with its simple
texture, simultaneous cadences and elementary
imitation. To round off the work of this
versatile composer we have a ballade with
Latin text in the most complex French style
for three voices and a 3-part *caccia*, ' Cacciando
per gustar ' with street cries of merchants
selling their wares in the *tenor*.
The motet ' Letetur plebs — Pastor ' is in
Charles van den Borren's ' Polyphonia Sacra '
(1932), the 2-part Gloria in J. Wolf, ' Eine
neue Quelle zur Musik des 15. Jahrhunderts ' in the Ilmari Krohn *Festschrift* (1927),
all but one of the *ballate* and the *caccia* in J.
Wolf's ' Der Squarcialupi-Codex ' (1955) and
the ballade in Wolf, ' Geschichte der Mensural-Notation ' (1904), Vols. II–III.
                                          G. R. (iii).

394   i   **ZÁDOR**
          OPERAS
          l. 6.   (?) *should read*:
(Saarbrücken, 1932).

          l. 8.   (1930) *should read*:
(Gera, 24 May 1930)

          l. 9 *should read*:
' Revisor ' (lib. after Gogol's comedy) (begun 1935;
re-written and completed 1952–57).

394 i ORCHESTRAL WORKS
Add after l. 12:
' Pastorale and Tarantella ' (1942).

ii ZAFRED
Add to Par. 3 (works) :
Concerto for harp.

395 i ZAJC
Par. 1, l. 2 *should read* :
Rijeka, 3 Aug. 1831 ; *d.* Zagreb, 16 Dec.

396 i ZAMPOGNA
l. 2 *should read* :
BAGPIPE (ITALY). *PLATE* 2, Vol. I, p. 352,
No. 9.

397 i ZANDONAI
Par. 1, l. 2. 12 June *should read* :
5 June

398 ii *Add before* ZANETTA :

ZANELLI (MORALES), Renato (*b.* Val-
paraiso, 1 Apr. 1892 ; *d.* Santiago de Chile,
25 Mar. 1935).
Chilean tenor singer. His father was an
Italian and his mother Chilean. He was
brought by his parents to Europe and educated
at Neuchâtel (Switzerland) and Turin. He
returned to Chile in 1910 to follow a business
career. At that time he had never had a
vocal lesson, though he often sang at social
gatherings. He was heard singing at a party
by Angelo Querez, a local teacher, who
advised him to study seriously, and Zanelli
spent three years with Querez who trained
him as a baritone. He made his début in
July 1916 at the Teatro Municipal, Santiago,
as Valentine in ' Faust '. After more local
appearances as Di Luna, Tonio and Renato,
he went to New York, where he was engaged
for a concert tour, and then for the Metropolitan for the 1919–20 season, where he
made his début as Amonasro.
There followed three unsatisfactory years,
during which he appeared to make little
progress, and he decided to go to Italy for
further experience. His brother, Carlos
Zanelli Morales, went with him and soon
established himself as a baritone, taking the
professional name of Carlo Morelli. Zanelli
was advised to change his voice to tenor,
and after a year's intensive study he made
his tenor début at Naples as Raoul in ' Les
Huguenots ', following it with Alfredo in ' La
Traviata ' and other lyric parts. He soon
found, however, that the baritone timbre of
his voice suited him more to heavy dramatic
parts, and in 1925 he began to coach Othello
with Leopoldo Mugnone, which he sang for
the first time at Turin in Oct. 1926. He
followed this with Lohengrin. In 1928 he

made his Covent Garden début as Othello
and engagements followed at the Teatro
Colón, Buenos Aires and Santiago, where
he was heard as Othello, Canio, Lohengrin
and Tristan. His Othello was generally considered the finest since Tamagno's, and his
Wagnerian interpretations were of a stature
rare among Italian-trained artists.
During the next few years he established
himself as the leading Wagnerian tenor in
Italy and was heard as Tristan, Lohengrin
and Siegmund. In 1931 he created the tenor
part in Pizzetti's ' Lo straniero ' in Rome,
and added Chénier, Radamès, Cavaradossi,
Manrico, Faust (Boito) and Pollione to his
repertory. He was encouraged to study Wagner
in German and was only prevented from
singing Tristan at Covent Garden in German
by ill health. In 1933 and 1934 his health
further deteriorated, and in Mar. 1935 he
was operated on for cancer of the kidney,
but died under the anaesthetic.

H. D. R.

398 ii ZANGIUS
Add at end :
See also Denkmäler (3), Vol. 87 (modern ed.).

ZANTEN
Par. 1, l. 2. 10 Jan. *should read* :
11 Jan.

404 i ZAVERTAL (1)
ll. 2–3. Litoměřice *should read* :
Litoměřice

ii ZAVERTAL (2)
l. 2. Litoměřice *should read* :
Litoměřice

406 i *Add after* ZECCHI, Adone :
ZECCHI, Carlo (*b.* Rome, 8 July 1903).
Italian pianist and conductor. He studied
the pianoforte under F. Baiardi and composition under Refice and Bustini at the
Conservatorio di Santa Cecilia in Rome. At
the age of seventeen he began a career as
concert pianist which took him on many
tours in Europe and the Americas. In 1938
he discontinued his appearances as soloist
and limited himself to chamber music for
pianoforte with string instruments : his duet
association with the cellist Enrico Mainardi
is particularly noteworthy. He also studied
conducting with Hans Münch and Antonio
Guarnieri, and in 1941 he began to appear
as concert conductor in Italy, beginning also
a busy and successful activity in other European countries and in America. He is in
charge of the finishing course in pianoforte
playing at the Accademia di Santa Cecilia
in Rome. G. M. G.

406 ii **ZEINALLY**
Par. 1, l. 2 *should read*:
baijan, 2 Apr. 1909; *d.* Baku, 27 Oct. 1932).

407 i *Add before* **ZEISLER**:
ZEISL, Eric (*b.* Vienna, 1905; *d.* Los Angeles, 18 Feb. 1959).
American composer of Austrian birth. He studied at the State Academy of Music in Vienna and later taught at the Conservatory there. He went to the U.S.A. in 1938 and in 1947 became professor of theory and composition at the Los Angeles City College. He has been a member of the Motion-Picture Academy since 1945 and is also a member of ASCAP, the screen composers' association.

Zeisl's very numerous and varied compositions include the operas 'Job' (on Josef Roth's novel) and 'Leonce and Lena' (on Büchner's play); the ballet 'Pierrot in Flask'; incidental music for Emil Ludwig's comedy 'The Return of Ulysses'; 'Requiem concertante' and 'Requiem ebraico' for solo voices, chorus and orchestra, 29th Psalm and 'Biblical Choruses' for chorus and orchestra; 'Little Symphony' and 'Passacaglia-Fantasy' for orch., 'Six Moods of November' for small orch., Suite and 'Scherzo and Fugue' for strings; 'Moon Pictures' (Christian Morgenstern) for baritone & orchestra; 2 string quartets and other chamber music; pianoforte music; songs, &c.
E. B.

408 ii **ZELINKA**
Title of 3rd opera *should read*:
'Paličatý švec'

410 ii **ZELTER**
Add to BIBL.:
HOLTZMANN, SIGRID (ed.), 'Carl Friedrich Zelter im Spiegel seines Briefwechsels mit Goethe' (Weimar, 1957).
ZELTER, KARL FRIEDRICH, 'Selbstdarstellung', ed. by Willi Reich (Zürich, 1956).

411 i **ZEMLINSKY**
Par. 3, l. 11. son-in-law *should read*:
brother-in-law

413 i **ZHELOBINSKY**
Par. 1, l. 2. Moscow *should read*:
Leningrad

Par. 2, ll. 10-11 *should read*:
Oct. 1933 his first opera, 'Kamarinsky Muzhik' ('The Swashbuckling Peasant'), was produced at the Leningrad

416 ii **ZIELEŃSKI, M. N.**
Par. 4, l. 3 *should read*:
Sacrae in Polonia', Vols. 1 & 2 (1885 & 1887) and in

416 ii **ZIELIŃSKI, J.**
Par. 1, l. 2. 1847; *should read*:
1844 [1];
Add footnote:
[1] His age was given as twenty when he enlisted in the Massachusetts Cavalry, according to the National Archives and Records Service, Washington, D.C., so that 1844 rather than 1847 seems to be the correct date of birth, and it fits in better with early biographical facts.

417 i Par. 1, ll. 4-5 *should read*:
in 1864 moved to the U.S.A. and on 13 Sept. enlisted as a bugler in the 4th Massachusetts Cavalry Union Army, serving there until the end

ii **ZILCHER**
Par. 1, l. 2. 17 Jan. *should read*:
1 Jan.

418 i **ZIMBALIST**
Par. 3, l. 2 *should read*:
singer Alma Gluck, the second (1943) Mary Louise

Add after **ZIMBALON**:
ZIMMERMAN, Franklin (Bershir) (*b.* Waneta, Kansas, 20 June 1923).
American musicologist. He studied at the University of Arizona from 1945 to 1946 and at the University of Southern California (1946–1953) where he specialized for a time in comparative musicology. Between 1953 and 1957 he continued his studies at Oxford, gaining the B.Litt. and Ph.D. for his work in the field of 17th-century music in England. His interest in Purcell led to the compilation of a Thematic Index of Purcell's music (London, 1961) and to the publication of various articles concerning Purcell's autographs and portraiture. He taught at the State Teachers' College (Potsdam, N.Y.) from 1958 to 1959, visited England for further research in 1959–1960, and was appointed Head of the Department of Music Theory at the University of Southern California in 1960. E. B.

ZIMMERMAN
Par. 1, l. 2 *should read*:
July 1873; *d.* Amsterdam, 6 Mar. 1954).

ii *Add before* **ZIMMERMANN, Pierre**:
ZIMMERMANN, Bernd Alois (*b.* Bliesheim nr. Cologne, 20 Mar. 1918).
German musicologist and composer. He studied at the Cologne High School for Music, with some interruptions by military service, and on leaving it in 1947 passed on to the University to study musicology. He is now a lecturer there, but devotes a good deal of his time to composition. His works include

a Concerto for orchestra (1949), a Sonata for violin and pianoforte (1950), a Sonata for unaccompanied violin (1951), a violin Concerto (1952), a Symphony in one movement (1952), chamber music and songs.   E. B.

422 i **ZIPOLI**
           Add at end:
See also Classici Musica Italiana, Vol. 36 (modern ed.).

425 i *Add before* **ZOELLER**:

ZODIACUS MUSICUS. The title of a book of suites for harpsichord published at Augsburg in 1698, containing 6 overtures (preludes) followed by various dances. It is described as a first part, but no second one seems ever to have appeared. The composer's name, shown by the initials J. A. S. only, is not known for certain, but has been conjectured [1] to be that of one J. A. Schmierer (or Schmicerer or Schmicorer).   E. B.

See also Denkmäler (2), Vol. 10 (modern ed.).

[1] By A. Göhler, ' Messakataloge ', Vol. III, p. 21.

427 i **ZORAS**
           Par. 2, l. 6. 1953 *should read*:
1935

           ZUCCALMAGLIO
           Par. 2, l. 4. Kretschmar *should read*:
Kretzschmer

      ii l. 1 *should read*:
1840, 2 vols., the second after Kretzschmer's death). It was on this book that

428 i **ŻUŁAWSKI**
           Par. 1, l. 2 *should read*:
Zakopane, 14 Feb. 1916; *d.* Mont Blanc de Tacul, French Alps, 18 Aug. 1957).

      ii **ZUMPE**
           Par. 3, l. 2. ' Anahna ' *should read*:
' Anahra '

432 ii **ZWEIG**
           Par. 2, l. 15 *should read*:
held until 1938. He was also active in Paris (1939–40) and New York (1940).

433 ii **ŻYWNY**
           Par. 2, l. 2 *should read*:
origin (Vojtěch Živný). He went to Poland as a youth during

           l. 8. Kuchář *should read*:
Kuchař

CHRONOLOGY OF COMPOSERS AND CONTEMPORANEOUS ARTISTS [1]

APPENDIX I

Page	Year	
445	1536	Rove, *should read*:
Rore,		
447	1555	Aracadelt *should read*:
Arcadelt		
		Delete Coperario.
449	1567	*Delete* Banchieri.
	1568	*Add*:
*Banchieri, 3 Sept.		
450	1575	Coperario, *c.* 20 *should read*:
c. Coperario		
452	1585	*Delete* Coperario.
	1587	*Delete* Banchieri.
453	1588	*Add*:
Banchieri, 20		
454	1595	Coperario, *c.* 40 *should read*:
c. 20		
	1597	*Delete* Banchieri.
		Add:
c. Rossi (Luigi)		
	1598	*Add*:
Banchieri, 30		
455		*Delete* Rossi (Luigi).
456	1605	Coperario, *c.* 50 *should read*:
c. 30		
	1607	*Delete* Banchieri.
	1608	*Add*:
Banchieri, 40		
458	1615	Coperario, *c.* 60 *should read*:
c. 40		
	1617	*Delete* Banchieri.
		Add:
Rossi (Luigi), *c.* 20		
	1618	*Add*:
Banchieri, 50		
		Delete Rossi (Luigi).
459	1623	Casti *should read*:
Cesti		
	1625	Coperario, *c.* 70 *should read*:
c. 50		

460 1626 Coperario, *c. 71 should read*:
c. 51

460 1627 *Delete* Banchieri.

Add:
Rossi (Luigi), *c.* 30

1628 *Add*:
Banchieri, 60

Delete Rossi (Luigi).

1630 Rossi (S.) *should read*:
†*c.* Rossi (S.), *c.* 60

461 1634 Banchieri *should read*:
†Banchieri, 66

462 1637 *Add*:
Rossi (Luigi), *c.* 40

1638 *Delete* Rossi (Luigi).

463 1645 *Delete* Muffat (Georg).

c. Staggins *should read*:
† *c.* Staggins (N.)

1647 *Add*:
Rossi (Luigi), *c.* 50

1648 *Delete* Rossi (Luigi).

464 1653 *Add*:
*Muffat (Georg)

Rossi (Luigi) *should read*:
†Rossi (Luigi), *c.* 56

466 1665 *Delete* Muffat (Georg).

467 1673 *Add*:
Muffat (Georg), 20

468 1675 *Delete* Muffat (Georg).

469 1683 *Add*:
Muffat (Georg), 30

470 1685 *Delete* Muffat (Georg).

471 1693 *Add*:
Muffat (Georg), 40

1695 *Delete* Muffat (Georg).

473 1703 *Add*:
Muffat (Georg), 50

1704 Muffat *should read*:
†Muffat (Georg), 50, 23 Feb.

481 1742 *Delete* Alessandri.

1743 Carey, 4 Oct. *should read*:
5 Oct.

482 1747 *Add*:
*Alessandri
†Bononcini (G.), 76, 9 July

483 1748 *Add*:
*Hölty, Ludwig. Po.

1750 *Delete* Bononcini.

484 1755 *Delete* Bononcini.

486 1762 *Delete* Alessandri.

487 1766 *Delete* Rössler.

1767 *Add*:
Alessandri, 20

488 1769 Hasse, 60 *should read*:
Hasse, 70

489 1772 *Delete* Alessandri.

490 1776 *Delete* Rössler.

Add:
†Hölty, Ludwig, 28. Po.

1777 *Add*:
Alessandri, 30

1778 *Add*:
†Perez, 67, 30 Oct.

491 1779 *Delete* Perez.

1782 *Delete* Alessandri.

493 1786 *Delete* Rössler.

1787 *Add*:
Alessandri, 40

494 1792 *Delete* Alessandri.

495 *Dezède *should read*:
†Dezède

Delete Rössler.

496 1797 *Add*:
Alessandri, 50

1798 Alessandri, 56 *should read*:
Alessandri, 51

507 1829 *Add*:
*Rubinstein, 28 Nov.

1830 *Delete* Rubinstein.

513 1844 *Add*:
*Widor, 21 Feb.

1845 *Delete* Widor.

514 1849 *Add*:
Rubinstein, 20

515 1850 *Delete* Rubinstein.

516 1855 Chausson, 21 Jan. *should read*:
20 Jan.

518 1859 *Add*:
Rubinstein, 30

1860 *Delete* Rubinstein.

520 1864 *Add*:
Widor, 20

521 1865 *Delete* Widor.

523 1869 *Add*:
Rubinstein, 40

1870 *Delete* Rubinstein.

525 1874 *Add*:
Widor, 30

1875 Harvé *should read*:
Hervé

Delete Widor.

527 1879 *Add*:
Rubinstein, 50

528 1880 Lassan *should read*:
Lassen

Delete Rubinstein.

1881 *Add after* †Hall:
*Jiménez, Juan Ramón. Po.

Add after *Ludwig, Emil:
*Macaulay, Rose. No. Li.

529 1883 *Add*:
*Różycki, 6 Nov.

530 1884 *Delete* Różycki.

Add:
Widor, 40

1885 *Add after* Glazunov:
*Harrison (J.), 26 Mar.

Delete Widor.

532 1889 *Add*:
Rubinstein, 60

533 1890 *Add*:
*Jemnitz, 9 Aug.

Delete Rubinstein.

Delete Macaulay, Rose.

534 1892 Hennikainen *should read*:
Hannikainen

535 1894 Rubinstein, 63 *should read*:
†Rubinstein, 64, 20 Nov.

Add:
Widor, 50

536 1895 *Delete* Widor.

537 1898 †Boudin, Eugène. Pa. *should read*:
†Boudin, Eugène, 73. Pa.

Add:
*Brecht, Bert(old). Dr.

538 1899 *Delete* Jemnitz.

540 1903 *Add*:
Różycki, 20

541 1904 *Delete* Różicki.

Skalkotas *should read*:
Skalkottas

Add:
Widor, 60

1905 *Add*:
*Hartmann (K. A.), 2 Aug.

542 *Delete* Widor.

544 1910 *Add*:
Jemnitz, 20

546 1913 *Add*:
Różicki, 30

547 1914 *Delete* Różicki.

Add:
Widor, 70

1915 *Delete* Widor.

549 1919 *Delete* Jemnitz.

*Lloyd *should read*:
†Lloyd

*Parker *should read*:
†Parker

550 1920 *Add*:
Jemnitz, 30

551 1922 *Veale *should read*:
*Veale, 15 June

552 1923 *Add*:
Różicki, 40

1924 *Delete* Różicki.

Skalkotas *should read*:
Skalkottas

553   *Add*:
Widor, 80

   1925   *Delete* Widor.

   1926   *Add*:
*Boulez, 25 Mar.

      Creson *should read*:
Creston

555   1929   *Delete* Jemnitz.

556   1930   *Add*:
Jemnitz, 40

      Verretti *should read*:
Veretti

   1931   Back (C.) *should read*:
Beck (C.)

558   1933   *Add after* Rolón:
† Schillings, 65, 23 July

      Add:
Różicki, 50

   1934   *Delete* Różicki.

      Skalkotas *should read*:
Skalkottas

      Add:
Widor, 90

559   1935   Hindsmith *should read*:
Hindemith

      Delete Widor.

560   1937   Widor, 92 *should read*:
Widor, 93

561   1939   Andreas, *should read*:
Andreae,

      Delete Jemnitz.

   1940   *Add*:
Jemnitz, 50

564   1943   *Add*:
Różicki, 60

      Delete Schillings.

   1944   *Delete* Różicki.

      Skalkotas *should read*:
Skalkottas

      Add after this:
†Smyth, 86, 9 May

564   1945   *Add*:
Boulez, 20

565   Hippias *should read*:
Hippius

   1946   *Delete* Boulez.

      Delete †Smyth, 86, 9 May

566   1948   *Delete* Bentzon.

      Viana da Mota, 1 June *should read*:
30 May

567   1949   *Delete* Jemnitz.

      Skalkotas *should read*:
Skalkottas

   1950   *Add*:
Jemnitz, 60

568   1951   *Add*:
†Bentzon (J.), 54, 9 July

      Add after Hovhaness:
†Ingenhoven, 75, 20 May

569   1953   Lotpatnikov *should read*:
Lopatnikov

      Nebokov *should read*:
Nabokov

      Różicki, 68 *should read*:
Różicki, 69

   1954   *Add before* Burian:
†Alfano, 78, 26 Oct.
†Braunfels, 71, 19 Mar.

      Ives *should read*:
†Ives (C.), 79, 19 May

      Add after Piston:
†Rogowski, 72, 14 Mar.

      Add:
†Benavente y Martínez, Jacinto, 88. Dr.
†Derain, André, 74. Pa.
†Matisse, Henri, 85. Pa.

569 ff.

1955

Alwyn, 50
Blitzstein, 50
Carneyro, 60
Carrillo, 80
Castelnuovo-Tedesco, 60
Dandelot, 60
David (J. N.), 60
Diamond, 40
†Dunayrusky, 55, 25 July
Farkas, F., 50

Février, 80
†Freitas Branco (L.), 65, 12 Oct.
Halffter (E.), 50
†Hannikainen, 63
Hindemith, 60
Höffer, 60
†Honegger, 63, 27 Nov.
Jacob, 60
Jolivet, 50
Josten, 70
Kamieński (L.), 70
Labey, 80
Liatoshinsky, 60
Martelli, 60
Menasce, 50
Milner, 30
Montemezzi, 80
Mulè, 70
Orff, 60
Rathaus, 60
Rawsthorne, 50
Riegger, 70
Rudhyar, 60
Searle, 40
Seiber, 50
Sikorski, 60
Sowerby, 60
Still, 60
Taylor (Deems), 70
Tippett, 50
Varèse, 70
Varvoglis, 70
Voormolen, 60
Weiner, 70
Wellesz, 70
Wirén, 50
Zádor, 60

Add :

†Claudel, Paul, 86. Li. Po. Dr.
†Mann, Thomas, 80. No.
†Vachell, Horace Annesley, 94. No.

1956
Alfano, 80
ApIvor, 40
Baudrier, 50
Boulez, 30
Capdevielle, 50
Carpenter, 80
Cilea, 90
Cooke (A.), 50
Creston, 50
Dutilleux, 40
Esplá, 70
Finney, 50
Frankel, 50
Gagnebin, 70
Gerhard, 60
†Gram, 64, 4 Feb.
†Grechaninov, 91, 3 Jan.
Guridi, 70
Hanson, 60

Henze, 30
Kenessy, 50
Labroca, 60
Leoz, 50
Levidis, 70
Lier (van), 50
Lopes Graça, 50
Lutyens, 50
Monnikendam, 60
Morawski, 80
Oldham, 30
Rivier, 60
Ruyneman, 70
Saikkola, 50
Sanders, 50
Schiske, 40
Sessions, 60
Shostakovich, 50
Stevens (B.), 40
Szeligowski, 60
Thomson, 60
†Vassilenko, 83, 11 Mar.
Vogel (V.), 60
Weinberger, 60
Wieniawski (A.), 80
Williams (G.), 50
Zuławski, 40

Add :

†Brecht (Bert(old)), 58. Dr.
†De la Mare, Walter, 83. Po. No.
†Milne, Alan Alexander, 74. Dr.
†Strong, Leonard Alfred George, 62. Li. Po.

1957
Angerer, 30
Arnell, 40
Atterberg, 70
Aubert, 80
Aubin, 50
Badings, 50
Cowell, 60
Dohnányi, 80
†Dresden, 66, 30 July
Fernström, 60
†Février, 81, 8 July
Fortner, 50
Gardner, 40
Gerster, 60
†Guessin, 74, 6 May
Höller, 50
†Kassern, 53, 2 Mar.
†Korngold, 60, 29 Nov.
Kósa, 60
Langlais, 50
Lindberg, 70
Lorenzo Fernândez, 50
Lualdi, 70
Maconchy, 50
Moeschinger, 60
Moreno Gans, 60
Nezeritis, 60
Palester, 50

†Rati, 73, 7 Feb.
Riisager, 60
Saeverud, 60
Saygun, 50
†Schoeck, 70, 8 Mar.
†Sibelius, 90, 20 Sept.
Szałowski, 50
Tansman, 60
Tiessen, 70
Toch, 70
Trapp, 70
Veress, 50
Villa-Lobos, 70
Vocht, 70
Vomačka, 70
†Żuławski, 41, 18 Aug.

Add:

†Dunsany, Edward John (Lord D.), 79,
   No. Dr.
†Murray, Gilbert, 91. Li. Po.

1958

†Bloch, 87, 24 Aug.
Boughton, 80
Damase, 30
Delannoy, 60
Durey, 70
Einem, 40
Eisler, 60
Ferguson, 50
Frazzi, 70
Frumerie, 50
Harris, 60
Harsányi, 60
Hessenberg, 50
†Holbrooke, 80, 5 Aug.
†Järnefelt, 88, 23 June
Knipper, 60
Lesur, 50
Linstead, 50
†Merikanto, 65, 28 Sept.
Messiaen, 50
Muradely, 50
Nielsen (R.), 50
Sklavos, 70
Suchoň, 50

Tarp, 50
Weis (F.), 60
Wordsworth, 50
†Vaughan Williams, 85, 26 Aug.
Zagwijn, 80

Add:

†Cabell, James Branch, 79. No.
†Jiménez, Juan Ramón, 76. Po.
†Macaulay, Rose, 77. No. Li.
†Morgan, Charles, 64. No. Dr.
†Noyes, Alfred, 77. Po. Li.

1959

Andreae, 80
Auric, 60
Bentzon (N. V.), 40
Campo, 80
Casal Chapí, 50
Chávez, 60
Dzerzhinsky, 50
Fitelberg (G.), 80
Gavazzeni, 50
Genzmer, 50
Gibbs (A.), 70
Haas, 80
Hadley (P.), 60
Høffding, 60
Holmboe, 50
Ireland, 80
Jemnitz, 60
Maklakiewicz, 60
Orr (R.), 50
Orrego-Salas, 40
Poulenc, 60
Santa Cruz, 60
Scott (C.), 80
Shaporin, 70
Sköld, 60
Souris, 60
Swanson, 50
Tcherepnin (A.), 60
Thompson, 60
Trunk, 80
Woytowicz, 60

Add:

† Housman, Laurence, 93. Po. Li. Pa.